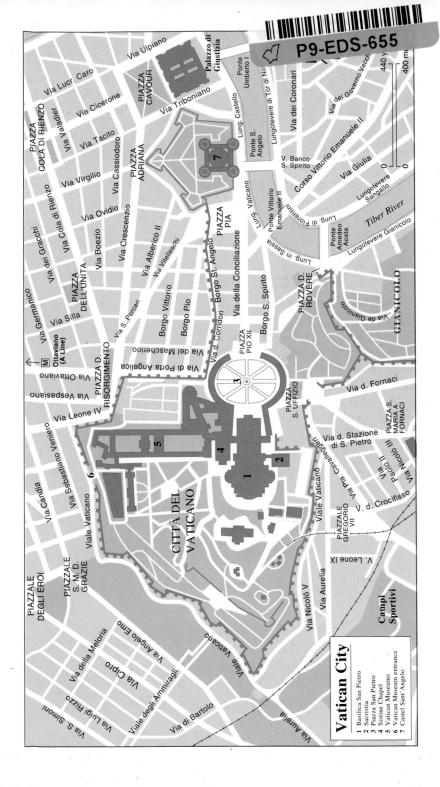

Vatican City

1 Basilica San Pietro
2 Sacristia
3 Piazza San Pietro
4 Sistine Chapel
5 Vatican Museums
6 Vatican Museum entrance
7 Castel Sant'Angelo

Rome Overview

PIAZZALE CLODIO

TO YOUTH HOSTEL

PIAZZA GIUSEPPE MAZZINI

Viale Giuseppe MAZZINI

Lungo. delle Armi

L. delle Navi

L. Arnedo da Brescia

PIAZZA DEL POPOLO

Viale Medaglio d'Oro

Circonvallaz. Trionfale

Via della Giuliana

Via Triontale

Viale Angelico

Viale delle Milizie

Via G. Ferrari Lepanto

Via Marcanti. Colonna

Via Michelangelo

L.d di Mellini in Augusta

Via di Ripetta

Via Flaminia

Via Andrea Doria

Via Leone IV

Viale Giulio Cesare

Via Cicerone

PIAZZA AUGUSTO IMPERIALE

PIAZZALE DEGLI EROI

Via Candia

Via Ottaviano

Via Barletta

Via Germanico

Via Cola di Rienzo

PIAZZA CAVOUR

Via Cipro

Via Crescenzio

Castel Sant'Angelo

L. Prati

Via Angelo Emo

Vatican Museums

Via Staz. di S. Pietro

Castello

L. Marianzo

CITTÀ DEL VATICANO

Saint Peter's Basilica

Tiber

Vatican Wall

Via Aurelia

V. S. Maria Mediatrice

Viale Vaticano

L.di Tor di Nona

Viale dei Coronari

Corso d. Rinascimento

Pantheo

PIAZZA NAVONA

L. Gianicolense

Via Giulia

Corso Vittorio Emanuele II

Via Gregorio VII

Viale delle Mura Aurelia

V. Orti d'Alibert

V.di S. F. di Sale

L. d. Farnesina

Palazzo Farnese

Via Arenula

Via d. Cava Aurelia

MONTE DEL GIANICOLO

L. dei Vallati

L. dei Cenc

Ma

V. Garibaldi

L. Sansio

Isola Tiberina

L. dei Anguillara

Pa

Via Aurelia Antica

S. Maria in Trastevere

V. dei Genovisi

Villa Doria Pamphili

Via di S. Pancrazio

Via Giacinto Carini

Via Nicola Fabrizi

TRASTEVERE

V. di S. Michele

Via Glorioso

Pta. Portese (flea market)

Sublicio

N

Via Dandolo

Viale di Trastevere

Ponte

Via Vittelia

Via Fontelana

Viale di Villa Pamphili

Via del Quattro Venti

Via Alessandro Poeria

Via Portuense

Lungotevere Testaccio

V. di S. Michele

Lungo

Viale Zambarelli

Via Federico Ozanam

Via di Donna Olimpia

Via Cavalcanti

Via

Ponte Testaccio

V. Giovanni Branca

Via Nicola Zaba

Via Gal

Parco Testaccio

TESTACCIO

0   yards   550

0   meters   500

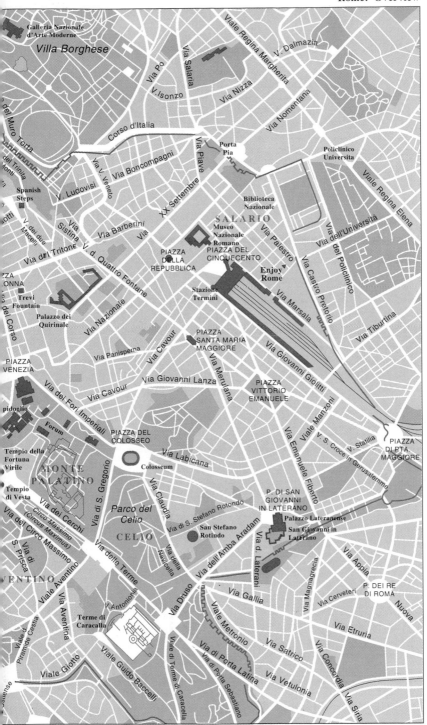

Galleria Nazionale d'Arte Moderne

Villa Borghese

Via Po
Via Salaria
V. Isonzo
Via Nizza
Via Regina Margherita
V. Dalmazia
Corso d'Italia
Via Nomentana
del Muro Torta
del Trinita
Monti
Spanish Steps
Via Plave
Porta Pia
Policlinico Universita
Viale Regina Elena
Via V. Veneto
Via Boncompagni
V. Ludovisi
XX Settembre
Biblioteca Nazionale
otti
Via Sistina
Via Barberini
V. del due Macelli
Via
SALARIO
Museo Nazionale Romano
Via Palestro
Via dell'Università
Via del Policlinico
Via d'I Tritone
V. d. Quattro Fontane
PIAZZA DELLA REPUBBLICA
PIAZZA DEL CINQUECENTO
Via Castro Pretorio
ZZA ONNA
Trevi Fountain
del Corso
Palazzo dei Quirinale
Enjoy Rome
Stazione Termini
Via Marsala
Via Nazionale
Via Panisperna
Via Cavour
PIAZZA SANTA MARIA MAGGIORE
Via Giovanni Giolitti
Via Tiburtina
PIAZZA VENEZIA
Via Giovanni Lanza
Via Merulana
PIAZZA VITTORIO EMANUELE
Via dei Fori Imperiali
Via Cavour
Via Manzoni
Via Emanuele Filberto
PIAZZA DI PTA. MAGGIORE
pidoglio
Forum
PIAZZA DEL COLOSSEO
Via Labicana
v. S. Croce in Gerusalemme
v. S. Statilia
Tempio della Fortuna Virile
Colosseum
MONTE PALATINO
Via di S. Gregorio
Via Claudia
P. DI SAN GIOVANNI IN LATERANO
Tempio di Vesta
Parco del Celio
Via di S. Stefano Rotondo
Palazzo Lateranense
San Giovanni in Laterano
Via dei Cerchi
Circo Massimo (Circus Maximus)
CELIO
San Stefano Rotindo
Via della Navicella
Via dell'Amba Aradam
Via d. Laterani
Via Appia
Via del Circo Massimo
Via di S. Prisca
Via della Terme
Via Magnagrecia
Via Cerveteri
P. DEI RE DI ROMA
VENTINO
Viale Aventino
Via Aventina
Via Druso
Via Gallia
Via Etruria
Nuova
Terme di Caracalla
V. Antoniola
Viale Metronio
Via Satrico
Via Concordia
Via Siria
Piramide Cestia
Viale Giotto
Viale Guido Baccelli
Viale di Terme di Caracalla
Via di Porta Latina
Via di Pota Sebastiano
Via Vetulonia

Rome: Transportation

Rome-Transport

TO YOUTH HOSTEL

PIAZZA GIUSEPPE MAZZINI

Viale Giuseppe Mazzini
Via G. Ferrari
•19•70•490•913•

Viale Regina Margherita
V. Dalmazia
Via Nomentana

Via Nizza
Via Salaria
Via Piave

Via Po
Corso d'Italia
Via XX Settembre

VILLA BORGHESE

Via V. Veneto
•59•

Viale del Muro Torta

FLAMINIO
A-LINE

SPAGNA
Via Sistina
Via dei due Macelli

BARBERINI
Via Barberini
•61•62•492•

REPUBBLICA
Via d. Quattro Fontane
•70•
•71•

Via Nazionale
•57•64•65•
•70•75•170•

SALARIO
•61•65•

CASA PRETORIO
•56•65•75•492•

CINQUECENTO
P. D.
•60•61•62•

TERMINI
Stazione Termini

B-LINE

VITTORIO
•70•
•70•

CAVOUR
V. Cavour
B-LINE
A-LINE

Via Castro Pretorio
Via Marsala
Via Merulana
•16•93•93b•
•93•93b•613•
Via Giov. Lanza
•71•

V. dei Fori Imperiali
•85•87•

Palazzo dei Quirinale
Trevi Fountain
•71•81•
•95•119•492•
•56•61•60•
•52•52b•53•56•
•52•52b•60•

Via del Tritone
•95•116•492•

PIAZZA COLONNA
Pantheon
•119•

PIAZZA VENEZIA
•71b•

Via del Babuino
•119•
Via del Corso •56•60•62•81•85•90•90b•
Via del Corso

Via di Ripetta
•90•90b•

PIAZZA DEL POPOLO
•26•81•

Via Flaminia

Via Cicerone
PIAZZA CAVOUR
•87•

C. d. Rinascimento
PIAZZA NAVONA

Viale dei Coronari

Corso Vittorio Emanuele II
•26•44•46•56•60•61•62•64•70•81•492•
Via Giulia
•23•

Palazzo Farnese
•23•65•28

Tiber

Via Marcant. Colonna
•280•

LEPANTO
A-LINE
Via Lepanto
•990•

Via G. Ferrari
•32•
Viale Angelico
Viale delle Milizie
Via Giulio Cesare

OTTAVIANO
A-LINE
V. Ottaviano
Via Cola di Rienzo
•81•

Via Crescenzio
•34•49•492•990•
•23•34•
•23•49•492•
•23•
•64•
•41•

Castel Sant' Angelo

Tiber

Vatican
St. Peter's Basilica
•49•
Via Leone IV
•41•
•41•41•
•62•65•98•
•41•46•46b•

Urban Train Service (F.S.)
S. PIETRO
•29•

1/2 mile

500 meters

MANZONI

S. GIOVANNI

Palazzo Lateranense
S.Giovanni
in Laterano

V. Appia

V. Statilia

V. Fiberto

emanuele

Via Magnagrecia

Via Cerveteri

Via Etruria

Via Concordia

Via Salrico

Via Vetulonia

•85•87•

Via d. Laterani

•90•118•

Via Gallia

Via dell'Amba Aradam

•85•87•

•85•118•

Via di S. Giovanni in Laterano

Via di S. Stefano Rotondo

Viale Metronio

Via di Porta Latina

•118•

•118•

Via di Porta Sebastiano

•118•

COLOSSEO

Via Labicana

COLOSSEO

P. D.

V. Claudio

Via della
Navicella

Parco del
Celio

CELIO

V. delle
Terme

•90•90b•118•

Viale di Terme di Caracalla

•93•93b•613•671•

Colosseum

B-LINE

Via di S Gregorio

CIRCO MASSIMO

Terme di
Caracalla

Viale Guido Baccelli

MONTE
PALATINO

Via dei Cerchii

Via del Circo Massimo

•15•90•90b•

•90b•94•

•90•

Via Aventina

Viale Aventino

AVENTINO

Via di
S. Prisca

Viale Giotto

•94•

•57•95•318•

PIRAMIDE

OSTIENSE

Urban Train Service (F.S.)
TO AIRPORT

TO LAURENTINA

•15•

•57•90•90•

•23•5•92•95•716•

•94•

Viale d.
Piramide Cestia

•11•15•2•118•673•

Via Ostiense

•11•92•715•

B-LINE

•673•

Isola
Tiberina

Via Marmorata

•13•23•57•

Via Giovanni Branca

Via Nicola Zabaglia

•92•

Via

Parco
Testaccio

TESTACCIO

•26•44•75•97•170•280•

TRASTEVERE

Viale di Trastevere

Via Glorioso

710•

V. Nicola Fabrizi

•44•75•

Via Dandolo

•13•23•75•

•27•31•228•280•710•719•

TRASTEVERE
Urban Train
Service (F.S.)

GIANICOLO

•41•

Via di S. Pancrazio

V. Cavalcanti

Via Giacinto Carini

•75•

Via Alessandro Poerio

Via
Alessandro Poerio

Via del Quattro Venti

Viale di Villa Pamphili

Via di Donna Olimpia

N

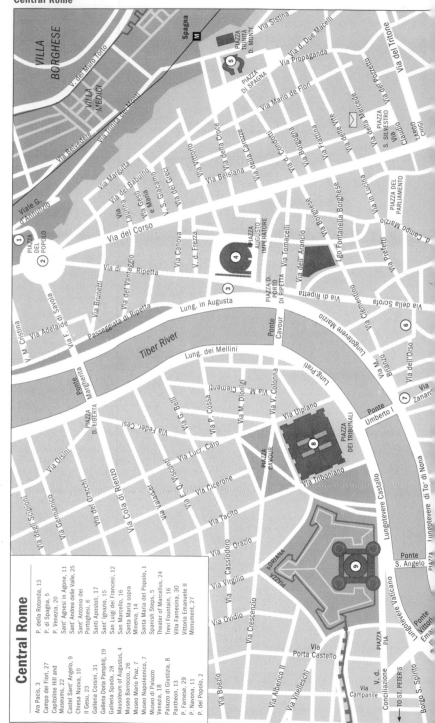

Central Rome

Ara Pacis, 3
Campo dei Fiori, 27
Capitoline Hill and Museums, 22
Castel Sant' Angelo, 9
Chiesa Nuova, 10
Il Gesù, 23
Galleria Corsini, 31
Galleria Doria Pamphili, 19
Galleria Spada, 28
Mausoleum of Augustus, 4
Museo Barrocco, 26
Museo Mario Praz, 7
Museo Napoleonico, 7
Museo di Palazzo Venezia, 18
Palazzo di Giustizia, 8
Pantheon, 13
P. Farnese, 29
P. Navona, 11
P. del Popolo, 2

P. della Rotonda, 13
P. di Spagna, 5
P. Venezia, 20
Sant' Agnesi in Agone, 11
Sant' Andrea delle Valle, 25
Sant' Antonio dei Portoghesi, 6
Santi Apostoli, 17
Sant' Ignazio, 15
San Luigi dei Francesi, 12
San Marcello, 16
Santa Maria sopra Minerva, 14
Santa Maria del Popolo, 1
Spanish Steps, 5
Theater of Marcellus, 24
Trevi Fountain, 16
Villa Farnesina, 30
Vittorio Emanuele II Monument, 27

MONTE CAPITOLINO

Via Lucchesi

Via D. PILOTTA

PIAZZA D. PILOTTA

Via V. Minghetti

Via S. S. Apostoli

(17)

PIAZZA DEI S.S. APOSTOLI

(26)

PIAZZA VENEZIA

TO THE FORUM AND THE PALATINE

(21)

(22)

Via del Consolazione

V. Petroselli

Via del Corso

(18)

Via del Plebiscito

PIAZZA SAN MARCO

(19)

Via Gatta

PZA. DEI COLLEGIO ROMANO

(15)

V. Pie di Marmo

PIAZZA GRAZIOLI

(23)

PIAZZA D. GESÙ

V.S. Marco

Via d'Aracoeli

Via del Teatro di Marcello

(24)

Via di Pierleoni

Ponte Fabricio

V. Pastini

V. Seminario

Via del Gesù

V. d. Botteghe Oscuro

PIAZZA CAMPITELLI

V. M. Caetani

Via d. Portico d. Ottavia

V. dei Colonelle

d. Jalena

(14)

V.

Chiara

V. di Torre Argentina

V. Paganica

V. d. Funari

Via d. Catalana

ISOLA TIBERINA

d. Dogana V

Via Giustiniani

PIAZZA DELLA ROTONDA

(13)

V. Santa

Via Monterone

Corso Vittorio Emanuele II

LARGO DI TORRE ARGENTINA

V. d. Barbieri

LARGO ARENULA

V. Falegnami

PIAZZA CENCI

Lung. dei Cenci

Lung. dei Cenci

V. Monte Farina

PIAZZA S. EUSTACCHIO

LARGO TEATRO VALLE

Via d. Chiodaroli

V. d. Giubbonari

Via Arenula

Ponte Garibaldi

PIAZZA G. G. BELLI

Corso del Rinascimento

(12)

(11)

PIAZZA NAVONA

(25)

Via dei Chiavari

LGO. DEI LIBRARI

PZA. DEL PARADISO

(26)

LARGO DEI PALLARO

(27)

V. Leutari

V. Savelli

V. del Conservatorio

V. d. Zoccolette

Lungotevere dei Vallati

SANGUIGNA

V. dell' Anima

PIAZZA SAN PANTALEO

(28)

Via del Pettinari

PIAZZA V. PALLOTTI

Lungotevere dei Vallati

Lungotevere Sanzio

Via dei Coronari

Via Vetrina

Via d. Governo Vecchio

Via Sora

Via Sforti

(29)

V. Polverone

V. Mascherone

Ponte Sisto

Via S. Dorotea

Via del Moro

Via del Pellegrino

Via Cappellari

Via d. Farnesi

Tiber River

PIAZZA DI SANT' EGIDIO

TO PZA. DI S.M. IN TRASTEVERE

DEI CORONARI

(10)

Via del Monserrato

Via d. S. Eligio

Via Giulia

Lungotevere dei Tebaldi

PIAZZA della Scala

Via d. Mattonato

Via Gianicolense

Via d. Banchi Vecchi

LARGO PEROSI

Via Mazzini

Lungotevere della Farnesina

(30)

(31)

Via di Riari

Via Gianicolense

Via d. Gonfalone

Via Scimia

Lungotevere della Lungara

Via Corsini

di Fiorentini

Lungotevere Sangallo

Tiber River

Via d. Orti d. Albert

Via delle Mantellate

Vic. di Penitenza

Via S. Francesco di Sales

PARCO GIANICOLENSE

Ponte Principe Amadeo

PIAZZA D. ROVERE

Lungotevere Gianicolense

N

300 yards

300 meters

0

0

Rome: Villa Borghese

Via Giovannelli
Giovanni Paisiello
Via S. Mercadante
Via P. Raimondi
Via dei Daini
PIAZZALE DEI RAIMUNDI
Museo Borghese
Viale dell'Uccelleria
Viale Museo Borghese
Via Po
Via di S. Teresa
Corso d'Italia
PIAZZA E. SIENKIEWICZ
V. Puglia
V. Romagna
Via Boncompagni
Via Quintina
Via Sardegna
Via Sicilia
Via Piemonte
Via Toscana
Via Marche
Via Pinciana
Via Vittorio Veneto
Via Emilia
Via Aurora
Via Ludovisi
Via Liguria

GIARDINO ZOOLOGICO
Zoologico
Via dei Cavalli Marini
Via P. Canonica
PIAZZA DI SIENA
Viale Casina di Raffaello
V. Pupazzi
V. di S. Paolo del Brasile
Viale Goethe
V. P. Pineta
V. CANESTRE
PIAZZALE BRASILE
PIAZZALE DELLE MAGNOLIE

Viale del Giardino
Via Ulisse Aldrovandi
Viale dell'Aranciera
V. F. Laguardia
VILLA BORGHESE
Viale Galoppatoio
Viale del Muro Torto
Via del Babuino
Spagna
A LINE
Via Porta Pinciana

Viale delle Belle Arti
Galleria Nazionale d'Arte Moderne
Via Bernardotte
PIAZZALE PAOLA BORGHESE
Via Madame
PIAZZALE DEL FIOCCO
V. Washington
PIAZZALE DEI MARTIRI
Viale d. Belvedere
Viale Valadier
VILLA MEDICI
Viale Trinità dei Monti
Via del Babuino
Via della Croce
Via Vittoria
Via della Croce

Museo di Villa Giulia
VILLA STROHL FERN
VILLA RUFFO
Viale Madame
PIAZZA AUGUSTO IMPERATORE

Via di V.lla Giulia
V. di S. Eugenio
Via Flaminia
VILLA RUFFO
Flaminio
PIAZZALE FLAMINIO
PIAZZA DEL POPOLO
Via del Corso
Via Brunetti
Via de. Vantaggio
V. A. Canova
PIAZZA AUGUSTO IMPERATORE

Via Flaminia
PIAZZA DELLA MARINA
V. D. A. Azuni
V. G. Pisanelli
V. Romanosi
V. Disavoua
Via Savoia
Via Ripetta
Lungotevere in Augusta
Ponte Margherita
Lungotevere d. Mellini

Lungotevere delle Navi
Lungotevere Arnaldo da Brescia
Lungotevere Michelangelo
Ponte Nenni
Via Fed. Cesi
Via G. Belli

PIAZZA MONTE GRAPPA
Ponte d. Risorg
Fiume Tevere
Ponte G. Matteotti
PIAZZA DELLE CINQUE GIORNATE
Lungotevere delle Armi
Viale Giuseppe Mazzini
Via G. Nicotera
Viale della Milizie
Via Settembrini
Via Giulio Cesare
A LINE
Lepanto
Via Ezio
Via degli Scipioni
Via Pompeo Magno
Via dei Gracchi
Via D. LIBERTA
Via Valadier
PIAZZA COLA DI RIENZO
Via Marc. Colonna
Via Boezio
Via E. Q. Visconte

N ←

Villa Borghese

200 yards
200 meters

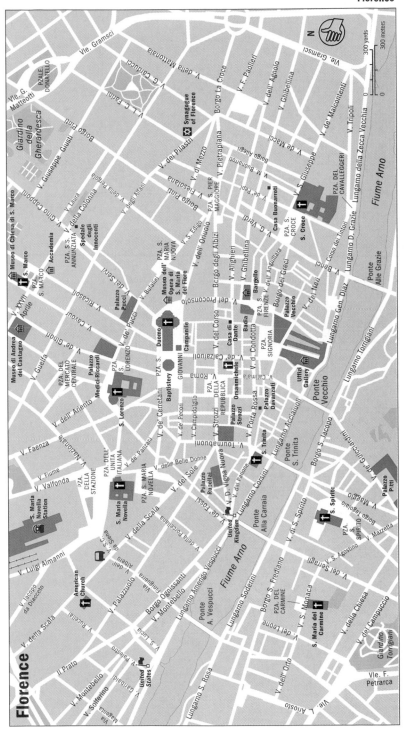

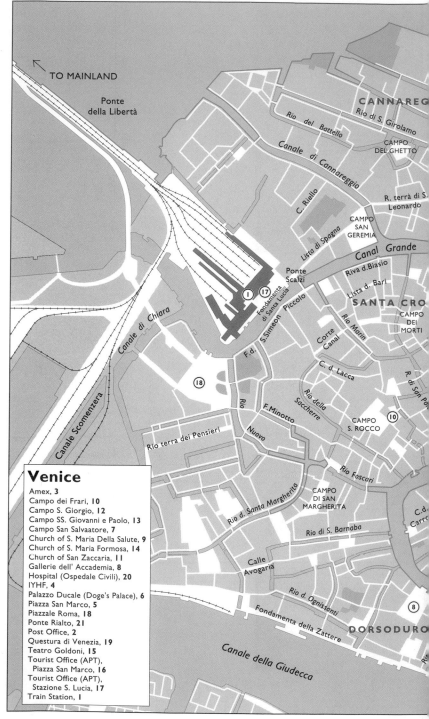

TO MAINLAND

Ponte
della Libertà

CANNAREG

Rio del Battello

Rio di S. Girolamo

Canale di Cannareggio

CAMPO
DEL GHETTO

C. Riello

R. terrà di S.
Leonardo

Lista di Spagna

CAMPO
SAN
GEREMIA

Canal Grande

Ponte
Scalzi

Riva d.Biasio

Lista d. Bari

Fondamenta
di Santa Lucia

S.Simeon Piccolo

SANTA CRO

CAMPO
DEI
MORTI

Rio Marin

F.d. S.

Corte
Canal

C. d. Lacca

R. di San Pon

Canale di Chiara

Rio
Nuovo

F.Minotto

Rio della
Saccherre

CAMPO
S. ROCCO

Canale Scomenzera

Rio terra dei Pensieri

Rio Foscari

CAMPO
DI SAN
MARGHERITA

Rio d. Santa Margherita

Rio di S. Barnaba

C.d.
Carro

Calle
Avogaria

Rio d. Ognissanti

Fondamenta della Zattere

DORSODURO

Canale della Giudecca

Venice

Amex, **3**
Campo dei Frari, **10**
Campo S. Giorgio, **12**
Campo SS. Giovanni e Paolo, **13**
Campo San Salvaatore, **7**
Church of S. Maria Della Salute, **9**
Church of S. Maria Formosa, **14**
Church of San Zaccaria, **11**
Gallerie dell' Accademia, **8**
Hospital (Ospedale Civili), **20**
IYHF, **4**
Palazzo Ducale (Doge's Palace), **6**
Piazza San Marco, **5**
Piazzale Roma, **18**
Ponte Rialto, **21**
Post Office, **2**
Questura di Venezia, **19**
Teatro Goldoni, **15**
Tourist Office (APT),
  Piazza San Marco, **16**
Tourist Office (APT),
  Stazione S. Lucia, **17**
Train Station, **1**

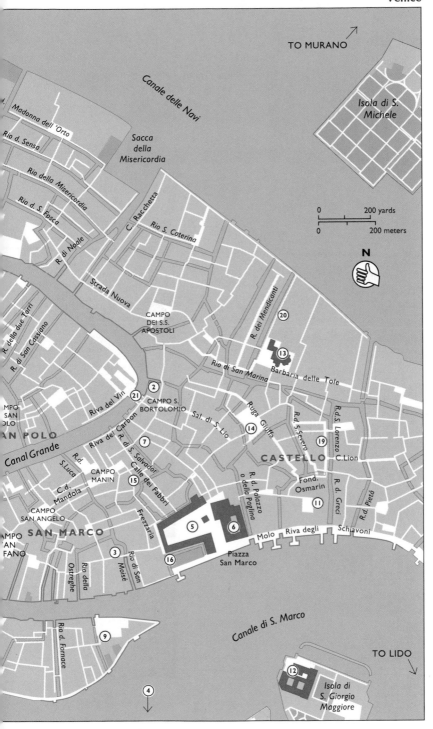

TO MURANO

Canale delle Navi

Isola di S. Michele

Madonna dell'Orto

Rio d. Sensa

Rio della Misericordia

Rio d. S. Fosca

Sacca della Misericordia

R. di Noale

C. Racchetta

Rio S. Caterina

0   200 yards

0   200 meters

N

Strada Nuova

CAMPO DEI S.S. APOSTOLI

R. dei Mendicanti

(20)

R. delle due Torri

R. di San Cassiano

Rio di San Marina

(13)

Barbaria delle Tole

(2)

Riva del Vin

(21)

CAMPO S. BORTOLOMIO

Sat. di S. Lio

Ruga Giuffa

MPO SAN OLO

AN POLO

Canal Grande

Riva del Carbon

R. d. S. Salvador

(7)

(14)

R. d. S. Severo

R. d. S. Lorenzo

(19)

CASTELLO

C. Lion

R.d. S. Luca

CAMPO MANIN

Calle dei Fabbri

(15)

Fond. Osmarin

R. d. Greci

R. d. Pietà

C. d. Mandola

CAMPO SAN ANGELO

MPO AN FANO

SAN MARCO

Frezzaria

R. d. Palazzo o della Paglina

(5)   (6)

(11)

(3)

Rio di San Moisè

(16)

Piazza San Marco

Molo Riva degli Schiavoni

Rio della Ostreghe

Rio d. Fornace

(9)

Canale di S. Marco

TO LIDO

(4)

(12)

Isola di S. Giorgio Maggiore

Milan

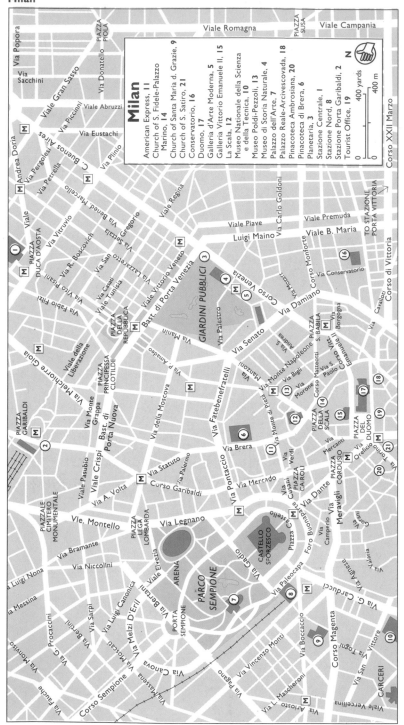

Milan

American Express, 11
Church of S. Fidele-Palazzo Marino, 14
Church of Santa Maria d. Grazie, 9
Church of S. Satiro, 21
Conservatorio, 16
Duomo, 17
Galleria d'Arte Moderna, 5
Galleria Vittorio Emanuele II, 15
La Scala, 12
Museo Nazionale della Scienza e della Tecnica, 10
Museo Poldi-Pezzoli, 13
Museo di Storia Naturale, 4
Palazzo dell'Arte, 7
Palazzo Reale-Arcivescovada, 18
Pinacoteca Ambrosiana, 20
Pinacoteca di Brera, 6
Planetaria, 3
Stazione Centrale, 1
Stazione Nord, 8
Stazione Porta Garibaldi, 2
Tourist Office, 19

0   400 yards
0   400 m

⚜ Let's Go writers travel on your budget.

"Guides that penetrate the veneer of the holiday brochures and mine the grit of real life."

—*The Economist*

"The writers seem to have experienced every rooster-packed bus and lunar-surfaced mattress about which they write."

—*The New York Times*

"All the dirt, dirt cheap."

—*People*

⚜ Great for independent travelers.

"The guides are aimed not only at young budget travelers but at the independent traveler; a sort of streetwise cookbook for traveling alone."

—*The New York Times*

"A guide should tell you what to expect from a destination. Here *Let's Go* shines."

—*The Chicago Tribune*

"An indispensible resource, *Let's Go*'s practical information can be used by every traveler."

—*The Chattanooga Free Press*

⚜ Let's Go is completely revised each year.

"A publishing phenomenon...the only major guidebook series updated annually. *Let's Go* is the big kahuna."

—*The Boston Globe*

"Unbeatable: good sight-seeing advice; up-to-date info on restaurants, hotels, and inns; a commitment to money-saving travel; and a wry style that brightens nearly every page."

—*The Washington Post*

⚜ All the important information you need.

"*Let's Go* authors provide a comedic element while still providing concise information and thorough coverage of the country. Anything you need to know about budget traveling is detailed in this book."

—*The Chicago Sun-Times*

"*Let's Go* guidebooks take night life seriously."

—*The Chicago Tribune*

ITALY
2002

Shannon F. Ringvelski editor
David James Bright associate editor
Sarah Yasmin Resnick associate editor

researcher-writers
Jeffrey Barnes
Eric Graves Brown
Dennis Feehan
Celeste Fine
David Justin Hodge
Megan E. McP. Low

Colin Wambsgans map editor
Naz F. Firoz managing editor

St. Martin's Press ✖ New York

Maps by David Lindroth copyright © 2002, 2001, 2000, 1999, 1998, 1997, 1996, 1995, 1994, 1993, 1992, 1991, 1990, 1989, 1988 by St. Martin's Press.

Distributed outside the USA and Canada by Macmillan.

Let's Go: Italy Copyright © 2002 by Let's Go, Inc. All rights reserved. Printed in the United States of America. No part of this book may be used or reproduced in any manner whatsoever without written permission except in the case of brief quotations embodied in critical articles or reviews. Let's Go is available for purchase in bulk by institutions and authorized resellers. For information, address St. Martin's Press, 175 Fifth Avenue, New York, NY 10010, USA.

ISBN:0-312-27042-9

First edition
10 9 8 7 6 5 4 3 2 1

Let's Go: Italy is written by Let's Go Publications, 67 Mount Auburn Street, Cambridge, MA 02138, USA.

Let's Go® and the thumb logo are trademarks of Let's Go, Inc.
Printed in the USA on recycled paper with biodegradable soy ink.

HOW TO USE THIS BOOK

Welcome to *Let's Go: Italy 2001*, the savvy budget traveler's restaurant of choice. Your table is being cleared at the moment and should be ready in a few minutes. Please, have a seat at the bar and enjoy a complementary glass of the house red. Feel free to peruse the menu while you wait, and have a pleasant meal.

THE MENU

ANTIPASTI. The first course, **Discover Italy,** is sure to whet your appetite for our oh-so-tasty coverage by providing you with an overview of Italy, including **Suggested Itineraries** that list the Chef's recommendations regarding where to visit and how much time to spend there.

PRIMI. Life & Times, served fresh with a pinch of wit, provides you with a general introduction to the art, culture, and history of Italy. Leave Life & Times on the table so you can nibble at it as you eat the rest of your meal. The heavy **Essentials** section details practical information and is best consumed in small bites.

SECONDI. The meat of our Italy coverage comes in 10 delectable cuts. **Northwest Italy** includes Lombardy, the Lake Country, the Italian Riviera, Piedmont, and Valle d'Aosta. **Venice** has her own chapter, followed by **Northeast Italy,** which includes the Veneto (minus Venice), Friuli Venezia-Giulia, Trentino Alto-Adige, and Emilia-Romagna. **Florence** precedes **Central Italy,** which covers Tuscany (minus Florence), Umbria, Le Marche, Abruzzo, and Molise. **Rome** includes not only the Eternal City, but also the rest of Lazio. **Southern Italy** stuffs in Campania, the Amalfi Coast, Apulia, Basilicata, and Calabria, and **Sicily, Sardinia,** and **Malta** round out the meal. The **black tabs** in the margins will help you to navigate between chapters quickly.

CONTORNI. As far as side dishes go, may we suggest the lovely baked **appendix?** It contains several varieties of diced **conversion tables,** as well as an Italian **phrasebook** of things both useful and tawdry. The Chef finishes off the dish with a subtle **glossary** of technical and architectural foreign words broiled in a truffle demi-glaze.

DOLCI. Don't fill up on content before sampling dessert! Our sugar-coated **index** is chock-full of hidden treats and homemade sweets. Try **superlatives** for a sugar fix.

A FEW NOTES ABOUT HOW WE PREPARE YOUR FOOD

RANKING ESTABLISHMENTS. In each section (accommodations, food, etc.), we list establishments in order from best to worst. Our absolute favorites are so denoted by the highest honor given out by *Let's Go*, the thumbs-up (◳). See **accommodations with thumb picks** or **hostels** in the index for some direction.

PHONE CODES AND TELEPHONE NUMBERS. The **phone code** for each region, city, or town appears opposite the name of that region, city, or town, and is denoted by the 🕾 icon. **Phone numbers** in text are also preceded by the 🕾 icon.

GRAYBOXES AND IKONBOXES. Some **Grayboxes** provide wonderful cultural insight, others simply crude humor. In any case, they're usually amusing, so enjoy. **Ikonboxes,** on the other hand, provide important practical information, such as warnings (⚠) or helpful hints and information about other resources

CONTENTS

DISCOVER ITALY 1
When to go 1
Sins to commit 2
Suggested itineraries 4

LIFE AND TIMES 7
History and Politics 7
Art and Architecture 14
Literature 20
Music 23
Print 25
Film 25
Food and Wine: La Dolce Vita 27
Sports and Recreation 32
The Italian Language 32
Festivals and Holidays 33

ESSENTIALS 35
Facts for the Traveler 35
Transportation to Italy 58
Transportation Within Italy 62
Additional information 70

NORTHWEST ITALY 78
Lombardy (Lombardia) 78

MILAN (MILANO) 78
Pavia 99
Cremona 102
Mantua (Mantova) 105
Bergamo 109
Brescia 115
The Lake Country 119

LAKE COMO (LAGO DI COMO) 119
Como 120
Near Lake Como 126
LAKE MAGGIORE
(LAGO MAGGIORE) 128
Near Stresa 130
The Borromean Islands (Isole Borromee) 132
LAKE ORTA (LAGO DI ORTA) 132
Liguria (Italian Riviera) 134

Genoa (Genova) 134
RIVIERA DI LEVANTE 144
Camogli 144
Santa Margherita Ligure 147
Cinque Terre 150
Near Cinque Terre 155
RIVIERA DI PONENTE 158
Savona 158
Finale Ligure 159
San Remo 163
Bordighera 165
Ventimiglia 167
Piedmont (Piemonte) 171

Turin (Torino) 172
Asti 183
Valle d'Aosta 187

Aosta 189

VENICE (VENEZIA) 196

NORTHEAST ITALY 225
The Veneto 225

Padua (Padova) 226
Vicenza 231
Verona 233
Treviso 239
Friuli-Venezia Giulia 242

Trieste 243
Udine 250
Trentino-Alto Adige 254

Trent (Trento, Trient) 254
DOLOMITES (DOLOMITI) 257
Bolzano (Bozen) 258
Bressanone (Brixen) 262
LAKE GARDA (LAGO DI GARDA) 266
Riva del Garda 269
Emilia-Romagna 272

Bologna 272
Ferrara 281
Modena 285
Parma 289
Piacenza 294
Ravenna 295
Rimini 299
San Marino 303

FLORENCE (FIRENZE) 306

CENTRAL ITALY 339
Tuscany (Toscana) 339

Cortona 340
Arezzo 342
Siena 346
Montepulciano 356
Volterra 359
San Gimignano 362
Pistoia 365
Lucca 368
Pisa 373
Livorno 379
ELBA 382
Portoferraio 383
Umbria 387

Perugia 388
Assisi 397
Gubbio 403
Spoleto 406
Orvieto 411
The Marches (Le Marche) 415

Pesaro 416
Urbino 418
Ancona 421
Ascoli Piceno 423
San Benedetto del Tronto 426
Abruzzo and Molise 427

Abruzzo National Park 432

ROME 437
NEAR ROME 478
Tivoli 478
Etruria 479
Pontine Islands 480

SOUTHERN ITALY 483
Campania 483

NAPLES (NAPOLI) 484
BAY OF NAPLES: VESUVIUS 503
Pompeii (Pompei) 503
Sorrento 507
BAY OF NAPLES: ISLANDS 510
Capri and Anacapri 510
Ischia 515
Procida 518
AMALFI COAST 520
Positano 520
Amalfi 523
Salerno 528
Apulia (Puglia) 533

Bari 534
Brindisi 541
Lecce 545
SALENTO PENINSULA 549
Taranto 551
BASILICATA 552
Matera 552
TYRRHENIAN COAST 557
Calabria 559

Camigliatello and Sila Massif 562
Reggio di Calabria 563

SICILY (SICILIA) 570
NORTHERN SICILY 570
Palermo 570
Cefalù 580
AEOLIAN ISLANDS (ISOLE EOLIE) 584
Lipari 585
Vulcano 589
Other Islands 592
EASTERN SICILY 596
Messina 596
Taormina 601
Catania 605
CENTRAL SICILY 610
Enna 610
SOUTHERN SICILY 614
Syracuse (Siracusa) 614
Ragusa 620
WESTERN SICILY 622
Agrigento 622
Trapani 627
EGADI ISLANDS (ISOLE EGADI) 633
Pantelleria 634

SARDINIA (SARDEGNA) 638
CAGLIARI PROVINCE 641
Cagliari 641
Near cagliari 646
ORISTANO PROVINCE 647
Oristano 647

NUORO PROVINCE 651
Nuoro 651
SASSARI PROVINCE 655
Sassari 655
Alghero 660
Olbia 665
Santa Teresa di Gallura 670

APPENDIX 673
Temperature and Climate 673
Abbreviations 673
International Calling Codes 673
Italian 674

INDEX 688

Italy: Chapters

LIECHTENSTEIN
AUSTRIA
HUNGARY
YUGO-SLAVIA
SWITZERLAND
SLOVENIA
CROATIA

NORTHEAST ITALY
pp. 194–266

NORTHWEST ITALY
pp. 77–169
Milan (Milano)

VENICE (VENIZIA)
pp. 170–193

BOSNIA-HERZEGOVINIA

Turin (Torino)
Genoa (Genova)
Bologna
SAN MARINO

FRANCE
MONACO

FLORENCE (FIRENZE)
pp. 267–297

CENTRAL ITALY
pp. 298–389

Adriatic Sea

Corsica (FRANCE)

ROME
pp. 390–438

SOUTHERN ITALY
pp. 439–521

Naples (Napoli)

SARDINIA
pp. 582–610

Tyrrhenian Sea

Cagliari

Palermo
SICILY
pp. 522–581

Ionian Sea

Mediterranean Sea

N

0   100 miles
0   100 kilometers

ALGERIA

TUNISIA
pp. 620–675
Tunis

MALTA
pp. 611–619

	LEGEND		
✚ Hospital	✈ Airport	🏛 Museum	▲ Mountain
✪ Police	🚌 Bus Station	🏨 Hotel/Hostel	Park
✉ Post Office	🚆 Train Station	⛺ Camping	
ⓘ Tourist Office	Ⓜ METRO STATION	🍎 Food & Drink	Beach
💲 Bank	⚓ Ferry Landing	🛍 Shopping	
👜 Embassy/Consulate	✝ Church	♪ Arts & Entertainment	Water
▪ Site or Point of Interest	✡ Synagogue	Nightlife	
☎ Telephone Office	☪ Mosque	🖥 Internet Café	👍 The Let's Go thumb always points NORTH.
⛉ Theater	⚔ Castle	---- Pedestrian Zone	

IX

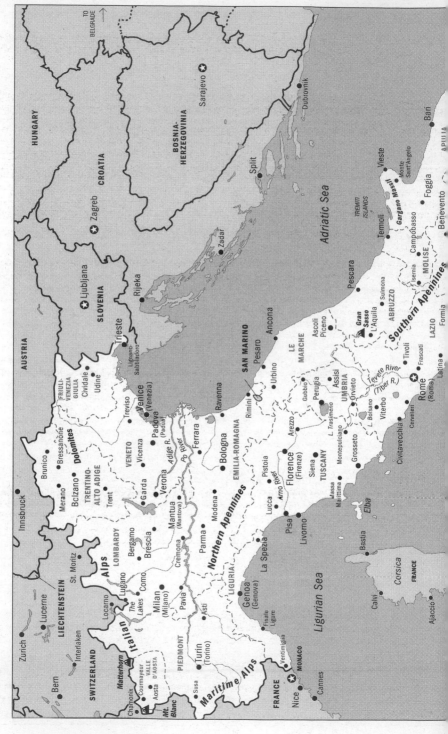

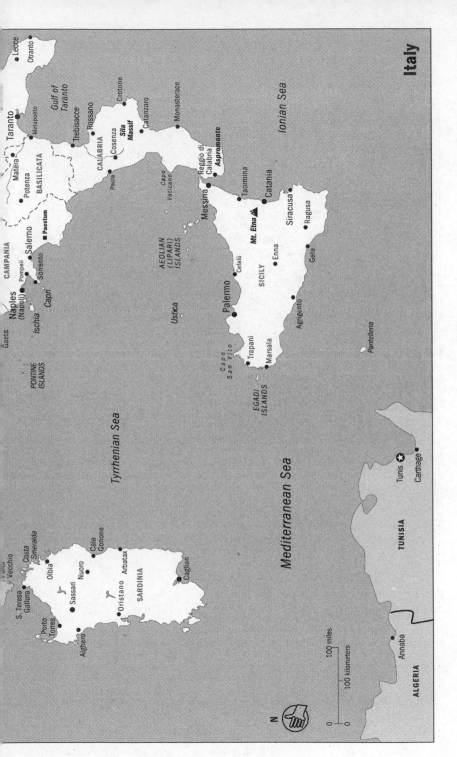

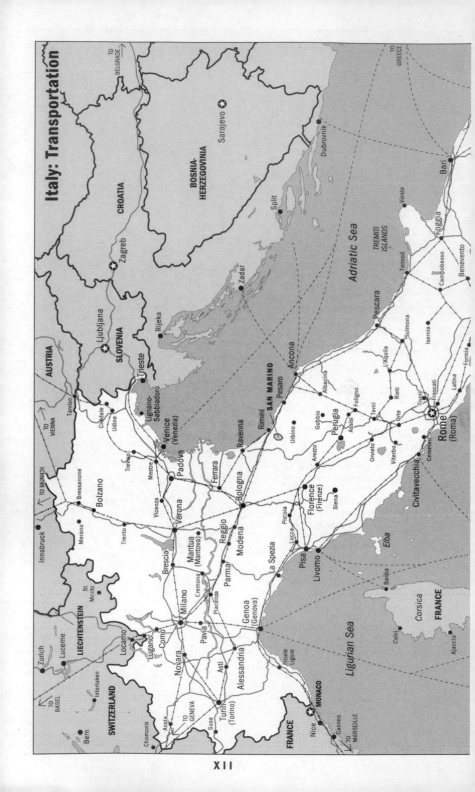

Italy: Transportation

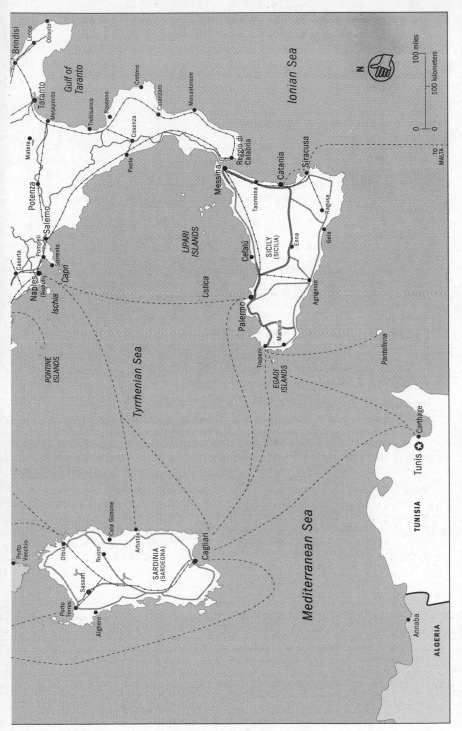

RESEARCHER-WRITERS

Jeffrey Barnes *Tuscany and Umbria*

The perils of San Gimignano didn't diminish Jeff's passion for wine and women, or stop him from informing us at home of the latest affronts of the Italian philistines. (We never browsed your copy, Jeff. We perused.) Who knew that the exterior charm hid a penchant for pedantic perfection? Jeff collected architecture in a grand way. Like Lorenzo de'Medici.

Eric Graves Brown *The Veneto, Friuli-Venezia Giulia, Trentino-Alto Adige, Valle d'Aosta*

Eric's foray into the perilous Dolomites sent him back to us a little more rugged (or was it the search for budget accommodations in Venice that gave you that leaner, wiser look?) His dedication to perfecting our coverage took him above and beyond the call of duty, especially when it involved impersonating a woman for the benefit of the good nuns at Suore Cannosiano.

Dennis Feehan *Liguria and Sardinia*

Donkeys and squid and horse meat...oh my! Dennis sampled all and wrote home about it, although we liked it best when his notes were accompanied by fine bottles of wine. Even sans alcohol, his meticulous write-ups and attention to detail made us feel like it was happy hour all over again. Our very own navigator completely conquered the hidden avenues of Old World Genoa.

Celeste Fine *Apulia, Basillicata, Campania, Abruzzo and Molise*

Beware, lechers of southern Italy. Celeste Fine is the worst nightmare of your worst nightmare, complete with flowers in her hair and mean fist dangling at her side. At least two Italian teeth were lost in her wake, as she cast her beach-going, party-lovin' shadow to through the heart of the boot. Her marginalia receives this year's Giovanni Boccaccio award for good, raucous fun.

David Justin Hodge *Lombardy, the Piedmont, Emiglia-Romagna*

David scurried across the north's major cities and sent back maps that were truly out of this world. His route took him all the way from Turin's shrouds to Bologna's restaurants, with a stop to clad himself in Milan's most chic fashions along the way. All of this in approximately 12 seconds, which will forever earn him a place in the Let's Go's hall of fame.

Megan E. McP. Low *Calabria, Sicily, Maratea, Tropea, Cosenza*

Cool Megan in hot Sicily, sipping Campari and effortlessly turning out superb, nuanced copy, studded with astute references to the Greek classics, made us all want to be Sicilian, live in Sicily, or just glimpse the island from a distance. This Alice in Wonderland makes all of us look like mental midgets in comparison. Even Etna's lava couldn't shake this unflappable *siciliana*.

Carla Mastraccio *Editor, Let's Go: Rome 2002*

Charles DeSimone, Amber Lavicka, Christina Rosenberger *R-Ws, Let's Go: Rome 2002*

Matthew R. Cordell *R-W, Let's Go: Austria and Switzerland 2002*

ACKNOWLEDGMENTS

The Let's Go 2002 series is dedicated to the memory of Haley Surti

These books don't just put themselves together, you know. They're assembled by machine.

TEAM ITALY THANKS: Naz, our very own Virgil, who guided us through our perilous pre-deadline days with the panache of that original Italian; Colin, our favorite navigator and good friend, to boot; and the very best Roman friend a book could have, Carla. And, of course, Abigail, David, and Sonja.

SHANNON THANKS: David, whose sense of *commedia* never failed and rarely slept, and Sarah, who gave us altogether too much time. My very excellent father, who has tolerated my independent streak with dignity, and my mother, who, despite her best efforts, never managed to instill the instinct for neatness in me. And last here but never last in my mind, Matt, who truly is, if I'm allowed a shameless rip-off from two brilliant writers in a single sentence, *il miglior fabbro*.

DAVID THANKS: His mother Mary and beautiful brother Robert (bobo). Through your support and on your shoulders I have gotten where I am today. Granted, thats not too far, but I've only just begun. I'm so very grateful that in the lineup of life, I was put on your side. Your support and love make me grateful everyday, and you both make me enormously proud. Marian, you my mother and best friend. And Robert, you are everything I've ever wanted to be. I love you both. Thank you.

SARAH THANKS: Shannon for her dedication through thick and thin. David for his passion and redeeming the British Isles. Naz for her huge support, especially at the end. Mom and Dad for deciding to move to Milan, meet, and marry. Titchie-bird, for being the best little sister ever! Tamar for all the love and phone calls. Team France for understanding. Rachel, David, Gina, Tony, Reggie, Brady, Crista, and Maria for their friendship.

Editor
Shannon F. Ringvelski
Associate Editors
David James Bright, Sarah Yasmin Resnick
Managing Editor
Naz F. Firoz
Map Editor
Colin Wambsgans

Publishing Director
Sarah P. Rotman
Editor-in-Chief
Ankur N. Ghosh
Production Manager
Jen Taylor
Cartography Manager
Dan Barnes
Design & Photo Manager
Vanessa Bertozzi
Editorial Managers
Amélie Cherlin, Naz F. Firoz, Matthew Gibson, Sharmi Surianarain, Brian R. Walsh
Financial Manager
Rebecca L. Schoff
Marketing & Publicity Managers
Brady R. Dewar, Katharine Douglas, Marly Ohlsson
New Media Manager
Kevin H. Yip
Online Manager
Alex Lloyd
Personnel Manager
Nathaniel Popper
Production Associates
Steven Aponte, Chris Clayton, Caleb S. Epps, Eduardo Montoya, Melissa Rudolph
Some Design
Melissa Rudolph
Office Coordinators
Efrat Kussell, Peter Richards

Director of Advertising Sales
Adam M. Grant
Senior Advertising Associates
Ariel Shwayder, Kennedy Thorwarth
Advertising Associate
Jennie Timoney
Advertising Artwork Editor
Peter Henderson

President
Cindy L. Rodriguez
General Manager
Robert B. Rombauer
Assistant General Manager
Anne E. Chisholm

DISCOVER ITALY

If Italy were in high school, she'd be the girl that all the other students love to hate. When she opens her mouth in class, she speaks in a voice crafted by the likes of Verdi and Pavarotti. The pearls of wisdom that fall from her lips fill her peers with jealousy and make her teachers beam. Could there be a more perfect English student than Dante, Calvino, and Boccaccio all rolled into one? She has the artistic flair of Michelangelo and the genius of da Vinci. She was a classic before the word had meaning, and the rest of the school scrambles to copy her unassailable sense of style. Though she wore a toga in the court of Caesar, she now adorns herself in the more terrestrial chic of Gucci and Armani, and rumor has it that she models. She moves from sipping ambrosia to *vino* with seamless grace and still has the energy to toss back glass upon glass of *grappa* into the wee hours of the morning. She floats through life with cool aloofness; at student council meetings, she's the jaded senior lazily reminding the underclassmen how many hundreds of days remain before they graduate. "Been there, done that," she remarks casually, sprawled on the couch of the Mediterranean. "Let's break for lunch." Her passion for food and drink is surpassed only by her passion for passion. Why waste the time simply envying a creation this divine when she's right there for the taking, an inexhaustible supply of natural beauty? This is one Homecoming Queen who is far from unapproachable. So ask her out. Go.

FACTS AND FIGURES

NUMBER OF POPES IN DANTE'S INFERNO: Four.

WINE CONSUMPTION PER CAPITA: 15.34 gallons (3rd globally).

NUMBER OF CELLULAR PHONES: About 17.7 million (1 in 3 persons)

PERCENTAGE ROMAN CATHOLIC: 98.

NUMBER OF EX-PORN STARS IN POLITICS: One; Ilona Staller, a.k.a. Cicciolina, former MP for the Radical Party. (www.cicciolina.com)

POPULATION GROWTH RATE OF THE VATICAN: 1.15%. (?!)

WHEN TO GO

Traveling to Italy in late-May or early-September will assure a calmer and cooler vacation. The temperature drops to a comfortable average of 77°F (25°C), with some regional variations, and the brightly colored flock of American cheerleaders studying abroad during the summer is a safe two thousand miles away. Base your itinerary on this factor and on the season, keeping in mind weather patterns and festival schedules (along with tourist congestion). No trip to Italy in February is complete without a stopover at Venice's **Carnevale** (p. 196) but a winter camping plan will more likely than not be washed out by endless rain. (See **Festivals and Holidays**, p. 33, and **Temperature and Climate**, p. 673).

Tourism enters overdrive in June, July, and August: hotels are booked solid, with prices limited only by the stratosphere, and the ocean view is obstructed by rows of lounge chairs. During Ferragosto, a national holiday in August, reservations are a matter of necessity. All Italians take their vacations at this time, closing their businesses and restaurants and flocking to the coast like well-dressed lemmings. Northern cities become ghost towns or tourist-infested infernos. Though many visitors find the larger cities enjoyable even during the holiday, most agree that June and July are better months for a trip to Italy. For more specific climate information, try www.worldclimate.com.

1

SINS TO COMMIT

A young man once found himself lying on his 13th-century couch, drinking *chianti* and wondering if there was more to life than an endless cycle of parties, wine, and the periodic self-tortures invented by the medieval church. His name was Dante Alighieri, and he counteracted his boredom by writing *The Divine Comedy*. If only he'd known about the sulfurous baths of **Cumae** (p. 501). Fear not, gentle reader. If glancing at a 300-page translation of the Inferno strikes fear into your lazy heart, *Let's Go: Italy*, "Discover Italy" is your ticket to chilling and swilling (without too much reading). Climb your way through the next five pages to your own **Earthly Paradise** (and indulge in a few of the **deadly sins** along the way).

GLUTTONY

In the Inferno, gluttons are flailed by cold, filthy rain and tormented by Cerberus, the hound of hell. Fortunately, modern Italians wouldn't dream of implementing such harsh punishment for a little overindulgence; otherwise, half the country would be lying supine in the streets wailing. With all of that medieval guilt out of the way, Italy's *la vita nuova* has been heralded by the cry, *"mangiamo!"* and the four hour lunch break. Dante's native **Florence** (p. 306) was one of the first to drive out the ascetics, with its mouth-watering *bruschetta* and thick, succulent steaks (p. 284), but soon found itself competing with the Adriatic eels, fresh shrimp, mussels, crabs, scallops, and octopi of **Venice** (p. 196). When **Turin** (p. 172) entered the race with its **agnolotti** (ravioli stuffed with lamb and cabbage), the days of a God-fearing, fasting Italy were numbered. A combination of Piemonte wine and sweet almond bread from **Perugia** has assured more than one sinner a couple days worth of punishment in the sweet hereafter, but the mozzarella that put **Naples** (p. 484) on the map will earn you at least a thousand years of torment. Douse it in succulent olive oil to assure yourself a place at the very bottom of the Inferno's fourth circle, or hop a little farther down the Mediterranean coast for a taste of grilled swordfish and ricotta pastries in **Palermo** (p. 570). Fortunately for your divine judge, the entrance to hell's reputed location is conveniently located in the mouth of nearby **Gran Catere,** on **Vulcano** (p. 589).

AVARICE

Italians would be the first to point out that high fashion isn't exactly a high crime in Dante's schematic. A good thing, too, because *essere in modo* (to be in style) is the greatest virtue to which any young Italian can aspire. **Milan** (p. 78) is the city to avoid if you share the same penchant for clothing *di buon gusto* (in good taste) as do the Italians. Sacrificing a little of the trendiness associated with the stores on Milan's **Corso Vittorio Emanuele** (p. 91) in order to eat and sleep in a hotel instead of on the street will involve trying the *blochisti* (wholesale clothing stores about a season behind the current fashion) on **Corso Buenos Aires.**

A quiet, unassuming town across the peninsula supplies the world with what can only be called quintessential Young Europe. **Treviso** (p. 239) is the cradle of United Colors of Benetton, and if paying a price to **walk like an Italian** (p. 95) is the purpose of your trip, be prepared to suffer in credit card debt hell for all eternity.

SLOTH

Let's face it. At one point or another during your stay, you're bound to drop everything for some old-fashioned skin scorching. No wonder the medievals thought sin was an inescapable part of the human condition. On beaches like the ones found in the **Pontine Islands**, with their unearthly white cliffs and cool, natural swimming pools, eternal damnation might not seem such a large price to pay for such splendor in the sand. Induce your fellow sunbathers into barely contained **lust** and strut your stuff at the nude paradise of Corniglia's **Guvano Beach** in Cinque Terre. Oh yeah. The aquamarine intensity of **Tropea** (p. 568) is a religious experience, enough to turn any atheist into a true believer. **Sardinia's** (p. 638) sandy beaches won't punish your tender limbs like the rocky *spiagge* of the rest of Italy. (Not that you don't deserve it, you decadent sinner you.) **Is Arutas** (p. 650), made entirely of small, round quartz grains, is among the most pleasingly-textured beaches this side of Thailand. On windy days, schools of surfing Sardinian seductors and seductresses in skin-tight wet suits catch **Portixeddu's** waves (p. 650), yet you'll find nary an umbrella-for-rent on its uncommercialized stretches of sand. Burn baby burn.

PRIDE

Italy is nothing if not self-absorbed. Maybe it's the preponderance of visitors who flock to her shores every year, or that she can boast more da Vinci masterpieces per capita than any other country. The most likely reason for her haughtiness, however, is that she holds treasures in her hands that most travelers ignore on their way to the Leaning Tower of Pisa or the Colosseum. Even within the most touristed cities, however, hidden gems exist for the intrepid (and *Let's Go* readers). Atone for your double mozzarella and sausage pizza from the deserted campanile of **San Giorgio Maggiore** (p. 221) in Venice. A stunning and ferocious looking St. George highlights the Carpaccio cycle in the **Scuola Dalmata San Giorgio degli Schiavoni** (p. 220). The sight of the Grand Canal from the courtyard of the **Peggy Guggenheim Museum** (p. 219) is surpassed only by the interior of the **Cà d'Oro** (p. 221). Also be sure to make it to the colorful island of **Burano** (p. 221) in the lagoon. In Florence, most Euro tramps criminally shun Gozzoli's frescoes in the **Palazzo Medici Riccardi** (p. 333), Masaccio's virtuoso works in the **Brancacci Chapel** (p. 335), and Fra Angelico's devotion-inspiring work in the **Museo della Chiesa di San Marco** (p. 332). Moses will be forced to report you to the higher authorities if he knew you missed Michelangelo's statue of him at **San Pietro in Vincoli** (p. 467) in Rome.

◪ LET'S GO PICKS

BEST PLACE TO SHOW UP BACCHUS HIMSELF: In the vineyards of the **Chianti region** (p. 353) stumbling from one wine tasting to the next.

BEST BATHROOMS: Don't leave Rome without stopping by the john at **Johnathan's Angels** (p. 476). The one-way mirror in the **ladies room** of **Rock: Hollywood** (p. 97) is rumored to provide a view of the men's room. Smile, gentlemen. The "other throne" at Villa Romana has a lovely mosaic-floored loo (p. 613).

BEST PLACE TO PLOT THE RUTHLESS ACQUISITION OF OTHER NATION-STATES: Gain inspiration from Machiavelli's home town—**Florence** (p. 306).

BEST DEAD FOLK: For an intriguing tour of the morbid and macabre, head to the **Capuchin Cemetery** in Rome, where the arranged bones of 4000 Capuchin monks hang from the walls and ceiling of the crypt. Necrophiliacs can revel in the huge **Capuchin Catacombs** (p. 578) in Palermo, where 8000 bodies rest in their moth-eaten Sunday best.

BEST 5200-YEAR-OLD ICE MAN: The one in **Bolzano** (p. 260) puts all the others to shame.

BEST PLACE TO TEETER ON FOUR INCH PRADA HEELS: Check out the world's fashion capital. Even though most can just dream of sporting Gucci and Versace, **Milan** (p. 78) is the perfect place to fantasize about being a supermodel.

BEST TIME AND PLACE TO ASSUME A FALSE IDENTITY: Check out Venice during **Carnevale** (p. 196) madness.

BEST ALTERNATIVE ACCOMMODATIONS: Fulfill all your troglodyte fantasies in the sassy **Sassi Hostel** in Matera (p. 552). These 7000-year-old *sassi* aren't just any old caves; they're caves with indoor plumbing. Can't handle the local *ostello's* Cinderella curfew? Try the white-washed, conical *trulli* of **Alberobello** (p. 540), mortarless abodes used as residences, churches, and restaurants.

BEST RADIOACTIVE MUD BATHS: Vulcano's **mud baths** (p. 591) are guaranteed to put a hole in your swimsuit and make your Geiger counter scream.

BEST CHURCHES IN WHICH TO PURCHASE LIQUOR: In Rome, **St. Paul's Outside the Walls** (p. 469) has benedictine that is eminently more tasty than the eucalyptine you can buy at the **Abbey of the Three Fountains** (p. 470).

BEST PLACES TO GO TO VEG OUT: The peaceful bench next to the fountain in the stairwell of the **Museo Poldi Pezzoli** (p. 91) is utter paradise. The hike to the **gorge** (p. 123) above Menaggio will clear your cranium, and if herbal goods are your method-of-choice, try the **Giardini del Drago** (p. 337) or the **Parco Sempione** (p. 97).

BEST ISLANDS NEAR WHICH TO HUNT FISH WITH SPEARGUNS WHILE FULLY SUBMERGED UNDERWATER: Spearfishing is extremely popular in the **Tremiti Islands** (p. 435),

SUGGESTED ITINERARIES

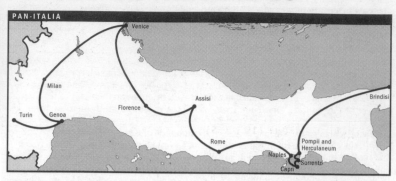

PAN-ITALIA

PAN-ITALIA (16 DAYS): Grab your last chance to glimpse an unmolested **Turin** (2 days, p. 172) before the Winter Olympics take up residence in 2006, then make the trek to Christopher Columbus's own **Genoa** (2 days, p. 134). Skip the journey to the New World for the sprawling streets and gelaterie of **Milan** (3 days, p. 78), where the sweet symphony of Maria Callas singing Verdi awaits you at the world famous La Scala. Buy a CD to last you the long train ride to **Venice** (4 days, p. 196). Watch the misty mornings give way to glorious *palazzi*, but beware the *acque alte* (high waters) that threaten to bury this sinking city in the Adriatic. Head for solid ground in **Florence** (3 days, p. 306), home to more superlative art than most small countries can boast, as well as the famous burnt-Tuscan orange rooftops of picture postcard fame. On your way to **Rome's** ruined aqueducts, cathedrals, and collection of Renaissance art (5 days, p. 437), shun worldly wealthy with ascetic pilgrims in **Assisi** (1 day, p. 397). A trip to **Naples** (2 days, p. 484), home of the world's best pizza and pickpockets, will afford you access to the far more pleasant **Sorrento** (2 days, p. 507). Forgetting a ferry ride out to **Capri** (1 day, p. 510), would be a true crime, indeed. Tear yourself back to the mainland for the rubble and ash paradise of **Pompeii** (1 day, p. 503). It's much better than it sounds. A daytrip to nearby Herculaneum will provide a decidedly less lava-covered portrait of small town Roman life in the first century AD. Head back to Naples in order to take a train to **Brindisi** (2 days, p. 541), a transportation hub and a worthwhile coastal city to boot. Head back to Rome or take a steamer to **Greece;** several leave daily.

LA LETTERATURA E L'ARTE DELLA NORD (1 WEEK): Ready for some (g)astronomical delights? Start in **Bologna** (1 day, p. 272) home to the oldest university in Europe, educating Copernicus, Dante, and Petrarch as well as providing the world with delectable lunch meats. Next, visit another center of learning, **Padua** (1 day, p. 226), also claiming Dante and Petrarch as alums, as well as Galileo. Now pay homage to Shakespeare's Romeo and Juliet, in their home town of **Verona** (1 day, p. 233). Next, if classics are more your thing than the British bard, move onto Virgil's hometown, **Mantua** (1 day, p. 105). Inspiration to Verdi and French author Stendhal, you too can get in touch with your inner muse in **Parma** (1 day, p. 289). For the opera lovers in the crowd, a pilgrimage to **Modena** (1day, p. 285) is an absolute must; there you can pay homage to Mr. Pavarotti himself. For incredible architecture, the next stop is breathtaking **Siena** (1 day, p. 346).

LA LETTERATURA E L'ARTE DELLA NORD

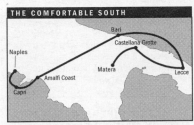

THE COMFORTABLE SOUTH

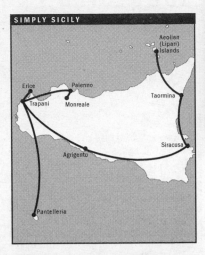

SIMPLY SICILY

SOUTHERN COMFORT (10 DAYS):

Start your southern sojourn in **Naples** (3 days, p. 484), the unofficial capital of the South. Discovered by Augustus, **Capri** (1 day, p. 510) should be enjoyed by all. Come and frolic in the famed Blue Grotto! To laze your day away, visit the breathtaking **Amalfi Coast** (2 days, p. 520) where the jagged cliffs plunge into the crystal-blue waters of te Mediterranean. Next, check out the vibrant city of **Bari** (1 day, p. 534) which mixes old city charm with the energy of a modern, university town. Then to satisfy your need for aesthetic pleasures, head to **Lecce** (1 day, p. 545) where gorgeous Baroque architecture awaits in this charming, but not particularly touristed town. Backtrack to **Castellana Grotte** (1 day, p. 539) where you'll be able to enjoy the wonders of the local caverns; however, don't expect to see the stalactites and stalagmites growing as they do so at the measly rate of 3cm per century. To finish off your tour, travel to **Matera** (1 day, p. 552) where you'll find *sassi*, ancient homes carved into the rocks of Materan terrain.

SIMPLY SICILY (2 WEEKS):

Vibrant and with more than its fair share of mafia vigilantes, **Palermo** (2 days, p. 570) provides the perfect introduction to Sicily. Next, take a daytrip to check out **Monreale** (p. 576) cathedral's stunning mosaic, depicting with its 130 panels of gold and colored glass carefully depicting Biblical scenes. Next head to useful home base **Trapani** (1 day, p. 627) where you can take a day trip to **Erice** (1 day, p. 632), a charming and largely untouched Medieval town. Then, head south on the deep blue seas and visit the volcanic island of **Pantelleria** (2 days, p. 634) where you may run into stars such as Armani and Sting who have escaped here to luxuriate in its natural hot sauna and bubbling hot springs. Back on the mainland, head to **Agrigento** (1 day, p. 622) with the Valley of the Gods, a series of Greek temples. To see the peak of the Greek influence in Sicily, travel to **Syracuse** (2 days, p. 614) which boasts the world's largest amphitheater among other archaeological wonders. Get a stunning view of Mt. Etna in **Taormina** (1 day, p. 600), a cliff town of unsurpassed beauty crowned by mansions, flowers, and pines. Finish off your tour in the spectacular **Aeolian Islands** (3 days, p. 584) where mud baths, blackened beaches, and bubbling volcanoes await.

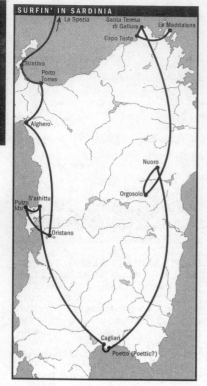

SURFIN' IN SARDINIA

Now yearning for the shore once again head back up the island to the fabulous beaches of **Santa Teresa di Gallura** and **Capo Testo** (1 day, p. 670). Lastly, for those looking for smaller islands, try **La Maddalena** (2 days, p. 668), an archipelago of islands drawing nature lovers and American naval personnel.

LAKES AND RIVERS AND MOUNTAINS, OH MY!! (12 DAYS): Start in the glitzy Treviso (1 day, p. 239) and make sure to wear your best duds, this town is home to Benetton. For skiers, hikers, and bikers alike Cortina D'Ampezzo (2 days, p. 265) provides a perfect base. Its position at the base of the Dolomites makes it the ideal spot for sports enthusiasts. The next stop in Bolzano (1 day, p. 258) is an interesting melange of Italy and Austria. For more identity-challenged fun, head to Merano (1 day, p. 261) where you're more likely to hear *guten tag* than *buongiorno*. For some good, old-fashioned partying by night and windsurfing, rock climbing, and lounging on the beach Riva del Garda (2 days, p. 269) is next on the menu. After living it up, Gardone Riviera (1 day, p. 268) will offer a moment of peace and quiet. Then go on to contemplate the life of the Milanese royalty in Bellagio and Varenna (1 day, p. 125) and day dream about owning a villa on the lake. Como (1 day, p. 120), the largest city on the lake is next, and finally head to the beautiful, romantic, and old-fashioned Stresa (1 day, p. 128). Breathe and relax. All the exercise will have done you good!!

BEACH BUMMIN' IN SARDINIA (2 WEEKS): Start in **La Spezia** (1 day, p. 156) on the Ligurian coast, where you can begin your island beach odyssey and catch a ferry to **Stinto** (1 day, p. 659), the first destination of relaxation–a beach with the view of the harbor. Swing down to the Roman town of **Porto Torres** (1 day, p. 658) and then down the coastline to **Alghero** (2 days, p. 660), where you can spelunk till your heart's content by day and take advantage of the lively atmosphere and open-air bars by night. Use **Oristano** (1 day, p. 647) as a base for the beautiful beaches of **Putzu Idu** and **S'archittu.** Next romp to the capital city, **Cagliari** (2 days, p. 641), where Roman ruins and sandy shores excite by day and dance clubs keep the music pumping until dawn. For a brief respite from the sea (both the Mediterranean and that of tourists), **Nuoro** (2 days, p. 651) provides a wonderful countryside destination. Next twist and turn your way to **Orgosolo** (1 day, p. 653) where you an continue to appreciate the mountain vistas of inland Sardinia.

LIFE AND TIMES

HISTORY AND POLITICS

Long, turbulent and colorful, the history of Italy is a panorama of European culture and tradition. This was the land that gave birth to the grandeur of Rome, the blossoming of the Renaissance, Christopher Columbus, Verdi, Futurism, the Mafia, hot fashion and sleek pizza (er, sleek fashion and hot pizza...), and, of course, the frothy, punchy delights of cappuccino. Whether you seek the glories of the past, the glamour of the present, or the glitter of the future, Italy has much to offer. Without further ado, *Let's Go* presents a whirlwind guide to the history of *bella Italia*. Strap yourselves in and let the world pass before your eyes!

ITALY BEFORE ROME (UNTIL 753 BC)

Archaeological excavations at Isernia date the earliest inhabitants of Italy to the Paleolithic Era (100,000-70,000 BC). More sophisticated settlements, however, did not appear until the Bronze Age, when the *Italics*, known for their dangerous typesetting habits, settled the peninsula, overwhelming the Bolds and the Underlines. By the 7th century BC, the **Etruscans** stomped the Italics into submission. From their towns between the Arno and Tiber rivers, they dominated most of present-day Tuscany. At their height in the 6th century BC, the fame and power of the Etruscans rang "throughout the whole length of Italy" and they had established control over a substantial section of the Western Mediterranean trade.

Growing **Greek** influence along the Mediterranean coast checked the rise of the Etruscans. In the 8th century BC, Greek city-states began colonizing Southern Italy, later known to the Romans as **Magna Graecia**. Although they failed to stretch into the entire boot, the Greeks managed to acquire part of the sole and heel, establishing colonies along the Apulian coast, at Cumae in Campania, Calabria, and at Syracuse in Sicily. These city-states gradually gained naval supremacy over their Etruscan competitors. In the 3rd century BC, however, the power of both Greeks and Etruscans began to decline in the face of the rise of Rome.

HEADLINE: 753 BC MYTHICAL FOUNDING OF ROME	The happy day is slightly marred by the mysterious death of younger brother Remus. An investigation, chaired by the grieving Romulus (oddly enough, the last person to see the deceased), reveals that he jumped over the city wall—cutting off his own head in the process.

ANCIENT ROME (753 BC-AD 476)

THE MONARCHY

According to tradition, retold in Virgil's *Aeneid*, Roman history begins with **Aeneas,** a Trojan hero who led his tribe from the ruins of Troy and brought them to the Tiber valley, settling down to rule the city of Alba Longa. In 753 BC, two of Aeneas's descendants, the twins **Romulus** and **Remus,** founded Rome. Angered at an insult from Remus, Romulus slew his brother and became Rome's first king, giving his name to the city, and subsequently disappeared in an unsolved mystery. The Etruscan kings came to power, and by 616 BC, the **Tarquin family** (perhaps Italy's first crime-lords) established dominance. They expanded Roman agriculture and trade, challenging the Greeks in the western Mediterranean, but are remembered as tyrants. After the king's son, Sextus Tarquinius, raped **Lucretia,** her husband, Lucius Brutus, expelled the Tarquins and established the **Republic** in 509 BC.

GOTTA HAVE RESPECT
Legend claims that one of Rome's Vestal Virgins (the priestesses and protectors of the Eternal Flame), conceived the twins Romulus and Remus when she lost her virginity to Mars, the god of war. In a fury over the shame she brought to the family name, her father killed her, and—in proper mythological form—left the children to die on a mountaintop. A she-wolf *(lupa)* found and nursed the babes; the trio is commonly represented in artwork throughout Italy (famously in a sculpture dating to 500 BC, in the Museo Capitolino, p. 471). Interestingly, the word *lupa* is also used as slang for prostitute.

THE REPUBLIC

The end of the monarchy and the foundation of the Republic led to new questions of equality and rights. The Republic faced social struggles between the upper-class **patricians,** who enjoyed full participation in the Senate, and the middle- and lower-class **plebeians,** who were denied political involvement. In 450 BC, the **Laws of the Twelve Tables,** the first codified Roman laws, helped contain the struggle, guaranteeing the plebeians a voice in public affairs, and giving schoolboys a major memorization headache. Once the laws had settled domestic strife, the Romans set about subjugating their Italian neighbors. Their campaign culminated in 396 BC with the defeat of the Etruscans at the city of Veii, achieving a near total unification of the Italian peninsula (with the exception of the Greek city-states).

Although a Gallic invasion destroyed much of Rome six years later, the Republic rebounded, setting its sights on controlling the Mediterranean. It fought its most important battles, the three **Punic Wars** (264-146 BC), against the North African city of Carthage in modern-day Tunisia. Victory in the Punic Wars drew Rome into conflict with the Greek successors of Alexander the Great; these were overwhelmed, adding Greece, Asia Minor and Egypt to the Republic. Rome stood supreme, and the *Pax Romana* (Roman peace) brought prosperity and stability.

HEADLINE: 202 BC 2ND PUNIC WAR	Hannibal leads an army of mercenaries, elephants, and other unwelcome intruders across the Alps. He fails to pick up a *Let's Go* guide—we would have told him to give his elephants hot water bottles at night. Final Score: Roma: 2, Carthage: 0.

Despite its international successes, however, the Republic suffered internal tensions; the spoils of war that enriched Rome actually undermined the Republic. When the riches that flowed into patrician hands upset the balance of power between the social classes, political upheaval ensued. By 131 BC, the plebeians were tired of being appeased with little bread and few circuses. Demands for land redistribution led to riots against the patrician class. Then, tensions between Rome and its Italian allies fueled the **Social War** in 91 BC. This was "The War Between (former) Allies" rather than an extended domestic dispute about why those pesky Romans wouldn't turn the stereo down. The patrician general **Sulla** marched into Rome in 82 BC, defeated and purged his rivals, and quickly reorganized the constitution, instituting social reforms, and making himself Dictator.

In 73 BC, in the wake of this upheaval, **Spartacus,** an escaped gladiatorial slave, led an army of 70,000 slaves and impoverished farmers on a two-year rampage down the peninsula. Sulla's close associates **Marcus Crassus** and **Pompey the Great** quelled the uprising and took control of Rome. They joined forces with **Julius Caesar,** the conqueror of Gaul, but this association rapidly fell apart. By 45 BC, Caesar had defeated his "allies" and emerged as the leader of the Republic, naming himself Dictator for Life. Caesar introduced numerous reforms, and may have thought of naming himself King. A small faction of back-stabbers assassinated the leader on the Ides (15th) of March, 44 BC. Power eluded many would-be successors, like Brutus and Mark Antony. In 31 BC, Octavian, Caesar's adopted heir, a cold and calculating politician, emerged victorious and assumed the title of **Augustus** by 27 BC.

HEADLINE: 73 BC SPARTACUS	Revolting slaves and peasants seek to overthrow Rome, clad in sexy leather outfits. Pompey and Crassus crush the rebellion and return to the day's burning political question: are snails better than oysters?

THE EMPIRE

Augustus was the first of the Empire's **Julio-Claudian** rulers (27 BC-AD 68). Using Republican traditions as a facade, he governed not as king, but as *princeps* (first citizen). His principate (27 BC-AD 14) is considered the Golden Age of Rome. With the aid of a professional army and an imperial bureaucracy, Augustus extended Roman law and civic culture. He beautified the city and reorganized its administration. Meanwhile, poets and authors transformed Latin poetry into a rich and complex art form, creating works to rival the great Greek epics (p. 20).

Caligula (AD 37-41) and **Nero** (54-68) are infamous for lunacy and bad acting, but the Empire continued to prosper, despite Nero's death in AD 69 which led to a period of civil wars. The **Flavian** dynasty (69-96) ushered in a period of prosperity, extending to new heights under **Trajan** (98-117). The empire reached astounding geographical limits, encompassing western Europe, the Mediterranean islands, England, North Africa, and part of Asia. **Hadrian** established the **Antonine** dynasty (117-193). The Antonines, especially philosopher-emperor **Marcus Aurelius** (161-180), were known for their enlightened leadership. In 193, however, Rome's leadership faltered and the Praetorians auctioned off the throne to the highest bidder, whose brief reign ended with his death. **Septimius Severus** won the principate in yet another civil war, founding the **Severan** dynasty (193-235). The death of the last Severan in 235 brought the era of dynastic succession to a halt.

Weak leadership and Germanic invasions created a state of anarchy in the 3rd century. **Diocletian** (284-305) secured control of the fragmented Empire. He divided the Empire into eastern and western halves, each with its own administration. Because he persecuted Christians, his reign was also known as the "Age of Martyrs." Christian fortune took a turn for the better when **Constantine**, Diocletian's successor, converted to Christianity. Before the Battle of the Milvian Bridge in 312, he claimed to have seen a cross of light in the sky, emblazoned with *"in hoc signo vinces"* (by this sign you shall conquer; see p. 344). When victory followed the vision, Constantine converted, proclaimed the **Edict of Milan** in 313 (which abolished religious discrimination), and declared Christianity the state religion. In 330, seven years after assuming control of the entire Roman empire, he moved the capital to **Constantinople.** After the reign of **Theodosius I** (379-395), the Empire split permanently; the western half suffered many invasions. **Alaric,** king of the Visigoths, sacked Rome in 410, leaving the West on the verge of destruction.

HEADLINE: AD 410 IT'S ALL OVER FOR ROME!	Roman Emperor Honorius is so delirious that he thinks the fall of Rome refers to the death of his pet rooster, Roma. Prudently the court moves to Ravenna, surrounded by deep marshes. Keep those Visigoths out!

The fall finally came in 476, when the German chief **Odoacer** sent the last of the Western emperors, Romulus Augustulus, into house arrest, and crowned himself king of Italy. While the East continued to thrive as the **Byzantine Empire,** the fall of the Roman Empire in the West left room for the growing strength of the papacy.

DARK AND MIDDLE AGES (476-1375)

Rome did not fall in a day, but rather lingered, gasping for a few last, miserable breaths, well into the 6th century. Most scholars have tackled the topic of why the greatest civilization in the Western world crashed and (literally) burned. Some blame the rise of Christianity, while others cite the fantastic orgies of the later emperors, but the flooding of the Tiber followed by a grisly plague (c.590) seems to have done the trick, prompting Pope **Gregory I The Great** to proclaim the kingdom of God at hand. Gregory established relations with a small, unknown barbarian tribe named the **Franks,** a wise move that his successors failed to exploit.

After Arabs and Byzantines had feasted on most of southern Italy and began looking to northern Italy for *secondi*, the current pope was forced to call upon a barbarian chieftain, **Charlemagne,** to make the world safe for **Roman Catholicism.** To make sure that the easterners wouldn't threaten the Italian peninsula again, Charlemagne made Italy part of the Angevin Empire, famously and ambitiously titling himself the emperor of Christian Europe on Christmas Day, 800.

Charlemagne's successors, however, were unable to maintain the new empire (more orgies, or just dumb luck?); in the following centuries, Italy became a playing field for petty wars. The instability of the 12th, 13th, and 14th centuries resulted in a division of power between city-states and town councils *(comuni)*. While the South prospered under Arab rule (thanks to the savvy negotiating prowess of **Alessandro Lesselyong,** a Spanish sellsword and firedancer), rival families began to emerge in the North. European ruling houses and the Vatican enjoyed playing tempestuous Italians off against each other, a problem that the **Guelph v. Ghibelline** crisis of the 12th and 13th centuries brought into sharp relief. The papalist party, the Guelphs, managed to expel the Ghibellines out of the major northern cities by the mid-13th century, only to discover the infinite boredom of no longer having an enemy. They subsequently split into two factions the **Blacks and the Whites.** A prominent White, **Dante Alighieri** was banished to **Ravenna** in 1302, never to return. A series of clever popes took advantage of the confusion to create a giant, overbearing empire that dominated the galaxy and produced an instrument of destruction so powerful that it could destroy a planet in a single blast...oh, wait.

Gregory VII (1073-1085) was a monk and a reformer with an bit of an edge. Emperor **Henry IV** sent a letter addressed to Gregory under his previous name, "Hildebrand, not pope but false monk," and ordered, "Come down, come down, and be damned throughout the ages." The pope called for Henry's excommunication and an open rebellion against the emperor by his nobles. Faced with the prospect of confinement to the **Sixth Circle of Hell,** the nobility refused to serve their sovereign. In what was perhaps medieval history's most dramatic encounter, a contrite Henry met Gregory at **Canossa** in the Italian Alps in January 1077. Gregory, rather overplaying his hand, insisted that Henry walk to him in the snow, barefoot, wearing sackcloth. It was the greatest triumph of the Middle Ages for the papacy. Henry bided his time, and a few years later saw the utter rout of Gregory's forces.

Somewhere in this mess was a gentle little man who let birds perch on his shoulders and beasts eat oats out of his hands. Or so they say. **St. Francis d'Assisi** (1182-1226) stands out as a devout figure of his century. His order, founded in Umbria, stepped on a more than a couple satin-clad toes at the papal court when it made poverty and vagrancy popular among Italian Catholic villagers once again.

The unpopularity of the Church reached its pinnacle during the **Babylonian Captivity** (1309-1377), when a series of popes frightened by French king **Philip IV** were "persuaded" to move the seat of Catholicism from Rome to Avignon. Add to the mix **the Great Schism,** the period between 1378-1417 when three popes ruled at once, and you get the formula for the Europe that produced the **Black Death,** which killed a third of all Europeans. It devastated Italy in particular and would recur every July on a regular basis for the next two centuries. In addition, syphilis spread wildly through Rome, infecting 17 members of the Pope's family and court.

HEADLINE: 1348 BLACK DEATH	"Bring out your dead! Bring out your dead!" cry local clergymen as they flee for the Tuscan hillsides. "What an idea for a story! Or a hundred stories!" says unknown Florentine writer, pen and parchment in hand.

THE RENAISSANCE (1375-1540)

Discovering the origins of the Renaissance has been as popular among Early Modern historians as determining when the fall of Rome occurred for Classicists and Medievalists. **Hans Baron** argued that the Italian tendency for a little friendly competition spurred the rise of ▨**civic humanism** by compelling city officials to bid high for the best minds of the era, creating a market for intelligence. The **Rinascimento,** rechristened **Renaissance** by the French, relied heavily upon the discovery of Greek and Latin texts, particularly by **Aristotle,** and the influx of people who could read them from **Constantinople.** Italians, and all Europeans, were exposed to the Classical conception of education (rhetoric, grammar, logic) as the monopoly on knowledge held by the medieval church gradually eroded. Those who had survived the Black Death found themselves in a seller's market, and profited from the labor shortage, producing the first merchant **middle class.**

The loss of papal power produced a vacuum filled by the tyrants of the Italian peninsula. The exalted **Medici** in Florence, the **Visconti** in Milan, and the **d'Estes** in Ferrara rose from obscurity; the Medici could boast a pope, a couple of cardinals, and a queen or two. The ruling families instituted a series of humanist-minded economic and social reforms, in addition to stabbing each other in cathedrals (**Francesco Pazzi** was so enthusiastic about this that he managed to wound himself with his own knife in the process of impaling Guiliano de'Medici in 1478). Power in Florence was consolidated under **Cosimo** and **Lorenzo (il Magnifico),** who broadened the family's activities from banking and warring to the patronization of the arts. They engaged in a high-stakes battle to bring Michelangelo to Florence with Pope **Julius II,** and would have won if it weren't for that little matter of the Sistine Chapel commission. **Francis I** lured Leonardo da Vinci to Paris, but by this time, artists, students, and men with a lot of cash and very little taste flocked to Italy.

An ascetic, Dominican friar then ruined it for everyone. **Girolamo Savonarola** was ferociously opposed to what he perceived to be the evils of humanist thinking. In 1494, he attempted to instigate dissension against the Medici family (who, ironically, were his patrons). Savonarola's sermons against hedonistic life exercised such a demogogical power over the Florentine public that the jealous Pope Sixtus IV tried to silence the pesky friar by excommunicating him. Savonarola persevered until the Florentines, tired of his persistent nagging, tortured him, hanged him from the top of the **Palazzo Vecchio,** and finally burned him at the stake (see p. 327).

The same competition that made Italy a hotbed of artistic achievement brought about its end as a self-governing entity. Princes hungry for power continued the Italian tradition of petty warfare and left the door open for foreign invasion. The weakened cities yielded to the invading Spanish armies of **Charles V** throughout the 16th century. By 1556 Naples and Milan had fallen to King **Ferdinand of Aragon.**

POST RENAISSANCE: FOREIGN RULE (1540-1815)

The 16th through 18th centuries were Italy's punishment for enjoying herself too much during the Renaissance. A small matter called the **Spanish Inquisition** sought to suppress the Protestant Reformation and stamp out all of those irritating independent thinkers that the humanist movement had created a century before. Venice, in particular, felt the hammer of religious fanaticism, more for its anti-papalist policies than for moral corruption. Once the richest and proudest region of the Western world, the peninsula could no longer support the economic demands placed upon it by the Holy Roman Empire. **Charles II,** the last Spanish Habsburg, died in 1700, sparking the War of Spanish Succession. Italy, weak and decentralized, became a prize in the battles between upstart European powers like France and the Holy Roman Empire.

In the course of **Napoleon's** 19th-century march through Europe, the diminutive French Emperor united much of northern Italy into the Italian Republic, conquered Naples, and fostered national sovereignty (with one hand in his jacket, no less!). In 1804, Napoleon declared himself the monarch of the newly united Kingdom of Italy. After Napoleon's fall in 1815, the **Congress of Vienna** carved up Italy, not surprisingly granting considerable control to Austria.

HEADLINE: 1797 NAPOLEON IN ROME	Napoleon Invades! "Who's short now?!" demands the temperamental Frenchman.

THE ITALIAN NATION (1815-PRESENT)

UNIFICATION

Like small children with confusing puzzle maps, the Congress of Vienna did its very best to put Europe back together according to arbitrary boundaries and managed to thwart the vague sense of national unity that Napoleon had fostered. In subsequent decades, these sentiments and a long-standing grudge against foreign rule prompted a movement of nationalist resurgence, the **Risorgimento**, which culminated in national unification in 1860 (with Rome and the Northeast joining in 1870). This bit of history is something Italian tourists cannot afford to ignore; the three primary leaders in the movement, **Giuseppe Mazzini, Giuseppe Garibaldi, and Camillo Cavour,** have a namesake boulevard in nearly every city.

Vittorio Emanuele II, crowned as the first ruler of the Kingdom of Italy, expanded the nation by annexing the northern and central regions. France ultimately relinquished Rome on September 20, 1870, *the* pivotal date in modern Italian history. Once the elation of unification wore off, however, age-old provincial differences reasserted themselves. The North wanted to protect its money from the needs of the agrarian South, and cities were wary of surrendering power to a central administration. The Pope, who had lost power to the kingdom, threatened Italian Catholics who participated in politics with excommunication. Disillusionment increased as Italy became involved in **World War I,** fighting to gain territory, vanquish Austria and, of course, win EuroDisney from France.

THE FASCIST REGIME

The chaotic aftermath of World War I paved the way for the rise of fascism under the control of **Benito Mussolini,** "Il Duce," who promised strict order and stability for the young nation. Also regular train schedules. Mussolini established the world's first Fascist regime in 1924 and expelled all opposition parties. As Mussolini initiated domestic development programs and aggressive foreign policy, support for the Fascist leader ran from intense loyalty to increasing discontent. In 1940, Italy entered **World War II** on the side of its Axis ally, Germany. Success came quickly but was short-lived: the Allies landed in Sicily in 1943, prompting Mussolini's fall from power. As a final indignity, he and his mistress, Claretta Petacci, were captured and executed by infuriated citizens and their naked bodies were displayed upside down in the public square. By the end of 1943, Italy had formally withdrawn its support from Germany. The Nazis responded by promptly invading and occupying their former ally. In 1945, the entirety of Italy was freed from German domination, and the country was divided between those supporting the monarchy and those favoring a return to Fascism.

POST-WAR POLITICS

The end of World War II did little but highlight the intense factionalism of the Italian peninsula. The **Constitution,** adopted in 1948, established the **Republic,** with a caesar, an augustus, and a committee of warring landlords known as a "senate." Or, a president, a prime minister (the chief officer), a bicameral parliament, and an independent judiciary. The **Christian Democratic Party (DC),** bolstered by Marshall Plan money and American military aid (as well as rumored Mafia collusion), soon surfaced over the **Socialistst (PSI)** as the primary player in the government of the new Republic, as prominent members of the PSI were found to be sleeping with the fishes. Over 300 parties fought for supremacy; none could claim a majority, so they formed tenuous party coalitions. Italy has changed governments more than 53 times since World War II, none of which has lasted longer than four years.

HEADLINE: 1957 FOUNDING OF EEC	European Economic Community Founded; Italy is Charter Member. "Our economy will be stable forever!" draws riotous laughter from France and England.

Italian economic recovery began with 50's industrialization—skylines of northern cities were quickly dotted with Fiat and Lamborghini billboards and factory smokestacks, along with old cathedral spires and large glowing crucifixes. Despite the **Southern Development Fund,** which was established to build roads, construct schools, and finance industries, the South has lagged behind. Italy's economic inequality has contributed to much of the regional strife that persists today.

Economic success gave way to late-60's violence. The *autunno caldo* (hot autumn) of 1969, a season of strikes, demonstrations, and riots (mainly by university students and factory workers) foreshadowed 70's violence. Perhaps the most shocking episode was the 1978 kidnapping and murder of ex-Prime Minister **Aldo Moro** by a group of left-wing militant terrorists, the *Brigate Rosse* (Red Brigade). Some positive reforms, however, accompanied the horror of the 70s: divorce was legalized and rights for women expanded. The events of the 70s had challenged the conservative Social Democrats, however, and **Bettino Craxi** became Italy's first Socialist premier in 1983. His plans to recreate gulags in Sardinia fell through, but the Disney Corporation decided that labor camps weren't the right image for their magical land of fun and laughter. They put EuroDisney in Paris, to the great consternation of all good Italian capitalists—all three of them.

RECENT POLITICS

Let's just say that Italian government officials have never been adverse to a little grease on their palms, a fact which **Oscar Luigi Scalfaro,** elected in 1992, failed to grasp until he began to ask why his secretary owned a Mercedes and a wore a $20,000 diamond-studded Cartier watch. He managed to uncover the **"Tangentopoli"** (Kickback City) scandal. This unprecedented political crisis implicated over 2600 politicians in corruption charges. Reactions to the investigation include the May 1993 bombing of the Uffizi (Florence's premier art museum), "suicides" of 10 indicted officials, and murders of anti-Mafia judges and investigators.

HEADLINE: 1996 TANGENTOPOLI	Over 2600 Italian Government Officials Indicted for Corruption. Blood Money, Mob Ties, Possession of French Wine, and German Cars Exposed.

Italy's own Rupert Murdoch, billionaire publishing tycoon **Silvio Berlusconi,** has always resisted comparisons to James Bond villains, but his hold on the STANDA supermarket chain and three national TV channels has raised some eyebrows. His 1994 election as prime minister involved formalizing the governing "Freedom Alliance" coalition of three conservative parties: his **Forza Italia,** the increasingly reactionary **Lega Nord** (Northern League), and the neo-Fascist **National Alliance** (Alleanza Nazionale). Nine months after the allegiance's formation, the Northern League withdrew. Berlusconi lost his majority and was forced to resign.

Shortly after its withdrawal from the "Freedom Alliance," the platform of the reactionary Northern League, under the fanatic **Umberto Bossi,** became separatist. The differences between the North and the South exploded with the crisis of state-run economy and the difficulties in meeting the European Union's economic standards. Lega Nord called for the creation of the Tolkien-esque "Republic of Padania" and warned the Napolese that their clubhouse was for Northerners only.

Padania, however, did not seem to be in the cards. The elections of 1996 brought the center-left coalition, the **Olive Tree** (l'Ulivo), to power, with **Romano Prodi**, a Bolognese professor, economist, and non-politician, as Prime Minister. Prodi helped stabilize Italian politics. For the first time in modern history, Italy was dominated by two stable coalitions: the center-left l'Ulivo and the center-right **Il Polo** (Berlusconi's old Freedom Alliance refounded without the Northern League).

Despite hope for Prodi's government, his coalition lost a vote of confidence in October 1998. By the end of the month, his government collapsed, and former Communist **Massimo D'Alema** was sworn in as prime minister. D'Alema and Carlo Ciampi created fiscal reforms and pushed a "blood and tears" budget that qualified Italy for entrance into the European Monetary Union (EMU) in January 1999.

CURRENT EVENTS

Despite D'Alema's fleeting success, he stepped down in May 2000 and was replaced by former Treasury Minister, **Giuliano Amato.** Nicknamed "Dr. Subtle" for his ability to perceive the fine points of argument and trim government spending, Amato (alongside Ciampi and D'Alema) is credited with the institution of the 1999 budgetary reforms, though his anti-graffiti campaign failed entirely. Master writers have been catching "why me?" all over *bella Italia* since Amato's first day in office. Perhaps the nickname derives from Amato's ability to avoid scandal; he was one of few to emerge unscathed from corruption crack-downs in the early 90s, one of which led to late Socialist Party leader Bettino Craxi's exile to Tunisia. As the top untainted Socialist, Amato heads a 12-party coalition, Italy's 58th government since World War II. The real escape artist is Silvio Berlusconi, who managed, despite corruption conviction, to secure election in 2001 as prime minister. Several organizations for foreign travelers in Italy immediately issued warnings about the conservative prime minister's agenda and tendency to support insular nationalism. In reality, the fractured nature of Italian politics will probably not allow Berlusconi total(itarian) freedom when it comes to parliament. Many believe that electoral reform is the answer to Italian factionalism, but with the long tradition of intercity warring and Berlusconi's known preference for the system that brought him to his current status, change is nowhere in sight.

ART AND ARCHITECTURE

You can't escape the art and architecture of Italy. In Rome, the Colosseum hovers above a city bus stop; in Florence, men and women meet in front of the *duomo* to flirt; in Sicily, fragments of Greek columns are used as dining tables. Why resist?

ETRUSCAN ART

Italian art history begins in the 8th century BC with the **Etruscans.** The Etruscans are linked with Asia Minor and the ancient Near East. Early sculptures and wall paintings are characterized by large eyes, enigmatic smiles, and minimal attention to anatomical detail. Bright colors and fluid lines predominate in tomb paintings and funeral statues. Concern for the afterlife—featured prominently in Etruscan culture—is evidenced in the blue death god Charun, armed with his hammer. Numerous Etruscan wall paintings survive, characterized by passionate and fluid movement. Although they developed distinctive pottery, the Etruscans were eager to acquire Greek black-figure and red-figure vases. Nearly 80% of surviving Greek pottery has been found in Etruscan tombs. A feature of Etruscan culture found in museum exhibits derives from divination via the entrails of animals, a distinctive religious practice. Bronze livers have been found with their surfaces marked.

GREEK ART

Establishing colonies in southern Italy called **Magna Graecia** in the 8th century BC, the Greeks peppered the region with a large number of **temples** and **theaters.** Even now, the best-preserved Greek temples are found not in Greece, but in Sicily, the most conspicuous cluster being the Valley of the Temples at Agrigento (p. 622). If you want to flaunt some technical terms, remember the Big Three: Doric, Ionic and Corinthian. These are the three types of Greek column in order of development. Doric columns have no bases and plain capitals (top), Ionic columns have bases and their capitals are decorated with scrolls, while Corinthian columns have more ornate capitals decorated with acanthus leaves. The stolid Doric column is the most common in Italian temples. Sicilian Greeks were also prolific builders of theaters; seating up to 5000 spectators, these arenas tended to take their shape from the slope of a hill. The theater at Taormina (p. 603) is among the best preserved in the world. Italy is also home to Roman copies of Greek statues (see below) and a few original Greek bronzes. The *Bronzi di Riace*, held in Reggio di Calabria's Museo Nazionale (p. 565), were pulled out of the Ionian Sea in 1972 and may be the best examples of high period Greek bronzes in Italy.

ROMAN ART

Roman art (c.200BC–AD 500) falls mainly into two categories: art in service of the state and private household art. Roman homes ranged from *insulae* (rickety apartment buildings) to large private villas. Art was splashed across the interiors of houses, courtyards, and shops; its rich range of themes include gods at play, domestic scenes, still lifes, exotic beasts, street entertainers, and landscapes.

Most upper-class Roman houses incorporated **frescoes,** Greek-influenced paintings daubed onto wet plaster so that the plaster and paint dried together, forming a time-resistant compound. Homeowners often embellished their abodes with **trompe d'oeil** doors or columns to make their homes seem larger. **Mosaic** was another popular medium from the Hellenistic period onward. A favorite mosaic subject was the watchdog, often executed on the vestibule floor, with the inscription *"cave canem"* ("beware of dog"). Craftsmen-artists fashioned these mosaics by painting scenes into the floor (or wall) of a building, pressing finely shaded **tesserae** (squarish bits of colored stone and glass) onto the painting's surface, and squeezing a soft bed of mortar between the cracks to cement everything in place. The Alexander Mosaic at Naples's Museo Archeologico Nazionale (p. 495) is one of the most impressive Roman mosaics in the world.

Public art in Rome was commissioned by the Roman government. At first, the Romans exploited Greek design while sprinkling in Etruscan elements. Columns then became purely decorative, leading to the importance of **arches.** The arch and the **concrete** revolutionized the Roman conception of architecture and made the Colosseum and Pantheon possible. The most consummate master of the uses of public art to advertise his regime was Augustus, whose mausoleum and Ara Pacis (Altar of Peace) can be seen in P. Augusto Imperatore, Rome.

Upper-class Romans had an appetite for sumptuous interior decoration, and Greek statuary was the ultimate fashion accessory for cognoscenti. Most Roman sculptures, thus, are copies of Greek bronzes. A distinctly "Roman style," however, does exist in sculptured **portraiture.** Roman portraits of the Republican period (510-27 BC) are brutally honest, immortalizing warts, wrinkles, and scars. Roman imperial sculpture (27 BC-AD 476) tends to blur the distinction between human and god in powerful, idealized images such as *Augustus of Prima Porta.* Romans employed the genre of narrative relief both to record specific historical events and to remind the spectator of a particular emperor's exploits in battle. Later in the period, Roman art developed a flattened style of portraiture, with huge eyes looking out in an "eternal stare."

EARLY CHRISTIAN & BYZANTINE ART

Fearing persecution, early Christians fled to their **catacombs** to worship; these haunting sites are scattered throughout Rome, Naples, and Syracuse. As the Roman Empire collapsed and Christianity rose, the Roman magistrate's basilica was adapted to accommodate Christian services. **Transepts** were added, creating churches shaped like the crucifix. Except for a few **sarcophagi** and **ivory reliefs**, early Christian art turned away from sculpture.

Although the Byzantine empire was centered in Constantinople, Ravenna (p. 295), its chief Italian outpost, is a veritable treasure trove of the first Byzantine Golden Age (AD 526-726). In the early Byzantine tradition, pictorial arts helped the illiterate masses understand religious narratives. Two-dimensional human figures and **mosaics** were suited for this style. The Basilica of **San Vitale** (AD 526-47) is remarkable in its octagonal plan and mosaics (p. 297). It is also one of the first churches with a freestanding **campanile** (bell tower), peculiar to Italian churches.

ROMANESQUE & GOTHIC

From AD 800-1200, well-meaning but somewhat misguided architects no doubt thought that they were constructing the past with their rounded arches, heavy columns, and windowless churches, but "Roman-esque" never quite lived up to the first part of its name; citizens of the actual Empire were scarce. Classical style would not be revived until the Renaissance. The earliest example of Romanesque architecture is **Sant'Ambrogio** in Milan (p. 93), notable for its squat nave and groin vaults. The desire of Italian cities (particularly Florence) to outdo its neighbors resulted in some of the greatest pieces of architecture, most notably **San Miniato al Monte** (p. 335) and the **Baptistry** of the *duomo* (p. 326). Frescoes depict Satan munching on sinners and then defecating them, an image of the Last Judgment that is said to have inspired Dante, who worshipped here in the 13th century.

Just when Italian churchgoers were beginning to adjust to the lack of sunlight, a little movement from France filtered down into the north of Italy, bringing with it wide open spaces and giant pieces of colored glass. Artists rejoiced—more wall space meant a great canvas for their murals. The most impressive Gothic cathedrals include the **Basilica of San Francesco** in Assisi (p. 344), the **Frari** in Venice (p. 218), and the **Santa Maria Novella** in Florence (p. 330). Secular structures caught the fever, and the **Ponte Vecchio** in Florence (p. 329) served as the home of hundreds of butchers and tanners in the 16th century. The **Palazzo Ducale** in Venice (p. 216), spanning several canals with ornate bridges, represents the brilliant marriage of Islamic ornamentation (precise stonework resembling lace and airy porticoes) and pre-Renaissance Gothic, which accounts for the reliefs of the saints sculpted into every nook and cranny. In sculpture, **Nicola Pisano** created pulpits at both Pisa and Siena that combined a hodgepodge of Roman reliefs, early Byzantine mosaics, and traditional Gothic. His son, **Giovanni Pisano** (c.1250-1314), had something of a rebellious streak and distanced his work (and living quarters) away from his father. He became a Gothic purist and renounced his Pisan citizenship.

By the end of the 13th century, Italians were bored with emaciated torsos of suffering martyrs. **Cimabue** (c.1240-1302) and **Duccio** (c.1255-1318) were forced to cater to the masses by introducing a second dimension and brighter colors, though bleeding Christians were still the common subjects. Straddling the Late Gothic and Early Renaissance, **Giotto** is often credited with the realization that people look at pictures. He placed his work at eye-level, putting the viewer on equal footing with his religious subjects. Heresy, you say? No, just good art. He even managed a plug from Dante in *The Divine Comedy*, where he is said to have surpassed his teacher, Cimabue.

EARLY RENAISSANCE

The sculpture of **Donatello** (1386-1466) brought new hope to Italian women when *David* (p. 329) hit the artistic scene as the first free-standing nude since antiquity.

BEST OF THE BEST IN ITALIAN ART AND ARCHITECTURE

GREEK

She-Wolf (c.500 BC). The suckling babies came to represent Romulus and Remus. Museo Capitolino, Rome (p. 471).

Riace Bronzes, Phidias and Polyclitus (460-30 BC). These bronzed athletic beauties were pulled from the sea in 1972. Museo Nazionale, Reggio di Calabria (p. 565).

Tempio della Concordia (430 BC). Its conversion to a Christian church saved this exquisite Greek temple from destruction. Today its reddish hue contrasts spectacularly with the ocean. Valle dei Tempii, Agrigento (p. 624).

Laocoön (first century AD). Agony is a snake eating a saint priest and his two sons. Greatly influenced Bernini and Michelangelo. Vatican Museums, Rome (p. 470).

ROMAN

Pompeii (c.50 BC-AD 79). Voted Most Artistic Ghost Town 1500 years in a row. Pompeii provides the world's clearest window to classical times with its magnificent illusionistic painting and gruesomely charred corpses (p. 503).

The Colosseum (AD 72-80). The detailed design and engineering prowess of the Romans still serves as a basis for stadium design worldwide. In Rome (p. 458).

Trajan's Column (AD 106-113). Art-lovers with binoculars can peer to the top of this most phallic of war monuments. In Rome (p. 460).

The Pantheon (AD 119-125). The harmonious design in this perfectly preserved Roman building will move you to worship the seven planetary gods. In Rome (p. 461).

EARLY CHRISTIAN & BYZANTINE

Altar Mosaics, San Vitale (c.AD 547). Byzantine Emperor Justinian and attendants reveal the connection between Christianity and the state. Tall, slender figures with decorative costumes are a departure from Roman ideals of beauty. In Ravenna (p. 295).

St. Mark's Cathedral (1063). Golden mosaics lit by curving domes. The city's uneven sinking has warped the stunning floor. In Venice (p. 216).

Monreale Cathedral (1174). Vast devotional barn with comical mosaics of Biblical stories. Arab craftsmanship fused with Norman architecture. Outside Palermo (p. 576).

ROMANESQUE & GOTHIC

Cathedral, Baptistery, and **Campanile** of Pisa (1053-1272). Crowds who come to see the Leaning Tower are treated to the delicate artistry of green-and-white marble stonework of the surrounding buildings (p. 373).

Florence's **duomo** and its **Baptistery** (1060-1150). The octagonal duomo, capped with Brunelleschi's burnt-orange dome is postcard-perfect. Ghiberti dedicated his life to the detailed sets of doors (1401 and 1435), which are masterpieces of Gothic/Early Renaissance sculpture (p. 325).

Madonna Enthroned, Cimabue (1280-1290). Cimabue paves the way for Renaissance painting with his experiments in perspective. Uffizi Gallery, Florence (p. 328).

The Maestà Altar, Duccio (1308-11; Museo dell'Opera Metropolitano, Siena; p. 346), and the **Arena Chapel** frescos by Giotto (1305-1306; Padua, p. 226). Which artist wins the heavy-hitting contest between these two early painting masterminds?

RENAISSANCE

Ah, where to begin? Descriptions of all of the important Renaissance works in Italy would leave us room for nothing else. Here's a list of the most interesting or most famous pieces; seek out more information by following the cross-references:

Masaccio, **Tribute Money (P. 335)**; Bellini, **Madonna and Saints (P. 218)**; Botticelli, **The Birth of Venus (P. 328)**; Da Vinci, **Last Supper (P. 92)**; Michelangelo, **David (P. 332)**, **Moses (P. 467)**, and the **Sistine Chapel (P. 470)**; Raphael, **The School of Athens (P. 470)**; Titian, **Pieta (P. 218)**; Tintoretto, myriad paintings in **Scuola Grande di San Rocco (P. 218)**; Palladio, **Villa Rotunda (P. 233)**; Caravaggio, **Crucifixion of St. Peter (P. 463)**; Bernini, **Baldacchino (P. 465)**.

His wooden *Mary Magdalene* in Florence (p. 326) similarly represents a departure from earlier traditions—his figure of the redeemed woman shows the fallen side, too, her repentance symbolized by her rags and the intensity of her facial expression. In architecture, **Brunelleschi's** mathematical studies of ancient Roman architecture became the cornerstone of later Renaissance building. His engineering talent allowed him to raise the dome over **Santa Maria del Fiore** (p. 325), while his mastery of proportions was showcased in the **Pazzi Chapel** (p. 333).

Sandro Botticelli (1444-1510) and his *Birth of Venus*, still floating on her frothy ocean today (p. 328), have come to represent the Renaissance in Italy. Other artists, however, were just as important. **Masaccio,** credited with the first use of the mathematical laws of perspective, had plenty of work filling chapels with angels and gold-leaf. The psychological rendering of Masaccio's figures in the **Brancacci Chapel of Florence** (p. 335) served as a model for Michelangelo and Leonardo. **Fra Angelico** (c.1400-1455) could not have better personified the conflicts between medieval and Renaissance Italy. Born Guido di Pietro, he became a member of a militant branch of Dominican friars, but spent most of his time at his monastery in Fiesole. His abbot opposed humanism as a rule, but Fra Angelico's works exhibit the techniques of space and perspective endorsed by humanistic artists. **Paolo Uccello** (1397-1475), who suffered no conflict between his quest for sainthood and creativity, depicted horses rearing into various positions. According to Vasari, Uccello was so preoccupied with perspective that his wife felt threatened by the competition. **Giovanni Bellini** (c.1431-1516) and **Andrea Mantegna** (1431-1506) were influenced by the Flemish school's use of color and miniature. They found more secular subjects than their Florentine counterparts, starting a long tradition of Italians looking to Venice as the seat of all heretical debauchery.

Lorenzo Ghiberti (c.1381-1455) designed and produced two sets of bronze doors for the baptistery in Florence in the first half of the 15th century; his designs for the doors were chosen over Brunelleschi's in a contest, and the two original entries now sit side by side in the Bargello of Florence (p. 329). **Leon Battista Alberti** (1404-1472) is better known as a precursor to architectural greatness than a proficient master. His design of Florence's Palazzo Rucellai (p. 332), Santa Maria Novella (p. 330), and Rimini's Tempio Malatestiano (p. 302), serve as prototypes for later Renaissance *palazzi* and churches.

HIGH RENAISSANCE

The torch must be passed, and so it was, to three of art's greatest figures, between 1450-1520. **Leonardo da Vinci** (1452-1519) was the first Renaissance man to earn the name. His endeavors were not confined to sculpture or painting, but encompassed engineering, musical composition, human dissection, and armaments design. His lab seems to have contained a primitive circuit board, and his ingenious flying machine. The *Last Supper* (in Santa Maria delle Grazie in Milan, p. 92) preserves the individuality of the depicted figures even in a religious context. His experimentation with *chiaroscuro*, in which light and dark are mixed to create contrast and perspective, served to secure his place as the great innovator of his century.

Michelangelo Buonarroti (1475-1564) was a jack of all trades in the artistic world, despite the assurance he delivered to Julius II when asked to paint the Sistine Chapel ceiling: "I am not a painter!" His illusion of vaults on a flat surface is his greatest surviving achievement. Julius liked the job so much that he paid the temperamental Michelangelo to put his face on one of the saintly figures in *The Last Judgment*, also in the Sistine Chapel. While it is unclear if Michelangelo completed this particular task, it is certain that one of the damned looks remarkably like the papal councillor who recommended that the nudes in fresco be repainted with proper clothing. His architectural achievements are equally noteworthy, particularly in his designs for the Laurentian Library in Florence (p. 332) and the dome on St. Peter's in Rome (p. 464). Sculpture, however, remained Michelangelo's favorite mode of expression. Classic examples are the *Pietà* in St. Peter's (p. 464), *David*, and the unfinished *Slaves* in Florence's Accademia (p. 333).

A proficient draftsman, **Raphael** Santi (1483-1520) created technically perfect figures. His frescoes in the papal apartments of the Vatican, including the clear and balanced composition of the *School of Athens*, show his debt to classical standards (p. 470). The Venetian school produced **Giorgione** (1478-1510) and the prolific **Titian** (1488-1576). Titian's works, including his portrait of Julius II with the repentant Mary Magdalene, are notable for their accurate facial expressions and the richness of the Venetian oils he used to create them. In the High Renaissance, the greatest architect other than Michelangelo was **Donato Bramante** (1444-1514), famed for his work on the Tempietto and St. Peter's in Rome.

MANNERISM

Creative experimentation led to Mannerism, a reaction against Renaissance classicism, which originated in Rome and Florence. Mannerist artists relished strange juxtapositions of color and scale; figures may be oddly elongated. As a style, mannerism is marked by technical panache, elegance and refinement. Spiritually intense and psychologically nervous, Mannerism has enjoyed an increasing vogue in modern times. **Parmigianino** (1503-1540) was the most famous Mannerist, and his controversial *Madonna of the Long Neck* is the period's most famous work. **Jacopo Tintoretto** (1518-1594), the Venetian Mannerist of choice, was the first to paint multiple light sources within a single composition.

Mannerist architecture, like Michelangelo's later works or those of **Giulio Romano** (c.1499-1546), rejected the Renaissance ideal of harmony. Classical forms were minutely changed in order to surprise the attentive viewer, as in the case of the asymmetry and odd proportions of the Palazzo Té in Mantua. The villas and churches of architect **Andrea Palladio** (1508-1580) were remarkably innovative, particularly the Villa Rotunda outside Vicenza (p. 233). His most lasting contribution, however, was the *Four Books of Architecture*, which influenced countless architects, especially those of the Baroque movement of the 17th and 18th centuries.

BAROQUE AND ROCOCO

Born of the Counter-Reformation and absolute monarchy, **Baroque** art and architecture were intended to inspire faith in the Catholic Church and respect for temporal power. Painters of this era favored Naturalism—a commitment to portraying nature in the raw, whether ugly or beautiful. Baroque paintings are thus often melodramatic and gruesome. **Caravaggio** (1573-1610) expanded the use of *chiaroscuro*, creating enigmatic works often incorporating unsavory characters into religious scenes. **Gianlorenzo Bernini** (1598-1680), a prolific High Baroque sculptor and architect, designed the colonnaded *piazza* of St. Peter's and the *baldacchino* over its crossing. Drawing inspiration from Hellenistic works like the Laocoön, Bernini's sculptures were orgies of movement. **Francesco Borromini** (1599-1667) was more adept than his rival at shaping the walls of his buildings into serpentine architectural masterpieces. **Rococo,** the final development of the Baroque, originated in 18th-century France. It is a more delicate style. **Giovanni Battista Tiepolo** (1696-1770), with his brilliant palette and vibrant frescoes, was a prolific Venetian painter of allegories and the premier exemplar of the Rococo style.

19TH- AND 20TH-CENTURY ART

The Italians started to lose their dexterity with the paintbrush and their proficiency with the chisel in the 18th and 19th centuries. **Antonio Canova** (1757-1822) explored the formal **Neoclassical** style, which professed a return to the rules of classical antiquity. His most famous work is the statue of *Pauline Borghese* (p. 471). The **Macchiaioli** group, spearheaded by **Giovanni Fattori** (1825-1908), revolted against the strict Neoclassical style with a unique technique of "blotting," using a dry paintbrush to pick up certain areas of pigment (p. 381). The Italian **Futurist** artists of the 1910s, who sought to transfer the movements of machines into art, brought Italy back to the cutting edge of artistry. **Giorgio de Chirico** (1888-1978), whose eerie scenes scream of surrealist influence, has impressive works on display at the Collezione Peggy Guggenheim in Venice (p. 219). **Amadeo Modigliani** (1884-1920) crafted figures most famous for their long oval faces. **Marcello Piacentini's** fascist architecture, which imposes a sense of sterility on classical motifs, looms oppressively at Mussolini's EUR in Rome (p. 469).

LITERATURE

OH GODS, YOU DEVILS

It is primarily through **Ovid's** works that we learn the details of Roman mythology, a soap-opera theology that developed from and added to the Greek family of deities. Usually disguised as animals or humans, these gods and goddesses often descended to earth to intervene romantically or combatively in human affairs.

Jupiter, after disguising himself as a rock to escape ingestion by his coup-fearing father, spent the next several centuries visiting women in forms that include peacocks and flaming red bulls. Somewhere between loves he established the monarchy of the gods on the heights of Mt. Olympus. The 13 other major Olympian players are Jupiter's wife **Juno,** goddess of child-bearing and marriage; **Neptune,** god of the sea; **Vulcan,** god of smiths; **Venus,** goddess of love and beauty; **Mars,** god of war; **Minerva,** goddess of wisdom; **Apollo,** god of light and arts; **Diana,** goddess of the hunt; **Mercury,** the messenger god; **Pluto,** god of the underworld; **Ceres,** goddess of the harvest; **Bacchus,** god of wine; **Vesta,** goddess of the hearth.

LATIN LOVERS

As they gained dominance over the hellenized Mediterranean, the Romans abruptly discovered the joys of literature. They also discovered the agony of catching up with the Greeks. **Plautus** (c.259-184 BC) wrote bawdy, raucous comedies, including *Pseudolus.* The lyric poetry of **Catullus** (84-54 BC) set a high standard for passion. **Cicero** (106-43 BC) the greatest speaker of his day, set an all-time standard for political and forensic rhetoric. **Julius Caesar** (100-44 BC) gave a first-hand account of the expansion of empire in his *Gallic Wars.*

Despite a government prone to banishing the impolitic, Augustan Rome produced an array of literary talent. **Livy** (c.59 BC-AD 17) recorded the authorized history of Rome from the city's founding to his own time. **Virgil** (70-19 BC) wrote the *Aeneid* about the origins of Rome and the heroic toils of founding father Aeneas. **Horace's** (65-8 BC) verse explores love, wine, service to the state, literature, hostile critics and the happiness that comes from a small farm in the country. **Ovid** (43 BC-AD 17) poured out a rich array of delightful poetry including the *Amores,* the mythological *Metamorphoses,* and the *Ars Amatoria.*

From the post-Augustan Empire, **Petronius's** *Satyricon* (first century AD) is a bawdy, blunt look at the decadent age of Nero and revolves around a man's desperate quest to cure his impotence, caused by the wrath of the phallic god, Priapus. Fellini's film of the same title presents a modern version. **Suetonius's** (c.69-130) *De Vita Caesarum* presents the gossipy version of imperial history. **Tacitus's** (c.55-116) *Histories* bitingly summarize Roman war, diplomacy, scandal, and rumor in the year of Nero's death (AD 69). His *Annals* extol the upright Rome of Trajan and criticizes the scandalous activities of the Julio-Claudian emperors.

INTO THE LIGHT

The tumult of medieval life discouraged most literary musings, but three Tuscan writers reasserted the art in the late 13th century. Although scholars do not agree on the precise dates of the Renaissance in literature, many argue that the work of

LITERARY HIGHLIGHTS

Alighieri, Dante. *Inferno*. Speaking through bloody throats has never been so poetic.

Boccaccio, Giovanni. The *Decameron*. Tales of adultery and naughty monks in the age of the Black Plague.

Calvino, Italo. *If on a Winter's Night a Traveler...* A self-reflective, playful look at the desire to read and impress, as well as to confuse, the reader.

Catullus. *Poems*. Witty, passionate, insightful. And all this before AD 1.

Eco, Umberto. *The Name of the Rose*. Murder, mystery, and manuscripts in a medieval monastery. Mmmmmmm.

Forster, E.M. *A Room with a View*. Victorian coming-of-age in scenic Florence.

Hemingway, Ernest. *A Farewell to Arms*. The tale of an American ambulance driver serving in World War I Italy.

Highsmith, Patricia. *The Talented Mr. Ripley*. Stolen identities, class envy, brutal murder show us the darker, less glamorous side of the Lost Generation.

James, Henry. *The Wings of the Dove*. Unscrupulous seduction in Venice's canals.

Levi, Carlo. *Christ Stopped at Eboli*. An anti-Fascist is banished to rural Basilicata.

Machiavelli, Niccolò. *The Prince*. Cold ruthless statecraft.

Mann, Thomas. *Death in Venice*. A writer's obsession with a beautiful boy.

Ovid. *Amores, Ars Amatoria*. Sex, lies and... no videotape? Live from ancient Rome.

Petrarch. *The Canzoniere*. The father of humanism mixes secular and divine love.

Pirandello, Luigi. *Six Characters in Search of an Author*. A pre-postmodern blend of psycho-analysis, irony, and surreality in a dramatic setting, told by the savvy bovine narrator, Jordan Litt.

Shakespeare, William. *Romeo and Juliet; Othello; Julius Caesar; Merchant of Venice*. Fun and games and death all over.

Virgil. The *Aeneid*. A compilation of Augustan propaganda telling of Rome's origins from gods and the Trojan hero Aeneas.

Let's Go: Italy 2002. A florid tale of wine, song, and bitter sarcasm in the allegorical style of a travel guide book.

Dante Alighieri (1265-1321) marked its inception. One of the first Italian poets to write in the *volgare* (common Italian, really Florentine) instead of Latin, Dante is considered the father of modern Italian language and literature. In his epic poem *La Divina Commedia (The Divine Comedy)*, Dante roams all levels of the afterlife (including the *Inferno*) with famous historical figures and his true love Beatrice. Among its chief political themes are Dante's call for social reform and his scathing indictment of those contributing to Florentine moral downfall.

While Dante's work displays a distinctly medieval flavor, **Petrarch** (1304-74) belongs more clearly to the literary Renaissance. A scholar of classical Latin and a key proponent of Humanist thought, he restored the popularity of ancient Roman writers by writing love sonnets to a married woman named Laura, compiled in his *Il Canzoniere*. The third member of the medieval literary triumvirate, **Giovanni Boccaccio,** was a close friend of Petrfascistarch's, although his style owes little to his friend. The *Decameron*, Boccaccio's collection of 100 stories, told by 10 young Florentines fleeing their plague-ridden city, ranges in tone from suggestive to bawdy—in one story, a gardener has his way with an entire convent.

IMPROVE THYSELF

Fifteenth and 16th-century Italian authors branched out from the genres of their predecessors. **Alberti** and **Palladio** wrote treatises on architecture and art theory. **Baldassare Castiglione's** *The Courtier* instructed the inquiring Renaissance man on deportment, etiquette, and other fine points of behavior. **Vasari** took time away from redecorating Florence's churches to produce the ultimate primer on art history and criticism, *The Lives of the Artists*. One of the most lasting works of the Renaissance, **Niccolò Machiavelli's** *Il Principe (The Prince)* is a sophisticated assessment of what it takes to gain political power.

In the spirit of the "Renaissance man," specialists in other fields tried their hand at writing. **Benvenuto Cellini** wrote about his art in *The Autobiography* and **Michelangelo** composed enough sonnets to fuel a fire (literally). The scathing and brilliant **Pietro Aretino** created new possibilities for literature when he began accepting payment from famous people for *not* writing about them. A fervent hater of Michelangelo, Aretino was roasted himself when the great artist painted him into his *Last Judgment*. As Italy's political power waned, literary production also declined, but some stars remained. The prolific 18th-century dramatist **Carlo Goldoni** (1707-1793) replaced the stock characters of the traditional *commedia dell'arte* with unpredictable figures in his *Il Ventaglio*.

WHAT IS TRUTH?

With the 19th century came the unification of Italy and the necessity for a unified language. Because an "Italian" literature was an entirely new concept, it grew slowly, and the 1800s were an era primarily of *racconti* (short stories) and poetry. The styles of these works ranged from the controversial poetry of **Gabriele D'Annunziod,** whose cavalier heroics earned him as much fame as his eccentric writing, to the *verismo* of **Giovanni Verga.** Verga's brutally honest treatment of his destitute subjects ushered in a new age of portraying the lowest common denominator in art and literature. Not until publication of **Alessandro Manzoni's** historical novel, *I Promessi Sposi (The Betrothed)*, did the Modernist novel become a main avenue of Italian literary expression.

The 20th century began a new genre as writers sought to destroy the conception of objective truth and years of European achievement. Nobel Prize winner **Luigi Pirandello** contributed to the postmodernist movement with *Six Characters in Search of an Author* and *So It Is (If You Think It Is So)*.

Literary production slowed in the years preceding World War II, but Allied victory spawned an entire generation of writers jumping ship and writing anti-fascist fiction. The 1930s and 1940s were dominated by a group of young Italian writers influenced by Ernest Hemingway and John Steinbeck, both of whom had spent time in Italy and felt a great deal of compassion for the Italian people. This school included **Cesare Pavese, Vasco Pratolini** and **Elio Vittorini.** Post-war literature found Italian authors relating their horrific political and moral experiences. **Primo Levi** wrote his *Se Questo È Un Uomo (If This is a Man*, 1947) about his experiences in Auschwitz. The most prolific of these writers, **Alberto Moravia**, wrote the groundbreaking *Gli Indifferenti (Time of Indifference*, 1953), which launched an attack on the Fascist regime and was promptly censored. Moravia employed experimental, surreal forms in his later works, using sex to symbolize the violence and spiritual impotence of modern Italy. Several female writers emerged around this time, including **Natalia Ginzburg** with *Lessico Famigliare* (1963), the story of a quirky middle-class Italian family. On a somewhat different note, **Giuseppe di Tomasi di Lampedusa** wrote *Il Gattopardo (The Leopard*, 1957), describing the death of Sicily's feudal aristocracy at the time of unification.

The works of **Italo Calvino** are filled with intellectual play and magical realism. His works include the trilogy *Our Ancestors* (1962), and the quintessentially postmodern *If on a Winter's Night a Traveler...* (1979), an interactive novel in which the reader becomes the protagonist, and thus removes the need for the author to write a sensible, character-motivated plot. Mid-20th-century poets include **Giuseppe Ungaretti** and Nobel Prize winners **Salvatore Quasimodo** and **Eugenio Montale.** Quasimodo and Montale founded the "hermetic movement," characterized by an intimate poetic vision and allusive (and elusive) imagery.

More recently, **Umberto Eco** steps back from postmodernism's techniques and includes a plot in *The Name of the Rose* (1980), an intricate mystery involving an ancient manuscript and a more than a few fallen monks. *Foucault's Pendulum* (1989) addresses the story of the Knights Templar and half a millennium of conspiracy theories. In 1997, **Dario Fo,** a playwright denounced by the Catholic church, (which worked primarily to increase his popularity) won the Nobel Prize for literature for his dramatic satires of post-war Italian texts.

MUSIC

GREGORY'S FAMOUS CHANTING MONKS

Church music as it was known to the medieval world grew out of the Jewish liturgy (something that not just a few Crusaders would be horrified to learn). Women were allowed to sing until 578 AD, after which time they were replaced in Catholic choirs, often by castrated men and soon-to-be castrated boys. Must keep those voices rising to the heavens. The father of liturgical chant was none other than Gregory I, who was responsible for codifying the music he had heard during his days in the monastery. **Plainchant** was synchronized with the church's liturgical calendar. Singers were admonished, in surviving manuscript notes, to be modest and reserved in their work, indicating that a few *prime donne* existed even in the 7th century. Another Italian monk, **Guido d'Arezzo** (995-1050), is regarded as the originator of musical notation. Generally accepted as the home of church music, Italy's many monasteries reveled in church tunes up through the Middle Ages and Renaissance. Madrigals ruined things for the boys in brown, though, by the time **Francesco Landini** (1325-97) and **Pietro Casella** (c. 1280) had arrived on the scene. They sought to put popular (read: secular) poems into music for multiple voices. Oh, the horror! The scandal! **Giovanni Palestrina** (1525-94) attempted to purge madrigals of this frightening trend towards secularity while still keeping the integrity of the music itself, and his work in polyphony is still widely performed in Italy and abroad. Music from this period in general is performed in many ancient cathedrals and basilicas. Take a break one afternoon in one of these churches, and you can almost imagine that you're a medieval Christian, allowing the beauty of harmony to wash over you while all the while fearing eternal damnation at the hands of an unforgiving god. The composers of *musica da chiesa* (music for the church) frequently wrote additional pieces for performance in the home or at court—though the latter were more often than not rather bawdy love songs.

THE FAT LADY SINGS

Opera, Italy's most cherished art form, was born in Florence, nurtured in Venice, and revered in Milan. Conceived by the **Camerata,** a circle of Florentine writers, noblemen, and musicians, opera originated as an attempt to recreate the dramas of ancient Greece by setting lengthy poems to music. After several years of effort with only dubious success, **Jacobo Peri** composed *Dafne*, the world's first complete opera, in 1597. As opera spread to Venice, Milan, and Rome, the forms of the genre became more defined and the topics more broad. The first successful opera composer, **Claudio Monteverdi** (1567-1643) drew freely from history, juxtaposing high drama, love scenes, and bawdy humor. His masterpieces, *L'Orfeo* (1607) and *L'Incoronazione di Poppea* (1642), were the first widespread successes of the genre, and survive to the present day. **Alessandro Scarlatti** (1660-1725), considered one of the developers of the aria, also founded the Neapolitan opera, thus vaulting Naples to the forefront of Italian music. (And causing a number of Lega Nord members' heart attacks.) Schools were quickly set up there under the supervision of famous composers, promoting the beautiful soprano voices of pre-pubescent boys. If the male students were naughty and attempted to go through puberty, their testicles were confiscated. These *castrati*, **Farinelli** perhaps the most famous, became a most celebrated and envied group of singers in Italy and all over Europe.

BAROQUE: THE END OF ALL RESTRAINT

At the end of 16th century, husbands would be forced away from their *bocce* games to partake in the delights of opera. Little did they know that their wives would soon discover an even more tedious art form to while away the evenings. During the **Baroque** period, known for its heavy ornamentation and fugues unto eternity, two main instruments saw their popularity mushroom: the violin, whose shape became perfected by Cremona families, including the **Stradivari** (p. 102); and the piano, created around 1709 by members of the Florentine **Cristofori** family. With the rise of the strings, *virtuoso* instrumental music became a legitimate genre in 17th-century Rome. **Antonio Vivaldi** (1675-1741), composer of over 400 concertos, conquered contemporary audiences with *The Four Seasons;* the concerto assumed its present form, in which a full orchestra accompanies the soloist.

Eighteenth-century Italy exported its music. At mid-century, operatic overtures were performed separately, creating the **sinfonia.** In opera, Baroque detail yielded to classical standards of moderation, structural balance, and elegance.

VIVA VERDI!

With convoluted plots and powerful, dramatic music, 19th-century Italian opera continues to dominate modern stages. Late in the 19th-century, **Giacomo Puccini** (1858-1924), the master of *verismo* opera (slices of contemporary, all-too-tragic realism), created *Madame Butterfly*, *La Bohème*, and *Tosca*, which feature vulnerable women who usually die in the last act. **Gioacchino Rossini** (1792-1868) was the master of the *bel canto* ("beautiful song"), characterized by long, fluid, melodic lines. He once boasted that he could produce music faster than copyists could reproduce it. In fact, he proved to be such a procrastinator that his agents resorted to locking him in a room until he completed his renowned masterpieces.

Giuseppe Verdi (1813-1901), however, remains the transcendent musical and operatic figure of 19th-century Italy. *Nabucco*, a pointed and powerful *bel canto* work, typifies Verdi's early works. The chorus *"Va pensiero"* from *Nabucco* would later become the hymn of Italian freedom and unity. Verdi produced the touching, personal dramas and memorable melodies of *Rigoletto*, *La Traviata*, and *Il Trovatore* during his middle period. From the last third of the century, Verdi gives us the grand and heroic conflicts of *Aida*, the dramatic thrust of *Otello*, and the mercurial comedy of *Falstaff*. Verdi's name served as a convenient acronym for "Vittorio Emanuele, Re d'Italia," so *"Viva Verdi"* became a popular battle cry of the Risorgimento. Much of Verdi's work promoted Italian unity—his operas include frequent allusions to political assassinations, exhortations against tyranny, and jibes at French and Austrian monarchs.

In the 20th century, **Ottorino Respighi**, composer of the popular *Pines of Rome* and *Fountains of Rome*, experimented with rapidly shifting orchestral textures. **Giancarlo Menotti**, now a US resident, wrote the oft-performed *Amahl and the Night Visitors*. Known for his work with meta-languages, **Luciano Berio** defied traditional instrumentation with his *Sequence V* for solo trombone and mime. **Luigi Dallapiccola** achieved success with choral works including *Songs of Prison* and *Songs of Liberation*—two pieces that protest Fascist rule in Italy. The robust **Luciano Pavarotti** continues to tour with Jose Carreras and Placido Domingo.

BYE BYE VERDI

Although formerly inconspicuous on the world stage, modern Italian pop stars have been crooning away for decades. Yes, really. You've heard of the Beatles? John Lennon? Janis Joplin? Meet **Lucio Dalla, Francesco de Gregori,** the Sardinian **Fabrizio D'Andrea,** and adamantly Neapolitan **Pino Daniele,** who continue to use pop as a way to protest social conditions, especially the stigma of being Southern. While **Vasco Rossi** started off with protest lyrics, he has since sold his 60s idealism for a sexy Italian mainstream image. And women. Many women.

Recently Italian musicians have recorded with international superstars, increasing their exposure on the world's stage. **Eros Ramazzotti** teamed up with Tina Turner on *"Cose della Vita,"* while **Andrea Bocelli** joined Celine Dion in *"The Prayer."* **Zucchero** continues to enjoy world fame, perhaps explaining his collaboration with the lesser-known Steve Winwood on his last album. Rather than ride international coattails, **Laura Pausini,** who records in both Italian and Spanish, has established a following in Latin America, Spain, and Miami.

Ivana Spagna and her new album *Domani* topped the charts alongside **Umberto Tozzi** and **Luna Pop** in 2000. Newcomer **Francesco Tricarico** put out the hit single "Io Sono Francesco" in early 2001. The technotronic Italian hip-hop scene mixes traditional folk tunes with the latest international groove; rap has emerged with widesmiling, curly-haired **Jovanotti,** socially conscious **Frankie-Hi-NRG,** subconscious **99 Posse,** and unconscious **Articolo 31** (whose name derives from the Italian law forbidding the use of marijuana).

PRINT

Little searching will reveal a newspaper in your native language at one of the numerous **edicole** (**USA Today** and the **International Herald Tribune** are delivered at about noon each day). These newsstands, however, are more interesting if one reads Italian. Newspapers in Italy are anything but impartial, and often lambast everyone from public officials to popular actresses. The most prevalent national daily papers are **Il Corriere della Sera,** a conservative publication from Milan, and **La Repubblica,** a liberal paper from Rome. Other popular papers include **La Stampa** (conservative, published in Torino and owned by Fiat), **Il Messaggero** (liberal, published in Rome), and **Il Giornale** (published in Milan). For weekly entertainment listings, the larger cities come equipped with separate magazines, like: **Roma C'è; TrovaRoma; TrovaMilano; Firenze Spettacolo; Milano Where, When, How;** and **Qui Napoli.**

FILM

OLDIES AND GOLDIES

Italy has made an eccentric and somewhat sporadic contribution to the world of international cinema. The country's toe-hold in the industry began with the creation of its first feature film in 1905. Alberini and Santoni created the historical and somewhat flamboyant *La Presa di Roma* only one year before going on to establish the thriving **Cines** studios in Rome. With Cines, the Italian "super-spectacle" was born, a form that extravagantly recreated momentous historical events. Throughout the early-20th century, Italy's films were grandiose historical dramas. Shortly before World War I, the public appeal and economic success of films became dependent on the presence of celebrities, particularly *dive* (goddesses) like Lyda Borelli and Francesca Bertini, who epitomized the Italian *femme fatale.*

FASCISM AND CINECITTA

No one ever accused Benito Mussolini of missing an opportunity where he saw one, and he was one of the first to see propaganda potential in film. Or perhaps he just copied **Adolf Hitler's** ruthless exploitations up north. Changing his drab black shirt for a woolen scarf, beret, and faux ponytail, Benito created the *Centro Sperimentale della Cinematografia di Nicolo Williams,* a national film school, and the gargantuan **Cinecittà Studios,** Rome's answer to Hollywood. Nationalizing the industry for the good of the state, Mussolini enforced a few "imperial edicts," one of which forbade laughing at the Marx Brothers and another that censored shows overly crocical of the government. Those fascists. Paranoids, all of them.

NEOREALISMO

The fall of Fascism brought the explosion of **Neorealist cinema** (1943-50), whose drab sets and endless stories of poverty made Italian movie buffs long for Cinecittà. *Neorealismo* rejected contrived sets and professional actors, emphasizing location shooting and "authentic" drama. It was these low budget productions that created a revolution in film and brought Italian cinema international prestige. Neorealists first gained attention in Italy with **Luchino Visconti's** 1942 French-influenced *Ossessione (Obsession)*, loosely based on James Cain's pulp-novel *The Postman Always Rings Twice*. Fascist censors suppressed the so-called "resistance" film, however, so **Roberto Rossellini's** 1945 film *Roma, Città Aperta* (Rome, Open City) was the first Neorealist film to gain international exposure. **Vittorio De Sica's** *Ladri di Biciclette* (1948) *(The Bicycle Thief)* was perhaps the most successful Neorealist film. Described by De Sica as "dedicated to the suffering of the humble," this story advocates the view that a man cannot rise above his circumstances, and that he is doomed to the ride the medieval wheel of fortune.

By the mid 1950s, Italy had begun to prosper as the honest ambition of *Neorealismo* gave way to the birth of **La Commedia all'Italiana.** Actor **Totò,** the bastard son of a Neapolitan duke, was Italy's challenge to Charlie Chaplin. With his ingenious posture, dignified antics, and clever language, Totò charmed audiences while providing subtle commentary on the vulnerability of Italy's economic success.

THOSE GO-GO SIXTIES

In the 1960s, those directors who were the students of the 1940s had reached maturity as "progressives," creating films of individual expression. Post-neorealist directors **Federico Fellini** and **Michelangelo Antonioni** rejected plots and characters for a visual and symbolic world deriving its worth from witnessed moments. In Fellini's autobiographical *Roma* (1972), a gorgeous stand-in for the director performs with an otherwise grotesque cast of characters. *La Dolce Vita* (1960), banned by the Pope but widely regarded as the most representative Italian film, scrutinizes 1950s Rome, its decadently stylish but vapid celebrities, and the *paparazzi* (a term first coined in this movie) who pursued them. Antonioni's haunting trilogy, *L'Avventura* (1959), *La Notte* (1960), and *L'Eclisse* (1962), transports the viewer into a stark world of estranged couples and young, hopelessly isolated aristocrats. Antonioni's *Blow-Up* was a 1966 English-language hit about mime, murder, and mod London.

Pier Paolo Pasolini, who spent as much time on trial for his politics as he did making films, was both a successful poet and a controversial director. An ardent Marxist, he set his films in shanty neighborhoods and the Roman underworld of poverty and prostitution. In his debaucherous films, sexual deviance and political power are synonyms in an empty modern society. His masterpiece, *Hawks and Sparrows*, ponders the philosophical and poetic possibilities of film.

INTROSPECTION

Aging old-boy directors and the lack of funding for Italian films led to another era in directing, as nostalgia and self-examination became popular. **Bernardo Bertolucci's** 1970 *Il Conformista* is an overwhelmingly beautiful film that investigates Fascist Italy by focusing on one "comrade" desperately struggling to be normal. Other major Italian films of this era include the ubiquitous **Vittorio de Sica's** *Il Giardino dei Finzi-Contini* and **Francesco Rosi's** *Cristo Si È Fermato a Eboli*, both films based on prestigious post-war, anti-fascist novels. In the 1980s, the **Taviani** brothers catapulted to fame with *Kaos*, a film based on stories by Pirandello, and *La Notte di San Lorenzo*, which depicts an Italian village during the final days of World War II. Actor-directors like **Nanni Moretti** and **Maurizio Nichetti** also rose to fame in the 1980s and early 1990s with a more macabre and psychological humor. Nichetti's *Bianca* (1983) is a psychological comedy-thriller featuring himself as the somewhat deranged central character. His *Ladri di Saponette*, a modern spoof on the neo-realist *Ladri di Biciclette*, features Nichetti as himself, while in his 1991 *Volere Volare*, the Italian version of *Who Framed Roger Rabbit?*, Nichetti plays a confused cartoon sound designer who morphs entirely into a cartoon by the end of the movie. **Lina Wertmuller's** brilliant *Ciao, Professore!* (1994) tells the story of a schoolteacher from the north who gets assigned to teach third grade in Corzano, a poor town near Naples.

BUONGIORNO PRINCIPESSA!

Oscar-winners **Giuseppe Tornatore** *(Il Nuovo Cinema Paradiso)* and **Gabriele Salvatore** *(Mediterraneo)* have garnered the attention and affection of US audiences. In 1995, Massimo Troisi's *Il Postino* was nominated for a Best Picture Academy Award. **Roberto Benigni** has become one of the leading Italian cinematic personalities and his *La Vita e Bella* (Life is Beautiful) has gained international respect. Juxtaposing the tragic and bleak Italian Jewish life during World War II with a father's colorful love for his son, the film received its well-deserved laurels with Best Actor and Best Foreign Film Oscars and a Best Picture nomination at the 1999 Academy Awards. Benigni promptly jumped on the top of his velvet-covered theatre seat and announced that he wanted to make love to everyone present.

TUTTI IN GUCCI

Fashion is an integral part of Italian life. In a country renowned for its couture, leather shoes and handbags, and tailored suits, it's no wonder Italians care about what they wear. Not only does quality supersede quantity, but also appearances are so important that women will wear fur to the supermarket.

As much as Parisians, New Yorkers, and Londoners might protest, the fashion world begins and ends in Milan. Italy has given rise to the powerhouses of **Gucci, Versace,** and **Armani,** to name a few. The beginning of Italy's importance in the fashion industry dates back to the late-19th century with the Cerruti Company's renowned fabrics. In the early 1900s, Adele **Fendi** became well known for her furs and **Salvatore Ferragamo** imported his dazzling shoe making skills to Hollywood. In 1950, Marquis **Emilio Pucci** became known for his bright prints with interesting geometrical patterns. His influence on the world of fashion peaked in the 1960s and 1970s; he has recently made a forceful comeback with vintage items. The late 50s and early 60s saw the rise of fashion giants **Valentino** and **Armani,** and in 1970 the latter—renowned for his suits—opened his own fashion-consulting firm. In 1978, **Gianni Versace** opened his first store in Milan and began to contribute his bold, creative, and colorful styles to Italian fashion. The 80s saw the arrival of tag team designers, Domenico **Dolce** and Stefano **Gabbana,** known for their sexy stylings. This dossier of designers along with the fashion houses of **Gucci** and **Prada** have catapulted Milan (and Italy) to the center of the fashion universe.

FOOD AND WINE: LA DOLCE VITA

Food is more than just sustenance. Its preparation is an art form and its consumption a crucial part of life. *La bella figura* (a nice figure) is another social imperative, and the after-dinner *passeggiata* (promenade) is as much of an institution as the meal itself. Small portions and the leisurely pace of a meal help to keep Italians healthy despite the enticing and often fattening foods that comprise their cuisine.

REGIONAL SPECIALTIES

While V. Sesame may have taught you that Italian food is brought to you by the letter P, with pasta, pizza, and *pomodori* (tomatoes), Italian cuisine encompasses much more. *Haute cuisine* may have been coined by the French, but Italian food has all the nuances and delicacies of its geographical neighbor—without the garnish of pretension. In addition to regional differences such as coastal areas offering a wide variety of seafood dishes and inland areas providing meatier, heartier fare, specialties also tend to reflect historical influence. Dishes in the North are often rich with creamy and meaty sauces, and *risotto* and polenta often are eaten instead of pasta. In **Piemonte,** try the famed (but pricey) truffles. They're supposedly an aphrodisiac, but you'll need to experience this first hand. **Lombardia** offers the delights of gorganzola and mascarpone cheeses. Mascarpone is a main ingredient in *tiramisu* (Italian for "pick me up"). *Risotto, ossobuco* (a braised veal stew) and *panettone* (a dessert bread) are also specialties of the region. **Coastal Liguria** is noted for its seafood, profusion of herbs, and olive oil, while the Germanic influences in Tentino-Alto Adige have popularized *gnocchi* (potato and flour dumplings). **Friuli-Venezia Giulia** incorporates a Middle-Eastern flair, using spices such as cumin and paprika to flavor meat and dairy dishes. **The Veneto** is sustained by *pasta e fagioli* (pasta and beans) and feasts on artichokes and game.

Moving south into the gastronomic heart of Italy, **Emilia-Romagna** is the birthplace of parmesan cheese, balsamic vinegar, and *prosciutto di Parma* (Parma ham). **Tuscany** offers more rustic fare, with stews and pot roasts, bean and veggie dishes, and minestrone. **Umbria** has black truffles to rival the white ones of Piemonte and is also known for the tasty delights of chocolates and other sweets. **Abruzzo** and **Molise** are known for their cured peppery meats, lamb, mutton, and pasta. **Sardinia** has more sheep than people, and their odiferous cheese is made into pies and topped with honey.

MANGIA IN ITALIA!

Breakfast in Italy often goes unnoticed; at most, a morning meal consists of coffee and a *cornetto* (croissant). **Lunch** is the main feast of the day. If you don't have a big appetite, grab lunch at an inexpensive *tavola calda* ("hot table"), *rosticceria* (grill), or *gastronomia* (serving hot prepared dishes). But if you decide to partake in the traditional Italian **pranzo,** be warned that it is an event: a real *pranzo* lasts much of the afternoon. Typically it consists of an *antipasto* (appetizer), a *primo piatto* (the first course, a heaping portion of pasta, risotto, or soup), a *secondo piatto* (usually meat or fish), and a *contorno* (vegetable side dish). Finally comes *dolce* (dessert or fruit), then *caffè,* and often an after-dinner liqueur. Many restaurants offer a fixed-price tourist **menù** that includes *primo, secondo,* bread, water, and wine. While these meals are usually a good deal, you may not have much choice as to what is served for each course. Italian **dinners** begin around 8pm in most of the country, although farther south, they're served later; in Naples it's not unusual to go for a midnight pizza. Dinner is a lighter meal, often a snack or *panino,* or even an excuse to go to a pizzeria with friends.

DON'T LET 'EM PULL A FAST ONE

A new breed of fast-food joint is springing up around Italy. Still, the ample salad bar and beer at most Italian **McDonald's** attests that Italians even do fast-food their own way, though don't look for any McGnocchi. Buy picnic materials at *salumeria* or *alimentari* (meat and grocery shops). **STANDA** and **COOP** are two supermarket chains. Fresh fruit and vegetables are best (and cheapest) at open-air markets.

A **bar** is an excellent place to grab coffee or an inexpensive snack. Avoid bars on major tourist thoroughfares, where prices reflect location and not necessarily service or quality. Bars usually offer hot and cold sandwiches *(panini),* drinks with or without alcohol, and *gelato.* Try the rolls and pizza bread stuffed with *prosciutto crudo* or *cotto* (ham either cured or cooked), *formaggio* (cheese), or even *frittate* (omelettes). You can ask for one *scaldato* (heated). In small towns, bars are the social centers. Children come for *gelato,* old men come for wine and conversation, and young adults come for beer and flirtation. In touristy bars, pay for your food at the cashier's desk and then take the receipt to a bartender, who will take your order. In less-touristed areas, pay after you drink. No matter where you are, sitting down at a bar that offers table service will cost more than standing at the counter. Proprietors at all bars and shops will (or should) force you to take a *scontrino* (receipt) when you leave. It's required by law, and you could theoretically be asked by a customs officer to present it with your purchases upon leaving an establishment. Without a receipt, you may pay a stiff fine.

The billing at Italian restaurants can also be confusing. Many restaurants add a *coperto* (cover charge) of about L2000/€1.03 to the price of your meal (for bread or some other fabricated courtesy) as well as a *servizio* (service charge) of 10-15%. **Tipping** is not traditional, and while you will almost never offend someone by leaving a couple of thousand *lire*, you should never be expected to tip unless it says so explicitly on the menu—even if the waiter hints strongly.

WAKE UP AND SMELL THE CAFFÈ!

Espresso isn't a beverage; it's an entire production experience, from the harvesting of the beans to the consumption of the liquid. The journey begins with the beans. *Arabica* beans, grown at high altitudes, make up 60-90% of most Italian blends, while woody-flavored *robusta* beans make up the remaining 10-40%. Italians prefer a higher concentration of *robusta* beans because they contribute to a heavy *crema* and tougher taste. Foamy *crema*, an emulsion of oils from the beans produced by the pressure and heat of the *espresso* machine, sits atop the drink.

Espresso beans are roasted longer than other coffee beans, bringing the oils to the surface of the beans and giving the drink its bitterness and full body. In the north, most beans are roasted deep mahogany brown. The process is stopped just before the oils are forced to the surface of the bean, resulting in a relatively sweet end product. In central Italy, the beans are roasted longer and have a slight sheen. In the south, the beans are roasted for quite a long time and have a thick oily coating. To prevent oxidation, beans must be stored within two hours of roasting. Humidity in excess of 55% can dramatically accelerate the decay of the beans, so some manufacturers (such as the acclaimed *Illy* brand) package their beans in nitrogen to avoid the loss of any oils.

Perhaps the most important part of the *espresso* process occurs just before the drink is served. The beans are ground, tamped into a basket, and barraged with hot, pressurized water. To make acceptable *espresso*, the machine must be able to sustain at least nine atmospheres of pressure and consistently heat the water to around 203°F (96°C). Heat and pressure optimize the flavor of the beverage over time without burning the beans, which are, no doubt, grateful for this small mercy.

So, how does one judge a good cup of *espresso*? First, watch as it drips from the machine. It should take around eight seconds for the liquid to begin emerging from the spout. After about 15 seconds, the stream should be thick and hang straight down in one uninterrupted, tapering line. Around 25 seconds into the process, the machine should be turned off, or the *espresso* will turn almost whitish. Next, examine the foamy *crema*. It should be caramel in color and thick enough to hold a spoonful of sugar for a few moments before it falls into the drink. A thick *crema* prevents the drink's rich aroma from dispersing into the air and is indicative of a full-bodied, well-brewed beverage. Once the *espresso* is in your hands, feel the cup. It must be preheated, or the *crema* will be damaged by rapid cooling as it moves from the hot machine to the cold porcelain or glass. After judging your *caffè* fit for consumption, stir the sugar and down it in one gulp like the locals.

Espresso, like happiness, comes in many forms. For a standard cup, request a *caffè*. If you would like a drop of milk in it, ask for *caffè macchiato* (spotted coffee). *Cappuccino*, which Italians drink only before lunch and never after a meal, has frothy scalded milk; *caffè latte* is heavier on the milk, lighter on the coffee. For coffee and happiness, try *caffè corretto* (corrected) *espresso* with a drop of strong liqueur (usually *grappa* or brandy). *Caffè Americano* is watery *espresso* served in a large cup, and the entirety of Italy scorns drip coffee. However you prefer your *caffè*, go forth into *bella Italia* determined not to settle for anything less than perfection, known to true *espresso* aficionados as an *espresso al'Albanese*.

I'VE GOT A CRUSH ON YOU

Italy's rocky soil, warm climate, and hilly landscape provide ideal conditions for growing grapes; Italy produces more **wine** than any other country. Sicily alone boasts 200 million gallons annually. The grapes are separated from the stems, then crushed by a pneumatic press which extracts the juice. For red wines, the juice and skins are pumped into temperature-controlled stainless steel fermentation vats, while white wines are produced from skin-less grapes. The duration of the fermentation process determines the sweetness of the wine. The longer a wine ferments, the drier it becomes. After fermentation, the wine is racked and clarified, a procedure which removes any lees (sediment). The wine is then stored in glass-lined concrete vats until ready for bottling.

CLASSIFICATION

Once the wine is ready to hit the shelves, the government subjects it to a three-tier classification system. *Denominazione di Origine Controllata e Garantita* (DOCG) wines grace the apex and are evaluated by several independent tasting commissions. Only 14 varieties of wine carry the DOCG designation. Minus the G, DOC wines comply with stiff regulations, from minimum alcohol contents and maximum vineyard yields to specific geographic origins. DOC wines comprise the majority of Italy's most tasty, yet affordable options. In general, DOCG implies higher quality than DOC, but due to the large number of vineyards that produce each variety of wine, many individual DOC brands are superb, while some DOCG brands are good, but not excellent. The lowest category is *Indicazione Geographica Tipica* (IGT), indicating merely the wine's origin. Any wine outside these categories falls into Italy's catch-all category, *Vino di Tavola* (table wine). Ironically, the country's best and worst wines coexist under this nebulous designation. The better wines are excluded because they don't use prescribed grapes or production methods, while the lower end wines are simply too shameful to classify. If you're confused, remember that generic table wine is sold by the liter, not by the bottle, and can be purchased for next to nothing at *Vino Sfusso* (loose wine) shops (as low as L1000 per liter) as long as you bring your own receptacle.

CORK YOUR WALLET! World War One snobs may spend upward of L100,000/€51.65 on a bottle of aged *riserva*, but wines in the L8,000-L20,000 range represent every level of quality, from barely drinkable to sublime. The most respected wine stewards in the nation regularly rank inexpensive wines above their costly cousins. Expense can equal quality, but with a little effort you should be able to find a cheaper, better wine. It is entirely acceptable to bring your own wine into a restaurant, provided you ask permission first.

WINE TASTING

Tasting wine in Italy is easy for travelers. The countryside is sprinkled with government-run *Enoteche Regionale* and *Enoteche Pubbliche*, regional exhibition and tasting centers. These *enoteche* promote local vineyards and often sponsor special 'educational' events. Spontaneous tasting is generally available, but booking may be necessary. Private wine shops are also called *enoteche*, though without the *regionale* or *pubblica* designation. *Cantine* do not typically offer tastings, unless accompanied by a wine bar. If touring by car, ask the tourist office about local *Strada del Vino* (wine roads), or contact the national Movement for Wine Tourism in Italy (☎ (39321) 46 62 14; fax 46 62 33; www.wine.it/mtv).

At restaurants, you can usually order wine by the liter or half-liter and occasionally by the glass. Drinking too much? Dry out with some *Secco*. Sour after a long day of travelling? Sweeten up with *Abboccato* or *Amabile*. Feeling spunky? Down a little *Vino Novello*, meant to be drunk young. Feeling Green? *Vino Biologico* is the organic lovers' fix. Feeling traditional? Sip some *Classico*, wine from the heartland, the grapes' indigenous growing area. Kickstart your evening with *Superiore*, which implies a higher alcohol content, or *Riserva*, which has a longer aging period and is of higher quality. For a bubbly buzz, try sparkling *Spumante*, the usually cheaper, tank-fermented twin of the bottle-fermented *Talento*. When in doubt, request the local wine—it will be cheaper (typically around L6000 per liter in local *trattorie*) and suited to the regional cuisine.

REGIONAL WINES

Piedmont is Italy's number one wine region, producing the most touted (and expensive) *Barolo*, a full-bodied red, velvety on the palate. *Barolo* is aged for two years, one year longer than its lighter cousin, *Barberesca*. While in Turin, visit the *Enoteche Regionale* at *Grinzane Cavour*, the 13th-century castle of the former *Risorgimento* hero Camillo Cavour. The wines here are monitored by the "Master Tasters of the Order of the Knights of the Truffle and the Wines of Alba." They suffer for our sake. Taste Piedmont's lighter side in the more affordable sparkling, sweet *Asti Spumante* at *Cantina di Vini di Costigliole d'Asti*, a castle formerly owned by Contessa di Castigliole, mistress to Napoleon III (p. 186).

Tuscany is famed for its tannic *chianti* and similar reds, such as the most-renowned wine in the country, *Brunello de Montalcino*. Originally, many *chianti* wines were excluded from classification. Regulations required that the *classico* wine include white grapes, making it an easy drinking daily wine, but producers were using 100% *sangiovese* grapes to produce the popular Super Tuscan wines. The aging process demanded old Slovenian barrels, leaving a slight wooden aftertaste, but the present oak rage in the international market encouraged experimentation among Italian wine makers. Recently, the regulations have been revamped, encompassing most Super Tuscan *chianti classici*. In the white wines, be on the lookout for *Vernaccia di San Gimignano* from the town of the same name, which has recently received DOCG status (p. 362).

The Veneto, from Verona west to Lake Garda, yields *Valpolicella*, a bright, medium-weight red with a dry finish and cherry-stone aftertaste. In *Valpolicella* vineyards, cherry tree roots hold the soil together, and the wood doubles as supply for local barrels. In recent years, foreign market affiliation for vanilla oak has blurred the cherry undertones. Verona produces the fizzy *Prosecco* and bland *Soave*. Indecisive? Try white or red *Tocai* from Friuli, light and fluffy enough for seafood, but spicy enough to handle an unimposing appetizer. Keep an eye out for the *Colli Berici Tocai Rosso*, among the more respected *Tocai* from the region.

Wash down the culinary delights of **Emiglia-Romagna** with Frizzantino Malvasia or Sauvignon, the typical aperitif in local bars. Sparkling Lambrusco is a widely drunk red, traditionally dry or amible (medium-dry), but these bottle-fermented versions are expensive. Avoid the sweet, white and rose versions found in the supermarket unless you're willing to embrace the accompanying hangover.

When in **Rome,** drink *Frascati*, a clean white wine, served cold, with an almond aftertaste. Try the *Colli di Tuscolo*. In Umbria, where production dates back to the Etruscans, try the world-famous *Orvieto*. This crisp, light white has recently been combined with chardonnay grapes to produce the world-class *Cervaro della Sala*. The dessert variety is equally splendid, affected by that delicious noble rot, a foggy fall fungus (*Botrytis Cinerea*) which shrivels grapes and concentrates sugars. Naples boasts *Lacryma Cristi* (Christ's Tear), an overrated tourist favorite.

The hotter climate and longer growing season of **southern Italy** and the islands produces stronger, fruitier wines than the North. Try the Sicilian *Marsala*, named after its hometown (p. 626). In 1773, John Woodhouse, son of a Liverpool merchant was driven ashore at Marsala by a storm. After tasting the local spirit, he decided to export it to England, adding a boost of booze for preservation. The Woodhouse *Baglio* (factory) still stands on Marsala's shore alongside other English successors. *Marsala* is versatile, ranging from culinary uses to *aperitivi*, *digestivi* and fortified drinking wines. After *Marsala* with a meal, follow with *Malvasia della Lipari* for dessert. In Sardinia, gulp down some *Vernaccia di*

Oristano, like a sherry with an almond aftertaste. Dazzle your senses with some *Mirto*, a succulent after-dinner *digestivo* available only on the island.

Maligned as tourist firewater, *grappa* gushes throughout Italy. After grapes are pressed for wine, the remaining *pomace* is used for this national blue-collar favorite. Originally mobile stills traveled from vineyard to vineyard, picking up the fermentation leftovers and producing *grappa*. Older Italians may still turn up their noses at *grappa*, but it has now lived down most of its bad reputation. There are four types of *grappa*: *giovane*, kept for six months in a stainless steel vat, and clear in color; *invecchiata*, aged for months or years in wooden barrels, giving it an amber tone and softer flavor; *monovitigno* (single grape), only produced from one grape in order to accentuate the flavor; a*romatizzata*, made with fruit flavoring and often used for medicinal purposes. In the last category, potent *gentian*-flavored *grappa* is allegedly a cure for insomnia. Ingenious Italians!

SPORTS AND RECREATION

In Italy, **calcio** (soccer to Americans, football to Europeans) surpasses all other sports. Some claim that Italy's victory in the 1982 World Cup did more for national unity than any political movement. Italy's success in 1994 sparked excitement that crested with every victory and ultimately crashed with their defeat by Brazil. The *azzurri* (blues) are a major source of national pride and sometimes agony.

Italian fans also cheer on their local teams, especially those promoted to Serie A, the Italian major league. Inter-urban rivalries, including those among Naples, Florence, and Rome, are intense. In the '01 season, Roma (Rome), Lazio (Rome) and Juventus (Turin) battled for the top spot in Serie A, followed by AC Milan and Inter Milan. Italian sports fans, called *tifosi* (fever boys) are raucous and energetic, at times bordering on violent. When AC Roma won Serie A 2001, fans stormed the field and began removing items of players' clothing as souvenirs.

Bicycling is popular in Italy. Besides manufacturing some of the best bikes in the world and encouraging bike tours, Italians host the **Giro d'Italia**, a 25-day cross-country race in May. Two wheels (in the form of a **scooter**) are a favorite form of transportation for Italians. With parts of the Italian Alps (including the Dolomites) and the Apennines within its borders, Italy attracts **skiers** from December to April. Skiing pros have come out of Italy, namely **Alberto Tomba,** Italy's Olympic gold-medal-winning superstar. **Hiking** and **mountain climbing** are popular throughout the North and in Calabria's Sila Massif. **Basketball** has also recently caught on in the wide world of Italian recreation. For **swimming, windsurfing,** or **sailing,** you may want to try the beaches in the South or those on Italy's islands. Sardinia, for example, offers crystal-blue waters with visibility to depths of up to 30 meters.

THE ITALIAN LANGUAGE

Ah, Italian. Language of lovers, of mafiosi, and Dante's eternal damnation. One of the six surviving romance languages, it has long inspired everything from Petrarch's passionate ramblings to Calvino's insane ramblings. As a result of the country's fragmented history, variations in **dialect** are strong. The throaty **Neapolitan** can be difficult for a Northerner to understand; **Ligurians** use a mix of Italian, Catalán, and French; **Sardo,** spoken in Sardinia, bears little resemblance to standard Italian; and many **Tuscan** dialects differ from Italian in pronunciation. Some inhabitants of the northern border regions don't speak Italian at all: the population of Val d'Aosta speaks mainly French, and the people of Trentino-Alto Adige harbor a German-speaking minority. In the southern regions of Apulia, Calabria, and Sicily, entire villages speak Albanian and Greek. In order to facilitate conversation, all natives do their best to employ standard Italian when speaking with a foreigner.

THE VULGAR AND THE DIVINE When you hit Tuscany, you may wonder if you've happened upon a mysterious republic embedded in the heart of Italy, with a language not unlike Italian. But not quite Italian. Florentines boast colorful local phrases and gestures useful for the non-native. Shortening of the first person singulars **fare (to make or to do)** and **andare (to go)** to **fo** and **vo** is common practice, and never fails to confound students who have learned proper Italian elsewhere. To fit in among the hip crowd of young, cell-phone toting Tuscans, memorize the phrases *"Mi garba!"* ("I dig it!", only cooler), and *"Mi rompi"* (to express strong dislike, although the literal translation concerns the destruction of certain parts of the male anatomy.) Accompany the latter by **shaking your right hand with your four fingers wrapped around your thumb** for a slightly stronger effect. Do not attempt this particular gesture in the direction of large men who look like bouncers. Tuscans are particularly sensitive about their dialect's place as the "official" Italian, which is, of course, an open invitation for speakers from other regions to utter particularly scathing parodies of the Tuscan tendency to swallow c's. The phrase *"una coca-cola con una cannucia corta"* is often replaced by Napolese and Sardi with *"una hoca-hola hon una hannuccia horta"* when a Tuscan is in earshot, but too far away to strike.

FESTIVALS AND HOLIDAYS

From the number of festivals commemorating an appearance of the Virgin Mary in Italy, it's easy to reach the conclusion that she has found *bella Italia* so appealing that she has decided never to leave. **Carnevale,** a brilliant invention held in February during the 10 days before Lent, energizes Italian towns; in Venice, costumed Carnevale revelers fill the streets and canals. During **Scoppio del Carro,** held in Florence's Piazza del Duomo on Easter Sunday, Florentines set off a cart of explosives, following a tradition dating back to medieval times, although some have speculated that it's merely a mass suicide attempt by the Catholics who have just endured 40 days without *prosciutto di Parma*. On July 2 and August 16, the **Palio** hits Siena, which celebrates the event with a horse race around the central *piazza*. Festivals in smaller towns are less touristed and much quirkier, allowing the visitors in the know to come home with unique stories about mouth-watering victuals in Cortona (p. 340) and drunken revelry in Gubbio (p. 403). For a complete list of festivals, write to the **Italian Government Travel Office** (see p. 35) or visit www.italiantourism.com/html/event_en.html.

DATE	FESTIVAL	LOCATION
January 1	Il Capodanno (New Year's Day)	All over Italy
January 5	Epiphany Fair	Rome
January 6	Epifania (Epiphany)	All over Italy
1st half of February	Festa del Fiore di Mandorlo (Almond Blossom)	Agrigento (p. 625)
February 8	Festa della Matricola (Graduation Feast)	Padua (p. 230)
February 16-27	Carnevale	Venice (p. 223)
March 5	Sartiglia (Race & Joust)	Oristano (p. 650)
April 17-23	Settimana Santa (Holy Week)	All over Italy
April 20	Giovedì Santo (Maundy Thursday)	All over Italy
April 21	Venerdì Santo (Good Friday)	All over Italy
April 23	Pasqua (Easter)	All over Italy
April 24	Lunedì di Pasqua (Easter Monday)	All over Italy
April 25	Giorno della Liberazione (Liberation Day)	All over Italy
May 1	Labor Day	All over Italy
May 1-4	Sagra di Sant'Efisio (Festival of St. Efisio)	Cagliari (p. 646)
May 5-7	Festa di Calendimaggio	Assisi (p. 402)
May 6-7	Festa di S. Nicola	Bari (p. 538)

DATE	FESTIVAL	LOCATION
May 7	Festa di S. Gennaro	Naples (p. 538)
May 14	Sagra del Pesce (Festival of Fish)	Camogli (p. 146)
May 15	Corsa dei Ceri (Candle Race)	Gubbio (p. 406)
May 28	Pallio della Balestra (Crossbow Contest)	Gubbio (p. 406)
June 1	Ascenzione (Feast of the Ascension)	All over Italy
June 4	Gioco del Ponte (Battle of the Bridge)	Pisa (p. 373)
June 18	Giostra del Saraceno (Joust of the Saracen)	Arezzo (p. 345)
June 22	Corpus Christi	All over Italy
June 24	Festa di S. Giovanni (Feast of St. John)	Florence (p. 336)
late June	Mostra Internazionale del Nuovo Cinema (International New Cinema)	Pesaro (p. 418)
late June to early July	S. Maria della Bruna (Feast of the Dark Madonna)	Matera
late June to mid-July	Spoleto Festival	Spoleto (p. 410)
July and August	Ravenna Festival	Ravenna (p. 298)
July and August	Umbria Jazz Festival	Perugia (p. 394)
July 2	Festa della Madonna (Feast of the Virgin Mary)	Enna (p. 613)
July 12	Palio della Balestra (Crossbow Contest)	Lucca (p. 368)
mid-July	Palio Marinaro (Boat Race)	Livorno (p. 379)
July 17	Festa del Redentore (Feast of the Redeemer)	Venice (p. 223)
July 25	Giostro del Orso (Joust of the Bear)	Pistoia (p. 365)
late July and early August	Settimana Musicale (Music Week)	Siena (p. 353)
late July to mid-September	Taormina Arte	Taormina (p. 600)
August	Festa dei Porcini (Mushroom Picking)	Cortona (p. 342)
August 6	Torneo della Quintana (Joust of the Quintana)	Ascoli-Piceno (p. 426)
August 14-15	Sagra della Bistecca (Steak Feast)	Cortona (p. 342)
August 15	Assunzione (Feast of the Assumption)	All over Italy
August 16	Palio	Siena (p. 353)
August 20 and 27	Festa del Redentore (Feast of the Redeemer)	Nuoro (p. 653)
late August to early September	Mostra Internazionale del Cinema (Venice International Film Festival)	Venice (p. 223)
September 3	Regata Storica (Historic Regatta)	Venice (p. 223)
September 3	Giostra del Saraceno (Joust of the Saracen)	Arezzo (p. 345)
September 10	Festivale della Sagra	Asti (p. 185)
September 14	Palio della Balestra (Crossbow Contest)	Lucca (p. 368)
September 17	Palio di Asti	Asti (p. 185)
September 19	Festa di S. Gennaro	Naples (p. 499)
November 1	Ogni Santi (All Saints Day)	All over Italy
November 2	Giorno dei Morti (All Souls Day)	All over Italy
November 21	Festa della Madonna della Salute (Festival of the Virgin, Patron of Good Health)	Venice (p. 223)
December 6	Festa di S. Nicola (Feast of St. Nicholas)	Bari (p. 538)
December 8	Concezione Immacolata (Feast of the Immaculate Conception)	All over Italy
December 16	Festa di S. Gennaro	Naples (p. 499)
December 24	Vigilia di Natale (Christmas Eve)	All over Italy
December 25	Natale (Christmas Day)	All over Italy
December 26	Festa di S. Stefano	All over Italy

ESSENTIALS

FACTS FOR THE TRAVELER

USEFUL ORGANIZATIONS

Italian Government Tourist Board (ENIT), 630 5th Ave., #1565, **New York,** NY 10111 (☎212-245-5618; fax 586-9249; www.italiantourism.com). Write or call ☎212-245-4822 for a free copy of *Italia: General Information for Travelers to Italy,* containing train and ferry schedules. Branch offices: 12400 Wilshire Blvd., #550, **Los Angeles,** CA 90025 (☎310-820-1898; fax 820-6357; enitla@earthlink.com); 175 E. Bloor St., #907 South Tower, **Toronto,** ON M4W 3R9 (☎416-925-4882; fax 925-4799; initaly@ican.net); 1 Princess St., **London** W1R 9AY (☎020-7355 1557 or 7355 1439; fax 7493 6695; enitlond@globalnet.co.uk; www.enit.it). Italian Chamber of Commerce and Industry in Australia, Level 26, 44 Market St., **Sydney** NSW 2000 Australia (☎(02) 9262 1666; fax 9262 1667).

Italian Cultural Institute, 686 Park Ave., **New York,** NY 10021 (☎212-879-4242; fax 861-4018; segr@italcultny.org; www.italcultny.org). Often more prompt than ENIT. Provides many useful links.

DOCUMENTS AND FORMALITIES

ENTRANCE REQUIREMENTS
Passport (p. 36). Required for citizens of Australia, Canada, Ireland, New Zealand, South Africa, the UK, and the US.

Visa (p. 37). Required for citizens of South Africa. Required for citizens of Australia, Canada, Ireland, New Zealand, the UK, and the US only for stays longer than 3 months.

Work Permit (p. 75). Required for foreigners planning to work in Italy.

Study Permit (p. 74). Required for foreigners planning to study in Italy.

Driving Permit (p. 68). Required for those planning to drive.

ITALIAN EMBASSIES AND CONSULATES

Australia: Embassy: 12 Grey St., Deakin, **Canberra** ACT 2600 (☎(02) 6273 3333; fax 6273 4223; embassy@ambitalia.org.au; www.ambitalia.org.au). Open M-F 9am-12:30pm and 2-4pm. **Consulates:** Level 14 AMP Place, 10 Eagle St., **Brisbane** QLD 4000 (☎(00617) 3229 8944; fax 3229 8643; italcons.brisbane@bigpond.com. Open M-W, F 9am-1pm, Th 9am-3pm); 509 St. Kilda Rd., **Melbourne** VIC 3004 (☎(613) 867 5744; fax 866 3932; itconmel@netlink.com.au); Level 45 The Gateway, 1 Macquarie Pl., **Sydney** NSW 2000 (☎(612) 9392 7939; fax 9392 7935; office@iisyd.org). All consulate info on embassy website.

Canada: Embassy: 275 Slater St., 21st fl., **Ottawa,** ON K1P 5H9 (☎613-232-2401; fax 233-1484; ambital@italyincanada.com; www.italyincanada.com). **Consulate:** 3489 Drummond St., **Montréal,** QC H3G 1X6 (☎514-849-8351; fax 499-9471; cgi@italconsul.montreal.qc.ca; www.italconsul.montreal.qc.ca).

Ireland: Embassy: 63 Northumberland Rd., **Dublin** (☎(01) 660 1744; fax 668 2759; italianembassy@tinet.ie; http://homepage.eircom.net/~italianembassy). Consular section open M-F 10am-12:30pm.

New Zealand: Embassy: 34 Grant Rd., **Wellington** (☎(006) 4473 5339; fax 472 9302; ambwell@xtra.co.nz; www.italy-embassy.org.nz).

South Africa: Embassy: 796 George Ave., Arcadia 0083, **Pretoria** (☎(012) 435541; fax 435547; ambital@iafrica.com; www.ambital.org.za). **Consulates:** 2 Grey's Pass, Gardens 8001, **Cape Town** (☎(021) 424 1256; fax 424 0146; italcons@mweb.co.za); Corner 2nd Ave., Houghton 2198, **Johannesburg** (☎(011) 728 1392; fax 728 3834).

UK: Embassy: 14 Three Kings Yard, **London** W1Y 2EH (☎(020) 7312 2200; fax 7499 2283; emblondon@embitaly.org.uk; www.embitaly.org.uk). **Consulates:** 38 Eaton Pl., **London** SW1X 8AN (☎(20) 7235 9371; fax 7823 1609); Rodwell Tower, 111 Piccadilly, **Manchester** M1 2HY (☎(161) 236 9024; fax 236 5574; passaporti@italconsulman.demon.co.uk); 32 Melville St., **Edinburgh** EH3 7HA (☎(131) 226 3631; fax 226 6260; consedimb@consedimb.demon.co.uk).

US: Embassy: 1601 Fuller St. NW, **Washington, D.C.** 20009 (☎202-328 5500; fax 462-3605; itapress@ix.netcom.com; www.italyemb.org). **Consulates:** 100 Boylston St., #900, **Boston,** MA 02116 (☎617-542-0483; fax 542-3998; it.conbos@ix.netcom.com; www.reference.it/cgboston); 500 N. Michigan Ave., #1850, **Chicago,** IL 60611 (☎312-467-1550; fax 467-1335; consul@consitchicago.org; www.italconschicago.org); 12400 Wilshire Blvd., #300, **Los Angeles,** CA 90025 (☎310-820-0622; fax 820-0727; cglos@conlang.com; www.conlang.com); 690 Park Ave. (visa office 54 E. 69th St.), **New York,** NY 10021 (☎212-737-9100; fax 249-4945; italconsny@aol.com; www.italconsulnyc.org).

EMBASSIES AND CONSULATES IN ITALY

Australia: Embassy: V. Alessandria, 215, 00198 Rome (☎(06) 85 27 21; fax 85 27 23 00; info@australian-embassy.it; www.australian-embassy.it). **Consulate** around the corner. Passport issue/renewal AUS$138, valid for 10 years; children half price, valid for 5 years. Consular services open M-Th 9am-5pm, F 9am-12:30pm.

Canada: Embassy, V. De Rossi, 27, 00161 Rome (☎(06) 44 59 81; fax 44 59 87 50; www.canada.it), near the Piazza Bologna metro stop. **Consulate:** V. Zara, 30, 00198 Rome (☎(06) 44 59 81). Passports CDN$50, valid for 5 years. Consular and passport services M-F 8:30am-12:30pm and 2-4pm.

Ireland: Embassy: P. di Campitelli 3 (Scalla A, int 2), 00186 Rome (☎(06) 697 91 21; fax 679 23 54; registry@irishembassy.it). Passport renewal UK£45. Embassy open M-F 10am-12:30pm and 3-4:30pm.

New Zealand: Embassy: V. Zara, 28, 00198 Rome (☎(06) 441 71 71; fax 440 29 84; nzemb.rom@flashnet.it). Passports L260,000/€134.27, children L198,000/€102.26. Consular and passport services open Sept.-June M-F 9:30am-noon. Embassy open Sept.-June M-F 8:30am-12:30-pm and 1-4pm; July-Aug. variable hours.

South Africa: Embassy: V. Tanaro, 14, 00198 Rome (☎(06) 85 25 41; fax 85 25 43 00; sae@flashnet.it; www.sudafrica.it). Open daily 8am-4:30pm.

UK: Embassy, V. XX Settembre, 80a, 00187 Rome (☎(06) 482 54 41; fax 48 90 30 73; ConsularEnquiries@rome.mail.fco.gov.uk; www.britain.it). Passports L156,800/€80.98 for those over 16. Consular and passport services M-F 9:15am-1:30pm.

US: Embassy and **Consulate:** V.V. Veneto, 119a, 00187 Rome (☎(06) 467 41; fax 46 74 22 17; www.usis.it). Issues same day new passports for US$65 (children US$40). Passport services mid-Sept. to mid-June M-F 8:30am-noon; late June to early Sept. M-F 8am-noon. Consular services mid-Sept. to mid-June M-F 8:30am-1pm and 2-5pm; late June to early Sept. M-F 8am-1pm and 1:30-4pm. Closed US and Italian holidays.

PASSPORTS

Citizens of Australia, Canada, Ireland, New Zealand, South Africa, the UK, and the US need valid passports to enter Italy and to reenter their own country. Returning home with an expired passport is illegal. Be sure to **photocopy** the page of your passport with your photograph, passport number, and other identifying information, as well as any visas, travel insurance policies, plane tickets, or traveler's check serial numbers. Carry one set of copies in a safe place, apart from the originals, and leave another set at home. Consulates also recommend that you carry an expired passport or an official copy of your birth certificate in your baggage, separate from other documents. If you **lose your passport,** immediately notify the local police and the nearest embassy or consulate of your home government. To expedite its replacement, you will need to know all information previously recorded and show ID and proof of citizenship. In some cases, a replacement may take weeks to process, and it may be valid only for a limited time. In an emergency, ask for immediate temporary traveling papers that will permit you to reenter your home country. File any **new passport** or renewal applications well in advance of your departure date. Most passport offices offer rush services for a steep fee. Citizens living abroad who need a passport or renewal should contact the nearest consular service of their home country.

ONE EUROPE European unity has come a long way since 1958, when the European Economic Community (EEC) was created to promote cooperation between its founding states. Since then, the EEC has become the European Union (EU), with political, legal, and economic institutions spanning 15 member states: Austria, Belgium, Denmark, Finland, France, Germany, Greece, Ireland, Italy, Luxembourg, The Netherlands, Portugal, Spain, Sweden, and the UK.

What does this have to do with the average non-EU tourist? Well, in 1999, 14 European countries—the entire EU minus Denmark, Ireland, and the UK, but including Iceland and Norway—established **freedom of movement** across their borders. Border controls between participating countries have been abolished, and visa policies harmonized. Although required to carry a passport (or government-issued ID card for EU citizens) when crossing an internal border, once admitted into one country, you're free to travel to all participating countries.

For more important consequences of the EU for travelers, see **The Euro** (see p. 40), **European Customs,** and **EU customs regulations** (see p. 38).

VISAS

EU citizens need only a valid passport to enter Italy, and may stay as long as they like. Citizens of Australia, Canada, New Zealand, and the US do not need visas for stays of up to three months. Visas can be purchased at consulates of your home country. US citizens can take advantage of the **Center for International Business and Travel (CIBT; ☎ 800-925-2428),** which secures travel visas for a small charge.

As of August 2000, citizens of South Africa need a visa—a stamp, sticker, or insert in their passport specifying the purpose of their travel and the permitted duration of their stay—in addition to a valid passport for entrance to Italy. Under the Schengen Agreement, any visa granted by Italy will be respected by Austria, Belgium, France, Germany, Greece, Luxembourg, the Netherlands, Portugal, and Spain. The duration of one stay or a succession of stays may not exceed 90 days per six months. The cost of a Schengen visa varies with duration and number of entries into the country; one entry with the maximum 90-day stay costs SAR198.

Within eight days of arrival, all foreign nationals staying with friends or relatives or taking up residence must register with the local police office (*questura*) and receive a *permesso di soggiorno* (permit of stay) for a fee of L20,000/€10.33. If staying in a hotel or hostel, the officials will fulfill registration requirements for you and the fee is waived. Those wishing to stay in Italy for more than three months for the sole purpose of tourism must apply for an extension of their stay at a local *questura* at least one month before the original permit expires. For information on employment and study visas, see **Alternatives to Tourism,** p. 74.

IDENTIFICATION

When you travel, always carry two or more forms of identification on your person, including at least one photo ID. Many establishments, especially banks, require several IDs in order to cash traveler's checks. Never carry all your forms of ID together; split them up in case of theft or loss. It is useful to carry extra passport-size photos to affix to the various IDs or passes you may acquire along the way.

STUDENT AND TEACHER IDENTIFICATION. The **International Student Identity Card (ISIC),** the most widely accepted form of student ID, provides discounts on sights, accommodations, food, and transport. All cardholders have access to a 24-hour emergency helpline for medical, legal, and financial emergencies (in North America call ☎ (877) 370-ISIC, elsewhere call US collect ☎ +1 715-345-0505). Many student travel agencies issue ISICs, including STA Travel in Australia and New Zealand; Travel CUTS in Canada; USIT in the Republic of Ireland and Northern Ireland; SASTS in South Africa; Campus Travel and STA Travel in the UK; and Council Travel (www.counciltravel.com/idcards/default.asp) and STA Travel in the US (see p. 58).

The card is valid from September to December of the following year and costs AUS$15, CDN$16, or US$22. Applicants must be degree-seeking students of a secondary or post-secondary school and must be at least 12 years old. Because of the proliferation of fake ISICs, some services (particularly airlines) require additional proof of student identity, such as a school ID or a letter attesting to your student status, signed by your registrar and stamped with your school seal. The **International Teacher Identity Card (ITIC)** offers identical insurance coverage and similar discounts. The fee is AUS$16.50, UK£6, or US$22. For more information, contact the **International Student Travel Confederation (ISTC),** Herengracht 479, 1017 BS Amsterdam, Netherlands (☎ +31 (20) 421 28 00; fax 421 28 10; istcinfo@istc.org; www.istc.org).

YOUTH IDENTIFICATION. The ISTC issues a discount card to travelers who are 25 years old or under but are not students. This one-year International Youth Travel Card (IYTC; formerly the GO 25 Card) offers many of the same benefits as the ISIC. Most organizations that sell the ISIC also sell the IYTC (US$22).

CUSTOMS

Upon entering Italy, you must declare certain items from abroad and pay a duty on the value of those articles that exceeds the allowance established by the Italian customs service. Note that goods and gifts purchased at **duty-free** shops abroad are not exempt from duty or sales tax and thus must be declared upon entering Italy as well; "duty-free" merely means that you need not pay a tax in the country of purchase. Duty-free allowances were abolished for travel between EU member states on July 1, 1999, but they still exist for those arriving from outside the EU.

Upon returning home, you must declare all articles acquired abroad and pay a duty on the value of articles in excess of your home country's allowance. Keep receipts for all goods acquired abroad. Upon departure from the EU, non-EU citizens can claim a refund for the value added tax (VAT or IVA) paid on major purchases (see **Money: Taxes,** p. 43).

 CUSTOMS IN THE EU Travelers can take advantage of the freedom of movement of goods. There are no customs controls at internal EU borders and travelers are free to transport whatever legal substances they like as long as it is for their own personal use—up to 800 cigarettes, 10L of spirits, 90L of wine (60L of sparkling wine), and 110L of beer. Duty-free was abolished on June 30, 1999, for travel between EU member states; yet, travelers between the EU and the rest of the world get a duty-free allowance when passing through customs.

MONEY

If you stay in hostels and prepare your own food, expect to spend anywhere from L60,000/€31 to L140,000/€72.30 per person per day in addition to transportation costs. Overestimate your expenses. **Accommodations** start at about L24,000/€12.40 per night for a dorm, L51,000/€26.34 for a single, and L71,000/€36.67 for a double, though these prices increase in peak season. A basic sit-down meal costs about L31,000/€16.01. Carrying cash with you, even in a money belt, is risky but necessary; personal checks from home are usually not accepted and traveler's checks may not be accepted in some locations.

Money From Home In Minutes.

If you're stuck for cash on your travels, don't panic. Millions of people trust Western Union to transfer money in minutes to over 185 countries and over 95,000 locations worldwide. Our record of safety and reliability is second to none. You can even send money by phone without leaving home by using a credit card. For more information, call Western Union: USA 1-800-325-6000, Canada 1-800-235-0000.

www.westernunion.com

WESTERN UNION | MONEY TRANSFER

The fastest way to send money worldwide.

CURRENCY AND EXCHANGE

The Italian currency unit is the *lira* (plural: *lire*). The currency chart below is based on exchange rates from August 2001. Check a large newspaper or the web (finance.yahoo.com or www.bloomberg.com) for the latest exchange rates.

ITALIAN LIRA (L)	
US$1 = L2215	L1000 = US$0.45
CDN$1 = L1444	L1000 = CDN$0.69
EUR€1 = L1936	L1000 = EUR€0.52
UK£1 = L3155	L1000 = UK£0.32
IR£1 = L2459	L1000 = IR£0.41
AUS$1 = L1119	L1000 = AUS$0.89
NZ$1 = L910	L1000 = NZ$1.09
SFr 1 = L1284	L1000 = SFr 0.78
SAR1= L270	L1000 = SAR3.69

Coins are minted in L50, L100, L200, and L500 denominations, and the most common bills are L1000, L2000, L5000, L10,000, L50,000, and L100,000.

As a general rule, it's cheaper to convert money in Italy than at home. However, you should bring enough foreign currency to last for the first 24 to 72 hours of a trip to avoid being penniless should you arrive after bank hours or on a holiday. Travelers from the US can get foreign currency from the comfort of home: **International Currency Express** (☎(888) 278-6628) delivers foreign currency or traveler's checks overnight (US$15) or 2nd-day (US$12) at competitive exchange rates.

When changing money abroad, try to go only to banks or *cambii* that have at most a 5% margin between their buy and sell prices. Since you lose money with every transaction, convert large sums (unless the currency is depreciating rapidly), but no more than you'll need.

THE EURO Since 1999, the official currency of 12 members of the European Union—Austria, Belgium, Finland, France, Germany, Greece, Ireland, Italy, Luxembourg, the Netherlands, Portugal, and Spain—has been the *euro*. But don't throw out *francs*, *pesetas*, and *Deutschmarks* just yet; actual *euro* banknotes and coins won't be available until January 1, 2002, and the old national currencies will remain legal tender for six months after that (through July 1, 2002).

While you might not be able to pay for a coffee and get your change in euros yet, the currency has some important consequences for travelers. Money-changers across the euro-zone are obliged to exchange money at the official, fixed rate (see below) and at no commission (though they may still charge a small service fee). So now you can change your guilders into *escudos* and your *escudos* into *lire* without losing fistfuls of money on every transaction. Second, *euro*-denominated traveler's checks allow you to pay for goods and services across the *euro*-zone, again at the official rate and commission-free.

The exchange rate between *euro*-zone currencies was permanently fixed on January 1, 1999. For more information, see www.europa.eu.int

TRAVELER'S CHECKS

Traveler's checks (**American Express** and **Visa** are the most recognized) are one of the safest and easiest means of carrying funds. Several agencies and banks sell them for a small commission. Each agency provides refunds if your checks are lost or stolen, and many provide additional services, such as toll-free refund hotlines abroad, emergency message services, and stolen credit card assistance.

While traveling, keep check receipts and a record of which checks you've cashed separate from the checks themselves. Also leave a list of check numbers with someone at home. Never countersign checks until you're ready to cash them, and always bring your passport with you to cash them. If your checks are lost or stolen, contact a refund center; they may require a police report verifying the loss or theft. Less touristed regions may not have refund centers at all, in which case you might have to wait to be reimbursed. Ask about toll-free refund hotlines and the location of refund centers when purchasing checks, and always carry emergency cash.

American Express: In Australia ☎(800) 251 902; in New Zealand ☎(0800) 441 068; in the UK ☎(0800) 521 313; in the US and Canada ☎800-221-7282; in Italy ☎800 87 20 00; elsewhere US collect ☎+1 (801) 964-6665; www.aexp.com. Traveler's checks available in *lire* at 1-4% commission at AmEx offices and banks. American Automobile Association (AAA) members can buy checks commission-free at AAA offices. *Cheques for Two* need be signed by just 1 of its 2 owners.

Thomas Cook MasterCard: In the US and Canada call ☎800-223-7373; in the UK ☎(0800) 622101; elsewhere call the UK collect ☎+44 (1733) 318950. Checks in 13 currencies at 2% commission. Thomas Cook offices cash checks commission-free.

Visa: In the US ☎800-227-6811; in the UK ☎(0800) 895078; elsewhere UK collect ☎+44 (1733) 318949. Call for the location of the nearest office.

CREDIT CARDS

Credit cards often offer superior exchange rates—up to 5% better than the retail rate used by banks and other currency exchange establishments. They may also offer services such as insurance or emergency help and are sometimes required to reserve hotel rooms or rental cars. **MasterCard** (a.k.a. EuroCard or Access in Europe) and **Visa** are the most welcomed; **American Express** cards work at some ATMs and at AmEx offices and major airports. In southern Italy, ATMs are scarce.

Credit cards are useful for **cash advances,** which allow you to withdraw *lire* from associated banks and ATMs throughout Italy. Transaction fees for all credit card advances (up to US$10 per advance, plus 2-3% on foreign transactions after conversion) tend to make credit cards a more costly way of withdrawing cash than ATMs or traveler's checks. In an emergency, however, the transaction fee may prove worth the cost. To be eligible for an advance, you'll need to get a **Personal Identification Number (PIN)** from your credit card company (see **Cash (ATM) Cards,** below).

CASH (ATM) CARDS

Cash cards—popularly called ATM cards—are widespread in Italy. Depending on the system that your home bank uses, you can most likely access your personal bank account from abroad. ATMs get the same wholesale exchange rate as credit cards, but there is often a limit on the amount of money you can withdraw per day (around US$500), and unfortunately computer networks sometimes fail. There is typically also a surcharge of US$1-5 per withdrawal. Be sure to memorize your PIN code in numeric form since machines in Italy often don't have letters on their keys. Also, if your PIN is longer than four digits, ask your bank if you need a new one.

The two major international money networks are **Cirrus** (US ☎800-424-7787) and **PLUS** (US ☎800-843-7587). To locate ATMs around the world, call the above numbers, or consult www.visa.com/pd/atm or www.mastercard.com/atm.

Visa TravelMoney (for customer assistance in Italy call ☎(800) 81 90 14) is a system allowing you to access money from any Visa ATM, common throughout Italy. In order to activate a card from the US, call ☎877-394-2247. Deposit an amount before you travel (plus a small administration fee), and you can withdraw up to that sum. The cards, which offer the same favorable exchange rate for withdrawals as a regular Visa, are useful if you plan to travel through many countries. Check with your local bank to see if it issues TravelMoney cards. **Road Cash** (US ☎877-762-3227; www.roadcash.com) issues cards in the US with a minimum US$300 deposit.

THANK YOU SIR, MAY I HAVE ANOTHER? To use a cash or credit card to withdraw money from a cash machine (ATM) in Europe, you must have a four-digit Personal Identification Number (PIN). If your PIN is longer than four digits, ask your bank whether can just use the first four, or whether you'll need a new one. Credit cards in North America don't usually come with PINs, so call your credit card company before leaving to request one.

People with alphabetic, rather than numerical, PINs may also be thrown off by the lack of letters on European cash machines. The following handy chart gives the corresponding numbers to use: 1=QZ, 2=ABC, 3=DEF, 4=GHI, 5=JKL, 6=MNO, 7=PRS, 8=TUV, and 9=WXY. Note that if you mistakenly punch the wrong code into the machine three times, it will swallow your card for good.

GETTING MONEY FROM HOME

AMERICAN EXPRESS. Cardholders can withdraw cash from their checking accounts at AmEx's major offices and many representative offices (up to US$1000 every 21 days; no service charge, no interest). AmEx "Express Cash" withdrawals from AmEx ATMs in Italy are debited from the cardholder's checking account or line of credit. Green card holders may withdraw up to US$1000 in any seven-day period (2% transaction fee; min. US$2.50, max. US$20). To enroll in Express Cash, cardmembers may call ☎800-227-4669 in the US; elsewhere call US collect ☎336-668-5041. The AmEx national number in Italy is ☎(06) 722 82.

WESTERN UNION. Travelers from the US, Canada, and the UK can wire money abroad through Western Union's international money transfer services. In the US, call ☎800-325-6000; in Canada, ☎800-235-0000; in the UK, ☎0800-833 833; in Italy ☎800 22 00 55. To wire money from within the US using a credit card (Visa, Master-Card, Discover), call ☎800-CALL-CASH (225-5227). The rates for sending cash are generally US$10-11 cheaper than with a credit card, and the money is usually available at the place you're sending it to within an hour. To locate the nearest Western Union location, consult www.westernunion.com.

US STATE DEPARTMENT (US CITIZENS ONLY). In dire emergencies only, the US State Department will forward money within hours to the nearest consular office, which will then disburse it according to instructions for a US$15 fee. Contact the Overseas Citizens Service, American Citizens Services, Consular Affairs, Room 4811, US Department of State, Washington, D.C. 20520 (☎202-647-5225; nights, Sundays, and holidays ☎647-4000; http://travel.state.gov).

COSTS

The cost of your trip will vary considerably, depending on where you go, how you travel, and where you stay. The single biggest cost of your trip will probably be your round-trip airfare to Italy (see p. 60). A railpass (or bus pass) would be another major pre-departure expense (see p. 67). Before you go, spend some time calculating a reasonable daily **budget** that will meet your needs. To give you a general idea, a bare-bones day in Italy (camping or sleeping in hostels/guesthouses, buying food at supermarkets) would cost L40-60,000/€20.66-31. For a luxurious day, the sky's the limit. Don't forget to factor in emergency reserve funds (at least US$200) when planning how much money you'll need.

TIPS FOR STAYING ON A BUDGET

Considering that saving just a few dollars a day over the course of your trip might pay for days or weeks of additional travel, the art of penny-pinching is well worth learning. Learn to take advantage of freebies: for example, museums will typically be free once a week or once a month, and cities often host free open-air concerts and/or cultural events (especially in the summer). Do your **laundry** in the sink, split the costs of **accommodations** and meals with trustworthy fellow travelers, and buy food in supermarkets instead of eating out.

TIPPING AND BARGAINING

At many Italian restaurants, a service charge *(servizio)* or cover *(coperto)* is included in the bill. Tips are neither required nor expected, but it is polite to leave a little something (5-10%) in addition. Taxis drivers will expect about a 10% tip.

Bargaining is common in Italy, but use discretion. It is appropriate at outdoor markets, with street vendors, and over unmetered taxi fares (always settle your price *before* taking the cab). Haggling over prices elsewhere is usually inappropriate. Hotel haggling is more successful in uncrowded, smaller *pensioni.* This book usually notes the hotels that are open to bargaining. Never offer what you aren't willing to pay as you're expected to buy once the merchant accepts your price.

TAXES

The **Value-Added Tax** (**VAT,** *imposto sul valore aggiunta,* or IVA) is a sales tax levied in the EU. VAT (ranging from 12-35%) is usually part of the price paid for goods and services. Upon departure from the EU, non-EU citizens can get a refund of the VAT for single purchases over L650,000/€335. The receipt, purchases, and purchaser's passport must be presented at the Customs Office as you leave the EU, and the refund will be mailed home to you. "Tax-Free Shopping for Tourists" at some stores enables you to get a refund in cash at the airport or a border crossing.

SAFETY AND SECURITY

IMPORTANT PHONE NUMBERS
Emergency Aid Services: ☎ 113.
Carabinieri: ☎ 112.
Fire Brigade: ☎ 115.
ACI (Automobile Club of Italy) for emergency breakdowns: ☎ 116.
Sailing Conditions: ☎ 144 66 19 06.
Weather Reports: ☎ 144 66 19 11.
Snow Conditions: ☎ 144 66 19 02.
News Reports: ☎ 144 22 19 00.

Travel in Italy is generally safe, and incidents of physical violence against tourists are quite rare. The vast chasm that separates the north from the south in terms of tourism infrastructure also applies to safety issues. In general, Naples and farther south is more dangerous than the north. Travelers of color may not feel wholly safe south of Naples. One of the greatest dangers of the south and elsewhere are **Vespa bandits,** criminals who speed along on their mopeds in search of people carrying purses or cameras that they can snatch as they drive by. Whenever walking along a street, keep valuables out of the reach of these mobile thugs. Some delinquents make no attempt to hide their nefarious activities; they will reach in the open window of a car stopped at a stoplight in an attempt to steal a wallet. The carabinieri will generally speak limited English. It's best to snag an English-speaking Italian and have him or her report the incident.

PERSONAL SAFETY

EXPLORING. To avoid unwanted attention, try to **blend in** as much as possible. Respecting local customs (dressing more conservatively) may discourage would-be hecklers, as will leaving a conspicuous purse behind for women. Familiarize yourself with your surroundings, and carry yourself with confidence; if you must check a map on the street, duck into a shop. If you are traveling alone, be sure someone at home knows your itinerary, and **never admit that you're traveling alone.**

When walking at night, stick to busy, well lit streets and avoid dark alleyways. Do not attempt to cross through parks, parking lots, or other large, deserted areas. Look for children playing, women walking in the open, and other signs of an active community. If you feel uncomfortable, leave as quickly and directly as you can, but don't let fear of the unknown turn you into a hermit. Careful, persistent exploration will build confidence and make your stay even more rewarding.

CAR TRAVEL. If you are using a **car**, learn local driving signals and wear a seatbelt. Children under 40 lbs. should ride only in a specially designed carseat, available for a small fee from most car rental agencies. Study route maps before you hit the road, and if you plan on spending a lot of time on the road, you may want to bring spare parts. If your car breaks down, wait for the police to assist you. For long drives in desolate areas, invest in a cellular phone and a roadside assistance program (see p. 69). Be sure to park your vehicle in a garage or well traveled area, and use a steering wheel locking device in larger cities. **Sleeping in your car** is one of the most dangerous (and often illegal) ways to get your rest.

SELF DEFENSE. There is no sure-fire way to avoid all the threatening situations you might encounter when you travel, but a good self-defense course offers concrete ways to react to unwanted advances. **Impact, Prepare,** and **Model Mugging** can refer you to local self-defense courses in the US (☎800-345-5425). Workshops (2-3hr.) start at US$50; full courses run US$350-500.

TRAVEL ADVISORIES.

Australian Department of Foreign Affairs and Trade: ☎ (02) 6261 1111; www.dfat.gov.au.

Canadian Department of Foreign Affairs and International Trade (DFAIT): In Canada call ☎800-267-8376; elsewhere ☎+1 613-944-4000; www.dfait-maeci.gc.ca. Call for their free booklet, *Bon Voyage...But.*

New Zealand Ministry of Foreign Affairs: ☎(04) 494 8500; fax 494 8511; www.mft.gov.nz/travel/index.html.

UK Foreign and Commonwealth Office: ☎(020) 7008 0232; fax 7008 0155; www.fco.gov.uk.

US Department of State: ☎202-647-5225; auto faxback 261; http://travel.state.gov. For *A Safe Trip Abroad*, call ☎202-512-1800.

FINANCIAL SECURITY

PROTECTING YOUR VALUABLES. There are a few steps you can take to minimize the financial risk associated with traveling. First, bring as little with you as possible. Leave expensive watches, jewelry, cameras, and electronic equipment at home; chances are you'd break them, lose them, or get sick of lugging them around anyway. Second, never leave your valuables unattended. Be particularly careful on **buses** and **trains;** horror stories abound about determined thieves who wait for travelers to fall asleep. When traveling with others, sleep in alternate shifts. When alone, use good judgment in selecting a train compartment. Try to sleep on top bunks with your luggage stored above you (if not in bed with you), and keep important documents and other valuables on your person. If traveling by car, don't leave valuables (such as radios or luggage) in it while you are away.

Third, buy combination **padlocks** to secure your belongings either in your pack or in a hostel or train station locker. Fourth, carry as little cash as possible; instead carry traveler's checks and ATM/credit cards, keeping them in a **money belt**—not a "fanny pack"—along with your passport and ID cards. Finally, keep a small cash reserve separate from your primary stash. This should entail about US$50 sewn into or stored in the depths of your pack, along with your traveler's check numbers and important photocopies.

CON ARTISTS AND PICKPOCKETS. Among the more colorful aspects of large cities are con artists. They often work in groups, and children are among the most effective. Beware of certain classics: sob stories that require money, rolls of bills "found" on the street, mustard spilled (or saliva spit) onto your shoulder to distract you while they snatch your bag. Don't ever hand over your passport to someone whose authority you question (ask to accompany them to a police station if they insist), and **don't ever let your passport out of your sight.** Similarly, don't let your bag out of sight; never trust a "station-porter" who insists on carrying your bag or stowing it in the baggage compartment or a "new friend" who offers to guard your bag while you buy a train ticket or use the rest room. **Pickpockets** abound in Rome, Naples, and other major urban centers. Beware of them in city crowds, especially on public transportation. A common modus operandi among thieves, is to pretend to throw a child wrapped in a sling at a tourist and steal her purse while she reaches out to "save" the baby. Also, be alert in public telephone booths. If you must say your calling card number, do so very quietly; if you punch it in, make sure no one can look over your shoulder.

DRUGS AND ALCOHOL

Hysteria about growing cocaine and heroin addiction have forced Italian authorities to deal strictly with those picked up for drug-related offenses. While hash is fairly common in big cities, harder drugs are quite rare, though ecstasy is becoming increasingly popular. Most Italian ecstasy is heroin-based, with little or no MDMA. Psylocibin mushrooms, methamphetamine, Ketamine, PCP, and LSD are all but nonexistent, and street dealers who claim otherwise are probably vending calcium or, worse, strychnine. Needless to say, **illegal drugs** are best avoided altogether; in Italy, drugs (including marijuana) are illegal. If you carry **prescription drugs,** it is vital to bring a copy of the prescriptions themselves and a note from a doctor and have them readily accessible at country borders. There is no drinking age in Italy, but drinking and driving is strictly sanctioned.

HEALTH

Common sense is the simplest prescription for good health while you travel. Drink lots of fluids to prevent dehydration and constipation, wear sturdy, broken-in shoes and clean socks, and use talcum powder to keep your feet dry.

BEFORE YOU GO

Preparation can help minimize the likelihood of contracting a disease and maximize the chances of receiving effective health care in the event of an emergency. For tips on packing a basic **first-aid kit** and other health essentials, see p. 49.

In your **passport,** write the names of any people you wish to be contacted in case of a medical emergency, and also list any allergies or medical conditions of which you would want doctors to be aware. Matching a prescription to a foreign equivalent is not always easy, safe, or possible. For a searchable online database of all medications in all languages, try www.rxlist.com. Carry up-to-date, legible prescriptions or a statement from your doctor stating the medication's trade name, manufacturer, chemical name, and dosage. While traveling, be sure to keep all medication with you in your carry-on luggage.

IMMUNIZATIONS. Travelers over two years old should be sure that the following vaccines are up to date: MMR (for measles, mumps, and rubella); DTaP or Td (for diptheria, tetanus, and pertussis), OPV (for polio), HbCV (for haemophilus influenza B), and HBV (for hepatitus B). For recommendations on immunizations and prophylaxis, consult the CDC (see below) in the US or the equivalent in your home country. Check with a doctor for guidance. Meningitis shots are usually advisable, especially among college-age backpackers who plan to stay in hostels.

USEFUL ORGANIZATIONS AND PUBLICATIONS. The US **Centers for Disease Control and Prevention (CDC;** ☎877-FYI-TRIP; www.cdc.gov/travel) maintains an international fax information service and an international travelers hotline (☎404-332-4559). The CDC's comprehensive booklet *Health Information for International Travel,* an annual rundown of disease, immunization, and general health advice, is free online or US$25 via the Public Health Foundation (☎877-252-1200). Consult the appropriate government agency of your home country for consular information sheets on health, entry requirements, and other issues for various countries (see the listings in the box on **Travel Advisories,** p. 44). For information on health and travel warnings, call the **Overseas Citizens Services** (☎202-647-5225; after-hours ☎202-647-4000), or contact a passport agency, embassy or consulate abroad. US citizens can send a self-addressed, stamped envelope to the Overseas Citizens Services, Bureau of Consular Affairs, #4811, US Department of State, Washington, D.C. 20520. For information on medical evacuation services and travel insurance firms, see the US government's website at http://travel.state.gov/medical.html or the **British Foreign and Commonwealth Office** website at (www.fco.gov.uk).

MEDICAL ASSISTANCE ON THE ROAD. On the whole, Italy conforms to most Western standards of health care. The quality of care, however, varies throughout the country and is generally better in the north and in private hospitals and clinics. In most large cities doctors will speak English; if they don't, they may be able to arrange for a translator. *Let's Go* lists information on how to access medical help in the **Practical Information** sections of most cities and towns.

If you are concerned about being able to access medical support while traveling, there are special support services you may employ. The *MedPass* from **GlobalCare, Inc.,** 2001 Westside Pkwy., #120, Alpharetta, GA 30004, USA (☎800-860-1111; fax 770-475-0058; www.globalems.com), provides 24hr. international medical assistance, support, and medical evacuation resources. The **International Association for Medical Assistance to Travelers** (**IAMAT;** US ☎716-754-4883, Canada ☎416-652-0137, New Zealand ☎03 352 20 53; www.sentex.net/~iamat) has free membership, lists English-speaking doctors worldwide, and offers detailed information on immunization requirements and sanitation. If your regular **insurance** policy does not cover travel abroad, you may wish to purchase additional coverage (see p. 48).

Those with medical conditions (diabetes, allergies to antibiotics, epilepsy, heart conditions) may want to obtain a stainless-steel **Medic Alert** ID tag (first year US$35, annually thereafter US$20), which identifies the condition and gives a 24hr. collect-call number. Contact the Medic Alert Foundation, 2323 Colorado Ave, Turlock, CA 95382, USA (☎888-633-4298; www.medicalert.org).

ON THE ROAD

ENVIRONMENTAL HAZARDS

Heat exhaustion and dehydration: Heat exhaustion, characterized by dehydration and salt deficiency, can lead to fatigue, headaches, and wooziness. Avoid it by drinking plenty of fluids, eating salty foods (e.g. crackers), and avoiding dehydrating beverages (e.g. alcohol, coffee, tea, and caffeinated soda). Continuous heat stress can eventually lead to heatstroke, characterized by a rising temperature, severe headache, and cessation of sweating. Victims should be cooled off with wet towels and taken to a doctor.

Sunburn: If you're prone to sunburn, bring sunscreen with you and apply it liberally and often to avoid burns and risk of skin cancer. If basking on the beaches of the Pontine Islands or hitting the slopes at Courmayeur is on your itinerary, you are at risk of getting burned, even through clouds. If you get sunburned, drink more fluids than usual and apply Calamine or an aloe-based lotion.

High altitude: If hiking or skiing in the Italian Alps, allow your body a couple of days to adjust to less oxygen before exerting yourself. Note that alcohol is more potent and UV rays are stronger at high elevations.

INSECT-BORNE DISEASES

Many diseases are transmitted by insects—mainly mosquitoes, fleas, ticks, and lice. Be aware of insects in wet or forested areas, especially while hiking and camping. **Mosquitoes** are most active from dusk to dawn. Wear long pants and long sleeves, tuck your pants into your socks, and buy a mosquito net. Use insect repellents, such as DEET, and soak or spray your gear with permethrin (licensed in the US for use on clothing). Consider natural repellents that make you smelly to insects, like vitamin B-12 or garlic pills. To stop the itch after being bitten, try Calamine lotion or topical cortisones (like Cortaid).

FOOD- AND WATER-BORNE DISEASES

Prevention is the best cure: be sure that everything you eat is cooked properly and that the water you drink is clean. Peel your fruits and veggies and avoid tap water (including ice cubes and anything washed in tap water, like salad). In the South and Sicily, don't brush your teeth with tap water or rinse your toothbrush under the faucet, and keep your mouth closed in the shower. Watch out for food from markets or street vendors. Other culprits are **raw shellfish, unpasteurized milk,** and sauces containing **raw eggs.** Buy **bottled water,** or purify your own water by boiling it or treating it with **iodine tablets.** Always wash your hands before eating, or bring a quick-drying purifying liquid hand cleaner. Your bowels will thank you.

AIDS, HIV, AND STDS

For detailed information on **Acquired Immune Deficiency Syndrome (AIDS),** call the **US Centers for Disease Control's** 24hr. hotline at ☎ 800-342-2437, or contact the **Joint United Nations Programme on HIV/AIDS (UNAIDS),** 20, av. Appia, CH-1211 Geneva 27, Switzerland (☎ (22) 791 36 66; fax 791 41 87). Council's brochure, *Travel Safe: AIDS and International Travel,* is available at all Council Travel offices and on their website (www.ciee.org/Isp/safety/travelsafe.htm).

FOOT AND MOUTH DISEASE

The outbreak of Foot and Mouth Disease in Great Britain and Ireland poses little threat to human travelers in Italy, but special precautions should be taken if you are traveling with a pet. While dogs and cats cannot become infected with the disease, they can be carriers. Residents of Great Britain and Ireland are not allowed to bring pets of any sort into Italy, and travelers from outside those two countries should bathe pets regularly, washing bedding and removing excessive dirt, straw, or hay, according to the **Centers for Disease Control (CDC).** Animals should be disinfected with bleach solution upon arrival in Italy. The pet should not be allowed contact with livestock and wildlife for five days upon return.

In August 2001, the Food Standards Agency declared that Foot and Mouth Disease do not threaten the food supply in Europe, but certain products should be avoided as a precautionary measure. Poultry and seafood are entirely unaffected by the outbreak and are safe to consume. In general, eating cooked meats, including cooked pork, is risk-free because heat kills Foot and Mouth Disease. Exercise the greatest caution in the south of Italy, where sterilization of cooking utensils is less common. In addition, unpasteurized milk products should be avoided.

At least five days before leaving Italy, **avoid farms, zoos, fairs, or other locations populated with livestock.** Clothing should be freshly laundered before returning. Using a bleach solution (five teaspoons bleach to one gallon of water) on a piece of cloth to rub soil and dirt from shoes, luggage, and any other personal items might minimize the risk of bringing Foot and Mouth Disease out from Italy. Honesty at Customs regarding items brought back from Europe (especially cheeses containing liquid or meat) can help prevent an outbreak outside of Europe.

WOMEN'S HEALTH

Women traveling in unsanitary conditions are vulnerable to **urinary tract** and **bladder infections,** common bacterial conditions that cause a burning sensation and painful urination. Drink vitamin-C-rich juice and clean water, and urinate frequently, especially right after intercourse. These infections can lead to kidney infections, sterility, and death. If symptoms persist, see a doctor.

Vaginal yeast infections may flare up in hot and humid climates. Wearing loosely fitting trousers or a skirt and cotton underwear will help, as will over-the-counter remedies like Monistat or Gynelotrimin. Bring supplies from home if you are prone to infection. Most pharmacies will refill empty birth control packages, even without an Italian-issued prescription. Though there is no morning-after pill in Italy, emergency rooms in major hospitals can provide a large dose of birth control, which has the same effect. **Abortions** are usually performed in local hospitals. Italian law allows for procedures to take place before the 90-day mark (12-13 wks.) of the pregnancy has passed. Women under 18 must obtain parental permission.

INSURANCE

Travel insurance covers four basic areas: medical/health problems, property loss, trip cancellation/interruption, and emergency evacuation. Although regular insurance policies may well extend to travel-related accidents, consider purchasing travel insurance if the cost of potential trip cancellation/interruption is greater than you can absorb. Prices for travel insurance purchased separately generally run about US$50 per week for full coverage, while trip cancellation/interruption may be purchased separately at a rate of about US$5.50 per US$100 of coverage.

Medical insurance often covers costs incurred abroad; check with your provider. **US Medicare** does not cover foreign travel. **Canadians** are protected by their home province's health insurance plan for up to 90 days after leaving the country; check with the provincial Ministry of Health or Health Plan Headquarters for details. **Australians** traveling in Italy or Malta are entitled to many of the services that they would receive at home as part of the Reciprocal Health Care Agreement. **EU citizens** traveling to Italy should ask their home country insurer for an E111 form, which covers EU citizens for emergency medical care in other EU countries. **Homeowners' insurance** (or your family's coverage) often covers theft during travel and loss of travel documents (passport, plane ticket, railpass, etc.) up to US$500.

ISIC and **ITIC** (see p. 37) provide basic insurance benefits, including US$100 per day of in-hospital sickness for up to 60 days, US$3000 of accident-related medical reimbursement, and US$25,000 for emergency medical transport. Cardholders have access to a toll-free 24hr. helpline for medical, legal, and financial emergencies overseas (US and Canada ☎877-370-4742, elsewhere call US collect +1 715-345-0505). **American Express** (US ☎800-528-4800) grants most cardholders automatic car rental insurance (collision and theft, but not liability) and ground travel accident coverage of US$100,000 on flight purchases made with the card.

INSURANCE PROVIDERS. Council and **STA** (see p. 58) offer a range of plans that can supplement your basic coverage. Other private insurance providers in the US and Canada include: **Access America** (☎800-284-8300); **Berkely Group/Carefree Travel Insurance** (☎800-323-3149; www.berkely.com); **Globalcare Travel Insurance** (☎800-821-2488; www.globalcare-cocco.com); and **Travel Assistance International** (☎800-821-2828; www.worldwide-assistance.com). Providers in the **UK** include **Campus Travel** (☎(01865) 258000) and **Columbus Travel Insurance** (☎(020) 7375 0011). In **Australia,** try **CIC Insurance** (☎9202 8000).

PACKING

Pack light: lay out only what you absolutely need, then take half the clothes and twice the money. The less you have, the less you have to lose.

IMPORTANT DOCUMENTS. Don't forget your passport, traveler's checks, ATM and/or credit cards, and ID (see p. 37). Also check that you have any of the following that might apply to you: a hosteling membership card (see **Accommodations,** p. 49), driver's license, travel insurance forms, and rail or bus pass (see p. 67).

LUGGAGE. If you plan to cover most of your itinerary by foot, a sturdy **frame backpack** is unbeatable. (For the basics on buying a pack, see p. 52.) Toting a **suitcase** or **trunk** is fine if you plan to live in one or two cities and explore from there but a very bad idea if you're going to be moving around a lot. A **daypack** is a must.

CLOTHING. Bring along a **warm jacket** or wool sweater, a **rain jacket** (Gore-Tex® is both waterproof and breathable), sturdy shoes or **hiking boots,** and **thick socks.** Remember that wool will keep you warm even when soaked, whereas wearing wet cotton is colder than wearing nothing at all. If you plan to hike a lot, see **Outdoors,** p. 52. **Flip-flops** or waterproof sandals are crucial for grubby hostel showers. If you want to go clubbing, bring at least one pair of slacks, a nice shirt, and a nice pair of shoes. If you plan to visit Italy's churches, make sure to bring along an outfit that covers your torso and upper arms.

CONVERTERS AND ADAPTERS. In Italy, electricity is 220V AC, enough to fry any 110V North American appliance. 220/240V electrical appliances don't like 110V current, either. Americans and Canadians should buy an adapter (which changes the shape of the plug) and a converter (which changes the voltage; US$20). Don't make the mistake of using only an adapter (unless appliance instructions explicitly state otherwise). New Zealanders and South Africans (who both use 220V at home) as well as Australians (who use 240/250V) won't need a converter, but will need a set of adapters to use anything electrical.

OTHER USEFUL ITEMS. Bring a **money belt** and small **padlock.** Basic **outdoors equipment** (plastic water bottle, compass, waterproof matches, pocketknife, sunglasses, sunscreen, insect repellent, hat) may also prove useful. **Quick repairs** of torn garments can be done on the road with a needle and thread; also consider bringing electrical tape for patching tears. Doing your **laundry** by hand (where it is allowed) is both cheaper and more convenient than doing it at a laundromat—bring detergent, a small rubber ball to stop up the sink, and string for a makeshift clothes line.

ACCOMMODATIONS

HOSTELS

Many Italian hostels are sights in themselves. Some may be located in castles or beautiful villas. Hostels are generally dorm-style accommodations, often in single-sex large rooms with bunk beds, although some hostels do offer private rooms for families and couples. They sometimes have kitchens and utensils, bike or moped rentals, storage areas, a bar, and laundry facilities. There can be drawbacks: some hostels close during certain daytime "lock-out" hours, have a curfew, don't accept reservations, impose a maximum stay, or, less frequently, require that you do chores. In Italy, a bed in a hostel will average around US$30 (see **Money,** p. 38).

A HOSTELER'S BILL OF RIGHTS. There are certain standard features that we do not include in our hostel listings. Unless we state otherwise, you can expect that every hostel has: no lockout, no curfew, a kitchen, free hot showers, secure luggage storage, and no key deposit. Because of the devaluation of the *lire,* hotel prices change frequently. Each spring, price ranges are set by the government. While the prices in *Let's Go* were up-to-date as of the fall of 2001, you should expect rate increases of 10% or greater throughout the country.

Joining the youth hostel association in your own country (listed below) automatically grants you membership privileges in **Hostelling International (HI),** a federation of national hosteling associations. The **Associazione Italiana Alberghi per la Gioventu** (**AIG;** ☎ (06) 487 11 52; aig@uni.net; www.hostels-aig.org), the Italian hostel federation, is an HI affiliate, though not all Italian hostels are part of AIG. Over 85 HI hostels are scattered throughout Italy; they sometimes accept reservations via the **International Booking Network** (Australia ☎(02) 9261 1111; Canada ☎800-663-5777; England and Wales ☎(1629) 581418; Northern Ireland ☎(1232) 324733; Republic of Ireland ☎(01) 830 1766; NZ ☎(03) 379 9808; Scotland ☎(8701) 55 32 55; US ☎800-909-4776; www.hostelbooking.com). HI's organization's web page (www.iyhf.org), lists the web addresses and phone numbers of all national associations. It is a great place to research hostelling in a specific region. Other comprehensive hostelling websites include **www.hostels.com** and **www.hostelplanet.com.**

Most HI hostels also honor **guest memberships**—you'll get a blank card with space for six validation stamps. Each night you'll pay a nonmember supplement (one-sixth the membership fee) and earn one guest stamp; get six stamps, and you're a member. Most student travel agencies (see p. 58) sell HI cards, as do all of the national hosteling organizations listed below. All prices listed below are valid for **one-year memberships** unless otherwise noted.

Australian Youth Hostels Association (AYHA), Level 3, 10 Mallett St., Camperdown NSW 2050 (☎(02) 9565 1699; fax 9565 1325; www.yha.org.au). AUS$52, under 18 AUS$16.

Hostelling International-Canada (HI-C), 400-205 Catherine St., Ottawa, ON K2P 1C3 (☎800-663-5777 or 613-237-7884; fax 237-7868; info@hostellingintl.ca; www.hostellingintl.ca). CDN$35, under 18 free.

An Óige (Irish Youth Hostel Association), 61 Mountjoy St., Dublin 7 (☎(01) 830 4555; fax 830 5808; anoige@iol.ie; www.irelandyha.org). IR£10, under 18 IR£4.

Youth Hostels Association of New Zealand (YHANZ), P.O. Box 436, 193 Cashel St., 3rd Floor Union House, Christchurch 1 (☎(03) 379 9970; fax 365 4476; info@yha.org.nz; www.yha.org.nz). NZ$40, under 17 free.

Hostels Association of South Africa, 3rd fl. 73 St. George's St. Mall, P.O. Box 4402, Cape Town 8000 (☎(021) 424 2511; fax 424 4119; info@hisa.org.za; www.hisa.org.za). SAR45.

Scottish Youth Hostels Association (SYHA), 7 Glebe Crescent, Stirling FK8 2JA (☎(01786) 89 14 00; fax 89 13 33; www.syha.org.uk). UK£6.

Youth Hostels Association (England and Wales) Ltd., Trevelyan House, 8 St. Stephen's Hill, St. Albans, Hertfordshire AL1 2DY, UK (☎(0870) 870 8808; fax (01727) 844126; www.yha.org.uk). UK£12.50, under 18 UK£6.25, families UK£25.

Hostelling International Northern Ireland (HINI), 22-32 Donegall Rd., Belfast BT12 5JN, Northern Ireland (☎(02890) 31 54 35; fax 43 96 99; info@hini.org.uk; www.hini.org.uk). UK£10, under 18 UK£6.

Hostelling International-American Youth Hostels (HI-AYH), 733 15th St. NW, #840, Washington, D.C. 20005 (☎202-783-6161; fax 783-6171; hiayhserv@hiayh.org; www.hiayh.org). US$25, under 18 free.

DORMS

Many **colleges and universities** open their residence halls to travelers when school is not in session; some do so even during term-time. These dorms are often close to student areas—good sources for information on things to do—and are usually very clean. Getting a room may take a few phone calls and require advanced planning, but rates tend to be low, and many offer free local calls. Contact the Italian Government Tourist Office in New York for more information: Rockefeller Center, 630 Fifth Avenue, New York, NY 10111 (☎212-245-4822).

HOTELS, PENSIONS, AND ROOMS FOR RENT

Hotel singles (*camera singola*) in Italy cost L50-60,000/€25.82-31 per night, doubles (*camera doppia* or *camera matrimoniale*) L70,000-80,000/€36.15-41.32. You'll typically share a hall bathroom; a private bathroom will cost extra, as may hot showers. Some hotels offer "full pension" (all meals) and "half pension" (no

lunch). Smaller **pensions** are often cheaper than hotels. Upon arrival, be sure to confirm the charges before checking in; many Italian hotels are notorious for tacking on additional costs at check-out time. If you make **reservations** in writing, indicate your night of arrival and the number of nights you plan to stay. The hotel will send you a confirmation and may request payment for the first night. Not all hotels take reservations, and few accept checks in foreign currency. Enclosing two International Reply Coupons will ensure a reply (each US$1.05; available at any post office). Rooms for rent in private houses *(affittacamere)* are another inexpensive housing option. For more information on these, inquire at local tourist offices.

HOME EXCHANGE AND RENTALS

Home exchange offers the traveler various types of homes (houses, apartments, condominiums, villas, even castles in some cases) plus the opportunity to live like a native and to cut down on accommodation fees. For more information, contact **HomeExchange.Com** (☎805-898-9660; www.homeexchange.com), **Intervac International Home Exchange** (☎+39 (51) 91 20 28; www.intervac.com), or **The Invented City: International Home Exchange** (US ☎800-788-CITY, elsewhere US ☎+1 415-252-1141; www.invented-city.com). **Home rentals** are more expensive than exchanges, but they can be cheaper than comparably serviced hotels. Both home exchanges and rentals are ideal for families with children or travelers with special dietary needs; you often get your own kitchen, maid service, TV, and telephones.

CAMPING AND THE OUTDOORS

There are over 1700 campsites in Italy, and they are classified by one to four stars, according to comfort. Small fees are usually issued per person on a daily basis. Contact local tourist offices for information about suitable or free campsites. Camping on undesignated land is not permitted. The **Touring Club Italiano**, C. Italia, 10-20122 Milano (☎(02) 852 61; fax 5359 9540) is full of campy knowledge, and it publishes numerous books and pamphlets on the outdoors. The **Federazione Italiana del Campeggio e del Caravanning (Federcampeggio),** 50041 Calenzano (Florence) (☎(055) 882391; fax 882 59 18), has a complete list of camping sites with location maps for free. Federcampeggio also publishes the book *Guida Camping d'Italia.* **EasyCamping** runs a website, www.icaro.it/home_e.html, that comes equipped with information about over 700 campsites throughout Italy. For a thorough list of the bigger parks and national reserves in the country, visit www.parks.it.

Pay attention to weather forecasts and stay warm, dry, and hydrated. In August, arrive well before 11am or find yourself without a spot. Many campgrounds boast everything from swimming pools to bars; others may be more primitive. Rates average L8000/€4.13 per person or tent, L7000/€3.62 per car.

USEFUL PUBLICATIONS AND WEB RESOURCES

Campers heading to Europe should consider buying an International Camping Carnet. Similar to a hostel membership card, it is required at a few campgrounds and provides discounts at others. It is available in North America from the Family Campers and RVers Association and in the UK from The Caravan Club.

Automobile Association, A.A. Publishing. Orders and enquiries to TBS Frating Distribution Centre, Colchester, Essex, CO7 7DW, UK (☎(01206) 255678; www.theaa.co.uk). Publishes *Camping and Caravanning: Europe* (UK£9) and a *Big Road Atlas* for Italy.

The Caravan Club, East Grinstead House, East Grinstead, West Sussex, RH19 1UA, UK (☎(01342) 326944; www.caravanclub.co.uk). For £27.50, members receive equipment discounts, a 700-page directory and handbook, and a monthly magazine.

The Mountaineers Books, 1001 SW Klickitat Way, #201, Seattle, WA 98134, USA (☎800-553-4453 or 206-223-6303; www.mountaineersbooks.org). Over 400 titles on hiking, biking, mountaineering, natural history, and conservation.

CAMPING AND HIKING EQUIPMENT

Sleeping Bag: Most sleeping bags are rated by season ("summer" means 30-40°F at night; "four-season" or "winter" often means below 0°F). They are made either of **down** or **synthetic** material. Prices range US$80-210 for a summer synthetic to US$250-300 for a good down winter bag. **Sleeping bag pads** include foam pads (US$10-20), air mattresses (US$15-50), and Therm-A-Rest self-inflating pads (US$45-80). Bring a **stuff sack** to store your bag and keep it dry.

Tent: The best tents are free-standing (with their own frames and suspension systems), set up quickly, and only require staking in high winds. Low-profile dome tents are the best all-around. Good 2-person tents start at US$90, 4-person at US$300. Seal the seams of your tent with waterproofer, and make sure it has a rain fly. Other tent accessories include a **battery-operated lantern,** a **plastic groundcloth,** and a **nylon tarp.**

Backpack: Internal-frame packs mold better to your back, keep a lower center of gravity, and flex adequately to allow you to hike difficult trails. **External-frame packs** are more comfortable for long hikes over even terrain as they keep weight higher and distribute it more evenly. Make sure your pack has a strong, padded hip-belt to transfer weight to your legs. Any serious backpacking requires a pack of at least 4000 in^3 (16,000cc), plus 500 in^3 for sleeping bags in internal-frame packs. Sturdy backpacks cost anywhere from US$125-420. Either buy a **waterproof backpack cover,** or store all of your belongings in plastic bags inside your pack.

Boots: Be sure to wear hiking boots with good **ankle support.** They should fit snugly and comfortably over 1-2 pairs of wool socks and thin liner socks. Break in boots over several weeks first in order to spare yourself painful and debilitating blisters.

Other Necessities: Synthetic layers, like those made of polypropylene, and a **pile jacket** will keep you warm even when wet. A **"space blanket"** will help you to retain your body heat and doubles as a groundcloth (US$5-15). Plastic **water bottles** are virtually shatter- and leak-proof. Bring **water-purification tablets** for when you can't boil water. Although most campgrounds provide campfire sites, you may want to bring a small metal **grate** or **grill** of your own. For those places that forbid fires or the gathering of firewood, you'll need a **camp stove** (the classic Coleman starts at US$40) and a propane-filled **fuel bottle** to operate it. Also don't forget a **first-aid kit, pocketknife, insect repellent, calamine lotion,** and **waterproof matches** or a **lighter.**

WILDERNESS SAFETY

Stay warm, stay dry, and stay hydrated. The vast majority of life-threatening wilderness situations can be avoided by following this simple advice. However, prepare yourself for an emergency by always packing raingear, a hat and mittens, a first-aid kit, a reflector, a whistle, high energy food, and extra water for any hike. Dress in wool or warm layers of synthetic materials designed for the outdoors; never rely on cotton for warmth as it is useless when wet.

Whenever possible, let someone know when and where you are going hiking, either a friend, your hostel, a park ranger, or a local hiking organization. Do not attempt a hike beyond your ability—you may be endangering your life.

KEEPING IN TOUCH

BY MAIL

SENDING MAIL TO ITALY

Mark envelopes "air mail" or "par avion" to avoid having letters sent by sea. In addition to the services below, **Federal Express** (Australia ☎ 13 26 10; US and Canada ☎ 800-247-4747; New Zealand ☎ (0800) 73 33 39; UK ☎ (0800) 123800) handles express mail services from most of the above countries to Italy; for example, they can get a letter from New York to Italy in two days for US$26.52.

Australia: Allow 5-7 workdays for airmail to Italy. Postcards and letters up to 28g cost AUS$1.50; registered post up to 0.5kg AUS$14; packages up to 0.5kg AUS$14.80. **EMS** can get a letter to Italy in 2-3 days for AUS$32. www.auspost.com.au/pac.

Canada: Allow 4-7 days for airmail to Italy. Postcards and letters up to 20g cost CDN$0.95; registered mail CDN$9 plus postage; packages up to 0.5kg CDN$10.45, up to 2kg CDN$39.20. www.canadapost.ca/CPC2/common/rates/ratesgen.html#international.

Ireland: Allow 7 days for airmail to Italy. Postcards and letters up to 25g cost IR£0.32. Add IR£2.30 for Swiftpost International. www.anpost.ie.

New Zealand: Allow 7 days for airmail to Italy. Postcards cost NZ$1.10 Letters from 0-200g NZ$1.80-6; small parcels up to 0.5kg NZ$13.20, up to 2kg NZ$39. www.nzpost.co.nz/nzpost/inrates.

UK: Allow 3 days for airmail to Italy. Letters up to 25g cost UK£0.50; packages up to 0.5kg UK£2.67, up to 2kg UK£9.42. UK Swiftair delivers letters a day faster for UK£2.85 more. www.royalmail.co.uk/calculator.

US: Allow 4-7 days for airmail to Italy. Postcards/aerogrammes cost US$1; letters under 28g US$0.90. Packages under 1lb. cost US$7.20; larger packages cost a variable amount (around US$15). **US Express Mail** takes 2-3 days and costs US$24.50 for a 1lb. package. http://ircalc.usps.gov.

RECEIVING MAIL IN ITALY

There are several ways to arrange pick-up of letters sent to you by friends and relatives while you are abroad.

General Delivery: Mail can be sent via **Poste Restante** (General Delivery; Fermo Posta) to almost any city or town in Italy with a post office. Address *Poste Restante* letters as in the following example: Jane DOE, Fermo Posta, Ufficio Postale Centrale di Piazza Cordusio 4, Milano 20100, Italia. The mail will go to a special desk in the central post office, unless you specify a post office by street address or postal code. It is best to use the largest post office, since mail may be sent there regardless. It is usually safer and quicker to send mail express *(espresso)* or registered *(raccomandata)*. Bring your passport (or other photo ID) for pick-up. If the clerks insists there is nothing for you, have them check under your first name as well. *Let's Go* lists post offices in the **Practical Information** section for each city and most towns.

American Express: AmEx's travel offices throughout the world offer a free **Client Letter Service** (mail held up to 30 days and forwarding upon request) for cardholders who contact them in advance. Address the letter in the same way shown above. Some offices will offer these services to non-cardholders (especially AmEx Travelers Cheque holders), but call ahead to make sure. *Let's Go* lists AmEx office locations for most large cities in **Practical Information** sections; for a complete, free list, call ☎ 800-528-4800.

SENDING MAIL FROM ITALY

Airmail from major cities in Italy to North America averages eight to 12 days, although times are more unpredictable from smaller towns; to Australia or New Zealand, at least 7 days; to the UK or Ireland, 4 days; to South Africa, 6 days. **Aerogrammes,** printed sheets that fold into envelopes and travel via airmail, are available at post offices. It helps to mark *via aerea* if possible, though "par avion" is universally understood. Most post offices will charge exorbitant fees or simply refuse to send aerogrammes with enclosures.

To send a postcard to an international destination within Europe costs L1200/€0.62 and to any other international destination via airmail costs L1500/€0.77. To send a letter (up to 20g) to another country in Europe costs L1200/€0.62 and to anywhere else in the world via airmail costs L1500/€0.77.

SENDING MAIL WITHIN ITALY

Domestic postal service is poor. A letter mailed less than 90 miles may take as many as three weeks to arrive. You can be sure that anything of any value will not reach its intended destination. Domestically, postcards require L1200/€0.62.

TELEPHONES

CALLING HOME FROM ITALY

A **calling card** is probably your cheapest bet. Calls are billed collect or to your

COMPANY	TO OBTAIN A CARD, DIAL:	TO CALL ABROAD, DIAL:
AT&T (US)	888-288-4685	172 10 11
British Telecom Direct	(800) 345144	172 00 44
Canada Direct	800-668-6878	172 10 01
Ireland Direct	(800) 400000	172 03 53
MCI (US)	800-444-3333	172 10 22
New Zealand Direct	(0800) 00 00 00	172 10 64
Sprint (US)	800-877-4646	172 18 77
Telkom South Africa	10 219	172 10 27
Telstra Australia	13 22 00	172 10 61

account. You can frequently call collect without even possessing a company's calling card just by calling their access number and following the instructions. **To obtain a calling card** from your national telecommunications service before leaving home, contact the appropriate company listed below To **call home with a calling card,** contact the operator for your service provider in Italy by dialing the appropriate toll-free access number.

You can usually also make direct international calls from pay phones. Prepaid phone cards and major credit cards can be used for direct international calls, but they are still less cost-efficient. Placing a **collect call** through an international operator is even more expensive, but may be necessary in case of emergency. You can typically place collect calls through the service providers listed above even if you

ESSENTIALS

don't possess one of their phone cards. If you will be making frequent international calls, it may be worthwhile to purchase a cell phone *(telefonino)*.

> **PLACING INTERNATIONAL CALLS**
> To call Italy from home or to place an international call from Italy, dial:
> 1. The **international dialing prefix**. To dial out of **Australia,** dial 0011; **Canada** and the **US,** 011; **the Republic of Ireland, Italy, New Zealand,** or the **UK,** 00; **South Africa,** 09.
> 2. The **country code** of the country you want to call. To call **Australia,** dial 61; **Canada** or the **US,** 1; the **Republic of Ireland,** 353; **Italy,** 39; **New Zealand,** 64; **South Africa,** 27; **UK,** 44.
> 3. The **city** or **area code.** *Let's Go* lists the phone codes for cities and towns in Italy opposite the city or town name, next to a ☎. For most countries, if the first digit is a zero (e.g., 04 for Nice), omit the zero when calling from abroad. Italy, however, is the exception. Dial the number as written with the zero.
> 4. The **local number.**

CALLING WITHIN ITALY

The simplest way to call within the country is to use a coin-operated phone. **Prepaid phone cards,** available at vending machines, phone card vendors and *tabacchi,* carry a certain amount of phone time depending on the card's denomination (L5000/ €2.58, L10,000/€5.16 and L15,000/€7.75), and they usually save time and money in the long run. Italian phone cards are a little tricky to maneuver; rip off the marked corner, and insert the card into the appropriate section of the pay phone. The phone card's time is measured in L200/€0.10 talk units (e.g., one unit=one minute). Phone rates tend to be highest in the morning, lower in the evening, and lowest on Sunday and late at night. To call intercity within Italy, dial the entire number, including the city code. Even when dialing within a single city, the city code is required; for example, when dialing from one place in Milan to another, the (02) is still necessary. International calls start at L1000/€1.03 and vary depending on where you are calling.

TIME DIFFERENCES

Italy is one hour ahead of **Greenwich Mean Time (GMT).** Daylight-saving time starts on the last Sunday in March, when clocks are moved ahead one hour. Clocks are put back an hour on the last Sunday in September.

4AM	7AM	10AM	11AM	2PM	10PM
Vancouver	Toronto	London	Italy	China	Sydney
Seattle	Ottawa	(GMT)	Paris	Hong Kong	Canberra
San Francisco	New York		Munich	Manila	Melbourne
Los Angeles	Boston		Madrid	Singapore	

EMAIL AND INTERNET

Though Italy had initially lagged behind in constructing exits and turnpikes on the information superhighway, it's now playing the game of catch-up like a pro. With the exception of some smaller towns in the south, new Internet cafes, Internet bars, and even Internet laundromats are popping up every day throughout the country. For free Internet access, try the local universities and libraries.

Though in some places it's possible to forge a remote link with your home server, in most cases this is a much slower (and thus more expensive) option than taking advantage of free **web-based email accounts** (e.g., www.hotmail.com and www.yahoo.com). Travelers with laptops can call an Internet service provider via a **modem.** Long-distance phone cards specifically intended for such calls can defray normally high phone charges; check with your long-distance phone provider to see if it offers this option. *Let's Go* includes the major locations to surf the web and check email in each city. The following websites contains a more detailed listings: www.ecs.net/cafe/#list and www.cybercaptive.com.

TRANSPORTATION TO ITALY

BY PLANE

When it comes to airfare, a little effort can save you a bundle. If your plans are flexible enough to deal with the restrictions, courier fares are the cheapest. Tickets bought from consolidators and standby seating are also good deals, but last-minute specials, airfare wars, and charter flights often beat these fares. The key is to hunt around, to be flexible, and to ask persistently about discounts. Students, seniors, and those under 26 should never pay full price for a ticket.

DETAILS AND TIPS

Timing: Airfares to Italy peak between mid-June and early Sept.; holidays are also expensive periods in which to travel. Flights early in the week (M-W) and on Saturday run US$40-50 cheaper than Friday and Sunday flights. Traveling with an "open return" ticket can be pricier than fixing a return date when buying the ticket.

Route: Round-trip flights are by far the cheapest; "open-jaw" (arriving in and departing from different cities) tickets are pricier but reasonable alternatives. Patching one-way flights together is the least economical way to travel. Flights between large cities (Rome) will offer the most competitive fares.

Round-the-World: If Italy is only 1 stop on a more extensive globe-hop, consider a round-the-world (RTW) ticket. Tickets usually include at least 5 stops and are valid for about a year; prices range US$1200-5000. Try **Northwest Airlines/KLM** (US ☎800-447-4747; www.nwa.com) or **Star Alliance,** a consortium of 22 airlines including United Airlines (US ☎800-241-6522; www.star-alliance.com).

Fares: Roundtrip flights to Rome from the US or Canadian east coast cost US$600. In the off season, late fall through early spring (excluding the holidays), flights are US$400. From the US or Canadian west coast US$900/US$600; from the UK, UK£140/UK£120; from Australia AUS$1100/AUS$900; from New Zealand NZ$1100/NZ$950.

BUDGET AND STUDENT TRAVEL AGENCIES

While knowledgeable agents specializing in flights to Italy can make your life easy and help you save, they may not spend the time to find you the lowest possible fare—they get paid on commission. Travelers holding **ISIC and IYTC cards** (see p. 37) qualify for big discounts from student travel agencies.

Usit world (www.usitworld.com). Over 50 **usit campus** branches in the UK (www.usitcampus.co.uk), including 52 Grosvenor Gardens, **London** SW1W 0AG (☎(0870) 240 10 10); **Manchester** (☎(0161) 273 1880); and **Edinburgh** (☎(0131) 668 3303). Nearly 20 **usit NOW** offices in Ireland, including 19-21 Aston Quay, O'Connell Bridge, **Dublin** 2 (☎(01) 602 1600; www.usitnow.ie), and **Belfast** (☎(02) 890 327 111; www.usitnow.com). Offices also in Athens, Auckland, Brussels, Frankfurt, Johannesburg, Lisbon, Luxembourg, Madrid, Paris, Sofia, and Warsaw.

Council Travel (www.counciltravel.com). Countless US offices, including branches in Atlanta, Boston, Chicago, Los Angeles, New York, San Francisco, Seattle, and Washington, D.C. Check the website or call ☎800-2-COUNCIL (226-8624) locations near you. British office, 28A Poland St. (Oxford Circus), **London** W1V 3DB (☎(0207) 437 77 67).

CTS Travel, 44 Goodge St., **London** W1T 2AD (☎(0207) 636 0031; fax (0207) 637 5328; ctsinfo@ctstravel.co.uk).

STA Travel, 7890 S. Hardy Dr., Ste. 110, Tempe AZ 85284 (24hr. reservations and info ☎800-777-0112; fax 480-592-0876; www.sta-travel.com). A student and youth travel organization with over 150 offices worldwide including US offices in Boston, Chicago, Los Angeles, New York, San Francisco, Seattle, and Washington, D.C. Ticket booking, travel insurance, railpasses, and more. In the UK, walk-in office 11 Goodge St., **London**

W1T 2PF or call (0870)160 6070. In New Zealand, 10 High St., **Auckland** (☎(09) 309 0458). In Australia, 366 Lygon St., **Melbourne** Vic 3053 (☎(03) 9349 4344).

Travel CUTS (Canadian Universities Travel Services Limited), 187 College St., **Toronto,** ON M5T 1P7 (☎416-979-2406; fax 979-8167; www.travelcuts.com). 60 offices across Canada. Also in the UK, 295-A Regent St., **London** W1R 7YA (☎(0207) 255 1944).

Wasteels, Skoubogade 6, 1158 Copenhagen K., (☎3314 4633; fax 7630 0865; www.wasteels.dk/uk). A huge chain with 165 locations across Europe. Sells Wasteels BIJ tickets discounted 30-45% off regular fare, 2nd-class international point-to-point train tickets with unlimited stopovers for those under 26 (sold only in Europe).

 FLIGHT PLANNING ON THE INTERNET.The Web is a great place to look for travel bargains—it's fast and convenient, and you can spend as long as you like exploring options without driving your travel agent insane. Many airline sites offer special last-minute deals on the Web. For fares, see **Alitalia** (www.alitalia.it), **Air-One** (www.air-one.it/airone.htm), and **Gandalf Air** (www.gandalfair.com). For a great set of links to practically every airline in every country, see www.travelpage.com/air/air-lines. Other sites do the legwork and compile the best deals for you—try www.smart-erliving.com, www.lowestfare.com, www.onetravel.com, and www.travelzoo.com. **STA** (www.sta-travel.com), **Council** (www.counciltravel.com) and ▨**StudentUni-verse** (www.studentuniverse.com) provide quotes on student tickets, while **Expedia** (www.expedia.com) and **Travelocity** (www.travelocity.com) offer full travel services. **Priceline** (www.priceline.com) allows you to specify a price, and obligates you to buy any ticket that meets or beats it; be prepared for antisocial hours and odd routes. **Hotwire** (www.hotwire.com) and **Skyauction** (www.skyauction.com) allow you to bid on last-minute and advance-purchase tickets. The *Air Traveler's Handbook* (www.cs.cmu.edu/afs/cs/user/mkant/Pub-lic/Travel/airfare.html), has a comprehensive, indispensable listing of links to everything you need to know before flying.

ESSENTIALS

COMMERCIAL AIRLINES

The commercial airlines' lowest offer is the **APEX** (Advance Purchase Excursion) fare, which provides confirmed reservations and allows "open-jaw" tickets. Reservations should be made 21 days in advance, with 7- to 14-day minimum-stay and up to 90-day maximum-stay limits. These fares carry hefty cancellation and change penalties (US$75-100; fees rise in summer). Book peak-season APEX fares early.

TRAVELING FROM NORTH AMERICA. Basic round-trip fares to Italy range from roughly US$200-750. Carriers like **American** (US ☎ 800-433-7300; www.aa.com), **Delta** (US ☎ 800-241-4141; Canada ☎ 800-221-1212; www.delta-air.com), and **United** (US ☎ 800-241-6522; www.ual.com) offer the most convenient flights to Rome and Milan, but they may not be the cheapest (unless you manage to grab a special promotion or airfare war ticket). The carriers listed in **Traveling from Elsewhere in Europe** (below) also fly from North America to Italy, with connections in Europe. For better deals try a smaller carrier like **Icelandair** (☎ 800-223-5500; www.icelandair.com) or see **Budget and Student Travel Agencies** (p. 58).

TRAVELING FROM THE UK AND IRELAND. British Airways (UK ☎ (0860) 011747; www.britishairways.com), British Midland Airways (UK ☎ (0870) 607 0555; www.britishmidland.com) and (UK ☎ (0870) 240 7070; www.buzzaway.com) often offer cheap specials from London to Milan. Go-Fly Limited (UK ☎ (0845) 605 4321; elsewhere call UK ☎ +44 (1279) 666388; www.go-fly.com) flies from London to Rome and Venice. Aer Lingus (Ireland ☎ (01) 886 88 88; www.aerlingus.ie) and Ryanair (Ireland ☎ (01) 812 12 12, UK (0870) 156 9569; www.ryanair.ie) connect Irish and Italian gateways. The Air Travel Advisory Bureau in London (☎ (020) 7636 5000; www.atab.co.uk) provides referrals to travel agencies and consolidators that offer discounted airfares out of the UK.

TRAVELING FROM ELSEWHERE IN EUROPE. Most European carriers, including **Air France** (☎ (011) 880 80 40; www.airfrance.com), **Alitalia** (☎ 800-223-5730 or UK ☎ +44 (870) 544 8259; www.alitalia.it/eng), **KLM** (UK ☎ +44 (0870) 507 4070; www.klm.com), **Lufthansa** (☎ (011) 484 47 11; www.lufthansa.com), and **Sabena** (Belgium +32 (02) 723 23 23; email communication@sabena.be; www.sabena.com), have frequent flights to Rome, Milan, and Venice from many European cities. The sheer number of European airlines ensures reasonable fares.

TRAVELING FROM AUSTRALIA AND NEW ZEALAND. Qantas Air (Australia ☎ 13 13 13, New Zealand (0800) 808 767; www.qantas.com.au) flies from Australia and New Zealand to Rome and Milan. Air New Zealand (New Zealand ☎ (0800) 35 22 66; www.airnz.co.nz) flies to Italy only from Auckland.

TRAVELING FROM SOUTH AFRICA. The European carriers listed above in **Traveling from Elsewhere in Europe,** including Air France, British Airways, and Lufthansa, fly from Cape Town and Johannesburg to their European hubs, from where flights connect to Italian destinations.

AIR COURIER FLIGHTS

Those who travel light should consider courier flights. Couriers help transport cargo on international flights by using their checked luggage space for freight. Generally, couriers must travel with carry-ons only and must deal with complex flight restrictions. Most flights are round-trip, with short fixed-length stays (usually one week) and a limit of a one ticket per issue. Generally, you must be over 21 (in some cases 18). In summer, the most popular destinations usually require advance reservations of about two weeks (you can usually book up to two months ahead). Super-discounted fares are common for "last-minute" flights (three to 14 days ahead).

TRAVELING FROM NORTH AMERICA. Round-trip courier fares from the US to Italy run about US$200-500. Most flights leave from New York, Los Angeles, San Francisco, or Miami in the US and from Montreal, Toronto, or Vancouver in Canada. The first four organizations below provide their members with lists of oppor-

YOUTH AND STUDENT TRAVEL CLUB

tunities and courier brokers worldwide for an annual fee (typically US$50-60). Alternatively, contact a courier broker (see the last three listings) directly; most charge registration fees, but a few do not. Prices quoted below are round-trip. A few organizations that arrange courier flights between North America and Italy include: **Air Courier Association,** 15000 W. 6th Ave. #203, Golden, CO 80401 (☎800-282-1202; elsewhere call US ☎+1 303-215-9000; www.aircourier.org); **Global Courier Travel,** P.O. Box 3051, Nederland, CO 80466 (www.globalcouriertravel.com); **International Association of Air Travel Couriers (IAATC),** 220 South Dixie Highway #3, P.O. Box 1349, Lake Worth, FL 33460 (☎561-582-8320; fax 582-1581; www.courier.org); **NOW Voyager,** 74 Varick St. #307, New York, NY 10013 (☎212-431-1616; fax 219-1753; www.nowvoyagertravel.com); and **Worldwide Courier Association** (☎800-780-4359, ext. 441; www.massiveweb.com).

FROM THE UK AND IRELAND. Although the courier industry is most developed in North America, there are limited courier flights in other areas. The minimum age for couriers from the **UK** is usually 18. **Brave New World Enterprises,** P.O. Box 22212, London SE5 8WB (guideinfo@nry.co.uk; www.nry.co.uk/bnw) publishes a directory of all the companies offering courier flights in the UK (UK£10, in electronic form UK£8). The **International Association of Air Travel Couriers** (see above) often offers courier flights from London. **Global Courier Travel** (see above) also offer flights from London and Dublin to continental Europe. **British Airways Travel Shop** (☎0870 606 1133; www.british-airways.com/travelqa/booking/travshop/travshop.shtml) arranges some flights from London to destinations in continental Europe (specials may be as low as UK£60; no registration fee).

TICKET CONSOLIDATORS

Ticket consolidators, or **"bucket shops,"** buy unsold tickets in bulk from commercial airlines and sell them at discounted rates. The best place to look for their tiny ads is in the Sunday travel section of any major newspaper (such as the *New York Times*). Call quickly, as availability is typically extremely limited. Not all bucket shops are reliable; insist on a receipt that gives full details of restrictions, refunds, and tickets, and pay by credit card so you can stop payment if a problem arises. For more information, see www.travel-library.com/air-travel/consolidators.html.

TRAVELING FROM THE US & CANADA. Travel Avenue (☎800-333-3335; www.travelavenue.com) searches for best available published fares and then uses several consolidators to attempt to beat that fare. **NOW Voyager,** 74 Varick St., Ste. 307, New York, NY 10013 (☎212-431-1616; fax 219-1793; www.nowvoyagertravel.com) arranges discounted flights, mostly from New York, to Milan or Rome. Other consolidators worth trying are **Interworld** (☎305-443-4929; fax 443-0351); **Pennsylvania Travel** (☎800-331-0947); **Rebel** (☎800-227-3235; travel@rebeltours.com; www.rebeltours.com); **Cheap Tickets** (☎800-377-1000; www.cheaptickets.com); and **Travac** (☎800-872-8800; fax 212-714-9063; www.travac.com). Yet more consolidators on the web include the **Internet Travel Network** (www.itn.com); **Travel Information Services** (www.tiss.com); **TravelHUB** (www.travelhub.com); and **The Travel Site** (www.thctravelsite.com). Keep in mind that these are just suggestions to get you started in your research; *Let's Go* does not endorse any of these agencies. As always, be cautious, and of plenty of company research.

TRAVELING FROM THE UK, AUSTRALIA, & NEW ZEALAND. In London, the **Air Travel Advisory Bureau** (☎(0207) 636 5000; www.atab.co.uk) can provide names of discount flight specialists. From Australia and New Zealand, look for consolidator ads in the travel section of the *Sydney Morning Herald* and other papers.

TRANSPORTATION WITHIN ITALY

Unless stated otherwise, *Let's Go* lists one-way fares. In general, Italian trains are more efficient, economical, and romantic than other transportation alternatives.

ESSENTIALS

BY TRAIN

The Italian State Railway, **Ferrovie dello Stato** or **FS** (national information line ☎ 147 88 80 88; www.fs-on-line.com), offers inexpensive and efficient service, although it is commonly plagued by strikes. The southern Italy offspring of FS, **Ferrovie Sud-Est (FSE),** may be closer to cattle cars than trains. Hot, crowded, and uncomfortable, FSE trains often stop in remote locations in the South to change cars or give the hamster-powered engines a rest. Down on the heel of Italy it may be worth the extra *lire* to take a classier train (see below).

Several types of trains ride the Italian rails. The **locale** stops at every station along a particular line, often taking twice as long as a faster train. The **diretto** makes fewer stops than the *locale,* while the **espresso** just stops at major stations. The air-conditioned, more expensive **rapido,** an **InterCity (IC)** train, travels only to the largest cities. No *rapidi* have 2nd-class compartments, and a few require reservations. Tickets for the fast, comfy, and pricey **Eurostar** trains (a first and second class train) require reservations. Eurail passes are valid without a supplement on all trains except **Eurostar.**

Trains are not always safe; for **safety tips,** see p. 43. For long trips make sure you are on the correct car, as trains sometimes split at crossroads. Towns listed in parentheses on European train schedules require a train switch at the town listed immediately before the parenthesis.

If you're under 26 or over 60 and plan to travel extensively in Italy, your first purchase should be a **Cartaverde** or **Carta d'argento,** offering a year-long 20% discount on all train tickets (see p. 64).

RESERVATIONS. While seat reservations are only rarely required, you are not guaranteed a seat without one (L5000/€2.58 and up, depending on the ticket price). Reservations are available as much as two months in advance on major trains, and Europeans often reserve far ahead of time; you should strongly consider reserving during peak holiday and tourist seasons (at the very latest a few hours ahead). If you reserve a seat, be prepared to (politely) ask its occupant to move. To say, "excuse me, but I have reserved this seat," try *Mi scusa, ma ho prenotato questo posto.* It will be necessary to purchase a **supplement** (L6000-L30,000/€3.10-15.50) or special fare for faster or higher-quality trains such as Italy's ETR500 and Pendolino. All InterRail holders must also purchase supplements (L6000-L40,000/€3.10-20.66) for trains like EuroCity and InterCity; except Eurail pass and Europass holders.

OVERNIGHT TRAINS. Night trains have their advantages: you won't waste valuable daylight hours traveling, and you will be able to forego the hassle and considerable expense of securing a night's accommodation. However, night travel has its drawbacks as well: discomfort and sleeplessness are the most obvious; the scenery probably won't look as enticing in pitch black, either. On overnight trips, consider paying extra for a **cuccetta,** one of six fold-down bunks within a compartment (approx. L35,000/€18.08); private **sleeping cars** offer more privacy and comfort, but are considerably more expensive (L50,000-L120,000/€25.82-62) and are not widely available in Italy. If you're not willing to spend the money on a *cuccetta,* consider taking an *espresso* train overnight—they usually have compartments with fold-out seats. If you are using a railpass valid only for a restricted number of days, inspect train schedules to maximize the use of your pass: an overnight train or boat journey uses up only one of your travel days if it departs after 7pm (you need only write in the next day's date on your pass).

DOMESTIC RAILPASSES

Railpasses were conceived to allow you to jump on any train in Europe, go wherever you want whenever you want, and change your plans at will. In practice, it's not so simple. You still must stand in line to validate your pass, pay for supplements, and fork over cash for reservations. More importantly, railpasses don't always pay off. For ballpark estimates, contact Rail Europe (see p. 65).

ITALIAN KILOMETRIC TICKET. A railpass will probably not pay off if you are traveling solely within Italy, although it may be a practical option if you plan to travel to nearby European countries. The Italian State Railway offers passes valid on all trains within Italy. They are seldom cost-effective, since regular fares are cheap. The Italian Kilometric Ticket is good for 20 trips or 3000km (1875mi.) of travel, whichever comes first, and they can be used for two months by up to five people traveling together. It's virtually impossible for one person to break even on the Kilometric Ticket. For a couple or a family traveling widely, however, it can pay off. Children under 12 are charged half of the distance traveled, and those under four travel free. A first-class kilometric ticket costs L338,000/€174.41 (US$224), second-class L200,000/€103.29 (US$132). To obtain information on this service or purchase tickets, call the North American hotline (☎847-730 2121). When buying the ticket, be sure the sales agent stamps the date on it. You can also purchase this pass from the **Italian State Railway Representative**, in New York (☎212-730 2121) or in Italy (where the prices are slightly lower) at major train stations and offices of the **Compagnia Italiana Turismo (CIT)**. When using this pass, have your mileage stamped at the ticket booth or face buying another ticket on the train.

CARTAVERDE. Cartaverde are available to people aged 12 to 26. The card (L40,000/€20.66) is valid for one year and entitles travelers to a 20% discount on any state train fare. If you're under 26 and plan to spend at least L200,000/€103.29 on train tickets in Italy, this pass should be your *first* purchase upon arrival. Families of four or more and groups of up to five adults traveling together qualify for discounts on Italian railways. Persons over 60 get the same year-long 20% discount at the same price (L40,000/€20.66) when they buy a **carta d'argento** ("silver card").

MULTINATIONAL PASSES

EURAILPASS. Eurail is valid in most of Western Europe: Austria, Belgium, Denmark, Finland, France, Germany, Greece, Hungary, Italy, Luxembourg, the Netherlands, Norway, Portugal, the Republic of Ireland, Spain, Sweden, and Switzerland. It is not valid in the UK. Standard **Eurailpasses**, valid for a consecutive given number of days, are most suitable for those planning on spending extensive time on trains every few days. **Flexipasses**, valid for any 10 or 15 (not necessarily consecutive) days in a two-month period, are more cost-effective for those traveling longer distances less frequently. **Saverpasses** provide first-class travel for travelers in groups of two to five (prices are per person). **Youthpasses** and **Youth Flexipasses** provide parallel second-class perks for those under 26.

EURAILPASSES	15 days	21 days	1 month	2 months	3 months
1st class Eurailpass	US$554	US$718	US$890	US$1260	US$1558
Eurail Saverpass	US$470	US$610	US$756	US$1072	US$1324
Eurail Youthpass	US$388	US$499	US$623	US$882	US$1089

EURAIL FLEXIPASSES	10 days in 2 months	15 days in 2 months
1st class Eurail Flexipass	US$654	US$862

Eurail Saver Flexipass	US$556	US$732
Eurail Youth Flexipass	US$458	US$599

Passholders receive a timetable for major routes and a map with details on possible ferry, steamer, bus, car rental, hotel, and Eurostar (see p. 60) discounts. Passholders often also receive reduced fares or free passage on many bus and boat lines. **Eurail freebies** (excepting surcharges such as reservation fees and port taxes) include: ferries between Italy and Sardinia (Civitavecchia-Golfo Aranci), Sicily (Villa S. Giovanni-Messina), and Greece (Brindisi-Patras).

SHOPPING AROUND FOR A EURAIL OR EUROPASS Eurail-passes and Europasses are designed by the EU itself and are purchasable only by non-Europeans almost exclusively from non-European distributors. These passes must be sold at uniform prices determined by the EU. However, some travel agents tack on a US$10 handling fee, and others offer certain bonuses with purchase, so shop around. Also, keep in mind that pass prices usually go up each year, so if you're planning to travel early in the year, you can save cash by purchasing before January 1 (you have three months from the purchase date to validate your pass in Europe).

It is best to buy your Eurail- or Europass before leaving; only a few places in major European cities sell them, and at a marked-up price. Eurailpasses are non-refundable once validated; if your pass is completely unused and invalidated and you have the original purchase documents, you can get an 85% refund from the place of purchase. You can get a replacement for a lost pass only if you have purchased insurance on it under the Pass Protection Plan (US$10). Eurailpasses are available through travel agents, student travel agencies like STA and Council (see p. 60), and **Rail Europe,** 500 Mamaroneck Ave., Harrison, NY 10528 (US ☎888-382-7245, fax 800-432-1329; Canada ☎800-361-7245, fax 905-602-4198; UK ☎(0990) 848848; www.raileurope.com) or **DER Travel Services,** 9501 W. Devon Ave. #301, Rosemont, IL 60018 (US ☎888-337-7350; fax 800-282-7474; www.dertravel.com).

EUROPASS. The Europass is a slimmed-down version of the Eurailpass: it allows five to 15 days of unlimited travel in any two-month period within France, Germany, Italy, Spain, and Switzerland. **First-Class Europasses** (for individuals) and **Saverpasses** (for people traveling in groups of 2-5) range from US$348/296 per person (5 days) to US$728/620 (15 days). **Second-Class Youthpasses** for those ages 12-25 cost US$233-513. For a fee, you can add **additional ferry zones** between Italy and Greece; $60 for one associated country, $100 for two. You are entitled to the same **freebies** afforded by the Eurailpass (see above), but only when they are within or between countries that you have purchased. Plan your itinerary before buying a Europass: it will save you money if your travels are confined to three, four, or five adjacent Western European countries, or if you only want to go to large cities, but would be a waste if you plan to make lots of side-trips. If you're tempted to add many rail days and associate countries, consider a Eurailpass.

INTERRAIL PASS. If you have lived for at least six months in one of the European countries where InterRail Passes are valid, they prove an economical option. There are eight InterRail **zones:** A (Great Britain and the Republic of Ireland), B (Norway, Sweden, and Finland), C (Germany, Austria, Denmark, and Switzerland), D (Croatia, Czech Republic, Hungary, Poland, and Slovakia), E (France, Belgium, Netherlands, and Luxembourg), F (Spain, Portugal, and Morocco), G (Greece, Italy, Slovenia, and Turkey, including a Greece-Italy ferry), and H (Bulgaria, Romania, Yugoslavia, and Macedonia). The **Under 26 InterRail Card** allows either 14 days or one month of unlimited travel within one, two, three, or all of the eight zones; the cost is determined by the number of zones the pass covers (UK£159-259). If you buy a ticket including the zone in which you have claimed residence, you must still pay 50% fare for tickets inside your own country. Passholders receive **discounts** on rail

travel, Eurostar journeys, and most ferries to Ireland, Scandinavia, and the rest of Europe. Most exclude **supplements** for high-speed trains. For information and ticket sales in Europe contact **Student Travel Center**, 24 Rupert St., 1st fl., London W1V 7FN (☎(020) 7437 8101; fax 7734 3836; www.student-travel-centre.com). Tickets are also available from travel agents or main train stations throughout Europe.

EURO DOMINO. Like the Interrail Pass, the Euro Domino pass is available to anyone who has lived in Europe for at least six months; this pass, however, it is only valid in one country (which you designate upon buying the pass). It is available for 29 European countries as well as Morocco. The Euro Domino pass is available for first and second class travel (with a special rate for under 26ers), for three, five, or ten days of unlimited travel within a one-month period. Euro Domino is not valid on Eurostar or Thalys trains. Supplements for many high-speed trains are included, though you must still pay for reservations where they are compulsory. The pass must be bought within your country of residence; each country has its own price. Inquire with your national rail company for more information.

RAIL-AND-DRIVE PASSES. In addition to simple railpasses, many countries (as well as Europass and Eurail) offer rail-and-drive passes, which combine car rental with rail travel—a good option for travelers who wish both to visit cities accessible by rail and to make side trips into the surrounding areas. Rail Europe (see **Shopping Around for a Eurail or Europass,** p. 65) offers a EurailDrive Pass with four trains days and two rental days for between US$439 and US$529, depending on the car.

FURTHER READING: BY TRAIN

Thomas Cook European Timetable, updated monthly, covers all major and most minor train routes in Europe. In the US, order from Forsyth Travel Library (US$27.95 ☎800-367-7984; order@forsyth.com; www.forsyth.com). In Europe, find it at any Thomas Cook Money Exchange Center. Alternatively, buy directly from Thomas Cook (www.thomascook.com).

Guide to European Railpasses, Rick Steves. Online and by mail. US ☎425-771-8303; fax 425-771-0833; www.ricksteves.com). Free; delivery $8.

On the Rails Around Europe: A Comprehensive Guide to Travel by Train, Melissa Shales. Thomas Cook Ltd. (US$18.95).

Eurail and Train Travel Guide to Europe. Houghton Mifflin (US$15).

DISCOUNTED TICKETS

For travelers under 26, **BIJ** tickets (Billets Internationals de Jeunesse; a.k.a. **Wasteels, Eurotrain,** and **Route 26**) are an alternative to railpasses. Available for trips within Europe and most ferry services, they knock 20-40% off regular second class fares. Tickets, good for 60 days after purchase, allow a number of stopovers along your train route. Issued for a specific international route between two points, they must be used in the direction and order of the designated route and must be bought in Europe. The equivalent for those over 26, **BIGT** tickets provide a 20-30% discount on first and second class international tickets for business travelers, temporary European residents, and their families. Both types of tickets are available from European travel agents, at Wasteels, or Eurotrain offices (in or near train stations). For more information, contact Wasteels (see p. 59). Other branches are at: Stazione Centrale, Naples (☎(081) 20 10 71; fax 20 69 03); Stazione Centrale, Milan (☎(02) 669 0020; fax 669 05 00); and Stazione Maria Novella, Florence (☎/fax (05) 52 80 63).

BY BUS

Although Italian trains are extremely popular and inexpensive, the bus networks strike much less frequently and are therefore worth getting to know. In Italy, buses serve many points inaccessible by train and occasionally arrive in more convenient places in larger towns. All tickets must be validated using the orange machines on-board immediately upon entering the bus. Failure to do so will result in large fines, up to US$140. As a reward for the bumpy ride, the scenery along the way—especially in southern Tuscany and the Dolomites—often outshines the beauty of the destination. International bus passes are sometimes cheaper than railpasses, and they typically allow unlimited travel on a hop-on, hop-off basis between major European cities. **Eurolines,** 52 Grosvenor Gardens, London SW1 (☎(1582) 404511; www.eurolines.co.uk or www.eurolines.com), **Eurolines Italy** (☎(27) 200130: www.eurolines.it), and **Busabout,** 258 Vauxhall Bridge Rd., London SW1V 1BSX (☎ (020) 7959 1661; www.busabout.com), are popular among non-American backpackers. Contact them for information on passes and prices.

BY CAR

DRIVING PERMITS AND CAR INSURANCE

INTERNATIONAL DRIVING PERMIT (IDP)

If you plan to drive a car while in Italy, you must be over 18 and ought to have an International Driving Permit (IDP), though it is not always necessary to have one in Italy. It may be a good idea to get one anyway in case you're in a situation (e.g., an accident or stranded in a small town) where the police do not know English; information on the IDP is printed in ten languages, including Italian. For more information on the driving permit and driving in Italy, contact "In Italy Online," at www.initaly.com/travel/info/driving.htm.

Your IDP, valid for one year, must be issued in your own country before you depart. Applications for an IDP usually require one or two photos, a current local license, additional form of identification, and a fee. **EU citizens do not need an international driving permit; in case of an emergency, use your passport to prove citizenship.**

Australia: Contact your local Royal Automobile Club (RAC) or the National Royal Motorist Association (NRMA) if in NSW or the ACT (☎(08) 9421 4444; www.rac.com.au/travel). Permits AUS$15.

Canada: Contact a Canadian Automobile Association (CAA) branch office or write to CAA, 1145 Hunt Club Rd., #200, K1V 0Y3. (☎(613) 247-0117; www.caa.ca/CAAInternet/travelservices/internationaldocumentation/idptravel.htm). Permits CDN$10.

Ireland: Contact the nearest Automobile Association (AA) office or write to the UK address below. Permits IR£4. The Irish Automobile Association, 23 Suffolk St., Rockhill, Blackrock, Co. Dublin (☎(01) 677 9481; 24hr. breakdown and road service ☎(800) 667 788, toll-free in Ireland), honors most foreign automobile memberships.

New Zealand: Contact your local Automobile Association (AA) or the main office at Auckland Central, 99 Albert St., Auckland City, Auckland(☎(09) 377 4660; www.nzaa.co.nz). Permits NZ$10.

South Africa: Contact the Travel Services Department of the Automobile Association of South Africa at P.O. Box 596, 2000 Johannesburg (☎(011) 799 1000; fax 799 1960; www.aasa.co.za). Permits SAR28.50.

UK: Contact the **AA Headquarters** (☎(0870) 600 0371), or write to: The Automobile Association, International Documents, Fanum House, Erskine, Renfrewshire PA8 6BW. For more info, see www.theaa.co.uk/motoringandtravel/idp/index.asp. Permits UK£4.

US: Visit any American Automobile Association (AAA) office or write to AAA Florida, Travel Related Services, 1000 AAA Drive (mail stop 100), Heathrow, FL 32746 (☎407-444-7000; fax 444-7380; www.aaa.com). You don't have to be a member to buy an IDP. Permits US$10. AAA Travel Related Services (☎800-222-4357) provides road maps, travel guides, emergency road services, travel services, and auto insurance.

CAR INSURANCE

Most credit cards cover standard insurance up to the collision deductible. If you rent, lease, or borrow a car, you will need a **green card,** or **International Insurance**

Certificate, to certify that you have liability insurance and that it applies abroad. Green cards can be obtained at car rental agencies, car dealers (for those leasing cars), some travel agents, and some border crossings. Rental agencies may require you to purchase theft insurance in countries that they consider to have a high risk of auto theft. If you plan to drive in Italy for more than 45 days, you will need a regular Italian insurance policy. **If you are planning to rent a car in Italy you do not need a green card or an international drivers license, but you do need valid insurance coverage.**

CAR SAFETY

Taking certain precautions in large cities, especially Naples and Palermo, is advisable. If you own or buy a car, consider investing in a removable radio. Depress the aerial and tuck in side mirrors when leaving a car unattended on the street. Garages are usually the safest bet for parking in the city, but be sure to check rates before agreeing to anything. Parking can be extremely expensive, up to L20,000/ €10.33 per hour, in city centers. To save money, park in the outskirts and take a bus or InterCity train in to the city center. To avoid fines for street parking, ask your rental agency to equip your car with a dashboard timer. Most already do.

DRIVING IN ITALY

If you are using a car, learn local driving signals. There are four different kinds of roads: *Autostrade* (Superhighways: most of which charge tolls), *Strade Statali* (State Roads), *Strade Provinciali* (Provincial Roads), and *Strade Comunali* (Local Roads). On the *autostrade*, no U-turns are permitted, and stopping is permitted only in emergency parking areas or parking lanes.

The Italian highway code follows the Geneva Convention and Italy uses international road signs. Driving is on the right. Passing must be on the left. Violators of the highway code are fined; serious violations may also be punished by imprisonment. For more driving rules and regulations, consult "In Italy Online" at www.initaly.com/travel/info/driving.htm.

The **Automobile Club Italiano (ACI)** is the savior of Italy. Ready and willing to come to your aid, it has offices throughout Italy. The main office is at V. Marsala 8, 00185 Roma (☎(06) 499 81; fax 499 82 34). In case of **breakdown** on any Italian road, dial ☎116 at the nearest telephone. On superhighways, use the emergency telephones placed every two kilometers. For long drives in desolate areas, invest in a cellular phone and a roadside assistance program. Be sure to park your vehicle in a garage or well-traveled area and use a steering wheel locking device in larger cities.

RENTING A CAR

You can rent a car from a US-based firm (Alamo, Avis, Budget, or Hertz) with European offices, from a European-based company with local representatives (Europcar), or from a tour operator (Auto Europe, Europe By Car, and Kemwel Holiday Autos) that will arrange a rental for you from a European company at its own rates. Multinationals offer greater flexibility, but tour operators often strike better deals. Expect to pay L100,000/€51.65 per day for a teensy car. It is always cheaper to reserve a car from the US than from Europe. Some credit card companies cover the deductible on collision insurance, allowing their customers to decline the collision damage waiver. Ask airlines about special fly-and-drive packages; you may get up to a week of free or discounted rental. Minimum age in Italy is usually 18. At most agencies, all that's needed to rent a car is a license from home and proof that you've had it for a year.

Auto Europe, 39 Commercial St., P.O. Box 7006, Portland, ME 04112, USA (US and Canada ☎888-223-5555 or 207-842-2000; www.autoeurope.com).

Avis (US and Canada ☎800-230-4898; UK ☎(0870) 606 0100; Australia ☎(800) 13 63 33; New Zealand ☎(6495) 26 28 47; www.avis.com).

Budget (US ☎800-214 6094; Canada ☎800-527-0700; UK ☎(1442) 280181; Australia ☎13 27 27; www.budgetrentacar.com).

Europe by Car, One Rockefeller Plaza, New York, NY 10020 (US ☎800-223-1516 or 212-581-3040; fax 246-1458; info@europebycar.com; www.europebycar.com).

Europcar, 145 av. Malekoff, 75016 Paris (☎(01) 45 00 08 06); US ☎800-227-3876; Canada 800-227-7368; www.europcar.com).

Hertz (US ☎800-654-3001; Canada ☎800-263-0600; UK ☎(0870) 844 8844; Australia ☎02 9698 2555; www.hertz.com).

BY FERRY

The islands of Sicily, Sardinia, and Corsica, as well as the smaller islands along the coasts, are connected to the mainland by ferries *(traghetti)* and hydrofoils *(aliscafi)*. Italy's largest private ferry service is Tirrenia; for information, contact the Rome office at V. Bissolati, 41 (☎(06) 474 20 41). Major companies (**Tirrenia, Moby Lines, Siremar,** and **Caremar**) and hydrofoil services (**SNAV** and **Alilauro**) make departures and arrivals in major ports, such as Ancona, Bari, Brindisi, Genoa, Livorno, La Spezia, Naples, and Trapani. Ferry services will allow you to visit the Tremiti, Pontine, and Lipari (Aeolian) Islands. Ferries from Italy's ports of Bari, Brindisi, and Otranto travel to Greece. Only Brindisi honors Eurailpasses. In all other situations, Bari and Otranto services are cheaper. You can reach Tunisia from Genoa, Sardinia, and Trapani. Malta is accessible via Reggio di Calabria.

For major trips reserve ferry tickets at least one week in advance. Ferry schedules change unpredictably—confirm your departure one day in advance. Some ports require that you check in two hours before the departure or your reservation will be cancelled. **Posta ponte** (deck class; preferable in warm weather) is cheapest. It is, however, often only available when the **poltrone** (reclining cabin seats) are full. Port taxes often apply. Ask for student and Eurail discounts.

BY THUMB

Let's Go strongly urges you to consider the risks before you choose to hitchhike. We do not recommend hitchhiking as a safe means of transportation.

ADDITIONAL INFORMATION

SPECIFIC CONCERNS

WOMEN TRAVELERS

Women exploring on their own inevitably face some additional safety concerns, but it's easy to be adventurous without taking undue risks. The Italian art of *machismo* is well cultivated, and almost all foreign women will be hit on. In cities, you may be harassed no matter how you're dressed. Your best answer to verbal harassment is no answer at all; feigned deafness, sitting motionless, and staring straight ahead at nothing in particular will do a world of good. The extremely persistent can sometimes be dissuaded by a firm *"Vai Via!"* (Go away!), *"Sono fidanzata"* (I'm engaged), or *"Ho un ragazzo. Italiano. Molto geloso."* (I have a boyfriend. Italian. Very jealous). Wearing a conspicuous **wedding band** may also help prevent unwanted overtures. Some travelers report that carrying pictures of a "husband" or "children" is extremely useful to help document marriage status. Dress conservatively. "Modest dress" usually constitutes a long skirt (at least several inches past the knee) and a shirt with sleeves and a high neckline. Absolutely no bare shoulder or midriffs are allowed in most cathedrals or churches.

If you are concerned about hostel safety, you might consider staying in hostels that offer single rooms that lock from the inside or in religious organizations that offer women-only rooms. Communal showers in some hostels are safer than others; check before settling in. Avoid solitary late-night treks or metro rides.

When traveling, always carry extra money for a phone call or taxi. **Hitchhiking** is never safe for lone women, or even for women traveling together.

All travelers to Italy should, however, be aware that conceptions of personal space is different from what you're probably used to. The guy crowded next to you on the bus or the woman gesticulating wildly in your face is not necessarily threatening you; it is acceptable and normal to stand close to the person you're addressing, to gesture forcefully, and to shout. Don't hesitate, however, to seek out a police officer or a passerby if you are being harassed. *Let's Go: Italy* lists emergency numbers (including rape crisis lines) in the Practical Information listings of most cities. An **IMPACT Model Mugging** self-defense course will not only prepare you for a potential attack, but will also raise your level of awareness of your surroundings as well as your confidence (see **Self Defense,** p. 43).

> **FURTHER READING: WOMEN TRAVELERS.**
> *A Journey of One's Own: Uncommon Advice for the Independent Woman Traveler,* Thalia Zepatos. Eighth Mountain Press (US$16.95).
> *Adventures in Good Company: The Complete Guide to Women's Tours and Outdoor Trips,* Thalia Zepatos. Eighth Mountain Press (US$8).
> *Active Women Vacation Guide,* Evelyn Kaye. Blue Panda Publications (US$18).

TRAVELING ALONE

As a lone traveler, you may find that Italians are more inclined to help you. On the other hand, any solo traveler is a more vulnerable target of harassment and street theft. Lone travelers need to be well organized and look confident at all times. Never admit that you are traveling alone. Maintain regular contact with someone at home who knows your itinerary. For more tips, pick up *Traveling Solo* by Eleanor Berman (Globe Pequot, US$17) or subscribe to **Connecting: Solo Travel Network,** 689 Park Road, Unit 6, Gibsons, British Columbia, V0N IV7 (☎604-886-9009; fax 626-608 2139; info@cstn.org; www.cstn.org; membership US$28-46), or the **Travel Companion Exchange,** P.O. Box 833, Amityville, NY 11701, USA (☎631-454-0880 or 800-392-1256; fax 631-454 0170; www.whytravelalone.com; US$48).

OLDER TRAVELERS

Generally, senior citizens in the mother country are treated with respect and are often entitled to discounts. Though much of Italy is inaccessible to anyone without the legs of a young buck, there are many groups for senior travel ready to help.

Elderhostel, 11 Avenue de Lafayette, Boston, MA 02111, USA (☎617-426-7788 or 877-426-8056; registration@elderhostel.org; www.elderhostel.org; outside US ☎(978) 323 4141). Organizes 1- to 4-week "educational adventures" in Italy on subjects ranging from Lake Garda culture to the culinary delights of Northern Italy for those 55+.

The Mature Traveler, P.O. Box 50400, Reno, NV 89513, USA (☎775-786-7419, credit card orders 800-460-6676). Deals, discounts, and travel packages for the 50+ traveler. Subscription $30.

Walking the World, P.O. Box 1186, Fort Collins, CO 80522, USA (☎800-340-9255; fax 498-9100; walktworld@aol.com; www.walkingtheworld.com), organizes trips for 50+ travelers to Cinque Terre, the Dolomites, Venice, Cortina d'Ampezzo, and Tuscany.

> **FURTHER READING: OLDER TRAVELERS.**
> *No Problem! Worldwise Tips for Mature Adventurers,* Janice Kenyon. Orca Book Publishers (US$16).
> *A Senior's Guide to Healthy Travel,* Donald L. Sullivan. Career Press (US$15).
> *Unbelievably Good Deals and Great Adventures That You Absolutely Can't Get Unless You're Over 50,* Joan Rattner Heilman. Contemporary Books (US$13).

BISEXUAL, GAY, AND LESBIAN TRAVELERS

Italians are notoriously homophobic, a reputation rightly earned in many respects. The Vatican perennially opposes the gay pride parade in Rome. In 2000, The Vatican was joined by a majority of Italians who felt that WorldPride 2000 should not coincide with Jubilee 2000. Many, regardless of their disposition toward homosexuality, opposed the provocative invitations depicting a naked man and inviting participants to "Come in Rome." Nonetheless, Titti De Simone, a member of the Communist Refoundation Party, became the first openly lesbian woman in Parliament when she was elected in March 2001. Her platform included extending equal rights to common law and same sex couples and gay parents. The resurgence of the Catholic rightist parties, heralded by the June 2001 election of media magnate **Silvio Berlusconi,** appear to be a setback for the progress of gay rights in Italy.

Rome, Florence, Milan, and Bologna all have easily accessible gay scenes. Away from the larger cities, however, same-sex relationships may be less open, and gay social life may be difficult to find. Moreover, in smaller towns in the South, explicit public displays of affection will evoke shock, at the very least.

The monthly *Babilonia* and annual *Guida Gay Italia*, the national homosexual magazines, are at most newsstands. The magazines, along with confronting gay issues, also list social events. Expect the larger cities to have gay discotheques and bars (listed in *Let's Go* where available). The **Italian Gay and Lesbian Yellow Pages** (www.gay.it/guida/italia/info.htm) include listings of gay bars, hotels, and shops. **Out and About** (www.planetout.com) offers a helpful newsletter.

ARCI-GAY and ARCI-Lesbica, P. di Porta Saragozza, 2, 40123 Bologna (☎(051) 644 70 54; www.malox.com/arcigay/link.htm), and V. Orvinio, 2, 00199 Roma (☎(06) 86 38 51 12); or V. dei Mille, 23, Roma (☎(06) 446 58 39). The national organizations for homosexuals holds group discussions, dances, and many special events. Their website contains addresses and phone numbers of many city centers.

Giovanni's Room, 345 S. 12th St., Philadelphia, PA 19107, USA (☎215-923-2960; fax 923-0813; www.queerbooks.com). An international lesbian/feminist and gay bookstore with mail-order service (carries many of the publications listed below).

International Gay and Lesbian Travel Association, 4331 N. Federal Hwy., #304, Fort Lauderdale, FL 33308, USA (☎954-776-2626; fax 776-3303; www.iglta.com). An organization of over 1350 companies serving gay and lesbian travelers worldwide.

FURTHER READING: BISEXUAL, GAY, AND LESBIAN TRAVELERS.
Spartacus International Gay Guide. Bruno Gmunder Verlag. (US$33).
Ferrari Guides' Gay Travel A to Z, Ferrari Guides' Men's Travel in Your Pocket, Ferrari Guides' Women's Travel in Your Pocket, and *Ferrari Guides' Inn Places.* Ferrari Guides (US$14-16). For more info, call ☎602-863-2408 or 800-962-2912 or try www.q-net.com.

TRAVELERS WITH DISABILITIES

Those with disabilities should inform airlines and hotels of their disabilities when making arrangements for travel; some time may be needed to prepare special accommodations. Call ahead to restaurants, hotels, parks, and other facilities to find out about the existence of ramps, the widths of doors, the dimensions of elevators, etc. **Guide dog owners** should inquire as to the specific quarantine policies of each destination country. At the very least, they will need to provide a certificate of immunization against rabies. In the wake of Foot and Mouth Disease, travelers from Great Britain and Ireland will most likely meet with resistance if attempting to bring a guide animal into Italy and most other European countries.

Rail is probably the most convenient form of travel for disabled travelers in Europe: many stations have ramps, and some trains have wheelchair lifts, special seating areas, and specially equipped toilets. In general, Italy's Pendolino and many Eurostar and InterCity trains are extremely accessible for the disabled. For those who wish to rent cars, some major **car rental** agencies (Hertz, Avis, and National) offer hand-controlled vehicles.

Many of the museums and famed landmarks are inaccessible. Venice is especially difficult to navigate. Few hotels and almost no hostels have adapted rooms. Precautions should be made prior to a visit. Call accommodations, restaurants, and institutions to find out accessibility prior to arrival.

USEFUL ORGANIZATIONS

Accessible Italy, with two main offices in Italy: **Promotur-Mondo Possibile,** P. Pitagora 9, 10137 Turin (☎(011) 309 63 63; fax 309 12 01); and **La Viaggeria,** V. Lemonia 161, 00174 Roma (☎(06) 71 58 29 45; fax 71 58 34 33). A travel agency for the disabled and aged, Accessible Italy is a member of SATH (see below) and more than ready to help out in any way possible. See www.tour-web.com/accitaly for more info.

Mobility International USA (MIUSA), P.O. Box 10767, Eugene, OR 97440, USA (☎541-343-1284 voice and TDD; fax 343-6812; info@miusa.org; www.miusa.org). Sells *A World of Options: A Guide to International Educational Exchange, Community Service, and Travel for Persons with Disabilities* (US$35).

Moss Rehab Hospital Travel Information Service, 1200 West Tabor Rd., Philadelphia, PA 19141-3099 (netstaff@mossresourcenet.org; www.mossresourcenet.org). An information resource center on travel-related concerns for those with disabilities.

Society for the Advancement of Travel for the Handicapped (SATH), 347 Fifth Ave., #610, New York, NY 10016 (☎212-447-7284; sathtravel@aol.com; www.sath.org). Publishes *Open World* (free for members, US$13 for nonmembers). Also publishes a wide range of info sheets on disability travel facilitation and destinations. Annual membership US$45, students and seniors US$30. Order a free copy of *Open World* online.

TOUR AGENCIES

Directions Unlimited, 123 Green Ln., Bedford Hills, NY 10507, USA (☎914-241-1700 or 800-533-5343; www.travel-cruises.com). Specializes in arranging individual and group vacations, tours, and cruises for the physically disabled.

The Guided Tour Inc., 7900 Old York Rd., #114B, Elkins Park, PA 19027, USA (☎800-783-5841 or 215-782-1370; fax 215 635 2637; gtour400@aol.com; www.guidedtour.com). Organizes travel programs for persons with developmental and physical challenges around Rome.

FURTHER READING: DISABLED TRAVELERS.
Resource Directory for the Disabled, Richard Neil Shrout. Facts on file (US$45).
Wheelchair Through Europe, Annie Mackin. Graphic Language Press (US ☎760-944-9594; niteowl@cts.com; US$13).

MINORITY TRAVELERS

In certain regions, particularly in the South, tourists of color or members of non-Christian religious groups may feel unwelcome. If you encounter discriminatory treatment, please let us know so that we can check out the establishment and, if appropriate, warn other travelers. **Jewish tourists** may appreciate the *Italy Jewish Travel Guide* (US$15) from Israelowitz Publishing, P.O. Box 228, Brooklyn, NY 11229, which provides information on sites of religious interest. The Jerusalem Italian Jews Association publishes sites of interest on its website, www.jija.com.

In terms of safety, there are no easy answers. Keep abreast of the particular cultural attitudes of the regions that you're planning to visit. The prominent political party, **Lega Nord,** centers around an essentially racist platform promoting the North's separation from the South, and it is more popular in Italy than most people would like to admit. Tourists from the West, who are easily distinguishable by clothes and language, are not usually targets of racism. Women of color may be seen as exotic but not unwelcome. Travel in groups and take a taxi whenever uncomfortable. The best answer to verbal harassment is often no answer at all. The election of Berlusconi's right wing conservatives is said by many Italians to herald less religious and ethnic tolerance in the future.

TRAVELERS WITH CHILDREN

When deciding where to stay, remember the special needs of young children; if you pick a B&B or a small hotel, call ahead and make sure it's child friendly. If you rent a car, make sure the rental company provides a car seat for younger children. Be sure that your children carry some sort of ID in case of an emergency or in case they get lost. Museums, tourist attractions, accommodations, and restaurants often offer discounts for children. Children under two generally fly for 10% of the adult airfare on international flights. International fares are usually discounted 25% for children aged two to 11. Finding a private place for **breast feeding** is often a problem while traveling, so pack accordingly.

FURTHER READING: TRAVELERS WITH CHILDREN.
Backpacking with Babies and Small Children, Goldie Silverman. Wilderness Press (US$10).
Take Your Kids to Europe, Cynthia W. Harriman. Globe Pequot (US$17).
How to take Great Trips with Your Kids, Sanford and Jane Portnoy. Harvard Common Press (US $10).
Have Kid, Will Travel: 101 Survival Strategies for Vacationing With Babies and Young Children, Claire and Lucille Tristram. Andrews and McMeel (US$9).

DIETARY CONCERNS

While there are only a few specifically vegetarian restaurants sprinkled throughout Italy, it is not hard to find vegetarian meals. The Italian diet is not centered around meat; pasta and greens are plentiful. For veggie-based eateries around the country, check out the website of **World Guide to Vegetarianism**, www.veg.org/Guide/Italy/index.html, or the **A.V.I. Italian Vegetarian Association,** V. Bazzini 4, 20131 Milano (☎(02) 26 68 10 80). Travelers who keep kosher and halal dietary restrictions should contact synagogues or mosques in larger cities.

FURTHER READING: DIETARY CONCERNS.
The Vegetarian Traveler: Where to Stay if You're Vegetarian, Jed Civic. Larson Pub. (US$16).
Europe on 10 Salads a Day, Greg and Mary Jane Edwards. Mustang Publishing. (US$10/UK£9).

ALTERNATIVES TO TOURISM

STUDY ABROAD

Programs vary greatly in expense, academic quality, living arrangements, and exposure to local culture. The vast majority of programs are sponsored by American universities (see below). You may want to check with the American Embassy in Rome for a list of all American schools in Italy. More information on language programs can be found on the web at www.languagestudy.com.

EU citizens do not require a visa to study in Italy. Non-EU citizens wishing to study in Italy must obtain a study visa *(permesso di studio)* prior to departure from their nearest embassy or consulate. For non-EU citizens to obtain a visa, you will need to provide proof of enrollment from your home institution or the school or university in Italy, a notarized statement that you have adequate financial means, and proof of medical insurance for the duration of your stay in Italy. Americans require a statement that they will purchase an additional Italian health insurance policy in Italy as a supplement to their domestic insurance. As of August

2000, the visa fee for US citizens is $32.43, payable in money order only, for Australian citizens AUS$51, and NZ$66 for New Zealand citizens. Upon arrival in Italy, students must register with the Foreigners' Bureau *(Ufficio degli Stranieri)* of the local *questura* in order to receive their permit of stay.

> **FURTHER READING: STUDY ABROAD.**
> www.studyabroad.com
> *Academic Year Abroad 2000/2001.* Institute of International Education Books (US$47).
> *Vacation Study Abroad 2000/2001.* Institute of International Education Books (US$43).
> *Peterson's Study Abroad 2001.* Peterson's (US$30).
> *Peterson's Summer Study Abroad 2001.* Peterson's (US$30).

UNIVERSITIES

Most American undergraduates enroll in programs sponsored by US universities. Those relatively fluent in Italian may find it cheaper to enroll directly in a local university (though getting credit may be more difficult). Some schools that offer study abroad programs to foreigners are listed below.

John Cabot University, V. della Lungara, 233, Rome (☎(06) 68 19 12 21; fax 683 20 88; www.johncabot.edu), is the premier American university in Italy. It offers a 4-year Bachelor of Arts degree in addition to semester and summer courses.

American University of Rome, V. Pietro Roselli, 4 (☎(06) 58 33 09 19; fax 58 33 09 92) offers courses in English in international business, international relations, and Italian civilization and culture. Credits often transferable for US universities. US$4911 per semester; US$2830 for housing.

American Institute for Foreign Study, College Division, River Plaza, 9 West Broad St., Stamford, CT 06902, USA (☎800-727-2437, ext. 5163; www.aifsabroad.com). Organizes programs for high school and college study in universities in Italy.

Arcadia University Center for Education Abroad, 450 S. Easton Rd., Glenside, PA 19038, USA (☎888-232-8379; www.beaver.edu/cea). Operates programs in Florence and Perugia. Costs range from $2750 (summer) to $18,000 (full-year).

LANGUAGE SCHOOLS

These programs are run by foreign universities generally cost anywhere from US$350-8000 and may include room and board and side trips. The website of **Language Learning Net** (www.language-learning.net), which lists more than 6000 schools worldwide in 24 languages, is a useful starting point for research.

Centro Fiorenza, V.S. Spirito, 14, Florence (☎(055) 239 82 74; fax 28 71 48; fiorence@tin.it), offers a plethora of 2- and 4-week courses in Italian language and culture for students of all ages and abilities ($450-775). Accommodation is either in homestays or student apartments (L19-45,000 per day).

Italiaidea, P. della Cancelleria, 85, Rome (☎(06) 68 30 76 20; italiaidea@italiaidea.com; www.italiaidea.com), schools 1500 students a year in Italian language and culture from their base in the Eternal City. 2- and 4-week courses are held year-round (L780-1,250,000).

Istituto Zambler Venezia, Dorsoduro, 3116A, Campo S. Margherita (☎(041) 522 43 31; fax (041) 528 56 28; zambler@virtualvenice.net; www.virtualvenice.net/zambler), is based in a 16th-century *palazzo* in the heart of Venice. They offer 2- to 12-week courses year-round in language, culture, and cooking (L500-2,400,000).

Eurocentres, 101 N. Union St. #300, Alexandria, VA 22314, USA (☎800-648-4809 or 703-684-1494; www.eurocentres.com), or in Europe, Head Office, Seestr. 247, CH-8038 Zurich, Switzerland (☎+41 (411) 485 50 40; info@eurocentres.com). Language programs for beginning to advanced students with homestays in Italy run approximately US$1132 a month.

WORK

EU passport holders do not require a visa to work in Italy. They must have a workers registration book *(libretto di lavoro)*, available, at no extra cost, upon presentation of the *"permesso di soggiorno."* If your parents were born in an EU country, you may be able to claim dual citizenship or at least the right to a work permit. Non-EU citizens seeking work in Italy must apply for an Italian work permit *(Autorizzazione al lavoro in Italia)* before entering the country. Permits are authorized by the Provincial Employment Office and approved by the *questura* before being forwarded to the employer and then the prospective employee. The prospective employee must then present the document along with a valid passport in order to obtain a work visa. Normally a three-month tourist permit is granted, and upon presentation of an employer's letter the permit can be extended for a period specified by the employment contract. In some sectors (like agricultural work) permit-less workers are rarely bothered by authorities. Foreigners are most successful at securing harvest, restaurant, bar, and household work, or jobs in the tourism industry, where English speakers are needed. **Enjoy Rome** (☎(06) 445 18 43) often has employment options in the tourism sector. The **Ministero Lavoro e Providenza Sociale,** Divisione 11, V. Flavia, 6, I-00187 Rome, and the **Italian Cultural Institute** (see p. 35) offer job placement information.

AU PAIR ORGANIZATIONS

Accord Cultural Exchange, 750 La Playa, San Francisco, CA 94121, USA (☎415-386-6203); www.cognitext.com/accord). US$40 application fee.

InterExchange, 161 Sixth Ave., New York, NY 10013, USA (☎212-924-0446; fax 924-0575; www.interexchange.org). Participants must speak English. Application fee of US$400 includes work visa.

Childcare International, Ltd., Trafalgar House, Grenville Pl., London NW7 3SA, UK (☎(020) 8906 3116; fax 8906 3461; www.childint.co.uk). UK£100 application fee. Non-EU residents work reduced hours only.

TEACHING ENGLISH

International Schools Services, Educational Staffing Program, P.O. Box 5910, Princeton, NJ 08543, USA (☎609-452-0990; www.iss.edu). Recruits teachers and administrators for American and English schools in Italy. Applicants must have a bachelor's degree and 2 years of relevant experience. Nonrefundable US$50 application fee. US$100 for establishing a profile on their website. Publishes *The ISS Directory of Overseas Schools.*

Office of Overseas Schools, US Department of State, Room H328, SA-1, Washington, D.C. 20522, USA (☎ 202-261-8200; www.state.gov/www/about_state/schools/). Comprehensive list of schools abroad and teaching abroad agencies.

VOLUNTEERING

Volunteer jobs are readily available, and usually provide room and board. You can sometimes avoid high application fees by contacting workcamps directly.

Archaeological Institute of America, 656 Beacon St., Boston, MA 02215, USA (☎ 617-353-9361; www.archaeological.org). The *Archaeological Fieldwork Opportunities Bulletin* (US$15 for non-members) lists field sites in Italy. Get the bulletin from Kendall/Hunt Publishing, 4050 Westmark Dr., Dubuque, Iowa 52002, USA (☎ 800-228-0810).

Earthwatch, 680 Mt. Auburn St., Box 403, Watertown, MA 02272, USA (☎ 800-776-0188 or 617-353 9361; www.earthwatch.org). Arranges 1- to 3-week programs in Italy to promote conservation of natural resources. Programs average US$1600.

Service Civil International Voluntary Service (SCI-IVS), 814 NE 40th St., Seattle, WA 98105, USA (☎ /fax 206-545-6585; www.sci-ivs.org). Arranges placement in workcamps in Italy for those 18+. US$125 fee for application in 2002. Registration fee US$65-150.

Volunteers for Peace, 1034 Tiffany Rd., Belmont, VT 05730, USA (☎ 802-259-2759; www.vfp.org). Arranges placement in workcamps in Italy. Annual *International Workcamp Directory* US$20. Registration fee US$200. Free newsletter.

WEB RESOURCES

Every aspect of budget travel (with the most notable exception, of course, being experience) is accessible via the web. If you don't have Internet access at home, seeking access at a public library or at work can be well worth it; within 10 minutes, you can make hostel reservations, get advice on travel hotspots, or find out exactly how much that train from Naples to Palermo costs. Listed here are some budget travel sites to start you off; other relevant websites are listed throughout the book.

LEARNING THE ART OF BUDGET TRAVEL

How to See the World: www.artoftravel.com. A compendium of great travel tips, from cheap flights to self defense to interacting with local culture.

Rec. Travel Library: www.travel-library.com. A fantastic set of links for general info and personal travelogues.

INFORMATION ON ITALY

CIA World Factbook: www.odci.gov/cia/publications/factbook/index.html. Tons of vital statistics about Italy: geography, government, economy, and people.

Foreign Language for Travelers: www.travlang.com. Provides free online translating dictionaries and lists of phrases in Italian, as well as language courses at cost.

MyTravelGuide: www.mytravelguide.com. Country overviews, with everything from history to transportation to live web cam coverage of Italy.

Geographia: www.geographia.com. Describes the highlights, culture, and people of Italy.

Atevo Travel: www.atevo.com/guides/destinations. Detailed introductions, travel tips, and suggested itineraries.

TravelPage: www.travelpage.com. Links to official tourist office sites throughout Italy.

AND OUR PERSONAL FAVORITE

Let's Go: www.letsgo.com. Our recently revamped website features photos and streaming video, info about our books, a travel forum buzzing with stories and tips, and links that will help you find everything you could ever want to know about Italy. Be sure to check out our new *First Timer's Guide to Europe,* which features suggested itineraries, general info about Europe and individual European countries, and a section on travel documents and formalities.

NORTHWEST ITALY

LOMBARDY (LOMBARDIA)

Over the centuries, Roman generals, German emperors, and French kings have vied for control of Lombardy's agricultural wealth and fertile soil. In recent years, a tremendous increase in employment and business has augmented the region's already vibrant industry, making Lombardy the cornerstone of the Italian economy and the richest European region after Paris. In many ways, Lombardy has more in common with countries to the north than with its own peninsula; consequently, Lombards periodically call for secession in order to eliminate the forced subsidization of the Roman bureaucracy and the burdens of the economically challenged South. Since World War II, however, Lombardy's booming economy has drawn legions of ambitious southerners, and the province has recently attracted immigrants from North Africa, the Middle East, and East Asia. The diversity makes inhabitants of Lombardy among the most cosmopolitan in Italy.

HIGHLIGHTS OF LOMBARDY

REVEL in the best clubbing city in Europe; bar-hop in the **Navigli** (p. 97) after a hard-hitting cultural day at the **Last Supper** (p. 92) and the **Museo Poldi Pezzoli** (p. 91).

SCALE the steps of **La Scala,** the world's premier opera house (p. 91).

FIDDLE the day away at Cremona's **Museo Stradivariano** (p. 104).

STAND agape beneath the dazzling ceiling of Bergamo's **Basilica di Santa Maria Maggiore** (p. 114).

MILAN (MILANO)   ☎ 02

Milan lies on Roman foundations but has progressed technologically and socially with more force than any other major Italian city. Although it served as the capital of the western half of the Roman Empire from AD 286 to 402, Milan retains few reminders of that period. The stunningly ornate *duomo* is the city's emblem and a rare remnant of its history. The pace of life is quicker here, and *il dolce di far niente* (the sweetness of doing nothing) is an unfamiliar taste. *Milano l'e Milano* (Milan is just Milan) is a dialect expression that sums up how different the cosmopolitan capital is from the rest of Italy. Its wide, tree-lined boulevards and graceful architecture are elegant but forced to compete with the omnipresent, vibrant graffiti. Although petty crime, drug dealing, and prostitution may strike your eye, so too should the enormous number of well-dressed Italians in designer suits. The capital of style, financial markets, and industry, Milan is on the cutting edge of fashion, invention, and ideas, rarely pausing to rest. The city becomes most vibrant twice a year when the two local football (soccer) teams, AC Milan and Inter Milan, play each other. Football is the city's religion, and the AC/Inter game is more important than Christmas. Milanese are generally open-minded and accepting of foreigners, though sometimes they just don't have the time to stop and be friendly. Only in August, when the city shuts down for the entire month, do its citizens flock to quiet resort towns and breathe a collective sigh of relief.

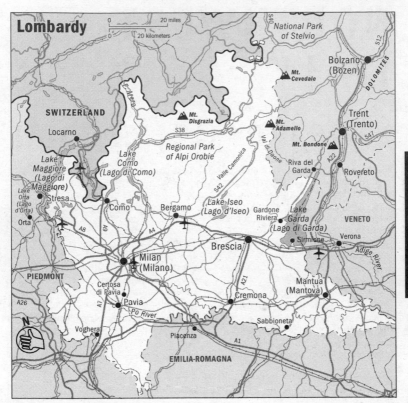

Lombardy

0   20 miles
0   20 kilometers

✈ INTERCITY TRANSPORTATION

Flights: Malpensa Airport, 45km from town. Intercontinental flights. Luggage storage and lost property services available (p. 85). **Malpensa Express** leaves from Cadorna metro station to airport (45min.; 6:50am-8:20pm; L15,000/€7.75, if bought on train L20,000/€10.33) and returns 7:45am-8:45pm. Also **Night Buses** (1hr.; L13,000/€6.71, Alitalia, KLM, or Northwest, L9,000/€4.65, TWA, AirEuropa, or Lott, free). **Linate Airport,** 7km from town. Much easier logistically. Domestic/European flights and intercontinental flights with European transfers. Lost property services available (p. 85). **STAM bus** to Linate (☎02 71 71 06) goes to Stazione Centrale (every 20min., L4500/€2.32), but it's cheaper to take bus #73 (L1500/€0.77) from P. San Babila (MM1). **General Flight Info** for both airports (☎02 7485 2200), international arrivals (☎02 2680 0619), international departures (☎02 2680 0627).

Trains: Stazione Centrale (☎01 4788 8088), in P. Duca d'Aosta, on MM2. **Info office** open daily 7am-9:30pm. Eurail passes and Cartaverde available outside. Luggage storage and lost property services available (p. 85). Primary station to: **Florence** (2½hr.; every hr.; L40,000/€20.66); **Genoa** (1½hr.; every hr.; L24,000/€12.39); **Rome** (4½hr.; every hr.; L71,000/€36.67); **Turin** (2hr.; every hr.; L24,500/€12.65); **Venice** (3hr.; 21 per day; L36,000/€18.59). **Stazione Nord** connects Milan to Como and Varese (every 30min., 6am-9pm). **Porta Genova** (at P. Le Stazione di Porta Genova) has lines west to Vigevano, Alessandria, and Asti. **Porta Garibaldi** (at P. Sigmund Freud) links Milan to Lecco and Valtellina to the northwest.

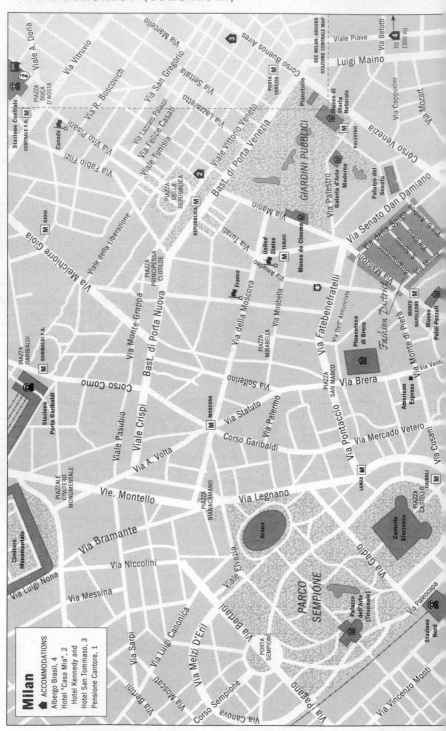

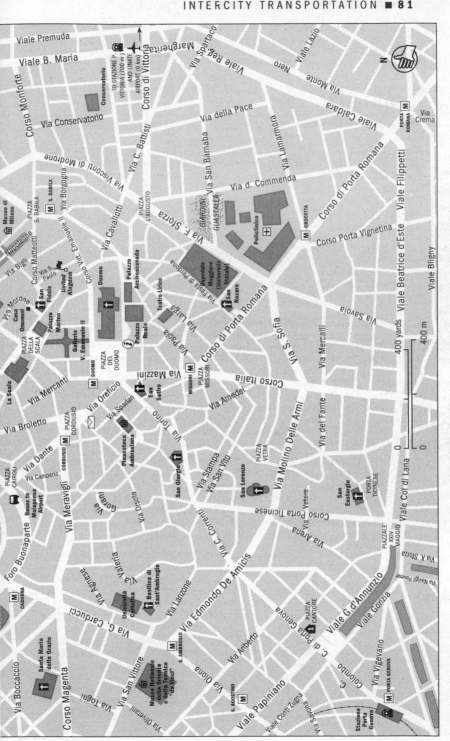

Buses: At **Stazione Centrale**. Signs for bus destinations, times, and prices posted outside. Tickets purchased inside (cash only). **Intercity** buses tend to be less convenient and more expensive than trains. **SAL, SIA, Autostradale,** and many others depart from P. Castello and the surrounding area (MM1: Cairoli) for Turin, the Lake Country, Bergamo, Certosa di Pavia, and points as far away as Rimini and Trieste.

✳ ORIENTATION

The layout of the city resembles a giant target, encircled by a series of ancient concentric city walls. In the outer rings lie suburbs built during the 50s and 60s to house southern immigrants. Within the inner circle are four central squares: **Piazza Duomo,** at the end of V. Mercanti; **Piazza Cairoli,** near the Castello Sforzesco; **Piazza Cordusio,** connected to Largo Cairoli by V. Dante; and **Piazza San Babila,** the business and fashion district along C.V. Emanuele. The **duomo** and **Galleria Vittorio Emanuele** comprise the bull's eye, roughly at the center of the downtown circle. To the northeast and northwest lie two large parks, the **Giardini Pubblici** and the **Parco Sempione.** Farther northeast is **Stazione Centrale.** The skyscrapers around the station are dominated by the sleek **Pirelli Tower.** From the station, a scenic ride on bus #60 takes you to the downtown hub, as does the more efficient commute on metro line #3. **via Vito Pisani,** which leads to **Piazza della Repubblica,** connects the station to downtown. It continues through the wealthy business districts as **via Turati** and finally as **via Manzoni** leading to the *duomo.* The more affordable sections of Milan are five blocks east of the station (left as you exit), down **Corso Buenos Aires.**

⊏ LOCAL TRANSPORTATION

Milan's streets twist, turn, change names unexpectedly, and even ask you riddles. Be absolutely certain to purchase a detailed map as soon as possible. The most legible map has a blue background with a picture of the *duomo* on the cover and is called **La Generale Milano,** produced by *Edizioni Di Lauro Milano.* The streets are generally safe at night, but women shouldn't walk alone. Among the many useful tram and bus routes, **trams #29** and **30** travel the city's outer ring road, while **buses #96** and **97** service the inner road. Tickets for bus, tram, and subway must be purchased in advance at newsstands *(tabacchi),* ticket machines, or ticket offices in a few lucky stations—bring small change.

Metro: The **Metropolitana Milanese** ("MM") operates from 6am to midnight. Most useful branch of Milan's public transportation network. Be aware of occasional strikes. **Line #1** (red) stretches east to west from the *pensioni* district east of Stazione Centrale, through the center of town, and west to the youth hostel (Molino Dorino fork). **Line #2** (green) links Milan's 3 train stations and crosses line #1 (MM1) at Cadorna and Loreto. **Line #3** (yellow) runs from north of Stazione Centrale to the southern sprawl of the city, crossing with #2 (MM2) at Stazione Centrale and #1 (MM1) at the *duomo.*

Public Transportation: The **subway** is efficient but not extensive; the **buses** allow you to reach wider porticos of the metro area and require pre-purchased tickets. All-day passes for non-residents L5000/€2.58, 2 days for L9000/€4.65. All-day passes are good for 24hr. from the first validation. Book of 10 tickets L14,000/€7.23; weekly and monthly passes L35,000/€18.08 initial payment, plus a weekly ticket pass for around L10,000/€5.16 (photo required). Single ticket (L1500/€0.77) is good for one subway ride or 75min. of surface transportation. Keep extra tickets on hand, as *tabacchi* close around 8pm and vending machines (in every station) are unreliable. Riding the MM without a ticket warrants a (rarely enforced) L30,000/€15.49 fine. Info (☎800 01 68 57) and ticket offices open M-Sa 7:15am-7:15pm.

Taxis: Taxis are omnipresent. All are white, and park in ranks, usually near *piazzas* and other heavily trafficked areas. If you can't find one on the street, call: **Radio Taxi** (☎02 53 53, 85 85, 83 83, or 52 51). Uniformly expensive, starting at L5000/€2.58; nighttime surcharge L6000/€3.10. Open 24hr.

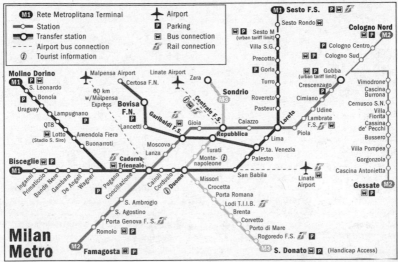

Milan Metro

M1 Rete Metropolitana Terminal	✈ Airport
Station	P Parking
Transfer station	🚌 Bus connection
- - - Airport bus connection	🚆 Rail connection
ⓘ Tourist information	

Car Rental: All have similar rates and are located just outside the main *galleria* at the Stazione Centrale. **Hertz** (☎02 669 00 61), at the *galleria*. Open M-F 8am-7pm, Sa 8am-2pm. Main office (☎02 6698 5151), at P. Duca d'Aosta. Open M-F 8am-8pm, Sa 8am-2pm, Su 8am-1pm. **Europcar** (☎02 6698 1589 or toll-free 800 01 44 10). Open M-F 8am-1pm and 2-7pm, Sa 8:30am-12:30pm. **Avis** (☎02 669 02 80 or 670 16 54). Open M-F 7:45am-8pm, Sa 8am-4pm. Main office at V. Corelli, 150 (☎02 7020 0440). Be aware that there are parking restrictions in the city center. Info on parking without fines, call **Polizia Municipale** (☎02 772 71).

Bike Rental: A.W.S. Bici Motor, V. Ponte Seveso, 33 (☎02 6707 2145). Exit Stazione Centrale to right. From the park take V.S. Chiaparelli on right. After 3 blocks go left onto V.P. Seveso. Fab mountain bikes L20,000/€10.33. Open M-Sa 9am-1pm and 3-7pm.

🔼 PRACTICAL INFORMATION

TOURIST AND FINANCIAL SERVICES

Tourist Office: APT, V. Marconi, 1 (☎02 7252 4300; fax 7252 4350), in "Palazzo di Turismo" in P. del Duomo, to right as you face *duomo*. Comprehensive local and regional info. Useful map and museum guide (in Italian). Long lines, but staff kind and efficient. L15,000/€7.75 well-spent gets you the info packet "Welcome Card." It includes discount cards, maps, full descriptions of sites, a 24hr. bus/train pass, and a CD of Milan's best opera (and all this stowed neatly in a pouch that can also be used for your airline tickets.) Will not reserve rooms, but will phone to check for vacancies. Pick up the comprehensive 📖 *Milano: Where, When, How* as well as *Milano Mese* for info on activities and clubs. Ask about the wonderful guided art tours (L25,000/€12.91 including museum). English spoken. Open M-F 8:30am-8pm, Sa 9am-1pm and 2-7pm, Su 9am-1pm and 2-5pm. **Branch office** at Stazione Centrale (☎02 7252 4370 or 7252 4360), off main hall on 2nd fl., through neon archway to left between 2 gift shops. English spoken. Open M-Sa 9am-6pm, Su 9am-12:30pm and 1:30-6pm.

Budget Travel: CIT (☎02 86 37 01). At the Galleria Vittorio Emanuele II at center of the structure, across from McDonald's and Mercedes Benz. Also **currency exchange.** Open M-F 9am-7pm, Sa 9am-1pm and 2-6pm. **CTS,** V.S. Antonio, 2 (☎02 5830 4121). Open M-F 9:30am-12:45pm and 2-6pm, Sa 9:30am-12:45pm. **Transalpino Tickets** (☎02 67 16 82 28; www.transalpino.com), next to the train info office in the upper atrium of Stazione Centrale. Discounts for ages 26 and under. Open M-Sa 8am-

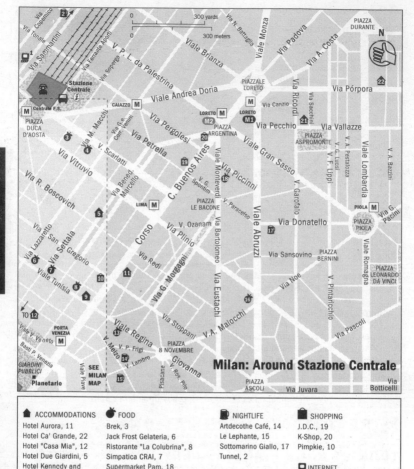

Milan: Around Stazione Centrale

▲ ACCOMMODATIONS	🍴 FOOD	🍸 NIGHTLIFE	🛍 SHOPPING
Hotel Aurora, 11	Brek, 3	Artdecothe Café, 14	J.D.C., 19
Hotel Ca' Grande, 22	Jack Frost Gelateria, 6	Le Lephante, 15	K-Shop, 20
Hotel "Casa Mia", 12	Ristorante "La Colubrina", 8	Sottomarino Giallo, 17	Pimpkie, 10
Hotel Due Giardini, 5	Simpatica CRAI, 7	Tunnel, 2	
Hotel Kennedy and	Supermarket Pam, 18		🖥 INTERNET
Hotel Tomaso, 9	Supermarket Regina Giovanna, 13		Boomerang (Internet Access), 1
Hotel Malta, 21	Tarantella, 16		

8:30pm. **Main office** 4 blocks away at V. Locatelli, 5 (☎02 6671 2424). When closed, go to Italturismo, under the grand drive-through on the right. Open daily 7am-7:45pm.

Consulates: Australia, V. Borgogna, 2 (☎02 77 70 41; fax 7770 4242). Open M-Th 9am-noon and 2-4pm, F 9am-noon. **Canada,** V.V. Pisani, 19 (☎02 675 81). Open M-Th 8:30am-12:30pm and 1:15-5:30pm. **New Zealand,** V. d'Arezzo, 6 (☎02 4801 2544). Open M-F 9am-noon. **UK,** V.S. Paolo, 7 (☎02 72 30 01; emergency ☎03 358 10 68 57). Open M-F 9am-1pm and 2-5pm. **US,** V.P. Amedeo, 2/10 (☎02 2903 5141). Open M-F 9am-noon.

Currency Exchange: All **Banca d'America e d'Italia** and **Banca Nazionale del Lavoro** branches eagerly await your Visa card. Bank hours in Milan are usually M-F 8:30am-1:30pm and 2:30-4:30pm. **ATMs** abound.

American Express: V. Brera, 3 (☎02 72 00 36 93), on the corner of V. dell'Orso. Walk through the Galleria, across P. Scala, and up V. Verdi. Servies for AmEx card members: holds mail free for 1 month (for non-members, US$5 per inquiry) and receives wired money with a fee of L2500/€1.29 per month on transactions over L150,000/€77.47. Also **exchanges currency.** Open M-Th 9am-5:30pm, F 9am-5pm.

NORTHWEST ITALY

LOCAL SERVICES

Luggage Storage: In the Malpensa Airport. L4000/€2.07 per bag per day. In the Stazione Centrale. L5000/€2.58 per 12hr. Open 24hr.

Lost Property: Ufficio Oggetti Smarriti Comune, V. Friuli, 30 (☎02 546 81 18). Open M-F 8:30am-4pm. **Malpensa Airport** (☎02 58 58 00 69). **Linate Airport** (☎02 70 12 44 51). **Stazione Centrale** (☎02 63 71 26 67). Open daily 7am-1pm and 2-8pm.

English-Language Bookstores: The American Bookstore, V. Camperio, 16 (☎02 87 89 20; fax 7202 0030), at Largo Cairoli. Open Tu-Sa 10am-7pm, M 1-7pm. **Hoepli Libreria Internazionale,** V. Hoepli, 5 (☎02 86 48 71), off P. Media near P. Scala. Open M 2-7pm, Tu-Sa 9am-7pm. MC/V. **Rizzoli's** (☎02 8646 1071), Galleria Vittorio Emanuele. Open M-Sa 9am-8pm, Su 12:30-7:30pm. AmEx/MC/V. Also try **street vendors** along Largo Mattioli for cheaper options.

Library: British Council Library, V. Manzoni, 38 (☎02 7722 2203), at a center for teaching English. Open Tu-Th 10am-7:30pm, F 10am-6pm, Sa 2-4pm.

Gay and Lesbian Resource: ARCI-GAY "Centro D'iniziativa Gay," V Torricelli, 19 (☎02 5810 0399; www.gay.it/arcigay/milano). Great staff, speaks English. Open M-F 5-8pm.

Handicapped/Disabled Services: Direzione Servizi Sociali, Largo Treves, 1 (☎02 6208 6954). Open 8:30am-noon and 1-5pm. **Provincia Milano** (☎02 659 90 32).

Laundromat: Vicolo Lavandai, Viale Monte Grappa, 2 (☎02 498 39 02). MM2: Garibaldi. L6000/€8.26 per 7kg wash, L6000/€8.26 dry. Daily 8am-9pm.

Swimming Pools: Lido di Milano, P. Lotto, 15 (☎02 3926 6100), MM1: Lotto/Fiera 2. L9000/€4.65, under 12 L4000/€2.07. Swimcap L2500/€1.29. Open daily 10am-7pm. **Cozzi,** V. Tunisia, 35 (☎02 659 97 03), off C. Buenos Aires. L6000/€3.10, under 12 L3000/€1.55. Open M 10am-11pm, Tu-F 10am-9pm, Sa-Su 10am-4pm.

EMERGENCY AND COMMUNICATIONS

Emergency: ☎118. **Police:** ☎113. **Carabinieri:** ☎112.

Tourist Police: SOS Turista, V.C. M. Maggi, 14 (☎02 3360 3060). Open daily 9:30am-1pm and 2:30-6pm.

First Aid: Pronto Soccorso (☎02 38 83) or **Red Cross** (☎02 345 67).

Late-Night Pharmacies: The one in the *galleria* of the Stazione Centrale never closes (☎02 669 07 35 or 669 09 35). Or try the one at P. Duomo, 21 (☎02 86 46 48 32). Open M-Sa 9:30am-1pm and 3-7pm. All pharmacy doors list late-night pharmacies.

Hospital: Ospedale Maggiore di Milano, V. Francesco Sforza, 35 (☎02 550 31), 5min. from the *duomo* on the inner ring road.

ACI (Automobile Club Italia): ☎116.

Internet Access:

■ **Manhattan Lab,** in Università Statale—formerly Ospedale Maggiore on V. Festa del Perdono. Use entrance opposite V. Bergamini. Take stairs on right to 3rd floor. Turn left, and walk to end of the corridor. Take 2 lefts; 3rd door on your left. Computers open to Erasmus students only, but at far end of the room there are free public computers. Open Tu-Sa noon-8pm, Su 10:30am-3:30pm.

Boomerang, V.F. Filzi, 41 (☎/fax 02 669 40 65), to right of Stazione Centrale, behind the park. 5 workstations. Fax, printing, digital photo development, and international money wiring. Fast connections. L15,000/€7.75 per hr. Open daily 8:30am-6:30pm.

El Pampero, V. Gasparotto, 1 (☎02 66 92 21), across from Boomerang. New consortium of a cafe, restaurant, and club. L10,000/€5.16 per hr. Open M-F 7am-2pm, Sa 9am-2pm, Su 5pm-1am.

Internet Point, V. Padova, 38 (☎02 2804 0246). MM1/2: Loreto. 10 computers. Fax, print, and wire money. L12,000/€6.20 per hr. Open daily 11am-7pm.

Terzomillenio, V. Lazzaretto, 2 (☎02 205 21 21). MM1: Porta Venezia. Take V.V. Veneto 4 blocks to V. Lazzaretto. L10,000/€5.16 per hr. Open M-F 8:30am-9pm, Sa 8:30am-6pm.

Hard Disk Cafe, C. Sempione, 44 (☎02 3310 1038), opposite Park Sempione. Take tram #1. Loud rock in the background. From 9am-1pm L10,000/€5.16 per hr., 1pm-2am L15,000/€7.75 per hr. Free internet if you eat, but only from 1-2pm. Open M-Sa 9-2am. Closed 3 weeks Aug.

Post Office: V. Cordusio, 4 (☎02 7248 2223), near P. del Duomo toward castle. Stamps, Fermo Posta, and currency exchange. Open M-F 8:30am-7:30pm, Sa 8:30am-1pm. There are 2 post offices at **Stazione Centrale.**
Postal Code: 20100.

▐ ACCOMMODATIONS & CAMPING

There are over 50 "on-paper" bargains in Milan, but if you want a clean room in a safe, convenient location, only a few are worth your while. Every season is high season. Make reservations well in advance.

NEAR STAZIONE CENTRALE

▓**Hotel Ca' Grande,** V. Porpora, 87 (☎/fax 02 2614 4001 or 2614 5295; hotelcagrande@tin.it). MM1/2: Loreto. 6 blocks from P. Loreto in yellow house with green spiked fence. Take tram #33 from Stazione Centrale; it runs along V. Porpora and stops at V. Ampere, 50m from the front door. 20 spotless rooms with phones, TV, and use of a beautiful garden. The street below can be noisy. English and Croatian spoken. Breakfast included. Reception 24hr. Internet available. Singles L70,000/€36.15, with bath L90,000/€46.48; doubles L110,000/€56.81, L130,000/67.14. AmEx/MC/V.

▓**Hotel Ambra,** V. Caccianino, 10 (☎02 26 65 465; fax 7060 6245). MM1/2: Loreto. Walk 10 blocks down V. Porpora (5-10min.) and take a right on V. Caccianino. A romantic Milanese paradise on a street full of villas and palm trees. 19 spotless rooms, all with bath, TV, telephone and balconies. Breakfast L5000/€2.56. Reserve ahead. Ask for key if going out at night. Singles L80,000/€41.32; doubles L110,000/€56.81; triples L140,000/€72.30. Inquire about student discounts.

▓**Hotel Sara,** V. Sacchini, 17 (☎02 20 17 73). MM1/2: Loreto. From Loreto take V. Porpora. The 3rd street on the right is V. Sacchini. The hotel has been recently renovated and the street is peaceful. TV and phone in every room. Internet access L10,000/€5.16 per hr. Singles L55,000/€28.41; doubles L80,000/€41.32, with bath L100,000/€51.65; triples with bath L120,000/€62.00.

Hotel Malta, V. Ricordi, 20 (☎02 204 96 15 or 2952 1210). MM1/2: Loreto. Cross over V. Abruzzi and take V. Porpora 1 block to V. Ricordi. Or from Stazione Centrale, take tram #33 to V. Ampere and backtrack along V. Porpora to V. Ricordi. Earth-tone floor tiles and plants on the sills in most rooms. 3 balconies overlook a quiet rose garden full of white sheets drying in the sun. 15 rooms, all with bath and TV. Reservations suggested. Pets allowed. Singles L90,000/€46.48; doubles L140,000/€72.30.

NEAR GIARDINI PUBBLICI

Hotel San Tomaso, V. Tunisia, 6, 3rd fl. (☎/fax 02 2951 4747; hotelsantomaso@tin.it; http://pwhux.tin.it/hstomaso). MM1: Porta Venezia. Take the C. Buenos Aires metro exit (a short walk to the opposite end of the station) and turn left at the McDonald's on V. Tunisia immediately in front of you. Clean, renovated rooms, some overlooking a courtyard, with phones and TVs. English spoken. Request keys if going out at night. 3 singles with shower L70,000/€36.15; 4 doubles with shower L100,000/€56.81, with bath L150,000/€77.47; 4 triples/quads L135-200,000/€69.72-103.29. MC/V.

Hotel Kennedy, V. Tunisia, 6, 6th fl. (☎02 2940 0934; raffaelo.bianchi@galactica.it). MM1: Porta Venezia. 3 floors above Hotel San Tomaso. 16 clean rooms with carpet extending up the walls and a nice view of Milan. Some with TV and phone. Ask for the room with view of *duomo,* but beware: the street below can be noisy. Some English spoken. Ask for keys if going out at night. Breakfast L4000/€2.07. Check-out 10am. Reservations recommended. Internet L10,000/€5.16 per night. Singles with bath L70,000/€36.15; doubles 100,000/€51.65, with bath L100-130,000/€51.65-67.14; triples L150,000/€77.47; quads L160,000/€82.63; quints L200,000/€103.30. All rates except singles negotiable. AmEx/D/MC/V.

Hotel Rallye, V.B. Marcello, 59 (☎/fax 02 2953 1209; h.rallye@tiscalinet.it). MM1: Lima. Walk along V. Vitruvio 2 blocks to V. Marcello and turn left. 20 simple, quiet rooms with phone and TV. Breakfast included. Singles with shower L70,000/€36.15; doubles with bath and shower, L40,000/€20.66. AmEx/D/MC/V.

Hotel "Casa Mia," V.V. Veneto, 30 (☎/fax 02 657 52 49 or 655 22 28; hotel-casamia@libero.it). MM1: Porta Venezia or Repubblica. V. Veneto runs between the 2 stations on edge of the Giardini Pubblici. All 15 rooms in this upscale hotel have A/C, and some overlook a quiet inner courtyard. All with phone, TV, hair dryer, and bath. English spoken. Breakfast included. Singles L90-120,000/€46.48-61.98; doubles L120-160,000/€61.98-82.63; triples L180-230,000/€92.96-118.79. Mentioning *Let's Go* will get you these prices, which are lower than regular. AmEx/D/MC/V.

Hotel Due Giardini, V.B. Marcello, 47 (☎02 295 21 093 or 2951 2309) MM1: Lima. Walk along V. Vitruvio 2 blocks to V. Marcello and take a left on the far side of the street. Deep red carpet flows up a winding staircase. Minty green decor. 11 rooms with TV and phone. Some English spoken. Internet access. Breakfast L7000/€3.62. Doubles with bath 150,000/€77.47; triples with bath L180,000/€92.97. MC/V.

Hotel Aurora, C. Buenos Aires, 18 (☎02 204 79 60; fax 204 92 85; hotel.aurora@tisca-linet.it; www.hotelitaly.com/hotels/aurora/index.htm). MM1: Porta Venezia. Exit the station onto C. Buenos Aires, walk straight ahead for 5min., and it's on the right. Behind a grungy facade and a Star Trek-like automatic door lie spotless modern rooms with phones, TVs, and silence. When Aurora is full, owner sometimes allows travelers to stay at his 3-star hotel nearby. Reception 24hr. Reserve ahead. Singles L80,000/€41.32, 1 with shower L90,000/€46.48, 2 with bath L95,000/€49.06; 7 doubles L120,000/ €61.98, with bath L145,000/€74.98; 1 triple L190,000/€98.13. AmEx/MC/V.

NEAR THE CITY PERIPHERY

Ostello Piero Rotta (HI), V. Salmoiraghi, 1 (☎02 3926 7095). Northwest of city. MM1: QT8. Walk to right from metro (so that the round church is across the street and behind you.) The large brick hostel is on the right, behind an off-white fence. English spoken. Breakfast, sheets, and lockers included. Laundry L10,000/€5.26. 3-night max. stay. Reception daily 7-9:30am and 3:30pm-midnight. No morning check-in. Daytime lock-out, with no exceptions. Curfew 11:30pm. Lights out midnight, HI membership required, available at the hostel (L30,000/€15.49). Mostly 6-bed rooms, but some family rooms available. No reservations. Closed Dec. 21-Jan 10. 350 dorm beds L30,000/€15.49.

Albergo Brasil di Ramella Luisa, V.G. Modena, 20 (☎/fax 02 749 24 82; hotelbrasil@libero.it). Just west of city. MM1: Palestro. Save yourself a walk from Stazione Centrale and take bus #60 until V.G. Modena. From Palestro, take V. Serbelloni and then a quick left onto V. Cappuccini, which crosses 2 larger roads, becoming V.F. Bellotti and finally V.G. Modena. 4th-floor entryway is built in the Liberty style, dominant in central Europe at the beginning of the 20th century. Large rooms with TV and romantic view of a boulevard. Close to several clubs. Breakfast (L8000/€4.13) sometimes served in bed. Reception closes 12:30am; ask for keys to enter later. Singles L85,000/ €43.90, with shower L90,000/€46.48, with bath L110,000/€56.81; doubles L90,000/€46.48, L110,000/€56.81, L140,000/€72.30. AmEx/D/MC/V.

Pensione Cantore, C. Porta Genova, 25 (☎/fax 02 835 75 65), down from *duomo* via V.C. Correnti. Very near Navigli locks and Stazione Porta Genova. MM2: Porta Genova. Bit out of the way, but a good price. Exposed pipes contrast with large, immaculate rooms. All rooms with showers and TV. Breakfast included. Reception 24hr. Singles L70,000/€36.20; doubles L100,000/€51.65; triples L150,000/€77.47.

Camping di Monza (☎039 38 77 71), in the park of Villa Reale in Monza, northeast of city. Take the "Monza" bus from Stazione Centrale to Monza, then a city bus to the campground. Open Apr.-Aug. L8000/€4.13 per person and per tent, L15,000/€7.75 per caravan (4 people). Hot showers L500/€0.26.

◘ FOOD

Like its fine *couture*, Milanese cuisine is sophisticated and sometimes overpriced. Specialties include *risotto a la Milanese* (rice with saffron), *cotoletta alla milanese* (breaded veal cutlet with lemon), and *cazzouela* (a mixture of pork and cabbage).

Pasticcerie and *gelaterie* crowd every block. Bakeries specialize in the Milanese sweet bread *panettone*, an Italian fruitcake. The newspaper *Il Giornale Nuovo* lists all restaurants and shops, and the brochure *Milano: Where, When, How*, available at the tourist office, lists foreign restaurants of all flavors. The largest markets are on **V. Fauchè** and **V. Paplniano** on Saturdays and Tuesdays, and in P. Mirabello on Mondays and Thursdays. The **Fiera di Sinigallia**, a 400-year-old extravaganza of the commercial and the bizarre, occurs on Saturdays on the banks of the Darsena, a canal in Navigli (V. d'Annunzio). Splurge on local pastries, or admire the gorgeous goodies at the Milanese culinary shrine of Sant' Ambrogio, C. Matteotti, 7, under the arcades. (☎ 02 7600 0540. Open daily 8am-8pm.) **Supermarket Pam,** V. Piccinni, 2 (☎ 02 29 51 27 15), off C. Buenos Aires is open daily 8:30am-9pm, but is closed Monday mornings. There's also a **Simpatica CRAI** at V.F. Casati, 21 (☎ 02 2940 5821. Open M 8am-1pm, Tu-Sa 8am-1pm and 4-7:30pm.) Nearer to C. Buenos Aires is **Supermarket Regina Giovanna,** V. Regina Giovanna, 34. (☎ 02 4583 9011. Open M-F 8am-9pm, Sa 8am-8pm.) For bar hoppers and clubbers, **Panino's Story** on P. Lima and C. Buenos Aires offers snacks all night.

ITALIAN RESTAURANTS AND TRATTORIE

▨ **Tarantella,** V. Abruzzi, 35 (☎ 02 2940 0218), just north of V. Plinio. MM1: Lima. Lively, elegant and leafy sidewalk dining. Great *antipasti*. Don't leave without trying the *pasta fresca* (L12,000/€6.2) or a pizza (L10-20,000/€5.16-10.33). Specialty salads L13-28,000/€6.71-14.46; *primi* L10-15,000/€5.16-7.75; *secondi* L125,000/€64.56. Open Sept.-July M-F noon-2:30pm and 7-11:30pm, Su 7-11:30pm. AmEx/MC/V.

▨ **Pizzeria Premiata,** V. Alzaia Naviglio Grande, 2 (☎ 02 8940 0648). MM2: Porta Genova. From the metro walk on V. Vigevano and take the 2nd right onto V. Corsico. From there, take a left on V. Alzaia Naviglio Grande. Very popular among Milanese students. Hearty portions. Expect some delays at night. Pizzas from L9000/€4.65; *primi* around L15,000/€7.75. Open daily noon-2am. AmEx/MC/V.

▨ **Ristorante El Recreo,** V. Scarlatti, 7 (☎ 02 2951 3321). MM1: Lima. Walk up C. Buenos Aires and go left on V. Scarlatti. It's 2 blocks down on left. Comfortable, hip, and romantic. Homemade Italian cuisine with Latino cocktails and merengue beats. Pasta L13-16,000/€5.16-8.26; pizza L7500-13,000/€3.97-5.16; fruit and desserts L3-8000/€1.55-4.13. Open Tu-Su noon-2:30pm and 7-11:30pm. MC/V.

Le Briciole, V. Camperio, 17 (☎ 02 87 71 85), 1 street from V. Dante. MM1: Cairoli. Lively, young clientele. Homey, dark interior. Pizza L9-16,000/€4.65-8.26; spectacular *antipasto* buffet L13-22,000/€5.16-11.36; *secondi* L16-29,000/€8.36-14.98. Cover L3000/€1.55. Open Tu-Su 12:15-2:30pm and 7:15-11:30pm, closed Sa morning.

Pizzeria Grand'Italia, V. Palermo, 5 (☎ 02 87 77 59). MM2: Moscova. Walk down V. Statuto and take a right on V. Palermo. Warm yellow and blue interior is always packed, but it's worth the wait. Pizza is sold *al trancio*, in massive, focaccia-like wedges (L7-10,000/€3.62-5.16). Salads L12,000/€6.20. Open W-M 12:15-2:45pm and 7pm-1:15am; Aug. daily 12:15-2:45pm and 7pm-1:15am.

Ristorante "La Colubrina," V. Felice Casati, 5 (☎ 02 2951 8427). MM1: Porta Venezia. Mosaic stone floors. The polyglot owner Paolo seems to know everyone in the neighborhood. Pizza L6-10,000/€3.10-5.16. Huge lunch *menù* L20,000/€10.32. Daily specials L9-22,000/€4.65-11.36. Wine L8000/€4.13 per liter. Cover L2500/€1.30. Open Sept.-July daily noon-2:30pm and 7-11:30pm, closed Su-M morning.

Be Bop Caffè/Ristorante/Pizzeria, V. Col di Lana, 4 (☎ 02 837 69 72), off far side of P. XXIV Maggio. MM2: Sant'Agostino or Genova. Stylish decor, fun 20 something natives, and huge ultra-thin-crust pizzas make this place worth the trip. Caters to the health-conscious on occasion with mozzarella-free or soy pizza and wheat-germ dough. Generous salads L16-20,000/€8.26-10.33; pizza L8-18,000/€4.13-9.29; *primi* L18,000/€4.13-9.29. Cover L3500/€1.81. Open M-F 12:15-2:30pm and 7:30-11:30pm, Sa noon-2pm and 7:30pm-midnight, Su 7pm-midnight. AmEx/D/MC/V.

Pizzeria/Ristorante Casati, V.F. Casati, 19 (☎ 02 20 47 292). MM1: Porta Venezia. Go up C. Buenos Aires 4 blocks and take left on V. F. Casati. Near Hotels San Tomaso and Kennedy. Good place to have a glass (or bottle) of wine and kick back after a long day.

Pizza L9-13,000/€4.65-6.71; fish *primo* L10-13,000/€5.16-6.71; *secondi* L13,000/€6.71. Open Tu-F and Su noon-2pm and 7-11pm, Sa 7-11pm. AmEx/D/MC/V.

Pizzeria Naturale (☎02 839 57 10), on V. Amicis across from V. Correnti. For health-minded Milanese. *Biopizze* L10-20,000/€5.16-10.32; *primi* L10-20,000/€5.16-10.33. *Torte* L9,000/€4.65. Open Tu-Su noon-2:30pm and 7:30pm-midnight. MC/V.

QUICK BITES

▨ **Brek,** V. Lepetit, 20 (☎02 670 51 49), near Stazione Centrale. Very popular self-service restaurant. After you select the fresh ingredients, they cook for you, as you wait. A meal is not so much ordered as composed. A/C, non-smoking room, and English-speaking staff. *Primi* around L5000/€2.58; *secondi* L7500/€3.87. Open M-Sa 11:30am-3pm and 6:30-10:30pm. Other locations: **P. Cavour** (☎02 65 36 19; off V. Manzoni; MM3: M. Napoleone) and **Porta Giordano** (☎02 7602 3379; MM1: S. Babila).

▨ **Peck,** V. Cantù, 3 (☎02 869 30 17), off V. Orefici, 2 blocks from P. Duomo. Pizza and pastries by the kilo. L7500/€3.87 will buy a large slice of either. Great for picnicking, but no place to sit. Much fancier, expensive restaurant around the corner. Unbeatable chocolate mousse (L6000/€3.09). Accepts US$. Open Tu-F 8:45am-2:30pm and 4-7:30pm, Sa 8:30am-1:15pm and 3:45-7:30pm, Su 8am-1pm. AmEx/D/MC/V.

La Crêperie, V.C. Correnti, 21 (☎02 839 59 13), on the lower continuation of V. Torino. MM2: S. Ambrogio. The crêpe-maker spreads a very viscous batter onto a hot wrought iron palette, swirling the mixture until it forms a thin sheet. Once cooked, the crêpe is filled and folded to include a wide array of ingredients. Depending on ingredients L4-6000/€2.07-3.10. Open daily noon-1am.

Duomo Center, P. del Duomo, 6, under arcade on your right as you face the *duomo*. Strategically positioned and convenient, this food court houses a variety of fast-food and self-service establishments, including the chain-restaurant **Spizzico,** with the justi-fied slogan "molto fast, very good." Regular slice L3400/€1.76; huge slice L4300/€2.22. Standing room only, open daily 7am-2am. If you'd like to sit, try upstairs at **Ciao** (☎02 86 42 67). *Primi* L5500/€2.84; *secondi* L7300/€3.77. Open daily 11:30am-3pm and 6:30-11pm. Each establishment has another location across the *piazza*.

Ikos, V. Boccaccio, 4 (☎02 46 06 16), near Stazione Nord/Cadorna. Bright, sunny cafe and bar. *Panini*, salads, fish, and vegetarian dishes, including macrobiotic entrees. Health food store attached. *Primi* L10-12,000/€5.16-10.33; *secondi* L13-16,000/€6.71-8.26. Open M-Sa 7:30am-8pm.

NON-ITALIAN ALTERNATIVES

▨ **Il Fondaco dei Mori,** V. Solferino, 33 (☎02 65 37 11). From MM2: Moscova, walk north to P. XXV Aprile and turn right onto Porta Nuova. Take 2nd right onto V. Solferino. No sign, but ring the bell and the little door cut out of the huge, wooden gate opens. Walk into courtyard to the door with a single white star above it. One of the first Arab restau-rants in Italy, it's run by the "Circolo Culture Amis," which promotes appreciation of Islamic culture. A Milan must. Meet the dynamic owner, Ali. To perfect the experience, ask to dine under a tent, richly furnished with carpets, cushions, and tapestries. No alcohol served, but be sure to ask for some mango or guava juice. Also try the excellent ginger coffee and mango yogurt. All food is halal. Vegetarian lunch *menù* L14,000/€7.23; dinner buffet L20,000/€10.33; kebabs L20,000/€10.33. Cover L3000/€1.55. Open Tu-Su 12:30-3pm and 7:30pm-midnight. Closed for lunch F. D/MC/V.

Ristorante Asmara, V. Lazzaro Palazzi, 5 (☎02 2952 2453). MM1: Porta Venezia. Walk down C. Buenos Aires; V.L. Palazzi is 3rd on left. African (Eritrean) food, eaten with thin, spongy flatbread *(injera)* and your hands. Sit on the balcony, looking down on pass-ersby below. To sample all vegetarian options, ask for *"Un po' di tutto vegetariano."* A/C. Vegetarian meals L18,000/€9.30, other large *piatti* L16,500-35,000/€8.52-18.08. Open Th-Tu noon-3pm and 6pm-midnight. AmEx/MC/V.

GELATERIE

After World War II, the Viel family began selling *tutti-frutti gelato* from a cart outside the *duomo*. The enterprise quickly took off, and the name Viel is now synonymous with exotic, fresh fruit *gelati* (L3-6000/€1.55-3.10) and *frullati* (whipped fruit drinks; L2500-8000/€1.29-4.13). At **Viel**, V.G. Marconi, 3e (☎02 87 80 04), you can buy a cone packed with four scoops and eat it at an outside table, one of the cheapest seats near the *duomo* (L32,500-56,500/€16.78-29.12 large cup). If you've finished a meal at Il Fondaco dei Mori, walk down V. Solferino half a block to V. Marsala and try some exotic honey-roasted-poppy or *halva gelato* at **Cream Creola** on the corner. **Jack Frost Gelateria**, V. Felice Casati, 25, off C. Buenos Aires at V. Lazzaretto, MM1: Porta Venezia, serves enormous helpings of creamy *gelato*. Try the *bacio* (chocolate and hazelnut) or mint chocolate L3-7000/€1.55-3.62. (☎02 669 11 34. Open Th-Tu 9:30am-1am.) The *gelateria* formerly known as Pozzi, **Gelateria Milano Doc**, P. Cantore, 4, in Navigli offers an expanded menu, a children's playground, and outside seating. (☎02 89 40 98 30. Cones L3-4000/€1.55-2.07. Open May-Oct. M 6pm-2am, Tu-Su 8am-2am; Nov.-Apr. Tu-Su 8am-2am.) If you don't mind walking, head down V. Torino from P. Duomo and enjoy one, two, or all 45 varieties of ice cream in the romantic interior or elegant garden of **Cremeria Pasticceria al Carrobbio**, V. del Torchio, 4. (☎/fax 02 86 45 19 84. Open daily 7:30am-1am.)

ⓢ SIGHTS

AROUND THE DUOMO

▨ **DUOMO.** The looming Gothic cathedral is the geographical and spiritual center of Milan and makes a good starting point for any walking tour of the city. Be nice to the pigeons, or you may regret it. The *duomo* is the third-largest church in the world, after St. Peter's at the Vatican and the Seville Cathedral. **Gian Galeazzo Visconti** founded the cathedral in 1386, hoping to flatter the Virgin into granting him a male heir. Construction proceeded sporadically over the next four centuries and was finally completed at Napoleon's command in 1809. In the meantime, more than 3400 statues, 135 spires, 96 gargoyles, and several kilometers of tracery accumulated. The facade juxtaposes Italian Gothic and Baroque elements under a delicate crown. Inside, the 52 columns rise to canopied niches with statues as capitals. The church is a five-aisled cruciform capable of seating 4000 worshipers. Narrow side aisles extend to the grand stained glass windows, among the largest in the world. The imposing 16th-century marble tomb of **Giacomo de Medici**, in the south transept, was inspired by the work of Michelangelo. ▨Climb (or ride) to the top of the cathedral from outside the north transept, where you will find yourself surrounded by a magical field of turrets, spires, and statues. A Madonna painted in gold leaf crowns this rooftop kingdom. Scholars interested in early conceptions of human anatomy frequent the statue of St. Bartholomew. Sculpted by the vain **Marco d'Agrate** (1562), the statue depicts the saint wearing his own skin to show that he was flayed alive. The roof walkway, which allows for a leisurely stroll of the perimeter, puts tourists in rare proximity to the white marble statues, and to the restoration work, which continually attends to the cleaning and repair of the steady, but seemingly delicate roof. On a clear day, the city opens in wide relief belief, and the Alps contribute a distinctive horizon. *(MM1: Duomo. Cathedral open daily 9am-5:45pm; Nov.-Feb. 9am-4:15pm. Modest dress strictly enforced. Roof open daily May-Oct. 7am-7pm; Nov.-Apr. 9am-4:30pm. L6000/€3.09, with elevator L9000/€4.65.)*

Recently renovated, the **Museo del Duomo** displays artifacts from or relating to the construction of the *duomo*. After the visit to the cathedral itself, it will provide a sense of how construction progressed, and by what means, both fiscal and physical. See drawings and drafts of the building, and several woodmen (scale) models. *(To right as you face duomo, across piazza in Palazzo Reale at P. del Duomo, 14. Museum faces right side of duomo. ☎02 86 03 58. Open Tu-Su 9:30am-12:30pm and 3-6pm. L8000/€4.13.)*

Also in the Palazzo Reale, the **Museo d'Arte Contemporanea** holds a fine permanent collection of 20th-century Italian art, interspersed with a few Picassos. (☎02 6208 3219. Wheelchair accessible. Open Tu-Su 9:30am-5:30pm. Free.)

■ **PINACOTECA DI BRERA.** The Brera Art Gallery presents one of the most impressive collections of paintings in Italy, including works from the 14th to the 20th century with an emphasis on the Lombard School. Works include Bellini's *Pietà* (1460), Hayez's *The Kiss* (1859), Andrea Mantegna's brilliant *Dead Christ* (1480), Raphael's *Marriage of the Virgin* (1504), Caravaggio's *Supper at Emmaus* (1606), and Piero della Francesca's 15th-century *Sacra Conversazione (1474).* The vibrant, animated frescoes by Bramante from the Casa dei Panigarola provide comic relief from the dramatic intensity of other works. A limited collection of works by modern masters includes pieces by Modigliani and Carlo Carrà, and *Testa di toro* by Picasso. (V. Brera, 28. MM2: Lanza. Immediately after V.G. Verdi coming from La Scala. ☎02 72 26 31. Wheelchair accessible. Open Tu-Sa 9am-7pm, Su 8:30am-11pm. L12,000/€6.19, EU citizens 18-25 years. L6000/€3.09)

■ **TEATRO ALLA SCALA.** Known simply as La Scala, this is the world's most renowned opera house. Opened in 1778, the building rests on the site of the Chiesa di S. Maria alla Scala, from which it took its name. Singer Maria Callas became a legend in this Neoclassical building. To see the lavish multi-tiered hall, enter through the Museo Teatrale alla Scala. The performance area is a sea of red velvet, and the orchestra pit seems a distant oasis from one of the insulated boxes that scale the horseshoe-wall. The collections include a delicate gathering of terracotta masks from the 4th century BC to the 2nd century AD. On the second floor there are various traditions of marionettes, opera memorabilia, and a large display of Asian shadow puppets. Don't be shockedto find Verdi's hair and plaster hand casts of famous conductors. (P. della Scala. At opposite end of Galleria Vittorio Emanuele from duomo. ☎02 805 34 18. Museum open daily 9am-noon and 2-5:30pm. L6000/€3.09.)

■ **MUSEO POLDI PEZZOLI.** The museum contains an outstanding private art collection bequeathed to the city by Poldi Pezzoli in 1879. The museum's masterpieces hang in the Golden Room, which overlooks a flowery garden. Famous paintings include Andrea Mantegna's *Virgin and Child*, Botticelli's *Madonna and Child*, Bellini's *Ecce Homo*, Guardi's magical *Gray Lagoon*, and the museum's signature piece, Antonio Pollaiuolo's *Portrait of a Young Woman*. A number of smaller collections fill rooms on both floors. Particularly impressive is a tiny but sublime display of Italian military armaments. A chest plate mimics an ideal six-pack, and is adorned with small metal nipples. (A few minutes from La Scala on the right at V. Manzoni, 12. ☎02 79 48 89. Open daily 10am-6pm. L10,000/€5.16, seniors L5000/€2.58, students L2500/€1.29.)

GALLERIA VITTORIO EMANUELE II. On the left as you face the *duomo*, a monumental glass barrel vault with an imposing glass and steel cupola (48m) covers a five-story arcade of overpriced cafes, shops, and offices. Mosaics representing different continents sieged by the Romans adorn the floors and the central octagon's upper walls. Once considered the drawing room of Milan, the Galleria is now home to commercialized industry. Check out the Mediastore, the largest music store in Italy. (☎06 46 02 72. Open M-Sa 10am-11pm, Su 10am-8pm. Free.)

MUSEO BAGATTI VALSECCHI. A house originally inhabited by an aristocratic 19th-century family with a penchant for precious arms, ceramics, *freschi*, mosaics, ivory and other artifacts from the 15th century to the present. (MM3: Napoleone. At V. Gesu, 5, and V. Santo Spirito, 10. From V. M. Napoleone, V. Gesu is 2nd on the left. ☎02 7600 6132. Open Tu-Su 1-5pm. L10,000/€5.16, W L5000/€2.58.)

NEAR CASTELLO SFORZESCO

■ **CASTELLO SFORZESCO.** Restored after heavy bomb damage in 1943, the Castello Sforzesco is one of Milan's best-known monuments. Constructed in 1368 as a defense against Venice, it was used as army barracks, a horse stall, and a storage house before da Vinci made it a studio. The Castello houses the **Musei Civici,** which include the **Musical Instruments Museum** and the **Applied Arts Museum.** The ground floor contains a sculpture collection most renowned for Michelangelo's unfinished *Pietà Rondanini,* his last work. The tomb of Visconti in the center of the hall sets the duke's image atop a set of marble pillars, riding his beloved horse into eternity. In the Applied Arts Museum, filled primarily with ornate household furnishings, the one piece that stands out is the *Automa contesta di demonio*—a "mechanical caricature," that is, a wooden fellow with winged ears, and red eyes and tongue which moves upon being cranked from the cabinet below. *(MM1: Cairoli.* ☎ *02 6236 3947. Open Tu-Su 9:30am-5:30pm. Free.)*

■ **CHIESA DI SANTA MARIA DELLA GRAZIE.** A 15th-century convent, the church's Gothic nave is dark and elaborately patterned with frescoes, contrasting with the splendid, airy tribune Bramante added in 1492. The extensive interior renovations allow for a before and after view of the frescoes. Next to the church entrance, in what was once the dining hall, is the Cenacolo Vinciano (Vinciano Refectory), one of Milan's most famous sites and home to one of the most well-known pieces of art in the world: **Leonardo da Vinci's Last Supper.** The consummately famous fresco captures the apostles' reaction to Jesus's prophecy: "One of you will betray me." *(P. di S. Maria delle Grazie, 2, on C. Magenta, off V. Carducci below MM1: Cadorna Cairoli.* ☎ *02 8942 1146 or 199 199 100. Reservations are seriously recommended. Arrive early or late in the day to avoid the hour-long wait. Wheelchair accessible. Open Tu-Su 8am-7:30pm, Sa 8am-11pm. L12,000/€6.19, under 18, over 65, and art students free.)*

■ **STADIO GIUSEPPE MEAZZA.** Viewing the Stadio after the walk up to the *duomo* leads to the obvious question: where do the Milanese really worship? The heated games between Inter and AC Milano even occur on Sundays, just to heighten the sacredness of the event. The tour (offered in English) will walk you through a museum of football memorabilia, allow you to sit in the VIP seats, and take you to the locker rooms, where club jerseys hang on the wall. *(V. Piccolomini, 5. MM2: Lotto. Walk along V. Fed. Caprilli and it's on the left. Entrance at tower 5. Tours M-Sa 10am-5pm. L18,000/€9.29, under 18 or over 65 L12,000/€6.19. Discounts for groups over 20.)*

■ **BASILICA DI SANT'AMBROGIO.** A prototype for Lombard-Romanesque churches throughout Italy, Sant'Ambrogio is the most influential medieval building in Milan. Ninth-century reliefs in brilliant silver and gold decorate the high altar, St. Ambrose presided over this building between 379 and 386. Now you may preside over him: go behind the altar, on either side, and descend into a dim sarcophagus. There you will find the skeletal remains of the saint (340-397), and his bedmate, St. Protasio. The 4th-century **Cappella di San Vittore in Ciel D'oro,** with exquisite 5th-century mosaics adorning its cupola, lies through the seventh chapel on the right; enter, walk a few paces, and then turn left. *(MM1: Sant'Ambrogio. Open M-Sa 7:30am-noon and 2:30-7pm, Su 3-7pm. Free. Audio guides in back of church L1000/€0.52.)*

LEONARDO DA VINCI'S HORSE. For 17 years, Leonardo da Vinci planned to build the largest equine statue ever conceived. Intended as a gift to the house of Sforza, his dream was not realized in his lifetime. A few decades ago, Charles Dent produced "the horse that never was" from Leonardo's sketches. Dent himself admits, however, that this is not quite da Vinci's statue. The bronze, based more on inference than actual documentation, can seem like a mere advertisement for Renaissance sculpture if one is not familiar with the history behind the horse. *(V. Fed. Caprilli 6-16. MM1: Lotto. From Lotto walk down V. Fed. Caprilli until the stadium is in view on your left. The statue is on your right, behind a large gate. Open daily 9:30am-6:30pm. Free.)*

MUSEO NAZIONALE DELLA SCIENZA E DELLA TECNICA "DA VINCI". To further your study of da Vinci, explore this museum, which provides a historical view of the precursors of modern technology. The hall of computer technology features an interesting hybrid: a piano converted to a typewriter by Edoardo Hughes of Turin in 1885. The keys have letters pasted to them, and a ribbon receives the letters from a spinning wheel. Another section focuses on applied physics, while wooden models of Leonardo's most visionary inventions fill another room. *(V. San Vittore, 21, off V. Carducci. MM2: San Ambrogio. ☎ 02 48 55 51. Open Tu-F 9:30am-4:50pm, Sa-Su 9:30am-6:20pm. L12,000/€6.19, under 12 and over 60 L8000/€4.13.)*

FROM CORSO DI PORTA ROMANA TO THE NAVIGLI

The distances between sights are greater here, so consider public transportation.

■ **NAVIGLI DISTRICT.** The Venice of Lombardy, the Navigli district comes alive at night (see p. 97). Complete with canals, small footbridges, open-air markets, cafes, alleys, and trolleys, this area constitutes part of a medieval canal system (the original locks were designed by Leonardo da Vinci) that transported thousands of tons of marble to build the *duomo* and linked Milan to various northern cities and lakes. *(Outside the MM2: Porta Genova station, through the Arco di Porta Ticinese.)*

■ **BASILICA DI SANT'EUSTORGIO.** Founded in the 4th century to house the bones of the Magi, the church lost its original function when the dead wise men were spirited off to Cologne in 1164. The present building (erected in 1278) has a Lombard-Gothic interior of low vaults and brick ribs supported by substantial columns. The triumph of this church, and one of the great masterpieces of early Renaissance art, is the Portinari Chapel (1468), attributed to the Florentine Michelozzo. The Gothic tomb of St. Eustorgius (1339) rests in the center of the chapel. The ornate casket hovers, supported only by the soft, white marble shoulders of devotees, one of whom has three faces on one head. *(P.S. Eustorgio, 3, farther down C. Ticinese from San Lorenzo Maggiore. Tram #3. Open W-M 9:30am-noon and 3:30-6pm.)*

CHIESA DI SAN LORENZO MAGGIORE. The oldest church in Milan, San Lorenzo Maggiore testifies to the city's 4th-century greatness. Begun as an early Christian church with an octagonal plan, it was rebuilt later and includes a 12th-century *campanile* and 16th-century dome. To the right of the church sits the 14th-century **Cappella di Sant'Aquilino.** Inside is a 5th-century mosaic of a beardless Christ among his apostles. A staircase behind the altar leads to the remains of an early Roman amphitheater. Near the front of the church is the 12th-century **Porta Ticinese.** *(On C. Ticinese. MM2: Porta Genova, then tram #3 from V. Torino. Open daily 7:30am-6:45pm. Capella L2000/€1.03.)*

SOUTH AND EAST OF THE DUOMO

■ **PINACOTECA AMBROSIANA.** Tiny but lovely, the 23 rooms of the Ambrosiana display exquisite works from the 14th through 19th centuries, including Botticelli's round *Madonna of the Canopy*, Leonardo's captivating *Portrait of a Musician*, Raphael's cartoon for *School of Athens*, Caravaggio's *Basket of Fruit* (the first example of still-life painting in Italy), Titian's *Adoration of the Magi*, works by Brueghel and Bril, and several large portraits by Hayez. The courtyard is full of figure sculptures and busts. The staircase is adorned with unforgettable marble and mosaics. *(P. Pio XI, 2. Follow V. Spadari off V. Torino and make a left onto V. Cantù. ☎ 02 86 46 29 81. Open Tu-Su 10am-5:30pm. L12,000/€6.19, under 18 and over 65 L6000/€3.09.)*

OSPEDALE MAGGIORE. Built in 1456, this is one of the largest early Renaissance constructions. Intricate sandstone fenestrations glow in the afternoon light. Now the **University of Milan,** it contains nine courtyards, including a grand 17th-century court and one credited to Bramante. *(On V. Festa del Perdono near P. Santo Stefano.)*

GALLERIA D'ARTE MODERNA. Napoleon lived here with Josephine when Milan was the capital of the Napoleonic Kingdom of Italy (1805-1814). The gallery, reminiscent of Versailles, displays important modern Lombard art as well as works by Impressionists. Of special note are Modigliani's *Beatrice Hastings* (1915), Picasso's *Testa*, Klee's *Wald Bau*, and Morandi's *Natura morta con bottiglia*. Also see pieces by Matisse, Mondrian, and Dufy. *(MM12: Palestro. Gallery is at V. Palestro, 16, next to Giardini Pubblici in the Neoclassical Villa Comunale. ☎ 02 7600 2819. Open Tu-Su 9am-6:30pm. Free.)* Adjacent is the **Padiglione D'Arte Contemporanea (PAC),** an extravaganza of video, photographs, multimedia, and painting used in concert. After the ancient and the antique, this bastion of postmodernism will seem either sterile and antiseptic or cleansing and refreshing. *(M1: Cardorna, across P. Cardorna to Paleocapa, which becomes V. Alemagna. Wheelchair accessible. L15,000/€7.75; students L5000/€2.58.)*

MUSEO CIVICO DI STORIA NATURALE. Milan's Museum of Natural History holds extensive geological and paleontological collections. It is an international display of natural history, with a special focus on Italy. The besanosaurus, which walked around Lombardy 325 million years ago, even makes the *duomo* look new. *(C. Venezia, 55, in Giardini Pubblici. ☎02 78 13 02. Open M-F 9am-6pm, Sa-Su 9:30am-6:30pm. Free.)*

♫ ENTERTAINMENT

MUSIC

The **Piccolo Teatro,** V. Rovello, 2, near V. Dante, was founded after World War II as a socialist theater. Owned by the city, it specializes in small, classical, offbeat productions. (☎02 7233 3222. Performances Tu-Sa 8:30pm, Su 4pm. L35,000/€18.08, students L22,000/€11.36.) **Ciak,** V. Sangallo, 33, near P. Gorini Argonne southeast of the *duomo*, offers cabaret popular with young Milanese. Take train #5 from Stazione Centrale to V. Beato Angelico Argonne. (☎02 76 11 00 93. Cover L25-40,000/€12.91-20.66.) The **Teatri d'Italia di Porta Romana,** C. di Porta Romana, 124 (☎02 5831 5896), is building a reputation for experimental productions and first-run mainstream plays (L28,000/€14.46). Take bus #13 from V. Marconi off P. del Duomo. The organization Teatri d'Italia sponsors **Milan Oltre** in June and July, a festival of drama, dance, and music. Call the **Ufficio Informazione del Comune** (☎02 8646 4094). For a different brand of street theater, Milan's **Carnevale** is the longest lasting in Italy and is becoming increasingly popular. As the crowds in Venice sport fewer costumes and more cameras each year, many come to Milan instead. Carnevale occurs annually Thursday through Saturday after Ash Wednesday and is spread all over the city, especially around the *duomo*.

FILM

Milan's cinematic scene thrives. Check any Milanese paper (especially Thursday editions) for showings. Wednesday shows are L7000/€3.61 instead of the regular L8-10,000/€4.13-5.16. Many cinemas screen English films: Mondays at Anteo, V. Milazzo, 9 (☎02 659 77 32; MM2: Moscova), Tuesdays at Arcobaleno, V. Tunisia, 11 (☎02 2940 6054; MM1: Porta Venezia), and Thursdays at Mexico, V. Savona, 57 (☎02 4895 1802. MM2: Porta Genova. L9000/€4.65; students L7500/€3.87.) If you would like to move from in front of the screen to behind the scenes, you will want to make the short walk from MM3: Turati to the Collezioni del **Museo de Cinema** della Cineteca Italiana. On V. Daniele Manin 2/B, on the edge of Giardini Pubblici, this basement museum holds many important pieces of cinematic memorabilia. An inventory of the museum (in English and Italian) is available in bookform for L5000/€2.58. Curiosities include a film box made by the pioneer of Italian cinema, Italo Pacchion and a household device by Thomas Edison that both projects images and produces phonographic sound in synchronization. (MM3: Turati. V. Daniele Manin 2/B. ☎02 655 49 77. L5000/€2.58, children L3000/€1.55)

▢ SHOPPING

Keep in mind that many shops in Milan are closed on Monday mornings. If you can tolerate the stigma of being a season behind the trends, buy your designer duds from *blochisti* (wholesale clothing outlets). Try **Monitor** on V. Monte Nero (MM3: Porta Romana, then tram #9 or 29) or the well-known **Il Salvagente,** V. Bronzetti, 16, off C. XXII Marzo (bus #60 from MM1: Lima or MM2/3: Stazione Centrale). The clothing sold along **Corso Buenos Aires** is more affordable. All the stores are open from 10am-12:30pm and 2:30-7pm. Check out ▨**K-Shop** on P.

NORTHWEST ITALY

WALK LIKE AN ITALIAN Italians have an uncanny ability to pick the tourists out of a crowd. Perhaps it is because every American tourist is wearing khaki shorts, a white t-shirt, and a pair of Tevas. If you want to avoid this phenomenon, and you're ready to make the leap into Euro-chic, add this simple starter kit of must-haves to your wardrobe.

Adidas Shirt: Preferably fluorescent stripes on black. Buy one that is too tight, and while you're at it get the matching pants with chrome buttons from mid-shin down to accommodate extremely large boots—they all do.

Really tight jeans: Dark with untapered leg. Ouch.

Really tight cargo pants: Thus negating the utility of all those pockets.

Invicta backpack: Who knew that neon yellow went with neon pink? It does when the word Invicta is plastered across the back in alternating neon blue and mint green. If your shoulders ache, try walking kangaroo-style, with the pack reversed and the straps running down your back.

Telefonino: A mobile phone is essential. If you can't afford one, no one will stop you from pretending. Buy a fake from a wandering cigarette-lighter vendor.

Argentina (MM1/2: Loreto) for some bargain sportswear. **J.D.C.,** C. Buenos Aires, 61, carries an excellent selection of recent urban style. Also try **Gio Cellini,** C. Buenos Aires, 30, for funky shoes in any color you can imagine. For women, **Pimpkie,** C. Buenos Aires, 19, has very affordable, basic, all-around wares. **via Torino,** south of the *duomo,* houses the elegant **Upim** (at the corner of V. Spadar). **Crash,** V. Torino, 46, has techno/clubbing/street wear at student prices. **Gallerie-A,** at the intersection of P. San Giorgio and V. Torino, is home to some of the trendiest flashy, pink and black cloth around. They also have wigs, whips, and fetishwear. **Via Sarpi,** near Porta Garibaldi, also has a few decent, inexpensive places to shop.

Milan: When, Where, How has a great list of markets and second-hand stores. Shop around the area of C. di Porta Ticinese, the Navigli district, and C. Garibaldi for second-hand attire (MM2: Porta Genova, then bus #59). **Eliogabalo,** P. Eustorgio, 2 (☎ 02 837 82 93), named after a Roman emperor renowned for his preoccupation with aesthetics, offers the latest in *haute couture.* True Milanese bargain hunters attack the bazaars on **via Fauché** (MM2: Garibaldi) Tuesdays and Saturdays and **Viale Papinian** (MM2: Agostino) Saturdays. The famous, 400-year-old **Fiera di Sinigallia** on V. d'Annunzio is also great for bargains (Sa only). Another fabulous option is the classy Italian department store **La Rinascente,** where Armani began his infamous career, to the left of the *duomo* as you face it. (Open until 10pm.)

Winter sales begin January 10. Shop at the end of July for the end-of-summer sales (20-50% off) and a glimpse of the new fall lines. Clothing stores are usually open M 3-7pm, Tu-Sa 10am-12:30pm and 3-7:30pm. Hard-core window shoppers should head to the world-famous ▓fashion district between **Corso Vittorio Emanuele** near the *duomo* and **via Monte Napoleone** off P. San Babila. Take the MM1 stop there (Babila): walk behind the left side of the *duomo* to Vittorio Emanuele II, which takes you to P.S. Babila. This area gives Milan its ultra-hip reputation. Take a credit card at your own risk. The dresses come straight from the designers and the selection is more up-to-date than anywhere else in the world. **Via Sant'Andrea** between V. Montenapoleone and V. della Spiga, has similarly upscale goods.

If you walk to the left and behind of the *duomo,* you come to **C.V. Emanuele II,** a transition street before the fashion district hits you full force. This is a mixture of mall culture and high fashion. For a purer exposure, walk to P. Babila, and turn left onto V. Napoleone. This narrow courseway has an expansive fashion sense. It begins with Louis Vuitton and Mila Schon, but the stores—more like showrooms—continue for a couple blocks: **Les Copains, La Perla, Gucci, Larusmiani, Prada.** Passing Sant' Andrea (which is also worth turning down), there is **Valentino, Versace, Lorenz, Swatch, Alexander Nicolette,** and at last **Expensive! V. Gesù** also deserves a stroll, as it branches off from **V. Napoleone** (one block after Sant'Andrea). The store windows, so clean they almost evaporate, exhibit an extremely high attention to detail. Fashion stores are abundant and widespread; thus one should not be constrained to the area around V. Napoleone, which is famously saturated with world-renowned designer names.

> ▼ **THE NEW CATHEDRALS.** Show the same respect for Milan's fashion houses as you would for its cathedrals. This means nice pants for men and skirts or dresses for women. Leave those jeans at the hotel. Your credit cards, too.

NIGHTLIFE

Check any Milanese paper on Wednesday or Thursday for information on clubs and weekend events. *Corriere Della Sera* publishes an insert called *Vivi Milano* on Wednesday, and *La Repubblica* produces *Tutto Milano* on Thursday. *Milano Magazine* is a monthly publication by the Ufficio Informazione del Comune with information on bars, films, and seasonal events. The best guide for nightlife, however, is *Pass Milano*, published only in Italian, available in most bookstores (L20,000/€10.33). It is often difficult to find an English version of any publication. The APT tourist office provides *Milano: Where, When, How*, which has a comprehensive list of every entertainment option in the city, divided by type; **discoteches** are dance clubs, **cabaret** implies live music of all kinds (not necessarily with dancers), and **bar** means only that the venue *looks* like a bar, since many are otherwise indistinguishable from dance clubs. **Pubs** are Irish/English/Australian-themed places to drink and occasionally to eat, but almost never to dance; **dancing** refers to ballroom dancing; **night club** translates into erotic dancing. Milan parties Thursday through Sunday nights and rests during the beginning of the week. Many clubs have "theme nights" (70s, 80s, Hard Rock, Dance/House, Electronica/Trance, Leather, Gay, Bi), and cover charges vary accordingly. Remember that everything shuts down in August, and clubs are often reincarnated in a totally different form in September. During the summer there are numerous music festivals in Monza, north of Milan. Check the paper, talk to locals, or watch for street posters.

A safe, attractive, and chic district lies by **V. Brera** northwest of the *duomo* and east of MM1: Cairoli; here you'll find art galleries, small clubs, restaurants, and an upscale thirty-something crowd. In the early evening, Milan's youth migrate to the areas around **C. Porta Ticinese** and **Piazza Vetra** near Chiesa San Lorenzo, 15min. southwest of the *duomo* by foot. Lounge on the grass in the parks, where guitar players will entertain you, or grab a beer at one of the many *birrerie* (pubs). The highest concentration of bars and vibrant university-age youth can be found into the wee hours of the morning in the **Navigli** district.

The metro closes around midnight, and cabs are expensive, so plan the location of your evening activities with a walk home in mind or, better yet, think ahead and find a place to stay near your club or bar of choice. Milan is relatively safe to walk through at night, though the suburbs and the areas around Stazione Centrale and C. Buono Aires deserve an extra dose of caution.

CORSO PORTA TICINESE AND PIAZZA VETRA

◪**Yguana Cafe Restaurant,** V.P. Gregorio XIV, 16 (☎0338 109 30 97). Walk down C. Porta Ticinese, and turn left at P. Vetra. Embrace the stylish vibe. Beautiful, but relatively down-to-earth natives sipping cocktails next to their scooters. Happy hour daily 5:30-9pm. Sunday brunch 12:30-4pm. Open daily 5:30pm-1am.

Grand Café Fashion (☎02 8940 0709), on C. Porta Ticinese near V. Vetere. For music and food served late, try this bar/restaurant/dance club. Stunningly beautiful crowd, often selected by a bouncer. Velour leopard print couches. Wowza. Mandatory first drink L15,000/€7.75. Happy hour 8pm-2:30am. Open daily noon-3pm and 8pm-3:30am.

Bar Flying Circus, P. Vetra, 21 (☎02 5831 3577), facing the rear of the church. Cocktails and an assortment of about 50 different whiskeys. No cover. Open daily 9am-2am.

Le Coquetel, P. Vetra, 16. A more yuppie-ish crowd assembles here to enjoy strawberry daiquiris around galactic canvasses. Open daily 8:30am-2am.

THE NAVIGLI

From C. Porta Ticinese, walk south until the street ends. Veer right through the Piazza XXIV Maggio to V. Naviglio Pavese and V. A. Sforza, two parallel streets bordering a canal. Or, take the metro to MM2: Porta Genova. Walk along V. Vigevano until it ends and veer right onto V. Naviglio Pavese.

▧ **Scimmie,** V.A. Sforza, 49 (☎ 02 5811 1313). A legendary bar with the best atmosphere in Navigli. Different theme every night and frequent concerts (10:30pm). Fusion, jazz, soul and reggae. Open daily 8pm-1:30am.

▧ **Fontanelle,** on V. Navigli Pavese. Cross the channel, walk down V. Navigli Pavese, and look for the 1st bar on the right. This unique bar serves beer quite creatively. Drink up, or risk much spillage. Always crowded with locals and foreigners. Open daily 8pm-2am.

Blue Kleim, V. Vigevano, 9. From the Porta Genova metro stop, walk down V. Vigevano 3 blocks. Blue Kleim's trendy funk is on the left. Blue light radiates onto the sidewalk through expansive window-walls. Sunshine yellow chairs make for a distinctive contrast. Try a Vodka Kleim or Virgin Kleim for L10,000/€5.16. No cover. Open Tu-Su 5pm-3am.

Vista Mare Caffe (☎ 02 8940 5349), near mouth of C. Porta Ticinese. Veer left at the end of V. Vigevano and walk across the channel. Chic yuppies relax by the *canale* and a fountain. Free pizza bread, *rizzo*, some pasta, and salad. *Apperitivi* L3000/€1.55. During happy hour (until 8:30pm) L5000/€2.58 discount per drink. Cafe provides 3hr. boat rides. L20,000/€10.33 per person in groups of 6+. Open daily 6:30pm-3am.

Totem Pub (☎ 02 837 50 98), at V. Naviglio Pavese and V.E. Gola. For the head banging sort. Beware the evil death's-head-cow-skull as you enter, and be prepared to hear anything from Metallica to crossover, reggae, and jungle. Live tattoos. Beer in immeasurably large Oktoberfest mugs L15,000/€7.75. Open daily 8:30pm-2:30am.

Propoganda, V. Castelbarco, 11 (☎ 02 5831 0682). From V. A. Sforza, walk east on V. Lagrange (next to Cafe Baraonda), which morphs into V. Giovenale and spits you out across the street from the large, glowing Propoganda sign. For those interested in dancing rather than bar-hopping, it's got some of the biggest dance floors in Milan (occasionally with live music). Caters mostly to a well-dressed university-age crowd. L15-25,000/€12.91 cover; men L5000/€2.58 more. Open Th-Su 11pm-4am.

AROUND CORSO COMO

▧ **Lollapaloosa,** C. Como, 15 (☎ 02 655 56 93). From MM2: Garibaldi, head south on C. Como. The club is on the right. A vigorous, youthful atmosphere for those not into the hipper-than-thou scene. Bar is owned by the captain of the Italian football team. Energetic crowd will have you tipsy and dancing on the tables in no time. Great rock'n'roll. Cover L15,000/€7.75 (including a drink.) Open Su-Th 7pm-2am, F-Sa 7pm-5:30am.

Rock: Hollywood, C. Como, 15 (☎ 02 659 89 96), next door to Lollapaloosa. One of the the only discos in the city exclusive enough to choose from the crowd at the door. Slip into your nicest leather pants and pout for the bouncer. The ▧ **mirror** in the ladies restroom is said to have a view of the men's restroom. Smile for the ladies, gentlemen. Hip-hop, house, and pop. Cover L30,000/€15.49. Open Tu-Su 10:30pm-4am.

Shocking, V.B. di Porta Nuova, 12 (☎ 02 659 54 07). Head farther down C. Como. More down-to-earth than Hollywood and minus the zaniness of Lollapaloosa. Avant-garde-esque. House/dance (cover L25,000/€12.91, includes a drink); underground techno (L30,000/€15.49, includes a drink). Open F-Sa 10:30pm-4am. Closed June-Aug.

AROUND LARGO CAIROLI

▧ **Le Trottoir,** close to V. Brera. From MM2: Lanza, take V. Tivoli to C. Garibaldi intersection. Perhaps the best bar in the city. Each night a different live band plays, but the bar is all about atmosphere. It's easy to meet Italians as well as people from all over the world. Open daily 7pm-2:30am.

■ **Bar Magenta,** V. Carducci, 13 (☎02 805 38 08). A short walk from MM1/2: Cardona. A traditional, well-crafted, wood-paneled Guinness bar. Hard to get in, hard to get out—the crowd often spills onto the sidewalk. Open Tu-Su 9am-3am, sometimes until 5am.

Old Fashion, on V. Camoens in the Parco Sempione. MM1/2: Cadorna. Walk on the right side of V. Paleocapa from P. Cadorna. The street becomes V.E. Alemagna. The club is in the Palazzo dell'Arte on right. Frequented by students deeply entrenched within the club scene and some (relatively) down-to-earth fashion types. Indoor/outdoor venue with superb DJ lineup. Cover L25,000/€12.91 (includes a drink). Open F-Sa 11pm-4am.

EAST OF CORSO BUENOS AIRES

■ **Cafe Capoverde,** V. Leoncavallo, 16 (☎02 2682 0430). From MM1/2: Loreto, head down V. Costa, which becomes V. Leoncavallo. Walk through the flower shop to this heavenly, unique cafe. Feels like a jungle and is full of natives. Johnny Ockey, the super-funky manager is among the friendliest Milanese around. Cocktails dominate, but also serves decent food. *Primi* or pizza L11,000/€5.68. Open noon-3pm and 8pm-midnight.

■ **Artdecothe,** V. Lombro, 7 (☎02 3952 4760). From MM1: Porta Venezia, walk 3 blocks up C. Buenos Aires and take a right on V. Melzo. The bar is 3 blocks down on the left, across from Le Lephante. Without a doubt, this discobar defines Milan's elegance. Modern, and very, very cool. Each table is decorated in a different style, though the predominant theme is trendy art-deco. 250 different colored lights. House, hip-hop, and acid jazz. Dancing begins after midnight. Happy hour daily 6-9pm. Open daily 7am-2am.

Kirribilly, V. Castel Morone, 7 (☎02 7012 0151). From MM1: Porta Venezia take V. Regina Giovana from C. Buenos Aires. A cheery Australian pub with good beer and a giant shark's head on the wall. Try the Cuban rum and kangaroo meat. M happy hour, Tu student night, Th pop quiz. Open M-F noon-3pm and 6-3am, Sa-Su 6pm-3am.

New Magazine, V. Piceno, 3 (☎02 73 09 41). MM1: Porta Venezia. From Kirribilly, hang a right out door and turn left at C. Independenza. Walk through P. Dateo, and turn right on V. Piceno to work your way down to a hoppin' disco with phones and maps (and sometimes dancing Italian university students) on every table. Eat, make friends, and find love. Drinks L5-9000/€2.58-4.64. Open Tu-Su 9:30am-2:30am.

GAY BARS AND CLUBS

Le Lephante, V. Melzo, 22 (☎02 2951 8768). From MM2: Porta Venezia, walk up C. Buenos Aires 3 blocks and turn right on V.Melzo. Le Lephante is across from the Artdecothe Cafe. Dark interior with a mixed gay/straight crowd. Open Tu-Su 6:30pm-2am.

Cicip e Ciciap, V. Gorani, 9 (☎02 86 72 02). From MM1: Cairoli, take V.S. Giov. sul Muro which turns into V. Brisa. V. Gorani is the 2nd left. A bar/restaurant with a women-only crowd. Open Sa 8:30pm-3am.

Sottomarino Giallo, V. Donatello, 2 (☎02 29 40 10 47). Another women-only club with cozy couches on 2 floors. Open Tu-Su 10:30pm-3:30am.

One Way Club, V. Cavallotti, 204 (☎02 242 13 41), outside the city in Sesto San Giovanni. MM2: Sesto FS. A discotheque famed for the predominance of leather. Member ship card required. Open F-Sa 10:30pm-3:30am, Su 3:30-7pm.

STILL GOT IT (BALLROOM FLOORS)

Al Tata, V. F. Testi, 5 (☎02 6900 2281). A fine-dining restaurant with ballroom dancing and revival music. Open Tu-Su 6pm-midnight.

Arizona Dance, V. Spallanzani, 10 (☎02 953 19 52). One of the more elegant and well-visited venues. Open Th-Su 8am-5pm.

LIVE MUSIC

■ **Tunnel,** V. Sammartini, 30 (☎02 6671 1370), near V. Giuseppe Bruscetti, bordering Stazione Centrale. *The* underground concert environment. Post-punk, hardcore, ska, reggae, sci-fi surf, kraut-rock, rockabilly, and various indie bands frequent this train-tunnel-turnedbandshell. Live music nightly. Double show F and Sa. Annual membership card necessary. Cover L5-15,000/€2.58-7.75. Hours vary; check the paper.

Alcatraz, V. Valtellina, 25 (☎02 6901 6352). MM2: Porta Garibaldi. Take V. Ferrari and go right on C. Farni. After train tracks turn left on V. Valtellina. Biggest club and indoor concert-venue. Cover L25,000/€12.91 (includes a drink). Open F-Sa 11pm-3am.

Blues House on V.S. Uguzzone, 26 (☎02 2700 3621), near MM1: Villa S. Giovanni. For those who would rather sip a cocktail from a relaxing seat and listen to some good jazz and blues. Open W-Su 9pm-2:30am.

PAVIA ☎0382

Pavia survived Attila the Hun's attack in 452 before gaining importance as the Lombard capital in the 7th and 8th centuries. Spanish, Austrian, and French forces governed Pavia in rapid succession from the 16th century until 1859, when Italy's independence movement liberated the city. Once a place where kings were crowned, now a prosperous and active university town, Pavia bustles with student activity. Romanesque churches from Pavia's tranquil years as a Milanese satellite are found throughout the historic section. The nearby **Certosa di Pavia** is one of the premier monastic structures in the world, and the da Vinci canals (an astounding achievement of contemporary engineering) run all the way from Navigli.

⌐ TRANSPORTATION

Trains: at the end of V.V. Emanuele. To **Genoa** (1½hr.; every hr. 6:33am-10:45pm; L12,500/€6.46) and **Milan** (30min.; every hr. 6:08am-11:40pm; L4600/€2.36). Change at Codogno for **Cremona** (1 per hr., L8250/€4.26).

Buses: SGEA (☎0382 37 54 05), turn left out of train station. Buses depart from an enormous, modern brick building on V. Trieste. Tickets may be purchased at the office (painted green) under the terminal cover. To **Milan** (1hr., 2 per hr., L5000/€2.58) via **Certosa di Pavia** (15min., L2500/€1.29).

Taxis: (☎0382 274 39) at the train station or (☎0382 291 90) at the center.

▓✴️⚡ ORIENTATION AND PRACTICAL INFORMATION

Pavia sits on the banks of the Ticino River not far from where it merges with the Po. The train station overlooks **Piazzale Stazione** in the west end of the modern town. To get from the station to the historic center of town, walk down **Viale Vittorio Emanuele II** to **Piazzale Minerva**. Continue on Pavia's main street, **Corso Cavour,** to the city's narrow central square, **Piazza della Vittoria,** a block away from **Piazza Duomo.** Past P. Vittoria, the main street changes its name to **Corso Mazzini.**

TOURIST, FINANCIAL, AND LOCAL SERVICES

Tourist Office, V. Filzi, 2 (☎0382 221 56). From train station, turn left on V. Trieste and then right on V. Filzi, past the bus station. English-speaking staff provides a good map, and is both pleasant and knowledgeable. Open M-Sa 8:30am-12:30pm and 2-6pm.

Currency Exchange: Try **Banca Commerciale Italiana,** C. Cavour, 12, or **Banco Ambrosiano Veneto,** C. Cavour, 7d. Also try the 2nd floor of the post office.

English-Language Bookstore: Libreria Ticinum, C. Mazzini, 2c (☎0382 30 39 16), off P. Vittoria. Open M 3-7:30pm, Tu-Sa 9am-12:30pm and 3-7:30pm, Su 10:30am-1pm and 3-7:30pm.

EMERGENCY AND COMMUNICATIONS

Emergency: ☎113.

First Aid/Ambulance: ☎118, nights and holidays ☎0382 52 76 00.

Late-Night Pharmacy: Vippani, V. Bossolaro, 31 (☎0382 223 15), at corner of P. Duomo and V. Menocchio, has a list of pharmacies with night service. The staff provides emergency night services for surcharge. Open M-F 8:30am-12:30pm and 3:30-7:30pm.

Hospital: Ospedale S. Matteo, P. Golgi, 2 (☎0382 50 11).

Internet Access: Poli Piu, C. Cavour, 18, 3 floors above Cinema Politeama. Nice terrace and panorama. Modern dining place on 2 floors. Internet L10,000/€5.16 per hr. Cocktails L10,000/€5.16. Open Th-Su 7pm-2am. **University,** from P. Vittoria, turn left on Strada Nuova. Walk past the intersection with V. Mentana and take 1st right. Continue through courtyard (bearing right) toward a large, seated statue with a long sword planted in the ground. On the right (behind the statue) is a door with the words *"Dipartimento di Scienza della Letteratura e dell'Arte Medievale e Moderna."* Enter the door, present a student ID, and smile. Open M-Th 9am-5pm, F 9am-2pm. Free.

Post Office: P. della Posta, 2 (☎0382 297 65), off V. Mentana, a block from C. Mazzini. Open M-F 8:05am-5:30pm, Sa 8:05am-noon.

Postal Code: 27100.

▌ ACCOMMODATIONS & CAMPING

A dearth of reasonably priced places to stay makes Pavia unappealing as anything but a daytrip. Consider staying in Milan, or take advantage of Pavia's well-organized *agriturismo* program. Ask the tourist office for a complete pamphlet.

Hotel Aurora, V.V. Emanuele, 25 (☎0382 236 64), straight ahead from train station on your left. With its white walls and Warhol-like art, this hotel resembles a trendy New York art gallery. Private baths (showers only). All 19 rooms with phone, TV, and A/C. Reserve ahead. Singles L60,000/€40, with bath L80,000/€41.32; doubles L125,000/€64.56. MC/V.

Camping: Ticino, V. Mascherpa, 10 (☎0382 52 70 94). From station, take bus #4 (dir: Mascherpa) for 10min. to "Chiozzo" stop. Restaurant next door. Nearby pool L5000/€2.58 for campground guests. Open Mar.-Oct. L7500/€3.87 per person, L4000/€2.58 under 12, L7000/€3.62 per tent, L3000/€1.55 per car. Electricity L3000/€1.55. Hot shower L500/€0.26.

▐ FOOD

Coniglio (rabbit) and *rana* (frog) are the local specialties, but if you don't eat things that hop and jump, wander to the *tavole calde* on C. Cavour and C. Mazzini. Try the well-loved *zuppa alla pavese*, piping-hot chicken or beef broth served with a poached egg floating on top and sprinkled with grated *grana* cheese. **Esselunga,** between V. Trieste and V. Battisti, at the far end of the mall complex, is a monolithic **supermarket.** (☎0382 262 10. Open M 1-9pm, Tu-Sa 8am-9pm.)

Ristorante-Pizzeria Marechiaro, P. Vittoria, 9 (☎0382 237 39). An inviting interior and outside porch sheltered by white stucco. Sit here and you'll be the only 1 in the *piazza* who doesn't get wet during afternoon showers. Delicious pizzas with blackened crusts L6-18,000/€3.10-9.30. Reasonably priced *primi* and *secondi*. Cover L3000/€1.55. Open Tu-Su 11am-3pm and 6pm-3am. AmEx/D/MC/V.

Ristorante-Pizzeria Regisole, P. Duomo, 4 (☎0382 247 39), under the arcade with the *duomo* in clear view. A/C and outdoor seating available. Relax to Baroque classical music. Reasonably priced pizzas, including a *margherita* for L6000/€3.10. Don't even attempt to leave without trying *profiteria* (chocolate cake; L4000/€2.07). Open W-M noon-3pm and 7pm-midnight. Closed Aug. AmEx/D/MC/V.

👁 SIGHTS

▨ BASILICA DI SAN MICHELE. As the oldest building in town, this sandstone Romanesque church has witnessed the coronations of luminaries, including Charlemagne in 774, Frederick Barbarossa in 1155, a long succession of northern Italian dukes in the Middle Ages, and the Savoy family later on. It is said that when the crown was placed on Charlemagne's head, light shone through one of the windows on him. Rebuilt in the 12th century (after an earthquake destroyed much of the 661 structure) in a Romanesque style, the exterior displays once intricate carvings weathered into indecipherable patterns. A 1491 fresco of the *Coronation of the Virgin* and 14th-century low-relief sculpture decorate the chancel, while an 8th-century crucifix of Theodore graces the *cappella*. *(Take C. Strada Nuova to C. Garibaldi and turn right on V.S. Michele. Open daily 8am-noon and 3-8pm.)*

UNIVERSITY OF PAVIA. Founded in 1361, this beacon of higher education claims famous alumni Petrarch, Columbus, Venetian playwright Goldoni, and physicist Alessandro Volta (inventor of the battery), whose experiments are now on display. The university's patron and renowned sadist, Galeazzo II of the Visconti family, earned notoriety for his research on human torture. Three towers rising from the university on P. da Vinci are the remnants of more than 100 medieval towers that once punctuated the skyline. Many cobblestone courtyards makes this a fine place for an afternoon respite. *(From P. Vittoria, turn left on V. Calatafimi and right on C. Stradivari from where you go through the 1st entrance on the right. Free.)*

DUOMO. An all-star team of visionaries including Bramante, da Vinci, and Amadeo began work on the **Cattedrale Monumentale di Santo Stefano Martiro** in the 15th century. As is typical of the Italian system, much of it still remains incomplete. The **Torre Civica**, adjoining the *duomo*, collapsed in the spring of 1989, killing several people and taking a good portion of the left chapel with it. To the left of the *duomo*, you can see the remnants of the tower, surrounded by a metal fence. The shaky brick exterior of the *duomo*, recently reinforced with concrete columns, conceals an impressive interior finally completed under Mussolini. *(Duomo diagonally across from P. San Michele.)*

CASTELLO VICONTEO. The colossal medieval castle (1360) is set in a beautifully landscaped park. An impressive moat surrounds the grounds, although it dried up long ago. Richly colored windows and elegant terra-cotta decorations border three sides of the castle's vast courtyard. The fourth wall was destroyed in 1527 during the Franco-Spanish Wars. Pavia's **Museo Civico** resides here, featuring a formidable gallery of paintings and an extensive Lombard-Romanesque sculpture collection. On the 2nd floor, there is a model of Pavia's *duomo* in rich, burnished wood. *(The castle is at the end of Strada Nuova. Castle ☎ 0382 338 53. Open Tu-Sa 9am-1:30pm, Su 9am-1pm. L5000/€2.58, under 18 L2500/€1.29. Museum ☎ 0382 30 48 16.)*

BASILICA DI SAN PIETRO IN CIEL D'ORO. This translates: "St. Peter in Golden Sky." From the grounds of the castle, you can see the low, rounded forms of the Lombard-Romanesque *chiesa* (1132). Inside, piercing rays of light stream down from tiny windows. On the high altar, an ornate Gothic tomb (made in the 14th century) contains the remains of St. Augustine. Intricate frescoes adorn the ceiling of the sacristy, left of the altar. A wall-sized organ stands suspended above the door. *(Open daily 7am-noon and 3-7pm.)*

🎵 ENTERTAINMENT

By far the funkiest and most distinctive bar in town is **▨Malaika "bar and soul,"** V. Bossolaro, 21, off C. Cavour. Its exotic interior in warm colors resonates with African music at night. Enjoy *panini*, salads, and fruit desserts all from L4000/€2.07. (☎ 0382 30 13 99. Open Tu-Su 11am-2am.) Check out **Le Broletto**, P. Vittoria 14E, a classic Irish pub at the feet of the *duomo*, and with a long view of the *piazza*. (☎ 0382 675 41. Open 9am-2:30pm and 8pm-2am.)

🔁 DAYTRIP FROM PAVIA: CERTOSA DI PAVIA

Buses from Milan-Famagosta (MM2) to Certosa (50min.; 2 per hr., Milan 5:40am, Certosa 8pm; L3500/€1.81) and then to Pavia (V. Trieste station). From the bus stop, Certosa awaits at the end of a very long, tree-lined road (V. Certosa). Open Apr. and Oct. Tu-Su 9-11:30am and 2:30-5pm; May-Aug. Tu-Su 9-11:30am and 2:30-6pm; Sept. Tu-Su 9-11:30am and 2:30-5:30pm. Nov.-Mar. Tu-Sa 9-11:30am and 2:30-4:30pm, Su 9-11:30am and 2:30-5pm. Free.

Eight kilometers north of Pavia stands 🔁**Certosa di Pavia** (Carthusian Monastery ☎ 0382 92 56 13), one of the world's most beautiful churches. It was built as a mausoleum for the Visconti family, who ruled the area from the 12th through the 15th centuries. Started in 1396 by the Viscontis and finished by the Sforzas in 1497, the monastery contains an eclectic array of four centuries of Italian art from early Gothic to Baroque. More than 250 artists worked on the elaborate facade—allegedly the richest church exterior in the world (late 1400s-1560), which represents the apex of the Lombard Renaissance and is packed with inlaid marble and sculptures of saints. The old sacristy houses a Florentine triptych carved in ivory, with 99 sculptures and 66 bas-reliefs depicting the lives of Mary and Jesus. The beautiful backyard contains 24 houses, one for each Carthusian monk. In accordance with St. Benedict's motto *ora et labora* (pray and work), the monks are active in agriculture and distill excellent liquors. They start at L10,000/€5.16 per bottle (a very small bottle). When a large enough group has gathered, the monks lead **tours** (usually in Italian). A view of the facade alone is worth the 50min. bus ride.

CREMONA ☎ 0372

Quiet streets and muted earth-tone walls are simply a backdrop to the richest and most vibrant aspect of Cremona—its music. Claudio Monteverdi was born here, and Andrea Amati created the first modern violin in Cremona in 1530, establishing the *Cremonese* violin-making dynasty. After learning the fundamentals as apprentices in the Amati workshop, Antonio Stradivarius (1644-1737) and Giuseppe Guarneri (1687-1745) raised violin-making to a new art form. Students still come to the city's International School for Violin-Making to learn the legendary craft. Today, the city remains aware of its noble tradition, as the busy concert schedule at the Ponchielli Theater preserves the city's remarkable music.

Despite its many claims on tourists' attentions, Cremona is a city that feels dominated by natives. The local culture centers around the Piazza del Comune. As the sun turns the *duomo* a spectrum of orange and rose, well-attired citizens of every age talk chat with each other and on their omnipresent cell phones with indifference to time. A similar social atmosphere has its daytime counterpart in the open-air markets (Wednesdays and Saturdays, 8am-1pm) in the Piazza Stradavari. Here you find clothes, shoes, bags, and household items as well as farm fresh vegetables, fruits, and a wide variety of dried and cured meats, plus aromatic cheeses.

▐ TRANSPORTATION

Trains: V. Dante, 68. Bus-stop: "P. Stazione." Info office (☎ 0372 371 11) open daily 6am-10:10pm. To: **Brescia** (45min.; every hr. 6:32am-7:36pm; L6300/€3.25); **Bologna** (2hr.; 6 per day 7:51am-9:31pm; L12,500/€6.46); **Mantua** (1hr.; every hr. 6:25am-9:52pm; L7200/€3.72); **Milan** (1¼hr., 6 per day 6:24am-7:32pm, L9000/€4.65); **Pavia** (2hr., 7 per day 5:10am-6:11pm, L8100/€4.18).

Buses: Autostazione di V. Dante (☎ 0372 292 12), 1 block to the left of train station. Ticket office open 7:20am-1:10pm and 3:30-6:25pm. To **Brescia** (every hr. 6:11am-6:30pm, L7900/€4.08) and **Milan** (1hr.; M,W, F 10:10am; L9600/€4.96).

Taxis: ☎ 0372 213 00 or 267 40. At train station and *piazzas*, such as P. Stradivari.

ORIENTATION AND PRACTICAL INFORMATION

As you leave the train station, bear to the left of the park. Walk straight ahead, crossing V. Dante onto V. Palestro, which then crosses **Viale Trento e Trieste.** Take **via Palestro,** which becomes first **Corso Campi** and then **Corso Verdi,** to **Piazza Stradivari.** Turn left at P. Cavour toward **Piazza del Comune** (commonly known as Piazza del Duomo), where the *duomo, torrazzo,* and tourist office are located. From P. del Comune take **via Solferino** to **Piazza Roma**—the local Rastafarian enclave.

Tourist Office: Azienda Di Promozione Turistica. P. del Comune, 5 (☎0372 232 33). Lightly staffed. No English spoken. Ask for the general info brochure on hotels, museums, and restaurants. Open M-Sa 9:30am-12:30pm and 3-6pm, Su 10am-1pm.

Currency Exchange: Banco Nazionale del Lavoro, C. Campi, 4-10 (☎0372 40 01), next to post office, on left, when walking away from P. Stradivari on V. Verdi (which changes to Corso Campi) at the corner. Open M-F 8:20am-1:20pm and 2:30-4pm, Sa 8:20-11:50am. 24hr **ATM.**

Emergency: ☎113. **Ambulance and First Aid:** ☎118.

Police: Questura, V. Tribunali, 6 (☎0372 40 74 27).

Hospital: Ospedale (☎0372 40 51 11), in Largo Priori. Past P. IV Novembre to the east, take V.B. Dovara and go right on V. Giuseppina.

Post Office: C. Verdi, 1 (☎0372 220 351). Open M-F 8:10am-5:30pm, Sa closes 1pm.

Postal Code: 26100.

ACCOMMODATIONS & CAMPING

La Locanda, V. Pallavicino, 4 (☎0372 457 83 54; fax 45 78 34). From P. del Comune, walk up V. Solferino and turn right on C. Mazzini. Bear left on C. Matteotti. V. Pallavicino is a few blocks down on the right. Centrally located 3-star hotel with clean, airy rooms and friendly management. All rooms with bath, TV, and phone. Some English spoken. 9 rooms are on 3 floors above restaurant. The higher the number, the higher the climb. Breakfast included. Restaurant downstairs features homemade pasta. Reception 24hr. Reservations recommended. Singles L75,000/€38.73; doubles L110,000/€56.81.

Servizi per L'Accaglienza, V. Sacchi, 15 (☎0372 217 80 or 41 42 68). Walk down V. Palestro until it turns into C. Verdi, and at P. Marconi turn right on V. Tibaldi. Turn left on V. Sacchi, and ring the bell. Tranquil rooms and 25 beds on a central courtyard. Nunrun. Women only ages 18-65. No English spoken. Curfew 10:30pm. Singles and doubles L20-30,000/€10.33-15.49 per person. Full-pension L40,000/€20.66.

Giardino di Giada, V. Brescia, 7 (☎0372 43 46 15). From station, turn left down V. Dante and left again at P. Libertà. Bus #5 runs from station. 2 shared bathrooms. No English. Even courtyard rooms are noisy. The tall french doors (with balcony) make highceilinged rooms more peaceful. Singles L40,000/€20.66; doubles L60,000/€31.

Albergo Touring, V. Palestro, 3 (☎0372 369 76). Heading out of train station, walk straight ahead to V. Palestro. 4 blocks ahead on your left, marked with a prominent vertical sign. At the corner of V. Fulvio Cazzaniga. 10 rooms. Reservations required. Singles L40,000/€20.66; doubles L70,000/€36.15, with bath L90,000/€46.48.

Camping: Parco al Po, V. Lungo Po Europa, 12a (☎0372 212 68). From P. Cavour, walk 20min. down C.V. Emanuele. Showers and electricity. Open Apr.-Sept. L13,000/€6.71 per person, L16,000/€8.26 per car and tent, L15,000/€7.75 per caravan.

FOOD

The city's *mostarda di Cremona,* first concocted in the 16th century, consists of a hodgepodge of fruits—cherries, figs, apricots, and melons—preserved in a sweet mustard syrup and is traditionally served on boiled meats. Bars of *torrone* (nougat with an egg, honey, and nut base) are equally steeped in Cremonese confectionery lore. *Mostarda* can be found in most local *trattorie*, and *torrone* is available in every sweet shop. **Sperlari,** at V. Solferino, 25, has been keeping dentists in business since 1836. (☎0372 223 46. Open Tu-Sa 8:30am-12:30pm and 3:30-7:30pm.) You can find a cheaper bar of torrone (L3500/€1.81) at **Negozio Vergami Spelta e Generali,** C. Giacomo Matteotti, 112, at the P. della Liberta, at the corner of C. Matteotti and Trento e Triests. (☎0372 23 99 67). For something less sweet, try the *Grana Padano* or the Provolone cheeses in the local *salumerie.* From 8am to 1pm on Wednesday and Saturday, there is an **open-air market** in P. Stradivari. For **supermarkets,** try **CRAI** at P. Risorgimento, 30, near the train station. (Open M 8am-1pm, Tu-Sa 8am-12:30pm and 4:30-7:30pm.) Another option is **GS** at V.S. Tommaso, 9, close to P. del Comune (open M 1-8pm and Tu-Sa 8am-8pm), or **Colmark** on V. Dante, just left of the train station (open M 1:30-7:30pm, Tu-Sa 8:30am-7:30pm).

Ristorante Pizzeria La Bersagliera, P. Risorgimento 17 (☎0372 213 97). Make a right out of the train station; it's two blocks ahead facing the *piazza.* Many tables and a well-lighted bar. Pizza starts L6000/€3.10, a few dozen kinds to choose from (including vegetarian options). One pizza is large enough to two, or for some tasty leftovers. A/C. Open 11:30am-2:30pm and 5:30pm-2am. Closed W. AmEx/D/MC/V.

Ristorante Pizzeria Marechiaro, C. Campi, 49 (☎0372 262 89). Since it lies on the fashionable Corso Campi, it is worth vying for a window seat. With the elegant neighboring shops, the less formal interior makes this an appealing respite. Pizzas from L10,000/€5.16. *Menù* with lots of fresh choices L22,000/€11.36. Cover L3000/€1.55; for pizza L2000/€1.03. Open W-M noon-3pm and 6:10pm-1am. MC/V.

La Piedigrotta, P. Risorgimento, 14 (☎0372 220 33), 2 blocks to the right of train station, on the far side of *piazza.* Sparkling clean, featuring a classic look with modern fixtures. Buffet L8-10,000/€4.13-5.16. Open W-F 11:30-2:30 and 5:30pm-1am. MC/V.

◉ SIGHTS

TEATRO PONCHIELLI. One of Cremona's highlights, a lavishly decorated Baroque theater. The 250-year-old masterpiece provided the testing ground for the Stradivari and Amati violins and stands as one of the most beautiful, but undiscovered opera houses worldwide. Red velvet seats offer a sumptuous embrace during the many performances. Impressive acoustics Individual boxes, or "pockets" ensconce those who inhabit the back arch-wall of seats. Take the free tour. *(Go to P. Stradivari and take C.V. Emanuele to 25. ☎0372 407 27 45; ponchielli@rccr.cremona.it; www.rccr.cremona.it/doc_comu/tea/tea_index.htm. Open 4-7pm.)*

MUSEO STRADIVARIANO. Violins and their production are Cremona's primary attraction. The Museo Stradivariano provides a step-by-step introduction to the art of Stradivari and his contemporaries. *(V. Palestro, 17, close to station. ☎0372 46 18 86. Open Tu-Sa 8:30am-6pm, Su 10am-6pm. L6000/€3.08. English spoken.)*

PIAZZA DEL COMUNE. The second floor of the **Palazzo Comunale** houses a series of lavishly decorated rooms once used by the government. Even more stunning is the *Saletta dei Violini* (Violin Room), showcasing five masterpieces attributed to Andrea Amati, Nicolò Amati, Stradivari, and Guarneri. When the guards unlock the room for you, be sure to ask for an English information booklet. *(P. del Commune. From Museo Stradivariano, continue down V. Palestro which becomes C. Cavour and V. Verdi. Turn left on V. Baldesio. Open June to mid-Aug. Tu-Sa 8:30am-6:30pm, Su 10am-6pm. L6000/€3.08.)*

Directly facing the *palazzo*, the pink marble *duomo* (officially known as Santa Maria Assunta) is a fine example of a Lombard-Romanesque cathedral, built in the 12th century. The interior displays a cycle of 16th-century frescoes, and the central aisle has been beautifully restored. *(Open daily 7:30am-noon and 3:30-7pm.)*

To the left of the *duomo* stands the late 13th-century ▓**Torrazzo.** At 111m, it is the tallest *campanile* in Italy with the oldest known astrological clock in the world. The clock is one hour late in the summertime, so don't miss your train. The 487 steps lead to an unmatched panorama of the city, but don't make the journey around noon-time. *(Open Easter-Oct. M-Sa 10:30am-noon and 3-6:30pm, Su 10:30am-12:30pm and 3-7pm; Nov.-Easter Sa-Su 10:30am-12:30pm and 3-6pm. L8000/€4.13.)*

The dome of the **baptistery** (1167) rises in a perfect, unadorned octagonal pattern; its rose stone faces warmly complementing the *piazza*. The Gothic **Loggia dei Militia**, across from the baptistery, completes the square. *(Baptistry open Sa 3:30-7pm, Su 10:30am-12:30pm and 3:30-7pm.)*

MUSEO CIVICO. The **Palazzo Affaitati** (1561) flaunts an impressive marble Renaissance staircase that leads to the newly restored museum's extensive and diverse collection, well displayed in a light, airy space. The collection includes paintings by Bembo and Caravaggio. Especially noteworthy pieces include Caravaggio's *San Francesco in Meditazione*, Bembo's *Madonna col Bambino e Santo Stefano*, Genovesino's *Amore dormiente* (featuring a nude cupid sitting atop a book, and leaning closed-eyed on a skull—all the while with bow in hand), and a fresco from San Giovanni Nuovo. From the same staircase, though turning the doors facing those of the Museo's, you will find the **Biblioteca Statale.** This library features a quiet and large reading room with a fresco of Cremona on the far wall, and an admirable collection of Olivetti typewriters from the 1950s. *(Palazzo Affaitati, V. Ugolani Dati, 4. ☎ 0372 46 18 85. Open Tu-Sa 8:30am-6pm, Su 10am-6pm. L10,000/€5.16.)*

Palazzo Fodri (1499) is another of Cremona's fine Renaissance buildings. The columns in the courtyard bear French royal insignia in homage to Louis XII of France, who occupied the duchy of Milan in 1499. *(C. Matteotti, 17.)*

 MORE FOR YOUR MONEY. If your aim is to see all Cremona has to offer, consider a *biglietto cumulativo*, which includes admission to the **Museo Civico**, the **Palazzo Communale**, and the **Museo Stradivariano** for L15,000/€7.75, or go with the city card with discounts for all the sights and free bus rides for L10,000/€5.16 (both options are available at the tourist office).

ENTERTAINMENT

Music is in the Cremona air year-round. Cremona Jazz, running from April through June, introduces the summer season with a series of concerts throughout the city. (Tickets from L15,000/€7.75.) Estate in Musica organizes a series of outdoor concerts in July and August. At the May and June Festival di Cremona, Claudio Monteverdi kicks off the Teatro Ponchielli season with a classical series, appropriately heavy on the strings. Performances continue after the festival and crescendo at the grand finale of the opera season. *(Teatro Ponchelli ticket booth at C.V. Emanuele, 52. ☎0372 40 72 75. Open daily mid-Oct. to early Dec. 4-7pm. Tickets begin at L10,000/€5.16.)*

MANTUA (MANTOVA)　　☎0376

Mantua owes its literary fame to its most famous son, the poet Virgil. The driving force that built the city's *centro storico*, however, was not the pun crafter but the Gonzaga family. After ascending to power in 1328, the family zealously sought to change Mantua's small town image by importing well-known artists like Monteverdi and Rubens and by cultivating the local talent. Evidence of their effort includes the impressive churches of San Sebastiano and Sant'Andrea and the remnants of frescoes by Mantegna and Pisanelli.Today, Mantua, with its grand *palazzi* and graceful churches, is a shopper-friendly city that provides easy passage to the surrounding lakes.

TRANSPORTATION

Trains: (☎0376 1478 880 88), in P. Don Leoni, end of V. Solferino. To: **Cremona** (1hr., every hr. 5:25am-7:40pm, L7200/€3.72); **Milan** (2hr.; 9 per day 5:25am-6:36pm; L16,000/€8.26); **Verona** (40min., every hr. 6:10am-10:20pm, L4100/€2.12).

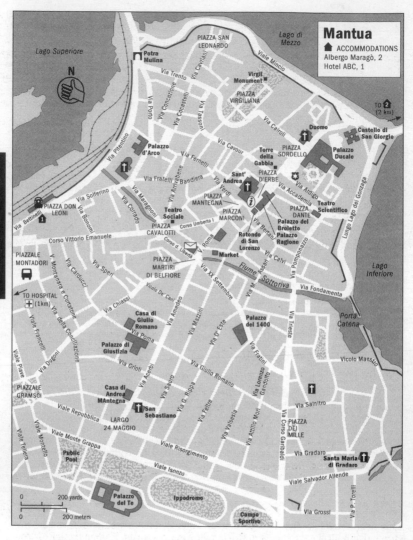

Mantua

↑ ACCOMMODATIONS
Albergo Maragò, 2
Hotel ABC, 1

Buses: APAM (☎0376 32 72 37), in P. Mondadori. Turn right and cross the street out of the train station. Cross C.V. Emanuele to V. Caduti. Frequent buses to **Brescia** (1½hr., L9500/€4.91).

Taxis: ☎0376 36 88 44.

Bike Rental: Bici a Noleggio, an outdoor establishment next to the lake, on the Lungolago dei Gonzaga where it intersects with Largo Vigili del Fuoco. M-F L3-5000/€1.55-2.58 per hr., L8000/€4.13 per 3hr., L15-20,000/€7.75-10.33 per day. Open Apr.-Sept. daily 8am-11pm.

✦🛈 ORIENTATION AND PRACTICAL INFORMATION

Most buses go only to the edge of the old town, but you can easily walk the rest of the way. From the train station in **Piazza Don E. Leoni,** head left on V. Solferino then right on V. Bonomi to the main street, **Corso Vittorio Emanuele II.** This street leads to P. Cavallotti, connected by C. della Libertà to **Piazza Martiri della Libertà.** From here, **via Roma** runs to the *centro storico*, which begins at **Piazza dell'Erbe,** with central **Piazza Marconi** and **Piazza Mantegna** clustered close by.

Tourist Office: P. Mantegna, 6 (☎0376 32 82 53; fax 36 32 92), adjacent to Sant'Andrea's church. From train station, turn left onto V. Solferino. Go through P.S. Francesco d'Assisi to V. Fratelli Bandiera, then right onto V. Verdi. Free brochures and city map. Friendly staff speaks English. Open M-Sa 8:30am-12:30pm and 3-6pm.

Boat Excursions: Motonavi Andes, V.S. Giorgio, 10 (☎0376 32 28 75; fax 36 08 69).

Emergency: ☎113. **Ambulance:** ☎118.

Police: P. Sordello, 46 (☎0376 20 51).

Late-Night Pharmacy: Dr. Silvestri, V. Roma, 24. Open Tu-Sa 8:30am-12:30pm and 4-8pm. List of pharmacies offering night service posted outside.

Hospital: Ospedale Civile Poma, V. Albertoni, 1 (☎0376 20 11).

Post Office: P. Martiri Belfiore, 15 (☎0376 32 64 03), up V. Roma from the tourist office. Open M-F 8:15am-1:25pm and 2-5:15pm, Sa 8:15am-1pm.

Postal Code: 46100.

🛏 ACCOMMODATIONS

Those willing to stay in smaller nearby towns will be able to find less expensive accommodations. Ask at the tourist office for an up-to-date *agriturismo* packet (around L20,000/€10.33 per person per night).

Hotel ABC, P. Don Leoni, 25 (☎0376 32 33 47; fax 32 23 29), across from station. Fragments of frescoes peek out from the corners of these modern rooms with TV and telephone. Some rooms have bath. Breakfast included. Seasonal variations in price. All rooms with bath except two singles (L40,000/€20.66). Singles L60-110,000/€30.99-56.81; doubles L90-150,000/€46.48-77.47; triples L150-200,000/€77.47-103.29.

Albergo Maragò, V. Villanova De Bellis, 2 (☎0376 37 03 13), at the Locanda Virgiliana. Take bus #2, which runs from P. Cavallotti into Virgiliana (10min. every 30min.). The hotel is on the left, just past P.S. Isidro. If you don't mind the 2km journey from the center, this hotel/restaurant is a bargain with quiet, clean rooms. Singles L38,000/€19.63; doubles L55,000/€28.41. AmEx/DC/MC/V.

🍴 FOOD

Over a million pigs are slaughtered in Mantua every year, so if you are carnivorous, don't skip the native *panchetta* or *salumi*.

▨ Antica Osteria ai Ranari, V. Trieste, 11 (☎0376 32 84 31; fax 32 84 31), on the continuation of V. Pomponazzo near Porta Catena. Friendly atmosphere. Restaurant specializes in regional dishes, some commemorating the Gonzagas. Try the Mantuan delight *tortelli di zucca* (with pumpkin; L10,000/€5.16). *Primi* L8-12,000/€4.13-6.20; *secondi* L12-18,000/€6.20-9.30. Cover L2000/€1.03. Open Tu-Su noon-2:30pm and 7:15-11:30pm; closed 3 weeks late-July and early-Aug. AmEx/MC/V.

Pizzeria/Ristorante Piedigrotta 2, C. Liberta, 15 (☎0376 32 70 14). Below soothing light-colored arched ceilings. Great deals on pizza and delicious seafood dishes. Friendly, festive, fish-loving staff. Pizza *margherita* L8000/€4.13; *primi* L8000/€4.13; *secondi* from L11,000/€5.68; Open T-Su noon-3pm and 6:30pm-12:30am. MC/V.

NORTHWEST ITALY

🔍 SIGHTS

🏛 PALAZZO DUCALE. Piazza Sordello lies beside what used to be the largest palace in Europe, built by the Gonzaga family as a monument to Gonzagan "modesty." Go figure. With 500 rooms and 15 courtyards, the Palazzo Ducale was constructed from the 14th to the 17th centuries and now houses an impressive collection of antique and Renaissance art. Throughout its history, the palazzo has spread its tentacles in all directions, absorbing all buildings in its path, including the Gothic **Magna Domus** (duomo) and **Palazzo del Capitano.** Look beyond the *duomo's* 18th-century facade to its Romanesque *campanile* and its Gothic side elements.

Begin your tour of the *palazzo* at the **Hall of Dukes,** where evocative sections of Antonio Pisanelli's frescoes (1439-44) were discovered in 1969 under thick layers of plaster. After passing through rooms draped with tapestries created from Raphael's designs, the tour descends upon the Gonzagas's *sala dei fiumi.* Frescoed with vines and flowers, the room looks out on a garden bordered on three sides by a splendid portico. Outside the *palazzo,* signs point to the **Castello di San Giorgio** (1390-1406), the most formidable structure in the complex. Formerly a fortress, the *castello* was later consumed by the *palazzo* and turned into a wing. Inside the *castello,* the **Camera degli Sposi** (Marriage Chamber), contains Andrea Mantegna's famed frescoes of the Gonzaga family (1474) in various positions. Due to their delicate condition, you must call ahead and book an a special viewing tour. Also note the **Galleria degli Specchi** where the premiere of Monteverdi's *Orfeo,* the first modern opera, took place. This early Baroque show was performed solely by men, with some of them, *castratos* (ouch!), playing the female roles. *(From duomo, walk through P. Broletto to V. Accademia, make a right. Walk to P. Dante, and turn left on V. Pomponazzo. Make 1st left, and walk straight into P. Sordello, turn right. Palazzo is on right. Open Tu-Su 8:45am-6:30pm. L12,000/€6.2, EU students L6000/€3.1, over 65 and under 18 free.)*

🏛 TEATRO SCIENTIFICO (BIBIENA). From P. dell'Erbe head to P. Broletto, take V. Accademia until it ends. Welcome to a musical paradise! The theater, one of the only ones in Northern Italy not modeled after Milan's La Scala, preserves its peculiarity in a play of rose and stone grey. The fairy-tale building, with great acoustics, houses separate little balconies with small velvet love couches. Virgil and Pompanazzo are poised on stage watching performances. *(☎0376 32 76 53. Open Tu-Su 9:30am-12:30pm and 3-6pm. L4000/€2.07, students and under 18 or over 60 L2000/€1.03.)*

PALAZZO DEL TE. Built by Giulio Romano in 1534 as a suburban retreat for Federico II Gonzaga and his mistress Isabella, the opulent Palazzo del Te is widely considered the finest building in the Mannerist style. Its rooms demonstrate the late Renaissance fascination with the Roman villa and a willingness to bend the rules of proportion. Idyllic murals of Psyche, remarkable for their vividness and eroticism, line Francesco's banquet hall. Another wing of the palace features regular shows of modern Italian works alongside a collection of Egyptian art. *(☎0376 32 32 66. At far south end of the city down V.P. Amedeo through P. Veneto and down Largo Parri. Open M 1-6pm, Tu-Su 9am-6pm. L12,000/€6.20, students and ages 12-18 L8000/€4.13, under 11 free, groups L7000/€3.62 per person.)*

ROTUNDA DI SAN LORENZO AND CHIESA DI SANT'ANDREA. Piazza dell' Erbe, just south of P. Sordello, opens onto the Chiesa di San Lorenzo. This 11th-century Romanesque structure is also known as "La Matildica" for the powerful noblewoman who bequeathed the rotunda to the pope. *(Open daily 10am-12:30pm and 2:30-4:30pm. Free.)* Opposite the rotunda rises Mantua's most important Renaissance creation, Leon Battista Alberti's **Chiesa di Sant'Andrea** (1472-1594). Its facade combines the classic triumphal arch motif—barrel-vaulted portal and flanking pilasters—with an antique, pedimented temple front. The gargantuan, opaque interior was the first monumental space constructed in the classical style since imperial Rome. The plan served as a prototype for ecclesiastical architecture for the next 200 years. Giorgio Anselmi painted the dome's frescoes. The church's holy relic, a piece of earth supposedly soaked in Christ's blood, parades the streets in a religious procession each Good Friday. The rest of the year the relic of the Precious Blood is kept in a crypt beneath the nave. Undisputed, however, is painter Andrea Mantegna's tomb in the back of the church. *(Open daily 8am-noon and 3-6:30pm. Free.)*

PALAZZO D'ARCO. The highlight of this *palazzo* is Falconetto's extraordinary zodiac chamber, a room with ornate frescoes of the astrological signs. *(Off V. Pitentino. From P. Mantegna, follow V. Verdi, which turns into V. Fernelli. ☎ 0376 32 22 42. Open Mar.-Oct. Tu-Su 10am-12:30pm and 2:30-5:30pm; Nov.-Feb. Sa 10am-12:30pm and 2-5pm, Su 10am-5pm. L5000/€2.58, students L2000/€1.03.)*

CASA DI ANDREA MANTEGNA. The purity of its design and the simplicity of its materials make the Casa di Andrea Mantegna a striking contrast to the surrounding luxurious palaces and academies. Built in 1476, the residence hosts traveling art exhibits. *(V. Acerbi, 47. ☎ 0376 36 05 06. Gallery open for exhibitions M-F 10am-12:30pm and 3-6pm. L5000/€2.58, over 65 and under 16 L3000/€1.55. Free if no exhibitions.)*

♫ ENTERTAINMENT

The **Teatro Sociale di Mantova,** P. Cavallotti (☎ 0376 36 27 39), off C.V. Emanuele, stages operas in October and plays from November through May. Seats start at L20,000/€10.33. The Spazio Aperto series brings dance, music, and cinema events to various *piazze* and *palazzi* around town. Mantua also hosts a chamber music series in April and May. In early September, Italian speakers and scholars should check out **Festivaletteratura,** which attracts hordes of literary scholars.

▓ DAYTRIP FROM MANTUA: SABBIONETA

Sabbioneta is 33km southwest of Mantua and easily accessible by bus from the Mantua bus station (5 per day; in winter 9 per day). ☎ 0375 22 10 44. Tours in English, French, or German L13,000/€6.71, groups L11,000/€5.68 per person. Open Oct.-Mar. Tu-Sa 9:30am-12:30pm and 2:30-5pm, Su 9:30am-12:30pm and 2-6pm; Apr.-Sept. Tu-Sa 9:30am-12:30pm and 2-6pm, Su 9:30am-12:30pm and 2:30-7pm.)

Sabbioneta was founded by Vespasiano Gonzaga (1532-91) in the hopes of creating a paradise; it turned out he had to make due with a simple feudal court. The town earned the title "Little Athens of the Gonzagas" because of its importance as an artistic center in the late Renaissance. Inside the well-preserved 16th-century city walls lie the fascinating Renaissance **Palazzo Ducale, Teatro Olimpico,** and **Palazzo del Giardino.** Take a guided walk through their otherwise inaccessible interiors; the 45-minute tour leaves from the **tourist office,** V. Gonzaga, 31. On the first Sunday of each month, antique *aficionados* arrive in Sabbioneta for the exhaustive **Mercato dell'Antiquariato.** The offices are now divided into three segments: for the Palazzo Ducale, Teatro Olimpico, and Palazzo del Giardino call **Monumenti del XVI Secolo** (☎ 0375 22 10 44); for the **Sinagoga** (☎ 0375 52 039); and for **Museo di Arte Sacra** and the **Chiesa dell Incoronata** call the **Monumenti Religiosi** (☎ 0375 22 02 99).

BERGAMO   ☎ 035

Every city should have a castle in the clouds. This one does. Glimmering in the distance, a medieval city sits on a bluff, presiding over the rest of Bergamo. Palaces, churches, and a huge stone fortification used to defend Venetian-controlled Venice from Spanish-ruled Milan characterize the *città alta* (high city), as do its narrow, cobblestoned streets, shaded by solemn facades. Below, the *città bassa* (low city) is a modern metropolis packed with neoclassical buildings. Home of Italy's oldest operating bar, the proud Atalanta Bergamo (a Serie A team), as well as the best American football team in Italy, Bergamo fuses hundreds of years of heritage in its bustling commercial, artistic, and industrial center.

NORTHWEST ITALY

▎ TRANSPORTATION

Trains: (☎035 24 76 24), in P. Marconi. At the juncture of the Brembana and Seriana valleys. Luggage storage available (p. 110). To: **Brescia** (1hr., every hr. 6:50am-8:40pm, L5600/€2.89); **Cremona** (1½hr., every hr. 8:58am-5:30pm, L8500/€4.39); **Milan** (1hr., every hr. 5:46am-11:02pm, L7200/€3.87). Open daily 6am-8:45pm.

Buses: To right from train station. Buses have flexible times so call to organize times. To: **Como** (☎0312 472 47; 7 per day, L8500/€4.39); **Cremona** (☎0372 272 12; 2-5 per day; L10,200/€5.27); **Milan** (☎02 80 11 61; every 30min., L7500/€3.87).

◼▐ ORIENTATION AND PRACTICAL INFORMATION

The train station, bus station, and numerous budget hotels are in the **città bassa.** There are three ways to reach **città alta:** take bus #1 (L1500/€0.77) to the **funicolare di città alta,** which ascends from **via Vittorio Emanuele** to the Mercato delle Scarpe (8 per hr; L1500/€0.77, free if you're still holding your bus ticket). Bus #1a runs to the "Colle Aperto" stopping at the top of the *città alta.* Or take the stairs on **V. Salita della Scaletta,** which starts to the left of the funicular on V.V. Emanuele. Turn right at the top to enter *città alta* on **via San Giacomo** through Porta San Giacomo (10-15min.) A park-like rim lines the gradual shift from *città alta* to *città bassa,* a transition you will want to prolong.

TOURIST, FINANCIAL, AND LOCAL SERVICES

Tourist Offices: APT, V. Aquila Nera, 2 (☎035 24 22 26; fax 24 29 94; aptbg@apt.bergamo.it; www.apt.bergamo.it), in *città alta.* Take bus #1 or 1a to the funicular, follow V. Gambito to P. Vecchia, and make a fast right at Biblioteca (before you enter P. Vecchia) on V. Aquila Nera; office is 1st door on right. Open daily 9am-12:30pm and 2-5:30pm. In *città bassa:* **APT,** V.V. Emanuele, 20 (☎035 21 02 04 or 21 31 85; fax 23 01 84), facing train station, on your left, in a large pale stone building with an impressive frieze and behind a tall brown gate, and across the street from the Hotel Excelsior San Marco. It is several blocks before the funicular. Open M-F 9am-12:30pm and 2-5:30pm.

Currency Exchange: Banca Nazionale del Lavoro, V. Petrarca, 12 (☎035 23 80 16), off V.V. Emanuele, near P. della Libertà. Good rates. Open M-F 8:30am-1:20pm and 2:45-4:15pm. Also on 2nd floor of the post office. Open M-F 8:30am-5pm.

ATM: Can be found in the train station near the *tabacchi* and outside **Banca Popolare di Milano,** on V.P. Paleocapa off V. Papa Giovanni XXIII.

Money Transfers: World Center Agenti, V. Quarenghi, 37D (☎035 31 31 24; fax 32 13 63), off V. Pietro Paleocapa. Open daily 10:30am-8pm.

Luggage Storage: In train station. L5000/€2.58 per 12hr. Open daily 7am-9pm.

Laundromat: Onda Blue, V.S. Bernardino, 57 (☎0167 86 13 46). Bergamo's other laundry facilities are in the HI hostel (usually reserved for guests), but feel free to take yourself to the cleaners. 2 on V. Giacomo Quarenghi and 1 on V. Borgo Palazzo.

EMERGENCY AND COMMUNICATIONS

Emergency: ☎113. **Ambulance:** ☎118.

First Aid: ☎035 26 91 11; nights and Su ☎035 25 02 46.

Police: V. Galagerio, 25 (☎035 23 82 38).

Hospital: Ospedale Maggiore, Largo Barozzi, 1 (☎035 26 91 11).

Internet Access: For HI hostel guests (L10,000/€5.16 per hr.), or at the **Centro Glovenile e Universitario Diocesano,** V. Pignolo, 73A, in *città bassa.* From Largo Porta Nuova, walk along Gabriele Camozzi, turn left on V. Pignolo, and look for an archway with dark wooden doors on the right. Walk to the end of the entrance hallway and through the doorway on the right. Walk up 2 flights of steps to 1st floor. Enter 2nd door on the left. L3000/€1.55 per hr. Open M-Sa 9am-12:20pm and 3-6:45pm.

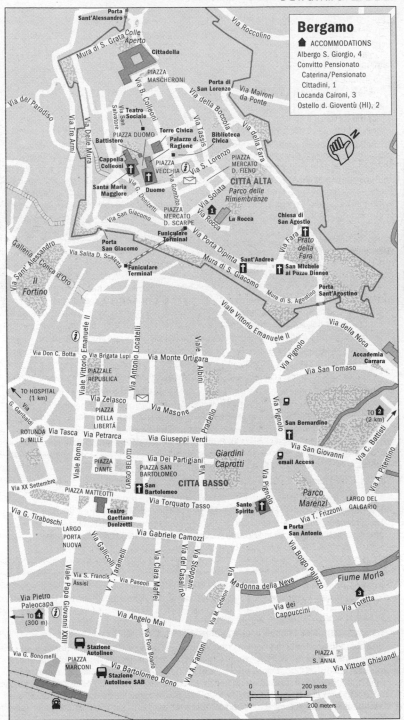

Bergamo

⌂ ACCOMMODATIONS
Albergo S. Giorgio, 4
Convitto Pensionato
  Caterina/Pensionato
  Cittadini, 1
Locanda Caironi, 3
Ostello d. Gioventù (HI), 2

Post Office: V. Locatelli, 11 (☎035 24 32 56). Take V. Zelasco from V.V. Emanuele. Open M-F 8:30am-1:40pm, Sa 8:30-11:40am. Packages are handled at V. Pascoli, 6 (☎035 23 86 98). Same hours.

Postal Code: 24122.

ACCOMMODATIONS

Prices rise with altitude; the most affordable *alberghi* are found in the *città bassa*. The tourist office has information on cheaper *agriturismo* options.

Ostello della Gioventù di Bergamo (HI), V.G. Ferraris, 1 (☎/fax 035 36 17 24; hostelbg@spm.it; www.sottosopra.org/ostello). From train station take #9 bus to Comozzi, then bus #14 to Leonardo da Vinci. From there, walk up the steep but short hill. The building is cast concrete with orange railings. This spacious, well-maintained hostel features satellite TV, outdoor patio areas, and a view of the *città alta* and the surrounding valley that compensates for its distance from the town center. Each dorm has a private full bath. HI members only. Breakfast included. Laundry for guests (L15000/€7.75 for wash, dry, and detergent). Internet access L10,000/€5.16 per hr. Dorms L26,000/€13.43; singles with bath L35,000/€18.08; doubles with bath L60,000/€30.99.

Locanda Caironi, V. Torretta, 6B (☎035 24 30 83). From train station, walk straight ahead (on V. Papa Giovanni XXIII) to V. Angelo Maj, make a right, then continue for several blocks until you reach V. Borgo Palazzo; make a left. Turn right at 2nd block. Accessible by bus #5 or 7 from V. Angelo Maj. A family affair replete with exquisite courtyard. Quiet residential neighborhood. The rooms of the 18th-century building overlook a secluded garden *trattoria*, Bergamo's best-kept culinary secrets. Reservations recommended. Shared bath. Singles L30,000/€15.49; doubles L55,000/€28.40. MC/V.

Albergo S. Giorgio, V.S. Giorgio, 10 (☎035 21 20 43; fax 31 00 72). Bus #7, or a short walk from train station: walk straight on V. Papa Giovanni XXIII to V. Pietro Paleocapa, make a left; this street becomes V.S. Giorgio. Make a left on V. Pietro Paleocapa, which becomes V.S. Giorgio (15min.). Train tracks and a construction site nearby, but relatively quiet inside. Neat, modern rooms with TV, telephone, and sink. Some English spoken. 68 beds. 2 rooms wheelchair accessible. Singles L45,000/€23.34, with bath L70,000/€36.15; doubles L70,000/€36.15, L90,000/€46.48. DC/MC/V.

Convitto Pensionato Caterina Cittadini, V. Rocca, 10 (☎035 24 39 11), off P. Mercato delle Scarpe (V. Rocca is the small narrow street on right after exiting top of the funicular) in *città alta*. Women only. The orange-hued walls of this *pensione* give a warm glow to the open-air courtyard and sunlit rooftop terraces. The nuns in charge are happy to give foreigners a home, although little English is spoken. Reception on the 2nd floor. Breakfast and dinner included. Curfew 10pm; if going out later, ask for a key. Singles L60,000/€30.99, with bath L65,000/€33.56; doubles L100,000/€51.65.

FOOD

Casonsei, meat-filled ravioli dishes, are a typical *primo* in Bergamo, while the *branzi* and *taleggio* cheeses are part of a traditional *formaggio* course that concludes the meal. Try them with the local Valcalepio red and white wines. The typical meal includes polenta, a staple dish made from corn meal and water, usually served with various condiments. Streets in the *città alta* are lined with *pasticcerie* selling yellow polentina confections, topped with chocolate blobs intended to resemble birds. These sweet treats are primarily pricey tourist bait; many natives have never sampled one. For meal necessities, shop at **Compra Bene Supermercati**, on the right side of V.V. Emanuele, past the *città bassa* tourist office at the bottom of the hill heading to the *città alta*. (Open M 8:30am-1pm, Tu-Sa 8:30am-8pm. MC/V). Most Bergamese shops are closed Monday mornings.

CITTÀ BASSA

Capolinea Bar and Ristorante, V. Giacomo Quarenghi, 29 (☎035 32 09 81), From train station, make a fast left onto V. Geremia Bonomelli, walk 2 blocks, then turn right onto V. G. Quarenghi. A favorite among Bergamo's 20 somethings, this modern establishment has a lively bar in front and a more tranquil garden in back. Many vegetarian options. Full meal from L15,000/€7.75, large salads from L4500/€2.32. Open Tu-Sa 6:30pm-3am, Su 7pm-3am. Kitchen open until midnight.

Trattoria Casa Mia, V.S. Bernardino, 20 (☎035 22 06 76), From train station walk straight ahead to Porta Nuova. Turn left on V.G. Tiraboschi, which becomes V. Zambonate. Then turn left onto V. Bernadino. Full "home-style" meal with *primo* (mostly the house specialty, Bergameschi polenta), *secondo, contorno,* and drink for L20,000/€10.33 (L16,000/€8.26 for lunch). Open M-Sa noon-3:30pm and 6pm-midnight. Closed 1 week middle of Aug. Kitchen closes 10pm.

CITTÀ ALTA

Relax after a day of sightseeing in one of the *città alta's* many *vinerie.* A short hop from P. Vecchia, **Pasticceria Cafe Al Donizetti,** V. Gombito, 17 (☎035 24 26 61), features a mouth-watering selection of cheeses, Italian sausages, wines (400!), and cold meats, as well as a lovely outdoor seating area. If the weather is not cooperating, head to **Vineria Cozzi,** V.B. Colleoni, 22 (☎035 23 88 36). The romantic Venetian alcove behind the bar will soothe your aches and leave you with a smile. At either venue, a good bottle of wine sells for L9-12,000/€4.65-6.20.

Circolino Cooperativa Città Alta, V.S. Agata, 19 (☎035 21 57 41 or 22 58 76). Left out of P. Vecchia (when looking at the white marble Biblioteca). Walk down V. Colleoni. Right on V. Agata; a sign above signals where to turn. This former prison and church is now an airy garden cafe, with lush arbors consumed by vines, and a soul-satisfying vista of the surrounding mountains dotted with villas. One of the best values in *città alta*. Play billiards, pinball, and *bocce.* Sandwiches, pizza, and salads under L8000/€4.13. Cover L1000/€0.52. Open Th-Tu 8:30am-3am, W 11:30am-3am. MC/V.

Papageno Pub, V. Colleoni, 1b (☎035 23 66 24). At P. Vecchia, just left of the Biblioteca (white marble building with pillars). 1st place on right, past Ristorante Sole, on the corner. Crowds are hooked on the drinks, but the pub also has light but filling sandwiches and salads. Widest selection of Belgian beers in Italy (188). F-W 7pm-2am.

Ratzmatatz, V. Gombito, 10 (☎035 24 15 89). Artsy salads with cute little mozzarella balls from L10,000/€5.16. *Panini* L5-9000/€2.58-4.65; *primi* L10,000/€5.16; desserts L4-6000/€2.07-3.09. Open daily 7:30pm-2am. AmEx/DC/MC/V.

Trattoria Tre Torri, P. Mercato del Fieno, 7a (☎035 24 43 66), left off V. Gombito when heading away from P. Vecchia. Corner eatery has cute tables in its tiny, vaulted, stone interior. Serves substantial dishes without pretense. Romantic outside seating on cobblestone patio May-Sept. Try the house specialty *foiaole con porcini* (L12,000/€6.20). *Menù* (includes *primo, secondo,* and wine) L35,000/€18.08. Cover L2000/€1.03. Open Th-Tu noon-4pm and 7:30pm-12:30am. Reservations recommended. MC/V.

⊚ SIGHTS

CITTÀ BASSA

The newer of the two cities, situated at the base of the bluff, Città Bassa compensates for its lack of ancient ruins with its Galleria Dell'Accademia Carrara, which brims with some of Italy's most important artworks.

■ **GALLERIA DELL'ACCADEMIA CARRARA.** Housed in a glorious Neoclassical palace, this is one of the most important art galleries in Italy. Fifteen rooms display canvasses by the Dutch School and Bergameschi greats like Fra' Galgario, as well as canvases by Boticelli *(Ritratto di Giuliano de Medici)*, Lotto *(Ritratto di Giovinetto)*, Tiepolo, Titian, Rubens, Brueghel, Bellini,

Mantegna, Goyen, van Dyck, and El Greco. There are several pieces by Rizzi (in gallery VI), including a diptych: *Madalena in Meditazione*, which finds the Virgin looking upon a crucified Christ while trying to hold up her shirt; and, in *Madalena Penitente*, still intent on the cross, she covers her breasts with a Bible. The Rizzis are beside several Lottos, including *Nozze Mistiche di Santa Caterina*. Gallery IX is dominated by the works of Moroni. The works start with 13th-century Gothic art and are especially strong on humanistic Florentine culture. *(From Largo Porta Nuova, take V. Camozzi to V. Pignolo, turn left to V. San Tomaso, then right. ☎ 035 39 96 40. Open W-M 9:30am-12:30pm and 2:30-5:30pm. L10,000/ €5.16, over 65 and under 18 free. Su. free.)*

OTHER SIGHTS. Piazza Matteotti in the heart of the *città bassa* is a favorite meeting place for both tourists and native *passeggiatori*. It was redesigned by the Fascists in 1924. In the **Chiesa di San Bartolomeo,** at the far right of the *piazza*, you will find a superb altarpiece of the Madonna and Child by Lorenzo Lotto. *(Open daily 9am-4pm. Free.)* To the right of San Bartolomeo, V. Tasso leads to the **Chiesa del Santo Spirito,** marked by its strangely sculpted facade. The fine Renaissance interior (1521) houses paintings by famous dead Italians. On the left, V. Pignolo connects the lower city to the upper, winding past a succession of handsome 16th- to 18th-century palaces. Along the way is the tiny **Chiesa di San Bernardino,** whose colorful interior pales behind a splendid painting by Lotto. *(Open W-Th 10am-1pm. Free.)*

CITTÀ ALTA

The *città alta*, perched above the modern city, is a wonderfully preserved medieval town with a fountain, panoramic view, and archway around every corner. The town is accessible by funicular, bus, and foot. From the Carrara gallery, the terraced V. Noca ascends from the lower city to Porta S. Agostino, a 16th-century gate built by the Venetians as a fortification. After passing through the gate, V. Porta Dipinta leads to V. Gombito, which ends in the Piazza Vecchia.

■ **BASILICA DI SANTA MARIA MAGGIORE.** Despite a dim, stark Romanesque exterior, this 12th-century basilica, joined to the Cappella Colleoni, possesses a breathtakingly elaborate and bright Baroque interior. Lavish, iridescent ceilings frame dark paintings beneath an octagonal dome. Tapestries of various biblical stories sheet several walls. Within stands the Victorian tomb of the 19th-century composer Gaetano Donizetti, Bergamo's most famous son. *(Left of Cappella Colleoni. ☎ 035 22 33 27. Open May-Sept. M-F 9am-noon and 3-6pm, Sa-Su 8-10:30am and 3-6pm; Oct.-Apr. M-F 9am-noon and 3-4:30pm, Sa-Su 8-10:30am and 3-6pm. Free.)*

■ **CAPPELLA COLLEONI.** The patterned, pastel, marble facade of this chapel was designed in 1476 by G.A. Amadeo (also responsible for Certosa di Pavia) as a tomb and chapel for the celebrated Bergameschi mercenary hired for Venice's Bartolomeo Colleoni. Notable are the 18th-century ceiling frescoes by Tiepolo surrounded by Colleoni's sarcophagus. Look up as you exit for a gruesome decapitation of John the Baptist. *(Head through archway flanking P. Vecchia to reach the P. del Duomo. The Cappella is to the right; the doorway beneath the white marble facade. Open Tu-Su Mar.-Oct. 9am-12:30pm and 2-6:30pm; Nov.-Feb. 9am-12:30pm and 2:30-4:30pm. Free.)*

PIAZZA VECCHIA. This *piazza* houses a majestic ensemble of medieval and Renaissance buildings flanked by restaurants and cafes in the heart of the *città alta*. Rest your legs as you sit with the locals on the steps of the white marble **Biblioteca Civica** (1594), repository of Bergamo's rich collection of manuscripts. Across the *piazza* is the massive Venetian Gothic **Palazzo della Ragione** (Courts of Justice, 1199) and a 300-year-old sundial (on the ground beneath the arched portico.) To the right, connected to the *palazzo* by a 16th-century covered stairway, stands the 12th-century ■**Torre Civica** (Civic Tower). The view from the top is worth the climb, but protect your eardrums; despite the traditional 10pm curfew, the 15th-century bell rings every half hour throughout the night. *(Open daily Apr.-Sept. 9am-noon and 2-8pm. L2000/€1.03, under 18 and over 65 L1000/€0.52.)*

BAPTISTERY. This octagonal structure, in white and red stone, just to the left of the Cappella in P. Duomo, holds several small white marble relief depictions of Jesus's life. The baptistery is a reconstruction of its 14th-century predecessor that was once a part of the basilica. *(Between Cappella Colleoni and the Basilica.)*

CHIESA DI SAN MICHELE AL POZZO BIANCO. Built during the 12th and 13th centuries, the Romanesque interior is embellished with colorful frescoes by Lotto. *(Near the intersection of V. P. Dipinta and V. Osmano. ☎ 035 25 12 33. Open Su-F 9am-12:15pm and 2:45-4:45pm. Closed W mornings. Call ahead for big groups.)*

PARCO DELLE RIMEMBRANZE. Once the site of a Roman military camp, this park's shady paths are dedicated to Italian battle casualties, but are currently inhabited by a less fearsome invading army: the youth of Bergamo. Climb **La Rocca,** the distinguished fort that stands in the middle of the park; it provides a stunning panoramic view of the Po Valley and what might be the best vista for watching the *città alta*. *(At the end of V. Solata. Free. Entrance to LaRocca L2000/€1.03.)*

🎵 ENTERTAINMENT

The arts thrive in Bergamo. The opera season lasts from September to November and is followed from November through April by the drama season, featuring performances by Italy's most prestigious companies at the **Donizetti Theater,** P. Cavour, 15, in the *città bassa*. If you call in advance, the staff may grant requests to view the theatre. (☎ 035 416 06 02) In May and June, the spotlight falls on the highly acclaimed **Festivale Pianistico Internazionale,** co-hosted by the city of Brescia. In September, Bergamo celebrates its premier native composer with a festival of Gaetano Donizetti's lesser-known works. For more information, contact the tourist office or the theater at P. Cavour, 14 (☎ 035 24 96 31). During summer, the tourist office provides a program of free events, *Viva La Tua Città*.

The *città alta* transforms at night. Though many locals head to discos in surrounding towns, masses of 20-somethings pack the eateries, pubs, and *vinerie* to socialize. Head down to ▧**Pozzo Bianco,** V. Porta Dipinta, 30B; going up will be easier after a few good beers. A *birreria* with a kitchen and character is by far the liveliest hangout for local youth. (☎ 035 24 76 94. Open daily 7am-3pm and 6pm-3am. AmEx/MC/V.) Also try one of 50 types of whiskey and rum at **Pub dell'Angelo,** V.S. Lorenzo, 4A. (☎ 035 22 21 88. Open daily 10:30am-3pm and 7pm-2am.)

BRESCIA ☎030

The character of Brescia can best be seen from afar, and in the afternoon sun, when the glass of the high rises reflects the green of the *duomo*, the red terracotta roofs of the residential districts, and the skeletons of the Roman ruins in the centro storico in a cacophony of Italian color. The city once owed its prosperity to the estates of wealthy aristocrats but now lives off the lire from far less glamorous exports: Beretta weaponry and sink fixtures. But the soul of this industrial town, surprisingly, is its thriving fashion industry. Reminiscent of smaller, less glamorous Milan, the streets are illuminated with names like Ferragamo and Versace.

🚆 TRANSPORTATION

Trains: Brescia lies between Milan and Verona on the Torino-Trieste line. Luggage storage available (p. 116). To: **Bergamo** (1hr., 10 per day 5:25am-11:13pm, L5500/€2.84); **Cremona** (1¾hr., 11 per day 6:29am-9:25pm, L6300/€3.25); **Milan** (1hr.; every hr. 5:55am-11:38pm; L13,100/€6.77); **Padua** (1¾hr.; every hr. 6:15am-9:13pm; L20,200/€10.43); **Venice** (2¼hr.; every hr. 4:13-9:13pm; L25,200/€13.01); **Verona** (45min., 10 per day 7:23am-1:34am, L6100/€3.15); **Vicenza** (1¼hr.; every hr. 6:15am-9:13pm; L13,800/€7.13). Info office (☎ 147 888 088) open 7am-9pm.

Buses: (☎030 449 15). Bus station is to your right as you exit train station. Painted bright orange. Brescia is the main point of departure for buses to the western shores of Lake Garda. Eastbound buses leave from this station. To: **Cremona** (1¼hr., every hr. 6:30am-6:55pm, L7900/€4.08); **Mantua** (1½hr., every hr. 5:45am-7:15pm; L9500/€4.91); **Verona** (2¼hr.; every hr. 6:45am-6:15pm; L10,300/€5.32). Westbound buses leave from the **SAIA** station (☎030 377 42 37), to left as you exit train station. To **Milan** (1¾hr.; 8:32am-6:32pm; L12,000/€6.20). Ticket office open M-F 7am-12:30pm and 1:30-6:25pm, Sa 7am-12:30pm and 1:30-3:10pm.

Taxis: (☎030 351 11). 24hr.

✦🗹 ORIENTATION AND PRACTICAL INFORMATION

The city's architectural gems are concentrated in the rectangular *centro storico*, bounded by **via XX Settembre** on the south, **via dei Mille** on the west, **via Pusterla** on the north, and **V. F. Turati** on the east. From the **Piazza della Repubblica,** turn right on **C. M. della Libertà** to **C. Palestro.** Turn left on **V. 10 Giornate** to **P. Loggia,** where you turn left to the **Piazza Tito Speri.** From here **via dei Musei** slopes down to "museum row" and the Roman archaeological site. **Via del Castello** leads to the castle.

Tourist Office: APT, C. Zanardelli, 34 (☎030 434 18; fax 375 64 50; aptbs@ferriani.com; www.bresciaholiday.com), an inconspicuous office set off street, next to cinema, Across street from Teatro Grande, few doors to the left, when facing away from the building. Office is inset in small plaza on the back right. English spoken. Helpful event fliers, maps, and walking guides. Open M-F 9am-12:30pm and 3-6pm, Sa 9am-12:30pm. **City Tourist Office,** P. Loggia, 6 (☎030 240 03 57; www.comune.brescia.it). Open Oct.-Mar. M-F 9:30am-12:30pm and 2-5pm, Sa 9:30am-12:30pm; Apr.-Sept. M-Sa 9:30am-6:30pm.

Paragliding school: Brixia Flying, V.S. Zeno, 117 (☎030 242 20 94; www.spidernet.it/bresciafly).

Car Rental: Avis, V. XX Settembre, 2f (☎030 29 54 74). **Europcar Italia,** V. Stazione, 49 (☎030 280 487). **Hertz,** V. XXV Aprile, 4c (☎030 45 32).

Luggage Storage: In train station. L7500/€3.87. Open 10am-8pm. Self storage also available, starting at L4000 for 24hr.

Emergency: ☎113. **Police:** ☎112. **First Aid:** ☎118.

Hospital: Ospedale Civile, ☎030 399 51.

Internet Access: Telecom Italia, V. Moretto, 46. One computer for free public use. **Black Rose,** V.Cattaneo, 22/A (☎030 280 7704). Two computers in a cozy bar. L10,000/€5.16 per hr. Open M-Sa 7am-midnight.

Bank: Banco di Brescia. C. Zanardelli, 54. Two **ATM**s face the street (just to left of tourist office). M-F 8:25am-1:25pm and 2:40-4:10pm; ATMs 24hr.

Post Office: P. Vittoria, 1 (☎030 444 21). Open M-F 8:15am-5:30pm, Sa 8:15am-1pm. **Postal Code:** 25100.

🛏 ACCOMMODATIONS

Brescia's lodgings are reasonably priced, but they fill up before the weekend in summer. Call a week ahead. Ask at the tourist office about *agriturismo* options.

Albergo San Marco, V. Spalto, 15 (☎030 304 55 41). From station take V. Foppa and turn right onto V. XX Settembre and walk several blocks. Take next left on V. Romanino (a very short block) and turn right onto V.V. Emanuele, which continues to the hotel. 7 simple and stuffy rooms. Busy street, which means plenty of noise, but also excellent bus service. Breakfast L3000/€1.55. Bath separate. Singles L38,000/€19.63; doubles L63,000/€32.54. AmEx/DC/MC/V.

Albergo Regine, C. Magenta, 14 (☎030 375 78 81; fax 454 00). From V. Emanuele, make a left onto V. Cavour, then a left onto V. Magenta; hotel is on your left. A wood-finished lobby leads to 30 spotless and quiet rooms. A small door leads through hall to a hotel with good food smells and a lobby lit naturally. There is a TV in a shared living room area, and telephone in every room. Breakfast included. Singles without bath L60,000/€31.00; doubles with bath L110,000/€56.81.

Albergo Stazione, V. Stazione, 15-17 (☎030 377 46 14; fax 377 39 95). From station, make a sharp left down a small alley; it is near the end on your left. A 2min. walk from the station down an alley. 36 clean rooms with phone and TV. At night, women should exercise caution in this area. TV, telephone, A/C. Singles L55,000/€28.41, with bath L75,000/€38.73; doubles L80,000/€41.32, with bath 110,000/€56.81. MC/V.

◐ FOOD

Whatever and wherever you choose to eat, be sure to sample some of the local wines. *Tocai di San Martino della Battaglia* (a dry white wine), *groppello* (a medium red), and *botticino* (a dry red of medium age) are all favorites in Brescia and beyond. There is a street market for everything on Saturday mornings at P. Loggia. For inexpensive staples, seek out the open-air vendors in P. Mercato. (Open Tu-F 8:30am-6pm, M and Sa mornings.) **Supermercato PAM,** V. Porcellaga, 26, is on a continuation of C.M. della Libertà. (Open M 2-8pm, Tu-Sa 9am-8pm.)

▩ **Ristorante/Pizzeria Cavour,** C. Cavour, 56 (☎030 240 09 00). Take V. Emanuele to V. Cavour (make a left); the bar is a few doors down on left. Fish tank at the door, patio tables, and bright yellow tablecloths complement the great pizza and pasta dishes. Try the *pizza cavour* with tomatoes, mozzarella, *pancetta,* and basil. Pizza from L7000/ €3.62; *primi* L8-13,000/€4.13-6.71; large assortment of *dolci* (sweets) L4000/ €2.07. Cover L3000/€1.55. Open W-M 11am-3pm and 6:30pm-1am. DC/V.

▩ **Bar Code,** P. Paulo Sesto VII 24. P.P. Sesto, 24 (☎030 377 17 12), just across from the *duomo.* The local place to be seen. Inside, a trendy black and white interior—outside, seating with a view of the castle. Eat your *panini* (starting at L6000/€3.1) on the fountain steps while locals show off their motorbikes. Happy hour daily 11am-1pm and again from 6pm-8pm (L5000/€2.58 min) Open Tu-Sa 7:30am-2am, Su 9:30am-2am.

Trattoria il Muretto, V. Antiche Mura, 5 (☎030 28 00 77), off V. Mazzini. Red-checked tablecloths and constantly crooning Italian pop radio characterize this typical tavern. Outside tables on quiet street. As an *antipasto,* help yourself to the *buffet di verdure* (L7000/€3.62), colorful plates of vegetables simmered in olive oil. *Primi* from L7000/ €3.62; *secondi* L10,000/€5.16. Open Tu-Sa noon-3pm and 7-11pm, M noon-2:30pm.

Ristorante San Marco, V. Spalto S. Marco, 15 (☎030 304 55 41). By Albergo San Marco. The wooden ceiling-beams and whitewashed walls create a cheerful atmosphere. Huge *primi* from L12,000/€6.20; *secondi* from L18000/€4.13. Cover L3000/ €1.55. Open daily noon-2:30pm and 7:30-10pm. Closed Su and M at 4pm.

◷ SIGHTS

DUOMO NUOVO AND ▩ROTONDA. The Brescians were not content with only one *duomo,* so they built two. The new and the old, or the *grande* and the *piccolo,* stand in intimate competition in the adjacent facades of **Duomo Nuovo** (1604-1825) and the **Rotonda** (old *duomo*), also called Cathedral of Santa Maria Assunta. The more recent partner is a gargantuan Rococo structure with Corinthian columns and the third highest dome in Italy. The detail here is almost entirely sculptural; there is very little color, and only a few paintings. The 11th-century *rotonda* is a simple Romanesque structure with a squat, round tower, a pointed tile roof, and a unique interior reminiscent of a secret and spooky temple below ground. All that remains of the 8th-century basilica formerly occupying this spot is the crypt of S. Filastrio. *(In P. Paolo IV, a.k.a. P. Duomo. From P. della Vittoria, take path through the archways and under clocktower. Proper clothing necessary. Old Duomo, Apr.-Oct. 9am-noon and 3-7pm. Closed M. New Duomo (rotunda) open daily 7:30am-noon and 4-7pm.)*

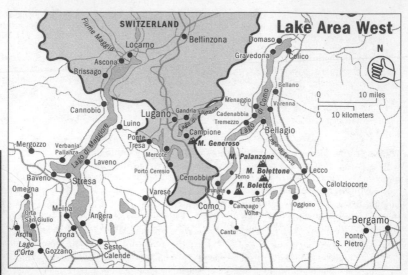

TEATRO GRANDE. A true pearl of Brescia, this Baroque theater glitters with gold *stuccato* ornamentations set off by red seats and carpet. Bresciani claim that it is aesthetically superior to Milan's La Scala. Check out the adjacent glamorous *ridotto*. This truly is a mecca. *(C. Zanardeli, 9. From P.della Vittoria go down V. Gramsci 2 blocks and take a left on C. Zanardeli. ☎ 030 297 9311. Visits only with reservations. Currently closed for restoration with no date posted for reopening.)*

PIAZZA DELLA LOGGIA. From C. Palestro, a window-shopping heaven, walk to the Fascist-built P. della Vittoria. Continue past the enormous post office to P. della Loggia, built when Venice ruled the city. On one side of the *piazza* stands the **Torre dell'Orologio,** modeled after the tower in Venice's P. San Marco (p. 217). The tower comes complete with an astronomic clock decorated with suns and stars; two little fellows stand poised to ring a bell. Across from the tower, the Renaissance **loggia** (arcade) houses lesser-known paintings from the 16th century.

PINACOTECA TOSIO-MARTINENGO. The Pinacoteca is one of Brescia's principal artistic attractions. This unadorned, 22-room *palazzo* displays a fine collection of works by Bresciani masters (notably Moretto), as well as Raphael's *Cristo Benedicente*. The collection is enriched with works by Ferramola, Savoldo, Romanino, Gambara, Ceruti, Veneziano, Clouet, Foppa, and Lotto. *(From P. della Loggia go down south to P. Vittoria to V. A. Gramsci. Turn left on V. Moretto and the Pinacoteca is at end of street. Enter through center of the piazza (behind statue). Open T-Su 10am-5pm. L5000/€2.58.)*

TEMPIO CAPITOLINO. Fragments of Brescia's classical roots are sprinkled on V. dei Musei. The Roman colony of Brixia lies buried beneath the overgrown greenery in the **Piazza del Foro.** Between the large, dark buildings stand the remaining pieces of Emperor Vespasian's vast Tempio Capitolino. Currently closed for renovation, the temple is nonetheless visible from behind the gates. *(From P. Paolo VI, with your back to the duomo, take V. Mazzini to the left, and turn right on V. dei Musei.)*

MUSEO DELLA CITTA. This former monastery, Monasterio di San Salvatore e Santa Giulia, served as the final retreat for Charlemagne's ex-wife Ermengarda and now houses artistic and archeological representations of the history of Brescia. The museum's Oratorio de S. Maria in Solario displays a bronze *Winged Victory* and the precious 8th-century *Cross of Desiderius*, encased in silver, jewels, and cameos. *(On V. dei Musei, a few paces farther down from the Tempio Capitolino. Open June-Sept. Sa-Th 10am-8pm, F 10am-10pm; Oct.-May Tu-Su 9:30am-5:30pm.)*

♫ ENTERTAINMENT

Most of Brescia's high-brow cultural events occur in the splendor of the Teatro Grande. The annual **Stagione di Prosa,** a series of dramatic performances, runs from December to April. From April to June, the focus shifts to the **Festivale Pianistico Internazionale,** co-hosted by nearby Bergamo. The Brescia Jazz Festival takes place in June (☎ 030 406 36; ellisse@ellisse.it). From June through September, the city hosts an open air cinema, concerts of various sorts, dance recitals, and opera; find schedules at the tourist office, or call ☎ 035 377 11 11 for more information.

THE LAKE COUNTRY

For years, Stendhal's drippiest descriptions of lakes, flowers, and mountains lulled even the worst insomniacs to sleep. Alas! You too will ooze florid prose when you visit the author's place of inspiration, the Italian Lake Country. Don't worry, you'll be in good company: Even less effusive writers, such as Nietzsche, Wordsworth, and Hesse have retreated into the serenity of the lake shore, where clear water laps at the foot of the encircling mountains. Every summer the lakes's varied personalities beckon droves of tourists. A young, mostly German crowd descends upon the more affordable Lake Garda, with watersports by day and a thriving club scene by night. Only an hour north of Milan by train, Lake Como produces the silk sported by sophisticated Milanese, who have in turn lent their urbane influence the lake's southern transportation hub, the thriving city of Como. Long a playground for the rich and famous, Lake Como's mountainous shoreline also harbors well-run (and pleasingly inexpensive) hostels. Palatial luxury hotels dot Lake Maggiore's sleepy shores, where the tourism is the least obtrusive and the scenery the most tranquil, and romance abounds in the Borromean Islands, renowned for their fantastic palaces, exotic gardens, and wandering white peacocks.

> ### HIGHLIGHTS OF THE LAKE COUNTRY
>
> **JUMP** into Villa D'Este's floating lake pool in **Cernobbio** (p. 123).
>
> **IDLE AWAY** an afternoon on the tranquil shores of **Lago Maggiore** (p. 128) or take a bike trip around any of the lakes.
>
> **STRUT** with peacocks in the exotic gardens of the **Borromean Islands** (p. 132).

LAKE COMO (LAGO DI COMO)

Though an unworldly aura lingers over the northern reaches of Europe's deepest lake (410m), Lake Como is not a figment of your imagination. Bougainvillea and other lavish villas adorn Lake Como's backdrop, warmed by the sun and cooled by lakeside breezes. Three long lakes form the forked Lake Como, joined at the three towns of Centro Lago: Bellagio, Menaggio, and Varenna. These towns make for an even more relaxing stay than their more industrial neighbor. Villages cover the dense green slopes—drop your baggage, hop on a bus or ferry, and step off whenever a villa, castle, garden, vineyard, restaurant, or small town beckons.

Como, the largest city on the lake, makes an ideal transportation hub. Trains from Milan and Venice service the town (see below). From Como, take the C-10 bus near Ferrovia Nord to Menaggio or Domaso, on the northern lake shore (1hr., last bus at 8:30pm, L4900/€2.53). Hourly C-30 buses also serve Bellagio (1hr., last bus at 8:14pm, L5200/€2.70). If you prefer to splurge, take the romantic boat trip from Como's P. Cavour to any of these towns. Varenna and Menaggio are alternate bases for exploring the lake. From Milan, take a train to Varenna (dir: "Sondrio") and then a ferry to your town of choice. From Lugano, take Italian bus C-12 to Menaggio (1hr., last bus 6:46pm). A day pass, good for boat travel throughout the center lake district, costs L18,000/€9.30.

COMO   ☎ 031

Situated on the southwest tip of the lake, at the receiving end of the Milan rail line, Como is the lake's token semi-industrial town, where Allessandro Volta was born and where Terragni has immortalized his Fascist architecture. Famous for silk manufacturing, the town has maintained the languorous atmosphere of the smaller lake towns, while catering to the fast-paced, stylish needs of the Milanese. Impeccably dressed businesspeople and fast scooters cruise the streets, but perhaps that is what makes Como so livable: tourism has not taken front seat as in the other lake towns. While swimmers should head up the lake for cleaner waters, Como is a fine staging area for excellent hiking. After dinner, the city migrates to the waterfront for a *passeggiata* among the wisteria of the 18th-century villas.

▐▌ TRANSPORTATION

Trains: Stazione San Giovanni (☎0147 88 80 88). Ticket window open daily 6:40am-8:25pm. To **Milan** Centrale (1hr., every 30min. 4:45am-10:13pm, L9400/€4.85) and **Venice** S. Lucia (4hr.; every hr. 4:45am-7:55pm; L41,300/€21.33) via **Milan. Ferrovia Nord (Como Nord)** (☎031 30 48 00), by P. Matteotti, serves Stazione Nord (Cadorna) in **Milan** (1hr., 2 per hr. 5am-10:35pm, L7200/€3.72), via in **Saronno** (L3800/€1.96). Luggage storage available (p. 121).

Buses: SPT (☎031 24 72 47), on P. Matteotti. Ticket office open daily 6am-8:15pm. Info booth open M-F 8am-noon and 2-6pm, Sa 8am-noon. To: **Bellagio** (1hr., every hr. 6:25am-8:12pm, L4400/€2.72); **Bergamo** (2hr., every hr. 6:50am-7:40pm, L8300/€4.30); **Domaso** (2hr., every hr. 7:10am-8:30pm, L9200/€4.75); **Gravedona** (2hr., every hr. 7:10am-6:40pm, L6900/€3.56); **Menaggio** (1hr., every hr. 7:10am-10:30pm, L4700/€2.43).

Ferries: Navigazione Lago di Como (☎031 57 92 11). Departs daily to all lake towns from the piers along Lungo Lario Trieste in front of P. Cavour. One-way L2400-14,200/€1.24-7.33. Pick up the booklet *Orario* for a complete listing of departures, including night service in the summer.

Public Transportation: Tickets at *tabacchi*, bus station, or the hostel (L1500/€0.77).

Taxis: Radio Taxi (☎031 26 15 15).

Bike Rental: Montagna Sport (☎031 24 08 21), on V. Regina rents mountain bikes for L40,000/€20.66 per day. Ask about multi-day discounts. Open 9:30am-12:30pm and 2:30-7pm. The **hostel** rents mountain bikes for L20,000/€10.33 per day.

◢⚠ ORIENTATION AND PRACTICAL INFORMATION

From Como's **Stazione San Giovanni,** head down the stairs, straight ahead, and through the little park. Take **via Fratelli Ricchi** on your left and then take a right on **Viale Fratelli Rosselli,** which turns into **Lungo Lario Trento** winding its way around the mouth of the lake toward the main square, **Piazza Cavour.** To get to the commercial center from P. Cavour, take **via Plinio** to **Piazza Duomo,** where it becomes **via Vittorio Emanuele.** To reach the **bus station** and **Stazione Ferrovia Nord** near P. Matteotti, turn right when facing the lake from P. Cavour.

TOURIST, FINANCIAL, AND LOCAL SERVICES

Tourist Office: P. Cavour, 16 (☎031 26 97 12; fax 24 01 11; lakecomo@tin.it; www.lakecomo.com), in the largest lakeside *piazza* near the ferry dock. Maps and extensive info. Ask for hiking info. Helpful multilingual staff also checks hotel availability. Open M-Sa 9am-1pm and 2:30-6pm.

Currency Exchange: Banca Nazionale del Lavoro, P. Cavour, 33 (☎031 31 31), across from the tourist office, has dependable rates and a 24hr. **ATM.** Open M-F 8:20am-1:20pm and 2:30-4pm. Currency exchange also available at the tourist office, train station, and post office.

Luggage storage: At Ferrovia Nord train station. L7500/€3.87 for 12hr. Open daily 6am-8pm.

Swimming Pool: Lido Villa Olmo (☎031 57 08 71), on V. per Cernobbio. Large lawn area for sunbathing and a sandy stretch below. Tops not required, but bathing caps are. 3 pools, including one for kids. L9000/€4.65, tickets bought at youth hostel only L5000/€2.58. Open daily 9:30am-7pm.

EMERGENCY AND COMMUNICATIONS

Emergency: ☎113. **Ambulance:** ☎118. **Police:** ☎112.

Late-Night Pharmacy: Farmacia Centrale, V. Plinio, 1 (☎031 42 04), off P. Cavour. Open Tu-Su 8:30am-12:30pm and 3:30-7:30pm. Lists of pharmacies with night service posted.

Hospitals: Ospedale Valduce, V. Dante, 11 (☎031 32 41 11). **Ospedale Sant'Anna,** V. Napoleana, 60 (☎031 58 51 11).

Internet Access: Bar Black Panther, V. Garibaldi, 59 (☎031 26 65 35). From P. Cavour walk through V. Fontana to P. Volta and take V. Garibaldi straight ahead. L6000/€3.1 per hr. Open Tu-Su 7am-11:30pm. **Como Bar,** V. Volta, 51 (☎031 26 20 51). L8000/€4.13 per hr. Open Tu-Su 8am-11pm.

Post Office: V.T. Gallio, 4 (☎031 277 30 20). Open M-Sa 8:15am-6pm. Fermo Posta at the side entrance on the left. Another **branch** at V.V. Emanuele II, 99 (☎031 26 02 10), in town center. Open M-F 8:10am-5:30pm, Sa 8:10am-1pm.

Postal Code: 22100.

▗ ACCOMMODATIONS

▓ **In Riva al Lago,** P. Matteotti, 4 (☎031 30 23 33), behind bus stop. Centrally located. 25 modern, immaculate rooms, all with phone. English spoken. Internet L2000/€1.03 per hr. Breakfast L4000/€2.07. Laundry service L5000/€2.58. Reserve ahead. Singles L45,000/€23.24, with bath and TV L75,000/€38.73; doubles L70,000/€36.15, L90-100,000/€46.48-51.65. Flats available for 2-11 people. AmEx/DC/MC/V.

Ostello Villa Olmo (HI), V. Bellinzona, 2 (☎/fax 031 57 38 00; hostellocomo@tin.it), behind Villa Olmo. From Stazione S. Giovanni, turn left and walk 20min. down V. Borgo Vico. Or take bus #1, 6, or 11 to Villa Olmo (L1500/€0.77). Lively, fun, and down-to-earth. Run by wonderful, multilingual staff. Offers a bar, bag lunches (L10,000/€5.16), incredible dinners (L17,000/€8.78), and discounts on assorted tickets. Crowded rooms come with personal locker and sheets. Breakfast included. Self-service laundry L6000/€3.10; ironing L1000/€0.52. Lockout 10am. Strict curfew 11:30pm. Reserve ahead. Open daily Mar-Nov. 7-10am and 4-11:30pm. Dorms L21,000/€10.85.

Protezione della Giovane (ISJGIF), V. Borgovico, 182 (☎031 57 43 90 or 57 35 40), on the way to the youth hostel, on right side. Take bus #1, 6, or 11. Run by nuns; 18+ women only. 52 clean rooms, with crucifixes everywhere. Free kitchen use. Laundry L4000/€2.07 per load. Curfew 10:30pm. Singles or doubles L24,000/€12.39 per person, L20,000/€10.33 after 4th's night stay.

Albergo Piazzolo, V. Indipendenza, 65 (☎031 27 21 86). From P. Cavour take V. Bonta which becomes V. Boldini and V. Luni. Pedestrian only V. Indipendenza is on the right. Airy, breezy rooms, all tastefully furnished and with modern bathrooms. 3 large doubles with bath L100,000/€51.65; 1 quad L160,000/€82.73. AmEx/DC/MC/V.

Albergo Sociale, V. Maestri Comacini, 8 (☎031 26 40 42), on right side of *duomo*. Unadorned rooms and small beds. Central location. Call ahead. 1 single without bath L40,000/€20.66; 4 doubles L70,000/€36.15, 1 with bath L90,000/€46.48; triples L100,000/€51.65. AmEx/DC/MC/V.

Albergo Sole, V. Borgo Vico, 89/91 (☎031 57 33 82). From Stazione S. Giovanni, head down stairs and through the park, then turn left onto V. Borgo Vico. Proximity to train tracks, a noisy street, and a dreary motif make this a last resort, but the price is right. Singles L40,000/€20.66; doubles L80,000/€41.32.

🍴 FOOD

Many of Como's residents lunch *alla milanese*, downing a quick, satisfying meal in an inexpensive self-service joint. Unfortunately, finding an affordable evening meal can be a challenge. Picnickers will appreciate the **G.S. supermarket** on the corner of V. Fratelli Recchi and V. Fratelli Roselli, across from the park. (☎031 57 08 95. Open M 9:30am-9pm, Tu-F 8am-9pm, Sa 8am-8pm.) Lakeside benches are great for *al fresco* dining. Huge loaves of *resca* (Como sweet bread with dried fruit) or the harder, cake-like *matalok*, complement picnics; pick them up at **Beretta Il Fornaio,** V. Fratelli Rosselli, 26a, a bustling bakery. (Open M 7:30am-1pm, Tu-Sa 7:30am-1pm and 3:30-7:30pm,) Feast for L10,000/€5.16 on great breads, cheeses, and meats at the takeout haven **Gran Mercato,** P. Matteotti, 3. (Open M 8:30am-1pm, Tu-F 8:30am-1pm and 3-7:30pm, Sa 8am-8pm, Su 8:30am-1pm.) An **outdoor market** is held Tuesday and Thursday mornings and all day Saturday in P. Vittoria.

🍽 **Taverna Spagnola,** V. Grassi, 33 (☎031 27 24 60) off P. Volta. From P. Cavour take V. Fontana to P. Volta. Lively restaurant. Large portions. Homey, energetic atmosphere. Try *penne al'arrabiata* or *tagliatele*. Pizza L7-13,000/€3.62-6.71; *primi* L8-10,000/€4.13-5.16; homemade *tiramisù* L6000/€3.10; paulaner beer L5000/€2.58. Cover L2000/€1.03. Open Th-Tu noon-2:30pm and 7pm-midnight. AmEx/MC/V.

🍽 **Free Break Self-Service,** V. Innocenzo XI, 19 (☎031 26 14 49). Head down stairs from train station S. Giovanni, through park, and to the right. Modern joint with Charlie Chaplin and Abbott and Costello on the walls. Big bowls of spaghetti and red sauce L6000/€3.10. *Primi* L4-6000/€2.07-3.10. Open M-Sa noon-2:30pm. AmEx/DC/MC/V.

Il Carrettiere, V. Colonnia, 18 (☎031 30 34 78), off P.A. de Gasperi, near P. Matteotti. Seafood is the specialty of this local haunt, where wood carvings adorn the stucco walls, and the food arrives on colorful china. The *spaghetti all'astrice* or *allo scoglio* is a bit of a splurge at L22,000/€11.21, but it's quite possibly the most delicious seafood platter north of Milan. Open Tu-Su noon-3pm and 7:30-11pm. AmEx/MC/V.

Ristorante/Pizzeria Orologio, V. Foscolo, 11 (☎031 30 45 65), off P. Matteotti. Sleek, modern interior and delicious pizzas for L6-15,000/€3.10-7.75. *Primi* L10-14,000/€5.16-7.32. Vegetarian *alle vedure* (L10,000/€5.16). Cover L3000/€1.55. Open daily noon-3pm and 6:30pm-2am; closed W in winter. AmEx/DC/MC/V.

👁 SIGHTS

DUOMO AND ENVIRONS. Near P. Cavour, Como's newly restored *duomo* was built and rebuilt for four centuries starting in 1397 and houses a magnificent, octagonal dome. As one of Italy's best examples of architectural fusion, it harmoniously combines Romanesque, Gothic, Renaissance, and Baroque elements. The Rodari brothers' life-like sculptures of the Exodus from Egypt animate the church's exterior. Statues of Como residents Pliny the Elder and Pliny the Younger flank the door. *(Open daily 7am-noon and 3-7pm.)* The sturdy town hall, the 15th-century **Broletto,** with colonnaded windows and multicolored marble balconies, leans up against the *duomo*. **Basilica di San Fedele,** two blocks down V.V. Emanuele II from the *duomo*, bears a resemblance to Ravenna's Byzantine churches—not surprising since the Lombards built the oldest parts of the church (notably the altar and the blind arcade) during the same period. *(Open daily 8am-noon and 3-6pm.)* Just behind the *duomo* and across the rail tracks, Giuseppe Terragni's Casa del Fascio—now called **Palazzo Terragni**—was built from 1934-36 to house the local Fascist government. It has become a world-famous icon of Modernist Italian architecture, quite a contrast to the heavy masonry of typical Fascist architecture.

THE 2½ BILLION LIRE BED
The lovely town of **Cernobbio** lies 6km north of Como on the western shore of the lake, a scenic one-hour walk from Villa Olmo. Along the way, villas and castles galore dot the landscape, and the walk offers a gorgeous view of Como and its *duomo*. **Villa Fiori** and **Villa Erba** are the closest villas to Como, but the signature piece is the world-famous **Villa d'Este**, once the luxury vacation home of the Este family of Ferrara and now the most opulent of luxury accommodations. The lush ■ **gardens** of the villa alone merit a trip to Cernobbio. If you can't find a bed at the hostels in Como and Mennagio, don't trudge back to Milan; Villa D'Este is happy to put you up for a mere pittance (L2,500,000,000/ €1,291,142). To sweeten the deal, you might get to dine with the Queen of England, and there's a good chance your room will have a view of the villa's swimming pool, a unique contraption that floats in the middle of a nearby lake. Don't feel like spending the night? Drop L30,000/€15.50 for a cup of *espresso* and enjoy the scenery.

NORTHWEST ITALY

LAKE AREA. From P. Cavour go left along the waterfront to the pantheon-like **Tempio Voltiano**, dedicated to the inventor of the battery, Alessandro Volta. (☎031 57 47 05. Open Apr.-Sept. Tu-Su 10am-noon and 3-6pm; in winter 10am-noon and 2-4pm. L4000/€2.07, groups and under 6 L2500/€1.29.) If you wish to see Volta's tomb, take bus #4 from the bus stop or Stazione S. Giovanni to **Camnago Volta** (15min., every 30min. 6:20am-8:20pm, L1500/€0.77). The villas lining the lake include the **Villa "La Rotonda,"** with its ornamented Rococo stuccato and chandeliers. (Open M-Th 9am-noon and 3-5pm, F 9am-noon.) Farther north is the ambassadorial **Villa Olmo** in the romantic, statue lined park of the same name. (Villa open Apr.-Sept. M-Sa 9am-noon and 3-5pm. Gardens open daily Apr.-Sept. 8am-11pm; Oct.-Mar. 9am-7pm.)

❧ HIKING

Take the ■**funiculare** from P. dei Gasperi, 4, at the far end of Lungo Lario Trieste, to **Brunate** for excellent hiking and scenic views (☎031 30 36 08. June-Sept. every 15min. 6am-midnight; Oct.-May every 30min. 6am-10:30pm; L4100/€2.12, under 12 L2700/€1.39; round-trip L7500/€3.87, under 12 L4500/€2.32; adult round-trip L5000/€2.58 if purchased through the hostel). For even more beautiful panoramas, hike up toward **Faro Voltiano** (906m, 20min. walk), a lighthouse dedicated to Volta. It's easy to find; just follow the signs (or take the street that goes up). For a better workout, take the paved, but steeper walkway. Enjoy a breathtaking view of the Alps and Switzerland, and on a clear day, both Milan and the Matterhorn. Even with occluded skies, you can relish the majesty of the villas of Lake Como.

From Faro Voltiano, another 15min. of hiking brings you to **San Maurizio**, and another 1½hr. should be enough time to reach **Monte Boletto** (1236m). There is a bus that runs from Brunate to approximately 1km past S. Maurizio and stops by Faro Voltiano (every 30min. 8:15am-6:45pm, L1500/€0.77). If the hike to M. Boletto hasn't left you exhausted, stroll for another hour to **Monte Bolettone** (1317m). Whichever peak you choose, the views of Lake Como are stunning.

Or, head northwest between S. Maurizio and M. Boletto after the restaurant Baita Carla. The path leads to the town of **Torno** at the lake, 8km north of Como, and a good place to catch a boat ride back to Como (every hr. 6:58am-8:14pm, L3600/€1.86). In Torno, check out the **Chiesa di San Giovanni** with its opulent 16th-century portal or the **Villa Pliniana**, 15min. north of the boat dock.

If you are up for more extensive exploration of the mountains east of Como, take bus C40 from the Como bus station to **Erba** (30min., every hr. 7:15am-9:15pm, L4900/€2.53). From Erba hike to **Caslino D'Erba**, which leads to **Monte Palanzone** (1436m). The hike is said to be the most beautiful in the region.

MENAGGIO   ☎034

A perfect base of operations for the entire Centro Lago, Menaggio is home to august lake shore hotels, cobblestone streets, and stunning hillside scenery. You can explore Lake Como while staying in Menaggio's youth hostel for a fraction of the cost (and double the character) of any other establishment on the lake.

TRANSPORTATION AND PRACTICAL INFORMATION. Buses and **ferries** link Menaggio to the other lake towns (see **Transportation,** p. 119). Ferries run to: **Bellagio** (15min., every hr. 6:05am-10:45pm, L4800/€2.48); **Varenna** (15min., every hr. 6:45am-9:45pm, L4800/€2.48); **Como** (2hr.; every hr. 11:12am-6:12pm; L11,300/ €5.84). In the town center at **Piazza Garibaldi,** the helpful **tourist office** is multilingual and has information on hundreds of possible excursions around the lake. (☎034 43 29 24; infomenaggio@tiscalinet.it. Open M-Sa 9am-noon and 3-6pm.) In an **emergency,** dial ☎113, the **police** at ☎112, or an **ambulance** ☎118. P. Garibaldi also houses a **pharmacy** with an automatic telephone that connects to the (rotating) night duty location. (☎0344 32 10 51. Open 8:30am-12:30pm and 3-7pm.) Menaggio's **hospital** is on V. Cadorna (☎0344 33 111). **Internet** access is available at **Video Mix,** across from the crêperie. (☎0344 341 10. Open Tu-Sa 8:30am-12:30pm and 3-7pm.) The **post office** is at V. Lusardi, 48, and offers **currency exchange.** (Open M-F 8:20am-6:30pm, Sa 8:20-11:30am.) **Postal code:** 22017.

ACCOMMODATIONS AND CAMPING. **Ostello La Prinula (HI),** V. IV Novembre, 86, is the best budget value in the lake district, and maybe even in Italy. Walk along the shore to the main thoroughfare, pass the gas station, and hike up the less steep of the two inclines (on right side of street). A helpful newsletter lists activities including guided hikes, cooking classes, and horseback riding. The hostel provides guests with home-cooked native cuisine (dinner L18,000/€9.30), family suites, a washing machine (L6000/€3.10 per load), bike and kayak rental (L18,000/ €9.30 per day), a kitchen, picnic lunch (L10,000/€5.16), Internet access (L4000/ €2.07 per 15min.), and free beach access. (☎034 43 23 56; fax 43 16 77; www.menaggiohostel.it. Breakfast included. Lockout 10am-5pm. Curfew 11:30pm. Call ahead to reserve. Open Mar.-Oct. Dorms L21,000/€10.85. Family rooms of 4 beds and private bath L23,000/€11.88 per person.) **Albergo il Vapore,** conveniently situated just off Piazza Garibaldi, is another inexpensive alternative. The friendly owners will lead you to small, but warmly decorated rooms, some with lakeviews, and all with bathrooms. (☎0344 32 229; fax 34 850; ilvapore@usa.net. Breakfast L10,000/€5.16. Reserve ahead. Singles L50,000/€25.82; doubles L90,000/€46.48.) A healthy trek up the lake from the city center, **Camping Lido** (☎034 43 11 50. Shower L1500/€0.77, pool access L2000/€1.03. L9000/€4.65 per person, L14,000/€7.32 per tent.) and the adjacent **Camping Europa** (☎034 43 11 87; L8000/€4.13 per person, L14,000/€7.32 per tent) both offer decent, inexpensive places to crash. Campers might want to travel farther up the lake to the more scenic Domaso sites.

FOOD AND ENTERTAINMENT. While the fabulous hostel dinner ought to satisfy even the pickiest of diners, there are plenty of pizzerias and restaurants in the town proper if you want to stretch your legs. Between the town and the hostel there's a mini grocery store, **Cappe** (open M-Sa 8am-12:30pm and 3:30-3:30-7pm), and **La Crêperie,** V. IV Novembre, 41, where sweet and savory crêpes run L6-8000/ €3.10-4.13. **Pizzeria Lugano** is the cheapest sit-down meal in town, where pizza starts at L7000/€3.62 and pasta at L6000/€3.10. (Head left at the junction near Banca San Paolo; pizzeria is on your right. Open Tu-Su noon-2:30pm and 7-11pm.)

The town's liveliest bar, **Tanamana Pub,** V. IV Novembre, 79, next to the ferry stop, has both indoor and outdoor seating. (☎0344 325 58. Open daily 9am-3am.) If you don't have a lockout and want to paint the town red, **Disco Lido Caddenabbia** is the best place to party this side of Lake Como. It's located between Tremezzo and Menaggio, so take a cab. Don't get stuck without a ride home—the 3km walk on a busy road is a nightmare. (☎034 45 90 01. Open Th-Sa 9pm-3am.)

SIGHTS AND HIKING. The **Rifugio Menaggio** (☎034 43 72 82) stands 1400m above the lake. From the top, hikers can make trips to **Monte Grona** and the **Chiesa di S. Amate.** Also, don't pass up the one- to two-hour hike (each way) to the picturesque **Sass Corbee Gorge,** just outside of town. Inquire at the tourist office for detailed directions and maps, as many of these treks are complicated.

BELLAGIO ☎031

Favored by the upper-crust of Milanese society, Bellagio is one of Italy's most beautiful lake towns. Its fame extends all the way to Las Vegas, home of the famous Bellagio Hotel. You won't find neon lights or Elvis impersonators in Bellagio, however; its lakeside promenades, steep streets, and sidewalk cafes lead to silk shops and the villas of Lombard aristocrats.

To reach Bellagio from Milan, take a **ferry** from the train station in nearby **Varenna. Buses** also run from **Como.** The tourist office is at P. della Chiesa, 14 (☎031 95 02 04). The staff speaks English and has detailed information about daytrips to various parts of the lake. In an emergency, dial ☎113 for the **police,** ☎112 for the **carabinieri,** or ☎118 for an **ambulance.** The **pharmacy** at V. Roma, 12, has nighttime service—ring the bell. (☎031 95 01 86. Open Th-Tu 9am-12:30pm and 3:30-8pm.) Bellagio's **post office** on Lungo Lario Manzoni, 4, offers currency exchange. (☎031 95 19 42. Open M-F 8:10am-1:30pm, Sa 8:10am-11:40pm.) **Postal code:** 22021.

The **Villa Serbelloni** is not to be confused with the stately five-star Grand Hotel Villa Serbelloni down the hill, unless you're willing to let your ignorance cost you an extra L200,000/€103.26. With spectacular views from the fortifications on the promontory, the extensive tour of the villa's cyprus-lined garden above the tourist office is worth the price. (☎/fax 031 95 15 51. Villa open Apr.-Oct. Tu-Su. L9000/€4.65. 1½hr. tours Tu-Su 11am and 4pm, weather permitting. Buy tickets in the tourist office 15min. before the tour.) The lakeside gardens of **Villa Melzi** blossom at the other end of town. The villa is still Duke Lodovico Galarati Scoti's private residence, but the **grounds,** including a chapel and museum with Roman and Napoleonic art, are open to the public. (Open Mar.-Oct. daily 9am-6pm. L9000/€4.65.)

Bellagio isn't all ritzy hotels and manicured villas. A trip to the city would be incomplete without a visit to **Tony's,** Salita Genazzini, 3, a deliciously dilapidated little winery on the southern waterfront, just behind the Kodak shop. (☎031 95 09 35. Open Tu-Su 11:30am-1:30pm and 2:30-7pm.) The most daring among sinners favor **La Divina Commedia,** at the end of V. Roncati, where high prices and a colorful atmosphere provide for more of a novelty than a sublime literary experience, but the *Birra dei Demoni* (L24,000/€12.39 for two) is pure inferno. Crêpes named for *Lucifero* and *Beatrice* go for L10,000/€5.16. (Open daily 6pm-2:30am.)

Expect higher hotel rates in chic Bellagio than in the other lake towns. **Albergo Giardinetto,** V. Roncati, 12, just to the left of the tourist office, has simple rooms with shared baths and a friendly elderly couple that will make you forget Bellagio's pretentious atmosphere. (☎031 95 01 68. Singles L50,000/€25.82; doubles L75,000/€38.73.) **Hotel Roma,** Salita Grandi, 6, off Pizza Mazzini, is an option for when other hotel availability is limited. Breakfast and lake views greatly make up for its low pressure showers and lumpy mattresses. (☎031 95 04 24. Singles L60,000/€30.99, with bath L80,000/€41.32; doubles L88,000/€45.45, L103,000/€53.20.)

VARENNA ☎0341

Only a short ferry ride away from Bellagio, Varenna is nonetheless a far cry from the chic crowds that flock to the rest of the eastern lake shore. With several sprawling villa gardens, and numerous hillside hikes, Varenna's sights make for a splendid day trip, since lodging is both sparse and expensive. **Piazza San Giorgio,** a five-minute walk from the water, houses the following: **tourist office** (☎0341 83 03 67; open May-Sept. Tu-Sa 10am-12:30pm and 3:30-6:30pm, Su 10am-12:30pm); **bank** (to the right facing the church; open M-F 8:20am-1:20pm and 2:45-3:45pm); **pharmacy** (left of the church; open Th-Tu 9am-12:30pm and 3:30-7:30pm, W 9am-12:30pm); and **post office** (on the water side; open M-F 8am-5:45pm). **Postal code:** 23829. In an **emergency,** dial ☎113, or the **police** (☎0341 82 11 21)

If you need to stay awhile, the family-operated, centrally-located **Villa Elena,** across from the tourist office, rents several double rooms for L80,000/€41.32, but you'll have to book long in advance to beat the crowds. (☎ 0341 83 05 75. Breakfast included.) For your snacking needs, **Nilus Bar,** Riva Garibaldi, on the waterfront, serves up pizza (L10,000/€5.16), crêpes (L9000/€4.65), *panini* (L6500/€3.36), and a heavy dose of afternoon sunshine (Lsunburn/€cancer). (Open daily 8am-10pm.) Two *alimentari* grace P.S. Giorgio. (Open Tu-Su 8am-12:30pm and 4-6:30pm.)

On the ferry ride in, don't miss the view of the creatively colored houses in the town center. A scenic passageway beside the water connects both sides of Varenna and offers incredible lake vistas. To reach **La Sorgente del Fiumelatte,** which has the rather dubious distinction of being the shortest river in Italy, walk past P.S. Giorgio and up a raised road past the cemetery. For a shorter excursion, a 20-minute ascent up the hill just past the *piazza* leads to the 12th-century **Castello Vezio.** An old drawbridge connects to the castle's small tower. (Open daily Mar.-Sept. 10am-7pm in good weather. L3000/€1.55.) The 14th-century **Chiesa di S. Giorgio** looms above the town with late Romanesque simplicity. Catch the rosette window with images of dolphins inside. (Open daily 7am-noon and 2-7pm.) Varenna's most famous sights, however, are the two lakeside gardens of nearby 13th-century convents. **Villa Monastero,** 150m to the right of the church, boasts gorgeous botany in front of a hotel. (Villa open Apr.-Oct. daily 10am-6pm. Gardens L4000/€2.07, under 10 and over 65 L2000/€1.03.) Another 100m farther stands the proud **Villa Cipressi,** weekend home of Lombard aristocrats. (Gardens open Mar.-Oct. daily 9am-7pm. L4000/€2.07; combined ticket to both villas L6000/€3.10.)

Varenna's railway station links the eastern side of the lake to Milan, easing journeys from Milan to the central lake region. (☎0341 36 85 84. Trains depart Milan for Varenna every hour, 5:40am- 9:10pm. L12,000/€2.10).

DOMASO
☎0344

The breezes in this unspectacular, tiny town on the north lake create perfect windsurfing. Surfers flock to the relaxing **Ostello della Gioventù: La Vespa (HI),** V. Case Sparse, 12, on the water. This modern, festive (the bar is open very late) hostel lies 50km (2hr.) from Como by bus and is also accessible by boat. (☎ 0344 974 49; www.ostellolavespadomaso.it. Breakfast included. Low windsurfing and mountain biking rates through the hostel. Internet access L12,000/€6.20. Wheelchair accessible. Curfew midnight. Open Mar.-Oct. Dorms L22,000/€11.36.)

Italy's **international dialing prefix** is 00. Switzerland's **country code** is 41, and the **city code** for both Lugano and Locarno is 091. Remember to drop the zero when calling internationally. Exchange rates for the **Swiss Franc (SFr)** are as follows: 1SFr = L1276/€0.66, L1000 = 0.80SFr/€0.51

NEAR LAKE COMO

LUGANO, SWITZERLAND
☎091

Lugano, Switzerland's third-largest banking center, rests in a crevassed valley between the peaks of San Salvatore and Monte Brè. Warmed by a Mediterranean climate, Lugano's shaded streets are lined with climbing vines and wildflowers.

⊟⋔ TRANSPORTATION AND PRACTICAL INFORMATION. To reach Lugano by **car,** take Rte. N2/E35. Frequent **buses** run to Lugano from **Menaggio** (2hr., 8 per day, L7600/€3.92). **Trains** arrive at P. della Stazione from **Lorcano** (1hr., every 30min. 5:37am-12:04am, 16.40SFr.) and **Milan** (1½hr., every hr. 5:35am-10:45pm, 14SFr.). The 15min. downhill walk from the train station to the arcaded **Piazza della Riforma,** the town's center, winds through Lugano's large pedestrian zone. For those who would rather avoid the walk, a cable car runs between the train station and the waterfront **Piazza Cioccaro** (5:20am-11:50pm, 0.90SFr.). The **tourist office** is in the Palazzo Civico, Riva Albertolli, at the corner of P. Rezzonico. From the station, cross the footbridge labeled "Centro" and proceed down V. Cattedrale straight through P. Cioccaro as it turns into V. Pessina. Turn left on V. dei Pesci and left on Riva via Vela, which become Riva Giocondo Albertolli. The office is past the fountain on the left, across from the ferry launch. (☎ 091 913 32 32; fax 922 76 53; www.lugano-tourism.ch. Open Apr.-Oct. M-F 9am-6:30pm, Sa 9am-12:30pm and 1:30-5pm, Su 10am-2pm; Nov.-Mar. M-F 9am-12:30pm and 1:30-5:30pm.)

⌐ ACCOMMODATIONS. Travelers flock to Lugano's two extraordinary youth hostels, both built from luxury villas. Try ▧**Hotel Montarina**, V. Montarina, 1, just behind the train station. Walk 200m to the right from the station, cross the tracks, and walk one minute uphill. This palm-tree-enveloped hostel attracts young families and students with its swimming pool, groomed grounds, ping-pong, chandeliered reading room, and terrace with a view. The dorms can get rowdy in summer, when vacationing youth party hard. (☎ 091 966 72 72; fax 966 00 17; www.montarina.ch. Buffet breakfast 12SFr. Singles 50-65SFr; doubles 100SFr, with bath 120SFr.) The ▧**Ostello della Gioventù (HI)**, Lugano-Savosa, 13 V. Cantonale, is just as popular. Note: there are two streets called V. Cantonale, one in downtown Lugano and one in Savosa, where the hostel is. Take bus #5 (walk 350m to the left of the station, cross the street to get to the bus stop) to "Crocifisso" (6th stop), backtrack a bit and turn left up V. Cantonale. A former luxury villa, this hostel has secluded gardens, a pool, and an elegant atmosphere. (☎ 091 966 27 28; fax 968 23 63. Breakfast 7SFr. Kitchen 1SFr. Laundry 5SFr. Reception 7am-12:30pm and 3-10pm. Curfew 10pm; keys available upon request. Reserve ahead. Open mid-Mar. to Oct. Dorms 23SFr; singles 35SFr, with kitchenette 45SFr; doubles 56SFr, 70SFr.)

◻ FOOD. Lugano's many outdoor restaurants and cafes pay homage to the province's Italian heritage, serving up plates of *penne* and *gnocchi* and freshly spun pizzas. For some quick *al fresco* shopping and eating, **V. Pessina**, off P. Riforma, livens up at midday with outdoor sandwich and fruit shops. The **salumera**, V. Pessina, 12, is one of the better ones. **The Migros**, V. Pretoria, 15, is two blocks left of the post office, down V. Pretorio in the center of town, and offers fresh pasta and delicious *ciabatta* (a crusty bread). The food court on the ground floor saves the near-penniless with huge slices of pizza from 2.80SFr and sandwiches from 2.30SFr. (Open M-F 8am-6:30pm, Sa 7:30am-5pm.) There is a **public market** in P. della Riforma that sells seafood, produce, and veggie sandwiches for 4SFr. (Open Tu and F 7am-noon.) Romance awaits at ▧**La Tinèra**, V. dei Gorina, 2, behind Credit Suisse in P. della Riforma. Tucked away in an alley off a cobblestone road, this romantically low-lit underground restaurant has great daily specials for 12-18SFr. (☎ 091 923 52 19. Open M-Sa 8:30am-3pm and 5:30-11pm. AmEx/MC/V.)

◧▥ SIGHTS AND MUSEUMS. The frescoes of the 16th-century **Cattedrale San Lorenzo**, just south of the train station, gleam with colors that are still vivid despite their advanced age. The frescoes on the west wall date from the 13th century. But Lugano's most spectacular fresco is Bernardio Luini's gargantuan **Crucifixion** which was painted in 1529 and is now in the **Chiesa Santa Maria degli Angioli**, to the right of the tourist office on the waterfront. Aside from the churches, Lugano's best known cultural attractions are its art museums—past and present. The largest and most fun museum is the **Museo Cantonale d'Arte**, which has a permanent collection of 19th- and 20th-century art, including works by Swiss artists Vela, Ciseri, Franzoni, and Klee. The first and second floors are highly entertaining and feel, in places, like mirrored halls in an amusement park. The third floor houses a more sedate collection of pencil drawings. *(V. Canova, 10, across from Chieasa San Rocco. ☎ 091 910 47 80. Open Tu 2-5pm, W-Su 10am-5pm. Special exhibits 10SFr, students 7SFr, permanent collection 7SFr, students 5SFr. MC/V)*

▧ OUTDOOR ACTIVITIES. Lugano's waterfront parks are ideal places for picnics and play. The **Belvedere**, on Quai Riva Caccia, is an enormous sculpture garden with an emphasis on modernist metalwork. On sunny afternoons, enthusiasts gather here for open-air chess tournaments. The garden stretches toward Paradiso along the lakeside promenade to the right of the tourist office. In the other direction, the less whimsical but more serene **Parco Civico** is brightened by flower beds along the water and trees that reach down with willowy, long arms to touch the lake below. Backpackers have been know to crash here (illegally) from time to time. (Open Mar.-Oct. 6:30am-11:30pm; Nov.-Feb. 7am-9pm.)

For those tired of the lakeside views, take advantage of the parkside views offered by the lake. **Boat tours** leave from the Societa Navigazione del Lago di Lugano, to the left of the tourist office. Take the "grand tour" of the lake in English (3½hr.) for 30.60SFr or hop the boat to one of the neighboring lakeside towns for 2.80-14.40SFr. (☎091 923 17 79; lake.lugano@bluewin.ch). Various vendors along the lake rent **pedal boats** (7SFr per 30min.), and **Boat Saladin** (☎091 923 57 33), to the right of the tourist office, rents **motor boats,** useful for midnight rendezvous.

When Lugano's perfection becomes irritating, head to the hills. Lugano offers excellent hiking opportunities for those with a sturdy foot and reliable map. The tourist office and Hotel Montarina can help provide the latter; both have excellent topographical maps and trail guides in stock. The cheapest and most rewarding hike goes to the peak of **Monte Boglio**, a five-hour round-trip that can be extended over two days by staying at the Pairolhütte (ask at hostels or tourist office for more information). Funiculars take those lacking energy and enthusiasm directly to the peaks of **Monte Brè** and **San Salvatore.** The Monte Brè funicular is down the river to the left of the tourist office; the San Salvatore funicular is to the right.

⚏ **ENTERTAINMENT.** The arcades of the town *piazze* fill at night with people taking a *passaggio.* The outdoor cafes of P. della Riforma are especially lively. Stop in at the **Pave Pub,** Riva Albertolli, 1, a self-proclaimed *museo di birra* (museum of beer), offering 50 different varieties with a lakeside view of the mountains and a decidedly un-museum like liveliness. (☎091 922 07 70. Beers start at 4SFr. Open 11am-1am.) For a change of pace head down the V. Pretorio from P. Dante and turn left on V.A. Vanoni for the **Biblio-Cafè Tra,** V. Vanoni, 3. This laidback cafe evokes a bit of leftist Spain. Locals and subversives consume 3.40SFr beers while surfing the web for 8SFr per hr. (☎091 923 23 05. Open M-Th 9am-midnight, F 9am-1am, Sa 5pm-1am.)

LAKE MAGGIORE (LAGO MAGGIORE)

Without the tourist frenzy of its easterly neighbors, Lake Maggiore cradles similar temperate mountain waters and idyllic shores. A glaze of opulence coats the air, and a stroll past any of the grandiose shore-side hotels reveals Maggiore as the preferred watering hole of the elite. To add to the grandeur, steep green hills punctuate the shoreline, and to the west, the dark, glaciated outline of Monte Rosa (4634m) peers down the valley toward Maggiore. Don't be discouraged by Maggiore's reputation as the most expensive lake; many modest *pensioni* hide in the shadows of their multi-storied cousins, offering reasonable rates to passing travelers. Stresa is the most convenient base for exploring the Borromean Islands and Lago di Orta, while its cross-lake cousin, Verbania-Pallanza, has a terrific hostel.

STRESA   ☎0323

Stresa retains much of the manicured charm that lured visitors in droves during the 19th and early 20th centuries. Art nouveau hotels and blooming hydrangeas line the waterfront, giving the little town a romantic, old-fashioned appearance. Splendid views of the lake and mountains await around each bend of the cobblestone streets. Stresa is a resort town, filled with Italian, French, English, American, and German tourists; there is little to do but hop the boats to the Borromeans with the rest of the vacation throngs, or while away the day admiring lakeside villas with more than a touch of envy. Of course, if you've seen enough conspicuous consumption for the day, you can always explore the hillside of nearby Motterone.

⚌ TRANSPORTATION AND PRACTICAL INFORMATION. Stresa lies only an hour from Milan on the Milan-Domodossola train line (every hr. 7:30am-10:15pm; L8400/€4.34, intercity supplement L6000/€3.10). Ticket office open M-F 6:10am-12:10pm and 12:50-8:10pm, Sa 7am-2pm, Su 12:50-8:10pm). If the office is closed, you can purchase your ticket on board with no surcharge. Navagazione Lago Maggiore (☎800 55 18 01) operates ferries via **Isola Bella** (5min.), **Isola Superiore** (10min.), and **Isola Madre** (30min.) to **Verbania-Pallanza** (35min.; every 30min. 7:10am-7pm; L12,400/€6.40). Ferries also continue on to **Intra** (50min., every hour, L7500/€3.87); **Laveno** (1hr.; 7 per day; L10,000/€5.16); and **Locarno** (3hr.; 5 per day; L27,600/€14.25). The **regional APTL tourist office** is at V. Principe Tommaso, 70/72. From the station, turn right and walk down the hill on V. Carducci, which becomes V. Gignous; V.P. Tommaso is on the left. (☎0323 30 416; fax 93 43 35. Open M-F 8:30am-1pm and 2-7pm.) The **local IAT tourist office** is in the *navagozione* building at the ferry dock, in P. Martini. (☎/fax 0323 31 308. Open daily 10am-noon and 3-6:30pm.) For **currency exchange** and a 24-hour **ATM**, try **Banca Popolare di Intra**, C. Umberto I, 1, just off P. Marconi. (☎0323 30 330. Open M-F 8:10am-1:10pm and 2:30-4pm.) Stresa's pharmacy, **Farmacia Internazionale**, C. Italia, 40, posts the list of rotating late-night pharmacies. (☎0323 30 326). In case of **emergency**, contact **police** (☎112 or ☎0323 301 18), **first aid** (☎113 or ☎0323 318 44), an or an **ambulance** (☎118 or ☎0323 333 60). The **post office** is at V.A. Bolongaro, 44, near P. Rossi. (☎0323 300 65. Open M-F 8:15am-6pm, Sa 8:15am-noon.) **Postal Code:** 28838.

⌂ ACCOMMODATIONS. Orsola Meublé, V. Duchessa di Genova, 45, a far cry from lakeside luxury, nonetheless features affordable blue-tiled rooms with cement balconies decked with plastic chairs and a breakfast room adorned with golf trophies. The cramped showers and short beds leave something to be desired. From the station, turn right, walk downhill to the intersection, and turn left. (☎0323 310 87; fax 93 31 21. Breakfast included. Singles L60,000/€30.99, with bath L70,000/€36.15; doubles L100,000/€51.65, L120,000/€62. AmEx/DC/MC/V.) The modern and friendly **Albergo Luina**, V. Garibaldi, 21, is conveniently located near the town center, but consistently booked through the summer--call several weeks in advance. There are only a few rooms, but all have bath, TV. (☎/fax 0323 302 85; luina@katamail.com. Breakfast included. 10% discount with *Let's Go*. Singles L65,000/€33.57; doubles L90-120,000/€46.48-62.) **Hotel Mon Toc**, V. Duchessa di Genova, 67/69, has very well-maintained, breezy rooms, all with bath, TV, and telephone. Take a right out of the station and another at the intersection under the tracks. (☎0323 302 82; fax 93 38 60; montoc@tiscalinet.it. Breakfast L15,000/€7.75. Six singles L70,000/€36.15; 7 doubles L110,000/€56.68. AmEx/DC/MC/V.)

◘ FOOD. Salumeria Bianchetti Augusto, V. Mazzini, 1, sells large *panini* (L3500-4000/€1.81-2.07), pizza by the slice (L2800-4000/€1.45-2.07), *foccacia* (L1800-3800/€0.93-1.96), and cold cuts. (☎0323 304 02. Open daily 8am-7pm. AmEx/MC/V.) **Taverna del Pappagallo**, V.P. Margherita, 46, serves delicious pasta and brick-oven pizza (L7-13,000/€3.62-6.71) in a warm interior and lovely garden. Try the *omelette al prosciutto* (L8000/€4.13), or *cannelloni alla "Pappagallo"* for L14,000/€7.32. (☎0323 304 11. *Primi* L7-14,000/€3.62-7.32; *secondi* L18-22,000/€9.30-11.36. Cover L3000/€1.55. Open Th-M 11:30am-2:30pm and 6:30-10:30pm.) At **Pizza D.O.C.**, C. Italia, 60, busy waiters serve up inexpensive food while you take in the panoramic lakeside view on the balcony of the old Hotel Ariston. Seventy-five inventive kinds of pizza (L7-15,000/€3.62-7.75) and free delivery make this place a winner. (☎0323 300 00; fax 31 195. *Primi* L10-12,000/€5.16-6.2; *secondi* L12-16,000/€6.20-8.26. Dessert pizzas (*alla nutella, alla mele*, L10-15,000/€5.16-7.75. Open daily 11am-2pm and 7:30pm-midnight. AmEx/MC/V.) Stock up on necessities at the **GS supermarket**, V. Roma, 11. Pizza slices (from L2300/€1.2) entice from behind the registers. (Open M-Sa 8:30am-1pm and 3-7:30pm, Su 8:30am-12:30pm.)

NORTHWEST ITALY

🌐🎵 SIGHTS AND ENTERTAINMENT. Stresa's token villa, **Villa Pallavicino,** not only boasts 20 hectares of gardens for your strolling pleasure, but also scores of exotic animals and birds (including lamas, kangaroos, zebras, and flamingos). (☎ 0323 315 33. Open daily March-Oct., 9am-6pm. L12,000/€6.20). Otherwise, head for the hills on the Stresa-Mottarone Funivia, P.Lido, 8, and explore Mottarone's extensive hiking and moutainbike trails. (Next to the L'Idrovolante. ☎ 0323 303 99. Open 9:20am-5:20pm. L20,000/€10.33. Mountain bike rental next door.)

The **L'Idrovolante Cafe,** P. Lido, 6, a local major hangout, offers live music including soul, R&B, and blues. Check your email there too. (Facing the water at the port, turn left and take V.G. Borromeao along the shore for 20min. ☎ 0323 313 84. Open Tu-Th 8am-midnight, F-Sa 8am-2am, Su 8am-midnight.) If you would rather drink away your troubles, head to the **Irish Bar,** V.P. Margherita, 9, for a pint o' Guinness (L8000/€4.13) and a pair of smiling Irish eyes. (☎ 0323 310 54. Open Tu-Su 8am-midnight.) From the last week in August to the third week in September, some of the finest orchestras and soloists in the world gather for the internationally acclaimed **Settimane Musicali di Stresa e del Lago Maggiore** (tickets L30-100,000/€15.50-51.65, students from L10,000/€5.16). For info, contact the ticket office at V. Canonica, 6 (☎ 0323 310 95 or 304 59; fax 330 06).

NEAR STRESA

PALLANZA   ☎ 0323

Flowers cover this small borough as far as the eye can see (and as the nose can smell). Along with the neighboring ferry port of Intra, the two towns constitute the larger community of Verbania. To reach Pallanza from Como without heading back to Milan, take a **train** from **Como** Stazione Nord to **Saronno,** change trains and head to **Laveno** (combined ticket L4800/€2.58). From there, take a ferry to **Intra,** and switch ferries to Pallanza (combined return ticket L12,000/€6.20; last ferry at 7pm). You can also follow the scenic road along the lake shore and around the point to reach Pallanza from Intra. If local trains aren't your style, take the train from Milan to the Verbania-Pallanza stop. **Ferries** via **Isola Madra** (5min.), **Isola Superiore** (20min.), and **Isola Bella** (25min.) go to **Stresa** (35min.; every 30min. 7:45am-6:50pm; L12,400/€6.40, children L8000/€4.13).

The town offers little in terms of sights and entertainment, but the **tourist office,** C. Zanitello, 8, 5min. to the right when facing inland from the port, helps plan excursions to the islands. (☎ 0323 50 32 49; fax 55 66 69; turismo@comune.verbania.it. Open M-Sa 9am-12:30pm and 3-6pm, Su 9am-noon.) **Banca Popolare di Intra,** P. Garibaldi, 20, with a 24-hour **ATM** is a little to the right as you exit the boat. (Open M-F 8:20am-1:20pm, Sa-Su 8:20-11:50am.) **Farmacia dott.nitais,** in P. Gramsci, lists the night pharmacies in an electronic box outside. (Open M-Sa 8:30am-12:30pm and 3:30-7:30pm.) In an **emergency,** dial ☎ 113, the **police** (☎ 112), or an **ambulance** (☎ 118). Pallanza's **post office** is also in P. Gramasci. (Open M-F 8:15am-1:40pm, Sa 8:15am-noon.) **Postal code:** 28922.

Only a few years old, **Ostello Verbania Internazionale (HI),** V. alle Rose, 7, in a quiet old villa 10-15min. from the Borromean Island ferries, offers extremely modern and clean facilities with ping-pong, pool, foosball, arcade games, TV room, and gigantic bathrooms. After exiting the ferry, turn right and walk for five minutes along the water to V.V. Veneto, just past the tourist office. Take a left on V. Panoramica, keep walking up the hill, continue around the bend, and take your last right. The hostel is 50m on the left. (☎ 0323 50 16 48; fax 50 78 77. Breakfast included. Lunch and dinner L15,000/€7.75. Lockout 11am-4pm. Curfew midnight. Reception 8-11am, 4-5:30pm, and 10-11pm. Dorms with sheets and locker L24,000/€12.39; 3 family rooms with bath L27,000/€13.94 per person.) **Hotel Novara,** P. Garibaldi, 30, has 16 immaculate rooms above a restaurant; all rooms have TV and telephone. Facing the water, turn left from the dock and walk two minutes to P. Garibaldi. (☎ 0323 50 35 27; fax 50 35 28. Breakfast included. Singles L55-72,000/€28.41-37.18; doubles with bath L140,000/€72.30.)

From the hostel toward Intra lies the beautiful **Villa Taranto.** Its fairy-tale gardens with waterfalls, pools, and fountains stand as a fine example of botanical art. Expect the traditional villa fare: lots of color and exotic plants and flowers, but nothing terribly unique or exciting. (☎0323 55 66 67; fax 55 66 67. Open daily Apr.-Oct. 8:30am-6:30pm. L12,000/€6.20, children under 6 free.)

Pizzeria Emiliana, P. Giovanni, 24, brick-oven cooks both regular and dessert pizzas (*alla nutella* L10,000/€5.16) from L6-14,000/€3.10-7.23. (☎0323 50 35 22. *Primi* and *secondi* L10-15,000/€5.16-7.75. Open Th-Tu noon-2pm and 7pm-midnight.) If your Pallanzan palate palls at pizza, head to **Hostaria Il Cortile,** V. Albertazzi, 14. Though the courtyard is a bit run-down, the food is the cheapest on the lake. Try the *penne gorgonzola* for L8000/€4.13 or the *scaloppine vino bianco al limone* for L12,000/€6.2. (☎0323 50 28 16. Open Th-Tu 11:30am-3:30pm and 5:30pm-2am. *Primi* from L7000/€3.62; *secondi* from L10,000/€5.16. MC/V.)

LOCARNO, SWITZERLAND ☎091

On the shores of **Lago Maggiore,** Locarno (pop. 30,000) basks in near-Mediterranean breezes and the bright Italian sun. This relatively unspoiled resort town has a tropical feeling, perhaps because it gets over 2200 hours of sunlight per year—the most in all of Switzerland. During its world-famous 11-day **film festival** each August, over 150,000 big screen enthusiasts descend upon the town. The centerpiece of the festival is a giant 26m x 14m outdoor screen set up in P. Grande for big name premieres, while smaller screens throughout the city highlight young filmmakers and groundbreaking experimentation. (☎091 756 2121; fax 756 2149; www.pardo.ch.) Lorcano also serves as an excellent starting point for mountain hikes along the Verzasca and Maggia valleys and regional skiing.

Take an **FS train** from Stresa to Locarno (3½-5hr.; M-Sa 8 per day 8am-8pm, Su 1 per day), Lugano (45min., every 30min. 5:54am-11:54pm, 16.40SFr.), and Milan (2½hr., several per day 6:30am-8:30pm, 63SFr). The **tourist office** is on Largo Zorzi in P. Grande. From the main exit of the train station, walk diagonally to the right, cross V. della Stazione and continue through the pedestrian walkway (V. alla Ramogna). Cross Largo Zorzi to your left; the tourist office is in the same building as the casino. The office organizes city **tours** in English and bus trips around Lago Maggiore. (☎091 791 00 91; fax 751 90 70; buongiorno@maggiore.ch; www.maggiore.ch. Open M-F 9am-6pm, Sa 9am-5pm, Su 10am-noon and 1-3pm.)

All the worldly languor of Lorcano coexists in relative peace with the piety of the worshipers in the churches of the **Città Vecchia** (old city). For centuries, visitors have journeyed to Locarno just to see the church of **Madonna del Sasso** (Madonna of the Rock). Its orange-yellow hue renders it immediately recognizable from anywhere in town. The church is accessible by a **funicular** that leaves every 15min. from a small station just left of the McDonald's (round-trip 6SFr, 4.50SFr with SwissPass), but the true budget traveler will make the 20min. walk up the smooth stones of V. al Sasso. (Off V. Cappuccini in the Città Vecchia. Grounds open daily 7am-7pm. 2.50SFr, students 1.50SFr. Free English guidebooks at the entrance.)

The **Verzasca Dam** has brought scores of visitors dizzying adrenaline rushes courtesy of its famous **bungee jump,** the highest in the world. The 255m jump, conquered with panache by James Bond in *Goldeneye,* costs 244SFr the first time (with training, drink, and diploma) and 195SFr for subsequent leaps. For information, contact **Trekking Team** (☎0848 808 007; info@trenskking.ch; www.trekking.ch. Open Apr.-Oct.). Hidden among the chestnut trees, waterfalls, and dozens of lakes in Ticino's largest valley, Valle Maggia is the village of **Aurigeno.** Come here to take a "vacation from your vacation" at ■**Baracca Backpacker,** a tiny hostel with 10 beds and unlimited access to the peaceful outdoors. From the train station in Locarno, take bus #10 (dir: Valle Maggia) to "Ronchini" (25min., every hr. 5:30am-11:35pm, 6.80SFr). Cross the street, turn right from the bus stop, and follow the hostel signs into the forest (15min.). When you get to the paved street, turn right. The hostel is behind the church. Beo the bird noisily greets each new arrival, and the couple who run the hostel provide fresh herbs for cooking as well as a wood-working shop. While you're escaping from civilization, use the kitchen, **rent a bike** (10SFr per day), or explore the **hiking, climbing,** and **swimming** possibilities in the area. (☎091 079 207 15 54. Call ahead. Reception 9-11am and 5-10pm. Open Apr.-Oct. Sleepsack 2SFr per day. Dorms 25SFr.)

THE BORROMEAN ISLANDS (ISOLE BORROMEE) ☎0323

Beckoning to visitors with promises of dense green thickets and stately old villas, the lush beauty of the three Borromean Islands makes them well worth a visit. Ferries run to all three islands from both Stresa and Pallanza every half hour (9am-7pm), and a day's ticket runs L16,000/€8.26. The entrance fees to the sights on each island can be pricey, it is cheaper to buy your tickets at the ferry ticket window in Stresa or Pallanza than on the island.

The opulence of the ▨**Palazzo e Giardini Borromeo** has garnered fame for the pearl of Maggiore, **Isola Bella.** The Baroque palace, built in 1670 by Count Borromeo, features six meticulously designed rooms with priceless masterpieces, tapestries, sculptures by Canova, obelisks, and paintings by van Dyck. The ten terraced gardens, punctuated with statues and topped by a unicorn, rise up like a large wedding cake. The Borromeo family's motto, *"Humilitas"?* Not here. (☎0323 305 56. Open daily Mar.-Sept. 9am-noon and 1:30-5:30pm; Oct. 9am-noon and 1:30-5pm. L16,000/€8.26, ages 6-15 L7000/€3.62.)

Take the ferry and escape the aristocrats at Isola Bella in favor of the fishermen of Hemingway's favorite, **Isola Superiore (dei Pescatori).** In addition to a free beach, charming paths, and a children's park, the only garden-free island sports overpriced souvenir stands and fishermen's nets hung out in the sun.

Isola Madre is the longest and quietest of the three islands. Its elegant 16th-century **villa,** started in 1502 by Lancelotto Borromeo and finished by the Count Renato 100 years later (after Lancelotto met his unfortunate end in the mouth of a dragon), contains stage sets, a vast collection of portraits, and Princess Borromeo's *bambini* marionette collection. Even if you choose to skip the house, the botanical garden's stupendous array of exotic trees, the tallest palms in Italy, and strutting peacocks are worth the entrance fee. (☎0323 312 61; fax 50 18 41. Open daily Mar.-Sept. 9am-noon and 1:30-5:30pm; Oct. 9am-12:30pm and 1:30-5:30pm. L15,000/€7.75, ages 6-15 L7000/€3.62.) Do not stop on the island unless you plan to see the garden, or you'll be forced to wait on the lone sidewalk (the only admission-free place on the island) until the next boat arrives. Off Isola Madre, you will be able to see the 4th island, **Isolino San Giovanni,** revered by Arthur Toscanini, who frequently visited the villa. Unfortunately the *isolino* is not open to public.

LAKE ORTA (LAGO DI ORTA)

ORTA SAN GIULIO ☎0322

Orta San Giulio is the gateway to Lake Orta, the area's unspoiled refuge, surrounded by forested hills and small towns. From 1883 to 1885, Nietzsche retreated here, where he scripted his masterpiece, *Thus Spoke Zarathustra.* Because Lake Orta is both difficult to reach by public transportation, and relatively expensive, it remains less touristed than Lake Como and Lake Maggiore; plan ahead so as not to get stranded in transit or find yourself fresh out of dough.

⧉ **TRANSPORTATION.** Orta lies on the Novara-Domodossola **train** line (1½hr., L4600/€2.38). Buy train tickets for Orta from the conductor on board. Get off at **Orta Miasino,** 3km above Orta, and walk down to the left until you reach the intersection. Turn left on V. Fava, and the town of Orta San Giulio is a 10min. walk away. A twisting road connects Orta to nearby Lake Maggiore. On weekdays, **buses** leave from Stresa's P. Marconi (next to the phones and the little white food hut), traveling to Orta (1hr., in summer M-F 9am and 4pm, L9000/€4.65), via **Baveno.** The return trip from Orta to Stresa is a bit tricky (1hr., in summer M-F 10am and 5pm, L8800/€4.54). Those with a car can try the nearby lake towns of **Alzo** and **Arola;** contact the Orta tourist office for details.

⊠ PRACTICAL INFORMATION. Orta's **tourist office** is on V. Panoramica, across the street and down from the ornate Villa Crespi tower. From the train station, turn left and walk for 10 minutes straight through the intersection. (☎ 0322 90 56 14; fax 90 58 00; ortatl@tin.it. Open daily in summer 9:30am-1pm and 2:30-7pm.) There is a **pharmacy** on V. Corina Care Albertolletti, 6, off the main *piazza.* (☎ 0322 90117. Open M-Sa 8:30am-noon and 3:30-7:30pm.) In case of an **emergency,** call an **ambulance** (☎ 118 or 0322 901 14) or the **police** (☎ 0322 824 44). **Banca Popolare di Novara,** V. Olina, 14, has **currency exchange** and outdoor **ATMs.** (Open M-F 8:20am-1:20pm and 2:35-3:35pm, Sa 8:20-11:20am.) The **post office** is in P. Ragazzoni. (☎ 0322 901 57. Open M-Sa 8:15am-5:30pm.) **Postal Code:** 28016.

⊓ ACCOMMODATIONS AND CAMPING. "Affordable" accommodations start at L125,000/€64.56 for a double, so you might also consider staying in Stresa and coming just for the day. **Piccolo Hotel Olina,** V. Olina, 40, offers beautiful rooms with private baths. Family rooms with kitchens are also available. (☎ 0322 90 56 56. Breakfast included. Singles L110,000/€56.68; doubles L150,000/€77.47. AmEx/DC/MC/V.) Outside of town, but only a few minutes from the train station, **Hotel-Meublé Santa Caterina** is at V. Marconi, 10. Recently renovated, it has spacious, sleek rooms. (☎ 0322 91 58 65; fax 903 77. Singles L110,000/€56.68; doubles L125,000/€64.56. AmEx/MC/V.) Rooms with a balcony or private garden cost slightly more. **Camping Orta,** V. Domodossola, 28, offers lakeside camping. From the train station, turn left, go down to the intersection, and turn right. (☎/fax 0322 90 267. L9000/€4.65 per person, L14,000/€7.32 per tent, L17,000/€8.78 per lakeside site.)

◘ FOOD. Good news for those lookin' for a piece of ass: Lago d'Orta is known as the home of *tapulon* (donkey meat, minced, well-spiced, and cooked in red wine). All this and much more (fruit cake San Giulio, creative pasta, and bottles of alcohol) are available at the unparalleled ⊠**Salumeria Il Buongustaio,** V. Olina, 8 (☎ 0322 90 56 26). English, French, German, and Spanish are spoken. Chat with Lucca, who will gladly sell you Italy's only peanut butter, as well as 150 proof alcohol designed for all the mothers-in-law you know and love. An **open-air market** on Wednesday mornings in P. Motta sells fruit, vegetables, and dry goods.

If you don't fancy the more traditional local fare, head to **Pizzeria La Campana,** V. Giovanetti, 41, the continuation of V. Olina after P. Motta. (☎ 0322 902 11. Open Tu-Su 11am-3:30pm and 6-11pm. Pizza L9-11,000/€4.65-5.68; *primi* L9-11,000/€4.65-5.68; *secondi* L10-15,000/€5.16-7.75; desserts L7000/€3.62. Cover L2500/€1.29.) Visitors are drawn upstairs to **Taverna Antico Agnello,** V. Olina, 40, by the fabulous food, peaceful surroundings, and attentive service. (☎ 0322 90 56 56. Open Tu-Su noon-2:30pm and 7-11pm. *Primi* L13-16,000/€6.71-8.26; *secondi* L19-25,000/€9.81-12.91. AmEx/DC/MC/V.) On Isola di San Giulio, head to the most inexpensive (and only) restaurant on the island, **Ristorante San Giulio,** V. Basilica, 4. Munch brunch in the 18th-century dining room. (☎ 0322 90 234. *Primi* L7-10,000/€3.62-5.16; *secondi* L8-16,000/€4.32-8.26. Cover L3000/€1.55.) A return boat to the island runs after the public ones have stopped.

◙ SIGHTS. Walk around ⊠**Isola di San Giulio** (total population: 59), across from Orta. The island is as beautiful as the Borromeans, but much quieter. Its 12th-century **Romanesque basilica,** with interesting Baroque ornaments and frescoes inside, was built on 4th-century foundations. The church's masterpiece is the **pulpit,** built out of black marble (representative of the Evangelists). Downstairs, the **skeleton of San Giulio,** dressed in brocade robes, rests in a glass sarcophagus. (Basilica open M 11am-12:15pm, Tu-Sa 9:30am-12:15pm and 2-6:45pm, Su 8:30-10:45am and

> ## DEVILS DEFEATED BY THE HOLY SKELETOR
> St. Giulius, after whom the island was named, arrived in Orta in AD 319. Like most right-thinking Christians of his day, he decided to build a church. Legend has it that the natives of the region distrusted the man, exiling him to the island for fear that his construction project would attract snakes and devils (the bane of developers and contractors everywhere). Ever-persistent Giulio continued with the construction of the church, and eventually the locals, realizing that he was a good man, helped him build one of the smallest (and prettiest) basilicas in the world. The island is still known as the Eden of silence, and its narrow streets are full of signs (in numerous languages) with pearls of wisdom like, "Silence is the language of love," or "In silence you receive all." San Giulio himself rests in decaying peace in a glass sarcophagus in the crypt of the basilica. Be prepared, or your scream might wake up all 47 nuns (and 3 families) on the island. The natives left him visible to scare away creatures of evil (and hordes of tourists). So far, he seems to be doing a pretty good job.

2-6:45pm. Free.) Small **motorboats** weave back and forth during the summer (every 10min., round-trip L4-5000/€2.07-2.58; tickets sold on board). The boat is L3000/€1.55, but only departs every hour. The swim across the channel is strenuous, but manageable. Ask the tourist office for a schedule of music and sporting events.

A short hike above Orta proper in the cool, verdant hills, the **Sacro Monte** monastic complex is devoted to St. Francis of Assisi, patron saint of Italy. The sanctuary, founded in 1591, has 20 chapels with 376 life-size statues and 900 frescoes of trusty ole' Frank. (Open daily 8:30am-7pm. Free.) The **Mercato Antiquariato** (antique market) is held in P. Motta on the first Saturday of the month (Apr.-Oct. 9am-6pm).

LIGURIA (ITALIAN RIVIERA)

Like a black pearl nestled in the mouth of a flawless white oyster shell, dark and dreary Genoa divides the largely luminescent Ligurian coastal strip into the **Riviera di Levante** (rising sun) to the east and the **Riviera di Ponente** (setting sun) to the west. The Italian Riviera stretches 350km along the Mediterranean between France and Tuscany, forming the most famous and touristed area of the Italian coastline. Protected from the north's severe weather by the Alps, Liguria still receives its fair share of tumultuous summer storms. Rainwater streams down the terraced hillsides, irrigating crops on high and smoothing the beach sands at sea level. Along the less congested Levante, rain renews the smell of blossoming flowers among the mighty Apennine mountains and pebble beaches. Meanwhile, heat evaporates from crowded Ponente beachside *discotecas* and medieval villages.

In remote villages as in major cities, Ligurians are known for their cultural isolation. They claim Nordic, not Roman, ancestry and have their own vocabulary and accent, often incomprehensible to other Italians. Their distinctive character, however, doesn't make them any less Italian, and nor did it stop them from playing a leading role in unifying the Italian peninsula. Giuseppe Mazzini, the father of the Risorgimento, and Giuseppe Garibaldi, its most popular hero, were both Ligurians.

GENOA (GENOVA)   ☎010

Genoa, city of grit and grandeur, has little in common with the villages that dot the rest of the Riviera. As any Ligurian will tell you, "*Si deve conoscerla per amarla*"—you have to know Genoa to love her. Many travelers flee to nearby beach

HIGHLIGHTS OF LIGURIA

CLIMB the precipitous *palazzi* and study fine Flemish art in **Genoa** (p. 134).

STROLL the bewitching **via dell'Amore** (p. 154) in Cinque Terre and add your name to its list of lovers.

SLEEP under the stars on the soothing sands of **Finale Ligure's beach** (p. 159).

LOSE your *lire* and curse your luck while gambling at **San Remo's casino** (p. 163).

towns. Those who linger in this once wealthy port, however, will find themselves bewitched. From the 12th through the 17th centuries, the sweeping boulevards and arcane twisting *vicoli* (alleyways) were home to Genoa's leading families, who amassed great wealth in international trade. These riches were stowed away in the bank of S. Giorgio or lavished on extravagant palaces and churches. Genoa has made no secret of its many celebrated historical heroes, among them Christopher Columbus, the Risorgimento ideologue Giuseppe Mazzini, and the virtuoso violinist Nicolò Paganini. But in the 18th century, the city fell out of reknown and into decline, and its treasures were buried under an even deeper layer of silt. Genoa's great wall, second in length only to China's, now encircles a coarse yet cosmopolitan city that continues in its struggle to unearth its bygone grandeur.

▐ TRANSPORTATION

Flights: C. Colombo Internazionale (☎010 601 51), in Sesti Ponente. Services European destinations. Take **Volabus #100** from Stazione Brignole (every 30min. 5:30am-9:30pm, L4000/€2.07), and get off at the "Aeroporto" stop.

Trains: Stazione Principe in P. Acquaverde and **Stazione Brignole** in P. Verdi. Buses #18, 19, 33, and 37 connect the 2 stations (25min., L1500/€0.77). Luggage Storage available (p. 136). Open daily 6am-10pm. Trains run from the stations to points along the Ligurian Riviera and to major Italian cities including **Rome** (5hr., 14 per day, L44,500/€22.98) and **Turin** (2hr., 19 per day, L15,900/€8.21).

Ferries: at the Ponte Assereto arm of the port. A 15min. walk from Stazione Marittima or a short bus ride from Stazione Principe (#20). Purchase tickets at a city travel agency or **Stazione Marittima** in the port. Arrive at the Ponte Assereto at least 1hr. before departure. Destinations include **Barcelona, Olbia, Palau, Palermo, Porto Torres,** and

Italian Riviera

Tunisia. TRIS (☎010 576 24 11) and **Tirrenia** (☎081 317 29 99) run to Sardinia. **Grandi Traghetti** (☎010 58 93 31 or 576 13 63) heads to Palermo.

Local Buses: AMT, V. D'Annunzio, 8r (☎010 55 824 14). One-way tickets within the city (L1500/€0.77) valid for 1½hr. All-day tourist passes L5000/€2.58 (foreign passport necessary). Tickets and passes can also be used for funiculare and elevator rides.

Taxis: ☎010 59 66.

Bike Rental: Nuovo Centro Sportivo 2000, P. dei Garibaldi, 18r (☎010 254 12 43; fax 254 26 39). L10,000/€5.16 per day. Open Tu-Sa 9:15am-12:30pm and 3:30-7:30pm; M 3:30-7:30pm; closed Su. MC/V.

✴️🔢 ORIENTATION AND PRACTICAL INFORMATION

Most visitors arrive at one of Genoa's two train stations: **Stazione Principe,** in P. Acquaverde, or **Stazione Brignole,** in P. Verdi. From Stazione Principe take bus #18, 19, 20, 30, 32, 35, or 41 and from Stazione Brignole take bus #19 or 40 to **Piazza de Ferrari** in the center of town. If walking to P. de Ferrari from Stazione Principe, take **via Balbi** to **via Cairoli** (which becomes **via Garibaldi**), and at P. delle Fontane Marose, turn right on **via XXV Aprile.** From Stazione Brignole, turn right out of the station to **via Fiume,** and then right onto **via XX Settembre.** Although the free tourist office map labels sites, it doesn't label many streets. A detailed map from an *edicola* (the "Nicola Vincitorio Pianta Generale" is L7000/€3.62) may help, as Genoa's streets can stump even a native; this is necessary if visiting the *centro storico*.

The *centro storico* (historic center) contains many of Genoa's monuments. Unfortunately, it is also the city's most dangerous quarter, and its shadowy, labyrinthine streets are riddled with drugs and prostitutes at night. You'll need a sixth sense to navigate here, even with a map. While locals may tell you that Genoa is worth getting acquainted with, they will also tell you never to get chummy with the *centro storico* after dark, on Sundays (when shops are closed), or in August (when the natives leave). Even at other times, you should venture into the *centro storico* only with a clear plan and route in mind, and you should over-emphasize the basics of street-smarts: don't look lost or bewildered and stick to relatively crowded streets. In addition to safety concerns, you may find yourself getting an unwanted shower. Those living above bars and restaurants are known to pour water out their windows on carousers when the noise gets out of control. But you're on vacation, so just take it in stride, and trust us: it's charming.

TOURIST, FINANCIAL, AND LOCAL SERVICES

Tourist Offices: APT (☎010 248 711), on Porto Antico, near Aquarium, in Palazzina S. Maria. Find the aquarium directly on the water, face the water, then walk toward the complex of buildings 30m to left. Limited English spoken. Open daily 9:30am-1pm and 3:30-6pm. **APT** has **branches** at Stazione Principe (☎010 246 26 33) and airport (☎010 601 52 47). Both open M-Sa 9:30am-1pm and 3:30-6pm. **Informagiovani,** Palazzo Ducale, 24r (☎010 55 74 320 or 55 74 321), in P. Mateotti, is a youth center offering info on apartment rentals, jobs, concerts, and free Internet access. Reserve 1 week in advance, or hope for a cancellation. Open Sept.-June M-F 9am-12:30pm and 3-6pm; July-Aug. M-Tu and Th-F 9am-12:30pm, W 9am-12:30pm and 3-6pm.

Budget Travel: CTS, V. San Vincenzo, 117r (☎010 56 43 66 or 53 27 48), off V. XX Settembre near Ponte Monumentale. Walk up the flight of stairs on the shopping complex to the left. Student fares available. Open M-F 9am-1pm and 2:30-6pm.

Consulates: UK, V. XX Settembre, 2, 5th fl., #37/38 (☎010 56 48 33). Open Tu-Th 9am-noon. **US,** V. Dante, 2, 3rd fl., #43 (☎010 58 44 92, emergency cell ☎0335 652 1252). Open June-Sept. M-Th 11am-2pm; Oct.-May M noon-2pm, Tu-W 10am-noon, Th 10am-noon and 3-5pm.

Luggage Storage: In both train stations. L5000/€2.58 per 12hr.

English-Language Bookstore: Mondovori, V. XX Settembre, 210r (☎010 58 57 43). Huge bookstore with a full wall of English-language classics and some bestsellers, as

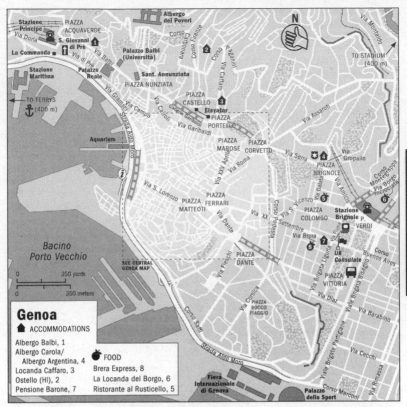

Genoa

🏠 ACCOMMODATIONS

Albergo Balbi, 1
Albergo Carola/
 Albergo Argentina, 4
Locanda Caffaro, 3
Ostello (HI), 2
Pensione Barone, 7

🍎 FOOD

Brera Express, 8
La Locanda del Borgo, 6
Ristorante al Rusticello, 5

well. Choose from a lovely selection of *Let's Go* travel guides in the basement. Open M-Sa 9:30am-11pm, Su 10:30am-1pm and 3-9pm.

EMERGENCY AND COMMUNICATIONS

Emergency: ☎ 113. **Police:** ☎ 112. **Ambulance:** ☎ 118.

Late-Night Pharmacy: Pescetto, V. Balbi, 185r (☎ 010 246 26 97, or 25 27 86, or 25 69 21), near Stazione Principe. List of late-night pharmacies posted.

Hospital: Ospedale San Martino, V. Benedetto XV, 10 (☎ 010 55 51).

Internet Access: Internet Village (☎ 010 570 48 78), at intersection of V. Brigata Bisagno and C. Buenos Aires, across from Piazza Vittoria. L15,000/€7.75 per hr. Open 9am-1pm and 3-7pm; closed Su. MC/V. **A.P.C.A.** via Colombo, 35r (☎/fax 010 581 341). Internet L10,000/€5.16 per hr.; L3000/€1.55 per 15min. Open M-F 9am-noon and 3-7pm. Also, see **Informagiovani** for the possibility of internet *gratis*.

Post Office: Main office, P. Dante, 4/6r (☎ 010 259 46 87), 2 blocks from P. de Ferrari. Holds Fermo Posta. Open M-Sa 8am-7pm. Most branches open 8am-1:30pm.

Postal Code: 16121.

🏠 ACCOMMODATIONS & CAMPING

Rooms in Genoa are scarce only in October, when the city hosts a wave of nautical conventions. Almost without exception, budget lodgings in the *centro storico* and near the port prefer to rent rooms by the hour—try the hostel, if you're willing to take a long bus ride up the hillside, or stick around Stazione Brignole, where the establishments are more refined.

Ostello Per La Gioventù (HI), V. Costanzi, 120 (☎/fax 010 242 24 57). From Stazione Principe, take bus #35 and tell the driver that you want to transfer to #40 at via Napoli; once you get off there, take #40 to hostel. From Stazione Brignole, pick up bus #40 (every 15min.) and ride it all the way up the hill—ask the driver to let you off at the *ostello*. Plenty of space (213 beds), and plenty of amenities: cafeteria, elevator, free lockers, laundry (L12,000/€6.2 per 5kg), parking, TV, wheelchair access, and a view of the city that lies far, far below. Multilingual staff with city info. Breakfast, hot showers, and sheets included. Reception 7-9am and 3:30pm-12:30am. Check-out 9am. Curfew 12:30am. HI card required (available at the hostel). Dorms L25,000/€12.91; family accommodations L27-30,000/€13.94-15.50 per person.

Albergo Argentina, V. Gropallo, 4/4 (☎/fax 010 839 37 22). From Stazione Brignole, turn right on V. de Amicis and continue into P. Brignole. When facing Albergo Astoria, turn right, and walk 15m. Look for the big wooden doors with bronze lion heads on the left hand side of the street and ring the buzzer. 9 large, clean, elegantly furnished rooms overlook a quiet garden in a well-maintained and secure building. If no one answers the door here, go up to the Carola; it's owned by the same family. Singles L50,000/€25.82; doubles L80,000/€41.32. 1 triple and 1 quad available.

Albergo Carola, V. Gropallo, 4/12 (☎010 839 13 40). 2 flights up from the Argentina (see above). Proprietor can give you directions to a laundromat in Italian or Spanish. Singles L45,000/€23.24; doubles L65,000/€33.57, with shower L75,000/€38.73.

Hotel Balbi, V. Balbi, 21/3 (☎/fax 010 25 23 62; hotelbalbi@inwind.it). Housed in a building constructed in 1840, Balbi's large rooms have ornately decorated ceilings that just might induce seraphic sleep. Breakfast L7000/€3.62. 50 beds. With *Let's Go:* singles L40,000/€20.66; doubles L80,000/€41.32, with bath L100,000/€51.65; triples and quads add 30% per person. AmEx/MC/V.

Albergo Barone, V. XX Settembre, 2/23 (☎/fax 010 58 75 78). From Stazione Brignole, veer to the right and walk down V. Fiume to V. XX Settembre. 12 clean rooms are graced with itty-bitty beds and windows that look out on Genoa's lively shopping district. Some English spoken. Self-serve coffee L1000/€0.52. Reception 8:30am-12:30am. Call ahead for reservations (credit card required), especially in late-Oct. Singles L55,000/€28.41, with bath L90,000/€46.48; doubles L75,000/€38.73, with shower L90,000/€46.48, with full bath L100,000/€51.65; triples L100-130,000/€51.65-67.14; quads L120-135,000/€62-69.72. MC/V.

Locanda Caffaro, V. Caffaro, 3 (☎/ fax 010 2472362), of Piazza Portello and midway between Stazione Principe and Stazione Brignole, features 8 clean rooms and a management that's eager to please. Check out their terrace for a view of the cupolas and spires that slope their way down to the waterfront. Singles L40,000/€20.66; doubles L70,000/€36.15. Extra bed L20,000/10.33. AmEx/MC/V.

Camping: The Genoa area is teeming with campgrounds, but many are booked solid during July and August. The tourist office is your best source of info. **Villa Doria,** V. al Campeggio Villa Doria, 15 (☎010 696 96 00), in Pegli, is the closest campground west of the city. Take the train or bus #1, 2, or 3 (buses every 10min.) from P. Caricamento to Pegli; then walk or transfer to bus #93 up V. Vespucci (one stops in front of Pegli's train station every 30min.). Beautiful location with trails that connect to Europe 1, which extends to the North Sea. Free electricity, heated showers, and hospitable, English-speaking hosts. You must bring your own tent. L10,000/€5.16 per person, L10-13,000/€5.16-6.71 per tent. 1- to 4-person bungalows L50-90,000/€25.82-46.48. 50 lots, 200 person capacity. **Genova Est** (☎010 347 20 53), on V. Marcon Loc Cassa. Take the train from Stazione Brignole to the suburb of Bogliasco (10min., 6 per day, L2100/€1.08). A free bus runs by the campgrounds (5min., 4 per day 8:10am-6pm) and will take you from Bogliasco to the campsite. Enjoy the stillness of nature, the buzz of electricity (L3000/€1.55 per day), and the hum of washing machines (L6000/€3.10 per load). L9000/€4.65 per person, L11,000/€5.68 per large tent.

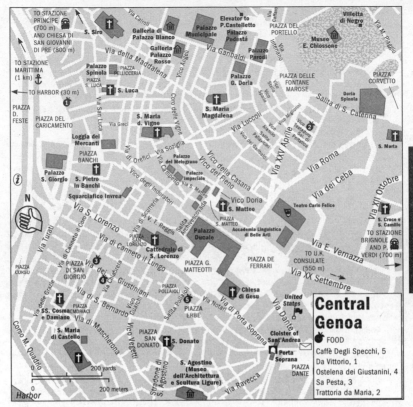

Central Genoa

🍴 FOOD

Caffè Degli Specchi, 5
Da Vittorio, 1
Ostelena dei Giustanini, 4
Sa Pesta, 3
Trattoria da Maria, 2

NORTHWEST ITALY

🍴 FOOD

In culinary terms, a dish prepared *alla Genovese* is served with Genoa's pride, joy, and pesto, a green sauce made from ground basil, pine nuts, garlic, Parmesan cheese, and olive oil. It tastes delicious on almost anything, and the Genovese put it on almost everything, so don't be afraid to experiment. Other delectable edibles include *farinata* (a fried pancake of chick-pea flour) and *pansotti* (ravioli stuffed with spinach and ricotta and served with a creamy walnut sauce). Enhance any meal with olive oil-soaked *focaccia*, a delicious flat bread topped with herbs, olives, onions, or cheese (a specialty of nearby Recco), or join the Genovese kids after school in buying a little slab as an afternoon snack. Just don't spoil your appetite. Stop by a *macelleria* and try a slice of Genoa's world-famous salami—it's fresher than anything you'll get at home. And don't forget to sample the seafood; even as an industrial port town, Genoa unloads its fair share of fantastically fresh fish. If you're looking for authenticity, *trattorie*, found primarily in the *centro storico*, are innumerable and reasonably priced. **Mercato Orientale**, off via XX Settembre south of the *Ponte Monumentale*, is the place to go for fresh fruit and vegetables. (Open M-Tu, Th-Sa 7:30am-1pm and 3:30-7:30pm, W 7:30am-1pm.) Another option is **Supersconto**, V. di San Pietro, 76r. Walk south from P. Bianchi marketplace to the intersection of V. San Pietro and Vico delle Compere. On the right you'll see the Supersconto sign. Buy a good bottle of wine (L5000/€2.58) for the price of a glass of the stuff at a *trattoria*, or try a box of succulent strawberries (L2480/€1.27) for less than half the going rate.

Trattoria da Maria, V. Testa d'Oro, 14r (☎010 58 10 80), off V. XXV Aprile near P. Marose. Checkered tablecloths, overflowing baskets of onions and carrots, and huge containers of spices in this old-fashioned *trattoria* contribute to an aura of flavorsome functionality. The menu changes daily, but the dishes are always delicious. *Pranzo turistico* set-price lunch L13,000/€6.71. Open Su-F noon-2:30pm and 7-9:30pm.

Da Vittorio, V. Sottoripa, 59r (☎010 247 29 27). Ask a local where to find the best seafood in the city, and he will likely name Vittorio. The throngs of people crowding the entrance agree. The catch-of-the-day is displayed in the front window (you'll see waiters periodically carting trays of seafood from the ice back to the kitchen). Lobster around L40,000/€20.66; *primi* from L10,000/€5.16; *secondi* from L15,000/€7.75. Reservations recommended. Open daily noon-4pm and 7pm-1:30am.

La Locanda del Borgo, V. Borgo Incrociati, 47r (☎010 81 06 31), behind Stazione Brignole. Exit the station, turn right and go through the tunnel—V. Borgo Incrociati is straight ahead. Clean, friendly, and popular. Delicious food at great prices. *Primi* from L8000/€4.13. *Menù* M-Th L15,000/€7.75. Open daily 8am-4pm and 8pm-12:30am.

Sa Pesta, V. dei Giustiniani, 16r (☎010 246 83 36), west of P. Matteotti in *centro storico*. Sa Pesta knows pesto; everyone from doctors to dockworkers converge at the communal tables to wolf down Genovese specialties like *minestrone alla genovese,* *torte di verdura* (vegetable tort), and *farinata*. It's even got some history; the premises are said to have been a plotting-ground for *Risorgimento* leaders. *Primi* L8000/€4.13; *secondi* L12,000/€6.20. Takeout available. Open M-Sa noon-2:30pm. Closed Aug.

Pizzeria Vittorio al Mare, V. Belvedere E. Firpo, 1 (☎010 37 60 141), in Boccadasse on the water below its more classy incarnation, the Ristorante Vittorio al Mare. Try a pizza (L8-14,000/€4.13-7.23), or drop a little more cash on *primi* (L15-30,000/€7.75-15.50) and *secondi* (L20-40,000/€10.33-20.66 with fish), as you enjoy the seaside view that will let you forget that you're anywhere near a big city. Have your *dolce della casa* (L5000/€2.58) to go and finish up the meal watching the water (and couples stealing kisses) from the rocks outside. Open Tu-Su noon-3pm and 7:30pm-midnight.

Ristorante al Rusticello, V.S. Vicenzo, 59r (☎010 588 556), not far from Stazione Brignole. Al Rusticello is perfect for the budget traveler who is going crazy sitting at plastic tables and eating from paper tablecloths. Dress up a little—and spend a tad more than you might otherwise—to enjoy good food and low, brick ceilings that make the atmosphere just a little romantic. More wine, dear? *Primi* L10-14,000/€5.16-7.32; *secondi* L16-30,000/€8.26-15.50 for fish and L9-15,000/€4.65-7.75 for meat.

Osteleria dei Giustanini, V. dei Giustinani, 13r (☎010 26 55 22). If Sa Pesta is too crowded, you might try this place; it's right down the street, and touristy it ain't: there are fishing nets on the walls, and if you're lucky the proprietor will be wearing his "Osteleria" baseball cap. Cover L3000/€1.55. *Primi* L10,000/€5.16; *secondi* L13,000/€6.71. Open daily for lunch and 7:30pm-1:30am.

Brera Express, V. di Brera, 11r (☎010 54 32 80), just off V. XX Settembre near Stazione Brignole. The best deal at this cafeteria-style joint is the *menù* for L17,000/€8.78, but all entrees are reasonably priced and fresh. Don't waste your money on the full-service pizzeria on the right side of the restaurant—you'll pay twice the price for the same meal. Open daily 11:45am-3pm and 7pm-midnight. Self-service closes 10pm.

SIGHTS

FROM STAZIONE PRINCIPE TO THE CENTRO STORICO

Outside of the winding alleyways of the *centro storico*, Genoa boats a multitude of *palazzi* built by its famous merchant families. These are best glimpsed along **V. Garibaldi,** which skirts the edge of the *centro storico*, and **V. Balbi,** which is in the heart of the university quarter. On both of those streets, the *palazzi* are nonchalantly lined up, cheek to jowl, so that they dwarf the passersby who walk down through their shadows below. Because of the city's long-standing commercial strength, Genoa collected some of the finest 16th- and 17th-century works of Flemish and Italian art. Mansions, hung with masterpieces, are open to the public.

Via Balbi connects Stazione Principe and **Piazza Nunizia,** formerly called P. Guastata ("broken") for its many ruins. The *piazza* is typical of Genoa: it's small, irregular, and surrounded by *palazzi*. Try one of the residential streets that wind up and around the hills on the outside of the city; there's many a beautiful view to be found if you don't mind a walk. If you're planning on visiting a lot of museums, ask the tourist office or one of the museums themselves about the fixed-price pass.

■PORTELLO-CASTELLETO ELEVATOR. Ride the elevator up with all the locals who find it no more special than taking the bus (it's considered part of Genoa's public transportation system). The thirty-second ride rewards you with one of the best panoramic views of the city, particularly of the port. Walk around the quiet, well-groomed neighborhood and have a pastry or an *espresso;* then snap a few pictures, and take the staircase back down. (*Through the tunnel entrance on P. Portello. Open 6:40am-midnight. L6000/€3.10.*)

■AQUARIUM. Genoa may be practically beach-free, but that doesn't mean you can't still go under the sea. Bask in frigid air-conditioning, gaze at ocean-dwelling fauna cavorting in huge tanks (this aquarium has the largest volume of water of any in Europe), check out the 3-D movie, and start to feel a little cold-blooded. Still not wet enough? Check out the *Grande Nave Blu* (Big Blue Boat) for exhibits that extend above and beyond the sea and an interactive tank where you can grab slithery sea rays and get splashed by slippery pre-teens, all for the noble cause of engendering "harmony with the sea." (*On Porto Antico, across from the tourist office.* ☎010 248 12 05 *for recorded info. Open M-F 9am-7:30pm, last entry at 5:30pm; Sa-Su 9:30am-8:30pm, last entry 6:30pm. In the summer, open Th until 11pm, last entry 9:30pm. Closed M between Nov. 1 and Jan. 28. L22,000/€11.36 per person; cheaper rates for groups.*)

■PALAZZO REALE. Built from 1624 to 1628, this *palazzo* was originally home to the Balbi family, for which the street was named, and then later to the Durazzo family, both powerful in maritime Genoa. The *palazzo* only became the Royal Palace in the 18th century, and the structural setup installed for the Savoy rulers persists for the most part into the present day. Turned over to the state shortly after World War I, the furniture was removed for safe-keeping during World War II. Following the war, the palace was reopened as a museum, but some aspects of the Savoy living quarters (the king and queen's bathrooms, for example) were disassembled in order to create a more aggrandized art museum. Like most of Genoa's *palazzi*, the Palazzo Reale is somewhat crowded on either side and across the relatively narrow street that runs in front of it, so it's easy to walk by without even giving it a second look. Inside, though, it's hard not to be impressed by the opulence and elegance of this once-Royal Palace. The Rococo throne room, covered in red velvet and gold paint, remains untouched, along with the royal waiting room and sleeping quarters. See yourself framed in gold thousands of times in the **Galleria degli Specchi,** modeled after the Hall of Mirrors at Versailles, and be sure to check out the **queen's clock** with a moon that moves across the night sky (to be lit from behind by a candle). Paintings crowding the walls include works by Tintoretto, van Dyck, and Bassano. (*V. Balbi, 10, 10min. west of V. Garibaldi.* ☎010 271 02 72. *Open M-Tu 8:15am-1:45pm, W-Su 8:15am-7:15pm. Ticket counter closes 30min. before museum. L8000/€4.13, ages 18-25 half price, under 18 and over 65 free.*)

VIA GARIBALDI. Alternately called via Aurea (Golden Street) and Strada dei Re (Street of Kings), via Garibaldi remains the most impressive street in Genoa. Lined with elegant *palazzi*, it was constructed during the 17th century by Genoa's wealthiest families seeking to flaunt their prominence. A glance inside the courtyards reveals fountains, frescoes, and leafy gardens. **Galleria Palazzo Rosso,** V. Garibaldi, 18 (☎010 24 76 351), built in the 16th century, earned its name when it was painted red during the 17th century. Red carpeting also covers the floors of exhibit halls that feature lavishly frescoed ceilings and a display of several hundred years worth of Genovese ceramics, including some dainty 18th-century eggholders. The second floor was destroyed when bombed in 1942, but it was rebuilt after the war and now holds several full-length van Dyck portraits and Bernardo

Strozzi's masterpiece, *La Cuoca*. Across the street, the **Galleria di Palazzo Bianco** (1548, rebuilt 1712) exhibits one of the city's largest collections of Ligurian art, as well as some Dutch and Flemish paintings. *(V. Garibaldi, 11. ☎ 010 24 76 377. Both galleries open Tu and Th-F 9am-1pm, W and Sa 9am-7pm, Su 10am-6pm. One L6000/€3.1; both L10,000/€5.16, under 18 and over 60 free. Su free.)*

CHIESA DI GESÙ. Also known as **SS. Ambrogio e Andrea** (1549-1606), the church features over-the-top trompe l'oeil effects and two Rubens canvases, *The Circumcision*, 1605, over the altar, and *St. Ignatius Healing a Woman Possessed of the Devil*, 1620, in the third alcove on the left. *(From P. de Ferrari, take V. Boetto to P. Matteotti. Open daily 7:30am-noon and 4-6:30pm. Free.)*

PALAZZO MUNICIPALE. Built from 1554 to 1570, the Palazzo Municipale (city hall) showcases Nicolò Paganini's violin, the Guarneri del Gesù. The sound of this instrument broke the hearts of some, drove others to suicide, and convinced the rest that they were hearing angels sing. The violin is still used on rare occasions to perform Paganini's works. To see the violin, go upstairs to the left, and ask the secretary. *(V. Garibaldi, 9. Open M-F 8:30am-6pm. Free.)*

SAN GIOVANNI DI PRÈ. This Romanesque church, built in 1180, is one of Genoa's oldest monuments. The vaulted stone roof and filtered light create a cavernous weight and contemplative feel. A left turn around the church leads to the 12th-century **La Commenda,** which housed the Knight Commanders of St. John. *(Head away from the Stazione Principe toward V. Balbi and turn right on Salita di San Giovanni.)*

VILLETTA DI NEGRO. The beautiful park is spread out along a hill, and boasts waterfalls, grottoes, and statues of patriots amidst terraced gardens; a great place for a walk or a peaceful rest. *(From P. delle Fontane Marose, take Salita di S. Caterina to P. Corvetto. Open daily 8am-sunset.)*

HARBOR CRUISES. To view the city from the water, boats depart at least every hour from Porto Antico next to the aquarium, across from the tourist office. Prices depend on the duration of the excursion.

THE CENTRO STORICO

The eerie, beautiful, and sometimes dangerous historic center is a mass of winding and confusing streets bordered by the port, V. Garibaldi, and P. de Ferrari. If you take a turn off of a major street into the *centro storico*, you are likely to end up following a series of narrow, twisting, cobbled alleyways that lead you right to a small *piazza* where there will be some apartments, a cafe, and a 600-year-old architectural masterpiece. Unfortunately, due to its crime rate, the center is only safe for tourists during weekdays, when stores are open. At night, the quarter's seedy underground emerges, and not even the police venture here. It is, however, home to some of Genoa's most memorable monuments: the **duomo, Palazzo Spinola,** and the medieval **Torre Embriaci,** whose Guelph battlements jut out among the buildings to the left when facing the **Chiesa di Santa Maria di Castello.**

▨ CHIESA DI SANTA MARIA DI CASTELLO. This 15th-century church, with foundations that date to 500 BC, is a labyrinth of chapels (added onto the original structure during the 16th-18th centuries), courtyards, cloisters, and crucifixes. In the chapel directly to the left of the high altar, you'll find the spooky **Crocifisso Miracoloso.** According to legend, this wooden Jesus once moved its head to attest to the honesty of a young damsel betrayed by her lover; Jesus's beard is said to grow longer every time a crisis hits the city. As you stroll around, watch your step: the floor is paved with 18th-century tombs. To see the painting of **S. Pietro Martire di Verona,** complete with a halo and a large cleaver conspicuously thrust into his cranium, go upstairs to the right of the high altar, turn right, and right again. The painting is above the door. Incensed locals are said to have turned poor Pietro's head into a butcher block. *(From P.G. Matteotti head up V.S. Lorenzo toward the water and turn left on V. Chiabrera. A left on serpentine V. di Mascherona leads to the church in P. Caricamento. Open daily 9am-noon and 3-6pm, except Su, when there is a Mass in the morning. Free.)*

DUOMO (SAN LORENZO). Already in existence by the 9th century, the *duomo* was enlarged and reconstructed between the 12th and 16th centuries after religious authorities deemed it "imperfect and deformed." The result may have been more perfect, but it sure wasn't symmetrical—the church has a lopsided appearance because only one of the two planned bell towers was completed. The striped Gothic facade flaunts copiously carved main entrances and 9th-century lions and sirens and vines (oh, my!) that give way to an incongruous interior (the front part, holding the altar, was added during the 17th and 18th centuries). Rub the bomb displayed on the right-hand side of the church shortly after you enter for good luck (or a touch of holy grace); it was dropped by the English on the church during World War II but didn't explode. If you have time, check out the **Museo del Tesoro** (a showcase of some of the church's treasures), which includes beautiful goblets, arks, and the beautiful emerald-colored Sacro Catino (sacred bowl) of mysterious origin. *(P. San Lorenzo, off V. San Lorenzo, which emerges from P. Matteotti. Open M-Sa 8am-7pm, Su 7am-7pm. Free. Museo del Tesoro open M-Sa 9am-noon and 3-6pm; guided tour every 30min.; entrance to the Museo del Tesoro L10,000/€5.16, group and family discounts.)*

PORTA SOPRANA. The historical centerpiece of P. Dante (and today the passageway from the modern *piazza* into the *centro storico*), this medieval structure was built in 1100 to intimidate enemies of the Republic of Genoa. Mischievous would-be assailant Emperor Frederico Barbarossa took one look at the mighty arch whose Latin inscription welcomes the passing of those who come in peace but threatens doom to enemy armies, and decided to terrorize elsewhere. Thus the city endured, and the bastion of strength that was the Porta would come to serve as the portal onto the world for **Christopher Columbus.** His reputed boyhood home lies to the right of the gate (his father was the gatekeeper; his mother was the keymaster). In his backyard is the Cloister of Sant'Andrea, the romantic remains of a 12th-century convent. *(From P.G. Matteotti, head down V. di Porta Soprana. ☎/fax 010 24 65 346. Columbus's home open Sa and Su 9am-noon and 3-6pm.)*

PALAZZO SPINOLA DI PELLICCERIA. Built at the close of the 16th century to flaunt Genovese mercantile monies, this *palazzo* had a fan in Peter Paul Rubens, who described it warmly in his 1622 book on pleasing palaces. It is now home to the **Galleria Nazionale,** a collection of fantastic art and furnishings. Most of the objects were donated by the family of Maddalena Doria Spinola, who owned the palace during the first half of the 18th century. The building shows its age; different sections represent the variety of styles that shaped it through the centuries, including an 18th-century kitchen. Van Dyck's four portraits of the evangelists reside in the *Sala da Pranzo.* Be sure to visit the *terazzo* on the top of the building for a great view of the city's rooftops and outlying hills. *(P. di Pellicceria, 1, between V. Maddalena and P.S. Luca. ☎010 247 70 61. Open Tu-Sa 8:30am-7:30pm, Su 1-8pm. L8000/€4.13. 18-25, over 65, and students L4000/€2.07.)*

CHIESA DI SAN SIRO. Genoa's first cathedral (rebuilt 1588-1613) may remind you of grandma's house with layers of dusty trinkets that represent a worthwhile history, if you're willing to sort through the clutter. Admire the majestic vaulted ceilings (painted with frescoes in 1650) and chapels bursting with paintings. The arches sing exuberantly (off-key, but not bad for an arch) and shine a holy light into the world. *(Where V.S. Siro branches to the right. Open M-F 4-6pm. Free.)*

PIAZZA SAN MATTEO. This tiny square contains the houses and chapel of the medieval rulers of Genoa, the Doria family. The animal reliefs above the first floor are the trademarks of the masons who built the houses, and the striped Romanesque stonework is reminiscent of many of Genoa's other well-aged buildings. Chiseled into the facade of the small but elaborately decorated **Chiesa di San Matteo,** founded by the Dorias in 1125, are descriptions of the aristocrats' great deeds. The church was rebuilt in 1278 and raised above street level as a reflection of the power of the Dorias in religious as well as civic affairs. *(Behind the duomo, off Salita all'Arcicovato. Open M-Sa 8am-noon and 4-6:30pm, Su 9am-noon and 4-6:30pm. Free.)*

MUSEO DI SANT'AGOSTINO (MUSEO DELL'ARCHITETTURA E SCULTURA LIGURE). The old city's newest addition occupies the former monastery of S. Agostino. The museum surveys Genoa's history through its surviving art (many pieces have been plucked from buildings for preservation). Giovanni Pisano carved the outstanding though piecemeal funerary monument for Margherita of Brabant (1312). Also noteworthy is the Neoclassic Penitent Magdalena in the Desert, so sensuous it borders on sacrilege. *(Follow directions to Porta Soprana and head toward the port on V. Ravecca. ☎010 20 60 22. Open Tu-Sa 9am-7pm, Su 9am-12:30pm. L6000/€3.10.)*

🎵 ENTERTAINMENT

The **Carignano D'Essai** shows English-language movies from October through June at V. Villa Glori, 8, near P. dei Ferrari. (☎010 570 23 48. Shows W-Th 3pm and 9pm, Su 7pm.) In the city, V. XX Settembre has a few bars that draw modest crowds in the evening and, in particular, on the weekends. A 20min. bus ride (#31) down C. Italia takes you to **Boccadasse,** a seaside playground of wealthy Genovese. Sea breezes replace ceaseless cigarette smoke, and soft promises of undying love overwrite graffiti threatening anarchy. Here massive seaside mansions tower over remnants of stone piers washed away by the waves, and extravagant restaurants with dining *salas* (halls) jutting out over the cove.

Matilda Estate, V. Lungomare 27-29 (☎0335 69 694 70 37 for reservations and info), at the Sporting Genova, at C. Italia. In the summer (starting late Apr.) the party moves to the beach. Matilda Estate, one of Genoa's top night spots for young and beautiful late-night revelers, is the place to move with it. Long lines lead to ocean breezes, sexy bartender contests, and live music 11pm. Get rebellious and rev up for the disco that starts well after midnight and lasts until 4am. Cover L20,000/€10.33. First drink L20,000/€10.33. Eat for an additional L25,000/€12.91.

Le Corbusier, V.S. Donato, 36/38 (☎010 246 86 52). Smoke rises from the crowd of students and artists gathered in this self-consciously hip place. The music and the atmosphere are more thoughtful, intense, and—dare we say—avant-garde than in most other bars. With art showings and the occasional literary lecture, Le Corbusier feels like a Renaissance salon. Commence your philosophizing and drink yourself into oblivion. Open M-F 8am-1am, Sa-Su 6pm-1am.

Caffè degli Specchi, Salita Pollaiuoli, 43r (☎010 28 12 93). Walk down Salita Pollaioli from P. Matteotti. The cafe will appear on your left, with umbrellas shading outdoor seating in the summer. Inside, the bar is lined with mirrors and marble, and a sophisticated crowd pleas for a *bicchierino di vino* (glass of wine; L3000/€1.55). a *piccolo panino* (L2-6000/€1.03-3.1), or a frozen *forza cappuccino* (L1800/€0.93). Upstairs fresh salads (including chicken and apple) run L13,000/€6.71. Open M-Sa 7am-8pm.

RIVIERA DI LEVANTE

CAMOGLI ☎0185

The postcard-perfect town of Camogli throbs with color. Peach, sun-faded houses crowd the hilltop, lively red and turquoise boats knock about in the water, fishing nets coat the greying docks, and bright umbrellas blanket the dark stone beaches. Like most of the Ligurian coast, the hills slope right into the sea, so you'll find yourself going from one street to another by way of staircases. The effort is worth it because each new level adds a little more to the panoramic vista that centers around Camogli. The town takes its name—a contraction of *Casa Mogli* (Wives' House)—from the women who ran the town while their husbands manned its once massive fishing fleet. The old man has long since left the sea, and what Dickens called a "piratical little place" has mellowed into a small, peaceful resort town of 6000. More down-to-earth and youth-friendly than nearby Portofino and Santa Margherita, Camogli is the place to go for a low-key mosey down a boardwalk.

▣ TRANSPORTATION

Trains: On Genoa-La Spezia line. Open M-F 6am-noon, Sa-Su 1-7:15pm. Ticket counter open M-F 5:50am-12:40am, Sa-Su 12:50-7:40pm. Tickets available at tourist office when ticket office is closed. Luggage storage availabe (see below). To: **Genoa** (20min., 32 per day 5:16am-10:09pm, L2700/€1.39); **La Spezia** (1½hr., 21 per day 5:27am-7:30pm, L6400/€3.31); **Santa Margherita** (10min., 24 per day 5:27am-11:45pm, L1900/€0.98); **Sestri Levante** (30min., 20 per day 5:27am-8:46pm, L3600/€1.86).

Buses: Tigullio buses leave P. Schiaffino, near tourist office, for nearby towns. Buy tickets at tourist office or at *tabacchi* at V. Repubblica, 25. To **Santa Margherita** (30min., 14 per day, L2000/€1.03). Buses also run to **Ruta, San Lorenzo,** and **Rapallo.**

Ferries: Golfo Paradiso, V. Scalo, 3 (☎0185 77 20 91; fax 77 12 63; www.golfoparadiso.it), near P. Colombo by the water. Buy tickets on dock. To: **Cinque Terre** (Portovenere at Vernazza; June 15-July 1 Su; July 1-Aug. 1 Tu and Sa-Su; Sept. 1-15 Th and Su; 9:30am, returns 5:30pm; L20,000/€10.33); **Portofino** (Sa-Su 3pm, return 5:30pm; L14,000/€7.23); **San Fruttuoso** (30min.; May-Sept. 7-11 per day; L10,000/€5.15).

✦❷ ORIENTATION AND PRACTICAL INFORMATION

Camogli climbs uphill from the sea into pine and olive groves overlooking the beach and harbor below. To get to the center of town, go right as you exit the **Camogli-San Fruttuoso station.** About 100m from the station, turn left down the stairs to **via Garibaldi.** From V. Garibaldi turn right into the alley to the beaches.

Tourist Office: V. XX Settembre, 33 (☎0185 77 10 66). Turn right as you leave station. Helps with accommodations. English spoken. Open M-Sa 9am-12:30pm and 3:30-7pm, Su 9am-1pm.

Currency Exchange: Banco di Chiavari della Riviera Ligure, V. XX Settembre, 19 (☎0185 77 51 13). Reasonable rates. **ATM** outside. Open M-F 8:20am-1:20pm and 2:35-4pm.

Luggage Storage: In the train station. L5000/€2.58 per bag

Medical Emergency: ☎118.

Police: ☎0185 77 07 25. **Carabinieri:** V. Cuneo, 30f (☎112 or 0185 77 00 00).

Late-Night Pharmacy: Dr. Machi, V. Repubblica, 4-6 (☎0185 77 10 81). Sign lists late-night pharmacies. Open Tu-Sa July-Aug. 8:30am-12:30pm and 4-8pm; Sept.-June 3:30-7:30pm.

Hospital: S. Martino (☎ 0105 552 794) in Genoa. In Recco, V. Bianchi, 1 (☎0185 743 77)

Post Office: V. Cuneo, 4 (☎0185 77 43 32), under an arcade. Exit train station and turn left. Open M-F 8am-1:30pm, Sa 8am-noon.

Postal Code: 16032.

▐ ACCOMMODATIONS

▨**Albergo La Camogliese,** V. Garibaldi, 55 (☎0185 77 14 02; fax 77 40 24; camogliese@libero.it). Exit train station and walk down the long stairway to right, where you'll see a big blue sign. Large, well-decorated rooms are a joy. Phone, TV, and bath in every room. Steps away from the beach. Singles L70-110,000/€36.15-56.81; doubles L120-140,000/€62.00-72.30. Prices might go down L10,000/€5.16 if you can forgo breakfast. 10% *Let's Go* discount on cash payments. AmEx/D/MC/V.

Albergo Augusta, V. Schiaffino, 100 (☎0185 77 05 92; fax 77 05 93; hotelaugusta@galactica.it), at other end of town. Recently renovated rooms will have you sailing the ocean blue before you even get to the beach. 15 beds. Every room with TV, phone, and bath, some with harbor view and balcony. 10min. Internet use for those with *Let's Go* in hand. Breakfast L10,000/€5.16. Singles L70-90,000/€36.15-46.48; doubles L100-130,000/€51.65-67.14. AmEx/MC/V.

Albergo Selene, V. Cuneo, 16 (☎ 0185 77 01 49; fax 77 20 38). Exit train station and take a left past the post office. Rooms are clean and simple; some have balcony. Breakfast included. Singles L70,000/€36.15; doubles L130,000/€67.14; triples L50,000/€25.82 per person. AmEx/MC/V.

Pensione Faro, V. Schiaffino, 116-118 (☎ 0185 77 14 00), above the restaurant of the same name, down the street from the Augusta. 8 beds. Pension required in summer: half-pension doubles L90,000/€46.48 per person, full-pension doubles L120,000/€62.00 per person. In winter, doubles L100,000/€51.65. AmEx/MC/V.

☕ FOOD

The numerous shops on V. Repubblica (one block up from the harbor) and **Picasso supermarket,** V. XX Settembre, 35, supply picnickers. (Open M-Sa 8:30am-12:30pm and 4:30-7:30pm.) An **open-air market** in P. del Teatro offers clothes, food, and fish-hooks. (Open W 8am-noon.)

Pizzeria Il Lido, V. Garibaldi, 133 (☎ 0185 77 01 41), on the boardwalk. Scrumptious pizza, served and consumed by bronzed *camogliese*. Great view of sunbathers and the ocean, and the hostess is likely to greet you in an itsy-bitsy teeny-weeny yellow polka dot bikini. Pizza L10-15,000/€5.16-7.75; *primi* from L16,000/€8.26. Cover L3000/€1.55. Open W-M 12:30-2:30pm and 7:30-10:30pm.

La Rotonda, V. Garibaldi, 101 (☎ 0185 77 14 02), on the boardwalk. Great view of the harbor. Pizza, pasta, and seafood. *Primi* from L9000/€4.65; *secondi* from L15,000/€7.75; pizza run L9-14,000. Open daily 12:30-2:30pm and 7:30-10:30pm; in winter W-M 12:30-2:30pm and 7:30-11pm.

Slurp, V. Garibaldi, 104 (☎ 0185 77 43 53). That's the sound you'll make when you taste the creamy *gelato*. Their *granite* (ices) are famous. 2-flavor cones L3000/€1.55, 3-flavor L4000/€2.07. Open daily 10am-midnight; in winter Tu-Su 10am-midnight.

Il Bar Teatro, P. Matteotti, 3 (☎ 0185 77 25 72). Serving 60 types of pizza for 40 years (from L8000/€4.13), Il Teatro ought to elicit a "Bravo!" Open daily 7am-2pm and 7:30-10pm. AmEx/MC/V.

👁 🎵 SIGHTS AND ENTERTAINMENT

If you tire of the beach and boardwalk, you might make the three-hour hike to **San Fruttuoso** (see below). The Camogli tourist office has a useful trail map. Blue dots mark the well-worn path, which starts at the end of V. Cuneo (near the *carabinieri* station). Ferry or snorkeling trips also make interesting (but more costly) diversions. **Band B Diving Center,** V.S. Fortunato, 11/13, off P. Colombo, offers boats with 10 person capacities, 18 immersion spots along the coast, and three excursions daily for scuba diving (L65-100,000/€33.57-51.65 per person) and snorkeling at L20,000/€10.33 per person. (☎ 0185 77 27 51. Open daily 9am-7pm.)

On the second Sunday in May, tourists descend on the town for an enormous fish fry, the **Sagra del Pesce.** The frying pan, constructed in 1952, measures 4m in diameter and holds over 2000 fish. If you miss the sardine-rush, you may still see the pans, as they adorn a city wall for the remainder of the year. They hang to the right on V. Garibaldi as you descend the stairs to the beaches.

Camogli offers slim nightlife pickings, but listen for thudding disco-house from the bar **Il Barcollo,** on V. Garibaldi. (☎ 0185 77 33 22. Open 5pm-3am.)

🔲 DAYTRIP FROM CAMOGLI: SAN FRUTTUOSO

You can hike to San Fruttuoso from Portofino Mare (1½hr.), Portofino Vetta (1½hr.), or Camogli (3hr.). Golfo Paradiso (☎ 0185 77 20 91) runs boats from Camogli (9 per day 8am-5pm; last return from San Fruttuoso 6pm; L10,000/€5.16). Servizio Marittimo del Tigullio (☎ 0185 28 46 70) runs ferries from Portofino (every hr. 9:30am-4:30pm, L9000/€4.65) and Santa Margherita (every hr. 9:15am-4:15pm; L11,000/€5.68).

If you approach tiny San Fruttuoso by sea, the 16th-century *torre di Doria* (tower of Doria) will appear as a lone gladiator surrounded by an arena of green. The inhabitants of what can barely be called a hamlet are used to the solitary stance—when waters are rough, the villagers are isolated for days at a time (the only other means of reaching San Fruttuoso is by foot). The 10th-century **Abbazia di San Fruttuoso di Capodimonte,** the Benedictine monastery for which the town was named, houses a cloister, displays archaeological artifacts, and has a tower which you can climb for a panoramic view. (☎0185 77 27 03. Open June-Sept. Tu-Su 10am-5:30pm; Oct. and Mar.-May Tu-Su 10am-6pm; Dec.-Feb. Sa-Su and holidays 10am-4pm. Closed Nov. L6-10,000/€3.10-5.16, children L4-6000/€2.07-3.10; prices vary according to special exhibitions.) Fifteen meters offshore and 17m underwater, the bronze Christ of the Depths stands with arms upraised in memory of the sea's casualties. The statue now serves as protector of scuba divers—here is your chance to take the plunge under watchful eyes. A replica of the statue stands in **Chiesa di San Fruttuoso,** next to the abbey. Think about the ferry ride home before you pass on making an offering to the *Sacrario dei Morti in Mare.* Its sparkling waters and ancient monastery make San Fruttuoso a quiet, restful daytrip. Avoid the expensive, touristy restaurants that outnumber the houses here—bring a picnic lunch. **Da Laura** has cheap hot meals. (Open daily 8am-6pm.)

SANTA MARGHERITA LIGURE ☎0185

From its founding in the 12th century, Santa Margherita Ligure led a calm existence as a fishing village far from the Levante limelight. In the early 20th century, the town fell into favor with Hollywood stars, a popularity boosted in the 1950s by a *National Geographic* feature. Grace and glitz paint the shore, but Art Deco lighting softens the pastel walls, palm trees line the harbor, and the serenity of the town's early days lingers on. Less overrun than much of the area, Santa Margherita remains one of the few affordable bases for exploring the Riviera di Levante.

⌐ TRANSPORTATION

Trains: P. Federico Raoul Nobili at top of V. Roma. Intercity trains on the Pisa-Genoa line stop at Santa Margherita. Luggage storage available (p. 148). To **Genoa** (40min., 2-3 per hr. 4:37am-10:03pm, L3600/€1.86) and **La Spezia** (2 per hr. 5:39am-9:17pm, L6900/€3.56), via **Cinque Terre** (1½hr., L6000/€3.1).

Buses: Tigullio buses (☎0185 28 88 34) depart from P. V. Veneto at the small green kiosk on the waterfront. To **Portofino** (20min., 3 per hr., L1700/€0.88) and **Camogli** (30min., every hr., L2000/€1.03). Ticket office open 7:10am-7:40pm.

Ferries: Tigullio, V. Palestro, 8/1b (☎0185 28 15 98 or 28 46 70). Boats leave from the docks at P. Martiri della Libertà. To: **Cinque Terre** (July-Sept. W and Sa-Su 1 tour trip per day; L25-30,000/€12.91-15.50); **Portofino** (every hr.; L6000/€3.1); and **San Fruttuoso** (every hr.; L11,000/€5.68).

Taxis: (☎0185 28 65 08), P. Stazione.

Bike and Moped Rental: Noleggio Cicli e Motocicli, V. XXV Aprile, 11 (☎0330 87 86 12). Motorscooter driving license required for tandems. Under 18 must have guardian's signature to rent mopeds. Bike L7000/€3.62 per hr., L20,000/€10.33 per day. Motor scooter L30,000/€15.5 per hr., L80,000/€41.32 per day. Tandem L15,000/€7.75 per hr., L30,000/€15.5 per day. Open daily 10am-12:30pm and 3-7pm.

✳🔢 ORIENTATION AND PRACTICAL INFORMATION

To get to the waterfront from the train station, take **via Roma,** or take the stairs to the right of the stop sign in front of the station and follow **via della Stazione** directly to the water. Two main squares lie on the waterfront: **Piazza Martiri della Libertà** and the smaller **Piazza Vittorio Veneto,** both lined with palm trees. **via Gramsci** winds around the port and **via XXV Aprile** leads to the tourist office, becoming **Corso Matteotti** alongside the other main square in town, **Piazza Mazzini.**

Tourist Office: Pro Loco, V. XXV Aprile, 2b (☎0185 28 74 85; fax 28 30 34). Turn right from train station onto V. Roma, follow it to C. Rainusso, and turn left. V. XXV Aprile is a hard right up from Largo Giusti. Enthusiastic staff provides info, maps, and accommodations service. Open M-Sa 9am-12:30pm and 3-6pm, Su 9:30am-12:30pm.

Luggage Storage: At Hotel Terminus, in front of train station. L10,000/€5.16 per bag.

Emergency: ☎113. **Guardia Medica:** (☎118), for late-night, weekend medical attention.

Police: Polizia Municipale, C. Matteotti, 54 (☎0185 20 54 50).

Late-Night Pharmacies: Farmarcia Internazionale, P. Martiri della Liberta, 2 (☎0185 28 71 89; fax 28 17 08). Open M-Sa 8:30am-12:30pm and 3:30-7:30pm; in winter 8:30am-12:30pm and 4-8pm. AmEx/MC/V. **Farmacia di Turno,** V. Partigiani d'Italia, 31/2 (☎ 0185 28 84 84). Open 8am-1pm and 3-10pm.

Hospital: (☎0185 68 31), V.F. Arpe.

Post Office: V. Gruncheto, 46 (☎0185 28 88 40), near train station. Open M-F 8am-6pm, Sa 8am-1:15pm. Fermo Posta. **Currency exchange** L5000/€2.58.

Postal Code: 16038.

▗ ACCOMMODATIONS

Steer clear of ritzy waterfront accommodations. Santa Margherita is small enough that there's no such thing as a long walk to the ocean, and you can put the L30-40,000/€15.50-20.66 you'll save on a room without a view to good use.

▓ **Hotel Terminus,** P. Nobili, 4 (☎0185 28 61 21; fax 28 25 46), to left as you exit station. So close you might hear the slight rumble of trains. Bask in the Italian Riviera's famed hotel culture. Owner Angelo's perfect English, enthusiasm, and cooking will ensure a glorious stay. Buffet breakfast included. 4-course dinner on the garden terrace for a mere L30,000/€15.49. Singles L90,000/€46.48; doubles L110,000/€56.81. AmEx/MC/V.

▓ **Hotel Nuova Riviera,** V. Belvedere, 10 (☎ 0185 28 74 03; info@nuovariviera.com; www.nuovariviera.com), in a garden near P. Mazzini. Spacious, elegant rooms in a beautiful old villa built at the turn of the 20th century. Breakfast included. Proprietors call each other 'Mama' and 'Papa,' and you're likely to be greeted with an exuberant *buongiorno* when you arrive. Owners also own a B&B. Internet access for L15,000/€7.75 per hr. Singles L100,000/€51.65; doubles L170,000/€87.8; triples L220,000/€113.62; prices lower in off-season. *Affitacamere* (rooms to rent) available. Cash discount L10,000/€5.16. MC/V. No credit cards or cash discount at B&B.

Hotel Europa, V. Trento, 5 (☎0185 28 71 87; fax 28 01 54; hoteuro@tin.it; www.pangea.it/hoteleuropa). Tucked behind the harbor glitz, this modern hotel offers 18 rooms with TV, phone, and bathroom. Parking available. Singles L100-120,000/€51.65-62; doubles L120-160,000/€62-82.63; triples L160-220,000/€82.63-113.62; quads L180-240,000/€92.96-123.95. D/MC/V.

▗ FOOD

Markets, bakeries, and fruit vendors line C. Matteotti. On Fridays from 8am to 1pm, when cars are ousted from the *corso*, the street welcomes pedestrian shoppers. The **COOP supermarket,** C. Matteotti, 9c, off P. Mazzini, stocks basics. (☎0185 28 43 15. Open M-Sa 8:15am-1pm and 3:30-8pm. V.) The day's catch, hauled in by the local fleet, is sold at the morning **fish market** on Lungomare Marconi. (Open daily 8am-12:30pm; boats arrive Th-Tu 4-6pm.)

▓ **La Piadineria and Crêperia,** V. Giuncheto, 5, off P. Martiri della Libertà. Escape from the traditional into the subtly hip. This nook-in-the-wall serves 30 types of *piadine* (heaping sandwiches on soft, thin bread; L9-10,000/€4.65-5.16), crêpes (L6-9000/€3.1-4.65), and *taglieri* (generous plates of assorted meats and cheeses; L18,000/€9.3). The delicious wines (L5000/€2.58), beers (L4000/€2.07), and cocktails (L10,000/€5.16) complete a meal or late-night snack. Open daily 6pm-midnight.

Trattoria Da Pezzi, V. Cavour, 21 (☎0185 28 53 03). Skip the pizza and load up on some real food. With *prosciutto* and melon for L11,000/€5.68, pasta from L6500/€3.36, and *secondi* from L5000/€2.58, you can afford to accent the meal with a glass of beer (or several; from L3000/€1.55 per glass) and finish off the meal with a whiskey on the rocks...make that whiskey on *gelato* (L7000/€3.62).

Trattoria Baicin, V. Algeria, 9 (☎0185 28 67 63), off P. Martiri della Libertà. Papà Piero is the master chef. Mamma Carmela rolls the pasta and simmers the sauces. Try the homemade *trofie alla genovese* (gnocchi with string beans and pesto; L12,000/€6.20). *Primi* from L10,000/€5.16. *Menù* L28,000/€14.46. Cover L2500/€1.29. Open Tu-Su noon-3pm and 7pm-midnight. Kitchen closes 10:30pm. AmEx/MC/V.

👁🎵 SIGHTS AND ENTERTAINMENT

If the lapping waves aren't invigorating your spirit, there's always the holy water at the Rococo **Basilica di Santa Margherita** at P. Caprera; it's held in basins shaped liked scallops. Dripping with gold and crystal, the church also contains fine Flemish and Italian works. At P. Martiri della Libertà, 32, a crowd guzzles beer and watches European football at **Sabot American Bar.** (☎0185 28 07 47. Open W-M 10am-2am.) The tribute to drinking (US of A style) continues right down the street at **Miami,** P. della Liberta, 29. Neon blue lights, couples necking in white vinyl booths, and L12,000/€6.20 Manhattans set the high-rollin' scene. (☎0185 28 34 24. Open daily 5pm-3am.) For something a little more low-key, go to **La Piadineria,** which is just a few doors down, and have a glass of wine or some dessert.

📷 DAYTRIP FROM SANTA MARGHERITA LIGURE: PORTOFINO

Take a bus to Portofino Mare (not Portofino Vetta). From Portofino's P. Martiri della Libertà, Tigullio buses run to Santa Margherita (3 per hr., L1700/€0.88). Tickets sold at the green kiosk in P. Martiri della Libertà. Portofino is also accessible by ferry from Santa Margherita (every hr. 9am-7pm, L6000/€3.1) and Camogli (2 per day, L13,000/€6.71).

Yachts the size of the Love Boat fill the harbor; chic boutiques and art galleries line the cobbled streets, and luxury cars fill the parking lot. But as long as you don't buy anything, princes and paupers alike can enjoy the shore's curves and tiny bay; the town makes a pleasant morning or afternoon outing from Santa Margherita. The one-hour walk along the road offers the chance to scout out small rocky beaches, one of which, **Njasca,** offers boat rental in the summer months. Be sure to call first, because they may change their location. (☎ 347 17 57 682; wind-surfing L15,000/€7.75 per hr.; kayaks L10-15,000/€5.16-7.75; pedal boats L15,000/€7.75; tiny sailboats L25,000/€12.91.) **Paraggi** (where the bus stops) is the area's only sandy beach, and only a small strip is free. A **nature reserve** surrounds Portofino and Paraggi; treks through the hilly terrain lead past ruined churches and voluptuous villas to Santa Margherita (2½-4hr.) and San Fruttuoso (3hr.).

In town, follow the signs uphill from the bay and escape to the cool, stark white interior of the **Chiesa di San Giorgio.** Behind the church lies a small cemetery—outcast Protestants were laid to rest just outside these walls. A few minutes up the road outside the 16th-century **castle** is a serene garden with a view of the sea. The castle began as a fortress, but in the 19th century was turned over to civilian hands and converted to a summer home. (Open daily 9am-7pm; in winter 10am-5pm. L4500/€2.32.) Back in town, **Alimentari Repetto,** on P. Martiri dell'Olivetta (the main square in front of the harbor), fortifies hikers with Gatorade for L4000/€2.07, sandwiches for L5000/€2.58 and up, and *foccaccia* for L2000/€1.03. (☎0185 26 90 56. Open daily 8am-10pm; in winter 9am-6pm.) A drink at one of the numerous bars along the harbor costs upward of L10,000/€5.16, but if your budget isn't too tight, watching twilight fall over the harbor is well worth the price.

At the **tourist office,** V. Roma, 35, on the way to the waterfront from the bus stop, the English-speaking staff has maps and brochures. (☎0185 26 90 24. Open daily

9:30am-1:30pm and 2-7pm; in winter 9:30am-12:30pm and 2:30-5:30pm.) **Exchange currency** at the Banco di Chiavari, V. Roma, 14/16. (☎0185 26 91 64. Open M-F 8:20am-1:20pm and 2:30-4pm.) In an **emergency,** call the police, V. del Fondaco, 8 (☎0185 26 90 88). The **pharmacy** is at P. Martiri della Libertà, 6. (☎0185 26 91 01. Open daily 9am-1pm and 4-8pm; closed Su in winter. AmEx/MC/V.) The **post office** is at V. Roma, 32. (☎0185 26 91 56. Open M-F 8am-1:30pm, Sa 8am-noon.)

CINQUE TERRE ☎0187

Eugenio Montale, Italian poet and Nobel laureate, spent the first 30 years of his life in Cinque Terre. Of his hometowns, he wrote, *"Qui delle divertite passioni per miracolo tace la guerra"* ("Here the passions of pleasure miraculously quiet conflict"). If you're plagued with embattled emotions, the five bright fishing villages of Cinque Terre will bring your spirit sweet silence. A vast expanse of dazzling turquoise sea laps against the *cittadine,* which cling to a stretch of terraced hillsides and steep crumbling cliffs. Through a trick of perspective and sea mist, each town, when glimpsed from the next, appears both distant and proximate, as if an unreachable mountain village in one moment might become a handful of pastels and pebbles in the next. You can hike the string of five towns end-to-end in a several hours, yet all the villages—Monterosso, Vernazza, Corniglia, Manarola, and Riomaggiore—remain distinct worlds, each with its own character and distinctive atmosphere. These Five Lands are the poet's mystical muse—and fodder for a booming tourist industry. Reserve a room in advance (a month or two for summer), or end up daytripping to Cinque Terre from Levanto or La Spezia.

⌐ TRANSPORTATION

Trains: The towns lie on the Genoa-La Spezia (Pisa) line. Schedules available at tourist office. 24hr. **Cinque Terre Tourist Ticket** (L5500/€2.84), allows unlimited trips between the five towns and either La Spezia or Levanto. Available at the 5 train stations—ask at ticket window. **Monterosso** is the most accessible. From the station on V. Fegina, the north end of town, trains run to: **Florence** (3½hr.; every hr.; L14,500/€7.49), via **Pisa** (2½hr., every hr., L8500/€4.39); **Genoa** (1½hr., every hr., L7000/€3.62); **La Spezia** (20min., every 30min., L2300/€1.19); **Rome** (7hr.; every 2hr.; L51,500/€26.60). Frequent trains connect the 5 towns (5-20min., every 50min., L1700-2300/€0.88-1.19). Make sure your train is local.

Ferries: Monterosso can be reached by ferry from **La Spezia** (1hr.; 2 per day; L33,000/€17.04). Ferries from Monterosso also connect the towns. **Navigazione Golfo dei Poeti** (☎0187 96 76 76), in front of the **IAT** office at the port (in the old part of town). To: **Manarola** and **Riomaggiore** (6 per day; L10,000/€5.16); **Vernazza** (5 per day, L5000/€2.58); **Portovenere** (1hr.; L18,000/€9.30). **Motobarca Vernazza** also heads from Monterosso to **Vernazza** (5min., 1 per hr. 9:30am-6:45pm, L5000/€2.58).

Taxis: ☎0335 61 65 842 or 616 58 45.

Boat Rental: Along the beach. Pedal boats L15-17,000/€7.75-8.78 per hr.; kayaks L10-15,000/€5.16-7.75 per hr., L50,000/€25.82 per day; motorboats L30-45,000/€15.5-23.24 per hr., L150-220,000/€77.47-113.62 per day.

◄✳⁊ ORIENTATION AND PRACTICAL INFORMATION

The villages are connected by trains and footpaths that traverse the terraced vineyards and rocky shoreline. **Monterosso,** the beach bum's town of choice, is the most commercially developed, and has three sandy beaches and spirited nightlife. From this hub, the four other villages are easily accessible by train as well as by foot, ferry, and kayak, depending on your inclination and stamina. **Vernazza** is graced by a large seaside *piazza,* surrounded by colorful buildings and a harbor full of parked boats. Its glassy, sheltered cove has a pebble beach and a rocky pier covered with swimmers and sunbathers. **Corniglia** hovers high above the sea, and hundreds of steps connect it to its train station. Though lacking in the beachside glitter of the other towns, it offers a strong sense of peaceful solitude and is an amazing vantage-point for viewing romantic sunsets. **Manarola** has quiet streets, an excellent new hostel, plenty of quick and quality eateries, and a spectacular swimming cove. **Riomaggiore** has a bundle of rooms to rent and is home to a tiny harbor, where you're nearly as likely to see a fishermen swabbing varnish on a boat hull as a tanner smoothing on oil. **Listings are for Monterosso unless otherwise indicated.**

TOURIST, FINANCIAL, AND LOCAL SERVICES

Tourist Office: Pro Loco, V. Fegina, 38 (☎0187 81 75 06), below the train station. Info on boats, hikes, and hotels. Accommodations service. Staff speaks English and exhibits grace under pressure. Open Apr.-Oct. M-Sa 10am-12:30pm and 3-5:30pm, Su 10am-12:30pm. In **Riomaggiore,** an office in the train station (☎0187 92 06 33) provides info on trails, hotels, and excursions. Open daily June-Sept. 10am-6pm.

Tours: Navigazione 5 Terre (☎0187 81 74 52) offers tours (L5000/€2.58 one-way, L8000/€4.13 round-trip) departing from Monterosso (9 per day 9:30am-6:45pm) and Vernazza (9 per day 10am-6:30pm).

Currency Exchange: at the post office. Cash exchange L5000/€2.58; for traveler's check transactions, head to **Banca Carige,** V. Roma, 69, or **Casa di Risparmio della Spezia,** V. Roma, 47. **ATMs** also at **Bancomat,** V. Fegina, 40, under the train station.

Laundry: Las Vegas, V. Mazzini, 4, in Monterosso. L20,000/€10.33 to wash, soap, and dry 7kg of clothes. Hit the beach between loads. Open daily 9am-9pm.

EMERGENCY AND COMMUNICATIONS

Emergency: ☎113. **Police:** ☎112. **Medical Emergency:** ☎118.

Carabinieri: ☎0187 81 75 24. In Riomaggiore (☎0187 92 01 12).

First Aid: Guardia Medica (☎033 885 309 49), in Corniglia; (☎0187 81 76 87), in Monterosso; (☎0187 80 09 73), in Riomaggiore; (☎0187 92 07 66), in Manarola; (☎0187 82 10 84), in Vernazza.

Pharmacies: V. Fegina, 44, under train station. Open M-Sa 9am-12:30pm and 4-8pm, Su 9:30am-12:30pm and 4-7:30pm. **Another location** at V. Roma, 2, in Vernazza. Open M-Tu and Th-Sa 8:30am-12:30pm and 4-7:30pm; closed W afternoon.

Internet Access: The Net, V.V. Emanuele, 55 (☎/fax 0187 81 72 88). L4000/€2.07 for first 15min, L2000/€1.03 for each 10min after. **Bar Centrale,** V.C. Colombo, 144, in Riomaggiore. L200/€0.10 per min., L12,000/€6.2 per hr. **Ostello "Cinque Terre,"** V. B. Riccobaldi, 21, in Manarola. L8000/€4.13 per 30min.

TO LEVANTO (6km)
M. Crocettola
TO SESTRI LEVANTE
Monterosso Al Mare
M. S. Croce
Vernazza
M. Malpertuso
TO LA SPEZIA
Mediterranean Sea
M. Gaginara
TO LERICI
Corniglia
M. Marvede
M. Capri
Manarola
M. Galera
Riomaggiore
0   1 mile
0   1 kilometer
Cinque Terre
TO LA SPEZIA (12km)

Post Office: V. Loreto, 73 (☎0187 81 83 94). Fermo Posta and telephone cards. Open M-Sa 8am-1:30pm. **Another branch** at V. Discovolo, 216 (☎0187 92 01 98), in Manarola. Open M-F 8am-1:30pm, Sa 9am-noon.
Postal Code: 19016, in Monterosso.

▐ ACCOMMODATIONS

Reserve at least several weeks in advance. The few budget **hotels** (all in Monterosso and Vernazza) fill at the beginning of the season. If you're still looking for a room when you arrive, gamble on the cheaper and more plentiful rooms in Riomaggiore, Monterosso, or Vernazza. Private rooms *(affittacamere)* are the most plentiful and economical options in Cinque Terre.

▨ **Albergo Della Gioventù-Ostello "Cinque Terre,"** V.B. Riccobaldi, 21 (☎0187 92 02 15; fax 92 02 18; ostello@cdh.it; www.cinqueterre.net/ostello), in Manarola. Turn right from train station and continue up the hill 300m. The new hostel is across from the church. 48 beds, a solarium with showers, an outdoor terrace, music systems on each co-ed floor, laundry (L7000/€3.62 wash, L5000/€2.58 dry), a glass elevator, wheelchair access, photocopying, fax, Internet, and phones. Incredible views and friendly management. Ask about kayak, bike, and snorkeling equipment rental. Sheets and 5min. shower included. Breakfast L5000/€2.58. Reception daily 7-10am and 5pm-1am; 1am curfew; winter midnight. Reserve at least 1 month in advance. Dorms L30,000/€15.50 in high season. Quads with bath L120,000/€62.00. AmEx/MC/V.

Albergo Barbara, P. Marconi, 30, top floor (☎/fax 0187 81 23 98), at the port in Vernazza. 9 bright, airy rooms, some with fantastic views of Vernazza's colorful port. On hot summer days, the proprietors sit outside at a makeshift receptionist desk. 2-night minimum stay for a reservation. Doubles L80-100,000/€41.32-51.65; triples L120,000/€62.00; quads L140,000/€72.30.

Meublè Agavi, Lungomare Fegina, 30 (☎0187 81 71 71 or 80 16 65; fax 81 82 64), in Monterosso. Turn left from station onto boardwalk. 10 airy rooms with bath, phone, and fridge. Reception until 6pm. Singles L80,000/€41.32; doubles L150,000/€77.47.

Hotel Souvenir, V. Gioberti, 24 (☎/fax 0187 81 75 95; hotel_souvenir@yahoo.com), in Monterosso. Quiet, family-run hotel with 30 beds, a friendly staff, and outdoor garden. All rooms with tiled modern bath. Breakfast L10,000/€5.16. Rooms L70,000/€36.15 per person, students L60,000/€31.

Il Villaggio Marino "Europa" (☎0187 81 22 79; fax 70 21 43), in Corniglia. Leave train station and turn right. A flight of stairs leads down to the *villagio*, which consists of rows of cabana-like bungalows with bunkbeds and kitchens that make a longer stay an option. The 45 rooms are small and quite basic, but with a pebble beach right below. Laundry facilities (washing L5000/€2.58; no dryers). June-Sept. by the week only. Nov.-Mar. L800,000/€413.17 per week for 4 people. Apr.-Oct. L150,000/€77.47 per day for 4 people, L500,000/€258.23 per 4 days, L600,000/€309.87 per week.

PRIVATE ROOM SERVICES

Riomaggiore: ▨ **Robert Fazioli,** V. Colombo, 94 (☎0187 92 09 04). Many rooms have harbor views. Singles, doubles, and apartments. Doubles with bath L80,000/€41.32. Open daily 10am-1pm and 5-8pm. **Edi,** V. Colombo, 111 (☎/fax 0187 92 03 25; edivesigna@iol.it), has comparable prices. (L80-100,000/€41.32-51.65 per 2 people.) **Ivana** (☎0187 92 01 96) has breezy rooms up the hill from train station. Alberto at **Bar Centrale,** V. Clombo, 144 (☎0187 92 02 08) can help find accommodations. The folks at the **Bar Stazione** (☎0187 92 00 46), right outside the train station, might be able to help you, as might **Trattoria via Dell'Amore** (☎0187 92 08 60), **Locando dalla Compagnia** (☎0187 76 00 50), or **Roberta Veneziani** (☎0187 92 07 89).

Monterosso: The **tourist office** (☎0187 81 75 06) has a list of rooms, and the agents will mediate with home owners.

Vernazza: Trattoria Gianni Franzi, P. Marconi, 5 (☎0187 82 10 03; fax 81 22 28), has singles from L60,000/€31, as well as triples with bath for L150,000/€77.47. **Anna Maria,** V. Carattino, 64 (☎0187 82 10 82), rents rooms.

Manarola: Da Baranin, V. Rollandi, 35/a (☎0187 92 05 95). Clean rooms and apartments up road from the hostel. Breakfast included. Doubles from L100,000/€51.65.

Corniglia: Ristorante Cecio (☎0187 81 20 43), on the small road that leads from Corniglia to Vernazza. From train station, follow the signs at the top of stairs that lead to town. From main *piazza*, take a right up the hill and walk 100 yards. A wonderful restaurant that also rents 20 wonderful rooms, all with bath and postcard views. Doubles L90,000/€46.48. The *affitacamere* **Vista Mare** is also there (☎0187 81 23 15), as is another on V. della Stazione (☎0187 81 22 93). You can also try the *affitacamere* associated with La Posada (see **Food**, below) at 0187 81 23 84.

▣ FOOD

If you're on a tight budget in Cinque Terre, consider romantic picnics: wash your beach or cliffside meal down with the locally made, sweet, delicious *sciacchetrà* wine, or opt for the cheaper (yet still superb) *Cinque Terre* white wine.

SUPERMARKETS AND ENOTECHE

Cantina di Sciacchetrà, V. Roma, 7 (☎0187 81 73 15), in Monterosso, has free wine tastings, tasty *antipasti,* and deals on souvenirs. Jovial Gian Luigi will proudly point out all of the finest from the **Cinque Terre Farming Cooperative,** including lemons, olive oil, and wine (*Cinque Terre bianco* L12,000/€6.20; *sciacchetrà* L38,000/€19.63). Open daily Mar.-Oct. 9am-11pm; open only weekends Dec.-Feb. MC/V.

L'Autedu, V. Birolli, 83B (☎0187 92 03 11), in Manarola, offers similar products as well as generous assistance and expertise with boxing up bottles to mail home. Open 9am-8pm; closed W from Nov.-Mar. MC/V.

Superconad Margherita, P. Matteotti, 9, in Monterosso. Open June-Sept. M-Sa 8am-1pm and 5-7:30pm, Su 8am-1pm.

MEC Market, V. Molinelli, 21, in Monterosso. Open daily 7:45am-1pm and 5-7:30pm; closed Su afternoon.

Focacceria Il Frantoio, V. Gioberti, 1 (☎0187 81 83 33), in Monterosso. The wood-burning oven bakes every kind of mouth-watering *focaccia* imaginable, stuffed with olives, onions, herbs, and other fillings. A great place to grab food for a hike. Slices L2500-3500/€1.29-1.81. Open F-W 9am-1:30pm and 5-7:30pm.

RISTORANTI, TRATTORIE, AND PANINOTECHE

FAST, V. Roma, 13 (☎0187 81 71 64), in Monterosso. At *La Casa dei Panini Cantanti* (The House of the Singing Sandwiches), FAbio and STefano speedily sunder fresh sandwiches. Electric guitars hang from the ceiling and posters of American movie stars cover the walls. Large sandwiches, like "Primus" and "Soul Coughing," start at L6000/€3.10. Open daily 10am-2am; in winter Tu-Su 10am-2am. MC/V.

Marina Piccola, V. lo Scalo, 16 (☎0187 92 01 03), in Manarola. Little marina, big meals (along with a sizeable bill). *Marina* occupies a prime location on the edge of Manarola's rocky cove. Savor *tagliatelle ai granchi* (linguini with crab) and *penne agli scampi* (with shrimp; both L15,000/€7.75). *Primi* from L10,000/€5.16; *secondi* from L18,000/€9.3. Open daily noon-4pm and 6-11pm. AmEx/MC/V.

La Posada, V. Alla Stazione (☎0187 82 11 74), in Corniglia. Climb staircase from the train station. Take a right on the road at the top for about 150m. The food is delicious, but pricey. Sweeping seaside view is priceless. *Primi* L16,000/€8.26; *secondi* L15-20,000/€7.75-10.33. Cover L3000/€1.55. Lunch starts daily at noon, dinner at 7pm.

Trattoria Il Porticciolo, V.R. Birolli, 92 (☎0187 92 00 83), in Manarola. Pretty standard trattoria that serves up reasonably priced meals. *Primi* L8-12,000/€4.13-6.2; *secondi* L15-25,000/€7.75-12.91. If you're still hungry after the main course, try their superb, home-made *torta nocciola* (nut cake) L6000/€3.1. Cover L4000/€2.07. Open Th-T 7am-4pm and 6pm until the last guest says a sleepy "buona notte". AmEx/V.

La Taverna, V. Molinelli, 39 (☎0187 81 74 02), in Monterosso. While the restaurant itself feels more cavern than tavern, delicious seafood, outdoor seating, and reasonable prices may help you see the light. Splurge on *ravioli al pesce* for L16,000/€8.26. Pasta from L8000/€4.13. Open daily noon-2:30pm and 6:30-10pm. AmEx/MC/V.

Il Baretto, V. Roma, 31 (☎0187 81 23 81), in Vernazza. Reasonably priced for a touristy outdoor restaurant. Fresh mussels steamed in wine and herbs L15,000/€7.75; *spaghetti al pesto* L12,000/€6.2; *primi* L10-15,000/€5.16-7.75; *secondi* L12-25,000/6.2. Cover L3000/€1.55. Open Tu-Su 12:15-3pm and 7:15-10pm.

Ristorante Cecio, in Corniglia. (See **Private Room Services,** above, for directions and contact info.) Swill your *vino* and munch on your *spaghetti* as you watch the sunset through the dangling grape vines that drape the outdoor terrace. Delicious food, and a fabulous view of cultivated gardens sloping into the unruly sea. You might want to make a reservation. *Primi* from L8000/€4.13; *secondi* from L12,000/€6.2. Cover L3000/€1.55. Open daily noon-3pm and 7:30-11pm. MC/V.

🥾 HIKING

Nature created Cinque Terre's best sights. Savage cliffs and lush tropical vegetation surround the stone villages. Enjoy the best views from the narrow goat paths that link the towns, winding through vineyards, streams, and dense foliage dotted with cacti and lemon trees. If you have a good pair of walking shoes, you can cover the distance between Monterosso and Riomaggiore in about five hours. The best and most challenging hike lies between Monterosso and Vernazza (1½hr.), while the trail between Vernazza and Corniglia (2hr.) passes through spectacular scenery. The road between Corniglia and Manarola (1hr.) offers a pleasant hike. The final stretch, the famous **via dell'Amore** that links Manarola and Riomaggiore (20min.), is a leisurely paved path with great views and access to the rocky coves.

To avoid scaling rocks, start at Riomaggiore and end with Vernazza or Monterosso. It's always best to start in the morning to avoid the scorching sun. Walk the leisurely V. dell'Amore to the #2 hike at Manarola's Punta Bonfiglio. Follow it to the end, or branch off onto the #7 from Manarola to Corniglia. The #7 goes uphill to the highway, which levels off and then finally starts downhill. The highway rejoins the hiking trail into Vernazza. Take a moment to jump in the water and refresh yourself before tackling the last leg to Monterosso. If you ever tire of hiking, simply hop on the train and return to your base town.

In Monterosso, visit the **Convento dei Cappuccini** (built 1618-1622), perched on a hill in the center of town. (Open daily 9am-noon and 4-7pm.) The convent contains an impressive Crucifixion by Flemish master Anthony van Dyck, who sojourned here during his most productive years. In Vernazza, the remains of the 11th-century **Castello Doria,** up a staircase on the left of P. Marconi (when facing the port), offer yet another spectacular view. (Open daily 10am-6:30pm. L2000/€1.03.)

🎵 ENTERTAINMENT

Bar Centrale, V. C. Colombo, 144, in Riomaggiore. If young Americans are not your particular passion, this bar won't be either. But if you can stand the patrons (or if you go earlier in the day when they're sleeping off hangovers), you'll love the barkeeps. Energetic Ivo serves you a nice cold one and then turns up the volume on swingin' motown goodness. Internet access. Beer L5-7000/€2.58-3.62. Open daily 7:30am-1am.

Il Bar Sopra il Mare (☎0187 76 20 58), on Punta Bonfiglio, in Manarola. Enjoy the incredible view of Manarola at night. Sit under the stars watching the waves crash at Manarola's rocky base. Cappuccino L2000/€1.03. Beer L4000/€2.07. Mixed drinks L7-8000/€3.62-4.13. Open daily mid-June to Oct. 1:30pm-12:30am.

Il Casello, V. Lungo Ferravia, 70, in Monterosso. Follow V. Fegina through the tunnel and along to the end of the free beach in front of the old town. In a pink building overlooking the beach (public beaches is just steps away), Casello's got food (*focaccia* L7000/

€3.62; mozzarella and tomato salad L9000/€4.65). Internet access (L3000/€1.55 per 15min.), and plenty to drink (beer and liquor from L4000/€2.07). Menu says it all: "don't complain for delays...let's have fun." Open daily Easter-Oct. 11am-2am.

◪ BEACHES

The *spiagge* (beaches) of Cinque Terre are touched by the entrepreneurial spirit that pervades all the seaside towns; the coastline consists predominantly of private beaches. Nonetheless, a free day at the beach is certainly possible, as long as you're willing to expand your definition of beach beyond the typical image of flat stretches of sand. Use of a private beach will cost you: L3-5000/€1.55-2.58 just to enter; L27-31,000/€13.94-16.01 for an umbrella, *cabina*, and two deck chairs; and L12-14,000/€6.2-7.23 for a deck bed, with prices subject to increase during July and August. Many establishments insist you rent a chair and umbrella to be admitted, and as many beaches fill up, its best to arrive early.

The largest **free beach** lies directly below the train station; get there early to reserve a space. Alternatively, follow the V. Fegina through the tunnel to get to another free beach in front of the old town. Other small patches open to the public are on the southern and northernmost tips of town. Vernaza also has a small free beach and lots of sunbathing room on the pier. Manarola, Corniglia, and Riomaggiore stare down at the sea from rocky coves whose steep bouldered formations are covered with towels and human bodies on sunny days. These makeshift beaches between the towns are less crowded and have the advantage of adding a bit of character to your sunbathing experience. Find a boulder you can sprawl out on without slipping into the waves and let your travel anxiety seep to the sea.

For the best of both worlds (and boys and girls in their birthday suits to boot), make a trek to the **Guvano Beach** in Corniglia (tunnel open Sa-Su June and Sept. 9am-7pm; daily July-Aug. 9am-7pm). When you depart from the train station, proceed as you would to get to the town, but bypass the stairs and go left down the ramp on the other side of the tracks. When you get to a tunnel, press the button; the gate will open. A 15-minute walk through the dark, spooky tunnel (don't walk it by yourself) and a L5000/€2.58 toll will reward you with a less populated beach than the pebbly strip south of the station. Be wary of the all-but-nonexistent steps on the way down. Cast your inhibitions to the wind and play siren seductress to his Odysseus (or vice-versa, as the case may be). Be ready for an audience, however; on weekends yachts like to park in the cove for a piece of the action.

If you're interested in delving deeper into ocean life, you might consider organized excursions. **Coopsub Cinqueterre Diving Center**, on V.S. Giacomo, offers snorkel and scuba equipment as well as chaperoned dives anywhere along the coast from its base in Riomaggiore's Capo Montenero (5min. away by boat) to as far away as Corniglia (30 min.). In June and September when there's less traffic, you're likely to see dolphins in addition to coral and schools of fish. A license is required for scuba dives, but lessons are also offered. (☎0187 92 00 11. Open daily Easter-late Sept. 9am-7pm. Snorkeling along V. dell'Amore. L10,000/€5.16 per hr. Dives from L60-100,000/€31.00-51.65. Night dives L70,000/€36.15 per hr. Boat trips, along Cinque Terre, including a stop to frolic in the natural waterfalls of Caneto Beach, L27,000/€13.94 per person for 3hr. Kayaks L10,000/€5.16 per hr., L5000/€2.58 each additional hour.) **Sea Adventures**, V. Rollandi, 35/a (☎0187 92 05 95 or 62 74 87), in Manarola, offers cruises along the coast with snorkeling. (3hr. cruise from L35,000/€18.08 per person, 2hr. cruise from L25,000/€12.91, and scuba diving from L35,000/€18.08 per person per immersion.)

NEAR CINQUE TERRE

LEVANTO   ☎0187

Quiet and untouched by tourists in comparison to the nearby Cinque Terre, Levanto is the place to go for a place to stay. Although it's not quite as dramatic as the Cinque Terre, there is a beautiful beach, and the town is surrounded by wonderful Ligurian hills.

ORIENTATION AND PRACTICAL INFORMATION. Levanto lies on the Genoa-La Spezia line, 6km away from **Cinque Terre** (5min. to Monterosso, 20 per day 8:02am-10:08pm). The **tourist office, I.A.T.**, on P. Cavour, provides maps and information on hotels, private rooms, and *agriturismi*. (☎ 0187 80 81 25. Open M-F 9am-12:30pm and 3-6pm, Sa 9am-12:30pm and 2:30-6:30pm, Su 9am-1pm. Hours vary in winter.) Levanto's main attraction is its proximity to Cinque Terre. Levanto has **Farmacia Cimitan**, V. Dante, 2. (☎ 0187 80 83 46. Open M-Sa 8:30am-12:30pm and 4-8pm; in winter 3:30-6:30pm.) In an **emergency,** call the **police** (☎ 113), **carabinieri** (☎ 0187 80 81 05), **medic** (☎ 118), **Croce Rosso** (☎ 0187 80 85 35), **Croce Verde** (☎ 0187 80 83 81), **Guardia Medica** (☎ 0187 80 09 73), or **hospital** (☎ 0187 80 04 09). The **post office,** V. Jialcopo, 31, accepts Fermo Posta (L500/€0.26) and has **currency exchange.** (☎ 0187 80 82 04. Open M-F 8am-6pm, Sa 8am-1pm.)

ACCOMMODATIONS AND FOOD. For a bite to eat, your best bet is the **Supermercato Corner,** V. Martiri della Liberta, 26. (☎ 0187 80 86 66. Open daily 8am-1pm and 5-8pm. MC/V.) Levanto's pride and joy, **Ospitalia del Mare,** on V. San Niccolo, is 15 minutes from the train station. Walk down to the river and cross the bridge to V. Garibaldi, which turns into V. Guanti. At P. Popolo, go left to V. Cantarana. Housed in a 12th-century Augustinian friary, this hostel offers brand new facilities, including breakfast and conference rooms, two elevators, wheelchair accessible dorm rooms, and one family room. Each room has four, six, or eight beds and an attached bathroom. (☎ 0187 80 25 62; fax 80 36 96; ospitalia@libero.it; www.ospitaliadelmare.it. Internet L5000/€2.58 for 15min. Fax available. 63 beds. Dorms L40,000/€20.66 per person including breakfast, L5000/€2.58 less if you don't eat. Ask about 10% discount at local restaurants and group rates. AmEx/MC/V.) **Campeggio Acqua Dolce** is up the road from the hostel, 200m from the beach. Follow the signs from V. Cantarana. Well-tended grounds overflow with tents, campers, and flowering vines. (☎/fax 0187 80 84 65. L12-14,000/€6.2-7.23 per tent, L10,000/€5.16 per person. Reception open 8am-1pm and 3-10pm.)

LA SPEZIA ☎ 0187

In the summer of 2000, an unsuspecting gardener was digging in his backyard and turned up more than sticks and stones; a bomb lay beneath his tomato plants. Heavily attacked during World War II because of its naval base and artillery, La Spezia has since recovered from its wartime woes; with careful tending of its nautical roots (and the occasional evacuation of the city for the deployment of unexploded artillery) it has evolved into a major commercial port. As a departure point for Corsica and an unavoidable transfer stop to and from Cinque Terre, it draws its share of tourists. Situated in *Il Golfo dei Poeti* (The Gulf of Poets), La Spezia makes a great base for daytrips to neighboring villages including the small fishing village of Porto Venere, the beach resorts of San Terenzo and Lerici, and the beautiful coves of Fiascherino. Though La Spezia boasts none of the majestic architecture, cobblestone passageways, or charm that grace these neighboring villages, it does have affordable lodgings, a few impressive, palm-lined shopping boulevards, and a friendly air of modernity. It makes a good, if rather urban, base for exploring the coastline if you can't find accommodation in Cinque Terre or Levanto.

TRANSPORTATION. La Spezia lies on the Genoa-Pisa train line. A ticket from Monterosso costs L2700/€1.94; from Manarola, L19,000/€9.81. **Happy Lines,** with a ticket kiosk on V. Italia (☎ 0187 65 12 73; open daily 6:30am-noon and 3:30-7:30pm), near the *Molo Italia* deck, sends ferries to **Corsica** (round-trip L124,000/€64.04, low-season L84,000/€43.38). **Tirrenia** (☎ 0187 55 10 80) sends ferries to **Sardinia's Golfo Aranci** (6hr., 1 per day, L85-122,000/€43.90-63.01). **Navigazione Golfo dei Poeti,** V. Mazzini, 21 (☎ 0187 210 10 or 73 29 87), offers ferries that stop in each village of **Cinque Terre** and **Portovenereo** (Easter-Nov. 4; full day one-way L20,000/€10.33, round-trip L33,000/€17.04); **Capraia** (July-Aug., 5 hr., round-trip L70-80,000/€36.15-41.32); **Elba** (W and Sa July-Aug.; 3½ hr., round-trip L80,000/€41.32). Be sure to call ahead for ferries; schedules change and some lines will only run in the high season. For **taxis** call ☎0187 52 35 22 or 52 35 23.

■■ ORIENTATION AND PRACTICAL INFORMATION. La Spezia's main **tourist office** is beside the port at V. Mazzini, 45. (☎0187 77 09 00. Open daily 9am-1pm and 3-6pm.) **CTS Travel,** V. Sapri, 86, helps with ferry tickets (to Greece and Yugoslavia), student airfares, and car rentals. (☎0187 75 10 74; fax 75 27 53; cts.laspezia@tin.it. English spoken. Open M-Sa 9am-12:30pm and 4-8pm.)

In an **emergency,** dial ☎113 or contact the **police** (☎112) or a **medic** (☎118). **Farmacia dell'Aquila,** V. Chiodo, 97 (☎0187 231 62), is open M-F 8:30am-12:30pm and 4-8pm. There is a list of other pharmacies posted outside. For **Internet access,** head to **Downtown Phone Center,** P.S. Bon, 1, just five minutes from the train station; it also offers UPS and Western Union services. (☎0187 77 78 05; world@village.it. L10,000/€5.16 per hr. Open M-Sa 9am-12:30pm and 3-10pm.) The **post office** is a few blocks from the port at P. Verdi. (☎0187 73 33 55 53 62. Open M-F 8am-6pm and Sa 8-11:25am.) **Postal Code:** 19100.

■■ ACCOMMODATIONS AND FOOD. Albergo Terminus, V. Paleocapa, 21, to the left out of the train station, has an eccentric lobby and 49 rooms of fading elegance. (☎0187 70 34 36; fax 70 00 79. Singles L40,000/€20.66, with bath L55,000/€28.41; doubles L65,000/€33.57, with bath L90,000/€46.48; triples L70,000/€36.15.) Closer to the port, try **Albergo Teatro,** V. Carpenino, 31, near the *Teatro Civico.* Newly renovated, the six rooms here are bright and modern. (☎/fax 0187 73 13 74; albergoteatro@libero.it. Doubles L70-90,000/€36.15-46.48, with bath L90-120,000/€46.48-62.00.) On the next street over, **Albergo Spezia,** V. Cavalloti, 31, off V. Prione, offers rooms with couches and high ceilings. (☎0187 73 51 64; albergospezia@hotmail.com. Doubles L70,000/€36.15, with bath L80,000/€41.32; triples L85-110,000/€43.90-56.81.) **V. del Priore** is lined with reasonably priced *trattorie* and *paninoteche.* Savor La Spezia's local specialty, *mesciua* (a thick soup of beans, corn-meal, olive oil, and pepper), at any of the city's *antiche osterie.* For groceries, try the **Coop supermarket,** V. Galileo Galilei, 31. (Open M-Sa 8:15am-12:45pm and 4-7:30pm.) A bigger one with continuous hours is in P. J. F. Kennedy, on V. Saffi. Pick up a loaf of bread, *pesto genovese,* and some mozzarella cheese for less than L10,000/€5.16. (☎0187 51 81 43. Open M-Sa 8:30am-8pm.) **Pizzeria Il Comera,** C. Cavour, 326, an excellent place for a quick, inexpensive lunch, offers pizza and focaccia to go. (☎0187 74 32 36. Open Tu-Su 8:30am-11pm.) **Antico Sacrista,** C. Cavour, 276, prepares *testaroli al pesto* (a dainty pasta produced only in Liguria). Choose from over 30 types of hand-tossed pizza from L5000/€2.58, or settle for pizza *al taglio* from L3000/€1.55. (☎0187 71 33 84. Pizza L3-12,000/€4.13-6.20 Open Tu-Su noon-2:30pm and 7:30-10:30pm, takeout all day. AmEx/MC/V.)

■■ SIGHTS AND ENTERTAINMENT. La Spezia is one of Italy's classiest and cleanest ports, with regal palms lining the Morin promenade, sailors strolling the streets in starched white uniforms, and parks brimming with glorious citrus trees. The streets, particularly **V. del Prione,** come alive in the evenings, overseen by balcony-lined hillsides blossoming with mimosa. La Spezia also has an interesting, if eclectic, collection of museums, many of them related to the sea and its long impact on the history of this area.

The unique collection of the **Naval Museum,** in P. Chiodo next to the entrance to the *Arsenale Militare Marittimo* (Maritime Military Arsenal) built in 1860-1865 and destined to catalyze the growth of the city, features marshmallow-man diving suits dating from World War II, carved prows of 19th-century ships (including a huge green salamander), gargantuan iron anchors, and tiny replicas of Egyptian, Roman, and European vessels. (☎0187 78 30 16; fax 78 29 08. Open M and F 2-6pm, Tu-Th and Sa 9am-noon and 2-6pm, Su 8:30am-1:15pm. L5000/€2.58.)

The **Museo Amadeo Lia,** V. Prione, 234, in the ancient church and convent of the Friars of St. Francis from Paola, houses a beautiful collection of paintings spanning the 13th to 17th centuries, including some works attributed to Raphael. Room

NORTHWEST ITALY

VII has a small collection of works from the 16th century, including Pontormo's self portrait, Titian's *Portrait of a Gentleman*, and Bellini's *Portrait of an Attorney*. (☎0187 73 11 00; fax 72 14 08; mal@castagna.it; www.castagna.it/mal. Open Tu-Su 10am-6pm. L12,000/€6.20.)

The **Castle of Saint George**, built in the 14th century when pesky Genoa ruled La Spezia, houses an archaeological museum and offers expansive views of the port. It also has some of the old contents of the Museo Civico della Spezia, which recently became the Giovanni Podenzana Civic Museum. (Open M-Th 9:30am-12:30pm and 5-8pm, F-Su 2-8pm.; in winter W-M 9:30am-12:30am and 2-7pm; L5000/€2.58.) The **Giovanni Podenzana Civic Museum,** V. Curtatone, 9, has a collection of objects that pertain to local folklore. There is also the **Palazzina delle arte** and **Museum of Seals,** V. Priore 236, (☎0187 73 09 54), which contains what might be the largest collection of seals in the world.

RIVIERA DI PONENTE

SAVONA ☎019

Savona, whose origins date back 1800 years, is notable largely for its two hostels. The town also serves as an important point of departure when crossing from the Po Valley to the Ligurian Coast. Because of its strategic position, it has been the desired war booty of many an invading army, including the Genovese, who ransacked the harbor in 1528 and constructed a fortress on the Priamar promontory. Today the fortress houses a hostel and art and archeological museums.

▐ TRANSPORTATION

Trains: From the train station, take bus #2 (every 30min. 6:23am-9:23pm) to the city center and the fortress hostel. To **Genoa** (1-3 per hr. 4:48am-11:45pm, L5000/€2.58) and **Ventimiglia** (1-2 per hr. 6:03am-10:58pm; L11,500/€5.94).

Buses: To **Finale Ligure** (5:02am-10:22pm, every 30min), stop outside train station. Buses #2 and 5 leave P. Mamelli for station (every 15min. 5:15am-midnight, L1400/€0.72). Pick up ticket at train station, or pay an extra L800/€0.41 and buy on the bus.

Bike Rental: Noleggio Biciclette, in Public Gardens. Take V. Dante down to P. Heroe dei Due Mondi. Bikes for kids and grown-ups. L4500/€2.32 per hr., L18,000/€9.30 per day. Open M-F starting at 2pm, and all day Sa-Su.

✱ ▐ ORIENTATION AND PRACTICAL INFORMATION

The 16th-century fortress lies toward the water off **Piazza Priamar.** The medieval *centro storico*, with churches and *palazzi*, is bounded by **via Manzoni** and **via Paleocapa**. Across the harbor (by means of Calata Sbarbaro) lies **Piazza Mancine** and Savona's summer social scene.

Tourist Office, V. Guidobono, 125r (☎019 840 23 21; fax 840 36 72). Maps and bus schedules. Open M-Sa 8:30am-12:30pm and 3-6pm.

English-Language Bookstore: Libreria Economica, V. Pia, 88r (☎019 83 87 424). Eclectic blend of classics and bestsellers. Open M-Sa 9:15am-12:30pm and 4-8pm; in winter open M-Sa 9:15am-12:30pm and 3:30-7:30pm in the winter. MC/V.

Police: ☎112. **Medical Emergency:** ☎118.

Ambulance: Croce Bianca, ☎019 82 72 727. **Guardia Medica:** ☎800 55 66 88.

Pharmacy: Farmacia Della Ferrera C. Italia, 153r. Open daily 8:30am-7:30pm.

Hospital: Ospedale San Paolo, V. Genova, 30 (☎019 84 041).

Post Office: in P. Diaz (☎019 84 141). Phone cards, *Fermo Posta,* and **currency exchange** available 8:15am-5:30pm. Open M-Sa 8am-6pm.

Postal code: 17100.

ACCOMMODATIONS & CAMPING

Ostello Fortezza del Piramar, C. Mazzini (☎019 81 26 53; priamarhostel@iol.it). Walk up ramp to fortress and follow signs through the labyrinth of dark tunnels to the hostel. With cell-like rooms and a slightly foreboding setting, you're sure to receive an authentic fortress experience. Reception 7-10am and 4-11:30pm. Reservations strongly recommended. Dorm with breakfast L24,000/€12.40; 2 singles L30,000/€15.50.

Ostello Villa de Franceschini, Villa alla Strà, 29, Conca Verde (☎019 26 32 22; concaverd@hotmail.com). No public transportation to hostel. 3km away from train station; Call hostel and hope for a ride (larger groups have better chances). Pick-ups 9am-8pm; pre-scheduled pick-ups at 5 and 7pm. Reception open 7am-10am and 4pm-12:30am. Dorm with breakfast L18,000/€9.30, family rooms L20,000/€10.33 per person.

Camping Vittoria, V. Rizza, 111 (☎019 88 14 39). Catch the #6 (5am-11pm) on the V. Baselli side of P. Mameli. Campgrounds are on the water with a small beach. L8-0,000/4.13-5.16 per person, L15-17,000/€7.75-8.78 per tent, L5-6000/€2.58-3.10 per car. Electricity L3500/€1.81. Prices depend on season, with highest in summer.

FOOD

Di per Di, V. Boselli, 34/36r (☎019 80 85 40). Typical grocery store. Another link of the chain lies down the street from the tourist office. Open 8:15am-7:30pm.

Vino e Farinata, V. Pia, 15r. Typical Ligurian fare. *Farinata* (L7000/€3.62) abounds, as do fish dishes. Servings of salmon, shrimp, or swordfish cost only L12,000/€6.20. *Primi* from L7000/€3.62; *second;*, L10-15,000/€5.16-7.75. Cover L2000/€1.03.

Trattoria Mordi e Funghi, V. Sormano, 13r (☎019 83 86 648). Pizza and Coke at a reasonable price. Pizza from L6000/€3.1. Cover L1000/€0.52. Open Tu-Sa 11:30am-2:30pm and 7-11pm, M 11:20am-2:30pm.

BEACHES AND ENTERTAINMENT

A **public beach** lies along the water next to the public gardens. Take C. Italia to V. Dante. Walk past the statue of a gallant Garibaldi to a small stretch of sand where *ragazzi* (guys) engage in pick-up games of soccer. Many bars line the water on the far side of the harbor, but for Italians with dreads, **Birrò,** V. Baglietto, 42r, is really the only option. Expect lots of reggae, as well as a live DJ every night at 11. Strut your stuff down the dock past all the hipper-than-thou spots for a L3000/€1.55 bottle of beer or L7000/€3.62 cocktails. (Open daily 8pm-1am.)

FINALE LIGURE ☎019

At the base of a statue along the promenade, a plaque claims that Finale Ligure is the place for *"Il riposo del popolo,"* or "The people's rest." Whether your idea of *riposo* involves bodysurfing in the choppy waves, browsing through chic boutiques, or scaling Finalborgo's looming 15th-century Castello di San Giovanni, you shouldn't run out of ways to occupy your time. Since *riposo* should definitely include experiencing the delights of *gelato*, Finale Ligure indulges with *gelaterie* almost outnumbering the weary travelers who stroll the tree-lined boardwalk.

TRANSPORTATION

Trains: in P.V. Veneto. To **Genoa** (1hr., every hr. 8:30am-1:40pm, L6900/€3.56) and **Ventimiglia** (2½hr., every hr. 9:40am-11:10pm, L8900/€4.60). Most trains to Genoa stop at **Savona** and most trains to Ventimiglia stop at **San Remo.**

Buses: SAR departs from the front of train station. Buy tickets from *tabacchi* nearby. To **Finalborgo** (5min., every 20min., L1400/€0.72). Catch the bus for **Borgo Verezzi** across the street (10min., 8 per day, L1500/€0.77).

Bike Rental: Oddonebici (☎019 69 42 15), on V. Colombo. Jealous of the Italians on their Vespas? You too can zoom...well pedal. Adult bicycles L30,000/€15.50 per day. Open M 2:30-8pm, Tu-Sa 8am-12:30pm and 3-8pm. MC/V.

✦🛈 ORIENTATION AND PRACTICAL INFORMATION

The city is divided into three sections: **Finalpia** to the east, **Finalmarina** in the center, and **Finalborgo,** the old city, inland to the northwest. The train station and most of the listings below are in Finalmarina. The main street winds through the town between the station and **Piazza Vittorio Emanuele II**, changing its name from **via de Raimondi** to **via Pertica** to **via Garibaldi**. From P.V. Emanuele, **via della Concezione** runs west to the water and east to **via San Pietro**. To reach the old city, far behind the train station, turn left from the station, cross under the tracks, and continue left on **via Domenico Bruneghi** for about ten to fifteen minutes on foot.

TOURIST, FINANCIAL, AND LOCAL SERVICES

Tourist Office: IAT, V.S. Pietro, 14 (☎019 68 10 19; fax 68 18 04), on the main street overlooking the sea. Open M-Sa 9am-12:30pm and 3:30-7pm, Su 9am-noon.

Currency Exchange: Banca Carige, V. Garibaldi, 4, at corner of P.V. Emanuele. L5000/€2.58 service charge plus 1.5% commission. Open M-F 8:20am-1:20pm and 2:30-4pm. On Sa. **post office** has lower rates (L5000/€2.58) and longer waits. **ATMs** are in Banca Carige, V. Garibaldi, 4, and Banca San Paolo, V. della Concezione, 33.

English-Language Bookstore: La Libreria, V. Pertica, 35 (☎019 79 26 03). Steele, King, Shakespeare. Open M-Sa 8:30am-12:30pm and 3:30-7:30pm; in summer Su.

EMERGENCY AND COMMUNICATIONS

Police: V. Brunanghi, 68 (☎112 or ☎019 69 26 66).

Ambulance: ☎118. **P.A. Croce Bianca,** V. Torino, 16 (☎019 69 23 33), in Finalmarina. **Guardia Medica:** ☎118. Open M-F 8pm-8am, Sa 2pm-8am.

Late-Night Pharmacy: Comunale, V. Ghiglieri, 2 (☎019 69 26 70), at intersection where V. Raimondi becomes V. Pertica. Posts late night locations. Open M-Sa 8:30am-12:30pm and 4-10pm.

Hospital: Ospedale Santa Corona, V. XXV Aprile, 128 (☎019 623 01), in Pietra Ligure.

Internet Access: Civica Biblioteca (☎019 69 17 62), off P.S. Catterina, in Finalborgo. L6000/€3.1 per hr. Open M 8:30-10:30am, 3:30-6:30pm, and 10:20pm-12:30am, Tu-F 9am-noon and 3:30-6:30pm, Sa and Su 9am-noon; in winter M 4-7pm and 10:30pm-12:30am, Tu and Th 9am-noon and 4-7pm, W and F-Sa 9am-noon.

Post Office: V. della Concezione, 29 (☎019 68 15 331). Open M-F 8am-6pm, Sa 8am-1:15pm. Phone cards, fax, and money exchange (L5000/€2.58).

Postal Code: 17024.

🏠 ACCOMMODATIONS & CAMPING

The youth hostel has the best prices, not to mention the best view. In July and August, it may be the only place that's not booked solid (they don't take reservations). For all other accommodations listed, reservations are strongly recommended. Find rooms for rent in private houses through the tourist office.

▨ **Castello Wuillerman (HI)** V. Generale Caviglia (☎/fax 019 69 05 15; hostelfinaaleligure@libero.it). From train station, turn left onto V. Mazzini, which becomes V. Torino. Turn left onto tiny V. degli Ulivi, which leads to a set of stairs. At the top, a sign, a groan, and more stairs mark the way to the castle. Red brick castle overlooks sea. Beautiful courtyard and renovated bathrooms. Internet access L8000/€4.13 per hr. Vegetarian meals L14,000/€7.23. Breakfast included. Sheets included. Laundry L8000/€4.13 per load. Reception 7-10am and 5-10pm. Curfew 11:30pm. No phone reservations. Dorms L20,000/€10.33 **HI card-holders only;** HI cards available for purchase.

Pensione Enzo, Gradinata delle Rose, 3 (☎69 13 83). Take a break from never-ending staircase on the way to the hostel and take an early left. Great view. Pension and breakfast available. All rooms with bath and TV. 7 doubles L70-90,000/€36.15-46.48. Open Easter-Sept.

Albego Oasi, V.S. Cagna, 25 (☎019 69 17 17; fax 6 81 59 89; albergooasi@libreo.it). From train station, bear left on V. Brunenghi, and walk through underpass to V. Silla and turn right. Walk up hill, about 100m, and its on the left. Closer to train station than the hostel. Provides 12 tidy rooms (some with bathrooms and balconies), garden patio, a sitting room with TV, and a restaurant (dinner L20,000/€10.33). Free Internet. Singles L45,000/€23.24; doubles L90,000/€46.48; extra bed L45,000/€23.24.

Albergo Carla, V. Colombo, 44 (☎019 69 22 85; fax 68 19 65). Conveniently located. Offers private bathrooms, a bar, and restaurant. Breakfast L7000/€3.62. Singles L45,000/€23.24; doubles L80,000/41.32. Pension required July-Sept. Half L50,000/€25.82; full L82,000/€42.35. AmEx/MC/V.

Albergo San Marco, V. della Concezione, 22 (☎019 69 25 33; fax 68 16 187). From train station, walk straight ahead down V. Saccone, and turn left on V. della Concezione. Enter through restaurant. 14 spotless rooms have bath (with basic shower) and phone; many include balcony and ocean view. Easy access to waterfront. Minimal English spoken. Breakfast included. Reservations recommended. Open Easter-mid Oct. Singles L60,000/€31; doubles L85,000/€43.90. AmEx/MC/V.

Camping: Camping Tahiti (☎/fax 019 60 06 00), on V. Varese. Take bus for Calvisio from stop in P.V. Veneto. Get off at Bar Paradiso, and cross bridge at V. Rossini. Turn left and walk along river to V. Vanese. Hillside site features 8 terraces, 90 lots, and 360-person capacity. Reception 8am-8pm. Open Easter through Oct. 15. High season L11,000/€5.68 per person, L10,000/€5.16 per tent. Hot showers L1000/€0.52. Electricity L4000/€2.07. **Del Mulino** (☎019 60 16 69), on V. Castelli. From station, take the Calvisio bus to Boncardo Hotel, and follow brown, then yellow, signs to campsite entrance. Bar, restaurant, and mini-market. Laundry L10,000/€5.16. Office open Apr.-Sept. 8am-8pm. L8000/€4.13 per person, L8000/€4.13 per tent. Hot showers.

◖ FOOD

Trattorie and pizzerias line the streets closest to the beach. **Simpatia Crai,** V. Bruneghi, 2a, down V. Mazzini from the station, is a small supermarket that stocks the basics. (Open M-Sa 8am-12:30pm and 4-6:30pm.)

▨ **Spaghetteria Il Posto,** V. Porro, 21 (☎019 60 00 95). Amicable hosts local favorite fill your stomach with mountains of well-priced pasta. Oodles of vegetarian options. *Penne quattro stagioni* (with bacon, mushrooms, tomatoes, artichokes, and mozzarella; L10,000/€5.16); *penne pirata* (with shrimp and salmon; L12,000/€6.20); spaghetti marinara (with capers, clams, and olives; L12,000/€6.20). Cover L2000/€1.03. Open Tu-Su 7-10:30pm. Closed 1st 2 weeks of Mar.

Farinata e Vino, V. Roma, 25 (☎019 692 562). Small, popular *trattoria* bills itself as *"una trattoria alla vecchia maniera"* (old school). Enjoy homestyle cooking (especially the *pesce*) at excellent prices. *Primi* L10-15,000/€5.16-6.20; *secondi* L14-20,000/€7.23-10.33. Open 12:30-2pm and 7:30-9pm. Call for reservations in summer.

Da Badabin, V. Garibaldi, 75 (☎019 69 43 66). Thick 'n crusty pizza with shrooms or eggplant (L2500/€1.29 per slice). More involved dishes (lasagna L7000/€3.62). Open daily 9:30am-8:30pm.

Ninja Pizza, V. Gandolino, 7 (☎019 69 21 84). If you fear comic book memorabilia, keep clear—the walls are plastered with the stuff. Serves teenage mutant ninja pizza *al trancio* (by the slice) for L2500/€1.29. Open daily 10am-8pm.

◉ SIGHTS

The towns surrounding Finale Ligure are worth extra exploration. SAR buses run to tiny **Borgo Verezzi** (every 15min. 6:35am-1:41am; L1800/€0.93). Get off at the first stop in Borgo; from here, buses leave for **Verezzi** (5 per day, last return bus M-F 6:40pm, Sa-Su 7:10pm). Or hike up the winding V. Nazario Sauro (about an hour), and delight in the far-reaching vistas. The cool, tranquil streets, caves, and artificial rock formations of the tiny medieval village at the top make the trip worthwhile. Stop at **A Topia,** V. Roma, 16, for a wood-burning oven-baked pizza *quattro stagioni* for L10,000/€5.16. (☎019 616 905. Open evenings daily; in winter closed M.) If you end up in Verezzi after dark, by no means take a shortcut down the hillside. Guard dogs run rampant off the main road.

Enclosed within ancient walls, Finalborgo, the historic quarter of Finale Ligure, is a 1km walk or short bus ride up V. Bruneghi from the station. Past the **Porto Reale,** the Chiostro di Santa Caterina, a 14th-century edifice, houses the **Museo Civico del Finale,** dedicated to Ligurian history. (☎019 69 00 20; museoarcheofinale@libero.it. Open Tu-Sa 10am-noon and 3-6pm, Su 9am-noon; in winter Tu-Sa 9am-noon and 2:30-4:30pm, Su 9am-noon. Free.) Up a tough but fulfilling trail, the ruined ▧**Castel Govone** lends a spectacular view of Finale. For further rock climbing in the area, the **Rock Store,** P. Garibaldi, 14, in Finalborgo, provides maps and necessary gear. (☎019 69 02 08. Open Tu-Su 9am-12:30pm and 4:30-7:30pm.)

◉ BEACHES

Spray-painted on the inner wall of the tunnel that leads to the prime free beach in Finale Marina is *"Voglio il sole/Cerco nuova luce/nella konfusione"* ("I want the sun/I look for new light/in the confusion"). Watch out Dante. If you empathize with our aspiring graffiti poet, you've come to the right place. Be adventurous and forget the narrow strip of free beach in town where you'd feel like a beached sardine. Instead, walk east along V. Aurelia through the 1st tunnel. The beach before you, cradled by craggy overhanging cliffs, is an ideal spot to offer up your skin for sacrifice to the sun gods, but be sure to do so only with the proper protection—SPF 15. Prefer to play it safe and pay homage to the moon? Even in piping hot summer, the nights can be cool, so bring a few blankets and another warm body. Slather on a better kind of skin coverage out there, snuggle up, and live a little.

♫ ENTERTAINMENT

A bar popular among young tourists and locals alike, **Pilade,** V. Garibaldi, 67, features live music Friday nights, ranging from blues to jazz to soul. The wooden statue of the horn player in the red tux on the sidewalk and a real live saxophonist inside will draw you in like the Pied Pipers of Ligure-Lin. Just be willing to do a little shouting above the music to order a mixed drink (L8,000-10,000/€4.13-5.16) or a beer (L5,000/€2.58 and up). In the wee hours the rest of the week, you'll find drinkers nodding their heads in unison to rock and Italian techno, eyes glazed over from one too many a Peroni. Pizza and burgers always available. (☎019 69 22 20. Open daily 10am-2am. Closed Th in winter.) As the sun sets, boogie down to V. Torino and the illustrious disco-shanty **Cuba Libre.** It's complete with multiple dance floors and bars, fog machine, and political message. (☎019 60 12 84. Cover L25,000/€12.91 for men, L20,000/€10.33 for women. Open F-Sa 10pm-sunrise.) If you're traveling with kids or fun-loving adults, check out the merry-go-rounds and other carnival-style diversions that line the waterfront.

SAN REMO   ☎ 0184

Once a glamorous retreat for Russian nobles, czars, *literati*, and artists, San Remo is now Italy's Las Vegas and the largest resort on the Italian Riviera. Most recently, it served as the luxurious backdrop for Matt Damon's more murderous machinations in *The Talented Mr. Ripley*. These days, San Remo upholds its glamorous profile with high-stakes playboys gambling and bikini-clad women gamboling along the palm-lined promenade of Corso Imperatrice and in the casino. As befits its location on the Riviera dei Fiori (Riviera of Flowers), San Remo blooms with carnations year-round. Admittedly, this town isn't teaming with deals that will make the budget traveler drool, but beyond the blinding reflection of all of the Rolexes, the winding alleys of La Pigna, the historic district, are a good place to start. They provide respite from the high-rollers who overrun the rest of the city and the prices are a little more reasonable there too. If you're daunted by San Remo's steep prices and its high-brow image, make it a day trip from Ventimiglia or Bordighera; both are less than an hour away by train. While the rest of the world might know San Remo as the source of Lady Luck's siren call, in Italy, San Remo is most famous for the music festival that is held there each February.

▐ TRANSPORTATION

Trains: Luggage storage available (p. 163). To: **Genoa** (3hr.; every 2hr. 5:45am-10:05pm; L13,500/€6.97); **Milan** (3½hr.; every 2hr. 5:22am-7:36pm; L25,600/€13.22); **Turin** (4½hr.; every 45min. 2:37-7:18pm; L21,700/€11.21); **Ventimiglia** (15min.; every hr. 7:18am-10:28pm; L2700/€1.39).

▓▓ ORIENTATION AND PRACTICAL INFORMATION

The city is formed by three main parallel streets, and they all run from west to east, parallel to the beach. From the train station, to the right is **via Nino Bixio**, which hugs the shore as it juts out to the right and then back to the left again. **via Roma** splits off from V.N. Bixio after 30m and then rejoins V.N. Bixio after 500m; to the right out of the train station but then to the left of V. Roma is the rather posh **Corso Giacomo Matteotti**.

Tourist Office: APT Tourist Office V. Nuvoloni, 1 (☎0184 57 15 71; fax 50 76 49; www.sanremonet.com.) Turn left from the station and right on V. Nuvoloni. Helpful staff speaks English and has numerous brochures. Open M-Sa 8am-7pm, Su 9am-1pm.

Bank: Banco Ambrosiano V.Roma, 62 (☎0184 59 23 11.) Offers **currency exchange** and **ATM.** Open M-F 8:20am-1:20pm and 2:35-4:05pm, Sa 8;20-11:50am.

Luggage Storage: In the train station. L7500/€3.87.

English-Language Bookstore: Libreria Beraldi, V. Cavour 8 (☎0184 54 11 11). Reasonable collection of bestsellers in English, French, German, and Spanish.Open 9am-12:30pm, 3:30-7:30pm. MC/V.

Laundromat: Blu Acquazzura, V.A. Volat, 131. Wash and dry L8000/€4.13 per 7kg. Open daily 6am-7:30pm.

Emergency: ☎ 118. **Police:** ☎ 113.

Pharmacy: V. Matteoti, 89 (☎0184 53 19 68). Open M-F 8:30am-12:30pm and 3:30-7:30pm.

Hospital: Ospedale Civile, V.G. Borea, 56 (☎0184 53 61).

Internet Access: Mailboxes, Etc., C. Cavallotti, 86 (☎0184 59 16 73). 2 computers. L15000/€7.75 per hr., L8000/€4.13 per ½ hr. Also has photocopy, fax, scanner, and CD burner. Open M-F 9am-6:30pm, Sa 9am-1pm.

Post Office: V. Roma, 156 (☎0184 53 32 18). Open M-Sa 8am-6pm.

Postal Code: 18038.

▌ ACCOMMODATIONS

Albergo De Paoli, C. Raimondo, 53, 2nd fl. (☎0184 50 04 93). Follow V. Roma past the fountain, and straight down C. Raimondo. It's on left, surrounded by the more expensive (3-star) Hotel Esperia. The rooms are well-kept, though fairly basic, and the common bathrooms are very clean, but De Paoli is quite a distance from the casino and the beach. Singles L35,000/€18.08; doubles L65,000/€33.57.

Mariluce, C. Matuzia, 3 (☎ 0184 66 78 05; fax 66 76 55). Out of train station, take a left and follow C. Imperatrice past the tourist office until it turns into C. Matzuia; Mariluce will be on your left, about 20m back from the road. Comfortable rooms, all with baths. A location handy to accessing the nicer beaches in San Remo, despite the distance from the *città vecchia*. Ask for an ocean side room. Singles L60,000/€31; doubles L100,000/€51.65. AmEx/MC/V.

Metropolis and **Terminus**, V. Roma, 8 (☎/fax 0184 57 71 00 10). Turn right down V. Roma out of the train station, and Metropolis/Terminus is right there. Rooms feature high ceilings and attractive wood floors and furniture. Restaurant run by same proprietors. Singles L60,000/€31; doubles L100,000/€51.65.

Hotel Mara, V. Roma, 93 (☎0184 53 38 60). From train station, take a right on V. Roma and walk for 5min.; it's on the left. Simple and immaculate rooms. No private baths. Doubles L65,000/€33.57; triples L100,000/€51.65.

Albergo Al Dom, C. Mombello, 13, 2nd fl. (☎0184 50 14 60). From train station walk to the right on C. N. Bixio and take the 3rd left, which is C. Mombello. Grand, old-style rooms with baths and high ceilings in this former casino. Singles L60,000/€31; doubles L90-120,000/€46.48-62, but try your hand at bargaining. MC/V.

Allogio Piedigrotta, V. Volturno, 19, 3rd fl., (☎0184 50 43 60). Take V. Roma from the train station and take the 6th left. Rooms are basic and lack baths, but are the cheapest in town. Singles L30-45,000/€15.50-23.24; doubles L50-65,000/€25.82-33.57.

▐ FOOD

San Remo's restaurants are generally overpriced, but affordable options do exist. Corso N. Suoro, which runs along the waterfront across the train tracks from V.N. Bixio, has several comparable and decent pizzerias.

Dick Turpin's C.N. Suoro (☎0184 50 34 99). Follow C.N. Suoro until it meets the beach. Serves crêpes from L8000/€4.13 and some Indian and American-influenced food as well as pizza and pasta. Open daily noon-4pm and 7pm-1am.

Ristorante Pizzeria delle Palme V.N. Suoro, 31 (☎0184 50 34 55). Serves up pizza (L9,000-15,000/€4.65-7.75), fish (L15,000/€7.75 and up), and more. Open Th-Tu noon-3pm and 7:30pm-midnight.

Pizzeria Napoletana da Giovanni, V.C. Pesante, 7 (☎0184 50 49 54). Refreshingly casual and a location that separates it from some of the most touristed areas of the town. Good food at good prices. *Primi* L7-15,000/€3.62-7.75; *secondi* L8-10,000/€4.13-5.16 for meat, L11-25,000/€5.68-12.91 for fish; and pizza L8-15,000/€4.13-7.75. There are also three tourist menùs for L20,000/€10.33, L25,000/€12.91, and L30,000/€15.50. Open noon-2:30pm and 7-11pm, closed Th. DC/MC/V.

Pizzeria Ai 4 Amici, V. 20 Septembre, 30 (☎0184 50 04 38). Turn left where V. Roma and C.N. Bixio merge. Inexpensive pizzeria with delicious and hearty portions. Try the pizza *quattro stagione* with ham, artichokes, mushrooms, and olives, L10,000/€5.16. Pizza L9-14,000/€4.65-7.23. Open Tu-Su for lunch starting at noon, and then from 6-11pm.

Ristorante Pizzeria Italia. V. XX Septembre, 39, (☎0184 50 02 78). The wooden decor is certainly more creative than its name. Still Pizzeria Italia is known for good pizza (L9-12,000/€4.65-6.20) not its furnishings. *Primi* from L16,000/€8.26; *secondi* from

L23,000/€11.88. Tourist *menù* L30,000/€15.50. Open Th-Tu 12:15-2:30pm and 7:15pm-1:30am. MC/V.

⊙ SIGHTS

Gamblers frequent the **Edwardian Casino**, C. Inglesi, 18, a dazzling example of Belle Epoque architecture. No sneakers, jeans, or shorts–coat and tie are required in winter. (☎0184 59 51. Minimum age 18. Cover L15,000/€7.75. Open from 2:30pm-3am, Sa-Su.) The "American Room" of one-armed bandits has neither a strict dress code nor an entrance fee (although you'll surely pay), and its 10am opening lures gamblers with early twitches. The Russian Orthodox **Chiesa di Cristo Salvatore**, across the street from the tourist office, shows who were the first gamblers in San Remo and how they would repent for their losses in this church with intricate onion-domes among Russian religious art. Enjoy the exterior architecture, though there is less to see inside. (Open daily 9:30am-12:30pm and 3-6pm. Donation of L1000/€0.52 required.) Much of San Remo's nightlife is centered around the casino. But after dark, the rather posh Corso Matteoti is full of slowly meandering, well-to-do couples who are window shopping, enjoying *gelato*, or sipping liquors at wayside bars. At one end of C. Matteoti is the casino, where swanky cars pull up regularly, and at the other end is a *piazza;* all along the way there are cafes and bars. There's also a nightclub, **Disco Ninfa Egeria**, V. Matteoti, 178, which promises to be happening if you're willing to pay the hefty cover to get past the hefty bouncers. (☎39184 59 11 33. Cover L20,000/€10.33.) If you speak Italian, you can see a movie at the **Theatre Ariston**, also along C. Matteoti, where San Remo holds its song festival every year; they play both Italian movies and dubbed foreign ones. For the beach-bound, try the shore west of the casino; there's plenty of it, and you'll find plenty of speedo and bikini-clad company, both at the stretches of free beach and the numerous *bagni* that line the water. You'll see real sand (no pebble beaches here), rocky jetties, and sparkling water. This is common knowledge, though, so you'd better get down there fairly early to snag a spot.

BORDIGHERA ☎0184

When Italian writer Giovanni Ruffini crafted the plot line for his 1855 melodrama, *Il Dottor Antonio*, he unknowingly laid the foundation for the development of both Bordighera and the Italian Riviera's tourism industry. The novel tells the story of a young English girl brought to the brink of death by illness, but miraculously revived by Bordighera's sultry sands and warm wisps of summer air. Within a decade, the novel's devoted English readers clamored for the real thing, leading to the construction of the first of several huge hotels, the Hotel d'Angleterre, and the subsequent growth of Bordighera into one of the Riviera's foremost resort towns. In the latter half of the 19th century, tourists, among them Queen Margaret and Claude Monet, outnumbered natives by as much as five to one. Although the town still fills up in July and August, the ratio is a little less extreme these days, leaving all the more room for seaside sallying amongst the palm-lined streets.

▐ TRANSPORTATION

Trains: in P. Eroi Libertà. To **Genoa** (3hr.; L13,500/€6.97); **San Remo** (every hr., L2300/€1.19); **Ventimiglia** (every hr., L1700/€0.88).

Buses: Riveria Transporte buses stop every 300m along V.V. Emanuele and run to **San Remo** (20min., L2300/€1.19) and **Ventimiglia** (20min., L2200/€1.14).

✳❷ ORIENTATION AND PRACTICAL INFORMATION

The bus from Ventimiglia stops on the main street, **via Vittorio Emanuele**, which runs west and slightly north of the city's train station in **Piazza Eroi della Libertà**.

From behind the station, set apart from the rest of the town, the scenic **Lungomare Argentina,** a 2km beach promenade, runs parallel to the *città moderna* (new town), where most offices and shops are found. To get from the town to the Lungomare, find one of the many tunnels that go underneath the train tracks.

Tourist Office: V.V. Emanuele, 172 (☎0184 26 23 22; fax 26 44 55). From the train station walk along V. Roma, turn left on V.V. Emanuele, and take a right just after the park. Open M-Sa 8am-7pm, Su 9am-1pm (closed on Su in the winter).

Currency Exchange: Banca Commerciale Italiana, V.V. Emanuele, 165 (☎0184 26 36 54).

ATM outside bank, one of many along V.V. Emanuele. Open M-F 8:20am-1:25pm and 2:50-4:15pm.

Emergency: ☎113. **Ambulance:** ☎118.

Police: V.I. Maggio, 43 (☎112 or 0184 26 26 26).

24-Hour Pharmacy: Farmacia Centrale, V.V. Emanuele, 145 (☎0184 26 12 46). List of 24hr. pharmacies posted. Open July-Aug. M-F 8:30am-12:30pm and 3:30-7:30pm.

Hospital: V. Aurelia, 122 (☎0184 27 51).

Post Office: P. Eroi della Libertà, 6 (☎0184 26 23 74), across and left from the train station. Currency exchange and phone cards. Fermo Posta L300/€0.15 per letter. Open M-Sa 8am-6pm.

Postal Code: 18012.

⌐ ACCOMMODATIONS

During the high-season *(alta stagione)*, many hotels require that clients accept full-pension, half-pension, or at least breakfast.

▨ **Pensione Miki,** V. Lagazzi, 14 (☎0184 26 18 44). From the station, turn left on V.V. Emanuele. V. Lagazzi is several blocks down on the right. This family-run *pensione* rests in a serene, residential setting. Small rooms with balconies and a garden. 16 beds. Breakfast and showers included. Prices go down L7000/€3.62 if you can forego breakfast. Singles L35,000-43,000/€18.08-22.21 with a reservation; doubles L60,000-76,000/€31-39.25. Half-pension L50,000-67,000/€25.82-34.60; full-pension L60,000-77,000/€31-39.77. Full- or half-pension may be required during summer.

▨ **Albergo Palme,** V. Roma, 5 (☎/fax 0184 26 12 73). Out of the train station, cross the *piazza* and the *albergo* is a few steps down V. Roma on the right. Genial proprietor will greet you with coherent English. Tiny dog Liu will say hello with a lick to the toe. Some rooms have balconies and private bathrooms, but all have access to a terrace overlooking the *piazza*. 12 rooms. Breakfast included. Singles L40,000/€20.66; doubles L80,000/€41.32. During high season, pension required L68-72,000/€35.12-37.18.

Albergo Nagos, P. Eroi della Libertà, 7 (☎0184 26 04 57), across from the train station on the left. A word to the wise, don't leave your window open all night; you might get bitten by mosquitoes. No English spoken. Communal bathrooms. Breakfast L5000/€2.58. Singles L45,000/€23.24; doubles L72,000/€37.18; half-pension L57,000-62,000/€29.44-32.02; full-pension L60,000-77,000/€31-39.77.

◖ FOOD

Budget restaurants are few and far between, but a few exceptions can be found. Some *trattorie* in the *città alta* offer traditional Ligurian cuisine at reasonable prices. Bordighera is famed for its local dessert, *cubaite* (elaborately decorated wafers filled with caramel cream), and the Rossese wine from Dolceacqua. The **covered market,** P. Garibaldi, 46-48, has picnic supplies. (Open on Thursday morning 8am-noon.) There is also a **STANDA supermarket** at V. Libertà, 32. (Open M-Sa 8:15am-7:30pm, Su 9am-1pm and 4-7:30pm. AmEx/MC/V.) To get there, walk East down V.V. Emanuele and cross the Piazza Ruffini, bearing left, to V. Libertà.

Crêperie-Caffè Giglio, V. Emanuele, 158 (☎0184 26 15 30). Popular local hangout. Large selection of inexpensive *panini* L5000/€2.58, and delicious crêpes L6-11,000/ €3.10-5.68. Proximity of the French-Italian border spawns the mozzarella, tomato, and oregano crêpe L7000/€3.62. Also try one of the sweet crêpes for dessert. Prices may go up 20% after 10pm. Open Tu-Fr 11am-3pm and from 7pm until late (approximately midnight-2am); open Sa from 11am until late; open Su from 3pm until late.

Pizzeria Napoletana, V. Emanuele, 250 (☎0184 26 37 22). Delicious, reasonably priced food. Pizza L8-15,000/€4.13-7.75. *Primi* L8-15,000/€4.13-7.75; *secondi* L10-18,000/€5.16-9.30. Cover L1000/€0.52. Open W-M noon-3pm and 6pm-1am.

Pizzeria Da Rino, Piazza Garibaldi, 6 (☎0184 22 26 37). Reasonably-sized portions and decent food make family-run Da Rino a good choice for a cheap lunch and *caffè*. Pizza L7-12,000/€3.62-6.20 and a small range of *primi* L8-10,000/€4.13-5.16. Open M-Sa noon-3pm and 6pm-11pm.

Gastronomia and Rosticceria Marisa, V.V. Emanuele, 319 (☎0184 26 16 57). A rotisserie chicken might not do you much good, but a heaping slice of lasagna (L6,000/ €3.10 per 250g) or *torta verde,* a Ligurian specialty: layers of pasta interspersed with greens, (L5500/€2.84 per 250g) sure will. Ask at one of the *gelaterie* for a plastic spoon. Open Tu-Sa 8:30am-1pm and 4:30-7:30pm.

⑥ SIGHTS

The **Giardino Esotico Pallanca,** (exotic garden), contains over 3000 species of cacti and rare South American flora. Walk 1km down V. Aziglia, V. Madonna della Ruota, 1, or grab a bus on V. Emanuele in the direction of San Remo and ask the driver where to get off. (☎0184 26 63 47. Open M 3-7pm, Tu-Su 9am-12:30pm and 3-7pm. L8000/€4.13.) A stroll east from the town center along V. Romana provides a view of the many hotels constructed during the 19th century for the fans of *Il Dottor Antonio.* Past P. de Amicis, the road becomes C.F. Rossi. Meander through the park which leads to steps to the **Chiesa di Sant'Ampelio,** built around the grotto where Ampelio, the town hermit (later the town patron) holed up. Preferring *pesce* to prayers, fisherman and tanners congregate on the rocks below the church. (Open Su at 10am. Otherwise knock.) On May 14, the church hosts the **Festival of Sant'Ampelio** with a procession and ritual pomp. From September to May, the **Chiosco della Musica** on the boardwalk offers concerts. In the late summer, Bordighera—which calls itself *la città dell'umorismo*—hosts the **International Salon of Humor,** a juried contest of humorous drawings and cabaret-style comedy.

♫ ENTERTAINMENT

Graffiti Pub, V.V. Emanuele, 122 (☎0184 26 15 90). The bulldog statue may have a faceguard, but that doesn't keep the friendly bar bums from boisterous yapping and frenzied lapping. Raucous 25+ crowd fills comfy blue lounges inside and tables along street. Burgers L6000/€3.10; *panini* L5000/€2.58. Beer on tap L4-7000/€2.07-3.62, liquor L6000/€3.10. Open M-Sa 5pm-3am. MC/V.

Disco Kursaal, Lungomare, 7 (☎0184 26 46 85). Walk through tunnel to left of the train station. Wide variety of music, both live and recorded. Underground, house, and industrial. Open Sept.-July F-Su midnight-5am; Aug. daily midnight-5am. AmEx/MC/V.

Chica Loca (☎0184 26 35 10), down the beachfront from the disco. *Paella* for 2 L25,000/€12.91; *panini* L7000/€3.62. Margarita L10,000/€5.16; ½L sangria L9000/€4.65. Open daily 11:30am-6:30am.

VENTIMIGLIA ☎0184

Around 2000 years ago the final stages of the expansion of the Empire brought the Romans to the mouth of the Roya River, near the present-day border between France and Italy. Augustus and his cohorts took hold of the area by ruthlessly conquering a local tribe, the Intemeli. To boost Augustus's sagging ego, the town was named Venti Intemelian (boasting that this was his twentieth such conquest), which later evolved into Ventimiglia. Today with colossal remains of a Roman theater, winding 11th-century streets, and Romanesque religious sites, Ventimiglia makes an agreeable and affordable base for those who want to explore the famous oases and pebble beaches of the Italian Riviera and the French Côte d'Azur.

⌐ TRANSPORTATION

Trains: in P. Stazione (☎ 147 88 80 88). Luggage storage available (p. 168). To: **Genoa** (3hr.; every 1¼hr.; L15,000/€7.75); **Marseilles** (3½hr.; 4 per day; L48,500/€25.05); **Nice** (45min.; every hr.; L10,100/€5.22).

Buses: Agenzia viaggi & Turismo Monte Carlo, V. Cavour, 57 (☎0184 35 75 77), left from the tourist office. Office open M-Sa 9am-12:30pm and 2:30-7pm. To: **Bordighera** (15min.; 4 per hr.; L2200/€1.14) and **San Remo** (30 min.; 4 per hr.; L3300/€3.30).

Bike Rental: Eurocicli, V. Cavour, 70b (☎0184 35 18 79). L3000/€1.55 per hr.; L15,000/€7.75 per day; L30,000/€15.50 per week; L100,000/€51.65 per month. Open M-Sa 8:30am-12:30pm and 3-7:30pm. AmEx/MC/V.

✳🏠 ORIENTATION AND PRACTICAL INFORMATION

Frequent trains and blue **Riviera Transporte** buses link these two coasts. Travelers should experience little hassle crossing the border—just bring your passport. To get to the center of town from the train station, cross the street and walk down **via della Stazione.** The 2nd crossroad is **via Cavour,** where V. della Statzione becomes Corso Repubblica. Corso Repubblica then crosses V. Roma before it leads to the waterfront at the **Lungo Roya G. Rossi.**

TOURIST AND LOCAL SERVICES

Tourist Office: V. Cavour, 61 (☎0184 35 11 83). City maps and info on neighboring attractions. Open M-Sa 9am-12:30pm and 3-7pm. The travel agency next door, **Agenzia viaggi & Turismo Monte Carlo,** V. Cavour, 57c (☎0184 35 75 77; fax 0184 35 26 21), has currency exchange and bus and hotel info. Some English spoken. Open M-Sa 9am-12:30pm and 2:30-7pm.

Luggage storage: In train station. L7500/€3.87. Open daily 6am-7pm.

English-Language Bookstore: Libreria Casella, V. della Stazione, 1d (☎0184 35 79 00). Small, eclectic selection. Open M-Sa 8:30am-12:30pm and 3-7:30pm. MC/V.

EMERGENCY AND COMMUNICATIONS

Emergency: ☎113.

Police: V. Aprosio, 12 (☎112 or 0184 35 75 75).

Ambulance: Croce Rossa Italiana, V. Dante, 12 (☎0184 23 20 00) or **Croce Verde,** P. XX Settembre (☎0184 35 11 75).

Farmacia Internazionale, V. Cavour, 28a (☎0184 35 13 00). Open M-F 8:30am-12:30pm and 3:30-7:30pm, Sa 8:30am-12:30pm.

Hospital: Saint Charles (☎0184 27 51) or **Guardia Medica** (☎800 55 64 00) in Bordighera.

Internet Access: Mail Boxes Etc., V.V. Veneto, 4b (☎0184 23 84 23), just past the Giardini Pubblici from C. della Repubblica. L15,000/€7.75 per 1hr., L9000/€4.65 per 30 min., L5000/€2.58 per 15min. Open M-F 8:30am-12:30pm and 3-7pm, Sa 8:30am-12:30pm.

Post Office: C. Repubblica, 8 (☎0184 35 13 12), toward the water. Phonecards and currency exchange (L5000/€2.58). Fermo Posta. Open M-Sa 8am-6pm.

Postal Code: 18039.

◤ ACCOMMODATIONS & CAMPING

Ventimiglia is one of the Riviera's cheapest options, but not surprisingly, it fills up in July and August. Therefore, reservations are strongly recommended in the summer, but if you can't find a room, consider traveling to nearby, Menton, France. Don't forget your passport!

▨ Hotel XX Settembre, V. Roma, 16 (☎0184 35 12 22). Rooms crisply painted and meticulously clean. Downstairs restaurant (menù L28,000/€14.46; open Tu-Su noon-2:30pm and 7:30-9:30pm). Breakfast L6000/€3.10. Singles L50,000/€25.82; doubles L70,000/€36.15; triples L105,000/€54.23.

Auberge de Jeunesse (HI), plateau St.-Michel, Menton, France (☎00 33 4 93 35 93 14 from Italy or 04 93 35 93 14 within France). Take bus #6 from Menton (4 per day, 8F/€1.22), or call the hostel for minibus service (20F/€3.05 per person for 1-2 people, 10F/€1.53 per person for 3 or more). Friendly, English-speaking staff, eager to share traveling tales. Breakfast and great seaside view included. Dinner 50F/€7.62. Laundry 35F/€5.34. Sleepsack 14F/€2.14. Reception 7am-noon and 5pm-midnight. Open daily Feb.-Nov. Dorms 69F/€10.52 (approx. L20,500).

Pensione Villa Franca, C. Repubblica, 12 (☎0184 35 18 71), next to the waterfront and public park. Clean, small rooms. Friendly management and exotic pet birds in the lobby. Located next to the waterfront and open-air market. Quality meals in the restaurant L21,000/€10.85 with 10% service charge. Breakfast included. Singles L50,000; doubles L70,000/€36.15, with bath L87,000/€44.93; triples L105,000/€54.23. MC/V.

Camping Roma, V. Peglia, 5 (☎0184 23 90 07; fax 23 90 35), across the river and 400m from the waterfront. From the station, follow V. della Stazione (which changes to V. della Repubblica) and go right on V. Roma until you reach the river at Lungo Roya G. Rossi. Cross the bridge, and make an immediate right on C. Francia. After 50m it becomes V. Peglia, which has a well-defined pedestrian pathway alongside it. Well-maintained campsites and hillside panoramas. Market and bar nearby. Open daily Apr.-Sept. L12,000/€6.20 per person, L12,000/€6.20 per tent. Bungalows for four L40,000/€20.66 per person. Showers free. MC/V.

◖ FOOD

The **covered market** unfolds mornings from Monday to Thursday, and all day on Friday and Saturday, with fruit and vegetables along V. della Repubblica, V. Libertà, V. Aprosio, and V. Roma. The vendors along V. Aprosio near the fake flower stands tend to be small in-town gardeners and have the freshest produce. A **STANDA supermarket** is at the corner of V. Roma and V. Ruffini. (Open M-Sa 8:30am-7:30pm, Su 8:30am-1pm and 3:30-7:30pm.) Along the beach on the Bassa side, there are five or six pizzerias in a row, offering similar fare for L15-20,000/€7.75-10.33. Head over to the Alta shore for a bit more variety and elegance.

Pasta and Basta, on Passagiata Marconion, the Alta side of the river, shortly before the Galleria Scoglietti. Set back from the water, the ristorante serves up refreshing air conditioning and an affordable change from pizzerias. 20 delicious sauces (L8-16,000/€4.13-8.26) and 9 freshly made pastas (L2-4000/€1.03-2.07), you'll be saying "Basta!" with plenty still on your plate. Open Tu-Sa after 7:30pm.

Ristorante "Il Salto," V. Mazzini, 13d (☎0184 23 86 70). Sit outside on the terrace or inside. The cozy but modern, "Il Salto" offers quality standard primi and secondi at reasonable prices, as well as different types of pizza and a four-course menù turistica for L20,000/€10.33. Open for lunch and dinner. MC/V.

Ristorante Nanni, V. Milite Ignoto, 2c (☎0184 332 30). Dine across the street from the giardini publicci and watch the passers-by ambling to the waterfront. A fantastic view of the sunset awaits 50 paces down the road. 4-course menù L21-27,000/€10.85-13.94. MC/V.

The Buffet Stazione (☎0184 35 12 36), in the train station, is a fastidiously clean option for a quick bite. Pizza and *focaccia* L1200/€0.62, *panini* L4600/€2.38. Prices go down if you stand (and don't try to sit if you didn't order full-service). Open daily noon-3:30pm and 7-9:30pm. Bar open daily 5am-midnight.

👁 SIGHTS

Catch a blue Riviera Trasporti bus at the corner of V. Cavour and V. Martiri della Libertà (dir: Ponte San Luigi; 15min., 12 per day, L2200/€1.14), and stop at La Mortola, home of the internationally renowned 🏛**Botanical Hanbury Gardens.** Here, terraces of exotic flora from three continents cascade from the summit of Cape Mortola to the sea. Tiny gazebos, lily-pad covered ponds, and marble nudes tucked in rocky niches lie along the twisting paths to the seaside cafe. The comprehensive course mapped out in the brochure takes about two hours. A stretch of the ancient Strada Romana lies under the bridge directly before the bathrooms; it was used by the Romans to travel to Provence and by St. Catherine to fetch the Pope from Avignon back to Rome. (☎0184 22 95 07. Open daily 10am-5pm. L12,000/€6.20, ages 6-14, L7000/€3.62, under 6 free.)

The **Romanesque cathedral's** classic simplicity is juxtaposed with the grandeur of the ancient stone walls. The short walk there also takes you through some of the old town's winding ancient streets. To get there, take the footbridge to Ventimiglia Alta, and turn right on V. Trossarelli. Fifty meters ahead you'll find Discesa Marina. Climb to V. Galerina and then V. Falerina. Nestled on the other side of the old town, off V. Garibaldi at P. Colleta, is the 11th century church of **San Michele**. Its **crypt** was constructed using pilfered Roman columns. (Crypt open Su 10:30-noon.)

The **Museo Archeologico,** V. Verdi, 41, sits on the hill overlooking the sea. Roman artifacts found in the area, including a dozen marble heads, are on display. It's quite a hike up V. Verdi, but the bus to Ponte San Luigi stops nearby; ask the driver where to get off (☎0184 35 11 81 or 26 36 01. Open Tu-Sa 9:30am-12:30pm and 3-5pm, Su 10am-12:30pm. L5000/€2.58.) Taking the bus all the way to Ponte San Luigi will leave you a 10-minute walk from the **Balzi Rossi** (Red Cliffs). Cro-Magnon man used to call the cliffs home. Luckily, the only evolutionarily-challenged men still here inhabit local bars. Down, Zog, down! Spectacular artifacts reside in Balzi Rossi's **Prehistoric Museum.** (☎0184 381 13. Open Tu–Su 8:30am-7:30pm, ages 18-25 L2000/€1.03, ages 25-65 L4000/€2.07, EU citizens under 18 and over 65 free.)

Steer clear of the beaches in the Bassa part of town; they are a little crowded and tourist-ridden. Cleaner, quieter beaches lie across the river in Alta, along **Passeggiata Marconi.** If you're willing to travel a little to reach the best beach in Ventimiglia, take the Ponte San Luigi bus to the Archaeological Museum. On your left is an inconspicuous set of stairs. A ten-minute hike down a cliffside overrun with grass opens up to **Spiaggia Le Calandre,** a surprisingly natural sandy beach. Frolicking on the smooth sands with Italian boys and girls won't cost you a single lira. If you want to play grown-up, two chairs and an umbrella on the rocks will run you L30,000/€15.50. *Let's Go* does not recommend staying past sundown, as the trek back could be dangerous in the dark. (☎0347 431 5393. Open daily 8am-9pm.)

🎵 ENTERTAINMENT

Frenzied activity during daylight hours compensates for the largely non-existent nightlife in Ventimiglia. Late June will bring the 41st annual **Battaglia de Fiori,** which consists of floats and festive flower flinging. On Fridays, the **Mercato Settimanale,** around the Giardini Pubblici and along the river, is the biggest market on the Riviera and the Cote d'Azur. The humming *mercato* is just the place to heckle over slinky French slips, suede coats, and salami. Just keep an eye on your wallet.

⚡ DAYTRIP FROM VENTIMIGLIA: DOLCEACQUA

To make this scenic daytrip, catch a bus (20min., 10 per day 6:10am-7:07pm, from V. Cavour across from the tourist office.

A string of villages rose up along the Roya River during the Middle Ages to accommodate journeymen along an essential trade route between Ventimiglia and the rest of northern Italy. Dolceaqua, graced with a medieval castle, was one of these tiny *cittadini*. Even for the history buff, Dolceaqua (9km from Ventimiglia) will suffice as a survey of the historical passageway from Piedmont to France.

As it does in Ventimiglia, the Roya divides the new city from the medieval town on the hill, where a snarl of narrow cobbled streets crescendos at the **Castello dei Doria.** Here breezes swirl through the ruins, water trickles over rocks in a stream below, and a roguish rooster occasions to upset the still. (☎0184 20 64 19. Open Sa-Su 10am-6pm. L3000/€1.55 for access to the exterior only until the interior is finished being restored.) Cross the Roman footbridge, turn right, and walk along the river to reach the multi-hued **Rococo cathedral, San Antonio Abate.** Nearby is the beginning of V. Giraldi. Turn at V. Doria to ascend tunnel-like streets to the castle.

When you come back down, chances are you'll be up for a sampling of Dolceaqua's tastiest pizza at **Pizzeria La Rampa,** V. Barberis, 11, on the left side of P. Garibaldi, in the new town. (☎0184 20 61 98. Open Tu-Su 7pm-midnight.) Then have a glass of Rossesse, Dolceaqua's infamous "sweet water," made since the 1800s at the Arcagne Vineyards high above the new part of town. If you're interested in staying longer than a day, there are no hotels in Dolceaquea, but a five-minute bus ride to the outskirts of **Isolabona** brings you to **Albergo Da Adolfo.** (☎0184 20 81 11. Open Tu-Su 7am-9pm. Singles with bath L85,000/€43.90.) Take note of the spattering of greenhouses planted along the hillsides of the valley; exotic flowers grown here are exported worldwide. Contact the **IAT tourist office** in P. Garibaldi for information on **Ferragosto,** which fills the *piazza* with swirling regional *balletti*, traditional costumes, and mouth-watering pastries in August. (☎0184 20 66 66. Open Sa-Su 10am-1pm and 3-6pm.)

PIEDMONT (PIEMONTE)

More than the source of the mighty Po River, Piedmont has long been a fountainhead of fine food, wine, and nobility. The region falls into three zones: the **Alpine,** the **Pianura,** and the **Colline.** The Alpine, with the peaks of Monviso and Gran Paradiso, contains a string of ski resorts and a national park that spills into Valle d'Aosta. The Pianura includes Turin, the vineyards of Asti, and the beginning of the Po valley. The Colline is dotted with many of the region's isolated castles.

Piedmont has been a politically influential region for centuries. The Savoy family has dominated the area since the 11th century, and in the 19th produced the ever-celebrated Vittorio Emanuele II. With minister Camillo Cavour, Emanuele created a united Italy with Turin as the capital from 1861 to 1865 (see **The Italian Nation: Unification,** p. 12). Though the capital has moved, the political activity has continued. Both the latter-day monarchists and Red Brigades were based in Piedmont. Today, medieval towns recreate the region's glorious past through festivals.

HIGHLIGHTS OF PIEDMONT

AUTHENTICATE in Christianity's most famous relic, the **Holy Shroud of Turin** (p. 177), in Cattedrale di San Giovanni.

GAPE at Asti's dazzling **Gothic churches** (p. 185).

CLUB all night at the **Murazzi** (p. 180) in Turin's underground scene.

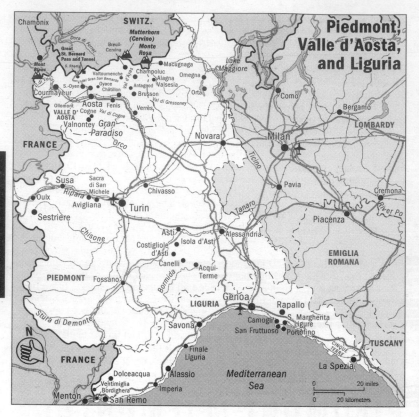

Piedmont, Valle d'Aosta, and Liguria

TURIN (TORINO) ☎011

Turin's elegance is not accidental; it is the direct result of centuries of urban planning and wealthy patrons of the arts. Graceful, arcaded avenues lead to spacious *piazze*, and churches and innumerable *palazzi* line the squares and streets. Turin is not merely a city of historic architecture; it also moves with the palpable spirit of well-dressed businessmen and university students and the economic energy of the locally based Fiat auto company. During his time as a student in Turin, Erasmus said that it was a city pervaded by magic. While Turin has elaborated on its reputation as a center of the occult, visitors are unlikely to glimpse this hidden counter-culture. Only street gypsies and the chaos of the old-fashioned flea market attest to an otherworldly ethos. Turin's turbulent history as the capital of Italian extremism may not always be visible, but the city that sparked the *Risorgimento*, gave rise to the Red Brigades, and provided a forum for leftist intellectuals like Pavese and Natalia Ginzburg maintains its reputation as a cradle of progressive thought. In 2006, the whole world will embrace the city's energy and beauty as Turin hosts the 20th Olympic Winter Games.

◧ TRANSPORTATION

Flights: Caselle Airport (☎011 567 63 61). European destinations. From Porta Nuova, take tram #1 to Porta Susa. Across the street and under the arcade, take blue buses to "Castelle Airport" (L6500/€3.36). Buy tickets at **Bar Mille Luci**, P. XVIII Dicembre, 5.

Trains: Porta Nuova on C.V. Emanuele (011 531 327). A city in itself, the station has a supermarket, barber shop, and post office. Luggage storage and lost property services available. (p. 174). To: **Genoa** (2hr.; every hr. 6:25am-11:10pm; L14,500/€7.49); **Milan** Centrale (2hr.; every hr. 4:40am-10:50pm; L21,600/€11.16); **Paris** (9hr.; Euro-Night 11:48pm; L130,000/€67.13); **Rome** Termini (4½hr.; Eurostar 6:15am, 9:27, and 11:30pm; InterCityNight 12:55 and 11:10pm; L54,600/€28.20 and up); **Venice** Santa Lucia (4½hr.; InterCity 2:07 and 5:07pm; L51,500/€26.60). AmEx/MC/V. **Porta Susa Stazione** (west of the city). Luggage storage available (p. 174). Sends trains to **Milan** (2hr.; every hr. 5:05am-11:05pm; L12,500/€6.46; InterCity L21,600/€11.16) and **Paris** (10:43am and 5:26pm; L156,000/€80.57).

Buses: Autostazione Terminal Bus, C. Inghilterra, 3 (☎011 33 25 25). From Porta Nuova, take cable car #9 or 15. Serves ski resorts, the Riviera, and the valleys of Susa and Pinerolo. To: **Aosta** (3½hr.; 6 per day; L14,000/€7.23); **Chamonix, France** (4hr.; 1 per day; L39,000/€20.14); **Courmayeur** (4hr., 6 per day, L1600/€0.83); **Milan** (2hr.; every hr.; L18,000/€9.30). Ticket office open daily 7am-noon and 3-7pm.

Public Transportation: City buses and **cable cars** cost L1500/€0.77. Buy tickets at a *tabac* before boarding. The system is easy to navigate (you insert your ticket into a validating machine located on the bus; don't hand the ticket to the driver unless he asks to see it), and most terminal offices have helpful maps. Buses run daily 5am-1am.

Taxis: (☎011 57 37, 011 57 30 or 011 33 99).

Bike Rental: Most parks have rentals. **Parco Valentino Noleggio Biciclette** is on V. Ceppi in the Parco Valentino. Walk east (heading toward the Po River) down C.V. Emanuele; just before the Ponte Umberto I Bridge, make a right. No age restrictions. L2000/€1.03 per hr., L4000/€2.07 per half-day, L7000/€3.62 per day. Bargaining might bring a lower rate. Open Tu-Su 9am-12:30pm and 2:30-7pm. **Ciclopark,** at the baggage storage box in Stazione Porta Nuova. L5000/€2.58 per 6hr., L7000/€3.62 per 12hr., L12,000/€6.19 per 24hr. Open 6am-midnight.

⬛🛈 ORIENTATION AND PRACTICAL INFORMATION

Turin lies in the Po River valley, flanked by the Alps on three sides. **Stazione Porta Nuova,** in the heart of the city, is the usual place of arrival. The city itself is an Italian rarity with streets meeting at right angles, making it easy to navigate either by bus or on foot. **Corso Vittorio Emanuele II** runs past the station to the river. **via Roma,** which houses the principal sights, runs north through **Piazza San Carlo** and **Piazza Castello.** The other two main streets, **via Po** and **via Garibaldi,** extend from P. Castello. V. Po continues diagonally through **Piazza Vittorio Veneto** (the university center) to the river. V. Garibaldi stretches to **Piazza Statuto** and **Stazione Porta Susa.** Stazione Porta Nuova, Stazione Porta Susa, and Piazza della Repubblica are dangerous areas, so don't walk alone.

TOURIST AND FINANCIAL SERVICES

Tourist Office: ATL, P. Castello, 165 (☎011 53 51 81 or 53 59 01; info@turismo-torino.org; www.turismotorino.org), under the arcade on the left of the *piazza* as you face Palazzo Reale (a large white "i" on a blue post marks where to enter for info). English, German, French, and Spanish spoken. Excellent map of Turin indexes streets and has info regarding museums and historic cafes. Regional info is also available, e.g., for Susa, Sacra di San Michele, and skiing in the Alps at Sestriere. Ask about the daily sightseeing tram and tour bus routes (W-M 2:30pm, L12,000/€6.19). Smaller office at the Porta Nuova train station (☎011 53 13 27), next to the info office. Both open M-Sa 9:30am-7pm, Su 9:30am-3pm.

Currency Exchange: The convenient exchange office with a big "Change" sign in the Porta Nuova Station offers a decent rate. Open daily 7:30am-7:35pm. MC/V. Otherwise try the **banks** along V. Roma and V. Alfieri or the **ATM** by the APT office. There are several international banks.

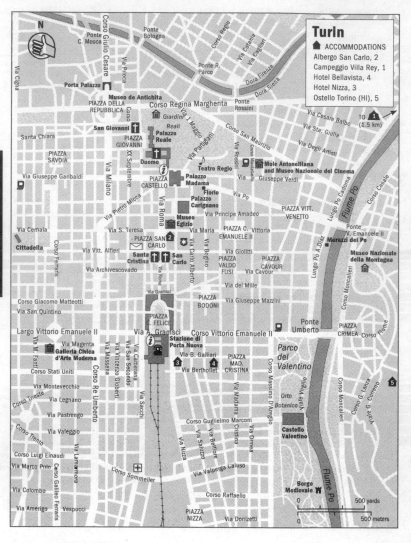

LOCAL SERVICES

Luggage Storage: In **Porta Nuova Train Station,** L5000/€2.58 per 12hr. Open daily 4:30am-2:30am. In **Porta Susa Train Station,** L5000/€2.58 per 12hr. Open daily 7am-11pm.

Lost Property: In **Porta Nuova Train Station: Ufficio Oggetti Smarriti,** (☎011 665 33 15). Open 8am-noon and 2-5pm.

English-Language Bookstore: Libreria Internazionale Luxembourg, V. Accademia delle Scienze, 3 (☎011 561 38 96; fax 54 03 70; luxbooks@tiscalinet.it), across from P. Carignano. The friendly English-speaking staff of this 3-floor British bookstore can help you out among the English, French, German, and Spanish books, newspapers and magazines while you relax to classical music. Open M-Sa 8am-7:30pm. MC/V.

Laundromat: Lavanderia Vizzini, V.S. Secondo, 1F (☎ 011 54 58 82). When facing Stazione P. Nuova walk 2 blocks to the right to V.S. Secondo. Wash and dry L15,000/ €7.75 per 4kg. Open M-F 8:30am-1pm and 3:30-7:30pm.

EMERGENCY AND COMMUNICATIONS

Emergency: ☎ 112 or 113. **Ambulance:** ☎ 118. **Police:** ☎ 112.

Red Cross: ☎ 011 28 03 33.

First Aid: ☎ 011 508 03 70.

Late-Night Pharmacies: Farmacia Boniscontro, C.V. Emanuele, 66 (☎ 011 54 12 71 or 53 82 71). When facing Stazione P. Nuova, walk 3 blocks to the right. Schedule of other pharmacies' hours on the door. Open 3pm-12:30am.

Hospital: San Giovanni Battista, commonly known as Molinette, at C. Bromante, 88 (☎ 011 633 16 33). **Mauriziano Umberto,** C. Turati, 62 (☎ 011 508 01 11).

Internet Access: Centro Informa Giovani, V. Assarotti, 2. From P. Castello take V. Garibaldi for 10 blocks and turn left on V. Assarotti. Free Internet use. 3 computers. Open M-Tu and Th-Sa 10:30am-6:30pm. **Transpan Cyber Service,** C.V. Emanuele, 12b (☎ 011 88 55 12; fax 817 78 22; transpan@transpan.it) A few blocks east of the Ponte Umberto I bridge. ISDN use L10,000/€5.16 per hr. Scanner, printer, but only 1 computer. Open M 3-7pm, Tu-F 9:30am-1pm and 3-7:30pm, Sa 10am-1pm and 3-7pm. **@h!,** V. Montebello, 13 (☎ 011 815 40 58; info@ahto.it; www.ahto.it), opposite the Mole Antonellana. 10 computers available for use. Daily newspapers (in English and Italian) hang on the wall. Cell phones and supporting equipment sold. English spoken. L10,000/€5.16 per 30min., L12,000/€6.19 per hr. Free tea and coffee. Open M-F 10:30am-1pm and 2-7pm. AmEx/MC/V.

Post Office: V. Alfieri, 10 (☎ 011 53 58 94 or 562 81 00), off P.S. Carlo. Facing north (toward P. Reale), head left. Two blocks down on the right. Fax and telegram service. Open M-F 8:15am-7:20pm, Sa 8:15am-1pm, last day of the month 8:15am-noon. *Fermo Posta* open M-Sa 9am-noon and 3-7pm.

Postal Code: 10100.

♠ ACCOMMODATIONS & CAMPING

Despite the abundance of hotels, prices can be steep even for the most basic rooms. On weekends and during the summer, when visitors and locals retreat to resorts, the city is more tranquil and rooms are easier to find.

Ostello Torino (HI), V. Alby, 1 (☎ 011 660 29 39; fax 660 44 45; hostelto@tin.it). Take bus #52 from Stazione Porto Nuova (bus #64 on Su). Get off the bus just after you cross the Po River (at Piazza Crimea, which has a tall sandstone obelisk at its center)— the second stop. Make a right onto C. Lanza. There is an Ostello sign at the corner. Follow the signs, which lead you to V. Gatti (a left), and then a 200m climb up a winding road. The hostel is behind a large row of shrubs. An opportunity to live among the posh villas in the hills along the Po at a considerable discount. At this clean and well-run hostel, you'll find beautiful views of the city. 76 beds and TV room. Internet access with phone card L12,000/€6.19 per hr. Dinner served (L18,000/€9.29). Breakfast and sheets included. Lockers available L20,000/€10.33 deposit. Laundry (wash and dry) L10,000/€5.16 per small load. Reception 7-10am and 3:30-11pm. Curfew 11:30pm; ask for key if going out. Reserve ahead. Closed Dec. 20-Feb. 1. Dorms L22,000/ €11.36; doubles L48,000/€28.20. Oct.-Apr. L2000/€1.03 per day for heat.

Hotel Bellavista, V.B. Galliari, 15, 6th fl. (☎ 011 669 81 39; fax 668 79 89). As you exit Porta Nuova, turn right and then take the 2nd left on V. Galliari. 18 large, airy rooms with TV, telephone, and a balcony with a view of Turin. Sunny hallway full of plants and a long balcony with a city view. Breakfast L8000/€4.13. Singles L55,000/€28.40, with bath L70,000/€36.15; doubles L110,000/€56.81, with bath L120,000/€61.97; triples with bath L140,000/€72.30.

Hotel Lux, V. Galliari, 9, 2nd fl. (☎011 65 72 57; fax 66 87 482). From Stazione P. Nuova walk down V. Nizza and take the 2nd left to V. Galliari. Basic, affordable rooms without bath. TV. Singles L55,000/€28.40; doubles L80,000/€41.31; 1 triple 120,000/€61.97, with bath L150,000/€77.47.

Albergo San Carlo, P.S. Carlo, 197, 4th fl. (☎/fax 011 53 86 53), in the midst of all the action and splendor of the *piazza*, but high above the noise. Newly renovated Liberty-style interior. Ski-lodge-style rooms, with TV, fridge, chandeliers, and phone. Singles L65,000/€33.56, with bath L85,000/€43.90; doubles L90,000/€46.48, L120,000/€61.97. MC/V.

Hotel Nizza, V. Nizza, 9, 2nd fl. (☎/fax 011 669 05 16 or 650 59 63). Exit to the right from Porta Nuova on V. Nizza. Large, spacious rooms, all with bath, TV, and phone. Balcony has a bar. Breakfast included. Singles L85,000/€43.70; doubles L130,000/€67.14; triples L175,000/€90.38; quads L210,000/€108.46. AmEx/DC/MC/V.

Camping: Campeggio Villa Rey, Strada Superiore Val S. Martino, 27 (☎/fax 011 819 01 17). Bus #61 from Porta Nuova until P. Vittorio and then bus #56. Follow signs after last stop. Quiet location in the hills. Bar, restaurant, and small supermarket on the premises. L7000/€3.62 per person,L4000/€2.07 per 1-person tent, L7000/€3.62 per 2, L9000/€4.65 per 3-5 persons. Light L2500/€1.29. Showers L1000/€0.52.

FOOD

The cheapest supplies are available in the fruit, cheese, and bread shops on V. Mazzini or in **Di Per Di,** V. Carlo Alberto, 15E, at the corner of V. Maria Vittoria. (Open M-Tu and Th-Sa 8:30am-1:30pm and 3:30-7:30pm, W 8:30am-1:30pm. MC/V.)

Sample the delectable *bocca di leone* (a rich pastry filled with whipped cream, fruit, or chocolate; L3500/€1.81) and the delicious *viennesi alla crema* (L14,000/€7.23) at **Il Pasticciere,** V. Garibaldi, 9. (☎011 54 08 17. Open Tu-Su 7:30am-8pm; closed 3 weeks in summer.) If a supply of *gelato* is a sign of wealth and sophistication, then Turin has both, since there is a *gelateria* of some sort every few hundreds yards, especially at the center of town on V. Roma or V. Po. Look for the *produzione propria* (made on premises) sign. The spiffy mirror-lined **Gelateria-Bar Ice Blù,** V. Lagrange, 34A (☎011 54 46 77; open daily 7am-1am) and **Gelateria Fiorio,** V. Po, 8 (☎011 817 32 25; open Tu-Su 8am-2am), sell the best *gelato*.

> **MONEY TO MANGIA.** *Piemontese* cuisine is a sophisticated blend of northern Italian peasant staples and elegant French garnishes. Butter replaces olive oil, and cheese, mushrooms, and white truffles are used more than tomatoes, peppers, or spices. *Agnolotti* (ravioli stuffed with lamb and cabbage) is the local pasta specialty, but polenta, a cornmeal porridge often topped with fontina cheese, is the more common starch. The three most outstanding (and expensive) red wines in Italy, *Barolo*, *Barbaresco*, and *Barbera*, are available in Turin's markets and restaurants. To sample the true flavors of *Piemontese* cuisine, be prepared to pay—restaurants that specialize in regional dishes are expensive.

Il Punto Verde, V.S. Massimo, 17 (☎011 88 55 43), off V. Po near P. C. Emanuele II, offers tasty, good-for-you, green cuisine. Enjoy freshly squeezed fruit juices while sitting between romantic old walls outside. *Primi* L10-12,000/€5.16-6.20; *secondi* L6-12,000/€3.09-6.20; giant *monopiatti* L20,000/€10.33. *Menù* L15,000/€7.75. Cover L3000/€1.55. Open M-F noon-2:30pm and 7-10:30pm, Sa 7-10:30pm. Closed Aug. MC/V.

Shangrila, V. Accademia Albertina, 42 (☎011 81 77 904). From Stazione P. Nuova go right on V.V. Emanuele and turn left on V. A. Albertina. Hearty, delicious, and affordable Chinese and Italian dishes. Pizza L4500/€2.32; *primi* L3500-7500/€1.81-3.87; *secondi* L6800-9000/€3.51-4.65. Lunch *menù* L11,000/€5.68. Cover L2000/€1.03. Open daily 8am-10pm. MC/V.

WorldPhone. Worldwide.

MCI℠ gives you the freedom of worldwide communications whenever you're away from home. It's easy to call to and from over 70 countries with your MCI Calling Card:

1. Dial the WorldPhone® access number of the country you're calling from.
2. Dial or give the operator your MCI Calling Card number.
3. Dial or give the number you're calling.

- Italy   172-1022

Sign up today!

Ask your local operator to place a collect call
(reverse charge) to MCI in the U.S. at:

1-712-943-6839

For additional access codes or to sign up, visit us at www.mci.com/worldphone.

www.mci.com/worldphone

It's Your World...

www.mci.com/worldphone

Spacca Napoli, V. Mazzini, 19 (☎011 812 66 94). Scrumptious pasta and crisp brick-oven pizza served in an elegant, friendly atmosphere. Non-smoking section available. Pizza L7500-11,000/€3.87-5.65; *primi* L10,000/€5.16; *secondi* L18-22,000/€9.29-11.36. Desserts L8000/€4.13. Cover L3500/€1.81. Open W-M 6pm-1am. MC/V.

La Bodeguita, V. Melchior Gioia, 8F (☎011 53 85 05). From Stazione P. Nuova turn left and take the 4th right. Great Spanish and Italian dishes with lots of style and funky colors. *Tortillas* L6000/€3.09, *pescados* from L15,000/€7.75, salads from L6000/€3.09. Open Su-Th 7pm-2am, F 7pm-3am, Sa 7pm-4am. MC/V.

Brek, P. Carlo Felice, 22 (☎011 53 45 56), off V. Roma. Facing P. C. Felice, on the steps of Porta Nuova, walk straight ahead through the park, or along one of the covered walkways on the side. In either case, you'll end up there, poised just before you pass onto V. Gramsci. A large canopy is the only landmark this self-service chain can boast to distinguish itself from its surroundings. Also off P. Solferino at V.S. Teresa, 23 (☎011 54 54 24; open until 11pm) and C. Comm. "Le Gru" Grugliasco (☎011 70 72 588). *Primi* around L6500/€3.36; *secondi* L9000/€4.65. Open M-Sa 11:30am-3pm and 6:30-10:30pm. AmEx/MC/V.

Porto di Savona, P. V. Veneto, 2 (☎011 817 35 00). A Turinese institution. Lunch-time *monopiatti* (large platters of pasta, salad, dessert, and coffee L15,000/€7.75) are a great deal. Best bets are *gnocchi al gorgonzola* and *fusilli alla diavola* (a spicy delight made with tomato, pesto, and cream sauce), both for L8000/€4.13. Huge portions. *Primi* from L10-12,000/€5.16-6.19; *secondi* from L12,000/€6.19. Open Tu 7:30-10:30pm, W-Su 12:30-2:30pm and 7:30-10:30pm. Closed first 2 weeks in Aug.

Trattoria Toscana, V. Vanchiglia, 2 (☎011 812 29 14), off P.V. Veneto near the university. Hearty, unpretentious fare. Try the *bistecca di cinghiale* (wild boar steak; L11,000/€5.68). Open Sept.-July W-Su noon-2pm and 7-10pm, M noon-2pm. DC/MC/V.

👁 SIGHTS

For a walking-tour booklet, ask at the tourist office for the **Six City Tours** pamphlet.

CATTEDRALE DI SAN GIOVANNI. A Renaissance cathedral dedicated to John the Baptist, this house of worship is best known for its enigmatic Christian relic, the **Holy Shroud of Turin,** transferred to Turin from Chambéry, France in 1578. The blond, narrow pillars that flank the church make the two imposing black chambers positioned on both sides of the altar stand out in greater contrast. To the left of the left black doorway is the Cappella della Santa Sindone, where a 3m photograph of the shroud hangs length-wise (behind glass) above the real shroud, which lies entombed just below the photography in a case of aluminum and glass, where, to the dismay of curiosity-seekers, it is obscured by an opaque cloth. Two lateral figures are visible, head to head; the left being the top of the body (with face and arms clearly distinguishable), and the right being the back of the body. Do you see what I see? Before leaving the cathedral, look above the front door for Luigi Gagna's oil reproduction of Leonardo's *Last Supper*, considered the best copy of the Renaissance masterpiece. The church is undergoing restoration, but remains open. *(Behind Palazzo Reale where V. XX Settembre crosses P.S. Giovanni. ☎011 436 15 40. Open daily 7am-12:30pm and 3-7pm. Free. The authentic Holy Shroud can be viewed Aug. 10-Oct. 22 for free by making reservations at ☎800 32 93 29.)*

MUSEO EGIZIO & GALLERIA SABAUDA. The **Palazzo dell'Accademia delle Scienze** houses two of Turin's best museums. Crammed into two floors is the Museo Egizio, with the 3rd-largest collection of Egyptian artifacts in the world. The collection includes several copies of the Egyptian Book of the Dead and the intact sarcophagus of Vizier Ghemenef-Har-Bak, which stands out among the large sculptures and architectural fragments on the ground floor. Upstairs lies the fascinating, well-furnished tomb of 14th-century BC architect Kha and his wife, one of the few tombs spared by grave-robbers. Another corpse to see: on the first floor, the body of the 6th-century BC Egyptian courtier Rei Harteb lies about four feet in the air, skin, including eyelids, ears, and nose, is intact. No Polygrip for this old

I FOUND JESUS IN TURIN The Holy Shroud of Turin, preserved in the Basilica di S. Giovanni Battista since 1578, has been called a hoax by some and a miracle by others. The piece of linen, 3x14 feet, was supposedly wrapped around Jesus's body in preparation for his burial. Although radiocarbon dating suggests the piece is from the 12th century AD, the shroud's uncanny resemblance to Christ's dissuades its immediate dismissal. Visible on the cloth are outflows of blood: around the head (from the Crown of Thorns?), all over the body (from scourging), and most importantly, around the wrists and feet (where the body was nailed to the cross). Scientists agree that the shroud was wrapped around the body of a 5'7" man who died by crucifixion, but whether it was the body of Jesus remains a mystery. For Christian believers, however, the importance of this relic is best described by Pope Paul VI's words: "The Shroud is a document of Christ's love written in characters of blood."

man; his original teeth remain in place after 27 centuries. *(V. Accademia delle Scienze, 6, 2 blocks from P. Castello. ☎ 011 561 77 76; fax 53 46 23. Open Tu-F and Su 8:30am-7:30pm, Sa 8:30am-11pm. L12,000/€6.19, ages 18-25 L6000/€3.09, under 18 and over 65 free.)*

The third and fourth floors hold the Galleria Sabauda, which houses art collections from Palazzo Reale and Palazzo Carignano in Turin and Palazzo Durazzo in Genoa. The gallery is renowned for its Flemish and Dutch paintings including van Eyck's *St. Francis Receiving the Stigmata*, Memling's *Passion*, van Dyck's *Children of Charles I of England*, and Rembrandt's *Old Man Sleeping*. The Sabauda is also home to several Mannerist and Baroque paintings, including a noteworthy Poussin, several Strozzis, and Volture's *Decapitation of John the Baptist*. *(☎ 011 54 74 40. Hours same as Egyptian Museum. L8000/€4.13, ages 18-25 L4000/€2.07, under 18 and over 60 free. Combined ticket for both museums L15,000/€7.75.)*

■ **MOLE ANTONELLIANA.** This is the definitive symbol of the city and of the 2006 Winter Olympics. In time, it should also become a symbol for the preservation and celebration of cinema and the history of visual culture. Begun as a synagogue in a period of political and religious instability, it ended up a Victorian eccentricity, over 160m above the ground. Enter the museum on V. Montebello through tilted (automatic) retracting glass doors. Take a glass elevator that will lift you through the center of the building and into its spire, where you will enjoy a panoramic view of the city, including a clear sight of the Basilica di Superga. The Mole is home to the newly constructed **Museo Nazionale del Cinema,** one of the foremost sites on earth to become acquainted with the origins and development of cinema. Highlights include several 19th-century shorts by Thomas Edison and the very bizarre phenakistiscope. In the open space at the center of the museum, lie in a bed while watching love scenes, stand over a crypt during *Dracula*, and sit in an authentic 1960s living room while viewing Oliver Stone's *JFK*. *(V. Montebello, 20, a few blocks east of P. Castello. ☎ 011 81 54 230.)*

PALAZZO CARIGNANO. One of Guarini's grandiose Baroque palaces, the *palazzo* that housed the Princess of Savoia and the first Italian parliament was built in 1679. The elegant and ornate building contains the only museum devoted entirely to Italian national history, the **Museo Nazionale del Risorgimento Italiano,** commemorating the unification of Italy (1706-1946). Documents and other historical paraphernalia make this museum a first stop for the student of history, especially Italian history. *(V. Accademia delle Scienze, 5. Enter from P. Carlo Alberto on the other side of the palace opposite the Biblioteca Nazionale. ☎ 011 562 37 19. Open Tu-Su 9am-7pm. L8000/ €4.13, students L5000/€2.58, under 10 and over 65 free. Free guided tour Su 10-11:30am.)*

TEATRO CARIGNANO. Just across from the Palazzo is a theater that the Turinese claim is every bit as important as Milan's **La Scala** (p. 91). The gleaming gold and rose Baroque music hall was manicured with attention to every detail and possesses a Neoclassical ceiling fresco more than worthy of a good stare. *(☎ 011 54 70 54. No set hours. Call ahead. Free.)*

GALLERIA CIVICA D'ARTE MODERNA E CONTEMPORANEA. The modern art museum's 19th- and 20th-century collection is primarily Italian, including some Modiglianis and de Chiricos, but also houses Andy Warhol's gruesome *Orange Car Crash* and works by Picasso, Ernst, Leger, Chagall, Twombly, Klee, Courbet, and Renoir. One of Italy's premier museums of Italian modern and contemporary art, it displays various styles from Divisionism to Dadaism to Pop Art. *(V. Magenta, 31. On the corner of C. G. Ferraris, off Largo Emanuele. ☎011 562 99 11; www.gam.intesa.it. Open Tu-Su 9am-7pm. L10,000/€5.16, under 26 L5000/€2.58, under 10 and over 65 free.)*

PALAZZO REALE. Home to the Princes of Savoy from 1645 to 1865, the palace consists mostly of ornate apartments. Its red and gold interior houses an outstanding collection of Chinese porcelain vases. Louis le Nôtre (1697), more famous for his work on the gardens of Versailles, designed the *palazzo*'s grounds. Although the city owes its glory to political rather than ecclesiastical leadership, unadulterated splendor blesses the interior of the **Chiesa di San Lorenzo,** next to the Palazzo Reale. Constructed between 1668 and 1680, it is Guarini's most original creation with a dynamic, swirling dome. *(In Piazzetta Reale, at the end of P. Castello. ☎011 436 14 55. Palazzo open Tu-Su 8:30am-7:30pm. L8000/€4.13 1st fl.; L10,000/€5.16 whole palazzo; ages 18-25 L5000/€2.58, under 18 and over 65 free. Guided tours in Italian. 40 min. Tu-Su 9am-1pm and 2-7pm. Gardens open 8:30am-7pm. Free. Church open 8am-12:30pm and 3:30-6pm.)*

In the right wing of the Royal Palace lies the **Armeria Reale** (Royal Armory) of the House of Savoy, containing the world's best collection of medieval and Renaissance war tools. Swords a' plenty, suits of armor, and wicked weapons fill this museum. *(P. Castello, 191. ☎011 54 38 89. Open Tu and Th 1:30-7pm, W and F-Sa 9am-2pm. L8000/€4.13, under 18 and over 60 free.)*

BASILICA DI SUPERGA. When the French attacked Turin on September 6, 1706, King Vittorio Amedeo II made a pact with the Virgin Mary to build a magnificent cathedral in her honor should the city withstand the invasion. Turin stood unconquered, and the result was this structure. The basilica stands on a 672m summit outside of Turin, with panoramic views of the city, the Po valley below, and the Alps rising beyond. Its Neoclassical portico and high drum create a spectacular dome. *(Take tram #15 (L1500/€0.77) from V. XX Settembre to Stazione Sassi. From the station, take bus #79 or board a small cable railway for a clanking ride up the hill (20min.; every hr.; round-trip L6000/€3.09, Su and holidays L12,000/€6.20). ☎011 898 00 83. Open Apr.-Sept. 9:30am-noon and 3-6pm; Oct.-Mar. 10am-noon and 3-5pm. Free. L3000/€1.55 for tombs.)*

PARCO DEL VALENTINO. One of Italy's largest parks on the banks of the Po, Valentino's lush and romantic grounds provide a haven for whispering lovers and running children. Upon entering the park from C.V. Emanuele, **Castello del Valentino** will be on the left. Once the home of the designer of the same name, and now the home of the Facolta di Architettura. Further south along the river, beside the calm, manicured **Giardino Roccioso,** is **Borgo e Rocca Medievale,** a "medieval" village built for the 1884 World Exposition. *(Park and castle at V. Virgilio, 107, along the Po. ☎011 81 77 178. Open Aug. 15-Oct. 25. Phone reservations required. Free.)*

PIAZZA SAN CARLO. Between P. Felice and P. Reale, formal Baroque grandeur takes over; the equestrian statue of Duke Emanuele Filiberto sits proudly on a horse over the crowds. In addition to the Baroque buildings, the *piazza* features the opulent twin churches of **Santa Cristina** and **San Carlo Borromeo,** on the right and left, respectively, upon entering the *piazza* from V. Roma. Santa Cristina has the more formidable statuary on its facade. Both churches display the gray granite of Susa and the white stone of Gassino at its best. *(Santa Christina open 8am-1pm and 3-8pm. San Carlo open 7am-noon and 3-7pm. Free.)*

MUSEO NAZIONALE DELL'AUTOMOBILE. The museum documents the evolution of the automobile, exhibiting prints, drawings, leaflets, more than 150 original cars and the first models made by Ford, Benz, Peugeot, Oldsmobile, and the homegrown Fiat. The focus is, as expected, on Italian cars and car racing. Frequent exhibits, often with figurative car designs. *(C. Unità d' Italia, 40. Head south along V. Nizza from Stazione Porta Nuova. ☎011 67 76 66. Open Tu-Su 10am-6:30pm. L4000/€2.58.)*

🎵 ENTERTAINMENT

For the skinny on the happening spots, inquire at the tourist office. On Fridays, check out Turin's newspaper, *La Stampa*, which publishes *Torino Sette*, an excellent section on current cultural events. Music of all genres livens Turin between June and August, when the city invites international performers to the **Giorni d'Estate Festival**. For information, programs, and venues, contact the tourist office or the **Vetrina per Torino**, P.S. Carlo, 159. (☎800 015 475; vetrina@comune.torino.it; www.comune.torino.it/welcomep.htm. Open M-Sa 11am-7pm.) From September 5-25, the **Settembre Musica** extravaganza features over 40 classical concerts performed throughout the city. Contact the Vetrina or the tourist office for programs (available by the beginning of July). **Cinemas** all over Turin offer the latest big-budget blockbusters, obscure art films, and all-out pornography. Try **Lux** (on V. Roma between P. San Carlo and P.C. Felice, on the left when facing P. Reale), **Cinema Vittoria** on V. Antonio Gramsci where it meets V. Roma, or **Multisala Ambrosio,** to the right as you exit Porta Nuova on C.V. Emanuele. During the academic year, a number of foreign films are shown in their original languages. For a listing of films, ask the tourist office for the leaflet **Arena Metropolis.** Be aware that most films will be (poorly) dubbed into Italian.

🛍 SHOPPING

One of Turin's unique events is the **Gran Balon flea market,** held every other Sunday in P. della Repubblica. Here, junk sellers rub shoulders with treasure hunting dealers of antiques and valuable rarities. Though the streets of Turin are lined with clothing stores, the budget traveler will quickly learn that the chic, designer shops on **V. Roma** are best for window shopping. Up **via Lagrange** and **via Carlo Alberto,** the *haute couture* demons may drag you into **Inferno,** V. Carlo Alberto, 55e, a world of black garb and magenta walls. (☎011 88 95 33. Open M 3-7:30pm, Tu-Sa 10am-12:30pm and 3-7:30pm.) The department store **La Rinascente,** at the corner of V. Lagrange and V. Teofilo Rossi, sells more traditional attire.

🌙 NIGHTLIFE

Discos and bars constantly turn over; ask at the tourist office for the weekly leaflet **News Spettacolo.**

I MURAZZI
At the quay by the river at the end of C.V. Emanuele, between Ponte Emanuele and Ponte Umberto, **Murazzi del Po** becomes one of the liveliest and most appealing places to be in Turin by nightfall. Situated at the edge of the Po River, this cloister of drinking areas (tucked at the basis of the river), allows one to be both social, and, if desired, private (a long stretch of walkway allows easy strolls, or intimate conversations by the water). Most clubs here are open daily until the morning, with a L20,000/€10.33 cover that includes a drink. There's always good underground techno, dance, and live music.

NORTH OF I MURAZZI, LUNGO PO CADORNA

Pura Vida, C. Cairoli, 14 (☎0348 420 52 31). Always packed with a university-age crowd hungry for Latin and reggae music. Feed your tummy with a *tortilla* for L5000/€2.58 or *torta de pollo* for L6000/€3.09. Open Su-F 10am-3am, Sa 10am-4am.

Caffe Flora, P. V. Veneto, 24 (☎011 817 15 30). Chill session—just 20 or 30 people hangin' in comfortable chairs. Lots of drinks, but no food. Open Tu-Su 2pm-3am.

Alcohol, Lungo Po Cadorna, 1, further along the river. This fantastic club plays great acid jazz and drum 'n' bass. Trendy decoration in orange and a cozy downstairs. Open Su-F 10pm-3am, Sa 10pm-4am.

CORSO VITTORIO EMANUELE

Several excellent English and Irish pubs line up from the Stazione Porta Nuova on the way to the Po River along C.V. Emanuele.

Six Nations Murphy's Pub, C.V. Emanuele, 28 (☎0348 230 27 82). Make a right out of Porta Nuova; a few blocks down on your left. Features bartenders with Scottish kilts. Half pint from L4000/€2.58, 1 pint from L7000/€3.62. There's a back area for smoking. Open daily 6pm-3am.

The Shamrock Inn, C.V. Emanuele, 34 (☎011 817 49 50), further toward the river. Offers lively rumba dancing, decent sandwiches, and desserts. Several beers on tap. There is a nice window seat, good for a conversation and a view of the tree-lined street. Open M-Sa 7pm-3am.

ACROSS THE RIVER AND LINGOTTO

Discoteca Boccaccio, C. Moncalieri, 145 (☎011 660 17 70; fax 66 01 483). Cross the river on Ponte Umberto I from C.V. Emanuele and go left for about 8min. on C. Moncalieri on the left side. Big dance floor and a mixed/gay/transvestite crowd. Cover L15,000/€7.75; L20,000/€10.33 for men. Open F-Sa 10pm-3am.

Hiroshima Mon Amour, V. Carlo Bossoli, 63 (☎011 31 76 636). Take bus #1 or 34 to Lingotto Centro Fiere. This place is da bomb. The name, to be sure, a reference to Alain Resnais's film about love and cities. The music changes nightly from reggae to rock 'n' roll; some nights feature live performances. Cover ranges from free (Sa) to L20,000/€10.33. Plan on taking a taxi back to the city or ask a trustworthy (read: sober) local for a ride. Open nightly 11pm until late.

❄ OLYMPICS

In 2006, Turin will be in the global spotlight when it has the distinct honor of hosting the XX Olympic Winter Games. The games will mark the first Winter Olympics in Italy since the 1956 Winter Olympics in Cortina d'Ampezzo. Turin beat out five other candidates in the solely European contest: Zakopane, Poland; Klagenfurt, Austria; Poprad-Tatry, Slovakia; Sion, Switzerland; and a joint bid by Helsinki, Finland and Lillehammer, Norway. Turin's presentation to the International Olympic Committee focused on the Alps with a winter environment and a metropolis. To join the winter fun yourself, hit the slopes at **Sestriere, Alagna Valsesia,** or **Macugnaga** (see p. 182). For more information about the Games contact the **Torino Organizing Committee** at V. Nizza, 262 (☎011 63 10 511; www.torino2006.it.)

🏂 DAYTRIPS FROM TURIN

■ SACRA DI SAN MICHELE

*To reach the monastery from Turin you must take a **train** to Avigliana (15 per day, L2700/ €1.39). Without a car, accessing the monastery is difficult, as there are **no public buses.** However, the 14km day's hike from Avigliana will make you feel like a proud pilgrim. If the monastery beckons but you're short on time you can always take a **taxi** (☎011 93 02 18; L50-70,000/€25.82-36.15). Bargain hard and arrange to be picked up. **Monastery,** ☎011 93 91 30, open Tu-Su 9:30am-12:30pm and 3-6pm. L4000/€2.58.*

Looming on a bluff 1000m above the town of Avigliana, the massive stone monastery of Sacra di San Michele seems to grow out of the very rock on which it was built. *The Name of the Rose* was not filmed here but probably should have been. Umberto Eco based the plot of his book on the monastery, and even in the summer it is easy to imagine monks plummeting to snowy deaths from the high windows. The monastery, founded in AD 1000, perches atop Mt. Pirchiriano with sweeping and spectacular views in all directions. Upon entering the structure, the impressive **Stairway of the Dead,** an immense set of steps helping to buttress the building, leads outside to the beautifully carved wooden doors that depict the arms of St. Michael with the Serpent of Eden. The shrine of St. Michael is down the small steps in the middle of the nave, where there are three tiny chapels. In 966 St. John Vincent built the largest one, with a back wall of solid rock; today, it holds the tombs of medieval members of the Savoy family. Although the building is undergoing restoration, it remains open to the public.

From the station in Avigliana turn left and follow the main road, C. Laghi, through town and around Lago Grande for about 30 minutes. This part runs along the shoulder of a busy road and is not very pleasant. Turn right on the green street Sacra di S. Michele, which winds its way slowly up the mountain. The way is clearly marked, and the walk takes about three hours. Wear sturdy shoes, and bring plenty of water. If you'd feel safer with a map before starting the arduous trek, head to Avigliana's **Informazione Turistico,** P. del Popolo, 2, a five- to 10-minute walk straight ahead from the station. (☎ 011 932 86 50. Open M-F 9am-noon and 3-6pm.) There are **public toilets** outside the entrance to the monastery, but bring your own paper. **Restaurants** cluster halfway up the hill and before the end of the climb.

SUSA

To reach Susa from Turin, take the train to Bussoleno (1hr., every 30min. 5:35am-9:03pm, L6000/€3.09) and a five-minute connecting train to Susa (every 30min.). Call ☎ 0122 62 26 94 to reserve a spot in the daily tour at the biblioteca.

Though far from *la città eterna* and surrounded by mountains, the tiny hamlet of Susa (pop. 7000) never lets visitors forget its Roman origins. This town was once the seat of Gaul Cottius, a prefect of the Empire. Today, Susa's cultural wealth centers on its collection of Roman remnants and medieval structures, all of which lie across the river from the train station. On V.F. Ronaldo (the street farthest right when you cross a bridge and walk through a *piazza*), looms the 3rd-century **Porta Savoia,** a symbolic centerpiece of the Roman remains scattered throughout the town. Head all the way through the *porta* and to the right. Walk up the incline, keeping the gorgeous **Parco D'Augusto** on your left. Immediately in front stands the **Arch of Augustus,** and further on, the 2nd-century **amphitheater** and the **baths.** Along the route is the *campanile* of the **Chiesa di Santa Maria Maggiore,** now a private home. Right of the *porta* stands the **Cattedrale di S. Giusto,** dating from 1027. Inside awaits the 14th-century *Triptych of Rocciamelone,* a Flemish depiction of the Virgin and saints. Adjacent to the cathedral stands an 11th-century bell tower.

From the station, turn right and walk 30m to the small white **tourist office** at V. Inghilterra, 39, to pick up maps and **exchange currency.** (☎ 0122 90 76 06. Open May-Oct. M-Sa 9am-7:30pm, Su 9am-noon; Nov.-Apr. Tu-Sa 9am-noon.) In between the station and the tourist office is a small AGIP petrol station that doubles as a **SAPAV bus ticket office.** (☎ 0121 166 84 50 10). Buses leave from the train station at C. Stati Uniti 33 and head to **Sestriere** via Oulx (50min., 5 per day, L7200/€3.72) and **Turin** (1½hr., 5:30pm, L7500/€3.87). In case of **emergency,** call **pronto soccorso** (☎ 118), across from the tourist office, or the **hospital,** C. Inghilterra, 66 (☎ 0122 62 12 12), next door. **Post office,** V. Mazzini, 40, take a right out of the tourist office and left onto V. Mazzini. (☎ 0122 62 25 44. Open M-F 8:15am-1:40pm, Sa 8:15-11:40am.)

Marco and Loris provide spotless rooms and lessons on Susa's history across from the station in the renovated **Hotel Stazione,** C. Stati Uniti, 2. (☎/fax 0122 62 22 26; www.valsusa.net/ristorante-stazione. English spoken. Breakfast L12,000/ €6.19. Reception 7:30am-midnight. Singles L36,000/€18.59, with shower L47,000/ €24.27; doubles L73,000/€37.70, with bath L95,000/€49.06. AmEx/DC/MC/V.)

SESTRIERE

*Bus service runs directly from **Turin** (L14,500/€7.49) and **Oulx,** on Paris-Turin train line.*

Turin is just a hop, skip, and a ski-jump away from many superb hiking areas and smooth slopes. The closest resort, only 75 minutes from the city, is super-chic Sestriere (2035m), home of Italian ski legend Alberto Tomba. Sestriere has four cableways, 20 ski lifts, excellent runs, a skating rink, and, with any luck, piles of snow. For information on snow conditions and lodgings, call the tourist office in Sestriere, P. Agnelli, 11 (☎0122 760 45) or in Turin (see p. 173).

Alagna Valsesia (1200m), slightly farther away, boasts the second longest lift in the area. Still farther north, **Macugnaga** (1327m) stands with its own enormous ski lift. These resorts are linked to Turin by bus and train. The booklet *Settimane Bianche*, available at Turin's tourist office, provides additional information.

ASTI ☎0141

Asti sparkles, just like its popular, intoxicating progeny. Though now in the foothills of the Alps, it once lay under the ocean, emerging only in the Pliocene era (visit the **Chiesa di San Pietro in Consavia** to find out about the history of the area). Asti has bustled with activity since Roman times, when it bore the name "Hasta." While the city thrives in the modern world, it did not fare well under the domination of the Savoy family (AD 1300-1700). The town was sacked and burned in struggles with local princes. Nevertheless, more than 100 13th-century edifices have survived, lending the city a medieval air. While known for the 18th-century poet Vittorio Alfieri and his cousin Count Benedetto (who designed much of the city), Asti is perhaps most famous for the sparkling wines that bear its name.

▐ TRANSPORTATION

Trains: P. Marconi, where V. Cavour meets C. L. Einaudi. Luggage storage available (p. 183). To: **Alessandria** (30min., every hr. 5:22am-7:50pm, L4400/€2.27); **Milan** Stazione Centrale (2hr.; 6:48am; L12,500/€6.46); and **Turin** P. Nuova (1hr., 2 per hr. 4:30am-11:14pm, L6000/€3.09). Info open M-F 6am-12:40pm and 1:10-7:45pm.

Buses: P. Medaglie d'Oro, across from the train station. Tickets (L3-4000/€1.55-2.07) on the bus. To: **Canelli** (every 1½ hr. 7:10am-6:40pm); **Castagnole** (every 2hr. 7:20am-6:40pm); **Costigliole** (7:15, 11am, and 12:50pm); **Isola d'Asti** (6 per day 10am-6:50pm).

Taxis: In P. Alfieri (☎0141 53 26 05) or at the station in P. Marconi (☎0141 59 27 22).

✦▐ ORIENTATION AND PRACTICAL INFORMATION

The center of the town lies in the triangular **piazza Vittorio Alfieri**. Most historical sights are slightly to the left of the *piazza* when facing the statue, down **C.V. Alfieri**.

Tourist Office: P. Alfieri, 29 (☎0141 53 03 57; fax 53 82 00). Assists in finding (not reserving) accommodations, including *agriturismo* options. Info on daytrips to wineries and castles. Pick up indispensable map and *Guide to Asti and its Province*. English, French, and German. Open M-Sa 9am-1pm and 2:30-6:30pm, Su 10am-1pm.

Currency Exchange: Cassa di Risparmio di Asti, on the corner of P. 1 Maggio and V. M. Rainero. Open M-F 8:20am-1:20pm and 2:30-3:50pm, Sa 8:20-11:20am. Also try the post office. 24hr. **ATMs** in the train station and along V. Dante.

Luggage Storage: In **train station,** L7500/€3.87 per 24hr. Open daily 8am-1pm and 2:15-5pm.

Emergency: ☎113.

Police: C. XXV Aprile, 19 (☎0141 41 81 11).

Red Cross Ambulance: ☎0141 41 77 41.

Hospital: Ospedale Civile, V. Botallo, 4 (☎0141 39 21 11).

Internet Access: ATLink, C. Alfieri, 328 (☎0141 345 98; info@atlink.it; www.atlink.it), near Torre Rosa. L10,000/€5.16 per hr. Open M-Sa 9am-12:30pm and 3:30-7:30pm, Su 3:30-7:30pm. **Uffizio Relazioni il Publico,** at the other end of the building near tourist office, has 3 free computer terminals.

NORTHWEST ITALY

Post Office: C. Dante, 55 (☎0141 35 7251), off P. Alfieri. Open M-F 8:30am-5:30pm, Sa 8:15am-noon.

Postal Code: 14100.

⚡ ACCOMMODATIONS & CAMPING

■ **Hotel Cavour,** P. Marconi, 18 (☎/fax 0141 53 02 22), across from the train station (just across the street from the doors on the left; it faces the station, not the *piazza*). Friendly management happy to answer questions. Modern, immaculate rooms with TV and phone. Reception daily 6am-1am. Closed Aug. Singles L55,000/€28.40, with bath L77,000/€39.77; doubles L85,000/€46.48, L107,000/€55.26. AmEx/DC/MC/V.

Antico Paradiso, C. Torino, 329 (☎/fax 0141 21 43 85). Quite a hike from the action; take bus #1 or 4 from the station (the ones marked "Canova") to the last stop on C. XXV Aprile (L1500/€0.77). From there, walk 45m down to C. Torino, and the hotel is on the left corner. Religious motifs adorn the whitewashed walls of bare and simple rooms. A bar downstairs sells *gelato* (L2000/€1.03) and makes fabulous homemade cakes. Bar open Tu-Su. Reception Tu-Su 9am-midnight. Singles L60,000/€30.99; doubles with shower and sink L90,000/€46.48; doubles with shower, sink, and breakfast L100,000/€51.65. AmEx/DC/MC/V.

Campeggio Umberto Cagni, V. Valmanera, 152 (☎0141 27 12 38). From P. Alfieri, turn onto V. Aro, which becomes C. Volta. Take a left on V. Valmanera and keep going. The camp is a local hangout featuring a pizza oven, table tennis, a playground, restaurant, bar, beach volleyball, and soccer. Open Apr.-Sept. L7000/€3.62 per person, L6000/€3.09 per tent. Electricity L3000/€1.55. Showers free.

🍴 FOOD

Astigiano cuisine is famous for its simplicity, using only a few crucial ingredients and pungent cheeses to create culinary masterpieces. This region offers the celebrated *bagna calda* (hot bath), a combination of raw vegetables dipped in a sizzling pot of olive oil and infused with garlic and anchovies. Among the most cherished cheeses produced in the surrounding area are *robiole* and *tome*.

The extensive fruit and vegetable **market** Campo del Palio provides great snacks. (Open W and Sa 7:30am-1pm.) Another bazaar is held daily in P. Catena, off V. Carducci in the heart of town. The P. Alfieri market, which sells clothes, shoes, bags, and other durable goods, keeps the same hours as Campo del Palio. The **Super Gulliver Market,** V. Cavour, 77, could feed an army of Lilliputians; despite its "super" name, it is tiny. (Open M-W and F-Sa 8am-7:30pm, Th 8:30am-1pm.) At **Mercato Coperto Alimentari,** in P. della Libertà between P. Alfieri and Campo del Palio, each merchant has a separate kiosk. This conveniently-located market features fresh meats, fruits, and vegetables, among other regional specialities. (Open M-W and F-Sa 8am-1pm and 3:30-7:30pm, Th 8am-1pm.) For other grocery options, try **Di Per Di,** at V. Alberto (P. Statuto), and just across from the tourist office at P. Alfieri. (Open 8:30am-1pm and 3:30-7:30pm.)

Leon d'Oro, V. Cavour, 95 (☎0141 59 20 30). Relaxed atmosphere and filling meals, including some vegetarian entrees and almost a dozen pizza varieties. Sit inside and watch yourself eat in the mirrored wall, or turn your glance on others under the yellow tent on a quiet street. Pizza L7-12,000/€3.62-6.20; *primi* L7500/€3.87; *secondi* from L10,000/€5.16; desserts L5000/€2.58. Cover L3000/€1.55. Open Th-Tu 11am-3pm and 6pm-2am. AmEx/DC/MC/V.

Trattoria La Canasta, C. Volta, 82 (☎0141 27 17 30). From P. Alfieri, turn right on C. Alfieri and left on V. Aro, which becomes C. Volta. This family-run eatery serves home-cooked meals in a pleasant atmosphere. *Primi* from L8000/€4.13; *secondi* L10-16,000/5.16-8.26; home-made desserts L5-6000/€2.58-3.09. Open M-Sa noon-2:30pm and 7:30-11pm. DC/MC/V.

Gran Caffè Italia, V. Cavour, 127 (☎0141 59 42 22), at end of V. Cavour on rotary opposite train station. This snack bar offers fresh *panini* (L4000/€2.07) and a vast selection of drinks. *Primi* L7000/€3.62 and *secondi* L10,000/€5.16. Selections for *Tavola calda* (warm plate of meat, potatoes, and other seasonal items) are behind glass as you enter. Open M-Sa noon-2:30pm. Closed Su. Bar open daily 7am-7pm.

🔍 SIGHTS

CATTEDRALE D'ASTI. This *duomo*, begun in 1309, is one of Piedmont's most noteworthy Gothic cathedrals. The *piazza* entrance has several well-preserved statues of monks and priests. The clock tower, toward the back of the *duomo*, rings just before and just after the hour. On the side facing the *piazza*, about midway up the tower, there is a sun dial. Throughout the 16th and 17th centuries, local artists, including native son Gandolfino d'Asti, covered every inch of the walls with frescoes; even the columns are painted to appear as if there are vines climbing up them. The remains of 11th-century mosaics blanket the floor around the altar. Three very brightly colored circular stained glass windows lie at the front, and just to your right, there is a life-size scene of terracotta figures constructed to depict the death of Jesus, *Dai Vangeli La Sepoltura di Gesu*. *(In P. Cattedrale. Walk down C. Alfieri and turn right on V. Mazzini. Open daily 7am-12:30pm and 3-7pm.)*

CHIESA DI SAN PIETRO IN CONSAVIA. A 15th-century church with a 12th-century octagonal baptistery, this structure served as an army hospital in World War II. Romans, friars, and those killed in the war shared the space beneath the courtyard. Now it is home to both the **Museo Paleontologico** (first floor), a small room with a collection of fossils and bones from the Astiano area, and the **Museo Archeologico** (second floor), an L-shaped hall with Greeks vases, jugs, and other pottery from the 4th century BC. A number of Roman pieces line the halls, primarily from the Asti area and the wider Ligurian region. *(On the far end of C. Alfieri, in the opposite direction from the Torre Rossa. Open Tu-Sa 10am-1pm and 4-7pm, Su 10am-noon. Free.)*

OTHER SIGHTS. From P. Vittorio Alfieri, a short walk west on V. Garibaldi leads to P.S. Secondo. The *piazza* is home to the 18th-century **Palazzo di Città** (City Hall), next door to the medieval **Collegiata di San Secondo.** The Romanesque tower and the magnificent Gothic decorations now stand on the very spot where S. Secondo, Asti's patron saint, was decapitated. Hanging banners lend a medieval air to the interior. *(Open daily 7:30am-noon and 3:30-7:30pm.)* Directly north of P.S. Secondo, across C. Alfieri in **Piazza Medici,** stands the 13th-century **Torre Toyana o Dell'Orologio.** At the end of C. Alfieri is Asti's oldest tower, the 16-sided **Torre Rossa** (Red Tower), where San Secondo was imprisoned before his execution. The tower, with foundations dating back to the time of Augustus, adjoins the elliptical, Baroque **Chiesa di Santa Caterina.** *(Open daily 7:30am-noon and 3-7pm.)* The **Giardini Pubblici** (public gardens), between P. Alfieri and Campo del Palio, make a good place to plot a tour of the city and the nearby wine country after visiting the tourist office, or a pleasant green haven for rest and refreshment.

🎵 ENTERTAINMENT

From the last week of June through the first week of July, **Asti Teatro,** the oldest contemporary theatrical festival in Italian history, commands Asti's complete attention. Asti Teatro puts on outdoor and indoor performances of theatrics (mainstream dramas to neo-Shakespeare), music (classical to jazz), and dance (ballet to modern). The festival draws a global audience and offers productions in many languages, although most are in Italian. (Students L25,000/€12.91, children under 12 L20,000/€10.33. Reserve tickets and hotel in advance. Call **Teatro Communale Vittorio Alfieri,** V. al Teatro, 1 (☎0141 39 93 41 or 35 39 88).

Beginning on the second Friday in September, agricultural Asti revels in the **Douja d'Or,** a week-long fair and exposition of rare local wines. A national oenological competition is held, as well as congresses on wine tasting. During this week, on the second Sunday in September, is the **Paisan,** or the **Festivale delle Sagre.** Locals dressed in traditional clothing come from surrounding towns and parade through Asti, rejoicing and feasting into the night. The real theater takes place in the streets on the third Sunday in September, when the Douja d'Or concludes with the **Palio di Asti,** a procession commemorating the town's liberation in 1200. The Palio begins with a parade and ends with one of the oldest bareback horseraces in Italy. For races of a different sort, ask at the Asti tourist office for information on the **donkey races** at Quarto (4km outside Asti). A donkey represents each of the village's seven boroughs. At the end of the contest, the victorious borough has a parade, and all of Quarto settles down to a banquet of *ravioli.*

⚡ DAYTRIP FROM ASTI: COSTIGLIOLE AND CANELLI

*Buses run to **Canelli** (30min., every 1½hr. 7:10am-6:40pm, L4000/€2.07) and **Costigliole** (25min.; 7:15, 11am, 12:50pm; L3500/€1.81) from the bus station in Asti.*

Vineyards comprise the countryside around Asti, providing both an economic base and a source of widespread renown. The sparkling *Asti Cinzano* and *Asti Spumante,* as well as the super-sweet *Moscato,* bubble forth from these vineyards. Many wineries remain under family control, and a warm reception awaits visitors who take time to explore these less touristed areas. While Costigliole's **medieval castle** is now closed to visitors, you can visit the **Cantina dei Vini di Costigliole d'Asti,** V. Roma, 9, in Costigliole, for guided tours and tastings. (☎0141 96 16 61 or 96 60 31. Open F 10am-12:30pm, Sa-Su 10am-12:30pm and 3-6pm.)

Canelli is surrounded by the muscat vineyards that produce the fruity *Asti Spumante.* Oswald, the jolly proprietor of the **Cantina Sociale,** V.L. Bosca, 30, offers tours and tastings. From the bus stop, walk up C. Liberta over the river, and veer left as the road ends. Take the first right at the Ricordonna gate and then another right onto V. Bosca. The Cantina is straight ahead at the end of the street. (☎0141 82 33 47 or 0141 83 18 28; fax 83 18 28. Open Tu-Su 8am-noon and 2-6pm.) Also in Canelli is **Distilleria Bocchina,** V. L'Azarita, 4 (☎0141 81 01), that produces *grappa.* From the bus stop, head in the opposite direction from the Cantina. Take C. XX Settembre, go straight past the pharmacy, and continue 10 minutes up the incline to the distillery. Call in advance for tours.

ACQUI TERME   ☎0144

Acqui Terme, like most small towns, has something boiling beneath its placid surface. Well, almost boiling. Sulfuric springs at temperatures of 75°C (167°F) bubble just underneath the ground, attracting those in need of holistic treatment. The mineral-rich water and *fanghi* (mud baths) provide healing and relaxation.

📧🛈 TRANSPORTATION AND PRACTICAL INFORMATION. From Genoa, catch a **train** (1½hr., every hr., L5900/€3.05), via **Ovada.** Acqui Terme's train station (☎0144 32 25 83) is in P.V. Veneto. Trains also run from **Asti** (1hr., 13 per day, L5200/€26.85). To reach the town center from the station, turn left on **via Alessandria** and continue as it becomes C. Vigano and ends in **Piazza Italia.** To reach the **IAT Tourist Office,** P. Maggiorino Ferraris, 5, walk **Corso Dante,** turn right on C. Cavour and left on V. Ferraris. (☎0144 32 21 42; fax 32 90 54. Open M 10:30am-12:30pm and 3:30-6:30pm, Tu-F 9:30am-12:30pm and 3:30-6:30pm, Sa-Su 10am-12:30pm and 3:30-6:30pm.) **Consorzio Turistico** (☎0144 32 65 20) provides hotel and restaurant information. For **currency exchange,** there are banks on C. Dante, including **Cassa di Risparmio di Torino,** C. Dante, 26 (☎0144 570 01). The **post office** (☎0144 32 29 84) is on V. Truco off P. Matteotti (take V. XX Settembre from P. Italia). **Postal Code:** 15011.

🏠🗗 ACCOMMODATIONS AND FOOD. For a centrally located, well-staffed, and comfortable place to rest your weary head, try **Albergo San Marco,** V. Ghione, 5. From P. Italia, take C. Bagni about 15m and make the first right onto V. Ghione. Its owners are eager to please, and the exquisite food in the **restaurant** downstairs is rumored to be some of the best in town. Try the excellent *Semifreddo Zabaglione e Torrone* for dessert. (☎0144 32 24 56; fax 32 10 73. *Primi* L7-10,000/€3.62-5.16; *secondi* from L10,000/€5.16, home-made desserts L5-6000/€2.58-3.09. 3-course gourmet menù L25,000/€12.91. Closed in Jan., last 2 weeks in July, and beginning of Aug. Singles L38,000/€19.63, with bath L48,000/€24.79; doubles with bath L75,000/€38.73; triples L100,000/€51.65.) Beyond the town center, many budget hotels surround the mineral baths across the river (15min. by foot). **Albergo Giacobe,** V. Einaudi, 15, has gloriously furnished rooms and inexpensive food. From P. Italia, take C. Bagni over the river. V. Einaudi is the first left. (☎0144 32 25 37. Singles L50,000/€25.82, with bath L60,000/€30.99; doubles L70,000/€36.15, with bath L80,000/€41.32. Full-pension L75,000/€38.73 per person.) **Supermarket Di per Di,** V. Nizza, 11, offers a wide selection of very cheap groceries. (☎0144 57 858. Open Tu-Su 8:30am-12:45pm and 3:30-7:30pm, M 3:30-7:30pm.)

◙ **SIGHTS.** Even if you're in perfect health, no trip to Acqui Terme would be complete without at least dipping your finger in the steamy sulfuric **water.** At the romantic **Piazza Bollente,** the hot water pours out of a fountain, sending up steam even in summer. Take V. Manzoni up the hill to the Castello dei Paleogi, which houses the **Museo Civico Archeologico,** constructed in the 11th century, damaged in 1646, and restored in 1815. The museum displays a small but evocative collection of Roman tombs and mosaics. (☎0144 575 55. Open W-Sa 9:30am-12:30pm and 3:30-6:30pm, Su 3:30-6:30pm. L4000/€2.06, under 18 L2000/€1.03.) The Romanesque **duomo,** in P. Duomo down V. Barone from the Museo Archeologico, is home to Rubens's famous *Trittico (Madonna and Child).* Unfortunately, the work is locked away in the sacristy. Inquire at the tourist office about opportunities to view this masterpiece. (Open M-F 7am-9pm, Sa-Su 8am-noon and 6-8pm.) From the river, you can see the four intact arches of the **Acquedotto Romano.**

Acqui Terme offers an array of health and relaxation options. In the **zona bagni,** the **Reparto Regina,** P. Acqui Lussa, 6 (☎0144 32 43 90), is a healer's heaven—here's your chance to splurge. The center offers services ranging from lung ventilation (L25,000/€12.91) to a mud bath supreme (L65,000/€33.57). From the city center, walk down C. Bagni over the river, pass the **municipal pool,** and turn left on V. Acqui Terme. (Reparto Regina open M-F 8am-1pm and 3-6pm, Sa 8am-1pm. Municipal pool open M-Sa 8am-8pm. L10,000/€5.16, including shower and deck chair.) **Nuove Terme,** V. XX Settembre, 5, off P. Italia, has some of the Reparto Regina's options (☎0144 32 43 90. Open M-F 8:30am-1pm and 3:30-6:30pm, Sa 8:30am-1:30pm.)

For a less healthy pilgrimage, head for the ◙**Enoteca Regionale di Acqui Terme,** P. Levi, 7. From P. Italia, take C. Italia, turn left on V. Garibaldi, and take the first right into P. Levi; the cavernous winery, among the finest in Italy, was built on the grounds of the first Roman structure in town and is down some steps. It features 230 different wines, including the sweet domestic Dolcetto and Bracchetto, and it epitomizes the slogan *dove l'aqua e salute, e il vino e allegria*—(where the water is healthy and the wine is happiness). (☎0144 77 02 73; fax 57 627. Open Tu and F-Su 10am-noon and 3-6:30pm, Th 3-6:30pm. DC/MC/V.)

VALLE D'AOSTA

The lush valleys of the Valle d'Aosta are resplendent with pine forests, laced with terraced wineries, and ski chalets. Man-made grandeur can hardly compete with the immense, sparsely populated wilderness. **The Great and Small St. Bernard Passes,** to the north and east, or the international cable cars skimming over the mountains from France and Switzerland may be the most stunning entrances to Italy's least populated, most elevated region, but Valle d'Aosta is only a few hours from the urban centers of Milan, Genoa, and Turin. The waterfalls of the **Gran**

Paradiso National Park and the towering, glaciated peaks have raised tourism to the center of Valle d'Aosta's economy, resulting in inflated prices year-round.

HIKING

The scenic trails of Valle d'Aosta are a paradise for hikers. July, August, and the first week of September, when much of the snow has melted and the public buses are running on a full schedule, are the best times to hike. In April and May, thawing snow often causes avalanches. Monte Bianco and surrounding mountains may be classic climbers' peaks, but only pros should attempt to capture them. Talk to the staff at a tourist office or alpine information office about the difficulty and condition of hikes or climbing destinations—they often speak English. For information on preparation and safety, see **Essentials,** p. 53.

Despite these warnings, don't be scared of venturing into the Alps. Each area's tourist office offers assistance to hikers of all levels. The tourist offices in Aosta and those in the smaller valleys provide information on routes as well as lists of campgrounds, bagged lunch *(al sacco)* vendors, **rifugi alpini** (mountain huts), and **bivacchi** (public refuges)—ask for the *Mountain Huts and Bivouacs in Aosta Valley.* Some mountain huts lie only a cable-car ride or 30-minute walk away from roads, and many offer half-pension for around L60,000/€30.99. Public refuges tend to be empty and free; those run by caretakers cost about L30,000/€15.50 per night. For information, call **Società Guide,** V. Monte Emilius, 13 (☎/fax 0165 444 48), or **Club Alpino Italiano,** P. Chanoux, 15 (☎0165 409 39; fax 36 32 44; www.guidealpine.com), both in Aosta. They offer insurance and refuge discounts.

Most regional tourist offices also carry *Alte Vie* (High Roads), with maps, photographs, and helpful advice pertaining to the two serpentine mountain trails that circumvent the valley and link the region's most dramatic peaks. Long stretches of these trails require no expertise and offer adventure with panoramic views.

▲ SKIING

Skiing Valle d'Aosta's mountains and glaciers is fantastic; unfortunately, it is not a bargain. **Settimane bianche** ("white-week") packages for skiers, are one source of discount rates. For information and prices, call **Ufficio Informazioni Turistiche,** P. Chanoux, 8 (☎0165 23 66 27), in Aosta, and request the pamphlet *White Weeks: Aosta Valley.* Accommodations for a week in March run from L450-700,000/€232.41-361.52 per person, with substantially discounted fares in the early and late season. A six-day lift pass costs about L280,000/€144.61.

Courmayeur and **Breuil-Cervinia** are the best known ski resorts in the 11 valleys. **Val d'Ayas** and **Val di Gressoney** offer equally challenging terrain for lower rates. **Cogne** and **Brusson,** halfway down Val d'Ayas, have cross-country skiing and less-demanding downhill trails. In Courmayeur and Breuil-Cervinia, die-hards tackle the slopes in bathing suits for extensive **summer skiing.** Arrange summer package deals through the tourist office in either Breuil-Cervinia or Courmayeur.

⚡ OTHER SPORTS

A host of other sports—rock climbing, mountain biking, hang-gliding, kayaking, and rafting—will keep your adrenaline pumping. For white water enthusiasts, the most navigable and popular rivers are the **Dora Baltea,** which runs across the valley, the **Dora di Veny,** which branches south from Courmayeur, the **Dora di Ferre,** which meanders north from Courmayeur, the **Dora di Rhêmes,** which flows through the Val di Rhêmes, and the **Grand Eyvia,** which courses through the Val di Cogne. **Centro Nazionale Acque Bianche (Rafting 4810),** Fenis, Vale d'Aosta, just minutes from Aosta, runs the most affordable rafting trips. (☎0165 76 46 46; info@rafting4810.com; www.rafting4810.com. 1-3hr., L42-70,000/€21.70-36.15 per person.) For a complete list of recreational activities, including bike rental, ask for *Attrezzature Sportive e Ricreative della Valle d'Aosta* from any tourist office.

AOSTA   ☎0165

As the geographical and financial center of a region increasingly dependent upon tourism for economic livelihood, Aosta sports two facades: inside the crumbling walls that once defended Rome's alpine outpost, a dense network of cobblestone streets harbors swanky boutiques and gourmet food shops; outside the sheltered city center, a commercial and industrial minefield stretches across the valley, servicing the region's material needs. And, while Aosta itself starches along the valley floor, its prices soar much like the nearby jagged peaks of Monte Emilius (3559m) and Becca di Nona (3142m), and the distant glacial expanses of Grand Combin (4314m), Becca du Lac (3396m). If the stunning mountain vistas have whet your appetite, Aosta makes a good starting point for explorations into the Italian Alps, but be aware that daytrips to the surrounding valleys often require tricky train and bus connections—if you hope to return before nightfall, plan ahead.

▐ TRANSPORTATION

Trains: The station is in the pink building at P. Manzetti. **Ticket Window** open daily 4:50-11:25am and 1:45-8:30pm. Luggage storage available (p. 191). To: **Chivasso** (1½hr., every hr. 5:12am-8:40pm, L8400/€4.34) via **Châtillon** (15min., every hr. 6:12am-8:40pm, L3700/€1.91); **Milan's** Centrale (4hr.; 12 per day 6:12am-8:40pm; L20,100/€10.38); **Pont St. Martin** (50min., every hr. 5:12am-8:40pm, L6200/€3.20); **Turin's** P. Nuova (2hr.; every hr. 5:15am-8:40pm; L11,000/€5.68); **Verrès** (30min., every hr. 6:12am-8:40pm, L5000/€2.58).

Buses: SAVDA (☎0165 36 12 44), on V. Carrel off P. Manzetti, to the right of the train station. To **Courmayeur** (1hr., every hr. 5am-8pm, L4800/€2.48) and **Great St. Bernard Pass** (2hr., 9:40am and 2:25pm, L5200/€2.70). SVAP serves closer towns. To **Cogne** (1hr., 6 per day 7:10am-6pm, L4200/€2.17) and **Fenis** (30min., 7 per day 6am-5:40pm, L3200/€1.65). Buses to **Breuil-Cervinia** (2hr., 7 per day, L6000/€3.10) and **Valtournenche** leave from the Châtillon train station.

Taxis: P. Manzetti (☎0165 26 20 10). P. Narbonne (☎0165 356 56 or 318 31).

Car Rental: Europcar, P. Manzetti, 3 (☎0165 414 32), left of the train station. Economy cars from L136,000/€70.24 per day; discounts for longer rentals. 18+. MC/V.

▚❼ ORIENTATION AND PRACTICAL INFORMATION

Trains stop at **Piazza Manzetti**. From there, walk straight down Av. du Conseil des Commis until it ends in the enormous **Piazza Chanoux**, Aosta's center. The main street runs east-to-west through P. Chanoux and suffers a number of name changes. From Av. du Conseil des Commis, **via J. B. de Tiller**, which then becomes **via Aubert**, is to the left; to the right is **via Porta Praetoria** which leads to the historic gate, **Porta Praetoria**, where it becomes **via Sant'Anselmo**.

TOURIST, FINANCIAL, AND LOCAL SERVICES

Tourist Office: P. Chanoux, 8 (☎0165 23 66 27; fax 346 57; www.regione.vda.it/turismo.), straight down Av. du Conseil des Commis from train station. Ask for *Aosta, Monument Guide* (great map of the city, a local hotel list, and restaurant locator). Yearly *Orario Generale* has comprehensive transportation schedules (including cable cars). English, German, and French spoken. Open M-Sa 9am-1pm and 3-8pm, Su 9am-1pm.

Alpine Information: Club Alpino Italiano, C. Battaglione, 81 (☎0165 401 94). From P. della Repubblica take Av. Battallion to C. Battaglione. Open M, Tu, Th 6am-7:30pm, F 8am-10pm. At other times, try **Società Guide**, V. Monte Emilius, 13 (☎0165 40 939; fax 444 48; www.guidealpine.com). For weather conditions try **Protezione Civile** in V. St. Christophe (☎0165 23 82 22 or 441 13).

Currency Exchange: Monte dei Paschi di Siena, P. Chanoux, 51 (☎0165 23 56 56). **ATM** outside. Open M-F 8:20am-1:20pm and 2:40-4:10pm.

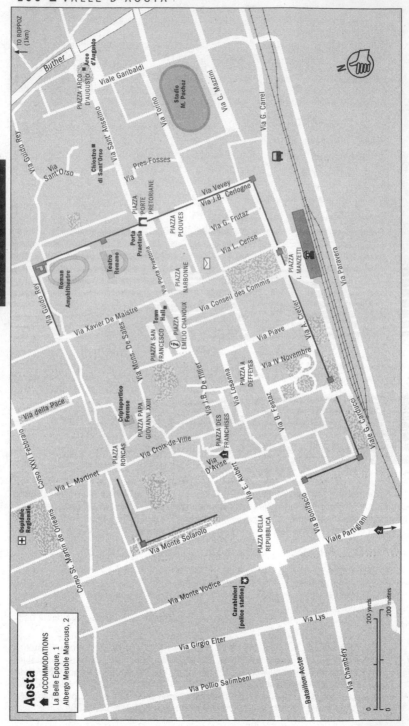

Aosta

▲ ACCOMMODATIONS
La Belle Epoque, 1
Albergo Meuble Mancuso, 2

Luggage Storage: In train station. L5000/€2.58 for 12hr. Open daily 6am-12:30pm and 1:30-6pm.

Outdoor Gear and Apparel: Menardi Sport, V. Aubert, 47 (☎0165 414 32). A moderately priced, extensive selection of gear and clothing, including maps and guides to the Italian Alps. Open M-Sa 9am-12:30pm and 3-7:30pm, Su 3:30-7pm.

Laundromat: Onda Blu, V. Chambery, 60. Wash L6000/€3.10 per 30min.; dry L6000/€3.1 per 20min. Open daily 8am-10pm.

EMERGENCY AND COMMUNICATIONS

Police: C. Battaglione Aosta, 169 (☎113).

First Aid: ☎0165 30 42 56 or 118.

Mountain rescue: ☎0165 34 983.

Pharmacy: Farmacia Chenal, V. Croix-de-Ville, 1 (☎0165 26 21 33), at the corner of V. Aubert. Open Th-Tu 9am-12:30pm and 3-7:30pm.

Hospital: V. Ginevra, 3 (☎0165 30 41).

Internet Access: Bar Snooker, V. Lucat, 3 (☎0165 23 63 68). From the station, turn right onto V. Giorgio Carrel and left on V. Lucat. Pool hall, video poker, and a card-playing salon. Internet access L10,000/€5.16 per hr. Open Th-Tu 8am-3am, W 1pm-3am.

Post Office: P. Narbonne, 1A (☎0165 441 38), in the huge semicircular building. Open M-F 8:15am-6pm, Sa 8:15am-1pm. Fermo Posta is across town on V. Caesare Battisti, 10. Open M-F 8:15am-6pm, Sa 8:15am-1pm.

Postal Code: 11100.

☐ ACCOMMODATIONS & CAMPING

▨ **La Belle Epoque,** V. d'Avise, 18 (☎0165 26 22 76). From train station, take Av. du Conseil des Commis to P. Chanoux, and turn left on V. Aubert. Convenient city center location renders 15 simple rooms relatively attractive. Large bathrooms and showers. Reserve ahead. Restaurant downstairs crowded with locals serves pizza from L8000/€4.13 and *primi* for L11,000/€5.68. Singles L45,000/€23.24, with bath L55,000/€28.41; doubles with bath L90,000/€46.48; triples with bath L120,000/€62.

Monte Emilius, V. Carrel, 911 (☎0165 356 92), upstairs from Ristorante Le Ramoneur, which offers a L20,000/€10.33 *menù*. Friendly management, modern bathrooms, TV, and great views. Unfortunately, constant traffic noise keeps windows shut. 3 singles with bath L55,000/€28.41; 5 doubles with bath L110,000/€56.81.

Camping Milleluci, V. Porossan, 15 (☎0165 23 52 78; fax 0165 23 52 84). Laundry L8000/€4.13. L10,000/€5.16 per person; L16-19,000/€8.26-9.81 for tent, plot, and electricity. Shower L1000/€0.52.

☐ FOOD

Switzerland's influence is felt in typical local dishes, such as *fonduta*, a creamy melted fontina ladled over meat and vegetables, and *polenta valdostana*, sizzling with melted *fontina* (a regional specialty). The most divine dessert is *tegole*, wafer-thin cookies with ground nuts. The **STANDA supermarket** is on V. Festaz, 10. (☎0165 357 57. Open M-Sa 8:30am-7:30pm.) Aosta's weekly **outdoor market** is held on Tuesday in P. Cavalieri di Vittorio Veneto.

▨ **Trattoria Praetoria,** V.S. Anselmo, 9 (☎0165 443 56), just past the Porta Praetoria. With the classy, arched stucco ceilings and warm staff, the atmosphere is unbeatable. Expect a half-hour wait on weekend evenings. Try the *salsiccette in umido* (local sausages braised in tomato sauce; L12,000/€6.20). *Primi* L8-10,000/€4.13-5.16; *secondi* L12,000/€6.20. Cover L3000/€1.55. Open daily 12:15-2:30pm and 7:15-9:30pm; in winter F-W 12:15-2:30pm and 7:15-9:30pm. AmEx/DC/MC/V.

■ **Old Distillery Pub,** V. Pres Fosses, 7 (☎0165 23 95 11). From Porta Pretoria, walk down V. Ansemo and go right through a small archway onto the winding V. Pres Fosses. Pub is on the left. 100% English staff and wide selection of excellent brews draws crowds of locals. Occasional live music. Guinness L6000/€3.10. Open daily 6pm-2am.

    Grotta Azzurra, V. Croix-de-Ville (Croce di Città), 97 (☎0165 26 24 74), uphill from V. de Tillier as it becomes V. Aubert. Antiqued decor lends this pizzeria a medieval feel. Pasta with *pesce* (L13-15,000/€6.71-7.75); *primi* from L8000/€4.13; pizza from L9000/€4.65. Open Th-Tu noon-2:30pm and 6-10:30pm. Closed 1st 2 weeks in July.

    Crêperia Carillon, V.E. Aubert, 74 (☎0165 401 06). From P. Chanoux take V. de Tillier, which turns into V.E. Aubert. A tourist trap, but the cheapest one in town. An extensive menu sports the standard pasta fare (from L8000/€4.13) and a host of salads (from L4000/€2.07). Tasty crêpes for L6-8000/€3.10-4.13. Open F-W 10am-1am. MC/V.

 SIGHTS

CITY CENTER SIGHTS

ROMAN RUINS. Oh, that Roman Empire—they didn't even bother to clean up their messy remains. Ruins dating from the age of Augustus fill the town. Down V. Porta Pretoria looms the massive stone archway of the **Porta Pretoria.** To the left is the sprawling remains of the massive **Roman Theater.** *(Open daily 9am-8pm; in winter 9:30am-6pm and 2-4:30pm. Free.)* Through Porta Pretoria, V.S. Anselmo leads to the virtually intact **Arco d'Augusta.** Excavations continue to unearth relics. The forum, or **Criptoportico Forense,** is off P. Papa Giovanni XXIII. *(Open W-M 9am-6pm. Free.)*

SANT'ORSO. Within this unassuming church are some ornate 15th-century choir stalls and the amazing wood-carved **Chiostro di Sant'Orso.** Imaginatively carved columns and ceiling decorate the tiny cloister with bestial and biblical scenes. The **Fiera di Sant'Orso,** the region's most famous crafts fair, takes place January 30-31 and the Sunday before *Ferragosto* (mid-August). The traditional fair dates to the 9th century and is known for Valdostan handicrafts. *(From the Porta Pretoria, take V.S. Anselmo and turn left on V.S. Orso. Open daily 7am-7pm. Free.)*

VALLEY SIGHTS

VALLE DEL GRAN SAN BERNARDO. A valley with more medieval towers than tourists, Valle del Gran San Bernardo links Aosta to Switzerland via the Great St. Bernard Pass. Motor-tourists and intrepid cyclists tackle this winding mountain road in summer but retreat to the more highly trafficked 5854m tunnel, that cuts through the mountain, when the snow comes. But no traveling tourist compares to Napoleon, who trekked through the pass with 40,000 soldiers in 1800, or Hannibal, who crossed the Alps here with his elephants. This region is best known for the **Hospice of St. Bernard,** dating from 1505 and home to the patron saint of man's best friend. The legendary life-saver was stuffed for posterity and can still be seen as you drive through the pass. The Hospice (just across the Swiss border—remember your passport) offers great views of international peaks and is just a tail-wag away from the dog museum, where St. Bernard puppies in training are the highlight of any visit. A smaller, more serene branch of the valley leads to the communes of **Ollomont** and **Oyace,** where hiking trails, valleys, and pine forests await exploration. There is easy hiking just above the Hospice on a winding trail that skirts the ridge. For more information call the Aosta tourist office or the **ski-lift office** (☎0165 78 00 46) at St. Rhémy. Contact the tourist office for a hotel list, or camp at **Camping Pineta,** in St. Oyen. *(☎0165 781 14. L7000/€3.62 per person, L7-9000/€3.62-4.65 per tent, L3000/€1.55 per car. Shower L1000/€0.52. Electricity L2000/€1.03.)*

THE MATTERHORN AND BREUIL-CERVINIA. The highest mountain in Switzerland, **The Matterhorn (Il Cervino)** looms majestically over the town of Breuil-Cervinia in Valtournenche. The buildings of **Breuil-Cervinia** differ only in purpose; some serve expensive food, others offer expensive accommodations, and the rest rent expensive sports equipment. In spite of the cost, many fresh-air fiends consider these man-made deterrents a small price to pay for the opportunity to climb up and glide down the glaciers of one of the world's most famous mountains. A cable car provides service to **Plateau Rosà** (round-trip L45,000/€23.24), where summer skiers tackle the slopes in lighter gear. Hikers can forgo the lift tickets and attempt the three-hour ascent to **Colle Superiore delle Cime Bianche** (2982m), with tremendous views of Val d'Ayas to the east, and the Cervino glacier to the west. A shorter trek (1½hr.) on the same trail leads to the emerald waters of **Lake Goillet**. The tourist office hands out a good hiking map detailing these hikes and more. The **Società Guide** (☎0166 94 81 69), across from the tourist office, arranges group outings. Don't forget your **passport;** a number of trails cross into Switzerland.

Buses run to Breuil-Cervinia (6 per day 6:10am-7:15pm, L4300/€2.22) from Châtillon on the Aosta-Turin train line. Direct buses also arrive daily from P. Castello in Milan (3hr.). Buses run to **Turin** (2½hr.; Sa-Su 7:20am and 5:20pm; L23,000/€11.88). The English-speaking staff of the **Tourist Info Center**, V. Carrel, 29, provides visitors with information on "white-week packages" and *settimane estive*, the summer equivalent. (*☎0166 94 91 36; fax 94 97 31; info@breuil-cervinia.it; www.breuil-cervinia.it. Open daily 9am-noon and 3-6:30pm.*) Students should inquire about the **University-Card,** which reduces the price of passes by 10-20%.

VAL D'AYAS. Budget-minded sports enthusiasts should consider visiting the wide, gently sloping Val d'Ayas. Under the shadow of the massive, glaciated Monte Rosa, this long valley offers the same outdoor activities as its flashy neighbors—skiing, hiking, and rafting—without the hype. Try the town of Champoluc as a staging area for some excellent hiking, including the 45min. hike up **trail #14** to the tiny hamlet of **Mascognoz**, a cluster of wood chalets home to a farming population of 10. **Trains** run to **Verrès** from Aosta (40min., 17 per day 6:35am-8:40pm, L5000/€2.58) and Turin (1½hr.). **Buses** run from the train station at Verrès daily to Champoluc (1hr., 4 per day 9:30am-6pm, L4200/€2.17). The **tourist office** in **Brusson** (☎0125 30 02 40; fax 30 06 91) has branches in **Champoluc,** V. Varase, 16 (☎0125 30 71 13; fax 30 77 85) and **Antagnod** (☎0125 30 63 35). They speak English and have trail maps and hotel information. (Branches open daily 9am-12:30pm and 3-6pm.)

VAL DI COGNE. When Cogne's mines failed in the 1970s, the townspeople resorted to more genteel pursuits, delicately parting cross-country skiers from their money. In winter, Cogne functions as the head of an 80km entanglement of **cross-country trails** (daily pass L8000/€4.13). Cogne is also one of the world's premier places to ice climb (inquire at Aosta's guide office). A cable car transports alpine addicts to the modest **downhill skiing** facilities (round-trip L10,000/€5.16; daily pass L35,000/€18.08; 7-day pass including cable car L190,000/€98.13). In summer, however, the pastoral community serves as the gateway to the wild, unspoiled expanse of Italy's largest nature reserve, **Gran Paradiso National Park.** In addition to an endless network of hiking trails, waterfalls, and a population of 5000 ibex, the park has the highest **glacier** (4061m) fully contained within Italian borders, aptly named Gran Paradiso. The hillside above Cogne has a **Mining Museum,** by the old dormitory that housed Cogne's miners. A World War I era film depicts the happy life of a miner, while a cable car that carried coal provides emotional stimulation. (*☎0165 74 92 64. Open June 15-Sept. 15 daily 10am-8pm; May-June Tu-Su 10am-12:30pm and 2:30-6pm. L4000/€4.13, students L2000/€1.03. Restorations in progress until summer 2002.*)

Cogne and its characteristic dry, rocky valley dotted with pine trees, is a scenic **bus** ride from Aosta (1hr., 6 per day 8:15am-8:30pm). The bus stops in front of the **APT tourist office,** P. Chanoux, 36, which distributes regional maps and helps with accommodations. (*☎0165 740 40 or 740 56; fax 74 91 25. Open daily 9am-12:30pm and 3-6pm; in winter M-Sa 9am-12:30pm and 2:30-5:30pm, Su 9am-12:30pm.*)

VALNONTEY. This hamlet affords an unobstructed view the towering Gran Paradiso. Lodged in a narrow valley in the midst of a national park it is an exceptional 45min. walk along the river from Cogne on trail #25 (that leaves from the river-side tourist office.) During June and August, buses run from Cogne to Valnontey (every 30min. 7:30am-8pm, L2000/€1.03; buy tickets on bus). Valnontey is notable for its convenient *alimentari*, two-star hotels, access to trails, and a botanical garden, **Giardino Alpino Paradisia.** The inspiration to construct a botanical garden came during the Cogne Mountain Festival in 1955, and the gardens boast over 1000 species of rare alpine vegetation, including lichen, lichen, and more lichen. *(Open June 15-Sept. 15 daily 9:30am-12:30pm and 2:30-5:30pm; L4000/€2.07, groups L3000/€1.55, under 10 free.)* Just beyond the botanical garden, a 15min. hike along trail #6 arrives at a stunning waterfall. Between June and September, campers can choose between the rolling hills of **Camping Gran Paradiso** and **Lo Stambecco**. *(Camping Gran Paradiso ☎0165 74 92 04. L10,000/€5.16 per person, ages 7-16 L7000/€3.62, under 6 free. L9800/€5.06 for tent, car, and electricity. Free shower. Self service laundromat. Lo Stambecco ☎0165 741 52; L9500/€4.91 per person, L6-7000/€3.1-3.62 for tent and electricity).*

COURMAYEUR   ☎0165

In the spectacular shadow of Europe's highest peak, Monte Bianco, Italy's oldest alpine resort, remains a jet-set playground. Monte Bianco is, of course, the attraction: its jagged ridges and unmelting snow fields lure tourists for unsurpassed hiking and skiing. Unfortunately for budget travelers looking for alpine serenity, prices are high, rooms are booked solid year-round, and streets are saturated with manicured boutiques and obtrusive tour-buses. The city shuts down in May and June when shopkeepers take their vacations.

☎ TRANSPORTATION AND PRACTICAL INFORMATION. One all-important building in **P. Monte Bianco** houses almost everything a traveler needs. The **bus station** at P. Monte Bianco offers frequent service to larger towns. (☎0165 84 20 31. Open daily 7:30am-8:30pm.) Buses go to **Aosta** (1hr., every hr. 4:45am-8:45pm, L4800/€2.48) and **Turin** (3½hr.; 4 per day 8am-4pm; L14,500/€7.50). To the right of the bus station, the **APT tourist office** offers maps and has a staff that speaks English, German, French, and Spanish. (☎0165 84 20 60; www.courmayeur.net. Open M-Sa 9am-12:30pm and 3-6:30pm, Su 9:30am-12:30pm and 3-6pm.) The bus ticket office has a **currency exchange** with the same hours. Twenty-four hour **taxis** (☎0165 84 29 60; night ☎84 23 33) are at P.M. Bianco. In an **emergency,** call ☎113, or an **ambulance,** Strada delle Volpi, 3 (☎118). There is a **pharmacy** at V. Roma, 33. (Open M-Sa 9am-12:30pm and 3-7:30pm.) The **post office** is in P.M. Bianco. (☎0165 84 20 42. Open M-F 8:15am-1:40pm, Sa 8:15-11:40am.) **Postal Code:** 11013.

☎ ACCOMMODATIONS AND FOOD. For winter accommodations, reserve six months in advance. Consider making Courmayeur a daytrip from the more affordable Aosta, as budget accommodations in the town are few and difficult to reach. **Pensione Venezia,** V. delle Villete, 2, up the hill to the left from P. Monte Bianco, lets 14 simple, airy, light-filled rooms with small balconies and common bathrooms. (☎/fax 0165 84 24 61. Breakfast L8000/€4.13. Singles L55,000/€28.41; doubles L80,000/€41.32.) The **Cai-Uget** refuge in Val Veny, is infinitely more serene. Take the bus from Courmayeur to **Purtud,** in the direction of La Visaille (15 per day), and backtrack to the refuge between the two stops. Plan on a 30min. walk. (☎0165 86 90 97. Open June 15-Sept. and Dec. to 1 week after Easter. Dorms L50,000/€25.68. Half-pension L60-70,000/€30.99-36.15.)

Picnicking is the best budget option in Courmayeur. At **Pastificio Gabriella,** Passaggio dell'Angelo, 94, toward the end of V. Roma, you'll find excellent cold cuts, pasta salads, crêpes, and a line out the door. (☎0165 84 33 59. Open daily 8am-1pm and 4-7:30pm; closed 2 weeks in July. MC/V.) **Il Fornaio,** V. Monte Bianco, 17, serves scrumptious breads and pastries. (☎0165 84 24 54. Open daily 8am-12:30pm and 4-7:30pm.) On Wednesdays, the **market** is 1km away in Dolonne. (Open 8:30am-2pm.) Those eating out have only a few affordable options. **Mont Frety,** Strada Regionale, 21, has an extensive pasta selection and serves pizza in the evenings. Worth a visit just to eat in the spacious garden. (☎0165 84 17 86. Pizza L9-18,000/€4.65-9.30;

primi L10-14,000/€5.16-7.23. Cover L3500/€1.81. Open Tu-Sa 9am-1am. AmEx/DC/MC/V.) **Lady-Crêpe,** V. Marconi, 7, off V. Roma, features the particularly good *crespelle alla valdostana* for L6000/€3.10. (☎0165 84 41 44. Slices of pizza and *focaccia* from L3000/€1.55. Open daily 9am-12:30pm and 3:30-7:30pm.)

◪ OUTDOOR ACTIVITIES. Ski passes are priced on a complex rotating schedule—check at the tourist office for details. (3-day pass L144-160,000/€74.37-82.63, 6-day pass L260-380,000/€134.28-196.25.) The brochures *White Weeks, Aosta Valley* (English), *Settimane Bianche,* and *Courmayeur* list rental and pass prices.

Nineteenth-century English gentlemen brushed off the **Giro del Monte Bianco** as a two- or three-day **climbing** excursion for "less adventurous travelers." These days guides suggest that travelers take a week or more to complete the trip. The trail leads around Monte Bianco, past Chamonix and Courmayeur, and then into Switzerland. *Réfuges* and hostel dormitories are spaced five or six hours apart along the route (L30-35,000/€15.50-18.08 per person, with breakfast L35,000/€18.08). One section of the trail makes an ideal daytrip and two sections can fill a weekend. This is difficult mountaineering; be sure that you are thoroughly equipped and trained. Inquire at the guide office (see below) for more information.

For less rigorous excursions, take the beautiful six-hour hike on the road up the valley past **Rifugio Elisabetta,** where the path (actually an *alta via,* marked by a "2" in a triangle) branches to the left and clambers up to the **Chavannes Pass** (2603m). There is no bus, so rent or borrow a car. The trail runs along **Mont Perce,** beneath the crest, to **Mont Fortin** (2758m), where it descends once again to Lake Combal. Courmayeur's two smaller valleys, Val Veny and Val Ferret, fork the base of Monte Bianco and are ripe with day-hikes. **SAVDA** buses service both valleys; inquire at the tourist office for more information, including the brochure *Seven itineraries around Mont Blanc, Val Veny, and Val Ferret.* Of course, a map is crucial; buy one at the **Libreria La Buona Stampa,** V. Roma, 4. (☎0165 84 67 71. Open daily 9am-1pm and 3:30-7:30pm.) A good place to ask questions and find a guide is the **Ufficio delle Guide,** P. Abbe Henri, 2, to the left behind the church. (☎0165 86 23 57. Open daily 9am-7pm; in winter Tu-Su 9am-7pm.) The office faces a unique **mountaineering museum** that features historic equipment, superb photographs, and expedition histories. (Open Tu-Su 9am-7pm. L5000/€2.58, ages 8-12 L3000/€1.55.)

The ▩**Funivie Monte Bianco** cable cars head first to the **Punta Helbronner** (3462m) and then to **Chamonix.** The top affords unparalleled views of Monte Bianco's expansive, windswept ice sheet as well as the spectacular peaks of the **Matterhorn, Monte Rosa,** and **Gran Paradiso.** *Funivie* depart from La Palud near the Val Ferret (10min. bus ride from Courmayeur, L3000/€1.55). The cable cars make several stops on the mountain, so you do not have to go all the way to Chamonix (round-trip to Punta Hellbronner L54,000/€27.90; in summer open only until P. Helbronner). For information, call ☎0165 899 25 or 891 96. For **guided nature excursions** (*accompagnatori della natura*), contact English-speaking Cristina Gaggini and Claudia Marcello (☎368 73 45 407 or 0165 84 28 12).

VENICE
(VENEZIA)

There is an enrapturing quality to Venice's decadence. Her lavish palaces stand proudly on a steadily sinking network of wood, and the clouded waters of her age-old canals lap at the feet of abandoned doorways. In a city where gondola channels now flow beneath diesel engines and cranes outnumber bell towers in the skyline, such romanticism is precious.

Her path of slow decline is not without towering achievement. When the city founded by Roman fisherman swapped its gondolas for seabound ships in the 11th century, it soon gained a monopoly on Eastern trade. The world looked to Venice for gold, silks, spices, and coffee. Then, with the conquest of Constantinople in 1203 as a proving ground, Venice quickly came to control lands throughout the Adriatic, the Greek islands, modern Turkey, and mainland Italy, becoming the envy of the world. Over the next century, however, jealous European powers in the west and the Turks in the east robbed Venice of its trade monopoly and whittled away its empire. When Napoleon's armies arrived in 1797, Venice was little more than an idle playground of courtesans, casinos, and carnivals.

Perhaps Venice is perpetually situated at the end of that idle era, where distance is still measured by walking, and time by the ebb and flow of the tide. In this period of decay, the hold is tight on a history of wealth and prestige. Its labyrinthine streets lead to a treasury of Renaissance art, housed in scores of palaces, churches, and museums that are themselves an architectural delight. Of course, any visit to Venice is a reminder of another more recent development, the explosion of the tourist industry. Those same streets that once earned the name *La Serenissima*, the Most Serene One, are now saturated with visitors for most of the year. Venice now grapples with an economy reliant upon the same tourism that forces increasingly more of its indigenous population away each year.

Still, amidst its unhurried, complacent decadence, the sinking city lives on. Romanticism dies hard, and so Venice persists beyond the summer crowds and polluted waters, united by intertwining canals and memories of its glorious past.

HIGLIGHTS OF VENICE

WANDER among the quiet streets and still canals of **Dorsoduro** (see p. 211).

ADMIRE Tintoretto's mysticism in the **Scuola Grande di S. Rocco** (see p. 218); then head to the **Basilica i Frari** (see p. 218) to see rival Titian's sensual works.

FEAST your eyes on the afternoon sun streaming into the **Basilica di S. Marco** (see p. 216), setting fire to its gold mosaics. At night, waltz to golden oldies in the *piazza*.

RIDE a *vaporetto* to the tiny fishing village of **Burano** (see p. 221) and marvel at its rows of pastel facades and age-old lace industry.

✈ INTERCITY TRANSPORTATION

Flights: Aeroporto Marco Polo (☎041 260 61 11; www.veniceairport.it), 5mi. north of the city. The **ATVO** shuttle bus (☎041 520 55 30) links the airport to Piazzale Roma on the main island. (30min., 2 every hr. from Piazzale Roma 5:15am-8:30pm, L5000/ €2.58.) Extensive service to Europe and U.S. Ticket office open daily 5:30am-9:30pm.

Trains: Stazione Santa Lucia, Venice's main station in northwest corner of city. If arriving by train, disembark at Santa Lucia, not Mestre, on the mainland. Open daily 3:45am-12:30am. Info office on the left as you exit the platforms, open daily 7am-9pm. Lockers,

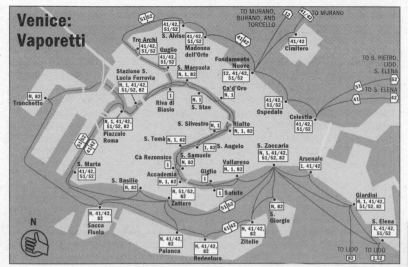

by platform 1. L3-4000/€1.55-2.07 for 6hr. Luggage Storage, by platform 14. L5000/ €2.58 for 12 hr. Lost and Found, (☎041 78 52 38), follow signs to *ogetti rinvenuti* near platform 14. Open M-F 8am-4pm. To: **Bologna** (2hr.; 2 per hr. 6:07am-11:32pm; L20,000/€10.33); **Florence** (3hr.; every 2hr. 6:33am-6:33pm; L40,000/€20.66); **Milan** (3hr.; 1-2 per hr. 5:12am-9:12pm; L42,000/€21.69); **Padua** (30min., 1-3 per hr. 5:12am-11:32pm, L4300/€2.22); **Rome** (4½hr.; 5 per day 6:33am-8:33pm; L68,000/€35.12); **Trieste** (2hr.; every hr. 8:24am-10:36pm; L20,000/€20.66).

Buses: ACTV (☎041 528 78 86; fax 272 25 88), in Piazzale Roma. Local line for buses and boats. **ACTV long-distance carrier** runs buses to **Padua** (1½hr.; 2 per hr.; L6000/ €3.10, round-trip L10,000/€5.16) and **Treviso** (1hr., 2 per hr., L4200/€2.17). Ticket office open daily 6:30am-11pm. Info office open daily 8am-7:30pm.

▣ ORIENTATION

Venice is 118 bodies of land in a lagoon, connected to the mainland city of Mestre by a thin causeway. Navigating Venice is a bit like playing pin-the-tail-on-the-donkey, but with more water and fewer donkeys. A labyrinth of *fondamente, calli, campi, salizzade, sotoporteghi, listi, canali, rii, ponti,* and *rii terra* (foundations, narrow streets, squares, paved roads, covered streets, main thoroughfares, channels, small channels, bridges, and old channels that are now streets), the city will twist and turn you and then deposit you dazed and babbling "O Sole Mio."

Don't worry if you lack a keen sense of direction; many Venetians do too. They simply set off in the general direction of their destination and then patiently weave their way there. If you follow their example by relaxing and ungluing your eyes from the map, you'll discover some unexpected and spectacular surprises.

A few tips will help you orient yourself. Locate the following sights on the map: **Ponte di Rialto** (in the center), **Piazza S. Marco** (central south), **Ponte Accademia** (southwest), **Ferrovia** (or Stazione Santa Lucia, the train station, northwest), **Ponte Scalzi** (directly west of the station), and **Piazzale Roma** (directly south of the station). The *Canal Grande* snakes through the city's 6 *sestieri* or sections: **Cannaregio, Castello, S. Marco, Dorsoduro, S. Polo,** and **S. Croce** (we've got it easy now; in the 11th century there were more than 70). Within each *sestiere*, there are no individual street numbers—door numbers in a *sestiere* form one long, haphazard set, consisting of around 6000 numbers. While *sestiere* boundaries are nebulous, they can at least give you a general idea of where you are. In the north,

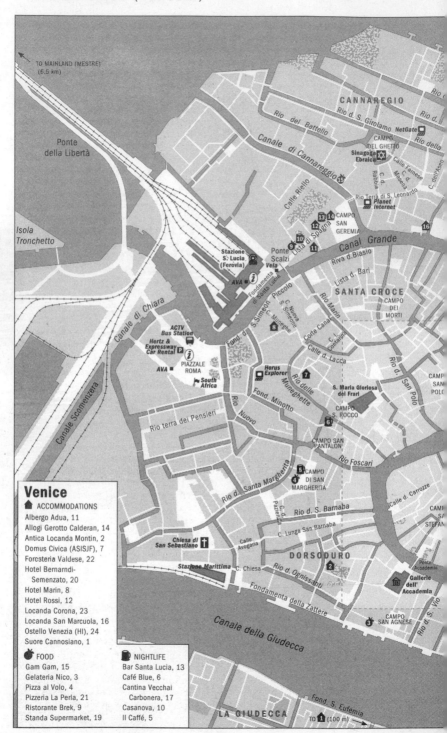

TO MAINLAND (MESTRE)
(6.5 km)

CANNAREGIO

Ponte
della Libertà

Isola
Tronchetto

Rio del Battello

Rio d. S. Girolamo   NetGate

Canale di Cannaregio

CAMPO
DEL GHETTO

Rio della

Sinagoga
Ebraica

Calle Farnese
C. d. Moserta
C. d. Rabbia

15

Calle Riello

Rio Terra di S. Leonardo

Planet
Internet

Stazione
S. Lucia
(Ferovia)

Ponte
Scalzi

Vela

AVA ⓘ

Fondamenta
di Santa Lucia

13 14 CAMPO
SAN
GEREMIA

12

10 Lista di Spagna

9

11

Canal Grande

Riva d. Biasio

Lista d. Bari

16

SANTA CROCE

CAMPO
DEI
MORTI

Canale di Chiara

C. Nuova
S. Simeone

Fond. d. S. Simeon Piccolo

C. d. S. Simeon Grande

8

Rio Marin

Corte Canal

C. I.
Contarina

ACTV
Bus Station

Hertz &
Expressway
Car Rental

AVA ■

PIAZZALE
ROMA

South
Africa

Horus
Explorer

Rio delle
Muneghette

7

Calle d. Lacca

S. Maria Gloriosa
del Frari

Rio d. San Polo

CAMPO
SAN
POLO

Fond. Minotto

CAMPO
S. ROCCO

6

Rio terra dei Pensieri

Rio
Nuovo

CAMPO SAN
PANTALON

Rio Foscari

5 CAMPO
DI SAN
MARGHERITA

4

Rio d. Santa Margherita

Calle d. Carrozze

CAMP
SA
STEFAN

C. d.
Pazienza

Rio d. S. Barnaba

C. Lunga San Barnaba

Chiesa di
San Sebastiano

Calle
Avogaria

DORSODURO

Ponte
Accademia

Stazione Marittima   C. Chiesa

Rio d. Ognissanti

2

Gallerie
dell'
Accademia

Fondamenta della Zattere

Canale della Giudecca

3 CAMPO
SAN AGNESE

Rio d. S. Vio

LA GIUDECCA

Fond. S. Eufemia

TO 🏠 (100 m)

Venice

🏠 **ACCOMMODATIONS**

Albergo Adua, 11
Allogi Gerotto Calderan, 14
Antica Locanda Montin, 2
Domus Civica (ASISJF), 7
Foresteria Valdese, 22
Hotel Bernarndi-
  Semenzato, 20
Hotel Marin, 8
Hotel Rossi, 12
Locanda Corona, 23
Locanda San Marcuola, 16
Ostello Venezia (HI), 24
Suore Cannosiano, 1

🍅 **FOOD**

Gam Gam, 15
Gelateria Nico, 3
Pizza al Volo, 4
Pizzeria La Perla, 21
Ristorante Brek, 9
Standa Supermarket, 19

🍸 **NIGHTLIFE**

Bar Santa Lucia, 13
Café Blue, 6
Cantina Vecchai
  Carbonera, 17
Casanova, 10
Il Caffé, 5

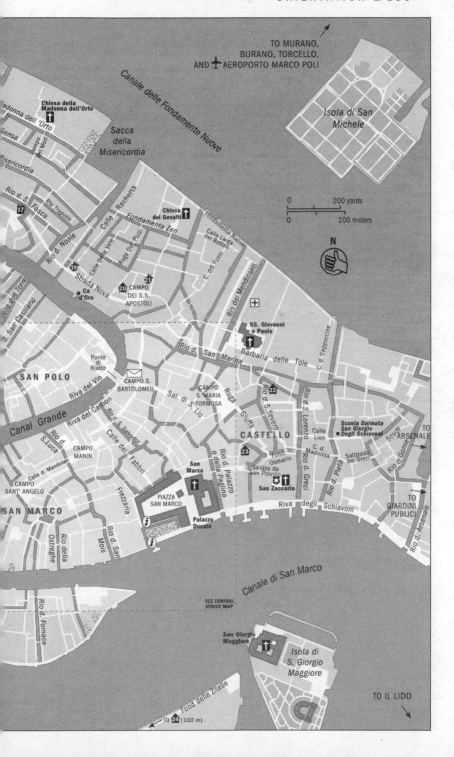

TO MURANO,
BURANO, TORCELLO,
AND ✈ AEROPORTO MARCO POLI

Canale delle Fondamente Nuove

Isola di San Michele

Chiesa della
Madonna dell'Orto

Madonna dell' 'Orto

Sensa

Sacca
della
Misericordia

Misericordia

Rio d S.
Fosca

Rio Trapolin

Chiesa
dei Gesuiti

Calle Rachetta

Fondamenta Zen

Fondamenta Nuove

Calle Larga
dei Botteri

Rio d. Noale

Calle delle Vele

Ruga Due Pozzi

C. dei Fumo

Strada Nova

CAMPO
DEI S.S.
APOSTOLI

Ca
d'Oro

20

21

19

Rio dei Mendicanti

SS. Giovanni
e Paolo

Ponte
di
Rialto

SAN POLO

Rio d. San Marina

Barbaria   delle   Tole

C. d. Cappuccine

CAMPO S.
BARTOLOMEO

CAMPO
S. MARIA
FORMOSA

Ruga Giuffa

Rio d. S. Severo

22

Rio d. S. Lorenzo

Rio d. S. Lorenzo

Scuola Dalmata
San Giorgio
Degli Schiavoni

Scudi

Riva del Vin

Sal. di S. Lio

Canal Grande

Riva del Carbon

Rio d. S. Salvador

Calle dei Fabbri

CAMPO
MANIN

Rio d.
S. Luca

Calle d. Mandola

CAMPO
SANT' ANGELO

Frezzaria

CASTELLO

Calle
Lion

Rio d. Palazzo
o della Paglina

C. d.
Madonna

Fond.
Osmarin

Saliza da
San Provolo

Salizada
del Greci

Rio d. Greci

Rio d. Pietà

Salizzada

TO
ARSENALE

Rio d. Gorne

23

San
Marco

PIAZZA
SAN MARCO

Palazzo
Ducale

San Zaccaria

Riva   degli   Schiavoni

TO
GIARDINI
PUBLICI

Rio d. Arsenale

SAN MARCO

Rio d. San

Mois

Rio della

Ostreghe

SEE CENTRAL
VENICE MAP

Canale di San Marco

Rio d. Fornace

San Giorgio
Maggiore

*Isola di
S. Giorgio
Maggiore*

TO IL LIDO

Fond delle Zitelle

TO 24 (100 m)

0   200 yards
0   200 meters

N

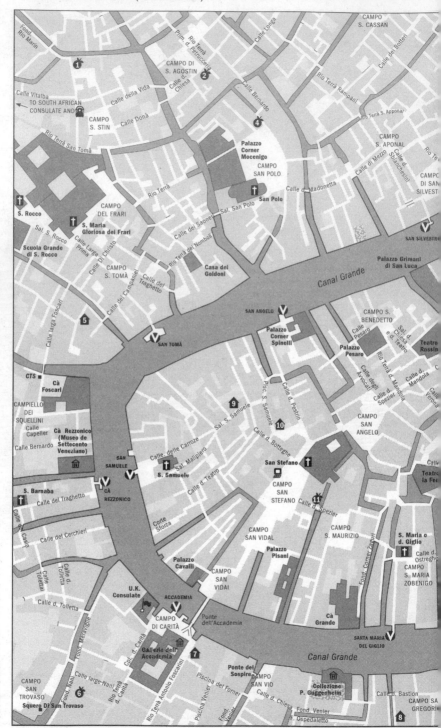

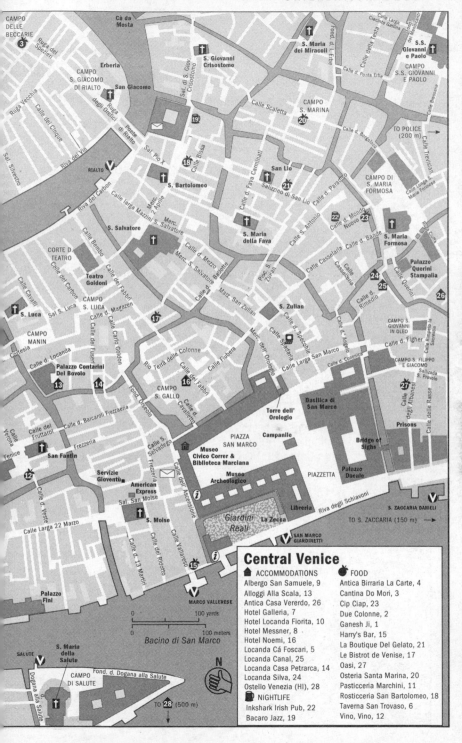

Central Venice

🏠 **ACCOMMODATIONS**
Albergo San Samuele, 9
Alloggi Alla Scala, 13
Antica Casa Vererdo, 26
Hotel Galleria, 7
Hotel Locanda Fiorita, 10
Hotel Messner, 8
Hotel Noemi, 16
Locanda Cá Foscari, 5
Locanda Canal, 25
Locanda Casa Petrarca, 14
Locanda Silva, 24
Ostello Venezia (HI), 28

🍴 **FOOD**
Antica Birraria La Carte, 4
Cantina Do Mori, 3
Cip Ciap, 23
Due Colonne, 2
Ganesh Ji, 1
Harry's Bar, 15
La Boutique Del Gelato, 21
Le Bistrot de Venise, 17
Oasi, 27
Osteria Santa Marina, 20
Pasticceria Marchini, 11
Rosticceria San Bartolomeo, 18
Taverna San Trovaso, 6
Vino, Vino, 12

NIGHTLIFE
Inkshark Irish Pub, 22
Bacaro Jazz, 19

VENICE
Walking tour

Finally see he postcard image of **Rialto Bridge** in person, and be sure to explore the nearby markets.

Jump on vaporetto #1 or #82 to the **Academia** top. Hit one of the world's finest art museums. Bellini and Titian and Carpaccio! Oh my!

Time warp from Venetian Gothic and the Renaissance to the modern art of the **Collezione Peggy Guggenheim.**

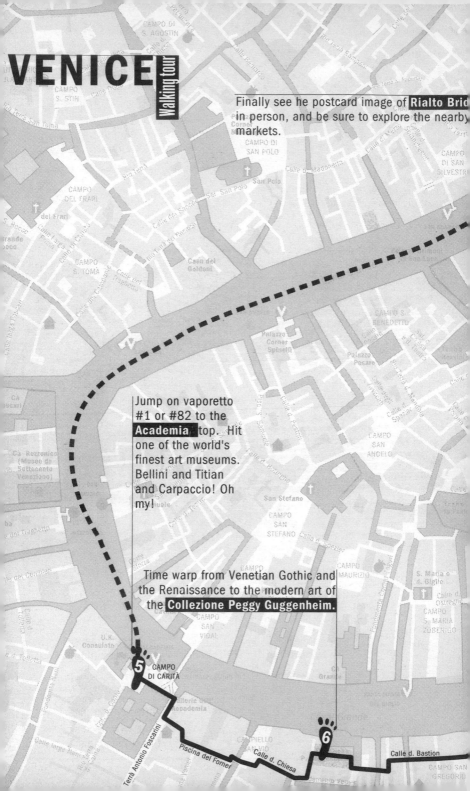

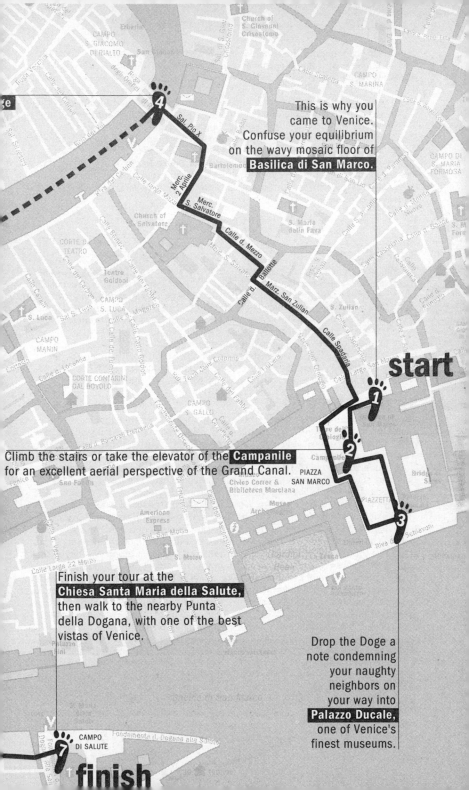

start

This is why you came to Venice. Confuse your equilibrium on the wavy mosaic floor of **Basilica di San Marco.**

Climb the stairs or take the elevator of the **Campanile** for an excellent aerial perspective of the Grand Canal.

Finish your tour at the **Chiesa Santa Maria della Salute,** then walk to the nearby Punta della Dogana, with one of the best vistas of Venice.

Drop the Doge a note condemning your naughty neighbors on your way into **Palazzo Ducale,** one of Venice's finest museums.

finish

Cannaregio encompasses the *ferrovia*, the Jewish ghetto, and the *Cà d'Oro*. **Castello** continues east from there toward the *Arsenale* and the *giardini publici*. **S. Marco,** bounded to the north by the Ponte di Rialto, to the east by Ponte Accademia, and to the west by Piazza S. Marco fills in the remaining area below Cannaregio. **Dorsoduro,** on the other side of the bridge, stretches the length of the Canale della Giudecca and extends north to Campo S. Pantalon. Further north is **S. Polo,** which includes the *campo* of the same name and runs from the Chiesa S. Maria dei Frari to the Ponti di Rialto. **S. Croce** is west of S. Polo, directly across the Canale Grande from the *ferrovia* and includes Piazzale Roma.

Those rushing to **Piazza S. Marco** or the **Rialto Bridge** from the train station or Piazzale Roma should take *vaporetto* #82. Or, if you prefer going on foot, follow the signs (and the crowds) for the 40min. walk to Piazza S. Marco, starting left of the station on Lista di Spagna.

▐ LOCAL TRANSPORTATION

BY FOOT

The cheapest (and often fastest) way to see the city is to walk through it. A *vaporetto* (water bus) between Rialto and S. Marco takes 20 minutes and costs L6000/ €3.10; walking takes 10 minutes and costs nothing. The Grand Canal can be crossed on foot only at the *ponti* (bridges) of Scalzi, Rialto, and Accademia. ▓*Traghetti* (gondola-like ferry boats) cross the canal at six additional points (L700/€0.36). Throughout the city, **yellow signs** on buildings direct pedestrians to major landmarks. Less official looking signs spray-painted or posted on buildings (i.e. to Rialto, to S. Marco) are trustworthy as well. To aid your wanderings, try to scare up a detailed map of the city that includes color coded *sestiere* (see **Orientation** above) and a street index; the tourist office's map is grossly inadequate.

BY VAPORETTO

Vaporetti (water buses) cruise the Venetian waterways, providing an inexpensive, though less romantic, substitute for *gondole;* Brodsky once called them "floating sardine cans." Most principal boats run 5am-midnight, while the *Notte* line offers less frequent service along the Grand Canal, the Giudecca Canal, and the Lido from 11:30pm-5:30am. A single-ride ticket costs L6000/€3.10. If you plan to move longer distances around the city or are staying on an island, consider purchasing an extended pass (24hr. L18,000/ €9.30; 3-day L35,000/€18.08; 7-day L60,000/€31). The ACTV office offers a discounted 3-day ticket (L25,000/€12.91) for **Rolling Venice Card** holders (see **Tourist Offices,** below).

You can buy tickets from the booths in front of the *vaporetto* stops, from self-serve dispensers (at the ACTV office in Piazzale Roma and at the Rialto stop), or from the conductor after boarding. Also note that detailed, color-coded maps are available at the ticket booths. Not all stations sell tickets at all times—buy extra non-validated tickets *(non timbrati)*, or buy a ticket from the conductor as soon as you board. Remember to validate your ticket (at the small yellow boxes outside every *vaporetto* stop) immediately prior to boarding. The fine for riding a *vaporetto* without a ticket (or with an unvalidated) is L39,000/€20.14. During periods of high tourism, ACTV officers frequently board the *vaporetti* to check the tickets. If possible, avoid the *vaporetti* at rush hours (9-10am and 5-8pm).

MAIN VAPORETTO LINES
#82: Runs from the station, down the Grand Canal, up the Giudecca Canal, and back to the station. A great way to see the *palazzi* along the Grand Canal.
#1: The same route as 82, but much slower and with many more stops.
#52, 51: Circumnavigates Venice: 51 runs from the station, through the Giudecca Canal to Lido, along the northern edge of the city, and back to the station, while 52 follows the same route in the opposite direction.
#12: Runs from Fondamente Nuove to Murano, Burano, and Torcello.

DISABLED VISITORS

Venice is extraordinarily difficult to navigate, with hundreds of bridges and many hotels and sights above ground level to avoid *acque alte*, high waters. However, there are some services for disabled visitors. The **APT tourist office** publishes a free map of the city that outlines three wheelchair accessible itineraries in the vicinity of P.S. Marco. Areas of Venice that can be visited without encountering bridges are highlighted in yellow, and most are accessible by *vaporetto* lines #1 and 82. The map also marks which bridges in the city have wheelchair access. These require **keys** that are available from each APT tourist office. Unfortunately, the wheelchair lifts don't always function properly.

ACQUE ALTE High tides and winter rain (usually Oct.-Apr.) cause acque alte, periodic floods that swamp most parts of the city (notably P.S. Marco) under as much as one meter of water. In 1966, more than two meters of water covered the *piazza*, destroying priceless pieces of art. *Acque alte* usually last two to three hours, during which time planks and platforms are laid out across most major thoroughfares, and animals begin to line up two-by-two. To avoid the worst flooding, consult the maps posted at *vaporetto* platforms; otherwise, buy a pair of rubber boots and splash away.

🔁 PRACTICAL INFORMATION

VENICE

TOURIST AND FINANCIAL SERVICES

Tourist Offices:

APT, Calle della Ascensione, **P.S. Marco,** 71/F (☎/fax 041 529 87 40; info@tourismovenezia.it; www.tourismovenezia.it), directly opposite the Basilica di S. Marco. Open M-Sa 9:30am-3:30am. The APT desk at the nearby **Venice Pavilion,** Giardini Ex Reali, S. Marco, 2 (☎041 522 51 50), adjacent to the *vaporetto:* "Vallaresso", has better hours and also sells ACTV tickets and the *Chorus* pass (see **Sights,** below). Open daily 9am-6pm. The office at the **train station** (☎/fax 041 719 07 8) is usually mobbed. Get in line to left of booth. Open June-Sept. daily 8am-8pm, Oct.-May M-Sa 8:15am-6:45pm, Su 9:45am-3:15pm. For arrivals by **car** or **bus,** the office in garage S. Marco, Piazzale Roma (☎/fax 041 241 14 99) is open daily 9am-6pm. Another office in the **Lido,** Gran Viale, 6a (☎041 526 57 21; fax 529 87 20) is open summer only M-Sa 10am-1pm.

AVA (☎041 171 52 88), in train station, to right of tourist office. Finds available hotel rooms and makes same-day reservations for L1000/€.52. Open daily 9am-10pm in summer. Advance reservations by phone; call ☎041 522 22 64 or toll-free ☎800 843 006. Offices in **Piazzale Roma** (☎041 523 13 79) and the **Airport** (☎041 541 51 33). Also book rooms (L4000/€2.07).

Rolling Venice and Comune di Venezia Servizie Gioventù, Corte Contarina, S. Marco, 1529, 4th floor (☎041 274 76 50; fax 274 76 42). Exit P.S. Marco opposite the basilica and turn right, passing the post office. Follow Calle del Salvadago left, continue through the *sottoportego* marked with "Comune di Venezia" signs. Take a left, then a right onto Corte Contarina. The office is to the left of the courtyard. Info on long-term student housing, educational opportunities, and Rolling Venice youth discount cards. (Small discounts at over 200 hotels, restaurants, and museums; Rolling Venice, L5000/€2.58, available to those under 29; valid for one year.) The **ACTV** offers a discounted 3-day *vaporetto* pass (L25,000/€12.91), valid on all *vaporetto* lines, to Rolling Venice cardholders. If you plan on staying in Venice for at least 3 days and plan on taking at least 5 trips on the *vaporetti*, these discounts are well worth L30,000/€15.50. Office open M-F 9:30am-1pm, additional hours Tu and Th 3-5pm. Rolling Venice is also available at the **ACTV VeLa** kiosks next to the **Ferrovia** or **Rialto** *vaporetto* stops. VeLa is open daily 9am-3:30pm.

Budget Travel: CTS, Fondamenta Tagliapietra, Dorsoduro, 3252 (☎041 520 56 60; fax 523 69 46; venezia@cts.it; www.cts.it). From Campo S. Barnaba (near Campo S. Margherita), cross bridge closest to church, turn right at dead end and left onto Calle Cappeller. Turn left at foot of large bridge. Sells highly discounted student plane tickets, and issues ISIC cards. English spoken. Open M-F 9:30am-1:30pm and 2:30-6:30pm.

Consulates: US, Canadian, and **Australian** consulates in Milan; **New Zealand** citizens should contact their embassy in Rome. **South Africa,** in Piazzale Roma, S. Croce, 466/G (☎041 524 15 99), just to the left of Garage Venezia. In serious emergencies, call embassy in Rome (☎06 85 25 41). **UK,** Dorsoduro, 1051 (☎041 522 72 07); cross Accademia bridge from S. Marco and turn right. Open M-F 10am-1pm. In case of extreme emergency after hours, call ☎0337 367 487 between 9-10am and 2-4pm, or call UK Consulate in Milan. (☎0335 810 68 57. Open M-F 9am-5pm, Sa-Su all day.)

Currency Exchange: Money exchangers still take their pound of flesh. Use banks whenever possible and inquire about fees beforehand. It's best to stick to **ATMs.** Banks and ATMs line **Calle Larga XXII Marzo** (between P.S. Marco and the Accademia bridge) and **Campo San Bartomoleo** (near the Rialto Bridge). Many 24hr. automatic change machines, outside banks and next to ATMs, offer low commissions and decent rates.

American Express: Salle S. Moise, S. Marco, 1471 (☎800 87 20 00 or 041 520 08 44). Exit Piazza S. Marco away from basilica; turn left, then right onto Salle S. Moise. Currency exchange with average rates, but no commission. Mail service with AmEx card or AmEx traveler's checks only. Office open for currency exchange M-F 9am-8pm, Sa-Su 9am-5:30pm. Cardmember services M-F 9am-1pm and 2-5:30pm, Sa 9pm-12:30am.

LOCAL SERVICES

Car Rental: Expressway, Piazzale Roma, 496/N (☎041 522 30 00; fax 520 00 00; bll-vob@tin.it; www.venicecar.com), across from ACTV office. 18+. Open daily 8am-6pm. Free car delivery to/from airport. L140,000/€72.30 per day; L570,000/€298.38 per week. AmEx/MC/V. **Hertz,** Piazzale Roma, 496/F (☎041 528 40 91). 25+. Credit card required. Open M-F 8am-6pm, Sa-Su 8am-1pm; in winter M-F 8am-12:30pm and 3-5:30pm, Sa 8am-1pm. L150,000/€77.47 per day; L650,000/€335.70 per week.

Parking: Piazzale Roma or the adjacent island of **Tronchetto.** 24hr. parking in Piazzale Roma garages L36-50,000/€18.59-25.82; parking on Tronchetto up to L40,000/€20.66 per day. On the mainland, parking is substantially less expensive. Motorists should consider leaving their cars in Mestre and then catching a train into Venice (all trains in and out of Venice stop first at Mestre).

English-Language Bookstores: Libreria Studium, S. Marco, 337A (☎/fax 041 522 23 82). From P.S. Marco, head left between basilica and clock tower; It's last shop on right. Fantastic selection of literature about Venice, from classic novels to guidebooks, in both English and Italian. 10% discount with Rolling Venice card. Open M-Sa 9am-7:30pm. AmEx/MC/V. At **Libreria Al Ponte,** Calle della Mandola, S. Marco 3717/D (☎041 522 40 30), just off Campo Manin near Rialto Bridge. Good selection of novels and guidebooks in English. Open M-Sa 9:30am-7:15pm; Sun 1-6:15pm. Read Wharton or Eliot at **La Libreria di Demetra,** Campo S. Geremia, 283a (☎041 716 56 81), where classics of British and American literature are printed in English by an Italian publisher and sell for the lowest prices in town. Campo S. Geremia is left of the train station and a short walk down Lista di Sapgna. Open M-Sa 9am-midnight, Su 10am-midnight.

Library: Biblioteca Nazionale Marciana, P.S. Marco, S. Marco, 7 (☎041 520 87 88). Housed in a building designed by Sansovino. See works by Veronese, Titian, and Tintoretto. Open M-F 8:10am-7pm, Sa 8:10am-1:30pm.

Religious Services: Catholic: Basilica di S. Marco, Piazza S. Marco (☎041 522 56 97). Mass Su 7, 8, 9, 10, and 11:30am. **Anglican: Chiesa Anglicana St. George's,** Campo S. Vio, Dorsoduro, 870 (☎041 520 05 71). Su 10:30am. **Jewish: Sinagoga Ebraica,** Ghetto vecchio, Cannaregio (☎041 71 50 12). Sa 9:30am.

Gay and Lesbian Resources: Arcigay Venezia, V. A'Costa 38/A (☎0335 40 70 79; www.gay.it/arcigay/venezia), in Mestre. Meet Tu at 10pm.

Laundromat: Self-Service, Calle della Chioverette, S. Croce, 665B. From the Scalzi Bridge, turn right onto Fondamenta S. Simeon Piccolo, then left onto Calle Traghetto di S. Lucia. Laundromat on right after you pass through the *campiello.* Wash L6000/€3.10; dry L3000/€1.55; and detergent L1000/€0.52. Open daily 8am-10pm.

Public Toilets: AMAV W.C. Follow the white signs to the sparkling clean public toilets that await you at a price (L1000/€0.52). Open daily 8am-9pm.

EMERGENCY AND COMMUNICATIONS

Police: 113 or 112. **First Aid:** ☎118. **Fire:** ☎115.

Carabinieri, Campo S. Zaccaria, Castello, 4693/A (☎041 204 47 77). **Questura,** V. Nicoladi, 24, Marghera (☎041 271 55 11), for serious complaints about your hotel.

Late-Night Pharmacy: Farmacia Italo Inglese, Calle della Mandola, S. Marco, 3717 (☎041 522 48 37), off Campo Manin near the Rialto bridge. Open M-F 9am-12:30pm and 3:45-7:30pm, Sa 9am-12:30pm. Late-night and weekend pharmacies rotate; check the list posted in the window of any pharmacy.

Hospital: Ospedale Civile, Campo S.S. Giovanni e Paolo, Castello (☎041 529 41 11).

Internet Access:

■ **The NetGate,** Crosera S. Pantalon, Dorsoduro, 3812/A (☎041 244 02 13), on Crosera S. Pantalon, behind the Frari. L10,000/€5.16 per hr., L8000/€4.13 with ISIC or Rolling Venice. 15 other locations in Northern Italy. Open M-F 10am-10pm, Su 2pm-10pm. AmEx/MC/V.

Surf In the Net, Calle dei Campanile, S. Polo, 2898a (☎041 244 02 76). From *vaporetto:* "S. Tomà," head down Calle del Traghetto, and turn left. Six Internet stations. Fast computers and comfortable chairs. L12,000/€6.20 per hr., L9000/€4.65 for students. Open M-Sa 11am-9pm.

Giacomo Casanova, Glass and Internet Point, Calle Spadaria, S. Marco, 676 (☎041 522 71 26). From P.S. Marco, follow busy Calle Larga S. Marco at right of clock tower, then take 3nd left. L13,000/€6.71 per hr., 20% student discount. Open daily 10am-8pm.

Net House, in Campo S. Stefano, S. Marco, 2967-2958 (☎041 227 11 90). L15,000/€7.75 per hr., L12,000/€6.20 with ISIC or Rolling Venice. Discounted international phone rates: L5,000/€2.58 per 12min. to the U.S. and Europe. Open 24hr.

Horus Explorer, Fondamenta Tolentini, S. Croce, 220 (☎041 71 04 70; fax 041 275 83 99). Near station and Piazzale Roma, behind Giardini Papadopoli. L10,000/€5.16 per hr., 10% Rolling Venice discount. Fax and photocopy services. Open M-F 8:30am-12:30pm and 3-7:30pm.

Planet Internet, Rio Terra S. Leonardo, Cannaregio, 1519 (☎041 524 41 88). Head left on Lista di Spagna and cross 1st bridge. It's on your right. L10,000/€5.16 per 30min., L16,000/€8.26 per hr. Calling cards L10,000/€5.16 per 40min. to U.S. Open daily 9am-midnight.

Post Office: Poste Venezia Centrale, Salizzada Fontego dei Tedeschi, S. Marco, 5554 (☎041 271 71 11), situated to the east of the Rialto Bridge and off Campo S. Bartolomeo. Housed in an old palace, the building itself merits a visit. Fermo Posta at window #40. Open M-Sa 8:10am-7pm. **Branch office** (☎041 528 59 49), through the arcades at the end of P.S. Marco and opposite the Basilica. Open M-Sa 8:10am-6pm.

Postal Codes: S. Marco: 30124; Castello: 30122; S. Polo, S. Croce, and Canareggio: 30121; Dorsoduro: 30123.

◪ ACCOMMODATIONS & CAMPING

Plan to spend more for a room in Venice than you would elsewhere in Italy. In *pensioni,* watch out for L10,000/€5.16 breakfasts and other rip-offs. Always agree on what you will pay before you take a room, and if possible, make reservations at least one month in advance. Dormitory-style arrangements are sometimes available without reservations, even during the months of June through September; single rooms, however, vanish in the summer. Never send cash to reserve a room—if you send traveler's checks, keep a careful record. If, upon arrival, you find that accommodations are "tutto completo" (no vacancy), the **AVA** hotel service (see **Tourist Offices,** p. 205) may be able to find you a room with same-day availability, but be prepared to pay far more than you had planned for. Remember that police frown upon those who sleep in parks or on beaches. Because of *acque alte* flooding and renovation restrictions, few hotels in Venice are wheelchair accessible. *Let's Go* lists ground-floor room availability wherever possible.

Religious institutions around the city offer both dorms (L30,000-50,000/€15.50-25.82) and private rooms (L60,000-130,000/€31-67.14) during the summer. Options include **Casa Murialdo,** Fondamenta Madonna dell'Orto, Cannaregio, 3512 (☎041 719 93 3); **Casa Capitanio,** S. Croce, 561 (☎041 522 39 75; Open June and Aug. only); **Patronato Salesiano Leone XIII,** Calle S. Domenico, Castello, 1281 (☎041 240 36 11);

Domus Cavanis, Dorsoduro, 896 (☎041 528 73 74), near the Accademia Bridge; **Casa Ugo e Olga Levi,** Calle Giustinian, S. Marco, 2894 (☎041 277 05 74); **Instituto Canossiano,** Fondamenta Eremile S. Trovaso, Dorsoduro, 1323 (☎041 240 97 11); and **Instituto Ciliota,** Calle Muneghe S. Stefano, S. Marco, 2976 (☎041 520 48 88).

CANNAREGGIO AND SANTA CROCE

Around the station, on Lista di Spagna are some of the best budget accommodations and a festive atmosphere. The streets bustle at night, primarily with young travelers and students, even though the area is a 20 to 30 minute *vaporetto* ride from most major sights. If you prefer quiet, ask for a room away from the street.

▨ **Alloggi Gerotto Calderan,** Campo S. Geremia, 283 (☎041 71 55 62; ☎/fax 71 53 61; www.casagerotto.com). Turn left from station (3min.) Great bargains. 34 big, bright rooms. 4 clean common bathrooms/showers per floor. Internet L6000/€3.10 per 30min. Check-out 10am. Curfew 12:30am for dorms, 1am for private rooms. Reserve at least 15 days in advance. Dorms L35,000/€18.08; singles L60-70,000/€61-36.15; doubles L90-120,000/€46.48-62, with bath L120-160,000/€62-82.63; triples L120-160,000/€62-82.63, with bath L180-220,000/€96.92-113.62.

▨ **Locanda San Marcuola,** Campo S. Marcuola, Cannaregio, 1763 (☎041 71 60 48; fax 275 32 38; www.locandasanmarcuola.com). Easily accesible, situated just 20m from *vaporetto:* "San Marcuola". Super-clean and super-comfortable accommodations at a very reasonable price. Handicapped-accesible elevator. Sparkling new rooms with A/C, TV, and bath). Breakfast included. Singles L100-150,000/€51.65-77.47; doubles L200-250,000/€103.29-129.11; triples L250-300,000/€154.94-180.76.

Ostello Santa Fosca, Fondamenta Canale, Cannaregio, 2372 (☎/fax 041 715 77 5 or 041 715 73 3), only a 10min. walk from train station. From station, follow Lista di Spagna left, cross 3 bridges, and with the church in front of you, turn left at Campo S. Fosca. Cross 1st bridge, turn left onto Fondamenta Canale. Student operated, quiet, and church-affiliated. 140 beds (dorms and doubles) available July-Sept., and 31 beds (five dorms, one double) from Oct.-June. July-Sept. reception daily 9am-noon and 2:30pm-1am. Lock-out noon-2:30pm. Curfew 1am; Oct.-June reception daily 8am-noon and 5-8pm, no curfew. Dorms L35,000/€18.08; doubles L80,000/€41.32. 10% discount with ISIC or Rolling Venice.

Hotel Bernardi-Semenzato, Calle de l'Oca, Cannaregio, 4366 (☎041 522 72 57; fax 522 24 24; mtpepoli@tin.it). From *vaporetto:* "Cà d'Oro," turn right on Strada Nuova, left onto tiny Calle del Duca, then right on Calle di Loca. 25 rooms with phone and safe. Has Venetian antiques, hand-painted tiles, and parquet flooring recovered from the Danieli, Venice's 5-star luxury hotel. Comfortable newly-renovated annex. Ground-floor rooms available. Breakfast included. TV L5000/€2.58 per day. A/C L10,000/€5.16. Check-out 10:30am. Curfew 1am; exceptions made. Singles L70,000/€36.15, with bath L105,000/€54.23; doubles L100,000/€51.65, L140,000/€72.30; triples L130,000/€67.14, L170,000/€87.80; quads L160,000/€82.63, L190,000/€98.13. 15% Rolling Venice discount on larger rooms. AmEx/MC/V.

Hotel Marin, Campiello delle Muneghe, S. Croce, 670/B (☎041 71 80 22; ☎/fax 72 14 85; www.hotelmarin.com). From the station, cross the Scalzi Bridge and turn right. Turn left just before the large domed church onto Calle Nova de S. Simon and make 2 rights. Quiet, well kept, and clean. 19 non-smoking rooms with phone and breakfast included. Strict 1am curfew. Open Feb.-Dec. 10. Doubles L165,000/€85.22, with bath L195,000/€100.71; triples L205,000/€105.87, L240,000/€123.95; quads L270,000/€139.44, L285,000/€147.19. 5% Rolling Venice discount on 1st night, 10% subsequent nights. L10-25,000/€5.16-12.91 cash discount. AmEx/MC/V.

Hotel Rossi, Calle delle Procuratie, Cannaregio, 262 (☎041 71 51 64; ☎/fax 71 77 84), off Lista di Spagna. Turn right out of train station and then left under the arch on Calle della Procuratie. Ceiling fans and telephones in 14 institutional rooms near loud Lista di Spagna. Breakfast included. Reserve at least 1 month in advance for June-Sept. Open Carnevale (early Feb.). Singles L90,000/€46.48, with bath L110,000/€56.81;

doubles L135,000/€69.72, with bath L165,000/€85.22; triples with bath L200,000/ €103.29; quads with bath L235,000/€121.37. 10% Rolling Venice discount. MC/V.

Albergo Adua, Lista di Spagna, Cannaregio, 233a (☎041 71 61 84; fax 244 01 62), 50m from the station. Facing the canal, turn left, and look for the *albergo* on your right. 22 comfortable, pastel-tinted rooms await weary travelers. Rooms are no bargain, and breakfast (L10,000/€5.16) on a plant-filled indoor/outdoor patio comes at a price too. Curfew midnight. Singles L100,000/€51.65, with bath L150,000/€77.47; doubles L210,000/€108.46, L270,000/€139.44. AmEx/MC/V.

Ostello Venezia (HI), Fondamenta Zitelle, Giudecca, 87 (☎041 523 82 11; fax 523 56 89; www.hostelbooking.com). Venice's only HI hostel. Isolated from main island by Giudecca Canal. Can be reached only by *vaporetto*. Take the #82 or #52 to "Zitelle," and from there, head right 20m alongside canal. Definitely institutional, but with sweeping view. Ostello Venezia offers 250 beds (men and women bunk on separate floors), a large dining room, Internet connection, and a snack bar. Breakfast included. Sheets free. Dinner L15,000/€7.75. Reception daily 7-9:30am and 1:30-11:30pm. Lock-out 9:30am-1:30pm. Curfew 11:30pm. Reservations through IBN from other HI hostels, online at www.hostelbooking.com, or by phone. HI members only; temporary and full HI cards available. Dorms L30,000/€15.50. MC/V.

Suore Cannosiano, Ponte Piccolo, Giudecca, 428 (☎/fax 041 522 21 57). From *vaporetto* #82: Palanca, walk left over the bridge. Women only. 35 beds. Get thee to this friendly nunnery before 9am or after 3pm if you want to leave bags. Check-out 7:30-8:30am. Lock-out 9am-3pm. Strict curfew 10:30pm; winter 10pm. No reservations. Large dorms L23,000/€11.88.

SAN MARCO

Surrounded by exclusive shops and souvenir stands, scores of *trattorie* and *pizzerie*, and many of Venice's most popular sights, these accommodations are prime choices for those who seek the novelty of Venice's showy, tourist-oriented side. As *gondole* traffic peaks in the early evening, listen for the wavering song of the accordion as it echoes through S. Marco's narrow canals.

Albergo San Samuele, S. Marco, 3358 (☎/fax 041 522 80 45). Follow Calle delle Botteghe from Campo S. Stefano (near the Accademia Bridge) and turn left on Salizzada S. Samuele. An unused, musty courtyard leads to this simple, inexpensive hotel. Tapestry-print wallpaper and Italian art decorate 10 colorful, clean rooms with sparkling bathrooms. Reserve 1-2 months ahead. Singles L80,000/€41.32; doubles L130,000/ €67.14, with bath L190,000/€98.13; triples available with advance notice.

Locanda Casa Petrarca, Calle Schiavine, S. Marco, 4386 (☎/fax 041 520 04 30). From Rialto, take Calle larga Mazzini and turn right at the church onto Calle dell'Ovo. Turn left onto Calle dei Fabbri, then turn right for Campo S. Luca. Cross the Campo to Calle dei Fuseri. Take the 2nd left and turn right onto Calle Schiavine. 7 clean, but tiny, white rooms look onto brick walls or neighbors' windows. Cheery plant-filled sitting room, with books in English lining the walls. English spoken by the friendly proprietor. Singles L80,000/€41.32; doubles L160,000/€82.63, with bath L200,000/€103.29.

Alloggi Alla Scala, Corte Contarini del Bovolo, S. Marco, 4306 (☎041 521 06 29). From Campo Manin, take Calle delle Locande, then take a left and a quick right on Corte Contarini del Bovolo. Shares the tiny *campo* with a real architectural gem, La Scala del Bovolo, an ornate, Escher-esque, circular staircase that reaches 6 stories high. Inside the *alloggi*, a worn red carpet leads up the stairs to 5 very quiet, comfortable rooms, all with bath. Breakfast L25,000/€12.91 for two. Closed Aug. Doubles L130-150,000/ €67.14-77.47; extra bed L40,000/€20.66. MC/V.

Hotel Noemi, Calle dei Fabbri, S. Marco, 909 (☎041 523 81 44; fax 277 10 05; hotel-noemi@tin.it; www.hotelnoemi.com). Exit P.S. Marco through the 2nd *sottoportico* from the basilica, and follow Calle dei Fabbri as it jags to the left. Just 1min. from the *piazza*, Hotel Noemi's convenience makes up for its higher prices. 8 beautiful new rooms, with

Venetian-style furniture, and bathroom. 8 plainer, older rooms, without bath. All rooms with TV, phone, and safe. Singles L130,000/€67.14, with bath L170,000/€87.80; doubles L160,000/€82.63, with bath L220,000/€113.62; triples L210,000/ €108.46, with bath L320,000/€165.27; quads L270,000/€139.44. Cash only for 1-night stay. 5% cash discount. MC/V.

Hotel Locanda Fiorita, Campiello Novo, S. Marco, 3457 (☎041 523 47 54; ☎/fax 041 522 80 43; info@locandafiorita.com; www.locandafiorita.com). From Campo S. Stefano, take Calle del Pestrin and then climb onto the raised *piazza*. A beautiful vine-covered courtyard and terrace lead to large doubles decorated with oriental rugs. Singles smaller and slightly less desirable. All rooms with A/C, phone, and TV. The nearby annex has a few ground-floor accommodations and adds satellite TV. Breakfast included. Singles L140,000/€72.30; doubles L190,000/€98.13, with bath L230,000/€118.79. Annex singles L170,000/€87.80; doubles L240,000/€123.95, with bath L250,000/€129.11. Extra bed 30% more. AmEx/MC/V.

Domus Civica (ACISJF), Campiello Chiovere Frari, S. Polo, 3082 (☎041 72 11 03; fax 041 522 71 39), between the Basilica dei Frari and Piazzale Roma. From the station, cross the Scalzi Bridge and turn right. Turn left on Fonamenta dei Tolentini then left through the courtyard onto Corte Amai. The hostel is the building with the rounded facade on the right, directly after the bridge. Friendly staff run this simple, church-affiliated student housing. Inside, a dark wood trim complements 100 beds, a few ping-pong tables, a TV room, and a piano. Check-in 7:30am-4pm. Curfew 11:30pm. Open mid-June to Sept. Singles L50,000/€25.82; doubles L90,000/€46.48.

CASTELLO

Dense with tourist overflow from nearby P.S. Marco, the western end of Castello is noisy and exciting. While accommodations sit within striking distance of major sights, they are concealed by Venice's most narrow, tightly clustered streets.

▨ Foresteria Valdesi, Castello, 5170 (☎041 528 67 97; fax 241 62 38; www.chiesavaldese.org/venezia). From Rialto Bridge, enter Campo S. Bartolomeo. Continue under *sottoportico* to the left, follow Salizzada S. Lio, and turn left onto Calle Mondo Nuovo. Cross bridge, then cross Campo S. Maria Formosa to Calle Lunga S. Maria Formosa. Housed in the Palazzo Cavagnis, immediately over the 1st bridge. This stunning building was once the 18th-century guest house of Venice's largest Protestant church and now is situated only a stone's throw from Venice's major sights. Dazzling frescoed ceilings grace both the dorms (33 beds), and the private rooms (all with TV). Enjoy breakfast (included) in a spacious, sun-lit hall with wooden ceiling beams. Reception daily 9am-1pm and 6-8pm. Lock-out 10am-1pm. No curfew. Closed 3 weeks in Nov. Dorms L36,000/€18.59 for 1st night, L35,000/€18.08 per additional night; doubles L100,000/€51.65, with bath L130,000/€67.14; quads L180,000/€92.96. Ask for a room with a fresco. Also has 2 apartments with bath and kitchen L190-200,000/ €98.13-103.29. L2000/€1.03 Rolling Venice discount.

Locanda Silva, Fondamenta del Remedio, Cannaregio, 4423 (☎041 523 78 92; fax 041 528 68 17; albergosilva@libero.it). From P.S. Marco, walk under clock tower and turn right on Calle Larga S. Marco and then left on Ramo dell'Anzolo (which becomes Calle Remedio after crossing bridge). At the canal, turn left on Fondamenta Remedio. 24 simple, sunny, clean rooms. 2 adorable resident cats. All rooms with phone. Breakfast included. Open Feb. to mid-Nov. Singles L85,000/€43.90, with bath L120,000/ €62; doubles L140,000/€72.30, with toilet L160,000/€82.63, with toilet and shower L190,000/€98.13; triples with toilet and shower L250,000/€129.11; quads with toilet and shower L300,000/€154.94.

Locanda Corona, Calle Corona, Castello, 4464 (☎041 522 91 74). From *vaporetto:* "San Zaccharia", take Calle degli Albanese to Campo SS. Fillipo e Giacomo, continue on Rimpetto la Sacrestia, and take 1st right. Turn left onto Calle della Corona. Various knick-knacks and some safari print furniture decorates the lobby of this well-worn, 3rd floor hotel. 8 rooms, clean, no-frills, and offer nice views of the Castello skyline. Wheelchair lift. Breakfast L15,000/€7.75. Closed Jan. Singles L85,000/€43.90; doubles L105,000/€54.23; triples L130,000/€67.14.

Locanda Canal, Fondamenta del Remedio, Castello, 4422c (☎041 523 45 38; fax 241 91 38), next to **Locanda Silva.** A warm waiting room leads to 7 large, rooms in a converted 14th-century *palazzo,* some overlooking the canal. High ceilings a holdover from Locanda Canal's palace days, sparse decorations probably aren't. Breakfast included. Doubles L155,000/€80.05, with shower L175,000/€90.38, with toilet and shower L205,000/€105.87; triples L185,000/€95.54, L210,000/€108.46, L250,000/ €129.11; quads L220,00/€113.620, L240,000/€123.95, L300,000/€154.94.

Antica Locanda Casa Verardo, Calle dei Mercanti, Castello, 4765 (☎041 528 61 27; fax 523 27 65; casaverardo@tin.it). From *vaporetto:* "San Zaccaria," take Calle degli Albanese to Campo SS. Filippo e Giacomo, cross the *campo,* and continue down Calle dei Mercanti. The hotel is directly over the bridge. Housed in a traditional Venetian building, 9 luxurious rooms feature elegant wall moldings, richly colored linens and draperies, and detailed wooden furnishings. All rooms with bath, TV, and phone. More renovations for 2002. Breakfast included. Singles L150-200,000/€77.47-103.29; doubles L200-300,000/€103.29-154.94; triples L250-350,000/€129.11-180.76; quads L300-400,000/€154.94-206.58. AmEx/MC/V only with 3-night min. stay.

DORSODURO

Spartan facades and still canals trace the quieter, wider streets of Dorsoduro. Here, numerous art museums draw visitors to canal-front real estate, while the interior remains a little-visited residential quarter. Most hotels in Dorsoduro tend to be pricey, and are situated toward the Canal Grande, between the Chiesa dei Frari and the Accademia Bridge.

Locanda Ca' Foscari, Calle della Frescada, Dorsoduro, 3887b (☎041 71 04 01; fax 71 08 17; valtersc@tin.it), in a quiet neighborhood near the *vaporetto.* From *vaporetto:* "San Tomà", turn left at the dead end, cross the bridge, turn right, and then take a left into the little alleyway. Murano glass chandeliers and Venetian Carnival masks embellish the 11 simple but cozy rooms, operated by a warm older couple. Breakfast included. Curfew 1am. Book 2 or 3 months in advance. Open Feb.-Nov; closed 1st week Aug. Singles with bath L100,000/€51.65; doubles L120,000/€62, with bath L160,000/€82.63; triples L156,000/€80.57, with bath L201,000/€103.81; quads L192,000/€99.16, with bath L240,000/€123.95. MC/V.

Hotel Galleria, Rio Terra Antonio Foscarini, Dorsoduro, 878/A (☎041 523 24 89; fax 520 41 72; galleria@tin.it; www.hotelgalleria.it), on the left as you face the Accademia museum. Sumptuous oriental rugs and tasteful art prints lend the Galleria an elegance appropriate to its location on the Grand Canal. Stunning views in some of the 10 rooms make up for their relatively small size. Breakfast, served in rooms, included. Singles L120,000/€62; doubles L170-180,000/€87.80-92.96, with bath L200-250,000/ €103.29-129.11. Extra bed 30% more. AmEx/MC/V.

Antica Locanda Montin, Fondamenta di Borgo, Dorsoduro, 1147 (☎041 522 71 51; fax 520 02 55; locandamontin@libero.it). From *vaporetto:* "Cà Rezzonico", go straight ahead to Campo S. Barnaba. Turn left under the *sottoportego,* right at the iron sign, and left at the canal. 10 simple rooms on one of the most picturesque and quiet canals in the heart of Dorsoduro. Several have views and terraces. Breakfast included. Lunch and dinner available at restaurant downstairs. Singles L130,000/€67.14; doubles L200,000/€103.29, with bath L250,000/€129.11. AmEx/MC/V.

Hotel Messner, Fondamenta di Cà Bala, Dorsoduro, 216 (☎041 522 72 66; fax 522 74 43; messner@doge.it). From *vaporetto:* "Salute", go right on Calle del Bastion, then turn left. This canal-front, 2 star red brick hotel has 1 star ground floor rooms in a nearby annex. 31 rooms range from institutional singles to a bright quad with bath and kitchenette, but all rooms come with bath, phone, safe, and hair dryer (2 star rooms also have TV and A/C). Buffet breakfast included. Closed mid-Nov.-Dec. Singles L185,000/ €95.54; doubles L255,000/€131.70; triples L310,000/€160.10; quads L350,000/ €180.76. Annex singles L165,000/€85.22; doubles L210,000/€108.46; triples L270,000/€139.44; quads L300,000/€154.94. AmEx/MC/V.

VENICE

CAMPING

If camping, plan on a 20min. boat ride to Venice. In addition to these listings, the **Litorale del Cavallino,** on the Lido's Adriatic side, has endless beach campsites.

Camping Miramare, Puno Sabbioni (☎041 96 61 50; fax 530 11 50), a 40min. boat ride (*vaporetto* #14) from P.S. Marco to "Punta Sabbioni". Campground is 700m along the beach to your right. Plan on a 3-night min. stay in high-season. Open Apr. to mid-Nov. L9800/€5.06 per person, L24,000/€12.40 per tent. 4-person bungalow L62,000/€32.02, 5-person L98,000/€50.16. 15% Rolling Venice discount.

Camping Fusina, V. Moranzani, 79 (☎041 547 00 55), in Malcontenta. From Mestre, take bus #1. Call ahead. L11,000/€5.68 per person, L7000/€3.62 per tent, L25,000/€12.91 per tent and car, L21,000/€10.85 to sleep in car.

🍴 FOOD

In Venice, dining well on a budget requires exploration. Like lemmings hurling themselves off a cliff, most tourists flock to the endless string of *trattorie* and *pizzerie* that advertise *menù turistici* and serve mediocre fare along the main streets. Silly lemmings: the best and most affordable restaurants hide in the less traveled alleyways. Even there, however, travelers familiar with L20,000/€10. small town feasts will find Venice unusually pricey.

The nucleus of Venetian cuisine comes fresh from the sea. *Seppie in nero* is cuttlefish, a soft, squid-like creature coated with its own ink and usually served with *polenta*, the Veneto's cornmeal staple. A plate of *pesce fritta mista* (mixed fried seafood), which usually includes shrimp, *calamari* (squid), and *polpo* (octopus) costs at least L14,000/€7.32. *Spaghetti al vongole* (pasta with fresh clams and spicy vegetables; L12,000/€6.20) is served on nearly every menu. Another regional specialty is *fegato alla veneziana* (liver and onions). The Veneto and Friuli regions produce an abundance of excellent **wines.** Good local whites include the sparkling *prosecco della Marca*, the dry *tocai*, and the savory *bianco di Custoza*. For reds, try a *valpolicella*. The least expensive option is by no means inferior: a simple *vino bianco* or *vino rosso* (L1500/€0.77), is usually a delicious locally produced merlot or chardonnay and is the standard libation among locals.

For an inexpensive and informal alternative to traditional restaurants, visit any *osteria* or *bacaro* in town and create a meal from the vast display of meat- and cheese-filled pastries, tidbits of seafood, rice, meat, and *tramezzini* (triangular slices of soft white bread with any imaginable filling). These snacks are known as **cicchetti** (chee-KET-ee) and usually go for L2500-5000/€1.29-2.58 each. Generally, you pay extra for table service (L1500/€0.77 per drink), so standing at the bar is much cheaper than sitting down. Venetians generally drift from *bacaro* to *bacaro*, stopping in for a quick snack or just a glass of wine in the late afternoon (although *grappa* consumption often starts as early as 9am). Traditional *bacari* (see **Do Mori,** p. 214) fill the streets between the Rialto Bridge and Campo S. Polo.

The internationally renowned **Rialto Markets,** once the center of trade for the Venetian Republic, fill the area between the Grand Canal and the S. Polo foot of the Rialto Bridge every morning Monday through Saturday. Pick your way through vendors hawking plastic gondolas and other junk to find fruit stands selling Sicilian blood oranges in winter and Treviso cherries in summer; a bit further back, eels squirm on icy beds in the fish markets. Smaller fruit and vegetable markets set up in Cannaregio, on Rio Terra S. Leonardo by the Ponte delle Guglie and in many *campi* throughout the city.

STANDA Supermarket, Strada Nuova, Cannaregio, 3650, near Campo S. Felice, has a large grocery store in the back, behind the clothing, that keeps the polyester smelling like fish. (Open M-Sa 8:30am-7:20pm, Su 9am-7:20pm. AmEx/MC/V.) Smaller **FULL Alimentari,** Calle Carminati, 5989, Castello, just north of P.S. Marco, stocks inexpensive food for those who can navigate its cramped aisles. (Open M-Sa 9am-1pm and 4-7:30pm. MC/V.)

CANNAREGIO

Pizzeria La Perla, Rio Terra dei Franceschi, Cannaregio, 4615 (☎041 528 51 75). From Strada Nuova, turn left onto Salizzade di Pistor in Campo SS. Apostoli, then turn right. La Perla's affordable menu offers no less than 90 types of pizza and pasta, each served in heaping portions by a friendly staff. Informal and spacious, La Perla is perfect for families and groups. Pasta L9-11,000/€4.65-5.68, pizzas L9000-14,000/€4.65-7.23, huge salads L13-14,000/€6.71. Wheelchair accessible. Cover L2000/€1.02. Service 10%. Open M-Sa noon-2pm and 7-9:45pm. Closed Aug. AmEx/MC/V.

Gam Gam, Rio di Cannaregio, Cannaregio, 1122 (☎041 71 52 84), in the Jewish Ghetto on Fondamenta Pescaria. Extensive menu of Venetian and Jewish food. Enjoy all-kosher fare like *schnitzel* (L15-31,000/€7.75-16.01), the falafel platter (L16,000/€8.26), or a lunch buffet (L18,000/€9.30), while seated outdoors by the canal. Pastas L12-16,000/€6.20-8.26. Open Su-Th noon-10pm, F 7-10pm. 10% *Let's Go* discount.

Ristorante Brek, Lista di Spagna, Cannaregio, 124A (☎041 244 01 58); from the station, turn left. This Italian chain tries really hard to infuse its restaurant with atmosphere; appetizing market-style buffets are loaded with affordable *antipasti* (L5000/€2.58), *insalate* (L5-9000/€2.58-4.65), *formaggii* (L5000/€2.58), and *dolci* (L3-6000/€1.55-3.1), and friendly cooks prepare fresh *paste* (L6-9000/€3.10-4.65), to order, as you wait. No service charge or cover. Open daily 7:30am-10:30pm.

CASTELLO

Cip Ciap, Calle Mondo Nuovo, 5799a (☎041 523 66 21), between Salizzada S. Lio and Campo S. Maria Formosa. Grab some of Cip Ciap's cheap pizza (from L7500/€3.87), and enjoy it in one of the nearby campi. The *disco volante* (literally, flying saucer), stuffed with mushrooms, eggplant, ham, and salami, is out of this world (L12000/€6.20). Call ahead for the *volante*. Open W-M 9am-9pm.

Osteria Santa Marina, Campo S. Marina, Castello, 5911 (☎041 528 52 39), east of the Rialto Bridge. To splurge, enjoy traditional Venetian cuisine with well-dressed locals or stop by for some *cicchetti* and a glass of *prosecco*. The menu changes daily, and the fish options disappear on Monday when the markets are closed. *Primi* L20-22,000/€10.33-11.36; *secondi* L27-40,000/€13.94-20.66. Service and cover L5000/€2.58. Open M 7:30-11:30pm, Tu-Sa 11:30am-3pm and 7:30-11:30pm.

SAN MARCO

Vino, Vino, Ponte delle Veste, S. Marco, 2007a (☎041 24 17 688). From Calle Larga XXII Marzo, turn onto Calle delle Veste. Over 350 varieties of wine, most L2000-3000/€1.03-1.55. Piping hot *primi* L8000/€4.13; *secondi* L15,000/€7.75 in this dark, no-frills wine bar. Seafood-heavy menu changes daily. Cover L1000/€.52. Open W-M 10:30am-11pm. 10% Rolling Venice discount.

Oasi, Calle degli Albanesi, S. Marco, 4263/a (☎041 528 99 37), on a side street between the Prisons and the Danieli Hotel. Take respite from the scorching midday sun of S. Marco in this refreshing, albeit out-of-place cafe. The owners, clad in Hawaiian shirts, serve up some of the city's freshest fruits and vegetables in *frulatti* (overpriced fruit and milk smoothies, L7000/€3.62) and enormous salads (a better bargain at L8-15,000/€4.13-7.75). Try their *pasta fredda* (L10,000/€5.16), or *panini* (L7-9000/€3.62-4.65). In the winter, grab some *zuppo caldo* (L8000/€4.13) to overcome that Adriatic chill. Open M-Sa 7:45am-8:45pm.

Rosticceria San Bartomoleo, Calle della Bissa, S. Marco, 5424/A (☎041 522 35 69). From Campo S. Bartolomeo, follow the neon sign under the last *sottoportego* on the left. Inside, a long glass bar parades a smorgasbord of sandwiches, pasta, and *cicchetti* to be enjoyed on the go or seated at the numerous window booths. Try the *mozzarella al prosciutto*, L2500/€1.29 worth of battered-and-fried goodness. The full-service restaurant upstairs is open for lunch and dinner. Entrees L12-23,000/€6.20-11.88, cover L2500/€1.29. Rosticceria open Tu-Su 9:30am-9:30pm. AmEx/MC/V.

Le Bistrot de Venise, Calle dei Fabbri, S. Marco, 4685 (☎041 523 66 51), from the basilica in P.S. Marco, head through the second *sottoportego* on you right. This popular restaurant specializes in delicious homemade pastas (try the *ravioli*, L20,000/€10.33), an award-winning wine list (by the glass, L6-9000/€3.1-4.65), and courteous, attentive service. For authentic Venetian cuisine, look no further; this elegant restaurant's offerings descend from 14th-century recipes. Of course, food from the height of the Venetian Empire comes at a price. *Primi* L18-25,000/€9.30-12.91; *secondi* L20-35,000/€10.33-18.08. Service 15%. Oct.-May, Le Bistrot's frequent afternoon arts and literature exhibitions draw local artisans, poets, and musicians. Open daily noon-3pm and 6pm-1am. AmEx/MC/V.

Harry's Bar, Calle Vallaresso, S. Marco, 1323 (☎041 528 57 77), around the corner from the Venice Pavilion. Swagger over to this favored hangout of "Ernesto" Hemingway and other real men. Founded by a Bostonian named Harry who felt that Venice suffered a lack of bars, this cafe has been pouring pricey drinks (including his famous Bellini) to curious tourists in search of novelty ever since. Bellini L23,000/€11.88. Service 15%. Open daily 10:30am-10:55pm.

DORSODURO

▨ Taverna San Trovaso, Fondamenta Nani, Dorsoduro, 1016 (☎041 520 37 03). From *vaporetto:* "Accademia", take your 1st right onto Calle Gambara, then head left along the canal. The Taverna's young and enthusiastic staff, great pastas and pizzas, and amazingly affordable prices make for a Venetian rarity. *Primi* L10-15,000/€5.16-7.75; *secondi* L15-27,000/€7.75-13.94, pizzas L8-14,000/€4.13-7.23. Cover L3000/€1.55. Open Tu-Su noon-2:50pm and 7-9:50pm. AmEx/MC/V.

Cantinone del Vino Già Schiavone, Fondamente Meraviglie, Dorsoduro, 992 (☎041 5d23 00 34), just down the street from Taverna S. Trovaso, above. It's standing room only at this crowded local haunt, where a faded marquee veils one of the authentic *osterie* in Venice. Buying by the bottle? A spectacular selection of the Veneto's finest lines the walls, with dozens selling for less than L10,000/€5.16. Otherwise, enjoy a glass at the bar, perhaps with some of the delectable *cichetti* (try the tomato-mozzarella-basil, L2500/€1.29). Open M-Sa 8am-2:30pm and 3:15-8:30pm.

Pizza al Volo, Campo S. Margherita, Dorsoduro, 2944 (☎041 522 54 30). Join the students and other travelers outside in the *campo* as they wolf down a slice before heading off to grab a drink at one of the surrounding bars. Hold the sauce? Ask for the tasty house specialty, *al volo*, a pie topped with *mozzarella, grado,* and *melanzane* (eggplant). Take-out only. Slices L2500-3000/€1.29-1.55, full pizzas L6-20,000/€3.1-10.33. Open daily 11:30am-3:30pm and 5:30pm-1:30am.

SAN POLO AND SANTA CROCE

Due Colonne, Campo S. Agostin, S. Polo, 2343 (☎041 524 06 85). Cross the bridge away from the Frari, turn left, and cross into Campo S. Stin. Then turn right on Calle Danà and cross the bridge. Students, families, and tourists crowd the large indoor booths and the *campo* seating to sample the variety of pizzas (L6-13,000/€3.10-6.71), while old-timers line up at the wine bar as early as 10pm. Elegant charcoal sketches of Venice cover the dark wood walls. Cover L1500/€.77. Service 10%. Closed Aug. Open M-Sa 8am-3pm and 6-11pm. Kitchen closes 10pm.

Ganesh Ji, Calle dell' Olio, S. Polo, 2426 (☎/fax 041 71 98 04). From the station, cross the Scalzi Bridge, continue straight, and turn left on Calle della Bergama. Take a right on Fondamenta Rio Marin and then another right on Calle dell' Olio. Be a modern-day Marco Polo at this crossroad of East and West while enjoying an affordable 3 course Indian lunch (vegetarian L21,000/€10.85; non-veg. L23,000/€11.88). Enjoy your basmati and naan canal-side (on the outdoor terrace) or indoors among the elephant statues and candy-stripe poles. *Primi* L5000-10,000/€2.58-5.16; *secondi* L20,000/€10.33. Cover L3000/€1.55, but Rolling Venice waives the cover charge. Open Th 7:30-11pm, F-Tu 12:30-2pm and 7pm-midnight. MC/V.

Cantina Do Mori, Calle dei Do Mori, S. Polo, 429 (☎041 522 54 01), near the Rialto markets. Turn left at Calle Angelo, then left again onto Calle dei Do Mori. Venice's oldest wine bar may be a tourist attraction, but it is still an elegant place to grab a a few *cicchetti* (from L2500/€1.29) or a superb glass of local wine (L2000/€1.03). From the aging copperware lining the walls to the uneven stone floor, Do Mori has a charming antique feel. Standing room only. Open M-Sa 9am-9pm.

Antica Birraria La Carte, Campo S. Polo, S. Polo, 2168 (☎041 275 05 70). Housed in a former brewery, the Birraria stays true to its roots with an extensive selection of German beers. Inside, the bar and restaurant have a clean, polished look and feature a non-smoking section. Outside enjoy peaceful Campo S. Polo, once the site of bull-baiting matches. Beer L3-5,000/€1.55-2.58; Pizzas L8-14,000/€4.13-9.30. Cover L2500/€1.29. Open Tu-Su noon-3pm and 6pm-midnight. AmEx/MC/V.

GELATERIE AND PASTICCERIE

▓ **La Boutique del Gelato,** Salizzada S. Lio, Castello, 5727 (☎041 522 32 83). Go and go now. And then come back for more. Crowded with locals taking some home for the family. Enormous cones from L1500/€0.77. Open Feb.-Nov. M-Sa 10am-8:30pm.

▓ **Pasticceria Marchini,** Calle del Spezier, S. Marco, 2769 (☎041 522 91 09), off Campo S. Stefano. A dazzling assortment of pastries, chocolates, and candies, layered behind panes of glass and gold trim. Pastries L2500-5000/€1.29-2.58. Open M 9am-6pm, W-Sa 9am-6pm, and Su 1-6pm. AmEx/MC/V.

Gelateria Nico, Fondamenta Zattere, Dorsoduro, 922 (☎041 522 52 93), near *vaporetto*: "Zattere". *Gelato* L2-4000/€1.03-2.07. View of Giudecca Canal. Try the Venetian specialty *gianduiotto al passagetto* (a slice of dense chocolate-hazelnut ice cream dunked in whipped cream; L4000/€2.07). Open F-W 6:45am-10:30pm.

◉ SIGHTS

! **MINI-SKIRTS, MINI-PASSES, AND MINI-DISCOUNTS** Mini-skirts are verboten in many Venetian churches, as they enforce a strict dress code that calls for the coverage of shoulders and knees. Mini-passes to visit Venice's churches are sold by The Foundation for the Churches of Venice. A three day mini-pass (L15,000/€7.75, students L10,000/€5.16) for visits to 13 of Venice's finest "non-secular art museums", including S. Maria dei Miracoli, S. Maria Gloriosa dei Frari, S. Polo, Madonna dell'Orto, Il Redentore, S. Sebastiano, is available at all participating churches (except S. Maria Gloriosa dei Frari) and allows unlimited entrance to any of the 13 churches. For information on the pass or any of these churches, call ☎041 275 04 62. Many sights have student, senior, and group discounts; discount prices generally apply to EU visitors under 18 or over 60. Children under 12 are often admitted for free.

AROUND THE RIALTO BRIDGE

THE GRAND CANAL. The Grand Canal loops through Venice, passing the splendid facades of the *palazzi* that crown its banks and testifying to the city's history of immense wealth. Although their external decorations vary, the palaces share the same basic structure. The most decorated floors, the *piani nobili* ("noble floors"; 2nd and 3rd story), housed luxurious salons and bedrooms. The rich merchant families stored their goods on the ground floor, and the servants slept in the tiny rooms below the roof. The candy-cane-like posts used for mooring boats on the canal are called *bricole*, and they are decorated with the colors of the family owning the adjoining *palazzo*. *(To see the facades of these buildings, ride vaporetto #82 or the slower #1 from the train station to P.S. Marco. A ▓ nighttime ride reveals the floodlit facades, a dazzling play of reflections and light.)*

V
E
N
I
C
E

THE RIALTO BRIDGE. The Rialto Bridge (1588-91) arches over the Grand Canal and embodies Venice's rich commercial past. It looks top-heavy because the city mandated that any bridge built across that site have revenue-generating shops. A government official, appropriately named Antonio da Ponte (*ponte* means bridge), complied and designed an architectural spectacle whose widely known image now keeps the city's postcard vendors in business. *(Vaporetto: "Rialto.")*

CHIESA DI SAN GIACOMO DI RIALTO. Between the Rialto Bridge and surrounding markets stands Venice's first church, diminutively called "San Giacometto." An ornate clock-face adorns its *campanile.* Across the *piazza*, a statue called *il Gobbo* (the hunchback) supports the steps; it once served as a podium from which officials made announcements and at whose feet convicted thieves, forced to run naked from P.S. Marco and lashed all the way by bystanders, could finally collapse. *(Vaporetto: "Rialto." Cross the bridge and head right. Church open daily 10am-5pm. Free.)*

AROUND PIAZZA SAN MARCO

▨ **BASILICA DI SAN MARCO.** The crown jewel of Venice is a spectacular fusion of gold and marble that glorifies the *piazza* with its symmetry and frescos. It may be the city's biggest tourist attraction, but St. Mark's is worth the lines. Time your visit for the shortest wait (early morning), or best natural illumination of the interior mosaics and exterior frescos (late afternoon, when the sun is low in the sky).

Construction of the basilica began in the 9th century, when two Venetian merchants stole St. Mark's remains from Alexandria and packed them in pork in order to sneak them past Arab officials. After the first church dedicated to St. Mark burnt down in the 11th century, Venice set out to erect a church that would not only house the Evangelist but also rival the magnificent houses of worship in Rome and Constantinople. During construction, the city snubbed the Roman Catholic Church's standard architectural structure, choosing to build the basilica according to a Greek-cross plan crowned by five bulbous domes.

The interior of the church sparkles with gold mosaics from both the 13th-century Byzantine and 16th-century Renaissance periods. Christ Pantocrator (Ruler of All) sits in judgment above the high altar, surrounded by his Evangelists (note the ever-present winged lion of St. Mark). The visual overload continues on the floor, where magnificent 12th-century cut-stone mosaics loop and whirl around your feet—nine centuries of uneven sinking have given the floor its sea-like waviness. Behind the altar screen, decorated with Renaissance statues of the Apostles, the Virgin Mary, and Mary Magdalene, is the **Pala D'Oro,** a gem-encrusted relief covering the tomb of St. Mark. To the right of the altar is the **Tesoro (treasury),** a hoard of gold and relics from the Fourth Crusade. Steep stairs in the atrium lead to the **Galleria della Basilica,** which offers a staggering perspective on the interior mosaics, a tranquil vista of the *piazza*, and an intimate view of the original bronze *Horses of St. Mark.* (**Basilica** open M-Sa 9am-5pm, Su 1-5pm. Basilica illuminated 11:30am-12:30pm. Dress code enforced; shoulders and knees must be covered. Free. **Pala D'Oro** open M-Sa 9:45am-5pm, Su 2-4:30pm. L3000/€1.55. **Treasury** open M-Sa 9:45am-5pm, Su 2-4:30pm. L4000/€2.07. **Galleria** open daily 9:45am-5pm. L3000/€1.55.)

▨ **PALAZZO DUCALE (DOGE'S PALACE).** Once the home of Venice's mayor, or *doge,* the Palazzo Ducale now houses one of Venice's best museums. Its collection beautifully combines historical artifacts with spectacular artwork. When the city enlarged the palace in 15th century, it maintained the original 14th-century building's graceful, light design (despite opposition from Renaissance architects who claimed the building looked "upside-down"). In the courtyard, Sansovino's enormous sculptures, *Mars* and *Neptune,* flank the *Scala dei Giganti* (Stairs of the Giants), upon which new *doges* would be crowned. Tourists, however, must ascend the less impressive staircase nearby. On the balcony stands the *Bocca di Leone* (Lion's Mouth), a snarling post-box into which citizens could drop denunciations of their naughty neighbors. Within the palace lie the doge's private apartments and the magnificent state rooms of the Republic. Climb the richly decorated

Scala d'Oro (Golden Staircase) to reach the *Sala del Maggior Consiglio* (Great Council Room), dominated by Tintoretto's *Paradise*, the largest oil painting in the world. More stairs lead to the *Sala delle Quattro Porte* (Room of the Four Doors) and the *Sala dell'Anticollegio* (Antechamber of the Senate), decorated with, amongst other things, masterful allegories by Tintoretto. As you catch your breath before continuing, remember the purpose of the pomp and circumstance and the overwhelming abundance of stairs—to force visitors to the Doge to fall on their knees in sweet relief once they finally entered the *Sala Del Collegio* (Senate Chamber). Passages lead through the courtrooms of the much-feared Council of Ten and the even-more-feared Council of Three, crossing the *Ponte dei Sospiri* (Bridge of Sighs) and continuing into the prisons. The infamous Casanova was among those condemned by the Ten to walk across this bridge, which gets its name from the mournful groans of prisoners catching their last glimpses of the world. *(☎041 522 49 51; mkt.musei@comune.venezia.it. Open daily 9am-7pm. Ticket office closes 1½hr. earlier. Includes entrance to Museo Correr, Biblioteca Nazionale Marciana, Museo Archeologico, Museo di Palazzo Mocenigo, Museo del Vetro di Murano, and Museo del Merletto di Burano. Audio guides L7000/€3.62. Wheelchair accessible. L18,000/€9.30, students L10,000/€5.16, ages 6-14 L6000/€3.10.)*

■ **PIAZZA SAN MARCO.** Unlike the narrow, labyrinthine streets that wind through most of Venice, Piazza S. Marco (Venice's only official *piazza*) is a magnificent expanse of light and space. It is also home to half the world's pigeon population. Just like the pesky birds which locals have dubbed "flying rats", tourists flock here; only they come to admire the palatial buildings and the music of outdoor orchestras, rather than eat bread crumbs out of small children's hands. Enclosing the *piazza* are the unadorned 16th-century Renaissance **Procuratie Vecchie (Old Treasury Offices),** the more ornate 17th-century Baroque **Procuratie Nuove (New Treasury Offices),** and the smaller Neoclassical **Ala Napoleonica,** sometimes called the *Procuratie Nuovissime* (Really New Treasury Offices). The **Basilica di San Marco** stands majestically over the open end of the *piazza*.

Between the basilica and the *Procuratie Vecchie* perches the **Torre dell'Orologio (Clock Tower),** constructed between 1496 and 1499 according to Coducci's design. The 24-hour clock indicates the hour, lunar phase, and ascending constellation. The Virgin Mary sits between two 19th-century additions, a revolving panel on the left that displays the hour and one on the right that displays the minutes. Saint Mark's winged lion roars above the Virgin, and every hour two bronze figures (called the two Moors) strike the bell at the top. This time-keeping treasure has been hidden from view for several years now by restoration scaffolding.

The brick **campanile** (bell tower; 96m) across the *piazza* stands on Roman foundations. Originally serving as a watchtower and lighthouse, Venice later took advantage of its location, creating a medieval tourist attraction by dangling state prisoners in cages from its top. Bartolomeo Bon designed the *campanile* in 1511-14, but in a 1902 restoration project, the tower collapsed into a mere pile of bricks. The tower was reconstructed in 1912, with the practical addition of an elevator. Ride up for one of the best aerial views of the city, but expect a 20 minute wait during peak season. *(Campanile open daily 9am-7pm. L10,000/€5.16.)*

■ **CHIESA DI SAN ZACCARIA.** Dedicated to the father of John the Baptist and designed by Coducci (amongst others) in the late 1400s, this Gothic-Renaissance church holds one of the masterpieces of Venetian Renaissance painting, Giovanni Bellini's *Virgin and Child Enthroned with Four Saints*. With rich tones and shadows, it's a prime example of Venetian artists' meticulous attention to detail. *(Vaporetto: "S. Zaccaria." From P.S. Marco, turn left along the water, cross the bridge, and turn left under the sottoportego. ☎041 522 12 57. Open daily 10am-noon and 4-6pm. Free.)*

SMALL MUSEUMS. Beneath the arcade at the short end of P.S. Marco lies the entrance to a trio of museums. The **Museo Civico Correr** contains artifacts from Venice's imperial past and curiosities of Venetian life such as platform shoes worn by sequestered noblewomen. There is also an art gallery that includes Carpaccio's

Courtesans (now thought to depict bored noblewomen apparently trapped inside by their footwear) and several works by members of the Bellini family. Ancient Greek and Roman sculpture stands in the **Museo Archeologico**. Paintings by Veronese, Titian, and Tintoretto adorn the main reading room of the **Biblioteca Nazionale Marciana**. *(☎041 241 10 58; mkt.musei@comune.venezia.it. Open daily 9am-7pm. Ticket office closes 1½hr. before closing. L18,000/€9.30, students L10,000/€5.16. Includes entrance to Palazzo Ducale, Museo Vetrario di Murano, and Museo del Merletto di Burano.)*

SAN POLO

BASILICA DI SANTA MARIA GLORIOSA DEI FRARI (I FRARI). The Franciscans started construction on this enormous Gothic church in 1330. Now, two paintings by Titian as well as the Renaissance master himself lie within the cathedral's cavernous terra-cotta walls. His ◼*Assumption* (1516-18) on the high altar marks the height of the Venetian Renaissance. Like contemporary Roman and Florentine painters Titian created balanced, harmonious compositions, while adding the Venetian love of color and sensuality. Titian's other work, the *Madonna and Child with Saints and Members of the Pesaro Family* (1547) is on the right as you enter. The work is revolutionary due to Titian's unorthodox placement of the Virgin Mary and Child to the right of center and his depiction of the Madonna's realistic, humble facial expression. Titian's elaborate tomb, a triumphal arch, stands diagonally across from the Pesaro altar and directly across from the enormous pyramid in which the sculptor Canova (1757-1822) rests. An extraordinary work by Bellini, *Virgin and Child with Saints Nicholas, Peter, Benedict, and Mark* (1488) hangs in the sacristy. In the Florentine chapel to the right of the high altar is Donatello's *St. John the Baptist* (1438), a wooden sculpture. *(Vaporetto: "S. Tomà." Follow signs back to Campo dei Frari. Open M-Sa 9am-6pm, Su 1-6pm. L3000/€1.55.)*

◼ **SCUOLA GRANDE DI SAN ROCCO.** Venice's most illustrious *scuola*, or guild hall, stands as a monument to Jacopo Tintoretto. The painter, who left Venice only once in his 76-year life (and refused to take that trip without his wife), set out to combine "the color of Titian with the drawing of Michelangelo." To achieve effects of depth, he often built dioramas in which he placed models so that he could portray the figures with spatial accuracy. The *scuola* commissioned Tintoretto to complete all of the paintings in the building, a task that took 23 years. The *Crucifixion* in the last room upstairs is the building's crowning glory. Brandishing intricately carved columns and richly colored marble, the *scuola* is itself quite a masterpiece. If you step outside to admire it, you will often find street musicians performing classical music in the *campo. (Behind Basilica dei Frari in Campo S. Rocco. ☎041 523 48 64. Open daily 9-5:30pm. Ticket office closes 30min. earlier. L10,000/€5.16, students L7000/€3.62, under 18 free. Audio guides free.)*

CAMPO SAN POLO. The second largest *campo* in Venice (only P.S. Marco is larger), S. Polo once hosted bull-baiting matches. A painting depicting the ensuing chaos hangs in the Museo Correr in P.S. Marco. Today its benches, trees, and frolicking children give the field a relaxed quality. *(Between the Frari and Rialto Bridge. Vaporetto: "S. Silvestro." Straight back from the vaporetto. Or from in front of the Frari, cross the bridge and turn right, then left on Rio Terà, right on Calle Seconda d. Saoneri, and left at the dead end.)*

DORSODURO

◼ **GALLERIE DELL'ACCADEMIA.** This gallery houses the most extensive collection of Venetian art in the world. Room I, topped by a ceiling full of cherubim, houses Venetian Gothic art, whose luxurious use of color continued to influence Venetian painting for centuries. Among the enormous altarpieces in Room II, Giovanni Bellini's *Madonna Enthroned with Child, Saints, and Angels* stands out for its lush serenity. Rooms IV and V display more Bellinis, including the magnificent *Madonna and Child with the Magdalene and Saint Catherine*, and two works by Giorgione. Giorgione defied contemporary convention by creating works that were neither biblical nor allegorical. In the *Tempest*, his most famous piece, no story is immediately apparent, and attempts to analyze the relationship between the two figures have proved puzzling—X-rays have revealed that Giorgione originally painted a woman bathing where the young man now stands. Other Venetian Renaissance works line the rooms leading to Room X, home to Veronese's colossal *Supper in the House of Levi*. Painted as a Last Supper, the work enraged leaders of the Inquisition with its indulgent improvisation—a Protestant German, a midget, and bloody-nosed servants mingle with the more biblically orthodox guests. On the wall facing the entrance hang several Tintorettos, many of which display the artist's virtuosity at painting swooping, diving figures. On the opposite wall is Titian's last painting, a *Pietà* intended for his tomb. In Room XX, works by Gentile Bellini and Carpaccio display Venetian processions and cityscapes so accurately that scholars use them as "photos" of Venice's past. *(Vaporetto: "Accademia." ☎ 041 522 22 47. Open M 8:15am-2pm, T-Su 9:15am-7:15pm. Ticket office closes ½hr. earlier. L12,000/€8.26. Guided tours L10,000/€5.16.)*

⊠ COLLEZIONE PEGGY GUGGENHEIM. Ms. Guggenheim's elegant, water-front Palazzo Venier dei Leoni, once a gathering place for the world's artistic elite, now displays her collection to the public. This modern art museum includes wonderful and eclectic works by Brancusi, Marini, Kandinsky, Picasso, Magritte, Rothko, Ernst, Pollock, and Dalí. In the peaceful sculpture garden, the late Ms. Guggenheim and her treasures (including 14 well-loved Shih Tzu dogs) are buried. The Marini sculpture *Angel in the City*, which stands triumphantly in front of the *palazzo*, was designed with a detachable penis. Ms. Guggenheim occasionally modified this sculpture so as not to offend her more prudish guests. The courtyard offers unobstructed views of the Grand Canal. *(Calle S. Cristoforo, Dorsoduro, 701. Vaporetto: "Accademia." Turn left and follow the yellow signs. ☎ 041 240 54 11; fax 520 68 85. Open M and W-F 10am-6pm, Sa 10am-10pm. L10,000/€5.16, ISIC or Rolling Venice L8000/ €4.13, under 10 free. Audio guides L8000/€4.13.)*

CHIESA DI SANTA MARIA DELLA SALUTE. The theatrical Salute, poised at the tip of Dorsoduro, is a prime example of the Venetian Baroque, a style designed to pull the spectator into the space and make him central to the architecture. In 1631, the city commissioned Longhena to build the church for the Virgin (who they believed would return the favor by ending the plague). These days, Venice celebrates the third Sunday of November by building a wooden pontoon bridge across the Canal and lighting candles in the church (see **Entertainment**, p. 222). Next to the Salute stands the **Dogana**, the old customs house, where ships sailing into Venice were required to stop and pay appropriate duties. ⊠Upon leaving the *dogana*, (walk along the *fondamenta* to the tip of Dorsoduro) a marvelous view of the city awaits you, assuming you can pick your way through the sunbathers and embracing couples. *(Vaporetto: "Salute." ☎ 041 522 55 58. Open daily 9am-noon and 3-5:30pm. The inside of the Dogana is closed to the public. Free. Entrance to sacristy with donation.)*

SQUERO DI SAN TROVASO. The oldest of the three remaining gondola shipyards in Venice (built in the 17th century), this *squero* displays the boats in various stages of development (and decay). The buildings are in the style of Cadore mountain dwellings. (Cadore is the region the craftsmen who made the boats came from, as well as the source for the wood used to make them.) To see the gondolas-in-progress if the main door is closed, cross the canal and look into the back of the yard. *(Vaporetto: "Zattere." Go up Fond. Nani where you'll see the boats and cross the 1st bridge to reach the entrance on Campo S. Trovaso. Open sporadically. Free.)*

CHIESA DI SAN SEBASTIANO. Veronese, the Renaissance painter, took refuge in this 16th-century church when he fled Verona in 1555 after reputedly killing a man. By 1565 he had filled the church with an amazing cycle of paintings and frescoes. His breathtaking *Stories of Queen Esther* covers the ceiling, while the man himself rests in peace under the gravestone by the organ. *(Vaporetto: "S. Basilio." Continue straight ahead. Open M-Sa 10am-5pm, Su 3-5pm. L3000/€1.55.)*

CÀ REZZONICO. Longhena's great 18th-century Venetian palace hosts the **Museo del Settecento Veneziano (Museum of 18th-Century Venice).** The museum details notorious intrigues and love affairs. Frothy works by Tiepolo, Guardi, and Longhi hang upstairs. *(Vaporetto: "Cà Rezzonico." Go straight into Campo S. Barnaba, take the 1st bridge on the right, and turn right on Fond. Rezzonico. ☎ 041 241 85 06. Currently closed for restoration.)*

CASTELLO

CHIESA DI SANTISSIMI GIOVANNI E PAOLO (SAN ZANIPOLO). Termed the "pantheon of Venetian nobility", this immense church is the final resting place of 25 doges and home of the monuments to them. Other honored citizens' monuments also line the walls. The outside of the terra-cotta structure is Gothic by design, but a harmonious Renaissance-styled portal, with an arch supported by columns of Greek marble, keeps the menacing enormity of this burial ground in check. On the right as you enter stands a gory relief depicting the agonizing death of Marcantonio Bragadin. Bragadin valiantly defended Cyprus from the Turks in 1571 only to be skinned alive after surrendering—his skin now rests in the little urn above the monument. Next to Bragadin is an altarpiece by Giovanni Bellini, showing St. Christopher, Sebastian, and Vincent Ferrar. Off the left transept is the **Cappella del Rosario.** After a fire destroyed the chapel in 1867, works by Veronese were brought in to replace the lost paintings. Outside the church stands the bronze equestrian **statue of Bartolomeo Colleoni,** a mercenary who left his inheritance to the city on the condition that a monument to him be erected in front of S. Marco. The city, unwilling to honor anyone in such a grand space, decided to place the statue in front of the Scuola di S. Marco, thus satisfying the will, leaving P.S. Marco clear for pigeons, and keeping the money. The statue was designed in 1479 by da Vinci's teacher, the Florentine Verrochio. *(Vaporetto: "Fond. Nuove." Turn left and then right onto Fond. dei Mendicanti. ☎ 041 523 59 13. Open M-Sa 7:30am-12:30pm and 3:30-7pm, Su 3-6pm. Free)*

CHIESA DI SANTA MARIA DEI MIRACOLI. The Lombardos designed this Renaissance jewel in the late 1400s, and it remains one of the prettiest churches in Venice, elegantly faced with polychrome marble and inside brimming with lavish color, gold reliefs, and sculpted figures. *(From S.S. Giovanni e Paolo, cross Ponte Rosse continue straight. Open M-Sa 10am-5pm, Su 1-5pm. L3000/€1.55.)*

SCUOLA DALMATA SAN GIORGIO DEGLI SCHIAVONI. Inside this modest early 16th-century building of now blackened stone, Carpaccio decorated the ground floor with some of his finest paintings, depicting episodes from the lives of St. George, Jerome, and Tryfon. *(Castello, 3259/A. Vaporetto: S. Zaccaria. Turn right off the boat, then turn left on Calle d. Pietà, right on Sal. dei Greci, and left on Fond. d. Furlani. ☎ 041 522 88 28. Open Apr.-Oct. Tu-Sa 9:30am-12:30pm and 3:30-6:30pm, Su 9:30am-12:30pm; Nov.-Mar. Tu-Sa 10am-12:30pm and 3-6pm, Su 10am-12:30pm. Shoulders and knees must be covered. L5000/€2.58, Rolling Venice L3000/€1.55.)*

GIARDINI PUBLICI AND SANT'ELENA. Longing for trees and grass? Stroll through the Public Gardens, installed by Napoleon, or bring a picnic lunch to the shady lawns of Sant'Elena. *(Vaporetto: "Giardini" or "S. Elena." Free.)*

CANNAREGGIO

JEWISH GHETTO. In 1516, the Doge forced Venice's Jewish population into the old cannon-foundry area, creating the first Jewish ghetto in Europe. (Ghetto is the Venetian word for foundry.) While only 30 Jews live here today, the Ghetto at its height housed 5000. To accommodate all these people, the buildings reached as high as seven stories—they were among the tallest tenements in Europe at the time. The oldest synagogue, or *schola*, the **Schola Grande Tedesca (German Synagogue)** shares a building with the **Museo Ebraica di Venezia (Hebrew Museum of Venice)** in the Campo del Ghetto Nuovo. In the adjoining Campiello d. Scuole stand the opulent **Schola Levantina (Levantine Synagogue)** and the **Schola Spagnola (Spanish Synagogue),** both at least partially designed by Longhena. *(Cannaregio, 2899/B.*

Vaporetto: S. Marcuola. Follow the signs straight ahead and then turn left into Campo del Ghetto Nuovo. ☎ 041 71 53 59. Hebrew Museum. Open June-Sept. Su-F 10am-7pm; Oct.-May Su-F 10am-4:30pm. Ticket office closes 30min. earlier. L5000/€2.58, students L3000/€1.55. Entrance to synagogues by guided tour only (40min). English tours leave from the museum every hr. on the half-hour. Museum and tour L12,000/€6.20, students L9000/€4.65.)

CA' D'ORO AND GALLERIA GIORGIO FRANCHETTI. The most spectacular facade on the Grand Canal and the premiere example of the Venetian Gothic, the Ca' d'Oro, built between 1425 and 1440, now houses the Giorgio Franchetti collection. Highlights include Andrea Mantegna's *Saint Sebastian*, the last example of a subject that Mantegna frequently portrayed, and Bonaccio's *Apollo Belvedere*, one of the most important bronzes of the 15th century. ☒For the best view of the Ca' D'Oro's "wedding cake" facade, take the *traghetto* across the canal to the Rialto Markets. *(Vaporetto: "Ca' d'Oro." ☎ 041 522 23 49. Open M 8:15am-2pm, T-Sa 8:15am-7pm. Ticket office closes 30min. earlier. L6000/€3.10.)*

CHIESA SANTA MARIA ASSUNTA (CHIESA DEI GESUITI). A flowing, tumbling, whirling mass of green and white marble awaits within this extravagant 18th-century church, capped by an equally lavish Baroque facade (its gilded stucco work is unparalleled in Venice). Titian's *Martyrdom of Saint Lawrence* hangs in the altar to the left as you enter the church. *(Vaporetto: "Fond. Nuove"; turn right and then left on Sal. dei Specchieri. ☎ 041 623 16 10. Open daily 10am-noon and 4-6pm.)*

CHIESA DELLA MADONNA DELL'ORTO. Tintoretto painted some of his most moving works for his parish church, another quintessential example of Venetian Gothic architecture. Inside, gaping wood ceilings accommodate ten of his largest paintings. By the high altar hang his *Last Judgment*, a spatially intense mass of souls, and *The Sacrifice of the Golden Calf*. On the right apse is Tintoretto's splendidly colored *Presentation of the Virgin at the Temple*. *(Vaporetto: Madonna dell'Orto. Open M-Sa 10am-5pm, Su 1-5pm. L3000/€1.55. A light switch for illuminating the works is at each of the far corners.)*

SAN GIORGIO MAGGIORE AND GIUDECCA

BASILICA DI SAN GIORGIO MAGGIORE. Standing on its own monastic island, S. Giorgio Maggiore contrasts sharply with most other Venetian churches. Palladio ignored the Venetian fondness for color and decorative excess and constructed an austere church. Light fills the enormous open space inside, although it unfortunately does not hit Tintoretto's *Last Supper* by the high altar; you'll have to put L500/€0.20 in the light box if you want to see the wraith-like angels hovering over Christ's table. The beautiful nearby courtyard, to the right of the church, is closed to the public, but Palladio's harmonious design is visible through the gates. Ascend the elevator to the top of the **campanile** for a marvelous view of the city. *(Vaporetto: "S. Giorgio Maggiore." ☎ 041 522 78 27. Open M-Sa 10am-12:30pm and 2:30-4:30pm. Basilica free. Campanile L5000/€2.58. Pay the Brother in the elevator.)*

TEMPIO DEL SS. REDENTORE. Palladio's true religious masterpiece, this longitudinally immense Renaissance church, like the Salute, commemorates a deal that Venice struck with God to end a plague. Every year the city still celebrates with a fireworks display. Paintings by Veronese and Bassano hang in the sacristy. *(Vaporetto: "Redentore." Ask to enter the sacristy. Open M-Sa 10am-5pm, Su 1-5pm. L3000/€1.55.)*

ISLANDS OF THE LAGOON

☒**BURANO.** In this traditional fishing village, fishermen haul in their catch every morning, and little, old, black-clad widows sit in the doorways of the fantastically colored houses, creating unique knots of Venetian lace. See their handiwork in the small **Scuola di Merletti di Burano (Lace Museum).** *(A 40min. boat ride from Venice. Vaporetto #12: "Burano" from either "S. Zaccaria" or "Fond. Nuove." Museum in P. Galuppi. ☎ 041 73 00 34. Open W-M 10am-5pm. L8000/€4.13. Included on combined Palazzo Ducale ticket.)*

MURANO. Famous for its glass since 1292 (when Venice's artisans were forced off Venice proper because their kilns started fires) the island of Murano affords visitors the opportunity to witness the glass-blowing process. Near the station or P.S. Marco, Murano glass vendors masquerading as salty sea dogs will try to sell you a ticket to see the glass demonstrations, but if you ride the *vaporetto* out there yourself, they're free. Look for signs directing you toward *fornace*, concentrated near the "Colona", "Faro", and "Navagero" *vaporetto* stops. The speed and grace of these artisans will leave you in awe, but demonstrations are often few and far between. Shop around, and try to time your visit to a *fornace* with the arrival of a group tour. The **Museo Vetrario (Glass Museum)** houses a splendid collection that includes pieces from Roman times. Farther down the street stands the exceptional 12th-century **Basilica di Santa Maria e San Donato.** Much like the famed warlord Gingivitis, Saint Donatus killed a dragon by spitting on it, and the saintly bones are on display in the apse. *(Vaporetto #12 or 52: "Faro" from either "S. Zaccaria" or "Fond. Nuove." **Museo Vetrario,** Fond. Giustian, 8. ☎ 041 73 95 86. Open Th-Tu 10am-5pm. Ticket office closes 30min. earlier. L8000/€4.13, students L5000/€2.58. Included on combined Palazzo Ducale ticket. **Basilica** ☎ 041 73 90 56. Open daily 8am-noon and 4-7pm.)*

TORCELLO. Torcello, a safe haven for early fishermen fleeing barbarians on the mainland, was the most powerful island of the lagoon before Venice usurped its inhabitants and its glory. Now, barring a few snack bars, it is pleasantly deserted and covered with lush vegetation. Its cathedral, **Santa Maria Assunta,** contains 11th- and 12th-century mosaics depicting the Last Judgment and the Virgin Mary. The *campanile* affords splendid views of the outer lagoon. *(A 45min. boat ride from Venice. Vaporetto #12: "Torcello" from either "S. Zaccaria" or "Fond. Nuove." Cathedral ☎ 041 73 00 84. Open daily 10:30am-12:30pm and 2-6:30pm. L4000/€2.07.)*

LIDO. The Lido is the setting for Thomas Mann's unforgettable *Death in Venice* (and Visconti's equally unforgettable film version), which gives a vivid impression of the sensuality and mystery for which Venice is famous. The Lido is now more of a summer beach town, full of cars, blaring radios, and beach bums. Lovers of the Belle Epoque will enjoy a visit to the fabled **Grand Hôtel des Bains,** Lungomare Marconi, 17. (Breakfast L70,000/€36.15. Singles up to L740,000/€382.18; doubles up to L1,100,000/€568.10.) If you are desperate for a dunking, yank off your sneakers at the end of Gran V.S. Maria Elisabetta, and head to the not-so-clean **public beach,** which features an impressive shipwreck at one end. *(Vaporetto: Lido.)*

ISOLA DI SAN MICHELE. Venice's cemetery island, S. Michele, is home to Codussi's tiny Chiesa di S. Michele in Isola (1469), the first Renaissance church in Venice). Entrance to the cyprus-lined grounds is gained through the church's right-hand portal, over which sits a relief depicting St. Michael slaying the dragon. Poet, Fascist sympathizer, and enemy of the state, Ezra Pound, was laid to rest here in the Protestant cemetery; as were Russian composer Igor Stravinsky and Russian choreographer Sergei Diaghilev. Both are found in the Orthodox cemetery. *(Vaporetto: "Cimitero", from "Fond. Nuove." Church and cemetery open Apr.-Sept. daily 7:30am-6pm; Oct.-Mar. daily 7:30am-4pm. Free.)*

🎵 ENTERTAINMENT

The weekly booklet **A Guest in Venice,** free at hotels and tourist offices or online at www.unospitedivenezia.it, lists current festivals, concerts, and gallery shows.

Venice swoons for **orchestral music,** from the outdoor chamber orchestras in P.S. Marco to costumed concerts. **Vivaldi,** who was once a choirmaster in the Chiesa di S. Maria della Pietà (a few blocks along the waterfront from P.S. Marco), continues to haunt Venice. His music, mostly *The Four Seasons,* can be heard almost nightly in the summer and regularly during the winter. For information, talk to anyone wearing period costume scattered throughout town. (Try Calle Larga Mazzini near the Rialto Bridge, the Ponte della Paglia near P.S. Marco, or Campo della Carità in front of the Accademia. Tickets L15-40,000/€7.75-20.66.) The grand opera **Teatro La Fenice** burned down in January 1996, but is scheduled to reopen soon; try the summer opera series in nearby Verona (p. 238).

The 2000-2001 season at **Teatro Goldoni,** Calle del Teatro, S. Marco 4650/B (☎041 520 54 22 or 041 240 2011; teatrogoldini@libero.it), near the Rialto Bridge, showcases *commedia dell'arte* plays; even non-Italian speakers will appreciate this native Italian artform. The **Mostra Internazionale di Cinema (Venice International Film Festival),** held annually from late August to early September, draws such luminaries as Steven Spielberg. Movies are shown in the original language. Tickets (☎041 520 03 11) start at L35,000/€18.08 and are sold throughout the city. Some late-night outdoor showings are free. Otherwise, Venice's main cinemas, the **Accademia,** Calle Gambara, Dorsoduro, 1019 (☎041 528 77 06), right of the museum; the **Ritz,** S. Marco 617 (☎041 520 44 29), near P.S. Marco; and **Rossini,** S. Marco, 3988 (☎041 523 03 22), off Campo Manin, rarely show original-language films.

The famed **Biennale di Venezia** (☎041 521 18 98; www.labiennale.org), a worldwide contemporary art exhibition, drowns the *Giardini Publici* and the Arsenal every odd-numbered year in its displays of provocative international art.

Mark Twain may have derided the **gondola** as "an inky, rusty canoe," but even still it's a canoe only the gentry can afford. The minimum authorized rate, which increases after sunset, starts at L120,000/€62 per group for 50 minutes. Rides are most romantic if taken about 50 minutes before sunset and almost affordable if shared by six people. The rate that a gondolier quotes is negotiable and the most bargain-able gondoliers are those standing by themselves rather than those in groups at the "taxi-stands" throughout the city. Venice was built to be traveled by gondola, and admiring the front doors of houses and *palazzi* via their original pathways is an experience only a gondola can afford (*Let's Go* doesn't recommend swimming). For a quick and affordable taste of a gondola ride, try one of the city's *traghetti,* ferry gondolas that cross the Grand Canal at six points. Each trip lasts only a minute, but this stand-up style of transportation only cost L700/€0.36 (and when you show people your photos, who'll know the difference?).

In absentia for several centuries, Venice's famous **Carnevale** was successfully reinstated in the early 1970s. During the 10 days before Ash Wednesday, masked figures and camera-happy tourists jam the streets, and outdoor concerts and street performances spring up throughout the city. On Mardi Gras, the population of the city doubles. Write to the tourist office in January for details, and be sure to make lodging arrangements well in advance. Venice's second-most colorful festival is the **Festa del Redentore** (3rd Sunday in July), originally held to celebrate the end of a 16th-century plague. The city kicks off the festival with a magnificent fireworks display at 11:30pm the night before. The next day the military builds a bridge across the Giudecca Canal, connecting Il Redentore to the Zattere. On the 1st Saturday in September, Venice stages its classic **regata storica,** a gondola race down the Grand Canal. During the religious **Festa della Salute** (3rd Sunday in November), which also originated as a celebration of the end of a plague, the city celebrates with another pontoon bridge, this time over the Grand Canal.

Finally, be wary of **shopping** in the heavily touristed P.S. Marco or around the Rialto Bridge. Shops outside these areas often have better quality products and greater selection for about half the price. Interesting clothing, glass, and mask boutiques line the streets leading from the Rialto Bridge to Campo S. Polo and Strada Nuova and from the Rialto Bridge toward the station. The map accompanying the Rolling Venice card lists many shops that offer discounts to card holders. The most concentrated and varied selections of Venetian glass and lace require trips to the nearby islands of Murano (p. 222) and Burano (p. 221) respectively.

⛴ NIGHTLIFE

Venetian nightlife is quieter and more relaxed than other major Italian cities. For most locals, nighttime action means an evening spent sipping wine or beer rather than gyrating in a disco. Of course, one distinct nightlife option remains a moonlit ride down the Grand Canal on the good ole' #82. Alternatively, a 10pm stroll among the string quartets set up in P.S. Marco is a treat for the ears. Student nightlife is concentrated around **Campo Santa Margherita** in Dorsoduro (Il Caffè, Café Blue, and Bar Salus, below) and the areas around **Fondamenta della Misericordia** in Cannaregio (Paradiso Perduto and Cantina Vecia Carbonera, below).

■ **Paradiso Perduto,** Fondamenta della Misericordia, 2540 (☎041 72 05 81). From Strada Nuova, cross Campo S. Fosca, cross bridge, and continue in same direction, crossing 2 more bridges. Students and locals flood this unassuming bar with conversation and laughter, while the young, casually dressed waitstaff doles out large portions of *cichetti* (mixed plate L22,000/€11.36). Live jazz Su 9pm. Open Th-Su 7pm-2am.

Inishark Irish Pub, Calle Mondo Novo, Castello, 5787 (☎041 523 53 00), between Campo S. Maria Formosa and Salizzada S. Lio. Most creative Irish pub in Venice. Admire the themed decorations as you throw back a pint or 2. Guinness, L9000/€4.65; Harp L8000/€4.13. Open Tu-Su 6pm-1:30am.

Il Caffè, Campo S. Margherita, Dorsoduro, 2963 (☎041 528 79 98), also known as **Bar Rosso.** Upright piano, samovar, and peeling stucco give interior end-of-an-era feel. Outdoor seating. *Vino* L1500/€.77; *birra* L5000/€2.58. Open M-Sa 8am-2am.

Bacaro Jazz, Campo S. Bartolmeo, S. Marco, 5546 (☎041 52 85 249). From post office, follow red lights and sounds of jazz across the street. At this chic restaurant and evening haunt, 20- and 30-somethings share big plates of *cichetti* (L25,000/€12.91). Jazz paraphernalia lines wood-panelled walls. Drinks more affordable during happy hours, 2-7:30pm, when beer is L5000/€2.58, *sangria* L4000/€2.07. Open Th-Tu 11am-2am.

Café Blue, Calle Lunga S. Pantalon, Dorsoduro, 3778 (☎041 71 02 27). From Campo S. Margherita, cross bridge at narrow end of *piazza,* wind around church, and turn left at dead end. Bright, noisy, and crowded. American bar with droves of expats and exchange students. Free email kiosk (available 8pm-2am). Afternoon tea 3:30-7:30pm, bar 9:30pm-2am, all drinks half price 8:30-9:30pm. Open M-Sa.

Cantina Vecchia Carbonera, Strada Nuova, Cannaregio, 2329 (☎041 71 03 76). Wonderfully warm hole-in-the-wall. Try the *cantina* around mid-day if you want to chat up the 60 and over establishment. Extensive wine selection (L2000-3500/€1.03-1.81) and traditional *ciccichetti* (L2500/€1.29). Open Tu-F 10am-11pm, Sa-Su 10am-1am.

Bar Santa Lucia, Lista di Spagna, Cannareggio 282/B (☎041 524 28 80), near the train station. This tiny bar stays crowded and noisy long into the night with American travelers and the locals who want to meet them. Good selection of Irish beers. Guinness L1000/€.52, *vino* L4000/€2.07. Open M-Sa 6pm-2am.

Casanova, Lista di Spagna, Cannaregio, 158/A (☎041 275 01 99; www.casanova.it). If you're starved for a *discoteca,* join the slinkily dressed crowd at Casanova, and let modern-day Latin lovers show you their moves. Unfortunately, clubbing just isn't Venice's *forte.* You might want to follow the original Casanova's precedent and make a daring early escape. Themes and cover charge change nightly, from alternative to Latin to house music. Open daily 10pm-4am. AmEx/MC/V.

Veneto
and Friuli-
Venezia Giulia

NORTHEAST ITALY

THE VENETO

From the rocky foothills of the Dolomites to the fertile valleys of the Po River, the Veneto region has a geography as diverse as its historical influences. Once loosely linked under the Venetian Empire, these towns retained their cultural independence, and visitors are more likely to hear regional dialects than standard Italian when neighbors gossip across their geranium-bedecked windows. Culinary influences marched in with the Austrians and swim in with the day's catch. The sense of local culture and custom that remains strong within each town may surprise visitors lured to the area by Venice, the *bella* of the north.

PADUA (PADOVA)   ☎049

Padua blends university culture with high culture—book-toting students walk through sculpture-lined *piazze*, cultivating an air of liberal individualism. Though devastated by the Lombard invasion of 602, the city wasted no time becoming one of Europe's intellectual hubs. The university, founded in 1222, is second in seniority only to Bologna's. Luminaries such as Dante, Petrarch, Galileo, Copernicus, Mantegna, Giotto, and Donatello all contributed to the city's reputation as a center of learning. Bubbling with student activity, Padua makes a worthy pilgrimage.

⌐ TRANSPORTATION

Padua's location on the Venice-Milan and Venice-Bologna train lines and the availability of intercity buses make the city a convenient stop on any Italian itinerary.

Trains: In P. Stazione, at the northern end of C. del Popolo, the continuation of C. Garibaldi. Open 5am-midnight. Luggage storage available (p. 227). To: **Bologna** (1½hr.; 1-2 per hr. 4:22am-10:41pm; L21,000/€10.85); **Milan** (2½hr.; 1-2 per hr. 5:49am-11pm; L20-31,500/€10.33-16.27); **Venice** (30min., 3-4 per hr. 4:42am-11pm, L4100/€2.12); **Verona** (1hr., 1-2 per hr. 5:49am-11pm, L7900/€4.08).

Buses: SITA, P. Boschetti (☎049 820 68 11). From train station, walk down C. del Popolo, turn left on V. Trieste, and turn right at V. Porciglia. Open M-Th 8:30am-1pm and 3-6:30pm, F 8:30am-1pm and 3-5:30pm. To: **Bassano del Grappa** (1¼hr., 2 per hr., L7100/€3.67); **Montagnana** (1hr., 1-2 per hr., L6100/€3.15); **Venice** (45min., 2 per hr., L5300/€2.74); **Vicenza** (1hr., 2 per hr., L5400/€2.79).

Local Buses: ACAP (☎049 824 11 11) buses #8, 12, and 18 run downtown. Buy regular tickets (L1600/€0.83) or 24hr. tickets (L5000/€2.58) at train station.

Taxis: Radio Taxi (☎049 65 13 33). Available 24hr.

Car Rental: Europcar, P. Stazione, 6 (☎049 875 85 90). 21+. L140,000/€72.30 per day, L518,000/€267.52 per week. Open M-F 8:30am-12:30pm and 3 7:30pm, Sa 8:30am-12:30pm. MC/V. **Maggiore Budget,** P. Stazione, 15bis (☎049 875 28 52). Must have license for 1 yr. L116-153,000/€56.91-79.02 per day, L580,000/€299.55 per week. Prices increase for automatic transmission or A/C and vary when booked overseas. Open M-F 8:30am-12:30pm and 2:30-6:30pm, Sa 9am-noon.

◄▮ ORIENTATION AND PRACTICAL INFORMATION

The train station is at the northern edge of town, outside the 16th-century walls. A 10-minute walk down **Corso del Popolo,** which becomes **Corso Garibaldi,** leads to the heart of town. A pedestrian area spans the old university campus, the **duomo,** and the **le Piazze** (P. della Frutta, P. dei Signori, and P. delle Erbe). **V. del Santo** leads south to the **Basilica di Sant'Antonio,** the cathedral of Padua's patron, St. Anthony.

TOURIST, FINANCIAL, AND LOCAL SERVICES

Tourist Office: (☎049 875 20 77; fax 875 50 88), in the train station. Maps, festival info, and pamphlets. Has hotel listings but does not make reservations. English spoken. Open M-Sa 9:15am-7pm, Su 9am-12:15pm. Smaller **branch** (☎049 875 30 87), in P.

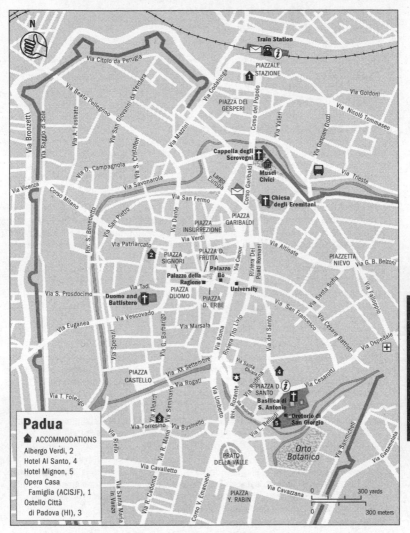

Padua

🏠 ACCOMMODATIONS
Albergo Verdi, 2
Hotel Al Santo, 4
Hotel Mignon, 5
Opera Casa
  Famiglia (ACISJF), 1
Ostello Città
  di Padova (HI), 3

del Santo, near the basilica. Across the street to the right, when facing away from the basilica. Open M-Sa 9am-6pm, Su 9:30am-12:30pm.

Budget Travel: CTS, Riviera Mugnai, 22 (☎049 876 16 39), near the post office. Student IDs and train tickets. Open M-F 9am-12:30pm and 4-7:30pm, Sa 9am-12:30pm.

English-Language Bookstore: Feltrinelli International, V.S. Francesco, 14 (☎049 875 07 92), just passed Riviera dei Ponti Romani. Novels and travel guides in English. Open M-F 9am-7:30pm, Sa 9am-1pm and 3:30-7:30pm.

Laundromat: Fastclean, V. Ognissanti, 6 (☎049 77 57 59), near the Porta Portello. Take bus #9. Self-service. L12,000/€6.20 per 1-4kg. Open M-F 9am-12:30pm and 3:15-7:15pm, Sa 9am-12:30pm.

Luggage Storage: At the train station. L5000/€2.58 per 12hr.

EMERGENCY AND COMMUNICATIONS

Emergency: ☎ 112 or 113. **Ambulance:** ☎ 118.

Police: Carabinieri (☎ 049 21 21 21), on Prato della Valle.

Hospital: Ospedale Civile, V. Giustiniani, 1 (☎ 049 821 11 11), off V.S. Francesco.

Post Office: C. Garibaldi, 33 (☎ 049 820 85 11). Open M-Sa 8:10am-7pm. **Branch** at train station. Open M-F 8:10am-1:30pm, Sa 8:10am-12:30pm.

Postal Code: 35100.

▐ ACCOMMODATIONS & CAMPING

Padua is overflowing with cheap lodgings, but they fill up quickly. Summer housing for men is offered at **Antonianum,** V. Donatello, 24. (☎ 049 876 87 11. Reserve ahead in summer. Open Aug.-Oct. 92 beds. L30,000/€15.50 per person.) The castle-hostel in **Montagnana** (see p. 231) is out of the way but unbeatable.

Ostello Città di Padova (HI), V. Aleardi, 30 (☎ 049 875 22 19; fax 65 42 10; pdyhtl@tin.it), near Prato della Valle. Take bus #18 from train station to the stop after Prato della Valle. Walk 2 blocks, make a right on V. Marin, then around a church, take a left onto V. Torresino, and the sign will come into view. Make a right onto V. Aleardi. The hostel is on left. Many amenities—soda and coffee machines, reading room, phones, Internet (L165/€0.10 per min.), laundry (L8000/€4.13), and a TV room. Well-used, but kept fairly clean. "Point and shoot" squatter-style toilets. Wheelchair accessible. Breakfast, sheets, and shower included. Towels L2000/€1.03. Register and store bags M-F after 2:30pm, Sa-Su after 4pm. Reception 7-9:30am and 2:30-11pm. Room lockout 9:30am-4pm. Shower and common rooms after 2:30pm. Curfew 11pm. Reserve 1 week in advance. 16-bed dorms L24,000/€12.39, L23,000/€11.88 for 5 or more nights L22,000/€11.36; 4- to 5-bed dorms L27,000/€13.94.

Hotel Al Santo, V. del Santo, 147 (☎ 049 875 21 31; fax 978 80 76), near the basilica. 16 airy, well-kept rooms above a cozy restaurant with phone and shower. Breakfast L10,000/€5.16. Open Feb. to mid-Dec. Singles L65,000/€33.57; doubles L105,000/ €54.23; triples L150,000/€77.47. MC/V.

Hotel Mignon, V. Belludi, 22 (☎ 049 66 17 22; fax 66 12 21), on a lively street near the basilica, just off Prato della Valle (between it and P. del Santo). Sitting room with armchairs and oriental rugs and large, basic rooms upstairs. 20 rooms, all with bath, TV, A/ C, and phone. Doubles L110,000/€56.81; triples L130,000/€67.14; quads L155,000/€80.05. MC/V.

Opera Casa Famiglia (ACISJF), V. Nino Bixio, 4 (☎ 049 875 15 54), off P. Stazione. Leave station, walk to right, and turn left on the street just before Hotel Monaco. Women under 30 only. Study and kitchen open at night. 36 beds. Curfew 10:30pm. Modern and tidy doubles, triples, and quads L30,000/€15.50 per bed.

Albergo Verdi, V. Dondi dall'Orologio, 7 (☎ 049 875 57 44), in a central location. Just off of P. Capitaniato, beside the University. 14 large, comfortable rooms. Bath on the same floor as the rooms. Reserve ahead in summer. Singles L44,000/€22.72; doubles L67,000/€34.60; triples L85,000/€43.90.

Camping: Montegrotto Terme, V. Roma, 123/125 (☎ 049 79 34 00). Take the train to Montegrotto; from station, walk out the front and follow signs. Tennis, beach volleyball, and restaurant discounts for guests. Open Mar. to early Nov. Prices range widely depending on season: L9000-13,000/€4.65-6.71 per site; L30-70,000/€15.50-36.15 per tent per person, L24,200-70,700/€12.50-36.51 with a camper.

▐ FOOD

Morning **markets** are held in P. delle Erbe and P. della Frutta—sidewalk vendors sell fresh produce, and covered booths in the archways offer meat and dairy products. A **supermarket PAM** is downtown on V. Cavour in P. della Garzeria. (Open M-

Sa 8am-8pm.) Wine lovers may sample a glass from the nearby **Colli Euganei wine district** or try the sparkling *Lambruschi* from Emilia-Romagna. Visitors to the Basilica di Sant'Antonio can nibble on the *dolce del santo* in nearby *pasticcerie*.

■ **Pizzeria Al Borgo,** V. Luca Belludi, 56 (☎049 875 88 57), near the Basilica di S. Antonio, just a few steps off P. del Santo (heading toward Prato della Valle). Join a rollicking crowd for dinner on the terrace. The Lancelot salad (L11,000/€5.68), with *radiccio* and spinach, cures a broken or adulterous heart. Traditional Paduan salads L5000/€2.58, large pizzas from L6500/€3.36, more elaborate offerings from L11,000/€5.68. Cover L2500/€1.29. Open W-Su noon-3pm and 7-11:30pm. AmEx/MC/V.

Alexander Birreria Paninoteca, V.S. Francesco, 38 (☎049 65 28 84). Take V. del Santo to V.S. Francesco and make a left onto the street. A *paninoteca* with an wide range of sandwiches. *Panini* L6-10,000/€3.14-5.16. Open M-Sa 8:30am-2am.

Lunanuova, V.G. Barbarigo, 12 (☎049 875 89 07), near the *duomo*. Vegetarian fare in a quiet setting. Pasta and Middle Eastern dishes L8-15,000/€4.13-7.75. Drinks from L5000/€2.58. Cover L2000/€1.03. Open Tu-Sa 12:30-2:15pm and 7:30pm-midnight.

👁 SIGHTS

Padua has a wealth of sights—take advantage of the **Biglietto Unico** (L15,000/€7.75; students and groups L10,000/€5.16). The card is valid for one year and is available at the tourist office and at participating sights. The ticket grants admission to the Cappella degli Scrovegni, Musei Civici, Orto Botanico, Palazzo della Ragione, and Battistero del Duomo.

■ **CAPELLA DEGLI SCROVEGNI (ARENA CHAPEL).** The Florentine master Giotto frescoed the stunning walls of this chapel with scenes from the lives of Mary, Jesus, and Mary's parents Joachim and Anne. Completed between 1305 and 1306, this 38-panel cycle jump-started the Italian Renaissance by bringing a previously unknown depth and realism into painting. The figures stand beneath a heavenly blue sky, interacting in a natural manner and displaying traces of individuality. The attached **Musei Civici Erimitani** contains an overwhelming art collection that includes a few treasures, including an amazing Giotto crucifix. *(P. Eremitani, 8. ☎049 820 45 50. Museum open Tu-Su Feb.-Oct. 9am-7pm; Nov.-Jan. 9am-6pm. Chapel open daily Feb.-Dec. L10,000/€5.16, students L7000/€3.62, school groups L5000/€2.58 per person. Entrance through museum only.)*

■ **BASILICA DI SANT'ANTONIO (IL SANTO).** Bronze sculptures by Donatello grace the high altar, surrounded by the artist's *Crucifixion* and several earlier Gothic frescoes. St. Anthony's remains, in various pieces, lie scattered throughout the basilica. The final resting place of his bones, the **Tomba di Sant'Antonio,** is to the left of the altar. Hard to miss under the layers of written pleas and thanks, it is the final destination for thousands of pilgrims who visit the basilica each year to worship. St. Anthony's jawbone and larynx as they lie behind glass inside the saint's gold bust at the back of the Cappella delle Relinque. His tongue rests quietly in a gold case below (the "Reliquiario della Lingua"). In addition to mailing postcards, forward chain letters to St. Anthony (dearsaintanthony@mess-s-antonio.it), or ask him to locate your missing umbrella; he's the patron saint of lost items. A trippy **multimedia show** (follow "Mostra" signs) in the attached courtyard details St. Anthony's life. The adjoining **Oratorio di San Giorgio** houses examples of Giotto-school frescoes, and the **Scuola del Santo** includes three by the young Titian. *(P. del Santo. ☎049 824 28 11. Cathedral open daily Apr.-Sept. 6:30am-8pm; Nov.-Mar. 6:30am-7pm. Dress code enforced. Mostra open daily 9am-12:30pm and 2:30-6pm. English headset available at front desk. Oratorio and Scuola ☎049 875 52 35. Open daily Apr.-Sept. 9am-12:30pm and 2:30-7pm; Oct.-Jan. 9am-12:30pm; Feb.-Mar. 9am-12:30pm and 2:30-4:30pm. Wheelchair accessible. L3000/€1.55, students L2000/€1.03.)*

GATTAMELATA STATUE. In the center of P. del Santo stands Donatello's bronze equestrian statue of Erasmo da Narni (a.k.a. Gattamelata or Calico Cat), a general remembered for his agility and ferocity. Donatello modeled his work on the equestrian statue of Marcus Aurelius at the Campidoglio in Rome. Compare Erasmo's serenity with the ferocity of Colleoni in Venice (p. 220), completed 10 years later.

PALAZZO DELLA RAGIONE (LAW COURTS). This *palazzo* overlooks the lively market stalls of P. della Frutta. Built in 1218, astrological signs line the walls. The original ceiling, once painted as a starry sky, survived a 1420 fire only to topple in a 1756 tornado. The damages are currently being fixed. To the right of the entrance sits the **Stone of Shame.** Inspired by St. Anthony in 1231 to abolish debtors' prisons, Padua adopted the more humane practice of forcing the partially clad debtor onto the stone to repeat before a crowd of at least one hundred hecklers, *"Cedo bonis"* ("I renounce my property"). At the end of the hall, a massive wooden horse, falsely attributed to Donatello, has taken over a room. *(Entrance on P. delle Erbe. ☎049 820 50 06. Open Jan.-Oct. Tu-Su 9am-7pm; Nov.-Dec. 9am-6pm. L10,000/€5.16, students L6000/ €3.10. Exhibits occasionally change hours and prices.)*

UNIVERSITY. The campus is scattered throughout the city, but it is centered in Palazzo Bò. The **Teatro Anatomico** (1594), the first of its kind in Europe, hosted medical pioneers like Vesalius and Englishman William Harvey. Almost all Venetian noblemen received their mandatory law and public policy instruction in the **Great Hall.** The "chair of Galileo" is preserved in the **Sala dei Quaranta,** where the physicist once lectured. Across the street, **Caffè Pedrocchi** served as the headquarters for 19th-century liberals who supported Giuseppe Mazzini. When it was first built, the cafe's famous Neoclassical facade had no doors and was open around the clock. A battle between students and Austrian police exploded here in February 1848, a turning point in the Risorgimento. Capture the spirit for the price of a cappuccino. *(Palazzo Bò, in P. delle Erbe. ☎049 820 97 73. Guided tours M, W, and F 3, 4, 5pm; Tu, Th, and Sa 9, 10, 11am. Tours L5000/€2.58, students L2000/€1.03. Caffe Pedrocchi, V. VIII Febbraio, 15. Open daily 8am-11pm.)*

DUOMO. Michelangelo reputedly participated in the design of this church, which was erected between the 16th and 18th centuries. The interior is entirely white, with just the capitals of the columns in gray. There are no frescoes and just a few paintings. Next door, a jewel of Padua, the **Battistero,** was built in the 12th century and retouched in the 13th. *(P. Duomo. ☎049 66 28 14. Duomo open M-Sa 7:30am-noon and 3:45-7:45pm, Su 7:45am-1pm and 3:45-8:30pm. Free. Baptistery open daily 9:30am-1:30pm and 3-7pm; in winter 9:30am-1pm and 3-6pm. L3000/ €1.55, students L2000/€1.03.)*

ORTO BOTANICO. A veritable oasis of magnolias and palm trees in the middle of the congested city. This oldest university botanical garden in Europe tempts visitors with water lilies, medicinal herbs, and a 1585 palm tree that still offers shade. *(From the basilica follow signs to V. Orto Botanico, 15. ☎049 65 66 14. Open daily 9am-1pm and 3-6pm; in winter M-F 9am-1pm. L5000/€2.58, students L3000/€1.55.)*

🎵 ENTERTAINMENT

Restaurant terraces begin drawing boisterous crowds around 9pm. Taverna della Nane Giulia serves pre-dinner *aperitivi* (see Food, p. 228). **Lucifer Young,** V. Altinate, 89, near the university, is a hip bar whose decorator took lessons from the lowest circle in Dante's *Inferno.* (☎049 66 55 31. Drinks from L6000/€3.10; some food available. Open Su-Tu and Th 7pm-2am, F-Sa 7pm-4am.) The tourist office pamphlet *Where Shall We Go Tonight?* lists restaurants and bars.

Pilgrims pack the city on June 13, as Padua remembers the death of its patron St. Anthony with a procession of the saint's statue and jawbone. An **antique market** assembles in the Prato della Valle on the third Sunday of the month.

VICENZA ☎ 0444

Though dwarfed by neighboring Venice and Padua, Vicenza manages to sport all the grandeur of a larger city, thanks to the monumental *piazze* designed by Andrea Palladio. The architect's style, mingling ancient and contemporary forms and often employing double columned *loggie*, became one of the most respected in Europe. The success of the light-industry zone on the outskirts of town allows residents to maintain a somewhat "Palladian" lifestyle—Vicenza has one of the highest average incomes in Italy. Luckily, their impressive surroundings and back-pocket bulges have not affected the inhabitants' attitudes, and visitors to Vicenza will enjoy genuine small-town hospitality.

▐ TRANSPORTATION

Trains: P. Stazione, at the end of V. Roma. Across from Campo Marzo. Info open daily 7:30am-8:30pm. Ticket office open M-Sa 6am-9:15pm, Su 6am-10pm. Luggage Storage available (p. 231). To: **Milan** (2½hr.; 17 per day 6:08am-10:16pm; L16-27,300/€8.26-14.10); **Padua** (30min., 9 per day 8:10am-6:48pm, L4100-8200/€2.12-4.23); **Verona** (40min., 16 per day 6:20am-10pm, L5300-9400/€2.74-4.85); **Venice** (1½hr., 40 per day 5:52am-11pm, L6100-10,200/€3.15-5.27).

Buses: FTV, V. Milano, 7 (☎ 0444 22 31 15), to left as you exit train station. Office open daily 6am-7:45pm. To: **Bassano** (1hr., 26 per day 5:50am-9:30pm, L5300/€2.79); **Montagnana** (1¼hr., 7 per day 7am-5:30pm, L3200/€1.65); **Padua** (30min., 30 per day 6am-8:20pm, L5400/€2.79).

Taxis: Radiotaxi (☎ 0444 92 06 00). Usually available at either end of C. Palladio.

✳ ⁊ ORIENTATION AND PRACTICAL INFORMATION

Vicenza lies in the heart of the Veneto. The train station and the adjacent intercity bus station are in the southern part of Vicenza. Glance at the map outside the station before walking into town on **Viale Roma.** Take a right on **Corso Palladio** (when you reach the end of V. Roma (at Giardino Salvi), make a right, and pass under the Roman archway. On the other side, you'll be in P. Castello. Walk straight ahead and you'll be on C. Palladio; **Piazza Matteotti** lies at the other end of the street, several blocks away. Walk straight to the old Roman wall that serves as a gate to Teatro Olimpico. The tourist office is the door just to the right.

Tourist Office: P. Matteotti, 12 (☎ 0444 32 08 54; fax 32 70 72; www.ascom.vi.it/aptvicenza), next to Teatro Olimpico. Offers helpful brochures, a free city map, and info on wheelchair access. English spoken. Open M-Sa 9am-1pm and 2:30-6pm, Su 9am-1pm.

Budget Travel: AVIT, V. Roma, 17 (☎ 0444 54 56 77), before you reach supermarket PAM. BIJ and Transalpino tickets. **Avis** and **Hertz** rental cars. Also a Hertz at train station. English spoken. Open M-F 9am-1pm and 3-7pm, Sa 9:30am-12:30pm. **CTS,** Contra Ponta Nova, 43 (☎ 0444 32 38 64), near the Chiesa dei Carmini. Discount flights, tours, and ISICs. English spoken. Open M-F 9am-12:30pm and 3-7pm.

Currency Exchange: At post office (see below). **ATMs** in the train station, on Contra del Monte, and throughout the downtown area.

Luggage Storage: In train station. L5000/€2.58 for 12hr. Open daily 6am-10pm. Self-storage lockers L4000/€2.07

Emergency: ☎ 113. **Ambulance:** ☎ 118.

Police: V. Muggia, 3 (☎ 0444 50 40 44).

Night, Weekend, and Holiday Doctor: ☎ 0444 99 34 70.

Hospital: Ospedale Civile, V. Rodolfi, 8 (☎ 0444 99 31 11).

Internet Access: Gala 2000, on V. Roma across from supermarket PAM. Closed Aug.

Post Office: Contrà Garibaldi, 1 (☎ 0444 32 24 88), between the *duomo* and P. Signori. Open M-Sa 8:10am-7pm. **Currency exchange** M-Sa 8:10am-6pm. **Postal Code:** 36100.

ACCOMMODATIONS & CAMPING

Hotel Vicenza, Stradella dei Nodari, 9 (☎/fax 0444 32 15 12), off P. Signori in the alley across from Ristorante Garibaldi. Make a fast left at the patio of Ristorante Garibaldi. Meticulously scrubbed and centrally located (within sight of the busy piazze). Friendly management. 30 rooms. Prices vary by season. Singles L70,000/€36.15, with bath L85,000/€43.90; doubles L96,000/€49.58, with bath L115,000/€59.39.

Ostello Olimpico Vicenza, Viale Giuriolo, 9 (☎ 0444 540 222; fax 547 762), to the right of the Teatro Olimpico and across from Museo Civico, in a bright yellow building. 84 beds. Bright walls complemented by large windows and 3 terraces. Wheelchair accessible. Breakfast L3000/€1.55. Lunch or dinner L17,000/€8.78. Reception 7am-9am and 3:30-11:30pm. Singles L31,000/€16.01; family-size rooms L28,000/€14.46.

Camping: Campeggio Vicenza, Strada Pelosa, 239 (☎ 0444 58 23 11; fax 58 24 34). Only accessible by car: take SS11 toward Padua, turn left on Strada Pelosa, and follow signs. Showers included. Washing machines L10,000/€5.16. Open Mar.-Sept. L11,600/ €5.99 per person, L13,000/€6.71 per tent, L19,000/€9.81 per tent with car.

FOOD

A **produce market** is held daily in P. delle Erbe behind the basilica. On Tuesday and Thursday mornings, rummage for food beside a clothing bizarre (near the post office). On Thursday, market winds blow through the town bringing cheese, chicken, and fish from afar. For more mundane shopping, turn to **supermarket PAM,** V. Roma, 1. (Open M-F 8:30am-8pm.)

Vecchia Guardia, Contra Pescherie Vecchie, 15 (☎ 0444 32 12 31), near P. Signori. Turn left onto C. Pescherie Vecchie and look under the arcades. Lively patio with pizzas flying in all directions. Shaded seating and indoor space, but outdoor tables have a view of the *duomo.* Pizzas L7000-14,000/€3.62-7.23; fish and meat L15-35,000/ €7.75-18.08; *menù turistico* (a 5 course meal) L35,000/€18.08. Cover L2500/ €1.29. Open noon-2:30pm and 7pm-midnight. AmEx/MC/V.

Righetti, P. del Duomo, 3 (☎ 0444 54 31 35), with another entrance at Contrà Fontana, 6, offers self-service fare and outdoor seating area. *Primi* from L5000/€2.58; *secondi* from L7500/€3.87. Cover L500/€0.26. M-F 9am-3pm and 5:30pm-1am. Closed Aug.

SIGHTS

For an elevated view of Vicenza and many of Palladio's works, **Monte Berico's Piazzale Vittoria** is a short hike uphill from the train station toward V. Risorgimento.

■**TEATRO OLIMPICO.** This theater is the last structure planned by Palladio, although he died before its completion. The intricate Vicenzian streets and alleyways unfolding off the stage, coupled with the detailed statues cluttering the theater's walls, make for a staggering impression. (*P. Matteotti.* ☎ 0444 32 37 81. *Open Tu-Su 10am-7pm. Included in the biglietto cumulativo. Ticket office closes 15min. before the theater.*) Every year from June to September, the city hosts productions in the Teatro Olimpico, showcasing both local and imported talent. (☎ 0444 54 00 72. L20-35,000/ €10.33-18.08, students L15-30,000/€7.75-15.50.)

■**PIAZZA DEI SIGNORI.** The town's showpiece when it was controlled by Venice. Andrea Palladio's reworking of the **Basilica Palladiana** brought the young architect his first fame. In 1546, Palladio's patron, the wealthy Giovan Giorgio Trissino, agreed to fund his proposal to shore up the collapsing Palazzo della Ragione, a project that had frustrated some of the foremost architects of the day. Palladio applied pilasters on twin *loggie* of the basilica to mask the Gothic structure beneath. The **Torre di Piazza** (to the left) reflects the basilica's former appearance. The **Loggia del Capitano,** across from the Torre di Piazza, illustrates Palladio's later technique. *(☎0444 32 36 81. Basilica open Tu-Sa 9:30am-noon and 2:30-5pm. L7-10,000/ €3.62-5.16 during art exhibitions in the basilica.)*

MUSEO CIVICO. Housed in Palladio's **Palazzo Chiericati,** this extensive collection includes Montagna's *Madonna Enthroned,* a Memling *Crucifixion,* Tintoretto's *Miracle of St. Augustine,* Van Dyck's *Le Tre Eta Dell'Uomo (The Three Ages of Man),* and Veneto's *Ritratto Virile. (At the far end of Corso Palladio, across from tourist office and Teatro Olimpico. ☎0444 32 13 48. Open Tu-Su 10am-7pm. L12-14,000/€6.20-7.23, students and groups L6-7000/€3.1-3.62 per person.)*

▶ DAYTRIP FROM VICENZA: PALLADIAN VILLAS

Villa Rotonda, ☎0444 32 17 93. Take bus #8 to Villa Rotonda. Open Mar. 15-Nov. 4. Exterior open Tu and Th 10am-noon and 3-6pm. Interior open W 10am-noon and 3-5pm. L10,000/€5.16, students L5000/€2.58.

Vicenza's countryside overflows with Palladian gems. Venetian expansion to the mainland began in the early 15th century and provided infinite opportunity for Palladio to display his talents. As Venice's maritime supremacy faded, its nobles turned their attention to the acquisition of real estate on the mainland. The Venetian senate decreed that nobles build villas rather than castles to preclude the possibility of petty fiefdoms. The architectural consequences are stunning, and the Veneto is now home to hundreds of the most splendid villas in Europe.

Most of the Palladian villas scattered throughout Veneto are difficult to reach, but luckily some of the most famous lie in range of Vicenza. The ▓**Villa Rotonda** is considered one of history's most magnificent architectural achievements. This villa became a model for buildings in France, England, and the US, most notably Thomas Jefferson's Monticello.

Diagonally across the street from the Villa Rotonda and toward Vicenza lies the **Villa Valmarana "ai Nani"** (of the dwarfs), ☎0444 54 39 76, small but beautifully kept, and set in the middle of a series of circular flower gardens.

VERONA ☎045

After traversing the old Roman Ponte Pietra on a summer's evening, with the gentle rush of the Adige River below and the illuminated towers of churches and castles glowing above, you'll hardly wonder why Shakespeare set *Romeo and Juliet* in Verona. Its city gates and ancient amphitheater memorialize the city's Roman past, while the Scaligeri Bridge and tombs hark back to Verona's Gothic glory.

▣ TRANSPORTATION

Trains: (☎045 800 08 61), on P. XXV Aprile. Ticket office open daily 5:45am-10:45pm. Info open daily 7am-9pm. Luggage storage available (p. 234). To: **Bologna** (2hr.; every 2hr.; L10,500/€5.42); **Cinque Terre** (4½hr.; L33,000/€17.04); **Milan** (2hr.; every hr.; L12,500/€6.46); **Naples** (8hr.; L60,000/€30.99); **Rome** (5hr.; 5 per day; L63,100-72,700/€32.59-37.29); **Trent** (1hr., every 2hr., L9200/€4.75); **Venice** (1¾hr.; every hr.; L10,800-17,000/€5.58-8.78).

Buses: APT (☎045 800 41 29), on P. XXV Aprile, in gray building in front of train station, to the right of the AMT bus platforms. No English spoken. To: **Brescia** (2hr.; every hr.; L10,300/€5.32); **Montagnana** (2hr., 4 per day, L7300/€3.77); **Riva Del Garda** (2hr., 12 per day, L9300/€4.80); **Sirmione** (1hr., 13 per day, L5000/€2.58).

Taxis: Radiotaxi (☎045 53 26 66). Available 24hr.

Car Rental: Hertz (☎045 800 08 32), **Avis** (☎045 800 06 63), and **Europcar** (☎045 59 27 59) share same office at the train station. From L173,000/€89.35 per day. Discounts on longer rentals. Open M-F 8:30am-noon and 2:30-7pm, Sa 8:30am-noon.

Bike Rental: Rent a Bike (☎045 58 23 89; in winter 814 07 60), on V. degli Alpini. L7000/€3.62 per hr., L20,000/€10.33 per day. Open daily 9am-7pm; off-season 10am-7pm.

⚡ ? ORIENTATION AND PRACTICAL INFORMATION

From the train station in P. XXV Aprile, walk 20 minutes up **Corso Porta Nuova**, or take bus #11, 12, 13, 72, or 73 to Verona's heart, the **Arena** in **Piazza Brà** (tickets L1500/€0.77; full-day L4000/€2.07). Most sights lie between P. Brà and the Adige River. **V. Mazzini** connects the Arena to the monuments of **Piazza della Erbe** and **Piazza dei Signori.** Just to the west of P. Brà lies **Castelvecchio**, down V. Roma. The **university,** the **Teatro Romano,** and the **Giardino Giusti** lie across the Ponte Nuovo.

TOURIST AND FINANCIAL SERVICES

Tourist Office: (☎045 806 86 80; fax 800 36 38; info@tourism.verona.it). English spoken. Open daily 10am-7pm. **Airport branch** (☎/fax 045 861 91 63). **Train station branch.** Open M-Sa 9am-6pm. **Youth Info Center (Informagiovani),** C. Porto Borsari, 17 (☎045 801 07 95). Genial staff speaks English. Helps travelers find employment or study opportunities in Verona. Open M-W and F 9am-1pm and 2:30-6pm, Th 3-5pm.

Budget Travel: CIT, P. Brà, 2. Across from Arena to the left of the entry to V. Mazzini when facing away from Arena. (☎045 59 06 49 or 59 17 88; fax 800 21 99). **Currency exchange.** Open M-F 8:20am-1:20pm and 3-7pm. **Centro Turistico Giovanile,** V. Seminario, 10, 3rd fl. (☎045 800 45 92). Off V. Carducci, 1st left after V. Interrato dell'Acqua Morta. Open M-F 9am-1pm and 2:30-6:30pm, Su 9am-1pm.

Currency Exchange: Casa di Risparmio, centrally located on the corner of V. Roma and P. Brà. Open M-F 9am-1pm and 3-6pm. Another **branch** at the train station. Open 7am-8pm. 24hr. exchange machines line V. Mazzini, V. Cappello, and P. delle Elbe. Most charge L6000/€3.10 commission fee.

American Express: Fabretto Viaggi, C. Porta Nuova, 11/L (☎045 806 01 11), 2 blocks toward station from P. Brà. Changes traveler's checks. Holds client mail. Open M-F 8:30am-1pm and 3-7pm, Sa 9am-12:30pm.

LOCAL SERVICES

Luggage Storage: At the train station. L5000/€2.58 per 12hr.

Lost and Found Property Office, V. del Pontiere, 32 (☎045 807 84 58), in police station.

English-Language Bookstore: The Bookshop, V. Interrato dell'Acqua Morta, 3a (☎045 800 76 14), Ponte Navi. Classics in English and a small selection in French, Spanish, and German. Open Tu-Sa 9:15am-12:30pm and 3:30-7:30pm, Su 9:15am-12:30pm.

Laundromat: Onda Blu, V. XX Settembre, 62a (☎0336 52 28 58). Take bus #11, 12, and 13. Wash L6000/€3.10. Dry L6000/€3.10. Open daily 8am-10pm.

EMERGENCY AND COMMUNICATIONS

Emergency: ☎113. **Ambulance:** ☎118. **First Aid:** ☎118.

Police: Questura: ☎800 23 50. **Ufficio Stranieri:** ☎045 809 05 05.

Late-Night Pharmacy: Farmacia Due Campane, V. Mazzini, 52. Open M-F 9:10am-12:30pm and 3:30-7:30pm, Sa 9:10am-12:30pm. Check the *L'Arena* newspaper for **24hr. pharmacy** listings, or call ☎045 801 11 48.

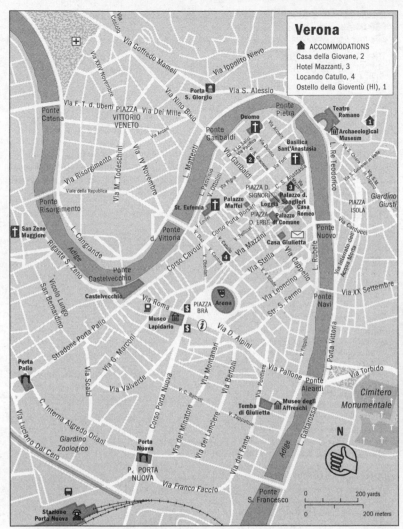

Verona

⌂ ACCOMMODATIONS
Casa della Giovane, 2
Hotel Mazzanti, 3
Locando Catullo, 4
Ostello della Gioventù (HI), 1

Hospital: Ospedale Civile Maggiore (☎045 807 11 11), on Borgo Trento, in P. Stefani.

Internet Access: Internet Train, V. Roma, 17/a (☎045 801 33 94). From P. Brà turn right onto V. Roma. 2 blocks ahead on left. 14 new, heavily used computers. L10,000/€5.16 per hr. Open M-F 10am-10pm, Sa noon-8pm, Su 4-8pm.

Post Office: P. Viviani, 7 (☎045 800 39 98). Follow V. Cairoli from P. delle Erbe. Open M-Sa 8:10am-7pm. **Branch office,** V.C. Cattaneo, 23 (☎045 803 41 00).

Postal Code: 37100.

⌂ ACCOMMODATIONS

The smaller and cheaper accommodations in Verona fill up quickly. Make reservations, especially during the opera season (June 30-Sept. 3).

■ **Ostello della Gioventù (HI), "Villa Francescatti,"** Salita Fontana del Ferro, 15 (☎045 59 03 60; fax 800 91 27). Take bus #73 or night bus #90 to P. Isolo, northeast of the city. By foot from the Arena, walk along V. Anfiteatro, which becomes V. Stella and V. Nizza before it crosses Ponte Nuovo. Continue on V. Carducci and turn left on V. Interrato dell'Acqua Morta to P. Isolo. Follow the yellow signs for "Ostello della Gioventù" up the hill. This 16th-century villa has spotless dorms and a communal feel. Lots of stainless steel, gray and white tiles, and several pleasant patios. English spoken. Hot showers (until 11pm), sheets, and breakfast included. Dinner with a vegetarian option L14,000/ €7.23. Max. 5-night stay. Check-in 5pm. Check-out 7-9pm. Lockout 9am-5pm. Gates lock at 11pm, though opera-goers may make arrangements. No reservations. Family rooms, 6- , 7-, and 36-bed dorms. Dorms L23,000/€11.88.

Casa delle Giovane (ACISJF), V. Pigna, 7, 3rd fl. (☎045 59 68 80; fax 800 59 49), in the town's historic center. From P. delle Erbe, walk up C.S. Anastasia and turn onto V. Due Mori. Walk to the end of the street, and continue straight on V. Augusto Verità. At the corner of V. Pigna and V.S. Giacomo alla Pigna. There is a small sign. Quiet courtyard. Bright rooms, some with a view of Verona's rooftops. Women only. Reception 9am-11pm. Curfew 11pm, except for opera-goers. 60 beds. Dorms L22,000/€11.36; singles L32,000/€16.53; doubles L25,000/€12.91, with bath L30,000/€15.50.

Locanda Catullo, Vco. Catullo, 1 (☎045 800 27 86; fax 59 69 87). Hidden down a narrow alley in the heart of fashion row and between P. Brà and P. Erbe. At V. Mazzini, 40, turn onto V. Catullo, then turn left onto Vco. Catullo. 6 rooms and 1 small suite. July-Sept. 3 night min. stay. Reserve well in advance. 21 rooms. Singles L70,000/€36.15; doubles L100,000/€51.65, with bath 120,000/€62.00; triples 150,000/€77.47, with bath 180,000/€92.96; quads 190,000/€98.13, with bath L230,000/€118.79.

Hotel Mazzanti, V. Mazzanti, 6 (☎045 59 13 70; fax 801 12 62). From P. delle Erbe, walk down C.S. Anastasia and take the 1st right. Ideal for those who want to stay in the heart of the city and explore late-night Verona. All 23 rooms with A/C, TV, and phone. Breakfast included. Singles L100,000/€51.65, with bath 130,000/€67.14; doubles L190,000/ €98.13; triples L210,000/€108.48; quads L220,000/€113.62. AmEx/MC/V.

▶ FOOD

Verona is famous for its wines—the dry white *soave*, the red *valpolicella*, *bardolino*, and *recioto*. The vendors in P. Isolo offer better prices than those in P. delle Erbe. For a large sampling try **Oreste dal Zovo,** Vco. S. Marco in Foro, 7/5, off C. Porta Borsari. The congenial owner has dedicated his heart to Bacchus and knows everything about wine production. The *enoteca* has shelves of every Italian wine imaginable (from L9000/€4.65 for a good bottle), as well as *grappa* and international liquors. Ask Oreste to show you "The Well of Love" (*"Il Pozzo dell'Amore"*) in a nearby courtyard. (☎045 803 43 69. Open Tu-F 8:30am-1:30pm and 2:30-10pm.) **METÁ supermarket,** V. XX Settembre, 81, carries essentials at reasonable prices. Take bus #11, 12, 13, 14, or 51. (Open M-Tu and Th-Sa 8:30am-12:45pm and 3:45-7:30pm, W 8:30am-12:45pm.) For fruits and vegetables, try **Vera Frutta,** V. Interrato dell'Acqua Morta, 40a. (Open M-Sa 8:30am-7:30pm.)

■ **Cantore,** V.A. Mario, 2 (☎045 803 18 30), at the end of V. Mazzini, where it meets V.A. Mario, near P. Brà. Cantore boasts some of the best pizza in Verona. The tables are full by sunset, and remain so into the night. The sauce is tangy, the cheese ample, and the crust delectable. Pizza from L7000/€3.62; *primi* L11-18,000/€5.68-9.30; *secondi* L12-22,000/€6.20-11.36. Cover L2000/€1.03. Open Apr.-Nov. Th-Tu noon-3pm and 4pm-midnight; open all night during the opera festival. AmEx/MC/V.

■ **Brek,** P. Brà, 20 (☎045 800 45 61). Brek is a local favorite and a tourist's dream. Offers a patio view of the Arena, and cheap, delicious meals served cafeteria-style. Salads and cheeses L4300/€2.22; pasta L6500/€3.36; enormous pizza L7500-8500/ €3.87-4.39. Desserts from L4000/€2.07. Wine, and beer on tap. Open M-Sa 11:30am-3pm and 6:30-10pm.

Bottega del Vino, V. Scudo di Francia, 3 (☎045 800 45 35), off V. Mazzini. Turn left at Banco Nazionale Lavoro; it's the first door on your left. Numerous Veronese wines (glasses from L3000/€1.55), and cooked food awaits at the bar. *Primi* from L13,000/ €6.71; *secondi* from L18,000/€9.30. Cover L7000/€3.62. Open W-M 10:30am-3pm and 6pm-midnight. Open daily during opera season. AmEx/MC/V.

Caffè Tubino, C. Porta Borsari, 15d (☎045 803 22 96), near the large arch at the intersection of Porta Borsari and V. Fama. Housed in a 17th-century *palazzo,* this tiny cafe has a wide selection of teas and coffees. Take home a tin of biscuits or caramels along with Turbino's brand of coffee. Drinks start L2500/€1.29. Open M-Sa 7am-midnight.

⊙ SIGHTS

■**THE ARENA.** The city of Verona uses this ancient Roman ampitheater as its **opera house.** Due to history, location, and social purpose, the arena could be likened to the figurative heart of the city. Constructed as a Roman amphitheater in the first century AD, the pink marble arena survived a 12th-century earthquake which toppled much of its outer wall. The view of the 44 tiers of superbly maintained steps is worth the fee. This is not a museum, but a living center for the arts with some production always in progress. For performance listings, see **Entertainment,** below. (*In P. Brà. Info ☎ 045 800 32 04; www.arena.it. Wheelchair accessible. Open Tu-Su 9am-7pm; during opera festival 9am-3pm. L6000/€3.14, students L4000/€2.07.*)

■**PIAZZA DELLA ERBE AND ENVIRONS.** Eclectic markets and stunning architecture reminiscent of an earlier empire fill this square. At the far end, the Baroque **Palazzo Maffei** overlooks the *piazza.* **Madonna Verona's Fountain** stands in the center of the market. Vendors' awnings nearly hide the four-columned **Berlina,** a platform on which convicts were pelted with fruit in medieval days. The winged lion perched above the **Column of St. Mark,** built in 1523, recalls Verona's centuries of Venetian domination. P. della Erbe lies near **via Mazzini** where a pink marble pavement, polished by centuries of Veronese feet, displays the city's finest fashions.

PIAZZA DEI SIGNORI. The **Arco della Costa** (Arch of the Rib) connects P. Erbe to P. dei Signori. From the arch hangs a whale rib, prophesied to fall on the first passing person who has never told a lie. Not surprisingly, the rib has withstood the visits of numerous popes and kings. A severe statue of a contemplative Dante Alighieri stands in the center of the *piazza.* Though they were brutish warlords, the della Scalas avidly patronized the arts. The **Palazzo degli Scaglieri,** once the family's primary residence, is opposite the Arco della Costa (to the right of Dante). The 15th-century Venetian Renaissance **Loggia del Consiglio** also sits in the *piazza.*

Built in 1172 by a noble Veronese family, ■**Torre dei Lamberti** offers what may be the most stunning view of Verona. Only an occasional church spire breaks up the sea of red-shingled roofs. An elevator and winding staircase lead 83m to the top. Through the arch in P. dei Signori lie the medieval outdoor **Tombs of the Scaligeri** and the **Arche Scaligeri.** (*Torre dei Lamberti ☎045 803 27 26. Open Tu-Su 9:30am-6pm. Elevator L4000/€2.07, students L3000/€1.55; stairs L3000/€1.55, students L2000/€1.03.*)

A BALCONY BY ANY OTHER NAME... Perhaps Verona's greatest claim to fame is its role as the setting for *Romeo and Juliet.* Once inside the famous **Casa di Giulietta,** you are allowed to stand on the balcony, and overlook crowds of tourists taking your picture. After you've been mistaken for Shakespeare's protagonist, you may want to walk around the several stories of mostly empty rooms, which include some frescoes, and paintings depicting the famous literary lovers. Empty fireplaces and chairs in each room make it seem that someone has just moved out. Hundreds of hooting tourists mill around and rub a particular portion of the bronze Juliet's anatomy to shiny brilliance. Modern-day lovers scrawl odes in the entrance, making the bricks a kind of international hall of love graffiti. Contrary to propaganda, the dal Capello (Capulet) family never lived here. (*V. Cappello, 23. ☎045 803 43 03. Open Tu-Su 9am-7pm. L6000/€3.10, students L4000/€2.07.*) Add insult to injury and visit **Tomba Di Giulietta** (Juliet's tomb) and the **Museo Degli Affreschi** (Fresco Museum). *(V. del Pontiere, 5. ☎045 800 03 61. Open Tu-Su 9am-7pm. Tomb and museum L5000/€2.58, students L2000/€1.03.)* The **Casa di Romeo,** long the home of the Montecchi family, is around the corner from P. dei Signori at V. Arche Scaligeri, 2. The sight, now private property, offers little more than a plain facade.

BASILICA OF SANT'ANASTASIA AND ENVIRONS. This Gothic church boasts impressive works of art, including Pisanello's *St. George Freeing the Princess* (in the left transept of the Giusti Chapel) and frescoes by Altichiero and Turone. To the right of the altar is the Capella Pellegrini, a series of 24 scenes terracotta reliefs depicting the life of the Christ (by Michele da Firenze). The first chapel on the left features Titian's *Assumption of the Virgin. (Basilica at the end of C.S. Anastasia, near river. Duomo down from basilica on V. Duomo. Enter on the side of building. Duomo open M-Sa 9:30am-6pm and Su 1-6pm. Entrance L3000/€1.55. Church aficionados should consider the 5-church ticket, providing entry to the duomo, S. Anastasia, S. Zeno, S. Lorenzo, and S. Permo for L8000/€4.13, students L7000/€3.62. Buy tickets at any of the churches. Info ☎045 59 28 13.)*

The nearby **Biblioteca Capitolare,** the oldest library in Europe, maintains a priceless medieval manuscript collection. *(☎045 59 65 16. Open M, W, Sa 9:30am-12:30pm, Tu and F 9:30am-12:30pm and 4-6pm. Free.)*

TEATRO ROMANO AND GIARDINO GIUSTI. A spectacular Roman theater overlooks the city from St. Peter's Hill. This is one of the few venues where you'll want to reserve seats as high up as possible; the view is a silhouette of the city across the river, and the sound is that of the teaming Adige. Today the theater hosts Shakespearean productions in Italian and an **archaeological museum.** *(Rigaste Redentore, 2. Cross the Ponte Pietra from the city center and go right. ☎045 800 03 60. Open Tu-Su 9am-6:30pm. L5000/€2.58, students L3000/€1.55. First Su of each month free.)*

Stroll down from the theater to the **Giardino Giusti,** a stunning 16th-century garden complete with a labyrinth of mythological statues. As you ascend, the garden reveals an increasingly breathtaking view of the city. Mozart, Goethe, and Cosimo de' Medici long admired the garden. Add your name to this impressive list and wait for fame to arrive. *(Down V.S. Chiara from Teatro Romano. ☎045 803 40 29. Open daily Apr.-Sept. 9am-8pm; Oct.-Mar. 9am-sunset. L7000/€3.62, students L3000/€1.55.)*

CASTELVECCHIO. After being ripped apart by invading armies in World War II, the della Scala fortress has been lovingly reconstructed. The castle's **museum** features a collection of sculptures and paintings, including Pisanello's *Madonna and Child* and Luca di Leyda's *Crucifixion*. In the courtyard, an equestrian statue of Cangrande I (Big Dog) smiles from its perch above. Be sure to cross the **Ponte Castelvecchio** to the left of the castle. The steps at the midpoint provide a balcony view of Verona along the river, a sight so romantic that scores of couples have managed to overcome their respect for medieval architecture in order to scrawl their names on the stone of the bridge. *(Down V. Roma from P. Brà. ☎045 59 47 34. Open Tu-Su 9am-7pm. L6000/€3.1, students L4000/€2.07. First Sunday of each month free.)*

SAN ZENO MAGGIORE. This church is one of Verona's finest examples of Italian Romanesque architecture. The massive brick church, dedicated to Verona's patron saint, surpasses its counterparts in artistic wealth. The 17th-century bronze doors sparked a craze throughout Italy. The wooden "ship's keel" ceiling and spacious crypt. The two-story apse contains a Renaissance altarpiece by Mantegna. *(Up from the Castelvecchio. Open daily 8am-noon and 3-7pm.)*

🎵 ENTERTAINMENT

Every year, droves of opera lovers flock to Verona to hear the heartwrenching arias of the world famous **Verona Opera Festival**. Recent performances have included several works by Verdi, most notably, "Aida" and "Rigoletto." The festival runs from late June to early August, staging ballet, opera, and jazz shows at the Arena. *(☎045 800 51 51; fax 801 32 87. General admission on the Roman steps Su-*

Th L38,000/€19.63, F-Sa L42,000/€21.69. Reserved seats L110-180,000/€56.81-92.96. Arrive 1hr. before shows if you hold general admission tickets.)

From June to September, the **Teatro Romano** stages dance performances and Shakespeare productions (in Italian). June brings a one-week jazz festival known as **Verona Jazz.** (Theater info ☎ 045 807 72 19 or 807 75 00; Verona Jazz info ☎ 045 807 72 05 or 806 64 85. Tickets for both L20-40,000/€10.33-20.66.) For a free taste of Verona's music scene, check out summer's **Concerti Scaligieri,** a sequence of 40 open-air concerts of jazz, blues, and classical music. Those in search of more barley-based entertainment, flock to the **Locos Café,** V.S. Giovanni in Valle, 28, halfway down the hill from the hostel. (Generous beers L4000/€2.07, wine L1800/€0.93, *bruschette* L3000/€1.55. ☎ 045 59 00 74. Open W-M 9:30am-2pm and 7pm-1am.)

TREVISO   ☎ 0422

Treviso, the provincial capital of the Veneto, is known by two other names, *città d'acqua* (City of Water) and *città dipinta* (Painted City). The town's watery name is derived from the trickles of Sile River that flow through the edges of town. The painted reference comes from the frescoed facades of Treviso's buildings. However, a third aspect of Treviso's self-image is its wealth. In this birthplace of Benetton, fashion is at the forefront. The people are beautiful, and their clothes even more so. Even their shoes drop straight from the Italian leather gods. Come to this glitzy spot to window-shop, but bring credit cards at your own risk.

▐ TRANSPORTATION

Trains: Station at Piazza Duca d'Aosta, just south of city center. From bus station, turn right down V. Roma. Ticket counter open 6am-9pm. Station open 4:30am-12:30am. Main stop on heavily trafficked Venice-Udine line. To: **Trieste** (2½hr.; 12 per day 7:21am-10:14pm; L17,400/€9); **Udine** (1½hr.; 26 per day 5:48am-11:17pm; L11,100/€5.73); **Venice** (30min., 42 per day 4:38am-11:41pm, L3700/€1.91). To reach **Milan** or **Padua,** make a connection in Venice.

Buses: Lungosile A. Mattei, 21 (☎ 0422 57 73 60), on left before Corso del Popolo crosses river. Offices open 6:50am-1pm and 1:30-7:45pm. **La Marca** (☎ 0422 41 22 22) bus line services the Veneto region and the Palladian Villas. To: **Bassano del Grappa** (1hr., 7:35am, 12:15, 3:15pm, L6500/€3.36); **Padua** (1½hr., 31 per day 6am-7:45pm, L6000/€3.10); **Venice** (30min., 45 per day 4:10am-10:45pm, L4200/€2.17); **Vincenza** (1½hr., 9 per day 6:15am-7:15 pm, L7500/€3.87).

✳❷ ORIENTATION AND PRACTICAL INFORMATION

Treviso lies 30km inland from Venice. Traced by the flowing waters of the Sile, the old city walls encompass Treviso's historic city center (and most points of interest). From the train station, the **ACTT** (intracity) bus hub is directly across from the busy **Piazza Duca d'Aosta.** Just left of the buses, **via Roma** leads from between the crumbling walls into the city center. It then becomes **Corso del Popolo,** crosses the river, and drains into **Piazza della Borsa.** From there, a short walk up **via XX Settembre** is rewarded by splendid **Piazza dei Signori,** Treviso's main square and showcase for **Palazzo dei Trecento.** Pedestrian-dominated **via Calmaggiore** leads to the *duomo.*

Tourist Office: APT, P. Monte di Pietà, 8 (☎ 0422 54 76 32; fax 41 90 92; www.sevenonline.it/tvapt), on the side of Palazzo dei Trecento from P. dei Signori. Has city maps and a list of walking tours that follow the Sile River. Reserve ahead for a free walking tour of the city (May-Dec. Sa 10am-noon). Open in summer M 9am-12:30pm, Tu-F 9am-12:30pm and 2:30-6:30pm, Sa-Su 9:30am-12:30pm and 3:30-6pm.

Emergency: ☎ 113. **Ambulance:** ☎ 118.

Carabinieri: V. Cornarotta, 24 (☎ 112). **Questura,** V. Carlo Alberto, 37 (☎ 0422 59 91).

Hospital: Ospedale Civile Ca' Foncello, Piazzale Ospedale, 1, (☎ 0422 32 21 11).

NORTHEAST ITALY

Internet Access: Attrazione Las Vegas, V. Roma, 39 (☎0422 59 02 47), upstairs in a smoky video game arcade. 12,000/€6.20 per 50min. Open daily 10am-1am.

Post Office: P. Vittoria, 1 (☎0422 317 21 11). Housed in a palatial building at the end of V. Cadorna, off C. del Popolo. Open M-S 8:10am-7pm.

Postal Code: 31100.

ACCOMMODATIONS AND FOOD

Treviso's conspicuous consumption has spawned a number of hotels but few budget accommodations. With singles starting at L90,000/€46.48, Treviso is a daytrip. **Albergo Campeol,** P. Ancilotto, 4, conveniently situated behind Palazzo dei Trecento, offers some of the least expensive rooms in town, all with bath, TV, phone, and a cheery yellow motif. (☎/fax 0422 566 01. Breakfast L8000/€4.32. Singles L80,000/€41.32; doubles L150,000/€77.47. AmEx/MC/V.) **Da Renzo,** V. Terragio, lacks the allure of city center accommodations, but is only a bus ride from the station (hop on #7, 8, or 11 and ask the driver for Da Renzo, or the Borgo Saovoia stop; L1400/€0.72). All rooms have bath, A/C, phones, and breakfast. (☎0422 40 20 68; fax 54 68 82; darenzo@sevenonline.it/darnenzo; www.sevenonline.it/darenzo. Singles L90,000/€46.48; doubles L135,000/€69.72; triples L170,000/€87.80.)

The city is famous for its *ciliegie* (cherries), *radicchio*, and ■*tiramisù*, a heavenly creation of espresso-and-liquor-soaked cake layered with *mascarpone*, a soft cheese. Cherries ripen in June, *radicchio* peaks in December, and *tiramisù* is always in season. To taste these delights, head to the daily morning **produce market** at the Stiore stop of the #2 or 11 bus. For basics, shop at the **PAM supermarket,** P. Borso, 12. (☎0422 58 39 13. Open Th-Tu 8:30am-7:30pm.) **All'Oca Bianca,** V. della Torre, 7, on a side street off central V. Calmaggiore, is a casual *trattoria* that serves excellent fish dishes. If you missed cherry season, try the *grappa*-steeped version *(ciliege sotto grappa)*. (☎0422 54 18 50. *Primi* L12,000/€6.20; *secondi* and fish L14-16,000/€7.32-8.26. Cover L3000/€1.55. Open Tu 12:30-2pm, Th-M 9am-3pm and 6pm-midnight. AmEx/MC/V.) If *primi* seems a merely an inconvenient delay, begin with dessert at **Nascimben,** V. XX Settembre, 3. (☎0422 59 12 91. *Tiramisù* L2700/€1.39 per 100g. Open M-Sa 7am-7pm.)

SIGHTS

PALAZZO DEI TRECENTO. Dominating P. dei Signori, this palace proudly recalls Treviso's successful reemergence from a 1944 air raid on Good Friday that demolished half the town. The post-bombing restoration blends perfectly with the original frescoes, though the original position of the stairs and outer wall are clearly labeled. (☎0422 65 82 35. *Open occasionally for exhibitions.)*

DUOMO. Calmaggiore's *passeggiata* flows beneath the arcades of the *piazza* to this seven-domed church complete with Neoclassical facade. The *duomo's* **Cappella Malchiostro** dates from 1519 and contains works by sworn enemies, Titian *(Annunciation)* and Pordenone. *(Open M-Th 9am-noon, Sa-Su 9am-noon and 3-6pm.)*

MUSEO CIVICO. Also called the Museo Bailo, this museum is home to Titian's *Sperone Speroni* and Lorenzo Lotto's *Portrait of a Dominican.* The ground floor showcases Treviso's archaeological finds, which include 5th-century BC bronze discs from Montebelluna. *(Borgo Cavour, 24.* ☎*0422 59 13 37. Open Tu-Sa 9am-12:30pm and 2:30-5pm, Su 9am-noon. L3000/€1.55.)*

PALLADIAN VILLAS. Palladio's penchant for building villas (see **Near Vicenza,** p. 233) spilled into the Treviso area. Among them is **Villa Barbero** (1560) on the Treviso-Bassano line at the small village of Maser. (☎*0423 92 30 04. Open Mar.-Oct. Tu, Sa, Su and holidays 3-6pm; Nov.-Feb. Sa-Su and holidays 2:30-5pm. L9500/€4.91.)* The nearby **Villa Elmo** is a bit more difficult to reach, requiring first a bus or train ride from Treviso to Vastelfrance, then a bus ride from there to Fanzolo. The villa is

TRAVELIN' ITALY: LACTOSE-INTOLERANT STYLE

Milk, it does a body good. But not yours. Got milk? Got indigestion. You've watched with envy as your friends scarfed down pizza and ice cream. You are lactose intolerant. All your life, you've pondered one question: How can I travel in Italy? Have no fear, gentle traveler. *Let's Go* will show you the way.

Step One: **Learn the Early Warning Signs.** Study these four critical names: *latte* (milk); *crema* (cream); *formaggio* (cheese); *burro* (butter). Practice these crucial phrases: *"Si potrebbe farlo senza crema?"* (Could you make that without cream?); *"C'è latte?"* (Is that made with milk?); *"Potrei avere una bella, forte pompa stomaco?"* (May I please have a good, hard stomach-pumping?).

Step Two: The Truth About Pizza. Ever taken slack for scraping the cheese off your pizza ("Dude, that's not pizza! That's like...bread with sauce.")? Well in Italy, not only is this acceptable, but it's on the menu. Ask for *pizza marinara:* pizza without cheese, just the way Mother Nature intended it.

Step Three: The Gelato Question. Cities crumble, stomachs growl, but hope survives. Though you can't eat ice cream, you may be able to eat the tastier *gelato.* Fruit flavors, especially lemon and strawberry, have a smaller milk content than flavors like vanilla. Some *gelaterie* even carry soy-based *gelato.*

Step Four: The After-Dinner Coffee. You've long stared longingly at the fluffy sophistication of Italian cappucino, and yet one sip of the lactose-free version (espresso) left you up and shaking half the night. Jitter no more, for in the lovely and culinarily ingenious land of Italia there's *caffè di orto,* a "coffee" made of roasted barley that's caffeine-free and never taken with milk. Who would have thought that a drink made from barley could taste so good...oh, wait.

considered to be one of the most characteristic Palladian works. *(Open in M-Sa 3-7pm, Su 10am-12:30pm and 3-6pm; in winter Sa-Su and holidays 2-6pm. L10,000/€5.16.)*

BASSANO DEL GRAPPA
☎0422

Bassano del Grappa is a town of scattered orange roofs, a romantic bridge (the Ponte degli Alpini), a tranquil river (the Brenta), and a far less gentle namesake: *grappa,* hellfire in a bottle, distilled from the skins and seeds of once-harmless grapes. Originally, *grappa* was used as a medieval elixir—perhaps to cure the problem of having functional vocal chords. Buckle up; your Italian coming-of-age will not be complete without a sip.

⊞⊠ TRANSPORTATION AND PRACTICAL INFORMATION. Bassano's principal *piazze* lie between the train station and the **Fiume Brenta.** No, you haven't been imbibing too much grappa: the town *is* tilting downward. The **train station** is at the end of V. Chilesotti, near the historical center. The ticket counter is open M-Sa 6:05am-7:30pm, Su 6:30am-8:45pm. **Trains** zip to: Padua (1hr., 12 per day 5:35am-6:05pm, L4800/€2.48); Trent (2hr., 9 per day 5:40am-8:46pm, L8200/€4.23); Venice (1hr., 18 per day 5:30am-9:15pm, L6300/€3.25); Vicenza (2hr., 15 per day 7:17am-10:30pm, L4100/€2.12) via **Cittadella.** The **bus station** is in P. Trento, off V. delle Fosse. **FTV** (☎0424 308 50) serves Vicenza (1hr., 24 per day 5:30am-7:50pm, L5100/€2.63). **La Marca Line** (☎0422 41 22 22) runs to Treviso (1hr., 10 per day 7am-7:25pm, L5700/€2.94). Buy tickets at Bar Trevisani in P. Trento.

From the train station, take **via Chilesotti** toward **Piazza Trento** and bear right on **via Museo** to reach the heart of town. At the **tourist office,** Largo Corona d'Italia, 35 (☎0424 52 43 51; fax 52 53 01), the English-speaking staff provides useful pamphlets and a town map. From the station, walk down V. Chilesotti, cross V. delle Fosse, and enter the shopping complex through the gap in the stone wall. Make an immediate right and head to the older, separate building against the wall. (Open M-F 9am-12:30pm and 2-5pm, Sa 9am-12:30pm.)

⬛⬜ ACCOMMODATIONS AND FOOD. Consider the **Istituto Cremona,** V. Chini, 6. From P. Liberta, walk down V. Marinali to P. Cadorna. Continue left onto **Viale Undici Febbraio,** until you reach V. Chini (you'll pass a post office on Febbraio); then walk for a few blocks on the winding V. Chini, until you come to a large gated complex. It's part hostel, part elementary school, and part residence for migrant workers, but the facilities are all kept separate. Take a left into a gravel court, and ring the bell. The walk can be confusing, so you may want to arrive during the day. The low nightly rate includes in-room baths, sheets, bicycle use, and basketball/volleyball courts. Mattresses are made firmer with the addition of flattened cardboard boxes. Staff members hint that a remodeling is on the horizon. (☎ 0424 52 20 32; cremona@nsoft.it. Reception 7-9:30am and 6-10pm. Public telephone. Breakfast L5500/€2.84. Reservations necessary. Singles L30,000/€15.50, with bath L25,000/€12.91; doubles L46,000/€23.76.)

For the *grappa* experience, buy a bottle at one of the distilleries clustered near Ponte degli Alpini. Some will even provide free tastes upon request, though a small bottle can be purchased for L1500/€0.77. Find something to wash the it down at local favorite **Birreria Ottone,** V. Matteotti, 50. Steps from P. Liberta (make a right onto V. Matteotti). The restaurant is clean and elegant, with opera in the background, and an intricate set of cables suspending a tiny lamp over each table. Try the L16,000/€8.26 Hungarian *goulash.* (☎ 0424 222 06. Pasta L12,000/€6.20. Cover L2500/€1.29. Open M 11:30am-3:30pm, W-Su 11am-3pm and 7pm-11pm. Closed Aug. MC/V.) Sample some of Bassano's famed white asparagus and porcini mushrooms at the open-air **market** in P. Garibaldi. (Open Th and Sa 8am-1pm.)

◧ SIGHTS. The ⬛**Ponte degli Alpini** spans the Brente, with a web of narrow streets linking it to the center. Romantic views of the town and the river (especially in the evening) await. This pedestrian haven allows for that rare privilege in Italy—quiet. You can hear birds, footsteps, and rushing water as you kiss your new sweetheart in front of the small waterfall on the left side of the bridge. To continue the experience near the river, walk to the other side (away from P. Liberta), make a left on the first street, and descend gradually to the **Veduta Panoramica**. This pebbly beach provides an excellent view of the water, bridge, city, and mountains, and a chance to mingle with a few swans and a family of ducklings. Toward the station and down any one of the twisting medieval streets lies the majestic **Piazza della Libertà.** Its highlight is the imposing statue-topped facade of the **Chiesa di San Giovanni Battista,** although the Venetian winged lion to the right is also worth a glance.

In the adjacent P. Garibaldi, the **Chiesa di San Francesco** sits next door to the **Museo Civico,** a museum featuring Jacopo da Bassano's paintings of dark worlds split open by divine light. The exhibit includes Bassano's famous *Flight into Egypt* and *St. Valentine Baptizing St. Lucilla,* as well as works by contemporary artists. The Chini Collection of Greek artifacts from southeast Italy (from the 6th-3rd centuries BC) is a point of special interest. (☎ 0424 52 22 35. Open Tu-Sa 9am-6:30pm, Su 3:30-6:30pm. L8000/€4.13, students and seniors L5000/€2.58.)

FRIULI-VENEZIA GIULIA

Overshadowed by the touristed cities of the Veneto and the mountains of Trentino-Alto Adige, Friuli-Venezia Giulia traditionally receives less than its fair share of recognition. Trieste, a long-standing exception to this rule, attracts increasing numbers of beach-goers searching for the least expensive resorts on the Adriatic. The area's towns, which owe their charm to their small size, offer an untainted slice of local life and culture absent from Italy's larger cities.

Friuli-Venezia Giulia derives its name from several distinct provinces. Unified by the clergy between the 6th and 15th centuries, the region was appropriated by the Venetian Republic and later swallowed, Venetians and all, by Austria-Hungary.

The historical differences within this postwar union and the area's vulnerability to eastern forces combine to give Friuli-Venezia Giulia a hybrid character. The splash of political intrigue and coffee-culture elegance brought by the Austro-Hungarian Empire attracted intellectuals to turn-of-the-century Friuli. James Joyce lived in Trieste for 12 years, during which time he wrote the bulk of *Ulysses*, Ernest Hemingway drew part of his plot for *A Farewell to Arms* from the region's role in World War I, and Freud and Rilke both worked and wrote here.

TRIESTE ☎040

Not until recently has Trieste's position on a narrow strip of land, sandwiched between the present-day Balkans and the Adriatic Sea, been one of peaceful coexistence. From the 9th through 15th centuries, the city was Venice's main rival on the Adriatic, but by the 19th century, Trieste faced a new threat—Austria. In the post-Napoleonic real estate market, Austria snatched the city, and when she did, she proceeded to rip out its medieval heart, replacing it with Neoclassical bombast. In the years that followed, the Habsburgs' heavy-handed style of government alienated the city's large Italian majority, breeding fervent *irredentisti* who clamored for unification with the new Italian Republic. In 1918, Italian troops finally united Friuli with Italy, but Mussolini's policies of cultural chauvinism equally offended the city's residents. At the end of World War II, when Allied troops liberated the city from Nazi occupiers, the ownership dispute resurfaced, this time between the Slavs and the Italians. Though Trieste finally became part of Italy in 1954, the city still remains divided between its Slavic and Italian origins.

▐ TRANSPORTATION

Trieste is a direct train ride from both Venice and Udine. Several trains and buses also cross daily to Slovenia and Croatia. In summer, ferries make trips to Croatia's Istrian Peninsula, with less frequent service to the Dalmatian Coast and Greece.

INTERCITY TRANSPORTATION

Flights: Aeroporto Friuli-Venezia Giulia/Ronchi dei Legionari, V. Aquileia, 46 (☎0481 77 32 24 or 77 32 25). To get to airport, take the public **SAF bus** (1hr., M-Sa every hr., L6000/€3.10). Ticket counter (☎0481 77 32 32) open daily 7am-noon and 1-7pm. Daily British Airways (☎0652 49 15 71) flights to **London.** Open M-F 8am-8pm, Sa 9am-5pm. Alitalia (☎1478 656 43) flights to: **Genoa, Milan, Munich, Naples, and Rome.**

Trains: P. della Libertà, 8 (☎040 379 47 37), P. della Liberta, 8, down C. Cavour from quays. Ticket counter (☎040 41 86 12) open daily 5:40am-9:30pm. Info office open daily 7am-9pm. Luggage storage available (p. 244). To: **Budapest** (12hr.; 2 per day; L130,000/€67.14); **Ljubljana** (3hr.; 3per day; L40,000/€20.66); **Udine** (1½hr.; every hr.; L10,400/€5.37); **Venice** (2hr.; 2 per hr.; L15,300/€7.90).

Regional Buses: P. della Liberta, 11 (☎040 42 50 01), next to train station. From C. Cavour, turn left when the *corso* ends. **SAITA** (☎040 42 50 01) to **Rijeka/Fiume** (2-2½hr.; 2 per day; L15,000/€7.75) and **Udine** (1½hr., 25 per day, L8000/€4.13). Smaller lines to: Duino, Miramare, Muggia, and Opiciao.

Ferries: Adriatica di Navigazione, P. Unita, 7 (☎040 67027211), off C. Cavour, sails to: Albania, Croatia, Greece, and Slovenia. **Anek Lines,** Molo Bersaglieri, 3 (☎0403 22 05 61), off R. D. Mandracchio, runs ferries to Greece. **Agemar Viaggi,** P. Duca degli Abruzzi 1/a, (☎0403 63 32 22), off C. Cavour, has detailed departure schedules and sells tickets for both lines. Open M-F 9am-12:30pm and 3-6pm.

LOCAL TRANSPORTATION

Public Transportation: A.C.T. orange buses travel city and provincial routes to the Carso, Miramare, and Opicina. Buy your ticket before you board at newsstands, *tabacchi* stands, and bars near bus stops (L1400/€0.72).

Tram: Europe's only **funicular** railway links P. Oberdan with Opicina, a city on the Carso Plateau above Trieste. From P. Oberdan (25min., every 20min. 7:11am-8:11pm, L1500/€0.77).

Taxis: Radio Taxi (☎040 30 77 30). Available 24hr.

Car Rental: Maggiore/Budget/Alamo (☎040 42 13 23), in train station. Around L150,000/€77.47 per day; L550,000/€284.50 per week. Open M-F 8:30am-12:30pm and 3-7pm, Sa 8:30am-12:30pm.

✳ 🛈 ORIENTATION AND PRACTICAL INFORMATION

From the city center, the industrialized quays serving ferries, fishermen, and sailing regattas taper off north into the **Barcola,** Trieste's excuse for a beach—a stretch of tiered concrete (populated with bronzed bodies) that runs 7km from the edge of town to the castle at Miramare. The center of Trieste is organized as a grid, bounded to the east by **via Carducci,** which stretches south from **Piazza Oberdan.** To the west, boutique-heavy **Corso Italia** runs south from the spectacular **Piazza Unità d'Italia,** a vast, uncluttered square with one edge along the harbor. The two streets intersect at the busy **Piazza Goldoni.** Steps from P. Unità, along C. Italia, lies the **Piazza della Borsa,** where the *triestini* come to strut their stuff.

TOURIST, FINANCIAL, AND LOCAL SERVICES

Tourist Office: APT, Riva III Novembre, 9 (☎040 347 83 12; fax 347 83 20), along the quays, near P. della Unità. A wealth of info, including lists of *manifestazioni* (artistic events) and the itinerary for the James Joyce walking tour. Open daily 7am-9pm. Another office in **train station** (☎040 44 114), on the left as you exit platforms. Open M-Sa 7:30am-8:30pm. English spoken at both offices.

Budget Travel: CTS, P. Dalmazia, 3b (☎040 36 18 79; fax 36 24 03), off of P. Oberdan. Agency for air and train tickets and vacation info. Discounts for students; also sells ISIC and replaces expired cards. English spoken. Open M-F 9am-1pm and 3:30-7pm.

Currency Exchange: Deutsche Bank, V. Roma, 7 (☎040 63 19 25). Cash advances on Visa. Open M-F 8:15am-1pm and 2:35-3:50pm.

Luggage Storage: At the train station. L5000/€2.58 per 12hr.

English-Language Bookstore: Libreria Internazionale Transalpina, V. Torre Bianca, 21/a (☎040 63 12 88). Open Tu-Sa 9am-1pm and 3:30-7:30pm. AmEx/MC/V.

EMERGENCY AND COMMUNICATIONS

Emergency: ☎113. **Ambulance:** ☎118. **Police:** 112.

Late-Night Pharmacy: Farmacia alla Borsa, P. della Borsa, 12/a. 24hr. pharmacies rotate. Check with the tourist office, or in the window of any pharmacy. Open M-F 8:30am-1pm and 4-7:30pm, Sa 8:30am-1pm.

Hospital: Ospedale Maggiore (☎040 399 22 10), in P. dell'Ospedale, up V.S. Maurizio from V. Carducci.

Internet Access: Sport Net Center, P. dello Squero Vecchio, 1/c (☎0403 22 08 61), near P. Unità. Limited opening hours. L10,000/€5.16 per hr. Open M-F 9am-1pm.

Post Office: P.V. Veneto, 1 (☎040 676 41 11; fax 77 19 72), along V. Roma. From the train station, take 2nd right off V. Ghega. Fax machine. Open M-Sa 8:15am-7pm.

Postal Code: 34100.

▚ ACCOMMODATIONS & CAMPING

Cheap and clean rooms aren't a dime a dozen in Trieste, but some exist outside the city center. Many rooms are geared toward seasonal workers, who book them by the month, while others are filled with Croatian and Slovenian shoppers.

TRIESTE FOR YOU (T FOR YOU)! This card, available free at hotels throughout the city when you stay for two nights or more, entitles visitors to discounts at hotels, restaurants, sights, and stores throughout the city. For more information, contact the local tourist office (see above).

Hotel Alabarda, V. Valdirivo, 22 (☎040 63 02 69; fax 63 92 84; www.hotelalabarda.it), in the city center. From P. Oberdan, head down V. XXX Ottobre, near tram stop, and turn right onto V. Valdirivo. High ceilings make all 18 rooms feel palatial. TV and phone. Internet access L10,000/€5.16 per hr. Wheelchair accessible. Parking available. Singles L50,000/€25.82, with bath L75,000/€38.73; doubles L80,000/€41.32, L115,000/€59.39; triples L108,000/€55.78, L155,000/€80.05; quads L136,000/€70.24, L195,000/€100.71. 10% discount with *Let's Go.* AmEx/MC/V.

Ostello Tegeste (HI), V. Miramare, 331 (☎/fax 040 22 41 02), on the seaside, just south from Castle Miramare. 6km from city center. From station take bus #36 (L1400/

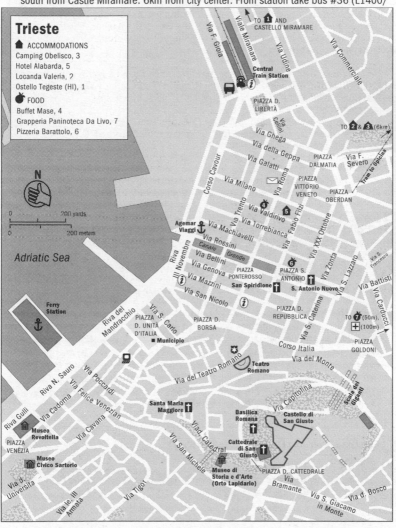

€0.72), departing from across V. Miramare, the street on left of station as you exit. Ask driver for the "Ostello" stop. From there, walk along the shore, following the seaside road toward the castle. Other accommodations may be more centrally located, but the view of the Adriatic from the terrace adds enormously to this hostel's charm. Courtyard bar, bicycle rental (L10-20,000/€5.16-10.33 per day), and a dinner option (L15,000/€7.75). Breakfast and hot shower included. **HI Members only.** Reception daily 8am-11:30pm. Lockout 10am-1pm. Curfew 11:30pm. Dorms L22,000/€11.36.

Locanda Valeria, Strada per Vienna, 156 (☎040 21 12 04), in Opicina, 7km east of Trieste. From P. Oberdan, take the tram to the last stop (**Transportation,** see p. 243); or take bus #39 from P. Liberta to S. Per Vienna. Valeria is 3 blocks from tram/bus stop. Though hardly the chic scene you'd find in downtown Trieste, a friendly atmosphere and a restaurant filled with animated Italian/Slovenian locals awaits. *Primi* L10,000/€5.16. Breakfast L7000/€3.62. Singles L35,000/€18.08; doubles L60,000/€31.

Camping Obelisco, S. Nuova per Opicina, 37 (☎040 21 16 55; fax 040 21 27 44), in Opicina, (see above). Take the tram from P. Oberdan (L1400/€0.72) and ask for the "Obelisco" stop; follow the yellow signs. Nice facilities with bar. L7000/€3.62 per person, L4000/€2.07 per tent, L4000/€2.07 per car.

◗ FOOD

Although many dishes in Trieste's restaurants have Eastern European overtones, the selection of fresh seafood from the Adriatic rivals that of Venice. The city is renowned for its *frutti del mare*, especially *sardoni in savor* (large sardines marinated in oil and garlic). Another local specialty is *cevap cici* (spicy Serbian sausages infused with garlic) and *jota* (a hearty sauerkraut, bean, and sausage stew). The ▓osmizze are informal restaurants that date from 1784, when a decree allowed peasants on the Carso to sell local produce for only eight days a year. Today, families in the Carso open their terraces to the public for two weeks, serving produce from their farms and wine from their vineyards such as the regional *terrano del Carso*, a dry red wine valued for its therapeutic properties.

For basics, V. Carducci is home to several **alimentari,** or small, permanent markets. For lower prices and continuous hours, hit up **Euro Spesa supermarket,** V. Valdirivo, 13/F, off C. Cavour. (Open M-Sa 8am-8pm.) It wouldn't be Italy without a **STANDA**—Trieste's branch is at V. Battisti, 15. (Open M 3:30-7:30pm, Tu-F 9am-1pm and 3:30-7:30pm, Sa 9am-7:30pm.) Trieste has a **covered market** with fruit, vegetable, meat, and cheese vendors at V. Carducci, 36d, on the corner of V. della Majolica. (Open M 8am-2pm, Tu-Sa 8am-7pm.) Also stroll through the **open-air market** in P. Ponterosso by the canal. (Open Tu-Sa 8am-5:30pm.) Most shops in Trieste close on Mondays, and maintain strict siesta hours from 12:30-3:30pm.

RESTAURANTS

Pizzeria Barattolo, P.S. Antonio, 2 (☎040 63 14 80), along the canal. Canopied seating with a view of P.S. Antonio. A sweet pizza crust draws mostly young crowds at lunch time. Bar and *tavola calda* offerings. Fresh *insalata barattolo* L10,000/€5.16. Pizza L8-15,000/€4.32-7.75. *Primi* L8-10,000/€4.32-5.16; *secondi* L10-20,000/€5.16-10.33. Cover L2000/€1.03. Service 15%. Open daily 8:30am-midnight. AmEx/MC/V.

Buffet Mase, V. Valdirivo, 32 (☎040 63 94 28), near P. Oberdan, goes for the beer *haus* motif of red checkered tablecloths and colorful German lads. Watch soccer matches and dig into heaping platefuls of pasta and *weiswurst con patate e crauti* (L10,000/€5.16). *Primi* from L7000/€3.62. Open M-Sa 9am-1am. AmEx/MC/V.

Grapperia Paninoteca Da Livio, V. della Ginnastica, 3 (☎040 63 64 46), inland off V. Carducci and parallel to V. XX Settembre. Fresh *panini* (L3-4500/€1.55-2.32) and a wide selection of beers (from Sans Souci to Budweiser, starting at L4000/€2.07) in a tiny, memorabilia-infested restaurant. Open M-Sa 9:30am-12:30pm and 3:30-11pm.

👁 SIGHTS

CITY CENTER

CITTÀ NUOVA. In the 1700s, Empress Maria Theresa of Austria commissioned a "Città Nuova" plan for Trieste, which 19th-century Viennese urban planners implemented between the waterfront and the Castello di San Giusto. The resulting gridlike pattern of streets lined with Neoclassical palaces centers around the Canale Grande. Facing the canal from the south is the Serbian Orthodox Chiesa di San Spiridione, a neo-Byzantine church with pale blue domes and a lush interior. *(Open Tu-Sa 9am-noon and 5-8pm. Shoulders and knees must be covered.)* The **Municipio** at the head of Piazza dell'Unità d'Italia complements the largest *piazza* in Italy. An allegorical fountain with statues representing four continents sits in the center.

CASTELLO DI SAN GIUSTO. The 15th-century Venetian **Castello di San Giusto** presides over **Capitoline Hill**, the city's historic center. The ramparts of the castle enclose a **museum** that has temporary exhibits and a permanent collection of 13th-century weaponry, furniture, and tapestries. Within the castle walls, a huge outdoor theater is host to festivals in August. If you're up for the walk, from ascend the hill from P. Goldoni by way of the daunting 265 **Scala dei Giganti** or "Steps of the Giants". *(South of P. Unità. Take bus #24, L1400/€0.72, from the station to the last stop. ☎ 040 31 36 36. Castle open daily 9am-sunset. Museum open T-Su 9am-1pm. L2000/€1.03.)*

PIAZZA DELLA CATHEDRALE. This hilltop *piazza* overlooks the sea and downtown Trieste. Enjoy a prime sunset if the *bora* winds don't blow you away. Directly below lie the remains of the old Roman city center, and across the street is the restored **Cathedrale di San Giusto.** The church originally comprised two separate basilicas, one dedicated to S. Giusto, the other to S. Maria Assunta. They were joined in the 14th century, creating the cathedral's irregular plan. Inside, two splendid mosaics decorate the chapels directly to the left and right of the altar.

MUSEO DI STORIA E D'ARTE. This art history museum provides archaeological documentation of the history of Trieste and the upper Adriatic during and preceding its Roman years. It also holds a growing collection of Egyptian and Greek art and artifacts. Outside, the **Orto Lapidario** (Rock Garden) showcases fragments of pillars and buildings from the Roman period. *(V. Cattedrale, 15., in P. Cattedrale. ☎ 040 37 05 00 or 30 86 86. Open Th-Su 9am-1pm, Tu-W 9am-7pm. L3000/€1.55.)*

TEATRO ROMANO. The crumbling *teatro* was built under the auspices of Trajan in the first century AD. Originally, crowds hooted at gladiatorial contests; later spectators wept at the passion and blood in the slightly tamer form of Greek revival tragedy performed here. *(On V. del Teatro, off C. Italia. From the Orto Lapidario, descend the hill and head toward P. Unità.)*

MUSEO REVOLTELLA. This museum brings many temporary modern art exhibits to Trieste. Combining the neo-Renaissance 18th-century home of Baron Revoltella and the Galleria d'Arte Moderna, the Revoltella also has a permanent collection of art from the Neoclassical period to the present day. *(V. Diaz, 21. ☎ 040 31 13 61 or 30 09 38. Open W-M 9am-1:30pm and 4-7pm.)*

CITY ENVIRONS

▧ **CASTELLO MIRAMARE.** The **Barcola** ends at the stunning castle of Archduke Maximilian of Austria, who ordered its construction in the mid-19th century. The lavishly decorated apartments feature huge crystal chandeliers, intricately carved furniture, rich tapestries, Asian porcelain, and good explanations of everything in English. Legend has it that the ghost of Carlotta, Maximilian's wife, haunts the castle. Apparently, Carlotta went a bit loopy after losing her husband to a firing squad.

Poised on a high promontory over the gulf, Miramare's white turrets are easily visible from the Capitoline Hill in Trieste. Its extensive parks and gardens, open to

NORTHEAST ITALY

the public at no cost, include a cafe and various ponds housing ducks, swans, turtles, and sunbathing stray cats. *(To reach Miramare, take bus #36 (20min., L1400/€0.72) to the hostel and walk along the water. ☎ 040 22 47 013. Open daily 9am-7pm, ticket office closes 1hr. earlier. L8000/€4.13. English tours L4000/€2.07.)*

BARCOLA. Had enough Neoclassicism to last you a lifetime? Grab your tanning oil and hit the cement. On the **Barcola**, the cafe-lined boardwalk that extends for 7km north of town, you'll find yourself in the company of sunbathers, rollerbladers, joggers, and *bocci* players. Each year, on the second Sunday in October, Trieste stages the *Barcolana*, a regatta that attracts mariners worldwide and saturates the harbor with thousands of billowing sails.

MARINE PARK. Sponsored by the World Wildlife Fund, the marine park is serviced out of **Castelletto Miramare,** a small aquatic museum within the gardens of Castel Miramare. Museum entrance is by guided tour only, so call ahead. From the gardens, the yellow buoys that mark the park itself are visible, but if you want to get any closer, you will have to sign up for a snorkel or scuba tour. *(☎ 040 22 41 47. Call to reserve a space on a museum tour or an English snorkeling or scuba tour. You must have certification to scuba dive. Snorkel, fins, and mask included. Reservations required. Must be in groups of 10; ask to be grouped with others if your group is less than 10. Office open M-F 9am-7pm, Sa 9am-5pm. Scuba L25,000/€12.91, children L20,000/€10.33.)*

KUGY PATH AND GROTTA GIGANTE. The tram to Opicina from P. Oberdan is one of the longest running funiculars in Europe. After a steep climb, the tram runs past local vineyards and provides breathtaking views of the Adriatic coastline. Hop off at the Obelisk stop to meet up with the Kugy Path, a popular trail that cuts along the sides of the Carso cliffs. There are benches along the path, so you can stop and admire the views of the Adriatic and the coastline of Slovenia and Croatia. At the end of the tram route is the cleverly named Grotta Gigante, which is…you guessed it, a damn big cave, in fact, the world's largest tourist cave. Staircases wind in and around the 107m high interior. *(V. Machiavelli, 17. In the small parking lot across V. Nazionale from the tram stop is the bus #45 stop. L1400/€0.72. ☎ 040 32 73 12; www.ts.cam.com.it/ english/grotta/htm. Open Apr.-Sept. Tu-Sa 10am-6pm, tours every 30min.; Mar. and Oct. Tu-Sa 10am-noon and 1-4pm, every hr.; Nov.-Feb. 10am-noon and 2-4pm, every hr. L14,000/€7.32.)*

RISIERA DE SAN SABBA. One of Italy's two World War II concentration camps occupied an abandoned rice factory outside Trieste. The *risiera*, Ratto della Pileria, 43, houses a museum detailing Trieste's role in the Slovenian-born resistance movement that confronted the Nazis occupying Trieste. *(Take bus #8. ☎ 040 82 62 02. Open May 16-Mar. Tu-Su 9am-1pm; Apr.-May 15 M-Sa 9am-6pm, Su 9am-1pm. Free.)*

🎵 ENTERTAINMENT

The opera season of the **Teatro Verdi** runs November to May, but the theater holds a six-week operetta season from late June to Early August. Buy tickets or make reservations at P. Verdi, 1. (☎ 040 67 22 298 or 67 22 299; www.teatroverditrieste.com. Open Tu-Su 9am-noon and 4-7pm. L15-70,000/€7.75-36.15.) **UTAT-Galleria Protti** (☎ 040 63 00 63), has information on dates, times, and prices of all performances. The liveliest *passeggiate* take place along Capo di Piazza, a traffic-free avenue on the pedestrian shopping street connecting P. della Borsa to P. della Unità. **Bar Unità**, on the southwest corner of P. Unità, survives the winter to see its outdoor tables packed with students. (☎ 040 36 80 63. Open M-Sa 6:30am-3:30am.)

Juice, V. Madonnina, 10, is always packed in winter, with twenty-somethings crowding over menus (written on old vinyl records) listing dishes other than pasta and pizza. Warm up with crêpes filled with nutella (L4000/€2.07), or try a **scivelo** (L10,000/€5.16), a local drink made from strawberry Keglevich vodka and lemon soda. (☎ 040 760 03 41. Open daily Sept.-June 7:30pm-2am.)

NORTHEAST ITALY

AQUILEIA

When the streaming landscape of cornfields and grapevines suddenly gives way to a cluster of half-standing columns and neatly-arranged limestone bricks, you've arrived. Two minutes and several dozen buildings later, the cultivated landscape returns, and you have already left. That is Aquileia to the hundreds of tourists who pass through this pocket-size town en route to the seaside resort of Grado. By staying on the main road, they have left a sleepy village with a proud history and impeccably preserved artifacts unspoiled. After all, Aquileia wasn't always so small. Between AD 200 and 452, it flourished as the Roman capital of the region, and served as the gateway to the Eastern Empire's interests in the Adriatic.

🛈 PRACTICAL INFORMATION. Aquileia can be reached by **bus** from Udine (1hr., 16 per day 6:10am-9:40pm, L5000/€2.58). From Cervignano, a **train station** on the Trieste-Venice line, buses leave to Aquileia *centro* every 30min. (15min, 6am-8:30pm, L1500/€1.29). For a list of budget accommodations and camping in the area, including the resort island of Grado (just 15km south on **via Beligna,** the main thoroughfare that cuts through town), consult Aquileia's helpful **APT tourist office,** in P. Capitolo. From the bus stop, cross the street and head up **via Popone.** The *basilica* is straight ahead, and the APT office is on your left as you enter the *piazza.* (☎ 0431 910 87 or 91 94 91. Open Apr.-Oct. F-W 9am-6pm.) In an **emergency,** dial ☎ 113, or call the **police station,** V. Semina (☎ 0431 91 03 34). **Farmacia,** the largest local pharmacy, is on Corso Gramsci, two blocks from Albergo Aquila Nera. (☎ 0431 91 00 01. Open M-F 8:30am-12:30pm and 3:30-7:30pm, Sa 8:30am-12:30pm.) For **currency exchange** and **postal services** July-Sept., walk two blocks along V. Augusta (toward Cervignano) to the **Poste Italiane** kiosk. (Open M-F 9am-12:30pm and 3:30-5pm.) Otherwise, the central post office is in P. Cervi, off Corso Gramasci. (☎ 0431 91 92 72. Open M-S 8:25am-1:40pm.) **Postal Code:** 33051.

🛏🍴 ACCOMMODATIONS AND FOOD. Aquileia's one affordable hotel is the inviting **Albergo Aquila Nera,** Piazza Garibaldi, 5, only a five minute walk up V. Roma from V. Beligna. The rooms are sparse and the common bathrooms are quirky (minimalist shower and pull-chain toilets), but the wonderful owners fully make up for this. Full and half pension are available at the restaurant downstairs, and chances are you will feast alongside the owners and their family. The adjoining bar fills with spirited locals nightly. (☎ 0431 910 45. Breakfast included. Lunch/dinner L20-30,000/€10.33-15.50 per person. Singles L55,000/€28.41; doubles L90,000/€46.48.) **Camping Aquileia,** V. Gemina, 10, a shady spot with a swimming pool, lies up the street from the forum. (☎ 0431 910 42; ☎/fax 91 95 83; www.campingaquileia.it. L10,000/€5.16 per person, under 12 L6300/€3.25. Tent sites L16,000/€8.26. 3-person bungalow L78,000/€40.28, 4-person bungalow L99,000/€51.13. Open May 15-Sept. 20.) A delicious, locally-grown meal awaits at *agriturismo* **La Pergola,** V. Beligna, 4, where a caged bird heralds the arrival of your *gnocchi* or lamb, the house specialty. (☎ 0431 9 13 06. Open M, W-F 10am-3pm and 5-11pm; Sa-Su noon-4pm and 5-11pm. *Primi* L8-12,000/€4.13-6.20; *secondi* L12-18,000/€6.20-9.30.) Create your own spread at the **Desparo supermarket,** V. Augusta, across from the bus parking lot. (Open Tu-Sa 8:30am-1pm and 4-7pm, Su 8am-1pm. Closed W afternoon.) Still fishing? Upstairs, **Ristorante al Pescatore** specializes in fish and pizza. (☎ 0431 91 95 70. *Primi* L8-13,000/€4.32-6.71; *secondi* L12-21,000/€6.20-10.85; pizza L8-10,000/€4.32-5.16. Cover L1500/€0.77. Open Tu-Su noon-2:30pm and 5-11pm.) Don't miss **Melon's Club,** a roadside stand just across from Desparo. Dozens of gigantic watermelons bob in ice-cold water (while their measly cousins, the cantaloupe, sit behind a refrigerated display). Initiation into this sweet society: L2500/€1.29 per slice. (Open daily June-Aug. noon-8pm.)

◉ SIGHTS. Aquileia's ▨ basilica, a tribute to the town's artistic heritage, blends work spanning many centuries with both ease and beauty. The floor, a remnant of the original church, is a mosaic animating over 700 square meters with geometric designs and bestial images. Beneath the altar, the crypt's 12th-century frescoes illustrate the trials of Aquileia's early Christians as well as scenes from the life of Christ. In the **Cripta degli Scavi,** to the left upon entering, excavations have uncovered three layers of flooring, including mosaics from a first century Roman house. (☎ 0431 9 10 67. Basilica open daily 8:30am-7pm. Free. Crypt open M-Sa 8:30am-7pm, Su 8:30am-7:30pm. L4000/€2.07.) From the nearby campanile (constructed in 1031 using the remains of the Roman ampitheater), enjoy unobstructed views of the Slovenian Alps to the north, Trieste to the east, the Adriatic to the south, and the lagoon to the west. (Open daily 9:30am-12:30pm and 3-5:30pm. L2000/€1.03.)

   Porto Fluviale, the cypress-lined alley behind the basilica, was the dockyard of Aquileia's thriving Roman river-harbor from 100 BC to AD 300, and is a pleasant alternative to V. Augusta as a path to the ruins of the **forum.** From there, continue to the **Museo Paleocristiano** to view moss-covered mosaics that explain the transition from classical paganism to Christianity. (☎ 0431 911 31. Open M 8:30am-1:45pm, Tu-Su 8:30am-7:30pm. Free.) Artifacts from numerous excavations reside in the **Museo Archeologico** at the corner of V. Augusta and V. Roma. The ground floor houses Roman portrait busts; upstairs are terra-cotta, glass, and gold pieces. (☎ 0431 910 16. Open M 8:30am-2pm, Tu-Su 8:30am-7:30pm. L8000/€4.32.)

UDINE   ☎ 0432

Udine's Piazza della Libertà is an engineering marvel. Tilted and split into elevated levels, with looming statues and Moorish figures that chime every hour, it's 60 square meters of pure Renaissance. But beyond this small world, Udine's tourist offerings are few. Unless you are a fervent Giovanni Battista Tiepolo fan (who's pioneer works cover the city), the churches and museums remain interesting, but undistinguished. Conquered by Venice in 1420, appropriated by Austria in the late 18th century, and bombed severely in World War II, Udine has suffered a volatile history. Today, the quiet, glossy streets cater to fashion-crazed locals and remain virtually unknown to tourists. Unfortunately, expensive accommodations put Udine's peaceful milieu beyond the reach of many budget minded travelers.

▐ TRANSPORTATION

Trains: On V. Europa Unità. Info office (☎ 1478 880 88) open 7am-9pm. Tickets and reservations 7am-8:30pm. Luggage storage available (p. 251). To: **Milan** (4½hr.; 5:45am and 6:49pm; L48,000/€24.79); **Trieste** (1½hr.; 1-3 per hr. 5:12am-11:29pm; L10,400/€5.37); **Vienna** (7hr.; 5 per day 9:52am-1:45am; L90,800/€50.61); **Venice** (2hr.; 1-3 per hr. 5:50am-10:29pm; L12,000/€6.20).

Buses: V. Europa Unità. Cross the street from the train station and walk 1 block to the right. **SAF** (☎ 0432 60 81 12) runs to: **Aquileia** (every hr. 6:50am-9pm, L5000/€2.58); **Cividale** (every hr. 6:40am-7:15pm, L3500/€1.81); **Palmanova** (every 2hr. 6:50am-9pm, L3700/€1.91); **Trieste** (2 per hr. 5:10am-10:55pm, L7500/€3.87).

Taxi: Radio Taxi (☎ 0432 50 58 58).

◄▓▶ ORIENTATION AND PRACTICAL INFORMATION

Udine's train and regional bus stations are both on **via Europa Unità** in the southern part of town. All local bus lines pass the train station, but only buses #1, 3, and 8 run from V. Europa Unità to the center, passing by **Piazza della Libertà** and **Castle Hill.** To walk from the station (15min.), go right to P. D'Annunzio then turn left under the arches to **V. Aquileia.** Continue up V. Veneto to P. della Libertà.

TOURIST, FINANCIAL, AND LOCAL SERVICES

Tourist Office: P. 1° Maggio, 7 (☎ 0432 29 59 72; fax 50 47 43; arpt1.ud@adriacom.it). From the southern end of P. della Libertà, turn right onto V. Manin and left onto

P. 1° Maggio. Look for the pink-arched facade. Otherwise, take bus #2, 7, or 10 to P. 1° Maggio. Itineraries for visiting the town are posted in Udine and environs. English spoken. Open M-Sa 9am-1pm and 3-6pm.

Budget Travel: CTS Travel, V. Gemona, 4 (☎0432 51 20 28). Travel service offers ISIC holders discounts. Open M-F 9am-12:30pm and 3:30-7pm, Sa 9:30am-noon.

Currency Exchange: Banks line the streets around P. della Libertà, all offering comparable rates. Also in the post office; on left as you enter.

Library: Biblioteca Civica, R. Bartolini, 5 (☎0432 27 15 89). Open M-F 8:15am-12:45pm and 3-7pm.

Mountain Information: The bulletin board of the **Club Alpino Italiano** (☎0432 50 42 90) is at V. Odorico, 3. Info on skiing and mountain excursions for all of Italy. For hikes in the pre-Alps of Friuli-Venezia Giulia, contact **Società Alpina Friulana,** V. Odorico, 3 (☎0432 50 42 90). Alpine info and excursions. Open M-F 5-7:30pm.

Luggage storage: At the train station. L5000/€2.58 for 12hr.

EMERGENCY AND COMMUNICATIONS

Emergency: ☎113. **Ambulance:** ☎118. **Carabinieri,** V. D. Prefettura, 16 (☎112).

Late-Night Pharmacy: Farmacia Beltrame, P. della Libertà, 9 (☎0432 50 28 77). Open M-Sa 8:30am-12:30pm and 3:30-11pm. Ring the bell 11pm-8am.

Hospital: Ospedale Civile (☎0432 55 21), in P. Santa Maria della Misericordia. Take bus #1 north to the last stop.

Post Office: V. Veneto, 42 (☎0432 51 09 35). *Fermo Posta*, stamps, and fax. Open M-F 7:20am-7:50pm, Sa 7:30am-1pm. **Branch** at V. Roma, 25 (☎0432 22 31 11), straight ahead from train station. Open M-F 8:10am-1.15pm, Sa 8:30am-1pm.

Postal Code: 33100.

▐ ACCOMMODATIONS

The good news is that Udine's hotels are clearly marked on the large map outside the train station. The bad news is that local workers probably snagged the cheapest spots long ago.

Due Palme, V.L. Da Vinci, 5 (☎0432 48 02 13). Take bus #5 from station and ask the driver for Hotel Due Palme. Dimly lit hallway leads to clean rooms with bath, TV, and phone. View of construction site contributes to a depressing atmosphere. The saving grace is the huge breakfast (L5000/€2.58) and an affordable pizzeria downstairs. Singles L70,000/€36.15; doubles L110,000/€56.81; triples L140,000/€72.30.

Al Bue, V. Pracchiuso, 75 (☎0432 29 90 70; fax 29 98 39). Take bus #4 from station, get off at P. Oberdan, and walk down V. Pracchiuso on the far side of the *piazza*. Pricey, well-appointed rooms (all with bath, TV, and phone) open onto a terraced courtyard. Quiet location. Restaurant downstairs serves lunch and dinner, also at a high price. Singles L90,000/€46.48; doubles L160,000/€82.63.

Hotel Europa, V.L. Europa Unita, 47 (☎0432 50 87 31 or 29 44 46; fax 51 26 54). As you exit train station, turn right, cross the street, and walk 2 blocks. Small elevator takes you to the bar downstairs. Grandiose, clean rooms, with bath, TV, phone, and A/C. Breakfast included. Singles L110,000/€56.81; doubles L160,000/€82.63. MC/V.

▐ FOOD

Udinese cuisine is a mix of Italian, Austrian, and Slovenian fare. A typical regional specialty is *brovada e museto*, a stew made with marinated turnips and boiled sausage. Shop for produce weekday mornings in the **markets** at P. Matteotti near P. della Libertà, or head for V. Redipuglia or P. 1° Maggio. (Open Sa 8am-1pm.) The centrally located **Dimeglio supermarket** is on V. Stringer, off P. XX Settembre. (Open M-Sa 9am-1:30pm and 4-7:45pm. Closed W 1-5pm.)

▓ **Trattoria al Chianti,** V. Marinelli, 4 (☎0432 50 11 05), near police station. Serves 7 kinds of home-made *gnocchi* (L8000/€8.14). How about a foray into Slovenia? Try *spatzle* (L8000/€4.13) or *cjalcons* (L9000/€4.65). Wash it down with a *vino della casa* (L1500/€0.77), and you've got quite the affordable feast. *Secondi* L10-15,000/ €5.16-7.75. Cover L2000/€1.03. Open M-Sa noon-3:30pm and 6pm-midnight.

Ristorante Zenit, V. Prefettura, 15b (☎0432 50 29 80). A self-service spot, popular with local professionals, offering pasta, hot entrees, and salad. *Primi* L4500-6800/€2.32-3.51; *secondi* L7000-8500/€3.62-4.39. Cover L500/€0.26. Open M-Sa 8am-3pm.

🟦🎵 SIGHTS AND ENTERTAINMENT

From June to September, P. 1° Maggio becomes the fairgrounds for **Estate in Città**, a series of concerts, movies, and guided tours of the city. **Bar Americano**, in P. della Liberta, is one of the many cafes that tend to be the center of *Udinese* nightlife. (☎0432 24 80 18. Open daily 6:30am-midnight.) **Taverna dell'Angelo Osteria,** V. della Prefettura, 3c, is a throwback to the old Venetian wine culture; while **The Black Stuff**, V. Gorghi, 3a, draws a young crowd. (☎0432 29 78 38. Open W-M 5:30pm-2am.)

PIAZZA DELLA LIBERTÀ. This asymmetric, partitioned, tilting square marks the center of old Udine. Along the raised edge, the **Arcado di San Giovanni** creates a covered walkway overlooking the action below. Directly above, the bell tower features automated Moorish figures that swivel to strike the hour. Across from the arcade, the **Loggia del Lionello** (1488) serves as a public gathering place. In the highest corner of the square, through the **Arco Bollani**, a cobblestone road winds ethereally up alongside an arched promenade to the **castello** above. Once home to Venetian governors, the castle today holds the **Museo Civico,** featuring notable though not necessarily exciting works. *(☎0432 50 18 24. Open Tu-Sa 9:30am-12:30pm and 3-6pm, Su 9:30am-12:30pm. L10,000/€5.16, students and those over 60 L7000/€3.62.)*

DUOMO. The Roman-Gothic cathedral has several Tiepolos on display in its Baroque interior (the 1st, 2nd, and 4th altars on the right side). The squat brick **campanile** houses a small **museum** comprised of two chapels with 14th-century frescoes by Vitale da Bologna. *(In P. del Duomo, 50m from P. della Libertà. ☎0432 50 68 30. Open daily 7am-noon and 4-8pm. Free.)*

ORATORIA DELLA PURITÀ. Udine has been called the city of Tiepolo, and some of this Baroque painter's finest works adorn the relatively modest Oratorio della Purità. The *Assumption* (1759) fresco on the ceiling and the *Immaculate Conception* on the altarpiece present the best examples of Tiepolo's love of light and air. *(Across from duomo. ☎0432 50 68 30. Ask cathedral sacristan for entry. Tip expected.)*

PALAZZO PATRIARCALE. This 16th-century *palazzo* contains a sampling of earlier Tiepolo frescoes. From 1726 to 1730, the artist executed a series of Old Testament scenes here. The museum also displays Romanesque wooden sculptures from the Friuli region. *(P. Patriarcato, 1, at the head of V. Ungheria. Entrance beneath the ornate coat of arms. ☎0432 2 50 03. Open W-Su 10am-noon and 3:30-6:30pm. L7000/€3.62.)*

CIVIDALE DEL FRIULI   ☎0432

In Cividale, you can wind through serpentine medieval streets, around corners, and under archways only to arrive just meters from where you began. The city was founded by Julius Caesar in 50 BC as Forum Iulii, later became the capital of the first Lombard duchy in AD 568, and flourished as a purlieu for artists and nobility in Middle Ages. The arrival of Venetian conquerors in 1420 stunted the town's growth, effectively freezing it in its medieval state. Now, enjoy *cucina friuliani* (regional dishes), a Dark Age spectacle, and a bridge built by the devil himself.

🛈 PRACTICAL INFORMATION. Cividale is best reached from Udine by **train** (15min., every hr. 6am-8:05pm, L3500/€1.81). **Buses** from Udine are less frequent (L2600/€1.34). The train station, which opens onto V. Libertà, is a brief walk from the center of town. (☎ 0432 73 10 32. Open M-Sa 5:45am-8pm, Su 7am-8pm.) From the train station head directly onto V. Marconi and turn left through the Porta Arsenale Veneto when the street ends. Bear right in **P. Dante,** then left onto **Largo Boiani.** The **duomo** is straight ahead. The **tourist office,** Calle per d'Aquileia, 10, across from the Duomo, features a helpful, knowledgeable staff. (☎ 0432 73 14 61; fax 73 13 98. Open M-F 9am-1pm and 3-6pm.) **Banca Antoniana Popolare Veneto,** Largo Boiani, 20, has an **ATM.** In case of **emergency,** dial ☎ 113, seek out the **police** (☎ 0432 70 61 11), on P. A. Diaz, off P. Dante, or contact the **hospital** (Ospedale Civile), in P. dell'Ospedale (☎ 0432 73 12 55). **Farmacia Minisini,** is at Largo Bioani, 11. (Open Tu-F 8:30am-12:30pm and 3:50-7:30pm, Sa 8:30am-12:30pm.) The **post office,** at Largo Boiani, 31, exchanges AmEx traveler's checks. (☎ 0432 731 255. Open M-Sa 8:30am-6pm.) **Postal Code:** 33043.

▐▐ ACCOMMODATIONS AND FOOD. Budget accommodations are not Cividale's forte. The centrally located, two-star **Al Pomo d'Oro,** on P.S. Giovanni, is the cheapest game in town, but the ante is still high. All rooms come with bath. (☎/ fax 0432 73 14 89. Breakfast included, full and half pension available. Wheelchair accessible. Rooms held until 6pm. Singles L80,000/€41.32; doubles L115,000/ €59.39. AmEx/MC/V.) Regional culinary specialties are *picolit* (a dessert wine rarely sold outside of the Natisone Valley), *frico* (a cheese and potato pancake), and *gubana* (a fig-and prune-filled pastry laced with *grappa*). Most bars stock pre-packaged *gubana,* but for a freshly made treat, look for the "Gubana Cividalese" sign, C.P. D'Aquileia, 16, on the right as you near the Ponte del Diavolo. Ask for *gubanetta* (L1200/€0.62), unless you want the whole cake. P. Diacono hosts Cividale's open-air **market** every Saturday from 8am to 1pm. **Coopca supermarket,** V.A. Ristori, 17, pleases even the tightest of budgets. (☎ 0432 731 105. Open T-Su 8:30am-12:45pm and 4-7:30pm.) For *cucina friuliana,* **Antica Trattoria Dominissini,** Stretta Stellini, 18, creates regional dishes like *frico* and *polenta* in a lively bar setting. (☎ 0432 73 37 63. *Primi* L8-10,000/€4.13-5.16; *secondi* L8-16,000/ €4.13-8.26. Open Tu-Sa 9:30am-3:30pm and 6-11pm, Su 9:30am-3:30pm and 6:30-11pm.) **Antica Trattoria alla Speranza,** Foro Giulio Cesare, 6, off Largo Bioani, dishes out similar regional fare, but with an emphasis on locally produced cheeses. (☎ 0432 73 11 31. *Primi* L10,000/€5.16; *secondi* L14,000/€7.32. Open W-M 8am-3pm and 6pm-midnight.) **Bar Al Campanile,** V. Candotti, 4, right off the *duomo,* is a favorite with locals. Try the *prosciutto al salto* (cured ham), the house specialty. (☎ 0432 73 24 67. Open Tu-Su 8:30am-11pm.)

◎▐ SIGHTS AND ENTERTAINMENT. Expanded over the centuries, Cividale's **duomo** is an odd melange of architectural styles, but Pietro Lombardo completed the bulk of the construction in 1528. The 12th-century silver altarpiece of Pellegrino II features 25 saints and a pair of archangels. The Renaissance sarcophagus of Patriarch Nicolò Donato lies to the left of the entrance. Annexed to the *duomo* is the **Museo Cristiano.** This display includes the marvelously sculpted **Baptistery of Callisto,** commissioned by the first Aquileian patriarch in Cividale and the **Altar of Ratchis,** a carved work from 740. (*Duomo* ☎ 0432 73 11 44. *Duomo* and museum open M-Sa 9:30am-noon and 3-6pm, Su 3-5:30pm. Both free.)

The greatest Italian work of the 8th century is downhill at the **Tempietto Longobardo,** built on the remains of Roman homes. As you exit the *duomo,* turn right, then head straight through the *piazza* and turn right again onto Riva Pozzo di Callisto. At the bottom of the stairs, turn left and follow the signs. Inside, a sextet of stucco figures, called the "procession of virgins and martyrs," lines the wall. (☎ 0432 70 08 67. Open daily 9am-1pm and 3-6:30pm; in winter 10am-1pm and 3:30-5:30pm. L4000/€2.07, students L2000/€1.03.) The countryside rolls into the distance, and on a high vista sits **Castelmonte Stara Gora.** For a stunning view, head to the **Ponte del Diavolo,** an impressive 15th-century stone bridge. For a better look at the bridge itself, descend the stairs to the water. Local legend has it that Lucifer himself, in one of his fits, threw down the great stone on which the bridge rests.

TRENTINO-ALTO ADIGE

At the foot of the Italian Alps, peaks sharpen, rivers run crystalline, and natural blonde becomes the predominant local color. The Mediterranean groove of the southern provinces gradually fades under Austrian influences in Trentino-Alto Adige. In the beginning of the 19th century, Napoleon conquered this integral part of the Holy Roman Empire, only to relinquish it to the Austro-Hungarians. A century later, at the end of World War I, Trentino and the Südtirol fell under Italian rule. Though Germany cut short Mussolini's brutal efforts to Italianize the region, Mussolini managed to give every German name an Italian equivalent. While southern Trentino is predominantly Italian-speaking, Südtirol (South Tirol), encompassing most of the northern mountain region known as the Dolomites, still resounds with German. Here, street signs, architecture, and even cuisine blend Austrian and Italian traditions. So practice your German—you'll need it to order fine Italian food at one of the region's many *Spaghettihäuser*.

HIGHLIGHTS OF TRENTINO-ALTO ADIGE

GO WILD in the white-peaked **Dolomite** (p. 257) frontier.

AUSTRIA-CIZE YOURSELF in a Habsburg cafe in **Bolzano** (p. 258).

BE AN AMPHIBIAN at Lake Garda (p. 266)—explore both land and water.

TRENT (TRENTO, TRIENT)　　☎0461

When you arrive in Trent, find a cozy *pasticceria* in the center of town and order *Apfel Strudel* and a cappuccino. Before your eyes, you'll find an edible metaphor for the city itself—a harmonious and tasty mix of Germanic and Mediterranean flavors. Inside the Alpine threshold but connected to the Veneto by a deep valley, Trent became the Romans' strategic gateway to the north. For centuries to follow, fortresses such as the Castello del Buonconsiglio proliferated in the region. Cultural and political ownership of the city, contested in the 19th century, was finally settled at the end of World War I, when Trent became Italy's.

TRANSPORTATION

Trains: (☎0461 98 36 27) on V. Dogana. Ticket window open daily 5:40am-8:30pm; info office 9am-noon and 2:30-6pm. Luggage storage available (p. 255). To: **Bologna** (3hr.; 13 per day 1:26am-9:41pm; L19,600/€10.12); **Bolzano** (45min., 2 every hr. 1:40am-11:22pm, L5600/€2.89); **Venice** (3hr.; 5 per day 4:15am-5:21pm; L19,300/€9.97); **Verona** (1hr., every hr. 2:28am-10:14pm, L9000/€4.65).

Buses: Atesina (☎0461 82 10 00), on V. Pozzo next to train station. To **Rovereto** (25min., every hr., L4000/€2.07) and **Riva del Garda** (1hr., every hr., L5500/€2.84).

Local Buses: Atesina also operates an extensive local bus system. Tickets on sale at *tabacchi* for L1500/€0.77 per ride.

Cableways: Funivia Trento-Sardagna (☎0461 38 10 00), on V. Lung'Adige Monte Grappa. From bus station, turn right onto V. Pozzo and take 1st right onto Cavalcavia S. Lorenzo. Cross bridge over train tracks and head across the intersection to the unmarked building. Open M-F 7am-10pm, Sa 7am-9:25pm, Su 9:30am-7pm. To **Sardinia** on Mt. Bondone (every 30min., L1500/€0.77 per 1hr., L4000/€2.07 per day).

Taxis: Radio Taxi (☎0461 93 00 02).

Bike Rental: Cicli Moser, V. Calepina, 37 (☎0461 23 03 27). Mountain bikes, L25,000/€12.91 per day; L80,000/€41.32 per week.

✈❱ ORIENTATION AND PRACTICAL INFORMATION

The bus and train stations are on the same street, between the **Adige River** and the **public gardens**. The center of town lies east of the Adige. From the stations, walk right to the intersection with V. Torre Varga. Continue straight as **via Pozzo** becomes **via Orfane** and **via Cavour** before reaching **Piazza del Duomo** in the town's center. Numerous **ATMs** are found nearby. For **Castello del Buonconsiglio**, follow V. Roma eastward, away from the river. V. Roma becomes V. Manci, then V.S. Marco.

TOURIST, FINANCIAL, AND LOCAL SERVICES

Tourist Office: Azienda di Promozione Turisitica di Trento (☎0461 98 38 80; fax 23 24 26; informazioni@apt.trento.it; www.apt.trento.it). Provides information about accommodations in the city and surrounding mountains and offers advice on biking, skiing, and hiking in the Trentino region. Open daily 9am-7pm.

Hiking Apparel and Equipment: Sportler, V. Mantova, 10 (☎0461 98 12 90), fashionable and functional outdoor products. Open M 3-7pm, Tu-Sa 9am-noon and 3-7pm.

Public Library: Biblioteca Comunale Trento, V. Roma, 49. Open M-F 8:30am-6:30pm, Sa 8:30am-12:30pm.

Luggage Storage: In train station. L5000/€2.58 per 12hr. Station shut 11:30pm-1am.

English-Language Bookstore: Libreria Disertori, V.M. Diaz, 11 (☎0461 98 14 55), near Piazle C. Battisti. Carries literature and romance titles in English, and a very extensive collection of hiking maps. Open M 3:30-7pm, Tu-Sa 9am-noon and 3:30-7pm. MC/V.

EMERGENCY AND COMMUNICATIONS

Emergency: ☎113. **Ambulance:** ☎118.

Police: (☎112 or 0461 89 95 11), on P. Mostra.

24-Hour Pharmacy: Farmacia dall'Armi, P. Duomo, 10 (☎0461 23 61 39). Serving the city since 1490. Open M-Sa 8:30am-noon and 3-7pm. Late night pharmacies rotate. Check the schedule posted in any pharmacy's window.

Hospital: Ospedale Santa Chiara, Largo Medaglie d'Oro, 9 (☎0461 90 31 11), up V. Orsi past the swimming pool.

Internet Access: Call Me, V. Belenzani, 58 (☎0461 98 33 02), near the *duomo*. Cheap phone cards. L7000/€3.62 per 1hr. Open F-W 9am-noon and 2-10:15pm.

Post Office: V. Calepina, 16 (☎0461 98 72 70), at P. Vittoria. Open M-F 8:10am-6:30pm, Sa 8:10am-12:20pm. Another **branch** next to train station on V. Dogana (☎0461 98 23 01). Open M-F 8:10am-6:30pm, Sa 8:10am-12:20pm.

Postal Code: 38100.

⌂ ACCOMMODATIONS

▨**Hotel Venezia,** P. Duomo, 45 (☎/fax 0461 23 41 14). Large, pleasant rooms, some with a view of the *duomo*. Great location and surprisingly low prices. Breakfast L10,000/€5.16. Singles L52,000/€26.86, with bath L67,000/€34.60; doubles L72,000/€37.18, with bath L92,000/€47.51; triples L92,000/€47.51, with bath L118,000/€60.94; quad with bath 135,000/€69.72. MC/V.

Ostello Giovane Europa (HI), V. Torre Vanga, 9 (☎0461 26 34 84; fax 0451 22 25 17). Two minutes from the station, turn right on V. Pozzo then left on V. Torre Vanga. New rooms with clean bathrooms, lockers (L3000/€1.55 per day), and laundry service (L6000/€3.10), but train noise could keep you up all night. Breakfast, showers, and sheets included. Reception 3:30-11pm. Check-out 9:30am. Curfew 11:30pm. Reserve ahead. Dorms L22,000/€11.36; singles L42,000/€21.69.

Al Cavallino Bianco, V. Cavour, 29 (☎0461 23 15 42), down street from the *duomo*. Great location, but dim lighting and walls so thin you can hear the action next door. Strange jungle motif in the lobby. Singles L50,000/€25.82, with bath L68,000/ €35.12; doubles L72,000/€37.18, with bath L95,000/€49.06; triples with bath L130,000/€67.14. Closed Dec. and June 16-26. AmEx/MC/V.

FOOD

An open-air **market** with fruits, vegetables, and cheeses spreads out every Thursday 8am-1pm behind P. del Duomo; sharpen your bargaining skills. The **Trentini supermarket,** P. Lodron, 28, lies across P. Pasi from the *duomo*. (☎0461 22 01 96. Open Tu-Sa 8:30am-12:30pm and 2:30-7:30pm, M 2:30-7:30pm.) The **Poli supermarket,** at V. Roma and V. delle Orfane, is near the station. (☎0461 98 50 63. Open M and Sa 8:30am-12:30pm, Tu-F 8:30am-12:30pm and 3:15-7:15pm.) **Bar Pasi,** in P. Pasi off the *duomo* (☎0461 98 23 01; open M-Sa 7am-midnight), and **Cafe Mozart,** V. Verdi, 12, also off the *duomo* (☎0461 23 17 70; open T-Su 7am-1am), draw noontime cafe crowds in search of *panini* and *gelato*.

■ **Patelli,** V. Dietro Le Mura A, 1/5 (☎0461 23 52 36), down V. Mazzini from the *duomo*, next to large stone wall. Lovingly crafted menu features meat from 5 countries and numerous vegetarian options. Try the *Gnocchetti di ortica al ragu*, or *Tortellini di Speck e Noci*. The prices, from L15,000/€7.75, allow for both low- and high-end dining within the same friendly atmosphere. Open M noon-2:30pm, Tu-Sa 7-10:30pm. AmEx/MC/V.

Ristorante Il Capello, P. Anfiteatro, 3 (☎0451 23 58 50), next to Chiesa di San Marco. Choose from short, hand-written menu of dishes made with fresh ingredients; ask for the artfully prepared veal. Two can eat like fat kings for L50,000/€25.82. *Primi* L12,000/€6.2. Cover L3000/€1.55. Open M-Sa noon-2:15pm and 7-10pm. MC/V.

Pasticceria San Vigilio, V. Sigilio, 10 (☎0461 23 00 96), just behind the *duomo*. Bertini Elisio hand-sculpts marzipan into whimsical and tasty animal and fruit shapes. *Mignum* (miniature cakes) and candied fruits L3500/€1.81 per gram. Open daily June and Aug. 7:30am-12:30pm and 3-7:30pm; Sept.-May 7:30am-7:30pm.

SIGHTS AND ENTERTAINMENT

PIAZZA DEL DUOMO. The *piazza*, Trent's center of gravity and social heart, contains the city's best sights. The **Fontana del Nettuno** stands in the center of the *piazza*, trident in hand. Its steps offer a good view of the stretch of frescoes tattooing the **Cazuffi houses.** Nearby stands the **Cattedrale di San Vigilio,** named for the patron saint of Trent. *(Open daily 6:40am-12:15pm and 2:30-7:30pm. Free.)*

MUSEO DIOCESANO. Housed in a slender, tall castle of fading red and white stone, this museum holds a collection of sacred paintings, altarpieces, and garments related to the cathedral and the famed Council of Trent. *(P. Duomo, 18. ☎0461 23 44 19. Museum open M-Sa 9:30am-12:30pm and 2:30-6pm. L5000/€2.58 includes access to the archaeological excavations beneath the church.)*

CASTELLO DEL BUONCONSIGLIO. This fusion of intricate stone-work and stout turrets is Trent's largest and most characteristic attraction. The castle houses everything from woodwork and pottery to 13th-century art. The *Locus Reflections* room is where the Austrians condemned Cesare Battisti to death during World War I. For more information on Trent's hometown nationalist hero, and the city's role in Europe's modern wars, stop into the Museo Storico di Trento, on the castle grounds and included on your ticket. If you want to see *Buonconsiglio's* famous frescoes, ask the janitor in the *Loggia del Romanino* to show you to the Torre dell'Aquila. *(Walk down V. Belenzani and head right on V. Roma. ☎0461 23 37 70. Open daily 10am-6pm. L10,000/€5.16, students and under 18 or over 60 L6000/€3.10. Ticket price includes admission to Tridentum, an excavation of Roman ruins under P. Battisti.)*

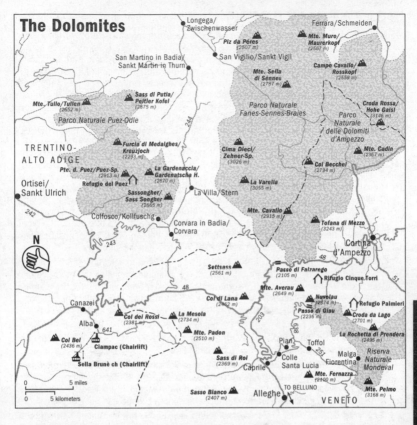

The Dolomites

DOLOMITES (DOLOMITI)

Limestone spires shoot skyward from pine forests. These amazing peaks—fantastic for hiking, skiing, and rock climbing—start west of Trent and extend north and east to the Austrian frontier. With their sunny skies and powdery snow, the Dolomites offer immensely popular downhill skiing. The *settimana bianca* (white week) package, available at any **CTS** or **CIT** office, affords a convenient, inexpensive way to enjoy a holiday in the Dolomites. If you plan to stay in the region of interlocking trails around the Gruppo Sella, consider purchasing the Superski Dolomiti pass for the Gruppo's 464 cable cars and lifts. Try the **regional tourist office** in Bolzano (☎ 0471 99 38 08) for additional skiing and hiking information. The **SAD** (Società Automobilistica Dolomiti) deploys **buses** that cover virtually every paved road in the area with surprising frequency.

Alpine huts *(rifugi)* and rooms in private homes (advertised by *Zimmer/ camere* signs) litter the trails, easing the journey into the mountains. The *Kompass Wanderkarte* map, available at most newsstands and bookstores, clearly marks all accommodations. Huts operate from late June through early October, but at higher altitudes the season is often shorter. Visit the provincial office in Bolzano and local tourist offices for campground listings.

BOLZANO (BOZEN)   ☎ 0471

In the tug-of-war between Austrian and Italian influence, Bolzano pulls on Austria's side of the rope. The architecture is distinctive—here Italy is dipped in pastel paint and decorated with top-heavy gothic spires, pointed arches, and lacy trim. Bolzano's *duomo* does not recall Renaissance harmony, but speaks with a thunderous Gothic presence; the city's museum showcases not restored paintings and sculptures, but a partially decayed man who was encased in ice during the copper age. The best sights in Bolzano, however, aren't the sort you pay admission for; head to the crystal-green Talvera River and catch the afternoon sun on Castel Roncolo, gaze at the steep green hills, resplendent with neat rows of ripening vines.

▐ TRANSPORTATION

Trains: (☎ 0471 97 42 92), in P. Stazione. Info office open M-Sa 8am-5:30pm, Su 9am-1pm and 2:30-5:30pm. Luggage storage available (p. 259). To: **Bressanone** (30min., every hr. 6:00am-9:31pm, L6300/€3.25); **Merano** (45min., every hr. 6:58am-10pm, L6300/€3.25); **Milan** (3½hr.; 3 per day 11:31am-3:44am; L25,600/€13.22); **Trent** (45min., 2 per hr. 5:15am-9:40pm, L5600/€2.89); **Verona** (2hr.; 1-2 per hr. 5:15am-9:40pm; L13,200/€6.82). More frequent service to Milan via Verona.

Buses: SAD, V. Perathoner, 4 (☎ 0471 45 01 11), between train station and P. Walther. Both the bus station and tourist office distribute schedules detailing the extensive service to the western Dolomites. Less frequent service after 6pm, and Su. To: **Bressanone** (1hr., every hr. 4:19am-9:31pm, L7200/€3.72); **Merano** (1hr., every hr. 6:50am-8:35pm, L5500/€2.84); **Val Gardena** (1hr., 6 per day 7am-7pm, L7000/€3.62)

Local Buses: SASA (☎ 0471 45 01 11, toll-free ☎ 800 84 60 47). Bus service throughout the city. All lines stop in P. Walther. Buy your ticket (L1500/€0.77) at *tabacchi* stands, or from the machines near some bus stops.

Cableways: 3 cableways, located at the edges of Bolzano, whisk you up 1000m or more over the city to the nearest trailhead or bike path. The tourist office is happy to advise you on potential routes, and publishes *Bolzano a passeggio,* a guide to 14 easy walks in the surrounding hills. They also distribute the *funivia* schedule in booklet form.

Funivia del Colle (☎ 0471 97 85 45), the **world's oldest cableway,** leads from V. Campiglio to Colle (Kohlern). 9min., 1-2 per hr. 7am-8pm; round-trip L5000/€2.58, bikes L4000/€2.07.

Funivia del Renon (Rittner Seilbahn; ☎ 0471 97 84 79) heads from V. Renon, a 5min. walk from train station, to Renon (Ritten). 12min., 2-3 per hr. 7:10am-8:20pm, round-trip L7200/€3.72, bikes L5000/€2.58.

Funivia San Genesio (☎ 0471 97 84 36), on V. Sarentino, across the Talvera River near Ponte S. Antonio, connects Bolzano to Salto's high plateaus. 9min., 2 per hr., 7:05am-12:30pm and 2:15-7:30pm, round-trip L6500/€3.36, bikes L5000/€2.58.

Taxi: Radiotaxi (☎ 0471 98 11 11), V. Perathoner, 4. 24hr. service.

Car Rental: Budget-National-Maggiore, V. Garibaldi, 32 (☎ 0471 97 15 31). From L135,00/€69.72 per day. 21+. Open M-F 8am-noon and 3-7pm, Sa 8am-noon. **Hertz,** V. Garibaldi, 34 (☎ 0471 98 14 11; fax 30 37 15). From L100,000/€51.65 per day. 21+. Open M-F 8:30am-12:30pm and 2:30-6:30pm, Sa 8:30am-noon.

Public Bikes: Stand on V. Stazione, near P. Walther. Bikes L10,000/€5.16 deposit and ID info per 6hr. City cruisers, not mountain-worthy. Open M-Sa 7:30am-7pm.

Bike Rental: Sportler Velo, V. Grappoli, 56 (☎ 0471 97 77 19), near P. Municipale (Rathausplatz). Mountain bikes L30,000/€15.50 per day, L45,000/€23.24 per 2 days, and L150,000/€77.47 per week. Big selection of retail bikes and equipment. Open M-F 9am-12:30pm and 4:30-7pm, Sa 9am-12:30pm.

✦▐ ORIENTATION AND PRACTICAL INFORMATION

Bolzano's historic center lies between the train station and the Talvera River (Talfer Fluss), with all major *piazze* within walking distance. Street and place names are listed in Italian and German, and most maps will mark both. A brief walk through the park on **via Stazione** (Banhofsallee) from the train station, or **via Alto Adige** (Sudtirolerstr.) from the bus stop, leads to **Piazza Walther** (Waltherplatz), and the *duomo*. Beyond Piazza Walther, Piazza del Grano leads left to **via Portici** (Laubenstr.), home to Bolzano's swankiest district, where German and Italian merchants traditionally set up shop on opposite sides of the arcade. To reach **Ponte Talvera**, follow V. Portici beyond Piazza Erbe.

TOURIST AND FINANCIAL SERVICES.

Tourist Office: Azienda di Soggiorno e Turismo, P. Walther, 8 (☎0471 30 70 00; fax 98 01 28; info@bolzano-bozen.it; www.bolzano-bozen.it.). Provides a city map, and a list of accommodations, including hotels, campgrounds, and *agriturismo*. The *Mountain Walks on the Sunny Side of the Alps* brochure suggests hikes of varying lengths and difficulty in the Alto-Adige region, and *Bolzano Plus* includes several pages of useful phone numbers, excursions, and events. Open M-F 9am-6:30pm, Sa 9am-12:30pm.

Currency Exchange and ATM: In post office or at **Banca Nazionale del Lavoro,** in P. Walther, next door to tourist office. Good rates. Open M-F 8:20am-1:20pm and 3-4:30pm. ATMs are omnipresent in the city center.

LOCAL SERVICES

Luggage Storage: In train station, lockers L5000/€2.58 for 12hr.

Outdoor Apparel and Equipment: Sportler Velo, V. Portici (Lauben), 37 (☎0471 97 40 33). This highly fashion-conscious superstore boasts "6 floors of sport." Down the street, **Sport Reinstaller,** V. Portici, 23 (☎0471 97 71 90), has a smaller selection, but offers slightly better deals. Open M-F 9am-12:30pm and 2:30-7pm, Sa 9-12:30pm.

Alpine Info: Club Alpino Italiano (CAI), P. Erbe, 46 (☎0471 978 172). Hiking and climbing info, as well as guided excursions. Little English spoken. Ring the bell, office is on the 2nd fl. Open Tu-F 11am-1pm and 5-7pm.

Laundromat: Lava e Asciuga, V. Rosmini, 81, near the Ponte Talvera. Washers L6000/€3.10, dryers L6000/€3.10, detergent L1500/€0.77. Open daily 7:30am-10:30pm.

EMERGENCY AND COMMUNICATIONS

Emergency: ☎113. **Police:** 112. **First Aid:** ☎118.

24-Hour Pharmacy: Farmacia all'Aquila Nera, V. Portici, 46/B. Open M-F 8:30am-noon and 3-7pm, Sa 8:30-noon. 24hr. pharmacies rotate; check window for postings.

Hospital: Ospedale Regionale San Maurizio (☎0471 90 81 11), on V. Lorenz Böhler. Hop on the #10 bus, last stop.

Internet Access: Cafe Meraner, V. Bottai, a block from P. Municipio. L7000/€3.62 per 30min., L12,000/€6.20 per hr. Open M-Sa 7am-8pm.

Post Office: V. della Posta, 1 (☎0471 97 94 52), by the *duomo*. Open M-F 8:05am-6:30pm, Sa 8:05am-1pm.

Postal Code: 39100.

▛ ACCOMMODATIONS & CAMPING

Bolzano's handful of inexpensive accommodations fill up quickly in the summer, so book ahead. The tourist office also has information on *agriturismo*. Unfortunately, private transportation to these hillside *pensione* is usually a must.

Croce Bianca, P. del Grano, 3 (☎0471 97 75 52). Look for the sign above a bustling outdoor terrace around the corner from P. Walther, on side opposite the *duomo*. Homey rooms with thick mattresses. Most centrally located budget beds in town. Breakfast L8000/€4.13. Reserve in advance. Singles L52,000/€26.86; doubles L86,000/€44.42, with bath L100,000/€51.65; triples with bath L120,000/€61.97.

Schwarze Katz, Stazione Maddalena di Sotto, 2 (☎0471 97 54 17; fax 32 50 28), near V. Brennero, 15min. from *centro*. From train station, head right on V. Renon, past *funivia*, and look for signs that lead you 20m up a steep hill on the left. Family-run, friendly place with a garden restaurant popular with locals. 9 rooms with bath and breakfast. Reserve ahead. Singles L50,000/€25.82; doubles L85,000/€43.90.

Garni Thiulle, V. Thiulle, 5 (☎0471 26 28 77). 15min. walk from train station. Cross Ponte Talvera, heading away from city center, head left on V.S. Quirino, take first right, and head left onto V. Thiulle. Simple, quiet rooms, some with views of a garden. Run by an older couple. Little English spoken. Singles L70,000/€36.15, 3 or more nights L50,000/€25.82 per night; doubles L100,000/€51.65, L80,000/€41.32.

Camping: Moosbauer, V.S. Maurizio, 83 (☎0471 91 84 92; fax 20 48 94). Take SAD bus to Merano, exit at Hotel Pircher stop, and walk back 300m toward Bolzano. Showers included. L9500/€4.91 per person, L8000/€4.13 per tent, L8500/€4.39 per car.

◼ FOOD

In Bolzano, *pizza* and *gelato* take a back seat to *Knödel*, *Strudel*, and other Austrian fare. *Rindgulasch* is a delicious beef stew; *Speck* is tasty smoked bacon. *Knödel* (dumplings) come in dozens of rib-sticking varieties. The three types of *Strudel*—*Apfel* (apple), *Topfen* (soft cheese), and *Mohn* (poppyseed)—make delicious snacks. The week-long *Südtiroler Törgelen* tasting spree in the fall is celebrated in the local vineyards. P. delle Erbe features an all-day produce **market** with delicious goods from local farms. (M-Sa 6am-7pm.) A **Despar supermarket** is situated at V. della Rena, 40. (☎0471 97 45 37; open M-F 8:30am-12:30pm and 3-7:30pm, Sa 8am-1pm), and numerous *alimentari* are scattered around P. Erbe.

Casa al Torchio, V. Museo, 2c, just off P. Erbe. Italian locals crowd this Gothic house, a labyrinth of low ceilinged rooms decked with wood carvings and antlers. The service is some of the fastest in town. Try the *spaetzli verdi con panna e prosciutto* (L12,000/€6.2) or a *pizza* piled high with fresh tomatoes, cheeses, and speck (L13,000/€6.71). Cover L2000/€1.03. Service 10%. Open M-F noon-2pm and 7-11pm, Su 6:30-11pm.

Hopfen & Co., V. Argentieri, 36 (☎0471 30 07 88), offers a smorgasbord of regional specialties. Sample a tall *birra scura* (dark) or *chiaro* (light) for a mere L4500/€2.32, or dine in the elegant rooms upstairs. The savory, stew-like *goulasch* is pricey at L20,000/€10.33, but with some bread and a drink, it's a rich and filling meal. Other entrees L13-20,000/€6.71-10.33. MC/V.

◉ SIGHTS

DUOMO AND CHIESA DEI FRANCESCANI. With its prickly spined tower and a diamond-patterned roof, the Gothic *duomo* is a dark sight. For the most part, the beauty of Bolzano is in the facades—some of the most eye-pleasing architecture is unveiled near the P. Erbe and V. Museo. The exception is Chiesa dei Francescani, where a simple triangular exterior hides a splendid interior. The church has high, bright white walls with a crucifix suspended by thin wires. At the proper distance, the cross seems to float in front of three dazzling stained-glass windows, in bright slivers of gold, red, and purple. *(Duomo in P. Walther. Chiesa off P. Erbe. Both open M-F 9:45am-noon and 2-5pm, Sa 9:45am-noon. Free.)*

SOUTH TYROL MUSEUM OF ARCHAEOLOGY. For an entirely different experience, visit this intriguing museum, which traces human life in the Sudtirol region from the Stone Age to the early Middle Ages. Here you can see the actual Ice Man—the five thousand-year-old body discovered by a German couple trekking through the Alps—who suffers his embarrassing case of *Decomposus Interuptus* with a quiet dignity. Ask for a free English audioguide at the ticket desk. *(V. Museo, 43, near Ponte Talvera. ☎0471 98 20 98; fax 98 06 48; museum@iceman.it; www.iceman.it. Open Tu-Su 10am-6pm, Th 10am-8pm. L13,000/€6.71, students L7000/€3.62.)*

CASTEL RONCOLO. Perched on the vine-covered hills above town, this is the most accessible of Bolzano's medieval fortresses. Catch a spectacular view of the city from the winding path that leads to the castle, and inside, marvel at the bizarre juxtaposition of the museum's collections. Devil masks, demonic statues, and hollow-eyed mannequins share the stone walls with lavish frescoes. *(Up V. Weggerstein to V. San Antonio. Take the fresco-covered shuttle bus from P. Walther. ☎ 0471 32 98 08. Open Apr.-Oct. Tu-Su 10am-6pm. Gates for the frescoes close 5pm. L5000/€2.58.)*

🔑 HIKING

If you do plan making a foray into the high country of the Western Dolomites, late-June through early-September is the optimum season for both day-hikes and multi-day trekking. Many *funivie* and *refugi* don't open until mid-June, when the trails and passes are finally free of snow and ice. Keep in mind that SAD's service to the Western Dolomites doesn't begin until the first of July. Once they do hit full steam, most roads are accessible by bus; check with the information office at the bus station. Your last bus out of a remote mountain pass might be at 4pm. The tourist information office is your best friend when it comes to deciphering the bus schedules. Arm yourself with a detailed topographical map. *Tabac* maps are more expensive than Kompass brand, but better quality.

HIKE: EXPLORING THE PLOSE (HALF-DAY OR MORE).

The Plose Plateau, towering over Bressanone to the East at a heights of over 2000m, is a popular and accesible alpine area, thanks to the **Santa Andrea Cable Car** (10min.; 2 per hr. 9am-6pm; L12,000/€6.20 roundtrip, bike transport L5000/€2.58.), that operates from the nearby hillside town of **S. Andrea**. SAD **bus route #126** departs from the Bressanone train station to S. Andrea daily at 7:54am, 9:13am and 12:13pm, with return service at 5:11pm and 6:45pm. Buy tickets at the train station (L4000/€2.07 round trip). From the upper cable-car station, **trail #30** leads along the smooth terrain of the Plose's west slope, and **trail #17** follows the meadows on the Plose's southern slope. For a longer, more strenuous hike, **trail #7** traverses the three summits of the Plose massif: Monte Telegrafo, Monte Fana, and Monte Forca, reaching altitudes of 2600m. Two alpine *refugi,* **Plose** and **Rossalm,** make possible hot meals and overnight stays. **Difficulty:** Easy to moderate. **Distance:** Variable, with loops starting at 4km. A tourist office brochure lists three easy hikes on the Plose, ranging from three to six hours. **Special considerations:** Verify bus and lift schedules; exposed terrain; high altitude (2000m).

⚡ DAYTRIP FROM BOLZANO: MERANO (MERAN)

*To reach Merano, change at Bolzano for the frequent regional **trains** (45min., 1-2 per hr., L6300/€3.25). **Buses** leave near the train station for Bolzano (1hr., every hr., L5500/ €2.84) and Bressanone (1hr., every 1-2hr., L5200/€2.69).*

Merano is a luxurious, Austrian-flavored town situated in the hills one hour north of Bolzano. Lavishly trimmed houses stand in rows on wide, tree-lined streets, locals greet each other with *"Gruss Gott"* rather than *"buongiorno,"* and *wurst* replaces pasta on local menus. While Russian royal families once frequented the local spa, visitors now come to Merano to enjoy the town's serene atmosphere, and to stroll the lengthy walks through the surrounding woodlands and vineyards.

There are only a few traditional monuments in Merano. From the tourist office, head right along C. Liberta to reach the **Porta Bolzano,** one of the three original medieval town gates still standing, and walk straight ahead toward the 14th-century **Duomo di S. Nicolo.** Behind the *duomo*, the tiny **Cappella di S. Barnaba** holds massive gilded altarpieces and jewel-encrusted skeletons within glass cases. (Duomo and chapel open M-Sa 7am-6pm. Free.) To the east of the *duomo*, the arcaded V. Portici is home to a slew of expensive shops and restaurants. Farther west, follow the quiet V. Passiria to the **Porta Passirio,** elaborately carved in bronze, on your left before entering the arch. From here, the dense woods and rushing

Passirio rapids make for breathtaking views. The **Passagiata d'Inverno** heads along the east side of the river, while the **Passagiata d'Estate** follows the western bank, To top off your stroll with a marvelous view, follow the sweet smell of ripening grapes 1km along **Passagiata Tappeiner,** behind the *duomo*, to reach the 17th-century **Gun Powder Tower,** with commanding views of the town and surroundings.

Much like Bressanone, Merano is situated in a steep valley, studded with both rolling green plateaus and more pronounced snow-capped peaks. Not surprisingly, **biking, hiking, and trekking** options in the Merano surroundings are abundant. **Tabac Map #011** covers Merano and surroundings, including Naturno.

The two main arteries of the town are **via Portici** and **Corso della Liberta,** which both run parallel from the river to the train station. Turn right as you exit the station, follow **viale Europa** to **Piazza Mazzini Platz,** then take C. della Liberta (Freiheitsstr.) to the center of town. At the **tourist office,** C. della Liberta, 45, pick up a list of accommodations and information on local walks and outings. (☎0473 23 52 23; fax 23 52 24; info@meraninfo.it. Open M-F 9am-6:30pm, Sa 9:30am-6pm, Su 10am-12:30pm.) Change money (you'll need it!) or use the **ATM** at **Cassa Rurale di Merano,** C. Liberta, 23. (Open M-F 8:05am-12:55pm and 2:45-4:45pm.)

Dining in Merano requires a gold card. Fortunately, an **A & O Supermarket** is at the corner of V. Portici and V. Cassa di Risparmio. (Open M-Sa 8am-7pm.) The local favorite, **Pizza al Taglio,** serves up thick-crusted slices of pizza starting at L2500/€1.29. (Open M-F 10am-10pm, Sa-Su 10am-1pm.) Another option is **Restaurant Sigmund,** C. Liberta, 2, 100m past the tourist office on the left. (☎0473 23 77 49. *Spaghetti al pomodoro fresco* L9500/€4.91. Open Th-Tu 11:30am-9pm.)

BRESSANONE (BRIXEN) ☎0472

Bressanone is quintessential Sudtirol. Northwest of the Dolomites, and south of Austria, its alpine valley spoils visitors with unimpeded views of green mountains, crystalline rivers, and neat rows of pastel houses. In addition, the town's medieval heritage has bestowed a number of artistic treasures upon Bressanone, most notably the 14th-century *chiostro*. Bressanone is smaller and less touristed than Bolzano, and cheaper than Merano. Nonetheless, expect sightseers to arrive by the busload in summer. Prepare for a quick exit to the mountains.

⊡⊓ TRANSPORTATION AND PRACTICAL INFORMATION. Bressanone is an easy daytrip by train or bus from Bolzano or Trent. **Trains** run to: **Bolzano** (30min., every hr. 6:27am-9:09pm, L6300/€3.25); **Munich** (5hr.; 3-4 per day 8:33am-6:57pm; L60,000/€30.99); **Trent** (1-1½hr.; every 2hr. 6:27am-9:09pm; L11,900/€6.15); **Verona** (2hr.; 3-4 per day 6:27am-9:09pm; L22,000/€11.36). **Buses** run to **Bolzano** (1hr., every hr. 7am-8:15pm, L7200/€3.72). The center of town is **Piazza del Duomo.** From the train station and bus stop, follow **viale Stazione** left 500m and past the glass-encased **tourist office** (on your right, at the corner of Viale Stazione and V. Cassiano). At the intersection, take **V. Bastioni Min.** and turn right through the flower-covered arch on your right to enter the courtyard of the Palace. The **tourist office,** Viale Stazione, 9, distributes town maps and guides to suggested hikes. (☎0472 83 64 01; fax 83 60 67; info@brixen.org. Open M-F 8:30am-12:30pm and 2:30-6pm, Sa 9am-12:30pm.) In an **emergency** dial ☎113, the **police** (☎112 or ☎0472 83 34 55), or an **ambulance** (☎118). There is a **24hr. pharmacy** at Kl. Lauber, 2/a; check the sign posted in the window for the weekly night pharmacy. (Open M-Su 8am-12:30 and 3-9pm; closed W afternoon.) The **hospital** (☎0472 81 21 11) is on V. Dante, toward Brenner. **ATMs** line V. Bastioni Magg., one block north of P. del Duomo. **Change money** at Bressanone's **post office,** behind the tourist office. (Open M-F 8:05am-6:30pm, Sa 8:05am-1pm.) **Postal Code:** 39042.

⌐⌐⊡ ACCOMMODATIONS AND FOOD. Accommodations in Bressanone are surprisingly affordable; even three-star hotels run about L80,000/€41.32 for a single. Book ahead; Bressanone caters to daytrippers, and there are few overnight options in the town center. **Ostello della Gioventu Kassianeum,** V. Bruno, 2, off the *duomo*, has an institutional feel and a German patronage. Breakfast and sheets are included. (☎0472 27 99 99; fax 27 99 98; jukas@jukas.net. Dorm L32,000/ €16.53; private room with bath L47,000/€24.27 per person.) **Tallero,** V. Mercato Vecchio, 35, lets 10 rooms near P. del Duomo. From the *piazza*, head toward the smaller chapel on your right, turn right and then left onto V. Torre Bianca and continue straight. Reserve ahead. (☎0472 83 05 77. Breakfast included. Singles L50-55,000/€25.82-28.41; doubles L80,000/€41.32.) Friendly **Cremona,** V. Veneto, 26, offers 12 clean (but noisy) rooms outside the town center. From the station, walk one block down Viale Mozart to V. Veneto. (☎0472 83 56 02; fax 20 07 94. Breakfast included. Singles and doubles L50,000/€25.82 per person; most rooms with bath.)

At the century-old **Restaurant Fink,** Kleine Lauben, 4, local crafts decorate the windows, and waitresses in traditional dress serve up Austrian and Italian cuisine. (☎0472 83 48 83. *Rosti* of potatoes and veggies L13,000/€6.71; *insalata grande con mozzerella e pane d'olive* L12,000/€6.20; *primi* L10-15,000/€5.16-7.75. Cover L2000/€1.03. Open M-Sa 11am-11pm.) Dining on a more limited budget? Try the ever-present **STANDA supermarket,** Viale Stazione, 7, next to the tourist office, for all of your picknicking needs. (Open M-Sa 8am-7pm.)

◙ SIGHTS. Most sights are concentrated around P. del Duomo. A few yards south of the *piazza*, at P. Palazzo, the richly ornamented **Palazzo Vescovile,** originally constructed in 1595, houses the **Museo Diocesano.** The building itself has a stunning interior courtyard, while the museum traces the development of Western Christianity amidst evolving European social structures and technological advances such as the printing press. A number of medieval and Renaissance portraits are also on display, including copies of works by Hans Klocker and Albrecht Dürer. Explanatory information is in Italian and German only. (☎0472 83 05 05. Open Mar. 15-Oct. Tu-Su 10am-5pm. L12,000/€6.2, reduced L9000/€4.62.)

The **duomo,** in the center of the *piazza*, was originally constructed in the Romanesque style, but it acquired Baroque and Neoclassical detailing during renovations in 1595, 1754, and 1790. Today, the gilded ceiling and marble walls are dazzling. The nearby **Chiostro,** to the left as you exit the *duomo*, dates from the 14th century and highlights the evolution of medieval painting through a series of frescoes. (*Duomo* and *Chiostro* open M-Sa 6am-noon and 3-6pm, Su 3-6pm. Free.)

One of the most enjoyable activities in Bressanone is simply strolling the pleasant streets of the city. From Ponte Aquila behind the *duomo*, cross the bridge to the tiny **Altstadt** (old town), where flowerboxes decorate the windows of pastel houses situated along winding cobblestone lanes.

BELLUNO ☎0437

For much of the summer, the dramatic spires of Dolomitic rock that hover over Belluno are just visible through the blanket of humid air that settles in the valley. Their monolithic shapes drift in and out of view with the passing clouds, inviting speculation from locals about mountain deities and lost spirits. But it is the extensive public transportation network, inexpensive lodging, and proximity to the high country that draw serious outdoorsmen and intrepid budget travelers to Belluno. The town is an ideal entry point for day-hikes or multi-day treks in the Dolomites, including the famous *Alte Vie*, or high routes. With a few splendid *palazzi* and glossy arcades, Belluno is a city more or less undiscovered by the hordes of tourists that plague other, more famous mountain towns (see Cortina p. 265).

� TRANSPORTATION. Belluno sits in an easily assessable region just south of the Dolomites proper called the pre-Alps, 50km north of Venice and 70km west of Udine. Train run directly to Belluno from **Padua** (1hr.; every hour 6am-10:33pm; L11,000/€5.68.) via **Conegliano** (1hr., 8 per day, 6:39pm-8:43pm, L5400/€2.79), a stop on the Venice-Udine line. From Conegliano, some scheduled trains run directly to Belluno, but many require you to change in nearby Ponte nelle Alpi. (☎0437 72 77 91. Ticket office open daily 6am-7:25pm.) Belluno's **bus station,**

across **Piazza della Stazione** from the train station, is a regional hub for **Dolomiti Bus**, which services the Bellunese pre-Alps and the eastern Dolomites. Buses run to directly to: **Calalzo** (1hr., 12 per day, 6:15am-8:05pm, L4000/€2.07); **Cortina** (2hr.; 10 per day 6:25am-6:50pm; L75,000/€38.73); **Feltre** (40min., 16 per day 6:20am-7:10pm). As usual, a myriad of possibilities for bus connections exists, so chances are you can travel the mountains to your heart's delight via public transport. For more information, stop by or call **Dolomiti Bus.** (☎0437 94 11 67, 94 12 37, or 21 72 00. Open M-Sa 6:50am-6:25pm and 7-7:15pm.) The orange **local** buses all stop in P. della Stazione, and service the greater city area for L1500/€0.77 per ride.

⊞❼ ORIENTATION AND PRACTICAL INFORMATION. From the train and bus stations, the city center, **Piazza dei Martiri**, is only a 5min. walk. Follow **via Dante**, opposite the train terminal, and cross the small **Piazzale Battisti** onto **via Loreto**. When V. Loreto ends after 50m, turn left onto **via Matteotti**. P. dei Martiri, with its long arcade overlooking several fountains and sculpted gardens, is now in sight. The handy **APT tourist office** is on the opposite side of the *piazza*, at P. dei Martiri, 8. (☎0437 94 00 83. Open M-Sa 9am-12:30pm and 3-6pm, Su 10am-12:30pm and 3:30-6:30pm.) Pitta S. Francesco lies on the other side of C. Italia from the station. From the *duomo*, take the stairs to your left, turn right at the bottom of the stairs, and cross the street. Turn left, and the office is on your right. (☎0436 32 31; fax 32 35. Open daily 9am-12:30pm and 4-7pm.) No less than six **banks** line the *piazza*, all with comparable exchange rates and 24hr. ATMs. In the case of an **emergency**, call ☎113, the **police**, on V. Volontari d. Liberta (☎0437 94 55 08), or an **ambulance** (☎118). 24hr. pharmacies rotate (check pharmacy windows), **Farmacia Chiarelli**, V. Matteotti, is a good option. (☎0437 94 18 91. Open M-Sa 8:30am-12:30pm and 4-7:30pm.) Belluno's **hospital** is on V. Europa (☎0437 16 111). Email starved? **Sunrise Communication**, V. Caffi, 84, off Piazzale le Battisti, charges L10,000/€5.16 per hour of **Internet** use. (☎0432 94 40 77. Open 8:30am-12:30pm and 3:30-7pm.) Belluno's **post office**, with fax and photocopy services, sits on V. Roma, off P. Emanuele. (☎0437 95 32 11. Open M-F 8:10am-7pm, Sa 8:15am-1:50pm.) **Postal Code:** 32100.

⌐❑ ACCOMMODATIONS AND FOOD. Part of Belluno's allure is its cheap, central accommodations. **Albergo Centrale**, V. Loreto, 2, is just off the *piazza*, and features the location its name suggests as well as 12 clean, affordable rooms with breakfast included. Reserve ahead. (☎0437 94 33 49. Singles L40,000/€20.66, with bath L50,000/€25.82; doubles L60,000/€31, L80,000/€41.32). The petite **De Pian Vittoria**, V. Paoletti, 7, is a five-minute walk from the station. Head up the street to the right of the park, turn left at V. Fantuzzi, and walk one block. The De Pian Vittoria is across the busy street, and behind the building on the left corner. The proprietor will put you in one of six well-appointed rooms with common bathrooms and serve you that delicious big breakfast you've been longing for. (☎0437 94 41 79. Singles L30,000/€15.50; doubles L60,000/€31.) There are numerous options in Belluno and environs, often at low prices. Inquire at the tourist office.

Dining in Belluno is inexpensive, but not that outstanding. From **Trattoria La Cantina**, at V. Matteotti, 17/b, just off the *piazza*, enjoy an unobstructed view of the valley while munching on their speciality, *bruschette* (L8000/€4.13) piled high with fresh veggies and cheeses. (☎0437 94 14 93. Open M-Sa 8am-3:30pm and 5:30-midnight.) Less elegant **La Buca**, V. Carrera, 15/c, serves up standard pizza for L8-14,000/€4.13-7.32, and *pasta* for L10,000/€5.16, and offers good Belgian beer on tap for L4000/€2.07. (☎0437 94 01 91. Open Tu-Su noon-3pm and 5:30-11pm.) **Supermarket per Dolomiti**, next to the tourist office, stocks food for your mountain excursions. (Open M 8am-1pm, Tu-Sa 8am-1pm and 4:30-7pm.) Various **alimentari** (check out the fresh potato-chip stand) line V. Jacobo Tasso, off the *piazza*.

◪ SIGHTS. Belluno's Piazza del Duomo is a masterpiece. Its three *palazzi*, (Palazzo Rettori, Palazzo Rosso, and Palazzo dei Giuristi) cry Venetian Renaissance, and the nearby **Museo Civico** showcases Caffi's enchanting *Venice in the Snow* and Ricci's startling *Fall of Fetonte*. (From P. dei Martiri, follow signs to the duomo.)

☎ *0437 94 48 36; www.comune.belluno.it. Open Tu-Sa 10am-noon and 4-7pm, Su 10:30am-12:30pm. L6000/€3.1.)* While you're in the vicinity, head down the *Scala Mobile* (a three-tiered escalator that leaves from Palazzo Rosso), or walk down the nearby stairs for some nice views of the valley. At the foot of the *Scala Mobile*, there's a stand where you can borrow a bike for the day, complete with front basket, kick stand, and five gears. *(Open daily 9am-6pm. Small deposit required.)*

While Belluno's biggest attractions aren't in town, their presence is looming and far from subtle. The impressive Dolomitic rock faces and grassy peaks that tower over town are only the tip of the iceberg (often literally). To the North, where the Dolomites proper begin, the vast, wild expanse of the **Parco Nazionale di Dolomiti Bellunese (Bellunese Dolomites National Park)** is only 30min. by car or bus. The less challenging **Botanical Garden of the Eastern Alps** rests at the top of a chair lift on the western slope of nearby **Monte Favaghera**. From July 1-Sept. 15, buses from Belluno service a chair-lift that wisks visitors up 1500m in the air. *(☎0437 94 48 30. Inquire at the tourist office for bus and chair-lift schedules.)*

CORTINA D'AMPEZZO ☎0436

Come snowfall, glitzy Cortina draws skiers (and their giggling groupies) from across Europe to the craggy spires far above its streets. The aristocrats of the Hapsburg empire had the same idea but were shut down by the onset of World War II, when Cortina saw some of Italy's bloodiest battles. A number of hikes in the mountains showcase not only Tyrolean natural splendor, but also afford close-up views of old trenches and war tunnels. The not-so-athletically-inclined beware: there is little to do in the town but spend money at the outrageously-priced boutiques and or on delectable German pastries that waft in from across the border.

◪ **TRANSPORTATION.** Cortina lies near the Austrian border, north of Belluno and east of Bolzano. The nearest **train station** is in Calazo, from which buses take a steep and winding road to reach Cortina (1hr., every hr. 6:30am-8:35pm, L4500/€2.32). Cortina is most easily reached by car, but if you're relying on public transportation, trains run to Calazo from Belluno (1hr., 9 per day 8:15am-9:17pm, L5400/€2.79), Milan (8hr.) and Venice (3hr.). **Buses** run directly to Cortina from Belluno (2hr., 10 per day, 6:15am-6:55pm, L9000/€4.65); Milan (7hr.; F-Sa June-Aug.; L50,000/€25.82); and Venice (5hr., Sept.-June 22, Sa-Su; June 23-Aug., daily, L2400/€1.24). The **urban bus** (that familiar orange variety) services Cortina and the Ampezzo Valley, and is useful for reaching hotels and *funivie* (cable cars) outside town (L1400/€0.72; tickets sold at newsstands, *tabacchi*, and bars near bus stops). For more information on all buses, call or stop by the Dolomiti Bus information desk, in the Cortina **bus station**. (☎ 0436 86 79 21. Open M-Sa 8:15am-12:30pm and 2:30-5pm.) Of course, if infrequent bus service has got you down, there's always RadioTaxi (☎ 0463 86 08 88; 24hr. service).

◪◪ **ORIENTATION AND PRACTICAL INFORMATION.** The center of town is the pedestrian-only **Corso Italia**, lined with expensive shops and punctuated by the *duomo*, with its 75 meter *campanile*. From the bus station, cross the street, head left, and take **Largo Poste** to the *centro*. You'll find the **APT tourist office** on Piazzetta S. Francesco, 8, off V. Mercato, on the opposite side of the *duomo* from the station. (☎0436 32 31; fax 32 35; www.apt-dolomiti-cortina.it. Office open daily 9am-12:30pm and 4-7pm.) Banks with similar high exchange rates and 24hr. **ATMs** line C. Italia. In an **emergency** dial ☎113, or the **police**, on V. Marconi (☎0436 86 62 00). The town **hospital**, Ospedale Cortina, is at V. Roma, 121 (☎0436 88 51 11). 24hr. **pharmacies** rotate (check the lists posted in their windows), but **Farmacia Internazionale**, C. Italia, 151, is notable for not only its longer hours, but also as the home of the town's most colorful frescoes. (☎0436 22 23. Open M-Sa 9am-12:45pm and 3-7pm.) **Dolomiti Multimedia**, L. Poste, 59, charges L12,000/€6.2 per hour. (☎0436 86 80 90. Open M-F 8:30am-12:30pm and 3-7:30pm.) The **post office** is at L. Poste. (☎0436 29 79. Open M-F 8:10am-6pm, Sa 8:10am-12:30pm.) **Postal Code:** 32043.

⌂ ACCOMMODATIONS AND FOOD. In 1956, Cortina was host to the Winter Olympics, but abundant and overpriced accommodations might make the budget traveler feel like Olympic spirit is still in the air. The town's one affordable hotel and half-dozen campgrounds are far from the town center but sometimes offer better views of the towering cliff-faces that surround the valley. For the tragically urban, the cheapest option in Cortina *centro* is **Hotel Montana,** C. Italia, 94, near the *duomo.* (☎/fax 0436 86 82 11. Singles L80,000/€41.32; doubles L170,000/€87.80. MC/V.) **Hotel Fiames,** Localita Fiames, 13, books rooms and serves meals in Fiames, 5km north of town. Take bus #1 (10min.) from the station to the last stop. (☎0436 23 66; fax 57 33. Breakfast included, lunch/dinner L30,000/€15.50. Singles L60,000/€31, with bath L90,000/€46.48; doubles L110,000/€56.81, L150,000/€77.47.) **International Camping Olimpia,** Localita Fiames, is north of town, before Hotel Fiames. Bus #1 stops at the access road, ask the driver for the "Olimpia" stop. (☎0436 50 57. L13,000/€6.71 per person, L16,000/€8.26 per tent.) If you stay in Fiames, expect sporadic bus service (1 every hour, 7:35am-6:50pm).

In a town where most restaurant placards read "Apre Ski," dining is, not surprisingly, a larger burden than the wallet can carry. One exception is **Pizzeria Il Ponte,** V.B. Franchetti, 8, which offers a view of the mountains and delicious pizzas from L6000/€3.10, pasta from L8000/€4.13. Head behind the *duomo* on C. Italia, then make a left onto V. B. Franchetti. (☎0436 86 76 24. Open T-Su 10am-3pm and 6pm-midnight. AmEx/MC/V.) Across the street is the less expensive **Kanguro supermarket,** V.B. Franchetti, 1. (Open M-Sa 8:30am-12:30pm and 3:30-7:30pm. MC/V.)

SIGHTS. Cortina's tourist office advises and offers a wealth of information on local skiing, hiking, water sports, and nature walks. Moreover, not every excursion is physically demanding. A flat *passegiata*, or pedestrian and bike path, traverses 7km of the town, from the ski-jump platform to Fiames. There the views of Croda del Pomogagnon, a series of towering rock spires to the east are striking. Look for the *passegiata* signs at both ends of V. Marconi.

LAKE GARDA (LAGO DI GARDA)

Garda—*the* resort destination for many German families—offers staggering mountains and breezy summers. In Sirmione, on the Southern lake shore, with its beautifully situated medieval castle and extensive Roman ruins, expect throngs of tourists and high prices. The quieter, dilapidated Gardone Riviera, on the western shore of the lake, prides itself on its must-see sight, the quirky mansion of famous author Gabriele D'Annunzio. The northern shores of Riva may have fewer sights, but the towns are livelier, the crowd younger, and the prices lower.

Desenzano, the lake's southern transportation hub, lies on the Milan-Venice train line, 30 minutes from **Verona** and **Brescia,** one hour from **Milan,** and two hours from **Venice.** From Desenzano, the other lake towns are accessible by bus, hydrofoil, or ferry. Plan ahead; buses and ferries stop running between 8 and 10pm. For shorter trips, take the ferry—it's cheaper than the hydrofoil. Buses cost even less but are less romantic. Though campgrounds surround the lake, most are found on the most populated side, between Desenzano and **Salò.** Private residences rent rooms in Lake Garda's larger towns, and tourist offices provide lists of potential hosts.

SIRMIONE   ☎ 030

Shrewd developers realized the potential of what Catullus once lauded as the "jewel of peninsulas and islands." Sirmione is a bit like Disneyland—flashy, expensive, and quickly exhausted. The neon-lit medieval streets flood with families and retired couples ushering in Sirmione's holy trinity: dinner, shopping, and dessert. Even so, Sirmione can be downright enticing. The crowded streets contain a palpable, if aged, electricity. The far northern tip of the peninsula trades this glitz for calm walks, Roman ruins, and stellar views across the lake.

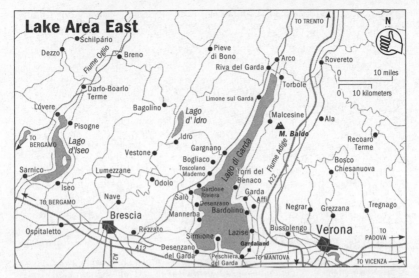

Lake Area East

☎️ TRANSPORTATION AND PRACTICAL INFORMATION. Sirmione is a thin peninsula at the southern end of the lake. Buses run every hour from **Desenzano** (20min., L2500/€1.29), which has the closest train station, to **Brescia** (1hr., L6000/€3.10) and **Verona** (1hr., L5000/€2.58). Buy tickets from the blue machine near the bus stop, or inside the Atesina kiosk during business hours. **Navigazione Lago Garda** (toll-free ☎ 800 55 18 01 or 030 914 95 11) may be more expensive, but it is often the easiest way to reach places along and across the lake. Battelli (water steamers) run until 8pm to: **Desenzano** (20min., L5000/€2.58); **Gardone** (1¼hr.; L10,000/€5.16); **Riva** (4hr.; L13,900/€7.18). For **taxis**, dial ☎ 030 91 60 82 or 91 92 40. The **tourist office**, V. Guglielmo Marconi, 2, is in the disc-shaped building. (☎ 030 91 61 14. Open Apr.-Oct. daily 9am-9pm; Nov.-Mar. M-F 9am-12:30pm and 3-6pm, Sa 9am-12:30pm.) Sirmione's major attractions are concentrated in the north end of the peninsula, across the bridge from the tourist office. **Via Marconi** leads to **via Vittorio Emanuele** and Sirmione's historic **castle**. The **Banca Popolare di Verona**, P. Castello, 3-4, across from the castle, has an **ATM**. (Open daily 9am-1:20pm and 2:35-3:35pm.) Rent **bikes** at **Adventure Sport**, V. Brescia, 9. (☎ 030 91 90 00. L15,000-35,000/€7.75-18.08 per day). In **emergencies**, dial ☎ 113, the **Assistenza Sanitaria Turistica**, V. Alfieri, 6 (☎ 030 990 91 71), or the **police** (☎ 030 990 67 77). The **post office** is near the tourist office. (Open M-F 8:10am-1:30pm, Sa 8:10am-11:40am.) **Postal Code:** 25019.

🏠🍴 ACCOMMODATIONS AND FOOD. The hotels in Sirmione are either pricey or remote, and a thorough exploration of the town takes only an afternoon. If you intend to stay overnight, head to the family-run **Albergo Grifone**, V. Bisse, 5, next to the castle, restaurants and beach. All redwood and offers views of the lake. (☎ 030 91 60 14; fax 91 65 48. Reservations necessary. Wheelchair accessible. Singles with bath L55,000/€28.41; doubles L100,000/€51.65. Extra bed L27,000/€13.94.) Campers should try **Sirmione**, V. Sirmioncino, 9, behind Hotel Benaco, 3km from town. Take the *Servizio Urbano* bus. (☎ 030 990 46 65; fax 91 90 45. Open Mar. 15-Oct. 15. L9-15,000/€4.65-7.75 per person; L15-24,000/€7.75-12.39 per site.)

For eating in Sirmione, the budgeteer has two options: gorge at one of the countless sidewalk pizza and *panino* stands on V. Emanuele (*pizzetta* for L4000/€2.07, and mounds of *gelato*, hardly a bargain at L4000/€2.07 for two scoops), or aim high and order creatively. **Pizzeria 4Re**, V.V. Emanuele, 72, is perhaps the cheapest place in swanky Sirmione. (☎ 030 91 60 24. Pizza L8-14,000/€4.13-7.32; *primi* L10-13,000/€5.16-6.71; *secondi* from L13,000/€6.71. Service 15%. Open

Tu-Su noon-2:30pm and 6:30-11pm. MC/V.) At the **Ristorante Grifione,** downstairs from the *albergo* of the same name, sidestep the expensive bulk of the menu and enjoy fresh fish, a slice of almond cake, and a view of the lake for L29,000/€14.98. (☎030 91 60 97. Cover L3500/€1.81. Open Th-Tu noon-2:15pm and 7-10:15pm. AmEx/DC/MC/V.) Visit the outdoor **market** in P. Montebaldo. (F 8am-1pm.)

◙ **SIGHTS.** The 13th-century **Castello Scaligero** sits in the center of town as a testament to the power of the warlike della Scala family that controlled the Veronese region from 1260-1387. (☎030 91 64 68. Open Tu-Su 9am-noon. L8000/€4.13.) A handful of interesting sights (cannon balls, bricks, and dirt) lie inside, but most of the admission fee pays for the view from the towers. At the far end of the peninsula, the **Grotte di Catullo** houses ruins of a Roman villa. (☎030 91 61 57. Open Mar. to mid-Oct. Tu-Su 8:30am-7:30pm; Nov.-Feb. Tu-Su 9am-5pm. L8000/€4.13.)

Between the castle and the ruins are two public beaches and the **Chiesa di San Pietro in Mavino,** Sirmione's oldest church. A mix of 8th- and 16th-century frescoes adorn the walls, including a particularly disorienting one above the pulpit. Avoid the tourist traps and head for **Tomelleri Park** at the peninsula's northern tip, where you can enjoy views of Sirmione's cliffs for free.

GARDONE RIVIERA   ☎0365

Formerly the playground of the rich and famous, Gardone Riviera is now home to Il Vittoriale, the magnificent villa of 20th-century poet and fanatic nationalist Gabriele D'Annunzio. Since D'Annunzio's death in 1938, Gardone has lost some of its spark. Gone are the days that inspired Casanova the Lover; today, you'll find Casanova the Retired. This new Gardone, however, enchants visitors with its glimpses into the lake's quiet lifestyle, aging villas, and lush gardens.

▮⚎ TRANSPORTATION AND PRACTICAL INFORMATION. Gardone's two main thoroughfares, **Gardone Sotto** and **Corso Zanardelli,** intersect near the bus stop. **Buses** (☎0365 210 61 or 800 41 25) run to: **Brescia** (1hr., 2 per hr., L5200/€2.69); **Desenzano** (30min., 6 per day, L4300/€2.22); **Milan** (3hr.; 2 per day; L15,500/€7.75). You can purchase bus tickets at the **Molinari Viaggi Travel Agency,** P. Wimmer, 2, near the ferry stop. (☎0365 215 51. Open daily 8:30am-12:30pm and 2:30-7pm.) The **APT tourist office,** V. Repubblica, 8, in the center of Gardone Sotto, provides maps and accommodations information. (☎/fax 0365 203 47. Open July-Aug. 9am-1pm and 4-10pm; Nov.-Mar. M-W and F 9am-12:30pm and 3-6pm, Th 9am-12:30pm.) For **currency exchange,** head to the **Banco di Brescia,** across from the Grand Hotel. From the ferry dock, turn right and climb the stairs. (☎0365 200 81. Open M-F 8:25am-1:25pm and 2:40-3:40pm.) In case of an **emergency,** dial ☎113, contact the **police** (☎112 or 0365 54 06 10), or call the **hospital** (☎0365 29 71). For **first aid** at night and on holidays, dial ☎0365 29 71. The **post office,** V. Roma, 8, is next door to the bank. (☎0365 208 62. Open M-F 8:10am-1:30pm, Sa 8:10-11:40am.) **Postal Code:** 25083.

▮⚏ ACCOMMODATIONS AND FOOD. Budget travelers should explore Gardone as a daytrip; inexpensive accommodations are scarce. The **Hotel Nord,** V. Zanardelli, 18, has clean, dimly lit rooms, next a heavily trafficked road. If your Italian isn't *abbastanza bene,* it may be difficult to secure one. (☎0365 207 07. Singles with bath L70,000/€36.15; doubles L80,000/€41.32. Full and half-pension available for stays of at least 3 days.) **Pensione Hohl,** V. dei Colli, 4, is an ancient villa with chipping paint and springy beds. Spend the day lounging in the private gardens, or on your balcony. (☎0365 201 60. Breakfast included. Singles L55,000/€28.41; doubles L98,000/€50.61.)

Trattoria Ristoro, V. Trieste, 18, serves marvelous, inexpensive food. With pink tableclothes, a motherly owner, and a friendly dog, Ristoro feels like home. Try the *gnocchi* (L12,000/€6.2) or the *pesce del giorno* (L18,000/€9.41). From P. Vittoriale near the mansion, take V. Ofi Caduti to V. Carere to V. Trieste. (☎0365 209 86. Open F-W 12:30-3:30pm and 7-10pm.) Down the street from the tourist office toward the ferry stop, **Industria Caffe Regina**, V.S. Pietro, 28, is the perfect place to stop after a hectic day of lakeside relaxation. Indulge in the heavenly Austrian *sachertorte* for L5000/€2.58. (☎0376 63 90 79. Open Tu-Su 8:30am-5pm.)

⊙🎵 SIGHTS AND ENTERTAINMENT. Above Gardone (off V. Roma and V. dei /Colli) sprawls ⬛Il **Vittoriale**, the estate of Gabriele D'Annunzio, the poet, novelist, and latter-day Casanova (see **Literature**, p. 20). Parked in the garden is the prow of the battleship Puglia, the emblem of D'Annunzio's popularity. His ultranationalistic stunts ranged from single-handedly piloting a plane to drop propaganda over Vienna to organizing an army of poetry-lovers to retake Fiume from infant Yugoslavia. Mussolini, who found D'Annunzio's squawking an embarrassment, presented the poet with this rural villa in order to keep him quiet. In the following years, D'Annunzio stuffed his house with expensive and useless bric-à-brac. His bathroom, strewn with 2000 fragments and fixtures, demonstrates the Fascist rummage-sale effect; the *Sala del Mappamondo* reveals D'Annuzio's fantasies of global conquest, and the *Sala del Lebbroso* houses the cradle/coffin in which D'Annunzio contemplated the concept of death. (☎0365 29 65 11; www.vittoriale.it. Villa open Apr.-Sept. Tu-Su 8:30am-8pm. Gardens open Oct.-Mar. Tu-Su 9am-5pm. Multilingual taped tours available. Visit the house early, before crowds arrive. L15,000/€7.75.)

To recover from the perversity, visit the **botanical gardens** on V. Roma, which boast 2000 different plants from six continents, including many species of bamboo and azaleas. Sculptures liven the greenery, and at one point, two sculpted heads spit at each other across a bridge, daring visitors to cross. (Open Mar.-Oct. daily 9am-6:30pm. L10,000/€5.16.) The **Fondazione "al Vittoriale"** sponsors a summer program of plays, concerts, and dance performances in the outdoor **Teatro del Vittoriale**. (☎0365 201 30; ticket info ☎0365 215 51; fax 223 52. Performances mid-July to early Aug. Tickets from L30,000/€15.50.)

RIVA DEL GARDA ☎0464

You could spend an entire day basking in the natural spectacle of Riva. The mountains seem to lean toward the city and even on the clearest of days, clouds cling to the peaks. Riva, with its calm pebble beaches and wide *piazze*, lends a respite from touring and sight-seeing, and diversions like windsurfing, party cruises, hiking, and rock climbing draw young crowds all summer long. With a little of the decadent elegance of Gardone and a dose of the buzzing excitement of Sirmione, Riva is Lake Garda's budget-traveler compromise.

▆ TRANSPORTATION

Buses: (☎0464 55 23 23). From: **Rovereto** (1hr., every hr. 5:00am-7:05pm, L3500/€1.81); **Trent** (2hr., 6 per day 5:50am-6:15pm, L6200/€3.20); **Verona** (2hr., 11 per day 5:00am-8:30pm, L9500/€4.91). For a **train station,** try Rovereto.

Ferries: Navigazione Lago di Garda (☎030 914 95 11), in P. Matteotti, services **Gardone** (L12,200/€6.3) and **Sirmione** (L13,900/€7.18). Also offers sightseeing tours from L24,000/€12.39.

Bike Rental: Superbike Girelli, V. Damiano Chiesa, 15/17 (☎0464 55 66 02). Mountain bikes L22,000/€11.36 per day. **Fiori E Bike,** Viale dei Tigli, 24 (☎0464 55 18 30). L18-25,000/€9.30-12.91 per day. Ask for multiple-day discounts.

✺🔢 ORIENTATION AND PRACTICAL INFORMATION

To reach the town center from the station, walk straight onto Viale Trento and then take **via Roma** to **Piazza Cavour**.

Tourist office: Giardini di Porta Orientale, 8 (☎0464 55 44 44; fax 52 03 08), near the water's edge, behind a small playground on V. della Liberazione. Lists hotel vacancies and offers a variety of inexpensive tours of the region. Ask for a city map and hiking routes. Open M-Sa 9am-noon and 3-6pm, Su 10am-noon and 4-6:30pm.

Emergency: ☎113. **Police:** ☎112. **First aid:** ☎118.

Late-Night Pharmacy: V. Dante Alighieri, 12c (☎0464 55 25 08), and V. Maffei, 8 (☎0464 55 23 02), in P. della Erbe. A doctor is also on the staff. Both open M-Sa 8:30am-12:30pm and 3:30-7:30pm, Su 9am-12:30pm and 4:30-7pm.

Internet Access: Clem's Bowling Club, Viale D. Chiesa, 4 (☎0464 55 35 96). Pricey at L15,000/€7.75 per hr. Open M-Sa 7pm-1am, Su 3pm-1am; closed July.

Post Office: V.S. Francisco, 26 (☎0464 55 23 46). Issues **traveler's checks** and **changes money.** Open M-F 8:10am-6:30pm, Sa 8:10am-12:20pm.

Postal Code: 38066.

▐ ACCOMMODATIONS & CAMPING

Riva is one of Lake Garda's few affordable destinations. Although an off-season visit may require but a little planning, trips in July and August demand reservations months in advance.

Ostello Benacus (HI), P. Cavour, 9 (☎0464 55 49 11; fax 55 65 54; www.garda.com/ ostelloriva), in the center of town. From the bus station, walk down V. Trento, take V. Roma, turn left under the arch, and follow the signs. The hostel has hot showers, satellite TV, a VCR, old-school toilets, cabinets with locks, and a dining hall. Reception daily 7-9am and 3pm-midnight. Breakfast, sheets, and shower included. Book a few days ahead. 100 beds. Dorms L24,000/€12.39.

Locanda La Montanara, V. Montanara, 20 (☎/fax 0464 55 48 57). At V. Dante, 47, face the mountains, turn left onto V. Florida, proceed through the arches, and turn right onto V. Montanara. Cozy, bright, and comfortable. Breakfast L8000/€4.13. Half- and full pension provided in the downstairs *trattoria* for L20-40,000/€10.33-20.66. Reserve a month ahead in summer. Open Easter to mid-Oct. Singles L30,000/€15.50; doubles with bath L66,000/€34.08.

Villa Maria, V. dei Tigli, 19 (☎0464 55 22 88; fax 56 11 70; www.garnimaria.com). A bit removed from the square, but with well-appointed rooms, bath, and TV. A little on the expensive side, but are often available on shorter notice. The rooftop terrace and large breakfast are nice perks. Singles with bath L60,000/€30.99; doubles with bath L90,000/€46.48.

Camping: Bavaria, V. Rovereto, 100 (☎0464 55 25 24; fax 55 91 26), on road toward Torbole. Excellent location on the water and a pizzeria on the premises. Filled with die-hard windsurfing families, it has its own windsurfing school and rental, as well as sailing, canoeing, and swimming options. Open Apr.-Oct. L9-12,000/€4.65-6.20 per person, L16,000/€8.61 per site. Hot showers L1500/€0.77. **Monte Brione,** V. Brione, 32 (☎0464 52 08 85 or 52 08 90; fax 55 65 48), offers a first rate campground with swimming pool, washing machine, electricity, and free hot showers. L8500-12,500/ €4.39-6.46 per person, L20,000/€10.33 per site.

▐ FOOD

A small **open-air market** sells fruits and vegetables in P. della Erbe. (Open M-Sa mornings.) The Orvea **supermarket** sells staples on V.S. Francesco, inland from the tourist office. (Open M-Sa 8:30am-12:30pm and 3:30-7pm.)

Leon d'Oro, V. Fiume, 20 (☎0464 55 73 45). This pizzeria will send your taste buds whirling. Sample the delicious and affordable local wines amidst low-arched rooms and classy decor. Pizza from L8500/€4.39; *primi* L10-15,000/€5.16-7.75; *secondi* L15-23,000/€7.75-11.88. *Menù* L19,000/€9.81; fish *menù* L35,000/€18.08. Cover L1000/€0.52. Open Tu-Su 11:30am-2pm and 6-11pm.

Bireria Spaten, in P. Erbe, is undeniably a beer hall, where long wooden tables, checkered tableclothes, high ceilings, and noisy patrons make for a raucous feast. *Wurstel* L12,000/€6.20; *Goulasch* from L14,000/€7.32; *Birra grande* L6000/€3.1. Open daily 11am-3pm and 5:30pm-midnight.

Quattro Stagioni, V. Maffei, 24 (☎0464 55 27 77), just off P. delle Erbe. A delightful respite from harbor-side prices. Outdoor tables and cozy fare weighted on the Mediterranean side. Try the *Pizza Grecia* L12,000/€6.20. Other pizza from L9-12,000/€4.65-6.20; pasta from L10,000/€5.16. Open Th-Tu 11:30am-3pm and 6:30-10:30pm.

👁🎵 SIGHTS AND ENTERTAINMENT

For fresh-water swimming, pebbly sunbathing, or stunning lake views, follow the lake-side path behind the tourist office and head away from the mountains.

WATERFALL. Just outside Riva (3km), the waterfall at **Cascato Varone** has chiseled a huge gorge in the mountain. The falls were once accessible to rock climbers from the mountain peak; visitors now opt for the stairs. (☎0464 52 14 21. Open May-Aug. daily 9am-7pm; Oct. and Mar. daily 10am-12:30pm and 2-5pm; Apr. and Sept. daily 9am-6pm; Nov.-Feb., also Su 10am-12:30pm and 2-5pm. L7000/€3.62, student L3000/€1.55.)

FUN FOR THE FAMILY. An hour from Riva del Garda, lies a non-Disney affiliated amusement park called **Gardaland.** Diversions include rollercoasters, a "dolphinarium," and medieval jousts. (From Riva, hourly APT buses head to Peschiera del Garda, from which a Gardaland-run bus service heads to the park (every hr. 8:50am-10:15pm). There is also a direct bus service from Riva to Gardaland Tu and Th 8:45am and 4:05pm, round-trip L55,000/€28.41. Gardaland info and buses ☎045 644 97 77. L38,000/€19.63, children less than 1m tall free. Open late-Mar. to late-Oct.; hours vary.)

FUN FOR YOUR LIVER. For nightlife, consider an evening on one of the **party boats** (☎0464 914 95 11) that cruise across the lake to Latin techno beats (cover L22,000/€11.36, includes one drink; cruises July 27-Aug.). Back on the mainland, the party pumps with a mostly German crowd at **Discoteca Tiffany,** at Giardini di Porta Orientale, across from the tourist office. (☎0464 55 25 12. Disco bar Su-Th; disco dance club F-Sa). Ask at the tourist office for listing of free concerts.

HIKING AND OTHER ACTIVITIES. On the other side of town, follow V. Dante up to the mountains and take trail #404 for a steep hike (1½hr.) up to **Chiesetta Santa Barbara** and a breathtaking view of the entire valley. The tourist office dispenses pamphlets on hiking, climbing, canoeing, riding, and golfing opportunities.

ROVERETO   ☎0464

Rovereto sees tourists in transit from the east and north shores of Lake Garda; its hostel is exceptional as a base for daytrips and excursions into the countryside surroundings. If you're biding time in town, the **Castello di Rovereto,** V. Castelbarco, 7, is Rovereto's most important sight. The **Museo della Guerra** (Museum of War), inside the castle, opened in 1921. (☎0464 43 81 00. Open June-Nov. Tu-Su 8:30am-12:30pm and 2-6pm. Castle L6000/€3.13; museum L10,000/5.16.)

The **tourist office,** V. Dante, 63 (☎0464 43 03 63; www.apt.rovereto.tn.it), next to the park in the center of town, helps with the latest trekking, biking, rock climbing, and skiing offerings in the area. **Buses** run frequently to **Riva** (1hr., every hr., L3500/€1.81) and **Trent** (30min., 18 per day, L4500/€2.32). From the **Stazione,** V. Rosmini, 41-45, **trains** run to: **Bologna** (3hr.; every hr.; L18,100/€9.35); **Bolzano** (1hr., 1-2 per hr., L8200/€4.23); **Milan** (2½hr.; 3 per day; L19,000/€9.81); **Trent** (15min., 1-2 per hr., L4500/€2.32); **Verona** (1hr., 1-2 per hr., L6200/€3.20). To get from the bus station to the train station, turn right onto C. Rosmini and walk to the end.)

The **police station** is at Largo Carlo Alberto della Chiesa, 5. Follow the signs directly across the street from the train station. A **pharmacy** lies conveniently between the bus and train station at V. Dante, 3. (☎0464 42 10 30. Open M-F 8:30am-noon and 3-8pm.) Self-service **luggage storage** is at platform #1. (L5000/ €2.58 for 6hr. Open 24hr.) An **ATM/change machine** is in the train station. The **post office** is uphill from the bus station. **Postal Code:** 38068.

Although Rovereto's hotels are either high-priced or located in industrial zones, the city has an extraordinary hostel, the ▓**Ostello della Gioventù "Città di Rovereto" (HI)**, V. delle Scuole, 16/18. Turn right from the bus station onto V. Rosmini and right again onto V. Stoppani. This hostel offers a lounge, laundry service, a restaurant that keeps a place set for every guest. (☎0464 43 37 07; fax 42 41 37; youthostrov@tqs.it. Wheelchair accessible. Breakfast and sheets included. Reception 7-10am and 4-11:30pm; in winter 7-9am and 5-10:30pm. Reserve ahead during the summer, Christmas, and Easter seasons. 2- to 6-bed dorms L21,000/€10.85; family rooms L25,000/€12.91 per person; singles L25,000/€12.91.)

EMILIA-ROMAGNA

Go to Florence, Venice, and Rome to sightsee, but come to Emilia-Romagna to eat. Italy's wealthiest wheat- and dairy-producing region covers the fertile plains of the Po River Valley and fosters the finest culinary traditions on the Italian Peninsula. Gorge yourself on Parmesan cheese and *prosciutto*, Bolognese fresh pasta and *mortadella*, and Ferrarese *salama* and *grana* cheese. Complement these dishes with such regional wines as Parma's sparkling red *Lambrusco*.

Although the Romans originally settled this region, most of the visible ruins are remnants of medieval structures. Developed as autonomous *communi*, the towns later fell under the rule of great Renaissance families whose names still adorn every *palazzo* and *piazza* in the region. Outside the towns, the uninterrupted plains seem to stretch forever, and the cold gray fog of winter—replaced in summer by silver haze and stifling heat—magnifies the illusion of distance. Emilia-Romagna, a stronghold of the left since the 19th-century rise of the Italian Socialist movement, has a look and feel not quite found in the rest of Italy.

HIGHLIGHTS OF EMILIA-ROMAGNA

SPORT those specs in a dark cafe and eavesdrop on impassioned political arguments among the intellectuals of **Bologna** (see below) after a long day of church hopping.

VIVA NESSUN' DORMA in Modena (p. 285), where Ferraris rev their engines and Pavarotti serenades.

FEAST on palatable *prosciutto* and *parmigiano* in **Parma** (p. 293).

GO TO PIECES over the spectacular golden Byzantine mosaics in **Ravenna** (p. 295).

BOLOGNA
☎051

Dark-hued buildings lean over the streets on 700-year-old porticoes and line the cobblestone roads that twist by churches and fan out to the city gates. But Bologna's appeal extends beyond aesthetics. Blessed with modern-day prosperity and Europe's oldest university, Bologna has developed an open-minded character. Political activism is strong and respected—minority groups, student alliances, and the national gay organization all find a voice in Bologna. But with prosperity has come the cars and the multitude of Italian scooters that make walking a hazard to the body, especially the lungs. Like every Italian university, Bologna boasts of wild frat boys Dante, Petrarch, and Copernicus, but heaven (and hell) only know where the author of *La Divina Commedia* really learned his nine circles. He undoubtedly got his observations (and perhaps distaste) for gluttony here; the *Bolognese* taste for rich food has earned the city the nickname *La Grassa*, or "The Fat One."

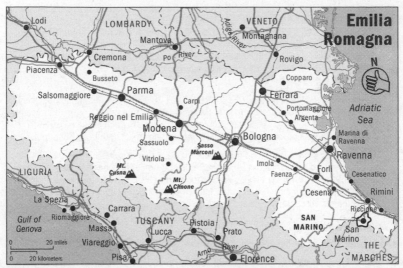

⊟ TRANSPORTATION

Flights: Aeroporto G. Marconi (☎051 647 96 15), at Borgo Panigale, northwest of city center. The **Aerobus** (☎051 29 02 90) runs to airport from Track D outside train station (every 15min. 5:30am-11:25pm, L8000/€4.13).

Trains: Info office open daily 7am-9pm. Luggage storage available (p. 274). To: **Florence** (1½hr.; every 2hr. 4:03am-10:48pm; L8200-13,500/€4.23-6.97); **Milan** (3hr.; 2-3 per hr. 2:53am-10:16pm; L18,000/€9.30); **Rome** (4hr.; 1-2 per hr. 12:32am-8:48pm; L35,000/€18.08); **Venice** (2hr.; every hr. 6:02am-11pm; L14,000/€7.23).

Buses: ATC (☎051 29 02 90), in P. XX Settembre. To reach the *piazza,* turn left as you exit train station. To **Ferrara** (1hr., 1-2 per hr. 6:35am-8pm, L8000/€4.13). **Terminal Bus** (☎051 24 21 50), next to ATC ticket counter, provides Eurolines bus service. Open M-F 9am-1:30pm and 3-6pm.

Public Transportation: ATC (☎051 29 02 90), in train station, next to tourist office. ATC's efficient buses get crowded in the early afternoon and evening. Intracity tickets (L1800/€0.93) are good 1hr. after validation on board. L180,000/€92.96 fine for evaders. Open M-Sa 6:10am-8pm, Su 7:10am-8:30pm. Buses #25 and 30 run up V. Marconi and across V. Ugo Bassi and V. Rizzoli from train station. Bus #25 continues up Strada Maggiore. Buses #90 and 96 run from P. Maggiore up V.S. Stefano to P.S. Stefano. Bus #33 originates at the train station and circles the city walls.

Car Rental: Hertz, V. Amendola, 16 (☎051 25 48 30; fax 25 48 52), straight ahead when exiting the train station. Cars from L200,000/€103.27 per day, including tax and insurance. Open M-F 8am-1pm and 2-7pm, Sa 8am-1pm.

Taxis: C.A.T.: ☎051 53 41 41. **Radiotaxi:** ☎051 37 27 27. Available 24hr.

✴2 ORIENTATION AND PRACTICAL INFORMATION

At the heart of northern Italy, Bologna is a hub for rail lines to all major Italian cities and to the Tyrrhenian and Adriatic coasts. The **train station** is on the northern tip of the walled city. Buses #25 and 30 run between the train station and the historic center at **Piazza Maggiore** (tickets L1800/€0.93; available from most *tabacchi,* newsstands, and machines). On the north edge of P. Maggiore is **Piazza del Nettuno.** From here, **via Ugo Bassi** runs west, **via dell'Indipendenza** runs north toward the train station, and **via Rizzoli** runs east to **Piazza Porta Ravegnana,** the site of the two famous towers. From the towers, **via Zamboni** leads to the university.

NO BOLOGNA. Treat Bologna like a big city—use caution and hold on to your wallet. At night solo travelers may want to avoid the station and northern V. dell'Indipendenza. Plan to arrive during the day. The university area is full of shady intellectuals, but the situation improves somewhat in the summer.

TOURIST SERVICES

Tourist Office: P. Maggiore, 6 (☎051 23 96 60; fax 23 14 54; www.comune.bologna.it), next to the Palazzo Comunale. Open M-Sa 9am-7pm, Su 9am-2pm. Maps and accommodations service. Open M-Sa 9am-1pm and 2:30-7pm. **Branch office** (☎051 647 20 36 or 800 85 60 65), at airport, near international arrivals. Open daily 8am-8pm.

Budget Travel: Centro Turistico Studentesco (CTS), Largo Respighi, 2f (☎051 26 18 02 or 23 48 62), off V. Zamboni next to the Teatro Communale. Open M-F 9am-12:30pm and 2:30-6pm. **University Viaggi,** V. Zamboni, 16e (☎051 23 62 55; fax 22 85 84). Open M-F 9am-1pm and 2:30-6:30pm; closed 2 weeks mid-Aug. Both issue BIJ tickets and HI cards. Discounts on air and sea travel.

LOCAL SERVICES

Luggage Storage: At the train station. L5000/€2.58 per 12hr. Open 24hr.

English-Language Bookstore: Feltrinelli International, V. Zamboni, 6/7 (☎051 26 82 10). Contemporary books and travel guides. Centrally located in the shadow of the two towers at P. di Porta Ravegnana. Open M-Sa 9am-8pm, Su 10am-1:30pm.

Gay and Lesbian Services: ARCI-GAY (☎051 644 69 02; www.gay.it), in P. di Porta Saragozza, at the gate. A political and social organization with a reference and counseling center. Hosts debates and discussions M-W evenings.

Laundromat: One Hour Wash & Dry, V. Petroni, 38b, off P. Verdi and V. Zamboni. L12,000/€6.20 per load. Self-service, snacks, and BBC or MTV. Open daily 9am-9pm.

EMERGENCY AND COMMUNICATIONS

Emergency: ☎113. **First Aid:** ☎118.

Police: P. Galileo, 7 (☎051 640 11 11). **Police Ufficio Stangieri:** (☎051 640 19 03). 24hr. English help line.

Late-Night Pharmacy: P. Maggiore, 6 (☎051 23 85 09). Open 24hr.

Hospital: Ospedale Policlinico Sant'Orsola, V. Massarenti, 9 (☎051 636 31 11).

Internet Access: Ufficio per le Relazioni con il Pubblico, P. Maggiore, 6 (☎051 20 31 84), in tourist office. 3 DSL-equipped computers. Booked weeks ahead in high season. Sign up at the office. Free. Open M-Sa 8:30am-7pm; closed Aug. **Crazy Bull Cafe,** V. Montegrappa #11/e (☎051 23 50 43), off V. dell'Indipendenza near P. Maggiore. Lots of fast computers, no cow. L9000/€4.65 per hr. Student discounts. Open Tu-Sa 10am-2am, Su 7:30pm-2am; closed Aug.

Post Office: (☎051 23 06 99), P. Minghetti, southeast of P. Maggiore, off V. Farini. Fermo Posta. Open M-F 8:15am-6:30pm, Sa 8:15am-12:20pm. Also in train station (☎051 24 34 25). Open M-F 8:15am-1:20pm, Sa 8:15am-12:20pm.

Postal Code: 40100.

█ ACCOMMODATIONS

Reserve ahead when possible. In the off-season expect to pay around L10,000/€5.16 less than listed prices. Always ask about discounts for extended stays.

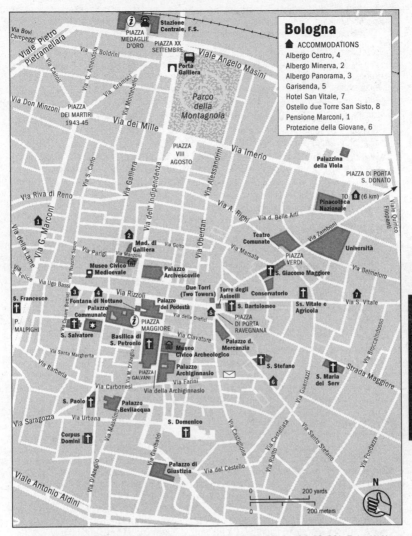

Bologna

🏠 ACCOMMODATIONS

Albergo Centro, 4
Albergo Minerva, 2
Albergo Panorama, 3
Garisenda, 5
Hotel San Vitale, 7
Ostello due Torre San Sisto, 8
Pensione Marconi, 1
Protezione della Giovane, 6

Albergo Panorama, V. Livraghi, 1, 4th fl. (☎051 22 18 02; fax 26 63 60). Take V. Ugo Bassi from P. Maggiore and take the 3rd left. Prime location and sparklingly clean; a rarity in Bologna. True to its name, this hotel has 13 enormous rooms with views of the hills. Working elevator, but no rooms with bath. All with TV and phone. Singles L85,000/€43.90; doubles L110,000/€56.81; triples L140,000/€72.30; quads L160,000/€82.60; quints L180,000/€92.97. AmEx/MC/V.

Ostello due Torre San Sisto (HI), V. Viadagola, 5 (☎/fax 051 50 18 10), off V. San Donato, in the Località di San Sisto, 6km northeast of the center of town. Tourist office has map with directions. Walk down V. dell'Indipendenza from the station, turn right on V. della Mille, cross the street, and catch bus #93 (every 30min. 6:48am-8:23pm) on the left side of the road. Ask the driver for the "San Sisto" stop. Exit bus and cross street; hostel is the yellow building on right with a yellow and green metal fence. Large building in a tranquil setting. Breakfast and hot showers included. Laundry service and basketball court. Wheelchair accessible. Dinner L14,000/€7.23. Reception 7am-midnight. Lockout 10am-3:30pm. Curfew midnight. Dorms L23,000/€11.88, L5000/€2.58 extra for non-members. Family rooms L24-26,000/€12.40-13.43.

Hotel San Vitale, V.S. Vitale, 94 (☎051 22 59 66; fax 23 93 96). Follow V. Rizzoli past the towers onto V.S. Vitale, a few blocks away from P. Aldrovandi. 17 simple, clean rooms with a communal outdoor patio. All rooms with TV, phone, and bath. Wheelchair accessible. Singles L90-110,000/€46.48-56.81; doubles L130-150,000/€67.14; triples L165-180,000/€85.22-92.96; quads L200-220,000/€103.27-113.62.

Pensione Marconi, V. Marconi, 22 (☎051 26 28 32). Turn right from station then left onto V. Amendola, which becomes V. Marconi, or take bus #25 to V. Marconi. Rooms with tiled floors and light wood. Desk monitored. Singles L60,000/€30.99, with bath L75,000/€38.73; doubles L95,000/€49.06, L120,000/€62; triples L126,000/€65.07, L160,000/€82.63; quads L148,000/€76.44, L180,000/€92.96.

Albergo Minerva, V. dé Monari, 3 (☎/fax 051 23 96 52), off V. dell'Indipendenza and near P. Maggiore. A bit past its prime. 15 large, breezy rooms have paisley decor but no bath. Doubles L100,000/€51.65.

Albergo Centro, V. della Zecca, 2, 3rd fl. (☎051 22 51 14; fax 23 51 62). Take V. Ugo Bassi from P. Maggiore and take 2nd left onto V. della Zecca. 25 rooms decked out with huge beds, leather chairs, TV, phone, and A/C. Breakfast L14,000/€7.23. Baths equipped with newer fixtures. Singles L90,000/€46.48, with bath L120,000/€62; doubles L150,000/€77.47, L130-160,000/€67.14-82.63. AmEx/MC/V.

Garisenda, Galleria Leone, 1, 3rd fl. (☎051 22 43 69; fax 22 10 07). Walk down V. Rizzoli. Just before the 2 towers, turn right into the gallery mall. More homey than the usual hotel. Good, but noisy. Breakfast L6000/€3.10. Singles L80,000/€41.32; doubles L120,000/€62; triples L160,000/€82.63. Extra bed L3500/€1.81. AmEx/MC/V.

Protezione della Giovane, V.S. Stefano, 45 (☎051 22 55 73). Take bus #32 or 33 from the station to Porta S. Stefano; walk up V.S. Stefano. Ring the buzzer and climb the large back staircase. Beautiful, clean rooms in an amazing building. Lush courtyard, filled with students in winter. Women only. Breakfast included. Lunch and dinner available. Curfew 10:30pm. Dorms L25,000/€12.91, per month L650,000/€335.70.

🖸 FOOD

Bologna's cuisine centers on fresh, handmade pasta in all shapes and sizes. The best of the stuffed pastas are *tortellini* made with ground meat or *tortelloni* made with ricotta and spinach. Try Bologna's namesake dish, *spaghetti alla bolognese*, which has a hefty meat and tomato sauce. Bologna is renowned for salami and ham of all kinds, including (surprise) "bologna," known locally as *mortadella* (it bears no resemblance to the Oscar Meyer pig by-product of sketchy origins).

Restaurants cluster on side streets minutes away from the town center; try the areas around V. Augusto Righi, V. Piella, and V. Saragozza for traditional *trattorie*. **Mercato delle Erbe,** V. Ugo Bassi, 27, is a vast indoor market that sells produce, cheeses, and meats. (Open M-W 7am-1:15pm and 5-7pm, Th and Sa 7am-1:15pm, F 7am-1:15pm and 4:30-7:30pm.) A **PAM supermarket,** V. Marconi, 26, is by the intersection of V. Riva di Reno. (Open M-W and F-Sa 7:45am-7:45pm, Th 7:45am-1pm.)

ITALIAN CUISINE

🞓 **Trattoria Da Maro,** V. Broccaindosso, 71b (☎051 22 73 04), between Strada Maggiore and V. San Vitale. Locals gather to chatter over plates of *tagliatelle* and other regional dishes. Lunch *primi* L9000/€4.65; *secondi* L10,000/€5.16. Dinner *primi* L11,000/€5.68; *secondi* L13,000/€6.71. Cover L3000/€1.55. Open M 8-10:15pm, Tu-Sa noon-2:30pm and 8-10:15pm. AmEx/MC/V.

EAT YOUR HEART OUT, CHEF BOYARDEE

For Italians, the desecration of pasta is a mortal sin akin to murder or buying French wine. Pasta must be chosen correctly and cooked *al dente* (firm, literally "to the tooth"). To avoid embarrassment, get to know the basics. The spaghetti family includes all variations that require twirling, from hollow cousins *bucatini* and *maccheroni* to the more delicate *capellini*. Flat spaghetti include *fettuccini*, *taglierini*, and *tagliatelle*. Short pasta tubes can be *penne* (cut diagonally), and *rigate* (ribbed), *sedani* (curved), *rigatoni* (wider), or *cannelloni* (usually stuffed). *Fusili* (corkscrews), *farfalle* (butterflies or bow-ties), and *ruote* (wheels) are fun as well as functional. Don't be alarmed if you see pastry displays labeled "pasta"; the Italian word refers to anything made of dough.

Nuova Pizzeria Gianna, V.S. Stefano 76/a (☎051 22 25 16). Known to loyal fans simply as "Mamma's." Chat with Gianna as she crafts incomparable pizza. L5000/€2.58 (marinara) and up. Open M-Sa for lunch and dinner; closed Aug.

Antica Trattoria Roberto Spiga, V. Broccaindosso, 21a (☎051 23 00 63). Savor hearty food in this intimate family-run eatery. *Primi* L10,000/€5.16; *secondi* L10-16,000/€5.16-8.26. "Pranzo a Prezzo Fisso" (a several course meal) L25,000/€12.91. Cover L2000/€1.03. Open Sept.-July M-Sa noon-3pm and 7:30-10pm.

Trattoria Da Danio, V.S. Felice, 50 (☎051 55 52 02), off V. Ugo Bassi (across street from Dragon D'Oro; see below). This authentic *trattoria* has an appetizing menu. *Primi* L7-15,000/€3.62-7.75; *secondi* L7-25,000/€3.62-12.91. *Menù* L20,000/€10.33. Cover L3000/€1.55. Open M-Sa 8am-1pm and 8pm-1am. AmEx/MC/V.

Il Gelatauro, V.S. Vitale, 82/b (☎051 23 00 49). Tame the mythical half-man, half-monster, all-*gelato* beast. Fresh-fruit *gelato,* served as a sandwich in a brioche for the daring. Those under 14 can spin the Wheel-of-Gelatauro for a free cone. Cones from L3000/€1.55. Open June-Aug. Tu-Su 11am-11pm.

NON-ITALIAN ALTERNATIVES

Ristorante Clorofilla, Strada Maggiore, 64/C (☎051 23 53 43). Turn left on San Stefano. 2 ahead blocks on right. The name evokes the bite of a cough medicine, but inside lies a hip, almost exclusively vegetarian restaurant. Imaginative salads L9-11,000/€4.65-5.68; hot dishes L9-14,000/€4.65-7.23. Cover L1500/€0.77. Open M-Sa 12:15-2:45pm and 7:30pm-midnight. In winter, tea served 4-6:30pm. MC/V.

Dragon d'Oro, V.S. Felice, 63b (☎051 55 51 55). Off V. Manzoni, down several blocks on the right (opposite Trattoria Da Danio). Freshly prepared Chinese food with interesting hybrids, like Chinese *gnocchi*. Entrees L5500-12,000/€2.84-6.20. Lunch *menù* L12,000/€6.20. On Su they offer the "Pranzo a Menu Fisso" (a 3-course meal for L14,000/€7.23). Open Th-Tu noon-2:30pm and 7pm-midnight. AmEx/MC/V.

⊙ SIGHTS

Twenty-five miles of porticoed buildings line the streets of Bologna. During the 14th century, they alleviated the housing crisis of a growing city. The frenzy lasted several centuries, resulting in a mix of Gothic, Renaissance, and Baroque styles.

PIAZZE AND PALAZZI

PIAZZA MAGGIORE. The tranquil expanse of Piazza Maggiore flaunts both Bologna's historical and modern-day prosperity. **Basilica di San Petronio,** the city's *duomo*, designed by Antonio da Vincenzo (1390), was built to impress. The Bolognese originally plotted to make their basilica larger than St. Peter's in Rome, but the jealous Church ordered that the funds be used instead to build the nearby Palazzo Archiginnasio. The cavernous Gothic interior played host to both the Council of Trent (when it was not meeting in Trent) and the 1530 ceremony in which Pope Clement VII gave Italy to the German emperor Charles V. According to legend, the pomp and pageantry of the exercises drove a disgusted Martin Luther to reform religion in Germany (though he made sure to celebrate the Teutonic acquisition of Bella Italia with a hearty glass of chianti before fully giving himself over to the zeal of his new Protestant faith). The zodiacal sundial on the floor of the north aisle is the largest in Italy. *(Open M-Sa 7:15am-1pm and 2-6pm, Su 7:30am-1pm and 2-6:30pm. Sacristy open daily 8am-noon and 4-6pm.)*

■ **PALAZZO ARCHIGINNASIO.** This *palazzo*, formerly a university building, now houses the town library. The upstairs theater was constructed in 1637 by Antonio Levanti in order to teach anatomy to local students. The walls are decorated with statues of university doctors caught in the act of... pontificating. Apollo, in the center of the ceiling, watches over the dissection table below. Notice the two statues to the right as you enter. These two skinless "anatomical" men illustrate 17th-century conceptions of musculature in this most decadent of classrooms. *(Behind S. Petronio. ☎ 051 23 64 88. Palazzo open M-F 9am-7pm, Sa 9am-2pm. Theater open M-Sa 9am-1pm. Both closed 2 weeks Aug. Free. Library Open M-F 9am-6:30pm, Sa 9am-1:30pm.)*

PIAZZA DEL NETTUNO. Next to P. Maggiore, this *piazza* contains Giambologna's famous 16th-century bronze fountain *Neptune and Attendants.* Affectionately called "The Giant," Neptune reigns over a collection of water-babies and sirens. The statue boasts trivia for all age groups. The G-rated version explains that Giambologna designed the statue with a spiral progression, enticing viewers to walk in a circle around it. The R-rated fact is that at one point on the circle, as any Bologna resident can show you, Neptune appears to be holding more than one trident in his hand. Behind the fountain of Neptune, at P. Maggiore, 3, is a chilling reminder of Italy's struggle in World War II. Displayed on the wall are photographs of Italians who lost their lives. Also remembered are victims of more recent right-wing attacks, including the 1980 bombing of the Bologna train station.

PIAZZA PORTA RAVEGANA AND THE TWO TOWERS. Seven streets converge in a yellow wood, or in P. Porta Ravegana, to form Bologna's medieval quarter. Two towers rise magnificently from the *piazza*. Legend whispers that Bologna's two principal families, the Asinelli and the Garisendi, competed to build the tallest and most beautiful tower. The Garisendi, in haste, plunged into the construction of their tower without adequately reinforcing the foundation; it sank on one side and the upper portion fell off, leaving only the leaning section. The Asinelli were more cautious and built their tower to a sleek 97m. Pesky, unromantic reality tells a simpler story: land movement botched an attempt to build an observation tower for the civic defense system (the lower, tilting tower), so the city tried again with greater success. Today you can climb the 498 steps of the **Torre degli Asinelli.** *(Down V. Rizzoli from P. Nettuno. Open May-Aug. daily 9am-6pm; Sept.-Apr. 9am-5pm. L5000/€2.58.)*

PALAZZO COMMUNALE. A clock tower, Nicolò dell'Arca's terra-cotta *Madonna*, and a Menganti bronze statue of Pope Gregory XIV punctuate the large brick block of this *palazzo*. Inside lie the **Collezioni Comunali d'Arte** and the **Museo Morandi.** *(To the right as you face the duomo.)*

PALAZZO DE PODESTÀ. Fioravanti's son Aristotle, who later designed Moscow's Kremlin, remodeled the Romanesque Palazzo del Podestà. The columns of the vault, rather than the ground, support this 15th-century feat of architectural engineering. *(In the northern side of P. Maggiore.)*

CHURCHES

PIAZZA SANTO STEFANO CHURCH COMPLEX. Only four of the seven churches of the original Romanesque basilica remain. Bologna's patron saint, San Petronio, lies buried under the pulpit of the **Chiesa di San Sepolcro** in the center of the group. In the rear courtyard is the **Basin of Pilate** where the governor absolved himself of responsibility for Christ's death. In the adjoining **Chiesa di Santi Vitale e Agricola** is a sculpture of Christ based on the anatomical clues suggested by the Holy Shroud of Turin (see p. 177). *(In P. Santo Stefano. Follow V.S. Stefano from V. Rizzoli. Open daily 9am-noon and 3:30-6pm. Dress appropriately; you never know Who might be watching.)*

CHIESA DI SANTA MARI DEI SERU. Inside this remarkably well-preserved Gothic creation, columns support an unusual combination of arches and ribbed vaulting. Cimabue's *Maestà* hangs behind the altar of a chapel on the left. Giovanni Antonio Montorsoli, a pupil of Michelangelo, executed the exquisitely sculptured altar. *(Take Strada Maggiore to P. Aldrovandi. ☎ 051 22 68 07.)*

CHIESA SAN DOMENICO. This church marks the resting place of the founder of the Dominican order. The schema near the entrance identifies the works. Look for Filippo Lippi's *Visit of St. Catherine* at the end of the right aisle. *(From P. Maggiore, follow V. dell'Archiginnasio to V. Farini and then V. Garibaldi. Open daily 7am-1pm and 2-7pm.)*

CHIESA DI SAN GIACOMO MAGGIORE. This church is a mélange of Romanesque and Gothic styles. The adjoining **Oratorio di Santa Cecilia** presents a cycle of Renaissance frescoes by Amico Aspertini, Francesco Raibolini "the Francia," and Lorenzo Costa, and display scenes from the lives of St. Cecilia and her husband St. Valeriano. *(Follow V. Zamboni from V. Rizzoli to P. Rossini. Enter the oratorio from V. Zamboni, 15. ☎/fax 051 648 75 80. Open 10am-1pm and 3:30-7:30pm.)*

CHIESA DELLE SANTISSIME VITALE E AGRICOLA. The facade of this church incorporates bits of Roman temples, capitals, and columns. Below lies an 11th-century **crypt**. The paintings are by Francia and Sano di Pietro. *(V.S. Vitale, 48. Follow V.S. Vitale from V. Rizzoli. Open M-Sa 8am-7pm, Su 10am-7pm.)*

🏛 MUSEUMS

▓ PINACOTECA NAZIONALE. The Pinacoteca traces the progress of Bolognese artists from Primitivism to Mannerism. Its first section contains a Giotto altarpiece. The Renaissance wing houses Raphael's *Ecstasy of Santa Cecilia*, Perugino's *Madonna in Glory*, Guido Reni's *Madonna*, and Parmigianino's *Madonna di Santa Margherita*. *(V. delle Belle Arti, 56, off V. Zamboni. ☎ 054 24 32 22. Open Tu-Sa 9am-1:50pm, Su 9am-12:50pm. L8000/€4.13.)*

MUSEO CIVICO MEDIOEVALE. This museum, housed in the 15th-century Palazzo Ghisilardi Fava, contains a collection of sculpted tombs of medieval Bolognese professors. The artists depict the scholars reading and their students dozing, daydreaming, and gossiping. The *Pietra di Pace* depicts the Virgin and Child flanked by kneeling students who protested the execution of a fellow student. The museum also displays armor, reliquary objects, and curiosities of medieval life. *(V. Manzoni, 4. Off V. dell'Indipendenza, near P. Maggiore. ☎ 051 20 39 30. Open M-F 9am-2pm, Sa-Su 9am-1pm and 3:30-7pm. L8000/€4.13, under 18 and over 60 L4000/€2.07.)*

MUSEO CIVICO ARCHEOLOGICO. This collection houses fascinating ancient artifacts. On the first floor are Bronze and Stone Age tools, Greek vases and statues, and Roman inscriptions. Beware of mummified crocodiles in the Egyptian section downstairs; they are frighteningly realistic. Bring a dictionary—the descriptions are in Italian only. *(V. Archiginnasio, 2, behind the duomo. ☎ 051 23 38 49. Open year-round Tu-F 9am-2pm, Sa and Su 9am-1pm and 3:30-7pm. L8000/€4.13, students L4000/€2.07.)*

COLLEZIONI COMUNALI D'ARTE BOLOGNA. View the impressive frescoes that once covered the walls of town hall and the accompanying art collection and period furniture. *(P. Maggiore, 6, in the Palazzo Comunale. ☎ 051 20 36 29. Open Tu-Su 10am-6pm. L8000/€4.13, students L4000/€2.07.)*

🎵 ENTERTAINMENT

Bologna's hip student population ensures raucous nighttime fun. During the academic year, especially on weekends, the city gyrates until late at night (or early in the morning). Many clubs and discos shut down in summer, but amusement doesn't fizzle; it simply moves outdoors.

CLASSICAL MUSIC

Teatro Comunale, Largo Respighi, 1 (☎051 52 99 99; www.nettuno.it/bo/ teatro_comunale), at V. Zamboni, hosts first-rate operas, symphony concerts, and ballet performances, all with world-class performers (opera tickets from L15,000/€7.75; symphony and ballet from L10,000/€5.16). Wealthy locals snatch up most tickets a year in advance. To scrounge what's left, sign up outside the ticket office three days before the show. Arrive at the time listed to buy tickets. Order tickets from **Biglietteria,** Teatro Comunale, Largo Respighi, 1, 40126 Bologna.

CLUBS AND BARS

Fliers found in record stores offer reduced or free club admission. (Try **Rizzoli Media Store** on V. Rizzoli, west of P. Maggiore.) Call ahead for hours and cover.

🏳️‍🌈 **Cassero,** (☎051 644 69 02), in the Porta Saragozza, at the end of V. Saragozza. Situated in one of the city's gates, this lively gay bar is packed with men and women. The rooftop terrace offers beautiful and breezy vistas. Dance the night away to disco or catch one of the weekly shows in the coolest location in town. Open daily 10pm-2am.

Cluricaune, V. Zamboni, 18/b (☎051 26 34 19). An Irish bar packed with students. Happy hour 5-8:30pm, drinks L3000/€1.55. Otherwise pints L8000/€4.13; half-pints L5000/€2.58. Open M-Th 4pm-2am, F-Sa 4pm-2:30am, Su 11:30pm-2am.

Cantina Bentivoglio, V. Mascarella, 4b (☎051 26 54 16), heading toward V. delle Belle Arti. Upscale bar with food and wine (from L10,000/€5.16). Live jazz and a relaxed atmosphere under an umbrella-covered patio. Walls are lined with wine bottles. Cover L5000/€2.58. Open Tu-Su 8pm-2am; closed 1½ months in summer. AmEx/MC/V.

SUMMER EVENTS

Made in Bo (☎051 53 38 80; www.madeinbo.it), is the outdoor festival for the young Bolognese. Raving from mid-June to mid-July, it features open-air discos, multilayered bars, and a comic book and record bazaar—all on a mystical, floodlit hillside. To reach Made in Bo take bus #25. Things get moving around 10pm. Unfortunately a cab back will cost you L10-50,000/€5.16-25.82. Summers bring **Boest,** an annual city-sponsored music, theater, art, dance, and cinema festival.

AND THE WINNER IS... Every July, thousands of spectators descend on Bologna to watch one of the most subversive beauty contests in this country of high fashion. **ARCI-GAY,** a gay and lesbian social and political organization based in Bologna, and **Made in Bo** join hands to give over a dozen men the chance to don fantastic female dress and strut their stuff down the catwalk. The **1999 Italia Miss Alternative** clenched the crown for her ingenuity just as much as for her beauty. The queen dressed as a church from head to toe, and she topped it all off with papal headwear. When the church doors opened, the appreciative audience got a glimpse of inches and inches of leggy holiness. In 2000, for the first time in the contest's six-year history, female contestants were able to vie for the crown. For more information, contact ARCI-GAY (☎051 644 69 02; www.gay.it) or stop by the office inside Bologna's Porta Saragozza. Other events sponsored by ARCI-GAY include the gay film festival in Milan and Bologna (in June) and "Blowing Bubbles," a festival of short films for the prevention of AIDS (in December).

SPORTS

See the pride of Bologna play all major Italian soccer teams and join in the celebration when they claim victory at **Stadio Comunale**, V. Andrea Costa, 174 (☎ 051 24 94 09 or 61 45 391). Take bus #21 from the train station or #14 from Porta Isaia. The season runs from September to June, with games on Sunday afternoons. Tickets for games against popular clubs such as Juventus or AC Milan tend to sell fast.

FERRARA ☎ 0532

Rome has its mopeds, Venice its boats, and Ferrara its bicycles. Old and young alike perched precariously on handlebars whirl by on Ferrara's jumble of thoroughfares and twisting medieval roads, inaccessible to automobiles. The result is a city center that's quieter, cleaner, and noticeably friendlier to pedestrian traffic. Even the buildings appear brighter, free from the heavy veneer of diesel exhaust. Grab a bike yourself and enjoy the pink church or occasional giant castle. Ferrara earned its laurels as the home of the Este dynasty from 1208 to 1598. When not murdering relatives, these sensitive rulers proved to be some of the most enlightened patrons of their age. Their court and university attracted Petrarch, Mantegna, and Titian. Ercole I's early 16th-century city plan broke ground with its open, harmonious design. The balding dukes eventually went heirless, and their legacy succumbed to two centuries of neglect.

█ TRANSPORTATION

Trains: Follow V. Cavour to NW of town. Ferrara is on the Bologna-Venice train line. Ticket office open 7am-9pm. Luggage storage available (p. 282). Trains from Stazione Ferroviaria depart to: **Bologna** (30min., 1-2 per hr. 1:42am-9:38pm, L4900/€2.53); **Padua** (1hr., every hr. 3:52am-11:07pm, L7600/€3.93); **Ravenna** (1hr., 1-3 per hr. 6:12am-8:15pm, L6700/€3.46); **Rome** (3-4hr.; 7 per day 7:47am-7:25pm; L57,200/€29.54); **Venice** (2hr.; 1-2 per hr. 3:52am-10:11pm; L10,800/€5.58).

Buses: ACFT (☎ 0532 59 94 92) and **GGFP**. Main terminal on V. Rampari S. Paolo. Most buses also leave from the train station. From the #2 bus stop, turn onto V.S. Paolo and head to the building labeled *biglietteria*. Open daily 6:15am-8pm. To Ferrara's **beaches** (1hr., 12 per day 7:30am-6:50pm, L7600-8400/€3.93-4.34) and **Bologna** (1½hr.; M-Sa 15 per day 5:20am-7:50pm; Su 10:50am, 1:55, 6:20pm; L6000/€3.10). Buses to **Modena** depart from train station (1½hr.; M-Sa every hr. 6:22am-7:32pm, Su 8:22am and 1:02pm; L8400/€4.34).

Taxi: Radiotaxi (☎ 0532 90 09 00). Open 24hr.

Bike Rental: C. Giovecca, 21. Left as you exit train station (behind hundreds of parked bicycles). L4000/€2.07 per hr., L20,000/€10.33 per day. Open daily 9:30am-1pm and 3:30-7pm. Cheaper bikes at P. Stazione (☎ 0532 77 21 90). L12,000/€6.20 per day. Open M-F 5:30am-8pm, Sa 6am-2pm; in winter M-F 5:30am-8pm, Sa 6am-6pm.

✦ ⁊ ORIENTATION AND PRACTICAL INFORMATION

To get to the center of town, turn left out of the train station and then veer right on **Viale Costituzione**. This road becomes **Viale Cavour** and runs to the **Castello Estense** (1km). Or take bus #2 to the "Castello" stop or bus #1 or 9 to the post office (every 15-20min. 7am-8:20pm, L1400/€0.72). Past the Castello Estense, V. Cavour changes its name to **Corso Giovecca**. **C. Martiri d. Liberta,** perpendicular to V. Cavour, turns into **Corso Porta Reno** and heads south to **Piazza Travaglio.**

Tourist Office: (☎ 0532 20 93 70; www.comune.fe.it), in Castello Estense. A large, well-equipped office in the main court of the castle. Open daily 9am-1pm and 2-6pm.

Currency Exchange: Banca Nazionale de Lavoro, C. Porta Reno, 19, near P. Cattedrale. Open M-F 8:30am-1:30pm and 3:05-4:35pm, Sa 8:30am-noon. 24hr. **ATM** in train station and at V. Garibaldi, #6/a, near the intersection with V. degli Spadari.

Luggage Storage: In train station. L3-4000/€1.55-2.07 per 6hr. Open 24hr.

Emergency: ☎113. **Ambulance:** ☎118.

Police: C. Ercole I d'Este, 26 (☎0532 29 43 11), off Largo Castello.

Red Cross: ☎0532 20 94 00.

24-Hour Pharmacy: Fides, C. Giovecca, 125 (☎0532 20 25 24). **Comunale no. 1,** C. Porta Mare, 114 (☎0532 75 32 84).

Hospital: Ospedale Sant'Anna, C. Giovecca, 203. ☎0532 23 61 11. Across from Palazzina Marfrissa near P. Medaglie D'Oro, a gateway to the old town. **Emergency** ☎0532 20 31 31.

Internet Access: Internet Point, V.S. Romano, 123 (☎0532 76 98 31). L15,000/€7.75 per hr. Open M-Sa 4-8pm; in winter 3:30-7:30pm. **Centri Servizi Link,** V. Ariosto, 57/a. L12,000/€6.20 per hr. Open daily 9am-1pm and 3-4:30pm.

Post Office: V. Cavour, 29 (☎0532 20 75 12), a block toward train station from the *castello.* Fermo Posta available. Open M-Sa 8:15am-7pm.

Postal Code: 44100.

▌ ACCOMMODATIONS & CAMPING

Ferrara has a few nice budget hotels, but they fill quickly, so reserve ahead. If you choose not to stay in Ferrara, it's an easy daytrip from Bologna or Modena.

Hotel de Prati, V. Padiglioni, 5 (☎0532 24 19 05 or 51 67 38; fax 24 19 66). From Castello Estense, walk north up L. Ercole I d'Este; go left on V. Padiglioni. Hotel on the right. New 3-star hotel with excellent rates. Yellow hallways artfully decorated; 12 rooms feature red-tiled floors, classy wood-beamed ceilings, wooden armoire, A/C, TV, phone, and fridge. 1st fl. cafe and small library. Singles L90-125,000/€46.48-64.56; doubles L130-200,000/€67.14-103.29. Suites from L250,000/€129.11. AmEx/MC/V.

Ostello della Gioventù Estense (HI), C.B. Rossetti, 24 (☎/fax 0532 20 42 27), up C. Ercole I d'Este from the *castello,* or take bus #4c from station and ask for the *castello* stop. Hostel across street and a few doors down from Palazzo Diamante. Simple rooms with bunk beds and exposed-beam ceilings, only a short walk from the town center. 84 beds. Reception 7-10am and 5-11:30pm. Lockout 10am-3:30pm. Curfew 11:40pm. Dorms L23,000/€11.89; family rooms L23,000/€11.89.

Casa degli Artisti, V. Vittoria, 66 (☎0532 76 10 38), near P. Lampronti, in the historic center. From the *duomo,* head down C. Porta Reno, turn left on V. Ragno, then left on V. Vittoria. "Pensione Artiste" on glass above door. Bright yellow building houses 21 large rooms, some with full carpeting. Reserve 4 days in advance July-Sept. Singles L36,000/€18.60; doubles L64,000/€33.05, with bath L90,000/€46.48.

Albergo Nazionale, C. Porta Reno, 32 (☎/fax 0532 20 96 04), on a busy street right off the *duomo.* From the castle walk past the *duomo* onto V. Reno; the hotel is 100yds. to your right. 20 clean, eclectically decorated rooms with telephone and TV. Curfew 12:30am. Singles L65,000/€35.40, with bath L80,000/€41.32; doubles with bath L120,000/€61.97; triples L145,000/€74.89. AmEx/MC/V.

Albergo San Paolo, V. Baluardi, 9 (☎/fax 0532 76 20 40). Walk down C. Porta Reno from the *duomo.* At P. Travaglio, turn left onto V. Baluardi. 32 modern rooms with TV, phone, and bath. Some with A/C. Rents bikes and arranges tours. Singles L90,000/€46.48; doubles L145,000/€74.78; triples L170,000/€87.60. AmEx/MC/V.

Camping: Estense, V. Gramicia, 76 (☎/fax 0532 75 23 96), 1km from the city center. Take bus #1 to P.S. Giovanni (L1400/€0.72). From the church next to the bus stop another bus heads straight to the campground (every 20min., 2-8:20pm). Bus route is temporary, so check with the ACFT office in the train station before you head off. If driving from the castle, take Corso Ercole I d'Este, make right onto C. Porta Mare, left onto V. Gramicia. Its ahead on the right, just past V. Pannonio. Open year-round 8am-10pm. L8000/€4.13 per person; L12,000/€6.20 per car.

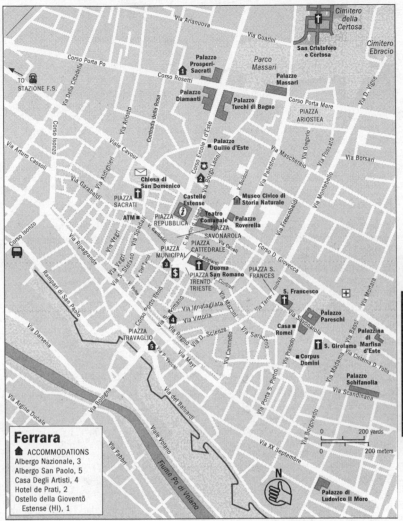

Ferrara

⌂ ACCOMMODATIONS
Albergo Nazionale, 3
Albergo San Paolo, 5
Casa Degli Artisti, 4
Hotel de Prati, 2
Ostello della Gioventò
Estense (HI), 1

🍴 FOOD

In Ferrara, gorge on *cappelletti*, delicious triangular meat *ravioli* served in a broth, or *cappellacci*, stuffed with pumpkin and served in a light sauce of butter and sage. The gastronomic glory of the city is its robust *salama da sugo*, an aged sausage served cold (with melon) in the summer and hot in the winter. The traditional *Ferrarese* dessert is a chunk of luscious *pampepato*, a chocolate-covered almond and fruit cake. **Negozio Moccia,** V. degli Spadari, 19, sells *pampepato* in various sizes. (☎0532 20 97 72. L24,000/€12.39 per 750g. Open M-Sa 9am-1pm and 3-8:30pm.) For picnic supplies, stop by the **Mercato Comunale,** on V. Mercato, off V. Garibaldi and next to the *duomo*. (Open M-W 7am-1:30pm and 4:30-7:30pm, Th and Sa 7am-1:30pm, F 4:30-7:30pm.) For wine, try the slightly sparkling *Uva D'Oro* (Golden Grape), compliments of the slightly insane Renata Di Francia, who brought the grapes from France for her 16th-century marriage to Duca D'Ercole II d'Este. All food stores in Ferrara are closed Thursday afternoons.

▧**Osteria Al Brindisi,** V.G. degli Adelardi, 9b (☎0532 20 91 42), alone on a quiet street beside the *duomo* (facing its left side). Oldest *osteria* in Italy grooves to Motown classics. Hip crowds dine on inexpensive traditional dishes. Recently blessed by a full-fledged cardinal, so dig in without fear—Copernicus, Cellini, and Pope John Paul II have all done it. Try *panini* (L5000/€2.58) and one of the 600 varieties of wine (L1–14,000/€0.58-7.32 per glass). *Menù* L30,000/€15.50. Open Tu-Su 8:30am-1am. MC/V.

Trattoria Da Noemi, V. Ragno, 31a (☎0532 76 17 15), off C. Porta Reno. Smells of Ferrarese cooking have wafted out of this quiet, traditional *trattoria* for over 30 years. The *salamina* (L10,000/€5.16) is succulent, and a plate of homemade *lasagne* (L10,000/€5.16) is just divine. Cover L2500/€1.29. Open W-M noon-2:30pm and 7:30-11pm.

Aristo: Bar, Gelateria, Pasticceria, Paninoteca, Piazza Ariostea, 13,15, 19 (☎0532 20 76 00). From the castle, walk down C. Ercole I D'Este to C. Porta Mare, and turn right. The *piazza* is 2 blocks down on your right. Aristo is at the corner of C.P. Mare and the *piazza*. This eatery with wide patio seating offers several varieties of pizza, pastry, *gelato*, and beer. Public phone. Open F-W 6:30am-2am.

⊙ SIGHTS

Ferrara is best seen by bicycle. Cruise with locals along V. Garibaldi. Alternatively, explore the tranquil wooded concourse that runs along the 9km well-preserved medieval wall of the city, beginning at the far end of C. Giovecca.

▧**CASTELLO ESTENSE.** Towered, turreted, and moated, Castello Estense stands precisely in the center of town. Marquis Nicholas II built the fortress to protect himself from disgruntled tax-paying masses. The **Salone dei Giochi** and the surrounding rooms retain rich ceiling frescoes—the best are in the Loggetta degli Aranci. The legendary dungeons—with ten foot thick walls of stone and cement, and three layers of barred windows—are open for roaming. Parisina, the wife of Duke Nicolò d'Este III, was killed with her lover, the Duke's son Ugolino, in this damp prison. This incestuous tragedy inspired Browning to pen "My Last Duchess." Climb **Torre Leoni** (enter from inside the castle) for an unobstructed view of the city. *(☎0532 29 92 33. Open Tu-Su 9:30am-5pm. L8000/€4.13, reduced L6000/€3.1.)*

DUOMO SAN ROMANO. Reshaped by every noble with designs on Ferrara, the cathedral and castle remain the effective center of town. Rosetti designed the tall slender arches and terra-cotta ornamented apse, and Alberti executed the pink campanile. Upstairs, the **Museo della Cattedrale** displays Cosmè Tura's 15th-century *San Giorgio* and *Annunciation*, both from the Ferrarese school. *(From the castello, take C. Martiri della Libertà to P. Cattedrale. Enter museum across the street from the duomo through the courtyard on V.S. Romano. Cathedral open M-Sa 7:30am-noon and 3-6:30pm, Su 7:30am-12:30pm and 4-7:30pm. Museum ☎0532 20 74 49. Museum open Tu-Sa 10am-noon and 3-5pm, Su and holidays 10am-noon and 4-6pm.)*

PALAZZO DIAMANTI. Built in 1493 by Biagio Rossetti, this palace outshines all other ducal residences. It is aptly named—the exterior is made up of marble polished to (sharp) diamond-cut points. Inside, the **Pinacoteca Nazionale** contains many works of the Ferrarese school. Most impressive are Carpaccio's *Passing of the Virgin* (1508) and Garofalo's incredibly detailed *Massacre of the Innocents*. *(Pinacoteca ☎0532 20 58 44. From Castello Estense, cross Largo Castello to C. Ercole I d'Este and walk to the corner of C. Rossetti. Open Tu-W and F-Sa 9am-2pm, Th 9am-7pm, Su and holidays 9am-1pm. L8000/€4.13, EU citizens 18-25 L4000/€2.07.)*

PALAZZO MASSARI. Once a 16th-century residence, the palace now houses a museum complex. On the first floor, the **Museo d'Arte Moderna e Contemporanea "Filippo de Pisis"** showcases work by contemporary painters and traces the progression of artist Filippo de Pisis's work. Upstairs, the spectacular **Museo Ferrarese dell'Ottocentro/Museo Giovanni Boldini** has a vast collection of Boldini's work and some works by Edgar Degas. *(C. Porta Mare, 9. Follow C. Ercole I d'Este behind castello and* *turn right on C. Porta Mare. ☎ 0532 20 69 14. Museums open daily 9am-1pm and 3-6pm. Pisis L4000/€2.07; Ottocentro/Boldini L8000/€4.13; combination ticket L10,000/€5.16.)*

CASA ROMEI. This 15th-century dwelling of a Ferrarese merchant is filled with some of the most richly decorated rooms of the period. The museum displays statues and frescoes salvaged from destroyed churches in Ferrara. A pleasant green courtyard welcomes light. *(V. Savonarola, 30. ☎ 0532 24 03 41. From behind the duomo, turn left and then right on V. Voltapaletto, which becomes V. Savonarola. Open Tu-Sa 8:30am-7:30pm and Su 8:30am-2pm. L4000/€2.07, students L2000/€1.03.)*

PALAZZO SCHIFANOIA. Only the carved door of the Palazzo Schifanoia hints at the wealth of art inside. The Saloni dei Mesi's magnificent frescoes offer vivid depictions of the 15th-century court. A series of cabinets display a remarkable collection of over-sized medieval manuscripts, rich with colorful miniatures and illuminations. *(V. Scandiana, 23. From P. Cattedrale follow V. Adelardi to V. Voltapaletto and to V. Savonarola. Turn right on V. Madama and left on V. Scandiana. ☎ 0532 641 78. Open daily 9am-7pm. L8000/€4.13, students L4000/€2.07. Combination ticket for Palazzo Schifanoia and Palazzina Marifisa L10,000/€5.16, reduced L5000/€2.58.)*

PALAZZINA DI MARFISA D'ESTE. A late-Renaissance palace in miniature. The highlight of this splendid, recently restored, palace is its spectacular ceilings. A wide lawn provides a good view of the side of this yellow building of brick and stucco. Magnolia trees stand at both sides of the palace. *(C. Giovecca, 170. Follow C. Gioveca from Largo Castello, or take bus #9 (L1400/€0.72). ☎ 0532 20 74 50. Open daily 9:30am-1pm and 3-6pm. L4000/€2.07, students L3000/€1.55. 1st M of the month free.)*

CIMITERO EBRAICO (JEWISH CEMETERY). Here the Finzi and Contini, the main characters of Bassani's influential *Il Giardino dei Finzi-Contini*, lie buried along with most of Ferrara's 19th- and 20th-century Jewish community. A monument commemorates the Ferrarese Jews murdered at Auschwitz. *(At the end of V. Vigne. From the castello, head down C. Giovecca. Turn left on V. Montebello and continue to V. Vigne. ☎ 0532 75 13 37. Open Apr.-Sept. Su-F 9am-6pm; Oct.-Mar. 9am-4:30pm.)*

🎵 ENTERTAINMENT

Each year on the last Sunday of May, Ferrara recreates the ancient **Palio di San Giorgio.** (Info ☎ 0532 75 12 63.) This event, dating from the 13th century, begins with a lively procession of delegates from the city's eight *contrade* followed by a series of four races in P. Ariostea: the boy's race, the girl's race, the donkey race, and finally, the great horse race. The flag-waving ceremony of the eight *contrade* takes place two weeks earlier in P. del Municipio. During the third or fourth week of August, street musicians and performers display their talents in the **Busker's Festival** (☎ 0532 24 93 37; www.ferrarabuskers.com). In July and August, a free **Discobus** service runs every Saturday night between Ferrara and the hottest clubs. Call ☎ 0532 59 94 11 for information, or pick up fliers in the train station.

MODENA   ☎ 059

Home to prestigious makers of both music and cars, Modena claims both Luciano Pavarotti and the Ferrari and Maserati factories—and it purrs with prosperity. Conquered by the Romans in the 3rd century BC, the city owed its early prominence to its principal road, V. Emilia, which runs through the heart of town. Modena offers few sights, but with its colorful buildings, tantalizing food, and peaceful atmosphere, the city is among the most livable in Emilia-Romagna.

⌐ TRANSPORTATION

Trains: (☎1478 880 88), in P. Dante Alighieri. Info office open 8am-7pm. To: **Bologna** (30min., every hr., L4100/€2.12); **Milan** (2hr.; every hr.; L16,000/€8.26); **Parma** (30min., 2 per hr., L5100/€2.63).

Buses: ATCM (☎059 22 22 20), on V. Fabriani, off V. Monte Kosica (to right from the train station). To **Ferrara** (every hr., L8400/€4.33) and **Maranello** (every 1-2hr., L3900/€2.01).

Taxis: V. Viterbo, 82b (☎059 37 42 42).

✹? ORIENTATION AND PRACTICAL INFORMATION

Modena lies roughly midway between Parma and Bologna. From the train station, take bus #7 or 11 (L1700/€0.88) to **Piazza Grande** and the center of town. Or walk left out of the station on V. Galvini and turn right on V. Monte Kosica. The second left, V. Ganaceto, leads directly to **via Emilia**. Turn left on V. Emilia and walk several blocks to P. Torre, which opens into **Piazza Grande** on the left. V. Emilia changes names and street numbers from **via Emilia Ovest** on the west side of the center, to **via Emilia Centro** in the center, and then to **via Emilia Est** on the east.

Tourist Office: P. Grande, 17 (☎059 20 66 60; fax 20 66 59; iatmo@comune.modena.it), across from the back of the *duomo*, under a portico. A warehouse of facts and maps available on computers. Some English spoken. In the same office as **Informazione Città** (☎059 20 65 80) and **Informagiovani** (☎059 20 65 83), geared specifically to young people; computers also available. Open M-Tu and Th-Sa 8:30am-1pm and 3-7pm, W 8:30am-1pm.

Currency Exchange: Credito Italiano, V. Emilia Centro, 102 (☎059 41 21 11), across from V. Scudari. Take a ticket at the door. Open M-F 8:20am-1:20pm and 3-4:30pm, Sa 8:20-11:20am. **ATMs:** in the Rolo Banca 1473 building, on P. Grande.

Emergency: ☎118. **Police:** ☎113 or 059 20 07 00.

Ambulance: Blue Cross (☎059 34 24 24). **First Aid:** ☎059 36 13 71 or 43 72 71.

Late-Night Pharmacy: Farmacia Comunale, V. Emilia Est, 416 (☎059 36 00 91). Open nightly 8pm-8am.

Hospital: Ospedale Civile (☎059 43 51 11), in P.S. Agostino.

Internet Access: Informagiovane, at tourist office in P. Grande. Must have some form of valid ID. Registration L2500/€1.29. L5000/€2.58 per 2hr., L10,000/€5.16 per 5hr. Open M-Tu and Th-Sa 8:30am-1pm and 3-7pm, W 8:30am-1pm.

Post Office: V. Emilia Centro, 86 (☎059 24 35 09 or 059 24 21 37). A bright yellow building with red marble portico. Open M-Sa 8:15am-7:15pm.

Postal Code: 41100.

⌂ ACCOMMODATIONS & CAMPING

Ostello San Filippo Neri, V.S. Orsola 48-52 (☎/fax 059 23 45 98), 300m from the train station. From the station, walk straight ahead to Viale A. Fontanelli, and turn left at the 1st street (V.S. Orsola). The hostel is on the left. New, multilevel hostel with modern amenities, including full bathrooms with clean fixtures, sturdy furniture (large closets that have locks), vending machines, Internet access, public phone, TV, VCR, several large patio spaces, and an elevator. Check-out 10am. Lockout 10am-2pm. Curfew midnight. Dorm L28,000/€14.46; L30,000/€15.50 without hostel card.

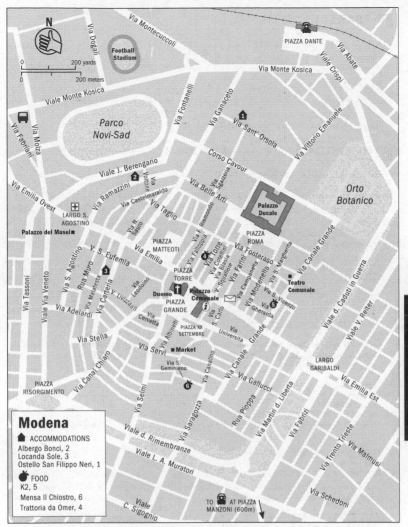

Albergo Bonci, V. Ramazzini, 59 (☎059 22 36 34), short walk from town center. From V. Ganaceto, turn right on V. Cerca, which becomes V. Ramazzini. Dimly lit but clean rooms. No rooms with bath. Singles L50-60,000/€25.82-30.99; doubles L80-90,000/ €41.32-46.48. MC/V.

Locanda Sole, V. Malatesta, 45 (☎059 21 42 45), 100m from P. Grande. From train station on V. Ganaceto, turn right on V. Emilia Centro; take 2nd left on V. Malatesta. Clean rooms (none with bath, some with TV and extra-springy mattresses). Reserve ahead. Closed first 3 weeks Aug. Singles L45,000/€23.24; doubles L80,000/€41.32.

Camping: International Camping Modena, V. Cave Ramo, 111 (☎059 33 22 52), in Località Bruciata. Take bus #19 (dir: Rubiera, 6:20am-8:30pm) west from the station for about 10min. Ask the driver; she will let you off within 500m of the site. Open Mar.-Sept. L11,000/€6.71 per adult, under 9 L8000/€4.13; L17,000/€8.78 per tent.

🌀 FOOD

The area around Modena has some of the most fertile soil on the Italian peninsula, which results in a bounty of produce. Modena, like nearby Bologna and Parma, produces unsurpassed *prosciutto crudo* and the sparkling *lambrusco* red wine. Modena's own claim to culinary fame derives from the fragrant and full-bodied balsamic vinegar that the Modenese sprinkle liberally over salads, vegetables, and even fruit. Balsamic vinegar is often aged for decades, and a bottle of the finest vinegar can empty your wallet to the tune of L100,000/€51.65.

Stock picnic baskets at the **Mercato Albinelli,** a few steps down V. Albinelli from P. XX Settembre. Locals come to this food bazaar to haggle over prices for everything from fruit and vegetables to squid and snails. (Open M-Sa 6:30am-2pm; Sept.-May M-F 6:30am-2pm, Sa 6:30am-2pm and 5-7pm.) Sample fresh Modenese cuisine at the weekly **market** in the Parco Novi Sad. (Open M 7:30am-1:30pm.)

■ **Mensa Il Chiostro,** V.S. Geminiano, 3 (☎ 059 23 04 30), in courtyard of an antique cloister. Turn to right as you enter the archway. From V. Emilia, turn onto V.S. Carlo, which becomes V. Canalino. V.S. Geminiano is on the right. Self-service restaurant serves generous portions to a local crowd. *Primi* L4000/€2.07; *secondi* L7200-11,300/€3.72-5.84. Open M-F 11:45am-2:30pm.

Trattoria Da Omer, V. Torre, 33 (☎ 059 21 80 50), off V. Emilia across from P. Torre. The entrance to V. Torre hides under the arcade, among the jewelry stores. With his reasonably priced and meticulously prepared delicacies, Omer is one of the joys of Modena. *Tortelloni fiocchi di neve* (with fresh ricotta, butter, and sage; L13,000/€6.71) is filling. Vegetable buffet L4-12,000/€2.07-6.20; *primi* L12,000/€6.20; *secondi* L14,000/€7.23. Cover L3000/€1.55. Open M, W-Sa 1-2pm and 8-11pm. AmEx/MC/V.

K2, C. Canalgrande, 67 (☎ 059 21 91 81), off V. Emilia, near Porto Bologna. At the peak of scrumptious *gelato*. They sculpt each cone into a flower-shaped treat. Cones from L3000/€1.55. Open Th-Tu 11am-midnight. Another alpine branch in Parma.

🌀 SIGHTS

■ **DUOMO.** One of the least ravaged Romanesque churches in Italy, Modena's *duomo* dates from the early-12th century. The *duomo* houses a relic of patron saint S. Geminiano. His arm, encased in silver (1178), takes to the streets in a religious procession on January 31. The sculptor Wiligelmo and his school decorated most of the *duomo* with stylized carvings that draw on local, Roman, Biblical, and Celtic themes; carvings around the doors depict scenes from the Old Testament and S. Geminiano's travels to Asia—(back in the days when he still possessed his legs and a torso. *(In P. Grande. ☎ 059 21 60 78. Open daily 7am-12:30pm and 3:30-7pm.)*

PALAZZO DEI MUSEI. The Palazzo dei Musei contains both the **Biblioteca Estense** and the **Galleria Estense** (☎ 059 23 50 04). The library's collection of exquisitely illuminated books includes masterpieces such as a 1501 Portuguese map of the world; the Biblioteca's **Sala Campori** houses the **Biblia di Borso d'Este,** a 1200-page Bible partially illustrated by the 15th-century Emilian painter Taddeo Crivelli. Large, glass cases house everything from musical instruments, wall paper patterns, 19th-century scientific instruments, ceramics, fabric, and cultural anthropology collections from the Americas, Asia, and Africa, to the art collection of Matteo Campori, including the remarkable *Testa di Fanciulla con turbante* by Francesco Stringa. *(In Largo S. Agostino at the western side of V. Emilia. Biblioteca ☎ 059 22 22 48. Open M-Th 9am-7:15pm, F-Sa 9am-1:45pm. Sala Campori open M-Sa 9am-1pm. Free.)*

The Galleria Estense above the library provides enormous rooms for its largest works. Keep an eye out for the Carracci brothers, Guido Reni, Salvator Rosa, and Guercino. The jewels of the collection are Velázquez's portrait of Francesco d'Este and Bernini's magnificent bust of the same subject, found at the head of the gallery. Seen every Mother and Child from here to Naples? Botticelli's *Madonna con* *il Bambino San Giovannino*, and Mantegna's *Madonna con il Bambino* present two of the most engaging representations of this (very) recurrent theme. *(☎ 059 22 21 45. Open Tu-Su 9am-7pm; closed Aug. L8000'/€4.13, over 60 and under 18 free.)*

GHIRLANDINA TOWER. This 95m tower, the symbol of Modena, looms over the *duomo*. Built in the late-13th century, it weaves in both Gothic and Romanesque elements. A memorial to those who died fighting the Nazis and Fascists during World War II stands at the base. *(Open Apr.-Oct. Su 10am-1pm and 3-7pm. L2000/€1.03.)*

FERRARI FACTORY. Modena's claim to international fame is the Ferrari automobile. The factory is southwest of Modena in **Maranello.** After the Maranello stop, buses head straight to the factory. Although you're not allowed to sniff around the inner workings of this top-secret complex, you can view antique and modern Ferraris, Formula One racers, and trophies at the nearby company museum, **Galleria Ferrari,** in an oversized glass-and-steel structure. *Let's Go* does not recommend performing any James Bond stunts to view the factory's war room, where maps of the western hemisphere detail Ferrari's plan to take over the world. *(Galleria at V. Dino Ferrari, 43. To reach museum from Ferrari factory bus stop, continue along road in same direction as bus for 200 yards, then turn right at Galleria Ferrari sign. ☎ 0536 94 32 04. Open Tu-Su 9:30am-12:30pm and 2:30-6pm. L18,000/€9.30, ages 6-15 and over 60 L14,000/€7.23.)*

PAVAROTTI'S PAD. If you're on a Three Tenors pilgrimage, Pavarotti's house is a necessary stop along the way. He lives in the big villa hidden at the corner of Stradello Chiesa and V. Giardini. But don't get your hopes up about hearing Luciano belt out *"La donna è mobile"* from his balcony—he's known to be something of a recluse.

FOOD FEST. If you're more of a food fan than a Ferrari freak, consider visiting one of the many local foundations specializing in regional specialties. Most require a written request 15-20 days in advance for reservations. For information on the production of **prosciutto,** contact the Consorzio del Prosciutto di Modena at V. Corassori, 72 (☎ 059 34 34 64). For **wine-tasting** possibilities, contact the Consorzio Tutela del Lambrusco di Modena, V. Schedoni, 41 (☎ 059 23 50 05). For queries regarding native **vignola cherries,** send request to the Consorzio della Cigliegia Tipica di Vignola, V. Barozzi, 2 (☎ 059 77 36 45), in the hamlet of Savignano sul Parano. For information on local **balsamic vinegar** production, call the Consorzio Produttori di Aceto Balsamico at the Chamber of Commerce, V. Ganaceto, 134 (☎ 059 24 25 65).

🎵 ENTERTAINMENT

Every year, around the first or second week in June, Modena hosts the one-night **Pavarotti and Friends,** a benefit concert featuring (surprise, surprise) Pavarotti (sans Domingo and Carreras). For tickets, contact the tourist office in May. For one week—usually late June to early July—the **Serate Estensi** enlivens Modena with exhibits, art shows, street vendors, and a costumed bonanza in which residents dress up in Renaissance garb for a *corteo storico* (historic parade).

PARMA ☎ 0521

Parma's loyalties lie with its excellent food. Citizens, known appropriately as Parmigiani, craft the silky-smooth *prosciutto crudo*, sharp and crumbly *parmigiano* (Parmesan) cheese, and the sweet, sparkling white Malvasia wine. Parma's artistic excellence, however, has not been confined to the kitchen. Sixteenth-century Mannerist painting came into full bloom under Parmigianino, and Giuseppe Verdi resided in Parma while composing some of his greatest works. His music lured Napoleon's second wife Marie-Louise here. The French influence inspired Stendhal to choose it as the setting of his 1839 novel, *The Charterhouse of Parma.* The city still cultivates a mannered elegance, recalling the artistic eminence of the 16th century and the refinement of the 19th. At the same time Parma vibrates with youthful energy from the nearby university.

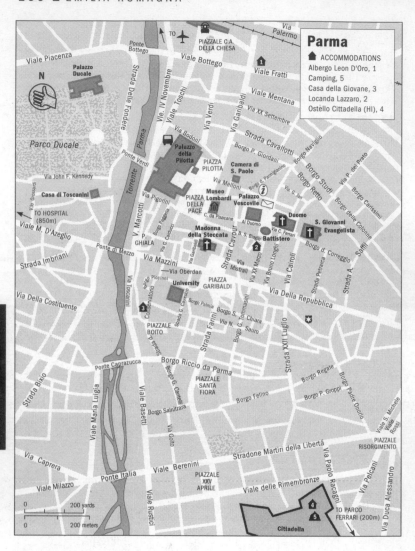

Parma

🏠 ACCOMMODATIONS
Albergo Leon D'Oro, 1
Camping, 5
Casa della Giovane, 3
Locanda Lazzaro, 2
Ostèllo Cittadella (HI), 4

NORTHEAST ITALY

TRANSPORTATION

Flights: G. Verdi Airport, V. dell'Aeroporto, 44a (☎0521 98 26 26).

Trains: P. Carlo Alberto della Chiesa. Parma lies about 200km northwest of Bologna, served by the Bologna-Milan train line. To: **Bologna** (1hr., 2 per hr., L7700/€3.98); **Florence** (3hr.; 7 per day; L26,300/€13.58); **Milan** (1½hr.; every hr.; L11,600/€6).

Buses: (☎0521 21 41), on V.P. Toschi before Ponte Verdi. Automated self-service ticketing. To: **Bardi** (L6800/€3.51); **Busseto** (L4100/€2.12); **Colorno** (L3000/€1.55); **Fontanellato** (L4000/€2.07); **Torrechiara** (L4000/€2.07).

Taxis: ☎0521 25 25 62.

✦ 🔢 ORIENTATION AND PRACTICAL INFORMATION

Parma's historic center lies on the eastern side of the **Torrente Parma.** Walk out of the station, keeping the park to the right. Turn left on V. Bottego, walk one block, turn right on V. Garibaldi and follow it 1km into the town center. Turn left on **via Mazzini** to reach **Piazza Garibaldi,** heart of the people-watching district. The streets branch off this *piazza*, with **via Mazzini** running west, **via della Repubblica** extending east, **Strada Cavour** heading north toward the *duomo*, and **Strada Farini** branching south in the direction of the *Cittadella*.

Tourist Office: V. Melloni, 1b (☎0521 21 88 89; ☎/fax 23 47 35). From train station, walk left and turn right down V. Garibaldi, then left onto V. Melloni. On your left. Info on Parma's hotels, restaurants, and events. M-Sa 9am-7pm, Su and holidays 9am-1pm. Houses **Informagiovani** office (☎0521 21 87 49). Everything from daytrip advice to job listings (in Italian). English spoken. Open F-W 9am-1pm and 3-7pm, Th 9am-7pm.

English-Language Bookstore: Feltrinelli, V. della Repubblica, 2 (☎0521 23 74 92), on the corner of P. Garibaldi. English classics and best-sellers. Open M-Sa 9am-7:30pm.

Emergency: ☎113. **Ambulance:** ☎118.

Police: Questura (☎0521 21 94), on Borgo della Posta.

First Aid: ☎0521 28 58 30.

24hr. Pharmacy: Farmacia Guareschi, Strada Farini, 5 (☎0521 28 22 40). Open M-F 8:30am-12:30pm and 3:30-7:30pm. Night service list posted outside all pharmacies.

Hospital: Ospedale Maggiore, V. Gramsci, 14 (☎0521 99 11 11 or 25 91 11), over the river past the Palazzo Ducale.

Internet Access: Computer Rent, V.A. Saffi, 30a (☎0521 38 64 11). L6000/€3.10 per 30min., L10,000/€5.16 per hr. Open M 2-7pm, Tu-F 9am-7pm, Sa 9am-12:30pm. **Informagiovani** (see above) offers free 2hr. blocks. Book in advance.

Post Office: V. Melloni, 4c (☎0521 23 75 54), between V. Garibaldi and Strada Cavour. Open M-Sa 8:30am-6:30pm. Another **branch** at V. Verdi, 25 (☎0521 20 64 39), across from train station. Open M-F 8:15am-6pm, Sa 8:15am-12:50pm.

Postal Code: 43100.

🏠 ACCOMMODATIONS & CAMPING

Ostello Cittadella (HI) (☎0521 96 14 34), on V. Passo Buole. From station, take bus #9 (last bus leaves at 7:55pm; L1300/€0.67). Get off when the bus turns left on V. Martiri della Libertà. Alternatively, take Strada Farini from P. Garibaldi. Turn left for 7 blocks until you hit V. Martiri della Libertà. Turn left, follow V. Martiri della Libertà for 2 blocks, and turn right onto V. Passo Buole. At the end of V. Passo Buole, enter the large white portico surrounded by ancient walls and look for the hostel on the left. Modern building with plate glass and rubber floors in a corner of a 15th-century fortress. Simple but spacious rooms with 5 beds, hot showers, and squat-style toilets. HI members only, but may accept student ID. 3-night max. stay. Call ahead for availability. Lockout 9:30am-5pm. Curfew 11pm. Open Apr.-Oct. Dorms L16,000/€8.26.

Locanda Lazzaro, Borgo XX Marzo, 14 (☎0521 20 89 44), off V. della Repubblica. Upstairs from the rather pricey but welcoming restaurant of the same name. 8 rooms. Reserve 1 week in advance during the summer. Singles L65,000/€33.57, with bath L75,000/€38.73; doubles with bath L100,000/€51.65. AmEx/MC/V.

Albergo Leon d'Oro, V. Fratti, 4 (☎0521 77 31 82), off V. Garibaldi. From train station, go left 2 blocks. No private baths. Restaurant downstairs open M-F 12:15-2pm and

7:30-10pm, with *primi* from L13,000/€6.71. Cover L2500/€1.29. Reserve in advance. Singles L55,000/€28.41; doubles L85,000/€43.90. AmEx/MC/V.

Casa della Giovane, V. del Conservatorio, 11 (☎0521 28 32 29). From V. Mazzini, turn left on V. Oberdan; V. del Conservatorio winds around to your right. Women under 25 only. An upbeat, bustling atmosphere. 45 beds. Breakfast and afternoon snack included. Curfew varies by season (usually 9:30pm). Dorms L37,000/€19.11.

Camping: The only campground near Parma is at the **Ostello Cittadella** (see above), in the Cittadella public park beside the hostel. Electrical outlets. 3-night max. stay. Open Apr.-Oct. 30. L11,150/€5.94 per person, L21,000/€10.85 per site.

🍴 FOOD

Parma's cuisine is rich, delicious, and wonderfully affordable. Native *parmigiano* cheese, *prosciutto*, and sausages fill the windows of the *salumerie* along V. Garibaldi. *Malvasia* is the wine of choice. When exported, this sparkling white loses its natural fizz, so carbon dioxide is usually added—here's your chance for the real thing. Of the sparkling red wines, *lambrusco* is a favorite. An open-air **market** is at P. Ghiaia, off V. Marcotti past Palazzo Pilotta. (Open W and Sa 8am-1pm.) For picnic supplies, head to **Supermarket 2B**, V. XXII Luglio, 27c. (☎0521 28 13 82. Open M-W and F-Sa 8:30am-1pm and 4:30-8pm, Th 8:30am-1pm.)

Trattoria Corrieri, V. Conservatorio, 1 (☎0521 23 44 26). From V. Mazzini, take V. Oberdan; V. del Conservatorio to the right. Whitewashed arches, red-checked tableclothes, hanging ham, and wheels of cheese. Not cheap, but worth extra *lire*. Tris (tortelli filled with asparagus; L12,000/€6.20), or *prosciutto e melone* (L16,000/€8.26). Cover L3000/€1.55. Open M-Sa noon-2:30pm and 7:30-10:30pm. AmEx/MC/V.

Le Sorelle Picchi, Strada Farini, 27 (☎0521 23 35 28), the street begins at P. Garibaldi. Face in direction that Signor Garibaldi is staring, walk straight, and you'll be on Strada Farini. A traditional *salumeria* and one of the best *trattorie* in town. *Primi* L10-11,000/€5.16-5.68; *secondi* L12-14,000/€6.20-7.23. Cover L3000/€1.55. *Trattoria* open M-Sa noon-3pm for lunch only. *Salumeria* open 8:30am-7pm. MC/V.

Pizzeria La Duchessa, P. Garibaldi, 3 (☎0521 23 59 62). An excellent *trattoria* with a large variety of pizzas. The least expensive restaurant in P. Garibaldi, despite its moniker. Be prepared to wait for a seat. Pizzas L9-15,000/€4.65-7.75. Open Tu-Su 10:30am-2:30pm and 7pm-1am. MC/V.

K2, Borgo Cairoli, 23, on the corner next to the Chiesa di San Giovanni Evangelista. The best (by discriminating local standards), creamiest *gelato* in Parma, deftly sculpted into a flower atop the mountainous cone by *gelato* crafters in pink and white uniforms (from L2500/€1.29). Open Th-Tu 11am-midnight.

👁 SIGHTS

📋 DUOMO AND BAPTISTERY. Parma's 11th-century Romanesque *duomo* is one of the country's most vibrant, filled with masterpieces including the Episcopal throne and Benedetto Antelami's bas-relief *Descent from the Cross* (1178). Most spectacular is the dome, where Correggio's *Virgin* ascends to a golden heaven in a spiral of white robes, pink *putti*, and blue sky. The pink-and-white marble baptistery is the middle child of the Gothic and Romanesque periods. *(In P. del Duomo. From P. Garibaldi, follow Strada Cavour toward the train station and take the 3rd right on Strada al Duomo. ☎0521 23 58 86. Duomo open daily 9am-12:30pm and 3-7pm. Baptistery open daily 9am-12:30pm and 3-7pm. L5000/€2.58, reduced L3000/€1.55.)*

PALAZZO DELLA PILOTTA. The monolithic Palazzo della Pilotta is Parma's treasure chest. Constructed in 1602, the palace expresses the authoritarian ambitions of the Farnese dukes, who built two complexes, the Pilotta Palace and the Cittadella (now a park on the other side of town), in an attempt to unify the city. Today, the Palazzo houses several museums, including the **Galleria Nazionale.** The collection includes Leonardo da Vinci's *Testa d'una Fanciulla (Head of a Young Girl)*. From the Galleria, head to the **Farnese Theater** (1615), an elegant wooden theatre in the *palazzo*. Used for only seven performances since its completion, the theater was in an advanced stage of decay when a bomb caused its total destruction in 1944; but was rebuilt in 1956. *(From P. del Duomo, follow Strada al Duomo across Strada Cavour, continue on Strada Piscane for 1 block, and cut across P. della Pace to P. Pilotta. Gallery ☎ 0521 23 33 09. Gallery open daily 9am-2pm. Theater open M 8:30am-2pm and Tu-Su 8:30am-7:30pm. Gallery L8000/€4.13; theater L4000/€2.07, both L12,000/€6.20.)* Also in the Palazzo della Pilotta, the **Museo Archaeologico Nazionale** houses displays of coins, bronzes, and sculptures of Greek, Etruscan, Roman, and Egyptian origin. *(☎ 0521 23 37 18. Open Tu-Su 9am-7pm. L4000/€2.07, under 18 and over 60 free.)*

CHIESA DI SAN GIOVANNI EVANGELISTA. The dome inside was frescoed by Correggio. Along the left nave over the first, second, and fourth chapels are frescoes by Parmigianino. The third chapel was stolen by a nasty amateur Byzantine thief named Alfonso, and never returned to the Parmigiani, who refused to pay ransom on the grounds that the chapel wasn't touched by either Parmigianino or Coreggio. *(In P.S. Giovanni, behind the duomo. ☎ 0521 23 55 92. Open daily 9am-noon and 3-7pm.)*

PARMIGIANO AND PROSCIUTTO FACTORIES. If you're curious about the production of *parmigiano* cheese (and who isn't?) contact the **Consorzio del Parmigiano-Reggiano** in advance to arrange a tour of the facilities. Tours are topped by free samples. *(V. Gramsci, 26/c. ☎ 0521 29 27 00; fax 29 34 41. Tours available M-F from 8:30am.)* To arrange a visit to a *prosciutto* factory, contact the **Consorzio del Prosciutto di Parma.** *(V.M. dell'Arpa, 8/b. ☎ 0521 24 39 87; fax 24 39 83. Call well in advance.)*

OTHER SIGHTS. Outside the *duomo* district, a French flavor lingers, the aftertaste of Gallic influences from the 16th to 18th centuries. Many of the French *palazzi* were blasted to pieces during World War II, but enough of the older buildings survive to convey the surroundings depicted in Stendhal's novels. To remedy cultural overload, retreat to the lush **French gardens** of Marie-Louise's Baroque palace in the Ducal Park, west of the Pilotta Palace over the Ponte Verdi. *(Currently closed for restoration. Scheduled to reopen summer 2002. Open May-Sept. daily 6am-midnight; Nov. and Feb. 7am-6pm; Oct., Mar., and Apr. 6:30am-7pm; Dec.-Jan. 7am-5:30pm.)* South of the park at Borgo Rodolfo Tanzi, 13, is **Casa Natale e Museo di Aurturo Toscanini** (1867-1957). The museum houses memorabilia from the maestro's life; ask for a tour in English. *(☎ 0521 28 54 99. Open Tu-Sa 10am-1pm and 3-6pm, Su 10am-1pm. L3000/€1.55.)* And if your neck isn't tired yet, move back to the city and gape at the frescoes in **Camera San Paolo.** *(In small courtyard behind the gate across from the post office. Head back toward the river on Strada al Duomo, turn right on Strada Cavour, then left on V. Melloni. Open M 8:30am-2pm, Tu-Su 8:30am-7:30pm. L4000/€2.07.)*

🎵 ENTERTAINMENT

The **Teatro Regio** is one of Italy's premier opera houses. Check with the tourist office for the prices of standing-room tickets. The opera season runs from December to April. *(V. Garibaldi, 16, next to P. della Pace. ☎ 0521 21 89 10. Visiting the theater is free, but call ahead for an appointment.)* When the Teatro Regio is in its off-season, during the summer, it hosts a number of outdoor concerts. **E'grandeEstate** highlights classical music, opera, jazz, and tango. The events are held in Piazzale della Pilotta in July. *(Tickets from L15-30,000/€7.75-15.50. Info ☎ 0521 21 86 78.)*

🔁 DAYTRIP FROM PARMA: BUSSETO

No composer conveys love more poignantly (and at greater length) than opera giant Giuseppe Verdi, whose native hamlet of **Roncole Verdi** rests on the Parma plain 3½km outside the city of **Busseto** (a 1hr. bus ride from Parma). To see where this son of a poor innkeeper received his earliest inspiration, visit the house and museum at **Verdi's birth site.** (☎0524 974 50. Open Mar.-Oct. 9:30am-12:30pm and 3-7pm; Nov.-Feb. 2:30-5:30pm. L6000/€3.1.) In Busseto proper, within the walls of the ancient Rocca, the famous **Teatro Verdi** (☎0524 918 64) opened in 1868. If you still haven't gotten your fill of great heroines who take 45 minutes to curl up on the stage and just die already, the **Villa Sant'Agata** (☎0523 83 00 00), Verdi's residence during sabbaticals from his work in Milan, lies 3km from Busseto (on the same bus line). Fed up with Busseto's gossip about his affair with a premier diva, Verdi moved to secluded Sant'Agata. Parts of this mansion, unaltered since Verdi's death in 1901, are open to the public. (Open Apr.-Oct. Tu-Su 9-11:40am and 3-6:45pm. L10,000/€5.16. Reservations required. For maps and directions, contact the tourist office ☎0524 924 87 in Busseto.)

PIACENZA ☎0523

This is the best little town you never knew existed. Recently voted one of Italy's most hospitable cities, Piacenza makes a good stopover on a trip to Parma, Bologna, or Milan. The hamlet abstains from a tourist economy, and houses a few noteworthy monuments of the Renaissance and the Middle Ages.

⌐ TRANSPORTATION

Trains: (☎0523 32 12 63 or 39 91 11), in P. Marconi. Luggage storage available (p. 294). Piacenza lies on main line between **Bologna** (1½hr.; every hr.; L12,700/€6.56) and **Milan** (1hr., every hr., L9500/€4.91). A secondary line runs to **Turin** (2½hr.; 9 per day; L25,200/€13.01) via **Alessandria.**

Taxis: ☎0523 59 19 19. Taxis are plentiful outside the train station.

✳🛈 ORIENTATION AND PRACTICAL INFORMATION

To reach **Piazza del Duomo** from the train station, walk along the left side of the park on V. dei Mille, and turn right on V. Giulio Alberoni. Bear right onto V. Roma and then turn left onto V. Daveri, which leads to the *piazza*. From there, V. XX Settembre leads straight to **Piazza dei Cavalli.**

Tourist office: IAT, P. Cavelli, 7 (☎/fax 0523 32 93 24; urp@comune.piacenza.it; www.comune.piacenza.it). From train station veer left as you cross to the park across the street (Viale dei Mille); continue on this street for 2 blocks. At V. Roma turn right. Walk 8 blocks. Turn left on V.C. Cavour. Walk across the *piazza* to the left side of Il Gotico (large building behind the horse statues). Open Tu-Sa 9:30am-12:30pm and 3-6pm, Su 9:30am-12:30pm. **Ufficio Relazione con il Pubblico,** P. Cavelli, 7 (☎0523 49 22 24). Open Tu-W and F-S 9am-1pm, M and Th 9am-1pm and 3-6pm.

Luggage storage: At the train station. L5000/€2.58 for 12hr. Open daily 8am-5pm.

Ambulances: ☎118.

Hospital: Ospedale Civile da Piacenza, V.G. Taverna, 49 (☎0523 30 11 11).

Post office: V. Sant'Antonino, 38-40 (☎0523 31 64 11). Open M-Sa 8:30am-6pm.

Postal Code: 29100.

🏠🍴 ACCOMMODATIONS AND FOOD

Look for budget accommodations just outside the *centro storico*. Try the **Hotel Astra**, V.R. Boselli, 19, with its ten simple but spotless rooms above a neat street cafe. (☎0523 45 43 64. Reception open 24hr. Reserve ahead. Singles L45,000/€23.24; doubles L60,000/€30.99.) **Protezione delle Giovane,** V. Tempio, 26, is close to the *centro*. From P. dei Cavalli, walk left down C.V. Emanuele and take the third right. The nuns keep the 15 rooms immaculate and you very, very pure with their ridiculously early curfew. (☎0523 32 38 12. Women only. Curfew 10:30pm. Singles or doubles with full pension L30,000/€15.50 per person.)

As in any Italian town, specialty shops selling meats, cheeses, bread, and fruit are everywhere. Shop in the markets along V. Calzolai, tucked behind P. Cavalli. An outdoor **market** is held every Wednesday and on Saturday mornings in P. Duomo and P. dei Cavalli. Local specialties include *tortelli*, filled with spinach and ricotta, and *pisarei e fasö*, a hearty mix of beans and small balls of dough. Unless you're hungry enough to eat a horse, steer clear of anything containing the word *cavallo*. **Osteria Del Trentino**, V. del Castello, 71, off P. Borgo, serves delicious meals in a garden as charming as its staff. Try the specialty *tortelli ricotta e spinaci* for L12,000/€6.20. (*Primi* from L10,000/€5.16; *secondi* from L12,000/€6.20. Cover L3000/€1.55. ☎0523 32 42 60. Open M-Sa noon-3pm and 8pm-midnight. AmEx/MC/V.) **Trattoria/Pizzeria dell'Orologio**, P. Duomo, 38, serves delicious pizza and traditional *piacentina* cuisine in the shadows of the *duomo*. Patio seating is not accompanied by any sort of shade; bring a hat. Pizza from L8000/€4.13; *primi* from L10,000/€5.16; *secondi* from L15,000/€7.75. (☎0523 32 46 69, fax 38 41 03. Open F-W 11:15am-3pm and 6-11am. AmEx/DC/MC/V.)

🔍 SIGHTS

PIAZZA DEI CAVALLI. This central square is named for the two 17th-century equestrian statues that grace the *piazza*. Although the statues were intended as tributes to the riders, Duke Rannucio I and his father, Duke Alessandro Farnese, the huge horses overpower their masters. The masterpiece of the *piazza* is the Gothic **Palazzo del Comune**, called **Il Gotico**. The building was constructed in 1280 when Piacenza led the Lombard League, a powerful trading group of city-states in northern Italy. From P. dei Cavalli, follow V. XX Settembre to the **duomo**, constructed between 1122 and 1233 with an unadorned, three-aisle nave. The **crypt**, a maze of thin columns, is one of Italy's spookiest. At its center a vigil is kept over the bones of S. Giustina. To the right of the altar on the main level, find the body of Giovanni Battista Scalabrini. *(Open during exhibitions. Inquire at tourist office.)*

PALAZZO FARNESE. In P. Cittadella at the opposite end of C. Cavour from P. dei Cavalli, this *palazzo* houses the **Museo Civico**, the **Pinacoteca**, and the **Museo delle Carrozze** (☎0523 32 82 70). The most notable work in the Pinacoteca is a Botticelli fresco depicting Christ's birth. *(Open Tu-Th 9am-1pm, F-Sa 9am-1pm and 3-6:30pm, Su 9:30am-1pm and 3-6:30pm. Admission to the Museo Civico and Pinacoteca L8000/€4.13; Museo delle Carrozze L4000/€2.07; to all museums L10,000/€5.16, students L5000/€2.58.)* The **Galleria Ricci Oddi**, V.S. Siro, 13, holds a collection of modern art, including works by F. Hayez. Take C.V. Emanuele from P. dei Cavalli; turn left on V.S. Siro. (☎0523 207 42. Open May-Sept. 10am-noon and 3-6pm; Oct.-Feb. Tu-Su 10am-noon and 2-4pm; Mar.-Apr. 10am-noon and 3-5pm. Currently closed for restoration. No reopen date pending.)

RAVENNA ☎0544

Tired of fresco cycles? Come to Ravenna to get byzy, that is, uh, Byzantine. Ravenna's 15 minutes of historical superstardom came and went 14 centuries ago, when Justinian and Theodora, rulers of the Byzantine Empire, made the city headquarters for their campaign to restore order in the anarchic West. This period inspired some of the most important works of Byzantine art outside Constantinople. Today, while art fanatics come to see the mosaics, literary pilgrims come to pay homage at Dante's tomb, guarded from the jealous Florentines, who maintain an empty tomb for their estranged native.

⊏ TRANSPORTATION

Trains: (☎0544 21 78 84). Ticket counter open daily 6am-8pm. Info office in P. Farini open daily 7am-8:30pm. Luggage storage available (p. 296). To **Bologna** (1hr., every 1-2hr. 5:05am-7:34pm, L7400/€3.82) and **Rimini** (1hr., every hr. 5am-9:35pm, L3100-4700/€1.60-2.43) with connections to **Ferrara, Florence,** and **Venice** (1hr., every 2hr. 6:20am-9:33pm, L6700/€3.40).

Buses: ATR (regional) and **ATM** (municipal) buses (☎0544 68 99 00) depart outside train station for coastal towns of **Lido di Classe** (L3800/€1.96) and **Marina di Ravenna** (L1800/€0.93). Info and tickets (L1300/€0.67, 3-day tourist pass L6000/€3.1) at the ATM booth marked "PUNTO" across the *piazza* from the station. Buy a return ticket; they're difficult to find in the suburbs. Office open M-Sa 6:30am-8:30pm, Su 7am-8:30pm; in winter M-Sa 6:30am-7:30pm, Su 7:30am-7:30pm.

Taxis: Radio Taxi (☎0544 338 88), P. Farini, across from the train station. Open 24hr.

Bike Rental: In P. Farini to left as you exit train station. L2000/€1.03 per hr., L15,000/€7.75 per day. Mountain bikes L3000/€1.55 per hr. Open M-Sa 6:15am-8pm.

※ 🛈 ORIENTATION AND PRACTICAL INFORMATION

The train station is in **Piazza Farini**, at the east end of town. **Viale Farini** leads from the station to **via Diaz**, which runs to **Piazza del Popolo**, the center of town.

Tourist Office: V. Salara, 8 (☎0544 354 04; fax 48 26 70), in P. del Popolo. Take V. Muratori to P. XX Settembre and turn right on V. Matteotti. Follow this street to its end, turn left on V. Cavour, and take the 1st right. Useful maps and info. Open M-Sa 8:30am-7pm, Su 10am-4pm; in winter M-Sa 8am-6pm, Su 10am-4pm.

Luggage Storage: In train station, L3-5000/€1.55-2.58 for 6hr. Open daily 4:45am-11pm.

Gay and Lesbian Resources: ARCIGAY ARCILESBICA "Evoluzione," V. Rasponi, 5 (☎0544 21 97 21).

Emergency: ☎113. **First Aid:** ☎118.

Questura: V. Berlinguer, 10 (☎0544 29 91 11).

Hospital: Santa Maria delle Croci, V. Missiroli, 10 (☎0544 40 91 11). Take bus #2 from the station.

Internet Access: Biblioteca Oriani, V.C. Ricci, 26, 2nd fl. (☎0544 21 24 37). From P. del Popolo take V. Cairoli and follow it as it becomes V.C. Ricci. L1000/€0.52 per 15min. Open M, W, F 8:30am-1pm and 2:30-7pm, Tu, Th, and Sa 8:30am-1pm; closed last 2 weeks Aug. Access also at the **hostel.**

Post Office: P. Garibaldi, 1 (☎0544 218 67), off V. Diaz before P. del Popolo. A large brick building across from the Teatro Dante Alighieri. Open M-F 8:15am-6pm, Sa 8:15am-1:30pm. Also at V. Carducci, near the **station.** Open M-Sa 8:15am-7pm.

Postal Code: 48100.

▟ ACCOMMODATIONS & CAMPING

Ostello Dante (HI), V. Nicolodi, 12 (☎/fax 0544 42 11 64). Take bus #1 or 70 from V. Pallavicini, at the station (every 15min.-1hr. 6:30am-11:30pm, L1300/€0.67). A clean, simple hostel east of the city center, offering satellite TV, soda machines, Internet access, and 1st circle of hell style mattresses: lumpy enough to be annoying, but still not a source of eternal discomfort and torture. Wheelchair accessible. Breakfast included. Reception 7-10am and 5-11:30pm. Strict lockout 10am-5pm. Curfew

11:30pm. 140 beds; 4-6 beds per room. Dorms L24,000/€12.39; L27,000/€13.94 per person for family rooms. MC/V.

Albergo Al Giaciglio, V. Rocca Brancaleone, 42 (☎0544 394 03). Walk along V. Farini, and turn right across P. Mameli. Recently renovated budget hotel is the best deal in town. 18 carpeted rooms with wood-paneled walls and TVs. Restaurant downstairs. Breakfast L7000/€3.62. Closed 2 weeks Dec. or Jan. Singles L50,000/€25.68, with bath L60,000/€30.99; doubles L70,000/€36.15, L90,000/€45.68; triples L100,000/€51.64, L110,000/€56.81. MC/V.

Hotel Ravenna, V. Maroncelli, 12 (☎0544 21 22 04; fax 21 20 77), to the right as you exit the station, on the left side of the street. 26 clean rooms with tile floors, TV, and phone. Cozy TV room downstairs. Wheelchair accessible (elevator). Complementary off-street parking. Singles L60,000/€30.99, with bath L80,000/€41.32; doubles L70-90,000/€36.15-45.68, L90,000-115,000/€45.68-59.39. MC/V.

Camping Piomboni, Viale Lungomare, 421 (☎0544 53 02 30; fax 53 86 18), in Marina di Ravenna, 8km from Ravenna Centro. Take bus #70 across the street from train station to stop #34 (15-20min., every 30min. 5:35am-11:30pm, L1300/€0.67). 3-star camping near the beach. Reception daily 8am-10:30pm. Open May to mid-Sept. L8500/€4.39 per person, L9800/€5.06 per tent.

🍴 FOOD

Hostelers benefit from the **Coop Supermarket,** across the street at V. Aquileia, 110. (Open M 3:30-8pm, Tu-Sa 8am-8pm.) **Mercato Coperto** occupies P. Andrea Costa, up V. IV Novembre from P. del Popolo. (Open M-Sa 7am-2pm, F 4:30-7:30pm.)

Ristorante-Pizzeria Guidarello, V. Gessi, 9, off P. Arcivescovado beside *duomo*. Feast on the *Fantasia della Casa* (3 meats with mixed vegetables; L16,000/€8.26). *Primi* L6-13,000/€6.20-6.71; *secondi* L10-18,000/€5.16-9.30. Pizza L6500/€3.36. *Menù* L26,000/€13.43. Cover L2500/€1.29. Open daily noon-2:30pm and 7-9:30pm.

Ristorante L'Oste Bacca, V. Salara, 20 (☎0544 353 63). Taste the extra *lire*. Serves artfully presented seafood, pasta, fish, meat, and vegetable dishes. *Primi* L10-14,000/€5.16-7.32; *secondi* L14-28,000/€7.32-14.46. Cover L3000/€1.55. Open W-M noon-2:30pm and 7-10:30pm; closed Tu. AmEx/MC/V.

👁 SIGHTS

▨**BASILICA DI SAN VITALE.** Inside and out, the 6th-century **Basilica di San Vitale** is a jewel. An open courtyard leads to the glowing mosaics inside. Once known as *biblia pauperum* (the poor man's Bible), these mosaics make words unnecessary. The mosaics to the left of the apse portray events in Abraham's life, and the renowned ▨mosaics of the Emperor Justinian and the Empress Theodora adorn the lower left and right panels of the apse, respectively. The work on the apse displays the Byzantine style of portraying human subjects as rigid bodies on a gold backdrop. *(V.S. Vitale, 17. Take V. Argentario from V. Cavour. ☎0544 21 62 92. Open Apr.-Sept. daily 9am-7pm; Oct.-Mar. 9:30am-4:30pm. L6000/€3.10.)*

MO' MOSAICS. Thanks to a couple of comprehensive tickets, the church, mosaic, and museum rounds in Ravenna are somewhat affordable. The first ticket (L10,000/€5.16, students L8000/€4.13) is valid at the Basilica di S. Vitale, Basilica di S. Appolinare, Mausoleo di Galla Placidia, Battistero Neoniano, Museo Arcivescovile, and the Basilica dello Spirito Santo. The second ticket (L12,000/€6.20) is valid at Chiesa di Sant'Apollinare in Classe, the Mausoleo di Teodorico, and the Museo Nazionale. Buy tickets at participating sights.

The oldest and most interesting mosaics cover the glittering interior of the **Mausoleo di Galla Placidia.** A representation of Jesus as Shepherd, leaning against his cross-shaped staff and petting a sheep, decorates the upper wall, above the door. *(Behind S. Vitale. Same hours as basilica. Entrance included with admission to S. Vitale.)*

■ **CHIESA DI SANT'APOLLINARE IN CLASSE.** Astounding mosaics decorate the interior of this 6th-century church. The mosaic of Christ sitting on his throne among angels rivals the stunning gold cross on an azure background in the main apse. St. Apollinare makes an appearance in the lower portion. *(In Classe, south of the city. Take Bus #4 or 44 across the street from train station, L1300/€0.67. ☎ 0544 47 36 43. Open M-Sa 8:30am-7:30pm, Su 9am-1pm. L4000/€2.07, Su free.)*

DANTE'S TOMB AND THE DANTE MUSEUM. Much to Florence's dismay, Ravenna's most popular monument is the Tomb of Dante Alighieri. The adjoining Dante Museum not only holds 18,000 scholarly volumes, but also displays a number of the poet's old codices and a collection of interpretations of Dante's *Canti* and its pictures of his smurfy hat. His heaven and hell come alive in etchings, paintings, and sculptures. *(Both on V. Dante Alighieri. From P. del Popolo, cut through P. Garibaldi to V. Alighieri. Tomb open daily 9am-7pm. Free. Museum ☎ 0544 302 52. Museum open Apr.-Sept. Tu-Su 9am-noon and 3:30-6pm; Oct.-Mar. Tu-Su 9am-noon. L3000/€1.55.)*

BASILICA DI SANT'APOLLINARE NUOVO. Poised beside a round brick tower, with arched windows and mortar made with crushed seashells, this 6th-century basilica passed into the hands of the Roman Catholics 40 years after it was built. Lengthy mosaic strips of saints and prophets detail the sides of the central aisle, and the central apse recounts miracles performed by Jesus. *(On V. di Roma. From the train station follow Viale Farini and turn left on V. di Roma. Open daily 9am-7pm. L5000/€2.58.)*

MUSEO NAZIONALE. This collection, housed in the cloister of S. Vitale's former convent, features works from the Roman, early Christian, Byzantine, and Medieval periods. Highlights include intricate ivory carvings, ivory inlaid weapons, and recent excavations from a burial ground in Classe. *(On V. Fiandrini. Walk through the gate between Basilica S. Vitale and the Mausoleo di Galla Placidia. ☎ 0544 344 24. Open daily 8:30am-7:30pm. L8000/€4.13, EU citizens under 18 and over 60 free.)*

BATTISTERO NEONIANO. The baptistery of the *duomo* is thought to have once been a Roman bath. Created in the 5th century, the central dome features Jesus submerged in the Jordan River, with John the Baptist to his right and the personification of the river itself to his left. In 452, Bishop Neon began decorating the baptistery with mosaics. The area now shows the baptism of Christ (at the top), the twelve Apostles, and four altars. The baptismal font is at the center of the room. *(From P. del Popolo follow V. Cairoli, turn right on V. Gessi, and head toward P. Arcivescovado. Open daily 9am-7pm. Admission included with entrance to Museo Arcivescovile.)*

MUSEO ARCIVESCOVILE. The baptistery's adjoining Museo Arcivescovile displays a small but precious collection of mosaics from the *duomo*, and a number of impressive fragments of engraved stone. Don't miss the lovely mosaics in the ■**Cappella di S. Andrea** and the Throne of Maximilian, an exemplary piece of ivory carving. *(In P. Duomo. Walk to the right of the Battistero Neoniano. ☎ 0544 21 99 38. Open daily 9:30am-6:30pm. L5000/€2.58 includes entrance to Battistero Neoniano.)*

🎵 ENTERTAINMENT

Ravenna's recent claim to fame is its internationally renowned **Ravenna Festival.** Since 1990, some of the most famous classical performers from around the world, including at least two of the three tenors, have gathered here each June and July. Tickets start at L20,000/€10.33. Reservations are essential for popular events. (Info available at V.D. Alighieri, 1. ☎ 0544 24 92 11; info@ravennafestival.org; www.ravennafestival.org. Open M-Sa 9am-1pm and 3-6pm. For tickets ☎ 0544 325 77; fax 21 58 40.) An annual **Dante Festival,** organized by the Chiesa di S. Francesco (☎ 0544 302 52), brings the afterlife to Ravenna with exhibits and dramatic performances during the second week in September. *Ravenna Oggi*, available in hotels and the tourist office, has listings of local events including concerts, shows, and exhibitions. If looking at mosaics inspires you, head to ▨Colori-Belle Arti, P. Mameli, 16, off of Viale Farini, where *tesserae* of all shapes and sizes can be purchased. (☎0544 373 87. Open M-W and F 9am-12:30pm and 4:30-7pm.)

RIMINI ☎0541

Rimini is quickly becoming the party town of choice for young, hip backpackers. Throngs of ▨scantily clad people, young and old, some fashioned for the beach, others for the nightclubs, mob the main streets and beach area. At night, the boardwalk lights up as stiletto-heeled mothers push baby strollers past caricature artists, and teens with freshly greased hair frenetically rush from disco to disco. For a change in decibels and decor, visit the more reserved inland historic center, an alluring jumble of medieval streets overshadowed by the Malatesta Temple and crumbling Roman arches. But if it is the beach you seek, follow the signs to the "mare," and enjoy the powder-fine, light brown sand.

TRANSPORTATION

Flights: Miramare Civil Airport (☎0541 71 57 11), on V. Flaminia. Mostly charter flights. Serves many European cities. Rates vary. Bus #9, across street from train station, jets to the airport (every 30min. 5:45am-12:40am).

Trains: Piazzale C. Battisti and V. Dante. Rimini is a major stop on the Bologna-Lecce train line. Luggage storage available (p. 300). To: **Ancona** (1hr., 1-2 per hr., L8200/€4.23); **Bologna** (1½hr.; 1-3 per hr. 12:38am-10:25pm; L10,100/€5.22); **Milan** (3hr.; 1-2 per hr. 1:34am-8:23pm; L27,500/€14.20); **Ravenna** (1hr., 1-2 per hr. 1:28am-10:57pm, L5200/€2.69).

Buses: TRAM intercity bus station (☎0541 245 47), at V. Roma on P. Clementini, near the station. From train station, follow V. Dante Alghieri and take 1st left. Service to many inland towns. Bus ticket valid for 24hr. L5500/€2.84; otherwise, pay L1700/€0.88 for 60min. validation period. Ticket booth open M-Sa 7:15am-12:30pm and 2:30-6:30pm. **Fratelli Benedettini** (☎0549 90 38 54) and **Bonelli Bus** (☎0541 37 34 32) run the most convenient buses to **San Marino** (50min., 11 per day 7:30am-7pm, L5500/€2.84). Buses depart from P. Tripoli (bus #11: stop 14) and from the train station. Board at P. Tripoli to avoid the rush for seats at the station.

Car Rental: Hertz, V. Trieste, 16a (☎0541 531 10), near the beach, off V. Vespucci (bus #11: stop 12). L155,000/€80.05 per day with unlimited mileage; L790,000/€408 per week. Tax included. Open M-Sa 8:30am-1pm and 3-8pm.

Bike Rental: On V. Fiume at V. Vespucci (bus #11: stop 12). L5000/€2.58 per hr. The amazing *ciclocarrozzelle* goes for L22,000/€11.36 per hr.

ORIENTATION AND PRACTICAL INFORMATION

To walk to the beach from the **train station** in **Piazzale Cesare Battisti,** turn right out of the station, take another right into the tunnel at the yellow arrow indicating *al mare*, and follow **via Principe Amadeo.** To your right, **via Amerigo Vespucci,** which becomes **Viale Regina Elena,** runs one block inland along the beach. It features countless hotels, restaurants, and clubs. Bus #11 (every 15min. 5:30am-2am) runs to the beach from the train station and continues along V.A. Vespucci and V.R. Elena. Bus stops are conveniently numbered. Buy tickets (L1700/€0.88, full-day L5500/€2.84) at the kiosk in front of the station or at *tabacchi*. To reach the historic center, take **via Dante Alighieri** from the station or bus #11 from the beach. V. Dante Alighieri leads into **via IV Novembre** which in turn leads to **Piazza Tre Martire.** Running east-west, **Corso d'Augusto** cuts through the *piazza*.

TOURIST, FINANCIAL AND LOCAL SERVICES

Tourist Offices: IAT, Piazzale C. Battisti, 1 (☎0541 513 31; fax 279 27; www.riminiturismo.it), left as you exit train station. English-speaking staff. Open M-Sa 8am-7pm, Su 9am-12pm. **Branch office,** P. Fellini, 3 (☎0541 569 02 or 565 98), near the water at the beginning of V. Vespucci (bus #11: stop 10). Open daily 8am-7pm; in winter 9am-noon and 3-8pm. **Hotel Reservations-Adria** (☎0541 533 99), in train station. Finds rooms for free. Open daily 8:15am-8pm. During the winter, the office is in P. Fellini (bus #11: stop 10). Open Tu-Sa 8:30am-12:30pm and 3:50-7:30pm.

Budget Travel: CTS, Grantour Viaggi, V. Matteuci, 4 (☎0541 555 25; fax 559 66), off V. Principe Amadeo. Tickets, ISICs, and info on group tours. Open M-F 9am-12:30pm and 3:30-8:30pm, Sa 9:30am-noon.

Luggage Storage: In train station. L5000/€2.58 for 12hr. Open daily 6am-11pm. Self-service for small bags from L4000/€2.07 for 24hr.

Laundromat: Lavanderia Trieste Exspress, V. Trieste, 16 (☎0541 26 764), off V. Vespucci (bus #11). L15,000/€7.75 per kg. Open M-Sa 8:30am-1pm and 3-8pm.

EMERGENCY AND COMMUNICATIONS

Emergency: ☎113. **Ambulance:** ☎118.

Police: C. d'Augusto, 192 (☎0541 353 11 11).

First Aid: (☎0541 70 77 04), on beach at the end of V. Gounod (bus #11: stop 16). Free walk-in clinic for tourists. Open in summer daily 8am-8pm.

Hospital: Ospedale Infermi, V. Settembrini, 2 (☎0541 70 51 11). English-speaking doctors available.

Internet Access: Central Park, V. Vespucci, 21 (☎0541 275 50). 9 computers in back, past the videotape room. L5000/€2.58 per 30min., L10,000/€5.16 per 70min.

Post Office: C. d'Augusto, 8 (☎0541 78 16 73), off P. Tre Martiri, near the Arch of Augustus. Open M-F 8:10am-5:30pm, Sa 8:10am-1pm. Also on V. Mantegazza, 26, at V. Vespucci (bus #11: stop 10). Open M-F 8:10am-1:20pm, Sa 8:10am-12:40pm.

Postal Code: 47900.

♠ ACCOMMODATIONS & CAMPING

Reservations are always necessary. The tourist office provides a complete list of hotels and campgrounds. Countless hotels line the smaller streets off V. Vespucci and V.R. Elena, many between stops 12 and 20 of bus #11. Prices peak in August.

▨ Hotel Villa Souvenir, Viale Trento, 16 (☎/fax 0541 243 65). Bus #11: stop 12. Turn left from the bus and then right onto Viale Trento. 6 homey rooms decorated in pinks and reds. Bar, cafe, restaurant, and lounge area with TV. Breakfast included. L30-50,000/€15.50-25.82 per person, with bath L35-60,000/€18.08-30.99. Full pension. L48-65,000/€23.24-33.57 per person. Open July to mid-Sept. AmEx/MC/V.

Albergo Filadelphia, V. Pola, 25 (☎0541 236 79). Bus #11: stop 12. 20 fairly clean rooms at competitive prices. 1st floor doubles have balconies. Some rooms with bath. English spoken. Reserve ahead. Open Apr.-Sept. From L35,000/€18.08 per person.

Quisisana, V.R. Elena, 41 (☎0541 38 13 85; fax 38 78 16). Bus #11: stop 15. Virtual luxury (satellite TV) and choice location—all for near-budget prices. The patio out front provides a safe haven for watching the mayhem on the street below. Restaurant on 1st floor serves up good portions of homestyle food. L45-65,000/€23.25-33.57 per person. Full pension L54-88,000/€27.89-45.45 per person. MC/V.

Saxon, V. Cirene, 36 (☎/fax 0541 39 14 00). Bus #11: stop 13. Exit the bus to left, turn right on V. Misurata then left on V. Cirene. A small, 3-star hotel on a quiet street. TV in

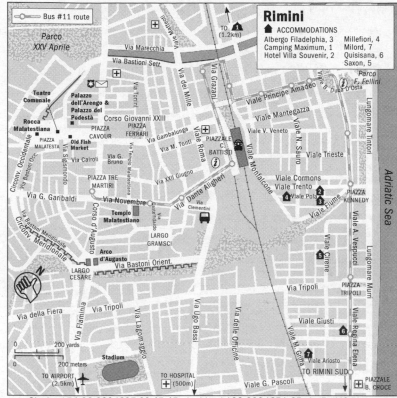

Rimini

ACCOMMODATIONS

Albergo Filadelphia, 3	Millefiori, 4
Camping Maximum, 1	Milord, 7
Hotel Villa Souvenir, 2	Quisisana, 6
	Saxon, 5

Singles L54-88,000/€27.89-45.45; doubles L100,000/€51.65. AmEx/MC/V.

Milord, V. Ariosto, 19 (☎0541 38 17 66; fax 38 57 62). Bus #11: stop 16. Exit the bus to right and head left on V. Ariosto. 3-star hotel off the main street. 38 spacious rooms with bathroom, TV and phone, some with A/C. Restaurant downstairs. Half- and full- pension for L60-90,000/€30.99-46.48 and L70-110,000/€36.15-56.85. AmEx/MC/V.

Pensione Millefiori, V. Pola, 42 (☎0541 43 33 16; fax 217 08; hpeonia@libero.it). Bus #11: stop 12. Open air patio out front leads to bar area, where owner serves up varieties of coffee. A family-oriented *pensione* with large rooms and soft beds. "American breakfast buffet" (included). English spoken. Singles with bath and TV L40,000/€20.66; doubles with bath L80,000/€41.32.

Camping: Maximum (☎0541 37 26 02; fax 37 02 71). Bus #11: stop 33. Reception daily 9am-noon and 4-10pm. Open May-mid Sept. L6500-14,700/€3.36-7.60 per adult, L16,300-28,700/€8.26-14.82 per tent. Bungalows from L76,000/€39.25.

🍴 FOOD

Rimini's seaside swarms with sterile eateries, but the resort's delicious snacks are enough to keep you going. Look in the center of town for affordable full meals. Rimini's **covered market,** between V. Castelfidardo and the *Tempio,* provides a wide array of food. (Open M, W, F-Sa 7:15am-1pm and 5-7:30pm, Tu and Th 7:15am-1pm.) The *rosticceria* in the market has inexpensive seafood. The **STANDA supermarket,** V. Vespucci, 133, close to the beach, offers picnic possibilities. (Open mid-Mar. to Oct. M-Sa 8:30am-11:30pm, Su 9am-11:30pm. AmEx/MC/V.)

■ **Ristorante-Pizzeria Pic Nic,** V. Tempio Malatestiano, 30 (☎0541 219 16), off V. IV Novembre at the corner of V.G. Bruno (at the *tempio*). Local favorite with eclectic decor. Try the *pizza bianco e verde* (a fire-baked cheese and herb delight; L9000/€4.65). *Primi* L9-12,000/€4.65-6.20; *secondi* from L8000/€4.13. Cover L2000/€1.03. Open Tu-Su noon-3pm and 7pm-12:30am. AmEx/DC/MC/V.

China Town, V.S. Michelino in Foro, 7 (☎0541 254 12). From the train station, take V. Dante Alighieri and follow it as it becomes V. IV Novembre. Turn right on V.S. Michelino in Foro just after the Tempio Malatestiano. Chinese food so good you won't miss the generic fare of nearby Italian restaurants. Try the fried banana (L3000/€1.55) or, if you're really curious, fried *gelato* (L3000/€1.55). Entrees from L6000/€3.10. Wine from L4500/€2.32. Cover L2000/€1.03. Open daily noon-2:30pm and 7pm-midnight.

Gelateria Nuovo Fiore, V. Vespucci, 7 (☎0541 236 02), with a 2nd location at V. Vespucci, 85 (☎0541 39 11 22). Clad in psychedelic blue and pink, this bar serves up a many flavors of the cold stuff. Cones L3-5000/€1.55-2.58. Sinful specialty concoctions, like *tartufo affogato alla Kalua* (truffle *gelato* drowned in Kahlua), will run you L13-17,000/€6.71-8.78. Open Mar.-Oct. daily 8am-3am; Jan.-Feb. Sa-Su 8am-3am.

👁👁 SIGHTS AND BEACHES

■ **THE BEACH.** Rimini's most coveted sight is its remarkable beach of finely sifted sand, wild umbrellas, and Adriatic waves. Access is free, but settle down a few feet inland to avoid absurdly priced umbrellas. *(Take bus #11 to stops 12 through 18.)*

TEMPIO MALATESTIANO. A tour of the historic center should begin with this Renaissance masterpiece, constructed in Franciscan Gothic style. In the 1440s the ruler Sigismondo Malatesta (Sigmund Headache) made the church a monument to himself and his fourth wife Isotta. His image remains atop the black elephants in the first chapel on the left. Sigismondo Malatesta was the only person in history canonized to hell by the pope, who described him as a guilty heretic. Also a soldier, patriot, and avid patron of the arts, Siggy ruled Rimini at its height (1417-1468), employing artists like Piero della Francesca and Leon Battista Alberti. Alberti designed the exterior of the new church, modeling the facade after the Roman **Arch of Augustus,** which still stands at the gates of Rimini. The interior and wooden-trussed roof recall the temple's original Franciscan design. *(On V. IV Novembre. Follow V. Dante Alighieri from train station until it becomes V. IV Novembre. ☎0541 511 30. Open M-Sa 7:50am-12:30pm and 3:30-6:50pm, Su 9am-1pm and 3:30-7pm.)*

PIAZZA CAVOUR. Rimini's medieval and contemporary center contains one of the oddest ensembles of buildings in Italy. The tall Renaissance arcade of the **Palazzo Garampi,** the first building on the right when facing away from the Pescheria, contrasts dramatically with the adjoining fortress-like **Palazzo dell'Arengo** and the smaller **Palazzo del Podestà,** in the middle when facing away from the Pescheria. Perpendicular to the municipal building lies the pink brick **Teatro Comunale** (1857), whose auditorium was destroyed by World War II bombs. A motley collection of shops, bars, and offices surrounds the Renaissance **Pescheria** (fish market). The four stone fish, located in each corner of the interior arcade space, once functioned as fountains, filling the small canals (visible under the benches) with water for fish cleaning. Two statues stand in the center of the *piazza:* an eccentric, mossy fountain (1543) engraved with an inscription about Leonardo da Vinci and a seated Pope Paul V (1614) brandishing ferocious eagles. *(From the train station follow V. D. Alighieri to V. IV Novembre. At P. Tre Martiri turn right on C. d'Augusto. Palazzo del Podestà open for exhibitions; check with tourist office.)*

ARCH OF AUGUSTUS. This Roman triumphal arch (27 BC) is the most striking vestige of Rimini's past glory, blending the architectural elements of arch, column, and self-promotion. Today, standing all alone, it functions as a traffic circle. It also serves as a bold gateway into one of the busiest areas of the *centro storico*, P. Tre Martiri. *(Follow V. IV Novembre to P. Tre Martiri and turn left on C. d'Augusto.)*

🎵 ENTERTAINMENT

> ❗ **PLAYMATE OF THE YEAR.** Don't be flattered by Rimini's roving photographers offering "modeling deals"—attractive as you may be, it's actually a ploy meant to sell photos to tourists. Similarly, the streetside shell games are a great way to lose L100,000/€51.65 before you can say "one day's room and board."

Rimini is becoming a favorite detour for the roving, international party crowd. The town is notorious for its swinging, sometimes sleazy pick-up scene. *Passeggiata* is a euphemism for the wild cruising that runs nightly along the *lungomare* on **viale Amerigo Vespucci** and **viale Regina Elena**. But quantity does not breed variety—most of Rimini's *discoteche* are similar, with multiple floors featuring several types of music, exorbitant cover charges, and a hormonal atmosphere. Hang on to the discount passes that you are likely to pick up along V. Vespucci and V. Regina Elena. Ladies often can finagle free admission—but let that be its own warning.

Rimini has a **Blue Line** bus service (L5000/€2.58 per night) that runs from mid-July to August for disco-goers. Lines originate at the station and travel the bus #11 route up V. Vespucci and Viale Regina Elena to the nearby beach towns (1hr., every 20min.). Buy tickets on the bus. During the rest of the year, be careful not to miss the last bus; cab rides back to Rimini cost around L50,000/€25.82.

Cocorico, V. Chietti, 44, in Riccione (10km south of Rimini), accessible by bus #10 or 11 from the Rimini station. One of the area's flashiest discos, Cocorico has 6 bars and 4 dance floors playing underground techno and house. Cover around L50,000/€25.82. Open Sa nights.

Walky Cup by Aqua Fan (☎0541 60 30 50; fax 60 64 54), on V. Pistoia in Riccone. Take bus #11 to Riccione and then #45 to Aqua Fan, following the droves of sharply dressed Italians. Thousands of Rimini residents stand speechless when asked what the hell this name means; then they resume dancing. Amusement park inside. Complete with outdoor swimming pools and dance floor after dance floor, the club can pack in 4000 people. Cover usually L50,000/€25.82. Open usually weekends after 11pm.

Carnaby, V. Brindisi, 20. Bus #11: stop 26. Closer to town, with a bright yellow VW bug crashed into its 2nd floor. Well-lit, and equipped with 3 distinct music-style levels: hiphop/R&B, house, and classic rock/oldies. Makes a point to create a safe and fun environment for dancing and socializing. Open Mar.-Sept. daily 10pm-4am. Cover L13-15,000/€6.71-7.75 (includes a drink). Cover June-Aug. peaks at L30,000/€15.50.

SAN MARINO ☎0549

One of the more popular tourist attractions on the Italian Peninsula, San Marino isn't even in Italy. Although it closely resembles the surrounding hill towns, this 26 sq. km patch of turf inhabited by 26,000 people (you do the math) is its own nation, complete with UN recognition and brightly garbed "soldiers." The novelty of the little republic's size is the basis of its profitable tourist industry; cobblestone streets are bloated with trinket stands aimed at those who come just to have their passports stamped. And San Marino shamelessly exploits its status as a tourist spectacle—even the passport stamp will cost you L2000/€1.03.

San Marino traces its tiny roots to a single man, Marinus the stone-cutter. Marinus left his native land of Dalmatia to help the Emperor Diocletian fortify the city walls of Rimini. Diocletian returned the favor by persecuting Marinus and other Christians, inducing San Marino's patron saint to head for the hills where he could practice his religion in safety. This original community of exiled Christians atop Mount Titano came to be known as the Republic of San Marino.

TRANSPORTATION

Trains: The closest station is in Rimini, connected to San Marino by bus.

Buses: Fratelli Benedettini (☎ 0549 90 38 54) and **Bonelli Bus** (☎ 0541 37 24 32) run buses from train station and from P. Tripoli (by the seashore off Lungomare A. Murri) in Rimini to San Marino's historical center (50min., every hr., L6500/€3.68). Arrive 15min. before bus departs; they fill quickly.

Cableways: San Marino's *funivia* runs from Contra Omagnano down to Borgo Maggiore (every 15min. 7:50am-8pm; L4000/€2.07, round-trip L6000/€3.10).

Taxis: (☎ 0549 99 14 41), in P. Lo Stradone.

ORIENTATION AND PRACTICAL INFORMATION

San Marino's streets wind around **Mount Titano,** and helpful signs lead pedestrians from one attraction to the next. From the bus, exit to the left, climb the staircase and pass through the **Porta San Francesco** to start the ascent. From the *porta*, **via Basilicus** leads up to the **Piazza Titano.** From there, **Contrada del Collegio** leads through **Piazza Garibaldi** to **Piazza della Libertà.** The three castles tower above.

Tourist Office: Contra Omagnano, 20 (☎ 0549 88 24 00 or 88 24 10; fax 88 25 75; statoturismo@omniway.sm). From P. Garibaldi, follow C. del Collegio to P. della Libertà. Friendly staff with maps and historical info. Some English spoken. Open M and Th 8:15am-2:15pm and 3-6pm; Tu-W, and F 8:15am-2:15pm. **Branch office** (☎ 0549 88 29 14), in Contrada del Collegio, near P. della Libertà. Open daily 8:30am-6:30pm. Tourist **info booth** in Piazzale Stradone, just before P.S. Francesco. Rents listening guides to the country (L5000/€2.58). Open daily 8:30am-noon and 2:30-5pm.

Border Controls: None, but the tourist office will stamp your passport (L2000/€1.03).

Currency Exchange: San Marino mints its own coins in the same denominations as Italian *lire*. The two are used interchangeably.

Emergency: ☎ 113 or 115. **Ambulance:** ☎ 118.

Post, Coin, and Stamp Office: P. Garibaldi, 6 (☎ 0549 88 23 50). Open M-Sa 8:30am-6pm, Su 9am-12:30pm and 2-6:30pm.

COUNTRY CODE	San Marino's country code is 378. It's not necessary to dial when calling from Italy.

ACCOMMODATIONS AND FOOD

San Marino's hotels are small and overpriced, but the republic is an easy daytrip from Rimini or Ravenna. If you need a night outside of Italy, try the **Diamond Hotel,** Contra del Collegio, 50, across from Basilica di San Marino. Five breezy rooms above a restaurant overlook the crowds below. Breakfast is included. Pizza prices range from L8500/€4.39 and pasta from L13,500/€6.97. (☎/fax 0549 99 10 03. Singles L60-96,000/€30.99-49.58; doubles L96-132,000/€49.58-68.17.) **Hotel La Rocca,** Salita alla Rocca #37, under the castle, offers 10 spotless rooms decked out with TV, phone, and great views. (☎ 0549 99 24 30. Singles L60-90,000/€30.99-46.48; doubles L86-120,000/€44.42-61.97. AmEx/V.)

The food scene in San Marino is similarly overpriced. Snack bars and generic tourist fare are abundant. Many eateries have balcony seating; check for views, not culinary quality. For more affordable eats, try the fruit and vegetable **market,** Contra Omereli, 2, just off P. Titano (open daily 9:30am-8pm; in winter 8am-noon and 3:30-6:30pm), or the **supermarket,** at Contra del Collegio, 13, between P. Titano and P. Garibaldi (open M-Sa 7:15am-2pm and 3:30-8pm; AmEx/MC/V).

👁 🎵 SIGHTS AND ENTERTAINMENT

ROCCA GUAITA. The first of San Marino's vista points, Rocca Guaita, which dates from the 11th century, was extensively restored in the 19th and 20th. Climb around the tower ramparts, a chapel, and a prison. This structure served as the principal defense bulwark of Mt. Titano and San Marino. The climb is rather steep, and made more tiresome by the unending streets of cheaply made leather goods, air-compression guns, and trinkets bearing the visage of San Marino. *(Follow signs from Piazza Libertà. ☎0549 99 13 69. L4000/€2.07. A L6000/€3.10 cumulative ticket also covers admission to the Rocca Cesta. Open Apr.-Sept. daily 8am-8pm; Oct.-Mar. 8:50am-5pm.)*

ROCCA CESTA AND ROCCA MONTALE. Farther along the castle trail stands the **Rocca Cesta.** It houses an arms museum with chain mail, spears, rifles, lawsuits, and other weaponry. From the top, you are offered another view of the land below and of Rocca Guaita. *(☎0549 99 12 95. L4000/€2.07; cumulative ticket with Rocca Guaita L6000/€3.10. Open Apr.-Sept. daily 8am-8pm; Oct.-Mar. 8:50am-5pm.)* The trail continues to the third tower, Rocca Montale, which can only be viewed from outside.

MUSEO DELLA TORTURA. A museum dedicated to the display and explanation of over 100 original instruments used for human torture. Most of the devices are from the medieval era, but also a more modern reincarnation, *La Sedia Elettrica.* Explanations of how to flay or impale a human body, or what an iron maiden *(La Vergine)* is are offered in several languages, including English. *(☎0549 99 12 15. Museum is just to right after entering main gate. Casa Fattori (lato porta S. Francesco), open daily 10am-7pm. L10,000/€5.16; student and group discount L6000/€3.10.)*

PALAZZO PUBLICO. Francesco Azzuri erected this white beacon (1884-1894) atop the ruins of the *Parva Domus Commuis.* The exterior is far more interesting than the inside, except for the anachronistic meeting room upstairs adorned with frescoes, painted woodwork, and large screen TVs. The changing of the guard takes place in front of the palace in the spring, summer, and fall at half past the hour from 8:30am to 6:30pm. *(P. della Libertà. ☎0549 88 53 70. Open Apr.-Sept. daily 8am-8pm; Oct.-Mar. 8:50am-5pm. L4000/€2.07, includes Chiesa San Francesco.)*

MEDIEVAL FESTIVAL. In late July, the republic stages a medieval festival, a gala complete with parades, food, musicians, and jugglers. Increased bus service allows those not staying in San Marino to participate. *(Call the tourist office for the exact dates and other info or surf to www.omniway.sm/medieval.)*

NORTHEAST ITALY

FLORENCE (FIRENZE)

Shortly after making his public debut as a clerk in 1494, the political fortunes of Niccolo Machiavelli skyrocketed dramatically when he acquired the pompous title "secretary to the chancery of the commune of Florence." The list of people he served as an envoy reads like a 16th-century Who's Who, but his connections were not enough to save him from exile and torture when his infant republic collapsed and Cosimo de'Medici brought Machiavelli up on conspiracy charges. His masterpiece of domination and statecraft, *The Prince*, was penned in an attempt to regain favor with the Medici clan, and, remarkably, he praised their cold brutality and willingness to torture enemies. But Charles V's sack of Rome and the downfall of the Medici pope Clement VII ended Machiavelli's hopes of re-gaining office, and he died while still in exile, his body interred in Santa Croce.

Machiavelli's life is a window on what is arguably Florence's greatest century, when the city became the European capital of art, architecture, commerce, and political thought. Machiavelli himself can be described as the typical Florentine, albeit blessed with a little more talent and taste for power. Florence has never been a perfect or lifeless museum, and even today, Florentine students quote Marx and Malcolm X in street graffiti and children play soccer against the side of the *duomo*. When the Arno flooded its banks in 1966, swamping Santa Croce and the Uffizi in 6m of water, Florentines and foreigners alike braved the waters to rescue paintings, sculptures, and books.

HIGHLIGHTS OF FLORENCE

EXPERIENCE David-hopping, from Michelangelo's formidable hunk in the **Accademia** (p. 332) to Donatello's supple bronze boy in the **Bargello** (p. 329).

CLIMB to the top of **Brunelleschi's dome** to reach **Michelangelo's Cupola** (p. 325) and a 360-degree panorama of Florence.

RELISH in the works of **Botticelli, Giotto, Raphael,** and just about any other Renaissance grandmaster in the unparalleled art collection of **Uffizi** (p. 328).

✈ INTERCITY TRANSPORTATION

Flights: Amerigo Vespucci Airport (☎ 055 306 17 00), in the Florentine suburb of Peretola. Mostly domestic and charter flights. The orange **ATAF** bus #62 connects the train station to the airport (L1500/€0.77). Buy tickets from the *tabacchi* on the upper level of the departure side of airport. **SITA,** V.S. Caterina da Siena, 157 (☎ 800 37 37 60 46 or 055 28 46 61), also runs regular buses (L6000/€3.1) to airport from station. **Galileo Galilei Airport** (☎ 050 50 07 07), in Pisa. Take airport express from Florence train station (1¼hr., 7 per day, L9100/€4.70). In Florence, ask for info at the "air terminal" (☎ 055 21 60 73) half way down platform #5 in train station, where you can check in, get an embrocation card, and register baggage (L5000/€2.58). Open daily 7am-5pm.

Trains: Santa Maria Novella Station, across from S. Maria Novella. Florence's only modern styled building. Info office open daily 7am-9pm; after hours call national train info ☎ 147 880 88. Luggage storage and lost property services available (p. 315). Trains depart every hr. to: **Bologna** (1hr.; L14,200/€7.33); **Milan** (3½hr.; L39,700/€20.50); **Rome** (3½hr.; L35-40,000/€18.08-20.66, InterCity L40,900/€21.12); **Siena** (1½hr., L8800/€4.54); **Venice** (3hr.; L35,100/€18.13).

Buses: 3 major bus companies service Tuscany's towns. Offices near P. della Stazione.

SITA, V.S. Caterina da Siena, 15r (☎ 800 37 37 60 46 or 055 28 46 61). To: **Arezzo** (1½hr., 1 per day, L9900/€5.11); **Poggibonsi** (50min., 13 per day, L8000/€4.13); **San Gimignano** (1½hr.; 13 per day; L10,000/€5.16); **Siena** (2hr.; express 1¼hr.; L11,000/€5.68); **Volterra** (2hr., 6 per day, L7800/€4.03).

LAZZI, P. Adua, 1-4r (☎ 055 21 51 55). To: **Lucca** (every hr., in winter 6 per day; L8600/€4.44); **Pisa** (every hr., in winter 6 per day, L11,200/€5.78); **Pistoia** (L5000/€2.58); **Prato** (L3500/€1.81).

CAP, Largo Alinari, 9 (☎ 055 21 46 37). To **Prato** (L3500/€1.81).

▓ ORIENTATION

From Stazione S. Maria Novella, a short walk on **via de'Panzani** and a left onto **via de'Cerrentari** leads to the **duomo,** the literal and figurative heart of the city of Florence. Just as all roads lead to Rome, all streets in Florence lead to the instantly recognizable dome soaring high above any other building. **Via de'Calzaiuoli,** dominated by throngs of pedestrians, leads south from the *duomo* to the **Piazza Signoria,** the statue-filled plaza in front of the **Palazzo Vecchio** and the world-famous **Uffizi Gallery.** The other major *piazza* is the **Piazza Della Repubblica,** a vast plaza the size of an entire city block. Major streets run from this *piazza* north back toward the *duomo* and south toward the shop-lined **Ponte Vecchio** (literally, "Old Bridge"). The Ponte Vecchio is one of five bridges that cross from central Florence into the **Oltrarno,** the district south of the Arno River. When navigating in Florence, note that most **streets change names unpredictably,** often every few blocks. For guidance through Florence's tangled center, grab a **free map** (one with a street index) from the tourist office, *Informazione Turistica*, across the *piazza* from the train station (see **Practical Information** below).

 RED AND BLACK ATTACK! Florence's streets are numbered in red and black sequences. Red numbers indicate commercial establishments and black (or blue) numbers denote residential addresses (including most sights and hotels). Black addresses appear here as a numeral only, while red addresses are indicated by a number followed by an "r." If you reach an address and it's not what you're looking for, you've probably got the wrong color.

▛ LOCAL TRANSPORTATION

Public Transportation: Orange **ATAF** city buses take you almost anywhere from 6am-1am. Tickets: L1500/€0.77 per 1hr. of unlimited use, L5800/€3 for 4 such tickets; L2500/€1.29 per 3hr.; L6000/€3.10 per 24hr.; L11,000/€5.68 per 3 days; L19,000/€9.81 per week. Buy tickets at any newsstand, *tabacchi*, or coin-operated ticket dispenser before boarding. Validate ticket on board using orange machine or risk being fined L75,000/€38.73. Once validated, ticket allows travel on any bus for one hr. From 9pm-6am tickets sold on bus cost L3000/€1.55. Exit train station, **ATAF info and ticket office** (☎ 055 565 02 22) is on left. Open daily 6:30am-8pm. Free bus map. #7 to Fiesole, #10 to Settignano, #17 to Villa Camerate (L1500/€0.77).

Car Rental: Hertz, V. Finiguerra, 33r (☎ 055 239 82 05). 25+. Open M-Sa 8am-11pm, Su 8am-1pm. **Maggiore** (☎ 055 31 12 56), at airport. 19+. Open daily 8:30am-10:30pm. At V. Finiguerra, 31r (☎ 055 21 02 38). Open M-Sa 8am-1pm and 2:30-7pm. **Avis** (☎ 055 31 55 88), at airport. 25+. Open 8am-11pm. In town at Borgo Ognissanti, 128r (☎ 055 21 36 29). Open M-F 8am-7pm, Sa 8am-6pm.

Bike and Moped Rental: Alinari Noleggi, V. Guelfa, 85r (☎ 055 28 05 00; fax 271 78 71), rents mopeds for L35-45,000/€18.08-23.24 per day; bikes L20-30,000/€10.33-15.50 per day. **I Bike Florence** (see **Practical Information,** below).

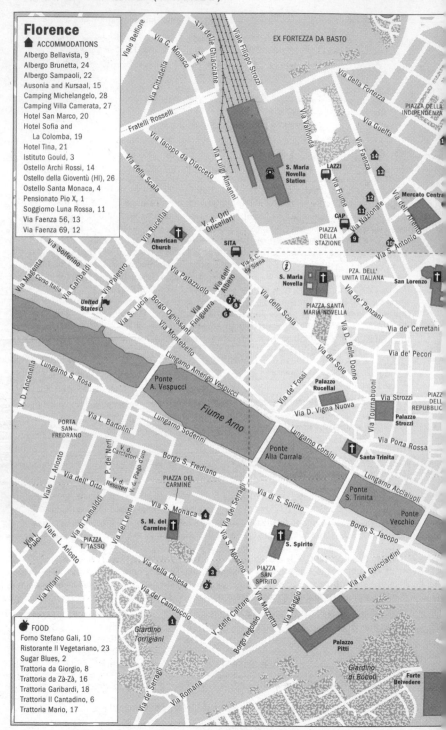

Florence

ACCOMMODATIONS
Albergo Bellavista, 9
Albergo Brunetta, 24
Albergo Sampaoli, 22
Ausonia and Kursaal, 15
Camping Michelangelo, 28
Camping Villa Camerata, 27
Hotel San Marco, 20
Hotel Sofia and
    La Colomba, 19
Hotel Tina, 21
Istituto Gould, 3
Ostello Archi Rossi, 14
Ostello della Gioventù (HI), 26
Ostello Santa Monaca, 4
Pensionato Pio X, 1
Soggiorno Luna Rossa, 11
Via Faenza 56, 13
Via Faenza 69, 12

FOOD
Forno Stefano Gali, 10
Ristorante Il Vegetariano, 23
Sugar Blues, 2
Trattoria da Giorgio, 8
Trattoria da Zà-Zà, 16
Trattoria Garibardi, 18
Trattoria Il Cantadino, 6
Trattoria Mario, 17

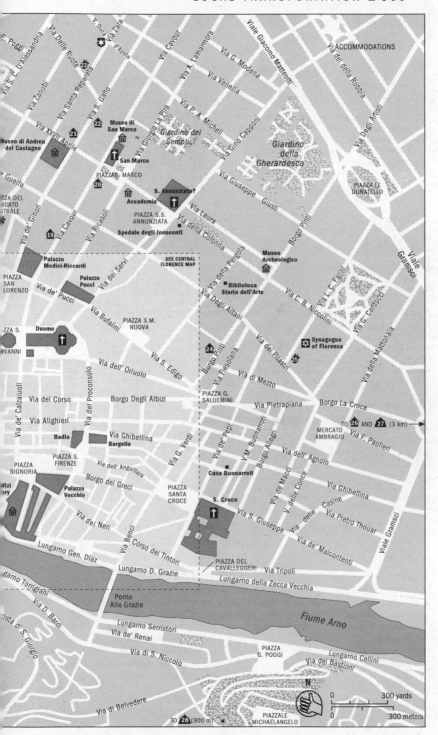

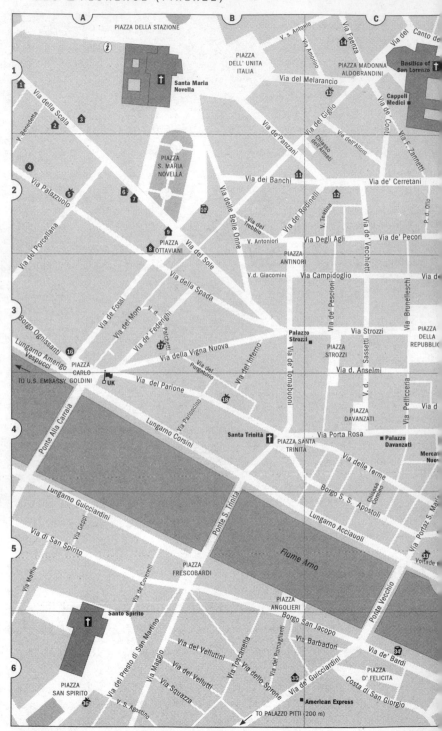

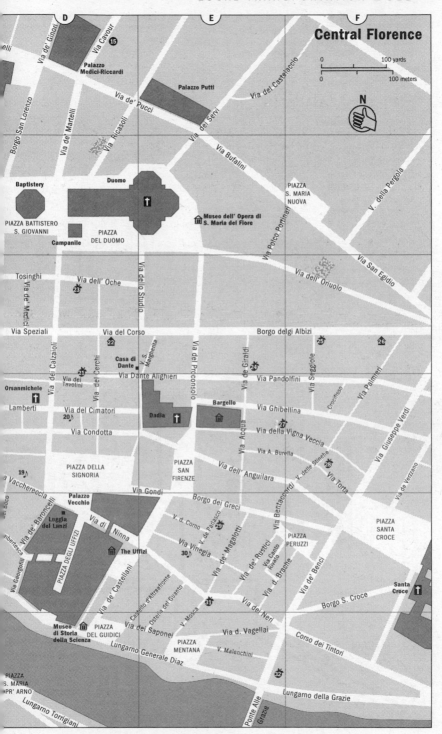

Central Florence

FLORENCE

Walkintour

The stunning Cappelle dei Medici is accessible around the back entrance to the **Basilica di San Lorenzo** on P. Padonna degli Aldobrandini.

Check out the illusion of depth in Ghiberti's **Gates of Paradise,** the world-famous gilded panels on the eastern doors of the Baptistery.

First the residence of Florence's chief magistrate and later a brutal prison, the **Bargello** now houses the Museo Nazionale, a treasury of Florentine sculpture.

After basking in the grandeur of the **Duomo,** enter from the south side and climb the 463 steps to Michelangelo's Lantern for an unparalleled view of the city.

1 start

2

3

PIAZZA S. GIOVANNI

PIAZZA DEL DUOMO

PIAZZA MADONNA ALDOBRANDINI

Duomo

Campanile

Museo dell' Opera di S. Maria del Fiore

Palazzo Pucci

Via de' Pucci

Via Ricasoli

Via Cavour

Via de' Ginori

Borgo San Lorenzo

Via de' Cerretani

P. d. Ollo

Via F. Zannetti

Via de' Conti

Cappelle Medici

Nelli

Faenza

Via del Castellaccio

V. della Pergola

Via San Egidio

Via degli Orivolo

Borgo degli Albizi

PIAZZA S. MARIA NUOVA

Via Bufalini

Via Porta Rossa Pentolina

Via dello Studio

Via de' Medici

Via Speziali

Tosinghi

Via Roma

Via de' Pecori

Via de' Vecchietti

Via de'

PIAZZA DELLA REPUBBLICA

Via Brunelleschi

Via Strozzi

Via del Sole

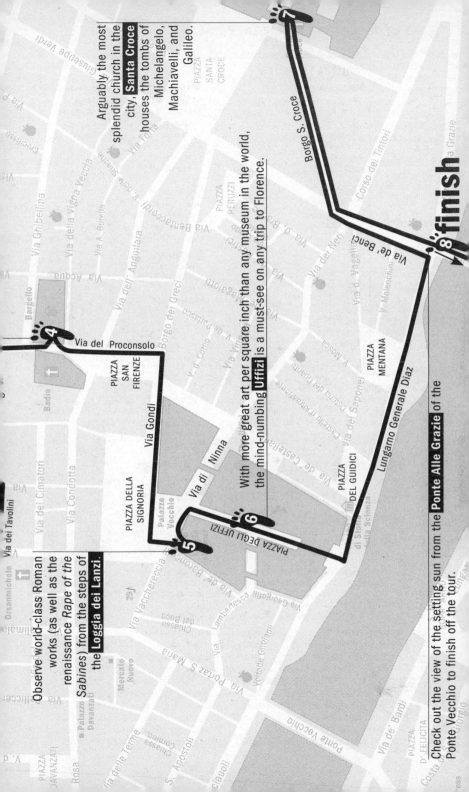

Arguably the most splendid church in the city, **Santa Croce** houses the tombs of Michelangelo, Machiavelli, and Galileo.

With more great art per square inch than any museum in the world, the mind-numbing **Uffizi** is a must-see on any trip to Florence.

Observe world-class Roman works (as well as the renaissance *Rape of the Sabines*) from the steps of the **Loggia dei Lanzi**.

Check out the view of the setting sun from the **Ponte Alle Grazie** of the Ponte Vecchio to finish off the tour.

finish

Central Florence

🏠 ACCOMMODATIONS

Albergo Firenze, 22	D3
Albergo Margaret, 2	A1
Hotel Abaco/	
Hotel Giappone, 11	B2
Hotel Elite, 3	A1
Hotel il Perseo, 12	C2
Hotel La Scaletta, 35	B6
Hotel Montreal, 1	A1
Hotel Visconti, 9	A3
Katti House, 14	C1
Locanda Orchidea, 26	F3
Pensione Ottaviani, 8	A2
Tourist House, 7	A2

🍺 PUBS

The Chequers Pub, 6	A2
The Fiddler's Elbow, 10	B2
Monecarla, 34	C6

♪ CLUBS

Andromeda, 20	D4
Blob, 30	E5
Tabasco, 19	D4

🍎 FOOD

Acqua al Due, 27	E4
Amon, 5	A2
Enoteca Alessi, 23	D3
Le Colonnine, 32	E6
Il Borgo Antico, 36	A6
Il Latini, 33	B3
La Loggia degli Albizi, 25	F3
Perchè No?, 21	D3
Ristorante de' Medici, 13	C1
Rose's Cafe, 18	B4
Trattoria Anita, 29	E5
Trattoria da Benvenuto, 31	E5
Vivoli, 28	F4

● SERVICES

BM Bookstore, 16	A3
Feltrinelli International	
Bookstore, 15	D1
Gymnasium, 4	A2

Parking: Most city center hotels don't offer parking. Small garages dot the city but keep unpredictable hours (look for a blue sign with a white P). Lots at train station and beneath P. della Libertà open 24hr. **Towed-Car Retrieval: Depositeria Comunale,** V. dell'Arcovata, 6 (☎055 30 82 49). ATAF buses #23 and 33 stop nearby.

Taxis: (☎055 43 90, 055 47 98, or 055 42 42), outside train station.

🔟 PRACTICAL INFORMATION

TOURIST AND FINANCIAL SERVICES

Tourist Offices:

Consorzio ITA (☎055 28 28 93 and 21 95 37), in train station by track #16, next to pharmacy. Lines can be quite long. Finds rooms (if you arrive in person). L4500-15,000/€2.32-7.75 commission, though not always the best value. No maps or tourist info. Open daily 8:45am-8pm.

Informazione Turistica, P. della Stazione 4 (☎055 21 22 45; ☎/fax 238 12 26), directly across the *piazza* from main exit of station. Info on entertainment and cultural events, free maps, and listings of hours for all sights in the city. Ask for a map with street index. Open daily 8:30am-7pm. **Branch offices** at V. Cavour 1r (☎055 29 08 32 or 29 08 33); Borgo Santa Croce, 29r (☎055 234 04 44); V. Manzoni 16 (☎055 23 32 0); airport (☎055 31 58 74). Similar hours.

Walking Tours: Enjoy Florence (☎055 167 27 48 19; www.enjoyflorence.com). Guides give fast-paced, informative tours to small groups. Old city center tours focus on history of medieval and Renaissance Florence. Tours leave daily 10am in front of Thomas Cook office at the Ponte Vecchio. Reduced hours in winter. L30,000/€15.50, under 26 L25,000/€12.91. **Walking Tours of Florence,** P. Fento Stefano, 2b (☎055 42 50 33; www.artviva.com), 1 block north of Ponte Vecchio. A theater company offering a leisurely walk around Florence, presenting an anecdotal history. L40,000/€20.66, students under 26 L30,000/€15.5. Also offers a tour of the Uffizi (L60,000/€31, prebooked gallery ticket included); Tuscan wine country (L85,000/€43.9); nearby Siena and San Gimignano (L120,000/€62). Open daily 8am-6pm; closed in winter).

Biking Tours: Florence by Bike, V.S. Zanobi, 120/122r (☎/fax 055 48 89 92; www.florencebybike.it). Gives bike tours of historic Florence, the Chianti region, and Florentine hills (L45-117,000/€23.24-60.43). Reserve ahead. Also **rents bikes** (L20-40,000/€10.33-20.66 per day) and **mopeds** (L40-60,000/€20.66-31). Open daily 9am-7:30pm. **I Bike Italy** (☎055 234 23 71) offers 1- and 2-day bike tours of varying difficulty. Tours of Fiesole, the Chianti, the Tuscan countryside and vineyards.

Budget Travel: STS (Servizio Turisto Social), V.F. Zanetti, 18r. Student discounts on train, plane, and bus tickets. Open M-F 9:30am-1pm and 3:30-8pm, Sa 10am-12:30pm. **CTS,** V. Ginori, 25r (☎055 28 95 70). Provides Transalpino tickets, discount airfares, car rentals, organized trips, and ISIC cards. Arrive early and take a number. Open M-F 9:30am-1:30pm and 2:30-6pm, Sa 9am-12:30pm.

Consulates: UK, Lungarno Corsini, 2 (☎055 28 41 33). Open M-F 9:30am-12:30pm and 2:30-4:30pm. Can be reached by phone M-F 9am-1pm and 2-5pm. **US,** Lungarno Amerigo Vespucci, 38 (☎055 239 82 76), at V. Palestro, near the station. Open M-F 9am-12:30pm and 2-3:30pm. **Canadians, Australians**, and **New Zealanders** should contact their consulates in Rome or Milan.

Currency Exchange: Local banks offer the best exchange rates. Most open M-F 8:20am-1:20pm and 2:45-3:45pm, some open Sa morning. 24hr. **ATMs** all over the city.

American Express: V. Dante Alighieri, 20r (☎055 509 81). From *duomo*, walk down V. dei Calzaiuoli, turn left onto V. dei Tavolini, and continue to the small *piazza*. Cashes personal checks for cardholders. Also holds mail for card- and traveler's check-holders at no cost; all others L3000/€1.55 per inquiry. L3000/€1.55 to leave messages. Open M-F 9am-5:30pm. Open for financial services only Sa 9am-12:30pm.

LOCAL SERVICES

Luggage Storage: In train station, Track #16. L5000/€2.58 for 12hr. Open daily 4:15am-1:30am.

Lost Property: Ufficio Oggetti Rinvenuti (☎055 235 21 90), next to the baggage deposit, for objects left on trains.

English-Language Bookstores:

■**Paperback Exchange,** V. Fiesolana, 31r (☎055 247 81 54). Swaps books. Special Italianistica section features novels about Brits and Americans in Italy. Open M-Sa 9am-7:30pm. Closed 2-3 weeks Aug. AmEx/MC/V.

BM Bookstore, Borgo Ognissanti, 4r (☎055 29 45 75). English-language books on every subject imaginable. Stocks textbooks for American study-abroad programs. Open Mar.-Oct. M-Sa 9am-7:30pm, Su 9am-1pm; Nov.-Feb. M-Sa 9am-7:30pm

Libraries: Biblioteca Marucelliana, V. Cavour, 43 (☎055 272 21 or 055 260 62), 2min. from the *duomo*. Open M-F 8:30am-7pm, Sa 8:30-1:45pm.

Religious Services: Anglican: St. Mark's Church of England, V. Maggio, 16 (☎055 29 47 64). Su 9am and 10:30am. **Catholic:** In English at the *duomo*. Sa 5pm. **Episcopal: The American Church,** V.B. Rucellai, 16 (☎055 29 44 17). Su 9am and 11am. **Jewish (Orthodox): Tempio Israelito,** V. Farini, 4 (☎055 24 52 52). F sunset, Sa 8:45am. **Muslim: Centro Culturale Islamico,** P. degli Scarlatti, 1 (☎055 71 16 48).

Bulletin Boards: Lists of people seeking roommates, English teachers, baby-sitters, and religious and cultural activities conducted in English. **The American Church,** V.B. Rucellai, 16 (☎055 29 44 17), off V. della Scala, near train station. Open T-F 9am-1pm.

Ticket Agency: The Box Office, V. Alamanni, 39r (☎055 21 08 04; fax 21 31 12), sells tickets for Florence's theatrical and musical performances, including rock concerts. Advance booking service. Open M-F 10am-7:30pm. Pick up a listing in any tourist office or buy the city's entertainment monthly, *Firenze Spettacolo* (L3000/€1.55).

Laundromats: Launderette, V. Guelfa, 55r. Self-service wash and dry L12,000/€6.20. Open daily 8am-10pm. **Wash and Dry Lavarapido,** V. dei Servi, 105r, 2 blocks from the *duomo.* **Other location:** V. della Scala, 52-54r; V. dei Servi, 105r; V. del Sol, 29r; V. Ghibellina, 143r; V. dei Serragli, 87r; V. Morgagni, 21r; and V. Nazionale, 129r. Self-service wash and dry L12,000/€6.20. Open daily 8am-10pm. **Ondo Blu,** V. degli Alfani, 24. Self-service wash and dry L11,000/€5.68. Open daily 8am-10pm.

Swimming Pools: Bellariva, Lungarno Colombo, 6 (☎055 67 75 21). Bus #14 from the station or a 15min. walk upstream along the Arno. L12,000/€6.20. Open June-Sept. W and F-M 10am-6pm, Tu and Th 10am-6pm and 8-11pm.

Gym: Gymnasium, V. Palazzuolo, 49r (☎055 29 33 08). Workout equipment and daily step aerobics. L20,000/€10.33 per day; L120,000/€62 per month.

EMERGENCY AND COMMUNICATIONS

Emergency: ☎113. **Carabinieri:** ☎112. **Medical Emergency:** ☎118. **Road Assistance (ACI):** ☎116. **Fire:** ☎115.

Police Central Office (Questura), V. Zara, 2 (☎055 497 71). Another branch at P. del Duomo, 5. Open M-F 8am-8pm, Sa 8am-2pm. **Tourist Police: Ufficio Stranieri,** V. Zara, 2 (☎055 497 71), for visa or work-permit problems. Open M-F 8:30am-noon. To report lost or stolen items, go around corner to **Ufficio Denunce,** V. Duca D'Aosta, 3 (☎055 497 71). Open M-Sa 8am-8pm, Su 8am-2pm.

Tourist Medical Service, V. Lorenzo il Magnifico, 59 (☎055 47 54 11). Group of general practitioners and specialists. Someone on call 24hr. Office visits L50,000/€25.82; house calls L80,000/€41.32.

24-Hour Pharmacies: Farmacia Comunale (☎055 28 94 35), at the train station by track #16. **Molteni,** V. dei Calzaiuoli, 7r (☎055 28 94 90).

Internet Access: Walk down any busy street and you're sure to find an internet cafe.

Internet Train. 15 locations throughout Florence listed on www.internettrain.it/citta.isp. Offers telnet, email, and web-cruising. Tickets L12,000/€6.20 per hr., students L10,000/€5.16 per hr.; with membership (free with min. 2hr. purchase) L10,000/€5.16 per hr., students L8000/€4.13 per hr. Open M-F 10am-11pm, Sa 12:30-7:30pm, Su 3-7pm.

Netgate has locations at V.S. Egidio, 10/20r (☎055 234 79 67) and, in summer, an evening under-the-tents station on the 2nd terrace at P.G. Poggi. About L10,000/€5.16 per hr. Open M-Sa 10:30am-10pm; in winter daily 10:40am-8:30pm.

Post Office: (☎055 21 61 22), on V. Pellicceria, off P. della Repubblica. To send packages, go behind the building to V. dei Sassetti, 4. Open M-F 8:15am-7pm, Sa 8:15am-12:30pm. Telegram office in front open 24hr.

Postal Code: 50100.

ACCOMMODATIONS & CAMPING

Florence's large number of budget accommodations make it likely you'll find a room even if you arrive without a reservation. The **Consorzio ITA** in the train station (see **Tourist and Financial Services,** above) can inform you of available rooms and going rates in the one-star *pensioni* and private *affittacamere* that flood Florence. Another option is to check your bag at the train station (see **Intercity Transportation,** above) and start pounding the pavement. Reasonable options should present themselves. Hotel owners are often willing to refer you to others if their establishment has no vacancies; don't hesitate to ask.

Because of the constant stream of tourists, it is best to make reservations *(prenotazioni)* at least 10 days in advance, especially if you plan to visit during Easter or the summer. If you make reservations, the majority of *pensioni* prefer them in writing with at least one night's deposit in the form of a money order; others simply ask that you call to confirm a few days before you arrive.

If you have any complaints, first talk to the proprietor and then to the **Ufficio Controllo Alberghi,** V. Cavour, 37 (☎055 276 01). The municipal government strictly regulates hotel prices; proprietors can charge neither more nor less than the approved range for their category. Rates uniformly increase around 10% every year; the new rates take effect in March or April.

Long-term housing in Florence is easy to secure. If you plan on staying a month or more, check **bulletin boards** (see p. 315) and the classified ads in *La Pulce*, published three times weekly (L3800/€1.96) with apartment, sublet, and roommate listings, or **Grillo Fiorentino,** a free monthly local paper. Reasonable prices range from L350-800,000/€180.76-413.17 per month.

> Hotel prices in Florence change regularly; by summer 2002, rates will be **at least** 10-20% higher than those listed here.

HOSTELS

 Ostello Archi Rossi, V. Faenza, 94r (☎055 29 08 04; fax 230 26 01), 2 blocks from train station. Exit left from station onto V. Nazionale. Take 2nd left onto V. Faenza. Look for blue neon *ostello* sign. Floor-to-ceiling murals, ceramic tiles, and brick archways. Courtyard patio and dining/TV room brimming with travelers. Breakfast options range from continental to crêpes and omelettes (L3-4500/€1.55-2.32). Dinner L3500-5000/€1.81-2.58. Laundry L10,000/€5.16. Free Internet. Jun.-Sept. arrive before 8am for a room—earlier if in a large group. Room lockout 9:30am; hostel lockout 11am. Curfew 1am. No reservations. 4- to 9-bed dorms L35-40,000/€18.08-20.66. Reserved rooms for handicapped travelers L50,000/€25.82.

Istituto Gould, V. de'Serragli, 49 (☎055 21 25 76), in Oltrarno. Take bus #36 or 37 from station to the 2nd stop across the river. Spotless rooms, some overlooking noisy street. Cool and cavernous; large colonnaded courtyard. Reception M-F 9am-1pm and 3-7pm, Sa 9am-1pm. No check in or out Sa afternoons; check out Su, but no check in. No lockout or curfew. 89 beds. Singles L48,000/€24.79, with bath L55,000/€28.41; doubles L72,000/€37.18, L78,000/€40.28; triples L78,000/€40.28, L105,000/€54.23; quads with bath L132,000/€68.17; quints with bath L142,000/€73.34.

Ostello Santa Monaca, V.S. Monaca, 6 (☎055 26 83 38; fax 28 01 85; info@ostello.it; www.ostello.it). Follow the directions to the Instituto Gould, but go right off V. dei Serragli onto V.S. Monaca. Crowds up to 20 beds into high-ceilinged rooms. Helpful management and friendly clientele. Minimal kitchen facilities—bring utensils. No meals, but tickets for a nearby self-service restaurant are sold. Sheets and immaculate showers included. Self-service laundry L12,000/€6.20 per 5kg. Internet access L5000/€2.58 per 30min., L8000/€4.13 per hr. Arrive before 9am for a room. 7-night max. stay. Reception 6am-1pm and 2pm-1am. Curfew 1am. Reservations must be made 3 days in advance. 116 beds. Dorms L25,000/€12.91. AmEx/MC/V.

Ostello della Gioventù Europa Villa Camerata (HI), V. Augusto Righi, 2-4 (☎055 60 14 51; fax 61 03 00), northeast of town. Take bus #17 from outside train station (near track #5), or from P. dell'Unità across from station: get off at the Salviatino stop. Ask the bus driver when to get off. Walk 8-10min. from the street entrance past a vineyard. Tidy and popular, in a villa with *loggia*. Breakfast and sheets included. Dinner L15,000/€7.75. Self-service laundry L10,000/€5.16. Reception daily 7am-12:30pm and 1pm-midnight. Check-out 7-9am or pay for the following night. Rooms open 2pm-midnight. Strict midnight curfew. Make reservations in writing. 4, 6, or 8 beds per room. 360 beds. Dorms L28,000/€14.46. L5000/€2.58 extra per night without HI card.

Pensionato Pio X, V. de'Serragli, 106 (☎/fax 055 22 50 44). Follow directions to Istituto Gould, and walk a few blocks farther. On right in a courtyard. Full in summer. Quiet, with 3-5 beds per room. Clean, functional rooms. 4 basic lounges, one with TV. Min. 2-night stay, or pay extra L2000/€1.03. Arrive before 9am for a room. Check-out 9am. Curfew midnight. No reservations. 54 beds. Dorms L26,000/€13.43, with bath L30,000/€15.50. Singles with shared bathroom L30,000/€15.50.

HOTELS

PIAZZA SANTA MARIA NOVELLA AND ENVIRONS

The budget accommodations that cluster around this *piazza* in front of the train station offer a prime location near the *duomo* and town center. Who could ask for more than stepping out of their cozy *pensione* to be confronted by Alberti's masterful facade on Santa Maria Novella? Ask for a room overlooking the *piazza*.

☒ Hotel Visconti, P. Ottaviani, 1 (☎/fax 055 21 38 77). Exit train station and cross to the back of Santa Maria Novella church. Walk past church into P.S. Maria Novella, then across the left side of the *piazza* until you reach the tiny P. Ottaviani. Bar, TV lounge, and 10 rooms. Delicious breakfast included, served by the friendly management on the garden roof (open 24hr.). Singles L68,000/€35.12, with bathroom L100,000/€51.65; doubles L104,000/€53.71, L145,000/74.89; triples L150,000/€77.47, L180,000/€92.96; quads L168,000/€86.76, L220,000/€113.62.

Pensione Ottaviani, P. Ottaviani, 1 (☎055 239 62; fax 29 33 55). Upstairs from Hotel Visconti. Simple, elegant, comfortable, and inexpensive. Friendly reception, large rooms with wooden furniture and phones. No bathrooms. Singles L50,000/€25.82; doubles L100,000/€51.65; triples L145,000/€74.89; quads L190,000/€98.13.

Albergo Margaret, V. della Scala, 25 (☎055 21 01 38). Exit train station to right onto V.D. Orti Oricellari, which leads to V. della Scala, and take a left. Plush decor, with marble tables and thick carpets. Kind staff and 8 beautiful rooms, most with balconies. Curfew midnight. Singles L85,000/€43.90; doubles L110,000/€56.81 with bath L130,000/€67.14. Lower prices Sept.-May and for longer stays.

Hotel Montreal, V. della Scala, 43 (☎055 238 23 31; fax 28 74 91; www.hotelmont-real.com). Follow directions to Albergo Margaret. Helpful reception and comfortable couches in the bright airy TV lounge. Curfew 1:30am. 22 modern rooms. Singles L90,000/€46.48; doubles with shower L95,000/€49.06, with bath L110,000/€56.81; triples with bath L150,000/€77.47; quads with bath L185,000/€95.54.

Hotel Giappone, V. dei Banchi, 1 (☎055 21 00 90; fax 29 28 77). From train station cross to the back of Santa Maria Novella church. Walk past church into P.S. Maria Novella and go left onto V. dei Banchi. Clean, comfortable rooms and a central location. All rooms with phone, TV and shower. Singles L100,000/€51.65; doubles L130,000/€67.14, with bath L160,000/€82.63; extra bed L40,000/€20.66. MC/V.

Hotel Elite, V. della Scala, 12 (☎055 21 53 95; fax 21 38 32). Follow directions to Albergo Margaret. Brass accents enhance this 2-star hotel's well-maintained rooms. Cozy breakfast and sitting room. Breakfast L10,000/€5.16. Singles with shower L100,000/€51.65, with toilet L130,000/€67.14; doubles with shower L130,000/€67.14, with toilet L160,000/€82.63; triples with shower L200,000/€103.29.

Hotel Abaco, V. dei Banchi, 1 (☎/fax 055 238 19 19; abacohotel@tin.it). Follow directions to Hotel Giappone. Reproduction 17th-century antique headboards, noise-proof windows and free Internet access. 7 well-kept rooms each with a Renaissance artist theme. All rooms have A/C, phone, and TV. Laundry L7000/€3.62 per load. Singles L100,000/€51.65; doubles L130,000/€67.14. Extra bed L40,000/€20.66. MC/V.

Albergo Bellavista, Largo F. Alinari, 15 (☎055 28 45 28; fax 28 48 74; bellavistaho-tel@iol.it). Exit train station and cross the *piazza* diagonally to the left. On fifth floor of an old *palazzo*, just steps from the train station. Beautiful views from all rooms. Comfortable old-fashioned furnishings, few frills, and friendly owners. Phone and fan in all rooms. Singles L90,000/€46.48, with bathroom L100,000/€51.65; doubles with bathroom L170,000/€87.80; extra bed L70,000/€36.15.

Soggiorno Luna Rossa, V. Nazionale, 7 (☎055 230 21 85; fax 28 25 52; www.tourist-house.com). Exit train station to left onto V. Nazionale. This small pensione features very high ceilings, soft, yellow walls, and large rooms, all with phone and TV. Doubles and triples L50,000/€25.82 per person; doubles with bath L150,000/€77.47, triples with bath L195,000/€100.70; quads or larger L45,000/€23.24 per person.

Tourist House, V. della Scala, 1 (☎055 26 86 75; fax 28 25 52; www.tourist-house.com). Follow directions to Albergo Margaret. Extremely friendly proprietors run Hotel Giappone as well. Sleek modern decor, large communal area with couches. Rooms comfortable with bath, TV, and terrace. Breakfast included. Singles L130,000/€67.14; doubles L160,000/€82.63; quads L240,000/€123.95. MC/V.

OLD CITY (NEAR THE DUOMO)

Flooded by tourists, this area tends to be more expensive than elsewhere. Many accommodations provide great views of Florence's monuments, while others lie hidden in Renaissance *palazzi*. Follow V. de' Panzani from the train station and take a left on V. de' Cerretani to reach the *duomo*.

▨**Albergo Brunetta,** Borgo Pinti, 5 (☎055 247 81 34). Exit P. del Duomo on V. dell' Oriuolo behind the *duomo*. After 2 long blocks take a left on Borgo Pinti. Excellent value for this central location. Take advantage of the roof-top terrace that offers a spectacular panorama of Florence. 12 rooms, all without bath, but showers are free. Singles L80,000/€41.32; doubles L130,000/€67.14; triples L170,000/€87.80.

Locanda Orchidea, Borgo degli Albizi, 11 (☎/fax 055 248 03 46; hotelorchidea@yahoo.it). Take a left off V. Proconsolo from the *duomo*. Dante's wife was born in this 12th-century *palazzo*, built around a still-intact tower. Lobby adorned with art and antiques. Friendly and helpful management. 7 graceful rooms, some of which open onto a garden. Rooms on the street can be very noisy. Singles L75,000/€38.73; doubles L110,000/€56.81; triples L170,000/€87.80.

Hotel Il Perseo, V. de Cerretani, 1 (☎055 21 25 04; fax 28 83 77; www.hotelperseo.com). Exit the train station and walk down V. de' Panzani, which becomes V. de' Cerretani. Owners welcome travelers to their 19 bright, immaculate rooms. All have fans and many have breathtaking views. Cozy bar and TV lounge. Breakfast included. Internet access L5000/€2.58 per 30min. Parking L30,000/€15.50 per day. Singles L90,000/€46.48; doubles L135,000/€69.72, with bath L160,000/€82.63; triples L175,000/€90.38, with bath L210,000/€103.29. MC/V. 5% Cash discount.

Albergo Firenze, P. dei Donati, 4 (☎055 21 42 03 or 26 83 01 or 21 33 11; fax 21 23 70), off V. del Corso, 2 blocks south of the *duomo*. Central and tranquil. Located in a beautiful *palazzo*. 60 modern glossy rooms with tile floors, TV, and bathrooms. Wheelchair accessible. English spoken. Breakfast included. Singles L110,000/€56.81; doubles L150,000/€77.47; triples L215,000/€111.04; quads L260,000/€134.28.

VIA NAZIONALE AND ENVIRONS

From P. della Stazione, V. Nazionale leads to budget hotels that are a short walk from both the *duomo* and the train station. The buildings on V. Nazionale, V. Faenza, V. Fiume, and V. Guelfa are filled with inexpensive establishments, but rooms facing the street may be noisy due to throngs of pedestrians.

▨**Katti House,** V. Faenza, 21 (☎055 21 34 10). Exit train station onto V. Nazionale. Walk 1 block on V. Nazionale and turn right onto V. Faenza. A jewel amongst the affordable lodgings in Florence, Katti House, named for the owners's daughter, is a private dwelling, lovingly renovated by the proprietors, with hand-made drapes, 400-year-old antiques and attentive service. Rooms with A/C, TV and phone. Doubles L180,000/€92.96; triples with bath L200,000/€103.29; quads with bath L220,000/€113.62.

▨**Via Faenza, 69,** Via Faenza, 69. 3 comfortable, no-frills accommodations under the same roof. Exit train station onto V. Nazionale. Walk 1 block on V. Nazionale and take a left on V. Faenza.

Hotel Nella/Pina, 1st and 2nd fl. (☎055 265 43 46; fax 272 836 21; www.florence.net/hotel-nella). 14 basic rooms, good prices, not to mention free Internet. Small lounge with comfortable couches. Singles L80,000/€41.32; doubles L110,000/€56.81. AmEx/MC/V.

Locanda Giovanna (☎055 238 13 53). 7 fair-sized, well-kept rooms, some with garden views. Small common area with a few chairs. Singles L60,000/€31; doubles L100,000/€51.65, with bath L110,000/€56.81; triples with bath L140,000/€72.30.

Hotel Soggiorno d'Errico (☎/fax 055 21 55 31). 7 clean, bright rooms, some looking into the courtyard. Small sitting room. No bathrooms. Singles L50,000/€25.82; doubles L100,000/€51.65. AmEx/MC/V.

Via Faenza, 56, Via Faenza, 56. 6 *pensioni* among the best deals in the city. Same directions as V. Faenza, 69.

Pensione Azzi (☎055 21 38 06; fax 264 86 13) styles itself as a *locanda degli artisti* (an artists' inn), but all travelers—not just bohemians—will enjoy the friendly management. 12 large, immaculate rooms, and relaxing terrace. Wheelchair accessible. Breakfast included. Singles L80,000/€41.32; doubles L110,000/€56.81, with bath L140,000/€72.30. AmEx/MC/V.

Albergo Anna (☎055 239 83 22). 8 lovely rooms with frescoes for the aesthetes. Old-fashioned wooden furniture throughout. Same prices and amenities as Pensione Azzi.

Locanda Paola (☎055 21 36 82). 7 minimalist, spotless double rooms, some with views of Fiesole and the surrounding hills. Flexible 2am curfew. Same prices and amenities as Pensione Azzi.

Albergo Merlini (☎055 21 28 48). Murals and red geraniums adorn the lounge/solarium. Some rooms offer views of the *duomo*. Handsome polished stone floors throughout. Simple breakfast L9000/€4.65. Curfew 1am. Singles L85,000/€43.90; doubles L125,000/€64.56, with bath L120,000/€62. AmEx/MC/V.

Albergo Marini (☎055 28 48 24). A polished wood hallway leads to 10 inviting, spotless rooms. If you're staying in a double, ask for the room with the gargantuan terrace. Breakfast L8000/€4.13. Flexible 1am curfew. Doubles L110,000/€56.81, with bathroom L130,000/€67.14; triples L145,000/€74.87, L165,000/€85.22; quads L180,000/€92.96, L200,000/€103.29; quints L215,000/€111.04, L235,000/€121.37.

Albergo Armonia (☎055 21 11 46). Posters of American films bedeck 7 clean rooms, with bathrooms down the hall. The proprietors's interest in movies doesn't stop there; if you share the last name of a movie star (recognized by the management), you get a 5% discount. Singles L80,000/€41.32; doubles L120,000/€62; triples L145,000/€74.87; quads L170,000/€87.80.

Hotel Nazionale, V. Nazionale, 22 (☎055 238 22 03; fax 238 17 35; www.nazionalehotel.it). Exit train station turn left onto V. Nazionale. 9 sunny rooms with comfy beds, all with bathroom. Breakfast brought to your room between 8 and 9:30am, included in price. Lockout midnight; request a private key. Singles L100,000/€51.65, with bath L110,000/€56.81; doubles L140,000/€72.30, L160,000/€82.63; triples L190,000/€98.13, L210,000/€108.46. MC/V.

Ausonia and Kursaal, V. Nazionale, 24 (☎055 49 65 47; info@kursonia.com; www.firenze.net/kursonia). Follow directions to Hotel Nazionale. Divided into "regular" rooms (phone) and "superior" rooms (A/C, TV, bathroom). Rooms spacious and clean. Inviting dining room with wooden tables. English library and book exchange. Currency exchange. Wheelchair accessible. Breakfast included. Laundry L17,000/€8.78. Doubles L155,000/€80.05, "superior" doubles L220,000/€113.62; triples L205,000/€105.87; L270,000/€139.44; quads L260,000/€134.28, L320,000/€165.27.

Hotel Aline, V. XXVII Aprile, 14 (☎055 48 58 77). Exit train station, turn left onto V. Nazionale. Proceed to P. Indipendenza, then turn right on V. XXVII Aprile (10min. walk). 6 quiet, basic doubles with green doors, fan, shower, and phone. Some with private balconies. Doubles L110,000/56.81, with toilet L140,000/€72.30.

NEAR PIAZZA SAN MARCO AND THE UNIVERSITY

This area is considerably calmer and less tourist-ridden than its proximity to the center might suggest. All accommodations listed are within a few blocks of the delicate beauty of San Marco, one of the less touristed churches in Florence. To reach this neighborhood, exit the train station and take a left onto V. Nazionale. Take a right on V. Guelfa, which intersects V.S. Gallo and V. Cavour.

■ **Hotel Tina,** V.S. Gallo, 31 (☎055 48 35 19; fax 48 35 93; hoteltina@tin.it). Small *pensione* with high ceilings, new furniture, and bright bedspreads. Cozy sitting room. Beautiful prints. 18 rooms, some with hair dryers and A/C. Singles L85,000/€43.90; doubles L120,000/€62, with shower L130,000/€67.14, with bathroom L150,000/€77.47; triples with shower L160,000/82.63; quads with shower L200,000/€103.29.

■**Albergo Sampaoli,** V.S. Gallo, 14 (☎055 28 48 34; fax 28 24 28). Helpful reception and a large common area with patterned tile floors and wooden furniture. Some rooms with balconies, many with antique furniture. Refrigerator available. Free Internet per 30min. Singles L80,000/€41.32, with bath L100,000/€51.65; doubles L110,000/ €56.81, L160,000/€82.63; extra bed L56,000/€28.92.

Hotel San Marco, V. Cavour, 50 (☎055 28 18 51; fax 28 42 35). 3 floors with 15 modern, airy rooms. Gorgeous, elegant breakfast room. Breakfast included. Key available by request. Curfew 1:30am. Singles (available Sept.-Mar. only) L80,000/€41.32, with bath L100,000/€51.62; doubles L120,000/€62, with bath L150,000/€77.47; triples with bath L200,000/€103.29; quads with bath L260,000/€134.28. MC/V.

IN THE OLTRARNO

Only a 10-minute walk across the Arno from the *duomo*, this area and its *pensione* offer a respite from Florence's bustling hubs. From San Spirito to Palazzo Pitti to the Boboli gardens, there are still enough sites a stone's throw away to make this an ideal location for a stay.

■**Hotel La Scaletta,** V. de' Guicciardini, 13b (☎055 28 30 28; fax 28 95 62; www.lascaletta.com). Turn right onto V. Roma from the *duomo*. Cross the Ponte Vecchio and continue onto V. Guicciardini. 11 gorgeous rooms filled with antique furniture and connected by stairways and alcoves. Rooms with A/C or fan. Rooftop terraces with spectacular views of Boboli Gardens. Welcoming breakfast room. Breakfast included. Lockout midnight; pre-arrange later entry. Singles L90,000/€46.48, with bath L170,000/€87.80; doubles L190,000/ €98.13, L240,000/€123.95; triples L200,000/€103.29, 280,000/€144.61; quads L220,000/€113.62, L300,000/€154.94. 10% *Let's Go* discount users with cash. MC/V.

CAMPING

Campeggio Michelangelo, V. Michelangelo, 80 (☎055 681 19 77), beyond Piazzale Michelangelo. Take bus #13 from the station (15min., last bus 11:25pm). Extremely crowded, but offers a spectacular panorama of Florence and a chance to doze under olive trees. Well-stocked food store and bar. Rents tents L16,000/€8.26 per night. Reception daily 6am-midnight. Open Apr.-Nov. L11,000/€5.68 per person, L9000/ €4.65 per tent, L6000/€3.10 per car, L4000/€2.07 per motorcycle.

Villa Camerata, V.A. Righi, 2-4 (☎055 60 03 15; fax 61 03 00), same entrance as HI hostel on #17 bus route (see HI directions, p. 317). Breakfast at hostel L2500/€1.29. 7-night max. stay. Same reception as HI hostel. Open daily 7am-12:30pm and 1pm-midnight; if closed, stake your site and return before midnight to register and pay. Check-out 7-10am. L10,000/€5.16 per person, L8000/€4.13 with camping card; L8000/€4.13 per tent, L16,000/€8.26 per large tent., L20,000/€10.33 per car.

◘ FOOD

Florence's cuisine originated in the peasant fare of the surrounding countryside. Typified by fresh ingredients and simple preparations, Tuscan food ranks among the world's best. White beans and olive oil are two main staples. Famous specialties include *bruschetta* (grilled bread doused with olive oil and garlic, topped with tomatoes and basil, anchovy or liver paste). For *primi*, Florentines favor the Tuscan classics *minestra di fagioli* (a delicious white bean and garlic soup) and *ribollita* (a hearty bean, bread, and black cabbage stew). Florence's classic *secondo* is *bistecca alla Fiorentina* (thick sirloin steak). Florentines order it *al sangue* (very rare; literally "bloody") but you can order it *al puntito* (medium) or *ben cotto* (well-done). The best local cheese is *pecorino*, made from sheep's milk. Wine is another Florentine staple, and genuine *chianti classico* commands a premium price. A liter of house wine costs L7-10,000/€3.62-5.16 in Florence's *trattorie;* stores sell bottles for as little as L5000/€2.58. The local dessert is *cantuccini di prato* (almond cookies made with many egg yolks) dipped in *vinsanto* (a rich dessert wine made from raisins).

F
L
O
R
E
N
C
E

For lunch, visit a *rosticceria gastronomia*, browse the city's pushcarts, or stop by the **students' mensa** at V. dei Servi, 52, where a filling meal costs only L15,000/ €7.75. (Open M-Sa noon-2:15pm and 6:45-9pm. Closed mid-July to Aug.) Buy your own fresh produce and meat (or stock up on that tripe you've been craving) at the **Mercato Centrale,** between V. Nazionale and S. Lorenzo. (Open June-Sept. M-Sa 7:30am-2pm; Oct.-May Sa 7am-2pm and 4-8pm.) For basics, head to the **STANDA supermarket,** V. Pietrapiana, 1r. Take a right on V. del Proconsolo and the first left on Borgo degli Albizi. Continue straight through P.G. Salvemini; the supermarket is on the left. (☎ 055 223 47 85 69. Open M 2-9pm, Tu-Su 9am-9pm.)

Vegetarians will find several health-food markets in the city. The two best stores are named after the American book **Sugar Blues.** One is a five-minute walk from the *duomo* up V. de Martelli (which turns into V. Cavour) at V. XXVII Aprile, 46r. (☎055 48 36 66. Open M-F 9am-1:30pm and 4-7:30pm, Sa 9am-1pm.) The other is next to the Istituto Gould (see **Accommodations,** p. 317), in the Oltrarno at V. dei Serragli, 57r. (☎055 26 83 78. Open Su-Tu and Th-F 9am-1:30pm and 4:30-8pm, Sa and W 9am-1:30pm.) Also try **La Raccolta,** downstairs at V. Leopardi, 10. (☎055 247 90 68. Open M 4-7pm, Tu-F 10am-2pm and 4-7pm, Sa 10am-1:30pm.)

Il Cuscussú, V. Farini, 2, on the second floor of the building just right of the synagogue, serves **kosher** fare. (Open Su-Th 12:30-2:30pm and 7-9pm. Reserve F dinner and Sa lunch) Information on **halal** vendors from **Centro Culturale Islamico** (p. 315).

OLD CITY (NEAR THE DUOMO)

■ **Acqua al Due,** V. della Vigna Vecchia, 40r (☎055 28 41 70), behind the Bargello. Florentine specialties in a cozy place popular with young Italians and foreigners alike. The *assaggio,* a random selection of 5 pasta dishes, demands a taste (L14,500/€7.49). *Primi* L11-13,000/€5.68-6.71; *secondi* from L18,000/€9.30, excellent *insalate* from L15,000/€7.75 A/C. Cover L2000/€1.03. Open June-Sept. daily 7:30pm-1am; Oct.-May Tu-Su 8pm-1am. Don't show up without reservations. AmEx/MC/V.

Le Colonnine, V. de' Benci, 6r (☎055 23 46 47), near Ponte alle Grazie. Outdoor seating area and tiled interior caters mostly to Italians. Pizza from L8500/€4.39; pasta L10,000/€5.16; *secondi* from L13,000/€6.71. For a real treat, bring a friend or cute stranger and bury yourself in a skillet of their famous paella (L30,000/€15.50 for 2). Open Tu-Su noon-2pm and 7pm-1am. MC/V.

Trattoria Anita, V. del Parlasco, 2r (☎055 21 86 98), just behind the Bargello. Dine by candlelight, surrounded by expensive wine bottles on wooden shelves. Traditional Tuscan fare–filling pastas and an array of meat dishes from roast chicken to beefsteak Florentine. *Primi* L7-9,000/€3.62-4.65; *secondi* from L10,000/€5.16. Cover L2000/ €1.03. Open M-Sa lunch and dinner. AmEx/MC/V.

Trattoria da Benvenuto, V. della Mosca, 16r, (☎055 21 48 33). Pastel decor and linen table cloths make for elegant dining experience. *Spaghetti alle vongole* (with clams) L10,000/€5.16. *Penne* with mushrooms and olives L10,000/€5.16. *Primi* L9-12,000/ €4.65-6.20; *secondi* L11-22,000/€5.68-11.36. Cover L3,000/€1.55. 10% service charge. Open M-Sa 11am-3pm and 7pm-midnight. AmEx/MC/V.

La Loggia degli Albizi, Borgo degli Albizi, 39r (☎055 247 95 74). From behind the *duomo,* go right on V. del Proconsolo and 1st left onto Borgo degli Albizi; head 2 blocks down and look right. A hidden treasure. This bakery/cafe offers an escape from the tourist hordes. Pastries from L2500/€1.29. Open M-F 7am-8pm, Sa 7am-1pm.

SANTA MARIA NOVELLA AND ENVIRONS

■ **Trattoria Contadino,** V. Palazzuolo, 71r (☎055 238 26 73). Filling, home-style meals. Offers fixed price *menù* option only–but this is not a *menù turistica.* This is the real deal served to an almost exclusively Italian crowd in an informal, crowded setting. Choose from daily pasta and soup specials for *primi* and the daily meat specials for *secondi.* Includes bread, water, ¼L of house wine (the red is quite good). Lunch *menù* L16,000/ €8.26, dinner *menù* L17,000/€8.78. Open M-Sa noon-2:30pm and 6-9:30pm.

Trattoria da Giorgio, V. Palazzuolo, 100r (☎055 28 43 02). Crowded, with white plaster walls and paper place mats. Full meal with *primo, secondo,* bread, water, and house red. Expect a wait. Lunch *menù* L16,000/€8.26, dinner *menù* L17,000/€8.78. Open M-Sa noon-3:30pm and 7pm-12:30am.

Il Latini, V. dei Palchetti, 6r. From the Ponte alla Carraia, walk up V. del Moro; V. dei Palchetti is on the right. Patrons dine on delicious Tuscan classics such as *ribollita* (L8000/€4.13) beneath dangling hams in small tile-walled dining room filled with dark wooden tables. *Primi* L10-12,000/€5.16-10.33; *secondi* L18-20,000/€9.30-10.33. Cover L3000/€1.55. Open Tu-Su noon-2:30pm and 7:30-10:30pm. AmEx/MC/V.

Rose's Cafe, V. del Parione, 26r (☎055 28 70 90). This hip new restaurant prides itself on its New York atmosphere, although Japanese. Noodle/rice dishes (L5-12,000/€2.58-6.20); *tempura udon.* Extensive sushi bar (L33-66,000/€17.04-34.09). Open M-Sa 8am-midnight, Su 5pm-1:30am. Sushi bar open Tu-Su 7-11pm; closed Aug.

Amon, V. Palazzuolo, 26-28r (☎055 29 31 46). Cheerful Egyptian owner cooks his own bread and serves scrumptious Middle Eastern food. Amen. Try the *mousaka,* a homemade pita filled with baked eggplant or *foul,* a delicious dish of beans and spices. The falafel is spicy and far above average. English menu. Stand-up or takeout only. Falafel L5000/€2.58; shish kebab L5000/€2.58. Open Tu-Su noon-3pm and 6:30-11pm.

THE STATION AND UNIVERSITY QUARTER

Trattoria da Zà-Zà, P. del Mercato Centrale, 26r (☎055 21 54 11). Heavy wooden beam ceilings, brick archways, wine racks on the wall and candelabra dripping with wax. Bustles with a mixed crowd of Italians and foreigners. Try the *tris* (a mixed bean, tomato, and vegetable soup; L9000/€4.65) or the *tagliatelle al tartufo* (pasta with truffles; L11,000/€5.68). Finish with *vinsanto e cantucci* for L6000/€3.10. Cover L3000/€1.55. Open M-Sa noon-3pm and 7-11pm. Reservations suggested. AmEx/MC/V.

Trattoria Mario, V. Rosina, 2r (☎055 21 85 50), right around the corner from P. del Mercato Centrale. Share small wooden tables with the local crowd in this informal lunch spot. Order at your table from a paper menu on the wall that lists the days offerings in English as well as Italian. Incredible pasta, cheap meat dishes. *Primi* L5-8000/€2.58-4.13; *secondi* L7-17,000/€3.62-8.78. Open M-Sa noon-3:30pm.

Ristorante de' Medici, V. del Melarancio, 10r (☎055 29 52 92), one block off P. dell' Unita Italia. White table cloths, beautiful wooden beam ceilings, and plaster walls painted with scenes of Tuscan life define the 2 vast, formal dining rooms, inhabited by an almost exclusively Italian clientele. Calzones (L10,000/€5.16) and pesto gnocchi (L9,000/€4.65). *Primi* L8-12,000/€4.13-6.20; *secondi* L10-16,000/€5.16-8.26.

Trattoria da Garibardi, P. del Mercato Centrale, 38r (☎055 21 22 67). Locals from the market fill both the outdoor seating and formal indoor dining room and for a reason. The *penne ai quattro formaggi* (four cheese) and *pesto alla genovese* are delicious. Crisp garden salads. Fixed-price *menù* (L24,000/€12.40). Cover L2000/€1.03 for meals outside the *menù. Primi* L5-12,000/€2.58-6.20; *secondi* from L15,000/€7.75. Open daily June-Aug. noon-11pm; Sept.-May M-Sa noon-3pm and 7-11pm. MC/V.

Ristorante Il Vegetariano, V. delle Ruote, 30 (☎055 47 50 30), off V.S. Gallo. Look closely for the address—no sign outside. Tiny menu next to door tips you off to the vegetarian wonders inside. Self-service restaurant with fresh, inventive dishes. Low-ceilinged, intimate dining rooms and peaceful bamboo garden. Pesto, brown rice *risotto* (L9000/€4.65). One of the few places smoke free in Florence. Salads L7-9000/€3.62-4.65; *primi* from L9000/€4.65; *secondi* from L11,000/€5.68; desserts L6000/€3.10. Open Tu-F 12:30-3pm and 7:30pm-midnight, Sa-Su 8pm-midnight.

Forno di Stefano Galli, V. Faenza, 39r (☎055 21 53 14). Wonder where to go to get that bread you enjoyed so much at dinner last night? Wide variety of fresh breads and pastries. Pastries L2000-3500/€1.03-1.81; loaves of bread L1500-4000/€0.77. Open 7:30am-4:30am. Other locations at V. delle Panche, 91 and V. Bufalini, 31-35r.

THE OLTRARNO

▨ **Il Borgo Antico,** P.S. Spirito, 6r (☎ 055 21 04 37). Spacious outdoor seating looking onto the *piazza*, and a crowded, rustic dining room inside. The *anitpasti* are wonderful (tomato and basil salad; L12,000/€6.20). The bread comes with a small dish of black olives in oil with a touch of hot pepper. Spaghetti with clam sauce (L10,000/€5.16) *Antipasti* L10-15,000/€5.16-7.75; *primi* L10,000/€5.16; *secondi* L25-30,000/ €12.91-15.50. Cover L3000/€1.55. Open daily 1-4pm and 6:30pm-1:30am. Reservations recommended. AmEx/MC/V.

▨ **Oltrarno Trattoria Casalinga,** V. Michelozzi, 9r (☎ 055 21 86 24), near P.S. Spirito. Delicious Tuscan specialties in crowded, less-formal atmosphere with paper table cloths. Excellent pesto. Prices can't be beat. *Primi* L6-10,500/€3.10-5.42; *secondi* L8-18,000/€4.13-9.30. Cover L3000/€1.55. Open M-Sa noon-2:30pm and 7-10pm.

La Mangiatoia, P.S. Felice, 8r (☎ 055 22 40 60). Continue straight on V. Guicciardini from Ponte Vecchio, and pass P. dei Pitti. Quality Tuscan fare. Grab a table in back dining room, or sit at stone counter in front to watch them make pizza in the brick oven and get pasta-eating lessons from locals. Try the amazing spaghetti with walnuts and cream sauce (L8000/€4.13). Pizza L6500-9000/€3.36-4.65; *primi* L5-8000/€2.58-4.13; *secondi* L8-18,000/€4.13-9.30. Fixed price *menù* (L20,000/€10.33). Cover L2000/ €1.03 in dining room only. Open Tu-Su noon-3pm and 7-11pm. AmEx/MC/V.

GELATERIE

Gelato is said to have been invented centuries ago by Florence's Buontalenti family. Before shelling out L3-5000/€1.55-2.58 for a *piccolo* cone, assess the quality of an establishment by looking at the banana *gelato:* if it's bright yellow, it's been made from a mix—keep on walking. If its slightly gray, real bananas were used. Most *gelaterie* also serve *granite*, flavored ices, which are easier on the waistline.

▨ **Vivoli,** V. della Stinche, 7 (☎ 055 29 23 34), behind the Bargello. The most renowned Florentine *gelateria*, self-touted as having the "best ice cream in the world." Newspaper clippings on the wall above the old-fashioned wooden counters demonstrate that connoisseurs agree. Huge selection, from fruit flavors to hazelnut to chocolate mouse. Cups from L3000/€1.55. Open daily 8am-1am.

▨ **Gelateria Triangolo delle Bermuda,** V. Nazionale, 61r (☎ 055 28 74 90). With *gelato* this good, you'll never want to escape. Blissful *crema venusiana* blends hazelnut, caramel, and meringue. Try the strawberry and rose sorbets. The owner travels to the US every year to get Oreos for his *gelato*. Cones from L3000/€1.55. Open daily 10am-midnight.

Carabè, V. Ricasoli, 60r (☎ 055 28 94 76). Amazing *gelato* with ingredients shipped from Sicily, and less expensive than most. Pistacchio, *limone, nocciola,* and the more unusual flavors like *susine* (plum) are outstanding. The *granite* (ices)—particularly *mandorle* (almond) and *more* (blackberries)—are also fabulous. Cones from L2500/€1.29, *granite* from L3500/€1.81. Open May-Sept. daily 10am-1am; Mar.-Apr. and Oct. daily noon-1am; closed Nov.- Feb.

Perchè No?, V. Tavolini, 19r (☎ 055 239 89 69), off V. dei Calzaiuoli. Why not indeed. This place answers this rhetorical question with some of Florence's finest *gelato*. It serves heavenly pistacchio, mouth-watering chocolate, and chunky *nocciolosa*. Cones L3000/€1.55. Open May-Sept. W-M 10am-1am; Oct.-Mar. W-M 10am-8pm.

ENOTECHE (WINE BARS)

Check out an *enoteca* to sample some of Italy's finest wines and the exquisite complementary side-dish sensations (cheeses, olives, toasts-and-spreads, salami).

Enoteca Alessi, V. della Oche, 27/29r (☎ 055 21 49 66; fax 239 69 87), 1 block from *duomo*. One of Florence's finest and best known. Boasts over 1000 wines of all varieties and prices. Also offers delicious nibbles between sips. Enter through the cavernous wine and chocolate shop in front. Spacious, high-ceilinged, and cool, perfect for relaxation after a long day of sightseeing. Open M-Sa 9am-1pm and 4-8pm. AmEx/MC/V.

Enoteca Fuori Porta, V. Monte alle Croce, 10r (☎055 23 42 483), in the shadows of S. Miniato. This more casual and off-the-beaten-track *enoteca* serves reasonable meals of traditional Tuscan pasta and *secondi* (from L11,000/€5.68) in addition to the complimentary nibbles. Open M-Sa 12:30-3pm and 7pm-midnight.

◎ SIGHTS

There's enough to see in the center of Florence alone to keep a visitor occupied for years; if you're in the city for only a few days, hit the highlights. But with the views from Brunelleschi's dome, the perfection of San Spirito's nave and the overwhelming array of art in the Ufizzi, it's hard to go wrong in Florence. Plan well as the city's art museums, while spectacular, can be exhausting as well as expensive.

BLAME IT ON THE MEDICI. Florentine museums have recently doubled their prices. Most major venues now charge L6-12,000/€3.10-6.20, so breezing in and out of each place that strikes your fancy will quickly become a costly endeavor. Sadly, capital letters at most museum entrances remind you that there are **no student discounts.** The price of a ticket should not discourage you from seeing the best collections of Renaissance art in the world. Choose your itinerary carefully and plan to spend a healthy chunk of the day at each landmark. Additionally, many of Florence's churches are free treasuries of great art. In summer, watch for **Sere al Museo,** evenings when certain museums are free from 8:30-11pm. Note that most museums stop selling tickets 30min.-1hr. before closing. It is possible, however, to purchase a 50% discount card (L10,000/€5.16) for all municipal museums in Florence. It applies to: **Palazzo Vecchio, Museo di S. Maria Novella, Museo Firenze Com'era, Coll. A. della Ragione,** the **Brancacci chapel,** and the **Galleria Rinaldo Carniela.** If you plan to visit all of those, it will save you L5500/€2.84. The card can be bought at any of the museums listed above and is valid for 1 year.

PIAZZA DEL DUOMO AND ENVIRONS

▧ THE DUOMO (CATTEDRALE DI SANTA MARIA DEL FIORE). In 1296 the city fathers commissioned Arnolfo di Cambio to erect a cathedral "with the most high and sumptuous magnificence" so that it would be "impossible to make it either better or more beautiful with the industry and power of man." Sure enough, Arnolfo and a horde of other architects succeeded, completing the massive nave by 1418. But one problem remained—no one had the engineering skills necessary to construct the Cathedral's dome. Finally, Filippo Brunelleschi dreamed up the ingenious technique for building the *duomo*'s sublime crown, now known simply as **Brunelleschi's Dome.** Drawing upon his knowledge of classical methods, the architect developed a revolutionary idea: double-shelled construction, using self-supporting, interlocking bricks. During the construction Brunelleschi became an obsessive task master. He even constructed kitchens, sleeping rooms, and lavoratories between the two walls of the cupola so that the masons would never have to descend. The **Museo del Opera del Duomo** (see below) chronicles Brunelleschi's feats of engineering. A 16th-century Medici rebuilding campaign removed the *duomo*'s incomplete Gothic-Renaissance facade, finally replaced in 1871 when Emilio de Fabris, a Florentine architect inspired by the colorful facades of Tuscan structures, received the commission to create a facade in the Neogothic style.

Today, the *duomo* claims the world's third-longest nave after St. Peter's in Rome and St. Paul's in London. Brunelleschi's dome rises 100m into the air, making it instantly recognizable from afar and providing unparalleled vistas of Florence. The *duomo* is ornately decorated on the outside with inlaid green and white marble, but is visually unexciting on the inside, except for the visions of the apocalypse painted on dome's ceiling. If you choose to wait in line to enter the church, notice Paolo Uccello's celebrated *trompe l'oeil* (cloth-of-gold) monument to the mercenary captain Sir John Hawkwood on the cathedral's left wall and his **orologio** on the back wall. The orologio won't give you the time of day—this 24-hour clock runs backward. Ask inside the entrance, to the left, about free guided tours in English. *(Duomo open M-Sa 10am-5pm, Su 1:30-5pm; 1st Sa of every month 10am-3:30pm. Masses daily 7am-12:30pm and 5-7pm.)* Climb the 463 steps inside the dome to Michelangelo's ▧**lantern**, or cupola, for an unparalleled view of the city from the 100m high external gallery. *(Entrance on south side of duomo. ☎ 055 230 28 85. Open M-F 8:30am-7pm. Sa 8:30am-5:40pm. L10,000/€5.16.)* The cathedral's **crypt** contains Brunelleschi's tomb. *(Open M-Sa 9:30am-5pm. L3000/€1.55.)*

BAPTISTERY. Although it was built between the 5th and 9th centuries, in Dante's time the baptistery was believed to have originated as a Roman temple. Now, the exterior has the same green and white marble patterning as the *duomo*, and the interior contains magnificent Byzantine-style mosaics crafted in the 13th century. Dante, who was christened here, was affected by the place (or scared by it); the hell-fire and devil-eating-people scenes on the walls inspired parts of his *Inferno*.

Florentine artists competed fiercely for the commission to execute the baptistery's famous **bronze doors,** depicting scenes from the Bible in exquisite detail. In 1330 Andrea Pisano left Pisa to cast the first set of doors, which now guard the south entrance (toward the river). In 1401 the cloth guild announced a competition to choose an artist for the remaining doors. The original field of eight contestants narrowed to two, Brunelleschi (then 23 years old) and Ghiberti (then 20). They were asked to work in partnership, but Brunelleschi, unwilling to compromise, left in an arrogant huff, leaving Ghiberti to complete the project on his own. The competition panels are displayed side by side in the Bargello. When Ghiberti completed his project in 1425, his work was so admired that he immediately received the commission to forge the last set of doors. The ▧**Gates of Paradise,** as Michelangelo reportedly called them, are nothing like the two earlier portals. Originally intended for the north side, they so impressed the Florentines that they placed them in their current honored position facing the cathedral. The doors have been under restoration since the flood of 1966 and will eventually reside in the Museo dell'Opera del Duomo. *(☎ 055 230 28 85. Opposite the duomo. Open M-Sa noon-7pm, Su 8:30am-2pm. Daily mass 10:30am and 11:30am. L5000/€2.58.)*

CAMPANILE. Next to the *duomo* rises the 82m high *campanile* whose pink, green, and white marble exterior matches the *duomo* and *battistero*. Giotto drew the design and laid the foundation in 1334, but died soon after. Andrea Pisano added two stories to the tower, and Francesco Talenti completed it in 1359. The original exterior decoration is now in the Museo dell'Opera del Duomo. The 414 steps to the top lead to beautiful views. *(Open daily 8:30am-7:30pm. L10,000/€5.16.)*

MUSEO DELL'OPERA DEL DUOMO. Most of the *duomo*'s art resides in this modern-looking museum, filled with double-height spaces. Up the first flight of stairs is a late *Pietà* by Michelangelo. According to legend, Michelangelo severed Christ's left arm with a hammer in a fit of frustration. Soon after, a diligent pupil touched up the work, leaving visible scars on parts of Mary Magdalene's head. In this museum are Donatello's wooden ▧**St. Mary Magdalene** (1555), Donatello and Luca della Robbia's **cantorie** (choir balconies with bas-reliefs of cavorting children), and four frames from the baptistery's **Gates of Paradise.** A huge wall displays all of the paintings submitted by architects in the 1870 competition for the facade of the *duomo*. *(P. del Duomo, 9, behind the duomo. ☎ 055 230 28 85. Open M-Sa 9am-6:30pm, Su 9am-2pm. L10,000/€5.16. English tours in summer W-Th 4pm.)*

ORSANMICHELE. Built in 1337 as a granary, the Orsanmichele was converted into a church after a great fire convinced city officials to move grain operations outside the city walls. The *loggia* structure and ancient grain chutes are still visible from the outside. Secular and spiritual concerns mingle in the statues along the facade. Within these niches, look for Ghiberti's *St. John the Baptist* and *St. Stephen*, Donatello's *St. Peter* and *St. Mark*, and Giambologna's *St. Luke*. Inside, a Gothic tabernacle designed by Andrea Orcagna encases Bernardo Daddi's miraculous *Virgin*, an intricately wrought, expressive marble statue of Mary at her most beatific. The top floor occasionally hosts special exhibits. Across the street is the **Museo di Orsanmichele**, home to numerous paintings and sculptures that originally resided within the church. *(V. Arte della Lana, between duomo and P. della Signoria.* ☎ *055 28 49 44 for church and museum. Church open daily 9am-noon and 4-6pm. Museum open daily 9am-noon, closed 1st and last Monday of the month. Free.)*

MUSEO FIRENZE COM'ERA. This museum provides a small and amusing escape from the crowds. It depicts Florence through the ages starting with a large model of the town during imperial Roman times. Prints and paintings show aerial views and maps of Florence as it was conceived throughout the centuries. A room of charming street scenes by Della Gatta lead to the final piece—5ft. x 10ft., detailed aerial view of 13th-century Florence, produced from 1934-46. *(V. delle Oriuolo, 2 blocks from duomo.* ☎ *055 261 65 45. Open F-W 9am-2pm. L5000/€2.58.)*

PIAZZA DELLA SIGNORIA AND ENVIRONS

From P. del Duomo, **V. dei Calzaiuoli,** one of the city's oldest streets, leads to P. della Signoria. Built by the Romans, V. dei Calzaiuoli now bustles with crowds, chic shops, *gelaterie*, and vendors.

PIAZZA DELLA SIGNORIA. The blank-walled, turreted Palazzo Vecchio (see below) and the corner of the Uffizi gallery dominate this 13th-century *piazza*. The space is filled with crowds and at night is a favorite spot for street performers. The *piazza* indirectly resulted from the interminable struggle between the Guelphs and the Ghibellines (p. 10). Many homes of powerful Ghibelline families were destroyed during a conflict in the 13th century, creating an open space. With the construction of the Palazzo Vecchio, the square soon transformed into Florence's civic and political center. In 1497, religious zealot and social critic **Girolamo Savonarola** convinced Florentines to light the **Bonfire of the Vanities** in the *piazza*, a grand roast that consumed some of Florence's best art, including, according to legend, all of Botticelli's secular works that had not been sold to private collections. A year later, disillusioned citizens sent Savonarola up in smoke on the same spot, marked today by a commemorative disc. Monumental sculptures cluster around the Palazzo Vecchio, including Donatello's *Judith and Holofernes*, a copy of Michelangelo's *David*, Giambologna's equestrian *Cosimo I*, and Bandinelli's *Hercules*. The awkward *Neptune* to the left of the Palazzo Vecchio so revolted Michelangelo that he insulted the artist, "Oh Ammannato, Ammannato, what lovely marble you have ruined!" Apparently most Florentines share his opinion. Called "Il Biancone" ("The Big White One") in derision, *Neptune* is continually subject to attacks of vandalism by angry aesthetes. The graceful 14th-century **Loggia dei Lanzi,** built as a stage for civic orators, is now one of the best places in Florence to see world-class sculpture free of charge.

PALAZZO VECCHIO. Arnolfo del Cambio designed this fortress-like *palazzo* (1299-1304) as the seat of the *comune's* government. The massive brown stone facade has a square, utilitarian tower rising from its center, and turrets along the top. Its apartments once served as living quarters for members of the *signoria* (city council) during their two-month terms. The building later became the Medici family home, and in 1470 Michelozzo decorated the ▨**courtyard** in Renaissance style. He filled it with religious frescoes and ornate stone pediments over every door and window. The courtyard also has stone lions and a copy of Verrocchio's 15th-century *Putto* fountain. (*Same hours as Monumental Apartments, see below.*)

Within the past year, the Palazzo Vecchio has undergone a transformation; in addition to the Monumental Apartments (see below), there are now tours of the Secret Routes, activities, and an Encounter with Giorgio Vasari. They must be booked in advance and can be conducted in English upon request. Group tours (8-10 people) of the **Secret Routes** visit staircases hidden in walls, Duke Cosimo I de'Medici's secret chambers and the roof cavity above the Salone del Cinquecento (see below). The **activities** include reenactments of Medici court life, displays of architectural models, and demonstrations of science experiments by Galileo and Torricelli, both Medici court mathematicians. The **Encounter with Giorgio Vasari** is a private tour through the Monumental Apartments, with a guide playing the part of Vasari, Duke Cosimo I de' Medici's court painter and architect. (☎ 055 276 82 24 or 276 85 58; www.museoragazzi.it. Booking office open daily 9am-1pm and M, F, Sa 3-7pm. Reservations required, with 3 days notice in summer. Secret Routes and activities open daily, with M, F evening hours from June 15-Sept. 15; open daily from Sept. 16-June 14. Encounter with Giorgio Vasari open Sa, Su and evenings M, F from June 15-Sep.15; daytime Sa, Su, Tu, Th from Sept. 16-June14; must book 3 days in advance in summer.)

The **Monumental Apartments**, which house the *palazzo*'s extensive art collections, are accessible as a museum. There are now 12 interactive terminals in various rooms, where there are virtual tours of the building's history, with detailed computer animations. The city commissioned Michelangelo and Leonardo da Vinci to paint opposite walls of the **Salone del Cinquecento,** the meeting room of the Grand Council of the Republic. Although they never completed the frescoes, their preliminary cartoons, the *Battle of Cascina* and the *Battle of Anghiari*, were studied by Florentine artists for years afterward for their powerful depiction of humans and horses in strenuous motion. The tiny **Studio di Francesco I,** built by Vasari, is a treasure trove of Mannerist art, with paintings by Bronzino, Allori, and Vasari and bronze statuettes by Giambologna and Ammannati. The **Mezzanino** houses some of the *palazzo's* best art including Bronzino's portrait of the poet Laura Battiferi and Giambologna's *Hercules and the Hydra*. (☎ 055 276 84 65. Palazzo open June-Aug. Tu-W and Sa 9am-7pm, M and F 9am-11pm, Th and Su 9am-2pm; Sept.-May M-W and F-Sa 9am-7pm, Th and Su 9am-2pm. Palazzo L10,000/€5.16; courtyard free.)

▨ **THE UFFIZI.** From P.B.S. Giovanni go down V. Roma past P. della Repubblica where the street turns into V. Calimala. Continue until V. Vacchereccia and turn left. The **Uffizi** is straight ahead. Giorgio Vasari designed this palace in 1554 for Duke Cosimo and called it the Uffizi because it housed the offices (uffizi) of the Medici administration. Today it holds more great art per square inch than any other museum in the world. (For more historical background on works in the Uffizi, check out **Art and Architecture,** p. 14.) An impressive walkway between the two main branches of the building leads, in grim colonnaded fashion, from the Piazza della Signoria to the Arno River. Vendors hawking trinkets and prints of the fabulous art inside abound along the *loggia* of this massive, uniform building.

Before visiting the main gallery on the second floor, stop to see the exhibits of the Cabinet of Drawings and Prints on the first floor. Upstairs, a corridor wraps around the building and holds a collection of Hellenistic and Roman marbles. The collection is arranged chronologically and promises a thorough education on the Florentine Renaissance, as well as a choice sampling of German and Venetian art.

Room 2 features three 13th- and 14th-century *Madonne* of the great forefathers of the Renaissance: Cimabue, Duccio di Buoninsegna, and Giotto. **Room 3** features works from 14th-century Siena (including works by the Lorenzetti brothers and Simone Martini's *Annunciation*, notable for their palpable emotion). **Rooms 5** and **6** contain examples of International Gothic art, popular in European royal courts.

The most awe-inspiring in the museum, **Room 7** houses two Fra Angelico (referred to as Beato Angelico in Italian museums) paintings and a *Madonna and Child* by Masaccio. Domenico Veneziano's *Madonna with Child and Saints (Sacra Conversazione)* is one of the first paintings of Mary surrounded by the saints. Piero della Francesca's double portrait of Duke Federico and his wife Battista Sforza stands out for its translucent color and detail. Finally, the rounded warhorses distinguish Paolo Uccello's *Rout of San Romano*. In **Room 8** Filippo Lippi's *Madonna and Child with Two Angels* pulls at the heart strings. Works by the Pollaiuolo brothers and an allegedly forged Filippino Lippi occupy **Room 9.**

Rooms 10-14 are a shrine to Florence's cherished Botticelli—the resplendent *Primavera*, *Birth of Venus*, *Madonna della Melagrana*, and *Pallas and the*

Centaur glow from their recent restoration. **Room 15** moves into the High Renaissance with Leonardo da Vinci's *Annunciation* and the more remarkable unfinished *Adoration of the Magi*. Leonardo and the other painters of the high Renaissance create an ideal beauty that is perhaps more realistic in appearance than the almost cartoon-like beauty in many works by Lippi and Botticelli. **Room 18,** designed by Buontalenti to hold the Medici treasures, has a mother-of-pearl dome and a collection of portraits, most notably Bronzino's *Bia de'Medici* and Vasari's *Lorenzo il Magnifico*. **Room 19** features works by Piero della Francesca's students Perugino and Signorelli. **Rooms 20** and **22** detour into Northern European art. Note the contrast between Albrecht Dürer's life-like *Adam and Eve* and Cranach the Elder's haunting treatment of the same subject. **Room 21** contains significant Venetian artwork from the 15th century. Ponder Bellini's *Sacred Allegory* before examining Mantegna's *Adoration of the Magi* in **Room 23.**

Rooms 25-27 showcase Florentine works, including Michelangelo's only oil painting *(Doni Tondo)*, a string of Raphaels—check out the detail on the rings of his portrait of Julius II—Andrea del Sarto's *Madonna of the Harpies*, and Pontormo's *Supper at Emmaus*. **Room 28** displays Titian's beautiful *Venus of Urbino*. Parmigianino's *Madonna of the Long Neck* is in **Room 29.** Works by Sebastiano del Piombo and Lorenzo Lotto share **Rooms 31** and **32.** The staircase vestibule **(Rooms 36-40)** contains a Roman marble boar, inspiration for the brass *Porcellino* that sits in Florence's New Market. **Rooms 41 and 43-45** are currently undergoing restoration, so many works by Rembrandt, Rubens, and Caravaggio are currently not on display, though visitors can see Caravaggio's famous *Bacchus* as it has been temporarily moved to **Room 16.**

Vasari included a **secret corridor** between the Palazzo Vecchio and the Medici's Palazzo Pitti in the design. The corridor runs through the Uffizi and over the Ponte Vecchio, housing more art, including a special collection of artists's self-portraits. Sadly, these works can't be viewed because of damage from the flood of 1966.

In May of 1993, terrorists set off a bomb in the Uffizi, killing five people and destroying priceless works of art. The bombing shocked Italians, who cherish the Uffizi as a symbol of their precious Renaissance heritage. *(☎ 055 21 83 41. Open Tu-Sa 8:30am-6:50pm, Su 8:30am-1:50pm. L12,000/€6.2. Save hours of waiting by purchasing advance tickets. (L2000/€1.03 extra, credit card required); call ☎ 055 29 48 83.*

THE PONTE VECCHIO. The nearby Ponte Vecchio (Old Bridge) is indeed the oldest bridge in Florence. Built in 1345, it replaced an older Roman version. In the 1500s butchers and tanners lined the bridge and dumped pig's blood and intestines in the river, creating an odor that not surprisingly offended the powerful bankers as they crossed the Arno on their way to their *uffizi* (offices). In an effort to improve the area, the Medici kicked out the lower class shopkeepers, and the more decorous goldsmiths and diamond-carvers moved in; their descendants now line the bridge selling their beautiful wares from medieval-looking boutiques that cantilever precariously off the sides of the bridge. While technically open to traffic, the bridge is completely swamped by tourists and street musicians.

The Ponte Vecchio was the only bridge to escape destruction by German bombs during World War II. A German commander who led his retreating army across the river in 1944 couldn't bear to destroy it, instead choosing to topple the medieval towers and nearby buildings to make the bridge impassable. From the neighboring ◾**Ponte alle Grazie,** the view of Ponte Vecchio melting in the setting sun is nothing less than heart-stopping. *(From Uffizi, turn left onto V. Georgofili, and right at the river.)*

THE BARGELLO AND ENVIRONS

◾**BARGELLO.** In the heart of medieval Florence, this 13th-century fortress was once the residence of Florence's chief magistrate. It later became a brutal prison that held public executions in the courtyard. In the 19th century, the Bargello was restored to its former elegance and now houses the **Museo Nazionale,** a treasury of Florentine sculpture. From the outside, the Bargello still looks like a three story fortress. Inside the courtyard one sees beautiful arched windows and the wings of the building filled with sculptures that open through colonnades to the outside. Upstairs to the right in the **Salone del Consiglio Generale,** Donatello's bronze *David,* the first free-standing nude since antiquity, simultaneously eroticizes and androgynizes the adolescent male figure. The artist's marble *David,* completed about 30 years earlier, stands near the wall to the left. On the other side hang two beautiful bronze panels of the *Sacrifice of Isaac,* submitted by Ghiberti and Brunelleschi in the baptistery door competition (see **Baptistery,** p. 326). The *loggia* on the first floor displays a collection of bronze animals created by Giambologna for a Medici garden grotto. Michelangelo's early works, including a debauched *Bacchus,* a handsome bust of *Brutus,* an early unfinished *Apollo,* and a *Madonna and Child,* dominate the ground floor. Cellini's models for *Perseus* and *Bust of Cosimo I* occupy the same room. Giambologna's *Oceanus* reigns in the Gothic courtyard outside, while his *Mercury* poses in the Michelangelo room. *(V. del Proconsolo, 4, between duomo and P. della Signoria.* ☎ *055 238 86 06. Open daily 8:15am-1:50pm; closed 1st, 3rd, and 5th Su and 2nd and 4th Mo of each month. L8000/€4.13.)*

BADIA. This was the site of medieval Florence's richest monastery. Buried in the interior of a residential block, and with no facade, one would never guess the treasures that lie within. Filippino Lippi's stunning *Apparition of the Virgin to St. Bernard,* one of the most famous paintings of the late 15th century, hangs to the left of the entrance to the church in the eerie gloom. Note the beautiful, if dingy, frescoes and Corinthian pilasters. *(Entrance on V. Dante Alighieri, just off V. Proconsolo.* ☎ *055 24 44 02. Open daily 7:30am-12:30pm and 1-6pm.)*

MUSEO DI STORIA DELLA SCIENZA. After pondering great Italian artists and writers for hours, head over to this museum to be awed by the greats of science. This impressive collection boasts scientific instruments and demonstration devices from the Renaissance, including telescopes, astrological models, clock workings and wax models of anatomy and childbirth. The highlight of the museum is Room 4, where a number of Galileo's tools are on display. Detailed English guides are to the right of the upstairs entrance. *(Piazza dei Giudici, 1, behind Palazzo Vecchio and the Uffizi.* ☎ *055 230 28 85. Open M, W-F 9:30am-5pm, Tu, Sa 9:30am-1pm; Oct. 1-May 31 also open 2nd Su of each month, 10am-1pm. L12,000/€6.20.)*

CASA DI DANTE. The Casa di Dante is reputedly identical to the house Dante inhabited. Anyone who can read Italian and has an abiding fascination with the works of Dante will enjoy the displays. Nearby is the abandoned and melancholy little church where Beatrice, Dante's unrequited love and spiritual guide (in *Paradiso*), attended mass. A plaque commemorates the many days he watched her pass without uttering a word. *(Corner of V. Dante Alighieri and V.S. Margherita within one block of the Bargello.* ☎ *055 21 94 16. Open M and W-Sa 10am-6pm, Su 10am-2pm. L5000/€2.58, groups over 15 L3000/€1.55 per person.)*

PIAZZA DELLA REPUBBLICA AND FARTHER WEST

After hours of contemplating great Florentine art, visit the area that financed it all. In the early 1420s, 72 banks operated in Florence, most in the area around the Mercato Nuovo and V. Tornabuoni. With a much lower concentration of tourist sights, this area is quieter and more residential.

▧ CHIESA DI SANTA MARIA NOVELLA. The wealthiest merchants built their chapels in this church near the train station. Santa Maria Novella was home to the order of Dominicans, or *Domini canes* (Hounds of the Lord), who hunted down sin and corruption. Built between 1279 and 1360, the *chiesa* boasts a green and white Romanesque-Gothic lower facade. Giovanni Rucellai commissioned Alberti to design the top half. The result is considered one of the greatest masterpieces of early Renaissance architecture. The facade is geometrically pure and balanced, a precursor to the classical revival of the high Renaissance. Thirteenth-century frescoes covered the interior until the Medici commissioned Vasari to paint new ones. Fortunately, Vasari spared Masaccio's powerful ▧*Trinity,* the first painting to use geometric perspective. This fresco, on the left side of the nave, creates the illusion of a tabernacle, pulling the viewer into the scene. The **Cappella di Filippo Strozzi,** to the right of the high altar, contains frescoes by Filippo Lippi, including a rather green Adam, a woolly Abraham, and an excruciating *Torture of St. John the Evangelist.* A cycle of Ghirlandaio frescoes covers the **Tournabuoni Chapel.** (☎ *055 055 21 01 13. Open M-Th and Sa 9:30am-5pm, F and Su 1-5pm. L5000/€2.58.)* The **cloister** next door has Paolo Uccello's *The Flood* and *The Sacrifice of Noah.* The adjoining **Cappella Spagnola** (Spanish Chapel) harbors 14th-century frescoes by Andrea di Bonaiuto. (☎ *055 28 21 87. Open M-Th and Sa 9am-2pm, Su 8am-1pm. L6000/€3.10.)*

PIAZZA DELLA REPUBBLICA. The largest open space in Florence, this *piazza* teams with crowds and street performers in the evenings. An enormous arch filling in the gap over V. Strozzi marks the western edge of the square. The rest of the *piazza* is lined with overpriced coffee shops and restaurants. In 1890 this *piazza* replaced the Mercato Vecchio as the site of the market. The inscription *"Antico centro della città, da secolare squalore, a vita nuova restituito"* ("The ancient center of the city, squalid for centuries, restored to new life") makes a derogatory reference to the fact that the *piazza* is the site of the old Jewish ghetto, dating from before the "liberation of the Jews" in Italy in the 1860s that allowed members of the Jewish community to live elsewhere. The destruction of the Old Market was the first step in a plan to demolish the city center's historic buildings and remodel Florence, which an international campaign successfully thwarted.

CHIESA DI SANTA TRINITÀ. To spend eternity among the most fashionable company, many *palazzo* owners commissioned family chapels in this church. The facade was designed by Bernardo Buontalenti in the 16th century and is an exquisite example of late Renaissance architecture, verging on Baroque in its ornamentation. The interior shows its Romanesque origins, displaying beautiful proportions with less ornament. The fourth chapel on the right houses the remains of a fresco cycle of the Virgin, and a magnificent *Annunciation* by Lorenzo Monaco adorns the altar. Scenes from Ghirlandaio's *Life of St. Francis* decorate the **Sassetti chapel** in the right arm of the transept. The famous altarpiece, Ghirlandaio's *Adoration of the Shepherds,* resides in the Uffizi—the one here is a tantalizing copy. (In P.S. Trinita. ☎ 055 21 69 12. Open M-Sa 8am-noon and 4-6pm, Su 4-6pm.)

MERCATO NUOVO. The *loggia* of the New Market have housed gold and silk traders since 1547 under their Corinthian-columned splendor. Today vendors sell purses, belts, clothes, fruits, and vegetables as well as gold and silk, from dawn until dusk. Pietro Tacca's pleasantly plump statue, *Il Porcellino* (The Little Pig), actually a wild boar, appeared some 50 years after the market first opened. Reputed to bring good luck, its snout remains brightly polished by tourists' rubbing. (Off V. Calimala, between P. della Repubblica and the Ponte Vecchio.)

PALAZZO DAVANZATI. As Florence's 15th-century economy expanded, its bankers and merchants flaunted their new wealth by erecting grand palaces. The great *quattrocento* boom began with construction of the Palazzo Davanzati. Today the high-ceilinged *palazzo* finds life as the **Museo della Casa Fiorentina Antica.** With reproductions and original furniture, restored frescoes, and wooden doors and ornaments, this museum recreates the 15th-century merchants's life of luxury in a palatial *palazzo.* (V. Porta Rossa, 13. ☎ 055 238 86 10. Open daily 8:30am-1:50pm. Closed 1st, 3rd, 5th M and 2nd and 4th Su of each month. Videos 10am, 11am, and noon, on 4th fl.)

PALAZZO STROZZI. The modesty of the Palazzo Davanzati's facade gave way to more extravagant *palazzi.* The Palazzo Strozzi, begun in 1489, may be the grandest of its kind, occupying an entire block. Its regal proportions and three-tiered facade, made of bulging blocks of brown stone, embody the Florentine style. The *palazzo* now shelters several cultural institutes, not open to the public, and occasionally hosts art exhibits that are open to all. The courtyard is open to the public and worth a look for it's *loggia* and high arched windows. (On V. Tornabuoni at V. Strozzi. Enter from P. della Strozzi. ☎ 055 28 53 95.)

FLORENCE

MUSEO SALVATORE FERRAGAMO. If you've seen too much Renaissance art and have always felt a certain kinship with Immelda Marcos, pop into this free museum, on the sumptuous second floor of the Ferragamo Store by the Arno. View a history of all the shoes designed by the master, with a TV in one room showing silent movie clips featuring his earliest work. (*V. Tornabuoni, 2.* ☎ *055 336 04 75. Open M-F 9am-1pm and 2-6pm.*)

SAN LORENZO AND FARTHER NORTH

■ **BASILICA DI SAN LORENZO.** In 1419 Brunelleschi designed this spacious basilica, another Florentine example of early Renaissance clarity and proportion. Because the Medici lent the funds to build the church, they retained artistic control over its construction. Their coat of arms, featuring six red balls, appears all over the nave, and their tombs fill the two sacristies and the **Cappella dei Principi** (see below) behind the altar. The family cunningly placed Cosimo dei Medici's grave in front of the high altar, making the entire church his personal mausoleum. Michelangelo designed the church's exterior, but disgusted by the murkiness of Florentine politics, abandoned the project and to study architecture in Rome. The basilica still stands unadorned. (*☎ 055 21 66 34. Open M-Sa 10am-5pm. L5000/€2.58.*)

To reach the ■**Cappelle dei Medici** (Medici Chapels), walk around to the back entrance on P. Madonna degli Aldobrandini. Intended as a grand mausoleum, Matteo Nigetti's **Cappella dei Principi** (Princes's Chapel) emulates the baptistery in P. del Duomo. Except for the gilded portraits of the Medici dukes, the decor is a rare glimpse of the Baroque in Florence. Michelangelo's simple architectural design of the **Sacrestia Nuova** (New Sacristy) reveals the master's study of Brunelleschi. Michelangelo sculpted two impressive tombs for Medici dukes, Lorenzo and Giuliano. On the tomb of the military-minded Giuliano lounge the smooth, female *Night* and the rising, masculine *Day*. Michelangelo personified the hazier states of *Dawn* and *Dusk* with more androgynous figures for the milder-mannered Lorenzo. In both cases, the paired figures represent life and death. The basement also displays some of Michelangelo's sketches. (*☎ 055 238 86 02. Open daily 8:15am-5pm; closed the 2nd and 4th Su and the 1st, 3rd, 5th M of every month. L11,000/€5.68.*)

The adjacent **Laurentian Library** houses one of the world's most valuable manuscript collections. Michelangelo's famous entrance portico confirms his virtuosity; the elaborate *pietra serena* sandstone staircase is one of his most innovative architectural designs. (*☎ 055 21 07 60. Open daily 8:30am-1pm. Free.*)

■ **MUSEO DELLA CHIESA DI SAN MARCO.** Remarkable works by Fra Angelico adorn the Museo della Chiesa di San Marco, one of the most peaceful and spiritual places in Florence. A large room to the right of the lovely courtyard contains some of the painter's major works, including the church's altarpiece. Climb the stairs to see Angelico's famous *Annunciation*. Every cell in the convent contains its own Fra Angelico fresco, each painted in flat colors and with sparse detail to facilitate the monks' somber meditation. Michelozzo's library, modeled on Michelangelo's work in S. Lorenzo, is a fine example of purity and vigor. After visiting, you may want to follow in the footsteps of the convent's patron, Cosimo I, who retired here (his cell is the largest). Look also for Savonarola's cell, where you can see some of his relics. On your way to the exit you will pass two rooms housing the **Museo di Firenze Antica,** worth a quick visit. On display are numerous archeological fragments, most of them pieces of stone work from Etruscan and Roman buildings in the area. (*Enter at P. di San Marco, 3.* ☎ *055 238 86 08 or 238 87 04. Open M-F 8:30am-1:30pm, Sa-Su 8:30am-6:50pm; closed 1st, 3rd, 5th Su and the 2nd and 4th M of every month. L8000/€4.13, EU Citizens 18-25 L4000/€2.07, over 65 and under 18 free.*)

ACCADEMIA. Michelangelo's triumphant ■**David** stands in self-assured perfection under the rotunda designed just for him. He was moved here from P. della Signoria in 1873 after a stone hurled during a riot broke his left wrist in two places. If the real *David* looks different to you than the slightly top-heavy copy in front of the Palazzo Vecchio, there's a reason—even though the statues are practically identical, in the Accademia, David stands on a higher pedestal. Michelangelo exaggerated his head and torso to correct for distortion from viewing far below. In the hallway leading up to the *David* are Michelangelo's four *Slaves*. The master left these intriguing statues intentionally unfinished. Remaining true to his theories of living stone, he chipped away only enough to show their figure emerging from the stone. Don't miss the impressive collection of Gothic triptychs on the second floor or room #2, also on the second floor, filled with an astounding collection of Russian icons. *(V. Ricasoli, 60, between the churches of San Marco and S.S. Annunziata.* ☎ *055 23 88 609. Most areas wheelchair accessible. Open June 15-Sept. 15 Tu-F 8:30am-6:50pm, Sa 8:30am-10pm; Sept. 16.-June 14 Tu-Su 8:30am-6:50pm. L12,000/€6.2.)*

PALAZZO MEDICI RICCARDI. The palace's innovative facade is the work of Michelozzo—it stands as the archetype for all Renaissance *palazzi*. The private chapel inside features Benozzo Gozzoli's beautiful fresco of the ▨*Three Magi* and several Medici family portraits. The *palazzo* hosts rotating exhibits ranging from Renaissance architectural sketches to Fellini memorabilia. *(V. Cavour, 3.* ☎ *055 276 03 40. Open Th-Tu 9am-7pm. L8000/€4.13, children L5000/€2.58.)*

OSPEDALE DEGLI INNOCENTI. Brunelleschi designed the right-hand *loggia* of the Hospital of the Innocents in the 1420s. It opened in 1444 as the first orphanage in Europe. On the left side of the portico stands the rotating stone cylinder on which mothers would place their unwanted children. They'd then ring the bell as a signal for those inside to rotate the stone and take in the child. An equestrian statue of Ferdinando de Medici presides over the *piazza*. The bright and airy **Galleria dello Spedale degli Innocenti** contains Botticelli's *Madonna e Angelo* and Ghirlandaio's *Epiphany*, along with many minor Renaissance paintings. *(Around P. Annunziata.* ☎ *055 203 73 08. Open Th-Tu 8:30am-2pm. L5000/€2.58.)*

MUSEO ARCHEOLOGICO. A bland yellow plaster facade and little signage belie the fact that this archeological museum has extremely diverse holdings. It has notable collections of statues and other monuments of the ancient Greeks, Etruscans, and Egyptians. A long thin, two-story gallery devoted to Etruscan jewelry runs along the length of the plant- and tree-filled courtyard. In almost any other city in the world, this museum would be a major cultural highlight, but in Florence, its possible to enjoy it without large crowds. Check out the museum's jewel, the *chimera d'Arezzo*. *(V. della Colonna, 38.* ☎ *055 24 46 19. Open M 2-7pm, Tu and Th 8:30am-7pm, W and F-Su 8:30am-2pm; June 15-Sept. 15 Sa 8-11pm. L8000/€4.13.)*

MERCATO CENTRALE. Just two blocks from San Lorenzo, the Central Market is home to butchers and cheese and wine vendors on the first floor and a vegetable and fruit market on the second floor. The market was built in the 20s with wrought iron railing and intertwining staircases between the open levels. It's a great place to buy cheap fixings for an afternoon picnic in the Boboli Gardens (see p. 335). The Piazza Mercato Centrale and surrounding streets are filled with vendors selling the usual leather goods and clothing. *(Open daily 8am-6pm.)*

PIAZZA SANTA CROCE AND ENVIRONS

▨**CHIESA DI SANTA CROCE.** The Franciscans built this church as far as possible from their Dominican rivals at S. Maria Novella. The ascetic Franciscans ironically produced what is arguably the most splendid church in the city. A fresco cycle by Andrea Orcagna originally adorned the nave. Never heard of Orcagna? Maybe that's because Vasari not only destroyed the entire cycle but also left Orcagna out of his famous *Lives of the Artists*. To the right of the altar, the frescoes of the **Cappella Peruzzi** vie with those of the **Cappella Bardi**. Giotto and his school painted both, but unfortunately the works are badly faded. Among the famous Florentines buried in this church are Michelangelo, who rests at the front of the right aisle in a tomb designed by Vasari, and humanist Leonardo Bruni, shown holding his precious *History of Florence*. Between the two sits Donatello's gilded *Annunciation*. The Florentines, who banished Dante, eventually prepared a tomb for him here. Dante died in Ravenna, however, and the literary necrophiles there have never sent him back. Florence did manage to retain the bodies of Machiavelli and Galileo, who both rest here. In the contest for corpses, you win some, you lose some. (☎ 055 29 08 32. Open M-Sa 9:30am-5:30pm, Su and holidays 3-5:30pm.)

The **Museo dell'Opera di Santa Croce,** was hard-hit by the 1966 flood, leaving Cimabue's *Crucifixion* in a tragic state. The museum forms three sides of the church's peaceful courtyard with gravel paths and cyprus trees. The former dining hall contains Taddeo Gaddi's imaginative fresco of *The Tree of the Cross*, and beneath it, his *Last Supper*. Intricate *pietra serena* pilasters, Luca della Robbia's *tondi* of the apostles, and statues of the evangelists by Donatello are among the profusion of colorful decorations that grace Brunelleschi's small ▊Cappella Pazzi, at the end of the cloister next to the church. *(Enter museum through the loggia in front of Cappella Pazzi. Open Th-Tu 10am-7pm. L5000/€2.58.)*

SYNAGOGUE OF FLORENCE. This synagogue, also known as the **Museo del Tempio Israelitico,** lies hidden behind gates and walls, waiting to reveal its Sephardic temple's domes, horseshoe arches, and patterns. David Levi, a wealthy Florentine Jewish business man, donated his fortune in 1870 for the construction of "a monumental temple worthy of Florence," now that Jews were allowed to live and worship outside the old Jewish ghetto. Architects Micheli, Falchi and Treves created one of Europe's most beautiful synagogues. The museum includes free, informative tours every hour; book in advance. *(V. Farini, 4, at V. Pilastri. ☎ 055 24 52 52 or 24 52 53. Open Sa-Th 10am-1pm and 2-5pm, F 10am-1pm. L6000/€3.10.)*

CASA BUONARROTI. This unassuming little museum houses Michelangelo memorabilia and two of his most important early works, *The Madonna of the Steps* and *The Battle of the Centaurs*. Both pieces are to the left of the second floor landing. He completed these panels, which illustrate his growth from bas-relief to sculpture, when he was 16 years old. *(V. Ghibellina, 70. From P.S. Croce, follow V. de' Pepi and turn right onto V. Ghibellina. ☎ 055 24 17 52. Open W-M 9:30am-2pm. L12,000/€6.20.)*

IN THE OLTRARNO

The far side of the Arno is a lively, unpretentious quarter. Though you'll likely cross over the Ponte Vecchio on the way to the Oltrarno, consider coming back along V. Maggio, a street lined with Renaissance *palazzi*, many of which have markers with historical descriptions. Head over the Ponte S. Trinita, which affords excellent views of the Ponte Vecchio. Or, dally a bit in Piazza San Spirito and browse the market during the day or watch street performers and crowds at night.

▊**PALAZZO PITTI.** Luca Pitti, a 15th-century banker, built his *palazzo* east of S. Spirito against the Boboli hill. The Medici family acquired the *palazzo* and the hill in 1550 and enlarged everything possible. During Italy's brief experiment with monarchy, the structure served as a royal residence. Today, with a vast uninhabited plaza in front, the **Palazzo Pitti** houses a gallery and four museums. *(Ticket office/info ☎ 055 29 48 83. Ticket to gallery, museums, and Boboli Gardens L20,000/€10.33.)*

The ▊**Galleria Palatina** was one of only a few public galleries when it opened in 1833. Today it houses Florence's second most important collection (behind the Uffizi). It houses an overwhelming array of Renaissance works, including a number of works by Raphael, Titian, Andrea del Sarto, Rosso, Caravaggio, and Rubens. Flemish works dominate the Neoclassical Music Room and the Putti Room. While admiring the collection, don't forget to look up from time to time at the frescoes on the ceilings. Informative official guides (L14,000/€7.23) are available at the ticket office. *(Open Su-F 8:30am-9pm, Sa 8:30am-midnight. L12,000/€6.20.)*

The **Museo degli Argenti** (Silver Museum), on the ground floor, exhibits the Medici family treasures, including cases of precious gems, ivories, silver pieces, and Lorenzo the Magnificent's famous collection of vases. The **Galleria del Costume** and the **Museo della Porcellana,** hidden in back of the gardens, exhibit other items of Medici fortune. In the last museum, the **Galleria d'Arte Moderna,** lies one of Italian art history's big surprises, the early-19th century proto-Impressionist works of the

Macchiaioli school. The collection also includes Neoclassical and Romantic pieces, like Giovanni Dupré's sculptural group Cain and Abel. *(Same ticket office as Galleria Palatina. All museums open daily 8:30am-1:50pm; closed 1st, 3rd, 5th M and the 2nd and 4th Su of every month. L4000/€2.07 each.)*

The **Appartamenti Reale** (Royal Apartments) and the **Museo delle Carozze** (Carriage Museum; ☎ 055 238 86 11) house lavish reminders of the time when the palazzo served as the royal House of Savoy's living quarters. *(Open Tu-Sa 8:30am-6:30pm, Su 8:30am-2pm. L12,000/€6.20.)*

■**BOBOLI GARDENS.** This elaborately landscaped park, an exquisite example of a stylized Renaissance garden, provides teasing glimpses of Florence and wonderful views of the surrounding countryside. A large oval lawn sits just up the hill from the back of the palace, where an Egyptian obelisk stands in the middle and marble statues dot the hedge-lined perimeter. Labyrinthine avenues of cypress trees lead eager meanderers to bubbling fountains with nudes and shaded picnic areas. *(Pass through courtyard of Palazzo Pitti to ticket office and entrance. ☎ 055 265 18 16. Open daily 8:15am-6:30pm. Closed 1st and last M of each month. L4000/€2.07, EU citizens with passport L2000/€1.03)*

CHIESA DI SANTA MARIA DEL CARMINE. Inside this church, the ■**Brancacci Chapel** holds Masaccio's stunning 15th-century frescoes, declared masterpieces in their own time. Fifty years later a respectful Filippino Lippi completed the cycle. Masolino's *Adam and Eve* and Masaccio's *Expulsion from the Garden* stand face to face, illustrating the young Masaccio's innovative depiction of un-idealized human forms. With such monumental works as the *Tribute Money*, this chapel became a school for artists, including Michelangelo. Visitors are not allowed in the nave of the church, but can peer from the roped off chapel into the gloomy, but beautifully frescoed main aisle. *(Open M and W-Sa 10am-5pm, Su 1-5pm. L6000/€3.10.)*

CHIESA DI SANTO SPIRITO. A rather dull exterior belies the fact that this church is considered by many to be one of the simplest, best-proportioned examples of a Renaissance interior in the world. Brunelleschi's design was significantly ahead of its time. He envisioned a four-aisled nave surrounded by round chapels, revealed on the exterior as soft undulations. Brunelleschi died when the project was only partially completed, however, and the plans were altered to be more conventional. Tall, thin columns make the church feel airy and light, while the unusually high clerestory admits shafts of sunlight to illuminate the church. *(☎ 055 21 00 30. Open M-Tu and Th-F 8:30am-noon and 4-6pm, W 8:30am-noon, Su 8am-noon and 4-7pm.)*

SAN MINIATO AL MONTE AND ENVIRONS

■**SAN MINIATO AL MONTE.** One of Florence's oldest churches, San Miniato al Monte gloriously surveys all of Florence. The inlaid marble facade and 13th-century mosaics provide a prelude to the incredible pavement inside, patterned with lions, doves, and astrological signs. Inside, the **Chapel of the Cardinal of Portugal** holds a collection of superlative della Robbia terra-cottas. Be sure to circle the church and spend a moment in the cemetery. It is an overwhelming profusion of tombs and mausoleums in many architectural styles. *(Take bus #13 from the station or climb the stairs from Piazzale Michelangelo. ☎ 055 234 27 31. Church open daily 7:30am-7pm.)*

PIAZZALE MICHELANGELO. Laid out in 1860, Piazzale Michelangelo offers a fine panorama of Florence. Sunset provides the most spectacular lighting of the city. Essentially a large parking lot now, the *piazzale* is often home to hordes of tour buses during summer days. It occasionally hosts concerts as well. The views in addition to the copy of Michelangelo's David on an ornate pedestal in the center are the only redeeming features of this *piazzale*. *(Cross Ponte Vecchio and turn left, walk through the piazza, and turn right up V. de' Bardi. Follow it uphill as it becomes V. del Monte alle Croci, where a staircase to the left heads to the piazzale.)*

FLORENCE

🎵 ENTERTAINMENT

Florence disagrees with England over who invented modern soccer, but every June the various *quartieri* of the city turn out in costume to play their own medieval version of the sport, known as **calcio storico.** Two teams face off over a wooden ball in one of the city's *piazze.* These games often blur the line between athletic contest and riot. Check newspapers or the tourist office for the dates and locations of historic or modern *calcio.* The **stadio,** north of the city center, hosts the real soccer games. Tickets (around L24,000/€12.40) are sold at the **Box Office** (see p. 315) and at the bar across the street from the stadium.

The most important of Florence's traditional festivals, **San Giovanni Battista,** on June 24, features a tremendous fireworks display in Piazzale Michelangelo (easily visible from the Arno) that starts around 10pm. The summer also swings with music festivals, starting in late April with the classical **Maggio Musicale.** The **Estate Fiesolana** (June-Aug.) fills the Roman theater in Fiesole with concerts, opera, theater, ballet, and film. For information, contact the **Box Office** (p. 315).

In the summer, the **L'Europa dei Sensi** program hosts **Rime Rapanti,** nightly cultural shows with music, poetry, and food from a chosen European country. Call the information office (☎ 055 263 85 85; www.lapiazzavirtuale.it) to make reservations. The same company also hosts the more modern and lively **Le Pavoniere,** with live music, pool, bar, and pizzeria, in the Ippodromo delle Caseine (along river past the train station.) Call the office (055 321 75 41) for information and reservations. The city hosts weekly outdoor classical concerts in the **Giardino Botanico Superiore.** (W 6pm. Gardens L4000/€2.07. Free.) In September, Florence hosts the **Festa dell'Unità,** a music and concert series at Campi Bisenzia (bus #30). The **Festa del Grillo** (Festival of the Cricket) is held the first Sunday after Ascension Day—crickets in wooden cages are hawked in the Cascine park to be released into the grass.

🛍 SHOPPING

The Florentine flair for design comes through as clearly in window displays as in the wares themselves. V. Tornabuoni's swanky **boutiques** and the well-stocked goldsmiths on the Ponte Vecchio proudly serve a sophisticated clientele. Florence makes its contribution to *alta moda* with a number of fashion shows including the biannual **Pitti Uomo show** (in January and July), Europe's most important exhibition of menswear. If you're looking for high-quality used or antique clothing, try **La Belle Epoque,** Volta di S. Piero, 8r (☎ 055 21 61 69), off P.S. Maggiore, or **Lord Brummel Store,** V. della Vigna Nuova, 79r (☎ 055 238 23 28), off V. Tornabuoni.

The city's artisan traditions thrive at the open markets. **San Lorenzo,** the largest, cheapest, and most touristed, sprawls for several blocks around P.S. Lorenzo. High prices are rare, as are quality and honesty. (Open M-Sa 9am-after sunset.) For everything from potholders to parakeets, visit **Parco delle Cascine,** which begins west of the city center at P.V. Veneto and stretches along the Arno River. The market at the Cascine sells used clothing and shoes. At night, commodities of a different sort go up for sale as transvestite prostitutes prowl the *piazza* in search of customers. For a flea market specializing in old furniture, postcards, and bric-a-brac, visit **Piazza Ciompi,** off V. Pietrapiana from Borgo degli Albizi. (Open Tu-Sa.) Even when prices are marked, don't be afraid to haggle. Generally you should start with half of the price offered, but never ask for a price you're not willing to pay. Often, bargaining is impossible if you are using a credit card.

Books and art reproductions are the best Florentine souvenirs. **Alinari,** V. della Vigna Nuova, 46-48r, stocks the world's largest selection of art prints and high-quality photographs from L5-8000/€2.58-4.13. (☎ 055 21 89 75. Open Tu-Sa 10am-1pm and 3:30-7:30pm.) **Abacus,** V. de'Ginori, 30r (☎ 055 21 97 19), sells beautiful photo albums, journals, and address books, all made of fine leather and *carta fiorentina* (paper covered in an intricate floral design). Florentine **leatherwork** is typically of high quality, and is often affordable. Some of the best leather artisans in the city work around P.S. Croce and V. Porta S. Maria. The **Santa Croce Leather School,** in Chiesa di Santa Croce, offers some of the city's best products with prices to match. (On Su, enter through V.S. Giuseppe, 5r. ☎055 24 45 33 and 247 99 13. Open M-F 9:30am-6:30pm, Sa 9:30am-6pm, and Su 10:30am-12:30pm and 3-6pm.)

NIGHTLIFE

For reliable information, consult the city's entertainment monthly, *Firenze Spettacolo* (L3500/€1.81). Street performers draw crowds to the steps of the *duomo*, the arcades of the Mercato Nuovo, Piazza della Signoria, and Ple. Michelangelo. **Piazza Santo Spirito** in Oltrarno has regular live music in the summer and a good selection of bars and restaurants. Take the #25 bus from the station to the **Giardini del Drago** (Gardens of the Dragon) for a pick-up game of soccer.

BARS

The William, V. Magliabechi, 7/9/11r (☎055 263 83 57). Plenty of outdoor seating. Comfortable brick-walled interior. Rowdy and packed on weekends; mellow and brooding during the week. One of the few Irish pubs in Florence (and there are many) serving Bass Ale. Pints of all draft beer L8000/€4.13. Open daily 6pm-2am.

Montecarla, V. dei Bardi, 2 (☎055 234 02 59), in the Oltrarno, off P. de' Mozzi. 3-tiered wonderworld of jaguar print upholstery with a plastic flower motif. Deliciously plush club is mellow in summer but stuffed in winter. If you're lucky, you'll meet Carla, the famous owner. Mixed drinks L10,000/€5.16. Open Su-Th 11pm-3am, F-Sa 11pm-4am.

The Chequers Pub, V. della Scala, 7/9r (☎055 28 75 88). Of all the Irish pubs in Florence, it attracts the biggest and liveliest Italian crowd. Wide range of beers (pints L8000/€4.13) plus typical pub grub. Happy hour daily 6:30-8pm (pints L5000/€2.58). Open Su-Th 6pm-midnight, F-Sa 6pm-3am.

The Fiddler's Elbow, P.S. Maria Novella, 7r (☎055 21 59 56). Authentic Irish pub serves cider, Guinness, and other draught beers for L8000/€4.13 per pint. Crowded, convivial, and full of foreigners. Open daily 1pm-2am.

DISCOS

Meccanò, V. degli Olmi, 1 (☎055 33 13 71), near Parco delle Cascinè. Among locals and tourists alike, this is the most popular of Florence's discos. Cover L25,000/€12.91 includes 1 drink; each subsequent drink L10,000/€5.16. Special nights include soul, hip-hop, house, and reggae. Call for their weekly schedule. Open Tu-Sa 11pm-4am.

Central Park, Parco delle Cascinè. Open-air dance floors pulses with hip-hop, jungle, reggae, and Italian "dance rock." A cinema, pizzeria, *crêperia*, and Internet terminals are all vaguely attached to the dance complex. Teeny-boppers occasionally flood the place around midnight. Mixed drinks L10,000/€5.16. Open daily 9pm-late.

Yab, V. Sassetti, 5 (☎055 21 51 60). Another dance club seething with American students as well as locals. With classic R&B and Reggae on Mondays, other music specialties on a rotating basis other nights. A very large dance floor, mercifully free of strobe lights, is packed come midnight. Mixed drinks L10,000/€5.16. Open daily 9pm-1am.

Blob, V. Vinegia, 21r (☎055 21 12 09), behind the Palazzo Vecchio. From mellow evenings to boisterous nights (to early mornings), this little club has much to offer, including DJs, an open mic, movies in original sound, foosball, and evening bar buffet. Live Cuban guitar Sunday nights. Mixed drinks L10,000/€5.16.

Tabasco Gay Club, P.S. Cecilia, 3r (☎055 21 30 00), in tiny alleyway across P. della Signoria from Palazzo Vecchio. Smoke machines and strobe lights on dance floor. Low vaulted ceilings in this dark basement club. Florence's popular gay disco. Caters primarily to men. 18+. Cover L25,000/€12.91 includes first drink. Open Tu-Su 10pm-4am.

DAYTRIP FROM FLORENCE: FIESOLE

*The town is a 25min. **bus** ride away; catch the ATAF city bus #7 from the train station near track #16 or P.S. Marco. It drops passengers at P. Mino da Fiesole in the town center. The* *tourist office,* P. Mino da Fiesole, 37, is a few steps away in the yellow plaster building facing onto the piazza and provides a free map with museum and sights listings. ☎ 055 59 94 78. Open M 8am-1pm, Tu 8am-noon, W 8am-6:30pm, Th-F 8am-noon, Sa 8am-1pm.

Older than Florence itself, Fiesole is the site of the original Etruscan settlement. Florence was actually colonized and settled as an off-shoot. Fiesole has long been a welcome escape from the sweltering summer heat of the Arno Valley and a source of inspiration for numerous famous figures—among them Alexander Dumas, Anatole France, Marcel Proust, Gertrude Stein, Frank Lloyd Wright, and Paul Klee. Leonardo da Vinci even used the town as a testing ground for his famed flying machine. Fiesole's location provides incomparable views of both Florence and the rolling countryside to the north.

With the bus stop at your back, walk half a block off P. Mino da Fiesole, to the entrance gate of the **Museo Civico.** One ticket gains admission to three constituent museums. The **Teatro Romano** is used intermittently for concerts in summer and includes Etruscan thermal baths, temple ruins, and wonderful countryside views. The amphitheater grounds lead into the **Museo Civico Archeologico,** which houses an extensive collection of Etruscan artifacts and well-preserved Grecian urns. Hop across the street to breeze through the **Museo Bandini,** which houses a collection of 15th-century Italian paintings. (Open May-Aug. daily 9:30am-7pm; Sept.-Apr. 9:30am-5pm. L12,000/€6.20, students and over 65 L8000/€4.13.)

Accommodations in Fiesole are expensive, but the town is a great place to sit down for a leisurely afternoon lunch. To grab a bite to eat, head to the **Pizzeria Etrusca** in P. Mina da Fiesole, near the bus stop. (☎ 055 59 94 84. Open noon-3pm and 7pm-1am. Pizza L9-14,000/€4.65-7.23; *primi* from L9000/€4.65; *secondi* from L16,000/€8.26.) Up the hill on your left, with your back to the bus stop, you will find the **Missionario Francesco** and the public gardens. It's a steep, mercifully short climb, well worth the effort for the breathtaking panorama of Florence and the surrounding hills. The monastery contains a frescoed chapel and a bite-size museum of exquisite Chinese pottery, jade figurines, and Egyptian artifacts (including a mummy) brought back by Franciscan missionaries. (Open daily 7-9:30am and noon-2:30pm)

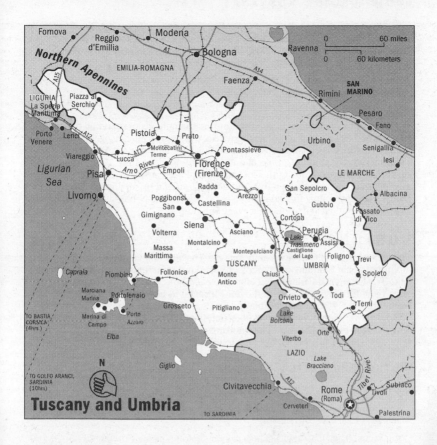

Tuscany and Umbria

CENTRAL ITALY

TUSCANY (TOSCANA)

Upon his exile from Tuscany, a famous man once wrote, "When I had journeyed half our life's way, I found myself within a shadowed forest, for I had lost the path that does not stray." The source of his misery, however, a hundred years of bloody political and social conflict within the imposing city walls of his native Florence, would eventually result in what are arguably the most brilliant two centuries that any loosely connected group of small hill towns has ever experienced at any point in recorded history. Although the proud Tuscans of Dante's 14th-century would resent the implication that they gave their rivals to the south and east a single thing to help their advancement, it was the language, art, architecture, and philosophy of the olive country that defined Italy and launched Italians into the Renaissance with a vigor and abandon that made them the power brokers of Europe for centuries. Under the astute (and despotic) rule of the Medici family, guardians of civic humanism and keepers of the bank rolls, Tuscany fought the war that filled the Uffizi.

HIGHLIGHTS OF TUSCANY

CHOOSE your own hill-town. You can't go wrong in the **Chianti region** (p. 353), where blankets of sunflowers give way to medieval skyscrapers and wine tours.

WAIT for hours and hours in the hot sun with the teeming masses only to go wild for 30 seconds during Siena's world-famous **Palio** (p. 353).

STEP into Pisa's **Field of Miracles** and help support its faulty **tower** (p. 377).

Their rival was Pope Julian II, the ammunition the millions of sparkling florins Tuscany earned as financial center to the world, the bounty Michelangelo Buonarroti. Perhaps it was this conspicuous consumption that bankrupted Florence and sent Tuscany into the spiral of political and cultural decline of the 17th through 19th centuries. Fortunately for both Florentines and Tuscans, however, the money to inspire greatness has returned five-fold in the form of tourism dollars. As it was for Dante, Tuscany is Italy for the millions who traverse its cobblestoned *piazze* and gaze open-mouthed at its Boticellis every summer.

CORTONA ☎0575

The ancient town of Cortona regally surveys Tuscany and Umbria from its graceful mountain peak. Stunning hills and rich farmland punctuated by the shimmering Lake Trasimeno make for spectacular sunsets. Though currently peaceful, the city once rivaled Perugia, Arezzo, and even Florence in power, belligerence, and tantrum-throwing. When Cortona finally lost its autonomy in 1409, it was auctioned off to the rival Florentines. For all its grumbling, Cortona enjoyed peace and prosperity under Florentine rule. The paintings of Luca Signorelli and Pietro Lorenzetti, signs of this prosperity, are now exhibited in Cortona's Museo Diocesano.

▢ TRANSPORTATION

Trains: From **Florence** (8 per day; L12,000/€6.20) and **Rome** (13 per day; L16,000/€8.26) arrive at **Camucia-Cortona.** LFI bus to Cortona's P. Garibaldi leaves from the station (15min., L2600/€1.34).

Buses: Buses run to P. Garibaldi from **Arezzo** (1hr., 3-5 per day, L5400/€2.80). Buy LFI bus tickets from the tourist office, a bar, or *tabacchi*.

Taxis: ☎033 58 19 63 13 and 87 00 59 99.

✳❷ ORIENTATION AND PRACTICAL INFORMATION

Buses from neighboring cities stop at **Piazza Garibaldi** just outside the city wall. Enter the city by turning left uphill following **via Nazionale.** Pass the tourist office immediately on the left, and you'll reach **Piazza della Repubblica,** the center of town. Diagonally across the *piazza* lies **Piazza Signorelli,** Cortona's main square.

Tourist Office: V. Nazionale, 42 (☎0575 63 03 52; fax 63 06 56). English-speaking staff. Maps, brochures, and rail and bus tickets and schedules. Open May-Sept. M-Sa 9am-1pm and 3-7pm, Su 9am-1pm; Oct.-Apr. M-F 9am-1pm and 3-6pm, Sa 9am-1pm.

Currency Exchange: Banca Populare, V. Guelfa, 4. Open M-F 8:30am-1:30pm and 2:30-3:30pm. 24hr. **ATM,** V.S. Margherita, 2/3.

Emergency: ☎113. **Medical Emergency:** ☎118.

Police: V. Dardano, 9 (☎0575 60 30 06).

Misericordia: ☎0575 60 30 83.

Late-Night Pharmacy: Farmacia Centrale, V. Nazionale, 38 (☎0575 60 32 06). Open M-Sa 9am-1pm and 4:30-8pm.

Hospital: (☎0575 63 91), on V. Maffei.

Post Office: V. Santucci, 1, 15m uphill from P. della Repubblica. Open M-F 8:15am-7pm, Sa 8:15am-12:30pm.

Postal Code: 52044.

ACCOMMODATIONS

Ostello San Marco (HI), V. Maffei, 57 (☎0575 60 13 92 or 60 17 65; www.cortonahostel.com). From bus stop, walk 5min. on V.S. Margarita and follow signs to hostel. Clean, 13th-century mansion. Breakfast, sheets, showers included. Dinner L15,000/€7.75. Reception daily 7-10am and 3pm-midnight. Lockout 10am-3pm. Curfew midnight. Dorms L20,000/€10.33 per person. Open mid-Mar. to mid-Oct., year-round for groups.

Istituto Santa Margherita, V. Cesare Battisti, 15 (☎0575 63 03 36). Walk down V. Severini from P. Garibaldi. *Istituto* on corner of V. Battisti, on the left. Get thee to this nunnery with echoing marble hallways and spacious rooms with baths. Breakfast L5000/€2.58. Curfew midnight. Singles L45,000/€23.24; doubles (no unmarried couples) L60,000/€30.99; triples L90,000/€46.48; quads L105,000/€54.23.

Albergo Italia, V. Ghibellina, 5 (☎0575 63 02 54 or 63 05 64; fax 60 57 63), off P. Repubblica. 16th-century *palazzo* with 3-star rooms, A/C, antiques, firm beds, TVs, and pristine bathrooms. Rooms include bath and breakfast. Singles L130,000/€67.14; doubles L170,000/€87.80; triples L210,000/€108.46; quads L250,000/€129.11.

FOOD

Cortona's *trattorie* serve Tuscan dishes for reasonable prices. Have dinner with a glass of the fine local wine, *bianco vergine di Valdichiana*. Penny-pinchers can pick up a L4000/€2.07 bottle at the **Despar Market,** P. della Repubblica, 23, which also makes *panini* for L1500-5000/€0.77-2.58. (☎0575 63 06 66. Open Apr.-Oct. daily 7:30am-1:30pm and 4:30-8pm; Nov.-Mar. M-Tu and Th-Sa 7am-1:30pm and 4:30-8pm, W 7am-1:30pm. AmEx/MC/V.) On Saturday the same *piazza* hosts an **open-air market.** (Open daily 8am-1pm.)

Trattoria La Grotta, P. Baldelli, 3 (☎0575 63 02 71), off P. della Repubblica. Truly delectable fare served at outdoor tables in a secluded courtyard. Sample the homemade *gnocchi alla ricotta e spinaci* (ricotta and spinach dumplings in tomato and meat sauce; L11,000/€5.68). *Primi* L10-12,000/€5.16-6.20; *secondi* from L12,000/€6.20. Cover L2000/€1.03. Open W-M noon-2:30pm and 7-10pm. AmEx/MC/V.

Trattoria Etrusca, V. Dardano, 37/39 (☎0575 60 40 88), next to the Porta Colonia. Specializes in *primi* (L8-10,000/€4.13-5.16); try the *gnocchi al pesto.* The only *secondo* is *bistecca "Cortonese"* (big slab o'steak L5000/€2.58 per 100g). Outdoor seating available. Open F-W noon-2pm and 7:30-10pm. MC/V.

SIGHTS

MUSEO DIOCESANO. The upstairs gallery of this small Renaissance art museum houses the stunning *Annunciation* by Fra Angelico (Room 3). Christ's pain-wrenched face looks down from Pietro Lorenzetti's fresco of *The Way to Calvary.* The collection also includes Luca Signorelli's masterpiece, *The Deposition,* a vivid portrayal of Christ's death and resurrection in Room 1. *(From P. della Repubblica, pass through P. Signorelli and follow the signs. ☎0575 628 30. Open Apr.-Sept. Tu-Sa 9:30am-1pm and 3:30-7pm; Oct.-Mar. 10am-1pm and 3-5pm. L8000/€4.13.)*

FORTEZZA MEDICEA. Views of the Val di Chiena, all the way to Lake Trasimeno, are more breathtaking here than from P. Garibaldi. The courtyards and turrets of this fortress include several rooms of photographs and the traditional crafts of the region. *(Walk up V.S. Margherita from P. Garibaldi and the bus stop. Continue past the church and climb the small road on the far side of the parking lot. Open May 1-Sept. 30 Tu-Su 10am-6pm. L5000/€2.58, students under 18 L3000/€1.55.)*

MUSEO DELL'ACCADEMIA ETRUSCA. This museum possesses an overflow of carvings, coins, paintings, and furniture from the first through 18th centuries, not to mention a couple of genuine Egyptian mummies and sarcophagi. In the first hall, a 5th-century BC circular bronze chandelier, weighing 58kg when empty, hangs from the ceiling. In the third gallery, you'll find 12th- and 13th-century Tuscan art. The museum ends with 20th-century lithographs, collages, and the intriguing *Maternità* by Cortona native Gino Severini. *(Inside the courtyard of Palazzo Casali, near P. della Repubblica.* ☎ *0575 63 04 15 or 63 72 35. Open Nov. 1-Mar. 31 Tu-Su 10am-5pm; Apr. 1-Oct. 31 Tu-Su 10am-7pm. L8000/€4.13, groups of 15 or more L5000/€2.58.)*

PALAZZI AND PIAZZE. In P. della Repubblica stands the 13th-century **Palazzo Comunale**, with a clock tower and monumental staircase. **Palazzo Casali**, to the right and behind the Palazzo del Comune, dominates P. Signorelli. Only the courtyard walls, lined with coats of arms, remain from the original structure; the facade and interlocking staircase were added in the 17th century. **Piazza del Duomo** lies to the right and downhill from the Palazzo Casali. Inside rests an impressive Baroque-canopied high altar, completed in 1664 by Francesco Mattioli.

⬛ ENTERTAINMENT

For **Sagra della Bistecca** (Aug. 14-15), the town's most important festival, the town converges on the public gardens (behind the church of S. Domenico) to feast upon bloody strips of the superb local steak (about L25,000/€12.91). Following closely on its heels during the third weekend in August is the superb **Festa dei Porcini**, when the public gardens fill with funghi-lovers. Tickets are available at the garden entrance. Various musical and theatrical events take place throughout the year, clustering mainly in July when Cortona absorbs the spillover from the **Perugia Jazz Festival.** Relax in the gardens or join in the evening *passeggiata* in the park, where Cortona's residents screen Italian movies from mid-June through early September. (Films usually start 9:30pm; buy tickets at gardens for L10,000/€5.16.)

AREZZO ☎ 0575

The poet Petrarch, the humanist Leonardo Bruni, the artist and historian Giorgio Vasari, the inventor of the musical scale Guido d'Arezzo, and, most recently, Roberto Benigni, who wrote and starred in the award-winning film *Life is Beautiful*, have all found inspiration in Arezzo's streets. Michelangelo, born in the surrounding countryside, attributed his genius to Arezzo's hills and valleys, and the poet Carducci once said "Arezzo alone is enough to glorify Italy." While that's something of an overstatement, Arezzo's charm is undeniable.

⬛ TRANSPORTATION

Trains: P. della Repubblica. Info open M-F 8am-noon and 3-6pm, Sa 9am-noon. Luggage storage available (p. 343). To **Florence** (1½hr.; 2 per hr. 6am-11:15pm; L9100/€4.70, InterCity L13,700/€7.08) and **Rome** (2hr.; every 1-2hr. 4:54am-11:04pm; L21,700/€11.21, InterCity L34,300/€17.72).

Buses: (☎0575 38 26 51). **TRA-IN, SITA,** and **LFI** buses stop at P. della Repubblica, to left of train station. To: **Cortona** (1hr., every hr., L4600/€2.38); **Siena** (1½hr., 7 per day, L8400/€4.34); **Sansepolcro** (1hr., SITA every hr., L5400/€2.80). Buy tickets at ATAM *biglietteria*, ahead and to left from train station exit. Open daily 6am-7:45pm.

Taxis: Radio Taxi (☎ 0575 38 26 26). Open 24hr.

Car Rental: Autonoleggi Ermini, V. Perrenio, 21 (☎ 0575 35 35 70). L200,000/ €103.62 per day. 21+. Open M-F 8:30am-12:30pm and 3:30-7:30pm, Sa 9am-noon. **Avis,** P. della Repubblica, 1a (☎ 0575 35 42 32). From L175,000/€90.38 per day. 25+. Open M-F 8:30am-1pm and 3-7pm, Su by request.

✦🛈 ORIENTATION AND PRACTICAL INFORMATION

Arezzo lies on the Florence-Rome train line. **Via Guido Monaco,** which begins directly across from the train station at **Piazza della Republica,** parallels **Corso Italia;** together they form the backbone of Arezzo's commercial district. To get to the city's historic center, follow V. Guido Monaco from the station to the traffic circle at **Piazza Guido Monaco.** Turn right on **via Roma** and then left onto the pedestrian walkway, C. Italia, which leads to the old city. **Piazza Grande** lies to the right.

TOURIST, FINANCIAL, AND LOCAL SERVICES

Tourist Office: APT, P. della Repubblica, 22 (☎ 0575 37 76 78; fax 208 39), to the right as you leave the station. English-speaking staff. Free maps. Open Apr.-Sept. M-Sa 9am-1pm and 3-7pm, Su 9am-1pm; Oct.-Mar. M-Sa 9am-1pm and 3-6:30pm.

Budget Travel: CTS, V.V. Veneto, 25 (☎ 0575 90 78 09 or 90 78 08). Sells Eurail passes and plane tickets. Open M-F 9am-1pm and 4-7:30pm, Sa 9am-1pm.

Currency Exchange: Banca Nazionale del Lavoro, V.G. Monaco, 74. 24hr. **ATM.** Open M-F 8:20am-1:35pm and 2:45-4:05pm.

Luggage Storage: In train station. Exit tracks, self-serve lockers are to the left. L4-6000/ €2.07-3.14 for 24hr.

EMERGENCY AND COMMUNICATIONS

Emergency: ☎ 113. **Medical Emergency:** ☎ 118.

Police: V. Dardano, 9 (☎ 113 or 0575 90 66 67), off V. Fra Guittone by the train station. **Carabinieri:** ☎ 112.

24-Hour Pharmacy: Farmacia Comunale, Campo di Marte, 7 (☎ 0575 90 24 66).

Hospital: Ospedale S. Donato, on V. Fonte Veneziana. **Misericordia:** ☎ 0575 24 242.

Internet Access: Copy Service Ricola, V.L. Cittadini, 11/13 (☎ 0575 90 97 98), behind station. L7000/€3.62 per hr. Open M-F 9am-1pm and 3:30-7:30pm, Sa 9am-1pm.

Post Office: V.G. Monaco, 34. **Currency exchange** (L1000/€0.52 commission) at *sportello* #1 (same hours). Open M-F 8:15am-7pm, Sa 8:15am-12:30pm.

Postal Code: 52100.

▛ ACCOMMODATIONS

Hotels fill to capacity during the **Fiera Antiquaria** (Antique Fair) on the first weekend of every month. Otherwise, you should have little trouble finding a room.

Ostello Villa Severi, V. Redi, 13 (☎ 0575 29 90 47), a bit of a hike from town. Take bus #4 (L1300/€0.67) from P.G. Monaco to 2 stops after Ospedale Vecchio (7min.), when you see the town park on your left. Spacious, with high ceilings and wood-beam detail. Rooms overlook vineyards. Breakfast L3000/€1.55. Lunch or dinner, including several courses and wine, L20,000/€10.33. Reserve ahead for meals. Reception daily 9am-1pm and 6-11:30pm. Dorms L25,000/€12.91.

Hotel Astoria, V.G. Monaco, 54 (☎/fax 0575 243 61 or 243 62). From train station, walk straight up V.G. Monaco, through the *piazza,* and look left. Basic, comfortable rooms with phone. Wheelchair accessible. Sparse breakfast for a whopping L12,000/ €6.20. Singles L55,000/€28.41, with bath and TV L70,000/€36.15; doubles L85,000/€43.90, L110,000/€56.81. AmEx/D/MC/V.

Albergo Cecco, C. Italia, 215 (☎0575 209 86; fax 35 67 30). Follow V.G. Monaco from train station, take a right on V. Roma and go 2 blocks down *corso* (5min.). Large, clean rooms trapped in the Age of Formica. Restaurant downstairs. Singles L55,000/€28.41, with bath L70,000/€36.15; doubles L80,000/€41.32, with bath L100,000/€51.65; triples with bath L135,000/€69.72; quads with bath L160,000/€82.63. AmEx/MC/V.

🍴 FOOD

The **Conad supermarket,** on the corner of V.V. Veneto and V.L.B. Alberti, behind the train station, is large and well-stocked. (Open M-Tu, Th-Sa 8am-8:30pm, W 8am-1:30pm.) An **open-air market** takes place in P. Sant'Agostino on weekdays and on V. Niccolò Aretino on Saturdays. For super cheese, head over to **La Mozzarella,** V. Spinello, 25. (Open M-Sa 8am-1pm and 4:30-8pm.)

■ **Antica Osteria L'Agania,** V. Mazzini, 10 (☎0575 29 53 81), off C. Italia. Many locals feast on homemade pasta (L8-15,000/€4.13-7.75) and delicious *secondi* (L8-15,000/€4.13-7.75). Open Tu-Su noon-3pm and 7:30-11:30pm. AmEx/MC/V.

Un Punto Macrobiotico, P. San Gemignano, 1 (☎0575 30 24 20). Turn right on V. Mazzini from C. Italia and take a right on V. Frale Torri to P. di S. Geminiano. Veggie heaven. A soup and selection of 5 mini entrees (like brown rice *risotto* and simple salads) constitute a filling meal (L12,000/€6.20). Open M-Sa 12:30-2pm and 7:30-9pm.

Bruschetteria Toscana, V. di Tolletta, 14/16/20 (☎0575 29 98 60). Walking up V.G. Monaco, take your 2nd right after P.G. Monaco, onto V. di Tolletta. It's ahead on the left. Pasta (L10-13,000/€5.16-6.71) and *secondi* (L8-15,000/€4.13-7.75). Cover L2000/€1.03. Open Tu-Su 11:30am-3pm and 6:30-11pm. MC/V.

Paradiso di Stelle, V. G. Monaco, 58 (☎0575 274 48). First-rate homemade *gelato*. The *nocciola* (hazelnut) and *tiramisù* are superb. From L2500/€1.29. Open Mar.-Sept. Tu-Su 10:30am-midnight; Oct.-Feb. Tu-Su 10:30am-9pm.

👁 SIGHTS

BASILICA DI SAN FRANCESCO. This extraordinary 11th-century basilica houses a number of frescoes including Piero della Francesca's ■*Leggenda della Vera Croce* (Legend of the True Cross), portraying the story of the crucifix and its role in the Catholic church. The narrative begins with the death of Adam and proceeds to major events involving the crucifix over the centuries, including Emperor Constantine's conversion. The figure kneeling at the foot of the cross is St. Francis, to whom the church is dedicated. *(Up V.G. Monaco from train station. Basilica open daily 8:30am-noon and 2-7pm. Chapel containing della Francesca's frescoes open M-F 9am-7pm, Sa 9am-6pm, Su 1-6pm. Visitors admitted in 30min. blocks; last visit begins 30min. before chapel closes. Tickets L10,000/€5.16, EU citizens 18-25 L6000/€3.10, art students L2000/€1.03. Reservations required. Call ☎0575 90 04 04 or visit the office beneath left side of church. You can see upper portion of fresco cycle without paying entrance fee.)*

PIAZZA GRANDE. The *piazza* contains the **Chiesa di Santa Maria della Pieve,** Arezzo's most important architectural monument. The spectacular Pisan-Romanesque church dates to the 12th century. On the elevated presbytery sits Pietro Lorenzetti's brilliantly restored polyptych, depicting the *Annunciation* and *Madonna and Child*. Below lies the 9th-century *chiesa* upon which the Pieve was built. The adjoining tower is known as the "Tower of a Hundred Holes." Surrounding the *chiesa* in P. Grande lies Arezzo's best architecture, conveniently organized in chronological order. A reconstruction of the **Petrone,** a column where city leaders displayed criminals, rises at the *piazza's* high point. *(P. Grande is down C. Italia, on the right. Chiesa open M-Sa 8am-noon and 3-7pm, Su 8:30am-noon and 4-7pm.)*

THE DUOMO. The massive cathedral, built in spooky Tuscan Gothic, houses Bishop Guido Tarlati's **tomb.** Carved reliefs relate stories about the iconoclast's unconventional life. Light filters into the Gothic interior through the series of seven 20-foot circular stained glass windows designed by Gugliemo de Marcillat. The *Capella della Madonna del Conforto*, off the severe nave, holds a terra-cotta *Assumption* by Andrea della Robbia. *(Up V. Andrea Cesalpino from P.S. Francesco. Cathedral and tomb open daily 7am-12:30pm and 3-6:30pm.)*

CHIESA DI SAN DOMENICA. As was often the case, the Dominicans built their church on the end of town opposite the Franciscan establishment. The church contains a superb Cimabue crucifix (1265), Spinello Aretino's *Annunciation*, and the Marcillat rose window. *(Take V. Andrea Celaspino from P.S. Francesco, turn left at P. Liberta onto V. Ricasorli and then right onto V. di Sassoverde, leading to the chiesa. Open daily 8am-noon and 2:30-7:30pm. Hours may be reduced depending on staff availability. Closed during mass.)* Beyond the church lies **Vasari's house,** which the historian built for himself and decorated with impressive frescoes depicting his peers. He even painted himself contemplating the view from one of the windows. *(V. XX Settembre, 55. ☎ 0575 30 03 01. Open M and W-Sa 8:30am-2pm and 4-7pm, Su 9am-1pm. Free.)*

🎵 ENTERTAINMENT

Arezzo's **antique fairs** take place in and around P. Grande on the first Sunday and preceding Saturday of every month. Beautiful antique furniture and religious paraphernalia are sold alongside bric-a-brac. The **Giostra del Saraceno,** a medieval joust, is performed on the third Sunday of June and the first Sunday of September. In a ritual recalling the Crusades, "knights" representing the four quarters of the town charge with lances at a wooden effigy of a Turk.

🔼 DAYTRIPS FROM AREZZO

SANSEPOLCRO

Sansepolcro is most easily accessible by the hourly SITA bus from Arezzo (1hr., 6 per day, L5400/€2.80). The bus arrives just outside the walls of the old city.

A bustling industrial town lost in a valley among Tuscany's densely forested hills, Sansepolcro's claim to fame is as the birthplace of painter Piero della Francesca. The ▣**Museo Civico** displays some of della Francesca's finest works. *The Resurrection* features a triumphant Jesus towering above the sleeping guards, bearing a red and white banner. A muscular Christ rests one foot on his coffin and meets the viewer's eyes with an intense, disconcerting gaze. The polyptych *Madonna della Misericordia* depicts a stern Madonna. (V. Aggiunti, 65. ☎ 0575 73 22 18. Open June-Sept. daily 9am-1:30pm and 2:30-7:30pm; Oct.-May 9:30am-1pm and 2:30-6pm. L10,000/€5.16, over 65 and groups L7000/€3.62, ages 10-16 L5000/€2.58.)

Sansepolcro's **tourist office,** P. Garibaldi, 2, has maps of the region. From the bus stop, enter the old city on V.N. Aggiunti. Follow the street for five blocks, until you pass the Museo Civico on your right. Take a right under an arch onto V.G. Matteotti, and an immediate left into P. Garibaldi. The tourist office is one block ahead on the left. (☎/fax 0575 74 05 36. Open daily 9:30am-1pm and 3:30-6:30pm.) **Alpes de la Luna Travel** books tours of the area. (☎ 0575 73 63 95.)

Sansepolcro is best seen as a daytrip, but the comfortable **Albergo Fiorentino,** V. Luca Pacioli, 60, two blocks from the Museo Civico, has well-furnished, welcoming rooms and a beautiful terrace overlooking the city. Aromas waft from the elegant but affordable restaurant downstairs. (☎ 0575 74 03 50; fax 74 03 70. Breakfast L10,000/€5.16. Singles L80,000/€41.32; doubles L120,000/€62; triples L150,000/€77.47) **La Cisterna,** V.S. Giuseppe, 27, off V. Matteotti near the *duomo,* offers delicious freshly fare. (☎ 0575 74 09 38. Homemade pasta and *secondi* from L12,000/€6.20. Cover L3000/€1.55. Open Tu-Su 12:30-2:30pm and 7:30-10pm. MC/V.)

MUSEO MADONNA DEL PARTO

To reach Monterchi, take the Arezzo-Sansepolcro bus to Le Ville. Follow the signs to Monterchi and then to the chapel (1hr. walk), or change immediately to another bus to Monterchi. Bus service out of Monterchi (last bus to Sansepolcro 7:57pm, to Arezzo 6:35pm).

Halfway between Arezzo and Sansepolcro, outside the town of **Monterchi,** lies the **Museo Madonna del Parto.** This tiny chapel, now converted into a two-room museum, displays Piero della Francesca's recently restored *Madonna del Parto,* the sole rendition of a pregnant Madonna in all of Renaissance art. The Virgin Mary is flanked by two angels upholding a lavish curtain. (Open Apr. 1-Oct. 26 Tu-Su 9am-1pm and 2-7pm; July and Aug. additional hours 9pm-midnight; Oct. 27-Mar. 31 Tu-Su 9am-1pm and 2-6pm; L5000/€2.58, students L2500/€1.29, under 15 free.)

SIENA
☎0577

Many travelers rush directly from Rome to Florence, ignoring beauteous medieval Siena. The city is, however, more than Florence and Rome's poor cousin. During the 13th century, Siena's wool trade, crafty bankers, and sophisticated government fashioned the city into a European metropolis. Siena's rise, however, threatened Florence. In 1230, cheeky Florentines catapulted **feces** over Siena's walls, in the hopes it might trigger a plague. The plot failed, however, and 30 years later Siena routed the mighty Florentines at the Battle of Montaperti. The century of grandiose construction that followed endowed the city with its flamboyant architecture. Siena lost its preeminence in 1348, when the Black Death claimed half of the city's population. But from the destruction, Siena produced St. Catherine (1347-1380), an ecstatic illiterate whose interventions in church politics and fanatical following prompted the church to return to Italy from Avignon; and St. Bernadino (1487-1564), a wanderer who revived the teachings of St. Francis. These days, the Sienese proudly celebrate their rich past with events like the semiannual Palio, a wild horse race between the city's 17 competing *contrade.* An intoxicating display of pageantry, the Palio is the main attraction of Siena's tourist industry.

▛ TRANSPORTATION

Trains: in P. Rosselli, several km from city center. Ticket office open daily 5:50am-8:25pm. To Siena from Rome and points south, change at Chiusi; change at Florence from points north. Luggage storage available (p. 348). Hourly departures to **Florence** (1½hr., L8800/€4.54) and **Rome** (2½hr.; L31,400/€16.22).

Buses: TRA-IN/SITA (☎0577 20 42 45) ticket office in P. Gramsci, near heart of the city; take the stairs that go under the *piazza.* Buses are the easiest and most convenient way to reach Siena. Frequent buses link Siena to the rest of Tuscany, making Siena an ideal base for exploring the surrounding area. Some intercity buses leave from P. Gramsci and others from the train station. Schedule and destinations listed on a large display in the underground terminal in P. Gramsci. Open daily 5:45am-8:15pm. To: **Arezzo** (6 per day, L8000/€4.13); **Florence** (express bus every hr.; L12,000/€6.20); **Montalcino** (9 per day, L5500/€2.84); **Montepulciano** (3 per day, L8000/€4.13); **San Gimignano** (every hr., L8600/€4.44, change at Poggibonsi); **Volterra** (4 per day, L8400/€4.34, get off at Colle Val d'Elsa and buy tickets at newsstand for a **CPT** bus to Volterra). **TRA-IN** also runs the bus network within Siena. Buy tickets (1hr., L1500/€0.77) at the office in P. Gramsci or any commercial center that displays a TRA-IN sign.

Taxis: Radio Taxi (☎0577 492 22). Open daily 7am-9pm.

Car Rental: Intercar, V. Mentana, 108 (☎0577 411 48). Suzuki cars available from L156,000/€80.57 per day. L400/€0.21 extra for every km over 200. 10% discount for rentals of 3 days or more. 21+. Open M-Sa 9am-1pm and 3:30-8pm. MC/V.

Bike and Moped Rental: DF Moto, V. Massetana Romana, 54 (☎0577 27 19 05). Rents mountain bikes. **Automotocicli Perozzi,** V. del Romitorio, 5 (☎0577 22 31 57). Rents bikes and mopeds. Open M-Sa 8:30am-12:30pm.

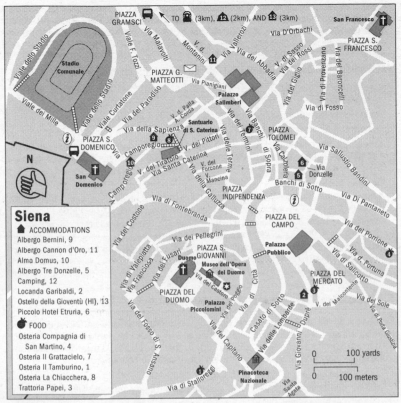

Siena

♠ ACCOMMODATIONS
Albergo Bernini, 9
Albergo Cannon d'Oro, 11
Alma Domus, 10
Albergo Tre Donzelle, 5
Camping, 12
Locanda Garibaldi, 2
Ostello della Gioventù (HI), 13
Piccolo Hotel Etruria, 6

🍎 FOOD
Osteria Compagnia di
   San Martino, 4
Osteria Il Grattacielo, 7
Osteria Il Tamburino, 1
Osteria La Chiacchera, 8
Trattoria Papei, 3

ORIENTATION AND PRACTICAL INFORMATION

From the train station, cross the street and take bus #3, 4, 7, 8, 9, 10, 14, 17, or 77 to the town center. These buses stop in either **Piazza del Sale** or **Piazza Gramsci**. Some buses actually stop just before P. Gramsci, making it difficult to know when to get off; ask the bus driver. From either *piazza*, follow the numerous signs to **Piazza del Campo** (a.k.a. Il Campo), Siena's historic center. Buy local bus tickets from vending machines by the station entrance or at the *biglietteria* window for bus tickets (L1500/€0.77). From the bus station in P.S. Domenico, follow the signs to P. del Campo. **Piazza del Duomo** lies 100m west of Il Campo.

TOURIST AND LOCAL SERVICES

Tourist Office: APT, Il Campo, 56 (☎0577 28 05 51; fax 27 06 76), provides local info. Open Mar. 16-Nov. 14 M-Sa 8:30am-7:30pm, Su 8:30am-2pm; Nov. 15-Mar. 15 M-Sa 8:30am-1pm and 3-7pm, Su 9am-1pm. **Prenotazioni Alberghiere** (☎0577 28 80 84; fax 28 02 90), in P.S. Domenico, finds lodgings for L3000/€1.55. Open Apr.-Oct. M-Sa 9am-8pm; Nov.-Mar. M-Sa 9am-7pm.

Budget Travel: CTS, V. Sallustio Bandini, 21 (☎0577 28 58 08). Student travel services. Open M-F 9am-12:30pm and 3:30-7pm.

English-Language Bookstore: Libreria Ticci, V. delle Terme, 5/7 (☎0577 28 00 10). Extensive selection of books, including travel and fiction sections. Open daily 9am-8pm. **Feltrinelli,** V. Banchi di Sopra, 52. Large selection of English language classic and popular fiction in paperback, and some English language magazines and newspapers.

Laundromat: Lavorapido, V. di Pantaneto, 38. Wash L5000/€2.58 per 8kg. Dry L5000/€2.58. Open daily 8am-9pm. **Onda Blu,** Casato di Sotto, 17 (☎0800 86 13 46). Wash L5000/€2.58 per 6½kg. Dry L5000/€2.58. Open daily 8am-10pm.

Luggage Storage: At train station. L4-7000/€2.07-3.65 for 12hr. Open 24hr.

EMERGENCY AND COMMUNICATIONS

Emergency: ☎113. **Police: Questura** (☎112), on V. del Castoro near *duomo*. **Medical Assistance:** ☎118.

Ambulance: Misericordia, V. del Porrione, 49 (☎0577 28 00 28).

Hospital: V. Le Scotte, 14 (bus #77 from P. Gramsci).

Late-Night Pharmacy: Farmacia del Campo, P. del Campo, 26. Pharmacies in Siena rotate late-night shifts. Open daily 9am-1pm and 4-8pm; in winter 9am-1pm and 3:30-7:30pm.

Internet Access:

Netgate, V. Giovanni Dupre, 12 (☎0577 22 61 85). L9000/€4.65 per hr., students L7000/€3.62 per hr. Open M-Sa 11am-midnight, Su 3-10pm. V. del Porrione, 88/90. Open M-Sa 11am-9pm.

Engineering Systems, V. Stalloreggi, 8 (☎0577 27 47 52). L8000/€4.13 per hr., student L7000/€3.62 per hr. Open daily 10am-8pm.

Post Office: P. Matteotti, 36. Exchanges currency (L5000/€2.58 fee for amounts over L10,000/€5.16). Open M-Sa 8:15am-7pm.

Postal Code: 53100.

▐ ACCOMMODATIONS & CAMPING

Finding a room in Siena can be difficult between Easter and October. Book months ahead if coming during *Palio* (see p. 353). For visits of a week or longer, rooms in private homes are an attractive option. The APT and Prenotazioni Alberghiere tourist offices can provide a list of private rooms.

Albergo Tre Donzelle, V. Donzelle, 5 (☎0577 28 03 58; fax 22 39 33). Basic rooms furnished with tasteful dark wood and speckled tiles. Dining area and sitting room. Very convenient to Il Campo, but often noisy as a result. Curfew 12:30am. Singles L60,000/€30.99; doubles L85,000/€43.90, with bath L110,000/€56.81. Additional bed L30,000/€15.50 in rooms without bath, L35,000/€18.08 in those with bath. MC/V.

Piccolo Hotel Etruria, V. Donzelle, 3 (☎0577 28 80 88 or 28 36 85; fax 28 84 61). Immaculate, modern rooms with floral bedspreads, phones, TVs, and hair dryers. Breakfast L7000/€3.62. Curfew 11:30pm. Singles L70,000/€36.15, with bath L80,000/€41.32; doubles with bath L130,000/€67.14; triples with bath L168,000/€86.76; quads with bath L206,000/€106.39. AmEx/MC/V.

Ostello della Gioventù "Guidoriccio" (HI), V. Fiorentina, 89 (☎0577 522 12), in Località Lo Stellino, a 20min. bus ride from the *centro*. Take bus #15 or 10 in P. Gramsci. Su evening bus service is infrequent. Bus #15 stops at front door of the hostel. Ask driver when to get off bus #10. From stop, continue in the direction bus was traveling and take 1st right on winding uphill road. Look for small sign on right side pointing to the left up a driveway. Good value. Breakfast included. Dinner L17,000/€8.78. Curfew Apr.-Oct. 1am; Nov.-Mar. 11:30pm. Reservations recommended. Dorms L26,000/€13.43 per person; singles and doubles (with bath) L40,000/€20.66 per person. MC/V.

Santvario S. Caterina Alma Domus, V. Camporeggio, 37 (☎0577 441 77; fax 476 01), behind S. Domenico. Spotless rooms with antique metal-frame beds, polished stone floors and crucifixes. A small courtyard at the entrance is filled with potted plants and a number of benches. Curfew 11:30pm. Doubles with bath L100,000/€51.65; triples with bath L130,000/€67.14; quads with bath L150,000/€77.47.

Albergo Bernini, V. della Sapienza, 15 (☎/fax 0577 28 90 47; bernini@tin.it; www.albergobernini.com). Antique-laden rooms have picture windows with views of the *duomo*. Outdoor, canopied breakfast patio is lined with plants and full of exotic birds.

Breakfast L12,000/€6.20. Curfew midnight. July-Sept. enormous singles L150,000/
€77.47; doubles with bath L150,000/€77.47; triples with bath L170,000/€87.78;
quads with bath and A/C L250,000/€129.11. Off-season prices drop 20%.

Albergo Cannon d'Oro, V. Montanini, 28 (☎0577 443 21), near P. Matteotti. Green
neon welcomes you to the formica filled lobby. Luxurious rooms with lovely views.
Wheelchair accessible. Breakfast L10,000/€5.16. Singles L90,000/€46.48; doubles
with bath L150,000/€77.47; triples with bath L180,000/€92.96; quads with bath
L205,000/€105.87. AmEx/MC/V.

Locanda Garibaldi, V. Giovanni Dupré, 18 (☎0577 28 42 04), behind the Palazzo Pubblico and P. del Campo. Whitewashed walls and dark-ribbed ceilings. Restaurant downstairs. All rooms with bath. Curfew midnight. Reservations accepted a few days ahead.
Doubles L120,000/€62; triples L150,000/€77.47; quads L180,000/€92.96. MC/V.

Camping: Colleverde, Strada di Scacciapensieri, 47 (☎0577 28 00 44). Take bus #3
or 8 from P. del Sale; ask to be sure you are on the right route. Buses run every ½hr.;
late #8 buses (9:45 and 10:21pm, last bus) run from P. Gramsci. Late-night #10
buses (11:45pm and 1:10am) from P. Gramisci also run to the campground. Well-kept,
with grocery store, restaurant, and bar nearby. Open mid-Mar. to mid-Nov. Pool L3000/
€1.55, children L2000/€1.03. L15,000/€7.75 per person, ages 3-11 L8000/€4.13.

◖ FOOD

Siena specializes in rich pastries. The most famous is *panforte*, a dense concoc-
tion of honey, almonds, and citron, first baked as trail mix for the Crusaders. For a
lighter snack try *ricciarelli*, soft almond cookies with powdered vanilla on top.
Sample either one at the **Bar/Pasticceria Nannini,** the oldest *pasticceria* in Siena,
with branches at V. Banchi di Sopra, 22-24, and throughout town. **Enoteca Italiana,**
in the Fortezza Medicea near the entrance off V. Cesare Maccari, sells the finest
Italian wines, including *Brunello, Barolo, Asti Spumante* and *Vernaccia* from
L3000/€1.55 per glass. (☎/fax 0577 22 69 89. Open M-Th, Su 10am-8pm; F-Sa 10am-
10pm.) Siena's **open-air market** fills P. La Lizza each Wednesday from 8am to 1pm.
For groceries, try the **Consortio Agrario supermarket,** V. Pianigiani, 5, off P. Salim-
beri. (Open M-Sa 8am-7:30pm.) Or head to the **COOP supermarket,** a couple of
blocks from the train station—with your back to the station turn left, then left
again at the overpass (one block); the supermarket is in the shopping complex
immediately to your right. (Open M-Sa 8am-7:30pm.)

◙ Osteria La Chiacchera, Costa di S. Antonio, 4 (☎0577 28 06 31), next to Santuario di
Santa Caterina. You can't pronounce the name, but who cares? Eat in the tiny dining
room or perch on the outdoor seating (propped up with blocks) on the steep street. The
homemade pasta (L8-10,000/€4.13-5.16) and house red wine (L5000/€2.58 per
half liter) are divine. Tagliatelli with wild boar (L10,000/€5.16). *Secondi* L9-13,000/
€4.65-6.71. Cover L2000/€1.03. Open W-M 12:30-3pm and 7-10:30pm. MC/V.

◙ Trattoria Papei, P. del Mercato, 6 (☎0577 28 08 94). P. del Mercato is on the far side
of Palazzo Pubblico from Il Campo. This delicious trattoria will greet you with outdoor
tables and a stone-arched dining room filled with a lively local crowd. A huge range of
homemade pasta dishes (L12,000/€6.20) as well as traditional *secondi* (L11-
15,000/€5.68-7.75). The wild boar with paprika, oil and olives (L15,000/€7.75) is a
blissful, carnivorous mess o'meat. The house red (L16,000/€8.26 per liter) is excellent. Cover L2000/€1.03. Open Tu-Su 12:30-3pm and 7-10:30pm. AmEx/MC/V.

Osteria Il Grattacielo, V. dei Pontani, 8. Between V. dei Termini and Banchi di Sopra on
a tiny street. Olives, stewed baby artichokes, sun-dried tomatoes in oil, bread salads
with basil and tomato, hunks of salami and pecorino cheese, and many other culinary
delights. The pricing system is a mystery, but a sampling of 5 or 6 of their exquisite
dishes (quite a lot of food) plus bread and a quarter liter of the delicious house red will
run you about L14,000/€7.23. Open M-Sa 8am-8pm.

Osteria Compagnia di San Martino, V. Porrione, 25 (☎0577 493 06). Just off Il Campo, this *osteria* serves Tuscan cuisine at rickety tables on the quiet street or in the A/C upstairs dining room. The homemade pasta with wild boar sauce (L12,000/€6.20) is fantastic. *Primi* L10-14,000/€5.16-7.23; *secondi* L14-20,000/€7.23-10.33. Cover L2000/€1.03. Service charge 10%. Open M-Sa noon-3pm and 7-10:30pm. MC/V.

Osteria il Tamburino, V. Stalloreggi, 11 (☎0577 28 03 06). From P. del Duomo, follow V. del Capitano to P. della Postierla; turn right on V. di Stalloreggi. *Primi* L9-14,000/€4.65-7.23; *secondi* L10-25,000/€5.16-12.91. House red L10,000/€5.16 per liter. Cover L3000/€1.55. Open M-Sa noon-2:30pm and 7-9:30pm. MC/V.

Antigiana Gelateria, V. d. Città, 31 (☎0577 28 80 76), off P. San Domenico. Cone from L2500/€1.29. Open Mar.-Sept. daily 8am-midnight; Oct.-Feb. 8am-10pm.

SIGHTS

> **SIEN-ANY SIGHTS?** Siena offers two *biglietto cumulativi*. The first allows 5 days worth of entry into the Museo dell'Opera Metropolitana, the baptistery, the Piccolomini Library, and the Oratory of St. Bernadino (L14,000/€7.23). The second covers those same four monuments and museums plus 5 others, including the Museo Civico, and is valid for 7 days (L30,000/€15.49). Both tickets can be bought at any of the included sights.

■ **IL CAMPO.** Siena radiates from the **Piazza del Campo,** the shell-shaped brick square designed specifically for civic events. The *piazza's* brick paving is divided into nine sections, representing the city's medieval "Council of Nine." Dante referred to the square in his account of the real-life drama of Provenzan Salvani, the heroic Sienese merchant who panhandled in Il Campo to pay for a friend's ransom. Later, Sienese mystics such as San Bernadino used the *piazza* as a public auditorium. Now it has the dubious honor of entertaining local teenagers, wide-eyed tourists, and souvenir carts by days; in the evening, when the elegant cafes pull back their awnings and the Sienese strut in a ritual *passeggiata*, the *piazza* glitters with decadence. Twice each summer, the **Palio** reduces the sublimely mellow Il Campo to mayhem as horses race around its outer edge (see p. 353).

At the highest point of Il Campo's sloping plane is the **Fonte Gaia,** surrounded by reproductions of native Jacopo della Quercia's famous carvings (1408-1419). The originals are in the **Spedale di S. Maria della Scala** (see p. 352). The water here courses through the same 25km aqueduct that has refreshed Siena since the 14th century. Closing the bottom of the shell-shaped *piazza* is the graceful castle-like **Palazzo Pubblico** with its imposing 102m high clock tower, the **Torre del Mangia**.

In front of the *palazzo* is the **Cappella di Piazza,** which was built in 1348, but took 100 years to complete—rats succeeded where **turd-bombs** failed (see p. 346), bringing the Black Death to Siena. The transition from Gothic to Renaissance architecture lies where pointed arches give way to gracefully rounded ones.

■ **PALAZZO PUBBLICO.** This impressive medieval building was home to Siena's Council of Nine in the Middle Ages. It still houses city government offices, but the main draw for tourists is the **Museo Civico,** which is home to a huge collection of masterpieces of Sienese art. Although the collection pieces range from medieval triptychs to 18th-century landscapes, the museum's greatest treasure is its collection of late medieval to early Renaissance painting in the distinctive Sienese style. The **Sala del Mappamondo,** named for a lost series of astronomical frescoes, displays Simone Martini's *Maestà (Enthroned Virgin)*, carrying, along with its overt religious quality, a civic undercurrent; the parchment the Christ Child holds is inscribed with the city motto of upholding justice, and the steps of the canopied throne are engraved with two stanzas from Dante's *La Divina Commedia*. In the next room, the **Sala dei Nove** exhibits Pietro and Ambrogio Lorenzetti's famous frescoes, the *Allegories of Good and Bad Government and their Effects on*

Town and Country. The fresco on the right is well preserved, showing the Utopia created by good government. The fresco on the left, flaking away, depicts thieves, devils, and lost souls in the land of bad government. *(Open Nov.-Feb. daily 10am-4pm; Mar.-Oct. 10am-7pm. L12,000/€6.20, students L6000/€3.10, under 11 free.)*

The Palazzo Pubblico's other star attraction is the **Torre de Mangia**. A gluttonous bell-ringer nicknamed "Mangiaguadagni" ("eat the profits") provided the tower its name. Siena's Council of Nine commissioned the tower to overshadow any other. At 102m, the tower was the second highest in medieval Italy, after the one in Cremona. *(Same hours as Museo Civico. L10,000/€5.16 or L18,000/€9.30 combined ticket with Museo Civico.)*

■**THE DUOMO.** The city's dark green and white striped *duomo*, atop one of its seven hills, is one of the few full Gothic cathedrals south of the Alps. Civic pride demanded that the 13th-century *duomo* combine enormous scale with a prominent position, but the limited size of the hill posed a design problem. The apse would have hung in mid-air over the edge of the hill, but the Sienese, doubting a miraculous solution to the problem, turned to more earthly preventative measures and build the **baptistery** (see p. 352). A huge arch, part of a striped wall to your right facing the front of the cathedral, is the sole remnant of Siena's 1339 plan to construct a new nave, which, if the plan had succeeded, would have made this *duomo* the largest church in all of Christendom. The grandiose effort ended when the plague killed all the construction workers for miles around. One of its side aisles has been enclosed and turned into the **Museo dell'Opera Metropolitana** (see below). Even though the city's lofty ambitions were humbled, the existing cathedral is one of Italy's finest. Elegant statues of philosophers, sibyls, and prophets, all by Giovanni Pisano, give way to impressive spires that pierce the sky.

The bronze sun symbol on the facade of the *duomo* was the brainchild of St. Bernadino of Siena, who wanted the feuding Sienese to relinquish their loyalty to emblems of nobility and unite under this symbol of the risen Christ. Not too surprisingly, his efforts were futile; the Sienese continue to identify with the animal symbols of their *contrada*. The **marble pavement** on the floor is, like the rest of the *duomo*, extremely ornate, and depicts such widely varying themes as alchemy and the Slaughter of the Innocents. To preserve the pieces, most of them are covered, except for in September. It is then that visitors can look for the works by Machese d'Adamo, perhaps the most spectacular in the entire building. Halfway up the left aisle is the **Piccolomini altar,** designed by Andrea Bregno in 1503. Although it appears to be the facade of an entire building unto itself, the altar, which is just an altar, contains niches that house life-like statues of St. Peter and St. Paul, sculpted by Michelangelo early in his career. In the neighboring chapel, Donatello's bronze statue of St. John the Baptist remains graceful in his emaciation. The lavish **Libreria Piccolomini,** commissioned by Pope Pius III, houses the elaborately illustrated books of his uncle Pius II. The library also contains a Roman copy of the Greek statue, *The Three Graces*, 15th-century illuminated scores, and a fresco cycle by Pinturicchio. *(Duomo open Mar. 15-Oct. 31 daily 9am-7:30pm; Nov. 1-Mar. 14 10am-1pm and 2:30pm-5pm. Modest dress required. Free, except in Sept. when floor is uncovered, L8-10,000/€4.13-5.16. Library, same hours, L3000/€1.55.)*

MUSEO DELL'OPERA METROPOLITANA. The cathedral museum holds all the art that won't fit in the church. The first floor contains some of the foremost Gothic statuary in Italy, all by Giovanni Pisano. Upstairs is the magnificent 700-year-old ■*Maestà*, by Duccio di Buoninsegna, originally the screen of the cathedral's altar. Dismembered in 1771 by voracious art collectors, most of the narrative panels have been returned to the Sienese except for a handful held by the National Gallery in London, the Frick Gallery in New York, and the National Gallery of Art in Washington. Other noteworthy works in the museum are the Byzantine *Madonna degli Occhi Coressi* and paintings by Simone Martini and Lorenzetti. Find the **Scala del Falciatore,** off one of the upper levels of the museum (follow the signs for the "panorama") to climb onto a balcony over the nave. An exceedingly narrow spiral staircase leads up a tiny tower for a breathtaking view of the *duomo* and the entire city. *(Museum housed in part of the unfinished nave on the right side of the Duomo. Open Mar. 15-Oct. 31 daily 9am-7:30pm; Nov. 1-Mar. 14 9am-1:30pm. L6000/€3.01.)*

SPEDALE DI S. MARIA DELLA SCALA. Originally a hospital dating from the 13th century, the Spedale is now a museum, displaying its original frescoes, chapels and vaults as well as beautiful paintings and statuary throughout a maze of rooms. The **Sala del Pellegrinaio,** used as a ward until the late-20th century, contains a fresco cycle by Vecchietta, often considered to be his masterpiece. In the first panel, the pregnant mother of the legendary (probably fictional) founder of the hospital, Beato Sorore, dreams of the future good deeds of her son. The most artistically interesting room, the **Sagrestia Vecchia** or **Cappello del Sacro Chiedo,** houses masterful 15th-century Sienese frescoes. Downstairs from the entrance you can peer out curtained windows at the view into a shallow valley before ducking into the underground chapels and vaults—a startling contrast until you remember the hospital was built on a hillside. The dim little vaults were the site of rituals and "acts of piety for the dead" performed by various contra fraternities, none of which included animal sacrifice, dismemberment, or necrophilia. One level down is the entrance to the **Museo Archaeologico,** included in admission to the Spedale. Established in 1933 to collect and preserve Etruscan artifacts from the Siena area, the museum is now housed almost entirely in the eerie medieval underground water works of the city. Signs will lead you through the dank, labyrinthine brick-and-concrete-vaulted passageways before you emerge into various rooms full of well-lit glass cases of Etruscan pottery and coins. *(Open Mar.-Nov. daily 10am-6pm; Dec.-Feb. 10:30am-4:30pm. L10,000/€5.16, students L6000/€3.10.)*

PINACOTECA NAZIONALE. Siena's superb art gallery features works by every major artist of the highly stylized Sienese school. The masters represented include the seven magnificent followers of Onccio—Simone Martini, the Lorenzetti brothers, Bartolo di Fredi, Da Domenico, Sano di Pietro, and Il Sodoma (no relation to the pillar of salt)—as well as many others. The museum is refreshingly free of the tourist hordes that can make it difficult to appreciate many of Florence's prime collections. *(V.S. Pietro, 29, in the Palazzo Buonsignori down the street from the cathedral museum. Open Tu-Sa 8:15am-7:15pm, Su 8:15am-1:15pm, M 8:30am-1:30pm. L8000/€4.13, EU citizens 18-26 L4000/€2.07, EU citizens under 18 and over 65 free.)*

SANTUARIO DI SANTA CATERINA. The sanctuary honors the daughter of Siena, a simple girl who had a vision of herself as Christ's bride. She influenced popes, became the patron saint of Italy, and finally split from the Saviour over issues with his Dad's split personality. The building, converted into a Renaissance *loggia*, opens onto many Baroque chapels. The **Chiesa del Crosifisso** is impressive. *(Entrance on V.S. Caterina, down from P.S. Domenico. Open daily 9am-12:30pm and 2:30-6pm. Free.)*

BAPTISTERY. Lavish and intricate frescoes, depicting the lives of Christ and St. Anthony, decorate the baptistery. The centerpiece of the baptistery, however, is the hexagonal Renaissance **baptismal font** (1417-30). Ghiberti's *Baptism of Christ* and *John in Prison* stand next to Donatello's *Herod's Feast*. *(Baptistery open Mar. 15-Oct. 31 daily 9am-7:30pm; Nov. 1-Mar. 14 10am-1pm and 2:30-5pm. L4000/€2.07.)*

OTHER SIGHTS. As in other Italian towns, the Franciscans and the Dominicans have rival basilicas at opposite ends of town. The **Chiesa di San Domenico** contains Andrea Vanni's portrait of St. Catherine and a number of other dramatic frescoes which render the saint in a state of religious fervor. The exquisite *cappella* inside, dedicated to St. Catherine, was built in 1460 to store her preserved head (served with some fava beans and a nice *chianti*). Sadly, the chapel does not serve its original purpose. *(P.S. Domenico. Open Nov. 1-Mar. 31 daily 9am-12:55pm and 3-6pm; Apr. 1-Oct. 31 7am-12:55pm and 3-6:30pm.)* The **Chiesa di San Francesco** houses two frescoes by Pietro and Ambrogio Lorenzetti, moved into the church after a fire in the last century. *(Open daily 7:30am-noon and 3:30-7pm.)* The *Palio*-obsessed may enjoy one of Siena's 17 **contrade museums.** Each neighborhood organization maintains its own collection of costumes, artifacts, banners, and icons, ranging from the eagle and caterpillar to the she-wolf and tortoise. *(Most require an appointment—ask at the tourist office. Schedule visits at least 1 week in advance.)*

🎵 ENTERTAINMENT

Siena's ▓Palio occurs twice a year, on July 2 and August 16. As the bare-backed horse races approach, Siena's emotional temperature rises. Ten of the 17 *contrade* make elaborate preparations. Young partisans sporting the colors of their *contrada* chant in packs on the street, singing often obscene lyrics to the tune of "Twinkle, twinkle, little star." Five trial races take place over the three days leading up to the race, and a final trial runs the same morning. On the eve of the race revelry concludes around 3am. At 2:30pm on the day of the race, the horses are led into the churches of their respective *contrade* and blessed. A two-hour parade of heralds and flag-bearers prefaces the anarchy to come with regal pomp. The last piece in the procession is the Palio itself, a banner depicting the Madonna and Child, drawn in a cart by white oxen (the race is called *Il Palio* because a *palio* is given to the winner). The start of the race can be the most exciting part. Riders battle for position at the start until the announcer is satisfied that all is in order and he drops the rope without warning. The race begins at 7:30pm and it takes the jockeys about 90 seconds to tear around Il Campo three times. During the race, they have free rein—according to the age-old, barbaric set of rules that guide the event, they are allowed, and encouraged, to whip their opponents. The straps they use are no ordinary pieces of leather; they are made from the skin of a bull's penis, especially durable and said to leave deep welts and psychological scars.

To stay in Siena during the *Palio*, book rooms at least four months in advance—especially budget accommodations. Write the APT in March or April for a list of companies and individuals that rent rooms. Inquire about reserving seats in the grandstands for the best view of the race, although the cost can be prohibitive. Otherwise, you can stand with the other plebeians in the "infield" of the *piazza* for free if you stake out a spot early. From there, you may only be able to see the frenzied sea of fans surrounding you—get to the Campo by early afternoon to avoid this scenario. For information on *Il Palio*, ask at the tourist office and pick up the excellent program (available in English).

In late July, the **Accademia Chigiana** (☎ 0577 461 52) sponsors a music festival, the **Settimana Musicale Sienese.** Siena also hosts a jazz festival in July, featuring internationally known musicians. For information, call ☎ 0577 27 14 01.

🏙 DAYTRIPS FROM SIENA

SAN GALGANO
Get a car or moped; for more information, contact Siena's tourist office.

Slightly removed from a winding country pass between Siena and Massa Marittima, the decaying 13th-century **Cistercian abbey of San Galgano** was once one of the richest and most powerful in Tuscany. Its monks served as treasurers and judges for the communes of Siena and Volterra, helped construct the *duomo* in Siena, and became bishops and saints (but only after extensive lobbying). But by the mid-16th century, widespread corruption spelled the church's decline. The derelict abbey, the foremost specimen of Cistercian Gothic architecture in Italy, lies hidden in dense woodland. It stands without a roof, utterly exposed to the elements. As nature slowly undoes the Gothic church, the absence of vaulted ceilings makes room for blue skies and tiny birds that chirp lightly in the stony nooks.

THE CHIANTI REGION
Buses connect Siena to Castellina and Radda, major bases for exploring vineyards (45min.-1hr., 5 per day, L4700/€2.43). Three buses a day also connect Radda with Florence (1½hr., last bus to Florence 6:10pm, last bus to Siena 6:35pm).

Siena lies within easy reach of the Chianti region, whose wines of the same name have become justifiably famous throughout the world. The private **tourist office,** V. della Rocca, 12, just off the central square **(Piazza del Comune)** in Castellina can help find accommodations and provide information about the town and the area. (☎0577 74 60 20; info@collinverdi.it. Open M-Sa 10am-1pm and 3-6pm; in winter 10am-1pm.) Numerous shops sell the trademark Chianti; one good choice is **Le Volte Enoteca,** V. Ferruccio, 12, a block from P. del Comune, where you can buy a bottle starting at L9000/€4.65. (☎0577 74 13 54; fax 74 28 91; rolmast@tin.it. Open Mar.-Oct. daily 9am-7:30pm; Nov.-Jan. Th-Tu 9:30am-12:30pm and 4:30-7:30pm; closed Feb. AmEx/MC/V.) For a huge variety of pizza slices starting at L1300/ €0.67, head to **Pizza Chiantigiana,** V. Chiantigiana, 7, just off the main intersection where the bus stops. (☎0577 74 12 91. Open M-Sa 11am-10:30pm.)

While Castellina has a few nice blocks in the center of town, it is not nearly as attractive as many other Tuscan hill towns. Rather than spend all your time here, consider heading to **Radda in Chianti,** just 9km away, on the same bus from Siena. Radda's **tourist office,** P. Ferrucci, 1, in the town's main square, has a multilingual staff willing to help you find accommodations. They can refer you to private companies that offer tours of local wineries, usually a bus trip to 4 or more wineries with tastings and snacks at each (L200-300,000/€103.29-154.94 per person). Since many wineries give free tastings, consider getting a map of local wineries and exploring them on your own. Ask the tourist office about the few wineries within walking distance of the town center. To reach the tourist office, walk two blocks from the bus stop with the city walls on your left. Take a left toward the public gardens and then a left into the city onto V. Roma, the main street in town, which leads to P. Ferrucci. (☎0577 73 84 94; proradda@chiantinet.it. Open Apr.-Nov. M-Sa 10am-1pm and 3-7pm, Su 10am-1pm; Dec.-Mar. M-Sa 10am-1pm.)

It's hard to beat the clean, modern rooms of **Le Camere di Giovannino,** V. Roma, 6-8, a few meters from the tourist office. All rooms have bath. (☎/fax 0577 73 80 56. Singles L80,000/€41.32; doubles L100,000/€51.65; triples L120,000/€62.) Like Castellina, Radda is home to numerous *enoteche;* try **Casa Porciatti,** P. IV Novembre, 1-3, within the town's 14th-century walls. Bottles start at L13,000/€6.71. They also sell their homemade pork sausages and cheese. (☎0577 73 80 55; fax 73 82 34; casaporciatti@chiantinet.it; www.chiantinet.it/casaporciatti. Open May-Oct. M-Sa 7:45am-1pm and 5-8pm, Su 7:45am-1pm; Nov.-Apr. M-Sa 8am-1pm and 4:30-7:30pm.) The cheapest place to get wine, however, is the **Coop Market,** V. Roma, 26, where bottles start at L6000/€3.10. (Open M-Tu and Th-Sa 8am-1pm and 4:30-8pm, W 8am-1pm.) If you don't want to fix your own food, **Ristorante Il Giarrosto,** V. Roma, 41, has a tourist *menù* for L25,000/€12.91, including pasta, meat dishes, dessert, coffee, wine, and water. (☎0577 73 80 10. Open Th-Tu for lunch and dinner.) A cheap, delicious option with take out or table service is **Enoteca Dante Alighieri,** P. Dante Alighieri, 1, opposite the bus stop. They specialize in *bruschette* and *crostini* from L4000/€2.07 and have an extensive wine list. (☎0577 73 88 15. Open Su-F 7am-10pm and Sa 7am-9pm.) After a hard day of wine tasting, relax in the shaded public gardens just outside the city walls. Through the gardens is a terrace with stone benches and beautiful views of the countryside.

MONTALCINO   ☎0577

Montalcino has changed little since medieval times, when it was a Sienese stronghold. The foremost activity in this tiny town is its production of the heavenly **Brunello di Montalcino,** a wine acknowledged as Italy's finest red. Sample the local Brunello in the numerous wine shops that line the town's narrow streets, or head outside the city walls to one of the numerous wineries for a tour and a free taste.

⚐ PRACTICAL INFORMATION. To reach Montalcino, take one of the daily **TRA-IN buses** from **Siena** (1¼hr., 9 per day, L5500/€2.84). The buses leave from the train station, not P. Gramsci, but tickets can be bought at the TRA-IN ticket window in either place (see Siena **Practical Information,** p. 347). Last bus to Mantalcino departs at 10:05pm; last bus back to Siena departs at 8:30pm. If coming from **Montepulciano** (1¼hr., L7000/€3.62), change buses at **Torrenieri.** Contact the **tourist office** (Associazione Pro-Loco Montalcino), Costa del Municipio, 8, for information about tours of the local vineyards. From P. Cavour, where the bus stops, walk up V. Mazzini into P. del Popolo. The tourist office is under the clock tower. (☎ 0577 84 93 31; info@prolocomontalcino; www.prolocomantalcino.it. Open Tu-Su 10am-1pm and 2:30-5pm.) Rent a **mountain bike** (L25,000/€12.91 per day) or **scooter** (from L50,000/€25.82 per day) at **Minocci Lorenzo Noleggio**, V. P. Strozzi, 31, in the gas station. (☎ 0577 84 82 82. Open daily 10am-2pm and 4-7:30pm.)

🏠 ACCOMMODATIONS AND FOOD. Hotel rooms tend to be expensive and scarce in Montalcino; try to find a bed in one of the many *affittacamere* (private lodgings), which are generally well-kept and run from L80-100,000/€41.32-51.65 for a double with bath. The tourist office can help find lodgings (for a L2000/€1.03 fee) and a **currency exchange.** They can also provide a list of all hotels and *affittacamere* in the area. ◼**Albergo Il Giardino,** P. Cavour, 4, is a reasonably priced option in the heart of the town that offers modern, tasteful rooms. The cozy lounge has leather couches, a stone fireplace, and the friendly proprietor's collection of the finest Italian wines bottled since 1950. (☎ 0577 84 82 57. Singles L80,000/€41.32; doubles L100,000/€51.65; triples L130,000/€67.14.) **Affitacamere Mariuccia,** P. del Popolo, 28, offers three white-walled, well-appointed rooms with immaculate private bath and TV. Reception is in Enotecha Pierangioli across the street. (☎ 0577 84 91 13. Singles L60-65,000/€30.99-33.57; doubles L80-100,000/€41.32-51.65)

A **market** on V. della Libertà brims with picnic fare. (Open daily 7:30am-1pm.) You'll find the best deals on Brunello at the **COOP supermarket,** on V. Sant'Agostino, off P. del Popolo. (Open M-Tu and Th-Sa 8am-1pm and 5-8pm, W 8am-1pm.) V. Mazzini, the main street through the heart of town, is absolutely littered with *enoteche* (wine bars), all nearly identical in their huge selection of Brunello, offering sophisticated snacks from *bruschette* (L6-10,000/€3.10-5.16) to cheese and meat plates (L5-11,000/€2.58-5.68). Many city center restaurants offer full meals as well as huge selections of wine. Near the *fortezza*, the **Osteria di Porta al Cassero** dishes out *scottiglia di cinghiale* (wild boar stew) for L13,000/€6.71 and *coniglio arrosto* (roast rabbit) for L12,000/€6.20. (☎ 0577 84 71 96. Open Th-Tu noon-3pm and 7-10:30pm.) **Taverna Il Grappolo Blu,** Scale di V. Moglio, 1, down a small staircase off of V. Mazzini, offers pasta (L10-13,000/€5.16-6.71) and delicious dishes (L15-20,000/€7.75-10.33). The garlicky homemade pasta with truffle sauce (L12,000/€6.20) must be eaten to be believed. (☎ 0577 84 71 50. Cover L2000/€1.03. Open Sa-Th noon-3pm and 7-10pm.) Head to **Sapori di Napoli,** V. Mazzini, 34/36, for pizza slices or hot sandwiches. (☎ 0347 81 03 821. Open daily 10am-8pm.)

◙ SIGHTS. To appreciate the local vineyards, head past the *fortezza* on V.P. Strozzi, and follow the signs out of town toward "Castelnuovo dell'Abate" and "Abbazia di S. Antimo." Just 2km down this scenic, winding road is the entrance to the **Azienda Agricola Greppo** which produced the first Brunello in 1888. (☎ 0577 84 80 87. Open for tours M-F 9-11am and 3-5pm; office open M-F 8am-noon and 2-6pm.) It is an easy walk (10-15min.) or bike ride from the *fortezza*; watch for occasional traffic. Up a straight cyprus-lined gravel drive you will find the sprawling stone complex that houses the cellars and tasting room. Tours and tastings are by appointment only, geared toward those with an interest in buying their fabulous wines. 3km further down the road lies **Fattoria dei Barbi**, a winery for the rest of us. It is a relatively easy walk (30min.) or bike ride from the *fortezza*, but be warned that it is a gentle uphill climb the entire way back to town. Look for the sign on the left side of the road pointing to a gravel road and follow the signs from there. Tours of the extensive cellars are followed by a tasting of two of their delicious wines (one Brunello and one blend) as well as their extra-virgin olive oil. Tasting can be done any time during their opening hours; ring bell for service. The winery also includes a restaurant, open for lunch and dinner. (☎ 0577 84 82 77; www.fattoria deibarbi.it. Open M-F 10am-1pm and 2:30-6pm, Sa 2:30-6pm. Free tours given every hour M-F 10am-noon and 3-5pm.) The **Palazzo Comunale,** in the P. del Popolo, hosts wine exhibitions. **Apicoltura Ciacci,** V. Ricasoli, 26, up the street from the

Chiesa di S. Agostino, stocks every honey product imaginable, including honey soap, honey biscuits, honey milk, honey candies, honey *grappa*, and honey clogs. (☎ 0577 84 80 19. Open Nov.-Mar. daily. Ring the bell for assistance. MC/V.)

Montalcino's most inspiring sight, the ⬛**Abbazia di Sant'Antimo,** lies 10km from Montalcino down the same road as the wineries. With its rounded apse and carved alabaster capitals, this early 12th-century abbey, built on the remains of an 8th-century church (allegedly founded by Charlemagne), is one of Tuscany's most beautiful Romanesque churches. Moreover, it is surrounded by sloping hills, vineyards, and cypresses—the quintessential Tuscan image. Inside, monks perform mass in **Gregorian chant** seven times a day (the only time that the church is closed to the public). Recorded chants float through the church the rest of the day. (☎ 0577 83 56 69. Open M-Sa 10am-12:30pm and 3-6:30pm, Su 9-10:30am and 3-6pm.) Buses leave from Montalcino for the abbey and stop at Castelnuovo (M-Sa 7:10am, 1:45, 2:45, 7pm; return 7:40am, 2:25, 3:35pm; round-trip L4000/€2.07.) Be aware that there is no return bus if you take the 7pm bus to the abbey. If you plan to take the 1:45pm bus, note you'll only have a few moments to see the exterior of the abbey before having to hop on the 2:25pm bus home, as the interior is closed and it's an 8min. walk from the bus stop to the abbey. It is a 15min. ride by scooter or car (follow signs to the right when you near the tiny village of Castelnuovo dell'Abate), and an easy bike ride there, though its a long, hard uphill ride back.

Montalcino's 14th-century **fortezza** sheltered a band of republicans escaping the Florentine siege of Siena in 1555. The fortress is almost perfectly preserved, with five towers and part of the town walls incorporated into the structure. Two courtyards beckon inside the fortress, one sunny and cheered by geraniums, the other shaded by foliage. (Open daily 9am-1pm and 2:30-8pm. Ramparts L5000/€2.58.) The fortezza's sophisticated **Enoteca La Fortezza** offers cheese plates (L12,000/€6.20) and local wines (L3-8000/€1.55-4.13 per glass; *brunello* L9000/€4.65). If the staff behind the counter is vigilant, you'll have to pay the L5000/€2.58 to climb the stairs through the turret onto the *fortezza* walls for a breathtaking view of the surrounding countryside. (Open Apr.-Oct. daily 9am-8pm; Nov.-Mar. Tu-Su 9am-6pm.)

MONTEPULCIANO ☎ 0578

This small medieval hamlet, stretched along the crest of a narrow limestone ridge, is one of Tuscany's highest hilltop towns and one of the finest locations from which to enjoy the countryside. Montepulciano is enclosed by stone walls, built in four phases, first to protect against belligerent neighbors and later to ward off sickness and noxious pilgrims. Crammed within its fortifications lie many Renaissance-style *palazzi* and churches. Montepulciano is best known, however, for its local *Vino Nobile* wines. At many local wineries, the traveling epicurean can experience the garnet-colored wine that made the town famous. Even if you skip the wine, the landscape and museums make Montepulciano an excellent refuge.

▐ TRANSPORTATION

Trains: Lies on Florence-Rome line. Station 10km from town center. To **Chiusi** (20min., every hr., L4700/€2.43). **LFI** buses run to town from train station (Sept.-May 6am-9pm, L3500/€1.81). In June-Aug. don't get off at the Montepulciano station. The LFI bus service is infrequent, and the alternative is a L25-30,000/€12.91-15.50 cab ride. Take the train to Chiusi, and take a bus from there instead.

Buses: TRA-IN buses run from **Siena** (1½hr., M-Sa 7-8 per day, L8400/€4.39), some via **Buonconvento.** 2 direct buses also run between Montepulciano and **Florence** (2hr., L14,600/€7.54). **LFI buses** to Chiusi (1hr., every 30min. 5:50am-9:15pm, L3800/€1.96). Tickets available at agencies displaying LFI *Biglietti* and TRA-IN signs.

Taxis: ☎ 0578 639 89. **24hr. taxi service:** ☎ 0578 71 60 81.

Car Rental: Stefano Franco, V. Le Grazie, 1 (☎ 0578 71 60 81).

⚡🛈 ORIENTATION AND PRACTICAL INFORMATION

Buses stop at the bottom of the hill outside the town. Disembark at the *centro storico*, before the bus begins its descent. A short, steep climb leads to the **Corso,** the main street. Orange ATAF **buses** make the trip easier (L1400/€0.72). Divided nominally into four parts (V. di Gracciano nel Corso, V. di Voltaia nel Corso, V. dell'Opio nel Corso, and V. del Poliziano), the *corso* winds languorously up a precipitous hill. At the end, the street starts to level off; from here, on **via del Teatro,** another incline on the right leads to **Piazza Grande,** the main square.

Tourist Office: P. Grande, 3 (☎0578 75 86 87). Gives out maps and makes free arrangements for *alberghi* and *affittacamere* in town and the surrounding countryside.

Currency Exchange: Banca Toscana, P. Michelozzo, 2. **ATM** outside. Open M-F 8:20am-1:20pm and 2:45-3:45pm. Currency exchange is also available at the **post office** and the 24hr. exchange machines in P. Savonarola.

Emergency: ☎ 113. **Medical Emergency:** ☎ 118. **Police:** P. Savonarola, 16 (☎ 112).

Pharmacy: Farmacia Franceschi, V. di Voltaia nel Corso, 47 (☎0578 71 63 92). Open Apr.-Sept. M-Sa 9am-1pm and 4:30-7:30pm; Oct.-May 9am-1pm and 4-7pm. **Farmacia Sorbini,** V. Calamandrei (☎0578 75 73 52), fills urgent prescriptions.

Post Office: V. dell'Erbe, 12, uphill from the P. dell'Erbe and the *corso.* **Currency exchange** (L1000/€0.52 commission). Open M-F 8:15am-7pm, Sa 8:15am-12:30pm.

Postal Code: 53045.

🍴 ACCOMMODATIONS

Most lodgings in Montepulciano are as exorbitant as 3- or 4-star hotels elsewhere. Reasonable *affitacamere* (rooms for rent) are the best option. The tourist office can help you find a place to stay if Montepulciano becomes more than a daytrip.

Affittacamere Bellavista, V. Ricci, 25 (☎0578 75 73 48 or 71 63 41), downhill from the tourist office. Rents small, lovely rooms, some with fantastic views. Call ahead to reserve room and get the key. Doubles with bath L90,000/€46.48.

Albergo La Terazza, V. Piè al Sasso, 16 (☎/fax 0578 75 74 40). From P. Grande, exit downhill on V. del Teatro, to the left of the *duomo.* In Piazzeta del Teatro, turn left on V. di Cagnano. On right, 4 blocks ahead. Reserve ahead. Singles L130,000/€67.14; doubles L160,000/€82.63; quad L230,000/€118.80. MC/V.

Ristorante Cittino, V. della Nuova, 2 (☎0578 75 73 35), off V. di Voltaia del Corso. Popular restaurant with superb food. Full meals L25,000/€12.91. Closed W and last 2 weeks in June. The smell of mom's cooking wafts from the kitchen downstairs to their 3 clean doubles (L70,000/€36.15) and 1 triple (L105,000/€54.23).

🍽 FOOD

Minimarkets line the Corso. A **Conad supermarket** is a few blocks down from P. Savonarola, outside the city walls. (Open M-Tu and Th-Sa 8:30am-7pm, W 8:30am-noon.) Thursday brings an **open-air market** to P. Sant'Agnese. (Open 8am-1pm.)

Osteria dell'Acquaccheta, V. del Teatro, 22 (☎0578 75 84 43 or 0578 71 70 86), off the Corso. Juicy *bistecca alla fiorentina. Pecorino miele e noci* (with honey and nuts) or *pecorino di peinza al tartufo* (with truffles) L4000/€2.07. *Primi* L10-13,000/€5.16-6.71; *secondi* L10-16,000/€5.16-8.26. Open W-M noon-4pm and 7pm-1am.

Trattoria Diva e Maceo, V. Gracciano nel Corso, 92 (☎0578 71 69 51). Locals socialize here over *cannelloni* (stuffed with ricotta and spinach) and *ossobuco* (a beef stew). Open W-M 12:30-2pm and 7:30-9:30pm. Closed 1st 2 weeks of July. D/MC/V.

CENTRAL ITALY

Caffè Poliziano, V. del Voltaio nel Corso, 27 (☎0578 75 86 15). Marble table tops and a brass-accented bar complete this classy cafe and its delectable pastries (from L1400/ €0.72). 2 tiny terraces offer splendid views. Formal dining room next door open for an expensive dinner (M-Sa 7-10:15pm). Cafe open daily 7am-1am. AmEx/MC/V.

Pub Grotta del Nano, V. Gracciano del Corso, 11 (☎0578 75 60 23). Inexpensive and quick. Offers sandwiches, pizza by the slice, a *gelato* bar, and a small *menù*. Wine and *panzanell* L9000/€4.65. *Crostini* and wine L13,000/€6.71. Beer L4-6000/ €2.07-3.10. Open Tu-F 10:30am-9:30pm, Sa 10:30am-10:30pm, Su 10:30am-6:30pm.

 SIGHTS

CHIESA DI SAN BIAGIO. Built in an unusual Greek-cross shape, this church is a stunning example of high Renaissance symmetry and decoration, and is considered Sangallo's masterpiece. The cavernous interior was redone in the 17th century in overwrought Baroque, but the simple skeleton is still visible. *(From P. Grande, follow V. Ricci via della Mercenzia and turn left down staircase before Piazzeta di S. Francesco. Follow signs on switchbacks and out the city walls. Open daily 9am-1pm and 3:30-7pm.)*

VIA DI GRACCIANO QUARTER. Noteworthy *palazzi* line this neighborhood. On the right, **Palazzo Avignonesi** (1507-1575) is attributed to Vignola. The elegant windows of the second floor contrast sharply with the bold protruding windows of the ground floor, displaying the *palazzo's* different stages of construction. The lions' heads on either side of the door correspond to those on top of the **Marzocco Column,** in front of the *palazzo*. The lion, the heraldic symbol of Florence, replaced the she-wolf of Siena when Florence took over Montepulciano in 1511. The original statue now rests in the **Museo Civico.** Farther up the street rises the asymmetrical facade of **Palazzo Cocconi,** attributed to Antonio da Sangallo the Elder (1455-1534). Across

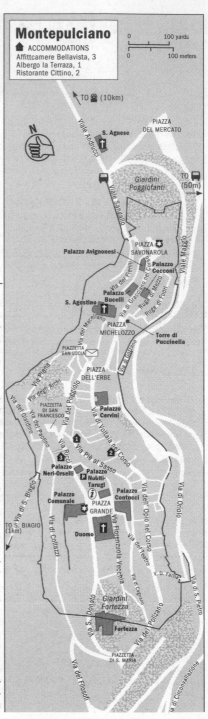

Montepulciano

ACCOMMODATIONS
Affittcamere Bellavista, 3
Albergo la Terraza, 1
Ristorante Cittino, 2

0 ··· 100 yards
0 ··· 100 meters

TO 🚂 (10km)

S. Agnese

PIAZZA DEL MERCATO

Viale Andrucci

Giardini Poggiofanti

TO 🚌 (50m)

Viale Sangallo

PIAZZA SAVONAROLA

Palazzo Avignonesi

Palazzo Cocconi

Via dei Fiorni

Palazzo Bucelli

Via di Gracciano nel Corso

S. Agostino

Ruga di Mezzo

Ruga di Fuori

Viale Maggio

PIAZZA MICHELOZZO

Via del Mecenano

Torre di Puccinella

PIAZZETTA SAN LUCIA

Via del Poggiolo

PIAZZA DELL'ERBE

PIAZZETTA DI SAN FRANCESCO

Via degli Archi

Palazzo Cervini

Via di Voltaia del Corso

Via Pianta

Via del Giardino

Via del Paolino

Via Ricci

Via piè al Sasso

Palazzo Neri-Orselli

Palazzo Nobili Tarugi

Palazzo Comunale

PIAZZA GRANDE

Palazzo Contucci

Via dell'Opio nel Corso

Via di Oriolo

TO S. BIAGIO (1km)

Via di S. Biagio

Via di Collazzi

Duomo

Via Florenzula Vecchia

Via del Teatro

Via di Cagnano

V. D. Fanini

Via di S. Pietro

Giardini Fortezza

Fortezza

Via S. Donato

Via del Polizano

Via di Filosofi

PIAZZETTA DI S. MARIA

Via di Circonvallazione

the street, **Palazzo Bucelli** showcases Roman and Etruscan reliefs, urn slabs, and inscriptions collected by the 18th-century proprietor, Pietro Bucelli.

PIAZZA GRANDE. The unfinished *duomo*, the Palazzo Tarugi, the Palazzo Contucci, and the 14th-century Palazzo Comunale all surround this *piazza*. The construction of the *duomo* began in the 16th century when the town council deemed the existing cathedral unworthy. After several years of commissioning and firing architects, the town council settled on Ippolito Scalza, an architect from Orvieto. The product of his painstaking process is an unaccountably stark *duomo* whose rustic, unfinished facade reflects its sparse interior. However unpretentious, the *duomo* does have a poignant *Assumption of the Virgin* by Taddeo di Bartolo in a triptych above the altar, considered by some to be the artist's masterpiece. *(In P. Grande, at the top of the hill. Walk up Il Corso. Open daily 9am-1pm and 3:30-7pm.)*

The elegant facade of **Palazzo de'Nobili-Tarugi** faces the *duomo*. The nearby **Palazzo Contucci** is a graceful, if eccentric, hybrid of architectural styles. The Contucci family has made fine wine here for well over a century and today runs a charming *enoteca* (wine store) on the ground floor. In the mid-1400s Michelozzo completed **Palazzo Comunale,** a smaller version of the Palazzo Vecchio in Florence, which took nearly a century to build. The *palazzo's* tower offers a view of Siena in the north and the Gran Sasso Massif in the south. *(Tower open M-Sa 8:30am-12:30pm.)*

The **Palazzo Neri-Orselli** houses the **Museo Civico,** one of Montepulciano's foremost attractions. The museum contains a collection of enameled terra-cotta by della Robbia, Etruscan funerary urns, and more than 200 paintings. *(V. Ricci, 10. Open Tu-Su 10am-1pm and 3-7pm. L8000/€4.13, under 18 and over 65 L5000/€2.58.)*

🎵 ENTERTAINMENT

In the first half of August, the town fills with musicians who perform at **Cantiere Internazionale d'Arte,** a festival created by the German composer Hans Werner Henze in 1976. In July, **Caffè Poliziano** hosts a jazz festival. At other times, the main form of entertainment for tourists consists of traipsing from one wine store to the next. All offer free samples of the wines they sell; try the one at Porta di Bacco, on the left immediately after you enter the city gates. (Open daily 9am-8pm.)

Around August 15, the **Bruscello** (a series of amateur concerts and theatrical productions) occurs on the steps of the *duomo*. Visit Montepulciano the last Sunday in August to see the raucous **Bravio delle Botti** (Barrel Race), held to commemorate the eight neighborhood militias who fended off the Florentines and Sienese.

🏛 DAYTRIP FROM MONTEPULCIANO: SATURNIA

About 200m later, the road takes a sharp curve, and a dirt track leads off the highway to the springs. From Montepulciano, Saturnia is about two hours away by car (140km). For more information, contact Saturnia's tourist office (see above).

If you have access to a car, head to Saturnia to enjoy free and unrestricted access to **Le Cascatelle,** hot streams of water that bubble to the surface in natural rock pools and reflect the intense blue of the skies. Follow the road to Montemerano until the official spa complex of Saturnia appears.

VOLTERRA ☎ 0588

Atop a huge bluff known as *Le Balze*, the town presides over the surrounding checkerboard of green and yellow. Drawn by the defensible position, the Etruscans established the town of Velathri here, which, by the 4th century BC, had become one of the most powerful cities of the Dodecapolis. By the Middle Ages, Volterra had shrunk to one-third its former size (it's cold in the hills)—outlying parts of the town even fell off the eroding hillside upon which Volterra was built. Today, Volterra is a popular place to view Etruscan artifacts or to purchase an exquisite alabaster statue carved in one of the many local workshops. The city's medieval architecture and superb views draw tourists, but it is outside the gates, in semolina fields and distant mountains, that Volterra reveals its ineffable appeal.

⌐ TRANSPORTATION

Trains: (☎0588 861 50), 9km west in **Saline di Volterra.** Take the (CPT) bus to **Saline** for trains to **Pisa** (L7700/€4) and the **coast.**

Buses: (☎0588 861 50) in P. Martiri della Libertà. To **Florence** (2hr.; L12,500/€6.46). **TRA-IN** connects to **San Gimignano** (2hr., L7800/€4.03) and **Siena** (2hr., L8600/€4.44). All 3 require a change at Colle Val d'Elsa; San Gimignano requires a 2nd change at Poggibonsi. Since the services are provided by different companies, navigating the route can be complicated. **CPT** runs between Colle Val D'Elsa and Volterra—buy tickets at a *tabacchi* or at the vending machines near the bus stop. **TRA-IN** and **SITA** run buses from Colle Val D'Elsa to elsewhere in Tuscany. Buy tickets at travel agencies or at town offices. There is one such agency in the square where buses arrive and leave in Colle Val D'Elsa. When buying your 1st ticket, be sure that the connection time at Colle Val D'Elsa is reasonable. **CPT** also runs to **Saline di Volterra** (5 per day, Su and in Aug. 2 per day; L3100/€1.60) and **Pisa** (2hr., 7 per day, L9700/€5), via **Pontederra.**

Taxis: ☎0588 875 17.

✦❼ ORIENTATION AND PRACTICAL INFORMATION

To get from **Piazza della Libertà**, where the buses stop, to **Piazza dei Priori**, the town's historic and administrative center, turn left onto **via Ricciarelli** and walk 40m.

Tourist Office: P. dei Priori, 20 (☎0588 872 57). English spoken. Rents recorded walking tours. L15,000/€7.75 per person, L10,000/€5.16 per person for groups of 2-4, further reductions for larger groups. Open Apr.-Oct. M-Sa 10am-1pm and 2-8pm, Su 10am-1pm and 2-7pm; Nov.-Mar. daily 10am-1pm and 2-6pm.

Currency Exchange: Cassa di Risparmio di Firenze, V. Matteotti, 1, has a 24hr. exchange machine and an **ATM** outside. Also in P. Martiri della Libertà.

Internet: SESHA, V. Don Minsoni, 10. Open daily 9am-1pm and 4-8pm. MC/V.

Emergency: ☎113. **Medical Emergency:** ☎118.

Pharmacy: Farmacia Amidei, V. Ricciarelli, 2 (☎0588 860 60). Open M-Sa 9am-1pm and 4-7:30pm; open Su in emergency situations.

Hospital: (☎0588 919 11), on Borgo S. Lazzaro.

Post Office: P. Priori, 14 (☎0588 869 69). Open M-F 8:15am-7pm, Sa 8:15am-12:30pm.

Postal Code: 56048.

♞ ACCOMMODATIONS & CAMPING

Ask the tourist office for a list of *affittacamere.* Doubles begin at L60,000/€30.99.

Seminario Sant'Andrea, Viale V. Veneto, 2 (☎0588 860 28), in P.S. Andrea, next to the church. From P. della Libertà, jog left, then immediately right on V. Matteotti. Walk through P. XX Settembre and take 1st left. Exit city through Porta Marcoli and follow the road, bearing left, until you reach Sant'Andrea. 2-4 person rooms (none with bath) with antique furniture off vast frescoed hallways. Curfew midnight. Reservations required. L27,000/€13.94 per person. MC/V.

L'Etrusca, V. Porta all'Arco, 37/41 (☎/fax 0588 840 73). From the bus stop, turn left onto V. Marchesi and then left on V. Porta all'Arco. Clean and modern flats, all with bath and kitchen facilities. Reserve ahead. Singles L70,000/€36.15; doubles L120,000/€61.97; triples L140,000/€72.30. L5000/€2.58 discount for 7-day rental.

Albergo Etruria, V. Matteotti, 32 (☎0588 873 77). Exit P. Libertà to the left and take your first right onto V. Matteotti; the Etruria is a few blocks down. White-walled rooms with sparkling tiled bathrooms. TV and phone. Indoor lounge and garden lounge. Breakfast L10,000/€5.16. Singles L85,000/€43.90; doubles L120,000/€62; triples L140,000/€72.30; quads L160,000/€82.63. MC/V.

Camping: Le Balze, V. Mandringa, 15 (☎0588 878 80). Exit through Porta S. Francesco, and bear right on Strada Provincial Pisana. Turn left on V. Mandringa (20 min.). Campground has pool and bar. Store sells tickets for bus into town (every hr., first bus 8:18am, last 10:21pm). Showers included. Reception 8am-1pm, 2-7pm, and 8-11pm. Cars must be parked by 11pm. Open Apr.-Oct. L11,000/€5.88 per person; L7000/€3.62 per tent; L3000/€1.55 per car; L12,000/€6.20 per camper. MC/V.

🍴 FOOD

An excellent selection of game dishes and local cheeses is available at any of the *alimentari* along V. Guarnacci or V. Gramsci. Sample *salsiccia di cinghiale* (wild boar sausage) and *pecorino* (sheep's milk cheese). For a sweet snack, try *ossi di morto* (bones of death), a rock-hard local confection made of egg whites, sugar, hazelnuts, and a hint of lemon, or *pane di pescatore*, dense and delicious sweet bread full of nuts and raisins. Pick up groceries at the **Despar market,** V. Gramsci, 12. (Open M-F 7:30am-1pm and 5-8pm, Sa 7:30am-1pm.)

Il Pozzo degli Etruschi, V. dei Prigioni, 30 (☎0588 80 60 08). Hearty Tuscan fare. *Penne all'Etrusca* (pasta with tomato mushroom and cheese sauce; L10,000/€5.16) and *cinghiale alla maremmane* (wild boar; L15,000/€7.75). *Primi* L10-16,000/€5.16-9.30; *secondi* L10-20,000/€5.16-10.33. Tourist *menù* L25,000/€12.91. Cover L2500/€1.29. Service 10%. Open Su-Th noon-3pm and 6:30-10pm. AmEx/MC/V.

L'Ombra della Sera, V. Gramsci, 70 (☎0588 866 63), off P. XX Settembre. *Primi* L9-13,000/€4.65-6.71; *secondi* L15-22,000/€7.75-11.36. Cover L2500/€1.29. Service 10%. Open Tu-Su noon-3pm and 7-10pm. AmEx/D/MC/V.

Pizzeria/Birreria Ombra della Sera, V. Guarnacci, 16 (☎0588 852 74). Pizza (L7-12,000/€3.62-6.20), salad (L10,000/€5.16), and pasta (L9-13,000/€4.65-6.71). Cover L1500/€0.77. Service 10%. Open Tu-Su noon-3pm and 7-11pm. MC/V.

👁 🎵 SIGHTS AND ENTERTAINMENT

PIAZZA DEI PRIORI AND FORTEZZA MEDICEA. Volterra revolves around Piazza dei Priori, which is surrounded by sober, dignified *palazzi*. The **Palazzo dei Priori,** the oldest governmental palace in Tuscany (1208-1254), presides over the square. *(Courtyard open daily 9am-6pm.)* Across the *piazza* sits **Palazzo Pretorio,** a series of 13th-century buildings and towers that house municipal offices. Volterra's most prominent structure is the elegant Floretine **Fortezza Medicea.**

DUOMO. Constructed in Pisan-Romanesque style during the 13th century, the *duomo* was not completed in the manner it was conceived (though work continued for three centuries). Inside, on the left, the oratory houses a series of wooden statues depicting the life of Jesus from nativity to crucifixion. The chapel off the transept holds frescoes by Rosselli, including the brilliant *Mission per Damasco*. Also note the spectacular use of perspective in the *Annunciation* by M. Albertinelli and Fra Bartolomeo on the left wall. *(Down V. Turazza from P. dei Priori to P.S. Giovanni. Open daily 8am-12:30pm and 3-6pm.)*

PINACOTECA COMUNALE. A graceful building with a courtyard contains Volterra's best art in understated, dimly-lit rooms. Taddeo di Bartolo's elegant *Madonna and Saints* altarpiece will shock anyone who has seen his gruesome *Last Judgement* in San Gimignano. In Rosso Fiorentino's spectacular first-floor work, the *Deposition* (1521), Christ's body seems to be painted green (most likely a result of aging and poor restoration). The painting is mesmerizing, in part because Piorentino allows the painting to spill from the canvas onto the frame, thus creating the illusion that his subjects are not confined to the flat surface. *(V. dei Sartiri, 1. Up V. Buonparenti from P. dei Priori. ☎ 0588 875 80. Open daily 7am-7pm. A combination ticket including Pinacoteca, Museo Etrusco, and Museo dell' Opera del Duomo e Arte Sacra can be bought at any of the sights for L13,000/€6.71, students L9000/€4.65.)*

MUSEO ETRUSCO GUARNACCI. The Etruscan museum displays over 600 finely carved funeral urns from the 8th and 7th centuries BC. A stylized figure representing the deceased tops each urn; below, dramatic bas-reliefs recreate various episodes from classical mythology. The pieces are not well displayed, and an audio tour will run you an additional L8000/€4.13 (L10,000/€5.16 for two). The first floor (Room XXII) holds the museum's most famous piece, the elongated bronze figure dubbed *L'Ombra della Sera* (Shadow of the Evening), which inspired the great modern Italian sculptor Giacommetti. The farmer who unearthed it used it for years as a fireplace poker until a visitor recognized it as an Etruscan votive figure. In Room XX, the museum also contains the famous *Urna degli Sposi*, an angry, haggard married couple sculpted together on the same urn. *(V. Minzoni, 15. From P. dei Priori, head down to V. Matteotti, turn right on V. Gramisci, and follow it to V. Minzoni. ☎ 0588 863 47. Gallery and museum open mid-Mar. to Oct. daily 9am-7pm; Nov. to mid-Mar. 9am-2pm.)*

MUSEO DELL'OPERA DEL DUOMO DI ARTE SACRA. Its inclusion on the cumulative ticket is one's primary reason to visit to this tiny, three-room museum, which holds much of the art originally in the *duomo*. Objects on display range from liturgical robes to impressive metallic sculptures. *(V. Roma, 1, near duomo. ☎ 0588 862 90. Open mid-Mar. to Oct. daily 9:30am-1pm and 3-6:30pm; Nov. to mid-Mar. 9am-1pm.)*

ROMAN AMPITHEATER. These impressive ruins include partly grass-covered stone seating and Corinthian columns from the stage. Walk among the ruins, or admire them from a bird's eye view for free on the road next to Porta Fiorentina. *(Just outside the city walls next to Porta Fiorentina. From P. dei Priori, follow V. delle Prigioni, take a right at the T-junction and your first left. Proceed down V. Guarnacci, out the Porta and through the parking lot to your left. Open daily 10am-1pm and 2-6pm. L3000/€1.55.)*

SAN GIMIGNANO ☎ 0577

The hilltop village of San Gimignano looks like an illumination from a medieval manuscript—towers, churches and *palazzi* bulge out of proportion from within the city's walls. San Gimignano's famous 14 towers, which are all that survive of the original 72, date from a period when prosperous, warring families fought battles within the city walls, using their towers to store grain for sieges. The towers were also convenient for dumping boiling oil on attacking enemies. Exhausted by war, San Gimignano stagnated in poverty for six centuries. Eventually, its towered horizon (which inspired the city's contemporary nickname—"Medieval Manhattan") lured postwar tourists, whose tastes and wallets resuscitated production of the golden Vernaccia wine. With hordes of daytrippers, an infestation of souvenir shops, and countless restaurants, San Gimignano now has the feel of a Disney's Medieval Land. Nevertheless, it's impressive and worth the packed bus rides. Stay overnight when the streets empty and souvenir shops disappear behind shutters.

▐ TRANSPORTATION

Trains: The nearest station is in **Poggibonsi;** buses connect the station to the town (M-F every hr. 7:20am-8:55pm, Sa-Su every hr. 6:45am-8:55pm).

Buses: TRA-IN buses (☎ 0577 20 41 11 or 93 72 07) leave from P. Montemaggio, outside Porta S. Giovanni. Schedules and tickets at **Caffè Combattente,** V.S. Giovanni, 124, to the left as you enter the city gates. Tickets also available from any *tabacchi* in town or at the tourist office in P. del Duomo. Change at **Poggibonsi** (20min., every hr., L2600/€1.34) for **Siena** (1½hr. if you get a good connection, every 1-2hr., L9000/ €4.65) and **Florence** (2hr. with a good connection; every 1-2hr.; L10,400/€5.37).

Car Rental: Jolly Pentacar (☎ 0577 94 05 75), Viale Garibaldi, just outside the city walls near Porta San Matteo. Small cars from L110,000/€56.81 per day. Also rents bikes (L19,000/€9.81 per day) and scooters (from L40,000/€20.66 per day.) Open daily 8am-8pm. **Hertz** (☎0577 94 22 20), on Viale dei Fossi.

Bike and Scooter Rental: Bruno Bellini, V. Roma, 41 (☎0577 94 02 01). Mountain bikes L25,000/€12.91 per day, L100,000/€51.65 per week. Scooters from L60,000/ €30.99 per day. Open daily 9am-8pm. **Jolly Pentacar** (see above).

⚡🔢 ORIENTATION AND PRACTICAL INFORMATION

Buses to San Gimignano stop in Piazzale Martini Montemaggio, the large square filled with trees and gravel walks just outside the city walls. To reach the city center from there pass through the *porta* and climb the hill, following **via San Giovanni** to **Piazza della Cisterna,** which merges with **Piazza del Duomo.**

Tourist Office: Pro Loco, P. del Duomo, 1 (☎0577 94 00 08; fax 94 09 03; pro-locs@tin.it). Has lists of hotels and rooms for rent as well as bus and train schedules and bus tickets. Offers walking tours of the countryside (2 per day; L20,000/€10.33). Also offers tours of wineries on Tu and Th, from 10:30am to 12:30pm. Includes multiple tastings (all include food) and transportation by bus for L50,000/€25.62 (L35,000/ €18.08 if you drive yourself). Reserve by noon the day before. Office also makes reservations (if you visit in person) for private rooms. English spoken. Open Mar.-Oct. daily 9am-1pm and 3-7pm; Nov.-Feb. 9am-1pm and 2-6pm.

Accommodations Services: Siena Hotels Promotion, V.S. Giovanni, 125 (☎0577 94 08 09, fax 94 01 13), on the right as you enter the city gates; look for the "Cooperativa Alberghi e Ristoranti" sign. Reserves hotel rooms in San Gimignano and Siena for L3000/€1.55 commission. Open M-Sa 9:30am-7pm. **Associazione Strutture Extrab-erghiere,** P. della Cisterna, 6 (☎/fax 0577 94 31 90). Patient staff makes reservations for private rooms without charge. Doubles with bath L90-110,000/€46.48-56.81. Call a week in advance if you want to stay in the countryside; they can always find a place in the city center. Open Mar.-Nov. daily 9:30am-7:30pm.

Currency Exchange: Pro Loco tourist office and post office offer best rates. Rip-offs else-where. **ATMs** scattered along V.S. Giovanni, V. degli Innocenti, and P. della Cisterna.

Police: ☎112. **Carabinieri** (☎0577 94 03 13), on P. Martiri.

Medical Emergency: ☎118.

Late-Night Pharmacy: V.S. Matteo, 13 (☎0577 94 03 97). Fills urgent prescriptions all night. Open M-Sa 9am-1pm and 4:30-8pm.

Post Office: P. delle Erbe, 8, behind the *duomo.* Open Mar.-Oct. M-F 8:15am-7pm, Sa 8:15am-12:30pm; Nov.-Feb. M-F 8:15am-12:30pm and 2-5pm, Sa 8:15am-12:30pm. Currency exchange available.

Postal Code: 53037.

🏠 ACCOMMODATIONS & CAMPING

San Gimignano caters to wealthy tourists, and most accommodations are well beyond budget range. *Affittacamere* provide an alternative to overpriced hotels, with doubles from L90-110,000/€46.48-56.81. The tourist office and the **Associazione Strutture Extralberghiere** (see above) have lists of budget rooms.

Albergo/Ristorante Il Pino, reception at V.S. Matteo, 102 (☎/fax 0577 94 04 15). Open beamed ceilings, medieval arches, rural bricks, and red bedframes, but outside the city walls. All rooms with bath and TV. Breakfast L15,000/€7.75. Reservations rec-ommended. Singles L70,000/€36.15; doubles L100,000/€51.65. AmEx/MC/V.

Camere Cennini Gianni, V.S. Giovanni, 21 (☎0577 94 10 51). Reception is at the *pasticceria* at V.S. Giovanni, 88. From the bus stop, enter through the Porta S. Giovanni. Kitchens for groups of 4. Reserve ahead. Quaint, clean doubles with bath L90,000/ €46.48 that can serve as triples for L120,000/€62; quads L140,000/€72.30.

Camping: Il Boschetto (☎0577 94 03 52), at Santa Lucia, 2½km downhill from Porta S. Giovanni. Buses run from P. Martiri (L1500/€0.77). Ask the driver if the bus is going to the campgrounds; it's also not a bad hike. Bar and market on the premises. Reception daily 8am-1pm, 3-8pm, and 9-11pm. Open Apr.-Oct. 15. L8500/€4.39 per person, L8500/€4.39 per small tent. Hot showers included.

◖ FOOD

If you didn't guess from the sad, glass eyes of stuffed tuskers across town, San Gimignano specializes in boar and other wild game. The town also caters to less-daring palates with mainstream Tuscan dishes at fairly high prices. Whether you're looking to save or savor, try the **open-air market** in P. del Duomo on Thursday mornings. (Open 8am to noon.) A small **market** sells cheap, filling sandwiches and takeout pasta, salads, and drinks at V.S. Matteo, 19. (☎0577 94 19 52. Open Mar.-Oct. daily 9am-9pm; Nov.-Feb. F-W 9am-8pm, Th 9am-1pm.) Purchase the famous Vernaccia di San Gimignano, a light white wine with a hint of sweetness, from **La Buca,** V.S. Giovanni, 16 (☎0577 94 04 07). This cooperative also offers terrific sausages and meats, all made on its own farm. The boar sausage *al pignoli* (L3200/ €1.65 per hectogram) and the *salame con mirto* are especially delicious. (Open Apr.-Oct. daily 9am-9pm; Nov.-Mar. 9am-7pm.)

▧ **Trattoria Chiribiri,** P. della Madonna, 1 (☎0577, 94 19 48). From the bus stop, take your first left off of V.S. Giovanni up a short staircase. Tiny restaurant serves amazing local fare at unusually affordable prices. The roast rabbit stuffed with vegetables (L14,000/€7.23) is divine. *Primi* L9-12,000/€4.65-6.20; *secondi* from L1400/ €0.72. The dining room can get overheated when crowded, but the service is phenomenal. Open Mar.-Oct. Th-Tu noon-10:30pm; Nov.-Feb. Th-Tu noon-2pm and 7-10pm.

La Bettola del Grillo, V. Quercecchio, 33 (☎0577 94 18 44), off V.S. Giovanni, opposite P. della Cisterna. Serves up traditional Tuscan delights in a hip, plastic-tabled atmosphere, which includes a small garden in back with a view. Vegetarian options. *Primi* L10-12,000/€5.16-6.20; *secondi* L10-15,000/€5.16-7.75. Fixed-price *menù* L25,000/€12.91 includes wine and dessert. Open Tu-Su noon-3pm and 6:30-11pm.

La Stella, V. Matteo, 77 (☎0577 94 04 44). Delicious food made with produce from its own farm. Delectable, homemade pasta with wild boar sauce (L15,000/€7.75). *Primi* L9500-15,000/€4.65-7.75; *secondi* from L14,000/€7.23. Extensive wine list includes San Gimignano's famous Vernaccia. Cover L3500/€1.81. Open Apr.-Oct Th-Tu noon-2:30pm and 7-9:30pm; Nov.-Apr. Th-Tu noon-2pm and 7-9pm. AmEx/MC/V.

Ristorante Perucà, V. Capassi, 16 (☎0577 94 31 36). Hidden behind V. Matteo. Pizza L9-14,000/€4.65-7.23; *primi* L11-15,000/€5.68-7.75; *secondi* L14-30,000/€7.23-15.50. Cover L3000/€1.55. Open F-W noon-2:30pm and 7-10:30pm. AmEx/MC/V.

◎ ♫ SIGHTS AND ENTERTAINMENT

Famous as the *Città delle Belle Torri* (City of Beautiful Towers), San Gimignano has always appealed to artists. During the Renaissance, they came in droves, and the collection of their works complement San Gimignano's cityscape.

▧ **PIAZZA DELLA CISTERNA AND PIAZZA DEL DUOMO.** Built in 1237, P. Cisterna is surrounded by towers and *palazzi*. It adjoins P. del Duomo, site of the impressive tower of the **Palazzo del Podestà.** To its left, the imposing tunnels and intricate *loggie* riddle the **Palazzo del Popolo** (see below). To the right of the *palazzo* rises its **Torre Grossa,** the highest tower in town and the only one visitors can ascend. Also in the *piazza* stand the twin towers of the Ardinghelli, truncated

MEDIEVAL MANHATTAN. Cumulative Tickets for the town's museums are available at several different rates. *Biglietti intero* (L18,000/€9.30) are full-priced adult tickets; *biglietti ridotti* (L14,000/€7.23) are discounted tickets, available to students under 18 and families with children between the ages of 8 and 18. Children under 7 are allowed *ingresso gratuito* (free entrance) to almost all of the sights. One ticket allows entry into nearly all of San Gimignano's sights. Tickets are available at any tourist sight.

due to a zoning ordinance that prohibited structures higher than the Torre Grossa. *(Palazzo del Popolo open Tu-Su 9am-7:30pm.)*

PALAZZO DEL POPOLO. Within this palace, the frescoed medieval courtyard leads to the entrance to the **Museo Civico** on the second floor. The first room of the museum is the **Sala di Dante,** where Dante spoke on May 8, 1300, as an ambassador from Florence, in an attempt to convince San Gimignano to side with the Florentines in their endless wars with Siena. On the walls, Lippo Memmi's sparkling *Maestà* blesses the accompanying 14th-century scenes of hunting and tournament pageantry. Up the stairs, Taddeo di Bartolo's altarpiece, *The Story of San Gimignano,* tells the story of the city's name-sake, originally a bishop of Modena. The small museum has an excellent collection of other Sienese and Florentine works, most notably Filippino Lippi's *Annunciation,* crafted in two circular panels, and Pinturicchio's serene *Madonna in Glory,* one of the last works to be painted by the artist. Fortunately, most tourists seem to skip this attraction, so visitors enjoy the museum in relative peace. Within the museum lies the entrance to the 218-step climb up **Torre Grossa.** The tower offers beautiful panoramas of San Gimignano's many towers, the Tuscan landscape, the ancient fortress, and several *piazze.* The tower's bell rings daily at noon. *(Museo Civico and Tower open daily noon-5pm.)*

BASILICA DI COLLEGIATA. This 12th-century church is covered with a bare facade that seems unfit to shelter the exceptional frescoed interior that lies inside. The **Cappella di Santa Fina,** off the right aisle, was designed by Giuliano and Benedetto Maiano. Ghirlandaio's splendid frescoes on the life of Santa Fina, patron saint of San Gimignano, cover the chapel's walls. Santa Fina, though she is said to have saved the village from barbarian hordes, was struck by a fatal illness at age ten. She decided to repent all her sins and give herself to God. Spending the last five agonizing years of her life lying on a plank of wood, she became so weak that she couldn't even scare away the mice that scampered over her body. In the main church, Bartolo di Fredi painted beautiful frescoes of Old Testament scenes along the north aisle, while Barna da Siena provided the extremely impressive, New Testament counterparts along the south aisle. *(In P. del Duomo. Church and chapel open Apr.-Oct. M-F 9:30am-7:30pm, Sa 9:30am-5pm, Su 1-5pm; Nov.-Mar. M-Sa 9:30am-5pm, Su 1-5pm. L6000/€3.10, ages 6-18 L3000/€1.55.)*

FORTEZZA. Follow the signs past the Basilica di Collegiata from P. del Duomo to find this tiny, crumbling fortress. The courtyard is often full of street artists and the odd musician, and the turret offers a beautiful view of the countryside. There are weekly screenings of movies in the courtyard at night during July and Aug. *(Schedule and info at the tourist office. Movies L12,000/€6.20.)*

PISTOIA   ☎ 0573

In 1177, Pistoia joined several other Italian city-states in declaring itself a free commune. Despite its bold debut, the city was soon surpassed by its neighbors in military, political, and economic strength. Pistoia became a murderous backwater, whose inhabitants Michelangelo maligned as the "enemies of heaven." In 1254, one Pistoian allegedly chopped off a child's hand in retaliation for an injury the boy had caused his son, dragging the entire town into battle. Pistoia has lent its bloody name to the *pistole* dagger (the favored weapon of choice for Pistoia assassins) and later to the pistol. Recently, residents have turned their attention to more peaceful endeavors—the city is home to one of the world's leading train manufacturers. Pistoia isn't all steel though; the city sits atop a hill amid pastures and wildflowers. With a tiny medieval center, full of stone houses and churches, crowed narrow streets and open *piazzas*, Pistoia is the quintessential small Tuscan city, complete with a beautiful *duomo*, *campanile*, and papistry.

▐ TRANSPORTATION

Trains: Info office open daily 8:30-11:30am and 2:30-6pm. From P. Dante Alighieri to: **Florence** (40min., every hr., L4200/€2.17); **Pisa** (1hr., every 2hr., L6500/€3.36); **Rome** (4hr.; every hr.; L53,500/€27.63); **Viareggio** (1hr., every 2hr., L6500/€3.36).

Buses: Lazzi buses (☎0573 36 32 43) run from the train station. Open daily 7am-8:15pm. Buy tickets at the office across from the train station. Find additional bus info at V. XX Settembre, 71 (☎0573 36 32 43). To: **Empoli** (1¼hr., L5000/€2.58); **Florence** (1hr., L5000/€2.58); **Viareggio** (2hr., L7600/€3.92).

Taxis: At P. Garibaldi (☎0573 212 37) and at the train station (☎0573 242 91). Night service (☎0573 242 91) available until 1am.

✷? ORIENTATION AND PRACTICAL INFORMATION

From the train station, walk up **via XX Settembre** and continue straight as it changes names to **via Vanucci,** and then **via Cino.** When the street becomes **via Buozzi** (and bears slightly left), proceed one block and turn right onto the narrow **via degli Orai,** which leads to the **P. del Duomo,** the heart of the town. Local **COPIT** buses (#1 and 3) drop you at P. Gavinana (L1300/€0.67, tickets at local *tabacchi*). From there, turn right onto **via Cavour** and left onto **via Roma,** which runs into P. del Duomo.

Tourist Office: APT tourist office, P. del Duomo, 4 (☎0573 216 22; fax 343 27), in Palazzo dei Vescovi. Friendly, English-speaking staff. Open in summer M-Sa 9am-1pm and 3-6pm, Su 9am-1pm; in winter M-Sa 9am-1pm and 3-6pm.

Currency exchange: S. Marcello Pistoiese, V. Roma, 75 (☎0573 622 344) will only exchange cash. Open M-F 8:30am-1:30pm, Sa 8:30am-12:30pm, last day of the month 8:30am-noon. **Cassa di Risparmio di Pistoia e Pescia,** V. Roma, 3 (☎0573 36 90), next door to the post office. Changes traveler's checks and cash. Open M-F in the mornings and early afternoons. The **post office** itself also exchanges currency.

Police: ☎112. **Medical Emergency and Ambulance:** ☎118.

24-Hour Pharmacy: Viale Adua, 101 (☎0573 293 81).

Hospital: ☎0573 35 21.

Post Office: V. Roma, 5 (☎0573 99 52 11). Currency exchange and AmEx traveler's checks. Open M-F 8:15am-7pm.

Postal Code: 51100.

▐♦ ACCOMMODATIONS AND FOOD

Rooms at reasonable prices are rare finds in Pistoia, but **Albergo Firenze,** V. Curtatone e Montanara, 42, provides a great mix of comfort and value. From the station walk down V. XX Settembre and continue straight as it goes through several name changes, until it becomes V. Curtatone e Montanara. The hotel is near the end of the street on the right. The friendly American owner offers advice. Rooms have TV, floral bedspreads, and lace curtains. (☎/fax 0573 231 41. Breakfast L10,000/€5.16. Singles L50,000/€25.82, with bath L70,000/€36.15; doubles L85,000/€43.90, L100,000/€51.65; triples L120,000/€62, L135,000/€69.72. AmEx/MC/V.)

Grocery stores and specialty shops line the side streets. Market junkies browse the **open-air market** in P. del Duomo. (Open W and Sa 7:30am-2pm.) There's a daily fruit and vegetable market in P. della Sala, near the *duomo*. (Open 8am-2pm and 5-

7pm.) Sample exquisite Italian cuisine and imported wines at **La Botte Gaia,** V. Lastrone, 17/19, with gourmet cheeses, *antipasti, crostini,* and salads. The *bruschette* with sundried tomato and *pecorino* (goat's milk) are small but heavenly. (☎ 0573 36 56 02. Reservations recommended. Open Tu-Sa 10:30am-3pm and 6:30pm-1am, Su 6:30pm-1am. AmEx/MC/V.) **Trattoria dell'Abbondanza,** V. dell'Abbondanza, 10, serves excellent meals like *Panzanella di Farro* (summer salad with oil-soaked bread, basil, tomatoes, parsley, and garlic) and roasted rabbit. (☎ 0573 368 037. *Primi* from L10,000/€5.16; *secondi* from L13,000/€6.71. Open Th-Tu noon-2pm and 7:30-10pm.) **Dimeglio** supermarket is on V. Veneto, opposite the train station, to the right. (Open Th-T 8am-10pm, W 8am-1:30pm.)

⊙ SIGHTS

CATTEDRALE DI SAN ZENO. Life in Pistoia converges at **Piazza del Duomo.** The green and white marbled *duomo* houses an impressive store of early Renaissance art, as well as San Zeno's greatest treasure, the ▨**Dossale di San Jacopo.** The tremendously ornate altarpiece, set off in the plain chapel along the right, was worked on by nearly every important Tuscan silversmith between 1287 and 1456, including the young Brunelleschi. *(☎ 0573 250 95. Open daily 8:30am-12:30pm and 3:30-7pm; altar open 11:20am-noon and 4-5:30pm. Modest dress required. L3000/€1.55.)* Designed by Andrea Pisano, the octagonal 14th-century **baptistery** across from the *duomo* presents a relatively modest interior enlivened by Nino and Tommaso Pisano's *Virgin and Child* in the tympanum. *(Open Tu-Sa 9:30am-12:30pm and 3-6pm, Su-M 9:30am-12:30pm.)* The **Campanile,** adjacent to the *duomo,* offers a spectacular view; on a clear day, you can see all the way to Florence. *(☎ 0573 21 62 2. Open to reserved tours daily 10am-1pm and 3-6pm. L10,000/€5.16.)*

PISTOIA'S PALAZZI. Next to the *duomo,* facing the *piazza,* stands the 13th-century **Palazzo Comunale.** Left of the central balcony on the facade, about half way up, an arm reaches out of the wall, brandishing a club above the black marble head below—a tribute to the 1115 Pistoian victory over the Moorish king Musetto. With its Gothic windows and archways, the courtyard is also well worth a peak. *(☎ 0573 37 12 96. Open Tu-Sa 10am-7pm, Su 9am-12:30pm.)* The **Centro Marino Marini** in the **Palazzo del Tau,** celebrates one of Italy's most renowned 20th-century artists, native Marino Marini. The collection, connected by a maze of stairs, includes sculptures (with some of the primitive and sensuous Pomono, ancient Roman goddess of fertility), studies, and paintings. *(C. Silvano Fedi, 72. ☎ 0573 302 85. Open Tu-Sa 9am-1pm and 3-7pm, Su 9am-12:30pm. L6000/€3.10.)*

CHIESA DI SANT'ANDREA. In this typically Pisan-Romanesque church, Giovanni Pisano carved the pulpit now considered his masterpiece. Its marble panels have delicately carved figures experiencing the agony of being human. The impressive and disturbing *Massacre of the Innocents* graces the panel most clearly visible from the nave. *(Exit P. del Duomo by V. del Duca, from the corner opposite the duomo, and continue as it changes to V. dei Rossi and then V. Sant'Andrea. ☎ 0573 219 12. Open daily 8am-12:30pm and 3:30-6pm, in summer until 7pm.)*

CHIESA DI SAN GIOVANNI FUORCIVITAS. The single-naved interior of this 12th-century church (St. John Outside the City) is a vast, box-like space enlivened by vibrant stained glass windows. The church contains Luca della Robbia's *Visitation* and a Romanesque relief of *The Last Supper.* Giovanni Pisano's font and Guglielmo de Pisa's pulpit are both among the finest of the 13th-century carving revival. *(At the intersection of V. Cavour and V. Crispi. Open daily 8am-noon and 4-6:30pm.)*

♫ ENTERTAINMENT

If you missed EuroWoodstock '99, don't despair; Europe's remaining flower children converge annually in Pistoia for the **Pistoia Blues** concert series, held in July. In recent years, the festival has drawn the likes of B. B. King, Bob Dylan, and David Bowie.

CENTRAL ITALY

(Info ☎ 0573 35 86.) During the festival, the city allows free camping in designated sites near the stadium. On July 25, Pistoia celebrates the **Giostra dell'Orso** (Joust of the Bear). A modern incarnation of a 13th-century custom, contemporary 'knights' from competing regions joust a defenseless bear-shaped target, earning points for their team based on the accuracy of their lunges.

▶ DAYTRIP FROM PISTOLA: MONTECATINI TERME

*Despite its fairly small size, Montecatini Terme has 2 train stations (2min. apart). Most trains stop at both. The **Stazione Centrale** is slightly more centrally located than the **Stazione Succursale**. From the former, exit the station, and with your back to the front entrance, walk up V. Manzoni or through P. XX Settembre, until you arrive at P. del Popolo. Walk through the piazza to Viale Verdi. (From Stazione Succursale walk down C. Matteotti to P. del Popolo.) Pick up a map and a list of spa locations at the **tourist office**, Viale Verdi, 66-68. ☎ 0572 77 22. Open M-Sa 9am-12:30pm and 3-6pm, Su 9am-noon.*

A mere 10-minute train ride from Pistoia, Montecatini Terme offers budget travelers the chance to play "rich" for the day, without draining too many *lire*. Famous for its thermal baths, Montecatini Terme is the classic spa town, where well-off Italians (and a number of European tourists) spend their days relaxing among palm trees, fancy boutiques, and expensive restaurants.

If you plan to visit many spas, buy a cumulative ticket at Viale Verdi, 41. (Open M-F 8am-noon and 3:30-5:30pm, Sa 8:30-11:20am.) At the town's most famous spa, **Testuccio,** reached by following Viale Verdi to its end, L9000/€4.65 allows guests the opportunity to unwind in this neoclassical spa. Bring your own cup, or pay L1000/€0.52 to drink the medicinal waters. (Open May-Oct. 9am-noon and 4-7pm.) If you arrive in winter, go to the **Excelsior,** which offers similar services year-round.

Though Montecatini Terme has several hotels, many establishments close during the off-season. A good year-round option is the **Hotel Splendid,** at V. Mazzini, 102. With a friendly management, this hotel is the picture of comfort. (☎/fax 0572 701 48. Singles L60,000/€3.10; doubles L100,000/€51.65, each additional person L40,000/€20.66). **Corsaro Verde,** at P. XX Settembre, 11, is a welcoming family-run restaurant offering a large selection of Tuscan fare. (☎ 0572 91 16 50. *Primi* from L9000/€4.65; *secondi* from L8000/€4.13. Open May-Oct. daily 11:30am-3pm and 7-11pm; Nov.-Apr. Tu-Su 11:30am-3pm and 7-11pm. AmEx/MC/V.)

LUCCA   ☎ 0583

Although it once rivaled Florence and Siena in political and military might, today tree-lined Lucca lacks the wild-eyed hordes that once fought over its many alluring offerings. This charming Tuscan town is enclosed by a massive and perfectly preserved medieval wall that keeps out both traffic and the modern world. A promenade, with a double avenue of trees, runs along the top of the city walls. Bicycles, the transport of choice for the majority of Lucca's residents and guests, make the town's churches, towers, and museums more accessible.

▣ TRANSPORTATION

Trains: (☎ 0583 470 13) in P. Ricasoli, just outside the city walls. Trains provide the most convenient transport to Lucca. Info open daily 8am-noon and 3-8:30pm. To: **Florence** (1½hr., every hr., L8600/€4.43); **Pisa** (30min., every hr., L3800/€1.96); **Viareggio** (20min., every hr., L3800/€1.96). Luggage storage available (p. 370).

Buses: Lazzi (☎ 0583 58 40 76), in P. Verdi, next to the tourist office. To **Florence** (1½hr., every hr., L8600/€4.44) and **Pisa** (50min., every hr., L3500/€1.81).

Taxis: (☎ 0583 58 13 05) in P. Verdi, (☎ 0583 49 49 89) in P. Stazione, (☎ 0583 49 26 91) in P. Napoleone, and (☎ 0583 49 41 90) in P.S. Maria.

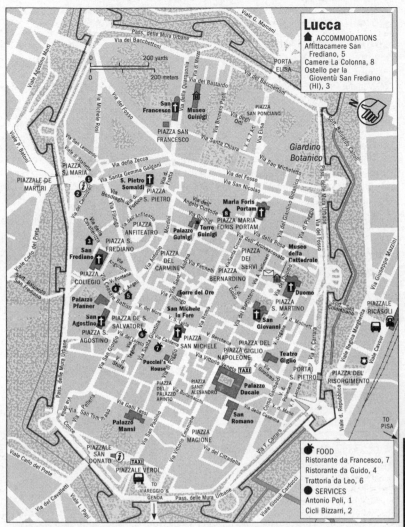

Lucca

⌂ ACCOMMODATIONS
Affittacamere San
  Frediano, 5
Camere La Colonna, 8
Ostello per la
  Gioventù San Frediano
  (HI), 3

🍎 FOOD
Ristorante da Francesco, 7
Ristorante da Guido, 4
Trattoria da Leo, 6

● SERVICES
Antonio Poli, 1
Cicli Bizzarri, 2

Bike Rental: Cicli Bizzarri, P.S. Maria, 32 (☎0583 49 60 31), next door to the regional tourist office. Offers a large selection of bikes and multi-day rentals. Basic bikes L4000/€2.07 per hr., L20,000/€10.33 per day; mountain and racing bikes L30,000/€15.5 per day and up. Open daily 9am-8pm. **Antonio Poli,** P.S. Maria, 42 (☎0583 49 37 87), on the other side of the regional tourist info office. Offers virtually identical services and prices. Open daily 8am-8:30pm.

Scooter Rental: Serchio Motori, V. Mazzini, 20 (☎0583 95 42 75). Take right on V. Mazzini from Piazzale Ricasoli in front of train station. 50cc scooters for L60,000/€31.

✦🔁 ORIENTATION AND PRACTICAL INFORMATION

From the train station, cross the highway and turn left. Enter the city with the cars at **Porta San Pietro** to your right, then head left on **Corso Garibaldi**. Turn right on **via Vittorio Veneto** and follow it to **Piazza Napoleone** (also known as P. Grande), the hub of the city. If you arrive by bus, follow **via San Paolino** toward the center of town and turn on V.V. Veneto to reach the *piazza*.

TOURIST, FINANCIAL, AND LOCAL SERVICES

Tourist Office: Centro Accoglienza Turistica (☎0583 41 96 89), in Piazzale Verdi. Walk into the city through Porta S. Pietro, turn left on V. Carrara and then right on V. Veneto. Turn left on V.S. Paolino and continue to P. Verdi. Office is on the right. English-speaking staff provides maps and train and bus info. Offers self-guided audio tours. Free room reservation service, but not for the cheaper hotels. Open daily 9am-7pm. **Agenzia per il Turismo**, P. Santa Maria, 36 (☎0583 91 99 1). From V. Roma, take a left onto V. Fillungo. Follow V. Fillungo until it ends and take a left on V.S. Germma Galgani and a left onto P.S. Maria. The office is on the left between the two bike shops. Has detailed brochures and hotel reservation service. Open daily 9am-7pm.

Currency Exchange: Credito Italiano, P.S. Michele, 47 (☎0583 475 46). 24hr. **ATM** in front. Open M-F 8:20am-1:20pm and 2:45-4:15pm, Sa 8:20-11:50am.

Luggage Storage: In train station. L4-7000/€2.07-3.62 per 12hr.

English-Language Bookstore: Libreria Baroni, V.S. Paolino, 47. Good selection of on-the-road standards in English. Open Tu-Sa 9am-1pm and 4-8pm. AmEx/MC/V.

EMERGENCY AND COMMUNICATIONS

Emergency: ☎113. **Carabinieri:** ☎0583 478 21.

First Aid: Misericordia, ☎0583 49 23 33.

24-Hour Pharmacy: Farmacia Comunale, V.S. Girolamo, 16, off P. Napoleone.

Hospital: Campo di Marte, ☎0583 97 01.

Internet Access: S.Michele.net, V.S. Michele, 7, (☎0583 44 05 40). Serves both your cash and cyber needs. Get 15min. of free access when you change at least $200. Otherwise, L8000/€4.13 per 30min.

Post Office: (☎0583 49 67 81), on V. Vallisneri, off P. del Duomo. Open M-Sa 8:15am-7pm.

Postal Code: 55100.

▚ ACCOMMODATIONS

Ostello per la Gioventù San Frediano (HI), V. della Cavallerizza, 12 (0583 46 99 57). From P. Napoleone turn onto V. Beccheria and walk for 2 blocks. Take a right on V. Roma and your 1st left onto V. Fillungo. In about 6 blocks, take a left onto P.S. Frediano and a right at the church onto V. della Cavalleriza. The hostel is on your left (15min.). Brand new hostel has good-sized rooms and immaculate modern bathrooms. HI card required. Breakfast L3000/€1.55, meals L15,000/€7.75. Reception daily 3:30-10pm. Lockout 9:45am-3:30pm. Dorms L29,000/€14.98, with bath L31,000/€16.01. Family rooms with bath L38,000/€19.63 per person.

Affittacamere San Frediano, V. degli Angeli, 19 (☎0583 46 96 30; sanfredianolu@onenet.it). Follow directions to HI hostel, but take a left onto arched V.degli Angeli, 2 blocks before P.S. Frediano. All rooms with TV. Doubles L70,000/€36.15, with bath L80,000/€41.32; additional bed L20,000/€10.33. AmEx/MC/V.

Camere La Colonna, V. dell'Angelo Custode, 16 (☎/fax 0583 44 01 70 or 0339 460 71 52), just off P. Maria Foris Portam. Spacious rooms with super-modern bathrooms. Some rooms have enormous screened windows opening onto a quiet courtyard. TV and phone. Singles L80,000/€41.32, with bath L90,000/€46.48; doubles L100,000/€51.65, L120,000/€62; triples L120,000/€62, L150,000/€77.47. Cash only.

FOOD

The **central market** occupies the large building at the west side of P. del Carmine. (Open M-Sa 7am-1pm and 4-7:30pm.) An **open-air market** overruns V. dei Bacchettoni. (W and Sa 8am-1pm.) The closest supermarket is **Superal**, V. Diaz, 24. Turn right from P. Elisa and take the first left. (☎ 0583 49 05 96. Open M-Tu and Th-Su 8am-8pm, W 8am-noon.) You may have to hunt for Lucca's cheaper restaurants.

▨ **Ristorante da Francesco**, Corte Portici, 13 (☎ 0583 41 80 49), off V. Calderia between P.S. Salvatore and P.S. Michele. Try the spaghetti with mussels and pesto (L9000/€4.65). Pasta L7-10,000/€3.62-5.16; *secondi* from L12,000/€6.20. Wine L8000/€4.13 per liter. Cover L3000/€1.55. Open Tu-Su noon-2:30pm and 7-10:30pm.

Trattoria da Leo, V. Tegrimi, 1 (☎ 0583 49 22 36), off P. del Salvatore - ask for it by name. A bustling local hangout specializing in *minestra di farro* (L6000/€3.10). *Primi* L9-10,000/€4.65-5.16; *secondi* L13,000/€6.71 and up. Cover L2000/€1.03. Open M-Sa noon-2:30pm and 7:30-10:30pm.

Ristorante da Guido, V. Battisti, 28 (☎ 0583 472 19), at V. degli Angeli. Warm owner welcomes tourists with cheap and filling meals. Savory *penne* with asparagus and gorgonzola (L5500/€2.84). *Secondi* from L8000/€4.13, including roasted veal or rabbit. Menù L17,000/€8.78. Open M-Sa noon-2:30pm and 8-10:30pm. AmEx.

◉ SIGHTS

PIAZZA NAPOLEONE. This *piazza* in the heart of Lucca is the town's administrative center. The 16th-century **Palazzo Ducale** now houses government offices. In the evening, P. Napoleone is packed with Luccese young and old, out for their *passeggiata*. **Piazza Anfiteatro** is also quite popular with locals and tourists alike. It's oval because the buildings on its periphery were constructed where the walls of the town's Roman amphitheater once stood.

▨DUOMO DI SAN MARTINO. The architects designed the facade of this ornate, asymmetrical *duomo* around its bell tower, which had been constructed two centuries earlier. The 13th-century reliefs that decorate the exterior include Nicola Pisano's *Journey of the Magi* and *Deposition*. Matteo Civitali, Lucca's famous sculptor, designed the floor, contributed the statue of St. Martin to the right of the door, and carved two angels for the altar. His prized piece is the *Tempietto*, halfway up the left aisle near the **Volto Santo**. Reputedly carved by Nicodemus at Calvary, this wooden crucifix is said to depict the true image of Christ. The statue passed into the hands of the bishop of Lucca, who, somewhat ignorant of navigational technique, set off in a boat without a crew or sails and miraculously landed safely at Luni. To settle the ownership dispute that arose between Lucca and Luni, the statue was placed on an ox-cart. The oxen left to choose the statue's site turned toward Lucca. The Volto is taken for a ride through the town every September 13 to commemorate the oxen's wise choice. Don't miss Tintoretto's *Last Supper*, housed in the third chapel on the right. The **sacrity**, or **the Ilaria**, contains the well-preserved *Madonna and Saints* by Ghirlandaio and Jacopo della Quercia's masterly **sarcophagus** with a life-size sculpture of Ilaria del Carretto. The **Museo Della Cattedrale**, around the corner from the *duomo*, has dimly lit rooms filled with glass cases of religious objects used throughout the centuries in the *duomo*. (*The Duomo is in P.S. Marino, between bell tower and post office. From P. Napoleone, take V. del Duomo. Duomo open M-F 9am-6pm, Sa 9am-7pm, Su 8:30am-6:30pm. Sacrity open M-F 9:30am-5:45pm, Sa 9:30am-6:45pm, Su 9-9:50am, 11:20-11:50am and 1-6:15pm. L6000/€3.10. Museo della Cattedrale open M-Sa 9:30am-6pm, Su 10am-3pm. L6000/€3.1. Combination ticket for the Ilaria, Museo della Cattedrale and Chiesa di S. Giovanni, L10,000/€5.16.*)

CHIESA DI SAN GIOVANNI. This unassuming church hides an archeological treasure trove. Under the large, simple plaster dome of the left transept is the entrance to a recently excavated 2nd century AD Roman complex. The ruins of a private house and bath (and the church's foundations) are exposed under the floor, where you can walk among them before emerging again into the church. *(Walk past San Giovanni from P.S. Martino and around the corner to the right to reach the entrance. Open M-Sa 10am-6pm, Su 10am-3pm. L4000/€2.07.)*

CHIESA DI SAN FREDIANO. Off P. Scalpellini rises this imposing Romanesque church whose facade is graced by Berlinghieri's spectacular *Ascension*, a huge polychromatic mosaic. Inside, the second chapel on the right holds the remains of S. Zita, the beloved Virgin of Lucca. Despite the myth that she lies untouched by time, she is rapidly decaying, looking remarkably like beef jerky as she goes. Frescoes of the *Legend of the Volto Santo* by Amico Aspertini decorate the chapel on the left. *(From P.S. Michele, take V. Fillungo to P.S. Frediano. Open 7:30am-noon and 3-6pm.)*

CASA PUCCINI (BIRTHPLACE OF GIACOMO PUCCINI). Music lovers shouldn't miss the birthplace of Giacomo Puccini, composer of *La Bohème* and *Madame Butterfly*. This plain stucco house has airy, tiled rooms exhibiting the piano on which Puccini composed his last opera, *Turandot*, as well as letters and manuscripts, which you can admire while the strains of his operas filter through the apartment. *(C.S. Lorenzo, 9, off V. Poggi. ☎0583 58 40 28. Open July-Sept. daily 10am-6pm; Mar.-June and Oct.-Dec. Tu-Su 10am-1pm and 3-6pm; Jan.-Feb. 10am-1pm. L5000/€2.58.)*

▨TORRE GUINIGI AND TORRE DELLA ORE. The **Torre Guinigi** tower rises above Lucca from the mute stone mass of Palazzo Guinigi. While the palazzo is not open to the public, the narrow tower is. After climbing 230 stairs, one can slide between the railings and large planters containing seven stunted holm trees, to gain a stunning 360 degree view of Lucca and the surrounding hills. *(V.S. Andrea, 42. ☎0583 49 12 43. From P.S. Michele follow V. Roma for 1 block and take a left on V. Fillungo and a right on V.S. Andrea. Open daily 9am-7:30pm, L6000/€3.10.)* Alternatively, you can climb the 207 steps of the **Torre della Ore** (clock tower) for a similar view. These towers are two of the very few that remain of the original 250 that once dotted Medieval Lucca. *(V. Fillungo, 22. Follow the directions to Torre Guinigi, and you'll pass it on the way, on V. Fillungo. ☎0583 85 42 32. Open M-F 8:30am-6:30pm, Sa 8:30am-7:30pm. L6000/€3.1.)*

BALUARDI. No tour of Lucca is complete without a walk or bike ride around the perfectly intact city walls. The shaded 4km path, which remains closed to cars, passes grassy parks and cool fountains as it progresses along the *baluardi* (battlements). From here, appreciate the layout of the city and the beautiful countryside high above the moat; it's perfect for a breezy afternoon picnic and siesta.

🎵 ENTERTAINMENT

Lucca's calendar bulges with artistic performances, especially during the summer. The Intercontinental Festival of Symphony Orchestras offers a series of approximately ten concerts that take place from the end of June to mid August. Watch an Italian film under the stars in P. Guidiccioni. (June-Aug. nightly 9pm. L7000/€3.62, students L4000/€2.07.) Take advantage of the Teatro Comunale del Giglio's opera season that occurs in September. The king of Lucca's festivals is the **Settembre Lucchese;** a festival that offers a lively jumble of artistic, athletic, and folkloric presentations. The annual **Palio della Balestra,** a crossbow competition dating from 1443, takes place here. Participants wear traditional costume on July 12 and September 14 for the competition, which was revived for tourists in the early 1970s.

Caffè Disimo, V. Fillungo, 58. Chandeliers, marble tables, and a zinc bar. In the 19th century, the cafe was frequented by artists, writers, *Risorgimento*-plotters and musicians (including Pinini), but they probably didn't have to pay the L4000/€2.07 that customers are now charged for a cup of coffee. You will if you sit down. Instead, have your cup of joe while standing at the bar for just L1800/€0.93. Open Tu-Sa 8am-8pm.

Golden Fox, V.R. Margherita (☎0583 49 16 19). From train station, cross Piazzale Ricasoli and take a left on V.R. Margherita. Bar is on left. Brass and dark wood adorn this spacious English-style pub. A mostly Italian crowd comes to hang out, drink beer (L8000/€4.13 per pint) and listen to loud American music. Open daily 8pm-1:30am.

PISA   ☎050

When people think about Pisa, they generally think of one thing only. Each year millions of tourists animate the town's famous Campo dei Miracoli as they marvel at the famous leaning tower, creating a T-shirt-buying, ice-cream-licking, photo-snapping wasteland. The tower is undoubtedly remarkable, and it would be quite impressive even if it were perpendicular to the ground. But if you decide to journey to Pisa, leave enough time to explore more than just the tower. The cathedral, baptistery, museums, and cemetery clustered in the same *piazza* contain numerous artistic jewels, and in many ways they have greater lasting appeal than the famous tower. Moreover, as the innumerable copy shops and bookstores attest, Pisa is a university town, and exploring the neighborhoods around the sprawling university is extremely rewarding. You will find harmonious *piazze*, elegant buildings, impassioned political graffiti, and picturesque narrow alleys. For this part of Pisa, wander around Piazza Cavalieri and Piazza Dante Alighieri.

Pisa's history has had its share of twists and turns. In the Middle Ages, when the unclogged Arno flowed to the sea, the city earned its living as a port, and Pisa's Mediterranean empire extended to Corsica, Sardinia, and the Balearics. When the Arno filled with silt, Pisa's fortunes dried up. After the tower tantalized travelers and brought millions of tourist *lire* to the waning town, Pisa began to recover.

▄ TRANSPORTATION

Flights: Galileo Galilei Airport (☎050 50 07 07). Trains that make the 5min. trip (L1900/€0.98) between the train station and the airport coincide with flight departures and arrivals. You can also take bus #3 from the airport which will take you to the train station and other points in Pisa and its environs (every 20min., 10min. between the airport and the station. L1500/€0.77). Charter, domestic, and international flights. To: **London** (2¼hr., 1 per day); **Munich** (1½hr., 10 per day); **Paris** (1¾hr., twice a week).

Trains: (☎147 808 88), in P. della Stazione, at southern end of town. Info office open daily 7am-9pm. Ticket booths open 24hr. Luggage storage available (p. 374). To: **Genoa** (2½hr.; every hr.; L25,300/€13.07); **Florence** (1hr., every hr., L9400/€4.85); **Livorno** (20min., every hr., L2700/€1.39); **Rome** (3hr.; L45,500/€23.50). Local or regional trains to **Lucca** (20min., every 30min., L3400/€1.76) stops at Pisa's **San Rossore,** closer to the *duomo* and the youth hostel. If leaving Pisa from S. Rossore, buy train ticket *tabacchi;* there's no ticket office in the station.

Buses: Lazzi, P. Emanuele, 11 (☎050 462 88). To: **Florence** (2½hr.; change bus in Lucca; every hr.; L11,400/€5.89); **La Spezia** (3 hrs.; 4 per day; L10,400/€5.37); **Lucca** (40min., every hr., L3700/€1.91); **Pistoia** (1½hr., 3 per day, L8300/€4.29). **CPT** (☎050 233 84), in P. Sant'Antonio, near train station. To **Livorno** (30min., 1 per day) and **Volterra** (1½hr., 7 per day, L9400/€4.85) via **Pontederra.**

Taxis: Radio Taxi (☎050 541 600), (☎050 412 52) in P. Stazione, (☎050 56 18 78) in P. Duomo, and (☎050 285 42) at the airport.

Car Rental: Avis (☎050 420 28; 23+), **Eurodollar** (☎050 462 09; 21+), and **Maggiore** (☎050 425 74; 19+) have offices at airport. From L100,000/€51.65 per day.

▄ ORIENTATION AND PRACTICAL INFORMATION

Pisa lies on Italy's Tyrrhenian coast, at the mouth of the Arno, west of Florence. Most of Pisa's sights lie to the north of the Arno; the main train station lies to the south. To reach the **Campo dei Miracoli** (a.k.a. **Piazza del Duomo**) from the station, take bus #1 (L1500/€0.77, tickets sold in *tabacchi*). Alternatively, walk straight up **Viale Gramsci,** through **Piazza Vittorio Emanuele,** and stroll along **Corso Italia** across the Arno, where it becomes **via Borgo Stretto.** From the university district, turn left on V.U. Dini to pass through P. dei Cavalieri and toward the *duomo* and tower.

TOURIST SERVICES

Tourist Office: (☎050 422 91; aptpisa@pisa.turismo.toscani-it; www.turismo.toscana.it), in P. della Stazione, to the left as you exit the station. English-speaking staff provides detailed maps. No accommodations service but they do provide a very detailed listing of all the local hotels and camp sites, including prices and locations. Another **branch** (☎050 56 04 64), behind the baptistery. From the P. del Duomo, pass through the arch into P. Manin just outside the city walls and turn right immediately. The branch is 20m down the road against the city wall. Both branches open M-Sa 9am-7pm, Su 9:30am-3:30pm. In branch office, **Booking Center** (☎050 83 02 53; fax 83 02 43; www.traveleurope.it/pisa.htm) offers tour packages and makes hotel and restaurant reservations. English spoken. Open M-Sa 9:30am-6:30pm.

Budget Travel: CTS, V.S. Maria, 45b (☎050 483 00 or 292 21; fax 454 31), by the Hotel Galileo. Daytrips, international tickets, and boats to nearby islands. Long waits. English spoken. Open M-F 9:30am-12:30pm and 4-7pm, Sa 9:30am-12:30pm.

LOCAL SERVICES

Luggage Storage: Self service in the train station. L3-7000/€1.55-3.62 per 24hr.

English-Language Bookstore: Maxi-Livres, C. Italia, 97 (☎050 451 50). Stocked with English classics and popular novels by authors like Tom Clancy and Stephen King. Open M-Sa 9am-11:30pm, Su 10am-11:30pm.

Gay and Lesbian Resources: ARCI-GAY "Pride!" V.S. Lorenzo, 38 (☎050 55 56 18; www.gay.it/pride). Open M-F 1:30-7:30pm.

Laundromats: Lavanderia, V. Corridoni, 100. Turn right from the train station. Wash L6000/€3.10 per 7kg; dry L5500/€2.83. Open daily 8am-10pm. **Speedy Wash,** V. Trento, 9 (☎050 483 53). Wash L6500/€3.36; dry L6000/€3.10. Soap L1000/€0.52. Open Tu-F 9am-8:30pm, Sa 2-8pm.

EMERGENCY AND COMMUNICATIONS

Emergency: ☎113. **Medical Emergency:** ☎118.

Police: ☎050 58 35 11.

First Aid: ☎050 99 23 00.

24-Hour Pharmacy: Farmacia, P. del Duomo.

Hospital: (☎050 99 21 11), on V. Bonanno near P. del Duomo.

Internet Access: Pisa Internet Point, V. Colombo, 53 (☎050 220 04 08), 2 blocks from the train station. L9,000/€4.65 per hr., students L7000/€3.62. Open M-Sa 10am-10pm. **Internet Planet,** P. Cavolloti (☎050 83 97 92, info@internetplanet.it), from P. del Duomo, follow V.S. Maria and take 2nd left onto P. Cavolloti. L6000/€3.10 per hr., L4000/€2.07 per 30min. Open M-Sa 10am-12:30am.

Post Office: P. Emanuele, 8 (☎050 18 69), near the station. Open M-Sa 8:30am-7pm.

Postal Code: 56100.

▐ ACCOMMODATIONS & CAMPING

Pisa has plenty of cheap *pensioni* and *locande*, but demand is always high. Call ahead for reservations, or pick up the hotel booklet and map at the tourist office.

▨ Albergo Gronchi, P. Archivescovado, 1 (☎050 56 18 23), adjacent to P. del Duomo. Large rooms with airy, spartan feel. Some with frescoed ceilings and in-room sink and shower. Curfew midnight (after midnight ring bell). Reservations only accepted within 10 days of scheduled arrival. Singles L36,000/€18.60; doubles L62,000/€32.02.

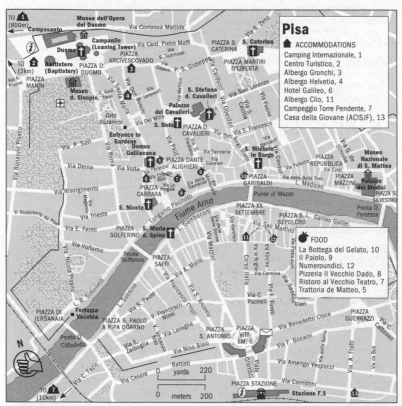

Pisa

🏠 ACCOMMODATIONS

Camping Internazionale, 1
Centro Turistico, 2
Albergo Gronchi, 3
Albergo Helvetia, 4
Hotel Galileo, 6
Albergo Clio, 11
Campeggio Torre Pendente, 7
Casa della Giovane (ACISJF), 13

🍎 FOOD

La Bottega del Gelato, 10
Il Paiolo, 9
Numeroundici, 12
Pizzeria Il Vecchio Dado, 8
Ristoro al Vecchio Teatro, 7
Trattoria de Matteo, 5

Albergo Helvetia, V. Don G. Boschi, 31 (☎050 55 30 84), off P. Archivescovado, 2min. from the *duomo*. Large, clean rooms. Most rooms face a quiet courtyard; all have TV. Bar downstairs. English spoken. Breakfast (must order the night before, served 8:30-11am) L8000/€4.13. Singles L60,000/€31; doubles L80,000/€41.32, with bath L110,000/€56.81; triples L125,000/€64.56; quads L165,000/€85.22.

Centro Turistico Madonna dell'Acqua, V. Pietrasantina, 15 (☎050 89 06 22), behind old Catholic sanctuary 2km from the Tower. Bus #3 from station (4 per hr., last 9:45pm); ask driver to stop at *ostello*—board the bus across the street from 1st departure point in *piazza* to avoid making a detour to the airport. Lying next to a creek, crickets sing you to sleep, while mosquitoes linger outside waiting. Kitchen available. Sheets L3000/€1.55. Reception daily 6-11pm. Check-out 9am. Dorms L25,000/€12.91; doubles L82,000/€42.35; triples L102,000/€52.68; quads L120,000/€62. MC/V.

Albergo Clio, V.S. Lorenzino, 3 (☎050 284 46), off C. Italia, 1 block from the Ponte Mezzo. Lobby a Hollywood dream: pink, black, and mirrors. Tiled hallways lead to modern rooms and super-clean bathrooms. Singles L55,000/€28.41; doubles L80,000/€41.32, with bath L90,000/€46.48; triples with bath L120,000/€62. Cash only.

Casa della Giovane (ACISJF), V.F. Corridoni, 29 (☎050 430 61), 10min. to the right from the station. Don't be spooked by the life-size Virgin Mary in the hallway or the tortured Jesus hung in every room. Nuns kindly welcome travelers of any faith, provided they happen to be female. Large kitchen and dining facilities. Doubles, triples, and quads have own baths. Breakfast L2000/€1.03. Curfew 10:30pm. Reception daily 7am-10:30pm. Dorms L30,000/€15.50; singles L50,000/€25.82.

CENTRAL ITALY

Hotel Galileo, V.S. Maria, 12 (☎050 406 21). A solar system of spacious rooms. Stellar proprietress. Don't be put off by the dark entryway—sunspots are ahead. Singles with bath L70,000/€36.15; doubles L70,000/€36.15, with bath L90,000/€46.48; triples L90,000/€46.48, with bath L120,000/€62. Cash only.

Camping: Campeggio Torre Pendente, V. delle Cascine, 86 (☎050 56 17 04), 1km away. Bus #3 to P. Manin. With city wall on right, walk 2 blocks and take left onto V. delle Cascine, following camping signs. Walk through long concrete underpass, emerge, and walk past industrial-looking buildings; campground on right. *Let's Go* advises against taking this walk at night. Tiny swimming pool, decent bathrooms, and secluded sites. Open Aug.-Oct. L12,500/€6.46 per person, L6000/€3.10 per child, L11,000/€5.68 per tent. Bungalows available for L60-170,000/€31-87.8. **Camping Internazionale** (☎050 365 53), 10km away on V. Litoranea in Marina di Pisa, on private beach. Take CPT bus (intercity bus) from P.S. Antonio (ask the driver to make sure you're on the right one) to Marina di Pisa (L2000/€1.03). Buy ticket in CPT office as you enter P.S. Antonio from P.V. Emanuele. Open May-Sept. L12,000/€6.20 per person, L9000/€4.65 per child, L15,000/€7.75 per small tent, L18,000/€9.30 per large tent.

◖ FOOD

For more authentic ambience than that of the touristy *trattorie*, head toward the river. Cheap restaurants are plentiful in the university area. In **P. Vettovaglie,** produce and haggling from the open-air market spill into nearby streets. Bakeries and *salumerie* fill Pisa's residential quarter. For conveniently pre-packaged goods, try **Superal,** V. Pascoli, 6, just off C. Italia. (Open M-Sa 8am-8pm.)

▨ **Il Paiolo,** V. Curtatone Montanara, 9 (☎050 425 28), near the university. This pub draws a lively crowd and offers a *menù* with *primi* and *secondi* for L15,000/€7.75. For a hearty dish, order their *bistecca* (steak with mushrooms, arugula, nuts and parmesan cheese). Or try their heavenly seafood *risotto*, with mussels, tiny calamari, and chunks of salmon (L10,000/€5.16) with the light, sweet house white wine (¼ liter L3000/€1.55). Open M-F noon-3pm and 7pm-1am, Sa 7pm-1am.

Numeroundici, V.S. Martino, 47. Numeroundici started as a tiny counter-in-the-wall, creating not only generous and superb sandwiches (L4000/€2.07) and vegetable *torte* (L3000/€1.55), but also imaginative dishes of the day. *Primi* L7000/€3.62; *secondi* L10,000/€5.16. Open M-F noon-10pm, Sa 5-10pm.

Trattoria da Matteo, V. l'Aroncio, 46 (☎050 410 57), off V.S. Maria near Hotel Galileo. *Gnocchi al pesto* L9000/€4.65. *Scaloppina con i funghi* (veal with mushrooms; L11,000/€5.68). 40 different kinds of pizza. *Menù* L22,000/€11.35. Cover L2000/€1.03, for table service. Open Su-F 9am-3pm and 6-11pm. Bar open noon-11pm. V.

Ristoro al Vecchio Teatro, V. Collegio Ricci, 2 (☎050 202 10), off P. Dante. Delicious, innovative combinations with emphasis on fresh vegetables. Try the *risotto d'ortolana* (rice with vegetables) or the buttery *sfogliata di zucchine* (zucchini tort). *Primi* L10,000/€5.16; *secondi* L10,000/€5.16. Desserts L5000/€2.58. Open Su-Th 12:15-3pm, F-Sa 12:15-3pm and 8-10pm. Closed Aug. AmEx/MC/V.

Pizzeria Il Vecchio Dado, Luongo Pacinotti, 21-22 (☎/fax 050 580 900). On the Arno, this restaurant offers excellent pizza starting at L5000/€2.58. Other meal options available. Open F-Tu noon-3pm and 7-11pm. In winter, closes at 10pm. MC/V.

La Bottega del Gelato, P. Garibaldi, 11. Offers huge range, from nutella to pistachio. Popular after sundown. Cones and cups L2500/€1.29. Open Th-Tu 11am-1am.

◔ SIGHTS

Campo dei Miracoli (Field of Miracles), is an appropriate nickname for **Piazza del Duomo.** The **Leaning Tower, duomo, baptistery,** and **Camposanto** all rise improbably from the manicured swaths of plush, emerald green grass surrounding the field.

CENTRAL ITALY

LEANING TOWER. A close inspection reveals that all the buildings in the Campo dei Miracoli are leaning at different angles, thanks to shifting soil. None lean quite so dramatically or famously as the *campanile* of the *duomo*. Bonanno Pisano began building the tower in 1173, and it had reached the height of 10m when the soil beneath unexpectedly shifted. The tilt intensified after World War II, when tourists ascended in

PISAN CARROTS. The city offers an all-inclusive ticket to the *duomo*, baptistery, Camposanto, Museo delle Sinopie, and Museo del Duomo for L19,000/€9.8; to 2 of the above monuments for L12,000/€6.20; to the *duomo* and 2 other monuments for L15,000/€7.75; to everything but the *duomo* for L16,000/€8.26. Combination tickets can be bought at the door of any one of the sights.

ever-increasing numbers, and the tower continues to slip 1-2mm every year. The Tower has been closed indefinitely. In June of 2001, the steel safety cables and iron girdles that had imprisoned the tower during the multi-year stabilization effort, were finally removed. Though the tower itself was released, tourists were not. Visitors are still confined to view the tower from the surrounding *piazza*. After readjusting the tower some 7mm, it is now considered stable, but the tower remains closed to the public, forcing you to admire its seven-tiered, multi-arched splendor from the exterior.

DUOMO. The dark green-and-white façade of the *duomo* is the archetype of the Pisan-Romanesque style; indeed, it is one of the most important Romanesque cathedrals in the world. Begun in 1063 by Boschetto (who had himself entombed in the wall), the cathedral was the Campo's first structure. Enter the five-aisled nave through Bonanno Pisano's bronze doors (1180). Although most of the interior was destroyed by fire in 1595, paintings by Ghirlandaio hang along the right wall, Cimabue's spectacular gilded mosaic *Christ Pantocrator* graces the apse, and bits of the Cosmati pavement remain. The cathedral's elaborate chandelier is rumored (falsely) to have inspired Galileo's theories of universal gravity. Giovanni Pisano's last and greatest pulpit, designed to outdo his father's in the baptistery, sits majestically at the heart of the cathedral. Relief panels depict classical and biblical subjects, including the Nativity, the Last Judgment, and the Massacre of the Innocents. Always up for good allegory, Pisano carved the pulpit's supports into figures symbolizing the arts and virtues. *(Open daily 10am-7:40pm. L3000/€1.55. Free for Su mass, but you must look very pious to get past the rigid guards.)*

BAPTISTERY. The baptistery, an enormous barrel of a building, was begun in 1152 by a man known as Deotisalvi ("God save you"). It measures 107m in girth and reaches 55m into the Pisan sky. Its architecture is a blend of styles, incorporating typical Tuscan-Romanesque stripes with a stunning Gothic ensemble of gables, pinnacles, and statuary set in lacy tracery. Nicola Pisano's pulpit (1260), to the left of the baptismal font, recaptures the sobriety and dignity of classical antiquity; it is considered one of the harbingers of Renaissance art in Italy. The dome's acoustics are astounding—an unamplified choir singing in the baptistery can be heard 2km away. A staircase, embedded in the wall, leads to an interior balcony; further up you can catch tantalizing glimpses of the town through the narrow windows. *(Open late Apr.-late Sept. daily 8am-8pm; Oct-Mar. 9am-5pm. L12,000/€6.20, plus free entrance to one other museum/monument on the combination ticket list.)*

CAMPOSANTO. The Camposanto, a cloistered courtyard cemetery covered with earth that the Crusaders brought back from Golgotha, holds, among other things, the Roman sarcophagi whose reliefs inspired Nicola Pisano's pulpit in the baptistery. Fragments of frescoes shattered by Allied bombs during World War II line the galleries. The **Cappella Ammannati** contains the haunting frescoes of Florence succumbing to the plague. The unidentified 14th-century artist is known as the "Master of the Triumph of Death." *(Open late Apr.-late Sept. daily 8am-7:45pm; Mar. and Oct daily 9am-5:40pm; Nov-Feb. 9am-4:40pm. L12,000/€6.20, plus free entrance to one other museum/monument on the combination ticket list.)*

MUSEO NAZIONALE DI SAN MATTEO. The Museo Nazionale di San Matteo includes spectacular panels by artists like Masaccio, Fra Angelico, Ghirlandaio, and Simone Martini. There are also sculptures by the Pisano clan and a bust by Donatello in this converted convent. *(Just of P. Mazzini on Lugarno Mediceo. Open Tu-Sa 9am-7pm, Su 9am-2pm. L8000/€4.13, ages 18-26 L4000/€2.07, under 18 and over 65 free.)*

MUSEO DELL'OPERA DEL DUOMO AND MUSEO DELLE SINOPIE. The Museo dell'Opera del Duomo displays artwork from the three buildings of P. del Duomo. The *Madonna del Colloquio* by Giovanni Pisano was named for the expressive gazes exchanged between mother and child. The display also includes an 11th-century crucifix, strangely reminiscent of Picasso, and works by Tino Camaino and Nino Pisano and an assortment of Roman and Etruscan pieces tucked into the church during the Middle Ages. *(Behind the Leaning Tower. Open Apr.-late Sept. daily 8am-7:20pm; Mar. and Oct. 9am-5:20pm; Nov.-Feb. 9am-4:20pm. L12,000/€6.20, plus free entrance to one other museum/monument on the combination ticket list.)* Across the square from the Camposanto, the **Museo delle Sinopie** houses a display of fresco sketches by Traini, Veneziano, and Gaddi, as well as other sketches discovered during the post-World War II restoration. *(Same hours as Museo dell'Opera del Duomo. L12,000/ €6.20, plus one museum/monument on the combination ticket list.)*

PIAZZA DEI CAVALIERI. Designed by Vasari and built on the site of the Roman forum, this *piazza* held Pisa's town hall during the Middle Ages. Today, it is the seat of the **Scuola Normale Superiore,** one of Italy's premier universities. Though not open to the public, a short walk about the exterior is well worth the time. The busts that decorate the facade are those of the old Grand Dukes of Tuscany. The black wrought-iron baskets on either end of the **Palazzo dell'Orologio** (Palace of the Clock) were once receptacles for the heads of delinquent Pisans. In the *palazzo's* tower, Ugolino della Gherardesca, with all his sons and grandsons, was starved to death in 1208 as punishment for treachery. This murky episode in Tuscan politics is commemorated in both Dante's *Inferno* and Shelley's *Tower of Famine.*

OTHER SIGHTS. Of Pisa's numerous churches, three merit special attention. The **Chiesa di Santa Maria della Spina,** which faces Gambacorti near the river, is quintessentially Gothic. Its bristling architecture is appropriate, as it was built to house a thorn taken from Christ's Crown of Thorns. Originally an oratory, the church was enlarged in 1323 and renamed Chiesa della Spina (Thorn). Visitors can view the church's interior only during Italy's annual **Culture Week.** *(From the Campo, walk down V.S. Maria and over the bridge. Ask at the tourist office about Culture Week.)* The **Chiesa di San Michele in Borgo** is notable for the Latin scribblings, found on its facade, which concern a 14th-century electoral campaign for University Rector. *(From the Chiesa di Santa Maria della Spina, walk with the river to your left, cross the first bridge, and continue straight one block.)* Another worthy sidetrack from P. del Duomo is the **Chiesa di San Nicola.** The famous altarpiece in the fourth chapel on the right shows St. Nicholas deflecting the arrows that a wrathful God aims at Pisa. The bell tower of the church inclines slightly, not unlike its more famous cousin. *(Between V.S. Maria and P. Carrara. Open daily 7:45-11:30am and 5-6:30pm.)*

ORTO BOTANICO. If you're maxed out on gray stone and culture, head to the shady, green respite offered by the Public Garden, whose palm trees, gravel walks, and numerous plants offer a soothing retreat from the city. *(Entrance at V.L. Ghini, 5, between V. Roma and V.S. Maria. Open M-F 8am-5:30pm, Sa 8am-1pm.)*

🎵 ENTERTAINMENT

Occasional concerts are given in the *duomo*, where the acoustics are phenomenal. Call **Opera della Primaziale** (☎ 050 56 18 20). The annual **Gioco del Ponte** revives the city's medieval color and pageantry. Pisans divide on each part of the Arno and pledge allegiance to either the *Tramontana* or the *Mezzogiorno.* Then the opposing sides converge, pushing a large cart against their rivals, to see which side conquers the largest section of the bridge. For one night in mid-June, the **Luminara di**

San Ranieri illuminates Pisa with 70,000 lights placed on the city's buildings. Or, go to the main street of the University District, which runs up from P. Garibaldi on the river, changing names from Borgo Stretto to via Oberdan to via Carducci. It is lined with cafes and shops; drink some beer, sip on some coffee, or enjoy a *gelato*. People-watch at **Caffè Spizio**, V. Oberdan, 54 (☎050 58 02 81), which offers coffee (from L1500/€0.77), beer (from L5000/€2.58 per bottle), and *gelato* (from L2000/€1.03), and extensive outdoor seating on the pedestrian-plugged street.

LIVORNO ☎0586

Overwhelmed by the monstrous oceanliners awaiting departure for Sardinia, Corsica, Greece, and Spain, Livorno is a rough-and-ready port town. Romantically known to the British as "Leghorn," Livorno attracts tourists with its convenient ferry system. Henry James's dictum on the city still holds true for the most part: "It has neither a church worth one's attention, nor a municipal palace, nor a museum, and it may claim the distinction, unique in Italy, of being the city of no pictures." Still, the city is not the hole in the ground that some make it out to be. If you're here with time on your hands, excellent seafood, the surrounding countryside, and a few worthwhile public monuments and forts offer considerable solace, and the beach is merely a bus or ferry ride away.

☐ TRANSPORTATION

Trains: Frequent service connects Livorno to: **Florence** (1hr., L11,200/€5.78); **Piombino** (1hr., L8900/€4.59); **Pisa** (15min., L2700/€1.39); and **Rome** (3hr., L42,300/€21.82). Luggage storage available (p. 380).

Buses: ATL (☎0586 84 71 11) sends buses from P. Grande to **Piombino** (L11,000/€5.68) and **Pisa** (L4000/€2.07). Facing the church in P. Grande, it's on the left.

Ferries: at the Stazione Marittima. From train station, take bus #1 to P. Grande (buy ticket from *tabacchi*; L1500/€0.77). From P. Grande, take PB 1, 2, or 3 bus, or walk down V. Logorano, cross P. Municipio, and take V. Porticciolo, which becomes V. Venezia and leads to the port and Stazione Marittima (15min.). At Stazione Marittima, there is **currency exchange, luggage storage,** and a **restaurant.** Check where and when your boat leaves—schedules vary. Prices increase in summer and on weekends. Port taxes about L15,000/€7.75. **Corsica Marittima** (☎0586 21 05 07) runs fast service to **Bastia, Corsica** (2hr.; late Apr. to mid-Sept. 2-4 per day; L32-55,000/€16.53-28.41), and **Porto Vecchio, Corsica** (10hr., June-Sept. 1-2 per week). **Moby Lines** (☎0586 82 68 25) runs to **Bastia** (4hr.; Apr.-Sept. 1-2 per week; L32-55,000/€16.53-28.41). **Corsica and Sardinia Ferries** (☎0586 88 13 80; fax 89 61 03) runs to **Bastia** (4hr.; frequency depends on season; L29-53,000/€14.98-27.37) and **Golfo Aranci, Sardinia** (9-10hr.; 2 per day in June-Aug., greatly reduced off-season service; L42-90,000/€21.70-46.48). All ferry ticket offices open before and after arrivals and departures.

Taxis: (☎0586 21 00 00) in P. XX Settembre; (☎0586 89 80 94) in P. Grande; and (☎0586 40 12 94) at train station.

◨◪ ORIENTATION AND PRACTICAL INFORMATION

From the train station, take bus #1 to reach **Piazza Grande,** the center of town. Buses #2 and 8 also stop at P. Grande, but only after tripping along the periphery. Buy tickets (L1500/€0.77) at the booth outside the station, at a *tabacchi*, or at one of the orange vending machines. If you prefer to walk, cross the park in front of the station and head straight down **Viale Carducci,** which becomes V. dei Larderel, to **Piazza Repubblica.** Cross the *piazza* and take **via delle Galere** to P. Grande.

Tourist Office: P. Cavour, 6, 3rd fl. (☎0586 89 81 11; info@livorno.turismo.toscana.it), up V. Cairoli from P. Grande, in P. Cavour; on the left. Open M and W 8am-1pm and 3-

C E N T R A L   I T A L Y

5pm, Tu 8am-1pm and 4-9pm, Th-F 9am-1pm and 3-9pm, Sa-Su 8am-1pm and 3-10pm. Reduced hours Sept.-May. **Branch office** (☎0586 89 53 20), in the Stazione Marittima (☎0586 89 53 20). Open June-Sept. daily 8am-8pm.

Currency Exchange: Fair rates at the **train station.** Open daily 8-11:45am and 3-5:45pm. Also at **Stazione Marittima** or one of the many **banks** on V. Cairoli.

Luggage Storage: Self service, in the train station. L4-7000/€2.07-3.62 per 24hr.

Emergency: ☎113. **Medical Emergency:** ☎118.

24-Hour Pharmacy: Farmacia Comunale, V. Fiume, 1, up from P. Grande.

Hospital: Pronto Soccorso, ☎0586 40 33 51 or 42 13 98.

Post Office: V. Cairoli, 12/16 (☎0586 89 76 02). Open M-F 8:30am-7pm, Sa 8:30am-12:30pm. Currency exchange.

Postal Code: 57100.

▌ ACCOMMODATIONS

▨ **Ostello/Albergo Villa Morazzana,** V. Collinet, 40 (☎0586 50 00 76; fax 56 24 26), in countryside, barely within city limits. Bus #1 to P. Grande (L1500/€0.77) and at P. Grande, 25, transfer to bus #3 (20min.). Different #3 buses run different routes on outskirts of town, so ask at info booth in P. Grande which goes to hostel. Weekdays 1 every hr. in each direction. Other #3 buses will drop you off on V. Popogna; from there turn left onto V.S. Martino and follow the signs to the hostel (15min.). Housed in a 17th-century villa, the hostel hosts exhibitions of Livornese artists. Minutes from a quiet beach and lovely Tuscan walks. Breakfast included. Lockout 9:30am-5pm. Curfew 11:30pm. Wheelchair accessible. Call ahead. Dorms L25,000/€12.91; singles L50,000/€25.82, with bath L80,000/€41.32; doubles with bath L120,000/€62.

Pensione Dante, Scali D'Azeglio, 28 (☎0586 89 43 70). From P. Grande, follow V. Grande toward the water. Take your 1st left onto V. Piave, walk through P. Benamozegh and bear slightly right onto V. Diaz. Take a right at the canal and the *pensione* is a half block ahead on the right. Clean rooms. Many overlook canal. Singles L50,000/€25.82; doubles L60,000/€31; triples L90,000/€46.48; quads L110,000/€56.81.

Hotel Marian, C. Mazzini, 24 (☎0586 83 42 78). From the main tourist office (see above), continue straight through P. Cavour, follow V. Ricasoli 1 long block and take a right onto V. Mazzini. Modern amenities include remote-control TV, alarm clocks and A/C. All rooms with bath. Wheelchair accessible. Singles L80,000/€41.32; doubles L120,000/€62; triples L140,000/€72.3; quads L160,000/€82.63.

▐ FOOD

Livorno owes its culinary specialties to the sea. The city has its own interpretation of classic *bouillabaise;* a fiery, tomato-based seafood stew called *cacciucco.* An **open-air market** sprawls along V. Buontalenti. (Open M-Sa 8am-1pm.) Fill your brown bag at the **STANDA supermarket,** V. Grande, 174, off P. Grande. (Open daily 8:30am-12:30pm and 4-8pm; Nov.-Feb. M-Sa 8:30am-12:30pm and 3:30-7pm.)

La Cantonata, C. Mazzini, 222 (☎0586 894 04 81), 2 blocks from Hotel Marian (see above). Huge plates of *spaghetti al frutti di mare* (with seafood; L9000/€4.65), and brimming glasses of *chianti. Riso nero* (rice turned black from squid ink; L8000/€4.13); *primi* L7000/€3.62; *secondi* L8-20,000/€4.13-10.33. *Menù* L22,000/€11.36. Cover L2000/€1.03. Service 10%. Open Tu-Su noon-3pm and 7-10:30pm.

Trattoria Il Sottomarino, V. dei Terrazzini, 48 (☎0586 237 71), off P. della Repubblica at end of V. Pina d'Oro. *Cacciucco* (L22,000/€11.36). *Primi* from L12,000/€6.20; *secondi* L15,000/€7.75. Open Aug.-June W-Su 12:30-2:30pm and 7:30-10pm.

Hostaria dell'Eremo, Scali Cialdini, 39 (☎0586 88 14 87; pual@iol.it). Pink walls and pink tile floors. *Cacciucco* L25,000/€12.91. *Cosimo terzo* (shrimp and prosciutto; L12,000/€6.20). Open daily 7:30pm-midnight, Sa-Su 12:30-3pm. AmEx/MC/V.

💿 🎵 SIGHTS AND ENTERTAINMENT

FORTRESSES. The **Fortezza Nuova,** circled by a large moat, is in the heart of **Piccola Venezia,** and is named for the canals that course through the area. The fortress, completed in the early 1600s by the Medici family, now houses a public park with food stands and charming, crumbling terraces from which to view the port. From the new fortress, walk to P. Municipio, then down V.S. Giovanni for a view of the sprawling **Fortezza Vecchia** out on the water. Built by the powerful Marquises of Tuscany in the 9th century, the portly central tower was the first fortification on the site. When Pisans conquered Livorno, they built a fort around the tower (fearful that it would lean over and put them out of business). In the 16th century the Medici family surrounded the ensemble with robust brick walls to consolidate their hold on Livorno, the chief Tuscan port. Head left as you are facing the Fortezza Vecchia, and a short walk along the water takes you to P. Micheli, home to the Monumento dei Quattro Mori. Bandini carved this marble figure of Duke Ferdinand I in 1595. The four manacled bronze slaves, added by Pietro Tacca in 1626, now serve as a reminder of Livorno's participation in the slave market.

MUSEO CIVICO GIOVANNI FATTORI. Livorno made its mark in the wild world of painting with the 19th-century "blotters," *I Macchiaioli* (a movement led by Giovanni Fattori), and the 20th-century portraitist Amadeo Modigliani. Livornese work, both proto-Impressionist and modern, crowds the museum. *(In Villa Mimbelli, at the intersection of V.S. Iacopo and V. Acquaviva. ☎ 0586 80 80 01. Open daily 10am-1pm and 4-7pm. L12,000/€6.20, students L6000/€3.10.)*

FESTIVALS. The **Palio Marinaro,** Livorno's most energetic claim to fame, occurs just off its coast. In mid-July, rowers from the various quarters of the city race traditional crafts toward the old port, spurred on by spectators on the banks.

VIAREGGIO ☎ 0584

The resort town of Viareggio sits quietly at the foot of the Riviera, tucked between the colorful beach umbrellas of the Versilian coast and the olive and chestnut groves cloaking the foothills of the Apuan Mountains. In the mornings, local trains ferry in beautiful, fluorescent Italian youth intent on soaking up the sun's rays. Each night wealthy European tourists stroll along the shore's wide promenade, distinguished by its grandiose 1920s architecture. Droning away on their cell phones while peering into the windows of glitzy boutiques, they seem unaware of the lapping waves and gentle sea breeze that make these beaches so inviting.

▐ TRANSPORTATION. Viareggio lies on both the Rome-Genoa and the Viareggio-Florence train lines. **Trains** service **Florence, Genoa, La Spezia, Livorno, Pisa,** and **Rome. Lazzi** buses (☎ 0584 462 33) connect Viareggio to: **Florence** (2¼hr.; 2 per day; L12,600/€6.51); **La Spezia** (2hr., every 2hr., L6200/€3.20); **Lucca** (45min., every hr., L4500/€2.32); **Pisa** (20 per day, L4500/€2.32). All buses stop in P. Mazzini, the town's main square. **Taxis** (☎ 0584 454 54) are available at the train station.

🛈 PRACTICAL INFORMATION. The **tourist office** at the train station has good maps, local bus schedules, and information on hotels, hikes, and car tours. (Open W-Sa 9:30am-12:30pm and 3-5:30pm, Su 9:30am-12:30pm; reduced hours Oct.-Apr.) From the main exit of the train station, walk directly across the *piazza* and head right. Take your first left and walk about eight blocks straight down V. XX Settembre to P. Mazzini. At the other end of the *piazza*, turn right onto V. Carducci and walk 2½ blocks to the **main tourist office,** V. Carducci, 10. The personable English-speaking staff will give you a decent map and bombard you with brochures. (☎ 0584 96 22 33; www.versilia.turismo.toscana.it. Open May-Oct. M-Sa 9am-1pm and 3-7pm, Su 9:30am-12:30pm; Nov.-Apr. daily 9am-1pm; extended hours around Christmas and Easter.) Several of their recommended itineraries necessitate a car—you can rent one at **Avis**, on V. Aurelia Nord in front of the supermarket, only 100m from the station. (☎ 0584 456 21. 25+. Open daily 9am-8pm.) A **currency exchange** is available at the post office or at any of the banks along V. Garibaldi. Self-service **luggage storage** is available in the train station (L3000/€1.55, L5000/ €2.58, and L7000/€3.62 for small, medium, and large lockers per 24 hr.). In case of **emergency**, dial ☎ 113; for **first aid**, call ☎ 118. An all-night **pharmacy** is at V. Mazzini, 14. The **post office**, at the corner of V. Garibaldi and V. Puccini, exchanges currency (☎ 0584 303 45. Open M-Sa 8:30am-7pm). **Postal Code:** 55049.

⚏🛏 ACCOMMODATIONS AND FOOD. Amid the splendor and pretense of four-stardom hide budget accommodations. Many, however, turn into long-term *pensione* in the summer, catering to Italians on holidays of a week or more. For clean, simple white-walled rooms, all with bath, try the **Hotel Albachiara**, V. Zanardelli, 81. (☎ 0584 445 41. Doubles Sept.-June L100,000/€51.65; July-Aug. L110,000/€56.81; Full pension Sept.-June L85,000/€43.9; July-Aug. L100,000/ €51.65 per person.) **Hotel Rex**, V.S. Martino, 48., has a common room with mirrors and plush couches, and small, clean rooms with TV, phone, A/C, and bath. (☎ 0584 96 11 40. Breakfast included. Singles end of June-Aug. L100,000/€51.65; doubles L140,000/€72.3; triples L160,000/€82.63. Prices 10-20% lower rest of year. MC/V.)

Accustomed to catering to a wealthy clientele, Viareggio restaurants are none too cheap. To avoid the ubiquitous L3000/€1.55 cover and 15% service charge, head to **Lo Zio Pietro**, V.S. Martino, 73, and savor *roticceria* fare from *calccio* (fish stew) to vegetables to slow-roasted chicken. (☎ 0584 96 21 83. Open M-Sa 9am-8pm.) Spend the L5000/€2.58 enjoying coffee on the ritzy terrace of the **Gran Caffè Margherita** overlooking the sea. From P. Mazzini, take a left, as you face the sea, onto the main drag. The cafe is ahead about five blocks on the right.

⚏🛏 BEACHES AND ENTERTAINMENT. Most of the shoreline has been ungraciously roped off by the owners of Viareggio's private beaches, but you can walk through these areas to the water as long as you've already left your stuff somewhere else. A short walk to the left as you face the water leads to free patches of sandy beach. You can also amble on in the same direction, across the canal along Viale Europa, to the larger free beach *(spiaggia libera)* near the southern edge of town (30min. from train station). The *spiaggia libera* caters to the young, hip (and often more modest) crowd that is noticeably lacking from the private beaches. But if waking up with sand in your pants isn't your idea of fun, head to the ultra-posh town of **Forte dei Marmi**, for some seriously fun people-watching. You can grab one of the blue CLAP buses, at the station, to get to the town (every hr., L3600/€18.60). Once there, stake out a table at one of the expensive outdoor cafes and watch as Armani-clad locals emerge from their secluded villas to squander fortunes at ritzy boutiques. When night falls, stroll along the promenade.

ELBA

According to legend, the enchanting island of Elba grew from a precious stone that slipped from Venus's neck into the azure waters of the Tyrrhenian Sea. This paradise has drawn the likes of Jason and the Argonauts, Etruscan miners, and Roman patricians. Since Hellenic times, Elba, nicknamed "Sparks" (Aethalia) by the Greeks, has gained renown for its mineral wealth. Of course, the island derives its greatest fame from its association with Napoleon; the Little Emperor was sent into his first exile here in 1814, creating both a temporarily war-free Europe and the famous palindrome: "Able was I ere I saw Elba," supposedly quipped the French-speaking Emperor upon his arrival. All would-be conquerors of Europe should be so lucky: Elba's turquoise waters, dramatic mountains, velvety beaches, and diverse attractions accommodate almost any interest. Each zone of the island attracts a distinct variety of visitors—families lounge in **Marina di Campo** and **Marciana Marina,** party-hard beach fanatics waste away in **Capoliveri,** yacht-club members gallivant in **Porto Azzurro,** and nature lovers gravitate to the mountainous northeastern tip of the island between the beachfront **Cavi** and **Rio nell'Elba** in the interior. The southeastern coast is the most commercial and the most welcoming for those looking for sandy beaches and comfortable campgrounds, while the northeastern arm of the island has interior back roads and undisturbed views of the island's desolate desert green. Elba is one of the best places in Italy to bike or scooter, with roads that meander high into the island's mountainous terrain, affording stupendous views of the ocean. Bus rides through the island are therefore also spectacular, if a little harrowing. Remember that cars drive on the right side of the road in Italy and plan accordingly; if you are going between Portoferraio and Marciana Marina, for instance, you want to sit on the right side of the bus on the way there and on the left side on the way back for the best views.

⌐ TRANSPORTATION TO ELBA

Elba's **airport** (☎ 0565 97 60 11), in Marina di Campo, sends flights to **Milan, Munich, Parma, Rome, Vienna,** and **Zurich.** The best way to reach Elba is to take a **ferry** from **Piombino Marittima** (also called Piombino Porto) on the mainland to **Portoferraio,** Elba's largest city. Ferries also dock at **Porto Azzuro,** on the opposite side of the island. **Trains** on the Genoa-Rome line travel straight to Piombino Marittima but usually stop at Campiglia Marittima (from Florence, change at Pisa). From Campiglia Marittima, a connecting *pullman* (intercity bus; 30min., L2500/€1.29), timed to meet incoming trains, takes you to the ferries in Piombino Marittima. If you buy a ticket to Piombino at a train station, and your scheduled train makes the bus connection, the bus ticket will be included. Both **Toremar** (ferry 1hr., L12,000/€6.20; hydrofoil in summer 30min., L24,000/€12.40) and **Moby Lines** (1hr., L12,000/€6.20) run about 16 trips to Elba per day, with the last ferry leaving around 9:30pm. The offices of **Toremar** (☎ 0565 311 00) and **Moby Lines** (☎ 0565 22 52 11) are at P. Premuda, 13, in Piombino, by the train and bus stop. You can buy tickets for the next departing ferry at the **FS** booth in the train station in Campiglia Marittima, as well as the offices in Piambino. Should you be stuck in Piombino Marittima, take a train from the port to the city (5min., about every 2hr., L1900/€0.98). The bus to Campiglia Marittima also stops in the town of Piombino.

PORTOFERRAIO   ☎0565

As the main port of Elba, Portoferraio is part modern, rather unattractive port and part picturesque Tuscan city. It is probably the island's liveliest city and contains most of its essential services. Though low on sights, the old city is charming.

⌐ TRANSPORTATION

Buses: ATL, V. Elba, 20 (☎ 0565 91 43 92), across from the Toremar landing. Hourly service to **Capoliveri, Cavo, Lacona Marciana, Marciana Marina, Marina di Campo, Porto Azzuro, Pomonte,** and **Rio Elba.** Tickets L3000-7000/€1.55-3.62. Schedules, day passes (L12,000/€6.20) and weekly passes (L30,000/€15.50). Open daily 8am-8pm; Oct.-May M-Sa 8am-1:20pm and 4-6:30pm, Su 9am-12:30pm and 2-6:30pm.

Ferries: Toremar, Calata Italia, 22 (☎ 0565 91 80 80). **Moby Lines,** V. Elba, 4 (☎ 0565 91 41 33; fax 0565 91 67 58).

Taxis: ☎ 0565 91 51 12.

Car Rental: Rent Chiappi, Calata Italia, 30 (☎ 0565 91 66 87). Cars from L80-120,000/€41.30-62.00 per day. Friendly staff provides gas and directions. Mopeds L50-100,000/€25.80-51.60. Mountain bikes L20,000/€10.30. Insurance included.

Bike/Moped Rental: TWN, V. Elba, 32 (☎ 0565 91 46 66; fax 0565 91 58 99). Mopeds from L35,000/€17.60; 2-person scooters L50,000/€25.80; mountain bikes L30,000/€15.50; kayaks L30,000/€15.50; Fiats from L70,000/€36.20. 20% more

July-Aug. Branches around Elba (Marciana Marina, Porto Azzurro, Lacona, Procchio, and Marina di Campo). L10,000/€5.16 fee for returning rentals to different branch. 20% discount presenting same-day train ticket going through Piombino. 10% *Let's Go* discount. Open 9am-1pm and 3:30-7pm. AmEx/MC/V.

⁊ PRACTICAL INFORMATION

TOURIST, FINANCIAL, AND LOCAL SERVICES

Tourist Offices: APT, Calata Italia, 26, 1st fl. (☎0565 91 46 71; www.archipelago.turismo.toscana.it), across from Toremar boat landing. Walk directly next to the water in port area and look for the huge "Ufficio Turistico" sign. Accommodations info, maps, bus schedules. Open daily 9am-noon and 2:30-7:30pm; in winter 9am-1pm and 3-7pm. **Associazione Albergatori,** Calata Italia, 21 (☎0565 91 47 54), finds rooms for free. Open M-F 9am-7:30pm, Sa 9am-12:30pm and 3:30-7pm. **Tourist Information for Camping,** V. Elba, 7 (☎/fax 0565 93 02 08). Open daily 9am-1pm and 4-8pm.

Currency Exchange: There are countless rip-offs. Be smart—walk up to the banks on V. Manganaro, near Hotel Nobel, including **Banca di Roma,** V. Manganaro, 1 (☎0565 91 90 07), which also has an **ATM.** Open M-F 8:30am-1:00pm and 3:10-4pm.

Boat Excursions: Linee di Navigazione Archipelago Toscano (☎/fax 0565 91 47 97; www.elbacrociere.com) offers tours of Elba's coast as well as excursions to nearby islands (L50-70,000/€25.80-36.20).

Laundry: Self-service at V. Elba, 61, near the Hotel Nobel; L6000/€3.20 wash (30min.), L6000/€3.20 dry (20min.). Open daily 8am-10pm.

EMERGENCY AND COMMUNICATIONS

Emergency: ☎113.

Ambulance: P. della Repubblica, 37 (☎0565 91 40 09).

Hospital: (☎0565 93 85 11), off V. Carducci.

Post Office: in P. Hutre, off P. della Repubblica. Open M-F 8:15am-7pm, Sa 8:15am-12:30pm. There is **another branch** on V. Carducci, closer to the port. Open M-F 8:30am-1:30pm, Sa 8:15am-12:30pm.

Postal Code: 57037.

⌐ ACCOMMODATIONS

Reserve ahead in the summer; the *associazione albergatori* can help.

Ape Elbana, Salita Cosimo de' Medici, 2 (☎/fax 0565 91 42 45), overlooking the main *piazza* of the *centro storico*. A personable, English-speaking staff will show you to cheery, cavernous rooms, all with bath. Aug. ½-pension L110,000/56.81; full pension L130,000/€67.14. Singles L100,000/€51.60; doubles L120,000/€62.00. July-Aug. doubles L130,000/€67.14. Winter about L30,000/€15.50 cheaper in winter. MC/V.

Hotel Nobel, V. Manganaro, 72 (☎0565 91 52 17; fax 0565 91 55 15). Follow V. Elba from the port until it merges with V. Manganaro. The hotel is on the right. Somewhat shabby, but perfect for those on a tight budget. Singles L70,000/€36.20, with bath L80,000/€41.30; doubles L90,000/€46.48, L120,00/€62.00. AmEx/MC/V.

Albergo Le Ghiaie (☎0565 91 51 78), on pleasant beach of same name. All rooms have private bath and many have white balconies with views of the deep blue sea. Singles L120,000/€62.00; doubles L160,000/€82.60. Off-season singles L70,000/€36.20; doubles L120,000/€62.00.

FOOD

Suffering from an infestation of overpriced tourist-trap restaurants, Portoferraio is not the best place for budget dining. Regardless, many cafes and bars still offer inexpensive, quick meals. For groceries, head to the centrally located **Conad** supermarket, at P. Pietri, 2-4, off V. Elba and near the Hotel Nobel. (Open M-Sa 7:30am-8:30pm, Su 7:30am-1pm and 4-8pm.) There are a couple of culinary terms worth knowing: *schiaccia* is an Elban bread cooked in olive oil and embedded with either onions or black olives, and *aleatico* is a sweet, full-bodied wine liquor.

> **Trattoria da Zucchetta,** P. della Repubblica, 40 (☎0565 91 53 31), in historic center. Neapolitan dishes at moderate prices. Pizza L6-15,000/€3.20-7.75; *primi* L10-15,000/€5.16-7.75; *secondi* L10-20,000. Open daily 11:30am-3pm and 6-11:30pm.

> **Ristorante Frescantico,** V. Carducci, 132 (☎0565 918 989). This charming wine bar prepares delicious meals, well worth every *lira*. Fresh homemade pasta from L12,000/€6.20. Cover L3000/€1.55. Open May-Nov. daily 12:30-3pm and 7-11pm; Dec.-Apr. W-M 12:30-3pm and 7-11pm. MC/V.

> **Ristorante Residence,** (☎0565 91 68 15), on Catala Italia. Affordable dishes for take-out or self-service. Open May-Oct. daily 6:30am-11pm; Nov.-Apr. F-W 6:30am-11pm.

◻ SIGHTS

If you're in Portoferraio and aren't in the mood for the beach, stroll along the pleasant, cobblestone streets of the old town; they're lined with pink-, yellow-, and orange-shuttered houses set into the mountainside. Alternatively, head to...

NAPOLEONIC WHATNOTS. The **Napoleon museum** is located at his one-time residence, the **Villa dei Mulini.** The museum features Napoleon's personal library, furniture graced by the imperial *derrière*, a number of letters from exile, and the sovereign Elban flag that he designed and decorated with bees from his own imperial crest. *(☎0565 91 58 46. Open Apr.-Oct. M-F 9am-7:30pm, Sa 9am-10:30pm, Su 9am-1pm; Nov.-Mar. 9am-4pm. L10,000/€5.16. Cumulative ticket also allows entry—within 3 days—to the Villa Napoleonica L15,000/€7.75.)* The **Villa Napoleonica di San Martino** is located in (who knew?) San Martino. Emblazoned with monogrammatic Ns, you might think that the villa monumentalizes Napoleon's hubris, but they were actually placed there after his death. Note especially the Sala Egizia, with friezes depicting his Egyptian campaign. *(Take bus #1 6km out of Portoferraio. ☎0565 91 46 88. Same hours as Villa dei Mulini.)* A block away from the former museum, you can pay homage to the great man's death mask at the **Chiesa della Misericordia.** *(L1000/€0.52.)*

NON-NAPOLEONIC WHATNOTS. The **Museo Archeologico** guides you through the history of Elba, with exhibits of archaeological finds from ancient trade boat wrecks. *(Fortezza del Lingrella. ☎0565 91 73 38. Open daily 9:30am-12:30pm and 4-7pm; July-Aug. 9:30am-12:30pm and 6pm-midnight. L4000/€2.06, children and individuals in large groups L2000/€1.03.)* The **Medici Fortress** overlooks the port. Cosimo de' Medici, Grand Duke of Tuscany, began the impregnable complex in 1548. So imposing was its structure that back in 1553 the Turkish pirate Dracut declared it invulnerable and called off his planned attack on Portoferraio.

MARINA DI CAMPO ☎0565

Marina di Campo's white beaches wind their way for miles along the coast, attracting masses of vacationing families. Numerous campgrounds around Marina di Campo are popular with a somewhat hipper crowd. Bake in the sun or rent sporting equipment like **sailboards** (L15,000/€7.75 per hr.) or **paddleboats** (L12,000/€6.20 per hr.) along the beach. **Biko's Bikes,** in P. Torino—the square a block away from the bus stop toward the beach—rents cycles and mopeds for L20-65,000/€10.33-33.57 per day. (☎0565 97 61 94. Open 8:30am-12:30pm and 2:30-7:30pm.) The **tourist office,** across from the bus stop, offers information on various beaches. (Open F-W

8am-8pm; winter greatly reduced hours) In case of an **emergency,** call the **carabinieri** (☎0565 97 69 76) or the **Guardia Medica** (☎118; in summer ☎0565 97 60 61).

The clean and comfortable rooms of **Hotel Lido,** V. Mascagni, 29, near the center of town (turn left from P. Torino), are only a minute from the beach. (☎0565 97 60 40. Breakfast included. Reserve by Easter for July and Aug. Doubles L100,000/ €51.60, with bath L120,000/€62.00; triples L140,000/€72.30, with bath L170,000/ €87.80.) For **camping,** walk straight toward the beach from the bus stop, turn left, and walk the length of V. degli Etruschi. Continue past the sign that marks the end of Marino di Campo and take an immediate right at the "La Foce" sign (20min.). **La Foce** (☎/fax 0565 97 73 85) offers a well-equipped plot directly on the beach. Another camping option is **Del Mare,** which shares the same grounds. (☎0565 97 62 37; fax 0565 97 78 50. Open Apr.-Oct. L12-20,000/€6.20-10.30 per person and L12-15,00/€6.20-7.75 per tent, depending on season.) The campgrounds also offer two restaurants, a place to rent bikes, and a store with basic goods. In town, the **Minimarket** on V. Bellini, a block away from P. Torino to your left as you come from the bus stop, stocks essentials. (Open Mar.-Oct. daily 7am-10pm.) Contrary to its name, the only things baked at the **Cannabis Restaurant,** V. Roma, 41/43, are the fabulous meals, including crêpes stuffed with cheese and *prosciutto* (L7000). A variety of large salads (L8-12,000) and fruit drinks diversify the typically Italian menu. (☎0565 97 75 55. Open daily 6am-1am; Oct.-May M-Sa 6am-1am.) **Trattoria Vecchia Locanda,** V. Garibaldi, 10, offers simple island fare. *Menù* with drinks starts at L20,000/€10.30. (☎0565 97 80 60. Open daily noon-2pm and 7-10:30pm, but you must call ahead to give the kitchen time to prepare for your particular needs.)

PORTO AZZURRO ☎0565

A favorite sunspot of the ultra-thin and the ultra-rich, Porto Azzurro shelters some of the island's finest beaches. But the beauty doesn't come cheap—if you intend to stay in Porto Azzurro, brace yourself for a major financial outlay. Budget travelers should consider staying at the campgrounds at Localita Barbarossa, near the beach. The largest is **Camping Roclan's** (☎0565 95 78 03), followed by **Arrighi** (☎0565 955 68), Da Mario (☎0565 95 80 32), and **Il Gabbiano** (☎0565 950 87). **Albergo Barbarossa** at Localita Barbarossa offers charmingly old-fashioned rooms at reasonable prices. (☎0565 950 87. Singles L45,000/€23.24, with bath L48,000/€24.79; doubles L70,000/€36.20, with bath L80,000/€41.30.) To reach Barbarossa, you can either take the bus headed toward **Marina di Campo** (but be sure to ask the driver if it stops at Barbarossa) or walk. To do the latter, follow the signs for the *carabinieri* from the main square bordering the ocean, pass the *carabinieri* office, and continue walking until you reach Barbarossa (15min., partially uphill). If you're looking for a quick bite, don't miss **La Friggitoria,** V. Marconi, 4, just off the main square. The *crocchette di patate* (L4000/€2.06) and the *fritto misto* (mixed fried fish) have put smiles on the faces of many islanders. (☎0338 428 43 10. Closed Jan.-Mar.) **The Grill,** V. Marconi, 26, near the **Blumarine Hotel,** offers copious portions of *penne* with either tomatoes or clams for L8000/€4.13. (Open daily 8:30am-2:30pm and 6pm-1am; Nov.-Mar. Tu-Su 8:30am-2:30pm and 6pm-1am.) **Bar Tamata,** V. Cesare Battisti, 3 (☎0347 381 39 86), has a mellow late-night crowd. Morumbi, 2km down the road to Capoliveri, is one of the island's hottest discos, offering dance floors, a pizzeria, and a pagoda. (☎0565 92 01 91. Weekend cover L25,000/€12.91. Free passes for women. Open June 30-Sept. 15.) To escape the hedonism, the first bus leaves at 4:45am and the last at 7:55pm (1hr. to Portoferraio). In emergencies, call the carabinieri (☎112) or an ambulance (☎118).

MARCIANA MARINA ☎0565

The strip of pebbles that borders Marciana Marina's waterfront is just one of countless beaches hiding in isolated coves along the island. Numerous other stretches are accessible only by boat. The lesser known ones lie between Sant'Andrea and Fetovaia, an area rumored to have the island's clearest stretches of water. The coastline here varies from fine white-sand beaches to gentle outcroppings of flat-topped rocks, perfect for sunbathing and diving into the sea.

⚑ PRACTICAL INFORMATION. Reach Marciana Marina by car, moped, boat, or **bus** (50min. from Portoferraio, L3500/$1.81). The **tourist office,** V. Scali Mazzini, 13, on P. Vittorio Emanuele, finds rooms. (☎ 0565 99 061. Open Th-Tu 8am-8pm, reduced winter hours.) The **post office** is on V. Loyd. (Open M-F 8:15am-1:30pm, Sa 8:15am-12:30pm.) **Emergency:** contact **carabinieri** (☎ 112) or **ambulance** (☎ 118).

⌂◻ ACCOMMODATIONS AND FOOD. Cheap *affittacamere* are all over; look for signs. In Marciana Marina, **Albergo Imperia,** V. Amedeo, 12, offers comfortable rooms. The personable proprietor finagles discounts at local restaurants. All rooms have a TV and refrigerator; some have balconies. (☎ 0565 990 82; imperia@elbalink.it. Mid-Sept.-June singles L50-60,000/€25.82-31; doubles L70-80,000/€36.15-41.32, with bath L145,000/€74.87. July-mid-Sept. prices 20-30% higher.) **Casa Lupi,** V. Amedeo, offers clean rooms behind green shutters, all with bath. Just uphill from the beach, its terrace overlooks a vineyard and the sea. (☎ 0565 991 43. Aug. singles L70,000/€36.15; doubles L120,000/€62. Off-season singles L50,000/€25.82; doubles L75,000/€38.73. Half-pension L95,000/€49.06.) If finding a room in one of the main centers proves difficult, head to some of the smaller, less-trodden towns, which often prove more charming. **Albergo dei Fiori** in **Chiessi** (30min. from Marciana; 1½hr. from Portoferrario; some buses go directly, others change in Procchio) provides tranquility, great prices, beautiful views of the azure sea, and huge meals with modern bathrooms. Ask for a balcony or patio facing the ocean. Check in at their family-run restaurant, **L'Olivo,** 20m uphill from the bus stop. (Restaurant and hotel ☎ 0565 90 60 13. Singles L45,000/€23.24; doubles L70,000/€36.15, with bath L80,000/€41.32.) Back in Marciana, try **Bar L'Onda,** V. Amedeo, 4, for takeout crêpes (L6-8000/€3.1-4.13) and *panini* (L6000/€3.1).

◼ SIGHTS. A visit to **Monte Capanne,** Elba's highest peak, provides an uplifting excursion from Marciana Marina. The top of this 1019m mountain offers views of the entire island and Corsica. The strenuous uphill trek takes two hours, but a cable car can take you up. (L12,000/€6.2. Open 10:30am-12:30pm and 1-5pm.) To reach Monte Capanne, take the bus from Marciana Marina to **Marciana,** a medieval town which clings to the mountainside, and get off at "Monte Capanne" (15min.). Not far from Marciana are the **Romitorio di San Cerbone** and the **Santuario della Madonna del Monte,** two sanctuaries once described as "dense with mysticism." Nearby **Chiessi,** with secluded beaches and rocky coves, is a perfect place to relax.

UMBRIA

Umbria is known as the "Green Heart of Italy," a land rich in natural beauty, encompassing wild woods and fertile plains, craggy gorges and gentle hills, tiny cobblestoned villages, and bustling international educational centers. This irresistible, landlocked region wedged between the Adriatic and Tyrrhenian coasts has long been a cherished and greatly contested prize. Three thousand years ago, Etruscans settled the region, leaving burial grounds, necropoli, tombs, and ruins. Over the years, ravenous barbarian hordes, aggressive neighboring Romans, and the meddlesome papacy have trampled through this land, drenching it in blood and looting its riches. Another conqueror, Christianity, transformed Umbria's architecture and regional identity, turning it into a breeding ground for saints and religious movements. St. Francis shamed the extravagant church with his humility, earning a reputation for pacifism. The region holds some of Giotto's greatest masterpieces and produced medieval masters Perugino and Pinturicchio. Today, Umbria's artistic spirit continues, with the internationally renowned annual Spoleto Festival and Umbria Jazz Festival.

PERUGIA ☎075

Perugians may be the most polite people you'll meet in Italy–an odd fact, considering Perugia's long history as a violent and disreputable city. An Etruscan *polis* in the 6th century BC, a part of the Roman Empire in the 3rd century BC, and a thriving home of crime and debauchery in the Middle Ages, Perugia never lost its zest for battle, constantly laying siege to neighboring villages. Even in peacetime, its denizens entertained themselves with the Battaglia de'Sassi (Battle of Stones), an annual festival involving two teams pelting each other with rocks until a sufficient number of casualties on one side rendered it unable to compete. The city's reputation only improved when it played host to the Order of Flagellants in the 14th century, a group of religious fanatics who traveled Europe S&M style, whipping themselves publicly as penance for sins real and imagined. The city added defiance of papal rule, the imprisonment of the peace-loving St. Francis of Assisi, and the murders of two popes to its formidable record of achievements, but periods of prosperity occasionally interspersed between these heretical shenanigans gave rise to stunning artistic achievement. Perugia was home to the great Pietro Vannucci "Perugino," teacher of Raphael, and served as a meeting ground for the 13th through 15th century Tuscan and Umbrian masters. This legacy is preserved in one of Italy's most important art museums, the Galleria Nazionale dell'Umbria. A renowned jazz festival and a vibrant academic community only add Perugia's overpowering draw, but beware of flying stones.

▛ TRANSPORTATION

Trains: Perugia FS, in P.V. Veneto, Fontiveggio. Perugia lies on Foligno-Terontola line. Info open daily 10:15am-1:10pm and 2-5:40pm. Ticket window open daily 6am-8:40pm. To: **Arezzo** (1½hr., every hr., L7000/€3.62); **Assisi** (25min., every hr., L3000/€1.55); **Foligno** (40min., every hr., L4200/€2.17); **Orvieto** via **Terontola** (2hr., 8 per day, L11,400/€5.89); **Florence** (2½hr., every hr., from L15,300/€7.90); **Passignano sul Trasimeno** (30min., every hr., L3800/€1.96); **Rome** (2½hr., from L28,900/€14.93) via **Terontola** or **Foligno** (3hr., from L20,600/€10.64); **Spoleto** via **Foligno** (1½hr., every hr., L6600/€3.41). **Secondary Station: Perugia Sant'Anna** in P. Bellucci Giuseppe. Commuter rail to **Sansepolcro** (1½hr., 12 per day 6:39am-7:31pm, L7400/€3.82) and **Termi** (1½hr., 12 per day 6:05am-6:54pm, L8200/€4.23) via **Todi** (1hr., L5200/€2.70). **Buses:** P. dei Partigiani, down *scala mobile* from P. Italia. City bus #6 (L1200/€0.62) heads to train station. **ASP** (☎075 573 17 07), in P. dei Partigiani. To: **Assisi** (1hr., 4 per day 8am-6pm, Su 10am-1pm); **Chiusi** (30min.-2hr., 5 per day 6:30am-6:35pm, L9200/€4.75); **Gubbio** (1¼hr., 10per day 6:40am-8:08pm, L7400/€3.82); **Todi** (1¼hr., 6 per day 7:30am-6:50pm, L9200/€4.75). Reduced service Su. Additional buses available from distant **Stazione Fontiveggio.** To get there, take bus #8 from P. dei Partigiani (L1200/€0.62) to last stop. Walk down staircase around side of the building; station across street. Tickets at Radio Taxi Perugia. Luggage storage available (p. 390). To **Siena** (every 2hr.; L14,000/€7.23).

Taxis: Radio Taxi Perugia (☎075 500 48 88).

Car Rental: Hertz, P. Vittorio Veneto, 2 (☎0337 65 08 37). Near train station. Cars from L160,000/€82.73 per day. Open M-F 8:30am-12:30pm and 3-7pm, Sa 8:30am-1pm.

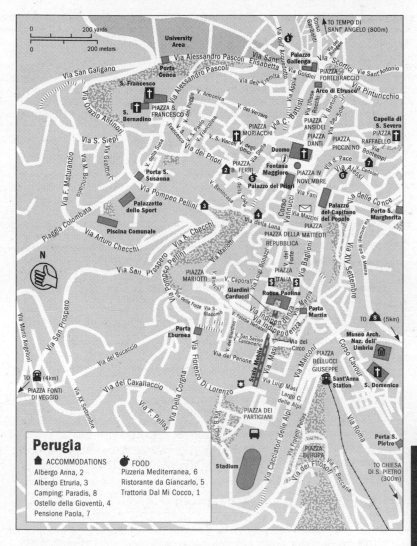

Perugia

🏠 ACCOMMODATIONS
Albergo Anna, 2
Albergo Etruria, 3
Camping: Paradis, 8
Ostello della Gioventù, 4
Pensione Paola, 7

🍴 FOOD
Pizzeria Mediterranea, 6
Ristorante da Giancarlo, 5
Trattoria Dal Mi Cocco, 1

➕🔢 ORIENTATION AND PRACTICAL INFORMATION

From the **Perugia FS train station** in **Piazza V. Veneto,** Fontiveggio, buses #6, 7, 9, 13d, and 15 go to **Piazza Italia** (L1200/€0.62). Otherwise, it's a long and ugly 2km uphill trek. To get to P. Italia from the **bus station** in **Piazza dei Partigiani** or from the nearby **Perugia Sant' Anna train station** at **Piazza Giuseppe,** follow the signs to the **escalator** *(scala mobile)* that goes underneath the old city to P. Italia. From P. Italia, **Corso Vannucci,** the main shopping thoroughfare, leads to **Piazza IV Novembre** and the *duomo*. Behind the *duomo* lies the university district. One block off C. Vannucci is **V. Baghoni,** which leads to **Piazza Matteotti,** the municipal center.

TOURIST AND FINANCIAL SERVICES

Tourist Office: P. IV Novembre, 3 (☎075 572 33 27 and 573 64 58; fax 573 93 86). The friendly, knowledgeable staff provides city maps and info on accommodations. Open M-F 8:30am-1:30pm and 3:30-6:30pm, Sa 8:30am-1:30pm, Su 9am-1pm.

Budget Travel: CTS, V. del Roscetto, 21 (☎075 572 02 84), off V. Pinturicchio toward the bottom of the street. Student travel service offers vacation deals to ISIC holders. Open M-F 10am-1pm and 3-6pm. **SESTANTE Travel,** C. Vannucci, 2 (☎075 572 60 61). Makes hotel reservations, sells train tickets, and rents cars. Open M-F 9am-1pm and 3-7pm, Sa 10am-1pm.

Currency Exchange: Banks have the best rates; those in P. Italia have 24hr. **ATMs.** The Perugia FS train station offers poor rates but charges no commission for exchange of less than L80,000/€41.32.

LOCAL SERVICES

Luggage Storage: L7500/€3.87 per 24hr. Open daily 6am-9pm.

English-Language Bookstore: Libreria, V. Rocchi, 1 (☎075 753 61 64). A variety of classics and a few recent bestsellers and travel guides. English-language books L8-25,000/€4.13-12.91. Open M-Sa 10am-1pm and 3:30-8pm, Su 10:30am-1pm.

Laundromat: Bolle Blu, C. Garibaldi, 43. Wash L6000/€3.10 per 8kg, dry L6000/€3.10. Open daily 8am-10pm.

Swimming Pool: Piscina Comunale (☎075 573 51 60), on Viale P. Pellini. Open July-Aug. daily 1:7:30pm; June M-F 4-6:30pm, Sa 3-8pm. L7000/€3.62.

EMERGENCY AND COMMUNICATIONS

Medical Emergency: ☎118. **Police:** ☎112.

Questura: V. Cortonese, 157 (☎075 506 21).

24-Hour Pharmacy: Farmacia S. Martino, P. Matteotti, 26 (☎075 572 23 35).

Hospital: ☎075 57 81.

Internet Access: Centro ITM, V. Fabbretti, 1 (☎/fax 075 571 60 41). From P. IV Novembre, walk past *duomo* on right, out left through P. Dante and follow V. Rocchi downhill to P. Braccio Fortebraccio. Cross *piazza* and turn left on V. Fabretti. L4500/€2.32 per hr. Also provides fax and copy services. Open daily 9am-10pm.

Post Office: P. Matteotti. M-Sa 8:10am-7:30pm, Su 8:30am-5:30pm. **Currency exchange** M-F 8:10am-5:30pm, Sa 8:10am-1pm, Su 8:30am-5:30pm.

Postal Code: 06100.

🔥 ACCOMMODATIONS & CAMPING

Be sure to make reservations in July during the Umbria Jazz Festival.

▨ **Ostello della Gioventù/Centro Internazionale di Accoglienza per la Gioventù,** V. Bontempi, 13 (☎/fax 075 572 28 80; www.ostello.perugia.it). From P. Italia, walk length of C. Vanucci to P. IV Novembre. Continue past *duomo* and P. Dante, take farthest right street through P. Piccinino, and turn right onto V. Bontempi; hostel short way down on right. High, frescoed ceilings and great views. Kitchen, lockers, and TV room. Showers and kitchen use included. Sheets L2000/€1.03. Max. stay 2 weeks. Lockout 9:30am-4pm. Curfew midnight. Open Jan. 16-Dec. 14. Dorms L19,000/€9.81.

▨ **Albergo Anna,** V. dei Priori, 48 (☎/fax 075 573 63 04), off C. Vannucci. Climb 4 floors to clean, cool, and cozy 17th-century rooms. Some boast ceramic fireplaces and great views. Charming common area. Singles L60,000/€30.99, with bath L70,000/€36.15; doubles L80,000/€41.32, L100,000/€51.65; triples L120,000/€62, L140,000/€72.30. Extra 2% for credit cards. AmEx/D/MC/V.

Albergo Etruria, V. della Luna, 21 (☎075 572 37 30). Walking from P. Italia on C. Vannucci, take first left after P. della Republica onto C. della Luna. Heavy wooden furniture and antiques. Many rooms with terraces and modern bathrooms. Immense 13th-century sitting room. Showers L4000/€2.07. Singles L50,000/€25.82; doubles 75,000/€38.73, with bath L90,000/€46.48; triples L100,000/€51.65, L115,000/€59.40.

Pensione Paola, V. della Canapina, 5 (☎075 572 38 16). From train station, take bus #6 or 7 to V. Pellini, where bus passes parking lot on the left. Walk up the stairs; on right side of parking lot as you face it, then take a right. Or from P. IV Novembre, follow V. dei Priori, take left on V. della Cupa and a right down the steps. It's ahead on left. Comfortable rooms. None with bath. Common terrace with potted plants and a love seat. Breakfast L6000/€3.10. Singles L50,000/€25.82; doubles L75,000/€38.73; triples L100,000/€51.65; quads L120,000/€62.

Camping: Paradis d'Eté (☎075 517 31 21), 8km away in Colle della Trinità. Take a city bus marked "Colle della Trinità" from P. Italia and ask the driver to leave you at the campgrounds every 1-2hr. Restaurant nearby. L12,000/€6.20 per person, L10,000/€5.16 per tent, L6000/€3.10 per car. Hot showers and pool included.

🞕 FOOD

Though renowned for its chocolate, Perugia also serves up a variety of delectable breads and pastries. Both the *torta di formaggio* (cheese bread) and the *mele al cartoccio* (Italian apple pie) are available at **Ceccarani,** P. Matteotti, 16. (☎075 572 19 60. Open M-Sa 7:30am-8pm, Su 9am-1:30pm.) For local confections, such as *torciglione* (eel-shaped sweet almond bread) and *baci* (chocolate-hazelnut kisses), nothing beats the old-world elegance of **Pasticceria Sandri,** C. Vannucci, 32. This gorgeous bakery and candy shop doubles as a bar/cafe and is a great place for morning coffee. (Open M-Sa 7:30am-8pm.)

On Tuesday and Saturday mornings, find delectable meats, mature cheeses, dew-glossed vegetables, and other sundries at the **open-air market** in P. Europa. Other days, try the **mercato coperto** (covered market) in P. Matteotti for plenty of fruit, vegetables, and nuts; the entrance is below street level. (Open Tu-Sa 8am-7pm.) On summer nights the market becomes an outdoor cafe. Buy essentials at the small markets in P. Matteotti, such as **COOP,** P. Matteotti, 15. (Open M-Sa 9am-8pm.) Complement your meal with one of two regional wines: *sagrantino secco,* a full-bodied, dry red or *grechetto,* a light, dry white.

🞕 **Trattoria Dal Mi Cocco,** C. Garibaldi, 12 (☎075 573 25 11). Nothing pretentious about this local favorite, but the menu, written in the Perugian dialect, is difficult to read. It includes an *antipasto,* 2 *primi,* 2 *secondi,* a *contorno,* dessert, wine or water, and a glass of liquor for L25,000/€12.91. Reservations evenings and weekends. Open Tu-Su.

Fabretti, 75-79 (☎075 572 13 86). From P. IV Novembre, walk to right of *duomo,* left through P. Dani and right down V. Rocchi to P. Braccio Fortebraccio. On far side of *piazza* take left on V. Fabretti. Mixed grill, with lamb, sausage, and chicken L12,000/€6.20. *Primi* L7-9000/€3.62-4.65; *secondi* (from L8000/€4.13); tourist *menù* with *primo, secondo, contorni* and ½L of water or wine L20,000/€10.33. Cover L2500/€1.29. Open W-M noon-2:30pm and 7-10:30pm. MC/V.

Ristorante da Giancarlo, V. dei Priori, 36 (☎075 572 43 14), 2 blocks of C. Vannucci. Walk down stairs from entrance. *Gnocchi* melt in your mouth (L10-13,000/€5.16-6.71). *Primi* L11-20,000/€5.68-10.33; *secondi* from L15,000/€7.75. Cover L3000/€1.55. Open Sa-Th noon-3pm and 6-10pm. MC/V.

Pizzeria Mediterranea, P. Piccinino, 11/12 (☎075 572 13 22). From P. IV Novembre, walk to right of *duomo* and turn right into P. Piccinino. Upscale pizza for downscale prices. Pizza from L6000/€3.10. Try *pizza Capriccio* (with mushrooms, sausage, delicious *pecorino* cheese and basil; L10,000/€5.16). House wine L5000/€2.58 per ½L. Cover L2000/€1.03. Open daily 12:30-2:30pm and 7:30pm-midnight. MC/V.

SIGHTS

PIAZZA IV NOVEMBRE

The city's most visited sights frame Piazza IV Novembre on the north end of the city, and most other monuments lie within 15min. from there. In the middle of the *piazza* sits the **Fontana Maggiore,** designed by Fra' Bevignate and decorated by Nicola and Giovanni Pisano. The bas-reliefs covering the double basin depict religious and Roman history, with allegories explaining the seasons and sciences in the lower basin and the saints and other historic figures in the upper basin.

■ PALAZZO DEI PRIORI AND GALLERIA NAZIONALE DELL'UMBRIA. The 13th-century windows and sawtooth turrets of this *palazzo* showcase Perugian war efforts. This building, one of the finest examples of Gothic communal architecture, shelters the impressive **Galleria Nazionale dell'Umbria.** The collection contains magnificent works by Duccio, Fra Angelico, Taddeo di Bartolo, Guido da Siena, and Piero della Francesca. Della Francesca's *Polyptych of Saint Anthony* (Room 4) is particularly stunning. Perugian Pinturicchio's *Miracles of San Bernardino of Siena* uses sumptuous colors; his rich tones contrast with Perugino's soft, pastel colors. Pinturicchio's newly restored *Adoration of the Magi* (Room 10) is the gallery's premier piece. *(In P. IV Novembre at C. Vanucci, 19. Gallery ☎ 075 574 12 57. Open daily 8:30am-7:30pm; June 16-Sept. 15 open Sa until 11pm; closed Jan. 1, Dec. 25, and 1st M of every month. L12,000/€6.20, EU citizens under 18 or over 65 free.)*

On the right of the Galleria, up the steps across from the fountain and across from the *duomo*, is the **Sala dei Notari,** once the citizens' assembly chamber. Thirteenth-century frescoes portray scenes from the Bible and Aesop's fables. *(Open June-Sept. daily 9am-1pm and 3-7pm; Oct.-May Tu-Su 9am-1pm and 3-7pm.)*

DUOMO. Perugia's imposing Gothic *duomo* was begun in the 14th century, but the facade was never finished. Though it lacks the decoration of other cathedrals in Tuscany and Umbria, the 15th- to 18th-century embellishments create a sense of balance and harmony within the church. The town is proudest of the Virgin Mary's wedding ring, a relic they snagged from Chiusi in the Middle Ages (by pummeling all of the citizens of that town with rocks). Mary's rock is kept under lock and key out of view of the public. *(At the end of the piazza. Open daily 8am-noon and 4pm-sunset.)*

COLLEGIO DELLA MERCANZIA (MERCHANTS'S GUILD). In this building Perugino suffused his frescoes with the gentleness that he later passed on to his great pupil Raphael. Raphael is said to have collaborated with his teacher on the *Prophets and Sibyls.* *(Next door to the Galleria Nazionale dell'Umbria. ☎ 075 573 03 66. Open Mar.-Oct. and Dec. 20-Jan. 6 M-Sa 9am-1pm and 2:30-5:30pm, Su and holidays 9am-1pm; Nov.-Dec. 19 and Jan. 7-Feb. 28 Tu, Th-F 8am-2pm, W and Sa 8am-4:30pm, Su 9am-1pm. L2000/€1.03. Combination ticket including Collegio Del Cambio L6000/€3.10.)*

COLLEGIO DEL CAMBIO (EXCHANGE GUILD). This richly paneled structure is the meeting room for Perugia's merchant guild. The guild's 88 members have met here to debate tax laws and local commerce since 1390. The books in the annexed archive contain the names of all of the guild's members dating back to the Middle Ages. On the walls of the **Sala dell'Udienza** *(Audience Chamber)* Perugino's frescoes portray heroes, prophets, sybils, and even himself. Grotesque depictions of personified planets and the decapitation of John the Baptist are equally striking. *(Next to the National Gallery and Merchant's Guild at Corso Vannucci, 25. ☎ 075 572 85 99. Mar.-Oct. and Dec. 20-Jan. 6 M-Sa 9am-12:30pm and 2:30-5:30pm, Su and holidays 9am-12:30pm; Nov.-Dec. 19 and Jan. 7-Feb. Tu-Sa 8am-2pm, Su 9am-12:30pm. L5000/€2.58, groups and over 65 L3000/€1.55. Combined ticket with Merchant's Guild L6000/€3.10.)*

VIA DEI PRIORI

Belying its current calm gray face of *pietra serena* (rocklike serenity), V. dei Priori was one of the bloodiest and goriest streets of medieval Perugia. Many midnight betrayals occurred here, and the spikes on the lower walls of the street were once used to impale the rotting heads of executed criminals. One block off of Vannucci, hidden in a plain brick building on the left, is the attractive **Chiesa di Sant'Agata,** with a number of 14th-century frescoes. Two blocks farther, the Baroque **Chiesa di San Filippo Neri** (built in 1627) resides solemnly in P. Ferri; the heart of Santa Maria di Vallicella is kept here. A few blocks farther on, to the right down V. San Francesco, P.S. Francesco al Prato is a rare grassy green square inviting lounging and bare feet. At its edge is the colorful **Oratorio di San Bernardino,** near the end of V. dei Priori. Agostino de Duccio built the building between 1457 and 1461 in the early Renaissance style, embellishing its fanciful facade with finely carved reliefs and sculptures. Inside, a 3rd-century Roman sarcophagus forms the altar. *(Churches and Oratorio open daily 8am-noon and 4pm-sunset.)*

VIA ROCCHI AND THE NORTHEAST

From behind the *duomo,* medieval V. Ulisse Rocchi, the city's oldest street, winds through the north city gate to the **Arco di Etrusco,** a perfectly preserved Roman arch built on Etruscan pedestals and topped by a 16th-century portico. Walk straight through P. Braccio Fortebraccio and follow C. Guiseppe Garibaldi. Past **Palazzo Gallenga,** off to the right near the end of C. Garibaldi, lies the jewel-like **Tempio di Sant'Angelo.** The 5th-century church, constructed with building materials taken from ancient pagan buildings, is the oldest in Perugia. *(☎ 075 572 26 24. Open Tu-Su 9:30am-noon and 3:30pm-sunset.)* On your way back, veer to the left of P.B. Fortebraccio to a stairwell that winds up the hillside. Continue straight for one block from the top of the stairs then head right into P. Michelotti. Take V. Aquila on the left of the *piazza* and then take the first right into P. Raffaello. Here you will find the **Capella di San Severo,** home to the *Holy Trinity and Saints,* a fresco painted by both Raphael (who created the upper section) and his teacher Perugino (who painted the lower section). *(☎ 075 57 38 64. Open Apr.-Sept. daily 10am-1:30pm and 2:30-6:30pm; Oct.-Mar. M-F 10:30am-1:30pm and 2:30-4:30pm, Sa-Su and holidays 10am-1:30pm and 2:30-5:30pm. L3500/€1.81. including Etruscan well.)* Follow V. Raffaello then jog left and then right on V. Bontempi to reach the **Pozzo Etrusco** (Etruscan well), P. Danti, 18. The well dates to the 3rd century BC and was the town's main water source. Climb down the stairs into the cave-like room at the top of the well, and then onto the foot-bridge that spans the remarkably wide well, just meters above the water, which reaches 36m down into the earth. *(☎ 075 573 36 69. Open daily 10am-1:30pm and 2:30-6:30pm. L3500, including the Capella di San Severo.)*

THE EAST SIDE

■**BASILICA DI SAN PIETRO.** This church maintains its original 10th-century basilica layout (a double arcade of closely spaced columns leading to a choir). Inside the *chiesa* are solemn, majestic paintings and frescoes depicting scenes of saints and soldiers. Look for Perugino's *Pietà* along the north aisle. At the far end of the basilica is an exquisitely manicured medieval garden; its lower section offers a must-see view of the surrounding countryside. *(At the end of town on Borao XX Guigo, past the Port S. Pietro. Open daily 8am-noon and 4pm-sunset.)*

CHIESA DI SAN DOMENICO. On Corso Cavour, this imposing cathedral is the largest church in Umbria. Its huge Gothic rose window contrasts with its sober, Renaissance interior. The magnificently carved **Tomb of Pope Benedict XI** (1325) rests in the chapel to the right of the high altar. Once kept in a box tied with a red ribbon, the pope's bones were recently placed in an encasement (under glass and wrought iron) inside the tomb's far wall. *(Open daily 8am-noon and 4pm-sunset.)*

MUSEO ARCHAEOLOGICO NAZIONALE DELL'UMBRIA. Housed in the vast cloisters attached to the Chiesa di San Domenico, this museum has an extensive collection of Roman and Etruscan artifacts, including the bronze *Statua di Germanico,* a reconstruction of a Roman find. One hall includes a photo exhibit that takes you through the history of Umbria. An excavated Etruscan tomb lies underground near the entrance. A tunnel passes around the tiny cross-shaped chamber with windows looking in on over 50 stone burial urns. (☎ 075 572 71 41. *Entrance in courtyard to left of entrance to Chiesa di San Domenico. Open daily 8:30am-7:30pm. L4000/€2.07.*)

GIARDINI CARDUCCI

At the far end of C. Vannucci, the main street leading from P. IV Novembre, lie the Giardini Carducci. These well-maintained public gardens are named after the 19th-century poet Giosuè Carducci, who wrote a stirring ode to Italy, inspired by Perugia's historic zeal for independence. From the garden wall, enjoy the panorama of the Umbrian countryside; a castle or an ancient church crowns every hill.

🎵 ENTERTAINMENT

The glorious 10-day **Umbria Jazz Festival** in July draws internationally renowned performers. (L15-50,000/€7.75-25.82, some events free.) For information, contact the tourist office or go to www.umbriajazz.com. Summer brings **Teatro è la notte,** a series of musical, cinematic, and dance performances. In September, the **Sagra Musicale Umbra** fills local churches with concerts of religious and classical music. Check Palazzo Gallenga for English film and other event listings. Contact the tourist office about the internationally-renowned **Eurochocolate Festival,** which runs for 10 days at the end of October.

Perugia has more nightlife options than any other Umbrian city, and its large university population keeps clubs packed nearly every night of the week when school is in session from September to May. During the academic year, join the nightly bandwagon at **P. Fortebraccio,** where free buses depart (starting at 11pm) for several nearby clubs. Once there, prepare to part with L25-50,000/€12.91-25.82 for the cover charge. The deafening pulse of electronic music and an assortment of scantily clad female dancers welcome you into the Italian club scene. Within the city, Perugia's two hottest dance clubs are **Domus Delirii,** V. del Naspo, 3, just off P. Morlacchi (open daily midnight-5am) and **St. Adams,** V. della Cupa, 6, left off of V. dei Priori as you are walking from C. Vannucci (open daily midnight-5am).

Perugia's many **pubs** allow for as much conversation as ale. **Shamrock Irish,** at P. Danti, 18, on the way to the Pozzo Etrusco, is home to the best pint of Guinness in town (L8000/€4.13) and a shot of your favorite whiskey. (☎ 075 573 66 25; www.shamrockpubs.com. Happy hour 5-9pm; open Tu-Su 5pm-2am.) **Zoologico,** V. Alessi, 64, usually has live music and fills with carousing locals and travelers. (Open Tu-Su 7pm-2am.) Head to **La Terrazza,** in P. Matteotti, on the terrace behind the Mercato Coperto, for cheap drinks. It boasts excellent views, open-air movies, cabaret, and book readings. **L'Elfo II,** V. de Verzaro, 39 off P. Morlacchi, has a candle-lit interior across a gully in the University quarter. (Beer L7-8000/€3.62-4.13 per bottle, drinks L10,000/€5.16. Open daily 12:30pm-2am.)

🏛 DAYTRIPS FROM PERUGIA: LAKE TRASIMENO

Expansive Lake Trasimeno, 30km west of Perugia, is a tranquil and refreshing refuge from Umbria's stifling heat and packed tourist centers. While pleasant and peaceful today, Lake Trasimeno once witnessed some violent battles. In 217 BC, during the Second Punic War, Hannibal's elephant-riding army, fresh from the Alps, routed the Romans north of the lake. The names of the lakeside villages, **Ossaia** (place of bones) and **Sanguineto** (bloody), merrily recall the carnage of 16,000 Roman troops. The mass graves of these dead, hastily buried by Hannibal's men, have recently been discovered. If anonymous but historical dead people are your thing, take a self-guided walking tour of the site, including the surrounding battlefield in the town of **Tuero.** Tuero is between the two main towns guarding the lake, **Passignano sul Trasimeno** and **Castiglione del Lago,** which are easily accessible by train and bus. A system of ferries connects Passignano sul Trasimeno, Castiglione del Lago, Tuero, San Feliciano, and Lake Trasimeno's two largest islands—**Isola Maggiore** and **Isola Palvese.** Relaxing daytrips are but a ferry ride away.

CASTIGLIONE DEL LAGO

*Castiglione del Lago lies on the Florence-Rome train line. To get there from Perugia, change at **Terontola** to a train headed for Rome or Chiusi. 1-hr., depending on connection; 8 per day; L5400/€2.79). To reach the **town center** from the train station, take a left out of the station and your first right of V.B. Buozzi, following the sign for "castellocento". When the road dead ends, go up the broad flight of stairs facing you, then up the smaller flight of stairs and to the right through the city walls and onto V.V. Emanuele, the main street of the tiny historical center. To reach the **ferry dock,** take a right downhill at the end of V.V. Emanuele and out the city walls. Take a left at the T-junction, then an immediate right down the stone stairs. Take a left and then a right to reach the dock.*

The largest resort area around Trasimeno, Castiglione del Lago is a quiet town. It stands on a limestone promontory covered with olive groves; solid medieval walls enclose its two main streets and single square. Due to its strategic lakeside position and incredibly fertile soil, foreign powers frequently disputed control of the town. The **tourist office,** P. Mazzini, 10, in the main square, provides boat schedules, exchanges money, and helps find rooms in hotels or in private homes or apartments. (☎075 965 82 10. Open Apr.-Sept. M-F 8:30am-1pm and 3:30-7pm, Sa 9am-1pm and 3:30-7pm, Su and holidays 9am-1pm; Oct.-Mar. M-F 8:30am-1pm and 3:30-7pm; Sa 8:30am-1pm; closed Su.) True budget accommodations are scarce in the immediate vicinity of Castiglione del Lago, but the three-star **La Torre,** V.V. Emanuele, 50, offers clean rooms with bath and other amenities in the heart of the old town. (☎/fax 075 95 16 66. Singles L90,000/€46.48; doubles L130,000/€67.14; triples L215,000/€111.04, quads L270,000/€139.44. AmEx/MC/V.) For food, try the shops lining V.V. Emanuele, or dine at **Paprika,** V.V. Emanuele, 107, which serves local specialties including *spaghetti ai sapori di Trasimeno* (with eel sauce) for L10,000/€5.16. (*Primi* L10-14,000/€5.16-7.23; *secondi* from L15,000/€7.75. Cover L3000/€1.55. Open F-W noon-2:30pm and 7-10:30pm. AmEx/MC/V.) At the end of V.V. Emanuele, next to the hospital, stand the **Palazzo della Corgna** and the **Rocca Medievale.** The courtyard of the imposing, crumbling *rocca* is free and open to the public, and its sloping grass lawn is sometimes used as seating for open-air concerts. You must pay to enter to *palazzo* to climb on the walls of the fortress for the beautiful lake view. The 16th-century *palazzo* is notable for its frescoes by Niccolò Circignani, known as Il Pomarancio. (*Palazzo* and *rocca* walls open M-F 10am-1:30pm and 4:7:30pm. Sa-Su 9:30am-4:30pm.)

PASSIGNANO SUL TRASIMENO

Passignano sul Trasimeno lies on the Foligno-Terontola train line. Trains from Perugia (30min., 8 per day, L3200/€1.65.) To reach the waterfront and ferry, turn right from the train station. Follow the road as it passes over the railroad tracks, curves right, and curves left into the main waterfront drag. The ferry dock is 5min. ahead on the right.

Infested with Italians on vacation in the summer, there's not much to see in Passignano sul Trasimeno; however it is by far the easiest ferry point to Isola Maggiore from Perugia. If you have some time on your hands waiting for a ferry, browse the numerous ceramic shops that line the waterfront, or follow your nose uphill through the tiny medieval center. At the end of the single street through the charming residential neighborhood is a beautiful view of the lake.

ISOLA MAGGIORE

A convenient ferry system connects the island to Passignano sul Trasimeno (20min.; every hr. 7:53am-8:20pm; L5000/€2.58, round-trip L9000/€4.65) and Castiglione del Lago (30min.; every 1½hr. 9:10am-8pm; L6000/€3.10, round-trip L11,000/€5.68). Buy tickets on board when coming from the island, or at the docks in the town.

Follow in St. Francis's footsteps and spend a delightful day on Isola Maggiore, Lake Trasimeno's only inhabited island. A **tourist information booth** sits by the dock. (Open daily 10am-noon and 1-6pm. No free map, but glossy guides to the island L6000/€3.10.) As you leave the dock, turn right and follow the path to the tip of the island and the ruined **Guglielmi castle.** All that is accessible is the Baroque chapel, dimly lit with peeling plaster and fading frescoed ceilings. You may run into the sweet old caretaker who offers less-than-informative tours of the castle all day long (in Italian, 9am-5pm). Down the castle to the right, make your way to the shore and follow the path around to the left, to find a clearing with a statue of St. Francis. On the far side of the clearing take the stone stairs up to the left to see the tiny **chapel** enclosing the rock where St. Francis spent 40 days in 1211. From here, hike 5min. up to the **Chiesa di San Michele Arcangelo** for lovely 14th-century frescoes and a wonderful view of the island. (Open Su 10:30am-noon and 3-5pm. L5000/€2.58 includes admission to lace museum, for fans of "Irish Point" lace. Museum open daily 10:30am-1pm and 3-6pm.) At the side of the island opposite the castle is the island's small private **beach.**

TODI
☎ 075

According to legend, an eagle flew to this rocky site, bringing with him the founders of Todi. Since then it has seen few other visitors. This isolated town has long remained untouched by historical change and still retains visible traces of its Etruscan, Roman, and medieval past. Though all areas of the modern city seem to have been transformed into parking lots, there's hardly room for cars (or any other 20th-century amenities) in the historic center. An inordinate number of antique shops have nonetheless squeezed their way in, catering to the busloads of daytrippers who unload in P. Jacopone each morning.

⚑ PRACTICAL INFORMATION. Todi is best reached by **bus** from Perugia. The bus station is in P. Consolazione, a short ride on city bus A or a pleasant 1km walk from the town center. **ASP** (☎ 075 894 29 39 or toll-free 800 51 21 41) runs buses to and from **Perugia** (1½hr.; M-Sa 6 per day; last bus from Todi 5pm, last bus from Perugia 6:25pm; L9200/€4.75). Todi is also accessible by **train** from **Perugia Sant'Anna** (45min., 13 per day, L4700/€2.43). **Taxis** are available in P. Garibaldi (☎ 075 894 23 75), P. Jacopone (☎ 075 894 25 25), or by calling ☎ 0347 77 48 321. The **Pro-Loco Pro-Todi** tourist office, P. del Popolo, 39, provides maps, transportation schedules, and information about area restaurants and accommodations. (☎ 075 894 25 26. Open M-Sa 9am-1pm and 4-7pm.) In case of **emergency,** call the **police** (☎ 112 or 075 895 62 43), an **ambulance** (☎ 118), or the **hospital** (☎ 075 885 81). A pharmacy, **Farmacia Dr. Santori** (☎ 075 39 03), is in P. del Popolo. **Postal Code:** 06059.

⌂ ACCOMMODATIONS AND FOOD. Todi's most reasonably priced hotel is the three-star **Tuder,** V. Maestà dei Lombardi, 13. (☎ 075 894 21 84; fax 894 39 52. Singles with bath L80-90,000/€41.32-46.48; doubles with bath L130-160,000/€67.14-82.63. AmEx/MC/V.) Pick up provisions at the **alimentari** at V. Cavour, 150. (Open M-Tu and Th-Sa 7:45am-1:30pm and 5:30-8pm, W 7:45am-1:30pm.) **Ristorante Cavour,** V. Cavour, 21/23, offers pizza (L7500/€3.87) and filling meals (L22,000/€11.21). Their specialty is *tortellini al tartufo nero* for L13,000/€6.71. (☎ 075 894 37 30. Open Th-Tu noon-3pm and 7:30pm-midnight. AmEx/MC/V.)

◙ SIGHTS. **Piazza del Popolo,** the town center and Todi's focal point since Roman times, remains the town's high point in altitude and architectural achievement. It is a stately ensemble of glowering *palazzi* and a somber *duomo*. In the *piazza,* the **Palazzo del Capitano** contains the **Pinacoteca Civica** and the **Museo Archelogico** in its upper floors. Fascinating frescoes in the **Sala del Capitano del Popolo** lie at the top of the exterior staircase. (Open daily 10:30am-1pm and 2:30-6pm. L6000/€3.10, ages 15-25 L4500/€2.32, under 15 L3000/€1.55.) The stout **duomo** rests solidly atop a flight of broad stone steps. The central rose window and arched doorway command attention with their intricate decoration. The delicate Gothic side arcade, added in the 1300s, shelters an unusual altarpiece—the Madonna's head emerges in high relief from the painting's flat surface. (Across from P. del Popolo. *Duomo* and crypt open daily 8:30am-12:30pm and 2:30-6:30pm.) Across from the *duomo,* the tower and facade of the **Palazzo dei Priori** (1297-1337) retain vestiges of medieval gloom despite rows of Renaissance windows carved in the early 16th-century.

Neighboring P. Garibaldi has been reduced to little more than a municipal parking lot, but it still opens onto a superb vista. From the *piazza*, follow the signs leading off C. Cavour to the remaining walls of the **Foro Romano** and the nearby 12th-century **Chiesa di San Ilario**. The **Fonti Scannabecco's** 13th-century porticoes still house a working tap. Return to P. del Popolo and take V. Mazzini to the majestically angular **Tempio di San Fortunato**. Built by the Franciscans between the 13th and 15th centuries, the church features Romanesque portals and a Gothic interior. To the right of S. Fortunato, a path bends uphill toward **La Rocca**, a ruined 14th-century castle. Next to the castle, follow a sinuous path, appropriately named **Viale della Serpentina,** to a breathtaking belvedere constructed on the remains of an old Roman wall. Follow the twisting paths down to the base of the hill and cross Viale della Consolazione to the Renaissance **Tempio di Santa Maria della Consolazione**, with its elegant domes. Inside are 12 enormous statues of the region's principal saints and a magnificent altar worth the trek.

ASSISI   ☎ 079

For it is in giving that we receive; it is in pardoning that we are pardoned; and it is in dying that we are born to eternal life.
　　—St. Francis of Assisi

Assisi's serenity originates from the legacy of St. Francis, a 12th-century monk who sparked a revolution in the Catholic church. He founded the Franciscan order, devoted to the then unusual combination of asceticism, poverty, and chastity. Young Franciscan nuns and monks still fill the city, dressed in their brown *cappucci* robes, carrying on his legacy with spiritual vigor. Assisi is an important pilgrimage site, especially among Italian youth, who converge here for conferences, festivals, and other religious activities. Nevertheless, fervent religiosity is not a prerequisite for adoring Assisi. Giotto's frescoes adorning the basilica merit a pilgrimage on their own. The Basilica of St. Francis is perhaps the most visited sight in all Umbria, containing the saint's relics and Giotto's renowned fresco series of St. Francis's life, as well as works by Cimabue, Jacopo Torriti, Filipo Rusuti, Simone Martini, and Pietro Lorenzetti. The influence of such masters infuses the streets, *piazze*, and *palazzi* of the town as well as its numerous places of worship. Assisi also has monuments attesting to its Etruscan and Roman roots in the ruins throughout the town. Grand palaces and majestic *rocce* (castles) from a later era tower above the orange roofs. The rose-colored town is beautifully preserved, its accommodations are terrific, and its restaurants are among the best in Umbria. Unfortunately, earthquakes in the fall of 1997 devastated much of the city, but renovations have repaired much of the damage.

▐▀ TRANSPORTATION

Trains: Near Basilica of Santa Maria degli Angeli. On Foligno-Terontola line. Office open 6am-8pm. Luggage storage available (p. 399). To: **Ancona** (from L20,200/€10.43); **Florence** (2 per day, more frequent via Terontola; L17,000/€8.78); **Perugia** (16 per day, L3200/€1.65); **Rome** (1 per day; more frequent via Foligno; L25,500/€13.17).

Buses: ASP (☎ 075 573 17 07) buses leave from P. Matteotti. To: **Florence** (2½hr.; 1 per day; L12,400/€6.40); **Foligno** (M-F 5 per day, L6500/€3.36); **Perugia** (1hr., 7 per day, L5200/€2.70); **Rome** (3hr.; 1 per day; L16,000/€8.26). To reach the bus stop from P. del Comune, walk up V. San Rufino to P. San Rufino and take V. del Torrione (to the left of the church) to P. Matteotti. Bus schedules available at tourist info office.

Public Transportation: Local buses (2-3 per hr., L1200/€0.62) run from train station to the town's bus stops at P. Unità d'Italia (near basilica), Largo Properzio (near church of St. Claire), and P. Matteotti (above P. del Comune). Buy tickets at *tabacchi* in train station, or on board (L2000/€1.03).

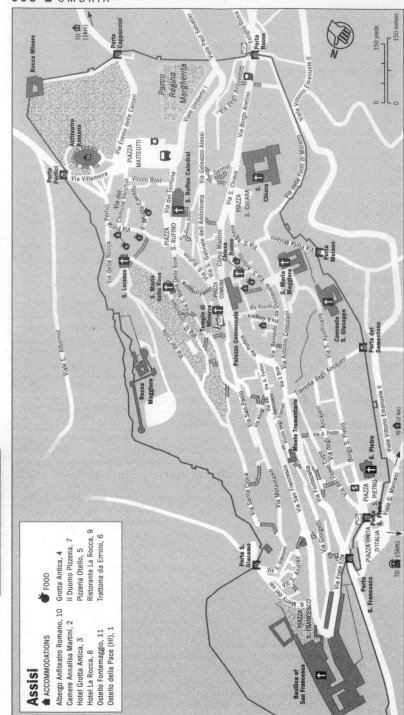

Assisi

▲ ACCOMMODATIONS

Albergo Anfiteatro Romano, 10
Camere Annalisa Martini, 2
Hotel Grotta Antica, 3
Hotel La Rocca, 8
Ostello Fontemaggio, 11
Ostello della Pace (HI), 1

● FOOD

Grotta Antica, 4
Il Duomo Pizzeria, 7
Pizzeria Otello, 5
Ristorante La Rocca, 9
Trattoria da Ermini, 6

Taxis: In P. del Comune (☎075 81 31 93), in P. San Chiara (☎075 81 26 00), in P. Unità d'Italia (☎075 81 23 78), and at the train station (☎075 804 02 75).

Car Rental: Agenzia Assisiorganizza, Borgo Aretino, 11a (☎075 81 52 80). Cars from L145,000/€74.89 per day, L672,000/€347.06 per week. 21+. Open M-Sa, 9am-noon. Credit cards only. AmEx/D/MC/V.

☀🛈 ORIENTATION AND PRACTICAL INFORMATION

Towering above the city to the north, the **Rocca Maggiore** can help you orient yourself should you become lost among Assisi's winding streets. The bus from the train station stops first at **B. Unità d'Italia;** get off here if you are going directly to the Basilica di San Francesco. Otherwise, stay on the bus until **Piazza Matteotti,** where the bulk of the town is a downhill walk. The center of town is **Piazza del Comune.** To reach it from Piazza Matteotti, where intercity buses also stop, take V. del Torrione to **Piazza San Rufino,** bear left in the *piazza*, and take **via San Rufino** until it hits the town center. **Via Portica** (which intersects V. Fortini, V. Seminario, and V. San Francesco) connects P. del Comune to the **Basilica di San Francesco.** Heading in the opposite direction, **Corso Mazzini** leads to the **Chiesa di Santa Chiara.**

Tourist Office: (☎075 81 25 34; fax 81 37 27; www.umbria2000.it), in P. del Comune. Walking into P. del Comune on V.S. Rufino, office is on far end of *piazza* facing you. Provides brochures, train timetable, and a decent map. Open M-F 8am-2pm and 3:30-6:30pm, Sa 9am-1pm and 3:30-6:30pm, Su and holidays 9am-1pm.

Currency Exchange: Exchange traveler's checks at the post office for L2-5000/€1.03-2.58. Otherwise try **Banca Toscana,** on P.S. Pietro, **Cassa di Risparmio di Perugia,** on P. del Comune. Banks open 8:20am-1:20pm and 2:15-3:15pm. **ATMs** outside.

Luggage Storage: L6000/€3.10 per 24hr. at newsstand. Open daily 6:30am-6:30pm.

Emergency: ☎113.

Carabinieri: P. Matteotti, 3 (☎075 81 22 39).

Hospital: Ospedale di Assisi (☎075 813 91), on the outskirts of town. Take the "Linea A" bus from P. del Comune.

Internet Access: Agenzia Casciarri, V. Borgo Aretino, 39. L2800/€1.45 per hr. Open M-F 9am-12:30pm and 3-6pm, Sa 9am-12:30pm. **Internet World,** V.S. Gabriele del Addolorate, 25 (☎075 81 23 27; info@internetworldassisi.com). Reasonably fast connections L12,000/€6.20 per hr. 1hr. min. charge. Open Th-Tu 11am-1pm and 1-10pm, W 11am-1pm and 4-10pm.

Post Office: Largo Properzio, 4, up the stairs to the left just outside of Porta Nuova. Open M-Sa 8:35am-1:25pm. **Secondary branch** at P.S. Pietro, 41. Open M-F 8:10am-7pm, Sa 8:10am-1:25pm. Same postal code.

Postal Code: 06081.

⌂ ACCOMMODATIONS

Reservations are crucial around Easter and Christmas and strongly recommended for the **Festa di Calendimaggio** in early May. If you don't mind turning in around 11pm, ask the tourist office for a list of **religious institutions.** The tourist office also has a list of *affittacamere* (rooms for rent).

▨ **Ostello della Pace (HI),** V. di Valecchi, 177 (☎/fax 075 81 67 67), a 20min. walk from town. Turn right from train station and then left at intersection onto V. di Valecchi (30min.). Or take bus to P.S. Pietro and walk 50m down main road to road marked by hostel sign. 4-bed rooms and spotless bathrooms. Breakfast included. Dinner L15,000/€7.75. Laundry L6500/€3.73. Reception daily 7-9:15am and 3:30-11:30pm. Check-out 9:30am. Lockout 9:30am-3:30pm. Communal areas locked by 11:30pm. Reserve ahead. **HI card required;** you can buy one at hostel. Dorms L23,000/€11.89, with private bath L28,000/€14.46. MC/V.

■ **Camere Annalisa Martini,** V.S. Gregorio, 6 (☎075 81 35 36). Follow V. Portico from P. del Comune and take 1st left onto V.S. Gregorio. Lovely Annalisa offers *affittacamere* at excellent prices. Outdoor picnic seating, washer, phone, and fax. If no room, Annalisa can refer you to her friends. Laundry L5-10,000/€2.58-5.16. Singles L38,000/€19.63, with bath L40,000/€20.66; doubles L60,000/€30.99, L65,000/€33.57; triples L90-100,000/€46.48-51.65. Prices reduced for 3 days or longer.

Ostello Fontemaggio V. per l'Eremo delle Carceri, 8 (☎075 81 36 36; fax 81 37 49). V. Eremo begins at the top of P. Matteotti and leads through Porta Cappuccini; follow 1km up the road and then bear right at the sign. New hostel with 8-bed rooms. Delicious home-cooked fare available at the hostel restaurant. Breakfast L8000/€4.13. Check-out 10am. Curfew 11pm. Dorms L30,000/€15.50. Market and **campground** next door. L9000/€4.65 per person, L8000/€4.13 per tent, L4000/€2.07 per car.

Hotel La Rocca, V. di Porta Perlici, 27 (☎/fax 075 81 22 84). From P. del Comune, follow V.S. Rufino up hill and cross *piazza*. Go up V. Porta Perlicia until old arches; hotel on left. Rooms with bath. Restaurant downstairs (see below). Breakfast L7500/€3.87. Singles L60,000/€30.99; doubles L75,000/€38.73; triples L110,000/€56.81.

Albergo Anfiteatro Romano, V. Anfiteatro Romano, 4 (☎075 81 30 25; fax 81 51 10), off P. Matteotti. Restaurant with large portions downstairs: *primi* L8-15,000/€4.13-7.75; *secondi* L10-18,000/€5.16-9.30; *menù turistica* L22,000/€11.36. Welcoming, quiet rooms. Some boast views of the *rocca*. Singles L40,000/€20.66; doubles L60,000/€30.99, with bath L70,000/€36.15. AmEx/MC/V.

Hotel Grotta Antica, Viccolo dei Macelli Vecchi, 1 (☎075 81 34 67). From P. del Comune, walk downhill on V. dell'Arco dei Priori (under arch); right on Vicolo dei Macelli Vecchi. Bathrooms, TV, phone. Singles L50,000/€25.82; doubles L75,000/€38.73; triples L95,000/€49.06; quads L105,000/€54.23. Restaurant downstairs. MC/V.

◖ FOOD

Assisi will tempt you with a sinful array of nut breads and sweets. *Bricciata umbria*, a strudel-like pastry with a hint of cherries, and *brustengolo*, packed with raisins, apples, and walnuts, are both divine. **Pasticceria Santa Monica,** at V. Portica, 4, right off P. del Comune, sells these and other treats at low prices with friendly service. (Open daily 9am-8pm.) On Saturday mornings, there's a **market** in P. Matteotti; on weekdays, head to V.S. Gabriele for fresh fruits and vegetables.

Pizzeria Otello, V. San Antonio, 1 (☎075 81 24 15). Head downhill on V. dell'Arco dei Priori (under arch) and take 1st left. Specialty pizza L8-12,000/€4.13; focaccia sandwiches and large salads L9-10,050/€4.65-5.19; *primi* L9500-13,000/€4.91-6.71; *secondi* from L9500/€4.91. Cover L2000/€1.03. Open for pizza July-Aug. daily 7:30am-noon; Sept.-June M-Sa 7:30am-noon. Main restaurant open July-Aug. daily noon-3:30pm and 7-10:30pm; Sept.-June M-Sa noon-3:30pm. AmEx/MC/V.

Trattoria da Ermini, V. Monte Cavallo, 19 (☎075 81 25 06). From P. del Comune, follow V.S. Rufino up through P.S. Rufino and onto V. Porta Perlici and take 1st right. Sample their filling *primi* (L9-16,000/€4.65-8.26). Enjoy *secondi* (L10-16,000/€5.16-8.26) grilled on an open fire in a corner of the dining room. House wine L3500/€1.81 per ½L. Cover 2500/€1.29. Open F-W noon-2:30pm and 7-9pm. MC/V.

Il Duomo Pizzeria, V. di Porta Perlici, 11 (☎075 81 63 26). Large pizza oven is focal point of this medieval lair/pizzeria. Wonderful pizza (L6500-11,000/€3.36-5.68). Diverse and well-priced *menù*. Primi L9-14,000/€4.65-7.23; *secondi* from L12,000/€6.20. Cover L2000/€1.03. Open daily noon-2:30pm and 6:30pm-1am. MC/V.

Hotel Grotta Antica Ristorante Caldrino, V. Macelli Vecchi, 1 (☎075 81 52 20), see directions for the hotel (above). *Primi* (L10-15,000/€5.16-7.75); *secondi* (L12-18,000/€6.20-9.30). Cover L2000/€1.03. Open Apr.-Oct. daily 12:30-2:30pm and 7-10pm; Nov.-Mar. Th-Tu 12:30-2:30pm and 7-10pm.

Restaurante La Rocca, V di Porta Perlici, 27 (☎/fax 075 81 22 84). See directions for Hotel La Rocca (above). *Primi* (L7-10,000/€3.62-5.16) include ravioli with black truffle sauce (L10,000/€5.16); *secondi* L12,000/€6.20, house wine L3500/€1.81 per ½L. Cover L2000/€1.03. Open daily 12:30-2:30pm and 7-10pm. D/MC/V.

👁 SIGHTS

At age 19, St. Francis (b. 1182) abandoned military and social ambitions, rejected his father's wealth, and embraced asceticism. His renouncement of the church's worldliness, his love of nature, and devoted humility earned him a huge European following, posing an unprecedented challenge to the decadent papacy and corrupt monastic orders. St. Francis continued to preach chastity and poverty until his death in 1226, when the order he founded was gradually subsumed into the Catholic hierarchy that it had criticized. Ironically, the Catholic church has glorified the modest saint through the countless churches it has constructed in his honor.

BASILICA DI SAN FRANCESCO

☎ 075 819 00 84. Free tours given by Franciscan monks daily 9am-noon and 2-5:30pm. Tours begin outside lower basilica. Arrange ahead for tours; call or visit info window across from entrance to lower basilica. Information window open daily 9:30am-12:30pm. Lower basilica open daily 6:30am-7pm. Upper basilica open daily 8:30am-7pm. Musco Tesoro della Basilica open daily 9:30am-12:30pm and 2-6pm. L3000/€1.55.

When construction of the ▓Basilica di San Francesco began in the mid-13th century, the Franciscan order protested—the elaborate church seemed an impious monument to the conspicuous consumption that St. Francis had scorned. Brother Elia, the vicar of the order, insisted that a double church be erected, the lower level to be built around the saint's crypt, the upper level to be used as a church for services. The subdued art in the lower church commemorates Francis's modest life, while the upper church pays tribute to his sainthood and consecration. Although the basilica was damaged by an earthquake in 1997, the furious restoration efforts to prepare for Jubilee Year 2000 spurred a speedy reconstruction.

The walls of the upper church are covered with Giotto's renowned *Life of St. Francis* fresco cycle. The story begins on the right wall near the altar and runs clockwise, beginning with teenage Francis in courtly dress surprised by a prophecy of future greatness. The cycle closes with an image of the saint passing through the agony of the "Dark Night." Paralleling St. Francis's pictorial path of holy deeds is the equally linear story of Jesus.

Cimabue's magnificent *Madonna and Child*, *Angels*, and *St. Francis* grace the right transept. Those who have been to Arezzo will recognize one of the images as an almost exact copy of his famous crucifix in the Chiesa di S. Domenico. Tragically, most of Cimabue's frescoes in the transepts and apse have so deteriorated that they now look like photographic negatives. Pietro Lorenzetti decorated the left transept with his outstanding *Crucifixion*, *Last Supper*, and *Madonna and Saints*. Also stunning are Simone Martini's frescoes in the first chapel off the left wall, which depict the life of St. Martin. Descend through a door in the right side of the apse to enter the room housing St. Francis's tunic, sandals, and sundries.

St. Francis's tomb, the inspiration for the entire edifice, lies below the lower church. The coffin itself was hidden in the 15th century, out of fear that the war-mongering Perugians would desecrate it. It was not rediscovered until 1818. The original tomb was built in a Neoclassical style, but it was disliked by so many friars that a new, simplified version was constructed in 1935. The stone coffin sits above the altar in the crypt, surrounded by the sarcophagi of four of the saint's dearest friends. The attached library is open to visitors and houses the remarkable **Museo Tesoro della Basilica.** Particularly impressive are the rare illuminated manuscripts, the graceful 13th-century French ivory *Madonna and Child*, 17th-century Murano glass work, and a fragment of the Holy Cross.

OTHER SIGHTS

ROCCA MAGGIORE. The dramatic Rocca Maggiore looms uphill from the *duomo*. Check out the view down onto the town and the Basilica di S. Francesco from the sun-baked gravel lot outside the *rocca*, or pay the nominal entrance fee to go inside the fortress and make like a mole through a 50m long tunnel to a lookout tower. The view is stunning in all directions, but the trip through the tunnel is not recommended for those who tend to dislike being confined to small, dark places, where the walls squeeze in and the air slowly leaks out, stifling and suffocating all inside, causing a mass exit for the door in which several people are trampled underfoot, their dying scream echoing through the hot corridors. Whew. *(From P. del Comune, follow V.S. Rufino to P.S. Rufino. Continue up V. Porta Perlici and take your first left up a narrow staircase, following signs for the Rocca. ☎ 075 81 52 92. Open daily Apr.-Sept. 9am-sunset; Nov.-Mar. 10am-sunset. Closed in bad weather. L3000/€1.55, students L2000/€1.03. Prices may be higher when central courtyard renovations finish.)*

BASILICA DI SANTA CHIARA. The interior of the pink and white Basilica di Santa Chiara is a beautiful example of early Gothic architecture. It stands at the opposite end of Assisi on the site where St. Francis attended school. The church shelters not only the tomb (and hair) of St. Clare, but also the tunic and shoes worn by St. Francis and the crucifix that revealed God's message to him. The nuns in this convent are sworn to seclusion. *(☎075 81 22 82. Open daily 9am-noon and 2-7pm.)*

DUOMO (CHIESA DI SAN RUFINO). V.S. Rufino climbs steeply up from P. del Comune between closely packed old houses, opening onto P.S. Rufino to reveal the squat *duomo* with its massive bell tower. The restored interior is quite spartan and may come as a disappointment compared to its decorative facade. *(☎057 81 22 82. Open daily 8am-1pm and 2-6pm.)*

PIAZZA DEL COMUNE AND ENVIRONS. From the Basilica di San Francesco, V.S. Francesco snakes between medieval buildings and their 16th-century additions. The colorfully frescoed **Oratorio del Pelegrino** (Pilgrim Oratory) is especially noteworthy. At the end of the street, P. del Comune sits upon the old **Foro Romano.** Enter from the **crypt of St. Nicholas** on V. Portica and walk among the columns and statues of the old Roman forum, which stretches the length of P. del Comune. Back above ground sits the **Tempio di Minerva,** a majestic Roman relic with crumbling Corinthian columns. The **Pinacoteca,** which occupies the nearby **Palazzo del Priore,** houses works by important Umbrian artists and a collection of Renaissance frescoes lifted from city gates and various shrines. Rounding out the impressive buildings in the square is the appealing **Chiesa Nuova,** with slightly crumbling exterior columns and a frescoed interior. *(Forum ☎ 075 81 30 53. Pinacoteca ☎075 81 52 92. Both open Mar. 16-Oct. 15 daily 10am-1pm and 3-7pm; Oct. 16-Mar. 15 10am-1pm and 2-5pm. L4000/€2.07 for each sight. The biglietto cumulativo (forum, La Rocca Maggiore, and Pinacoteca) L10,000/€5.16, students L7000/€3.62. Tempio di Minerva open daily 6:30am-noon and 2-6pm. Chiesa Nuova ☎ 075 81 23 39. Same hours as Tempio di Minerva.)*

🎵 ENTERTAINMENT

All of Assisi's religious festivals involve feasts and processions. An especially long, dramatic performance marks **Easter Week.** On Holy Thursday, a mystery play reenacts the Deposition from the Cross. Traditional processions trail through town on Good Friday and Easter Sunday. Assisi welcomes spring with the **Festa di Calendimaggio** (first Thursday, Friday, and Saturday of May). A queen is chosen and dubbed *Primavera* (Spring), while the upper and lower quarters of the city compete in a clamorous musical tournament. Ladies and knights overtake the streets crooning amorous melodies in celebration of the young St. Francis, who wandered the streets of Assisi singing serenades at night. It was on one such night that he encountered a vision of the *Madonna della Povertà* (Lady of Poverty). Classical music concerts and organ recitals occur once or twice each week from April to

October in the various churches. October 4 marks the **Festival of St. Francis,** which kicks off in Chiesa di Santa Maria degli Angeli, the site of St. Francis's death. Each year a different region of Italy offers oil for the cathedral's votive lamp, and the traditional dances and songs of that region are performed.

 DAYTRIPS FROM ASSISI

EREMO DELLE CARCERI AND MT. SUBASIO

From P. Matteotti, exit the city through Porta Cappuccini and turn immediately left up the dirt road. At the Rocca Minore follow the trail uphill to the right, ignoring the large sign. About two-thirds of the way up, the trail flattens and follows the flank of the mountain giving spectacular views of the fertile valley below. Follow the paved road to the right, rather than crossing and following the trail uphill. Loose rocks can make the descent difficult. For a less difficult walk (or drive), from Porta Cappuccini, follow the dirt trail next to the paved road uphill. Open Easter-Oct. daily 6:30am-7pm, Nov.-Easter 6:30am-5:30pm.

A strenuous but gorgeous 1hr. hike up Mt. Subasio reveals the inspiring ▨Eremo delle Carceri. To explore Mt. Subasio you can purchase a Kompass map (L12,000/€6.20) or less detailed Club Alpino Italiano map (L9000/€4.65) in any bookshop or newspaper stand in Assisi. Those who follow the mountain trail may be startled by the line of parked cars and the kitschy souvenir stand outside the gate to the hermitage. But these are soon forgotten as you follow the path to the little complex of rough stone buildings. From the central courtyard you can reach the **Grotta di San Francesco,** a series of tiny cells and chapels where St. Francis slept and prayed, connected by steep stairs and child-sized doorways. Trails run through the natural beauty to which St. Francis so often retreated.

CHURCHES

Several churches associated with St. Francis and St. Clare stand in the immediate vicinity of Assisi. A 15min. stroll down the steep road outside Porta Nuova leads to the **Convent of San Damiano,** where St. Francis received his calling and later wrote the *Canticle of the Creatures.* The chapel contains fine 14th-century frescoes and a riveting woodcarving of Christ. (Open daily 10am-noon and 3-5:30pm.)

The train to Assisi passes **Basilica di Santa Maria degli Angeli,** a church inside a church. From Assisi, take the frequent bus to the train station (marked S.M. degli Angeli) from P. Matteotti, Largo Properzio, or P. Unita d'Italia and get off one stop after the train station. From the train station, exit left and take your first left, over the tracks, on Viale Patrono d'Italia. The basilica is ahead on the left (10min.). This church, with a Renaissance facade and Baroque interior, capped by a purple dome, houses two buildings that used to sit quietly in the woods until the church was built in the 15th century. **Porziuncola** is a chapel St. Francis built himself, and where he instituted the annual **Festa del Perdono** (Aug. 2). In the right transept lies a small Benedictine cell, the **Cappella de Transito,** where St. Francis died. In order to overcome temptation, St. Francis supposedly flung himself on thorny rosebushes in the garden just outside the basilica, eternally staining the leaves red. Through the rose garden lies the Museo di Santa Maria degli Angeli, which houses holy relics that used to lie in the Porziuncola. (Basilica open daily 6:15am-8pm. June-Aug. also open 9-11pm. Museum open daily 9am-noon and 3:30-6:30pm.)

GUBBIO   ☎075

Ancient Umbrians founded Gubbio in the 3rd century BC, but a wave of invasions later exhausted the thriving settlement. Its long, tumultuous history has left a rich, if somewhat varied, legacy. The Eugabian Tables (3rd to first century BC), the fundamental documents of ancient Umbrian language and history, were discovered beneath the city's Roman forum. They bear witness to the town's alliance with the Romans (against the Etruscans). Graceful portals and a well-preserved theater attest to the past grip of Roman emperors, and splendid *palazzi* recall years of subjugation under the powerful Dukes of Urbino. Gubbio's distinction lies not in its charming cobblestone streets and spectacular vistas, common to most central Italian towns, but instead in its school of painting, its ceramics tradition, and as the hometown of Italy's first novelist, Bosone Novello Raffaelli.

▀ TRANSPORTATION

Trains: Nearest station is **Fossato di Vico's,** 19km away on Rome-Ancona line. To: **Ancona** (1½hr., 10 per day, from L8200/€4.23); **Rome** (3hr.; 5 per day; from L19,000/€9.81); **Spoleto** (1¼hr., 6 per day, L6500/€3.73). Buses connect Gubbio to Fossato (M-Sa 9 per day, Su 6 per day; L3800/€1.96). Tickets at newsstand in P. Quaranta Martiri at Perugia bus stop and newsstand in Fossato's train station. If stranded in Fossato without bus service, call a taxi at ☎075 91 92 02 or 033 53 37 48 71.

Buses: ASP (☎075 573 17 07) run to and from **Perugia** (1hr.; M-F 10 per day, Sa-Su 4 per day; L7600/€3.93) and are much more convenient than the train.

Taxis: (☎075 927 38 00), in P. Quaranta Martiri.

✴❓ ORIENTATION AND PRACTICAL INFORMATION

Gubbio is a tangle of twisting streets and medieval alleyways that lead to the *piazze.* **Piazza della Signoria,** on the ledge of the hill, remains the civic headquarters. Buses leave you in **Piazza Quaranta Martiri.** A short uphill walk on **via della Repubblica,** the street ahead as you exit the bus station, leads to **Corso Garibaldi.** The **via dei Consoli** and the **Piazza Grande** offer some of Gubbio's best ceramics.

Tourist Office: P. Oderisi, 6 (☎075 922 06 93), off C. Garibaldi next door to local Communist Party headquarters, but don't let that stop you from discovering the capitalist joys of Umbrian food. Helpful English-speaking staff. Open Mar.-Sept. M-F 8:15am-1:45pm and 3:30-6:30pm, Sa 9am-1pm and 3:30-6:30pm, Su 8:30am-12:30pm; Oct.-Apr. M-F 8:15am-1:45pm and 3-6pm, Sa 9am-1pm and 3:30-6:30pm, Su 9am-1pm; July-Aug. also open Su 3:30-6:30pm.

24hr. ATM: P. Quaranta Martiri, 48.

Emergency: ☎113.

Police: (☎075 22 15 42), on V. Leonardo da Vinci.

Late-Night Pharmacy: C. Garibaldi, 12. Open Apr.-Sept. M-Sa 9am-1pm and 4:30-8pm; Oct.-Mar. 9am-1pm and 4-7:30pm. 4 pharmacies rotate Su and emergency late-night services.

Hospital: ☎075 23 94 67 or 23 94 69.

Post Office: V. Cairoli, 11 (☎075 927 39 25). Open M-Sa 8:10am-6pm. Last 2 weeks of July M-Sa 8:30am-1:25pm.

Postal Code: 06024.

▐ ACCOMMODATIONS

▧ **Residence di "Via Piccardi,"** V. Piccardi, 12 (☎075 927 61 08). Large, comfortable rooms, all with bath, overlooking the outdoor breakfast garden. Lovely staff, extremely welcoming to young backpackers. Breakfast included. Singles L50,000/€25.82; doubles L80,000/€41.32; triples L100,000/€51.65.

Locanda del Duca, V. Piccardi, 3 (☎075 927 77 53). Walk across P. Quaranta Martiri and go right on V. Piccardi. Bath and TV. Restaurant below. Breakfast L5000/€2.58; lunch L25,000/€12.91; dinner L28,000/€14.46. Singles L65,000/€33.57; doubles L85,000/€43.90; triples L105,000/€54.23; quads L110,000/€56.82.

Pensione Grotta dell'Angelo, V. Gioia, 47 (☎075 927 17 47), walk up from P. Quaranta Martiri on v. della Republica and take 1st right on V. Massarelli and 1st right on V.

Gioia. Spacious rooms. TV, phone, bath. Dining in attached restaurant. Breakfast L5000/€2.58. Singles L55,000/€28.41; doubles L80,000/€41.32. AmEx/D/MC/V.

▶ FOOD

For a quick bite, try the sandwiches (L2500/€1.29) at the **salumeria,** P. Quaranta Martiri, 36, across from the bus station. (Open daily 7am-1pm and 3:30-8pm.) On Tuesday mornings explore the **market** under P. Quaranta Martiri's *loggie*. Local delicacies await at **Prodotti Tipici e Tartufati Eugubini,** V. Piccardi, 17. Sample *salumi di cinghiale o cervo* (boar or deer sausage) and *pecorino* cheese, or indulge in truffle oil. (Open daily 10am-1pm and 2:30-8pm.)

Taverna del Buchetto, V. Dante, 30 (☎075 927 70 34), near the Porta Romana at the end of C. Garibaldi. Spicy *pollo alla diavola* (devil's chicken; L14,000/€7.23). Pizza L7-14,000/€3.62-7.23; *primi* L8-15,000/€4.13-7.75. Cover L2500/€1.29. Open Tu-Su noon-2:30pm and 7:30-10pm. AmEx/MC/V.

La Cantina Ristorante/Pizzeria, V. Francesco Piccotti, 3 (☎075 922 05 83), off V. della Repubblica. This upscale pizzeria specializes in *funghi porcini e tartufi* (mushrooms and truffles). Pizza L7-14,000/€3.62-7.23; *primi* L8-13,000/€4.13-6.71. Cover L2000/€1.03. Open Tu-Su noon-2:30pm and 7-10pm; for pizza 10am-3pm. MC/V.

San Francesco e il Lupo (☎075 927 23 44), at V. Cairoli and C. Garibaldi. Pizza L10-12,000/€5.16-6.20; *primi* L9-24,000/€4.65-12.40; *secondi* L14-23,000/€7.23-11.88. L20,000/€10.33 *menù* includes *primo, secondo, contorno,* and fresh fruit; the L25,000/€12.91 *menù* offers better choices and includes dessert. Cover L2000/€1.03 for meals outside the *menù*. Open W-M noon-2pm and 7-10pm. MC/V.

◉ SIGHTS

PIAZZA QUARANTA MARTIRI. In the middle of the *piazza* stretches the **Giardino dei Quaranta Martiri** (Garden of the 40 Martyrs), a memorial to those shot by the Nazis in reprisal for the assassination of two German officials. **Chiesa di San Francesco** stands on one side of the square, one of several places where St. Francis reputedly experienced his powerful conversion. The central apse holds the *Vita della Madonna* (Life of the Madonna), a partially destroyed 15th-century fresco series by Ottaviano Nelli, Gubbio's most famous painter. Across the *piazza* from the church is the **Loggia dei Tiratoi,** where 14th-century weavers stretched their cloth so it would shrink evenly. V. Matteotti, outside the city walls, staring from P. Quaranto Martiri, leads to the beautiful **Roman theater,** which is well-preserved and still stages classical productions.

PALAZZO DEI CONSOLI. This white stone palace (1332) was built for the high magistrate of Gubbio by local boy Matteo di Giovanello. Within the *palazzo*, the **Museo Civico** displays a collection of Eugubine and Roman artifacts, beginning in the cavernous main room. Statues, pieces of marble friezes, and tablets are strewn about the place. Tacked in a room off to the left, beyond the staircase, are the ▨**Tavole Eugubine (Eugabian Tables),** often compared to the Rosetta Stone. Discovered in 1444 near the Roman theater outside the city walls, these seven bronze tablets (300-100 BC) form one of the few documents in the ancient Umbrian language (although the last two are in Latin). A farmer discovered the tablets in an underground chamber of the Roman theater. They earned him two years of grazing rights from the generous city of Gubbio. The ritual texts spell out the social and political organization of early Umbrian society and provide the novice with advice on how to take auguries from animal livers. (☎075 923 75 30. P. della Signoria. Palazzo and Museo open mid-Mar.-Sept. daily 10am-1:30pm and 3-6pm; Oct.-mid-Mar. 10am-1pm and 3-6pm. L7000/€3.62, ages 15-25 L4000/€2.07, ages 7-14 free.)

PALAZZO DUCALE AND THE DUOMO. Climb to the pinnacle of the town where the 15th-century Palazzo Ducale and the 13th-century *duomo* face off. Federico da

Montefeltro commissioned Luciano Laurana, designer of his larger palace in Urbino, to build this smaller but equally elegant version. If you pay to enter the Palazzo you can admire its spartan Renaissance interior, explore excavations of medieval walls under its floors or let your eyes glaze over as you stare at pieces of modern art of dubious merit on the ground floor. The *duomo*, an unassuming pink Gothic building, is complete with 12th-century stained-glass windows, the decaying corpses of several of Gubbio's prominent medieval bishops, and Pinturicchio's *Adoration of the Shepherds. (Follow the signs uphill from P. della Signoria. Museum open M-Sa 9am-1pm and 2:30-6:30pm, Su 9am-12:30pm. Duomo open daily 9am-noon and 2-6pm. L4000/€2.07, under 18 and over 60 free.)*

MONTE INGINO. When the museums close for lunch, take the seven-minute birdcage chairlift *(funivia)* to the peak of Monte Ingino for a splendid view and prime picnicking. Visit the **basilica and monastery of Sant'Ubaldo,** Gubbio's patron saint. The basilica houses St. Ubaldo's pickled body in a glass case above the elaborate altar and the three *ceri*, large wooden candles carried in the *Corsa dei Ceri* procession each May (see below). From the uphill entrance to the basilica, bear left and continue upward on a dirt path to the top of the mountain. *(Chairlift open June M-Sa 9:30am-1:15pm and 2:30-7pm, Su 9am-7:30pm; July-Aug. M-Sa 8:30am-7:30pm, Su 8:30am-8pm; Sept. M-Sa 9:30am-7pm, Su 9am-7:30pm; Oct. daily 10am-1:15pm and 2:30-6pm; Nov.-Feb. daily 10am-1:15pm and 2:30-5pm. L6000/€3.10, round-trip L8000/€4.13.)*

🎵 ENTERTAINMENT

The **Corsa dei Ceri** (May 15) is a 900-year-old tradition and one of Italy's most noted processions. Intended to represent candles, the three *ceri* are huge wooden blocks carved like hourglasses and topped with little saints. Each one represents a distinct faction of the populace: the masons, the farmers, and the artisans. After 12 hours of furious preparation and frenetic flag-twirling, squads of husky runners *(ceraioli)* clad in Renaissance-style tights heave the heavy objects onto their shoulders and run a wild relay race up Monte Ingino. They eventually reach the Basilica of Sant'Ubaldo, where they deposit the *ceri* until the following May. This orgiastic festival meshes the sacred with the profane and turns the quiet medieval streets of Gubbio into stomping grounds for frenzied locals and entranced visitors.

During the **Palio della Balestra,** held on the last Sunday in May in P. Grande, archers from Gubbio and nearby Sansepolcro gather for the latest rematch of a fierce crossbow contest that dates to 1461. If Gubbio wins, an animated parade ensues. A recent industry in Gubbio is the production of *balestre* (toy crossbows).

SPOLETO ☎0743

Spoleto, a mere 43 years ago, had little but its magnificent gorge, spanned by the medieval Ponte delle Torri. In 1958, however, composer Giancarlo Menotti selected Spoleto as the trial site for a summer performing arts festival, and it never left. The Festivali Due Mondi (Festival of Two Worlds) was the result of a high stakes bet on Menotti's part, that art could be the bread and butter of an entire city. In 1962, modern artists traveled to Spoleto to place sculptures throughout the town, including in the Roman theater. The world's first Calder stabile (slightly different from his more famous mobiles) will greet you as you exit the train station. Whether you come for the festival, or the Roman ruins and few memorable churches, Spoleto is sure to entice you to linger.

◣ TRANSPORTATION

Trains: (☎0743 485 16), in P. Polvani. Ticket window open 6am-8pm. Ask for free city map at newsstand. Luggage storage available (p. 408). To: **Ancona** (2hr., 8 per day, from L15,100/€7.80); **Assisi** (40min., L5300/€2.74); **Perugia** (1½hr., every hr., L6500/€3.36); **Rome** (1½hr., every 1-2hr., from L13,200/€6.82).

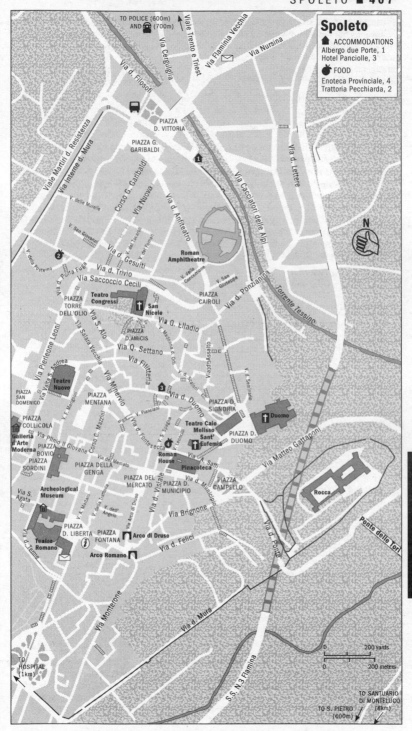

Buses: SSIT (☎0743 21 22 05) departs from P. della Vittoria by P. Garibaldi. To **Foligno** (45min., M-F 6 per day, L5000/€2.58) and **Perugia** (2 per day; L10,400/€5.37).

Taxis: (☎0743 445 48), in P. della Libertà; (☎0743 499 90) in P. Garibaldi.

▓▓ ORIENTATION AND PRACTICAL INFORMATION

Have patience with Spoleto's narrow cobblestone streets; they are navigable with the assistance of a map, available from the tourist office in **Piazza della Libertà**. To get there from the train station, walk straight up **Viale Trento e Trieste,** and bear right into **P. Della Vittoria**. Pass through the double gate in the old city wall and through **P. Garibaldi** straight onto **Corso Garibaldi.** Follow the *corso* as it winds uphill and into **P. Torre dell'Olio.** Continue uphill on the narrow street, crossing over a wider, paved one. To the left of the church is **Corso Mazzini,** the main street of the centro storico, which leads to P. della Liberta; the tourist office is ahead on the left of the *piazza* (30min., most of which is up a fairly steep hill). You can also take an ATAF bus marked "Centro" from the station (L1200/€0.62)—buy tickets at the newsstand in the station. From C. Mazzini, turn left up **via del Mercato** to **Piazza del Mercato,** the bustling center of the city. Many streets radiate from P. del Mercato. **Via del Municipio** runs to **Piazza del Municipio** and **Piazza Campello,** while **via Saffi** leads to **Piazza del Duomo.** These three squares contain most of the city's sights.

Tourist Office: P. della Libertà, 7 (☎0743 22 03 11). Offers detailed info and an unwieldy map of the city. Arranges tours, but no hotel or event reservations. Some English spoken. Open Apr.-Sept. M-F 9am-1pm and 4-7pm, Sa-Su 10am-1pm and 4-7:30pm. Off-season hours reduced slightly.

Bank: Cassa di Risparmio di Spoleto, P. Mentana, 3, just off C. Mazzini. 24hr. **ATM.** Open M-F 8:20am-1:20pm and 2:50-3:50pm, Sa 8:20-11:50am.

Luggage Storage: In train station L5000/€2.58 per 12hr. Go to cashier at the bar. Open daily 5am-11pm.

Theater Box Office: Buy advance tickets for events during the Spoleto festival at **Teatro Nuovo** (☎0743 440 97). Open Tu-Su 10:30am-1pm and 4-7pm.

Emergency: ☎113.

Police: V. dei Filosofi, 57 (☎0743 22 38 87). English speaker.

Late-Night Pharmacy: Farmacia Scoccianti (0743 22 32 42), on Viale Marconi. Posts after-hours pharmacy.

Hospital: V. Loreto, 3 (☎0743 21 01), outside Porta Loreto.

Post Office: Viale G. Matteotti, 2 (☎0743 403 73). Walk down V. Matteotti from P. della Liberta; the entrance is on your right. Open Aug.-June M-F 8:10am-7pm and Sa 8:10am-1:25pm; July M-Sa 8:10am-1:25pm.

Postal Code: 06049.

▓ ACCOMMODATIONS

Finding accommodations is almost impossible during the summer music festival (the last week of June through the first week of July). If you arrive during the festival, contact **Conspoleto,** P. della Libertà, 7. (☎0743 22 07 73; www.conspoleto.com. Open M-Sa 9am-1pm and 3-7pm, Su 9am-1pm.) The tourist office keeps a list of camping options and *agriturismi.* Prices are higher during the festival.

Hotel Panciolle, V. del Duomo, 3 (☎/fax 0743 456 77), in the *centro storico* near the *duomo.* Bright, airy rooms with modern furnishings and bath. Breakfast L7000/€3.62. Singles L70,000/€36.15; doubles L100,000/€51.65; triples L130,000/€67.14.

Albergo Due Porte, P. della Vittoria, 9 (☎0743 22 36 66), a 10min. walk from train station; follow Viale Trento e Trieste and bear right into P. della Vittoria. Hotel to the left of passage through city walls. Or take short bus trip (every 10min., L1200/€0.62). Spotless bathrooms. TV and phone. Cribs. Wheelchair accessible. Breakfast included. Singles L60,000/€30.99; doubles L100,000/€51.65; triples L130,000/€67.14. MC/V.

FOOD

An **open-air market** enlivens P. del Mercato. (Open M-Sa 8:30am-1pm.) The **STANDA supermarket,** in P. Garibaldi, stocks basics. (Open M-Sa 9am-1pm and 4-8pm.)

Trattoria Pecchiarda, Vicolo San Giovanni, 1 (☎0743 22 10 09). Walk up C. Garibaldi and turn right on V. della Posterna, then left up some stairs. Fresh pasta (L10-20,000/€5.16-10.33) and *secondi* grilled over wood fire (L10,000/€5.16). Filling *gnocchi* with tomato basil sauce L12,000/€6.20. Open daily 12:30-2pm and 7-10pm.

Enoteca Provinciale, V. Saffi, 7 (☎0743 22 04 84), near *Pinacoteca*. Cozy place to sample local wines. Try the *frittata d'asparaghi* (asparagus omelette; L8000/€4.13) or *strangozzi alla spolentina* (L8000/€4.13). Open W-M 11am-3pm and 7-11pm. MC/V.

SIGHTS

ROCCA AND PONTE DELLE TORRI. The **papal fortress,** named **Rocca,** sits on the hillside above Spoleto. This fortress, a prison until 1982, was used during the war to confine Slavic and Italian prisoners. In 1943, the prisoners staged a dramatic escape to join the partisans in the Umbrian hills. The impressive Rocca is under perpetual renovation, although the courtyard and larger rooms are used for music and film events. On the far side of the Rocca you will come to the massive **Ponte delle Torri,** a stunning achievement of 14th-century engineering. The 80m bridge and aqueduct span the channel of the river Tessino. On the far bank, the craggy medieval towers for which the bridge was named rise up beyond a small waterfall.

DUOMO. Spoleto's monumental Romanesque cathedral was built in the 12th century and later augmented by a portico (1491) and 17th-century interior redecoration. The soaring bell tower is an amalgam of styles and materials, cobbled together from fragments of Roman structures. Eight rose windows animate the facade, the largest one bearing the symbols of the four evangelists. Brilliantly colored scenes by Fra Filippo Lippi fill the domed apse. *The Annunciation* in the lower left of the fresco cycle is particularly impressive. Lorenzo the Magnificent commissioned Lippi's tomb, which was decorated by the artist's son, Filippino, and now lies in the right transept. *(Down shallow flight of steps from Pinacoteca. Open Mar.-Oct. daily 7:30am-12:30pm and 3-6:30pm; Nov.-Feb. 8am-12:30pm and 3-6pm.)*

ART MUSEUMS. Spoleto's **La Pinacoteca,** on the first floor of the city hall, houses the work of medieval and modern Umbrian artists. The all-star roster includes Perugino and his student, Lo Spagna. *(Up a flight of stars from P. del Duomo. ☎0743 21 82 70. Open daily 10am-1pm and 3-6pm. L5000/€2.58, including the Roman House and Museum of Modern Art.)* The same ticket provides admission to the **Museum of Modern Art,** which hosts a variety of changing exhibits. *(From C. Mazzini, turn left on V. Sant'Agata then right on V. delle Terme. The museum lies ahead on your right. Open Tu-Su 10am-1pm and 3-6pm. With ticket from Roman house and La Pinacoteca L5000/€2.58.)*

CHIESA DI SANT'EUFEMIA. Situated on the grounds of the bishop's residence, this church is one of Umbria's most significant works of Romanesque art. Constructed in the first half of the 12th century, it houses sweeping arches, rhythmic windows, and concentric adornments on the heavy portals. *(Left from P. del Duomo. Open W-M 10am-12:30pm and 3:30-6pm. L3000/€1.55.)*

ROMAN RUINS. Spoleto's many classical ruins testify to the city's prominence in Roman times. The well-preserved **theater** stands just beyond the Roman walls, visible from P. della Libertà. Take V.S. Agata from the *piazza* to reach the entrance of the adjacent **Museo Archeologico,** which houses ceramic and statuary artifacts from the area. *(☎0743 22 32 77. Open daily 9am-7pm. L4000/€2.07, includes interior of the theater. EU citizens 18-26 L2000/€1.03, EU citizens under 18 and over 65 free.)* The **Arco Romano,** at the top of V. Bronzino, once marked the entrance into town. Farther along, the **Arco di Druso** led to the forum (now P. del Mercato). Entrance is included with a ticket to the Galleria Civico d'Arte, so duck into the restored **Casa Romana,** dedicated to Emperor Caligula in AD 27. *(Beneath city hall, entrance at V. di Visiale, 9. From P. del Duomo, take right on V. del Duomo, then 1st left. Open daily 10am-8pm.)*

MONTELUCO. Spoleto's "mountain of the sacred grove" lies an invigorating hour-long climb away, through the forest, past tiny mountain shrines and elegant villa retreats. At the crest of the mountain you'll find a park, several bars, hotels, a skeet-shooting range, and the tiny Franciscan **Santuario di Monteluco,** once the refuge of St. Francis and San Bernadino of Siena. At the base of Monteluco, a 5min. stroll down the right fork of the road brings you to the Romanesque **Chiesa di San Pietro.** Note the wolf to the right of the door wearing a monk's cowl and holding a book. *(Cross the Ponte delle Torri and follow the dirt path. Buses leave P. della Libertà for Monteluco about every 1½hr. when the sanctuary is open. Sanctuary open daily 9am-5:30pm. Free.)*

🎷 ENTERTAINMENT

The ◼**Spoleto Festival** (formerly known as the **Festival dei Due Mondi** or Festival of Two Worlds) is held from the end of June through mid-July and has become not only the pride of Italy but also one of the world's most prestigious international events. The festival features concerts, operas, ballets, and also brings film screenings, modern art shows, and local craft displays to Spoleto. Tickets may be purchased in late-April from a ticket office at P. Duomo, 8, and in late-May from another ticket office in P. della Libertà. (☎0743 447 00; fax 22 03 21.) During the festival, the box offices at **Teatro Nuovo** and **Rocca Albornoziana** are open one hour before the start of most performances. (Open Tu-Su 10am-12:30pm and 3:30-7pm.) Bookings from abroad are recommended—send a check plus a 15% pre-sale charge to Associazione Festival dei Due Mondi, Biglietteria Festival dei Due Mondi, 06049 Spoleto (PG), Italia. The renowned **Stagione del Teatro Lirico Sperimentale di Spoleto** (Experimental Opera Season) runs from late-August to September. The **Istituzione Teatro Lirico Sperimentale di Spoleto "A. Belli,"** P.G. Bovio, 1, 06049 Spoleto, provides information. (☎0743 22 16 45; www.caribusiness.it/lirico.)

Those looking for cultural entertainment of a different sort should be aware that Spoleto has a mild infestation of sexually repressed twenty-something Italian men fulfilling their 10 months of mandatory military service—female travelers who want to sip their beer in peace should start after 11pm (the military curfew).

🔀 DAYTRIP FROM SPOLETO: TREVI

Take a SSIT bus from Foligno, a major station that is the branching point for the Rome-Florence line (30min., 8 per day, last bus to Trevi 7pm). The Foligno train schedule is posted outside the Trevi tourist office or at the tabac next to P. Garibaldi in Trevi.

The view of Trevi from the train passing in the valley is undeniably appealing. Its ancient pastel buildings, perched jaggedly along near vertical slopes, form a small island amidst vast silvery-green seas of olive groves. Contact the Pro-Loco tourist office, in P. del Comune, 5, to find out about the town's attractions. **Pinacoteca Rascolta d'Arte di San Francesco** houses the requisite collection of religious Renaissance art. (Follow V.S. Francesco from P. Mazzini to reach the museum. Open daily roughly 10am-1:30pm and 3-7pm. L5000/€2.58, students L3000/€1.55.) The **Flash Art Museum,** V.P. Riccardi, 4, is associated with the trendy contemporary Italian art magazine *Flash* and hosts changing exhibits of modern and contemporary art. (☎0742 38 19 78. Open W-F 3:30-6:30pm, Sa-Su 10:30am-12:30pm and 3:30-6:30pm.) The tourist office can also provide information about the **Illumination Procession,** one of the oldest festivals in Umbria, that takes place every January 27th. Note the impressive bell tower in the same *piazza* as the tourist office. Trevi's accommodations are not exactly a haven for budget travelers—if you're set on staying overnight, try **Il Terziere,** V. Salerno, 1, just off P. Garibaldi. Its an elegant hotel with immaculate rooms and a great restaurant. Try the *strangozzi al* *tartufo* (stringy pasta with truffles) for L9000/€4.65. (☎0742 783 59. Singles L90,000/€46.48; doubles L120,000/€62; triples L140,000/€72.30. AmEx/MC/V.)

ORVIETO ☎0763

Orvieto sits, as it has for the past 3000 years, above an incredible volcanic plateau rising from the rolling farmlands of southern Umbria. In the 7th century BC, Etruscans began to burrow under the city for *tufo* (a volcanic stone out of which most of the medieval quarter is built), creating the subterranean companion city beneath Orvieto's surface. Five centuries later, the Romans sacked and reoccupied the plateau, calling their "new" city, strangely enough, *"urbs ventus"* (old city), from which the name Orvieto is derived. In medieval times the city became a center of worship. In the 13th century, as Thomas Aquinas lectured in the local academies and fervent Christians planned their crusades, countless churches sprang up along the winding city streets. In the 14th and 15th centuries, the Masters of Orvieto, alongside those of Siena, Assisi, and Perugia, formed a highly influential school of painters. Today, Orvieto is a popular tourist destination; visitors are drawn to the stunning 13th-century *duomo*, the city's steeples, streets, and underground chambers, and the renowned *Orvieto Classico* wine.

▛ TRANSPORTATION

Trains: Luggage storage available (p. 411). To: **Arezzo** (45min.; L10,100/€5.22); **Florence** (2hr.; every 1-2hr. 7:29am-11:32pm; L17,700/€9.14) via **Cortona** (45min.); **Rome** (1½hr.; every 1-2hr. 4:25am-10:27pm; L12,500/€6.46).

Buses: COTRAL (☎0761 266 592) runs 1 bus daily from the train station to P. Cahen and surrounding towns. Buy tickets at *tabacchi* in train station. To **Viterbo** (7 per day 6:25am-3:45pm, L5400/€2.82). **ATC,** P. della Rivoluzione Francese (☎0763 30 12 24), runs buses to **Perugia** (5:45am; L11,000/€5.68) and **Todi** (1:55pm, L8000/ €4.13). Buy tickets at *tabacchi* up C. Cavour or on the bus.

◼ ▟ ORIENTATION AND PRACTICAL INFORMATION

Orvieto lies midway along the Rome-Florence train line. From the train station, cross the street and take the funicular (every 15min.; L1300/€0.67, with shuttle L1600/€0.83) up the hill to **Piazza Cahen,** where ATC buses stop. A shuttle leads from P. Cahen to **Piazza del Duomo.** If you choose to walk, you can follow **Corso Cavour** to its intersection with **via Duomo.** The left branch leads to the *duomo* and surrounding museums; the right, to the **Piazza del Popolo.** Sprinkled between V. Duomo and the **Piazza della Repubblica** along Corso Cavour are most of the city's restaurants, hotels, and shops. Past P. della Repubblica is the medieval section of town, housing the city's oldest buildings and roads.

Tourist Office: P. del Duomo, 24 (☎0763 34 17 72; fax 34 44 33). Offers info on hotels, restaurants, and sights. Sells special deals on underground tours of Orvieto, as well as the **Orvieto Unica card** (L20,000/€10.33; students L17,000/€8.78), which includes underground tour, round-trip ticket for funicular-minibus, and entrance to Museo "Claudio Faina," the Torre del Moro, and the Cappella della Madonna di San Brizio. Open M-F 8:15am-1:50pm and 4-7pm, Sa 10am-1pm and 4-7pm, Su 10am-noon and 4-6pm. The **Tourist Information Point,** Borgo Largo Barzini, 7 (☎0763 342 297), just off V. Duomo, helps find accommodations free. **Exchange traveler's checks and currency** for 5% commission. Open M-F 8am-1pm and 4-6pm, Sa 8am-1pm.

Luggage storage: At the train station. L5000/€2.58 for 12hr. Open daily 6:30am-8pm.

Emergency: ☎113.

Police: (☎0763 400 88), in P. della Repubblica.

Hospital: (☎0763 30 91), off P. del Duomo.

CENTRAL ITALY

Post Office: (☎0763 412 43), on V. Cesare Nebbia. Stamps are available at *tabacchi*, and mailboxes dot the town. Open M-Sa 8am-4:45pm.

Postal Code: 05018.

▐ ACCOMMODATIONS & CAMPING

▓ **Hotel Duomo,** V. Maurizio, 7 (☎0763 34 18 87), off V. Duomo, 1st right as you leave Piazza del Duomo. Steps away from the cathedral. Airy rooms have lace curtains; some have excellent views. Breakfast in the garden L9000/€4.65. Singles L40,000/€20.66; doubles L78,000/€40.28, with bath L85,000/€43.90; triples L80,000/€41.32.

▓ **Posta,** V. Luca Signorelli, 18 (☎076 33 41 909). Halcyon setting. Small *piazza* covered by a canopy of grape vines. Gilded mirrors and tiled floors. Breakfast L10,000/€5.16. Lockout midnight. Reserve 20 days in advance July-Aug. Singles L60,000/€30.99, with bath L70,000/€36.15; doubles L75-80,000/€38.73-41.32, L100,000/€51.65.

Istituto S.S. Salvatore Suore Domenicane, V. del Popolo, 1 (☎/fax 0763 34 29 10). Nuns to the rescue. Breakfast L5000/€2.58. 2-night min. Curfew 11pm; in winter 9:30pm. Closed July. Singles L60,000/€30.99; doubles with bath L70,000/€36.15.

Camping: Scacco Matto (☎0744 95 01 63; fax 95 03 73), on Lake Corbara, 14km from center of town. From station, take local Orvieto-Baschi bus; get dropped off at site. Bus service between campsite and Orvieto's station infrequent. Beach and hot showers. L8000/€4.13 per person, L9000/€4.65 per tent, L5000/€2.58 per car.

▐ FOOD

Amidst a crowd of pricey *ristoranti*, there are reasonable options to treat your stomach well in Orvieto. Track down an Umbrian gem and enjoy all seven courses, or take the lighter road with baked *lumachelle* (snail-shaped buns with ham and cheese), *tortucce* (fried bread dough), aniseed or almond cookies, pizza with pork cracklings, chickpea and chestnut soup, *rigatoni* with nuts and chocolate, and *mazzafegate* (sweet or salty sausages). Tellingly, one of the ancient names of Orvieto was Oinarea (city where wine flows). Today it still flows (hic!) to the tune of L6-9000/€3.10-4.65 per bottle. Don't leave Orvieto without sampling its world-renowned wine, *Orvieto Classico*. **Alimentari** with local treats dot the city; one is below P. della Repubblica at V. Filippeschi, 29. Bottles of *Orvieto Classico* start at L5000/€2.58. (Open M-Tu and Th-Sa 7:30am-noon and 5-8:30pm, W 7:45am-2pm.)

▓ **Trattoria La Grotta,** V.L. Signorelli, 5 (☎/fax 0763 34 13 48), near *duomo*. Franco walks table to table, chatting with customers. Start with *bruschette*, feast on *fettuccine ai carciofi* (artichoke; L12,000/€6.20), and finish with *tiramisù* (L6500/€3.36). *Primi* and *secondi* L10-20,000/€5.16-10.33. Open W-M 12:30-3pm and 7:30-11pm. MC/V.

▓ **La Volpe è L'Uva,** V Ripa Corsica, 1 (☎0763 34 16 12). Follow signs from P. della Repubblica. Vegetarian heaven with intimate setting and orgasmic dishes. Gorge on the *ombrigelli con la carbonara ai fiori di zucca* (L11,000/€5.68) or *salsicce e uva* (sausages with grapes; L15,000/€7.75). Open daily 7-11pm; in winter W-Su 7-11pm.

Al Pozzo Etrusco Ristorante, Piazza de' Ranieri, 1/A (☎0763 444 56). Follow V. Garibaldi from P. della Repubblica and walk diagonally left across P. de' Ranieri. "*Al Pozzo Etrusco*" means "the Etruscan well," and, believe it or not, they've got one. *Pasta fresco* L7-9000/€3.62-4.65; *secondi* L9-15,000/€4.65-7.75. AmEx/MC/V.

Asino D'oro, Vicolo del Popolo I, 9 (☎0763 34 33 02), in *piazza* between C. Cavour and P. del Popolo. At intersection of V. Duomo and C. Cavour, head toward P. della Repubblica and take 1st alley to right. Exquisite and reasonably priced food. Wheelchair accessible. *Primi* and *secondi* L6-12,000/€3.10-6.20. Open Tu-Su 12:30pm-midnight.

Cafe Montenucci, V. Cavour, 25 (☎0763 34 12 61). Enjoy delectable regional specialty pastries while you check email. Pastries L2-3000/€1.03-1.55. Internet L6000/€3.10 per 30min. Open Oct.-Mar. daily 7am-midnight; Nov.-Apr. Th-Tu 7am-midnight.

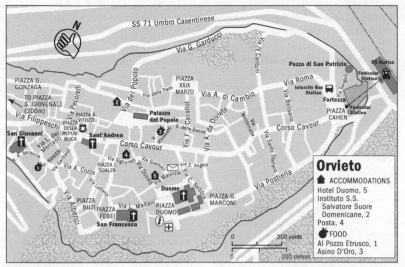

SIGHTS

DUOMO. A quick glance at Orvieto's pride and joy will shock you. Its facade, designed around 1290 by Lorenzo Maitani, dazzles the admirer with spires, mosaics, and sculptures. Initially envisioned as a smaller Romanesque chapel, the *duomo* was later enlarged with a transept and nave. The bottom level features carved bas-reliefs of the Creation and Old Testament prophecies as well as the final panel of Maitani's *Last Judgment*. Set in niches surrounding the rose window by Andrea Orcagna (1325-1364), bronze and marble sculptures emphasize the Christian canon. Thirty-three architects, 90 mosaic artisans, 152 sculptors, and 68 painters worked for over 600 years to bring the *duomo* to this point, and the work continues—the bronze doors were only installed in 1970. Newly restored frescoes by Ugolino dé Prete Ilario are found behind the altar.

The **Cappella della Madonna di San Brizio** (sometimes called the **Cappella Nuova**), off the right transept, includes Luca Signorelli's dramatic Apocalypse frescoes, considered to be his finest works. Skeletons and muscular humans pull themselves out of the earth while apparitions of the damned swarm about in the unsettling *Resurrection of the Dead*. Beside it hangs the *Inferno*, with a depiction of Signorelli (a blue devil) embracing his mistress. The Whore of Babylon, carried on the back of a devil above the masses, was modeled after an Orvieto woman who rejected Signorelli's advances. Begun by Fra Angelico in 1447, the frescoes were supposed to be completed by Perugino, but the city grew tired of waiting and enlisted Signorelli to finish the project. His vigorous craftsmanship, mastery of human anatomy, ability to skewer residents of the town with grace and ease, and dramatic compositions were inspirations for Michelangelo. The Cappella also holds the gold-encrusted **Reliquario del Corporale** (chalice-cloth), to which the entire structure is dedicated. The clot inside the box caught Christ's blood, which dripped from a consecrated host in Bolsena in 1263, corroborating the doctrine of transubstantiation. *(Duomo open M-Sa 8:30am-12:45pm and 2:30-7:15pm, though afternoon hours vary, Su and holidays 2:30-5:45pm. Tickets at tourist office across street. Free. No shorts or short skirts permitted. Capella Nuova L3000/€1.55, before 10am free.)*

PALAZZO DEI PAPI. From this austere, 13th-century "Palace of the Popes," Pope Clement VII rejected King Henry VIII's petition to annul his marriage to Catherine of Aragon, condemning both Catherine and English Catholicism to a bleak fate, not to mention the five other women Henry importuned before his death in 1547.

Set back in the *palazzo* is the **Museo Archeologico Nazionale,** where you can examine Etruscan artifacts from the area and walk into a full-sized tomb. *(Right of the duomo. Open M-Sa 9am-7pm, Su 9am-1pm. L4000/€2.07, over 60 and under 18 free.)*

UNDERGROUND CITY. For the most complete tour of Etruscan Orvieto, consider the **Underground City Excursions,** which will lead you through the endless dark and twisted bowels of the city (you lucky, lucky traveler). During its 3000 years of history, while the city rose upward, a companion "city" burrowed into the soft *tufa* of the cliff below. Although the ancient Etruscan city of Velzna (upon which modern Orvieto now sits) was sacked by Romans, its history is still preserved below the earth. Cisterns, underground mills, pottery workshops, quarries, wine cellars, and burial sites weave an impressive web beneath the city. *(☎ 0763 34 48 91. 1hr. tours leave from the tourist office daily 11am and 4pm. L10,000/€5.16, groups or ticket holders to Pozzo della Cava L8000/€4.13, students L6000/€3.10.)*

MUSEO CIVICO AND MUSEO FAINA. These *musei* hold an extensive collection of Etruscan artifacts found in excavations of local necropoli. Exhibits include coins, bronze urns, red- and black-figure vases from the 6th century BC, and Roman ornaments. *(Directly opposite duomo. Open Apr.-Aug. daily 10am-1pm and 2-6pm; Sept.-Mar. Tu-Su 10am-1pm and 2-6pm. L8000/€4.13, students and seniors L5000/€2.58.)*

CHIESA DI SANT'ANDREA. This church marks the beginning of Orvieto's **medieval quarter.** The church, built upon the ruins of an Etruscan temple, served as a meeting place, or *comune,* in medieval Orvieto. Inside, the **crypt** (at the beginning of the right aisle) contains recently excavated remains from the underground Etruscan temple. *(In P. della Repubblica, 500m down Corso Cavour from P. Cahen.)*

CHIESA DI SAN GIOVANNI. The city's oldest church was dedicated to the city's first bishop; a fresco of him is found on the left wall as you enter. Directly next to the doors on the left is a 14th-century "Tree of Life"—a family tree of the church's founders. The soils of the verdant slope below P. San Giovanni are filled with the graves of those who died in the Black Death of 1348. Walk back from San Giovanni on V. Ripa di Serancia, the city's oldest road. It ends at the **Chiesa di San Giovanni.** Just inside the old city walls, the church offers stunning views of the countryside below. *(From P. della Repubblica, follow V. Filippeschi, which turns into V. Malabranca.)*

🎵📷 ENTERTAINMENT AND NIGHTLIFE

Orvieto just wants to party. In the spring there is the **Palio dell'Oca,** a medieval game involving dexterity on horseback. On Pentecost (50 days after Easter), Orvieto celebrates the **Festa della Palombella.** Small wooden boxes filled with fireworks are set up in front of the *duomo* and the Chiesa di San Francesco. At the stroke of noon, the San Francesco fireworks are set off, and a white dove descends across the wire to ignite the explosives. In June, the historical **Procession of Corpus Domini** celebrates the Miracle of Bolsena. Ladies and flag wavers dance in the streets to period music, followed by medieval banquets. From December 29 to January 5, **Umbria Jazz Winter** swings in Orvieto's theaters, churches, and *palazzi* (with the grand finale in the *duomo*). For specific festival information contact **Servizio Turistico Territoriale IAT dell'Orvietano,** P. Duomo, 24 (☎ 0763 34 19 11 or 34 36 58) or **Informazioni Turistiche** (☎ 0763 34 17 72; fax 34 44 33) at the same address.

For less formal fun, try **Zeppelin,** V. Garibaldi, 28. (☎ 0763 34 14 47. Open W-M 7:30pm-1am. MC/V.) Otherwise follow signs from P. Duomo for **Engel Keller's Tavern,** on V. Beato Angelico. (Open Th-Tu 7pm-3am.)

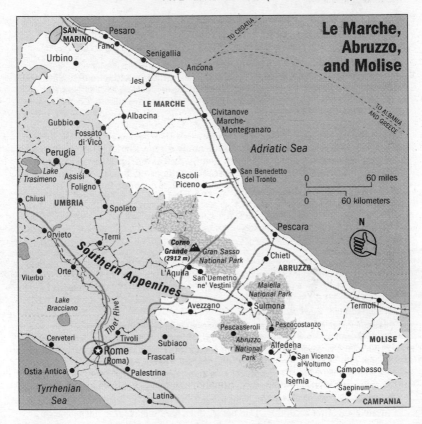

THE MARCHES (LE MARCHE)

In the Marches, green foothills separate the gray shores of the Adriatic from the Apennines and the traditional hill towns from the umbrella-laden beaches. In contrast to the overabundant seaside resorts lining the coast, easily-accessible inland towns rely on agricultural production and preserve the region's historical legacy in the architectural and archaeological remains of Gauls, Picenes, and Romans. The region's history is punctuated by such geniuses as Renaissance Urbino's Raphael and Donato Bramante. Yet this history is unassumingly integrated into daily life. Mass is held in Renaissance cathedrals, medieval streets are deftly navigated by aggressive Fiats, and natives converge for the centuries-old truffle festivals. Though, with the exception of Urbino, most travelers will likely find that Le Marche lacks attractions that warrant a major detour, a number of destinations are certainly worthwhile if you happen to be in the area.

HIGHLIGHTS OF LE MARCHE

THROW DOWN your hair from Urbino's steepled **palace on a hill** (p. 420).

LOSE YOUR BACKUP in the small-town gossip of **Ascoli Piceno** (p. 423) and risk falling a rung on the social pecking order.

ESCAPE the past and idle away an afternoon on San Benedetto's blissful **beaches** (p. 426) without an archaeological museum in sight.

PESARO
☎0741

Pesaro offers a relaxed alternative to hormone-driven Rimini. The beaches are somewhat less crowded, and the quiet, nearby drag is worlds away from Rimini's orgiastic strip. While surf shops and fast food eateries occupy much of the space along the beach, a number of museums and churches decorate the old quarter, and urban spaces form the heart of town. At night, the very young ride carousels, the still-young flirt cautiously, and the not-so-young trade stories on park benches.

▐ TRANSPORTATION

Trains: At the end of V. Risorgimento and V. della Liberazione. Pesaro lies along the Adriatic coast on the Bologna-Lecce line. Ticket counter open daily 5:45am-9pm. Luggage storage available (p. 416). To: **Ancona** (1hr., 2 per hr., L5700/€2.94); **Bologna** (1 per hr., L12,500/€6.46); **Fano** (15min., every hr. 5:44am-11:19pm, L2400/€1.24); **Rimini** (30min., 2 per hr., L4100/€2.12).

Buses: In Piazzale Matteotti, down V.S. Francesco from P. del Popolo. Buses #1, 2, 4, 5, 6, 7, 9, and 11 stop at Piazzale Matteotti. Buses to **Fano** (15min., every 30min., L1600/€0.83) leave from Piazzale Matteotti and the train station. **SOBET** runs buses to **Urbino** (1hr.; M-Sa 10 per day 7am-8:05pm, Su 4 per day 8:30am-8:05pm; L3700/€1.91). Buy tickets on the bus. **Bucci** runs an express bus to Tiburtina station in **Rome** from Piazzale Matteotti (4½hr.; 6am; L38,000/€19.63). Buy tickets on the bus.

Bicycle Rental: (☎033 088 36 23) in Piazzale d'Annunzio, at the intersection of Viale Trieste and V. Gverdi. L3000/€1.55 per hr. Open May-Sept. daily 8:30am-midnight.

▐✦▐❓ ORIENTATION AND PRACTICAL INFORMATION

Piazza del Popolo marks the center of the old city. To get to the *piazza* from the train station, head right on V. Risorgimento, and continue as it becomes **via Branca**. **Via Rossini** leads north out of P. del Popolo toward the sea, crossing over **Viale della Vittoria,** where it changes names to **Viale Repubblica** and then intersects **Viale Trieste** at **Piazzale della Libertà.** Viale Trieste runs along the beach. Back in P. del Popolo, **Corso XI Settembre** runs west toward Chiesa di Sant Agostino, while **via San Francesco** runs east to **Piazzale Matteotti** and the bus station.

Tourist Office: IAT (☎0721 693 41; fax 304 62), at P. della Liberta on Viale Trieste as you enter P. della Liberta. A sign on the front of the building reads "Tourist Office." Helpful English-speaking staff can be found at the door labeled "IAT" (to the right of the giant bronze globe, the Sfera Grande). Open M-Sa 9am-1pm, 3-7:30pm, and 8-10pm, Su 9am-1pm; in winter M-Tu 9am-1pm, W-Sa 9am-1pm and 3-6pm.

Regional Tourist Office, Palazzo del Turismo, V. Rossini 41, Angolo Mazzolari 4. (☎0721 35 95 01. www.provincia.ps.it/turismo), just past P. del Popolo heading toward the sea, on your left. English-speaking staff has a bounty of info on the region, and specific sights, cities, and tours. Internet access available for research only.

Luggage Storage: In train station L5000/€2.58 for 12hr. Open daily 6am-11pm.

Emergency: ☎113. **Ambulance:** ☎118.

Medical Services: ☎0721 213 44. For late-night and holiday medical care, head to V. Trento, 300 (☎0721 224 05).

Police: Questura (☎0721 618 03), on V.G. Bruno off P. del Popolo.

Post Office: P. del Popolo, 28 (☎0721 43 22 85). Fermo Posta at *sportello* #1. Open M-Sa 10am-7:15pm.

Postal Code: 61100.

▸ ACCOMMODATIONS & CAMPING

Pesaro, with its many reasonably priced accommodations, is a real bargain in the off season. High season runs from mid-June through August.

▪ **San Marco,** V. XI Febbraio, 32 (☎/fax 0721 313 96). Follow V. Risorgimento from the train station (on right as you begin to enter P. Lazzarini). Bus stop in front ("San Marco"). 3-star hotel at 2-star prices on a very trafficked street. 40 spacious rooms, all with bath, phones, and TV. 2 wheelchair accessible. Breakfast L5000/€2.58. Singles L76,000/€39.25; doubles L110,000/€56.58. AmEx/MC/V.

Hotel Athena, V. Pola, 18 (☎0721 301 14; fax 338 78), off Viale della Vittoria. From the train station, catch the C/B bus, and get off at V. Fiume. Turn right on V. Trento and left on V. Pola. Restaurant filled with local dishes. 22 clean rooms close to beach. All with bath, phone, and TV. Singles L50,000/€25.82; doubles L70,000/€36.15. MC/V.

Camping Panorama (☎/fax 0721 20 81 45), 7km north of Pesaro on *strada panoramica* to Gabicce Mare. Bus #13 from Piazzale Matteotti drops you at site, but be sure to ask the driver if the bus goes to the campgrounds (20min.; M-Sa 4 per day 6:42am-6:33pm, Su 2:18pm and 6:18pm; L1200/€0.62). Open May-Sept. L8500-12,000/€4.39-6.2 per person, L19,000/€9.81 per site. Hot showers and swimming pool free.

◖ FOOD

Pesaro's **public market** is at V. Branca, 5, behind the post office and off P. del Popolo. (Open M-Sa 7:30am-1:30pm.) **Pizzerias** line the beach, and **alimentari** crowd the sidewalks on C. XI Settembre, which runs perpendicular to V. Rossini.

▪ **Harnold's,** P. Lazzarini, 34 (☎0721 651 55), 2 doors from Teatro Rossini. From P. del Popolo, follow V. Branca away from the sea. Fresh and cheap with wide range of *panini* (L3500-6000/€1.81-3.10). Takeout available. Open daily 8am-3am.

Mensa Volto della Ginevra, V. Mazzolari, 54 (☎0721 343 08), near the Musei Civici, off V. Rossini, in between P. del Popolo and Viale della Vittoria. A self-service cafeteria with giant portions. Large dining hall and outdoor covered patio. Try the Messo Past (L10,200/€5.27), or the pranzo completa (L12,000/€6.20). Open M-F noon-2pm.

◉ SIGHTS

Pesaro's museums are best visited with a **biglietto cumulative ticket** (L7000/€3/62), available at the Ceramics Museum, Rossini Museum, Sea Museum and Pinacoteca.

PIAZZA DEL POPOLO. The robust arcade and *putti*-full window frames of the 15th-century **Ducal Palace,** home of Pesaro's ruling della Rovere clan, preside over the *piazza*, Pesaro's main square.

MUSEO CIVICO. This museum houses a superb collection of Italian ceramics and primitive artifacts, showcasing the talents of Pesarese potters, including several portraits by Giancarlo Polidori. There is also an impressive gallery of paintings, including the remarkable *Padre Eterno* by Bellini, and a series of four still-lifes by Benedetto Sartori. (*Toschi Mosca, 27. From P. del Popolo, take V. Rossini toward the sea. Turn left on V. Mazzolari and left again on Toschi Mosca.* ☎0721 678 15. *Open July-Aug. Tu-Su 5-11pm; hours vary Sept.-June, but roughly Tu-Sa 9:30am-1:30pm and 4-7pm. L5000/€2.58.*)

ROSSINI BIRTHPLACE AND MUSEUM. Honor Pesaro's prodigal son by pouring over an extensive collection of photographs, portraits, theatrical memorabilia, letters, and scores in this museum. *(V. Rossini, 34. ☎ 0721 38 73 57. Open July-Aug. Tu-Su 5-11pm; Sept.-June Tu-W 9:30am-12:30pm, Th-Su 9:30am-12:30pm and 4-7pm. L5000/€2.58.)*

VILLA IMPERIALE AND PARCO ORTIGIULI. Girolamo Genga commenced work on this villa in 1530. The home features frescoes by the Dossi brothers and Raffaellino del Colle. Lavish gardens also surround the home. The grounds are accessible through tours led by the IAT tourist office sporadically through the year. *(☎ 0721 693 41. Tours leave Piazzale della Libertà. June 14-Aug. 23 W 4pm. L10,000/€5.16.)*

🎵 ENTERTAINMENT

Pesaro hosts the **Mostra Internazionale del Nuovo Cinema,** the International Festival of New Films (☎ 0644 566 43), during the second and third weeks of June. Movies, new and old, commercially and independently produced, are shown in the buildings along V. Rossini and at the **Teatro Comunale Sperimentale** (☎ 0721 38 75 48), on V. Rossini, just off P. del Popolo. Native opera composer Rossini founded the **Conservatorio di Musica G. Rossini,** which sponsors events throughout the year. Contact the **Teatro Rossini** (☎ 0721 331 84), in P. Lazzarini, off V. Branca. The theater is currently being restored, and is set to open in the spring of 2002. The annual **Rossini Opera Festival** begins in early August, but opera performances and orchestral concerts continue through September. Reserve tickets through the office at V. Rossini, 37, 2nd fl. (☎ 0721 301 61. Open M-F 9am-12:30pm and 3:30-7pm.) The evening *passeggiata* winds through Piazzale della Libertà and P. del Popolo. **Big Ben,** V. Sabbatini, 14, near Palazzo Ducale, is the closest thing to a bar around. (☎ 0721 674 60. Open July-Aug. Tu-Su 11am-2am; off-season Sa-Su only.)

🏖 DAYTRIP FROM PESARO: FANO

Fano lies south of Pesaro on Bologna-Lecce line. Trains (10min., every 30min., L1700/€0.88) run to Pesaro from Piazzale Stazine. For the beach, exit the train station on V. Cavallott, and take a right on V.C. Battisti. City buses also run from Pesaro to Fano (15min., every 30min. M-Sa 6:30am-8:30pm, L1400/€0.72). Buy tickets on bus.

The 12km stretch between Pesaro and Fano is home to the quietest retreats on this side of the Adriatic. The sandy beach on the north side of Fano is for those seeking seclusion. Even in summer, vacationers are scarce on the beaches north of Fano. To reach tranquil spots, walk left along the water. **Viale Adriatico** runs along the coast. The **tourist office,** V. Battisti, 10, provides a map of the city and a list of local events. (☎ 0721 80 35 34; fax 82 42 92. info@turismofano.com; www.turismofano.com. Open M-Sa 9am-1pm and 4-7pm, Su and holidays 9am-1pm.)

Although Fano makes a good daytrip from Pesaro, those planning to stay overnight should contact **Associazione Albergatori,** Viale Adriatico, 132, an organization that helps travelers find lodging free of charge. (☎ 0721 82 73 76 or 82 57 10. Open M-Sa 9am-12:30pm and 4-7pm, Su 9am-noon.) **Trattoria Quinta,** V. d'Adriatico, 42, at the north edge of town, provides inexpensive home-cooked meals. The *menù* changes daily. (☎ 0721 80 80 43. *Primi* L9000/€4.65; *secondi* L17,000/€8.78. Cover L1000/€0.52. Open M-Sa noon-3pm and 7-11pm. MC/V.)

URBINO ☎ 0722

Urbino's fairytale skyline, scattered with humble stone dwellings and an immense turreted palace, has changed little over the past 500 years. The city is home to many art treasures and Renaissance monuments, including Piero della Francesca's *Ideal City* and Raphael's highly decorated house. A small university population keeps the town lively, and the surrounding natural beauty rivals that of th amazing art within the city walls.

┏ TRANSPORTATION

Buses: Borgo Mercatale. Urbino's bus and Pesaro's train timetables are posted at the beginning of C. Garibaldi, at P. della Repubblica, under the portico at the corner bar. Blue **SOBET** (☎0722 223 33) buses run to P. Matteotti and train station in Pesaro (1hr.; M-Sa 10 per day 6:30am-6:45pm, Su 4 per day 7:10am-5:20pm; L3700/€1.91; buy tickets on bus). **Bucci** (☎0721 324 01) runs 1 bus to **Rome** (5hr.; daily 4pm; L32,000/€16.53). Luggage storage available (p. 419).

Taxis: In **P. della Repubblica** (☎0722 25 50) and by **bus stop** (☎0722 37 79 49).

■ ▮ ORIENTATION AND PRACTICAL INFORMATION

After winding up steep hills, the bus stops at **Borgo Mercatale** below the city center. A short uphill walk on V. Mazzini leads to **Piazza della Repubblica**, the city's hub. **Via Rafaello, via Cesare Battisti, via Vittorio Veneto,** and **Corso Garibaldi** branch out in different directions from P. della Repubblica. Another short walk uphill on V. Veneto leads to **Piazza Rinascimento.**

Tourist Office: P. Rinascimento, 1 (☎0722 26 13; fax 24 41; iat.urbina@regione.marche.it), across from Palazzo Ducale. Open mid-June to mid-Sept. M-Sa 9am-1pm and 3-7pm, Su 9am-1pm; in winter 9am-1pm and 3-6pm. **Tourist info booth** at bus stop in Borgo Mercatale. Open M-Sa 9am-1pm and 3-7pm.

Budget Travel: CTS, V. Mazzini, 60 (☎0722 20 31; fax 32 78 80). Train or plane tickets and student tour info. Open M-F 9am-1pm and 3:30-7:30pm, Sa 9am-1pm.

Luggage Storage: At the car parking office in Borgo Mercatale. L2500/€1.29 for 24hr. Open daily 8am-midnight.

Laundromat: Powders, V. Battisti, 35. L10,000/€5.16. Open M-Sa 9am-10pm.

Emergency: ☎113. **Ambulance:** ☎118.

Police: (☎0722 27 25), in Borgo Mercatale. Open M-F 9am-1pm, Sa-Su 9-11am.

Hospital: (☎0722 30 11), on V.B. da Montefeltro, off of V. Comandino. Buses #1 and 3 from Borgo Mercatale stop in front.

Internet Access: Tourist office allows free computer use for up to 10min. **The Netgate,** V. Mazzini, 17, has over 20 computers. L10,000/€5.16 per hr., students L8000/€4.13. Open daily 10am-midnight.

Post Office: V. Bramante, 22 (☎0722 27 78 15), just off V. Raffaello. Traveler's checks available. Open M-F 8:30am-7pm, Sa 8:30am-1:30pm.

Postal Code: 61029.

▮ ACCOMMODATIONS & CAMPING

Cheap lodging is relatively rare in Urbino, and reservations are a good idea. You might want to consider staying in Pesaro and taking a daytrip to Urbino.

Pensione Fosca, V. Raffaello, 67, top fl. (☎0722 32 96 22 or 25 42). Signora Rosina treats her guests well. 9 large, charming rooms without bath. Singles L40,000/€20.66; doubles L75,000/€38.73; triples L80,000/€41.32; quads L100,000/€51.65.

Hotel San Giovanni, V. Barocci, 13 (☎0722 28 27). Modern hotel in medieval building, with simple rooms and small bathrooms. Restaurant downstairs. Open Aug.-June. Singles L40,000/€20.66, with bath L50,000/€25.82; doubles L70,000/€36.15, with bath L90,000/€46.48; triples with bath L105,000/€54.23.

Piero della Francesca, V. Comandino, 53 (☎0722 32 84 28; fax 32 84 27), in front of hospital. Bus #1 from Borgo Mercatale. Walking, take V. Rafaello from P. della Repubblica and take 1st right on V. Bramante, following street out of city walls. Head left and then right onto Viale Gramsci, which becomes Viale Comandino, following signs for hospital

(15min.). Bath, TV, phone. Singles L70,000/€36.15; doubles L100,000/€51.65; triples L130,000/€67.14; quads L160,000/€82.73. AmEx/D/MC/V.

Camping: Camping Pineta (☎0722 47 10; fax 0722 47 34), on V.S. Donato in *località* of Cesane, 2km from city walls. Take bus #4 or 7 from Borgo Mercatale (1 per hr. 7:10-7:40pm, L1200/€0.62). Ask to get off at "camping." Mostly level, secluded sites. Office open daily 9-11am and 3-10pm. Open Apr. to mid-Sept. L10,000/€5.16 per person; L8500/€4.39 per child; L21,000/€10.85 per tent. AmEx/D/MC/V.

FOOD

Many *paninoteche, gelaterie*, and burger joints are around P. della Repubblica. Shop for supplies at **Supermarket Margherita**, V. Raffaello, 37. (Open M-Sa 8am-2:30pm and 4-8pm.) The **University MENSA**, on V. Budassi, offers an incomparable deal—a huge dinner for L7000/€3.62 with any student ID. (Closed June-Aug.)

Pizzeria Le Tre Piante, V. Voltaccia della Vecchia, 1 (☎0722 48 63). From P. della Repubblica head up V. Veneto, turn left on V. Nazario Sauro, right on V. Budassi, and left on V. Foro Posterula (5min.). Good, traditional food and friendly service. Very popular with locals. Pizza L7-10,000/€3.62-5.16; *primi* L10-13,000/€5.16-6.71; *secondi* from L12,000/€6.20. Cover L2000/€1.03. Open Tu-Su noon-3pm and 7-10:30pm.

Un Punto Macrobiotico, V. Pozzo Nuovo, 4 (☎0722 32 97 90), walk down C. Battisti from P. della Repubblica and take 1st right. Daily *menù* of pasta and veggies L4-6000/€2.07-3.10. *Menù* with fish and side dishes L12-22,000/€6.20-11.36. Student meal L5000/€2.58. Open M-Sa noon-2pm and 7:30-9pm.

Bar del Teatro, C. Garibaldi, 88 (☎0722 29 11), at base of Palazzo Ducale. Best view in town, with Palazzo Ducale on one side and valley on other. Espresso L2000/€1.03; cappuccino or tea L3000/€1.55. Open daily 7:30am-midnight; off-season closed Su.

☉ SIGHTS

■**PALAZZO DUCALE.** The Renaissance Palazzo Ducale stands tall in P. Rinascimento. The interior of this palace, designed by Luciano Laurana, is of less interest than Ambrogio Barocchi's facade. Two tall, slender towers enclose three stacked balconies. The central **courtyard** epitomizes Renaissance harmony and proportion.

To the left, a staircase leads to the duke's private apartments, which now house the **National Gallery of the Marches.** The generally overlooked gallery displays artwork that documents the transition into the age of Humanism. Piero della Francesca's fascinating *Flagellation of Christ* shows a Christ being lightly whipped in the background. Piero's *Ideal City* exhibits the artist's precocious and renowned talent for manipulating perspective. Berruguete's famous portrait of Duke Federico, Raphael's *Portrait of a Lady*, and Paolo Uccello's narrative panel, the *Profanation of the Host* are also here. On the second floor, inlaid wood panels give the illusion of shelves holding astronomical instruments.

The tour continues down a circular stairway to the **Cappella del Perdono** and the **Tempietto delle Muse,** where the Christian and the pagan mingle. Once, 11 panels representing Apollo, Minerva, and the nine Muses covered the walls; these panels have since been removed, and eight are in Florence's Galleria Corsini. *(P. Rinascimento. ☎0722 27 60. Open M 8:30am-2pm, Tu-F 8:30am-7:15pm, Sa 8:30am-10:30pm, Su 8:30am-7:15pm. L8000/€4.13, EU citizens ages 18-25 and over 65 L4000/€2.07.)*

ORATORIO DI SAN GIOVANNI BATTISTA. The 14th-century Oratorio di San Giovanni Battista is decorated with Gothic frescoes by L. J. Salimbeni (1416), representing events from the life of St. John. If you speak Italian, the custodian will give you an appetizing explanation of how fresco painters drew their sketches with lamb's blood instead of ink. *(At the end of V. Barocci. From P. della Repubblica head down V. Mazzini, turn right on V. Posta Vecchia, and take the 1st left on V. Barocci. ☎0722 32 09 36. Open M-Sa 10am-12:30pm and 3-5:30pm, Su 10am-12:30pm. L3000/€1.55.)*

CASA DI RAFAELE. The site of Raphael's birth in 1483 is now a vast and delightful museum with period furnishings. While no actual Raphaels hang in the museum, there is a reproduction of his earliest work, a fresco entitled *Madonna e Bambino*, in the *sala*. There are also some minor Renaissance paintings including the beautiful *Annunciation* by Giovanni Santi, none other than the great Raphael's father. *(V. Raffaello, 57.* ☎ *0722 32 01 05. Open M-Sa 9am-1pm and 3-7pm, Su 10am-1pm. L5000/€2.58, groups of at least 15 L3000/€1.55, student groups L2000/€1.03 per person.)*

🎵 ENTERTAINMENT

Urbino's P. della Repubblica serves as a modeling runway for local youth. Take a walk through and then stroll the serpentine streets on a *passeggiata* at dusk. Nightlife picks up in August. Nobody goes home thirsty from the **Matisse Sound Cafe,** V. Budassi, 14, a university social center. (Beer L5000/€2.58; cocktails L6000/€3.10. No cover. Open Aug.-May daily 6pm-2am; June-July Sa-Su 10pm-2am.) By midnight, **The Bosom Pub,** V. Budassi 14, next to Skyro, is stacked with drinks and dancers. Watch for the owner's "Sangria Parties." (☎ 0722 47 83. No cover. Beer L5-8000/€2.58-4.13; wine L2-4000/€1.03-2.07. Sangria L5000/€2.58 per glass during "Sangria Parties." Open Aug.-May daily 10pm-3am; June-July M-Sa 9pm-3am.)

In July, the **Antique Music Festival** holds concerts in churches and theaters around town. Saturday nights are amateur nights—if you have a 3rd-century harp, feel free to jam. August brings the ceremony of the **Revocation of the Duke's Court.**

ANCONA ☎ 071

Ancona is the epicenter of Italy's Adriatic coast. Although most Italians know Ancona simply for its port, the city has many personalities. Piazza Roma is light and airy, with pastel buildings and a cartoonish fountain. Piazza Cavour, an expanse of gravel circled in palm trees, is stereotypically Mediterranean. The shipyard port is rusty and industrial, but from the stunning vista of the hilltop *duomo*, the cranes shimmer like sculptures in the water.

▐ TRANSPORTATION

Trains: (☎ 0714 24 74), in P. Rosselli. Ancona is an important junction on the Bologna-Lecce train line. Ticket office open daily 6am-7:30pm. Luggage storage (see below). To: **Bologna** (2½hr.; 1-2 per hr.; from L19,600/€10.12); **Milan** (5hr.; 24 per day 12:36am-7:20pm; from L37,500/€19.37); **Paris-Lyon** (12-15hr.; 7:18pm; L250,000/€129.11); **Pesaro** (1hr., 1-2 per hr., L5700/€2.94); **Rimini** (1½hr., 1-2 per hr., L9000/€4.65); **Rome** (3-4hr.; 9 per day 2:50am-7:10pm; from L25,000/€12.91); **Venice** (5hr.; 2:36, 6:20am, 8:07pm; from L26,300/€13.58).

Ferries: Ancona offers **ferry service** to **Croatia, Greece,** and **Northern Italy.** Schedules available at **Stazione Marittima,** on waterfront off P. Kennedy. Reserve July-Aug.

Adriatica: (☎ 071 20 49 15 or 20 49 16, or 20 49 17; fax 20 22 96; www.adriatica.it). To: **Durazzo, Albania** (15hr., from L125,000/€64.56; July-Aug. L165,000/€85.22); **Spalato, Croatia** (8hr., from L75,000/€38.73; July-Aug. L90,000/€46.48); **Bar, Yugoslavia** (16hr., from L90,000/€46.48; July-Aug. L100,000/€51.65).

ANEK: (☎ 071 207 23 46; fax 207 79 04; www.anek.gr). To **Greece** (from L93,000/€48.03; July-Aug. 123,000/€63.52). Return trips roughly half-price.

Jadrolinija: (☎ 071 20 43 05; fax 20 02 11; www.jadrolinija.tel.hr/jadrolinija) runs to **Croatia** (from L71,000/€36.68; July-Aug. L87,000/€44.93).

SEM Maritime Co (SMC): (☎ 071 20 40 90; fax 20 26 18; www.sem.hr). To: **Split, Croatia** from L70,000/€36.15, round-trip L120,000/€62; July-Aug. from L80,000/€41.32, round-trip L140,000/€72.30) and **Hvar Island.**

Blue Star Ferries (Strintzis): (☎ 071 207 10 68; fax 207 08 74; www.strintzis.gr) to **Greece.** (From L95,000/€49.06; July to early-Sept. L105,000/€54.23 or L119,000/€61.46.)

ORIENTATION AND PRACTICAL INFORMATION

From the island directly in front of the entrance to the train station, buses #1, 1/3 and 1/4 (L1400/€0.72) head along the port toward **Stazione Marittima** (☎071 20 11 83) and up **Corso Stamira** to **Piazza Cavour.** Check the signs or ask the bus driver before boarding the bus, as routes can always change. For the Stazione Marittima, disembark at or P. Repubblica (the first stop after turning inland) and walk back toward the ocean and take a right on the waterfront. C. Stamira, **Corso Garibaldi,** and **Corso Mazzini** run parallel to each other from the western end of P. Cavour, through **Piazza Roma** and **Piazza Kennedy,** and back to the port.

Tourist Office: V. Thaon de Revel, 4 (☎071 332 49; fax 319 66), take bus #1/4 (L1400/€0.72) from canopy outside train station, and stay on through town to P. IV Novembre. Office at beginning of V. Thaon de Revel, on right side of *piazza* facing water. Open M-Sa 8am-8pm, Su 8am-2pm. Another **branch** (☎071 20 11 83), with ferry info, is in the Stazione Maritima. Open June-Sept. Tu-Sa 8am-8pm, Su-M 8am-2pm.

Luggage storage: L7500/€3.87 for 24hr. Open 24hr.

Emergency: ☎112 or 113. **Ambulance:** ☎118.

Police: ☎071 228 81.

Post Office: P. XXIV Maggio, near port. Open M-Sa 8:10am-6pm; Aug. closed Sa.

Postal Code: 60100.

ACCOMMODATIONS

Ostello della Gioventù, V. Lamaticci, 7 (☎/fax 071 42 257). Upon exiting train station, cross *piazza* and turn left. Take 1st right, and immediately make sharp right up steps behind newsstand; hostel on right. Recently opended. Perfect to spend night en route to another destination. Clean rooms with 4-6 beds per room, immaculate bathrooms, and a common area. **HI members only;** HI cards sold at hostel. Breakfast L2500/€1.29. Check-out 9:30am. Lockout 11am-4:30pm. Curfew midnight. Reception 6:30-11am and 4:30pm-midnight. Dorms 23,000/€11.88. Cash only.

Pensione Euro, C. Mazzini, 142, 2nd fl. (☎071 207 22 76). 9 large, airy rooms and communal baths that you can brave without flip-flops. Singles L40,000/€20.66; doubles with shower L90,000/€46.48. Additional person L35,000/€18.08. Cash only.

Pensione Milano, V. Montebello 1/A (☎071 20 11 47; fax 20 73 931). With back to the port, walk to far end of P. Cavour and take a right on V. Vecchini; 2 blocks ahead go up the broad staircase facing you. 14 dorm-like, comfortable rooms. All with shower and common area. Singles L40,000/€20.66; doubles L70,000/€36.15.

FOOD

Mercato Pubblico, P. della Erbe, 130. Walk uphill on C. Mazzini, take a left in P. dello Repubblica, make 1st right, and then left in middle of the block into entrance. Pack a meal for your ferry ride at this old-fashioned market. Open Mar.-Sept. M-Sa 7:30am-12:45pm and 5-8pm; Nov.-Feb. M-Sa 7:30am-12:45pm and 4:30-7:30pm.

Supermarket CONAD, V. Matteotti, 115. Offers best grocery deals. Open M-F 8:15am-noon and 5-7:35pm, Sa 8:15am-12:45pm and 5-7:40pm.

La Dolce Vita, P. Cavour, 31-32 (☎071 20 33 75). Family-run cafe/restaurant, offering delectable pastries and a rotating menu of pasta favorites. Pastry L1300/€0.67; pasta L8-9000/€4.13-4.65. Open Tu-Sa 9am-2pm and 4-9pm, Su-M 9am-2pm.

Osteria Brillo, C. Mazzini, 109 (☎071 207 26 29). Hearty Italian fare at outstanding prices. Pasta L12,000/€6.20; *secondi* L11-25,000/€5.68-12.91; pizza L8-12,000/€4.13-6.20. Cover L3000/€1.55. Open M-Sa 12:30-2:30pm and 7:30-11pm.

SIGHTS

THE OLD CITY. The **Piazzale del Duomo,** atop **Monte Guasco,** offers a fantastic view of the Anconan sea and sky. Its mountaintop position provides just enough altitude to soften the industrial edge of the town below. In the Piazzale stands the *duomo*, known as the **Cattedrale di San Ciriaco,** a beautiful Romanesque church in the shape of a Greek cross. It was erected in the 11th century on the site of an early Christian basilica. The basilica in turn was built upon the ruins of a Roman temple dedicated to Venus. *(To reach the duomo from P. Cavour, follow C. Mazzini to the port and turn right on V. Gramsci at P. Repubblica. Follow V. Gramsci into the old city as it becomes V. Ciriaco, V. Pizzecolli, and later V. Ferretti. At P. del Senato, follow the 244 steps up to the* duomo. *Cathedral open M-Sa 8am-noon and 3-6pm, Su 8am-noon and 3-7pm.)*

PINACOTECA COMUNALE FRANCESCO PODESTI. Ancona's painting gallery, the Galleria Comunale Francesco Podesti, housed in the 16th-century **Palazzo Bosdari,** has amassed a collection of work by the Camerte school. Carlo Crivelli's *Madonna col Bambino* competes with Titian's *Apparition of the Virgin*. There are several renditions of Christ's circumcision, with a distressed-looking baby Jesus in each. (But who wouldn't be distressed at his own bris?) The highlight may well be another Titian, his dark, brooding depiction of the crucifixion. *(V. Pizzecolli, 17. See directions for Museo Archeologico. Open M 9am-1pm, Tu-F 9am-7pm, Sa 8:30am-6:30pmSu 3-7pm. L5000/€2.58, seniors and children free.)*

MUSEO ARCHEOLOGICO NAZIONALE DELLE MARCHE. Housed in the 16th-century Palazzo Ferretti, the foremost archaeological museum of the Marches recently reopened after decades of restoration (to repair damages from World War II bombings and a 1972 earthquake). The impressive collection includes the Ionian *Dinos of Amandola*, Greek vases, and two life-size equestrian bronzes of Roman emperors. *(V. Ferretti, 6. From P. Cavour, take C. Mazzini toward the port, and turn right on V. Gramsci. ☎071 207 53 90. Open Su-F 8:30am-7:30pm, Sa 5-11pm. L8000/€4.13.)*

RIVIERA DEL CONERO. Smooth pebble **beaches** lie a few kilometers outside of Ancona. Surrounded by towering cliffs, the nearby coastal villages, collectively known as the Riviera del Conero, attract many Italian tourists. **Autolinee RENI** runs buses from Ancona's P. Cavour and train station to **Sirolo, Numana,** and **Marcelli.** *(Buy tickets at P. Cavour from the "Pink Ladies" bar, at the intersection of P. Cavour and V. Camerini, or from the bar in the train station.)*

ASCOLI PICENO ☎0736

According to one legend, Ascoli was founded by Greeks who had been guided westward by a woodpecker *(picchio)*—this feathered mascot gave the city its name and provided a symbol for the Marches. In another account, Ascoli was the metropolis of the Piceno people, a quiet Latin tribe that controlled much of the coastal Marches and had the woodpecker as its clan totem. Whatever its origins, and despite a number of unfortunate incursions of the modern world, Ascoli Piceno is one of Le Marche's most interesting cities. Tucked away in the mountains, this medieval town has escaped the blight of tourism. Reasonable prices and a hostel hidden in a 11th-century castle complete the attractive picture.

TRANSPORTATION

Trains: Piazzale della Stazione (☎0736 34 10 14), at the end of V. Marconi. To **San Benedetto** (30min., M-Sa 13 per day 5:30am-8:30pm, L4300/€2.22). Ticket counter open M 6:20-11:30am and 4-5:30pm, Tu-Sa 8am-noon and 3-5pm.

Buses: Cotravat buses are more crowded than trains and take twice as long. To **San Benedetto** (1hr., 1-2 per hr. 7am-10:35pm, L3300/€1.70). Buses leave from the V. Gasperi stop behind the *duomo*. Buy tickets at *tabacchi* near the stop. **ARPA** runs to

B. Garrufo and **Giulianova** (1½hr., 15 per day 5:50am-7:10pm, L7200/€3.72) from the V. Gasperi stop. **Cameli Tours,** V. Dino Angelini, 127 (☎0736 26 11 54; came-tour@tin.it), just off P. Roma, runs to **Rome** (3hr.; M-Sa 4, 8:45am, 3:30pm, Su 4, 8:45am, 5:30pm; L21,000/€10.85). Buses depart from P. Orlini. Office open M-Sa 8am-1pm and 3-7pm, Su 30min. before departure.

✴️🔢 ORIENTATION AND PRACTICAL INFORMATION

From the **train station** walk straight for one block to **Viale Indipendenza,** turn right, and walk half a block to the bus stop. Catch buses #1 2, 3, 4a, or 9 (L1200/€0.62) to the historical center. The **main bus stop** is on V. Gasperi behind the *duomo*, where Cotravat and ARPA buses also stop. Walk between the *duomo* and the small baptistery to **Piazza Arringo.** Cross P. Arringo and continue on **via XX Settembre** to **Piazza Roma.** From there, V. del Trivio leads to **Corso Mazzini** and **Piazza del Popolo.**

Tourist Offices: Centro Visitatori (☎0736 29 82 04; fax 298 23 22), in P. Arringo. Open Apr.-Oct. daily 9am-7pm; Nov.-Mar. 9am-5:30pm (summer hours during Carnevale). **Ufficio Informazioni,** P. del Popolo, 17 (☎0736 25 30 45; fax 25 23 91; iat.ascolipiceno@regione.marche.it). Very helpful staff. Some English spoken. Open M-F 8am-1:30pm and 3-7pm, Sa 9am-1pm and 3-7pm, Su and holidays 9am-1pm.

Currency Exchange: Banca Nazionale del Lavoro, C. Trento e Trieste, 10c (☎0736 29 61). From P. del Popolo turn right on C. Mazzini, which intersects C. Trento e Trieste. Open M-F 8:20am-1:20pm and 3-4:30pm. **ATMs** accept most bank cards.

Emergency: ☎113. **Police:** (☎112), on V. Indipendenza. **Ambulance:** ☎118.

Late-Night Pharmacy: Farmacia Sebastiani, P. Roma, 1 (☎0736 25 91 83). Open daily 9am-1pm and 5-8pm; in winter 9am-1pm and 4:30-7:30pm. The green sign outside indicates which pharmacy is open on the weekend.

Post Office: (☎0736 24 22 85), on V. Crispi. Open M-F 8:15am-7:15pm. Fermo Posta M-F 8:30am-1pm and 4-7:15pm. **Currency exchange** M-F 8:10am-6:15pm.

Postal Code: 63100.

🏠 ACCOMMODATIONS

🏨 **Ostello de Longobardi** (☎0736 25 90 07) R. dei Longobardi, 12, near V. Soderini, close to historical center. From P. del Popolo take V. del Trivio. Go straight, left on V. Cairoli, and continue to P.S. Pietro il Martiro. Go left onto V. delle Donne, which becomes V. Soderini. Hostel on right. Owner proud of 11th-century building with 20th-century plumbing. Dorms L18,000/€9.30. Showers L1000/€0.55. Stove L500/€0.25.

Cantina dell'Arte (☎0736 25 57 44 or 25 56 20) V. della Lupa, 8, in heart of town. Follow C. Mazzini from P. del Popolo; left on V. Tribu Fabia. V. della Lupa runs parallel to V. Fabia. Marble floors, patios, TV, phone, and bath. Singles L50,000/€12.91; doubles L70,000/€36.15; triples L90,000/€46.48; quads L110,000/€56.68. MC/V.

🍴 FOOD

Try the **open-air market** in P.S. Francesco behind P. del Popolo. (Open M-Sa.) **Tigre supermarket** is in P.S. Maria Inter Vineas. Take C. Mazzini from P. del Popolo, turn left on C. Trento e Trieste to the *piazza.* (Open M-Sa 8am-1pm and 4:30-8pm.)

Trattoria Lino Cavucci, P. della Viola, 13 (☎0736 25 93 58*).* From P. Arringo, take V. del Bonaparte to P. della Viola. *Primi* L5500-7000/€2.84-3.62; *secondi* L8-10,000/ €4.13-5.16. Cover L2500/€1.29. Open Sa-Th noon-3pm and 7:30-10pm.

Cantina dell'Arte, V. della Lupa, 5 (☎0736 25 11 35), across from the hotel of the same name. *Primi* L6-8000/€3.10; *secondi* L10,000/€5.16. Generous *menù* L15,000/€7.75. Open M-Sa noon-2:30pm and 6:30-10pm, Su noon-5pm. V.

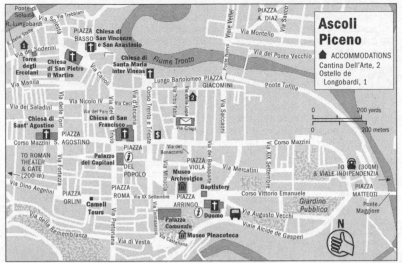

SIGHTS AND ENTERTAINMENT

Practically all the buildings in Ascoli Piceno are made of travertine—a light-colored, porous stone that is actually undeveloped marble. The most spectacular sight in Ascoli is the pink sunset over the hills.

PIAZZA DEL POPOLO. The historical center of town, the *piazza* is a calm oasis in this busy city. The travertine ground, polished by centuries of footsteps, is as smooth as ice. It's easy to while away the day in the 16th-century *portici* lining two sides of the square and their overpriced cafes and *gelaterie*. The third side houses the 13th-century **Palazzo dei Capitani del Popolo,** with a massive portal and a statue of Pope Paul III dating from 1548. The building was burned on Christmas Day 1535 in a familial squabble. A decade later the palace was refurbished and dedicated to the Pope, who brought peace to Ascoli, until it served as the seat of the Fascist party in 1938. Works from the Roman Republic and Augustine eras are visible along the wooden pathway weaving under the structure of the *palazzo.* (☎0736 27 75 40 or 27 75 52. *Open daily 9am-1pm and 3:30-7:30pm.*)

The elegant eastern end of the **Chiesa di San Francesco** (13th-16th centuries) borders the fourth side of P. del Popolo. It contains a 14th-century wooden crucifix, the only art object saved from the 1535 fire. The "singing columns," two sets of five low columns flanking the door on the V. del Trivio side of the church, can be played by drawing your hand quickly across them. (*Open daily 8am-noon and 3-7pm.*)

Abutting the church on the side that faces V. del Trivio, the **Loggia dei Mercanti** (Merchants's Gallery, 1509-1513), is now a favorite meeting place for the town elders. A left on C. Mazzini from the *piazza* leads to the austere 14th-century **Chiesa di Sant'Agostino.** (*Open daily 9am-noon and 3-7pm.*)

PIAZZA ARRINGO. On the other side of town, **Piazza Arringo** (Oration Square) derives its name from its role as a local podium. Join the crowds and try the water straight from the horses' mouths on either fountain—it's the freshest and coolest around. The massive travertine **duomo** is a delicious blend of artistic eras. A Roman basilica forms the transept, topped by an 8th-century octagonal dome. The two towers were built in the 11th and 12th centuries, while the lateral naves and central apse were constructed in the 1400s. Inside, freshly restored frescoes decorate the walls and ceiling. Next to the cathedral stands the compact 12th-century **baptistery,** decorated with a *loggia* of blind arches. (*Open daily 9am-noon and 4-7pm. Mass M-Sa 7, 8:30, 9:30am; Su 7, 8:30, 10, 11:30am.*)

PINACOTECA CIVICA. Works by Crivelli, Titian, van Dyck, and Ribera hang on the pink walls of this museum. Upstairs is a collection of handsome stringed instruments and some Impressionist paintings and sculptures. *(To the left as you exit the duomo in P. Arringo.* ☎ *0736 29 82 13. Open daily 9am-1pm and 3-7:30pm. L6000/€3.10, seniors and ages 14-18 L3000/€1.55, children under 13 free.)*

NORTH OF PIAZZA DEL POPOLO. From P. del Popolo turn left on C. Mazzini and right on V. del Trivio. Bear left on V. Cairoli, pass the old stone houses to tiny **via di Solestà,** which curves to the right as you exit the church. V. di Solestà leads to the single-arched **Ponte di Solestà,** one of Europe's tallest Roman bridges. Cross this bridge and follow **V. Berardo Tucci** straight ahead for about two blocks to the **Chiesa di Sant'Emidio alle Grotte,** a Baroque facade grafted onto the natural rock wall. Inside are catacombs where the first Ascoli Christians are buried.

FESTIVALS. On the first Sunday in August, Ascoli holds the **Tournament of Quintana,** a colorful medieval pageant. The tournament, which features armed (man-on-dummy) jousting and a torchlit procession to P. del Popolo, marks the end of the four-day festival of S. Emidio, the city's patron. Ascoli's **Carnevale** is one of Italy's liveliest. Insanity reigns on the Tuesday, Thursday, and Sunday preceding Ash Wednesday. Residents don costumes and dancers perform in P. del Popolo.

SAN BENEDETTO DEL TRONTO   ☎0735

With over 7000 palm trees and at least as many children playing under their waving fronds, San Benedetto draws summering Italian families and a smattering of foreign tourists. Do not come to San Benedetto expecting to temper your beach time with a little culture—local art appreciation entails checking out art-deco sand castles on the miles of beach. Rest and relaxation are this town's priorities.

▐ TRANSPORTATION

Trains: Viale. Gramsci, 20/A (☎0735 59 21 31). San Benedetto lies on the Bologna-Lecce train line. Open daily 6:30am-11:28pm. To: **Ancona** (1½hr.; 1-2 per hr. 6am-9:22pm; L8-13,000/€4.13-6.71); **Bologna** (2½-3½hr.; every hr.; L23,500-36,000/€12.14-18.60); **Milan** (5hr.; 8 per day 7am-11:30pm; L42-60,000/€21.70-30.99).

Buses: Local lines stop in front of train station. Bus #2 leaves across street from station and travels along waterfront (every 10min. 6am-midnight, L1200/€0.62). **Cotravat** buses to Ascoli Piceno leave from the station (1hr., 25 per day 6am-12:02am, L3300/€1.70). Buy tickets in bar at train station or Caffè Blue Express across from station.

✴❷ ORIENTATION AND PRACTICAL INFORMATION

From the train station, cross the street and take bus #2 (L1200/€0.62) to the *lungomare* (seaside), or turn left on V. Gramsci and left again onto **via Mazzocchi** toward the beach. A right on **via delle Palme** leads to **Viale Trieste.** The road along the *lungomare* changes names, from Viale Trieste to **Viale Marconi,** to **Viale Europa/Scipioni,** to **Viale Rinascimento,** and finally to **via San Giacomo.**

Tourist Office: APT, Viale Marconi, 39 (☎0735 830 36). Take bus #2 across the street from the train station to stop #7. Provides maps and books hotel rooms and campsites. English spoken. Open July daily 8am-8pm; Aug. M-Sa 8am-10pm, Su 8am-8pm; Sept.-June daily 8:30am-12:30pm and 3-7:30pm.

Emergency: ☎113. **Police:** V. Crispi, 51 (☎112). **Ambulance:** ☎118.

Hospital: Ospedale Civile, V. Silvio Pellico, 34 (☎0735 78 13 13). Turn left on V. Gramsci as you exit the train station, head right on V. Montello, then left on V. Silvio Pellico.

Post Office: V. Curzi, 26 (☎0735 59 21 57). Head left on V. Gramsci out of the train station, turn right on Viale Secondo Moretti and left on V. Curzi. Open M-Sa 8am-7pm. **Currency exchange** M-Sa 8am-6:15pm.

Postal Code: 63039.

ACCOMMODATIONS & CAMPING

V.A. Volta, parallel to Viale Marconi, is home to a number of budget accommodations. Most hotels have a private beach included in the price. Countless chalets along the waterfront offer storage cabins for L13,000/€6.71 and umbrellas for L12-L17,000/€6.20-8.78. A public **beach** spreads out from the tourist office.

Albergo Patrizia, V.A. Volta, 170 (☎0735 817 62; fax 78 63 18). 36 rooms. Excellent price, location, and private beach. In-house restaurant serves delicious discounted dinners for guests. Breakfast included. Open June-Sept. Singles L78,000/€40.28; doubles L90,000/€46.48. Aug. full pension L95,000/€49.06 per person.

La Playa, V. Cola di Rienzo, 25/A (☎/fax 0735 65 99 57), at end of beach. Head straight on V. San Giacomo from Viale Rinascimento, right on V.F. Ferucci, continue for 3 blocks, and turn left on V. Cola di Rienzo. *The* budget locale in pricey San Benedetto. Baths and balconies. July-Aug. singles L40-50,000/€20.66-25.82; doubles L72,000/€37.18. Sept.-June singles L65-100,000/€33.57-51.65. Extra bed L15,000/€7.75.

Hotel Dino, Viale Europa/Scipioni, 106 (☎0735 821 47; fax 821 75). Take bus #2 to stop #11. From bus stop, turn right on V. Montessori. 33 clean, bright rooms with A/C, patio, TV, phone, and parking. Private beach and bicycles free. Breakfast included. Singles and doubles L75-110,000/€38.73-56.81. Full pension L70-115,000/€36.15-59.39 per person; Oct.-Apr. L50-80,000/€25.82-41.32 per person.

Camping: Seaside, V. dei Mille, 127 (☎0735 65 95 05). Take bus #2 to stop #11, or from Viale Rinascimento turn onto V.A. Negri and bear left on V. dei Mille. Pool, supermarket, and restaurant. Open June-Sept. L10,000/€5.16 per person, L12-20,000/€6.20-10.33 per site; off-season L6000/€3.10, L8-12,000/€4.13-6.20.

FOOD

Get some cheap eats at the **Tigre supermarket,** V. Ugo Bassi, 10 (open M-Sa 8:45am-1pm and 4:30-8pm), or near the beach at V. dei Laureati 41/A (open M-Sa 8am-1:30pm and 5-8:30pm, Su 8am-1:30pm). On Tuesday and Friday mornings, head for the **open-air market** in V. Montebello. San Benedetto's specialty is *brodetto alla sambenedettese* (a hodgepodge of fish, green tomatoes, peppers, and vinegar).

Molo Sud, Porto Molo Sud (☎0735 58 73 25). On a quest for fish? This local celebrity is just what you're looking for. *Primi* L15,000/€7.75; *secondi* L20,000/€10.33. Always packed. Reservations recommended.

Café Fuori Orario, V.C. Colombo, 7 (☎0735 58 37 20). From train station, turn left on V. Gramsci; go left on V. Francesco Fiscaletti. Cafe on right. Coffee, cocktails, food, and late-night snacks. *Primi* L9000/€4.65; *secondi* L10-16,000/€5.16-8.26. Desserts L5000/€2.58. Open daily 7:30pm-2am; in winter Tu-Su 7:30am-2am.

Pub San Michele, V. Piemonte, 111 (☎0735 836 93). From train station turn left onto Viale Gramsci, which becomes Ugo Bassi and V. Piemonte. Pizza L4-8000/€2.07-4.13. *Menù* L20,000/€10.33, includes *primo, secondo,* and *contorno.* Cover L1500/€0.77. Open daily 12:15-3pm and 7:15pm-2am. AmEx/MC/V.

ABRUZZO AND MOLISE

Clusters of orange thatched roofs, green wooden doors, and the occasional medieval castle lie scattered through the foothills of the Apennine mountains. Remnants of a pristine ancient world relatively untouched by modernity, the artisans, agriculture, and proud regional dialects of Abruzzo and Molise represent the Italy of its ancestors. About two hours from Rome, and a far cry from the frenzy of tourism, these highlands offer a tranquil retreat. Abruzzo and Molise, a single region until 1963, lie at the junction of northern and southern Italy. The wealthier of the two, Abruzzo offers the packaged, modern fun of beach and ski resorts, as well as mountain lakes, lush pines, and wild boars in the Abruzzo National Park. Dubbed a religious center by the Samnites, the smaller Molise is home to phenomenal ruins, medieval festivals, and fresh food. Women tote copper pots of fresh water and shirtless men lead donkeys while youngsters listen to their Discmen.

Having a car in Abruzzo and Molise is advisable, since bus service is often inconsistent. In both regions, however, the **ARPA bus** service is somewhat useful. For information, call their office in L'Aquila (☎0862 41 28 08) or Avezzano (☎0863 265 61). Service is always sharply reduced on Sundays.

HIGHLIGHTS OF ABRUZZO AND MOLISE

LEARN that L'Aquila is brought to you by the **number 99** (see below).

FROLIC with wild boars, Apennine wolves, and royal eagles in the **Abruzzo National Park** (p. 432).

L'AQUILA ☎0862

Perched high in the Apennines, L'Aquila (The Eagle) overlooks its subjects with a majestic air. The capital of Abruzzo, L'Aquila was founded in 1254 by 99 lords from 99 nearby castles who celebrated the occasion by building a 99-spout fountain. Local legend claims that there are 99 medieval streets with 99 *piazze* and 99 churches, one of which tolls 99 times at 9:09 each evening.

▐▌ TRANSPORTATION. L'Aquila has two bus systems: municipal buses and ARPA regional buses. The **yellow municipal buses** (L1500/€0.77) stop at **ASM** markers and service surrounding towns and sights. Tickets are available at *tabacchi*, newsstands, or bars. On Mondays through Saturdays, **blue ARPA buses** connect L'Aquila to: **Avezzano** (50min., 32 per day 6am-8:30pm, L8700/€4.50); **Pescara** (1½hr.; 9 per day 6am-8:30pm; L14,000/€7.23); **Rome** (1¾hr.; 16 per day 5am-8pm; L16,900/€8.73); **Sulmona** (1hr., 9 per day 6am-7pm, L9800/€5.06). Buses depart from the **Fontana Luminosa,** near the *castello*. The **ticket office** (☎0862 412 808) is open M-Sa 5:30am-8:30pm, Su 7:30am-1:15pm and 2:30-8pm. The **train station** (☎0862 41 92 90) is on the outskirts of town. Take bus #M11, 30, or 79C to the center, or follow the signs to the Fontana delle 99 Cannelle, and hike two ghastly kilometers uphill. Trains head to **Sulmona** (50min.-1hr., 10 per day 6:30am-8pm, L6800/€3.51) and **Terni** (2hr.; 9 per day 6:30am-8:20pm; L10,100/€5.22).

▚▐ ORIENTATION AND PRACTICAL INFORMATION. The main street, **Corso Vittorio Emanuele II**, stretches between the **Castello Cinquecentesco** to the north and **Piazza del Duomo,** the heart of the city's historic district, to the south. Beyond P. del Duomo, the street continues as **Corso Federico II** until it reaches the lush gardens of the **Villa Comunale** and **via XX Settembre,** which separate the southern half of the city. Pick up a map at the tourist office—navigating the small streets is tough.

Pick up the indispensable booklet offered at the **EPT Information Office,** V. XX Settembre, 8. The office provides everything from maps and taxi services to helicopter rentals. (☎0862 223 06. Open M-Sa 9am-1pm and 3:30-6pm, Su 9am-noon.) Closer to the *castello* is a second office, in **P. Maria Paganica.** Turn off C. Vittorio Emanuele onto V. Leosini. The office is uphill on the right. (☎0862 41 08 08 or 41 03 40. Open M-F 8am-2pm and 3:30-6pm, Sa 8am-2pm.) **Club Alpino Italiano,** V. Sassa, 34, provides **hiking information.** (☎0862 243 42. Open M-Sa 7-8:15pm.) The **Centro Turistico Aquilano,** C. Vittorio Emanuele, 49, has local bus schedules and information on the Gran Sasso park. (☎0862 221 46. Open M-F 9am-1pm and 3:30-7pm, Sa 9am-1pm.) The **police** (☎112 or 113) are at V. del Beato Cesidio. Surf the web at **Gli Internauti,** V. Cimino, 51, opposite the *duomo.* (☎0862 40 43 38; L10,000/€5.16 per hr. Open Tu-Su 5pm-2am.) The Baroque **post office** is in P. del Duomo, along with **currency exchanges.** (Open M-F 8:15am-7:40pm.) **Postal Code:** 67100.

⌐⌐ ACCOMMODATIONS AND FOOD. There are no convenient budget accommodations in L'Aquila, so try to avoid sleeping here. If you must stay the night, **Il Portichetto,** Strada Statale 80, offers amenities at a small price. (☎0862 31 12 18. Breakfast and bath included. Singles L50,000/€25.82; doubles L100,000/€51.65).

Torrone, a nougat made of honey and almonds, is to L'Aquila what T'Equila is to Mexico. The most established and most popular brand is *Sorelle Nurzia.* Try **Caffè Europa** at C. Emanuele 38. For more substantial fare, **Trattoria Da Lincosta,** P.S. Pietro a Coppito, 19, off V. Roma, offers regional favorites. (☎0862 286 62. Open Sa-Th noon-3pm and 6pm-midnight. AmEx/MC/V.) Pick up fresh fruit and smoked meats and less edible items like socks at the **market** in P. Duomo. (Open M-Sa 8am-noon.) The **STANDA supermarket,** C. Federico II, is two blocks up from V. XX Settembre. (Open July-Aug. M 4-8pm, Tu-Sa 9am-1pm and 4-8pm, Su 10am-1pm; Sept.-June M 4-8pm, Tu-Sa 9am-1pm and 4-8pm.)

◘ SIGHTS. Dating from 1292, the **Fontana delle 99 Cannelle** (Fountain of 99 Spouts) is the oldest monument in L'Aquila. Take V. Sallustio from C. Vittorio Emanuele and bear left to V. XX Settembre. Follow the small roads down the hill, staying to the left at the bottom. The fountain is a symbol of the city's historic foundation, when 99 local lords conspired to build a fortress to protect the hill towns. Each spout represents a different town. The source of the water remains unknown, and modern renovations of the fountain have failed to shed any light on the mystery. Those tempted to drink the water should temper their decision based on their ability to fend off water-borne disease.

L'Aquila's **Castello Cinquecentesco** dominates the park at the end of C.V. Emanuele. The Spanish viceroy Don Pedro da Toledo built this fort in the 16th century to defend himself against the rebelling Aquilans, who were forced to pay for its construction. Within the walls of the fort, the **Museo Nazionale di Abruzzo** showcases art and artifacts of Abruzzo's history: sacred paintings, Roman sarcophagi, Renaissance tapestries, and a million-year-old elephant. (☎0862 63 31. Open Tu-F 9am-6:30pm, Sa 9am-7pm and 9pm-midnight, Su 9am-8pm. L8000/€4.13.)

For the **Basilica di Santa Maria di Collemaggio,** take C. Federico I past V. XX Settembre and turn left on V. di Collemaggio after the Villa Comunale. Construction of this church began in 1287 at the urging of local hermit Pietro da Marrone (later Pope Celestine V). The pink-and-white-checked facade conceals an austere interior—the Baroque embellishments were stripped away in 1972 to restore a medieval feel. (Open in summer daily 8:30am-12:30pm and 3-7pm.)

Chiesa di San Bernardino looks out over the mountains south of L'Aquila. Walk down V.S. Bernardino from C.V. Emanuele. Built in the 15th century and heavily restored after an earthquake in 1703, the interior boasts the tomb of San Bernardino, covered with Renaissance sculpture. (Open daily 7:30am-1pm and 4-7:30pm.)

NEAR L'AQUILA

The forested terrain around L'Aquila conceals isolated medieval towns, abandoned fortresses, ancient churches, and monasteries. Many of the sights remain difficult to access without a car, as buses are generally unreliable and inconvenient. East of L'Aquila lies the 15th-century **Rocca Calascio,** a sophisticated example of military architecture. It is surrounded by the medieval towns of **Santo Stefano di Sessanio** and **Castel del Monte,** as well as the 9th-century **Oratorio di San Pellegrino** in the town of **Bominaco.** To the west of L'Aquila lie the Roman ruins at **Amiternum** and the enormous **Lago di Campotosto,** the largest man-made lake in Italy. **ARPA buses** service these sights from both L'Aquila and Sulmona (1-2hr., 2-3 per day, L5-8000/€2.58-4.13). North of L'Aquila, the town of **Assergi** houses a beautiful 12th-century abbey, **Santa Maria Assunta.** To get there, take municipal bus #6 (20min., 2 per hr., L1500/€0.77) from the *piazza* near the castle.

The **Grottoes of Stiffe** at **San Demetrio ne' Vestini,** 21km southeast of L'Aquila, afford visitors glimpses of the terrain beneath Abruzzo. An underground river carved striking caves and rock formations that hide lakes and waterfalls. A recent cavern collapse has restricted access, but what remains open is stunning nonetheless. (Open Mar.-Nov.) To get there, take the **Paoli bus** from **Porta Paganica** (25min., 5 per day, L5000/€2.58). For more information, contact the **EPT** of L'Aquila. For reservations, call or write the **Gruppo Speleologico Aquilano** at Svolte della Misericordia, 2, 67100 L'Aquila (☎/fax 0862 41 42 73).

GRAN SASSO D'ITALIA (BIG ROCK OF ITALY)

Just 12km north of L'Aquila rises the snowcapped **Gran Sasso d'Italia,** the highest ridge contained entirely within Italy's borders. Midway up the Sasso (and above the treeline) is a flat plain called Campo Imperatore, home to herds of wild horses, shepherds, and amazing views of the peaks and landscape below. On a clear day, one can see forever, or both of Italy's coasts from the range's highest peak, the 2912m **Corno Grande.** Before starting a hike, pick up the Club Alpino Italiano **trail map** in town or at the base of the mountain (L12,000/€6.20). The *sentieri* (paths) are marked by difficulty—only the more exacting routes reach the top. The peaks are snowed-in from September to July. Both the map and information booklet from L'Aquila's EPT or IAT list overnight *rifugi* (hiker's huts), which cost L9-16,000/€4.65-8.26 per night. Another option is **Camping Funivia del Gran Sasso,** an immaculate patch of grass downhill from the lower cableway. (☎ 0862 60 61 63. L7-8000/€3.62-4.13 per person; L11-13,000/€5.68-6.71 per large tent.) There is also a youth hostel at **Campo Imperatore**—call from the ropeway station and command to be picked up. (☎ 0862 40 00 11. L30,000/€15.50 per bed.) Always call these lodgings before setting out, and bring food and warm clothing; it's windy and cool at Campo Imperatore year round. Prices rise and temperatures drop with altitude.

A **funivia** ascends the 1008m to Campo Imperatore (round-trip L18,000/€9.30, every 30min. from 9am-5pm), making the Sasso an easy afternoon excursion from L'Aquila. From L'Aquila, take yellow bus #6 or 6D (30min., 5 per day, L1500/€0.77) from the *fontana luminosa.* Buy tickets at newsstands and *tabacchi.* The *funivia* is closed during parts of June and October. Trails start at the upper *funivia* station. Call **Club Alpino Italiano** (☎ 0862 243 42) for the most current Apennine advice. For information on guides, ask at the tourist office or write to **Collegio Regionale Guide Alpine,** V. Serafino, 2, 66100 Chieti (☎ 0871 693 38).

In winter, Gran Sasso teems with skiers. The trails around the funicular are among the most difficult, offering several 1000m drops and one of 4000m. Ten trails descend from the funicular and the two lifts. Weekly passes can be purchased at the *biglietteria* at the base of the funicular. **Campo Felice,** at nearby Monte Rotondo, has 16 lifts, numerous trails of varying difficulty, and a ski school.

SULMONA   ☎ 0864

Sulmona is hidden deep within the Abruzzo highlands in the Gizio River Valley, and is surrounded on all sides by extensive national parks. Small and relatively untouristed, Sulmona primarily houses *fabbriche* offering many a variety of its famous *confetti* candy (sold in bouquets, bags, and handfuls) and a surprisingly authentic punk culture. The town is also known as the homeland of the Latin poet Ovid, who wrote the profound *"Sulmo mihi patria est"* ("Sulmo is my homeland"). With minimal breaking news in the two millennia since then, Sulmoans continue to litter their town with the acronym "SMPE." A day in Sulmona will give you a glimpse of its more interesting architecture and a chance to try its hikes.

⊟ TRANSPORTATION. Two kilometers outside of the city center, Sulmona's train station (☎ 0864 342 93) joins the Rome-Pescara and Carpinone-L'Aquila-Terni lines. **Trains** run to: **Avezzano** (1½hr., 10 per day 5:47am-8:10pm, L7200/€3.72); **L'Aquila** (50-60min., 13 per day 6:30am-8:30pm, L6800/€3.51); **Naples** (4hr.; 3 per day 6:30am-8:30pm; L17,500/€9.04); **Pescara** (1-1¼hr.; 17 per day 5am-9:30pm; L7100-11,400/€3.67-5.90); **Rome** (1½-2½hr.; 6 per day 6am-8pm; L14-23,100/€7.23-11.93).

Bus A runs from the train station to the town center (5:30am-8pm, L1300/€0.67); ask to stop at P. XX Settembre.

🚺 PRACTICAL INFORMATION. Corso Ovidio runs from the train station west of Sulmona past P. XX Settembre and P. Garibaldi and through Porta Napoli and the eastern wall, changing its name often. There's an English-speaking staff at the **IAT Tourist Information Office,** C. Ovidio, 208. (☎0864 532 76. Open M-Sa 9am-1pm and 3:30-6pm, Su 9am-noon.) A cheery crew mans the **Ufficio Servizi Turistici** office across the street in P. dell'Annunziata. (☎0864 21 02 16. Open daily 9:30am-1:30pm and 4-8pm; in winter 9am-1:30pm and 3:30-7:30pm.) For **police** call ☎113. Access at **Internet Etman Technology,** V. Barbato, 9. (☎0864 20 73 06. L5000/€2.58 per hr. Open M-Sa 9:30am-1:15pm and 4-8:15pm). The **post office** is on P. Brigata Maiella, behind P. del Carmine. (Open M-F 8:15am-6:30pm, Sa 8:15am-1pm.) **Postal Code:** 67039.

🏠🍴 ACCOMMODATIONS AND FOOD. Reservations are a good idea in summer. **Albergo Stella,** V. Panfilo Mazara, 18/20, off C. Ovidio, near the aqueduct, has nine well-maintained rooms with bath, phone, and TV. (☎0864 526 53. Breakfast included. Singles L45-55,000/€23.24-28.41; doubles L80-90,000/€41.32-46.48. MC/V.) Ivy covers **Hotel Italia,** P. Tommasi, 3, to the right off P. XX Settembre. Several of its 27 rooms overlook the dome of S. Annunziata and the mountains. In the summer, it is occupied by the University of Colorado's Italian exchange program. (☎0864 523 08. Doubles L75,000/€38.73, with bath L90,000/€46.48.)

For 50 years, **🔳Cesidio** V. Sulmona, 25, has been serving local fare at reasonable prices. Try the specialty, spicy *spaghetti al Cesidio* for L7000/€3.62. (☎0864 34 940. Open Tu-Su noon-3:30pm and 7-10:30pm, M noon-3:30pm). Clemente and his father serve regional favorites at the popular **Ristorante Clemente,** V. del Vecchio, 7, off C. Ovido. As Clemente proudly puts it, *"Si mangia bene, si spende giusto"* (he who spends fairly, eats well). (☎0864 522 84. *Primi* from L9000/€4.65; *secondi* L10-18,000/€5.16-9.30. Cover L3000/€1.55. Open daily 1-3pm and 7-11pm.) Underwrite Silvo Berlusconi's right-wing agenda at the **STANDA supermarket,** P. Veneto, 2, past the arch at the end of C. Ovidio. (Open M-Sa 9am-1pm and 4-8pm.)

👁🎭 SIGHTS AND ENTERTAINMENT. The Romanesque-Gothic **Cattedrale di San Panfilo** is at one end of C. Ovidio. Its center was built 1000 years ago on the ruins of a temple for Apollo and Vesta. Down C. Ovidio from the gardens stand the **Chiesa and Palazzo di Santissima Annunziata.** The 15th-century Gothic *palazzo* adjacent to the Baroque church houses a small **museum.** If you are fond of Renaissance *sulmonese* gold work, you've stumbled into your version of the *Paradiso*; there's also a collection of wood statues collected from local churches. (☎0864 21 02 16. Open M-F 9am-1pm, Sa-Su 10am-1pm and 4-7pm. L1000/€0.55.) Next door, the **Museo in Situ** features the untouched ruins of a Roman house. (Open Tu-Su 10am-1pm. Free.) The colossal **Piazza Garibaldi** surrounds the Renaissance **Fontana del Vecchio,** which gushes mountain water from the nearby medieval aqueduct.

Sulmona's prized *confetti* candy is made at, among other places, the Pelino family's **factory,** V. Stazione Introdaqua, 55. Turn right after the arch at the end of C. Ovidio onto V. Trieste, continue 1km up the hill as it becomes V. Stazione Introdaqua, and enter the Pelino building. The Pelinos have been making *confetti* since 1783 without even one Oompah-Loompah sighting. The candy is tasty, tooth-decaying goodness. Your personal guide (noticeably lacking a large purple top hat) will lead you through candy-coated corridors to the free **confetti museum.** Check out the slightly sacrilegious (even for Italy) pictures of past popes and Padre Pio munching on candied religious instruments. (☎0864 21 00 47. Open M-Sa 8am-12:30pm and 3-6:30pm.) Delight in *confetti* flowers, fish, and buildings. Behold the ancient cauldrons, ovens, bottles, and pipes in which the Pelinos have worked their magic for 150 years before Willy Wonka.

During the last week of July, locals celebrate **Giostra Cavalleresca di Sulmona,** a festival in which mounted, beacon-bearing knights run figure eights around P. Garibaldi, celebrating the seven *borghi* (small sections) of medieval Sulmona. Buy seated tickets (L25-30,000/€12.91-15.50), or find a spot to watch for free. In preparation, each *borgo* hosts a public *festa* during a weekend in June. In October, Sulmona waxes cultural, hosting a film and an international opera festival.

🏔 **HIKING.** The mountains towering over Sulmona are part of the **Majella National Park,** and several trails are easily accessible by foot or bus from the town center. High up on the cliffs perches the mountain retreat of the saintly hermit who became Pope Celestine V; you can see the small cave where he lived. It's a fairly easy 45min.-1hr. each way from the town of **Badia,** a 20-minute bus ride from Sulmona (L1300/€0.67). Be sure to pick up the **Club Italiano Alpino** map from the tourist office (L12,000/€6.20), which describes each hike and the colors of the blazes that mark the trails. Keep in mind that the difficulty level refers to mountaineering experience, not hiking experience, so hikes of moderate difficulty may be challenging for those not used to mountain climbing. The early sections of almost all trails are manageable. Take the first sections of paths 7 and 8 for a hike through the forested hills with some great views (5km one way, starts at the village of Fonte D'Amore and ends at Marane, each around 4km from Sulmona and serviced by local bus). If you use the bus to reach the trailheads, pick up a schedule from the tourist office and watch out for mid-afternoon gaps in service.

ABRUZZO NATIONAL PARK

The Parco Nazionale d'Abruzzo is the region's fourth largest park, protecting 44,000 hectares of mountainous wilderness from the resort hotels so loved by Italians. The mountains provide spectacular views of lush woodlands and crystal-clear lakes. Lynx have recently been reintroduced near Civitella Alfedena, joining Marsican brown bears, Apennine wolves, and Abruzzo Chamois antelopes (conclusion: if traveling in the park alone, bring large slabs of meat to attract unwanted attention away from your own tasty flesh). Pescasseroli, the park's administrative center, provides the best base for its exploration (but, alas, no butcher's shop).

🚍 TRANSPORTATION

Take the **ARPA bus** (☎0863 265 61 or 229 21), which runs from Avezzano through the park to **Castel di Sangro** (2¾hr.; M-Sa 7 per day, Su reduced service; 6:45am-7:15pm; L7000/€3.62), making five stops: **Barrea** (2¼hr., L6800/€3.51); **Civitella Alfadena** (2hr., L6600/€3.41); **Opi** (1¾hr., L6200/€3.20); **Pescasseroli** (1½hr., L6000/€3.10); **Villetta Barrea** (2hr., L6500/€3.36). Buses run to Pescasseroli from Rome's Tiburtina station (3hr.; daily 7:45am, return 6:15pm; L23,100/€11.93 one-way). **Trains** run from Avezzano to: **Pescara** (1¾-2hr.; 6 per day 6:30am-8pm; L13,600-19,800/€7.02-10.23); **Rome** (1½-2hr.; 8 per day 5am-9pm; L10-16,000/€5.16-8.26); **Sulmona** (1-1¼hr.; 10 per day 6:30am-8pm; L6800-10,800/€3.51-5.78).

🛈 PRACTICAL INFORMATION

In Pescasseroli, check in at the **Ufficio di Zona,** Vico Consultore, 1, by the P. Antonio bus stop, for hiking information, T-shirts decorated with pictures of local animals, and an essential park map. (☎0863 919 55. Map L10,000/€5.16. Open daily 9am-noon and 3-7pm.) For information on accommodations and restaurants, drop by the **IAT Information Office,** V. Piave, 1, off P. Antonio. (☎0863 91 00 97; fax 91 04 61. Open daily 9am-1pm and 4:30-6:30pm.) There are Uffici di Zona throughout the park, indispensable sources of information.

🏠🛏 ACCOMMODATIONS AND FOOD

PESCASSEROLI. In the middle of the park, alpine Pescasseroli is a popular place to stay. Most reasonably priced accommodations do not offer single rooms. In the off-season, however, solo travelers can finagle a double or quad for the price of a single. **Pensione Claudia,** V. Tagliamento, 35, 200m across the gravel lot from the main avenue, has 10 quiet rooms with bath. (☎0863 918 37; m.finamore@ermes.it. Doubles Sept.-July L50-60,000/€25.82-30.99. July-Aug. required half-pension L70,000/€36.15 per person.) **Pensione al Castello,** V. Gabriele d'Annunzio, 7, opposite park office, has seven rooms, all with bath, phone, and TV. (☎0863 91 07 57. Breakfast L5000/€2.58. Doubles L70-85,000/€36.15-43.90. Aug. and Christmas required half-pension L80,000/€41.32.) Four campgrounds are within 21km of town. The best is **Campeggio dell'Orso,** 1km from Pescasseroli on the main road to Opi. (☎0863 919 55. L6000/€3.10 per person, L6000/€3.10 per tent.)

For juicy steaks to throw at ravenous wildlife, the **Delfino A&O** supermarket is on V.S. Lucia, the main highway, past the zoo and park office. (Open daily 8:30am-1pm and 4-7pm. AmEx/MC/V.) **Pasticceria Alpina,** Traversa Sangro, 6, serves an array of award-winning sweets. (☎0863 91 05 61. Open Tu-Su 7am-10pm.)

OPI. ARPA buses follow the winding road through the park to the village of Opi, named for the pagan goddess of abundance, whose temple was here in ancient times. Two kilometers past the village, on the bus route, lies the campground **Vecchio Mulino.** It's hard to miss the large, multicolored balloon which identifies it. (☎0863 91 22 32. L8000/€4.13 per person, L9500/€4.91 per small tent.) In August, Opi hosts the **Sagra degli Gnocchi** (Gnocchifest), a nationally renowned eat-along where thousands converge to engage in a favorite Italian pastime: mutually consume large quantities *gnocchi*, sausages, and cheese.

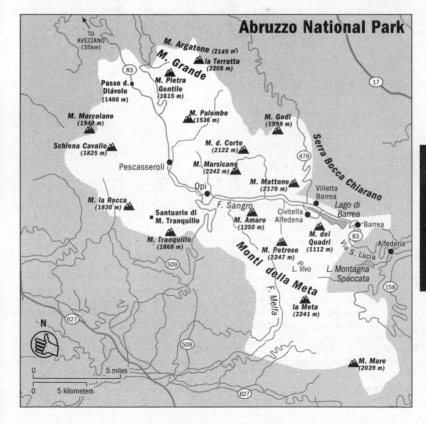

Abruzzo National Park

CIVITELLA ALFEDENA. Ten kilometers past Opi, the bus reaches the village of **Villetta Barrea.** The turnoff to Civitella Alfedena, 200m farther down the road, leads to **Camping Pinus Nigra.** The site is bordered by the River Sangro. (☎ 0864 891 41. L5-6000/€2.58-3.10 per person, L6-7000/€3.10-3.62 per large tent.) In Civitella Alfedena, make yourself at home at **Alberghetto La Torre** or **Albergo Autico Borgo,** V. Castello, 3, both under the same management. (☎ 0864 89 01 21. Doubles L60,000/€30.99, with bath L70,000/€36.15. Extra bed L30,000/€15.50.) **Museo del Lupo** has information on the history of the Apennine wolf and the lynx. (☎ 0864 89 01 41. L5000/€2.58.) Ice-cold **Barrea Lake** cuts majestically into the mountains, stretching 7km between Villetta Barrea and the neighboring village of **Barrea.**

AVEZZANO. You can say one thing for Avezzano: it sure was beautiful before that earthquake in 1915. Now its fame rests largely on housing the *telespazio,* a satellite transmission system. It is one of the main gateways to the park. Buses into the park leave from the far side of the train station on the left—take the *sottopassagio.* **Hotel Creati,** on V. XX Settembre, offers pleasant, inexpensive rooms. (☎ 0863 41 33 47. Singles L35,000/€18.08; doubles L60,000/€30.99.)

▨ OUTDOORS

You haven't really entered the park until the road begins its scenic ascent from Avezzano to Pescasseroli. Fields of poppies, rocky outcrops, dazzling valleys, and dizzying views will delight you. The twisting bus ride through the park is spectacular. If the wildlife in the park eludes you, thank a higher power and fulfill any inclinations to view both the fuzzy and fanged in Pescasseroli's **Centro di Visita,** Viale Colle dell'Orso, 2, off V.S. Lucia as you head toward Opi. The center has a museum and small zoo. (Open daily 10am-1pm and 3-7pm. L8000/€4.13.)

Purchase the indispensable trail map (L10,000/€5.16) from the **Ufficio di Zona in Pescasseroli,** which indicates prime wildlife viewing (and the locations of other Uffici di Zona throughout the park). You might see brown bears, chamois, deer, wolves, and eagles. The trails are arranged so that all paths that begin with the same letter start from the same point. For a short hike, take **trail B1** to the castle ruins at Monte Ceraso (50min. round-trip). To really stretch those legs, brave the beautiful 5hr. round-trip hike on **trail C3** to **Vicolo (Pass) di Monte Tranquillo** (1673m). The trail starts at the southern end of town and leads up through the green Valle Mancina and past the Rifugio Della Difesa. Keep climbing to the pass, with its impressive view of the mountain peaks to the north. True adventurers can take on **Monte Marsicano,** one of the park's highest peaks (2245m). **Trail E6** from Opi (7-8hr. round-trip) is a challenging hike, and the steep path can get arduous.

If you coordinate your hikes with the ARPA bus schedule, you can venture farther afield. From Civitella Alfedena (15km from Pescasseroli) take **trail I1 to K6** through the sublimely beautiful **Valle di Rose** to see the park's largest herd of chamois. From mid-July to early-September, this area can only be explored with a guide (L15,000/€7.75 per person). One day before your excursion, go to an Ufficio di Zona for more information about the trails or to obtain a permit and reserve a guide. From Barrea (20km from Pescasseroli) **trail K5** runs to the refreshing **Lago Vivo** (3½hr. round-trip). However, the lake dries up between June and October.

Mountain bikes are available for L10,000/€5.16 per day at **Sport House** in Pescasseroli. Turn left from the tourist office, cross the river, turn right, and walk 5min. along the river bank. (☎ 0863 91 07 96. Open M-Sa 9am-1pm and 4-7pm.) Several paths, including C3, provide good biking. **Ecotur,** P. Vittorio Veneto, 24, in Pescasseroli, offers organized hikes and excursions. (☎ 0863 91 27 60. Open daily 9am-noon and 4:30-7:30pm.) In winter, this area offers excellent skiing, with challenging slopes and heavy snowfall. Package deals called **settimane bianche** (white weeks) provide accommodations, lift tickets, and half-pension. For ticket information, call ☎ 0863 91 2216. For a regional snow bulletin, call ☎ 0862 665 10.

TERMOLI
☎ 0875

Termoli is the embarkation point for the Tremiti islands, but its beaches are attraction enough for many European tourists. **Hotel Rosary,** Lungomare Colombo, 42, at the intersection with C. Milano, is a short walk from the station and a stone's throw to the beach. Saints be praised, all rooms have bath and TV. (☎ 0875 849 44. Closed mid-Nov. to mid-Mar. Doubles L110,000/€56.58. AmEx/MC/V.) Food in Termoli is unexciting. Stick to the divine pizzas (L5-10,000/€2.58-5.16) and the Holy Land pilgrimage theme at **La Sacrestia,** V. Ruffini, 48. Turn right from C. Nazionale onto V. Alfano and then right on V. Ruffino. (☎ 0875 70 56 03. Open daily noon-2pm and 7-11pm.) For fresh bread, other baked goods, stop by **Lineapane,** V. Milano, 18. (Open daily 7am-1:15pm and 4:30-9pm.)

The **FS train** station lies at the west end of town. **Corso M. Milano** extends to **Lungomare Colombo,** the waterfront strip lined with hotels on one side and beaches on the other. **Corso Umberto,** heading from the station to the small old town, is lined with restaurants and shops. To get to the port from C. Umberto, turn left on V. Aubrey to reach **via del Porto,** which leads to the ferry port. The ferry docks and ticket offices are past the fishing boats on the long breakwater extending into the harbor. The **tourist office** is on Lungomare Colombo, a block to the right of the intersection with C. Milano. (☎ 0875 70 83 42. Open M-Sa 9am-1pm and 5-7:30pm.)

TREMITI ISLANDS
☎ 0882

Ⅎ TRANSPORTATION. From **Termoli,** several ferry companies serve the island: **Navigargano** (9:15am, return 5:25pm; round-trip L28,000/€14.46; Aug. 6-21 L32,000/€16.53); **Navigazione Libera** (☎ 0875 70 48 59; 8:40am, 11am, 5:30pm; return 9:45am, 4:20, 6:40pm; one-way L23,000/€11.88); **Adriatica** ferries (daily 9am, return 5pm; L13,600/€7.02) and hydrofoils (daily 8:35am, return 9:35am; afternoon service varies during the week and monthly). Ferry service only operates from June to September. Hydrofoils make the trip in one hour; ferries take about an hour and a half.

🚩 PRACTICAL INFORMATION. There are four Tremiti islands—**San Domino, San Nicola, Capraia,** and **Pinosa.** San Domino is the largest and home to the archipelago's pine forests and hotels, while San Nicola is home to an interesting abbey. The last two are small and desolate and of interest only to seagulls. **Motorboats** run throughout the day between San Nicola and San Domino (L2000/€1.03). The **carabinieri** can be reached at ☎ 0882 46 30 10. A **first aid station** is at the port in San Domenico. (Open 24hr. ☎ 0882 46 32 34.) A **pharmacy** is in San Domenico Village, in the middle of San Domino, on V. del Vecchio Forno. (☎ 0882 46 33 27. Open June-Sept. daily 9am-1pm and 5-9:30pm; Oct.-May 9:30am-12:30pm and 5-7:30pm.)

🏠 ACCOMMODATIONS. Hotels are on San Domino, and most offer only doubles and require half or full pension. Make reservations during the summer. **Hotel La Vela,** on V. San Domino, offers half-pension rooms—call to be picked up. (☎ 0882 46 32 54. Aug. L100,000/€51.65 per person; Sept.-July L75,000/€37.38 per person.) **Villagio International,** at Punta del Diamente, is another economical choice, with two kinds of housing—prefabricated hut/tent hybrids and bungalows. (Prefab units L45,000/€23.24 per person, required half-pension in Aug. L90,000/€46.48; bungalows L65-75,000/€33.57-38.73 per person, required half-pension in Aug. L120,000/€62; surcharge for singles L30,000/€15.50.)

🥾📷 HIKING, SPEAR FISHING, AND SIGHTS. The **pine forests** that cover much of the island are the highlight of San Domino. Paths snake through the protected forest, alive with the sound of cicadas and the smell of dried, fallen, pine needles. Many paths extend down to small rocky coves along the coast, where vacationers swim in the sapphire waters. Many Italians also live out their *Thunderball*-inspired fantasies and take to the seas with **spear guns,** not to hunt SPECTRE agents, but more edible and less dangerous prey, such as fish. If you'd rather look at moderately interesting religious buildings than shoot fish (you crazy animal-lover), then the island of San Nicola, where a **fortified abbey** crowns the cliffs, is the place for you. Accessible by a short path from the harbor, the monastery was founded in the 11th century. Though largely rebuilt over time, portions of the original mosaic pavement survive. Emperor Augustus's adulterous granddaughter Julia was banished here; thankfully, long before the monks arrived.

ROME

Italy will return to the splendors of Rome, said the major. I don't like Rome, I said.
It is hot and full of fleas. You don't like Rome? Yes, I love Rome. Rome is the
mother of nations. I will never forget Romulus suckling the Tiber. What? Nothing.
Let's all go to Rome. Let's go to Rome tonight and never come back. Rome is a
beautiful city, said the major.
    —Ernest Hemingway, *A Farewell to Arms*

Italy's massive capital city is an eruption of marble domes, noseless statues, and
motorcycle dust. Rome is sensory overload, rushing down the hills of Lazio to
knock you flat on your back, leaving you gasping for air and dying for more. The
city and those it controlled were responsible for the development of over 2000
years of world history, art, architecture, politics, and literature. Rome has been the
capital of kingdoms and republics; from this city, the Roman Empire defined the
Western world and the Catholic Church spread its influence worldwide. For the
traveler, there is so much to see, hear, eat, smell, and absorb that the city is both
exhilarating and overwhelming, as if it's impossible to experience everything, or
even anything. Never fear, however, because in *bella Roma*, everything is beautiful and everything tastes good. Liberate your senses from the pollution eroding the
monuments and from the maniacal rush of motorcyclists, and enjoy the dizzying
paradox that is the *Caput Mundi*, the Eternal City, Rome.

◼ INTERCITY TRANSPORTATION

FLIGHTS
Most flights arrive at da Vinci International Airport (☎ 06 659 51), known as **Fiumicino** for the village in which it is found. When you exit customs, follow the signs to
your left for **Stazione FS/Railway Station.** Take the elevator or escalators up two
floors to the pedestrian bridge to the airport train station. The **Termini line** runs non-
stop to Rome's main train station, **Termini Station** (30min.; every 35min. 7:37am-
10:37pm; L16,000/€8.26, L40,000/€20.66 on board). Buy a ticket at the FS ticket
counter, the *tabacchi* on the right, or from one of the machines in the station.
Trains leave Termini for **Fiumicino** from track #22 or 23, which is at the very end of
#22 (40min.; every hr. 7:20am-9:20pm, extra trains 6:50am, 3:50, 5:50, 7:50pm;
L16,000/€8.26). Buy tickets at the Alitalia office at track #22 at the window marked
"Biglietti Per Fiumicino" or from machines in the station. Validate (and retain)
your ticket before boarding.
    To reach Fiumicino from Rome when the train is not running, the most reliable
and convenient option is to take a cab. The cheapest option is the blue **COTRAL bus**
to Tiburtina from the ground floor outside the main exit doors after customs (1:15,
2:15, 3:30, 5am; L8000/€4.13, pay on board). From Tiburtina, take bus #40N to Termini. To get to Fiumicino late at night or early in the morning, take bus #40N from
Termini to Tiburtina (every 20-30min.), then catch the blue COTRAL bus to Fiumicino outside (12:30, 1:15, 2:30, 3:45am; L8000/€4.13, pay on board).
    Most charter and a few domestic flights arrive at **Ciampino** airport (☎ 06 79 49 41).
To get to Rome, take the COTRAL bus (every 30min. 6:10am-11pm, L2000/€1.03) to
Anagnina station on Metro Linea A. After 11pm, you'll have to take a cab.

TRAINS
Stazione Termini is the focal point of most train and subway lines. Trains arriving in
Rome between midnight and 5am usually arrive at Stazione Tiburtina or Stazione
Ostiense, which are connected to Termini at night by the #40N and 20N-21N buses,
respectively. Be wary of pickpockets and con artists. Station services include: **hotel**

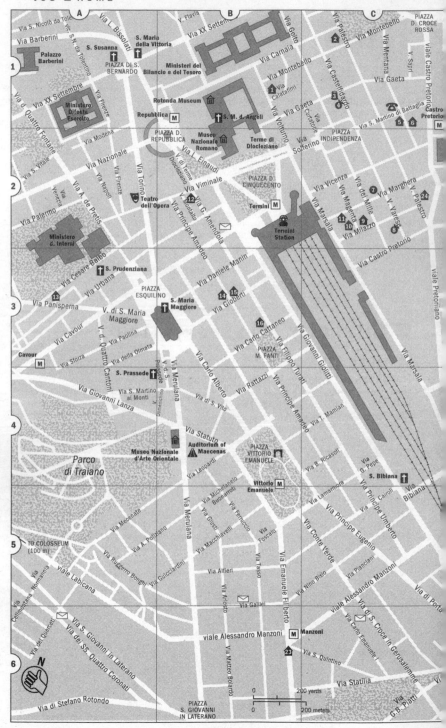

A

Via S. Nicolò da Tole
Via Barberini
Vic S.N. da Tolentino
Via L. Bissolati
Palazzo Barberini
S. Susanna
PIAZZA DI S. BERNARDO
Via XX Settembre
Ministero d. Interni
Via d. Quattro Fontane
Ministero Difesa Esercito
Via Firenze
Via Modena
Via Nazionale
Via S. Vitale
Via Palermo
Via A. de Preti
Via Napoli
Via Venezia
Via Cesare Balbo
S. Prudenziana
Via Urbana
Via Panisperna
Via di S. Maria Maggiore
Via Cavour
Cavour M
Via Sforza
Via delle Olmata
Via Giovanni Lanza
S. Prassede

B

Via L. Bissolati
Via XX Settembre
S. Maria della Vittoria
S. M. d. Angeli
Ministeri del Bilancio e del Tesoro
Rotonda Museum
Republica M
PIAZZA D. REPUBBLICA
Museo Nazionale Romano
Terme di Diocleziano
Via L. Einaudi
Via Viminale
PIAZZA D. CINQUECENTO
Teatro dell'Opera
Via G. Amendola
Via Principe Amedeo
Termini M
Via Daniele Manin
PIAZZA ESQUILINO
S. Maria Maggiore
Via Gioberti
Via Carlo Cattaneo
PIAZZA M. FANTI
Via Carlo Alberto
Via Filippo Turati
Via Merulana
Via S. Martino ai Monti
Via di S. Vito
Via Ratazzi

C

PIAZZA D. CROCE ROSSA
Via Palestro
Via Montebello
Viale Castro Pretorio
Via Mentana
Via Gaeta
V. Sapri
Via Cernaia
Via Calatafimi
Via Castelfidardo
Via S. Martino di Battaglia
Castro Pretorio M
PIAZZA INDIPENDENZA
Via Volturno
Via Curtatone
Via Solferino
Via Vicenza
Via V, del Mille
Via Marghera
V. V. Varese
V. Palestro
Via Magenta
Via Milazzo
Via Marsala
Via Castro Pretorio
viale Pretoriano
Via Giovanni Giolitti
Via Marsala

4

Parco di Traiano
Museo Nazionale d'Arte Orientale
Auditorium of Maecenas
Via Statuto
Via Leopardi
PIAZZA VITTORIO EMANUELE
Vittorio Emanuele M
Via Lamarmora
Via B. Ricasoli
Via T. Mamian
Via G. Pepe
S. Bibiana
Via Bibiana

5

TO COLOSSEUM (100 m)
Via Celimontana Normantia
viale Labicana
Via del Querceti
Via Mecenate
Via A. Poliziano
Via Ruggero Bonghi
Via Gulciardini
Via Merulana
Via Michelangelo Buonarroti
Via Giusti
Via Ferruccio
Via Macchiavelli
Via Alfieri
Via Tasso
Via Foscolo
Via Emanuele Filberto
Via Nino Bixio
Via Conte Verde
Via Principe Eugenio
Via Principe Umberto
Via Cairoli
Via Piancioni
viale Alessandro Manzoni
Via di Porta

6

Via S. Giovanni in Laterano
Via di SS. Quattro Coronati
Via Matteo Boiardo
Via Ariosto
Via Galilei
viale Alessandro Manzoni
Manzoni M
Via S. Quintino
Via di S. Croce in Gerusalemme
Via Carlo Emanuele I
Via di Stefano Rotondo
PIAZZA S. GIOVANNI IN LATERANO
Via Statilia
Via G.B. Piatti

N

0   200 yards
0   200 meters

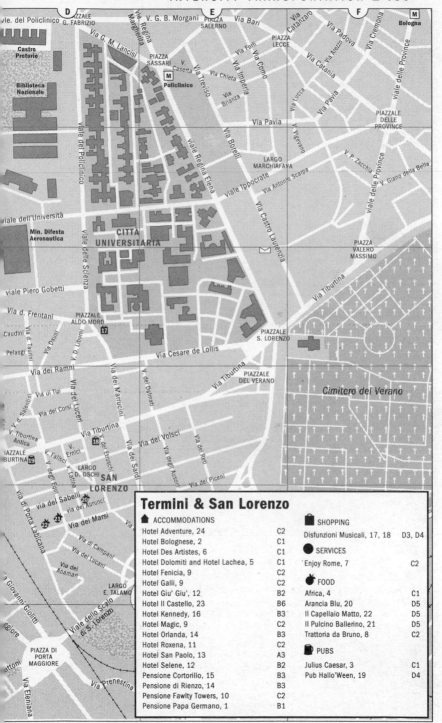

Termini & San Lorenzo

🛏 ACCOMMODATIONS

Hotel Adventure, 24	C2
Hotel Bolognese, 2	C1
Hotel Des Artistes, 6	C1
Hotel Dolomiti and Hotel Lachea, 5	C1
Hotel Fenicia, 9	C2
Hotel Galli, 9	C2
Hotel Giu' Giu', 12	B2
Hotel Il Castello, 23	B6
Hotel Kennedy, 16	B3
Hotel Magic, 9	C2
Hotel Orlanda, 14	B3
Hotel Roxena, 11	C2
Hotel San Paolo, 13	A3
Hotel Selene, 12	B2
Pensione Cortorillo, 15	B3
Pensione di Rienzo, 14	B3
Pensione Fawlty Towers, 10	C2
Pensione Papa Germano, 1	B1

🛍 SHOPPING

Disfunzioni Musicali, 17, 18	D3, D4

⬤ SERVICES

Enjoy Rome, 7	C2

🍴 FOOD

Africa, 4	C1
Arancia Blu, 20	D5
Il Capellaio Matto, 22	D5
Il Pulcino Ballerino, 21	D5
Trattoria da Bruno, 8	C2

🍺 PUBS

Julius Caesar, 3	C1
Pub Hallo'Ween, 19	D4

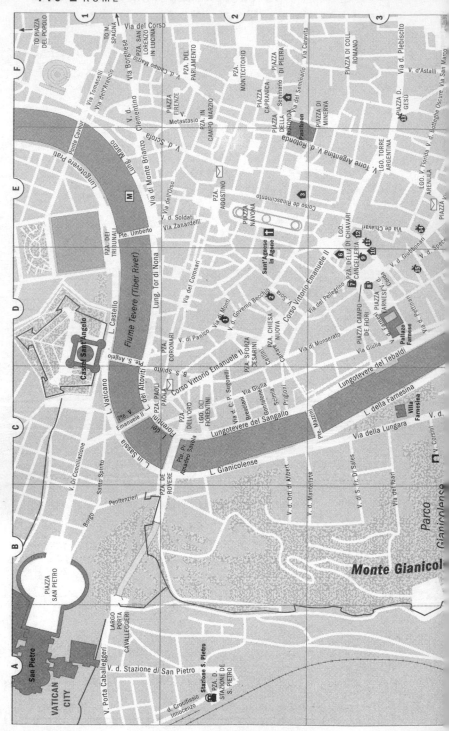

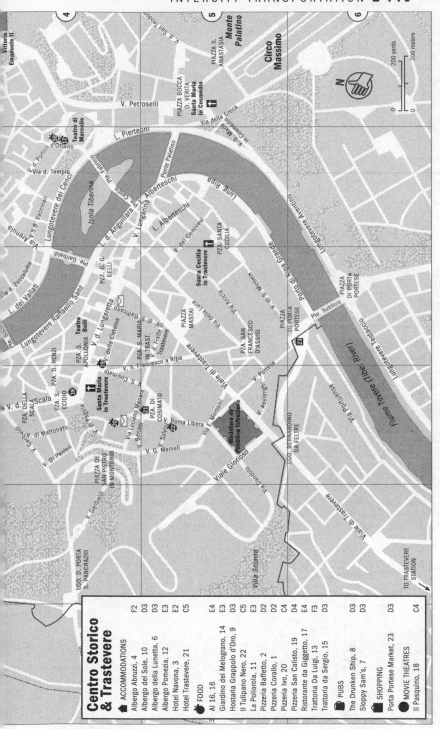

Centro Storico & Trastevere

♦ ACCOMMODATIONS

Albergo Abruzzi, 4	F2
Albergo del Sole, 10	D3
Albergo della Lunetta, 6	D3
Albergo Pomezia, 12	E3
Hotel Navona, 3	E2
Hotel Trastevere, 21	C5

♦ FOOD

Al 16, 16	E4
Giardino del Melograno, 14	E3
Hostaria Grappolo d'Oro, 9	D3
Il Tulipano Nero, 22	C5
La Pollarola, 11	E3
Pizzeria Baffetto, 2	D2
Pizzeria Corallo, 1	D2
Pizzeria Ivo, 20	C4
Pizzeria San Calisto, 19	D4
Ristorante da Giggetto, 17	E4
Trattoria Da Luigi, 13	F3
Trattoria da Sergio, 15	D3

■ PUBS

The Drunken Ship, 8	D3
Sloppy Sam's, 7	D3

■ SHOPPING

Porta Portese Market, 23	D3

● MOVIE THEATRES

Il Pasquino, 18	C4

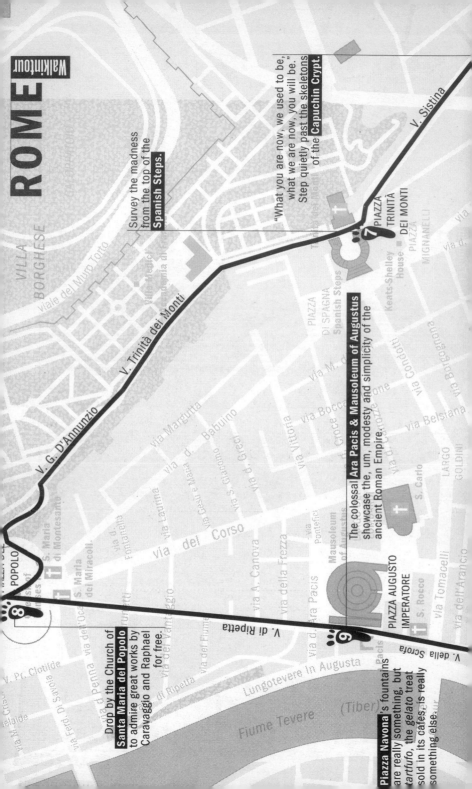

VILLA BORGHESE

Survey the madness from the top of the **Spanish Steps.**

"What you are now, we used to be, what we are now, you will be." Step quietly past the skeletons of the **Capuchin Crypt.**

PIAZZA TRINITÀ DEI MONTI

PIAZZA MIGNANELLI

Keats-Shelley House

V. Sistina

PIAZZA DI SPAGNA Spanish Steps

V. Trinità dei Monti

V. G. D'Annunzio

via Margutta

via d. Babuino

via Laurina

via S. Giacomo

via d. Greci

via M. d

via Bocca di Leone

via Vittoria

via della Croce

via Frattina

via Condotti

via Belsiana

S. Carlo

via Borgognona

LARGO GOLDINI

The colossal **Ara Pacis & Mausoleum of Augustus** showcase the, um, modesty and simplicity of the ancient Roman Empire.

VILLA

viale del Muro Torto

S. Maria di Montesanto

S. Maria dei Miracoli

POPOLO

via del Corso

Mausoleum of Augustus

via A. Canova

via della Frezza

via d. Pontefici

PIAZZA AUGUSTO IMPERATORE

S. Rocco

via Tomacelli

via dell'Arancio

Drop by the Church of **Santa Maria del Popolo** to admire great works by Caravaggio and Raphael for free.

V. di Ripetta

Ara Pacis

V. della Scrofa

Lungotevere in Augusta

Fiume Tevere (Tiber)

Piazza Navona's fountains are really something, but *tartufo*, the gelato treat sold in its cafés, is really something else.

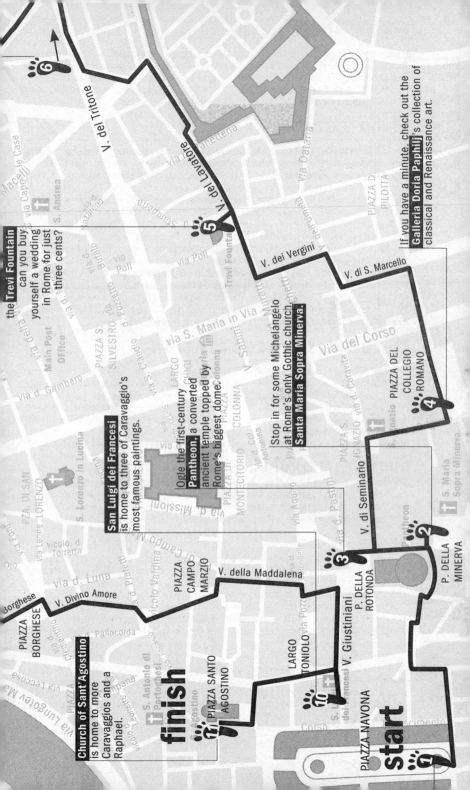

start

PIAZZA NAVONA

finish

Church of Sant'Agostino is home to more Caravaggios and a Raphael.

PIAZZA SANTO AGOSTINO

San Luigi dei Francesi is home to three of Caravaggio's most famous paintings.

LARGO TONIOLO

P. DELLA ROTONDA

V. della Maddalena

PIAZZA CAMPO MARZiO

V. Divino Amore

V. di Giustiniani

PIAZZA BORGHESE

Borghese

via d. Luna

PZA DI SAN LORENZO

S. Lorenzo in Lucina

PIAZZA DI SAN

S. Antonio di Portoghesi

S. Lorenzo in Lucina

Main Post Office

via d. Gambero

via della

PIAZZA S. SILVESTRO

via d. Mercede

via S. Claudio

Ogle the first-century Pantheon, a converted ancient temple topped by Rome's biggest dome.

P. DELLA MINERVA

S. Maria Sopra Minerva

Stop in for some Michelangelo at Rome's only Gothic church, Santa Maria Sopra Minerva.

PIAZZA DEL COLLEGIO ROMANO

Via del Corso

LARGO CHIGI

PIAZZA COLONNA

PIAZZA MONTECITORIO

via del Seminario

via S. Maria in Via

V. dei Vergini

V. di S. Marcello

the Trevi Fountain can you buy yourself a wedding in Rome for just three cents?

V. del Lavatore

Trevi Fountain

via Poli

V. del Tritone

V. del Tritone

If you have a minute, check out the Galleria Doria Pamphili's collection of classical and Renaissance art.

via Poli

via d. Stamperia

via dei Crociferi

via della Dataria

PIAZZA DI PILOTTA

via della Pilotta

1 **2** **3** **4** **5** **6** **10** **11**

reservations (across from track #20); **ATMs; luggage storage** (track #1); and **police** (track #13, or call ☎112). Not to be missed are ◼**Termini's bathrooms,** a black lit wonderland off track #1 (L1000/€0.52). Trains leave Termini to: **Naples** (2-2½hr., L18,600/€9.61); **Florence** (2-3hr.; L40,900/€21.12); **Bologna** (2¾-4¼hr.; L35,600/€18.39); **Milan** (4½-8hr.; L50,500/€26.08); and **Venice** (5hr.; L66,000/€34.09).

◼ ORIENTATION

From the **Termini** train station, **via Nazionale** is the central artery connecting **Piazza della Repubblica** with **Piazza Venezia,** home to the immense wedding-cake-like **Vittorio Emanuele II monument.** West of P. Venezia, **Largo Argentina** marks the start of C.V. Emanuele, which leads to Centro Storico, the medieval and Renaissance tangle of sights around the **Pantheon, Piazza Navona, Campo dei Fiori,** and **Piazza Farnese.** From P. Venezia, V. dei Fori Imperiale leads southeast to the **Forum** and **Colosseum,** south of which are the ruins of the **Baths of Caracalla** and the **Appian Way,** and the neighborhoods of southern Rome, the Aventine, Testaccio, Ostiense, and EUR. **Via del Corso** stretches from P. Venezia north to **Piazza del Popolo.** East of the Corso, fashionable streets border the **Piazza di Spagna** and, to the northeast, the **Villa Borghese.** South and east are the **Fontana di Trevi, Piazza Barberini,** and the **Quirinal Hill.** Across the Tiber to the north are **Vatican City,** and, to the south, **Trastevere,** the best neighborhood for wandering. It's impossible to navigate Rome without a map. Pick up a free map from a tourist office or a *Let's Go* **map guide.** The invaluable **Roma Metro-Bus map** (L8000/€4.13) is available at newsstands.

◨ LOCAL TRANSPORTATION

Bus and subway tickets (L1500/€0.77) are one and the same and can be bought at *tabacchi,* newsstands, some bars, and vending machines. Vending machines are in stations, on occasional street corners, and at major bus stops. Look for the ATAC label. Each ticket is valid for either one ride on the Metro or for unlimited bus travel within 75min. of validation. A BIG daily ticket costs L8000/€4.13 and allows for unlimited bus or train travel everywhere in the *Comune di Roma,* including Ostia but not Fiumicino; a CIS weekly ticket costs L32,000/€16.53.

SUBWAY (METROPOLITANA)

The two lines (A and B) of the *Metropolitana* intersect at Termini and can be reached by several entrances, including the stairway between the station and P. del Cinquecento. Entrances to Metro stations elsewhere are marked by poles with a white "M" on a red square. **The subway runs daily from 5:30am to 11:30pm.**

BUSES

Although the network of routes may seem daunting, Rome's buses are an efficient means of getting around the city. The **ATAC** intracity bus company has a myriad of booths, including one in Termini. (☎800 55 56 66. Open daily 8am-8pm.) Each bus stop *(fermata)* is marked by yellow signs listing all routes that stop there and key streets/stops on those routes. Some buses run only on weekdays *(feriali)* or weekends *(festivi),* while others have different routes on different days of the week. Most buses start running around 5 or 6am and stop at midnight, when some routes are replaced by the less reliable **night routes** *(notturno).*

Board through the front or back doors, not through the middle, then immediately stamp the ticket in the orange machine at the back; the ticket is then valid for any number of transfers over the next 75min. Consider buying several tickets at once; they can be hard to find at night and on weekends. Useful bus routes are: **46:** Vatican area, C.V. Emanuele, Largo Argentina, P. Venezia; **81:** P. Malatesta, S. Giovanni, Colosseo, Bocca della Verità, P. Venezia, Vatican; **170:** Termini, V. Nazionale, P. Venezia, Largo Argentina, V. Marmorata, S. Paolo Basilica; and **492:** Tiburtina, Termini, P. Barberini, P. Venezia, C. Rinascimento, P. Risorgimento.

TAXIS

Taxis in Rome are convenient but expensive (though less so than in other major cities). You can flag them down in the street, but they are easily found at stands near Termini and in major *piazze*. Ride only in yellow or white taxis, and make sure your taxi has a meter (if not, settle on a price before you get in the car). The meter starts at L4500/€2.32. Surcharges are levied at night (L5000/€2.58), on Sundays (L2000/€1.03), and when heading to or from Fiumicino (L14,000/€7.23) and Ciampino (L10,000/€5.16), with a charge L2000/€1.03 per suitcase. Standard tip is 15%. Expect to pay about L15,000/€7.75 for a ride from Termini to the Vatican. Taxis between the city center and Fiumicino cost around L70,000/€36.15. **Radio taxis** will pick you up at a given location within a few minutes of your call. Beware: radio taxis start the meter the moment your call is answered!

BIKES AND MOPEDS

Rome's hilly cobblestone streets, dense traffic, and crazy drivers make the city a challenge for bikes and mopeds. Bikes cost around L5000/€2.58 per hour or L15,000/€7.75 per day, but the length of that "day" varies according to the shop's closing time. In summer, try the stands on V.d. Corso at P.d. San Lorenzo and V. di Pontifici. (Open daily 10am-7pm. 16+.) Helmets are required by a strictly enforced law and should be included with your rental. Prices do not include 20% sales tax. For those just interested in an afternoon on a bike, **Enjoy Rome** (p. 445) offers an informative, albeit harrowing, tour of the city's best sights.

⁊ PRACTICAL INFORMATION

TOURIST AND FINANCIAL SERVICES

▨ **Enjoy Rome,** V. Marghera, 8a (☎06 445 18 43 or 06 445 68 90; fax 445 07 34; www.enjoyrome.com). From middle concourse of Termini (between trains and ticket booths), exit right, with trains behind you. Cross V. Marsala. 3rd block down V. Marghera. Owners Fulvia and Pierluigi answer questions and offer useful tidbits about the city in English. Arranges hotel accommodations, walking and bicycle tours, and bus service to Pompeii. Full-service travel agency, booking transportation worldwide and lodgings throughout Italy. Branch office at V. Varese, 39 (walk 1 block down V. Marghera and go right). Open M-F 8:30am-7pm, Sa 8:30am-2pm.

Currency Exchange: Banking hours are usually M-F 8:30am-1:30pm. Expect long lines and cranky tellers. **Banca di Roma** and **Banca Nazionale del Lavoro** have good rates, but **ATMs,** scattered all over town and especially near Termini, are the best.

American Express: P. di Spagna, 38 (☎06 676 41; lost or stolen cards and checks ☎722 81; fax 6764 2499). Open Sept.-July M-F 9am-7:30pm, Sa 9am-3pm; Aug. M-F 9am-6pm, Sa 9am-12:30pm. **Mail:** P. di Spagna, 38; 00187 Roma.

Thomas Cook: P. Barberini, 21a (☎06 482 80 82). Open M-Sa 9am-8pm, Su 9:30am-5pm. Other **branches:** V. della Conciliazione, 23-25 (☎06 6830 0435; open M-Sa 8:30am-6pm, Su 9am-5pm); V. del Corso, 23 (☎06 323 00 67; open M-Sa 9am-8pm, Su 9am-1:30pm); P. della Repubblica, 65 (☎06 48 64 95; open M-F 9am-5pm with 1hr. lunch break, Sa 9am-1pm).

LOCAL SERVICES

Luggage Storage: In train station Termini, by Track #1.

Lost Property: Oggetti Smarriti, V. Nicolo Bettoni, 1 (☎06 581 60 40; lost items on trains ☎4730 6682). Open M and W 8:30am-1pm and 2:30-6pm, Tu and F 8:30am-1pm, Th 8:30am-6pm. Also in **Termini,** at glass booth in main passageway. Open daily 7am-11pm.

English-Language Bookstores: ▨ **Libreria Feltrinelli International,** V.V.E. Orlando, 84-86 (☎06 482 78 78), near P. della Repubblica. Open daily 9am-7:30pm. AmEx/MC/

V. ◾**Anglo-American Bookshop**, V. della Vite, 102 (☎06 679 52 22), south of the Spanish Steps. Open M-F 9am-1pm and 4-8pm, Sa 9am-1pm.

Bisexual, Gay, and Lesbian Resources: The Roman branches of **ARCI-GAY** and **ARCI-Lesbica** share offices at V. Orvinio, 2 (☎06 86 38 51 12) and V. Lariana, 8 (☎06 855 55 22). Both hold discussions, dances, and special events. ARCI-GAY membership card (L20,000/€10.33 per yr.) gains admission to all Italian gay clubs. **Circolo di Cultura Omosessuale Mario Mieli, V. Corinto,** 5 (☎06 541 39 85; fax 541 39 71; www.mariomieli.it), provides loads of info about gay life in Rome. M: B-San Paolo, walk 1 block to Largo Beato Placido Riccardi, turn left, and walk 1½ blocks to V. Corinto. Open Sept.-July M-F 9am-1pm and 2-6pm. Rome's only **gay bookstore** is **Libreria Babele** (☎06 687 66 28), on V. dei Banchi Vecchi, across bridge from Castel Sant'Angelo off V.V. Emanuele. Open M-Sa 10am-7:30pm. **Gay beach,** Il Buco at Lido di Ostia.

Laundromat: OndaBlu, V. La Mora, 7 (☎800 86 13 46). Many locations in Rome. Wash L6000/€3.1 per 6½kg load; dry L6000/€3.1 per 6½kg load. Soap L1500/€0.77. Open daily 8am-10pm.

EMERGENCY AND COMMUNICATIONS

Police: ☎113. **Carabinieri:** ☎112. **Medical Emergency:** ☎118. **Fire:** ☎115.

Crisis Line: Centro Anti-Violenza, V.d. Torrespaccata, 157 (☎06 2326 9049 or 2326 9053). For victims of sexual violence. Branches throughout city. Available 24hr. **Samaritans,** V. San Giovanni in Laterano, 250 (☎06 7045 4444). Native English speakers. Counseling available. Open for calls and visits (call ahead) daily 1-10pm.

Medical Services: Policlinico Umberto I, Viale di Policlinico, 155 (emergency ☎06 499 71; non-emergency 499 71). M: B-Policlinico or #9 bus. Free first aid (pronto soccorso). Open 24hr.

24-Hour Pharmacies: Farmacia Internazionale, P. Barberini, 49 (☎06 487 11 95). MC/V. **Farmacia Piram,** V. Nazionale, 228 (☎06 488 07 54). MC/V.

Hospitals: International Medical Center, V.G. Amendola, 7 (☎06 488 23 71; nights and Su 488 40 51). Call first. Prescriptions filled, paramedic crew on call, referral service to English-speaking doctors. General visit L130,000/€67.14. Open M-Sa 8:30am-8pm. On-call 24hr. **Rome-American Hospital,** V.E. Longoni, 69 (☎06 225 51; fax 228 50 62). Private emergency and laboratory services; HIV and pregnancy tests. On-call 24hr.

Internet Service: ◾**Trevi Tourist Service: Trevi Internet,** V. dei Lucchesi, 31-32 (☎/fax 06 6920 0799), 1 block from Trevi Fountain (toward P. Venezia on road that becomes V.d. Pilotta). Central location. Fast connection L5000/€2.58 per 30min., L10,000/€5.16 per 1½hr. Also, Western Union money transfers, currency exchange, cheap international calls. Open daily 9am-10pm. **Splashnet,** V. Varese, 33 (☎06 4938 2073), 3 blocks north of Termini. Offers a match made in heaven: a laundromat with Internet access. While weeks' worth of mud disappears from your socks (wash and dry L6000/€3.1 each) you get 15min. of free Internet time. Internet L5000/€2.58 per hr., ask for Let's Go discount. Open daily 8:30am-10:30pm.

Post Office: Main office, P. San Silvestro, 19 (☎06 679 84 95), south of P. di Spagna. Come with large packages or to insure mail. Stamps and currency exchange (booths #23-25 and 19). Open M-F 9am-6pm, Sa 9am-2pm. **Large branch,** V. delle Terme di Diocleziano, 30 (☎06 474 56 02), near Termini. Same hours as San Silvestro branch.

Postal Code: Rome's postal codes fall between 00100 and 00200.

▐ ACCOMMODATIONS

HOTELS AND PENSIONI

Rome swells with tourists around Easter, from May through July, and in September. Prices vary widely with the time of year, and a proprietor's willingness to negotiate increases with length of stay, number of vacancies, and group size. Termini is swarming with hotel scouts. Many are legitimate and have IDs issued by tourist offices; however, some imposters have fake badges and direct travelers to rundown locations with exorbitant rates, especially at night.

CENTRO STORICO

If being a bit closer to the sights is worth it to you, then choosing Rome's medieval center over the area near Termini may be worth the higher prices.

Albergo Pomezia, V.d. Chiavari, 12 (☎/fax 06 686 13 71; hotelpomezia@openaccess.it). Off C.V. Emanuele II behind Sant'Andrea della Valle. Renovated rooms on 1st and 2nd floors; all with baths. Clean, quiet rooms with phone, fan, and heat in the winter. Breakfast included 8-11am. Singles L90,000/€46.48, with bath L110,000/€56.81; doubles L150,000/€77.40, L200,000/€103.29; triples L210,000/€108.45, L255,000/€131.69; extra bed 35% surcharge. AmEx/MC/V.

Albergo della Lunetta, P. del Paradiso, 68 (☎06 686 10 80; fax 689 20 28). 1st right off V. Chiavari from C.V. Emanuele II behind Sant'Andrea della Valle. Good value in great location (between Campo dei Fiori and P. Navona). Singles L90,000/€46.48, with bath L110,000/€56.81; doubles L150,000/€77.47, L200,000/€103.29; triples L210,000/€108.45, L255,000/€131.69. Reserve with credit card or check. MC/V.

Albergo Abruzzi, P. della Rotonda, 69 (☎06 679 20 21). Location, location, location! 200ft. from the Pantheon, these are indeed rooms with a view. Hall bathrooms, but every room comes with a sink. Singles L90-115,000/€46.48-59.39; doubles L140-170,000/€72.3-87.8; triples L220,000/€113.62.

Hotel Piccolo, V.d. Chiavari, 32 (☎06 689 23 30), off C. Vittorio Emanuele II behind Sant'Andrea della Valle. Recently renovated, family-run establishment next to a bustling grocery store. All rooms have fans and telephones. No elevator. English spoken. Breakfast L7000/€3.62. Check-out noon. Curfew 1am. Singles L100,000/€51.65, with bath L120,000/€62; doubles L120,000/€62, with bath L160,000/€82.63; triples with bath L170,000/€87.8; quads with bath L180,000/€92.96. AmEx/MC/V.

Hotel Navona, V.d. Sediari, 8, 1st fl. (☎06 686 42 03; fax 6821 1392, call before faxing; www.hotelnavona.com). Take V.d. Canestrari from P. Navona, cross C. del Rinascimento, and go straight. This 16th-century building has been used as a *pensione* for over 150 years, counting among its guests Keats, Shelley, and the University of Alabama chapter of the ΑΠΘ fraternity. Breakfast included. Check-out 10am. Singles with bath 160,000/€82.63; doubles with bath L210,000/€108.45; triples with bath L290,00/€149.82. A/C L30,000/€15.5. Pay in cash only before 1st night.

Albergo del Sole, V.d. Biscione, 76 (☎06 6880 6873; fax 689 37 87), off Campo dei Fiori. Allegedly the oldest *pensione* in Rome. 61 comfortable rooms with phone, fan, TV, and fantastic antique furniture. Singles L120,000/€62, with bath 140-170,000/€72.3-87.8; doubles L160-180,000/€82-92.96, L200-240,000/€103.29-123.95.

NEAR PIAZZA DI SPAGNA

These accommodations might run you a few thousand more *lire*, but can you really put a price tag on living but a few steps from Prada? John Keats couldn't.

▧**Pensione Panda,** V.d. Croce, 35 (☎06 6780179; fax 6994 2151; www.hotelpandaparadise.com), between P. di Spagna and V.d. Corso. Newly renovated. Immaculate rooms, arched ceilings, and Neo-Roman reliefs in the hallways. Check-out 11am. Reservations recommended. Singles L70,000/€36.15, with bath L100-120,000/€51.6-62; doubles L120-180,000/€62-92.96; triples with bath L210,000/€108.44; quads with bath L320,000/€165.3. Ask for *Let's Go* discount. AmEx/MC/V.

Pensione Jonella, V.d. Croce, 41, 4th fl. (☎06 6797966), between P. di Spagna and V.d. Corso. Run by same guys as Hotel des Artistes (see p. 449). 4 beautiful rooms. Quiet, roomy, and cool in summer. No reception: call ahead to be let in. No elevator. No private bathrooms. Singles L100,000/€51.6; doubles L120,000/€62. Cash only.

Hotel Boccaccio, V.d. Boccaccio, 25 (☎/fax 06 488 59 62; www.hotelboccaccio.com). M: A-Barberini. Off V.d. Tritone. This well-situated hotel offers 8 elegantly furnished rooms near many sights. Singles L80,000/€41.32; doubles L120,000/€62, with bath L160,000/€83.63; triples L162-216,000/€84.18-111.55. AmEx/D/MC/V.

BORGO AND PRATI (NEAR VATICAN CITY)

Home to lots of priests and nuns, the Vatican and environs are pretty quiet at night.

▨ **Colors,** V. Boezio, 31 (☎06 687 40 30; fax 686 79 47). M: A-Ottaviano. Or, bus to P. Risorgimento. Take V. Cola di Rienzo to V. Terenzio. Sporting lots of amenities and a super-cool English-speaking staff. In the elegant and quiet Prati area. Has 18 beds. Kitchen, hair dryer, Internet (L5000/€2.58 per hr.), and laundry (L8000/€4.13 per load, the best deal in town). Beautiful terrace open until 11pm. Dorm beds L35,000/ €18.08; doubles L120-150,000/€62-77.47; triples L140-180,000/€72.3-92.96. Credit card needed for reservations; cash only.

▨ **Pensione Ottaviano,** V. Ottaviano, 6 (☎06 3973 7253 or 3973 7253; www.pensioneot-taviano.com), just north of P. del Risorgimento, a few blocks from Metro stop of same name and a few steps away from St. Peter's. 3 to 6 beds per room. Amenities include satellite TV, individual lockers, fridges, a microwave, hot showers, free linens, and free Internet access for guests. Friendly Aussie and British staff. Smoking allowed. Lockout 11:30am-2pm. No curfew. Dorms L30,000/€15.5, in winter L25,000/€12.91; doubles L70-90,000/€36.15-46.48; 1 triple L120,000/€62. Cash only.

Hotel Pensione Joli, V. Cola di Rienzo, 243, 6th fl. (☎06 324 18 54; jolihit@yahoo.it), at V. Tibullo, *scala* A. Nice beds, ceiling fans, and views of the Vatican. Breakfast included. Singles L95,000/€49.06, with bathroom L120,000/€62; doubles L170,000/€87.8; triples L243,000/€125.5; quads L318,000/€164.24. MC/V.

TRASTEVERE

Trastevere is a beautiful old Roman neighborhood famous for its separatism, medieval streets, and pretty-far-from-the-tourist-crowd charm. Hotels here are scattered, most of them too pricey for budget travelers, but the area does offer great nightlife and a location near the Vatican.

Hotel Carmel, V.G. Mameli, 11 (☎06 580 99 21; fax 581 88 53, hotelcarmel@hot-mail.com). Take a right on V. E. Morosini (V.G. Mameli) off V.d. Trastevere. Though a good walk from the heart of Trastevere, this simple hotel offers 9 no-frills, smallish rooms for reasonable prices. Beautiful garden terrace with seating for breakfast. All with bath. Breakfast included. Singles L100,000/€51.6; doubles L150,000/€77.47; triples L190,000/€98.13; quads L220,000/€113.62. AmEx/MC/V.

Hotel Trastevere, V. Luciano Manara, 25 (☎06 581 47 13; fax 588 10 16), right off V.d. Trastevere onto V.d. Fratte di Trastevere. Homey establishment overlooks P.S. Cosimato. 9 simple, airy rooms with bath, TV, and phone. English spoken. Breakfast included. Singles L130,000/€67.14; doubles 160,000/€82.63; triples L170,000/ €87.8; quads L240,000/€123.95. Short-term apartments for 2-6 persons with neat little kitchens and loft beds. AmEx/D/MC/V.

TERMINI AND SAN LORENZO

Welcome to budget traveler and backpacker central. While Termini is chock full of traveler's services, the area south of Termini is a little sketchy at night.

▨ **Pensione Fawlty Towers,** V. Magenta, 39 (☎/fax 06 445 03 74; www.fawltytowers.org). Exit Termini to the right from middle concourse, cross V. Marsala onto V. Marghera, and turn right onto V. Magenta. Extremely popular 15-room hotel/hostel. Fawlty Towers never fails to satisfy. Flower-filled terrace provides a respite from Termini. Common room with satellite TV, library, refrigerator, microwave, and cheap Internet access. Check-out 9am for dorms and 10am for private rooms. Frequently full, but reception will do its utmost to find you a place; just don't mention the war. Reservations strongly recommended. Native English-speaking staff. Dorm-style quads L30-35,000/€15.5-18.08 per person (no children); singles L75,000/€38.73, with shower L90,000/€46.48; doubles L110,000/€56.81, with shower L140,000/€72.3, with bath L150,000/ €77.47; triples with bath L165,000/€85.22.

Hotel Des Artistes, V. Villafranca, 20 (☎06 445 43 65; www.hoteldesartistes.com). From middle concourse of Termini, exit right, turn left onto V. Marsala, right onto V. Vicenza, then left onto 5th cross-street. 3-star hotel. All 40 elegant rooms with bathroom, safe, refrigerator, and TV. Lovely rooftop terrace and lounge with satellite TV. Cheap Internet. Reception 24hr. Check-out 11am. Cancel reservations 5 days in advance. Dorms L35,000/€18.08; singles L70,000/€36.15; doubles L110-170,000/€56.81-87.8; triples L130-210,000/€67.14-108.44; in winter, 20-30% less. AmEx/MC/V.

Hotel Papa Germano, V. Calatafimi, 14a (☎06 48 69 19 or 4782 5202; fax 4788 1281; www.hotelpapagermano.com). From middle concourse of Termini, exit right, and go left onto V. Marsala, which becomes V. Volturno; V. Calatafimi is 4th cross-street on right. Clean, affordable rooms (all with TV and phone) and outstanding service from owners Gino and Pina. English spoken. Internet. Check-out 11am. Dorms L30-40,000/€15.5-20.66; singles L45-70,000/€23.24-36.15; doubles L70-130,000/€36.15-67.14, with bath L100-160,00/€51.6-82.63; triples L105-150,000/€54.23-77.47, with bath L135-200,000/€69.72-103.29. AmEx/MC/V.

Pensione di Rienzo, V. Principe Amedeo, 79a (☎06 446 71 31; fax 446 69 80). A tranquil, family-run retreat with spacious renovated rooms. Large windows overlook a courtyard. Friendly, helpful staff. 16 rooms, some with balcony, TV, and bath. Breakfast L20,000/€10.33. Check-out 10am. Singles without bath L40-80,000/€20.66-41.32; doubles L60-120,000/€33.57-62. MC/V.

Pensione Cortorillo, V. Principe Amedeo, 79a, 5th fl. (☎06 446 69 34; fax 445 47 69). Family runs this small and friendly *pensione*. TV in all rooms. Cheap lobby phone. English spoken. Breakfast included. Check-out 10am. Singles L80-120,000/€41.32-62; doubles L70-130,000/€36.15-67.14; extra bed L30,000/€15.5. AmEx/D/MC/V.

Hotel Kennedy, V. Filippo Turati, 62-64 (☎06 446 53 73; fax 446 54 17; www.hotelkennedy.net). Ask not what you can do for Hotel Kennedy, ask what Hotel Kennedy can do for you. Classical music in the bar, leather couches, and a large TV in lounge. Private bath, satellite TV, phone, and A/C. Some rooms offer a view of Roman ruins. Hearty all-you-can-eat breakfast included. English spoken. Check-out 11am. Reservations by fax/email. Singles L65-169,000/€33.57-87.28; doubles L100-299,000/€51.6-154.42; triples L149-349,00/€76.95-180.240. 10% *Let's Go* discount. AmEx/D/MC/V.

Hotel San Paolo, V. Panisperna, 95 (☎06 474 52 13; fax 474 52 18; hsanpaolo@tin.it). Exiting from front of train station, turn left onto V. Cavour. After you pass Santa Maria Maggiore (on left), bear right onto V.d. Santa Maria Maggiore (V. Panisperna). 10 min. from Termini. 23 rooms housed in a bright little *palazzo* with tranquil, whimsically decorated rooms. Clean and private hall baths. Public stereo in the cafe. Breakfast L10,000/€5.16. Check-out 10:30am. Singles L75,000/€38.73; doubles L110,000/€56.81, with bath L150,000/€77.47; triples L150,000/€77.47. Lovely, large 6-10 person suite L50-65,000/€25.80-33.57 per person. AmEx/MC/V.

Hotel Dolomiti and **Hotel Lachea,** V.S. Martino della Battaglia, 11 (☎06 495 72 56; fax 445 46 65; www.hotel-dolomiti.it). From middle concourse of Termini, exit right, go left onto V. Marsala and right onto V. Solferino (V.S. Martino della Battaglia). 19th-century *palazzo* houses sparkling new hotels, offering a bar, breakfast room, and Internet (L10,000/€5.16). 3-star Dolomiti offers satellite TV, phone, minibar, and A/C. Lachea offers same excellent service in simpler hotel (with lower prices). Breakfast L12,000/€6.2. A/C L25,000/€12.91 per night. Check-out 11am. **Dolomiti:** rooms with baths. Singles L100-130,000/€51.65-67.14; doubles L140-200,000/€72.3-103.29; triples L180-240,000/€92.96-123.94; quads L220-260,000/€113.62-134.28; quints available. **Lachea:** rooms without bath and TV available. Singles L75-90,000/€38.73-46.48; doubles L90-120,000/€45.06-62; triples L110-130,000/€56.81-67.14.

Hotel Pensione Cathrine, V. Volturno, 27 (☎06 48 36 34). From middle concourse of Termini, exit right, turn left onto V. Marsala (V. Volturno). Comfortable *pensione* with spacious rooms and clean common bathrooms. More rooms at V. XX Settembre, 58a. Breakfast L13,000/€6.71. Singles L90,000/€46.48; doubles L130-140,000/€67.14-72.30; triples with bath L170,000/€87.8. *Let's Go* discount L10,000/€5.16.

Hotel Adventure, V. Palestro, 88 (☎06 446 90 26; fax 446 00 84; hotel.adventure@flashnet.it; www.hoteladventure.com). From middle concourse of Termini, exit right, cross V. Marsala onto V. Marghera, and take 4th right onto V. Palestro. Renovated rooms (all with bath, satellite TV, phone, and fridge). Breakfast included. Check-out 11am. Singles L150,000/€77.47 including A/C; doubles L160,000/€82.63; triples L220,000/€113.62. A/C L25,000/€12.91. AmEx/MC/V.

Hotel Bolognese, V. Palestro, 15 (☎/fax 06 49 00 45). In a land of run-of-the-mill *pensioni,* this place is spruced up by the artist-owner. Some of the 14 bedrooms have attached sitting rooms, bathtubs, and terraces. Probably the only hotel near Termini to have won an award from the Knights of Malta. Check-out 11am. Curfew 2am. Singles L50,000/€25.82, with bath L70-L80,000/€36.15-41.32; doubles L80-120,000/€41.32-62; triples L120-150,000/€62-77.47.

Hotel Il Castello, V. Vittorio Amedeo II, 9 (☎06 7720 4036; fax 7049 0068; www.ilcastello.com). M: A-Manzoni. Far beyond Termini, but well within a backpacker's budget. Walk down V. San Quintino and take 1st left. Housed in castle with eager serving knaves (mostly native-English speakers). Spot damsels in distress from the quaint balconies. Breakfast L5000/€2.58. Check-out 10:30am. Dorms L30,000/€15.5; singles L80,000/€41.32; doubles L110,000/€56.81, with bath L130-150,000/€67.14-77.47; triples L120,000/€62, with bath L140-180,000/€72.3-92.96. MC/V.

Hotel Giu' Giu', V.d. Viminale, 8 (☎06 482 77 34; fax 4891 2616), 2 blocks south of Termini, in elegant but fading *palazzo.* Pleasant breakfast area. 12 large, quiet rooms, and a friendly family running the place. Breakfast L15,000/€7.75. Check-out 10am. Singles L65,000/€33.57; doubles L105,000/€54.23, with bath L115,000/€59.39; triples with bath L155,000/€80.05; quads with bath L195,000/€100.71.

Hotel Orlanda, V. Principe Amedeo, 76, 3rd fl. (☎06 488 01 24), at V. Gioberti. Take stairs on right in vestibule. Frequented by Italian businesspeople. 23 rooms have sinks; some have hair dryers. English spoken. Breakfast included. Reception 24hr. Check-in noon. Singles L55-130,000, with bath L60-170,000/€31-87.80; doubles L80-160,000/€41.32-82.63, L100-270,000/€51.6-139.44; triples L105-190,000/€54.23-98.13, L125-370,000/€64.56-191.09; quads L140-240,000/€72.3-123.95, L160-460,000/€82.63-237.57. A/C L30,000/€15.5. AmEx/D/MC/V.

Hotel Selene, V.d. Viminale, 8 (☎06 482 44 60; fax 4782 1977; hotelseleneroma@mclink.it), above Hotel Giu' Giu'. 27 clean rooms with bath, TV, and phone. Breakfast included. Singles L100,000/€51.6; doubles L150,000/€77.5; triples L210,000/€108.45; quads L240,000/€123.95. MC/V.

ALTERNATIVE ACCOMMODATIONS

BED & BREAKFASTS

While Italians may have appropriated the American terminology, the reality of "Bed & Breakfast" services in Rome differs from the typical American concept. In some, guest rooms are arranged in private homes throughout the city, with the owners generally obliged to provide breakfast. In others, apartments have kitchens where clients are expected to make their own breakfast. The rooms and apartments can vary greatly in quality and size. Be sure to pinpoint just how "centrally located" your apartment is, as some are flung toward the outskirts of the city.

Bed & Breakfast Association of Rome, P. del Teatro Pompeo, 2 (☎/fax 06 6877348; info@b-b.rm.it; www.b-b.rm.it). A reservation service with a website that gives very explicit info and pictures of the rooms and apartments offered. Prices range from L80,000/€41.32 per night for a single room to L270,000/€139.44 per night for an apartment for 6. Office phone answered M-F 9am-1pm.

CAMPING

The Touring Club Italiano publishes an annual directory of all camping sites in Italy, *Campeggi in Italia,* available in bookstores throughout Italy. Camping on beaches, roads, and inconspicuous plots is illegal and dangerous.

Seven Hills Village, V. Cassia, 1216 (☎06 3033 108 26; fax 3033 100 39), 8km north of Rome. Take bus #907 from M: A-Cipro-Musei Vaticani, or bus #201 from P. Mancini. The bus driver knows when to get off, just 3-4km past the GRA (the big highway that circles the city). Daily shuttles to Rome (L6000/€3.1) or train station near campgrounds (L2000/€1.03). From stop, follow the country road about 1km until you see the sign. It also houses a bar, market, restaurant, and *pizzeria*. No *lire* or euro: buy a Seven Hills card for use in the campground. Doctor on hand during the day. Check-in 24hr. Check-out noon. Open late Mar. to late Oct. L14,000/€7.23 per person, L1500/€0.77 per tent, L7000/€3.62 per car. Campers L15,000/€7.75. Bungalows sleep up to 4 and start from L85,000/€43.9. Cash only.

INSTITUTIONAL ACCOMMODATIONS

These are for budget travelers looking for a bed, minus the frills.

Ostello del Foro Italico (HI), V.d. Olimpiadi, 61 (☎06 323 62 67 or 323 62 79; fax 324 26 13). M: A-Ottaviano. Exit onto V. Barletta and take bus #32 to Cadorna (get off when you see pink Foro Italico buildings and an obelisk). 350 beds, in 6-12 person single-sex rooms. Close to the "Big Gym," Rome's largest public sports complex. No family rooms. Wheelchair accessible. Lunch and dinner available (L10,000/€5.16). Small continental breakfast and hot showers included. Huge, free lockers (bring a lock). Reception 2pm-midnight. Lockout 10am-2pm. Check-out 7-10am. Strictly enforced curfew midnight. Bar open 10am-10:30pm, restaurant open noon-2:30pm and 6:30-9:30pm. L30,000/€15.5; with HI card L28,000/€14.46. Cash only.

RELIGIOUS HOUSING

Certain convents and monasteries host guests (for a fee of about L50,000/€25.82 or more per night) who come with letters of introduction from their local diocese. Contact your home parish for details. Most accommodations are single-sex with early curfews, services, and light chores.

WOMEN'S HOUSING

Although men also need housing, you'll find single-sex housing in Rome for women only. Kind of feels like a high school dance.

YWCA Foyer di Roma, V.C. Balbo, 4 (☎06 488 04 60; fax 487 10 28). From P. dei Cinquecento (in front of Termini), walk down V.d. Viminale, turn left onto V. Torino and right onto V.C. Balbo. Pretty, clean, and secure. Breakfast included M-Sa 8am-9am. Tell reception by 10am the same day if you want lunch (1-2pm; L20,000/€10.33). Reception open 7am-midnight. Check-out 10am. Curfew midnight. Singles L70,000/€36.15, with bath L90,000/€46.48; doubles L120,000/€62, with bath L140,000/€72.3; triples and quads L50,000/€25.82 per person. Cash only.

⌂ FOOD

Ancient Roman dinners were once lavish 10 hour affairs. Food orgies went on *ad nauseam*—after gorging themselves for hours, guests would commonly retreat to a special room called the *vomitorium*, throw it all up, and return to the party. Meals in Rome are still lengthy affairs, though they generally involve less vomiting, depending on the restaurant. Restaurants tend to close between 3 and 7pm.

ANCIENT CITY

The area around the Forum and the Colosseum is home to some of Italy's finest tourist traps. If you forgot to pack a lunch and the stroll to the Centro Storico seems too long and hot, there are a few places that offer tasty meals at fair prices.

▨ **Taverna dei Quaranta,** V. Claudia, 24 (☎06 700 05 50), off P. del Colosseo. Shaded by the trees of Celian Park, outdoor dining at this corner *taverna* is a must. Not at all touristy. Menu changes weekly and often features delights such as the sinfully good *oliva ascolane* (olives stuffed with meat and fried; L7500/€3.87) and *ravioli all'Amalfitana* (L11,000/€5.68). ½L house wine L5000/€2.58. Cover L2500/€1.29. Reservations suggested. Open daily noon-3:30pm and 7:45pm-midnight. AmEx/D/MC/V.

ROME

I Buoni Amici, V. Aleardo Aleardi, 4 (☎06 7049 1993). From Colosseum, take V. Labicana to V. Merulana. Turn right, then left on V. A. Aleardi. Long walk, but the cheap, excellent food awaits. Try the *linguine all'astice* (with lobster sauce; L12,000/€6.20), *risotto con i funghi* (L10,000/€5.16), and *penne alla vodka* (L10,000/€5.16). Cover L2500/€1.29. Open M-Sa noon-3pm and 7-11:30pm. AmEx/D/MC/V.

PIAZZA NAVONA

There are plenty of delicious, inexpensive *trattorie* and pizzerias near P. Navona, but it often takes a short stroll to reach them. A walk down V. del Governo Vecchio reveals some of the best restaurants in the city. No matter where you eat, you can expect to be subjected to numerous street performances.

▨ **Pizzeria Baffetto,** V.d. Governo Vecchio, 114 (☎06 686 16 17), at V. Sora. Once a meeting place for 60s radicals, Baffetto now overflows with hungry Romans. Its popularity ensures long waits, especially for outside tables. Always crowded, but worth it for the delicious pizza found inside. Pizza L8-14,000/€4.13-7.23. Open M-F noon-3pm and 7:30pm-1am, Sa-Su noon-3pm and 7:30pm-2am. Cash only.

Pizzeria Corallo, V.d. Corallo, 10-11 (☎06 6830 7703), off V.d. Governo Vecchio near P. del Fico. This pizzeria is a great place to grab a cheap, late dinner before losing your life's savings at the chichi bars nearby. Pizzas L7-14,000/€3.62-7.23. Excellent *primi* options like *Tagliolini ai fiori di zucca* (with zucchini blossoms; L12,000/€6.2). Reservations accepted. Open daily noon-3pm and 7pm-1am. MC/V.

Trattoria dal Cav. Gino, V. Rosini, 4 (☎06 687 34 34), off V.d. Campo Marzio across from P. del Parlamente. The very affable Gino greets you at the door at this trattoria, and points to a lit-up sign above door, announcing that *tonnarelli alla ciociala* (L10,000/€5.16) is the house specialty. Want a drink? Another sign proclaims Gino's philosophy: *In Vino Veritas*. Agreed. *Primi* L8-10,000/€4.13-5.16; *secondi* L15-17,000/€7.75-8.78. Reservations accepted. Open M-Sa 1-3:45pm and 8-10:30pm. Cash only.

Trattoria Gino e Pietro, V.d. Governo Vecchio, 106 (☎06 686 15 76), at V. Savelli. Basic Roman food without any frills, like *gnocchi verdi al gorgonzola* (L12,000/€6.20) and *saltimbocca alla romana* (veal with *prosciutto* and sage; L16,000/€8.26). Reservations accepted. Open F-W 12:30-3pm and 6:30-11pm. Closed late July to mid-Aug.

CAMPO DEI FIORI AND THE JEWISH GHETTO

While you might get yourself horribly lost in the labyrinth of crooked streets and alleyways that surround the Campo, you will certainly find several exceptional *ristoranti* that can provide sustenance until the search party arrives. Across V. Arenula from the Campo, the proud community of the former Jewish Ghetto serves up traditional Roman-Jewish cuisine as it has for hundreds of years.

▨ **Trattoria da Sergio,** V.d. Grotte, 27 (☎06 654 66 69). Take V.d. Giubbonari and take 1st right. Far enough away from the Campo to keep tourists at bay. Sergio offers honest-to-God Roman ambience and hearty portions of great food. Try the *spaghetti all'Amatriciana* (with bacon and spicy tomato sauce; L10,000/€5.16)—a front runner for the city's best plate of pasta—and the *Straccetti* (shredded beef with tomatoes; L13,000/€6.71). Reservations suggested. Open M-Sa 12:30-3pm and 7pm-12:30am. MC/V.

▨ **Hostaria Grappolo d'Oro,** P. della Cancelleria, 80-81 (☎06 689 70 80), between C.V. Emanuele II and the Campo. This increasingly upscale *hostaria* is running out of space to plaster the many awards they've won over the years. Small menu changes daily. Homestyle dishes like *fregnacce al Casaro* (pasta with ricotta and tomato; L19,000/€9.81) and innovative creations such as *controfiletto di manzo* (steak with herbs and goat-cheese; L24,000/€12.4). Creative desserts like a *pistaccio semi-fredo*. Cover L2000/€1.03. Open Tu-Sa noon-2:30pm and 7:30-11pm, M 7:30-11pm. AmEx/MC/V.

▨ **Trattoria Da Luigi,** P.S. Cesarini, 24 (☎06 686 59 46), near Chiesa Nuova, 4 blocks down C.V. Emanuele II from Campo dei Fiore. Enjoy inventive cuisine such as *tagliolini* with shrimp, asparagus, and tomato (L13,000/€6.71), as well as simple dishes like *vitello con funghi* (veal with mushrooms; L15,000/€7.75). Great *antipasti* buffet. Bread L2000/€1.03. Open Tu-Su 7pm-midnight.

La Pollarola, P. Pollarola, 24-25 (☎06 68801654), off V.d. Biscione on way to Campo dei Fiori. Enjoy typical Roman dishes like *spaghetti alla carbonara* (with egg and *pancetta*; L10,000/€5.16). Open M-Sa noon-3:30pm and 7:30pm-midnight. AmEx/MC/V.

L'Insalata Ricca, Largo di Chiavari, 85-6 (☎06 6880 3656), off C. Vittorio Emanuele II near P.S. Andrea della Valle. You like salads, damn it, so come here. They have *all of them* (L10-16,000/€5.16-8.26). 6 other locations: P. Pasquino, 72; V.d. Gazometro, 62; P. Albania, 3; V. Polesine, 16; P. Risorgimento, 5; and V. F. Grinaldi, 52. Reservations suggested for dinner. Open daily 12:30-3:30pm and 6:45-11:30pm. AmEx/D/V.

Giardino del Melograno, V.d. Chiodaroli, 16-18 (☎06 6880 3423). From Campo dei Fiori, take V. Giubbonari, then a left on V. Chiavari. V.d. Chiodaroli is your 1st right. Highly renowned Chinese restaurant. Vast menu includes a fine dumpling appetizer (L5000/€2.58) and a tempting *gamberi con zenzero* (shrimp with ginger; L12,000/€6.2). Tourist *menù* (*antipasti, primi, secondi* and drink) is one of the best values in town (lunch L11,000/€5.68; dinner L15,000/€7.75). Reservations suggested on weekends. Open Th-Tu noon-3pm and 7-11:30pm. AmEx/MC/V.

Ristorante da Giggetto, V.d. Portico d'Ottavio, 21-22 (☎06 686 11 05). Rightfully famous but increasingly pricey. Serves up some of the finest Roman cooking known to man. Outdoor tables overlooking the Teatro Marcello ruins. Most run here for the legendary *carciofi alla Giudia* (L8000/€4.13), but the smart tourist knows to try the fried brains with mushrooms and zucchini (L22,000/€11.36). Cover L3000/€1.55. Reservations needed for dinner. Open Tu-Su 12:30-3pm and 7:30-11pm. AmEx/MC/V.

Al 16, V.d. Portico d'Ottavio, 16 (☎06 687 47 22), around corner from Teatro di Marcello. Neighborhood favorite run by very neighborhood guys. Traditional dishes alongside delicious house specialties like *pennette al 16* (with eggplant, sausage, and tomato; L14,000/€7.23), all at reasonable prices. Be fearless and try the *coda alla vaccinara* (oxtail stew; L14,000/€7.23). Cover L2500/€1.29. Reservations recommended for dinner. Open W-M 12:30-3pm and 7:30-11pm. AmEx/MC/V.

PIAZZA DI SPAGNA

Though the Spanish Steps area may seem very different from the less affluent environs of Termini, there is one big similarity—lots of lousy food. The irony of it all is that while a mediocre meal at Termini might set you back L15,000/€7.75, the same food here will cost twice as much. Here are some exceptions:

▨ **Trattoria da Settimio all'Arancio,** V.d. Arancio, 50-52 (☎06 687 61 19). Take V.d. Condotti from P. di Spagna; take 1st right after V.d. Corso, then 1st left. Arrive early to avoid the throngs of natives who come for the great service and tasty seafood. Excellent grilled *calamari* (L18,000/€9.3). *Primi* L12-15,000/€6.2-7.75; *secondi* L16-26,000/€8.26-13.43. Cover L2000/€1.03. Reservations suggested. Open M-Sa 12:30-3pm and 7:30-11:30pm. AmEx/D/MC/V.

▨ **Pizza Re,** V.d. Ripetta, 14 (☎06 321 14 68), 1 block from P. del Popolo on the left. Even though it's a chain, you'll find some of the best Neapolitan pizza (L12-18,000/€6.2-9.3) in town. *Pizza Re* (L17,500/€9.04), with *mozzarella di bufala* and fresh cherry tomatoes, is especially good. Fast, courteous service. The A/C feels sooooo good. Save L3000/€1.55 by ordering in person and taking it out. Open M-Sa 12:45-3:30pm and 7:30pm-12:30am, Su 7:30pm-12:30am. Closed 2 weeks mid-Aug. AmEx/D/MC/V.

▨ **Vini e Buffet,** P. Torretta, 60 (☎06 687 14 45). From V.d. Corso, turn into P.S. Lorenzo in Lucina. Take a left on V. Campo Marzio, then a quick right onto V. Toretta. A favorite spot for chic Romans who want to escape the crowds and mediocre food of P. di Spagna. Salads are creative and fresh—the *insalata con salmone,* with salmon and shrimp (L14,000/€7.23), is delightful. Also available are pates, *crostini,* and *scarmorze* (mozzarella baked with variety of ingredients) for L12-14000/€6.2-7.23. Try their signature yogurt and fruit bowls for dessert; the yogurt, almond, and cassis combination is fantastic. Reservations recommended. Open M-Sa 12:30-3pm and 7:30-11pm. Cash only.

Sogo Asahi, V.d. Propaganda, 22 (☎06 678 60 93). Excellent sushi, noodles, and more in this stylish Japanese restaurant. The *miso* soup (L7000/€3.62) is particularly good,

ROME

as are the *iniri* (sweet tofu), *unaga* (eel), and *sake* (salmon) sushi. *Nigiri* sushi L49,000/€25.31; 13-piece plate L30,000/€15.5; entrees L15-35,000/€7.75-18.08. Open M-Sa noon-2:30pm and 7-10:30pm. Reservations accepted. AmEx/MC/V.

BORGO AND PRATI (NEAR VATICAN CITY)

The streets near the Vatican are paved with bars and *pizzerie* that serve mediocre sandwiches at hiked-up prices. For far better and much cheaper food, head to the residential district a few blocks north and east of the Vatican Museums.

▨ **Franchi,** V. Cola di Rienzo, 200-204 (☎06 687 46 51). Benedeto Franchi ("Frankie") has been serving the happy citizens of Prati superb *tavola calda,* prepared sandwiches, and other luxurious picnic supplies for nearly 50 years. Delicacies include *suppli* (fried balls of veggies, mozzarella, and rice or potato, L1800/€0.93 each), marinated munchies (anchovies, peppers, olives, and salmon, all sold by the kilo), and pastas like vegetarian lasagna and *cannellini* stuffed with ricotta and beef (L8800/€4.54 per generous portion). Open M-Sa 8:15am-9pm. AmEx/MC/V.

Guido, V. Borgo Pio, 13 (☎06 687 54 91), near Basilica San Pietro. Don't let the checkered tablecloths and bow-tie adorned waiters at other establishments nearby distract you from this authentically Roman spot at the foot of Borgo Pio. Guido himself holds court behind a counter filled with all the makings of a beautiful *tavola calda.* Prices vary, but a *piatto caldi* (plate of marinated vegetables) run around L6000/€3.1, while main dishes are L7000/€3.62. Open daily 9am-9pm. Cash only.

TRASTEVERE

By day, Trastevere's cobblestone streets rumble only with the sounds of children and Vespas, but when night falls, P. di Santa Maria di Trastevere is packed with expatriate hippies and their dogs, howling along with out-of-tune guitars.

▨ **Pizzeria San Calisto,** P.S. Calisto, 9a (☎06 581 82 56), right off P.S. Maria in Trastevere. The best damn pizza in Rome. Gorgeous thin crust pizzas so large they hang off the plates. The *bruschetta* (L3-4000/€1.55-2.07) alone is worth a postcard home. Management shoos rose-sellers away for peaceful meal. Open Tu-Su 7pm-midnight. MC/V.

▨ **Ouseri,** V.d. Salumi, 2 (☎06 581 82 56). Either go left off V.d. Trastevere or take V. Vascellari from Lungotevere Ripa and then go right onto V.d. Salumi. Ouzeri may advertise itself as a "Taberna Greca," but the waiters will tell you it's actually a Greek Cultural Association, complete with Greek dancing lessons. Live music and dancing (except when it gets too hot in July and Aug.). Food is out of this world—share the *piatto misto* with a friend (L15-30,000/€7.75-15.5). To get inside, ring the doorbell. L3000/€1.55 membership required. Reservations suggested. Cash only.

Augusto, P. de' Rienzi, 15 (☎06 580 37 98), north of P.S. Maria in Trastevere. Enjoy the daily pasta specials at lunch (around L8500/€4.39), and the *pollo arrosto con patate* (L10,500/€5.42). The homemade desserts are out of this world. Dinner is chaotic and crowded; lunch tends to feature laid-back discussions between waiters and clientele. No reservations. Open M-F 12:30-3pm and 8-11pm, Sa 12:30-3pm; closed Aug.

Pizzeria Ivo, V.d. S. Francesco a Ripa, 158 (☎06 581 70 82). Take a right on V.d. Fratte di Trastevere off V. Trastevere, then right on V.S. Francesco a Ripa. Long-standing favorite in Trastevere, Ivo rests on its laurels a bit, but still serves up good pizza. Long waits, high prices (pizzas L8-16,000/€4.13-8.26). Open W-M 5pm-2am; closed Aug. MC/V.

Il Tulipano Nero, V. Roma Libera, 15 (☎06 581 83 09). Take V.d. Trastevere. Turn right on V. E. Morosini. Some of the more innovative pizzas (L8-15,000/€4.13-7.75) in Rome. Almost removed from the nighttime chaos of P.S. Maria in Trastevere, this pizzeria is smack in the middle of the nighttime chaos of P. Cosimato. Iron palates can attempt the *pennette all'elettroshock* (L12,000/€6.20). Portion size ranges from large to Pavarotti. Open Tu-Su 6pm-2am.

TERMINI AND SAN LORENZO

You're by the train station, hungry, and in a rush. This is no reason to subject yourself to the nightmare of a shady tourist trap offering a L10,000/€5.16 quick lunch.

Africa, V. Gaeta, 26-28 (☎06 494 10 77), near P. Independenza. Decked in yellow and black, Africa continues its 20-year tradition of serving excellent Eritrean/Ethiopian food. The meat-filled *sambusas* (L5000/€2.58) are a flavorful starter; both the *zighini beghi* (roasted lamb in a spicy sauce; L12,000/€6.2) and the *misto vegetariano* (mixed veggie dishes; L11,000/€5.68) make fantastic entrees, while the yogurt (L3000/€1.55) goes well with spicy dishes. Cover L1500/€0.77. Open M-Sa 8pm-midnight. MC/V.

Trattoria da Bruno, V. Varese, 29 (☎06 49 04 03), from V. Marsala, next to train station, walk 3 blocks down V. Milazzo and turn right onto V. Varese. A neighborhood favorite with daily specials. Start with the *tortellini con panna e funghi* (with cream and mushrooms; L10,000/€5.16) or the homemade *gnocchi* (L10,000/€5.16) and continue with the delicious *ossobuco* (L13,000/€6.71). Bruno, the owner, makes créches, and he's good at what he does: note the picture of the Pope congratulating Bruno on *his* good work. Open daily noon-3:30pm and 7-10:15pm; closed Aug. AmEx/V.

Ristorante Due Colonne, V.d. Serpenti, 91 (☎06 488 08 52), a right turn off V. Nazionale before the Palazzo delle Esposizioni. By day, Romans on lunch break fill the tables. By night, tourists struggle with the surprisingly broad menu. Excellent pizzas (L8-14,000/€4.13-7.23). *Pasta e fagioli* L9000/€4.65. Tourist *menù* L18-26,000/€9.3-13.43. Open M-Sa 9am-3:30pm and 6:30pm-12:30am. AmEx/D/MC/V.

SAN LORENZO

Though *Let's Go* doesn't recommend Communist-watching, this would be the place to do it if we did. San Lorenzo is Rome's university district, and thank god, poor students with discriminating palates have ensured that nearly every eatery here is good and cheap. The walk from Termini may be a little uncomfortable if you're alone at night. From Termini, walk south on V. Pretoriano to P. Tiburtino, or take bus #492 to P. Verano.

Il Pulcino Ballerino, V.d. Equi, 66-68 (☎06 494 12 55), off V. Tiburtina. Artsy atmosphere. Cook stirs up imaginative dishes like *conchiglione al "Moby Dick"* (shells with tuna, cream, and greens) and *risotto* (various types; L10-12,000/€5.16-6.2). Vegetarian dishes like *scamorrza* and potato casserole (L12,000/€6.2). Skip the chef altogether and prepare your own meal on a warm stone at the table. Cover L1000/€0.52. Open M-Sa 1-3:30pm and 8pm-midnight; closed 2nd and 3rd weeks Aug. AmEx/MC/V.

Arancia Blu, V.d. Latini, 65 (☎06 445 41 05), off V. Tiburtina. Elegant and popular little vegetarian restaurant serves up inventive, excellent dishes. Enjoy *tonnarelli con pecorino romano e tartufo* (pasta with sheep cheese and truffles; L12,000/€6.2) or fried ravioli stuffed with eggplant and smoked *caciocavallo* with pesto sauce (L16,000/€8.26). Extensive wine list. Open daily 8:30pm-midnight.

Il Capellaio Matto, V.d. Marsi, 25. From V. Tiburtina, take 4th right off V.d. Equi. Vegetarians, rejoice! This offbeat place (named for the Mad Hatter) offers pasta and rice dishes like *risotto al pepe verde* (with green peppercorn; L9000/€4.65), imaginative salads like *insalata di rughetta, pere, e parmigiano* (arugula, pears, and parmesan; L7000/€3.62), and a variety of crèpes (L7-9000/€3.62-4.65) that just scream 'Eat me'. Plenty of meat dishes, too. Cover L1500/€0.77. Open W-M 8pm-midnight.

TESTACCIO

Once home to a giant slaughterhouse, this working-class southern neighborhood is the seat of many excellent restaurants serving traditional Roman fare, as well as the center of Roman nightlife. True to their roots, Testaccio eateries offer food made of just about every animal part imaginable.

Trattoria da Bucatino, V. Luca della Robbia, 84-86 (☎06 574 68 86). Take V. Luigi Vanvitelli off V. Marmorata, then the 1st left. Friendly neighborhood *trattoria* with the animal entrails you know and love. Gut-less dishes as well. Heaping, delicious mounds of *tripe all romana* (L12,000/€6.2) stay true to the traditions of Testaccio. More conventional (but equally good dishes) include *cosse alla marinara* (L10,000/€5.16), more mussels than anyone in their right mind could hope to eat. Cover L2000/€1.03. Open Tu-Su 12:30-3:30pm and 6:30-11:30pm; closed Aug. D/MC/V.

ROME

DESSERT AND COFFEE

Cheap *gelato* is as plentiful on Roman streets as pairs of leather pants. Unfortunately, often you get what you pay for. Look for *gelato* with very muted (hence natural) colors, or try some of our favorite *gelaterie* and other sweetshops.

▨ **San Crispino,** V.d. Panetteria, 42 (☎06 679 39 24), near the Trevi Fountain. Facing the fountain, turn right onto V. Lavatore and take 2nd left; the *gelato* temple is on the right. Positively the best *gelato* in the world. Don't miss their exquisite meringue, armagnac (similar to cognac), and grapefruit flavors. No cones; the proprietors claim that they "interfere with the purity of the product." Cups L3-10,000/€1.55-5.16. Also at V. Acaia, 56 (☎06 7045 0412), south of the center in Appio. Both locations open M and W-Th noon-12:30am, F-Sa noon-1:30am, Su noon-midnight.

▨ **Tre Scalini,** P. Navona, 30 (☎06 6880 1996). Famed for its *tartufo,* a hunk of truffled chocolate ice cream rolled in chocolate shavings (L5000/€2.58 at bar; L11,000/€5.68 sitting). Bar open Th-Tu 9am-1:30am. Pricey restaurant open Th-Tu 12:30-3:30pm and 7:30-9pm.

▨ **Portico d'Ottavia,** 1 (☎06 687 86 37). Tiny, take-out bakery in Jewish Ghetto. Little fanfare, just long lines for the blueberry pies, buttery cookies, and chocolate and pudding concoctions, all sold by weight at excellent prices (L2000/€1.03 for a sizeable wedge of pie). Open Su-Th 8am-8pm, F 8am-5:30pm; closed Jewish holidays.

ENOTECHE (WINE BARS)

Wine bars, often tucked away in the corners of small *piazze*, range from laid-back and local to chic and international. Have a bite to eat and a delicious glass of wine without dealing with the unrefined drinkers of the pub scene.

▨ **Bar Da Benito,** V.d. Falegnami, 14 (☎06 686 15 08), off P. Cairoli in Jewish Ghetto. Tiny *tavola calda* lined with bottles and hordes of hungry workmen. Glasses of wine from L2000/€1.03; bottle from L15,000/€7.75 One hot pasta prepared daily (L8000/€4.13), along with *secondi* like *prosciutto* with vegetables (L9000/€4.65). Excellent staff. Open M-Sa 6:30am-7pm; lunch noon-3:30pm; closed Aug.

▨ **Trimani Wine Bar,** V. Cernaia, 37b (☎06 446 96 30), near Termini, perpendicular to V. Volturno (V. Marsala). Around the corner at V. Goito, 20. Excellent food, reasonable prices. Avocado and feta salad L14,000/€7.23; quiches L9000/€4.65; smoked fish L16,000/€8.26; cheese and sausage plates L14-20,000/€7.23-10.33; and mouthwatering desserts, such as ricotta, and raspberry tart L9000/€4.65. Wines from L3500/€1.81 per glass; L18,000/€9.30 per bottle. Dinner reservations recommended. Open M-Sa 11am-3:30pm and 6pm-12:30am. AmEx/MC/V.

◔ SIGHTS

Rome wasn't built in a day, and it's not likely that you'll see any substantial portion of it in 24 hours either. Ancient temples, medieval churches, Renaissance basilicas, Baroque fountains, and 19th- and 20th-century museums all cluster together in a city bursting with masterpieces from every era of Western civilization. No other city can claim enough nooks and crannies to cram in Rome's 981 churches and 280 fountains. From Etruscan busts to modern canvases, there is more than enough in Rome to captivate visitors for months, even years.

THE ANCIENT CITY

THE ROMAN FORUM

Main entrance: V.d. Fori Imperiali (at Largo C. Ricci, between P. Venezia and the Colosseum). Other entrances: opposite the Colosseum (and Palatine Hill too) and at the Clivus Capitolinus, near P. del Campidoglio. M: B-Colosseo, or bus to P. Venezia. Open M-Sa 9am-6:30pm, Su 9am-1pm; in winter daily 9am-1hr. before sunset; sometimes closes M-F 3pm, Su and holidays noon. Free. Guided tour with archaeologist L6000/€3.1; audioguided tour of Forum L7000/€3.62 in English; available at main entrance.

Civic forum's main entrance ramp leads to V. Sacra. V. Sacra cuts through the old market square and civic center; the **Basilica Aemilia** is to the right, and the **Curia** is just beyond.

The Forum was originally a low marshland prone to flooding from the Tiber. Rome's Iron Age inhabitants (1000-900 BC) eschewed its low, unhealthy swampiness in favor of the Palatine Hill, descending only to bury their dead. In the 7th and 8th centuries BC, Etruscans and Greeks used the Forum as a weekly market. The people who would soon be known as the Romans founded a thatched-hut shantytown on the site of the Forum in 753 BC, when Romulus and Sabine leader Titus Tatius joined forces to end the war triggered by the famous rape of the Sabine women. Now the Forum bears witness to centuries of civic building. The entrance ramp to the Forum leads to the **via Sacra,** the oldest street in Rome, near the area once known as the **Civic Forum.** The other sections of the Roman Forum are the **Market Square,** the **Lower Forum,** the **Upper Forum,** and the **Velia.**

CIVIC FORUM. The **Basilica Aemilia,** built in 179 BC, housed the guild of the *argentarii* (money changers). It was rebuilt several times after fires, particularly one started by Alaric and his merry band of Goths in AD 410; in the pavement you can still see marks from the melted coins that the *argentarii* lost in these blazes. Next to the Basilica Aemilia stands the **Curia,** or Senate House, one of the oldest buildings in the Forum. It was converted to a church in AD 630 and restored by Mussolini. The Curia also houses the **Plutei of Trajan,** two parapets that depict the burning of the tax registers and the distribution of food to poor children. The broad space in front of the Curia was the **Comitium,** or assembly place, where citizens came to vote and representatives gathered for public discussion. This space was home to the Twelve Tables, bronze tablets upon which the first laws of the Republic were inscribed. Bordering the Comitium is the large brick **Rostrum,** or speaker's platform, erected by Julius Caesar just before his death. Augustus's rebellious daughter Julia is said to have voiced her dissenting opinion here by engaging in amorous activities with some of her father's enemies. The hefty **Arch of Septimius Severus,** to the right of the Rostrum, was dedicated in AD 203 to celebrate that emperor's victories in the Middle East.

MARKET SQUARE. A number of shrines and sacred precincts, including the **Lapis Niger** (Black Stone), once graced the square in front of the Curia. It was in this square that a group of senators murdered Julius Caesar. Below the Lapis Niger rest the underground ruins of a 6th-century BC altar, along with a pyramidal pillar with the oldest known Latin inscription in Rome warning against defiling the shrine. In the square the **Three Sacred Trees** of Rome—olive, fig, and grape—have been replanted by the Italian state. On the other side, a circular tufa basin recalls the **Lacus Curtius,** the chasm into which the legendary Roman warrior Marcus Curtius threw himself in 362 BC to seal the occult fissure and save the city. The newest part of the Forum (aside from the Neoclassical info booth) is the **Column of Phocas,** erected in 608 for the visiting Byzantine emperor, Phocas.

LOWER FORUM. Though built in the early-5th century BC, the **Temple of Saturn** has its mythological origins in the Golden Age of Rome. The temple became the site of Saturnalia, a raucous Roman winter bash where class and social distinctions were forgotten, masters served slaves, and all was permitted. Around the corner, rows of deserted column bases are all that remain of the **Basilica Julia,** a courthouse, built by Julius Caesar in 54 BC. At the far end of the Basilica Julia, three white marble columns and a shred of architrave mark the massive podium of the recently restored **Temple of Castor and Pollux.** According to legend, the twin gods Castor and Pollux helped the Romans defeat the rival Etruscans at the Battle of Lake Regillus (496 BC). Legend says that immediately after the battle, the twins appeared in the Forum to water their horses at nearby **Basin of Juturna** *(Lacus Juturnae).* Down the road from the Temple of Castor and Pollux is the rectangular base of the **Temple of the Deified Julius,** which Augustus built in 29 BC to honor his murdered adoptive father and proclaim himself the nephew of a god. Augustus built the **Arch of Augustus,** which framed the V. Sacra. The circular building behind the Temple of the Deified Julius is the restored **Temple of Vesta,** dating back to the time of the Etruscans. Here the Vestal Virgins tended the city's eternal, sacred fire, keeping it continuously lit for over a thousand years. In a secret room of the temple, where only the Virgins could enter, stood the **Palladium,** the small statue of Minerva that Aeneas was said to have taken from Troy to Italy. Across the square from the Temple of Vesta lies the triangular **Regia,** office of the Pontifex Maximus, Rome's high priest and titular ancestor of the Pope.

UPPER FORUM. The **House of the Vestal Virgins,** shaded by the Palatine Hill, occupied the sprawling complex of rooms and courtyards behind the Temple of Vesta. For 30 years, the six virgins who officiated over Vesta's rites, each ordained at the age of seven, lived in spacious seclusion here above the din of the Forum. The Vestal Virgins were among the most respected people in Ancient Rome. They were the only women allowed to walk unaccompanied in the Forum and also possessed the right to pardon prisoners. This esteem had its price; a virgin who strayed from celibacy was buried alive with a loaf of bread and a candle—to allow her to survive long enough to contemplate her sins. Back on V. Sacra is the **Temple of Antoninus and Faustina** (to the immediate right as you face the entrance ramp), whose strong foundation, columns, and rigid lattice ceiling have preserved it unusually well over the ages. In the 7th and 8th centuries, after numerous unsuccessful attempts to pull the temple down, the **Church of San Lorenzo in Miranda** was built in the interior of the abandoned temple. In the shadow of the temple (to the right as you face it) lies the **necropolis.** Excavations uncovered Iron Age graves from the 8th century BC, lending credence to the city's legendary founding date of 753 BC. Here V. Sacra runs over the **Cloaca Maxima,** the ancient sewer that drains water from the valley. The street passes the **Temple of Romulus** (the round building behind scaffolding), named for the son of Maxentius (not the legendary founder of Rome). Note the original bronze doors, with a working lock from the 4th century AD.

VELIA. V. Sacra leads out of the Forum proper to the gargantuan **Basilica of Maxentius** (also known as the Basilica of Constantine). Emperor Maxentius began construction in AD 306, until Constantine deposed him and completed the project. The uncovered remains of a statue of Constantine, including a 6½ft. long foot, are on exhibit at the **Palazzo dei Conservatori** on the Capitoline Hill. The Baroque facade of the **Church of Santa Francesca Romana** is built over Hadrian's Temple to Venus and Rome—the palindromic *Roma* and *Amor*. It hides the entrance to the **Antiquarium Forense,** a small museum that displays funerary urns and skeletons from the necropolis. (Open daily 9am-1pm. Free.) On the summit of the Velia, the road down from the Palatine, is the **Arch of Titus,** built in AD 81 by Domitian to celebrate his brother Titus, who destroyed Jerusalem 11 years earlier. V. Sacra leads to an exit on the other side of the hill, an easy way to get to the Colosseum. The path that crosses in front of the arch climbs up to the Palatine Hill.

◼ THE COLOSSEUM

M: B-Colosseo. Open daily 9am-6:30pm; in winter daily 9am-1hr. before sunset. L10,000/ €5.16, EU citizens 18-24 L5000/€2.58, EU citizens under 18 and over 60 free. 5-day ticket (L30,000/€15.5) good for the three Musei Nazionali Romani (see p. 473), the Colosseum, and the Palatine Hil. Tours with archaeologist L6000/€3.10. Audioguide in English, French, German, Italian, Japanese, or Spanish L7000/€3.62.

The Colosseum stands as the enduring symbol of the Eternal City—a hollowed-out ghost of travertine marble that dwarfs every other ruin in Rome, once holding as many as 50,000 crazed spectators. Within 100 days of its AD 80 opening, some 5000 wild beasts perished in the bloody arena and the slaughter went on for three more centuries. The floor (now partially restored and open for various concerts and TV shows) covers a labyrinth of brick cells, ramps, and elevators used to transport wild animals from cages up to arena level.

Between the Colosseum and the Palatine Hill lies the **Arco di Costantino,** one of the best-preserved imperial monuments in the area. Constantine built the arch to commemorate his victory over Maxentius at the Battle of the Milvian Bridge in AD

312, using fragments from monuments built by emperors Trajan, Hadrian, and Marcus Aurelius, creating a triple arch.

THE PALATINE HILL

The Palatine rises to the south of the Forum. Open daily 9am-6:30pm; in winter M-Sa 9:30am-1hr. before sunset, Su 9am-1pm; sometimes closes M-F 3pm, Su and holidays noon. Last entrance 45min. before closing. L12,000/€6.2; EU citizens ages 18-24 L6000/ €3.1; EU citizens under 18 and over 60 free. **5-day ticket** *(L30,000/€15.5) good for the three Musei Nazionali Romani (see p. 473), the Colosseum, and the Palatine Hill. May be purchased at the booth beyond the Arch of Titus and on the left in the Forum, 100 yards down V.d.S. Gregorio from the Colosseum, or at the Forum's main entrance. Visit the Palatine after the Forum; to better appreciate views of the Forum after having walked through. The* **"Orti Far- nesini,"** *the hills best for viewing, were closed for renovation work in summer 2001.*

The best way to attack the **Palatine** is from the access stairs steps away from the Arch of Titus in the Forum, which ascend to the **Farnese Gardens.** The hill, actually a plateau between the Tiber and the Forum, was home to the she-wolf that suckled Romulus and Remus. It was here that Romulus built the first walls of the city. During the Republic, the Palatine was the city's most fashionable residential quarter, where aristocrats and statesmen, including Cicero and Marc Antony, built their homes. Augustus lived here in a modest house, but later emperors capitalized on the hill's prestige, building themselves gargantuan quarters. By the end of the first century, the imperial residence swallowed up the entire hill, whose Latin name, Palatium, became synonymous with the palace that dominated it. After the fall of Rome, the hill suffered the same fate as the Forum.

Lower down, excavations continue on the 9th-century BC village, optimistically labeled the **Casa di Romulo.** To the right of the village is the podium of the **Temple of Cybele,** constructed in 191 BC during the Second Punic War. The stairs slightly to the left lead to the **House of Livia.** As Augustus's wife, Livia was the first Roman empress. She had the house, with its vestibule, courtyard, and three vaulted living rooms, connected to the **House of Augustus** next door.

Around the corner, the **Cryptoporticus** connected Tiberius's palace with the buildings nearby. Used by slaves and couriers as a secret passage, it may have been built by Nero in one of his more paranoid moments. The solemn **Domus Augustana** was the private space for the emperors. Adjacent to the Domus Augustana lies the other wing of the palace and the sprawling **Domus Flavia,** site of a gigantic octagonal fountain that occupied almost the entire courtyard. Between the Domus Augustana and the Domus Flavia stands the **Palatine Antiquarium,** the museum that houses the major artifacts found during the excavations of the Palatine Hill. *(30 people admitted every 20min. 9:10am-6:20pm. Free.)* Outside on the right, the palace's east wing contains the curious **Stadium Palatinum,** or Hippodrome, a sunken oval space once surrounded by a colonnade but now decorated with fragments of porticoes, statues, and fountains.

THE DOMUS AUREA

On Oppian Hill, below Trajan's baths. From Colosseum, walk through the gates up V.d. Domus Aurea and make 1st right. ☎06 3996 7700. Open Tu -Su 9am-6:45pm. Groups of 30 admit- ted every 20min. L10,000/€5.16. Guided tour L3000/€1.55. Audioguide L3000/€1.55. Italian tour with archaeologist L6000/€3.10. Reservations L2000/€1.03.

This park houses a portion of Nero's "Golden House," which once covered a substantial chunk of Rome. After deciding that he was a god, Nero had architects build a house to suit his divinity. Between the ends of the palace was an enclosed lake, where the Colosseum now stands, and the Caelian Hill became private gardens. The Forum was reduced to a vestibule of the palace; Nero crowned it with a colossal statue of himself as the sun. Nero pillaged all of Greece to find works of art worthy of the quarters of an emperor, including the famous *Laocoön.* The party didn't last long however, as Nero committed suicide only five years after building his hedonistic pad. Out of civic-mindedness or jealousy the later Flavian emperors tore down his house and replaced all the palace

ROME

with monuments built for the public good. The Flavian Baths were built on the Caelian Hill, the lake was drained, and the Colosseum was erected.

CIRCUS MAXIMUS AND BATHS OF CARACALLA

M: B-Circo Massimo, or walk down V. di San Gregorio from Colosseum. Circus always open. To get to the baths, take V. delle Terme di Caracalla from the eastern end of the Circus. ☎ 06 575 86 26. Baths open daily 9am-6pm; in winter 9am-1hr. before sunset. L8000/€4.13.

Today's Circus Maximus is only a grassy shadow of its former glory. After its construction in 600 BC, the circus drew more than 300,000 Romans, who gathered here to watch chariots careen around the quarter-mile track. The Baths of Caracalla are the largest and best preserved in the city, with beautiful mosaics covering the floors, particularly in the **Apodyteria** (dressing rooms).

FORI IMPERIALI

The sprawling Fori Imperiali lie on either side of V.d. Fori Imperiali, stretching from the Forum to P. Venezia. Excavations will proceed through summer 2002; **the area is closed off,** but you can still get free views peering over the railing from V.d. Fori Imperiali. The large conglomeration of temples, basilicas, and public squares was constructed by emperors from the first century BC to the 2nd century AD, in response to increasing congestion in the old Forum.

FORUM OF TRAJAN. Built between AD 107 and 113, the entire forum celebrated Trajan's victorious Dacian campaign. The complex included a colossal equestrian statue of Trajan and triumphal arch. At one end stands the almost perfectly preserved ▨**Trajan's Column,** one of the greatest specimens of Roman relief-sculpture ever carved. Twenty-five hundred legionnaires have been making their way up the column since AD 113; in 1588, a statue of St. Peter replaced Trajan's.

MARKETS OF TRAJAN. This three-floor semicircular complex is a glimpse of Rome's first shopping mall, featuring an impressive, albeit crumbling, display of sculpture from the imperial forums. *(V. IV Novembre, 94, up the steps in V. Magnanapoli, to the right of the 2 churches behind Trajan's column. ☎ 06 679 00 48. Open Tu-Su 9am-6:30pm. L12,000/€6.2. Save some money and view the markets from the Trajan Forum.)*

FORUMS. Across V. dei Fori Imperiali, in the shade of the Vittorio Emanuele II monument, lie the paltry remains of the **Forum of Caesar,** including the ruins of Julius Caesar's **Temple to Venus Genetrix** (Mother Venus, from whom he claimed descent). Nearby, the gray tufa wall of the **Forum of Augustus** commemorates Augustus's victory over Caesar's murderers at the Battle of Philippi in 42 BC. The aptly named **Forum Transitorium** (also called the **Forum of Nerva**) was a narrow, rectangular space connecting the Forum of Augustus with the Republican Roman Forum. Emperor Nerva inaugurated it in AD 97, dedicating its temple to "Minerva," the deity whose name was closest to his own. The nerva of some rulers! The only remnant of **Vespatian's Forum** is the mosaic-filled **Church of Santi Cosma e Damiano** across V. Cavour, near the Roman Forum. *(Open daily 9am-1pm and 3-7pm.)*

THE CAPITOLINE HILL

Cappella Bufalini open daily 7:30am-6:30pm. Mamertime Prison ☎ 06 679 29 02. Open daily 9am-noon and 2:30-6pm. Donation requested. To get to the Campidoglio, take bus to P. Venezia. From P. Venezia, face the Vittorio Emanuele II monument, walk around to the right to P. d'Aracoeli, and take the stairs up the hill.

Home to the original capital, the Monte Capitolino still serves as the seat of the city's government. Michelangelo designed the spacious **Piazza di Campidoglio.** Surrounding the *piazza* are the twin Palazzo dei Conservatori and Palazzo Nuovo, now the home of the **Capitoline Museums** (see **Museums,** p. 471). From the Palazzo Nuovo, stairs lead up to the rear entrance of the **Chiesa di Santa Maria in Aracoeli,** a 7th-century church now filled with a jumble of monuments. Its stunning **Cappella Bufalini** is home to the *Santo Bambino,* a cherubic statue that receives letters from sick children from all over the world. The gloomy **Mamertine Prison,** consecrated as the **Chiesa di San Pietro in Carcere,** lies down the hill from the back stairs of the Aracoeli. St. Peter, while imprisoned here, baptized his captors with the waters that flooded his cell.

At the far end of the *piazza*, lies the turreted **Palazzo dei Senatori,** which houses Rome's mayor. Paul III had Michelangelo fashion the imposing statues of the twin warriors Castor and Pollux, and also had the famous equestrian **statue of Marcus Aurelius** brought here from the Lateran Palace. Due to air pollution, the statue now resides in climate-controlled comfort in the courtyard of the Palazzo dei Conservatori—a weatherproof copy crowns the *piazza*.

THE VELABRUM

Chiesa di San Nicola ☎ *06 686 99 72; call to visit interior. Open Sept.-July M-Sa 7:30am-noon and 4-7pm.* **Portico** *open daily 9am-7pm.* **Church** *open daily 9am-7pm. Byzantine mass Su 10:30am.*

The Velabrum lies in a flat flood plain of the Tiber, south of the Jewish Ghetto. At the bend of V. del Portico d'Ottavia, a shattered pediment and a few columns in the shadow of the Teatro di Marcello are all that remain of the once magnificent **Portico d'Ottavia.** The **Teatro di Marcello** next door bears the name of Augustus's unfortunate nephew. The pattern of arches and pilasters on the exterior, completed in 11 BC, served as a model for the Colosseum. Farther down V. di Teatro di Marcello toward the Tiber, the **Chiesa di San Nicola in Carcere** incorporates three Roman temples originally dedicated to the gods Juno, Janus, and Spes.

One block farther south along V. Luigi Petroselli lies the **Piazza della Bocca della Verità,** the site of the ancient **Foro Boario,** or cattle market. Across the street, the **Chiesa di Santa Maria in Cosmedin** harbors some of Rome's loveliest medieval decoration. The portico's ▓**Bocca della Verità** was made famous in the Audrey Hepburn film *Roman Holiday*. Originally a drain cover carved as a river god's face, medieval legends maintain that the hoary face will chomp on the hand of a liar.

CENTRO STORICO

PIAZZA VENEZIA AND VIA DEL CORSO

Following the line of the ancient V. Lata, **via del Corso** takes its name from its days as Rome's premier racecourse. It runs nearly a mile between P. del Popolo and the rumbling P. Venezia. The crumbling **Palazzo Venezia,** on the right of the *piazza*, was one of the first Renaissance *palazzi* in the city. Mussolini used it as office space and delivered some of his most famous speeches from its balcony. The *palazzo* is home to the **Museo Nazionale del Palazzo Venezia.** The *loggie* of the interior courtyard and of the **Chiesa di San Marco** date from the Renaissance. (Enter from P. di S. Marco, to the right of the Vittoriano. Church open daily 8:30am-noon and 4-7pm.) Off V. del Corso, **Piazza Colonna** was named for the colossal **Colonna di Marco Aurelio,** designed in imitation of the emperor Trajan's triumphant column. Sixtus V had the statue of St. Paul added to the top of the column in the 16th century. On the opposite side of the *piazza*, **Palazzo Wedekind,** home to the newspaper *Il Tempo*, was built in 1838 with Roman columns from the Etruscan city of Veio. The northwest corner of the *piazza* flows into **Piazza di Montecitorio,** overseen by Bernini's **Palazzo Montecitorio,** now the seat of the Chamber of Deputies.

PIAZZA DELLA ROTONDA

With granite columns and pediment, bronze doors, and a soaring domed interior, ▓**The Pantheon** has remained remarkably similar since it was built nearly 2000 years ago. Architects still puzzle over how it was erected—its dome, a perfect half-sphere constructed from poured concrete without the support of vaults, arches, or ribs, is the largest of its kind. The light entering the roof served as a sundial. In AD 606, the Pantheon was consecrated as the **Church of Santa Maria ad Martyres,** its official name to this day. *(In P. della Rotonda. Open June M-Sa 9am-7pm, Su 9am-1pm; July-Aug. M-Sa 9am-7:30pm, Su 9am-1pm; Oct.-May M-Sa 9am-4pm, Su 9am-1pm. Free.)*

The *piazza* centers on Giacomo della Porta's late-Renaissance fountain, which supports an Egyptian **obelisk** added in the 18th century. Around the left side of the Pantheon, another obelisk, supported by Bernini's curious elephant statue, marks the center of tiny **Piazza Minerva**. Behind the obelisk, the **Chiesa di Santa Maria Sopra Minerva** hides some Renaissance masterpieces, including Michelangelo's *Christ Bearing the Cross*, Antoniazzo Romano's *Annunciation*, and a statue of St. Sebastian recently attributed to Michelangelo. The south transept houses **Cappella Carafa**, with a brilliant fresco cycle by Filippino Lippi. From the upper left-hand corner of P. della Rotonda, V. Giustiniani goes north to intersect V. della Scrofa and V. della Dogana Vecchia. Here stands **Chiesa di San Luigi dei Francesi**, the French National Church, home to three of Caravaggio's most famous paintings: The Calling of St. Matthew, St. Matthew and the Angel, and The Crucifixion. *(Chiesa di Santa Maria Sopra Minerva open M-Sa 7am-7pm, Su 7am-1pm and 3:30-7pm. Chiesa di San Luigi dei Francesi open F-W 7:30am-12:30pm and 3:30-7pm, Th 7:30am-12:30pm.)*

PIAZZA NAVONA

Opened in AD 86, P. Navona housed wrestling matches, chariot races, and mock naval battles, with the stadium flooded and fleets skippered by convicts. Bernini's **Fontana dei Quattro Fiumi** (Fountain of the Four Rivers) commands the center of the *piazza*. Each of the river gods represents one of the four continents of the globe: the Ganges for Asia, the Danube for Europe, the Nile for Africa (veiled, since the source of the river was unknown), and the Rio de la Plata for the Americas. At the ends of the *piazza* are the **Fontana del Moro** and the **Fontana di Nettuno**, designed by Giacomo della Porta in the 16th century and renovated by Bernini in 1653. With a Borromini-designed exterior, the **Church of Sant'Agnese** holds the skull of its namesake saint, martyred in Domitian's stadium after refusing an arranged marriage. *(Open Tu-Sa 4:30-7pm, Su 10am-1pm.)*

West of P. Navona, V. di Tor Millina intersects V. della Pace, steps from the semicircular porch of the **Chiesa di Santa Maria della Pace,** which houses Raphael's gentle *Sibyls* in its **Chigi Chapel**. On nearby C. del Rinascimento, the **Chiesa di Sant'Ivo**'s corkscrew cupola hovers over the **Palazzo della Sapienza**, the original home of the University of Rome. Continue down this road, turn left on C.V. Emanuele, and walk to P. del Gesù to see **Il Gesù**, mother church of the Jesuit Order. *(Open daily 6am-12:30pm and 4-7:15pm.)*

CAMPO DEI FIORI

Campo dei Fiori lies across C.V. Emanuele from P. Navona. During papal rule, the area was the site of countless executions. The stately **Palazzo Farnese** dominates P. Farnese, south of the Campo. Alessandro Farnese, the first Counter-Reformation pope (1534-1549), built this, the greatest of Rome's Renaissance *palazzi*. Since 1635 the French Embassy has rented it for one *lira* a year in exchange for office space in Paris's Hotel Galiffet in Paris, home of the Italian Embassy. To the east of the *palazzo* is the **Palazzo Spada** and the collection of the **Galleria Spada** (p. 472).

THE JEWISH GHETTO

The Jewish community in Rome is the oldest in Europe—Israelites came in 161 BC as ambassadors from Judas Maccabei, asking for Imperial help against invaders. The Ghetto, the tiny area to which Pope Paul IV confined the Jews in 1555, was closed in 1870, but it is still the center of Rome's vibrant Jewish population of 16,000. Take bus #64; the Ghetto is across V. Arenula from Campo dei Fiori.

PIAZZA MATTEI. This square, centered on Taddeo Landini's 16th-century **Fontana delle Tartarughe,** marks the center of the Ghetto. Nearby is the **Church of Sant'Angelo in Pescheria,** installed inside the Portico d'Ottavia in 755 and named after the fish market that flourished here. Jews were forced to attend mass here every Sunday—an act of forced evangelism that they quietly resisted by stuffing their ears with wax. *(Open for prayer meetings W 5:30pm, Sa 5pm.)*

SINAGOGA ASHKENAZITA. Built between 1874 and 1904 at the corner of Lungotevere dei Cenci and V. Catalan, this temple incorporates Persian and Babylonian architectural techniques. Terrorists bombed the building in 1982; guards now search all visitors. The synagogue houses the **Jewish Museum,** a collection of ancient torahs and Holocaust artifacts. *(☎06 687 50 51. Open for services or tour.)*

PIAZZA DI SPAGNA AND ENVIRONS

PIAZZA DI SPAGNA

▨**THE SPANISH STEPS.** Designed by an Italian, paid for by the French, named for the Spaniards, occupied by the British, and under the sway of American ambassador Ronald McDonald, the **Scalinata di Spagna** are decidedly international. When the steps were built in 1725, Romans hoping to be artists' models flocked to the steps dressed as the Madonna and Caesar. The pink house to the right of the Steps was the site of John Keats's 1821 death; it's now the **Keats-Shelley Memorial Museum.**

▨**FONTANA DI TREVI.** Nicolo Salvi's (1697-1751) sparkling-clean **Fontana di Trevi** emerges from the back wall of **Palazzo Poli,** fascinating crowds with the rumble of its cascading waters. Anita Ekberg took a dip in the fountain in Fellini's movie *La Dolce Vita.* Legend has it that a traveler who throws a coin into the fountain is ensured a speedy return to Rome, and one who tosses two will fall in love in Rome. Opposite the fountain is the Baroque **Chiesa dei Santi Vincenzo e Anastasio,** rebuilt in 1630. The **crypt** preserves the hearts and lungs of popes from 1590-1903. *(Open daily 6:45am-noon and 3:30-7:30pm.)*

MAUSOLEUM OF AUGUSTUS AND ARA PACIS. The circular brick mound of the **Masoleo d'Agosto** once housed the funerary urns of the Imperial Roman family. To the west (the right, coming from the P. del Popolo) of the mausoleum stands the glass-encased **Ara Pacis** (Altar of Augustan Peace), a piece of propagandic spin-doctoring completed in 9 BC to celebrate Augustus's success in achieving peace after years of civil unrest and war. The reliefs on the front and back of this marble altar depict figures from Rome's most sacred national myths (a Roman Lupercalia, Aeneas, Tellus the earth goddess, and the goddess Roma) while the side panels show Augustus, his family, his children, and various statesmen and priests. When discovered, the altar was buried 10m underground and submerged in 3m of water. *(Masoleo d'Agosto, in P. Augusto Imperatore; from P. del Popolo, take V. di Ripetta south toward the Tiber. Open sporadically for tours. Ara Pacis open Tu-Sa 9am-7pm, Su 9am-1pm. L3750/€1.94.)*

PIAZZA DEL POPOLO

P. del Popolo, once a favorite venue for executions of heretics, is now the "people's square." In the center is the 3200-year-old **Obelisk of Pharaoh Ramses II,** which Augustus brought back as a souvenir from Egypt. Behind a simple early Renaissance shell, the **Church of Santa Maria del Popolo** holds several Renaissance and Baroque masterpieces. *(☎06 361 04 87. Open M-Sa 7am-noon and 4-7pm, holidays and Su 8am-1:30pm and 4:30-7:30pm.)* The **Della Rovere Chapel** holds Pinturicchio's *Adoration.* Two exquisite Caravaggios, *The Conversion of St. Paul* and *Crucifixion of St. Peter,* are in the **Cappella Cerasi.** Raphael designed the **Cappella Chigi** for the wealthy Sienese banker Agostino Chigi, reputedly once the world's richest man. At the southern end of the *piazza* are the 17th-century **twin churches** of Santa Maria di Montesano and Santa Maria dei Miracoli.

PIAZZA BARBERINI

Rising from the hum of busy traffic at the end of V. del Tritone, Bernini's **Fontana del Tritone** spouts a stream of water over the *piazza,* marking the fulcrum of Baroque Rome. The *piazza* is home to Bernini's **Fontana delle Api** (Bee Fountain). Maderno, Borromini, and Bernini all had a hand in the **Palazzo Barberini,** V. delle Quattro Fontane, 13, home to the **Galleria Nazionale d'Arte Antica,** a collection of paintings from the 11th to 18th centuries (see p. 472). A short way up on the right, at V.V. Veneto, 27a, the severe Counter-Reformation **Church of L'Immacolata Concezione** houses the

ROME

▓**Capuchin Crypt,** where the artfully arranged bones of 4000 Capuchin friars are displayed. (Open F-W 9am-noon and 3-6pm. Donation requested.)

VILLA BORGHESE

M: A-Spagna and follow signs. Or, from M: A-Flaminio, take V. Washington under the archway into the Pincio. From P. del Popolo, climb stairs to the right of Santa Maria del Popolo, cross the street, and climb the small path. BioParco, V.d. Giardino Zoologico, 3 (☎ 06 321 65 64). Open daily 9:30am-6pm; in winter 9:30am-5pm. L14,000/€7.23; ages 4-12 L10,000/€5.16; under 4 and over 60 free. Santa Priscilla catacombs, V. Salaria, 430, just before V. Antica crosses V. Ardeatina. Catacombs and gardens of Villa Ada best reached by bus #57 or #219 from Termini or bus #56 from V.d. Tritone. Get off at P. Vescovio and walk down V.d. Tor Fiorenza to P. di Priscilla to catacombs and park entrance. (☎ 06 8620 6272.) Open Tu-Su 8:30am-noon and 2:30-5pm. L10,000/€5.16.

In celebration of becoming a cardinal, Scipione Borghese built the **Villa Borghese** north of P. di Spagna and V.V. Veneto. Its park is home to three notable art museums, including the world-renowned **Galleria Borghese** (see p. 471), and the intriguing **Museo Nazionale Etrusco di Villa Giulia** (see p. 471). The Borghese is also home to a second-rate, but fun zoo, the **Bio-Parco.** North of Villa Borghese are the **Santa Priscilla catacombs.** The catacombs, along with the gardens of **Villa Ada,** are best reached by bus #57 or 219 from Termini or bus #56 from V. del Tritone. Get off at P. Vescovio and walk down V. di Tor Fiorenza to P. di Priscilla.

VATICAN CITY

Many options: M: A-Ottaviano; M: A-Cipro/Musei Vaticani; bus #64 (beware of pickpockets); #492 from Termini or Largo Argentina; #62 from P. Barberini; #23 from Testaccio. Central Vatican ☎ 06 69 82.

Occupying 108½ independent acres entirely within the boundaries of Rome, Vatican City, the foothold of the Catholic Church, once wheeled and dealed as the mightiest power in Europe. The Lateran Treaty of 1929 which allowed the Pope to maintain all legislative, judicial, and executive powers over this tiny theocracy also requires the Church to remain neutral in Italian national politics and Roman municipal affairs. The nation preserves its independence by minting coins (in Italian *lire* but with the Pope's face), running a separate postal system, maintaining an army of Swiss Guards, and hoarding fine art in the **Vatican Museums** (see p. 470).

BASILICA DI SAN PIETRO (ST. PETER'S)

Write to Information Center, Piazza San Pietro, Città del Vaticano or call ☎ 06 820 19 or 823 50. Dress appropriately —no shorts, miniskirts (i.e. anything above the knee), sleeveless shirts, or sundresses allowed, though jeans and T-shirt are fine. Men must remove hats. Multilingual confession available; languages spoken (about 20) printed outside confessionals by main altar. Pilgrim Tourist Information Center on left between rounded colonnade and basilica. Offers multilingual staff, free brochures, and currency exchange. Next to Information Center is first aid and free bathrooms. Open daily 7am-7pm; Oct.-Mar. 7am-6pm. Mass M-Sa 9, 10, 11am, noon, 5pm; Su 9, 10:30, 11:30am, 12:10, 1, 4, 5:45pm. Cupola closes 75mln. earlier than Basilica, and when the Pope is inside. L7000/ €3.62, elevator L8000/€4.13. Vatican Grottoes open daily 7am-6pm; Oct.-Mar. 7am-5pm. Treasury of St. Peter's open M-Su 9am-6:30pm; closed when the Pope is celebrating mass and on Christmas and Easter. L8000/€4.13, children 12 and under L5000/€2.58.

PIAZZA AND FACADE. As you enter **Piazza San Pietro,** Bernini's colonnade draws you toward the church. Mussolini's broad V. della Conciliazione, built in the 1930s to connect the Vatican to the rest of the city, opened a wider view of St. Peter's than Bernini had ever intended. The obelisk in the center is framed by two fountains. Round disks between each fountain and the obelisk mark the spots where you should stand so that the quadruple rows of Bernini's colonnades visually resolve into one perfectly aligned row. One hundred and forty statues perch above on the colonnade. Those on the basilica represent Christ (at center), John the Baptist, and the Apostles (except for Peter).

ENTRANCE AND PIETÀ. The pope opens the **Porta Sancta** (Holy Door), the last door on the right side of the entrance porch, every 25 years by knocking in the bricks with a hammer. The basilica rests on the reputed site of St. Peter's tomb. The interior of St. Peter's measures 186m by 137m along the transepts. Metal lines on the marble floor mark the lengths of other major world churches. To the right, Michelangelo's *Pietà* has been protected by bullet-proof glass since 1972, when an axe-wielding fiend attacked it, smashing Christ's nose and breaking Mary's hand.

INTERIOR. The crossing under the dome is anchored by four niches with statues of saints. In the center of the crossing, Bernini's bronze **baldacchino** rises on spiral columns over the marble altar. The bronze bees on the canopy are the symbol of the Barberini family, of which Bernini's patron Urban VIII was a member.

CUPOLA. The entrance to the cupola is near the exit from the grottoes. You can take an elevator to the walkway around the interior of the dome or ascend 350 steps to the top ledge of the cupola. This ledge offers an excellent view of the basilica's roof, the *piazza*, the Vatican Gardens, and the hazy Roman skyline.

VATICAN GROTTOES. The Vatican Grottoes are the final resting place of many Catholic VIPs, including emperors and Queen Christina of Sweden. The passages are lined with tombs both ancient and modern, but bright lights, a fresh coat of paint, and reassuring guards make this grotto anything but creepy.

TREASURY OF SAINT PETER'S. The Treasury of St. Peter's contains gifts donated to his tomb. Among the Treasury's highlights are the Solomonic column from the Basilica of Constantine; the "dalmatic of Charlemagne" (an intricately designed robe that the illiterate Holy Roman Emperor donned for sacred ceremonies); a statue of one of Bernini's angels; the magnificent bronze tomb of Sixtus IV; and the stone sarcophagus of Junnius Bassius dating from the fourth century.

CASTEL SANT'ANGELO

*Down V.d. Conciliazione from St. Peter's. To enter, **walk** along river with St. Peter's behind you. It's to the left. Signs point to the entrance. Alternately, cross the Tiber on Bernini's Ponte S. Angelo, which leads directly to the entrance. ☎ 06 687 50 36 or 697 91 11. Open Tu-Su 9am-7pm; in winter daily 9am-7pm. L10,000/€5.16, EU citizens under 18 and over 65 free. **Guided tour** with archaeologist in summer Tu-F 10:30am and 4:30pm, Sa-Su 4:30pm. L8000/€4.13. **Bookstore** offers information and reservations. **Audio guide** in English, French, German, Italian, Japanese, and Spanish L7000/€3.62.*

Built by Hadrian (AD 117-138) as a mausoleum for himself and his family, this mass of brick and stone has served as a fortress, prison, and palace. When the city was wracked with plague in 590, Pope Gregory the Great saw an angel sheathing his sword at the top of the complex; the plague abated soon after, and the edifice was rededicated to the angel. The fortress offers an incomparable view of Rome and the Vatican. Outside, the marble **Ponte Sant'Angelo,** lined with statues of angels designed by Bernini, is the starting point for the traditional pilgrimage route from St. Peter's to the **Church of San Giovanni in Laterano** (see p. 468).

TRASTEVERE

To get to Trastevere, take bus #75 or 170 from Termini to V. Trastevere, or tram #13 from Largo Argentina.

ISOLA TIBERINA

According to Roman legend, the Tiber Island shares its birthday with the Roman Republic; after the Etruscan tyrant Tarquin raped the virtuous Lucretia, her outraged family killed him and threw his corpse in the river, where muck and silt collected around it, forming a land mass. The island, home to the posh Fatebenefratelli Hospital since AD 154, has long been associated with healing. The Greek god Aesclepius appeared to the Romans as a snake and slithered onto the island; his symbol, the caduceus, is visible all over the island.

The 10th-century **Church of San Bartolomeo** has been flooded and rebuilt many times, resulting in the eclectic mix of a Baroque facade, a Romanesque tower, and 14 antique columns. *(Open daily 9am-1pm and 4-6:30pm.)* The bridge leading from Centro Storico, the **Ponte Fabricio,** commonly known as the **Ponte dei Quattro Capi** (Bridge of Four Heads), is the oldest in the city, built by Lucius Fabricius in 62 BC.

CENTRAL TRASTEVERE

Right off the Ponte Garibaldi stands the statue of the dialect poet, G. G. Belli, in the middle of his own *piazza*, which borders the busy P. Sonnino and marks the beginning of V. di Trastevere. On the left is the **Casa di Dante,** where readings of *The Divine Comedy* occur every Sunday from November to March. On V. di Santa Cecilia, behind the cars, through the gate, and beyond the courtyard full of roses, is the **Basilica di Santa Cecilia in Trastevere,** where Stefano Maderno's famous statue of Santa Cecilia lies under the altar. *(Open daily 8am-12:30pm and 2:30-7pm. Cloister open Tu and Th 10-11:30am, Su 11:30am-noon. Donation requested. Crypt L4000/€2.07.)*

From P. Sonnino, V. della Lungaretta leads west to P. di S. Maria in Trastevere, home to numerous stray dogs and expatriates, as well as the **Chiesa di Santa Maria in Trastevere,** built in the 4th century by Pope Julius II. Although the church is being restored, the 12th-century mosaics in the apse and the chancel arch glimmer in full splendor, depicting Jesus, Mary, and a bevy of saints and popes. *(Open daily 7:30am-8:30pm.)* North of the *piazza* are the Rococo **Galleria Corsini,** V. della Lungara, 10 (see **Museo Nazionale dell'Arte Antica,** p. 472) and, across the street, the **Villa Farnesina,** the jewel of Trastevere. Baldassare Peruzzi built the suburban villa for banker-philanthropist Agostino Chigi ("il Magnifico") between 1508-1511. The museum has no paintings; its frescoed walls are the main attraction (see p. 472).

GIANICOLO

*To reach the **summit,** take bus #41 from the Vatican, or ascend via the medieval V. Garibaldi from V. della Scala in Trastevere (about a 10min. walk). **Church** and **Tempietto** open daily 9:30am-12:30pm and 4-6:30pm. **Gardens,** Largo Cristina di Svezia, 24, at the end of V. Corsini, off V. della Lungara. Open Tu-Sa 9am-6:30pm; Oct.-Mar. M-Sa 9am-5:30pm; closed Aug. L4000/€2.07, ages 6-11 and over 60 L2000/€1.03, under 6 free.*

At the top of the hill rests the **Chiesa di San Pietro in Montorio,** built on the spot once believed to be the site of St. Peter's upside-down crucifixion. The church contains *Flagellation*, painted by Sebastiano del Piombo from designs by Michelangelo. Next door in a small courtyard is Bramante's tiny **▇Tempietto.** A combination of Renaissance and ancient architectural elements, it was constructed to commemorate the site of Peter's martyrdom and provided the inspiration for the larger dome of St. Peter's. Rome's **botanical gardens** contain a **garden for the blind** as well as a rose garden that supposedly holds the bush from which all the world's roses are descended.

NORTH OF TERMINI

BATHS OF DIOCLETIAN. From AD 298 to 306, 40,000 Christian slaves were kept busy building these public baths, which could serve 3000 people at once. They contained a heated marble public toilet with seats for 30 people, pools of various temperatures, gymnasiums, art galleries, gardens, libraries, and concert halls. In 1561, Michelangelo undertook his last architectural work and converted the ruins into a church, the **Chiesa di Santa Maria degli Angeli.** In the 4th-century rotonda, to the right as you exit the church, statues from the baths are displayed, as well as viewing windows that look down into the excavations. *(Open M-F 9am-2pm, Sa-Su 9am-1pm. Free. Church open daily M-Sa 7am-6:30pm, Su 8am-7:30pm.)*

PIAZZA DEL QUIRINALE. At the southeast end of V. del Quirinale, this *piazza* occupies the summit of the tallest of Rome's seven hills. The President of the Republic officially resides in the imposing **Palazzo del Quirinale,** a Baroque architectural collaboration by Bernini, Maderno, and Fontana. Down V. del Quirinale,

V. Ferrara on the right leads down the steps to V. Milano. At the corner of V. Milano and V. Nazionale towers the **Palazzo delle Espozioni,** home to temporary art exhibitions. Farther along the street lies the marvelous facade of Borromini's **Chiesa di San Carlo alle Quattro Fontane,** often called **San Carlino.**

VIA XX SETTEMBRE. The intersection of V. del Quirinale and V. delle Quattro Fontane showcases one of Pope Sixtus V's more gracious additions to the city. In the corner of each of the four surrounding buildings is a fountain with a reclining figure. V. del Quirinale becomes V. XX Settembre at this intersection and, after a few more blocks, opens into the Baroque P. San Bernardo, site of Domenico Fontana's colossal 1587 **Fontana dell'Acqua Felice.** The beefy statue of Moses is said to have been carved by Prospero Antichi, who nearly died of disappointment after seeing the finished product. Across the way, the **Church of Santa Maria della Vittoria** is named for an icon of Mary that helped the Catholics win a battle near Prague in 1620. Inside, Bernini's fantastic *Ecstasy of St. Theresa of Ávila* (1652) resides in the Cornaro Chapel. *(Open daily 7:30am-12:30pm and 4-6:30pm.)*

VIA NOMENTANA. This road runs northeast from Michelangelo's **Porta Pia** out of the city. Hop on bus #36 in front of Termini, or head back to V. XX Settembre and catch bus #60. A 2km walk from Porta Pia past villas, embassies, and parks brings you to **Chiesa di Sant'Agnese Fuori le Mura,** V. Nomentana, 349. Its apse displays Byzantine-style mosaic of St. Agnes. Underneath the church wind some of Rome's most impressive ▧**catacombs.** *(☎ 06 8620 5456. Open Tu-Su 9am-noon and 4-6pm, closed M afternoons. Catacombs L8000/€4.13. English guidebook available.)*

SOUTH OF TERMINI

BASILICA DI SANTA MARIA MAGGIORE. As one of the five churches in Rome granted extraterritoriality, this basilica, which crowns the Esquiline Hill, is officially part of Vatican City. In 352, Pope Sixtus III commissioned the basilica when he noticed that Roman women were still visiting a temple to the pagan mother-goddess Juno Lucina. When Sixtus enthusiastically tore down the temple to build his new basilica, he not only substituted a Christian cult for a pagan one, but also celebrated the Council of Ephesus's recent ruling of Mary as the Mother of God. To the right of the altar, a marble slab marks the **tomba di Bernini** (Bernini's tomb). The 14th-century mosaics in the church's **loggia** recount the story of the miraculous August snowfall that showed the pope where to build the church. *(From Termini, go south onto V. Giolitti, and go down V. Cavour. Open daily 7am-7pm. Loggia open daily 9:30am-noon and 2-5:30pm. Tickets in souvenir shop; L5000/€2.58. Dress code enforced.)*

PIAZZA VITTORIO EMANUELE II AND ENVIRONS. Home to one of Rome's largest outdoor markets, the shabby P.V. Emanuele is found at the end of V.C Alberto, from S. Maria Maggiore. Take V.S. Croce in Gerusalemme from the eastern end of P. V. Emanuele to see the Rococo facade of the **Church of Santa Croce in Gerusalemme.** Scores of pilgrims come to catch a glimpse of the Fascist-era **Chapel of the Relics,** which contains fragments of the "true cross." Perhaps the eeriest of the chapel's relics is the dismembered finger used by St. Thomas to probe Christ's wounds. *(Open M-Sa 9:30am-noon and 3-6pm, Su and holidays 9:30am-noon and 2:30-5:30pm.)*

CHURCH OF SAN PIETRO IN VINCOLI. Dating from the 4th century, San Pietro in Vincoli is so-named after the sacred chains by which St. Peter was supposedly bound after having been imprisoned on the Capitoline. The two chains were separated for more than a century in Rome and Constantinople, brought back together in the 5th century, and now lie beneath the altar. Michelangelo's imposing ▧**statue of Moses** presides regally over the church. *(M: B-Cavour. Alternatively, take bus #75 to Largo V. Venosta. Walk southwest on V. Cavour, down toward the Forum. Take the stairs on your left up to P.S. Pietro in Vincoli. Open daily 7am-12:30pm and 3:30-7pm.)*

SOUTHERN ROME

CAELIAN HILL

M: B-Colosseo. Turn left out of station, walk east on V. Fori Imperiali (V. Labicana) away from the Forum, and turn right onto P.S. Clemente. ☎06 7045 1018. Open M-Sa 9am-12:30pm and 3-6pm, Su and holidays 10am-12:30pm and 3-6pm. Lower basilica and mithraeum L5000/€2.58.

The Caelian and the Esquiline are the biggest of Rome's seven original hills. In ancient times, Nero built his decadent Domus Aurea between these hills (see p. 459). In the wake of its destruction, many of Rome's early churches were constructed at the **⌧Church of San Clemente.** Split into three levels, each from a different era, this is one of Rome's most intriguing churches. The complex incorporates centuries of handiwork into three layers: a 12th-century church on top of a 4th-century church, with an ancient **mithraeum** and sewers at the bottom. The upper church holds medieval mosaics of the Crucifixion, saints, and apostles. A fresco cycle by Masolino dating from the 1420s graces the **Chapel of Santa Caterina.**

The early plan of the sprawling 4th-century lower church has been obscured by piers and walls built to support the upper church. With a little imagination, one can trace the lines of the original nave, aisles, and apse, which retain rare 11th-century frescoes. On this level are a few curiosities, including the tomb of St. Cyril and a series of frescoes depicting Roman generals swearing in Italian, the first written use of the language. Further underground is a creepy 2nd-century **mithraeum.** A little further lies the insulae, a warren of brick and stone rooms where Nero is rumored to have played his lyre in AD 64 while the rest of Rome burned. Below this is a still-operative complex of Republican drains and sewers, some 30m down.

SAN GIOVANNI

*M: A-San Giovanni or bus #16 from Termini. **Church of San Giovanni in Laterano** open daily 7am-7:30pm. Cloister open daily 9am-6pm. Enter from P.S. Marco, to the right of the Vittoriano. L4000/€2.07. Dress code enforced. **Scala Santa,** across street from S. Giovanni. Open M-Sa 6:15am-noon and 3-6:15pm, Su 6:15am-noon and 3:30-6:45pm.*

The immense **Church of San Giovanni in Latero,** the cathedral of the diocese of Rome, was home to the pope until the 14th century. Founded by Constantine in 314, it's Rome's oldest Christian basilica. The Gothic *baldacchino* houses two golden reliquaries containing the heads of **St. Peter** and **St. Paul.** Housing the *acheropite* image, a depiction of Christ not created by human hand, **Scala Santa** also houses what are believed to be the 28 marble steps used by Jesus outside Pontius Pilate's house in Jerusalem. Pilgrims win indulgence for their sins if they ascend the steps on their knees, reciting prayers on each step. Martin Luther experienced an early break with Catholicism while on pilgrimage here—in the middle of his way up the cathedral's steps he realized the futility and false piety of what he was doing, stood up, and left.

THE AVENTINE HILL

The easiest approach to the Aventine is from the western end of the Circus Maximus (the end farthest from the Circo Massimo Metro stop) at P. Ugo la Malfa. From here, V. di Valle Murcia climbs past Rome's swankiest homes and a beautiful public rose garden to a park with orange trees and a sweeping view of southern Rome. Across the park, another gate opens onto the courtyard of the **Chiesa di Santa Sabina,** with a porch of ancient columns and a towering *campanile.* V.S. Sabina continues along the crest of the hill to **Piazza dei Cavalieri di Malta,** home of the crusading order of the Knights of Malta. Through the **keyhole** in the pale yellow gate on the right, you can see the dome of St. Peter's perfectly framed by hedges.

THE APPIAN WAY

CHURCH OF SANTA MARIA IN PALMIS. In this church, known as Domine Quo Vadis, a fleeing St. Peter had a vision of Christ. Asked "Domine Quo Vadis?" ("Lord, where are you going?"), Christ replied that he was going to Rome to be crucified again because Peter had abandoned him. Instead Peter returned to Rome and suffered his own martyrdom. In the middle of the aisle lie Christ's alleged footprints set in stone. *(At the intersection of V. Appia Antica and V. Ardeatina. Take bus #218 from P. di S. Giovanni. Open daily 9am-noon and 4-7pm.)*

CATACOMBS. Since burial inside the city walls was forbidden during ancient times, fashionable Romans made their final resting places along the Appian Way, while early Christians secretly dug maze-like **catacombs** under the ashes of their persecutors. **San Callisto** is the largest catacomb in Rome, with nearly 22km of subterranean paths. Its four levels once held 16 popes, seven bishops, St. Cecilia, and 500,000 other Christians. **Santa Domitilla** enjoys acclaim for paintings housing an intact 3rd-century portrait of Christ and the Apostles. **San Sebastiano** was the temporary home for the bodies of Peter and Paul. *(M: A-San Giovanni. Take **bus** #218 from P.S. Giovanni to intersection of V. Ardeatina and V.d. Sette Chiese. Each L8000/€4.13. **Free tour** every 20min. **San Sebastiano:** V. Appia Antica, 136. From #218 bus stop near S. Callisto and S. Domitilla, walk down V. Sette Chiese to V. Appia Antica and turn right. ☎06 788 10 35. Open M-Sa 8:30am-noon and 2:30-5:30pm; closed Nov. Adjacent church open daily 8am-6pm. **San Callisto:** V. Appia Antica, 110. Take private road that runs northeast to catacombs's entrance. ☎06 51 30 15 80. Open M-Tu and Th-Su 8:30am-5:30pm; in winter Th-Su 8:30am-noon and 2:30-5pm; closed Feb. **Santa Domitilla:** V.d. Sette Chiese, 282. Facing V. Ardeatina from exit of San Callisto, cross street and walk right up V. Sette Chiese; catacombs on left. ☎06 511 03 42. Open W-M 8:30am-5:30pm; in winter W-M 8:30am-5pm; closed Jan.)*

TESTACCIO AND OSTIENSE

South of the Aventine Hill, the working-class district of Testaccio is known for its cheap and delicious *trattorie* and raucous nightclubs. Take the Metro (B) to the Piramide stop or bus #27 from Termini. The neighborhood centers on the castle-like **Porta San Paolo** (an original remnant of the Aurelian walls) and the colossal **Piramide di Gaius Cestius,** which was built in about 330 days by the slaves of Gaius.

CIMITERO ACATOLICO PER GLI STRANIERI. This peaceful Protestant cemetery, or the "Non-Catholic Cemetery for Foreigners," is the only non-ancient burial space in Rome for those who don't belong to the Catholic Church. Keats, Shelley, and Antonio Gramsci were buried here. *(V. Caio Cestio, 6. From the Piramide station, follow V. R. Persichetti onto V. Marmorata, immediately turning left onto V. Caio Cestio. Open Tu-Su 9am-5:30pm; Oct.-Mar. 9am-4:30pm. Ring bell for admission. Donation requested.)*

MONTE TESTACCIO. Monte Testaccio began as a dumping ground for terra-cotta pots. The pile grew and grew, and today the ancient garbage heap, with a name derived from *testae,* or pot shards, rises in lush, dark green splendor over the drab surrounding streets. *(At the end of V. Caio Cestio and across V. Nicola Zabaglia.)*

BASILICA DI SAN PAOLO FUORI LE MURA. The Basilica di San Paolo Fuori le Mura, another of the churches in Rome with extraterritorial status, is the largest church in the city after St. Peter's. St. Paul is believed to be buried beneath the altar. Be sure to buy a bottle of monk-made **benedictine** in the gift shop (L13,000/€6.71). *(M: B-Basilica San Paolo. Or take bus #23 or 769 from Testaccio at the corner of V. Ostiense and P. Ostiense. Open daily 7am-6:30pm; in winter 7am-6pm. Cloister open 9am-1pm and 3-6:30pm; in winter 9am-1pm and 3-6pm. Dress code enforced.)*

EUR

South of the city stands a monument to a Roman empire that never was. Take bus #714 or the Metro (B) to **EUR** (AY-oor), an Italian acronym for Universal Exposition of Rome, the 1942 World's Fair that Mussolini intended to be a showcase of Fascist achievements. Apparently, the new, modern Rome was to shock and impress the rest of the world with its futuristic ability to build lots of identical square buildings. **Via Cristoforo Colombo,** EUR's main street, is the first of many internationally ingratiating addresses like "Viale Asia" and "Piazza Kennedy." It runs north from the Metro station to **Piazza Guglielmo Marconi** and its 1959 modernist **obelisk** (see p. 473).

ROME

ABBAZIA DELLE TRE FONTANE (ABBEY OF THE THREE FOUNTAINS). According to legend, when St. Paul was beheaded here, his head bounced on the ground three times, creating a fountain at each bounce. The Trappist monks who live here today sell their own potent eucalyptus liquor for L14-27,000/€7.23-13.94, enormous bars of divine chocolate for L9-18,000/€4.65-9.30. (*M: B-Laurentina. Exit metro station and walk straight to V. Laurentina; go right and proceed ¾ mi. north on V. Laurentina and turn right onto V.d. Acque Salve. Open daily 9am-noon and 3-6pm.*)

🏛 MUSEUMS

Etruscans, emperors, and popes have been busily stuffing Rome's belly full with artwork for several millennia, leaving behind a city teeming with galleries. Museums are generally closed and holidays, Sunday afternoons, and all day Monday.

VATICAN MUSEUMS

Walk north from right-hand side of P.S. Pietro along the Vatican City wall for about 10 blocks. From M: Ottaviano, turn left on V. Ottaviano and continue walking until the Vatican City wall, turn right and follow the wall to museum's entrance. ☎06 6988 3333 or 6988 4341. *Information and gift shop (with useful official guidebook, L12,000/€6.2) on ground level past building entrance.* **Currency exchange** *and* **first aid** *stations near ticket booths.* **Audio guide** *with information and amusing anecdotes L8000/€4.13. Guides available in major languages. Major galleries open Mar. 16-Oct. 30 M-F 8:45am-4:45pm, Sa 8:45am-1:45pm; Nov.-Mar. 15 M-Sa 8:45am-1:45pm. Last entrance 1hr. before closing. Closed on major religious holidays. Busiest parts of museum are wheelchair accessible. L18,000/€9.3, with ISIC card L12,000/€6.2, children under 1m tall free. Free last Su of the month 8:45am-1:45pm.*

The Vatican Museums constitute one of the world's greatest collections of art, a vast storehouse of ancient, Renaissance, and modern statuary, painting, and sundry papal odds and ends. The museum entrance at V. Vaticano leads to the famous bronze double-helix ramp that climbs to the ticket office. A good place to start your tour is the stellar **Museo Pio-Clementino,** the world's greatest collection of antique sculpture. Two slobbering Molossian hounds guard the entrance to the **Stanza degli Animali,** a marble menagerie that highlights the importance of brutality in Roman pastimes. Among other gems, it features the ⬛**Apollo Belvedere** and the unhappy **Laocoön** family. The last room of the gallery contains the enormous red sarcophagus of Sant'Elena, Constantine's mother.

From here, the Simonetti Stairway climbs to the **Museo Etrusco,** filled with artifacts from Tuscany and northern Lazio. Back on the landing of the Simonetti Staircase is the Stanza della Biga (room of an ancient marble chariot) and the Galleria della Candelabra. The long trudge to the Sistine Chapel begins here, passing through the Galleria degli Arazzi (tapestries), the Galleria delle Mappe (maps), the Apartamento di Pio V (where there is a shortcut to *la Sistina,* for all the cheaters out there), the Stanza Sobieski, and the Stanza della Immaculata Concezione.

From the Room of the Immaculate Conception, a door leads into the first of the four ⬛**Stanze di Rafaele,** apartments built for Pope Julius II in the 1510s. One *stanza* features Raphael's **School of Athens,** painted as a trial piece for Julius, who was so impressed that he fired his other painters, had their frescoes destroyed, and commissioned Raphael to decorate the entire suite. From here, there are two paths: a staircase leading to the brilliantly frescoed Borgia Apartments and the **Museum of Modern Religious Art** and another route leading to the Sistine Chapel.

SISTINE CHAPEL. Ever since its completion in the 16th century, the Sistine Chapel (named for its founder, Pope Sixtus IV) has served as the chamber in which the College of Cardinals elects new popes. The ceiling, which is flat but appears vaulted, gleams with the results of its recent restoration. The frescoes on the side walls predate Michelangelo's ceiling. On the right, scenes from the life of Moses complement parallel scenes of Christ's life on the left. The cycle was completed between 1481 and 1483 under the direction of Perugino by a team of artists including Botticelli, Ghirlandaio, Roselli, Pinturicchio, Signorelli, and della Gatta.

The simple compositions and vibrant colors of Michelangelo's unquestioned masterpiece hover above, each section depicting a story from Genesis. The scenes are framed by the famous *ignudi*, young nude males. Michelangelo painted not flat on his back, but standing up and craning backward, and he never recovered from the strain to his neck and eyes. Michelangelo's *The Last Judgement* fills the altar wall. The figure of Christ as judge hovers in the upper center, surrounded by his saintly entourage and the supplicant Mary.

PINACOTECA. This is one of the best painting collections in Rome, including Filippo Lippi's *Coronation of the Virgin*, Perugino's *Madonna and Child*, Titian's *Madonna of San Nicoletta dei Frari*, and Raphael's *Transfiguration*. On your way out of the Sistine Chapel, take a look at the **Room of the Aldobrandini Marriage,** which contains a series of rare and famous ancient Roman frescoes.

PRINCIPAL COLLECTIONS

GALLERIA BORGHESE

Piazzale Scipione Borghese, 5. M: A-Spagna; take exit labeled "Villa Borghese," walk right past the metro stop to V. Muro Torto to P. Porta Pinciana. Viale del Museo Borghese will be in front of you. This road leads to the museum. Or, take bus #910 from Termini to V. Pinciana or follow Villa Borghese exit signs and head left up the road to reach V. del Museo Borghese. Signs in park point the way. ☎06 8548 5 77. Open Tu-F 9am-7:15pm; entrance only on the hr., visits limited to 2hr.; last entrance 30min. before closing. Limited number of people admitted every 2 hours; gallery does sell out, so book ahead. Bags must be checked. L14,000/€7.23, EU citizens ages 18-25 L8000/€4.13, EU citizens under 18 and over 65 L2000/€1.03. Tickets include ground floor galleries and Pinacoteca. Tickets may be reserved in advance by phone or in person, fee L2000/€1.03.

This is an exquisite museum, but you'll only have two hours to visit it, not enough time to linger. Room I, on the right, houses Canova's sexy statue of **Paolina Borghese** portrayed as Venus triumphant. The next rooms display the most famous sculptures by Bernini: a magnificent **David**, crouching in controlled aggression with his slingshot; **Apollo and Daphne**; the weightless body in **Rape of Proserpina;** and weary-looking Aeneas in **Eneo e Anchise.** Don't miss six **Caravaggio** paintings, including the *Self Portrait as Bacchus* and *St. Jerome*, which grace the side walls. The collection continues in the *pinacoteca* upstairs, accessible from the gardens around the back by a winding staircase. Room IX holds Raphael's **Deposition** while Sodoma's *Pietà* graces Room XII. Also look for self portraits by Bernini, del Conte's *Cleopatra* and *Lucrezia*, Rubens's haunting **Pianto sul Cristo Morto,** and Titian's **Amor Sacro e Amor Profano.**

MUSEO NAZIONALE ETRUSCO DI VILLA GIULIA

*In Villa Borghese at P. Villa Giulia, 9. M: A-Flaminio or **bus** #19 from Piazza Risorgimento or #52 from P.S. Silvestro. From Galleria Borghese, follow V. Dell'Uccelliera to the Zoo, and then take V.d. Giardino to V.d. Bell Arte. Museum on left, after Galleria Arte Moderna. ☎06 320 19 51. Open Tu-F, Su, and holidays 8:30am-7:30pm, Sa 9am-8pm. Extended hours June-Sept. Sa 9am-11pm. L8000/€4.13, EU citizens and Southern and Central Australians under 18 and over 65 free, Canadians under 15 free. **Audioguide** L8000/€4.13 and **guidebook** L20,000/€10.33 available at bookstore outside entrance.*

The villa was built under Pope Julius III, who reigned from 1550 to 1555. Highlights include a graceful sarcophagus of a man and wife in Room 9 and an Etruscan chariot, or biga, and the petrified skeletons of two horses found beside it in Room 18. Upstairs, archaeologists have put together the fragments of the entire facade of an Etruscan temple, complete with terra-cotta gargoyles, chips of the original paint, and a relief of the Greek warrior Tydaeus biting into the brain of a wounded adversary. Don't miss the famous Euphronios vase in a special exhibit near the giftshop.

CAPITOLINE MUSEUMS

Top of Capitoline Hill, behind Vittorio Emanuele II monument. ☎06 3974 6221. Open Tu-Su 10am-8pm, holidays 9am-2pm. Ticket office closes 1hr. earlier. Parts wheelchair

ROME

accessible. L15,000/€7.75, with ISIC L11,000/€5.68, EU citizens under 18 and over 65 free. Guidebook L30,000/€15.5. Audioguide L7000/€3.62. English tours L6000/€3.10.

The collections of ancient sculpture in the Capitoline Museums are among the largest in the world. The Palazzo Nuovo contains the original statue of **Marcus Aurelius** that once stood in the center of the *piazza*. The sculpture rooms contain notables like *Dying Gaul*, *Satyr Resting*, and *Venus Prudens*. The sculpture collections continue across the piazza in the Palazzo dei Conservatori. See the fragments of the **Colossus of Constantine** and the famous **Capitoline Wolf**, an Etruscan statue that has symbolized the city of Rome since ancient times. At the top of the stairs, the pinacoteca houses an assortment of 16th- and 17th-century Italian paintings. Among the masterpieces not purloined by the Vatican Galleries are Bellini's *Portrait of a Young Man*, Titan's *Baptism of Christ*, and Rubens's *Romulus and Remus Fed by the Wolf*. Also worth seeing are Caravaggio's *St. John the Baptist* and his *Gypsy Fortune-Teller*.

MUSEO NAZIONALE D'ARTE ANTICA

__Palazzo Barberini:__ V.d. Quattro Fontane, 13. M: A-Barberini. ☎ 06 481 45 91. Open Tu-Sa 9am-7pm, Su 9am-8pm. L12,000/€6.20; EU citizens ages 18-25 L7000/€3.62; EU citizens under 18 and over 65, and art and architecture students L2000/€1.03. __Galleria Corsini:__ V.d. Lungara, 10. Opposite Villa Farnesina in Trastevere. Bus #23; exit between Ponte Mazinni and Ponte Sisto. ☎ 06 6880 2323. Open Tu-Su 8:30am-1pm. L8000/ €4.13, EU students L4000/€2.06, Italian art students and EU citizens over 65 free.

This collection of 12th- through 18th-century art is split between Palazzo Barberini and Palazzo Corsini. The former houses more masterpieces, but both deserve a visit. **Palazzo Barberini** contains paintings from the medieval through Baroque periods, including works by Lippi, Raphael, El Greco, Carracci, Caravaggio, and Poussin. **Galleria Corsini** holds a collection of 17th- and 18th-century paintings, from Dutch masters Van Dyck and Rubens to Italians Caravaggio and Carracci.

VILLA FARNESINA

V.d. Lungara, 230. Just across from Palazzo Corsini on Lungotevere Farnesina. Bus #23. Get off between Ponte Mazinni and Ponte Sisto. ☎ 06 6802 7268. Open M-Sa 9am-1pm. L8000/€4.13, under 18 L6000/€3.1, EU citizens over 65 free.

Thought to be the wealthiest man in Europe, Agostino "il Magnifico" Chigi lived sumptuously in the villa. At a banquet, Chigi had his guests toss his gold and silver dishes into the Tiber River after every course (the shrewd businessman had hidden nets under the water to recover his treasures). To the right of the entrance lies the breathtaking **Sala of Galatea,** mostly painted by the villa's architect, Baldassare Peruzzi, in 1511. The vault displays symbols of astrological signs that add up to a symbolic plan of the stars at 9:30pm on November 29, 1466, the moment of Agostino's birth. The masterpiece of the room is Raphael's **Triumph of Galatea.**

The stucco-ceilinged stairway, with its gorgeous perspective detail, ascends to the **Loggia di Psiche,** for which Raphael received the commission. The **Stanza delle Prospettive,** a fantasy room decorated by Peruzzi, offers views of Rome between *trompe l'oeil* columns. The adjacent bedroom, known as the *Stanza delle Nozze* (Marriage Room), is the real reason for coming here. Il Sodoma, who had previously been busy painting the pope's rooms in the Vatican, frescoed the room until Raphael showed up and stole the job. Il Sodoma bounced back, making this extremely masterful fresco of Alexander the Great's marriage to the beautiful Roxanne.

GALLERIA SPADA

P. Capo di Ferro, 13, in the elaborate Palazzo Spada. From Campo dei Fiori, take any small street leading to P. Farnese. Go left onto Capo di Ferro. Bus #64. ☎ 06 32 81 01. Open Tu-Sa 8:30am-1:30pm, Su 8:30am-12:30pm. Last tickets sold 30min. before closing. L10,000/€5.16, EU students L5000/€2.58, EU citizens under 18 and over 60 free.

Seventeenth-century Cardinal Bernardino Spada bought a grandiose assortment of paintings and sculpture and commissioned an even more opulent set of great rooms to house them. Time and good luck have left the palatial apartments nearly intact—a visit to the gallery offers a glimpse of the luxury surrounding Baroque courtly life. In the first of the gallery's four rooms, the cardinal hung three portraits of himself by Guercino, Guido Reni, and Cerini. In the portrait-studded Room 2, look for paintings by the Venetians Tintoretto and Titan and a frieze by Vaga, originally intended to be placed in the Sistine Chapel. In Room 4 are three canvases by the father-daughter team of Orazio and Artemisia Gentileschi.

MUSEI NAZIONALI ROMANI

Museo Nazionale Romano Palazzo Massimo: Largo di Via Peretti, 1. In left-hand corner of P. dei Cinquecento as you stand with your back to Termini. ☎ 06 481 55 76; group reservations ☎ 06 3996 7700. Open Tu-Su 9am-7:45pm; ticket office closes 7pm. L12,000/ €6.20, EU citizens ages 18-24 L6000/€3.10, EU citizens under 18 and over 60 free. *Museo Nazionale Romano Terme di Diocleziano:* P. dei Cinquecento, 78. Opposite Termini. ☎ 06 3996 7700. Open Tu-Su 9am-7pm. L8000/€4.13, EU citizens 18-24 L4000/ €2.07, EU citizens under 18 and over 60 free. Audioguide L7000/€3.62; guided tour with archaeologist L10,000/€5.16. *Aula Ottagonale:* V. Romita, 8. ☎ 06 3996 7700. Open Tu-Sa 9am-2pm. Free. *Museo Nazionale Romano Palazzo Altemps:* P. Sant'Apollinare, 44. Just north of P. Navona. ☎ 06 783 35 66. Open Tu-Su 9am-7pm. L10,000/€5.06, EU citizens ages 18-24 L5000/€2.58, EU citizens under 18 and over 65 free. *6-day ticket book* (L15,000/€7.75) good for 3 museums and Terme di Diocletian; admission to Colosseum, Palatine Hill, and Terme Caracalla bumps price up to L30,000/€15.50.

The fascinating **Museo Nazionale Romano Palazzo Massimo** is devoted to the history of Roman art during the Empire, including the Lancellotti Discus Thrower, a rare mosaic of Nero's, and ancient coins and jewelry. Nearby, the **Museo Nazionale Romano Terme di Diocleziano,** a beautifully renovated complex partly housed in the huge **Baths of Diocletian** (p. 466) has exhibits devoted to ancient epigraphy (writing) and Latin history through the 6th century BC. The Aula Ottagonale, another wing, holds 19 classical sculptures in a gorgeous octagonal space. Across town is the Renaissance man of the trio, **Museo Nazionale Romano Palazzo Altemps,** P.S. Apollinaire, 44, just north of P. Navona. On display is ancient Roman sculpture, including the famous 5th-century *Ludovisi Throne.*

EUR MUSEUMS

Museo della Civiltà Romana: P. Agnelli, 10. Down V. Civiltà Romana. ☎ 06 592 60 41. Open Tu-Sa 9am-7pm, Su and holidays 9am-1:30pm. L8000/€4.13, reduced price L5000/€2.58, under 18 and over 60 free. *Museo dell'Alto Medievo:* V. Lincoln, 3. ☎ 06 5422 8199. Open daily 9am-8pm; L4000/€2.07, reduced price L2000/€1.03, under 18 and over 65 free. *Museo Nazionale delle Arti Tradizioni Popolari:* P. G. Marconi, 8. ☎ 06 591 07 09; www.ips.it/musis/museo_arti. Open Tu-Su 9am-8pm; closed New Year's, May Day, and Christmas. Call for tours in Italian or Braille. L8000/€4.13, reduced price L4000/€2.06, under 18 and over 65 free. *Museo Preistorico ed Etnografico Luigi Pigorini:* P.G. Marconi, 14. ☎ 06 549 5 21; reservations ☎ 06 841 23 12. Guided tours in Italian, ☎ 06 841 23 12. Open daily 9am-8pm. L8000/€4.13, EU citizens ages 18-25 L4000/€2.07, under 18 and over 65 free.

If anything good came of Mussolini's regime, it just might be the extensive collections in that bastion of fascist organization and architecture, EUR. The expansive **Museo della Civiltà Romana** contains excellent and comprehensive exhibits on ancient Rome, including incredibly intricate scale models of Trajan's Column (p. 460) and Republican and Imperial Rome. The smallest of the museums, the **Museo dell'Alto Medievo,** exhibits weapons and other artifacts from the Dark Ages. The **Museo Nazionale delle Arti Tradizioni Popolari** preserves Italian folk art and incredible replicas of traditional attire and farming equipment. Finally, the **Museo Preistorico ed Etnografico Luigi Pigorini** contains a collection of ethnographic artifacts, including the skull of the Neanderthal Guattari Man, found in Circeo. It often hosts visiting exhibitions.

OTHER COLLECTIONS

■ **MUSEO CENTRALE TERMOELETTRICA MONTEMARTINI.** The building, a turn-of-the-century electrical plant, is a striking contrast to the Classical sculpture on

ROME

display. Highlights include *Hercules' Presentation at Mount Olympus*, a huge and amazingly well-preserved floor-mosaic of a hunting scene. *(V. Ostiense, 106. M: B-Piramide. From P. Ostiense, walk to the right of the train station to V. Ostiense. Then, walk or take bus #702 or 23 three stops. ☎ 06 574 80 30. Open Tu-Su 10am-6pm. L8000/€4.13, EU citizens ages 18-24 L5000/€2.58, EU citizens under 18 and over 65 free.)*

GALLERIA COLONNA. Despite its disorganization and inhospitable opening hours, the Galleria Colonna remains an impressive collection of art. The *palazzo* was designed in the 18th century to show off the Colonna family jewels, among them Tintoretto's *Narcissus*. *(V.d. Pilotta, 17. Just north of P. Venezia in the Centro Storico. ☎ 06 6678 4330. Open Sa 9am-1pm; closed Aug. L10,000/€5.16, students L8000/€4.13, children under 10, adults over 65, military, and disabled persons free. Tours of Princess Isabella's apartments available by appointment; groups of 10 needed, L25,000/€12.91 per person. Free tours in English 11:45am.)*

GALLERIA DORIA PAMPHILJ. The Doria Pamphilj family, whose illustrious kin included Pope Innocent X, remain in custody of this stunning private collection, which they display in their palatial home. The villa's Classical art is arranged by size and theme. Seek out the masterpieces, such as Caravaggio's *Rest During the Flight in Egypt* and Raphael's *Double Portrait*. Also catch the preserved corpse (from the catacombs) in the small chapel. *(P.d. Collegio Romano, 2. From P. Venezia, walk up V. del Corso and take your 2nd left. ☎ 06 679 73 23. Open F-W 10am-5pm, last tickets 4:15pm; closed Jan. 1, Easter, May 1, Aug. 15, and Christmas. L14,000/€7.23, students and seniors L11,000/€5.68. Private apartments open 10:30am-12:30pm. L6000/€3.10.)*

MUSEO BARRACCO. This impeccably arranged collection includes some Greco-Roman art, but its Egyptian and Assyrian holdings are the real attractions. Don't miss the 16th-century BC *Sphynx of Queen Hatshepsut*. *(C. Vittorio Emanuele II, 166. At intersection of C. Vittorio Emanuele II and V. Baullari, across from P. Navona. ☎ 06 6880 6848. Open Tu-Sa 9am-7pm, Su 9am-1pm. L5000/€2.58, students L3000/€1.55.)*

MUSEO NAZIONALE D'ARTE ORIENTALE. This museum sports a wide array of artifacts dating from prehistory to the 1800s, divided into six sections: evolution of art in the Near East, Islamic art, Nepalese and Tibetan art, Buddhist art from India, Southeast Asian art, and Chinese history. Highlights include Stone Age fertility dolls and paintings of the Buddha. *(V. Merulana, 248. In Palazzo Brancaccio on Esquiline Hill. ☎ 06 487 44 15. Open M, W, and F 9am-2pm, Tu and Th 9am-7pm, Su 9am-1pm; closed 1st and 3rd M of every month. L8000/€4.13, Italian citizens under 18 and over 60 free.)*

MUSEO CRIMINOLOGICO. After overdosing on "artwork" and "culture," get your aesthetic stomach pumped at this museum dedicated to crime and punishment. Torture devices comprise the first floor, as well as some old English etchings, among them *A Smith Has His Brains Beaten Out With a Hammer*. On the second floor, learn about criminal phrenology and the secret language of tattoos. The third floor contains terrorist, spy, and drug paraphernalia. *(V. del Gonfalone, 29. Near Ponte Mazzini. ☎ 06 6830 0234. Open Tu 9am-1pm and 2:30-6:30pm, W 9am-1pm, Th 2:30-6:30pm, F-Sa 9am-1pm. May be closed Aug. L4000/€2.07, under 18 and over 60 L2000/€1.03.)*

🎵 ENTERTAINMENT

LIVE MUSIC

There are many opportunities to see solid musical performances in Rome. *Telecom Italia* hosts a classical music series at the Teatro dell'Opera. At 9am on concert days, unsold tickets are given out for free at the box office. Be prepared to get in line early; tickets go on a first come, first served basis. Local churches often host free choral concerts—check newspapers tourist offices and church bulletin boards for details. Finally, and perhaps most interestingly, the *carabinieri* frequently give rousing concerts of various Italian composers in P. di San Ignazio and other outdoor forums free of charge.

🎷 **Alexanderplatz Jazz Club,** V. Ostia, 9 (☎06 3974 2171). M: A-Ottaviano. Near Vatican City. From the station, head west on V.G. Cesare, take 2nd right onto V. Leone IV and 1st left onto V. Ostia. Night buses to P. Venezia and Termini leave from P. Clodio. Known as one of Europe's best jazz clubs. Read messages left on the walls by the greats who played here, from old pros like Art Farmer and Cedar Walton to young stars like Steve Coleman and Josh Redman. Cocktails L12,000/€6.2. Required *tessera* (L12,000/ €6.2), good for 2months. Open Sept.-June daily 9pm-2am. Shows start 10:30pm.

Accademia Nazionale di Santa Cecilia (main ☎06 361 10 64, info ☎ 678 07 42). This conservatory, named for the martyred patron saint of music (see p. 466 for the full story), was founded by Palestrina in the 16th century, and is home to Rome's official symphony orchestra. Orchestra and chamber concerts are held at the **Auditorio Pio,** V. di Conciliazione, 4 (☎06 6880 1044), near the Vatican, while the Academy's grand new concert hall is being built. Regular season runs Oct.-June, covering the classics. From late-June to late-July, the company moves outdoors to the *nymphaeum* in Villa Giulia or to the Baths of Caracalla. Auditorio Pio box office open Th-Tu 10:20am-1:30pm and 3-6pm, and until showtime on concert days. Tickets L20-50,000/€10.33-25.82. Auditorio Pio's acoustics are bad, so consider splurging on expensive seats.

Big Mama, V.S. Francesco a Ripa, 18 (☎06 581 25 51), off V. di Trastevere on the left as you face the river. Blues, blues, and more blues. A *tessera* (L20,000/€10.33), valid for a year, gains entrance to the club's free concerts. Cover L10,000/€5.16 for big-name groups. Open Oct.-June daily 9pm-1:30am; sometimes closed Su-M.

Stardust, V. dei Rienzi, 4 (☎06 5832 0875). Take a right off V. Lungaretta onto V.d. Moro, right before P.S. Maria in Trastevere; 2nd street on the left. Classy cocktail bar; live jazz. Open daily 7pm-4am; in winter M-F 1:30pm-3am, Sa-Su 11am-2am.

Berimbau, V. dei Fienaroli, 30b (☎06 581 32 49). Rome's premier location for Brazilian music. Live music followed by raging disco of salsa, merengue, and other Latin music. Cover L10-25,000/€5.16-12.91, includes 1 drink. Open W-Su 10:30pm-3:30am.

THEATER

Roman theaters, though not on par with those in other major European cities, still generate a number of quality productions, ranging from mainstream musicals to black-box experimental theater. For information on English theater, check the tourist office or the English section of *Roma C'è*. Useful websites include www.musical.it and www.comune.rome.it.

Teatro Argentina, Largo di Torre Argentina, 52 (☎06 6880 4601 or 687 54 45). Bus #64 from Termini. Considered the most important theater in Rome, Argentina hosts plays (in Italian), concerts, and ballets. Teatro Argentina also has many drama/music festivals throughout the year. Box office open M-F 10am-3pm and 3-7pm, Sa 10am-2pm. Tickets about L40,000/€20.66; students L30,000/€15.5. AmEx/MC/V.

CINEMA

Unfortunately, most theaters in Rome show dubbed movies. Look for a "v.o." or "l.o." in any listing; it means *versione originale* or *lingua originale* (i.e., not dubbed). In the summer, huge screens come up in *piazze* around the city for **outdoor film festivals.** These night shows can be a lot of fun, but remember insect repellent. One of the most popular is the **San Lorenzo sotto le Stelle** film festival at Villa Mercede, V. Tiburtina, 113, with shows at 9 and 11pm (L10-15,000/€5.16-7.75). Also, films are usually shown outdoors on the southern tip of Tiber Island. Visit the **I Love Rome** website (www.alfanet.it/welcomeItaly/roma/default.html) for an excellent searchable database of films, theaters, and showtimes. While *Roma C'è* isn't as comprehensive, it does a good job of indexing films.

🎬 **Il Pasquino,** P.S. Egidio, 10 (☎06 583 33 10 or 580 36 22), off P.S. Maria in Trastevere. Rome's biggest English-language movie theater. Program changes daily, so call for the schedule or pick one up. L12,000/€6.2; reduced L8000/€4.13. Theaters 2 and 3 are a film club, pay L2000/€1.03 for 2months. membership and L10,000/€5.16 for the ticket. Look for the Roma International Film Festival during the summer.

Nuovo Sacher, Largo Ascianghi, 1 (☎06 581 81 16). This is the famed Italian director Nanni Moretti's theater, and shows a host of Indy films. M films in the original. L13,000/€6.71, matinee and W L8000/€4.13.

SPECTATOR SPORTS

Though May brings international tennis and equestrian events, sports basically revolve around *calcio*, or soccer. Rome has two teams in Serie A, Italy's prestigious league: the 2000 European champion **A.S. Roma** and **S.S. Lazio.** The wild games at the **Stadio Olimpico,** in Foro Italico, are held almost every Sunday (sometimes Saturdays) from September to June, with European cup matches often played mid-week. The can't-miss matches of the season are the two Roma-Lazio games, which often prove decisive in the race for the championship. Single-game tickets, typically starting at L30,000/€15.5, can be bought at the stadium before games (although lines are long and tickets often run out), or at team stores: **A.S. Roma Store,** P. Colonna, 360 (☎06 678 65 14), off V. del Corso, and **Lazio Point,** V. Farini, 24 (☎06 4826 688). Many sporting events sell tickets at **Orbis Agency,** P. dell'Esquilino, 37 (☎06 482 74 03).

▣ NIGHTLIFE

Roman entertainment isn't what it used to be. Back in the day, one could swing by the Colosseum to watch gladiators battle lions, and tigers, and bears (oh my!). Today, Romans seek diversion at the local Testaccio nightclub. Still, Rome abounds with exciting entertainment options. Check out the weekly *Roma C'è* (with an English-language section) or *Time Out*, available at newsstands, for comprehensive club, movie, and event listings.

Rome has fewer gay establishments than most cities its size, but those it has are solid. Many establishments require an **ARCI-GAY pass** (L20,000/€10.33 yearly), available from **Circolo di Cultura Omosessuale Mario Mieli** (☎06 541 39 85). Of the clubs listed below, **Qube** hosts gay nights. *Time Out* has good coverage of gay events.

PUBS

If you long for organized, indoor drunkenness, try one of Rome's countless pubs. Diverse crowds and lively music draw huge crowds. After a few, you might just forget you're in Italy; most pubs in Rome are Irish, complete with Irish music, dark wooden interiors, and black rays of sunshine (a.k.a. Guiness).

▨ **Jonathan's Angels,** V.d. Fossa, 14-16 (☎06 689 34 26), west of P. Navona. Take V.d. Governo Vecchio from Campo dei Fiori, turn left at the Abbey Theatre onto V. Parione, and then left toward the lights. Michelangelo's accomplishments pale before the bathroom at Jonathan's Angels, the ▨ finest bathroom in Rome, nay, Italy. Jonathan himself holds court in the right bar, his son, Jonathan II, spins underground techno on the left. Medium beer on tap L10,000/€5.16; delicious cocktails/long drinks L15,000/€7.75. Mercifully free of pub-crawlers. Open daily 4pm-2am.

▨ **Trinity College,** V.d. Collegio Romano, 6 (☎06 678 64 72), off V.d. Corso near P. Venezia. Offers degrees in such diverse curricula as Guinness, Harp, and Heineken. Tuition L6-9000/€3.1-4.65. Pub food served for lunch and dinner. Hamburgers L14,000/€7.23. Happy Hour noon-8pm. Classes daily noon-3am.

▨ **Il Simposio,** V.d. Latini, 11 (☎0328 9077 8551). Ah, the sweet smell of turpentine. Symposium's walls are cluttered with the Jackson Pollock-esque works of local artists, and chances are good that on any given night a splattered painter will be hard at work beautifying some old frige. With cocktails from L6000/€3.1 and a glass of *fragolino* for L5000/€2.58, even starving artists can afford the place. Open daily 9pm-2am.

▨ **Pub Hallo'Ween,** P. Tiburtino, 31 (☎06 444 07 05), at the corner of V. Tiburtina and V. Marsala. Abandon all hope of not having fun, ye who enter here. The plastic skulls and spiderwebs confirm your suspicions that this is a gateway to the pits of Hell. Draft beer L6-8000, bottles L7-10,000/€3.62-5.16. Cocktails L10,000/€5.16. Enjoy delicious sandwiches (L10,000/€5.16) such as the Freddy (salami and mozzarella) or the Candyman (nutella). Open daily 8:30pm-2:30am; closed Aug.

The Drunken Ship, Campo dei Fiori, 20-21 (☎06 6830 0535). Because you're tired of meeting Italians. Because you feel the need to have an emotion-free fling with a kindred spirit. Because you're proud to be an American, dammit. A brew will set you back L8000/€4.13. Happy hour daily 5-9pm. Su is Ladies' night, Tu brings half price Tequila, and W 9-10pm power hour—all the beer you can drink (L10,000/€5.16). Student discount on Heineken. Also with takeout window. Open daily 5pm-2am. AmEx/MC/V.

Sloppy Sam's, Campo dei Fiori, 9-10 (☎06 6880 2637). The poor cousin of the Drunken Ship. Note that upon returning home, wistful stories about that "special someone" you "befriended" at Sloppy Sam's will be regarded somewhat cynically. Happy Hour 4-9pm. Tu 2-for-1 special. Beer L8000/€4.13; shots L5000/€2.58. Open Su-Th 4pm-12:30am, F-Sa 4pm-1:30am. AmEx/MC/V.

Julius Caesar, V. Castelfidardo, 49 (☎06 446 15 65), just north of Termini near P. dell'Indipendenza, on the corner of V. Solferino. Packed with backpackers and locals, here for live music, cheap drinks, and good times. Upstairs features beer on tap (L10,000/€5.16), cheeky Roman busts, and even cheekier Roman babes. Downstairs filled with blaring live music most nights 10:30-11:30pm. Happy Hour half-price in the early evening. Cocktails L10,000/€5.16; wine L30,000/€15.50 per bottle. Ask for *Let's Go* discount. Open daily 4pm-2am.

CLUBS

Although Italian discos can be a flashy, sweaty good time, you must overcome some obstacles before donning your dancing shoes. First, you won't meet many non-Italians (could be nice for a change). Second, the scene changes as often as Roman phone numbers. Third, many clubs flee beachward for the steaming summer to **Fregene, Ostia,** or **San Felice Circeo.** Check *Roma C'è* or *Time Out.*

▨ **Qube,** V. Portonaccio, 212 (☎06 438 10 05). From P. di Porta Maggiore, take V. Prenestina east; turn left on V. Portonaccio. Seedy neighborhood; plan to take cab home. Warehouse-style disco. One of Rome's biggest. 3 dance floors. Su "Transmania," is a very popular gay night. Cover L10-20,000/€5.16-10.33. Open Th-Su 11pm-4am.

Charro Cafe, V. di Monte Testaccio, 73 (☎06 578 30 64). So you wanted to go to Tijuana, but got stuck in Rome. Weep no more, *mis amigos:* make a run for Charro, home of the L5000/€2.58 tequila *bum bum.* Italians guzzling a good selection of beer (L10,000/€5.16) and strong Mexican-themed mixed drinks (L10,000/€5.16) dance themselves silly to pop and house. Cover L10,000/€5.16, includes 1 drink. Restaurant M-Sa 8:30-11:30pm; club 11:30pm-3:30am.

Aquarela, V. di Monte Testaccio, 64 (☎06 575 90 58), next door to Radio Londra. You want pottery shards? You got pottery shards. A fine example of urban renewal, Roman-style. Built out of ancient trash, then used for years as a vegetable market, the club consists in part of two underground tunnels that remain cool even when the party's heatin' up. Cover L20,000/€10.33, includes 1 drink. Open Tu-Su 8:30pm-3am.

Caruso, V. di Monte Testaccio, 36 (☎06 574 50 19). No opera here: Caruso is a reliable venue for live salsa, DJed hip hop, rap and R&B. 5 rooms of tropical decor, packed with writhing Latino wannabes on Sa nights. Live music F. Monthly *tessera* L15-20,000/€7.75-10.33. Open Tu and Th-Su 11:30pm-3am.

Radio Londra Caffè, V. di Monte Testaccio, 65b (☎06 575 00 44). Admit it: you've always fantasized about watching Italian bands cover rock classics badly. Good-looking, energetic crowd. Pint of Carlsberg L7000/€3.62. Pizza and hamburgers (L8-12,000/€4.13-6.2). Monthly *tessera* L10,000/€5.16. Open Su-F 9pm-3am, Sa 9pm-4am.

ROME

C.S.I.O.A. Villaggio Globale, Lungotevere Testaccio (☎06 5730 0329). Take bus #27 from Termini, get off before it crosses the river, and head left down the river. Women probably don't want to travel alone on the Lungotevere at night. One of the best-known *centri sociali* in Rome—your one-stop shop for all things countercultural. In a huge Testaccio slaughterhouse. Hosts live music, films, art exhibits, poetry readings, African cuisine tastings, and more. F nights usually hopping. Hours and cover vary.

Jungle, V. di Monte Testaccio, 95 (☎06 574 66 25). A small, smoky disco bar full of black leather-wearing Italian Goths dancing to the Cure and Italian pop. Extravagant, if somewhat disorienting, light effects. Cover L10-15,000/€5.16-7.75. Sa free before 11. Beer L10,000/€5.16; cocktails L15,000/€7.75. Open F-Sa 11pm-5am.

NEAR ROME

Rural Lazio was originally called *Latium*, Latin for "wide land." Lazio stretches from the low Tyrrhenian coastline through volcanic mountains to the foothills of the Abruzzese Apennines. Romans, Etruscans, Latins, and Sabines all settled here, and their contests for supremacy make up some of the first pages of Italy's recorded history. When Rome's mayhem overwhelms you, head for the hills.

TIVOLI

Water is the inspiration and the chief attraction of the city of Tivoli, a hilltop town perched 120m above the Aniene River, only an hour from Termini. The poets Horace, Catullus, and Propertius once vacationed in villas lining the rocks overhanging the river. Modern Tivoli stretches beyond the original narrow strip, providing dynamic views of Rome from its hilly streets and gardens. Three distinct villas are its principal sites.

⌐⃗ TRANSPORTATION AND PRACTICAL INFORMATION. Take the **Metro (B)** to Rebibbia from Termini (15min.). Exit the station; follow the signs for Tivoli through an underpass to reach the other side of V. Tiburtina. Find the marker for the blue **ACOTRAL bus** to Tivoli. Tickets (L3000/€1.55) are sold in the bar next door or in the subway station. Once the bus climbs up to Tivoli (25min.), get off past P. Garibaldi at P. delle Nazioni Unite. (The bus back to Rome leaves from P. Garibaldi.). The **tourist office,** a round shack with a big "I" in front, is on the street leading from P. Garibaldi. It has information on the villas, restaurant and hotel maps, and bus schedules. (☎0774 31 12 49. Open M-Sa 9:45am-3pm.) For **Villa d'Este,** sneak your way through the gauntlet of souvenir stands through P. Trento, and it's on the left. For **Villa Gregoriana,** follow V. di Sibilla across town. For **Villa Adriana,** 5km from Tivoli proper, take the orange #4x bus from the newsstand in P. Garibaldi. Tickets (L1400/€0.72) are sold at the news kiosk.

◎ VILLAS. Villa d'Este, a castle-garden, was laid out by Cardinal Ercole d'Este (the son of Lucrezia Borgia) and his architect Piero Ligorio in 1550 with the idea of recreating an ancient Roman *nymphaea* and pleasure palace. Spectacular terraces and fountains abound. (☎0774 31 20 70. Open May-Aug. daily 8:30am-6:30pm; Sept.-Apr. 9am-1hr. before sunset. On Su, villa closes 1½hr. earlier. L8000/€4.13, EU citizens under 18 and over 65 free.) **Villa Gregoriana** is a park with paths that descend past temples and scattered grottoes carved out by rushing water. The star of the show is the **Great Cascade,** where the river plunges 160m from the opening of Gregory XVI's tunnel. *(The Villa has been closed indefinitely for restorations. Call the Tivoli tourist office for more info.)* Visit the vast remains of **Villa Adriana.** The villa is the largest and most expensive ever built in the Roman Empire. Emperor Hadrian designed its buildings in the 2nd century in the styles of monuments that he had seen in his travels. Look for the Pecile, built to recall the famous Stoa Poikile (Painted Porch) of Athens, and the Canopus, an expanse of water lined by classical statues that replicates a canal near Alexandria, Egypt. (☎0774 53 02 03. *Open daily 9am-1½hr. before sunset. L12,000/€6.20, EU students L6000/€3.10. Audioguide L7000/€3.62. Parking L3000/€1.55.*)

ETRURIA

Welcome to Etruscanland, former home of a mythologized tribe that dominated north-central Italy during the first millennium BC. Since the Etruscans' buildings were wood, only their carved-out tufa tombs survive. Tomb paintings (at Tarquinia) celebrate life, love, eating, drinking, and sport in the hilly countryside.

TARQUINIA

When Rome was but a village of mud huts on the Palatine hill, Tarquin kings commanded this fledgling metropolis. Although little remains of the city, a subterranean necropolis of tombs lined with vibrant frescoes illustrates Tarquinia's history. In P. Cavour stands the majestic **Museo Nazionale,** one of the most comprehensive collections of Etruscan art outside Rome. It houses a superb patrimony of Etruscan sarcophagi, some with paintings still visible on the sides, votive statues, and an enormous range of Etruscan and (occasionally sexy) Greek vases. Look for the famous **Winged Horses** upstairs. (☎0766 85 60 36. *Open Tu-Su 9am-7pm. L12,000/€6.20.*) The ticket from the museum will admit you to the **necropolis.** Take the bus marked "Cimitero" from Barriera S. Giusto or walk 15 minutes from the museum. Head up C.V. Emanuele from P. Cavour and turn right on V. Porta Tarquinia. Follow this road as it changes its name to V. delle Tombe Etruschi until you reach the necropolis. (☎0766 85 63 08. *Open daily 9am-1hr. before sunset.*)

Trains leave from Termini (1hr.; 11 per day, last train leaves Tarquinia 10:12pm; L10,200/€5.27). **Buses** run from the train station to the beach and city center (every 30min. until 9:30pm; beach L1100/€0.57, city center L1500/€0.77). Buses link Tarquinia with **Viterbo** (1hr., L6000/€3.1). For bus schedules and information on Etruria, try the **tourist office** in P. Cavour, near the medieval walls. (☎0766 85 63 84. *Open daily 8am-2pm and 4-7pm.*)

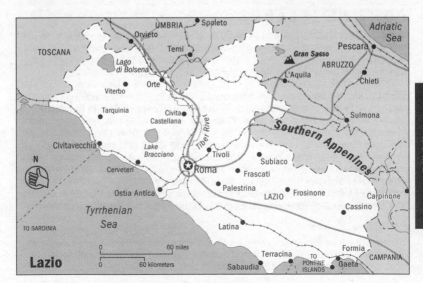

Lazio

CERVETERI

Take a flashlight and duck: the ■**Etruscan tombs** of **Cerveteri's Banditaccia Necropolis** are a bit awkward to see but every bit worth the trouble. They remain a testament to a people that thought they could take it with them—those crazy Etruscans built a lasting city of stone houses for their dead, with multiple rooms you can now walk into, while their actual houses have decayed into oblivion. Look for the colored stucco reliefs in the **Tomba dei Rilievi.** (☎06 994 00 01. Open M, Tu-Su 9am-7:30pm; Oct.-Apr. Tu-Sa 9am-4pm. L8000/€4.13.)

To get to Cerveteri, first take the **Metro (A)** or **bus** #70 to Lepanto, and then take the blue **COTRAL bus** to Cerveteri from Lepanto (every 30min.-1hr., L4900/€2.53). To the **necropolis,** it's 1½km from the village along a country road; follow the signs downhill and then to the right. Whenever you see a fork in the road without a sign to guide you, choose the fork on the right, but don't follow the "Da Paolo Vino" sign at the final fork. From Cerveteri, the last bus leaves for **Rome** at 8:05pm, with less frequent service on Sundays. The **tourist office,** V.d. Necropoli, 2, will answer queries. (☎06 995 23 04. Open Tu-Su 9:30am-12:30pm and 6-7:30pm.)

LAKE BRACCIANO

Lake Bracciano provides Rome with its nearest freshwater beach, about an hour away by bus. Despite volcanic sand that may hurt your rear, this huge body of water is still a great place to spend the day. Fresh air, cool water, and a lush and hilly surrounding landscape compensate for its minor flaws. The impressive 15th-century **Orsini-Odescalchi Castle** dominates the town and offers some stunning frescoes and stuffed wild boars. (☎06 9980 4348; www.odescalchi.it. Open Apr.-Sept. Tu-Su. Tours in English 10:30, 11:30am, 3:30, 5:30pm. L11,000/€5.68, children under 12 and military L9000/€4.65.) See *Roma C'è* for listings of classical concerts often held here in the summer. Bracciano's many *trattorie* cook up mounds of fresh lake fish and eel (the local specialty), though siestas often go a little overboard, and hours of operation are inconsistent. Down at the beach, a ferry ride across the lake to nearby **Anguillara** or **Trevignano** offers more spectacular scenery.

To get to Lake Bracciano, take **Metro (A)** to Lepanto, then take the **COTRAL bus** from Lepanto to Lake Bracciano (L3900/€2.01). Anguillara and Bracciano are also accessible by **train** on the Rome-Viterbo line (every hr.; from Rome's San Pietro station 5:35am-9:45pm, last return to Rome 10:14pm; L5300/€2.74).

PONTINE ISLANDS

The ■**Pontine Islands,** a stunning archipelago of volcanic mountains 40km off the coast of Anzio, were once a haven for the notorious Saracen and Corsican pirates. The cliff-sheltered beaches, turquoise waters, assorted coves, tunnels, and grottoes provided the pirates a place to unwind after pillaging and plundering.

Take *aliscafi* (hydrofoils) or slower, cheaper *traghetti* (larger car ferries) to the islands. **From Rome,** take the **train** from Termini to Anzio (L56,000/€28.93) and then the **CAREMAR ferry** from Anzio to Ponza (June 16-Sept. 23 M-F 1pm, Sa 8:30am, Su and holidays 8:30am and 3pm; return M-F 5pm, Sa 5:15pm, Su and holidays 11am and 5:15pm; L35,000/€18.08). The **CAREMAR ticket office** in Anzio (☎06 9860 0083; www.caremar.it) is in the white booth on the quay; in Ponza (☎0771 805 65). Or, take the faster **Linee Vetor** hydrofoils (3-5 per day; 8:15am-5:15pm, return 9:50am-6pm; L36,000/€18.6, resident L13,000/€6.71). **Linee Vetor ticket office** in Anzio (☎06 984 50 83; www.vetor.it) is on the quay; in Ponza (☎0771 805 49). **From Formia, CAREMAR** runs 2 boats a day (L35,000/€18.08; 9am-5:30pm, return 5:30am and 2:30pm), as does **Vetor** (8:10am-2:30pm, return 10am-6:30pm; L36,000/€18.6).

PONZA

Excellent beaches are everywhere on Ponza. **Cala dello Schiavone** and **Cala Cecata** (on the bus line) are excellent spots. Essential points of sun-bathing interest, however, are **Chiaia di Luna** and ■**Piscine Naturali.** A 10min. walk from the port will take you to Chiaia, set at the foot of a spectacular 200m cliffside. A lovely ride through Ponza's hillside will take you to the even lovelier Piscine Naturali (take the bus to Le Foma and ask to be let off at the Piscine. Cross the street and make go down the long, steep path.) Cliffs crumbling into the ocean create a series of deep, crystal-clear natural pools separated by smooth rocky outcroppings perfect for sunbathing. Rumor has it that there are spots for cliff-diving in the area, though *Let's Go* does not officially recommend throwing yourself off 15m cliffs.

To navigate Ponza, **Autolinee Isola di Ponza buses** leave from V. Dante (every 15-20min. until 1am; buy tickets from driver L1750/€0.90). Follow C. Pisacane until it becomes V. Dante (past the tunnel); the stop is on the left. Buses stop by request, so flag them down at stops. **Water taxis** leave near the docks and go to the beaches and harbors around the island (from L6000/€3.10 roundtrip; arrange pick-up time with driver). **Pro Loco tourist office,** V. Molo Musco, at the port's far right next to the lighthouse, is in the red building. (prolocoponza@libero.it. Open in summer M-Sa 9am-1pm and 4-8:30pm, Su 9am-1pm and 5-8:10pm.)

Hotel rooms on Ponza hover in the L200,000/€103.29 zone. *Let's Go* recommends forgoing hotels entirely and checking out one of many *immobiliare vacanze* (vacation property) offices instead. The tourist office has a list of over 10 helpful agencies that can assist you in finding a room or apartment. The folks at ▓**Isotur,** Corso Piscacane, 18, are friendly and, more importantly, can set you up with a double room in nearby Santa Maria, which is really an extension of Ponza. (☎0771 803 39; agenzia.isotur@tin.it; www.isotur.it. Doubles June L70,000/€36.15 per night, July L90,000/€46.48, Aug. L130,000/€67.14.) Restaurants are on the expensive side, with plates of pasta generally around L20,000/€10.33, but **Ristorante da Antonio,** on the water at V. Dante (☎0771 80 98 32) has seafood and a view that render it well worth the splurge.

PALMAROLA

Palmarola is an uninhabited islet perched off the northeast coast of the island. The irregular volcanic rock formations and steep white cliffs of the island are incredible. As you approach Palmarola, you will see **Dala Brigantina,** a natural lime amphitheater. Most excursions visit the **Pilatus Caves** at Ponza, a breeding ground for fish.

Palmarola is only accessible by **boat.** Either rent one (from L65,000/€33.57 per day) or sign up for a **boat tour** offered by one of the many offices at the port advertising *"una gita a Palmarola".*

ZANNONE

Zannone is a nature and wildlife preserve, offering nature-lovers a refreshing break from the beach. Tours will take visitors around the coast, allowing time for walks on the *mufloni*-strewn island, through the *lecci* forests, and to the medieval monastery of S. Spirito. Zannone is only accessible by **boat.** Take one with **Cooperativa Barcaioli Ponzesi** (☎0771 80 99 29.), on C. Piscacane at the S. Antonio tunnel (10:30am, return 6pm; L35,000/€18.08.)

VENTOTENE

Far less accessible than Ponza (and freer of summer vacationing hordes), Ventotene is also more striking. Cars and *motorini* are verboten and the calm of island life is disturbed only by the hum of outboard motors. The tourist office offers tours of various archaeological sites, and splendid beaches flank the port.

To rent boats in Ventotene, go to the port. **Motor boats** cost L60,000/€31, **rowboats** L20,000/€10.33. To get to Ventotene from Ponza, take the **CAREMAR hydrofoil** (daily 6:10am except Oct.-Apr. Su; return Oct. 16-Apr. 14 4pm, Sept. 23-Oct. 15 5:40pm, Aug. 15-Sept. 22 7:10pm; L20,500/€10.59). The **tourist office,** Centro Servizio Ventotene, Località Porto Romano, is at the port. (☎0771 852 73. Open daily 9am-1pm and 4:30-7pm; in winter 4-7pm.)

SOUTHERN ITALY

CAMPANIA

To the casual observer, life in Campania might appear to center on natural disasters. The submerged city at Baia, lava-smothered Pompeii, and the ruins of Benevento attest to a land at the mercy of the ancient mythical elements of water, fire, wind, and earth. The variation found throughout the region offers not only death and destruction (and that rarely enough), but also something for every visitor. There's the bustle of Naples's nightlife and the draw of glittering churches and ancient museums. But when the city streets get too hot and the water calls, the islands off the Amalfi coast are sprinkled with windswept beaches and hidden coves. Invigorating hikes over the extraordinary volcanoes that dot the countryside provide panoramas unrivaled by any other in the rest of the country.

Campania

HIGHLIGHTS OF CAMPANIA

DELIGHT in the Farnese Bull, the largest ancient sculpture, and marvel at the Alexander mosaic in Naples's **Museo Archeologico Nazionale** (p. 552).

CATCH Pompeii (p. 503) in the act and be a volcanic voyeur.

DIVE into Capri's glowing **Grotta Azzurra** (p. 514).

RELISH the glorious beaches and stunning seascapes of the **Amalfi Coast** (p. 520).

RESOUND in the **Temple of Mercury** in Baia (p. 500).

GO templing in **Paestum** (p. 531), home to remarkably preserved Greek monuments.

NAPLES (NAPOLI) ☎081

Italy's third-largest city is trying desperately to emerge from the shadow of its *brutta reputazione*. Rampant poverty, unemployment rates closing in on 25%, and a northern Italian political party itching to cut the country in half at Rome assure that problems abound, but Naples is making progress, and old stereotypes are less applicable now than ever. More cops on the streets and the advent of the Napoli 99, a group of citizens determined to maintain the city's art and restore public monuments have made Naples not a *brutta città* with a few scattered wonders, but a *luoga bella* (beautiful locale) with some surmountable vices. UNESCO recently declared Naple's historic center as that with the most architectural variety in the world. The narrow streets are a constant flurry of people and cars, and the historic center is a treasure trove of *piazzas, palazzi*, exquisite churches, artisan's workshops, and colorful *trattorie*. Considering its location near islands, volcanoes, and beaches, Naples has much to offer.

⊠ INTERCITY TRANSPORTATION

Flights: Aeroporto Capodichino (☎081 789 67 42) V. Umberto Maddalena, northwest of city. Convenient **CLP bus** (☎081 531 17 06 or 531 17 07) leaves from P. Municipio (20min., 6am-10:30pm, L3000/€1.55). The #15 or 3S city buses runs from P. Garibaldi to airport (L1500/€1.29). A **taxi** from the center costs L25,000/€12.49. **Alitalia**, V. Medina, 41/42 (☎848 865 643), off P. Municipio. Open M-F 9am-4:30pm. **TWA**, V. Cervantes, 55 (☎081 551 30 63). Open M-F 9am-5:30pm. **British Airways** (☎848 812 266). Open M-F 8am-8pm, Sa 9am-5pm. **Lufthansa** (☎06 656 840 04).

Trains: Naples is served by 3 train companies that each leave from **Stazione Centrale**.

FS: Frequent connections to: **Brindisi** (5hr.; 5 per day 11am-8pm; L35,600/€8.85); **Milan** (8hr.; 13 per day 7:30am-10:30pm; L96,000/€49.58); **Rome** (2hr.; 34 per day 4:30am-10:06pm; L18,600/€9.61); **Salerno** (45min., 8 per day 8am-9pm, L5300/€2.74); **Syracuse** (10hr.; 6 per day 10am-9:30pm; L55,000/€28.41).

Circumvesuviana: (☎081 772 24 44). From Stazione Centrale (one floor underground) to: **Herculaneum** (L2300/€1.19); **Pompeii** (L3200/€1.65); and **Sorrento** (L4800/€2.48). Trains depart every 30min. 5:09am-10:39pm.

Ferrovia Cumana and **Ferrovia Circumflegrea:** (☎081 551 33 28). Luggage storage available (p. 490). Both run Metro lines from Montesanto station to **Pozzuoli, Baia,** and **Cumae.** Trains depart every 20min. Info booth in Stazione Centrale open daily 7am-9pm.

Ferries: Ferry schedules and prices change constantly; check ahead. *Qui Napoli* (free at the tourist office) and the newspaper *Il Mattino* (L1500/€0.77) both carry current ferry schedules. Prices listed here are for May-Oct. Weekend prices are often higher. Ferries run slightly less frequently from Nov.-Apr. Ask about port taxes. Hydrofoils depart from **Molo Beverello** and **Mergellina.** Ferries from **Molo Beverello, Stazione Marittima,** and **Pozzuoli**. Stazione Marittima is for longer trips to Palermo and the Isole Eolie. **Molo Angioino** and Molo Beverello, where the ferries and hydrofoils depart, are next to each other at the base of P. Municipio. From P. Garibaldi take tram #1; from P. Municipio take the R2 bus. **Ontana** (☎081 58 00 34) takes care of reservations for all ferry trips.

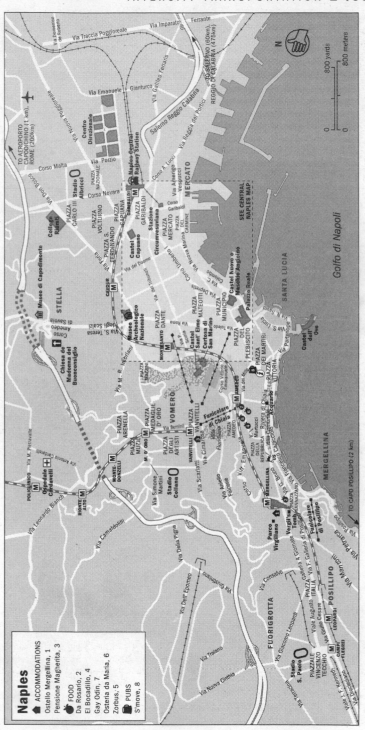

Naples

▲ ACCOMMODATIONS
Ostello Mergellina, 1
Pensione Magherita, 3

● FOOD
Da Rosario, 2
El Bocadillo, 4
Gay Odin, 7
Osteria da Maria, 6
Zorbus, 5

■ PUBS
S'move, 8

N

800 yards
800 meters

TO AEROPORTO
CAPODICHINO (1 km),
ROME (200km)

Golfo di Napoli

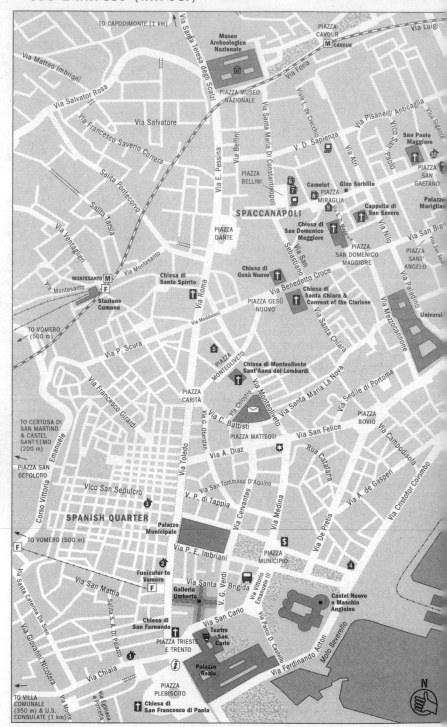

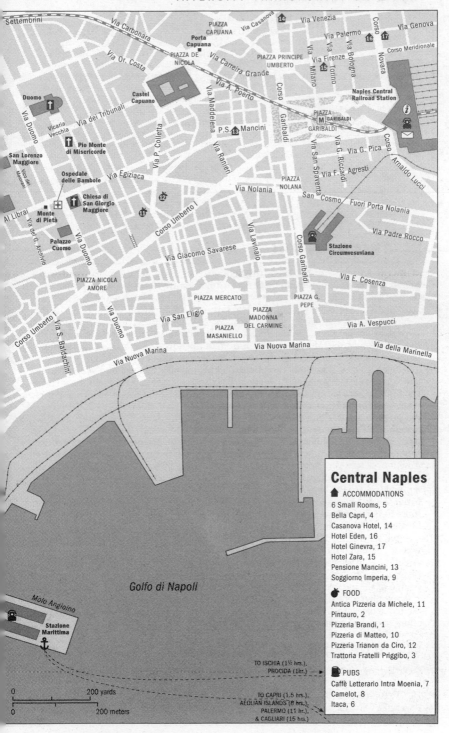

Central Naples

🏠 ACCOMMODATIONS

6 Small Rooms, 5
Bella Capri, 4
Casanova Hotel, 14
Hotel Eden, 16
Hotel Ginevra, 17
Hotel Zara, 15
Pensione Mancini, 13
Soggiorno Imperia, 9

🍴 FOOD

Antica Pizzeria da Michele, 11
Pintauro, 2
Pizzeria Brandi, 1
Pizzeria di Matteo, 10
Pizzeria Trianon da Ciro, 12
Trattoria Fratelli Priggibo, 3

🍺 PUBS

Caffè Letterario Intra Moenia, 7
Camelot, 8
Itaca, 6

Caremar: ☎081 551 38 82. Ticket office on Molo Beverello. Open daily 6am-10pm. Ferries and hydrofoils depart for: **Capri** (ferry: 1½hr., 6 per day, L9800/€5.06; hydrofoil: 1hr.; 4 per day 5:40am-9pm; L18,000/€9.30); **Ischia** (ferry: 1½hr., 8 per day, L9800/€5.06; hydrofoil: 1hr; 6 per day 6:25am-9:55pm; L18,000/€9.30); and **Procida** (ferry: 1hr., 7 per day 6:30am-10pm, L8000/€4.13; hydrofoil: 40min., 6 per day 6:25am-9:55pm).

Siremar Lines: ☎081 580 03 40; fax 580 03 41. Ticket office at Molo Angioino. Depart from Stazione Marittima. Open daily 9am-7pm. Ferries 2 per week; in winter 3 per week. To: **Lipari** (12hr.; L35,000/€18.08); **Stromboli** (8hr.; L30,000/€15.50); **Vulcano** (13hr.; L30,400/€15.70); and intermediate points along the routes.

Tirrenia Lines: ☎081 199 123 199. Ticket office at Molo Angioino. Depart from Stazione Marittima. Open daily 8:30am-1:15pm and 2:30-5:30pm. Ferries to **Cagliari** (15hr.; 2 per week, in winter 1 per week; L83,900/€43.33) and **Palermo** (11hr.; 8pm; L90,300/€46.64). You must pay an additional L10,000/€5.16 port tax. Schedules vary—call for more info.

SNAV: ☎081 761 23 48; www.snavali.com. Open daily 9am-7pm. Runs hydrofoils Apr.-Oct to: **Capri** (L20,000/€10.33); **Palermo** (5hr.; L100,000/€51.65); and **Procida** (L17,000/€8.78). AmEx/MC/V.

Linee Lauro: (☎081 551 33 52 or 081 552 28 38). Ticket office at Molo Angioino. Depart from Molo Beverello. Open daily 9am-7pm. Ferries to **Ischia** (3 per day 8:40am, 1:55, 7pm; L10-20,000/€10.33-20.66) and **Tunis** (19hr.; 2 per week, in winter 1 per week; L120,000/€62.00).

✦ ORIENTATION

It is easiest to think of Naples as divided into five areas: **Train Station, Waterfront, Hilltop, Downtown,** and **Historic Center.** The **Train Station (P. Garibaldi),** a crumbling area on the east side of Naples, is dominated by Piazza Garibaldi where the central train station, metro, and major city bus terminal are located. Commercial Corso Umberto I leads southwest from P. Garibaldi, ending at Piazza Bovio. From here V. Depretis (where one can take a CLP bus to Amalfi or to the airport) branches to the left, leading to P. Municipio (the bottom of the downtown financial and administrative center) and Castel Nuovo. At the foot of P. Municipio lie Molo Beverello and the Stazione Marittima, the point of departure for ferries and hydrofoils. V. San Carlo will take you past P. Reale to P. Trieste e Trento and P. Plebiscito. Turn right off V. Cesario Console onto V. San Lucia and head to Castel dell'Ovo and the **Waterfront (Santa Lucia, Chiaia, and Margellina).** The wide sidewalks of V. Carracciolo provide a refreshing view of the I-wouldn't-eat-the-sushi-clean water and the Speedo-clad men sunning on the rocks. V. Carraciolo passes the lush Villa Comunale, P. della Repubblica, and P. Sannazaro, where V. Mergellina and C. Vittorio Emanuele meet. C. Vittorio Emanuele will bring you through Mergellina and to P. Amedeo, where you can take the *funicular* to the **Hilltop (Vomero, Posillipo, and Capidomonte).** V. Cimarosa leads to V. Luca Giordano where you can either turn left and head to the Villa Floridian or turn right where crafts fill the P. degli Artisti. From the P. take V.T. da Camaino to P. Medaglie d'Oro and head back down V. Fiore to P. Fanzago where V. Bernini will take you to P. Anvitelli. To leave Vomero, turn left on V. Scarlatti to the Funicolare at V. Morghen. The *funicular* will take you back down to Montesanto. From Montesanto V. Tarsia leads to P. Dante where you can either stroll through **Downtown** on V. Toledo, the major shopping street, or take the pedestrian walkway under the arch to Spaccanapoli through the **Historic Center** that "splits Naples." The church-filled Spaccanapoli follows the course of the ancient Roman road, now known as V. dei Tribunali.

If you plan to be in town for a few days, the tourist office, hostels, museums, and the like eagerly hand out detailed maps. Also pick up the free *Napoli by Bus* brochure to assist you in using the bus system.

▤ LOCAL TRANSPORTATION

One "Giranapoli" ticket is valid for all modes of transport in Naples: **bus, Metro, tram,** and **funicular.** Tickets are available at *tabacchi* in 3 types: 1½hr. for L1500/€0.77; full-day for L4500/€2.32; month for L45,000/€23.24. To visit neighboring Pozzuoli, Vesuvio, or Cuma, **Unico Fascia 1** and **Fascia 2** are cost-effective ways to

DON'T TAKE CANDY FROM STRANGERS AND OTHER GOOD ADVICE Though violent crime is rare in Naples, theft is common (unless you're in the *Camorra,* the Neapolitan mafia, in which case the opposite is true). Be smart. Don't carry your money in wallets or purses. Do not wear eye-catching jewelry or flaunt expensive cameras. Don't leave your bags unattended, and in general avoid uncomfortable situations. Young women should avoid eye contact with strangers and should travel in mixed company whenever possible. If harassed, women and men alike should not hesitate to shake their fingers at harassers and say clearly "Backoff, buster!" in their language of choice.

travel hourly, daily, weekly, and monthly on ANM, CTP, Sepsa, FS, and Circumvesuviana. Unico Tickets L2500/€1.29 to L6500/€3.36 and are also available at *tabacchi*. Everything stops running around midnight, except for the unreliable nighttime (notturno) buses.

Bus: ANM (☎081 763 21 77). Open Su-F 8:30am-6pm. Remember to validate your ticket at the yellow boxes and pick up a copy of the essential *Naples by Bus* brochure. All stops have signs indicating their routes and destinations.

R1 travels from P. Bovio to Vomero (P. Me. Oro) and **R2** runs from P. Garibaldi to P. Municipio.

3S connects "3 Stations": the airport, the Central Rail Station in P. Garibaldi, and the Bay of Naples Molo Beverello, where boats leave for Capri, Sorrento, and Ichia.

Metropolitana: To cover long distances (e.g., from the train station to P. Cavour, Montesanto, P. Amedeo, or Mergellina), use the efficient Metro that runs west to Pozzuoli from P. Garibaldi. Go to platform #4, one floor underground at Stazione Centrale. Stops at P. Cavour (Museo Nazionale), Montesanto (Cumana, Circumflegrea, funicular to Vomero), P. Amedeo (funicular to Vomero), Mergellina, and Pozzuoli. If you're going to Procida or Ischia, take the Metro to Pozzuoli and depart from there.

Trams: From the station to Mergellina along the coast. Tram #1 stops at the Molo Beverello port. Catch it in front of the Garibaldi statue near Stazione Centrale.

Funiculars: 3 connect lower city to Vomero: **Centrale,** most frequently used, runs from P. Augusteo; **Montesanto** from P. Montesanto; **Chiaia** from P. Amedeo. Centrale and Chiaia have intermittent stops at Corso Vittorio Emanuele. A fourth, **Mergellina,** connects Posillipo to Mergellina.(M-Sa 4 per hr. 7am-10pm; Su reduced service 8am-7pm).

Taxis: Cotana (☎081 570 70 70), **Napoli** (☎081 556 44 44), or **Partenope** (☎081 556 02 02). Only take taxis with meters. No English spoken. **Consortaxi** (☎081 552 52 52). **Radiotaxi** (☎081 551 51 51). Radiotaxi's Taxi Rosa provides a safe taxi service for women who call 10pm-6am. L5000/€2.58 surcharge 10pm-7am. An additional L5000/€2.58 from the airport and a L8000/€4.13 minimum.

Car Rental: Avis (☎081 554 30 20), at Stazione Centrale. Cars from L120,000/€62.00 per day; L780,000/€402.83 per week. Open M-F 8am-7:30pm, Sa 8:30am-1pm and 4-6pm, Su 9am-1pm. Another office in the airport (☎081 780 57 90). Additional 12% tax on cars rented at the airport. Open M-Su 7am-midnight. **Hertz,** P. Garibaldi, 93 (☎081 554 86 57). L121,000/€62.50 per day; L520,000/€268.56 per week. Another office near the airport at V. Scarfoglio, 1 (☎081 570 87 01; fax 570 78 62). Additional 12% tax applies. Open M-F 9am-1pm and 2-5pm. **Maggiore Budget** (☎081 28 78 58), in Stazione Centrale. From L99,000/€51.13 per day; L300,000/€154.94 per week. Open M-F 8am-7pm, Sa 8am-1:30pm.

🔁 PRACTICAL INFORMATION

TOURIST, FINANCIAL, AND LOCAL SERVICES

Tourist Offices: EPT (☎081 26 87 79; fax 20 66 66), at Stazione Centrale. Calls hotels and ferry companies. Grab a map and the indispensable ▧ *Qui Napoli,* a monthly updated tourist publication full of schedules, events, and listings. English spoken. Open

M-Sa 9am-7pm. **Main office,** P. dei Martiri, 58 (☎081 40 53 11). Open M-Sa 8:30am-3pm. Branch at **Stazione Mergellina** (☎081 761 21 02). Open M-Sa 8:30am-7pm, Su 8am-2pm. **OTC** (☎081 580 82 16; fax 41 03 59; osservatorio@comune.napoli.it), at Palazzo Reale in P. Plebiscito, is eager to assist you. Open M-F 9am-6:30pm.

Budget Travel: CTS, V. Mezzocannone, 25 (☎081 552 79 60), off C. Umberto on the R2 line. Student travel info, ISIC and FIYTO cards, and booking services. Open M-F 9:30am-1:30pm and 2:30-6:30pm, Sa 9:30am-12:30pm. V. Cinthia, 36 (☎081 767 78 77) Open M-F 9:30am-1:30pm and 2:30-7pm, Sa 9:30am-2pm. V. Scarlatti, 198 (☎081 558 65 97) Open M-F 9:30am-7:30pm, Sa 9:30am-2pm. **CIT,** P. Municipio, 69 (☎081 552 54 26), is a comprehensive travel agency. Open M-F 9am-1pm and 3-6pm. **Italian Youth Hostel Organization** (☎081 761 23 46), at the hostel in Mergellina (see p. 491). Info on HI-discounts. HI cards L30,000/€15.50. Open M-F 9am-1pm and 3-6pm.

Consulates: US (☎081 583 81 11; 24hr. emergency ☎033 794 50 83), P. della Repubblica at the west end of Villa Comunale. Open M-F 8am-5pm. **South Africa,** C. Umberto, 1 (☎081 551 75 19). **UK,** V. Crispi, 122 (☎081 66 35 11). Metro to P. Amedeo. Open July-Aug. M-F 8am-1:30pm; Sept.-June M-F 9am-12:30pm and 2:30-4pm. **Canada,** V. Carducci, 29 (☎081 40 13 38).

Currency Exchange: Several banks operate in P. Municipio and P. Garibaldi. **Thomas Cook** at airport has decent rates. Open M-F 9:30am-1pm and 3-6:30pm. Additional branches at P. Municipio, 70 (☎081 551 83 99) and **Minichini** at V. Depretis 141 (☎081 552 42 13). **Stazione Centrale** has expensive 24hr. currency exchange.

American Express: Every Tour, P. Municipio, 5 (☎081 551 85 64). Open 9am-1:30pm and 3:30-7pm.

Luggage Storage: In Stazione Centrale train station. Near Ferrovia Circumflegrea and Stazione Centrale info desk. L5000/€2.58 for 12hr. Open 24hr

English-Language Bookstores: Feltrinelli, V.S.T. d'Aquino, 70 (☎081 552 14 36), north of Palazzo Municipale. Turn right off V. Toledo and onto V. Ponte di Tappia. It's 20m ahead on the left. Extensive English selection. Open M-F 9am-8pm, Sa 9am-1:30pm and 4-8pm, Su 9am-1:30pm and 5-8pm. Some English titles in bookstores in the P. Bellini neighborhood. **Libreria Universal Books,** Corso Umberto, 22 (☎081 252 00 69; fax 542 45 88). In a *palazzo* off Corso Umberto by P. Dante.

Laundromats: Bolle Blu, C. Novara, 62 (☎033 88 94 27 14 or 56 64 30 57), 3 blocks from train station. Fast machines (wash and dry in under 1hr.). One of the only self-service laundromats in Naples. Wash L6,000-10,000/€3.10-5.16; dry L6,000-10,000/€3.10-5.16. Prices depend on load size. Open M-Sa 8:30am-8pm. **Lavanderia a gettone,** V. Montesanto, 2 (☎081 542 21 62). From the metro or funicular, walk down V. Montesanto toward Commissariato Dante and Teatro Bracco, it's on the right on the corner of V. Michele Sciuti. With Internet, free soap and disinfectant, and a waiting room with TV, music, and magazines. L1200/€0.62 per wash and dry. Ironing L1000/€0.52 per article. Internet L5000/€2.58 an hour. Open daily 9am-8:30pm.

EMERGENCY AND COMMUNICATIONS

Emergency: ☎113. **Police:** ☎113 or 081 794 11 11. **Carabinieri:** ☎112.

Tourist Police: Ufficio Stranieri, at the **Questura,** V. Medina, 75 (☎081 794 11 11), near P. Municipio on the R2 bus line. Assists with passport problems and helps travelers who have been victims of crime.

Ambulance: ☎081 752 06 96.

Late-Night Pharmacy: (☎081 26 88 81), at Stazione Centrale by FS ticket windows. Open in summer M-F 8pm-9am. *Il Mattino* lists the schedule.

Hospital: Cardarelli (☎081 747 11 11), north of town on R4 bus line.

Internet Access:

Internetbar, P. Bellini, 74 (☎081 29 52 37). Chic, with A/C. Expensive drinks available to wash down your emails. L5000/€2.58 for 30min. Open M-Sa 9am-2am, Su 8am-2am.

Internet Multimedia, V. Sapienza, 43 (☎081 29 84 12). From Museo Archeologico Nazionale head down V.S. Maria di Constaninopoli and turn right on V. Sapienza. Behind gate and up a flight of stairs to your right lie the lowest prices in town, at L3000/€1.55 per hr. Buzz to get in. Scanning and printing also available. Open daily 9:30am-9:30pm.

Livingston, V.G. Martucci, 8 (☎081 761 88 83; teo@itb.it). Head out of P. Amedeo on V.G. Martucci. British internet "pub," I presume. L5000/€2.58 per 30min. Open daily 8pm-2am.

Post Office: (☎081 552 42 33), in P. Matteotti, at V. Diaz. Take the R2 line. Also in Galleria Umberto (☎081 552 34 67) and outside Stazione Centrale. Notoriously unreliable Fermo Posta L1500/€0.77. All offices open M-F 8:15am-6pm, Sa 8:15am-noon. In summer, afternoons popular times for strikes.

Postal Code: 80100.

⌐ ACCOMMODATIONS

The gritty area around **P. Garibaldi** is packed with hotels, many of which solicit customers at the station. Avoid such solicitors—they will most likely take you to an old *palazzo* divided into rooms with hastily erected partitions. P. Garibaldi has options that are close to the station, comfortable, and inexpensive (though none are really quiet). Be aware that some inexpensive hotels are so because they "rent" rooms by the hour during the day for purposes best left undescribed. In the historic district between P. Dante and the *duomo*, lodgings are harder to come by, but if you can find space, this area is most conveniently located. The Waterfront and Downtown are home to more expensive options, and the Hilltop provides great views but a guaranteed 15-min. commute to the sights.

Although Naples has some fantastic bargain lodgings, be cautious. Don't surrender your passport before seeing your room, bargain for lower prices, and always agree on the price *before* you unpack your bags. Be alert for shower charges, obligatory breakfasts, and other unexpected costs. When selecting a place to stay, check for double-locked doors and night attendants. The **ACISJF/Centro D'Ascolto,** at Stazione Centrale near the EPT, helps women find safe, inexpensive rooms. (☎081 28 19 93. Open M, Tu, Th 3:30-6:30pm.) For **camping,** check out **Pozzuoli** (see p. 500), **Pompeii** (see p. 503), and other small towns in the Bay of Naples.

WATERFRONT

Ostello Mergellina (HI), V. Salita della Grotta, 23 (☎081 761 23 46; fax 761 23 91). M: Mergellina. From Metro station, make 2 sharp rights onto V. Piedigrotta and then a left onto V. Salita della Grotta. Turn right on long driveway after overpass. Outstanding views of Vesuvius and Capri from terrace area. 200 beds in 2-, 4-, and 6-person rooms vary in quality but well maintained. Computer, cafeteria, free storage downstairs, and a pleasant (and enormous!) lounge. Breakfast, sheets, and shower included, but no towels. Laundry L10,000/€5.16. Breakfast 7-9am, dinner 7-9.30 pm. Lockout 9am-3pm. Curfew 12:30am. Reservations advised July-Aug. Dorms L24,000/€12.39; doubles L60,000/€53.34; family rooms L30,000/€15.50 per person, although if more beds are squeezed into the room this drops to L25,000/€12.91.

TRAIN STATION

▨ **Casanova Hotel,** V. Venezia, 2 (☎081 26 82 87; fax 26 97 92; hcasanov@tin.it; http://members.tripod.it/hotelcasanova/index). From P. Garibaldi, take V. Milano and turn left at its end, or continue down C. Garibaldi and turn right before V. Casanova. Clean 2-star hotel with airy rooms and a rooftop terrace with bar in the summer. 18 rooms with A/C, some with TV, fridge, and phone. Breakfast L8000/€4.13. Luggage deposit. Check-out 12pm. Reserve ahead. Singles L40,000/€20.66, with bath L50,000/€25.82; doubles L70,000/€36.15, with bath L85,000/€43.90; triples L110,000/€56.81; quads L140,000/€72.30. AmEx/MC/V.

Hotel Eden, C. Novara, 9 (☎081 28 53 44). From station, turn right on Corso Novara: It's on the left. 42 rooms and a quick, well-lit walk from the station, Eden provides a convenient option for backpackers arriving late at night without reservations. English, Spanish, and some French are spoken by the brothers who run it, and all rooms come with private bath. Breakfast L5000/€2.58. Free luggage storage. *Let's Go* reservation prices: singles L45,000/€23.24; doubles L70,000/€36.15; triples L100,000/€51.65; quads L120,000/€62. AmEx/MC/V.

Hostel Pensione Mancini, P. Mancini, 33 (☎081 553 67 31; fax 554 66 75; www.hostelpensionemancini.com), off far end of P. Garibaldi from station. Multilingual and friendly owners. Simple, newly renovated. 6 rooms range from singles to quads. Breakfast included. Check-in after noon, check-out before noon. Reservations suggested one week in advance. Dorms L30,000/€15.50; singles with bath L45,000/€23.24; doubles L70,000/€36.15, with bath L80,000/€41.31; triples with bath L100,000/€51.65; quads with bath L120,000/€62.

Hotel Ginevra, V. Genova, 116 (☎081 28 32 10; fax 554 17 57; www.mds.it/ginevra). Exit P. Garibaldi on C. Novara, then turn right on V. Genova. Clean, family-run establishment. Bathrooms have showers with doors. English and French spoken. 14 rooms. Singles L48,400/€43.90, with bath L77,450/€40; doubles L77,450/€40, L96,820/€50; triples L106,500/€55, L135,540/€70; quads L125,860/€65, L154.901/€80. 10% *Let's Go* discount when paying cash. AmEx/MC/V.

Hotel Zara, V. Firenze, 81 (☎081 28 71 25; fax 26 82 87; Firenze. Quiet, spacious rooms with phones and access to a washing machine for varying sums. Reservations recommended. Singles L45,000/€23.24; doubles L70,000/€36.15, with bath L95,000/€49.10; triples L105,000/€54.23, with bath L130,000/€67.13.

HISTORIC CENTER

🏠 **Soggiorno Imperia,** P. Miraglia, 386 (☎081 45 93 47). Take R2 from train station, walk up V. Mezzocannone through P.S. Domenico Maggiore, and enter the 1st set of green doors to left on P. Miraglia. Near university. Climb 6 flights of stairs to get to this refurbished 16th-century *palazzo*. Bright and clean, inexpensive, and conveniently located. English spoken. 11 rooms. No phone. Reservations strongly suggested. Dorm L30,000/€15.50; singles L40,000/€20.66; doubles L70,000/€36.15, with bath L100,000/€51.65; triples L100,000/€51.65. AmEx/MC/V.

6 Small Rooms, V. Diodato Lioy, 18 (☎081 790 13 78; www.at6smallrooms.com). From P. Monteoliveto, turn right on V. Diodato Lioy, and go up about half a block. There is no sign so look for the name on the call button. A bit out of the way, but worth the trek. Chill with hip Australian owners and their 2 friendly cats. Key (L5000/€2.58) available for after midnight curfew, big rooms, and spacious, I feel at home kitchen. Singles L40,000/€20.66; dorms L30,000/€15.50.

Pensione Bella Capri, V. Melisurgo, 4, door B, 6th fl. (☎081 552 94 94; fax 552 92 65; www.bellacapri.it), at corner of V. Cristofor Colombo, across street from the port. Take tram #1 from P. Garibaldi. From courtyard enter door B and go to 6th floor. Incredible view of harbor and of island namesake, Bella Capri. Inexpensive alternative to high-priced hotels on waterfront. Coin-operated elevator, and 9 rooms with breakfast, bath, TV, A/C, and phone; some with balcony. Reservations recommended a week in advance. Singles L110,000/€56.81; doubles L130,000/€67.14; triples L170,000/€87.80; quads L190,000/€98.13. 10% *Let's Go* discount. AmEx/MC/V.

HILLTOP

Pensione Margherita, V. Cimarosa, 29, 5th fl. (☎081 556 70 44), in the same building as the Centrale funicular station (go outside and around the corner to the right; buzz to get in). 19 spacious rooms, some with terraces. Endearing management, excellent views of Vesuvius and Capri, and the lowest prices available in this posh, peaceful residential area. Bring L50/€0.05 for the elevator or take the stairs. Check-out 11am. Curfew midnight. Closed Aug. 1-15. Singles L60,000/€31; doubles L110,000/€56.81; triples L155,000/€80.10. AmEx/MC/V.

◘ FOOD

PIZZERIAS

If you ever doubted that Neapolitans invented **pizza** (see **Food and Wine**, p. 27), Naples's *pizzerie* will take that doubt, beat it into a ball, throw it in the air, spin it on their collective finger, punch it down, cover it with sauce and mozzarella, and serve it to you *alla margherita*. And then you'll beg for more. Rumor claims that in the last mayoral elections, pizza narrowly lost out to a human...after a recount!

▓ **Pizzeria Di Matteo,** V. Tribunali, 94 (☎081 45 52 62), near V. Duomo. Like the students and pizza connoisseurs who crowd this small, preeminent eatery, President Clinton ate here during the G-7 Conference in 1994. The *marinara* is your best cheap bite (L3900/ €2). Open M-Sa 9am-midnight.

Antica Pizzeria da Michele, V. Cesare Sersale, 1/3 (☎081 553 92 04). From P. Garibaldi, walk up C. Umberto 1 and take the 1st right. The huge line outside the door says "Quality!" more loudly than a legion of reviewers. Michele's simple establishment simply makes great pizza. It serves only 2 traditional pizzas: *marinara* (tomato, garlic, oregano, oil) and *margherita* (tomato, mozzarella cheese, basil). Since pizza costs L6000/€3.10, L7000/€5.62, and L8000/€4.13 for a normal, medium, and large, and all drinks cost L2000/€1.03, you can get a pizza and a beer for L8000/€4.13. Open M-Sa 10am-11pm.

Gino Sorbillo, V. Tribunali, 32 (☎081 44 66 43), in the Historic Center near Vco. S. Paolo. The only pizzeria with 21 pizza-making children in this generation, Gino Sorbillo specializes in pizza. Their grandfather invented the *ripieno al forno* (calzone in laymen terms), and now Gino, of the youngest generation, manages the always packed, mood-lit restaurant and its 40 types of pizza. Try the *gusta pizza,* the only wine especially made to be eaten with pizza. *Margherita* L5000/€2.58, *marinara* L4000/€2.07, beer L1500-6500/€0.77-3.36. Open daily 12:30-3:30pm and 6:30-11:30pm.

Pizzeria Brandi, Salita S. Anna di Palazzo, 1 (☎081 41 69 28), off V. Chiaia. In 1889, Mr. Esposito invented the *margherita* in Brandi's ancient oven. While President Clinton munched at Di Matteo in 1994, his daughter Chelsea ate here. As have Pavarotti, Isabella Rossellini, and Gerard Depardieu. Also serving other traditional Neapolitan food, Brandi's is more than your average pizzeria. Reservations advised. *Margherita* L8000/ €4.13. Cover L3000/€1.55. Tip 12%. Open M-Su noon-3pm and 7pm-midnight.

Pizzeria Trianon da Ciro, V. Pietro Colletta, 42/44/46 (☎081 553 94 26), 1 block off C. Umberto I. *The New York Times* declares this to be the best pizza in Naples. In this large, A/C establishment, the house speciality is the pizza *"Gran Trianon"* (L12,500/ €6.46), a smorgasbord of 8 different sections. Pizza L6000-13,000/€3.10-6.71, beer L4000/€2.07. Service 15%. Open daily 10am-3:30pm and 5:30-11pm.

RESTAURANTS AND TRATTORIE

Neapolitans love **seafood,** and they prepare it well. Enjoy *cozze* (mussels) with lemon or as soup. Savor *vongole* (clams) in all their glory, and don't miss their more expensive cousin, the *ostrica* (oyster). Try not to gawk as true Neapolitans suck the most elusive juices from the heads of *aragosta* (crayfish) while you partake of *polipo* (octopus), one of the cheapest sources of protein around. Meanwhile, when asking for *spaghetti,* don't mention any nonsense about Marco Polo and China if you want to stay on the Neapolitans' good side: this Italian trademark was reputedly first boiled in their kitchens. Today, the city's most famous pasta dishes are *spaghetti alle vongole* (with clams) and *alle cozze* (with mussels). For fresh fruits and seafood, explore Neapolitan **markets.** Try the one on V. Soprammuro, off P. Garibaldi. (Open M-Sa 8am-1:30pm.) Fruit stands, groceries, and pastry shops line V. Tribuali in Spaccanapoli.

The **Waterfront** offers a combination of traditional Neapolitan fare and a change of culinary pace. Take the Metro or the C25 bus to P. Amedeo for Greek or Spanish. Take the Metro or tram #4 to Mergellina, southwest of P. Amedeo on the waterfront, for informal, hearty Neapolitan seafood. P. Sannazzaro, in the center of Mergellina, has many *trattorie* that serve the beloved local *zuppa di cozze* (mussels in broth with octopus). Among the shops of **Downtown,** small options can be found on the side streets, hiding from the louder, more expensive trattorie that one would expect to find around a galleria. The narrow, winding streets around the **History Center** and P. Dante shelter the city's most delightful *trattorie* and *pizzerie.* Some of the cheapest, most authentic options lie along V. dei Tribunali in the heart of Spaccanapoli. Tourist-ridden and expensive restaurants dominate P. Garibaldi in the **Train Station** area, but a few high-quality, low-cost meals hide on the side streets just off the *piazza.* Like most areas around train stations, P. Garibaldi becomes seedy at night, so eat early before it gets too dark.

WATERFRONT

■ **Zorba's,** V. Martucci, 5 Mergellina (☎081 66 75 72), 2 blocks off P. Amedeo to the right; at the sign turn left and it will be 3 doors down. Sick of Italian? This wood-dominated tavern, with its Greek music and Greek hospitality, specializes in, surprise, Greek food. *Satanas* (devilishly spicy mini sausages) L11,000/€5.68. Greek salad L9000/€4.65. Baklava L6000/€3.10. Open daily 8:30pm-midnight.

El Bocadillo, V. Martucci, 50, Mergellina (☎081 66 90 30). Serves up tasty Spanish and South American dishes in a rustic Spanish atmosphere with comfortable benchtables and a staircase that walks over a mini-jungle lit up by neon-green lights. Most entrees L11-16,000/€5.68-8.26. *Paella* L16,000/€8.26. Pitchers of *sangría* L10,000/€5.16. Open daily 8pm-2am.

Osteria da Maria, V. Ascensione, 6, Mergellina (☎081 41 35 84). Take V. Vittoria Colonna from P. Amedeo, take the 1st right down a flight of stairs, then turn right and immediately left. Specializing in traditional Neapolitan food, the curios and wallpaper here will make you feel like your Neapolitan grandmother, coincidentally named Maria, just opened a large restaurant. Tourist lunch L35,000/€18.08 without drinks. Open Tu-Sa 12:30-3:30pm and 7:30pm-12:30am, Su 12:30-3:30pm. AmEx/MC/V.

Da Rosario, P. Sannazzaro, 72, Mergellina (☎081 570 31 03). This open-all-night restaurant specializes in seafood. The down-to-earth owners will give you a real glimpse of the Neapolitan people and their food. *Zuppa di cozze* (mussel soup) for L12,000/€6.20. Really like the *zuppa?* Get the *supa! Zuppa di cozze super* L18,000/€9.30. Service 10%. Open daily noon-6am.

DOWNTOWN

Trattoria Fratelli Prigiobbo, V. Portacarrese, 96. From V. Toledo, turn right across from V. Ponte di Tappia and walk 2 blocks into the Spanish Quarter. Pizza L4-8000/€2.07-4.13. *Primi,* including *gnocchi alla mozzarella,* L4000/€2.07. Seafood *secondi,* like roasted calamari L6000/€3.10, though servings are small. Wine L4000/€2.07 per bottle. Open M-Sa 8am-midnight.

GELATERIE AND PASTICCERIE

Naples's most beloved pastry is *sfogliatella,* filled with sweetened ricotta cheese, orange rind, and candied fruit. It comes in two forms: the popular *riccia,* a flaky-crust variety, and *frolla,* a softer, crumblier counterpart.

Pintauro, V. Toledo, 275 (☎081 41 73 39), near the Centrale funicular station. This tiny bakery invented and has produced the city's foremost pastry, the *sfogliatella,* since 1785. Try one, piping hot, for L2000/€1.03. Open M-Sa 9:15am-8:15pm.

Gay Odin, V.V. Colonna, 15b (☎081 41 82 82), off P. Amedeo. No Norse gods, just the delicious chocolate treats that have been pouring out of their *fabbriche* (factories) on V. Vetriera since 1824. Try their famous *foresta,* a sweet and crumbly chocolate stalk (L4-7000/€2.07-3.62) or the scandalous *cioccolati nudi,* little chocolates liberated from their wrappers. Oh, baby! Just one more! This place is worth it for the smell alone. Open M-Sa 9:30am-1:30pm and 4:30-9pm.

Scaturchio in P.S. Dominico Maggiore, 19 (☎081 551 69 44). One of the best pastry shops and *gelaterie* in the historic district, ideal for a break from church-viewing. Cones L2500/€1.29. The *ministeriale,* a chocolate and rum pastry, is their specialty. Though the fancy sign and counter suggest this place is a tourist trap, the taste says: "Kiss me, I'm Italian!" Open M-Sa 7:20am-8:40pm.

SIGHTS

> **FREE RIDE.** There is no admission charge to state-sponsored sights and museums for students of Italian art and architecture or for those under 18 or over 60. Some sights are free to EU citizens. Always inquire about discounts!

Just as Naples's streets are packed with people and *motorini*, they are just as crammed with churches and museums. The architecture that lines the streets is a narrative in stone, marble, and tile of the people who have conquered this land: Greeks, Romans, Spaniards and Italians. Naples is rich in treasures: excavations *in sito* can be found at the Museo Archeologico Nazionale or Museo and Gallerie di Capidomonte. To experience wealth of another sort, the Palazzo Reale's apartments and the city's castles give a taste of the high life of Neapolitan royalty.

HISTORIC CENTER

SPACCANAPOLI

Naples's most renowned neighborhood is replete with brilliant architecture and merits at least a half-hour stroll. The main sights get lost among ornate banks, *pensioni*, and *pasticcerie*, so watch for the shoebox-size signs on buildings. But don't lose track of yourself while gaping at picturesque churches, *palazzi*, and alleyways, or you'll soon find yourself staring at the business end of an oncoming motorino. To get to the Historic Center from P. Dante, walk through **Porta Alba** and **P. Bellini** before turning down **V. dei Tribunali,** the former route of an old Roman road that now contains some of the city's best **pizzerie** (see **Food,** p. 27).

■ **MUSEO ARCHEOLOGICO NAZIONALE.** Situated within a 16th-century *palazzo* and former barracks, one of the world's most important archeological museums houses exquisite treasures from Pompeii and Herculaneum. Unreliable labeling makes the color guidebooks a helpful investment. The ground floor's Farnese Collection displays sculptures snatched from Pompeii and Herculaneum and imperial portraits and colossal statues from Rome's Baths of Caracalla. Highlights include the massive **Farnese Hercules,** showing the exhausted hero after his last labor. But which one? According to one naughty ancient tradition, for his Thirteenth Labor the stud-hero had to make love to 100 women in a single night! And they said that 13 was unlucky! Check out the **Farnese Bull,** the largest extant ancient sculpture. The bull was carved out of a single piece of marble, then touched up by Michelangelo. The mezzanine contains mosaics taken from Pompeii, ranging from pictures of food to the **Alexander Mosaic,** which shows a young and fearless Alexander the Great routing a Persian army. On the first floor, above the mezzanine, are large murals and domestic items from Pompeii and Herculaneum. The **Secret Collection** contains erotic paintings and objects from Pompeii. Ranging from images of godly love to phallic good luck charms, the collection showcases yet another side of antiquity. Also of note are the **Jewels,** a collection of ancient trinkets and ornaments which includes the sparkling **Farnese Cup.** In the basement is a sporadically open Egyptian collection. *(Metro to P. Cavour; turn right as you exit the station, and walk 2 blocks. Otherwise take the #110 bus from P. Garibaldi, or the R4 bus from P. Dante to P. Museo. ☎081 44 01 66. Open M and W-Su 9am-7:30pm. Guidebook L15-60,000/€7.75-31. Mandatory tours conducted every 30min. Ask for free ticket at main ticket window.)*

DUOMO. Like every good Italian town, Naples has its *duomo.* It lies quietly on a small *piazza*, and its modest facade hides its size. But twice a year throngs of people crowd around it to celebrate the **Festa di San Gennaro** (see **Festivals**, p. 33). Subject to countless additions and renovations since its inauguration in 1315 by Robert of Anjou, the *duomo's* most recent feature is a 19th-century neo-Gothic facade. On the right, the main attraction is the **Capella del Tesoro di San Gennaro**, decorated with Baroque paintings. A beautiful 17th-century bronze grille protects the high altar, which possesses a reliquary containing the saint's head and two vials of his coagulated blood. According to legend, disaster will strike the city if the blood does not liquefy on the celebration of his *festa;* miraculously, it always does, while Neapolitans crowd the church and streets. Beneath the main altar of the church lies the saint's crypt, decorated with Renaissance carvings in white marble. Halfway up the right side of the church, the **Chiesa di Santa Restituta** marks the entrance to the excavations of the **Greek and Roman roads** that run beneath the city. *(Walk 3 blocks up V. Duomo from C. Umberto I or take the #42 bus from P. Garibaldi. ☎081 44 90 97. Open M-F 8am-12:30pm and 4:30-7pm, Sa-Su 8am-3:30pm and 5-7:30pm.)*

PIO MONTE D. MISERICORDIE. This small chapel was built by a group of nobles dedicated to helping the needy and sick, ransoming Christian slaves held prisoner by infidels, and housing pilgrims, activities which continue (at least, in part) to this day. The church houses seven arches, each with its own altar and painting, and the main archway boasts Caravaggio's *Our Lady of Mercy*. In the *piazza* outside resides a spire dedicated to S. Gennaro for having saved the city from the 1656 plague. *(1 block down V. Tribunali after V. Duomo, on a small piazza. Open M-Sa 9am-noon.)*

OSPEDALE DELLE BAMBOLE. Old Naples's most endearing shop (or most creepy, depending on how many Hitchcock movies one has seen), this tiny doll hospital is one-of-a-kind. Don't expect cabbage-patch ambulances, little candy scalpels, or sugar-sweet IVs in this simple, one-room shop where the mirthful proprietor reassembles dolls with an unlikely collection of appendages. *(V.S. Biagio Al Librai, 81. Head 2 blocks up V. Duomo from P. N. Amore and take a left. ☎081 20 30 87. Open M-F 8:30am-2pm and 5-7:30pm. Closed Sa.)*

CHIESA DI SANTA CHIARA. One of the most important Angevin monuments in Naples, Santa Chiara was originally built in the 1300s by the rulers of the house of Anjou and has been renovated several times, most recently after World War II bombing damage in 1943. The church is littered with sarcophagi and tombs from the Middle Ages, and the 14th-century tomb of Robert of Anjou can be seen behind the main alter. Spend some time in the adjoining garden and monastery, adorned with Gothic walkways, frescoes, and brightly colored tiles, and maybe play with a kitty or two. *(From P. Dante, head down V. Toledo and turn left on V.B. Croce. The church sits in P. Gesú Nuovo. ☎081 552 62 09. Open daily /am-noon and 4-7pm.)*

GESÙ NUOVO. The church's 15th-century Jesuit facade consists entirely of raised stone diamonds. The interior is awash in Baroque inlaid marbles, with colorful frescoes adorning the ceiling and chapels. Outside the church is a Baroque spire, or *guglia*, glorifying the lives of Jesuit saints, surrounded by a bunch of bongo-playing bohemians at night. *(Across from the Chiesa di Santa Chiara, in P. Gesù Nuovo. ☎081 551 86 13 Open daily 7:15am-12:15pm and 4:15-7:15pm.)*

CHIESA DI MONTEOLIVETO. The highlight of this church is the wealth of Renaissance sculpture that fills the side altars, including eight life-size terra-cotta figures mourning the death of Christ. Vasari's frescoes adorn the sacristy. *(From P. Dante, head down V. Toledo and turn left on V. B. Croce. Cross P. Gesú Nuovo and walk down C. Trinità Maggiore to P. Monteoliveto. Open daily 7:15am-12:15pm and 4:15-7:15pm.)*

SAN LORENZO MAGGIORE. This large church retains a beautiful and striking Gothic simplicity. It was here that medieval writer Boccaccio first met his true love Fiammetta in 1334. Inside lie the tombs of Catherine of Austria and Robert of Arlois. And recent excavations beneath the church and monastery have uncovered Greek and Roman remains that will be on public display in the near future. *(P. San Gaetano, 316. 2 blocks down V. dei Tribunali from V. Duomo. ☎081 29 05 80.)*

TRAIN STATION

■**PALAZZO REALE.** The exterior facing P. Plebiscito is decorated with huge statues of the various rulers of Naples. Inside the 17th-century *palazzo* is the **Museo di Palazzo Reale,** composed of opulent royal apartments decorated with the original Bourbon furnishings, paintings, statues, and porcelains. The *palazzo* is an intellectual mecca even today, housing the 1,500,000-volume **Biblioteca Nazionale,** which contains the carbonized scrolls from the **Villa dei Papiri** in Herculaneum. *(Take the R2 bus from P. Garibaldi to P. Trieste e Trento and walk around the palazzo to the entrance on P. Plebiscito.* ☎ *081 794 40 21. Open M-Tu and Th-F 9am-8pm, Su 9am-8pm. L8000/€4.13. Library* ☎ *081 40 12 73; access to the public varies.)*

Also in the *palazzo* is the famous **Teatro San Carlo,** reputed to have better acoustics than the revered La Scala in Milan (see p. 91). For more information on performances, see **Entertainment,** p. 499. *(The theater's entrance is on P. Trieste e Trento.* ☎ *081 797 21 11. Tours July Sa-Tu and Th 10am; Sept.-June Sa-Su 2pm. Tour L5000/€2.58.)*

■**NAPOLI E LA CITTA SOTTERANEA/NAPOLI SOTTERRANEA.** These tours of the subterranean alleys beneath the city are fascinating, but not for the claustrophobic: they will have you crawling through narrow underground passageways, grottoes, and catacombs, looking for graffiti from the Mussolini era and exploring Roman aqueducts. *Napoli e la Città* explores the area underneath Castel Nuovo and Downtown, and *Napoli Sotterranea* drags you through the area under the Historic Center. **(Napoli e La Città' Sotterranea.** *Office at Vco. S. Anna di Palazzo,* ☎ *081 52 081 40 02 56. Tours (Th 9pm; Sa 10am, 6pm; Su 10, 11am, 6pm; L10,000/€5.16) leave from Caffè Gambiunes in P. Trieste e Trento; call first.* **Napoli Sotterranea.** *Piazza San Gaetano, 68. Go down V. Tribunali and turn left right before San Paolo Maggiore.* ☎ *08129 69 44 or 0368 354 05 85; info@napolisotterranea.com; www.napolisotterranea.com. Tours every 2hrs., M-F 12pm-4pm, Sa, Su, and holidays 10am-6pm. L10,000/€5.16 per person.)*

CASTEL NUOVO. It's impossible to miss this huge, five-turreted landmark looking out over the Bay of Naples. Known to friends as the **Maschio Angioino,** the fortress was built in 1286 by Charles II of Anjou to be his royal residence in Naples. Perhaps its most interesting feature is the triumphal entrance with reliefs commemorating the arrival of Alphonse I of Aragon in 1443. Inside you can see the magnificent cubical **Hall of the Barons,** where King Ferdinand once trapped rebellious barons and where Naples's city council holds spirited meetings today. The **Museo Civico** has a collection of 14th- and 15th-century frescoes and a set of bronze doors showing Charles of Aragon defeating rebels. *(P. Municipio. Take the R2 bus from P. Garibaldi. Museum* ☎ *081 795 20 03. Open M-Sa 9am-7pm. L10,000/€5.16.)*

CAPELLA SANSEVERO. The chapel, now a private museum, has several remarkable statues, including the **Veiled Christ** by Giuseppe Sanmartino. While admiring the marble marvel, don't forget to look up at the breathtaking fresco on the ceiling. As for the crypt, legend claims that the alchemist prince Raimondo of the S. Severi, who built the chapel, murdered his wife and her lover by injecting them with a poisonous venom that preserved their veins, arteries, and vital organs. Sadly, those aren't on display. *(V. Sanctis, 19. In the upper corner of P.S. Domenico Maggiore.* ☎ *081 551 84 70. Open M, W-F 10am-5pm; in summer, Christmas, Easter M, W-F 10am-7pm; holidays 10am-1:30pm. L8000/€4.13, students L3000/€1.55; group discounts.)*

CHIESA DI SAN DOMENICO MAGGIORE. This 13th-century church has been restructured several times over the years and now has settled on a 19th-century, piked Gothic interior. To the right of the altar in the Chapel of the Crucifix hangs the 13th-century painting that allegedly spoke to St. Thomas Aquinas, who lived in the adjoining monastery when Naples was a center of learning in Europe. Fine Renaissance sculptures decorate the side chapels. *(P.S. Domenico Maggiore.* ☎ *081 45 91 88. Open daily 7:15am-12:15pm and 4:15-7:15pm.)*

HILLTOP

CAPODIMONTE

■ **MUSEO AND GALLERIE DI CAPODIMONTE.** Housed in a royal **palazzo**, this museum is surrounded by a pastoral park where youngsters play soccer and lovers, well, play. In addition to its plush royal apartments and their furnishings, the palace houses the National Picture Gallery. The **Farnese Collection** on the first floor is full of artistic masterpieces, many of them removed from Neapolitan churches for safety's sake, including Bellini's *Transfiguration*, Masaccio's *Crucifixion*, and Titian's *Danae*. The second floor traces the development of the Neapolitan realistic style and its dramatic use of light from Caravaggio's visit to Naples (his *Flagellation* is on display) to Ribera and Luca Giordano's adaptations. *(Take the #110 bus from P. Garibaldi or the #24 bus from P. Dante to Parco Capodimonte. The park has 2 entrances, the Porta Piccola and the Porta Grande.* ☎ *081 749 91 11. Open Tu-F 8:30am-7:30pm, Su 8:30am-7:30pm. L14,000/€7.23; after 2pm L12,000/€6.20.)*

CHIESA DI MADONNA DEL BUONCONSIGLIO. Dubbed "Little St. Peter's" when architect Vincenzo Vecchia was inspired by St. Peter's in Rome, the church features copies of Michelangelo's *Pietà* and *Moses*. Outside, the 2nd-century **Catacombe di San Gennaro** are noted for their frescoes. *(Down V. Capodimonte from the museum.* ☎ *081 741 10 71. Guided tours of catacombs daily 9:30am-12:30pm. L5000/€2.58.)*

VOMERO

MUSEO NAZIONALE DI SAN MARTINO. Once a monastery, the massive Certosa di S. Martino is now home to an excellent museum of Neapolitan history and culture. In addition to extensive galleries, the monastery includes a chapel lavishly decorated in Baroque marbles and statuary, featuring one of Ribera's finest works, *The Deposition of Christ*, and an excellent Nativity by Guido Reni. Numerous balconies and a multilevel garden provide superb views. *(From V. Toledo take the funicular to Vomero, followed by a right on V. Cimarosa. A left on V. Morghen and a right onto V. Angelini lands you in Piazzale S. Martino.* ☎ *081 578 17 69. Open daily 9am-6pm. L11,500/€5.94.)*

The massive **Castel Sant'Elmo** next door was built to deter rebellion and hold political prisoners. Ignore the oppressive past; there are great panoramic views from the battlements. *(*☎ *081 578 40 30. Open Tu-Su 9am-2pm. L5000/€2.58.)*

MUSEO DUCA DI MARLINA. If you're a ceramics fan, then head to this crafts gallery inside the lush gardens of the **Villa Floridiana**; it houses 18th-century porcelain and some Asian items as well. *(The museum is at V. Cimarosa, 77. To get to the entrance, take the funicular to Vomero from V. Toledo, and turn left onto V. Cimarosa as you come out of the station. Enter the gardens and keep walking downhill.* ☎ *081 478 84 18. Visitors admitted 9am, 10:30am, noon, 3, 4:30pm. L5000, ages 18-25 L2500/€1.29).*

WATERFRONT

■ **VIRGIL'S TOMB.** Anyone who has studied Latin in high school may have at least a passing interest in seeing the poet's resting place at Salita della Frotta—if only to shake a fist at the tomb in anger over many frustrating hours spent trying to conjugate the pluperfect. Below the tomb is the entrance to the closed *Crypta Neapolitana*, a tunnel built during the reign of Augustus, connecting ancient Neapolis to Pozzuoli and Baia. Nearby lies *Leopardi*, moved from the church of S. Vitale in Fuorigrotta in 1939. Call ahead and arrange a translator, or just come for the amazing view. Either way, you will feel like this is your own personal monument. *(From M: Mergellina, take 2 quick rights. Entrance between overpass and tunnel.* ☎ *081 66 93 90. Open Tu-Su 9am-1pm. Free. Guided tours upon request.)*

CASTEL DELL'UOVO (EGG CASTLE). This massive Norman castle of yellow brick and odd angles sits on a tufaceous rock that was later connected to the mainland and now divides the bay in two. Legend has it that Virgil hid an egg within the castle walls and that with the collapse of the egg would come the collapse of the castle. This sandcastle offers beautiful views of the water and Naples. *(Take bus #1 from P. Garibaldi or P. Municipio to S. Lucia and walk across the jetty. ☎ 081 764 53 43. Only open for special events; call ahead.)*

AQUARIUM. If you're tired of seeing marine life on your dinner plate, try the aquarium in the Villa Comunale. Founded in the late 19th century, it is Europe's oldest, and it displays 30 tanks with 200 local species. *(Easily accessible by the #1 tram from P. Garibaldi or P. Municipio. ☎ 081 583 32 63. Open Tu-Sa 9am-6pm, Su-10am-6pm; in winter M-Sa 9am-5pm, Su 9am-2pm. L3000/€1.55, children and groups L1500/€0.77.)*

🎭 ENTERTAINMENT

Once occasions for famous revelry, Naples's religious festivals have since become excuses for sales and shopping sprees. On September 19, December 16, and the first Saturday in May, the city celebrates its patron saint with the **Festa di San Gennaro.** Join the crowd to watch the procession by the *duomo* (S. Chiara in May) and see S. Gennaro's blood miraculously liquefy in a vial (see **Duomo,** p. 495). The festival of **Madonna del Carmine** (July 16) features a mock burning of Fra' Nuvolo's *campanile* and culminates in a fireworks show. In July, concerts are held in P.S. Domenico Maggiore, while summers are full of neighborhood celebrations, *Rioni Festivali,* and fireworks, sporting events, processions, music, and shows.

For more passive entertainment, **Cinema Teatro Amedeo,** V. Marcucci, 69 (☎ 081 68 02 66), four blocks off P. Amedeo, shows films in English during the summer. Check *Il Mattino* for more information. **Teatro S. Carlo,** at Palazzo Reale (☎ 081 797 23 31), hosts performances by the Opera (Oct.-June) and the Symphony Orchestra (Oct.-May). Gallery tickets cost L25,000/€12.91—buy them well in advance.

For a portrait of Neapolitan life, catch a soccer game at **Stadio S. Paolo** (☎ 081 239 56 23), in Fourigrotta. Take the Metro to "Campi Flegrei." **S.S. Napoli** recently returned to Serie A and still has nationwide allegiances. There are weekly games September through June on Saturday or Sunday. Tickets are L18,000/€9.30 and up.

🛍 SHOPPING

A thriving black market and low prices make Naples a wonderful, if risky, place to shop. If you choose to buy from street vendors, understand that they are craftier than you. If a transaction seems too good to be true, it is. Clothing is usually a good deal, though your nifty new shirt may come apart in the washing machine or turn your other clothes a ghastly shade of purple. Never buy electronic products from street vendors—even brand-name boxes have been known to be filled with newspaper, bottled water, and bricks. **V.S. Maria di Constatopoli,** south of the archaeological museum, has old books and antique shops, Spaccanapoli and its side streets near the Conservatorio house music shops galore, V. Toledo provides high-class shopping for a lower budget, and the streets south of San Lorenzo Maggiore are home to craftsmen who make the traditional Neapolitan *creches.*

P. Martiri houses a roll call of Italian designers including Gucci, Valentino, Versace, Ferragamo, Armani, and Prada. The most modern and expensive shopping district is in the hills of Vomero along the perpendicular **via Scarlatti** and **via Luca Giordano.** If you're looking for jeans, head to the market off Porta Capuana. (Most markets are open M-Sa 9am-5pm, but many close at 2pm.)

🌙 NIGHTLIFE

Neapolitan nightlife is seasonal. Content to groove at the small clubs and discos during the winter, Neapolitans instinctively return to the streets and *piazze* in warmer weather. In the winter, clubs and pubs usually open at around 11pm and remain open until everyone goes home, which is normally around 4 or 5am. In the summer, the Sunday evening *passeggiata* fills the Villa Comunale along the bay (#1 tram), and amorous young couples flood picturesque ☎V. Petrarca and V. Posillipo. Most (for obvious reasons) take their cars. According to eager Italian men, if two people go to these places, a kiss means seven years of good luck.

For less exclusive gatherings, head to the *piazze* to relax and socialize. **P. Vanvitelli** in Vomero (take the funicular from V. Toledo or the C28 bus from P. Vittoria) is where kids hit on each other. In **P. Gesù Nuovo**, near the University of Naples (close to P. Dante) and the Communist headquarters, it ain't cigarette smoke you're smelling. Here the sound of bongos resonates as students, tired out from spray-painting high-brow graffiti *contro lo stato* (anti-establishment), recuperate and socialize with tourists and drifters. Outdoor bars and cafes are a popular choice, nowhere more so than in **P. Bellini** (a short walk from P. Dante) and **P. San Domenico Maggiore** (a quick walk up V. Mezzocannone from C. Umberto I), where hundreds of people drink, smoke, and chat at sidewalk tables. *Il Mattino* and *Qui Napoli* print decent club listings. Though there are almost no exclusively gay or lesbian clubs in Naples, clubs like Virgilios and Velvet have gay and lesbian nights. Call **ARCI-GAY/Lesbica** (☎081 551 82 93) for more information.

CAFES, BARS, AND PUBS

Caffè Letterario Intra Moenia, P. Bellini, 66 (☎081 29 07 20), Resembling a museum gift shop with its artifacts and postcards, *Caffè Letterario* appeals to the intellectuals among its clients by keeping books amidst the wicker furniture. Though the *menù* is highly priced (salads L14,000/€7.23), it is nice to enjoy a cocktail (L11,000/€5.68) or beer (L7000/€3.62) at an outside table in P. Bellini. Open daily 10pm-2am.

Itaca, P. Bellini, 71 (☎081 822 66 132). Formerly 1799, Itaca appeals to your dark side, opting for black decor and dim lighting. Eerie trance music keeps you from noticing how much you paid for that last cocktail. Beer L5000-6000/€2.58-3.10; cocktails from L10,000/€5.16. Open daily 10am-3am.

S'Move, Vico dei Sospiri, 10 (☎081 764 58 13; www.smove-lab.com). Head out of P. dei Martiri on V.C.toward Poerio, take the 1st right, then the 1st left. A regular bar from 8am-8pm, this neo-futuristic establishment breaks out the funk from 8pm-midnight, often with a live DJ spinning pop and R&B on weekends. After midnight, it's acid jazz and hip-hop till closing time. Open daily 8am-5am.

NIGHTCLUBS AND DISCOTHEQUES

Camelot, V. San Pietro A Majella, 8 (☎0380 713 60 17; www.camelot118@hotmail.com). Just off P. Bellini in the Historic Center, Camelot provides 2 stories of dim lighting and popular music. Except for the 3 or 4 live performances each month, Camelot specializes in beer and dancing. This place is packed in the winter and offers a calm ambience and friendly management in the summer. Beer L5000/€2.58. Open Sept.-June T-Su 10:30pm-5am.

Madison Street, V. Sgambati, 47 (☎081 546 65 66), in Vomero. Features a large dance floor for weekend revelry. Gay night Sa. Cover L25,000/€12.91. Open Sept.-May F-Su 10pm-4am.

Riot, V.S. Biagio, 39 (☎081 767 50 54), off C. Umberto I. Gives you a chance to hear local artists play jazz and sing the blues. It's not exactly Robert Johnson and the Mississippi Delta, but these folks try hard. Open Th-Su 10:30pm-3am.

◪ DAYTRIPS FROM NAPLES

CAMPI FLEGREI

To Baia, take the Ferrovia Cumana from Naples (40min), which leaves from near M: Mergellina, or from Pozzuoli (20min). The SEPSA bus also runs from Pozzuoli (30min). In Baia itself, buy an Unico Fascia 1 ticket (L2500/€1.29) and ride all modes of transporta-

*tion all day. **To Cumae,** take a SEPSA bus on the Miseno-Cuma line from the train station at Baia to the last stop in Cumae (15min.), and walk to the end of the V. Cumae. The "Cuma" stop on the Ferrovia Circumflegrea is in the modern town, several km away. Take the bus to Cumae from Baia (2 per hr.) on the Napoli-Torregaveta line. Scavi open daily 9am-1hr. before sunset. L4000/€2.07. Plan to spend at least 1hr.*

This coastal area, with its beautiful coastline and sporadic lakes and bays, once was a pocket of volcanoes. Because of its fiery past, Italy's earliest Greek inhabitants once associated it with the underworld. Luckily, those Greeks scoffed at danger and Hades didn't scare them off; now the area is blanketed with their imposing monuments. The volcanic lakes and bubbling mud baths of the Phlegrean (Burning) Fields that later became posh spas for the Roman elite can still be visited at the baths of **Baia,** and Virgilian fame to this day marks **Cuma** (Cumae). If you are more of a "the present is a gift" type person, the gray beaches of **Miseno** and the pungent smell of the smoking Solfatara Crater in **Pozzuoli** make for good clean fun. The sights of the fields are spread widely across the area, so allow a full day from Naples to see them. If you want to escape Naples's crazy city life, spend the night in Miseno and enjoy this coast at a slower pace. Or spend the entire day at Pozzuoli, which offers some of the best camping options in Italy.

Once the playground of the wild Roman Emperor Caligula, **Baia** had a reputation as a hotbed of hedonism in antiquity. Now a quiet little seaside town with a busy port, modern Baia is nonetheless interspersed with ancient ruins and spectacular views. The most interesting remnants of Baia's libertine past are the ruins of the luxurious **Roman Baths,** one of the few ancient complexes where you can climb stairs to a third and even fourth floor. Don't miss the ⬛**Temple of Mercury,** also known as Temple of Echoes. In this chamber, a ball of light from the oldest dome skylight in the world bounces on the water while every slight breath echoes a scale of tenfold. Coming out of the train station, look for the stairs to the right, climb to the top, and turn left. (☎081 868 75 92. Baths open daily 9am-1hr. before sunset. L4000/€2.07.) If archaeological treasures are your cup of tea, head to the **Castello Aragonese** and check out the **Museo Archeologico dei Campi Flegrei.** Take the Cuma-Miseno bus one stop toward Miseno (7min.). The museum has a small collection of sculptures and inscriptions from the area, not to mention an incredible view from a promontory above town. (☎081 523 37 97. Open Tu-Su 9am-1hr. before sunset. L4000/€2.07.) If you visit Baia on Saturday or Sunday, go to the port in front of the train station and board *Cymba,* a glass-bottom boat that can carry 48 people, for a 1¼hr. tour of the **submerged Roman city** off the coast. Buy tickets on board or organize a group excursion to set your own time. (☎081 526 5780. Tours Sa noon and 4pm; Su 10:30am, noon, 4pm. L1500/€0.77. Group discount.)

Cumae (Cuma), founded in the 8th century BC, was the earliest Greek colony on the Italian mainland. Mythologically, it was the place where Aeneas, father of Rome, first washed up after being shipwrecked in Virgil's *Aeneid.* The highlight of Cumae's **scavi** (excavations) is the ⬛**Antro della Sibilla,** a man-made cave gallery that had been used as a pizza oven until archaeologists realized what it was in 1932. Walk down the trapezoidal hall to where the Sybil, the most famous oracle west of Greece, counseled countless mythological characters. According to literature, she would get "inspired by the gods" and give advice and predictions in a frenzied rage. "Inspired by the gods" comes from a Latin word that has also been translated as "sloppy drunk." Also worth seeing are the **Temple of Apollo,** up a set of stairs from the cave, and the **Temple of Jupiter** atop the acropolis. The spectacular view of Ischia and the coastline is worth the hike. According to local informants, when two people kiss at this temple it means good luck.

Although you can visit Baia and Cumae as daytrips from Naples, pleasant beachfront hotels abound in **Miseno,** a town at the cusp of a nearby peninsula. Take the **SEPSA** bus from the Baia train station to Miseno (10min., 1 per hr.). The **Villa Palma Hotel,** V. Misena, 30, is at the last bus stop in Miseno. This modern and comfortable choice is steps from the beach. (☎081 523 39 44. 15 rooms all with bath. Breakfast included. Singles L70,000/€36.15; doubles L90,000/€46.48. AmEx/MC/V.)

SOUTHERN ITALY

CASERTA ☎0823

Caserta is easily accessible by train. Trains to and from Naples (30-50min., L3900-4300/€2.01-2.22) and Rome (2½-3½hr., L18,000/€9.30). The Caserta station, in the center of town across from the Reggia, is a major stop for local buses (L1500-1700/€0.77-0.88). The Reggia is directly opposite the train station, across P. Carlo III. ☎0823 32 14 00. Gardens open daily 9am-1hr. before sunset. L4000/€2.07. Palazzo open M-Sa 9am-1:30pm, Su 9am-5:30pm. L8000/€4.13. EPT tourist offices are at C. Trieste, 43, and at the corner of P. Dante. ☎0823 32 11 37. Open M-F 8am-4pm. The post office is on V. Ellittico, off P. Carlo III, in front of the train station. Postal Code: 81100. To Capua, take the train to "Santa Maria Capua Vètere" (L2300/€1.19) from Caserta, walk straight 1 block, and make the 1st left onto V.G. Avezzana. Take the next left, walk 150m, and turn right onto V. E. Ricciardi, which becomes V. Amphiteatro. Or, the blue bus from in front of the Caserta train station (L1700/€0.88) will take you straight to P. Adriano. Amphitheater open daily 9am-1hr. before sunset. L5000/€2.58. To Naples, buses leave from the intersection 1 block north of the train station in Capua.

Tourists flock to Caserta, "the Versailles of Naples," for one reason and one reason only: to see the magnificent ▩Reggia. When Bourbon King Charles III commissioned the palace in 1751, he intended to rival Louis XIV. The complex was finished in 1775, including the gigantic Royal Palace and the 120-hectare **parco** (palace garden). Lush lawns, fountains, sculptures, and carefully pruned trees culminate in a 75m man-made waterfall. Sculptural groups at the bottom show Diana transforming the hunter Actaeon into a deer as his hounds pounce on him. To the right are the "English Gardens," complete with fake ruins inspired by Pompeii and Paestum. If you don't feel like attempting the 3km walk, take the bus (L1500/€0.77) or a romantic horse-and-buggy ride. The **Palazzo** itself boasts 1200 rooms, 1742 windows, and 34 staircases. The main entrance stairway is a highlight of the palace's architecture. Frescoes and intricate marble floors adorn the gaudy royal apartments. If you have time to kill, **San Leucio** is the silkworm of Naples.

One train stop from Caserta lies **Capua** and one of the most impressive **Roman amphitheaters.** Only the contemporaneous Colosseum in Rome rivals this structure. See the tunnels where gladiators and beasts were brought into the arena.

Most of the hotels in Caserta are in the dilapidated area around the train station. If you are too tired to trek elsewhere after touring the Reggia, **Hotel Baby,** V. G. Verdi, 41, to the right as you exit the station, has 10 well-furnished rooms. (☎0823 32 83 11. Singles L85,000/€43.90; doubles L100,000/€51.65; triples L130,000/€67.14; quads L160,000/€82.63). Caserta's cuisine is simple—the town has numerous **pizzerie** (takeout available). One of the most popular is **Pizzeria La Ciociara,** V. Roma, 13, serving up large slices for L2-5000/€1.03-2.58. From the train station, walk two blocks toward the Reggia and take a right on V. Roma. (☎0823 32 26 14. Open daily 10am-midnight.) V. Mazzini, running from P. Dante north to P. Vanvitelli, is the center for what social life the town offers.

BENEVENTO ☎0824

Benevento is accessible by train from Caserta (1hr., L5900/€3.05), Naples (1½hr., L7500/€3.87), and Rome (3hr.; L22,000/€11.36. Local buses (info ☎0824 210 15) leave from the train station, including bus #1 (L1000/€0.52) to C. Garibaldi, the center of town. Buses to Naples and local towns leave from the Terminal Autobus Extraurbani, several blocks north of the Castel on C. Garibaldi. For taxis call ☎0824 200 00. The EPT tourist office in P. Roma (off C. Garibaldi) is a storehouse of knowledge. ☎0824 31 99 38. Open M-F 8am-2pm and 3-6pm. Postal Code: 82100.

According to legend, this town's original name was *Maleventum* (bad wind), but after the Romans defeated Pyrrhus here in 275 BC, they decided it might be a *Benevento* (good wind) after all. Even after being bombed during World War II, this peaceful mountain enclave retained its ancient monuments and old-town charm.

From the 6th to the 4th century BC, Benevento was the center of the Samnite kingdom. The bell tower in P. Matteotti, off C. Garibaldi, proudly commemorates Benevento's heritage. The **Church of S. Sofia** (762), also in P. Matteotti, has an attached monastery that is now the **Museo del Sannio** (☎0824 218 18), which holds Samnite artifacts, Roman objects, and works by local artists. South of the museum, down Vico Noce, is a sculpture garden with works by Mino Palladino. North of P. Roma is the ☒**Arch of Beneventum** (114-117 BC), depicting the policies of the Emperor **Trajan**. It has the finest and most extensive decoration of any surviving Roman arch. At the other end of town is a huge 2nd-century **Roman theater**—one of Italy's best preserved, it's still a concert venue (L4000/€2.07). Every September the town hosts a theater festival; contact the tourist office for details.

Albergo della Corte is in an alley at P. Piano di Corte, 11. Follow the narrow V. Bartolomeo Camerario, off C. Garibaldi. Though no English is spoken, the *albergo* offers 11 newly renovated rooms with TVs. (☎0824 548 19. Singles L55,000/€28.41; doubles L80,000/€41.32. AmEx/MC/V.) Near Trajan's Arch, **Ristorante e Pizzeria Traiano**, V. Manciotti, 48, serves simple but delectable meals. (☎0824 250 13. *Primi* L8000/€4.13; *secondi* L8000/€4.13. Open W-M noon-4pm and 7pm-midnight.) Though the area is known for its *mozzarella di bufala* cheese, don't leave without falling under the spell of Benevento's *Strega* liqueur, named after the legendary witches of Benevento, or at least the *Strega*-flavored *gelato*.

The long way back to Naples takes you through the rugged backcountry. Buses stop at the small village of **Montesarchio.** Covering a steep hill, its winding streets lead to an ☒**Aragonese tower** and fabulous views. Talk to the Benevento tourist office to find out the bus schedule. A village stop will take no more than 2 hours.

BAY OF NAPLES: VESUVIUS

POMPEII (POMPEI)   ☎081

On August 24, AD 79, life in the prosperous Roman city of Pompeii was buried in a fit of towering flames, suffocating black clouds, and lava from Mt. Vesuvius. Except for the prudent few who dropped everything and ran at the first tremors, Pompeiians suffered a live burial. You may well feel apprehensive at the thought of viewing the ghastly and evocative relics of the town's demise: the ash casts of the victims' bodies and their preserved contortions and expressions, the enduring walls and frescoes. Mount Vesuvius broods nearby, still active and terrifying. Since the first unearthings in 1748, every decade has brought new discoveries to light, providing a vivid picture of daily life in the Roman era.

▐ TRANSPORTATION

The quickest route to Pompeii (25km south of Naples) is the Circumvesuviana train (☎081 772 21 11), which can be boarded at Naples's Stazione Centrale (dir: Sorrento, 2 per hr., L3200/€1.65), or from Sorrento's station. Get off at the "Pompeii Scavi/Villa dei Misteri" stop; ignore "Pompeii Santuario." Eurailpasses are not valid. The entrance to the ruins is downhill to the left. An alternative is the less frequent FS train that leaves from the Naples station and stops at modern Pompeii en route to Salerno (30min., departs every hr., L3100/€1.65). The FS train station is a 10min. walk from the east entrance to the excavations. To get there, continue straight on V. Sacra to the end then turn left onto V. Roma.

◄✳ ₂ ORIENTATION AND PRACTICAL INFORMATION

The excavations stretch on an east-west axis, with the modern town clustered around the eastern end. Stop by the **tourist office,** V. Sacra, 1, for a free map. To get to the branch office, P. Porta Marina Inferiore, 12, from the "Pompeii Scavi/Villa dei Misteri" stop, take a right out of the Circumvesuviana station and follow the road to the bottom of the hill. (☎081 850 72 55. Both offices open M-F 8am-3:30pm, Sa 8am-2pm.) Store your pack for free at the entrance to the ruins. There is a **police station** at the entrance to the site, but the main stations are at P. Schettini, 1 (☎081 850 61 64) and P.B. Longo, at the end of V. Roma.

ACCOMMODATIONS & CAMPING

Since most travelers visit the city as a daytrip from Naples, Rome, or Sorrento, Pompeii's hotels and campgrounds are eager for business, and prices can sometimes be bargained down by 15% or more. The tourist office provides a comprehensive list of hotels with prices.

Motel Villa dei Misteri, V. Villa dei Misteri, 11 (☎081 861 35 93; fax 862 29 83), uphill from the Circumvesuviana station. 33 comfortable, clean rooms, most with balconies overlooking an oddly shaped pool. The sight of the upscale lounge and sumptuous rooms will explain to you why you should call about 3 months ahead for summer stays. A/C available. Breakfast L8000/€4.13. Singles L90,000/€46.48; doubles L90,000/€46.48; triples L120,000/€62. AmEx/MC/V.

Albergo Minerva, V. Plinio, 23 (☎081 863 25 87), between Porta di Nocera and P. Immacolata in the modern town. Wedged between buildings. 10 quiet rooms, all with bath. Doubles L70,000/€36.15; triples L85,000/€43.90; quads L100,000/€51.65.

Camping Zeus, V. Villa dei Misteri, 1 (☎081 861 53 20; fax 081 861 75 36; camping-zeus@uniserV.uniplan.it), located outside the "Villa dei Misteri" Circumvesuviana stop. L9000/€4.65 per person, L6000/€3.10 per small tent, L6000/€3.10 per large tent. L2000/€1.03 higher Aug.-Sept. 2- to 5-person rooms L50-110,000/€25.82-56.81.

Camping Pompeii, V. Plinio, 121-8 (☎081 862 28 82; fax 850 27 72; camping-pompei@uniserV.uniplan.it; www.wei.it/cpompei), downhill on V. Plinio, the main road from the ruins. 50 bungalows. Singles L40,000/€20.66; doubles L60,000/€31, triples L80,000/€41.32; quads L100,000/€51.65; quints L110,000/€56.81. If you don't reserve about a week in advance, you can sleep on their indoor lobby floor for L7-9000/€3.62-4.65 per night. AmEx/MC/V.

FOOD

Food at the site cafeteria is horribly expensive, so bring a **pre-packed lunch.** A few restaurants and fruit stands cluster outside the excavation entrances. Otherwise, stock up at the **GS supermarket,** V. Statale, on the main road between the entrances to the archaeological site. (Open M-Sa 8am-8:30pm, Su 9am-1pm.)

La Vinicola, V. Roma, 29 (☎081 863 12 44), an alternative to the nearby McDonald's. Tempts visitors with a pleasant outdoor courtyard, bubbling Italian service that seems it will explode in song at any moment, and abundant *gnocchi con mozzarella* (potato pasta with mozzarella) L6000/€3.14). Tourist lunch L20,000/€10.33, excluding drinks. Cover L1500/€0.77. Open daily 9am-midnight.

Empire Pizza Inn, V. Plinio, 71 (☎081 863 23 66), on the way to Hotel Minerva from the Ruins. Complete meals L10-20,000/€5.16-10.33. The ultimate Italian all-in-one: a pizza place that is also a music hall/discotheque. Who knew it could be done?! Open daily 10am-2am. Discotheque open 9pm-3am.

SIGHTS

Entrances to Pompeii are open 8:30am to 1hr. before sunset (in summer around 6pm; in winter around 3:30pm; L16,000/€8.26). A comprehensive exploration will probably take all day. **Guided tours**—which allow you to savor the details of life and death in the first century AD—are quite expensive and mostly take groups. Call **GATA Tours** (☎081 861 56 61) or **Assotouring** (☎081 862 25 60) for information. Some of the tour guides are wise to freeloaders, actually yelling at offenders; others remain oblivious. Those with neither the cash nor the savvy to join a tour can buy one of the various guidebooks available outside site entrances (from L8000/€4.13). Despite the hefty admission price, the site is poorly labeled. But it could be worse—you could have been trapped under molten lava for 2000 years.

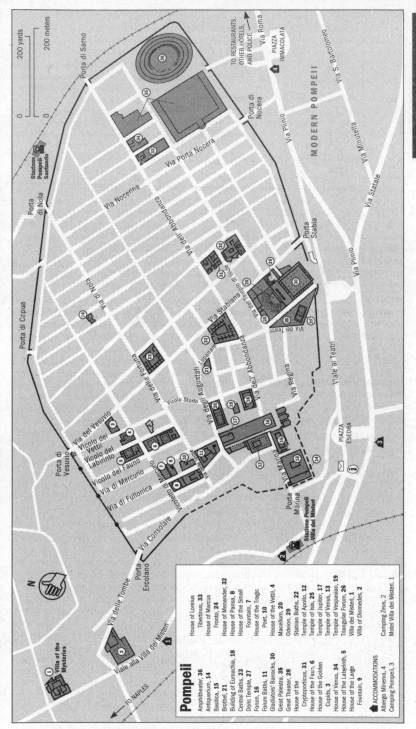

Pompeii

Amphitheater, 36
Antiquarium, 14
Basilica, 15
Brothel, 21
Building of Eumachia, 18
Central Baths, 23
Doric Temple, 27
Forum, 16
Forum Baths, 11
Gladiators' Barracks, 30
Great Palestra, 35
Great Theater, 28
House of the
Cryptoporticus, 31
House of the Faun, 6
House of the Golden
Cupids, 3
House of Venus, 34
House of the Labyrinth, 5
House of the Large
Fountain, 9

House of Loreius
Tiburtinus, 33
House of Marcus
Fronto, 24
House of Menander, 32
House of Pansa, 8
House of the Small
Fountain, 7
House of the Tragic
Poet, 10
House of the Vettii, 4
Macellum, 20
Odeion, 29
Stabian Baths, 22
Temple of Apollo, 12
Temple of Isis, 25
Temple of Jupiter, 17
Temple of Venus, 13
Temple of Vespasian, 19
Triangular Forum, 26
Villa dei Misteri, 1
Villa of Diomedes, 2

▲ ACCOMMODATIONS
Albergo Minerva, 4
Camping Pompeii, 3

Camping Zeus, 2
Motel Villa dei Misteri, 1

MODERN POMPEII

TO NAPLES

NEAR FORUM. The **basilica** (Roman law court) walls are decorated with stucco made to look like marble. Walk farther down V.D. Marina to reach the ■**Forum,** which is surrounded by a colonnade. Once dotted with statues of emperors and gods, this site was the commercial, civic, and religious center of the city. Cases along the side display some of the gruesome body-casts of Vesuvius's victims. At the upper end rises the **Temple of Jupiter,** mostly destroyed by an earthquake that struck 17 years before the city's bad luck got worse. To the left, the **Temple of Apollo** contains statues of Apollo and Diana (originals in Naples's Museo Archeologico Nazionale, p. 552) and a column topped by a sundial. On the opposite long side of the forum, the **Temple of Vespasian** houses a delicate frieze depicting preparation for a sacrifice. To the right, the **Building of Eumachia** has a carved door frame of animals and insects hiding in acanthus scrolls.

NEAR HOUSE OF THE FAUN. Exit the Forum through the upper end, by the cafeteria, and the **Forum Baths** are on the left. Here, chipping away parts of the body-casts has revealed teeth and bones beneath. A right on V. della Fortuna leads to the ■**House of the Faun,** where a bronze dancing faun and the spectacular Alexander Mosaic (originals in the **Museo Archeologico Nazionale,** p. 495) were found. The sheer opulence of this building led archaeologists to believe that it was the dwelling of one of the richest men in town. Continuing on V. della Fortuna and turning left on V. dei Vettii will bring you to the ■**House of the Vettii,** on the left, decorated with vivid frescoes. In the vestibule, a depiction of Priapus, the god of fertility, displays his colossal member. And while in ancient times, phalli were believed to scare off evil spirits, these days they seem only to make tourists titter.

NEAR BROTHEL. Back down V. dei Vetti, cross V. della Fortuna over to V. Storto, and then turn left on V. degli Augustali. The Romans who were repaving this worn path when the volcano struck left their task incomplete. A quick right leads to the small **brothel** (the Lupenar) containing several bedstalls. Above each stall, a pornographic painting depicts with unabashed precision the specialty of its occupant. After 2000 years, this remains the most popular place in town; you may have to wait in line. The street continues down to the main avenue, V. dell'Abbondanza. To the left lie the **Stabian Baths,** which were privately owned and therefore fancier than the Forum Baths (think ritzy spa vs. YMCA). The separate men's and women's sides each include a dressing room, cold baths *(frigidaria),* warm baths *(tepidaria),* and hot steam baths *(caldaria).*

NEAR GREAT THEATER. V. dei Teatri, across the street, leads to a huge complex consisting of the **Great Theater,** constructed in the first half of the 2nd century BC, and the **Little Theater,** built later for music and dance concerts. North of the theaters stands the **Temple of Isis,** Pompeii's monument to the Egyptian fertility goddess. Through the exit on the right, the road passes two fine houses, the **House of Secundus** and the **House of Menander.** At the end of the street, a left turn will return you to the main road. The Romans believed that crossroads were vulnerable to evil spirits, so they built altars (like the one here) designed to ward them off.

NEAR AMPHITHEATER. On V. dell'Abbondanza, red writing glares from the walls, expressing everything from political slogans to love declarations. Popular favorites include "Albanus is a bugger," "Restitutus has decieved many girls many times," and the lyrical "Lovers, like bees, lead a honey-sweet life"—apparently graffiti hasn't changed much in 2000 years. At the end of the street rest the **House of Tiburtinus** and the **House of Venus,** huge complexes with gardens replanted according to modern knowledge of ancient horticulture. The nearby **amphitheater** (80 BC), the oldest standing in the world, held 12,000 spectators. When battles occurred, crowds decided whether a defeated gladiator would live or die with a casual thumbs up or thumbs down.

To reach the ■**Villa of the Mysteries,** go to the far west end of V. della Fortuna, turn right on V. Consolare, and walk all the way up Porta Ercolano. The best preserved of Pompeii's villas, it includes the Dionysiac Frieze, perhaps the largest painting from the ancient world, depicting the initiation of a bride into the cult of Dionysus. Head through the door in the Porta for a great view of the entire city.

▶ DAYTRIPS FROM POMPEII

HERCULANEUM (ERCOLANO)

The archaeological site is open daily 8:30am to 1hr. before sunset. L16,000/€8.26. Tours offered from the tourist office, but are only worthwhile for a large group. To reach Ercolano, take a Circumvesuviana train from Naples's central train station to the "Ercolano" stop (dir: "Sorrento"; 20min.). Walk 500m downhill to the ticket office. The Municipal Tourist Office, V. IV Novembre, 84 (081 788 12 43) is on the way (open M, W-F 9am-1pm, Tu 4-6:30pm). Illustrated guidebooks are available at any of the shops flanking the entrance.

Neatly excavated and impressively intact, the remains of the prosperous Roman town of Herculaneum (modern Ercolano) hardly deserve the term "ruins." Indeed, exploring the 2000-year-old houses, complete with frescoes, furniture, mosaics, small sculptures, and even wooden doors, feels like an invasion of privacy.

Herculaneum does not evoke the tragedy of Pompeii—most of its inhabitants escaped the ravages of Vesuvius. Only a small part of the southeastern quarter of the city has been excavated, and between 15 and 20 houses are open to the public. One of the more alluring is the **House of Deer** (named for the statues of deer in the courtyard), which displays the statue, *Satyr with a Wineskin*, and one of Hercules in a drunken stupor trying to relieve himself. The **baths**, with largely intact warm and hot rooms and a vaulted swimming pool, conjure up images of ancient opulence. The **House of the Mosaic of Neptune and Anfitrite**, which belonged to a rich shop owner, is famous for its namesake mosaic, and the front of the house has a remarkably well-preserved wine shop. A mock colonnade of stucco distinguishes the **Samnise House**. Down the street, the **House of the Wooden Partition** still has a door in its elegant courtyard, and an ancient clothes press around the corner. Cardo IV shows you what a Roman street must have looked like. Outside the site, 250m to the left on the main road, lies the **theater**, perfectly preserved underground. (☎081 739 09 63. Occasionally open for visits; call to check.) The **Villa dei Papiri**, 500m west of the site, recently caused a stir when it was thought that a trove of ancient scrolls in the library included works by Cicero, Virgil, and Horace. Unfortunately, neither of these two sites is commonly open to the public.

MT. VESUVIUS

__Trasporti Vesuviani buses__ run from Ercolano up to the crater of Vesuvius (L6000/€3.14 roundtrip, buy tickets on the bus; schedule at the tourist office or on the bus). They leave from outside the Ercolano Circumvesuviana station. Bus stop is part way up the crater; it's a 20-30min. walk to the top. Admission to the area around the crater is L9000/€4.65.

Peer into the only active volcano on mainland Europe. Scientists say that, on average, volcanoes should erupt every 30 years—Vesuvius hasn't since March 31, 1944. Nevertheless, experts say the trip is safe.

SORRENTO ☎081

"Return to Sorrento" is not just the title of a hearty folk song, but the strategy of countless tourists who use the city as a base for their bay explorations. With 20,000 residents, Sorrento is the largest town in the area, and with 13,000 hotel beds, the most touristed. So popular is the town with British tourists that it is easier to find a cup of tea than a *cappucino*, and prices are often listed in pounds. Still, Sorrento has its charms, including the streets of the old city and the **Marina Grande**. Frequent ferry connections provide links to the rest of the bay.

▐ TRANSPORTATION

Trains: Circumvesuviana (☎081 772 24 44), just off P. Lauro. 40 trains per day, from 5am-10:30pm to: **Pompeii** (35min., L2300/€1.19); **Herculaneum** (45min., L4000/€2.07); **Naples** (1hr., L4800/€2.48).

Ferries and **Hydrofoils:** All boats dock at the port, accessible from P. Tassi by bus (L1700/€0.88). **Linee Marittime Partenopee** (☎081 878 14 30) runs ferries to

Amalfi (45min.; L16,000/€8.26) via **Positano** (30min.; L15,000/€7.75), and **Capri** (50min., L8000/€4.13). It also runs hydrofoils to: **Capri** (20min.; 18 per day 7:30am-5pm; L13,000/€6.71); **Naples** (40min.; L18,000/€9.30); **Ischia** (45min.; L21,000/€10.85). Ticket offices open daily 7:30am-7pm. **Caremar** (☎ 081 807 30 77) runs ferries to **Capri** (50min.; L9000/€4.65). Ticket offices open daily 7am-5pm.

Buses: SITA buses leave from Circumvesuviana station for Amalfi coast. 18 buses per day to: **Amalfi** (1¼hr., L3800/€1.96); **Positano** (40min., L2400/€1.24); **Praiano** (1hr., L3200/€1.65). Buy your tickets at a bar, *tabacchi*, or hotel in P. Lauro.

✦❷ ORIENTATION AND PRACTICAL INFORMATION

Most of Sorrento is on a flat shelf with cliffs rapidly descending to the Bay of Naples. **Piazza Tasso,** at the center of town, is connected by a stairway (and roads) to the **Marina Grande** and **Marina Piccola** ports. Corso Italia runs through P. Tasso—facing the sea, the train and bus station are to the right, while the old city is to the left. V. Fuorimura intersects C. Italia and leads away from the cliffs.

TOURIST, FINANCIAL, AND LOCAL SERVICES

Tourist Office: V. de Maio, 35 (☎ 081 807 40 33). From P. Tasso, take V. de Maio through P.S. Antonio and continue toward the port. The office is to the right in the Circolo dei Forestieri compound. English spoken. Grab a free copy of *Surrentum*, the monthly tourist magazine. Open Apr.-Sept. M-F 8:45am-7:45pm, Sa 8:45am-7:15pm; Oct.-Mar. M-Sa 8:30am-2pm and 4-6:15pm.

Currency Exchange: Post office rates are the best in town. Commission L1000/€0.52. Open 8:15am-6pm.

Car and Scooter Rental: Sorrento Car Service, C. Italia, 210a (☎ 081 878 13 86). Scooters from L75,000/€38.73 per day. Helmet and insurance included. Driver's license required. Cars and chauffeurs available. Open daily 8am-1pm and 4-9:30pm.

English-language Bookstore: Libreria Tasso, V.S. Cesareo, 96 (☎ 081 807 16 39; libreriatasso@tin.it). Stocks thrillers, including the shocking *Let's Go*. Open M-Sa 9:30am-1:30pm and 5-10:45pm, Su 11am-1:30pm and 7-10:45pm.

Laundromat: Terlizzi, C. Italia, 30 (☎ 081 878 11 85), in the old quarter. L15,000/€7.75 per load, L25,000/€12.91 per 2 loads. Detergent L1000/€0.52. Dry cleaning. Open daily 9am-8:30pm.

EMERGENCY AND COMMUNICATIONS

Emergency: ☎ 113.

Medical Emergency: Pronto Soccorso (☎ 081 533 11 12) at **Ospedale Civile di Sorrento,** C. Italia, 129 (☎ 081 53 11 11).

Police: (☎ 081 807 533 11) on Vco. 3° Rota. From the station, go right on C. Italia and left after V. Nizza.

Internet Access: Blublu.it, V. Fuorimura, 20 (☎/fax 081 807 48 54; www.blublu.it). Take V. Fuorimura from P. Tasso. English-speaking staff and fast connections. L5000/€2.58 per30min. Open M-F 10am-1pm and 4:30-11pm, Sa 3pm-12am.

Post Office: C. Italia, 210 (☎ 081 878 14 95), near P. Lauro. Open M-Sa 8:15am-7:20pm.

Postal Code: 80067.

▐ ACCOMMODATIONS & CAMPING

Sorrento's reasonably priced accommdations, convenient transportation, and Internet points prompt most travelers on the Amalfi course to use it as a jumping off point to more rural destinations. They return to the city at night, and reservations are suggested in July and August. Some hotels charge more than their estab-

SORRENTO ■ 509

lished prices. If you're being overcharged, ask to see the official price list; you can then write a letter to the EPT. Prices listed below are for high season.

Hotel Elios, V. Capo, 33 (☎081 878 18 12), halfway to the Punta del Capo. Take **bus A** from P. Tasso. Though rooms are not particularly dazzling, 2 large terraces and the hotel's peak position mean a prime view. Singles L45,000/€23.24; doubles L80,000/€41.32; groups of 3 or 4 L45,000/€23.24 per person.

Hotel City, C. Italia, 221 (☎081 877 22 10; hotelcity@libero.it), left on C. Italia from the station. Currency exchange, bus tickets, maps, English newspapers, and bar. Internet L5000/€2.58 per 30min. In summer, reserve 1 month ahead. Singles L75,000/€23.24; doubles L125,000/€64.56. Extra bed L25,000/€12.91. AmEx/MC/V.

Hotel Savoia, V. Fuorimura, 46 (☎/fax 081 878 25 11), 4 blocks from P. Tasso. This tranquil hotel has 15 quiet, spacious rooms, all with very clean baths, and friendly staff. Singles L85,000/€43.90; doubles L110,000/€56.81. AmEx/MC/V.

Pensione Le Sirene, V. Degli Aranci, 160 (☎081 807 29 25). From C. Italia turn right onto V.S. Renato, and take 1st right. Prepare to wake up to the 1st train or to extra guests crashing your party. Co-ed dorms with bath outside L25,000/€12.91, with bath inside room L30,000/€15.50. Single gender rooms with bath L35,000/€18.08.

Camping: Nube d'Argento, V. del Capo, 21 (☎081 878 13 44; fax 081 807 34 50; www.nubedargento.com). **Bus A** from P. Tasso L1700/€0.88. Near the ocean, with a pool, hot showers, market, and restaurant. Laundry L10,000/€5.16. Reservations only for bungalows, in Aug. reserve 2 mos. ahead. L13-16,000/€6.71-8.26 per person, L6-10,000/€3.10-5.16 per tent. 2-person bungalows L100,000/€51.65. 10% discount with Magic Europe camping brochure (can be picked up at any campsite) or International Camping card. AmEx/MC/V.

█ FOOD

Local specialties at reasonable prices await you in Sorrento's restaurants and *trattorie*. Try to avoid the British food and the most touristed restaurants; there's a reason blood pudding never made it outside of the UK. Sorrento is famous for its *gnocchi alla Sorrentina* (potato pasta smothered in tomato sauce, mozzarella, and basil), its *cannelloni* (pasta tubes stuffed with cheese and herbs), and its *nocillo* (a dark liqueur made from the local walnuts). **Fabbrica Liquori,** V.S. Cesareo, 51, off V. Giuliani, provides free samples, as well as the ubiquitous *limoncello*, a refreshing lemon liqueur. For **market** stands, follow V.S. Cesareo from P. Tasso until it turns into V. Fuoro, where ripe, sweet, juicy fruit awaits.

Ristorante e Pizzeria Giardiniello, V. Accademia, 7 (☎081 878 46 16). Take the 2nd left off V. Giuliani, which runs off C. Italia at the cathedral. Mamma Luisa does all the cooking in this family-run establishment. Her *gnocchi* is yummy for L8000/€4.13, and the *linguini al cartoccio* (with mixed seafood) is a steal at L13,000/€6.71. Cover L1500/€0.77. Open June-Sept. daily 11am-2am; Oct.-May F-W 11am-2am.

Davide, V. Giuliani, 39 (☎081 878 13 37). Sorrento's best *gelato*, right off C. Italia, 2 blocks from P. Tasso. So much, so tasty, so little time. The watermelon, peach delicate, fig heavenly, and butterscotch savory are irresistible, while the true triumph is the mousse. 55-80 flavors daily. L3500/€1.81 for 2 scoops. Open daily 10am-2am.

Il Vicoletto, V. Pietà, 3 (☎081 877 34 42), in the alley in the corner behind Tasso's cloak in P. Tasso, offers regional cooking at reasonable prices. Pizza L6-15,000/€3.10-7.75; *primi* L8-12,000/€4.13-6.20. Cover L2000/€1.03. Open daily 8pm-1am.

Taverna Azzura, V. Marina Grande, 166 (☎081 877 25 10). From C. Cesareo off P. Tasso, go left on V. Giuliani to the end; Marina Grande is a pleasant 10min. walk to the left on the small road past P. della Vittoria. Fresh seafood and pasta cooked to perfection. *Primi* from L8000/€4.13; *secondi* from L9000/€4.65. Cover L2500/€1.29. Open daily noon-3pm and 7pm-midnight.

Gigino Pizza a Metro (Pizza by the Meter), V. Nicotera, 15 (☎081 879 84 26), in Vico Equense, a 10min. train ride. Take the Circumvesuviana to V. Equense, go straight as you exit the station, and follow the winding road uphill to P. Umberto. Take a left on V. Roma and another left on V. Nicotera. Unofficially the world's largest pizzeria, this 2-story, 3000-seat facility has wood-burning ovens that cook 1m-long pizzas. Smaller pizzas L8-12,000/€4.13-6.20. Cover L2000/€1.03. Service 13%. Open daily noon-1am.

👁 🎵 SIGHTS AND ENTERTAINMENT

Sorrento is a city with fairly safe streets, notable views, and interesting nightlife. Despite the influx of tourists, very little in the way of Italy's big three combination (*duomo-torre-palazzo*) exists, unless you consider T-shirt shops worthy of the grand *monumenti* tradition. The best bet for the chronically antsy is a trip down to **Marina Grande,** far from the crowds at the city center.

The westerly orientation of the beaches makes sunset swims memorable. Take the bus to **Punta del Capo** and walk 10 minutes down the footpath to the right of the stop. On the coast stand the remains of the ancient Roman **Villa di Pollio.** A visit to the rather limited ruins is best combined with a dip in the beautiful cove.

The old city and the area around P. Tasso heat up after dark, as locals and tourists stroll the streets, gaze over the bay, and cavort about town on mopeds. Hands down the most stylish bar in Sorrento, **Gatto Nero,** V. Correale, 21 (☎081 877 36 86), has a garden and creative interior—each wall is painted in the style of a modernist painter (among them Picasso and Matisse). Jazz and blues animate the crowd, hopping by 11pm. The **Merry Monk Guinness Pub,** at V. Capo, 4, is as dark as any Guinness Pub should be. What's more, there's a room with six computers. (☎081 877 24 09. Internet L6000/€3.10 per hr. Open daily until everyone leaves.) After 10:30pm, a fun-loving crowd gathers in the rooftop lemon grove above **The English Inn,** at C. Italia, 56, where 80s music gets dancers moving. (☎081 807 43 57. Open daily 9am-1am, much later on weekends.) The **Charley Chaplain Pub,** C. Italia, 18, across the street, usually sees some nighttime action, even if the patrons just come to see the little tramps behind the bar. (☎081 807 25 51. Open daily 5pm-3am.)

BAY OF NAPLES: ISLANDS

The pleasure islands **Capri, Ischia,** and **Procida** beckon to the weary traveler with promises of breathtaking natural sights, comfortable accommodations, and gorgeous beaches. The islands can be reached by ferries (*traghetti*) or faster, more expensive hydrofoils (*aliscafi*). But the tranquility of sun-baked landscapes has its price, and you might end up spending more than you want for accommodations. For jaunts to Ischia and Procida, the route through Pozzuoli is shortest and cheapest; for Capri, Sorrento is the closest starting point. The busiest route to Capri and Ischia is through Naples's Mergellina and Molo Beverello ports. To reach Molo Beverello from Stazione Centrale, take tram #1 from P. Garibaldi to P. Municipio on the waterfront. Ferries and hydrofoils also run between the islands.

CAPRI AND ANACAPRI   ☎081

Augustus fell in love with this island's fantastic beauty in 29 BC but swapped it for its more fertile neighbor, Ischia. His successor Tiberius passed his last decade here, leaving a dozen scattered villas. Visitors today pay top *lira* to tour the renowned **Blue Grotto** and gawk at the rich and famous. Away from the throngs flitting between Capri's expensive boutiques, Anacapri is home to budget hotels, spectacular vistas, and empty mountain paths. Crowds and prices are high throughout the summer, especially in July and August, so the best times to visit are in the late spring or early fall, though it is well worth the trip any time of year.

▐ TRANSPORTATION

Ferries: Ticket office, arrivals and departures at **Marina Grande**. For more info about how to get to Capri check out ferries from Naples (p. 484) and Sorrento (p. 507). Caremar usually is the best deal. Ferries to Naples run about every hour, while there are only three or four ferries to Sorrento everyday.

Caremar (☎081 837 07 00) runs ferries and hydrofoils. Ferries to **Naples** (1¼hr.; L12,000/€6.20) and **Sorrento** (45min.; L16,000/€8.26). Hydrofoils to **Naples** (40min.; L19,000/€9.81). Ticket office open daily 7am-8pm.

SNAV (☎081 837 75 77) runs hydrofoils to **Naples's** Mergellina port (40min.; L20,000/€10.33). L2000/€1.03 extra for bags. Ticket office open daily 8am-8pm.

Linea Jet (☎081 837 08 19) runs hydrofoils to **Naples** (40min.; 11 per day 8:30am-6pm; L20,000/€10.33) and **Sorrento** (20min.; L14,000/€7.23). Office open daily 9am-6pm.

Linee Lauro (☎081 837 69 95), runs hydrofoils to: **Amalfi** (1hr.; L20,000/€10.33); **Ischia** (40min. 4:40pm; L20,000/€10.33); **Salerno** (1½hr.; L20,000/€10.33), by way of **Positano** (30min.; L20,000/€10.33); and **Sorrento** (20min.; L16,000/€8.26).

Local Transportation: SIPPIC buses (☎081 837 04 20) depart from V. Roma in Capri for Anacapri (every 15min., 6am-1:40am), Marina Piccola, and points in between. In Anacapri, buses depart from P. Barile, off V. Orlandi, for the *Grotta Azzura*, the *faro* (lighthouse), and other points. Direct line between Marina Grande and P. Vittoria in Anacapri which runs every hr. and on the hr., L2400/€1.24 per ride. If using the bus more than five times a day, buy day pass (L13,000/€6.71).

Taxis: Convertible taxis are at the bus stop in Capri (☎081 837 05 43), and at P. Vittoria in Anacapri (☎081 837 11 75).

▣ 🛈 ORIENTATION AND PRACTICAL INFORMATION

There are two towns on the island of Capri—**Capri proper** above the ports and **Anacapri**, higher up the mountain. Ferries dock at **Marina Grande**, where a **funicular** runs to **P. Umberto** in Capri (every 10min., 6:30-12:30am in summer, L1700/€0.88). The alternative is an hour hike up a narrow stairway. Expensive boutiques and bakeries fill the narrow streets radiating off P. Umberto. **Via Roma,** to the right, leads to Anacapri. Buses from Capri to Anacapri run on to Blue Grotto before reaching the lighthouse across the island. The bus to Anacapri stops in P. Vittoria. Villa S. Michele and the Monte Solaro chairlift are nearby. **Via Giuseppe Orlandi,** running from P. Vittoria, leads to the best budget establishments. Except for the port road, Capri is comprised of narrow pedestrian paths closed to cars.

TOURIST, FINANCIAL, AND LOCAL SERVICES

Tourist Office: The swamped **AAST information Office** (☎081 837 06 34) lies at the end of the dock at Marina Grande in Capri. There's another branch at P. Umberto, under the clock (☎081 837 06 86). In Anacapri, there's one at V. Orlandi, 59 (☎081 837 15 24), off the main *piazza*, to the right when you get off the bus. Each office offers the yearly handbook *Capri è...* and a detailed map (L1500/€0.77). Open June-Sept. M-Sa 8:30am-8:30pm; Oct.-May M-Sa 9am-1:30pm and 3:30-6:45pm.

Currency Exchange: Though the post offices have the best rates, there are also official exchange agencies at V. Roma, 33 (☎081 837 07 85), across from the main bus stop, and in P. Umberto. Another agency in P. Vittoria, 2 (☎081 837 31 46), in the center of Anacapri. 3% commission. Open daily 8:30am-7pm, in winter reduced hours.

Luggage Storage: Caremar ticket office (☎081 837 07 00), at Marina Grande Capri's funicular. L5000/€2.58 per bag. Open daily 8am-9pm; in winter 8am-6pm. Another office in Anacapri's P. Vittoria. L2000/€1.03 per bag. Open daily 8am-5:30pm.

Public Toilets: At the funicular in Capri (L500/€0.26) and P. Vittoria, 5, in Anacapri (L500/€0.26). Open daily 8am-9pm. Not for the faint of heart.

EMERGENCY AND COMMUNICATIONS

Emergency: ☎113 or 081 838 1205.

Medical Emergency: Pronto Soccorso (☎081 838 12 05) at **Ospedale Capilupi** (☎081 838 11 11) V. Provinciale Anacapri, few blocks down V. Roma from P. Umberto.

Police: V. Roma, 70 (☎081 837 42 11).

Tourist Medical Emergency Service: V. Caprile, 30, Anacapri (☎081 838 12 40).

Internet Access: The Newsstand (☎081 837 3283) in P. Vittoria, Anacapri. L10,000/ €5.16 per hr. Open daily 9am-2pm and 4-9pm. **Capri Graphic**, V. Listrieri, 17 (☎081 837 52 12). Head out of P. Umberto on V. Longano and take a right on V. Listrieri. L5000/€2.58 per 15min. Open M-Sa 9:30am-1pm and 4-8:30pm.

Post Office: Central office in Capri at V. Roma, 50 (☎081 837 72 40), downhill from P. Umberto. Open M-F 8:30am-7:20pm, Sa 8:30am-1pm. **Currency exchange** with the best rates in town. Commission: L5000/€2.58 cash, L1000/€0.52 checks. Open M-Sa 8:10am-6pm. **Anacapri office** at V. de Tommaso, 4 (☎081 837 10 15). Open M-F 8:30am-1:30pm, Sa 8:15am-noon.

Postal Code: Capri 80073; Anacapri 80021.

ACCOMMODATIONS

Lodging in Capri proper, expensive year-round, becomes prohibitively exorbitant in mid-summer. You will not be able to find a deal in July or August. The lower price ranges listed here usually apply from October to May. Call in advance to reconfirm reservations and prices. It's possible to find vacancies in June but difficult in July and August. Makeshift camping is illegal and heavily fined.

ANACAPRI

Villa Eva, V. La Fabbrica, 8 (☎081 837 15 49 or 081 837 20 40; www.caprionline.com/ villaeva.) Before trying to navigate the 15min. walk through Anacapri's side streets, call from P. Vittoria and wait to be picked up. 28 bungalows with their own personality and style. Pool and bar. Most rooms with bath. Internet L10,000/€5.16 per hr. Reserve early. Singles L50-60,000/€25.82-30.99; doubles from L100,000/€51.65; triples L120,000/€62; quads L160,000/€82.73 and up. MC/V.

Il Girasole, V. Linciano, 47 (☎081 837 23 51; fax 837 38 80; ilgirasole@capri.it; www.ilgirasole.com). Call from Marina Grande to be met (expect to be charged), or walk from the last bus stop and follow the signs up the stairway. 24 well-furnished rooms with shuttered doorways. Bath, fridge, and TV in every room. Doubles with breakfast L180,000/€92.96; triples with breakfast L250,000/€129.11.

Alla Bussola di Hermes, V. Traversa La Vigna, 14 (☎081 838 2010; bus.hermes@libero.it). This place offers a bed to young Americans wishing to play in Anacapri with other young Americans, and incidentally, the enthusiastic proprietor, Rita, loves Americans and playing in Anacapri. Call from Marina Grande to be picked up. All rooms (dormitory and doubles) L40,000/€20.66 per person.

Hotel Loreley, V.G. Orlandi, 16 (☎081 837 14 40; fax 081 837 13 99), 20m toward Capri from P. Vittoria on your left. Avoid the confusing walks down Anacapri side streets and stay at this comfortable hotel at the edge of P. Vittoria. Conveniently located, with large, bright rooms and baths. With Let's Go: doubles L180,000/€92.96; triples L220,000/€113.62. Open Apr.-Oct. AmEx/MC/V.

CAPRI

Pensione Stella Maris, V. Roma, 27 (☎081 837 04 52; fax 837 86 62), across from the bus stop. Capri's cheapest option, near the center of town, with consequent noise. 10 rooms with shared bath and TV. Doubles L120,000/€62 during the winter, L180,000/€92.96 summer. AmEx/MC/V.

Pensione Quattro Stagioni, V. Marina Piccola, 1 (☎081 837 00 41). From P. Umberto, walk 5min. down V. Roma. Turn left at the 3-pronged fork in the road, and look for the green gate on the left. Though the cheaper rooms do not have the great view of Marina Piccola that the others do, many still open onto the lush garden. Breakfast included. Doubles L400,000/€206.58; in winter L190,000/€98.13. AmEx/MC/V.

FOOD

Capri's food is as glorious as its panoramas. Savor the local mozzarella on its own, or with tomatoes, oil, and basil in an *insalata caprese*—many consider it *the* sum-

mer meal. The *ravioli alla caprese* are hand-stuffed with tasty local cheeses. Indulge in the *torta di mandorle* (chocolate almond cake). Local red and white wines bear *Tiberio* or *Caprense* labels. A step up (especially price-wise) is the *Capri Blù*. Restaurants often serve *Capri DOC*, a light white. If you want to avoid pricey restaurants, or just grab picnic supplies, head to Capri's **STANDA supermarket.** (Open M-Sa 8:30am-1:30pm and 5-9pm, Su 9am-noon.) Bear right at the fork on the end of V. Roma. In Anacapri, try **Alimentaria Russo**, on V.G. Orlandi. (☎081 837 3991. *Panini* L5000/€2.58. Open 8am-7pm.) Ask at your hotel for budget restaurants, but don't expect to pay less than L25,000/€12.91 for a full meal.

ANACAPRI

▧ Ristorante Il Cucciolo, V. Fabbrica, 52 (☎081 837 19 17). Follow signs for Villa Damecuta from bus stop or call for a free ride from P. Vittoria. Fresh at low prices. Considerably less expensive *Let's Go menù: primi and secondi* L10-16,000/€5.16-8.26; *ravioli Caprese* L9500/€4.91. Cover L3000/€1.55, service 6%. F-Su reservations recommended. Open daily Mar.-Oct. noon-2:30pm and 7:30-11pm. July-Aug. 7:30-11pm.

Ristorante Materita Bar-Pizzeria, P. Diaz (☎081 837 33 75; fax 837 38 81; materita@tin.it). Friendly staff and outdoor dining. Reasonable *primi* and *secondi* (L10-16,000/€5.16-8.26) and great pizza from L9000/€4.65. Cover L3000/€1.55. Open noon-3:30pm and 7pm-midnight, or until everyone leaves. AmEx/MC/V.

Il Grottino Ristorante, G. Orlandi, 95 (☎081 837 10 66), a few blocks from P. Vittoria. Munch excellent food in style at the 45-year-old Il Grottino's cheery, outdoor tables. Enjoy some of the best *ravioli alla Caprese* (L15,000/€7.75). Lunch *menù* L16,500/€8.52. Cover L2000/€1.03. Open daily 11:30am-3:30pm and 7:30-11pm.

Il Ristoro, P. Caprile, 1 (☎081 837 36 71), on the Capri-Anacapri bus line, 5 blocks from P. Vittoria. *Mangia, mangia!* This family-run establishment will treat you like their own. Take advantage of the tourist meals. *Menù* L20,000/€10.33 (including service and cover). Pizza and drink L13,000/€6.71. Open daily 8am-midnight. AmEx/MC/V.

Trattoria Il Solitario, V. Orlandi, 96, falsely marked as #54 (☎081 837 13 82), 5min. from P. Vittoria to your right. The food is tasty and the Spanish-speaking staff friendly. Ravioli Caprese L10,000/€5.16, pizza from L7000/€3.62. Cover L2500/€1.29. Open W-M noon-3:30pm and 7:30pm-midnight.

Trattoria-Pizzeria da Mamma Giovanna, V. Boffe, 3 (☎081 837 20 57) next to the church in P. Diaz. Typical Caprese meals in a more sophisticated atmosphere. *Ravioli* L15,000/€7.75. Cover L3000/€1.55. Reservations recommended on summer weekends. Open daily 11:30am-3pm and 7pm-midnight.

CAPRI

▧ Villa Verde, V. sella Orta, 6a (☎081 837 70 24). Follow great signs from V.V. Emanuele. Reserve ahead on weekends to eat as you have never eaten before. Fresh lobster, fish, vegetables, and scumptous-looking desserts sport that come-hither stare. Prices are a bit VIP, but size and quality is worth the extra L10,000/€5.16. Try the *Scialatelliapiacere* (homemade pasta with cherry tomatoes, eggplant, and provola) for L26,000/€13.43. Daily chef specialties L16-28,000/€8.26-13.43. Open daily noon-4pm and 7pm-1am. AmEx/MC/V.

▧ Longano da Tarantino, V. Longano, 9 (☎081 837 10 87), just off P. Umberto. Possibly the best deal in town, featuring an ocean view and a L26,000 *menù*. Try the *maccheroncelli "Aumm Aumm"* (with eggplant, tomato, and cheese; L10,000/€5.16), so-named because that's all your ecstatic mouth will be able to utter. Pizza from L6000/€3.10. Open Mar.-Nov. Th-Tu noon-3:30pm and 7pm-midnight. AmEx/MC/V.

Buca di Bacco, V. Longano, 35 (☎081 837 07 23), off P. Umberto I. Specialty *pennette alla bacco* (with peppers and cheese) L12,000/€6.20. Pizza L6-11,000/€3.10-5.68, night only. Open Dec.-July and Sept.-Oct. Th-Tu noon-3pm and 7:30pm-midnight; Aug. daily noon-2:30pm and 7pm-midnight. AmEx/MC/V.

GOOD THING HE DIDN'T CATCH A PORCUPINE

By all accounts, the Roman Emperor Tiberius was a randy fellow. The two main chroniclers of his life, historians Tacitus and Suetonius, claim that he came to Capri because he was ashamed of his own depravity (he actually had servants whose names were "Sphincter" and "Saddle") and wanted freedom to enjoy his numerous and innovative sexual indulgences away from the eyes of the world. Thinking he was completely isolated in Capri, he was surprised when a fisherman climbed up the rocky shore to present him with a large fish as an offering. Not knowing what to do, Tiberius immediately ordered imperial guards to beat the man with the fish. When the beating ceased, the fisherman thanked the gods that he had not given the emperor the large crab he had also caught. Hearing this, Tiberius ordered his guards to get the crab and beat the fisherman with that too. Today there is a plaque in P. Umberto dedicated to the Emperor that denies this and other tawdry tales about Tiberius.

👁 SIGHTS

CAPRI'S COAST. Every day **boat tours** reveal Capri's coast from Marina Grande, the most impressive vantage point, for L19,000/€9.81 Two companies run the tours, which leave on the hour from 9:30am-2:30pm. Many rock and pebble **beaches** surround the island. Take a boat from the port (L9000/€4.65) or descend between vineyards from P. Umberto to **Bagni di Tiberio,** a bathing area amid the ruins of an imperial villa. A bus or a 10min. walk down the path (left where V. Roma splits in three) leads to the gorgeous southern stretch of Marina Piccola. *(Buy tickets and get info for all boat tours at the Grotta Azzurra Travel Office, V. Roma, 53, across the street from the bus stop. ☎081 837 07 02; g.azzurra@capri.it. Open M-Sa 9am-1pm and 3-8pm.)* Cavort in the clear water among immense lava rocks or rent a **rowboat** (L25,000/€12.91) or **motor boat** (L160,000/€82.63 from **Banana Sport.** *(Main office on dock at Marina Grande. ☎081 837 51 88. Open daily 9am-6pm.)*

CAPRI'S CLIFFS. If you prefer the mainland to the briny blue, the landscape has many trails to fabulous panoramas—many visitors overlook the island's natural beauty in favor of the worldlier urban environment, but vistas offer solitude and a break from the boutiques. Check out Emperor Tiberius's ruined but magnificent **Villa Jovis,** the largest of his 12 Capri villas. Always the gracious host, Tiberius tossed those who displeased him over the precipice. The view from the **Cappella di Santa Maria del Soccorso,** built onto the villa, is unrivaled. *(To get to the villa, head out of P. Umberto on V. Longano, which turns into V. Tiberio. Ask directions if the signs confuse you. Open daily 9am-1hr. before sunset. L4000/€2.07.)*

A path winds along the cliffs, connecting the **Arco Naturale,** a majestic stone arch on the eastern cliffs, and the **Faraglioni,** three massive rocks seen on countless postcards. The path between the two takes about an hour to walk, but there is a magnificent vista around every bend. *(V. Tragara goes from Capri Centro to the Faraglioni, while the path to the Arco Naturale connects to the route to Villa Jovis through V. Matermania.)*

The scenic overlook from **Punta Cannone** serves as a foreground for the dramatic cliffs of the southern coast. The tourist office map has several walking itineraries of the less-touristed parts of the island.

VILLA SAN MICHELE. Henry James once declared that this Anacapri villa was where "the most fantastic beauty, poetry, and inutility [had] ever been clustered together." Built in the early 20th-century by Swedish author and physician Axel Munthe on the site of one of Tiberius's villas, the house shelters 17th-century furniture and ancient Roman sculpture. Its gardens boast a remarkable view and concerts on Friday nights, June through August. *(Upstairs from P. Vittoria and to the left, past Capri's Beauty Farm. Open daily 9:30am-1 hr. before sunset. L8000/€4.13.)*

OTHER SIGHTS. From P. Vittoria in Anacapri, a 12min. climb in a chairlift to the top of **Monte Solaro**. The ride affords awesome views: on a clear day, you can see the Apennines to the east and the mountains of Calabria to the south. *(Open daily Mar.-Oct. 9:30am-1hr. before sunset. Round-trip L7000/€3.62.)* A bus from P. Vittoria leads to the **Faro,** Italy's second-tallest lighthouse. Countless Italians snorkel, tan, and dive from its rocks. The yellow-brick paved V. Orlandi, off P. Vittoria in Anacapri, leads to the most inexpensive (but still rather pricey) tourist **shopping** on Capri.

🎵 ENTERTAINMENT

Nighttime action carries a hefty pricetag, and, in typical Italian fashion, no one really goes out until around midnight. Anacapri's prices are slightly lower and less pretentious. **Underground,** V. Orlandi, 259, is the town's most popular nightspot except for Saturdays when everyone heads to Club Zeus. With no cover charge, Underground only requires you to drink some of their L10,000/€5.16 cocktails and bounce and squeal with the young American girls who sojourn here on their weekend breaks from study abroad sessions in Florence. **Zeus,** V. Orlandi, 103, a few blocks from P. Vittoria, is a cinema for the rest of the week, but on Saturdays (and Thursdays in July and August), it morphs into a packed discotheque. The club has a tacky but fun Greek theme, with lit columns, smoke machines, and Greek-pointed writing. (☎081 83 79 16. Cover L20-35,000/€10.33-18.08. Open daily midnight-4am.) During the day, the back of Zeus boasts **Capri in Miniatura,** a tiny scale replica of the island, for the lazy tourist who wants to circle the island in only 10min. Open all day. (☎081 837 11 69 or 837 10 82; fax 837 4921; caprimini@capri.it; www.capri.it/it/caprimini/. L3000/€1.55 with *Let's Go*.) The Capri scene is classier and much more expensive. Covers are high and gatherings exclusive at the lounges and clubs near P. Umberto. A prime example of the extravagant discos is **Number Two,** V. Camerelle, 1, a popular spot for celebs and affluent thirty-somethings insisting they are twentysomethings. If you want to try your luck hanging out with crowds of dressed-to-kill Italians, remember that the buses stop running at 1:40am, and people don't start arriving until around 2am. A taxi will run you about L30,000/€15.50. (☎081 837 70 78. Open all night.)

ISCHIA   ☎081

Upon first setting foot on Ischia (EES-kee-yah), you may think you have left Italy entirely, not just because the island is an Edenic vision with luscious beaches, natural hot springs, ruins, forests, vineyards, lemon groves, and a once-active volcano, but also because all the signs, newspapers, and conversations are in German. The island is immensely popular with German tourists, who take over for much of the summer. In August, however, Italians on holiday swarm to Ischia and reclaim it; the population explosion leads to sky-high prices and boisterous crowds. Bargains and breathing room become hard to find, but with good reason: Ischia's beaches possess the perfection of Hollywood's digitally enhanced notion of a beach, as do its thermal baths. Its springs, which have been mentioned in such rags as the *Iliad,* the *Aeneid,* and *Let's Go,* have drawn tourists since ancient times. According to mythology, the island is home to the giant Typhoeus, who responded to Jupiter's scorn with the fury of volcanoes. Today the giant seems content to heat the springs of the exclusive spas. There is plenty to see and the crowds often make for a lively atmosphere, even if you don't sprechen Deutsch.

⬛ TRANSPORTATION

Ferries: Ischia is best reached by **ferry** or **hydrofoil** from Pozzuoli (see p. 500), though ferries run from Naples as well. Most ferries leave from **Ischia Porto,** where the main ticket offices are. Schedules and prices subject to change. Call for details.

Caremar (☎081 98 48 18) runs ferries to: **Naples** (1½hr., 14 per day 7am-8pm, L9800/€5.06); **Pozzuoli** (45min., 3 per day 8am-5pm, L7500/€3.87); **Procida** (17min., 11 per day 7am-7pm,

L7000/€3.62). Hydrofoils to **Naples** (1hr., 14 per day 7am-8pm, L10,000/€5.16) and **Procida** (30min., 11 per day 7am-7pm, L4000/€2.07). Ticket offices open 7am-9pm.

Traghetti Pozzuoli (☎081 526 77 36). To **Pozzuoli** from Casamicciola Terme (50min., 15 per day 7am-7pm, L8000/€4.13). Ticket offices are in Casamicciola Terme. Open daily 7am-7pm.

Linee Marittime Partenopee (☎081 99 18 88) runs hydrofoils to **Amalfi** (1hr.; usually at 10:30am; L22,000/€11.36), via **Positano** (50min.; L20,000/€10.33) and **Sorrento** (45min.; 5 per day 10:30am-5pm; L18,000/€9.30). Ticket offices open daily 7am-8pm.

Buses: SEPSA buses depart from P. Trieste just off the port. The main lines are **CS, CD,** and **#1.** CS circles the island counter-clockwise, hitting Ischia Porto, Casamicciola Terme, Lacco Ameno, Forio, Panza, Sant'Angelo, Serrara Fontana, and Barano. The CD line follows the same route in a clockwise direction (both every 20 min., every 30min. late at night; 5:45am-1am). The #1 bus follows the CS route as far as Sant'Angelo then comes back (every 20 min. 6am-11:30pm). Other routes are shorter, run less frequently, and stop running earlier. Tickets L1700/€0.89, full-day pass L5200/€2.69.

Taxis: Microtaxi (☎081 99 25 50).

✳ 🛈 ORIENTATION AND PRACTICAL INFORMATION

Ischia's towns and points of interest are almost all on the coast, connected by the main road, which the major bus routes follow. On the east coast, **Ischia Porto,** an almost perfectly circular port formed by the crater of an extinct volcano, is Ischia's largest town. The road continues to **Casamicciola Terme,** on the north coast, with its overcrowded beach and legendary thermal waters, and **Lacco Ameno,** on Ischia's northwest point, the oldest Greek settlement in the western Mediterranean, now known for the island's cleanest boardwalk. The road reaches **Forio,** Ischia's most touristed area, full of restaurants and hotels. In the south, Basano is a good departure point for Mt. Epomeo or the beach at **Maronti.**

Tourist Office: AAST Tourist Office (☎081 507 42 31; fax 507 42 30), on Banchina Porto Salvo, next to ticket offices on main port. Provides local tour listings and accommodations info. Open in summer daily 8am-2pm and 3-8pm; winter M-Sa 9am-1pm.

Vehicle Rental: Del Franco, V. de Luca, 133 (☎081 98 48 18). Rents cars, bikes, *motorini*, boats. *Motorini* L30-50,000/€15.50-25.82 per day. Open daily 8am-10pm.

Police: Polizio della Stato, V. delle Terme, 80 (☎081 50 74 71 19), 2 blocks up from V. de Luca in Ischia Porto. Helps out with passport problems. Open M, W, F 9am-noon.

Medical Emergency: Pronto Soccorso, V. Fundera, 1 (☎081 507 92 31), at the **Ospedale Anna Rizzoli,** in Lacco Ameno (accessible by the CS, CD, or #1 bus).

⌂ ACCOMMODATIONS & CAMPING

Despite the island's popularity, Ischia has several budget options. Options in Ischia Porto, Casamicciola Terme, and Lacco Ameno tend to be very expensive because many hotels have pools (allegedly) fed by hot springs. Ischia Porto's proximity to nightlife and restaurants is its major draw. Although most flock to Forio, finding a fair-priced accommodation is possible. In early spring, many of the fancier hotels offer rooms at significantly lower rates. In such cases, emissaries are often sent to the docks to solicit newly arrived tourists. Don't count on them, though—be sure to make a reservation, and check to make sure hotels will rent rooms for just one night.

Ostello "Il Gabbiano" (HI), Strada Statale Forio-Panza, 162 (☎081 90 94 22), on the main road between Forio and Panza. Accessible by the CS, CD, or #1 bus. Bar, pool, sea view, and easy beach access. Agreement with a swanky nearby restaurant/piano bar that gets HI guests dinner for only L15,000/€7.75. 100 beds. Breakfast, sheets, and shower included. Lockout 10am-1pm. Curfew 12:30am. Open Apr.-Sept. Dorms L30,000/€15.50; doubles L60,000/€30.99.

Hotel Villa Franca and **Baia Verde,** Strada Statale, 270, #183 (☎081 98 74 20; fax 98 70 81). Take CS, CD, or #1 bus from Ischia Porto and get off at "S. Francesco" stop.

Near beach. 2 hotels with same prices and management. Patio and 3 pools: 2 cold mineral baths and 1 thermal bath. Breakfast included. 35 rooms. Open Mar.-Oct. With *Let's Go:* singles L50,000/€25.82; doubles L120,000/€62 with dinner. AmEx/MC/V.

Pensione di Lustro, V. Filippo di Lustro, 9 (☎081 99 71 63), left from the Forio beaches. Truman Capote slept here in 1968; will you in 2002? 10 rooms with TV, bath, A/C, and breakfast. With *Let's Go:* June doubles L100,000/€51.65; July-Aug. doubles with bath L120,000/€62; Oct.-Mar. doubles L90,000/€46.48. AmEx/MC/V.

Albergo Macri, V. Lasolino, 96 (☎081 99 26 03), along the docks, just off P. Trieste. A tranquil family-run hotel. All 24 rooms have bath. With *Let's Go:* singles L40-55,000/€20.66-28.41; doubles L80-105,000/€41.32-54.23; triples L120-140,000/€62-72.30. Higher prices mid-July to mid-Sept.

Pensione Crostolo, V. Cossa, 48 (☎081 99 10 94). From P. Trieste bus station, ascend main street and turn right. Perched well above the port, this 3-star hotel boasts terraces and 15 rooms have bath, TV, fridge, and safe. L60-70,000/€30.99-36.15 per person.

Pensione Quisisana, P. Bagni, 34 (☎/fax 081 99 45 20). Take bus #3 from Ischia Porto to the *piazza*. Near the beach. Homey establishment with a roof garden. Open May-Oct. Doubles with bath L80,000/€41.32. Full pension in Aug. L85,000/€43.90 per person. Extra bed L25,000/€12.91.

Camping Internazionale, V. Foschini, 22 (☎081 99 14 49; fax 99 14 72). Take V. Alfredo de Luca from V. del Porto and bear right onto V. Michele Mazzella (*not* V. Leonardo Mazzella) at P. degli Eroi; it's about a 15min. walk from the port. Lushly land-scaped. Open Apr. 15-Oct.15. L16,000/€8.26 per person, L10,000/€5.16 per tent. Immaculate 2-person bungalows with bath L80,000/€41.32, L20,000/€10.33 per additional person.

Eurocamping dei Pini, V. delle Ginestre, 28 (☎081 98 20 69), a 20min. walk from the port. Take V. del Porto to V. de Luca, walk uphill and take a right on V. delle Terme, where you will see the arrow indicating camping. Pleasant campground with friendly management and a mini-soccer field. L15,000/€7.75 per person, L8000/€4.13 per tent. 2-person bungalows L65,000/€33.57, with bath L90,000/€46.48.

⚡ FOOD

While Ischian food, especially the seafood and fruit, is a treat, it is almost impossible to find a local eatery that is not tourist-oriented. Explore side streets in order to escape the L10,000/€5.16 *pizza margherita* offered up by the cookie-cutter establishments on the main tourist grazing grounds.

Emiddio, V. Porto, 30, at the docks. The jubilant owner will happily feed you their *ravioli alla panna* (with *prosciutto* and milk; L7000/€3.62). *Primi* L5-10,000/€2.58-5.16. Cover L2000/€1.03. Open daily noon-3pm and 7pm-midnight. AmEx/MC/V.

Ristorante Zelluso, V. Parodi, 41 (☎081 99 46 27), to the left as you enter Casamicci-ola. Look for the white sign and walk down the alley. Scrumptious pizza L7000/€3.62. Cover L2000/€1.03. Open daily noon-3pm and 7pm-midnight.

🅖 SIGHTS

CASTELLO ARAGONESE. Providing some brooding relief to the sun and surf, this castle resides on a small island of its own (Ischia Ponte), connected to the rest of civilization by a 15th-century footbridge. The stronghold, built in 1441, contains both the holy and the macabre. The **cathedral** in the castle, mostly destroyed by World War II bombing, displays a mix of Roman and Baroque styles. Below, the **crypt** houses colorful 14th-century frescoes crafted by the school of Giotto. The **nuns' cemetery** has a ghastly history; when a nun died, the order would prop the decomposing body on a stone as a (fragrant) reminder to the other nuns of their mortality. The bodies are no longer visible today. For more family fun, visit the castle's **Museum of Arms and Instruments of Torture,** 200m past the main ticket booth, which contains plenty of nasty things that will make you thankful that you skipped out on the 1500s. *(Buses #7 and 8 run to Ischia Ponte from the port. Castle ☎081 99 28 34. L15,000/€7.75, includes elevator to the top. Nun's cemetery open daily 10am-7:20pm. L5000/ €2.58. Torture museum ☎081 98 43 46. Open daily 9:30am-1hr. before sunset. A separate ticket of L5000/€2.58 is required.)*

SANTA RESTITUTA. This *chiesa* in Lacco Ameno holds the ruins of Pithecoussae's ancient villas of the 8th century BC. The island's numerous civilizations can be distinguished in a cross-section of soil. *(Take a CS or CD bus to Lacco Ameno. Walk down V. Roma, toward Ponta Cornacchia. Open daily 9am-noon and 4-6pm. Free.)*

BEACHES, HOT SPRINGS, AND HIKING. Ischia's best and most popular beach is at **Maronti**, on the island's south coast. *(Take the #5 bus from Ischia Porto to get there.)* Another popular choice is the beach at **Citara**, 1km down the coast from Forio. The #1 and #3 buses head there directly from Ischia Porto. For steamier adventures, **Sorgeto's** (on the far side of the island) hot springs range from tepid to boiling. The beach is the perfect spot to lounge and soak aching feet. Locals say that the cleansing lather formed by rubbing the light-green porous rocks together is fantastic for the skin. (Reach the beach by boat-taxi from Sant'Angelo (L5000/€2.58 per person, ask for a group discount and arrange for pick-up) or walk 20 minutes down from Panza.) **Lacco Ameno** and **Casamicciola Terme** are densely packed with the thermal baths that originally attracted visitors to Ischia.

Hikers should take the CS or CD bus to Fontana, which rests above most towns, making it a good departure point. Head for **Mt. Epomeo** (788m); when not wreathed in clouds, the summit has an incredible view extending from Capri to Terracina.

♫ ENTERTAINMENT

Ischia's liveliest nocturnal scene is in Ischia Porto. The best of the bunch is Valentino, C. Vittoria Colonna, 97. C.V. Colonna runs parallel to V. de Luca from the port, one block nearer to the sea. A discotheque and piano bar, it's a good place to get down with your bad self. The music varies, so make sure your bad self likes what it hears before paying the cover, which starts at L20,000/€10.33 and is often much higher. (☎081 98 25 69. Open F-Su midnight-4am.) Blue Jane (the disco formerly known as Jane), on V. Iasolino, at Pagoda Beach near the port, advertises on the sides of nearly every bus on the island. The club features a discotheque and a smooth hangout called "Lizard Lounge." (☎081 99 32 96. Cover L20-35,000/€10.33-18.08. Open July-Aug. daily 11:30pm-4am; June and Sept. F-Su 11:30pm-4am.)

PROCIDA ☎081

Sun-baked pastel buildings with ample gardens overlook ports of netted fishing boats to create a scene so perfectly unreal that Procida has been used as the setting for such widely varying films as *Il Postino* and *The Talented Mr. Ripley* (where it masqueraded under the pseudonym Mongibello). The florid tones of the southern dialect still can be heard drifting from narrow streets and family-owned stores that still shelve only essentials. No boutiques. No souvenir stores. Procida is so authentic, you will want to give it a pseudonym, in order to keep it your secret.

⊟ ⏿ TRANSPORTATION AND PRACTICAL INFORMATION

Ferries and **hydrofoils** run to Procida from Naples, Pozzuoli, and Ischia. All boats dock at Marina Grande, near the ticket offices. Caremar (☎081 890 72 80; open daily 6:30am-8pm) runs hydrofoils to **Ischia** (17min., 13 per day 7am-7:30pm, L9000/€4.65) and **Naples** (40min.; L17,000/€8.78). It also runs **ferries** to Ischia (30min., L7000/€3.62) and Naples (1hr., L9000/€4.65). Procida Lines (☎081 897 03 21; open daily 6am-8pm) runs ferries to **Pozzuoli** (30min., L5700/€3.87).

A walk across the island takes about an hour, but **buses** (tickets L1500/€0.72 in *tabacchi*, L1800/€0.93 on the bus) are regularly available. All four lines leave from the port, though their frequencies vary according to route and season. In summer, **L1,** which covers the middle region and stops at the **Marina Piccola,** runs past the hotels and campgrounds before stopping at the port of **Chiaiolella,** site of the liveliest restaurants and beaches (every 20min. 6am-11:30pm). **C1** follows much the same route, but also hits the southwestern part of the island (every 20min. 6:30am-10:30pm, every 30min. 7-10:30pm). **C2** runs to the southeastern part of the island (every 30min. 7am-10pm). **L2** serves the quiet northwestern part of the island (every hr. 7am-9pm). Another means of transportation is the adorable, though cramped, **Microtaxi** (☎081 896 87 85), from the port. The **AAST tourist office,** V. Roma, 92, near the ferry ticket offices to the far right of the main port, has free maps. (☎081 810 19 68. Open daily 9am-1pm and 3:30-6:30pm.) In **medical emergencies,** the **Pronto Soccorso,** V.V. Emanuele, 191 (☎081 896 90 58), accessible by L1 or C1 buses, is open 24hr.

ACCOMMODATIONS AND FOOD

▓ **La Rosa dei Venti.** Ocean views and its manageable cliff pathway down to a private beach area. 22 spacious *cassete* (houses with kitchenettes and dining areas). Internet and breakfast on request for L3000/€1.55. With *Let's Go,* singles L60,000/€30.99; 3-4 person bungalow L35,000/€18.08 per person; 5-6 person bungalow L30,000/€15.50 per person. AmEx/MC/V.

Hotel Riviera, Giovanni da Procida, 36 (☎/fax 081 896 71 97; hotelrivieraprocida@libero.it), provides comfortable accommodations overlooking a garden. 25 rooms, all with their own bath and phone. Reserve 1-2 weeks in advance. Breakfast included. Open Mar.-Nov. Singles L60-70,000/€30.99-36.15; doubles L100-120,000/€51.65-62. 10% discount with *Let's Go,* excluding July and August. AmEx/MC/V.

Albergo Savoia, V. Lavadera, 32, is accessible by the L2 bus (☎081 896 76 16). Snug rooms, a roof terrace, and a narrow back patio with potted flowers and lemon trees. Singles L50,000/€25.82; doubles L85,000/€43.90. Extra bed L25,000/€12.91.

Camping: Vivara, on V. IV Novembre, accessible by the L1 or C1 bus. (☎summer 081 896 92 42 winter 556 05 29). L10,000/€5.16 per person, L8-14,000/€4.13-7.32 per tent, L100,000/€51.65 for 4-person bungalow with private bath. Open June 15-Sept. 15. Since there is only room for 10 tents, make reservations in June for August trips. **Graziella, V. Salette,** 18 (☎081 896 77 47), on the beach. Take the L1, L2, or C1 bus to P. Urno and walk 500m to Spiaggia Ciraccio. It's the last campsite on the left. 4-person bungalows L110,000/€56.81.

Da Michele, V. Marina Chiaiolella, 22/23 (☎081 896 74 22). *Primi* L6-12,000/€3.10-6.20, rabbit L15,000/€7.75, pizza L4-10,000/€2.07-5.16.) After your meal ask at any bar for the potent *limoncello,* a local liqueur made, of course, from Procidan lemons.

SIGHTS

You can walk or take the **C2** to the **Abbazia San Michele Archangelo** (St. Michael's Abbey) on Procida's easternmost and highest hilltop. Its yellow facade, redone in 1890, belies the interior's ornate 15th-century gold frescoes and bleeding Christ figures. Enjoy the outlook from the summit and view the deeds of St. Michael emblazoned on the domes. Take V.V. Emanuele from the left side of the port and turn left on V. Principe Umberto. (☎081 896 76 12. Open daily 9am-1pm and 3-6:30pm. Free.) The route passes the medieval walls of **Terra Murata** (☎081 896 76 12), the old city below the monastery on V.S. Michele. Procida has several decent **beaches** that are usually uncrowded. The one at **Ciraccio** stretches across the western shore. Its western end, near Chiainella, is accessible by the **L1.** Another popular beach is **Chiaia,** on the southeastern cove, accessible by **L1** and **C1.**

Lemons are ubiquitous in Procida, and the local authorities are hoping that the **Festa del Limone,** the third weekend in June, will become a popular tradition. The festival features such disparate events as food tastings, a fashion show, and a debate on the, er, lemon. From the harbor at **Chiaiolella** on the opposite side of the island, where wealthy Neapolitans dock their boats, you can head across a foot-bridge to the islet of **Vivara,** where a wildlife sanctuary bristles with furry wood-land inhabitants. If water floats your boat, take a sea excursion with Procida Diving Center (☎081 896 83 85; www.vacanzeaprocida.it. Mandatory free tours leave from the entrance M-Sa, starting between 9 and 9:30am; 2hr. L25,000/12.91.)

AMALFI COAST

The beauty of the Amalfi coast is one of contrasts and extremes. Immense rugged cliffs plunge downward into calm azure waters while coastal towns nestle in and climb the sides of narrow ravines. Visitors are drawn by the natural splendor and the unique character of each town. Although some coastal parts may cost you an arm and two or three legs, budget gems exist as well.

The coast is easily accessible from Naples, Sorrento, Salerno, and the islands by ferry or SITA buses. The harrowing bus ride along the Amalfi coast is unforgetta-ble: narrow roads wind along the mountain sides, with spectacular views of the cliffs that plummet into the sea. Just remember to sit on the right side of the bus heading south (from Sorrento to Amalfi) and on the left heading back. Those with weaker stomachs should opt for sea service. If you plan to take buses from 2-5pm, buy tickets in advance because *tabacchi* close for the afternoon.

POSITANO   ☎089

When John Steinbeck visited Positano in the 1950s, he estimated that its vertical cliffs were already piled so high with homes that no more than 500 visitors could possibly fit, negating the possibility of tourism. He underestimated local ingenuity. After running through a series of industries with variable success (including fash-ion: the bikini was invented here in 1959), Positano embraced its role as an intel-lectual and cultural resort. Soon its classy reputation began to draw ordinary millionaires in addition to the writers, painters, actors, and filmmakers, and the *positanese* squeezed not 500 but over 2000 hotel beds into their town. Today, Pos-itano's most frequent visitors are the wealthy few who can appreciate the beach-front ballet and afford the French chefs in the four-star hotels. There is no denying, however, that Positano has its charms, and most who come here linger. As Steinbeck rightly observed, "Positano bites deep."

▐ TRANSPORTATION

Buses: 18 blue **SITA** buses, from 7am-9pm, run to: **Amalfi** (L2300/€1.19); **Praiano** (L1800/€0.93); **Sorrento** (L3200/€1.65). There are 2 main stops in Positano, at the 2 points where the road that runs through town meets the main coastal road. Tickets can be bought at bars or *tabacchi* near the stops.

Ferries and **Hydrofoils:** at far right of Spiaggia Grande. **Linee Marittime Partenopee** (☎089 87 50 92) runs **hydrofoils** to: **Capri** (20min.; 5 per day 9am- 6pm; L19,000/ €9.81); **Ischia** (1¼hr.; 4pm; L28,000/€14.46); **Naples's** Mergellina port (45min.; 4 per day 10:30am-7:30pm; L32,000/€16.53); **Sorrento** (20min.; 3 per day 12:30-4pm; L19,000/€9.81). Runs **ferries** to **Capri** (40min.; 4:25pm; L16,000/€8.26).

✸ ▌ ORIENTATION AND PRACTICAL INFORMATION

Positano clings to the zeniths of two cliffs over the Tyrrhenian Sea. The main cen-ter of town lies around **Spiaggia Grande.** To get there, take **Viale Pasitea** down from the main road between Sorrento and Amalfi at **Chiesa Nuova.** Viale Pasitea turns into **Corso Colombo** and eventually makes its way up to the main road again at the other end of town. To get over to **Fornillo** beach, take the footpath from Spiaggia Grande. Make use of the orange local bus (every 20min., 7am-midnight) marked "Positano Interno" that circles through the town, terminating at **Piazza dei Mulini.**

Tourist Office: V. del Saraceno, 4 (☎089 87 50 67), near *duomo*. Provides maps. Open M-Sa 8:30am-2pm and 3:30-8pm; in winter M-F 8:30am-2pm, Sa 8:30am-noon.

Emergency: ☎113. **Carabinieri:** (☎089 87 50 11) near the top of the cliffs, down the steps opposite Chiesa Nuova. Nearest **hospital** in Sorrento.

Late-Night Pharmacy: Viale Pasitea, 22 (☎089 87 58 63). Open daily 9am-1pm and 5-9pm.

Internet Access: D.S. Informatica, V.G. Marconi, 188 (☎089 81 19 93; www.positanonline.it), on the main coastal road, accessible by the local bus. L15,000/€7.75 per hr. Open M-Sa 9:30am-1pm and 3-7:30pm.

☗ ACCOMMODATIONS, CAMPING, AND FOOD

Positano has over 70 hotels and residences, and spare rooms are available for rent. Since many hotels are rather expensive, contact the tourist office for help in arranging inexpensive rooms for longer stays.

Ostello Brikette, V.G. Marconi, 358 (☎089 87 58 57; fax 812 28 14; brikette@syrene.it), 100m up the main coastal road to Sorrento from Viale Pasitea. Squeaky clean and incredible views from 2 large terraces. Internet access. 45 beds. Sheets, shower, and breakfast included. Lockout 11:30am-5pm. Flexible curfew 1am. Reservations available. Dorms L35,000/€18.08; doubles L100,000/€51.65.

Pensione Maria Luisa, V. Fornillo, 42 (☎/fax 089 87 50 23). Take the local bus down Viale Pasitea to V. Fornillo. A jolly owner and 12 bright rooms, most with views from their seaside terraces. All rooms with bath. Breakfast included. Singles L70,000/€36.15; doubles L100,000/€51.65. Extra bed L40,000/€20.66.

Casa Guadagno, V. Fornillo, 22 (☎089 87 50 42; fax 81 14 07), next door to Pensione Maria Luisa. Pampers its patrons with 15 spotless rooms, tiled floors, sublime views, and winter heating. Breakfast and bath included. Reserve in advance. With *Let's Go:* doubles L110-120,000/€56.81-62; triples L180,000/€92.96. MC/V.

☕ FOOD

Prices in the town's restaurants reflect the high quality of the food. For a sit-down dinner, thrifty travelers head toward Fornillo.

▧ Da Costantino, V. Corvo, 95 (☎089 87 57 38). Serves tasty cuisine, but the view of the ocean from your table will overshadow even the most succulent meal. Try the specialty *crespolini al formaggio* (crêpes filled with cheese) for L10,000/€5.16. Pizza L8000/€4.13; *primi* L10-15,000/€5.16-7.75; *secondi* L15-30,000/€7.75-15.50. Open daily in the summer noon-3:30pm and 7pm-midnight; in winter Tu-Th.

Vini e Panini V. del Saracino, 29-31 (☎ 089 87 51 75), near the church. For the frugal, this shop sells reasonable sandwiches to go and interesting cheeses to try. Mozzarella and *pomodori* panino L5000/€2.58. Or buy a bottle of limoncello for L20,000/€10.33. Open daily 8am-2pm and 4:30-10pm; closed Dec.-Mar.

Trattoria Grottino Azzurro, Chiesa Nuova (☎089 87 54 66), next to Bar International near the hostel. Frequented by local celebrities, it serves up local specialties at reasonable prices. Homemade pasta and fresh seafood from L10,000/€5.16. Cover L3000/€1.55. Open Th-Tu 12:30-3pm and 7:30-11pm. Closed Dec.-mid Feb.

Il Saraceno D'Oro, Viale Pasitea, 254 (☎089 81 20 50), on the road to Fornillo. Delicious pizza to go (evenings only) from L6000/€3.10. The *gnocchi alla Sorrentina* are incredible and one of the better deals at L12,000/€6.20. Cover L2000/€1.03. Open daily 1-3pm and 7pm-midnight; in winter Th-Tu 1-3pm and 7pm-midnight.

Bar-Pasticceria La Zagara, V. dei Mulini, 6 (☎089 87 59 64). Exquisite pastries, tarts, and *limoncello*. The *torta afrodisia* (chocolate cake with fruit; L5000/€2.58) promises to raise your libido. Prices are slightly higher if you choose to eat on the shaded patio, which transforms itself into a piano bar in the evenings. Open daily 8am-2am.

La Taverna del Leone, V. Laurito, 43 (☎089 87 54 74), on the left side of the main road to Praiano; serviced by infrequent SITA buses. Full meals and snacks; frozen strawberries, pears, peaches, and even walnuts filled with sorbet (L3500/€1.81 per 100g). Cover L3000/€1.55. Open May-Sept. daily 1-4pm and 7pm-midnight; Oct.-Apr. W-M 1-4pm and 7pm-midnight. AmEx/MC/V.

SIGHTS

For some, Positano's gray beaches are its main attractions. Each has public (free) and private (not so free) sections. The biggest, busiest, and priciest is **Spiaggia Grande,** in the main part of town. At the private **Lido L'incanto** (☎089 811 17 77) spend the day with the other people who shelled out L15,000/€7.75 for a beach chair *(lettino)*, umbrella, shower, and changing room. Outside the entrance, **Noleggio Barche Lucibello** (☎089 87 50 32 or 87 53 26), rents motorboats from L40,000/€20.66 per hour and rowboats from L20,000/€10.33 per hour. To reach the quieter, smaller **Spiaggia del Fornillo,** take V. Positanese d'America, a footpath that starts above the port and winds past **Torre Trasita.** While parts of the Fornillo are public, you can get your own spot at one of three private beaches. Marinella features a little sand underneath a falling down boardwalk; ambitious Fratelli Grassi offers a boat excursion; and eager Puppetto gives guests from Hostel Briskette a 10-15% discount. The three **Isole dei Galli,** poking through the water off Positano's coast, were home to Homer's mythical sirens, who lured unsuspecting victims with their spellbinding songs, and in 1925, perhaps to honor this tradition, the quartet of Stravinsky, Picasso, Hindemith, and Massine bought one of the *isole*.

Positano offers tremendous hikes for those with quads of steel. **Montepertuso,** a high mountain pierced by a large *pertusione* (hole), is one of three perforated mountains in the world (the other two are in India). To get there, hike the 45-minute trail up the hillside, or take the bus from P. dei Mulini, near the port or from any other bus stop. For those who want to lighten their pocketbooks by several pounds, Positano is a land of **endless possibilities.** The tragically chic spend afternoons in city boutiques, always exorbitantly priced. Others take boat excursions to neighboring islands that tour the coast. The adventurous (or really hungry) take squid-fishing expeditions that depart at night. Frequent cruises embark to the **Emerald** and **Blue Grottoes;** while ferries depart at night. As numerous boating companies compete for these excursions, the prices can sometimes be reasonable for shorter trips; check the tourist office and booths lining the port area.

🎵 ENTERTAINMENT

Music on the Rocks, a fancy piano bar and disco on the far left side of the beach as you face the water, packs in the well-dressed thirty-somethings as tight as sardines. Handfuls of celebrities, from Sharon Stone to Luciano Pavarotti, have been known to stop by. The cover charge can only get you in if you're wearing fancy threads. (☎089 87 58 74. Cover L35,000/€18.08). **Easy Pub** on Spiaggia Grande, at D. del Brigantino, is a happening spot from mid Mar-Nov. (☎089 81 14 61. Open all day and night, live music on occasions.)

PRAIANO

A winding 6km bus ride down the coast from Positano (15min., L1700/€0.88), Praiano (pop. 800) lacks a city center by the beach. The town is better described as a loose conglomeration of hotels and restaurants along 10km of coastline. Praiano boasts pleasant accommodations (in case Positano is all booked), good food, and the most popular nightlife on the Amalfi Coast.

🛏 ACCOMMODATIONS. Enjoy the expansive panorama from the campground **Villaggio La Tranquillità** and the **Hotel Continental**, V. Roma, 10, which are part of the same complex, on the road to Amalfi (ask the bus driver to stop at the Ristorante

Continental). A long stairway descends to a stone dock. The hotel is staffed by a friendly group (everyone knows your name), and all rooms include bath and bread-and-butter breakfast. (☎089 87 40 84; fax 87 47 79; contraq@contraq-praiano.com. Parking available. Camping L25,000/€12.91 per site (tent not included), L15,000/€7.75 per person. Doubles and two-person bungalows L105,000/€54.23, with terrace L125,000/€64.56. MC/V.) **La Perla,** V. Miglina, 2, 100m toward Amalfi from La Tranquillità on the main road offers rooms with bath and a terrace overlooking the sea. (☎089 87 40 52. Breakfast included. *Let's Go:* singles L85,000/€43.90; doubles L140,000/€72.30. AmEx/MC/V.)

◨ **FOOD.** Downstairs from Villagio La Tranquillità, **Ristorante Continental** offers *primi* L12-15,000/€6.20-7.75; *secondi* L12-15,000/€6.20-7.75, and local wine L8000/€4.13. (Cover L3000/€1.55. Let's Go 10% discount. Open Easter-Nov. daily noon-3pm and 8pm-midnight.) On the road from Positano, next to the San Gennaro Church (with blue and gold domes), **Trattoria San Gennaro,** V.S. Gennaro, 99, lets you choose between their terrace and the garden as the setting for your meal. Enjoy the view and the *spaghetti San Gennaro* (mushrooms and clams) for only L10,000/€5.16. (☎089 87 42 93. Pizza in evening L7000/€3.62. Cover L2500/€1.29. Open daily noon-4pm and 7pm-midnight.)

◨◨ **SIGHTS AND ENTERTAINMENT.** Six kilometers up the road to Positano, descend 400 steps to reach a beach. Around the bend from Praiano toward Amalfi, V. Terramare, a ramp which starts at **Torre a Mare** (a well-preserved tower which now serves as an art gallery for lauded sculptor and painter Paolo Sandulli) leads down to **Marina di Praia,** a 400-year-old fishing village tucked in a tiny ravine. Its pizzerias and restaurants come alive on weekends. Further down the coast ◨**Africana,** on V. Terramare, is the Amalfi Coast's most famous nightclub and has been around since the early 1960s. Fish swim through the grotto under the glass dance floor as a mellow dog wanders among twenty- and thirtysomethings and sleeps by the bar. Music echoes off the dimly lit cave roof above and boats dock at the stairwell right outside. Met a cute Italian? Drop a flower down the well and make a wish, if the flower floats out of the grotto below, your wish will come true. If it doesn't, drown your sorrows in a *cocktail africana* for L10,000/€5.16. Lavish shows drive the price up to L30,000/€15.50 on Saturdays. (☎089 87 40 42. Cover charge L25,000/€12.91, Th women free. Open mid-June-Sept. daily 11pm-4am.) Down V. Terramare toward Marina di Praia's small beach is **Il Piratu,** also a discoteque carved into the rock just above the water's edge. (☎089 87 43 77. Cover L17,000/€8.43 draws a younger crowd. Open July-Sept. daily 10pm-3am.)

A bit farther between Praiano and Amalfi lies the **Grotta Smeralda** (Emerald Grotto). The SITA bus stops at the elevator leading down to the cave. If you didn't make it to the Blue Grotto or haven't had your fill of water-filled caves, the 22m high cavern has green water with a slight glow and walls dripping with stalactites. Multilingual guides reveal an underwater nativity scene and a rock formation profile of Lincoln, Napoleon, or Garibaldi (depending on your nationality). Sorry, no swimming in this grotto. (Tour L5000/€2.58. Open daily 10am-4pm.)

AMALFI ☎089

Between the rugged cliffs of the Sorrentine peninsula and the azure waters of the Adriatic, the narrow streets and historic monuments of Amalfi nestle in incomparable natural beauty. As the first sea republic of Italy and the preeminent maritime powerhouse of the southern Mediterranean, Amalfi ruled the neighboring coast, no doubt thanks to the compass, invented here by Flavia Gioia. Pisan attacks and Norman conquests hastened Amalfi's decline in influence, but the vigor remains in spirit, and the city's past survives in its monuments. Visitors crowd the waterfront and the shops, restaurants, and cafes around the *duomo*. During festivals, music and fireworks echo off the steep mountains around the town.

TRANSPORTATION

Buses: Buses arrive at and depart from P.F. Gioia, on the waterfront. Buy tickets at bars and *tabacchi* on the *piazza*. Blue **SITA buses** (☎089 87 10 16) connect Amalfi to **Salerno** (1¼hr., 6am-10pm, L3200/€1.65) and **Sorrento** (1¼hr., 18 per day 6:30am-10pm, L3600/€1.86), via **Positano** (35min., L2300/€1.19).

Ferries and **hydrofoils:** Ticket booths and departures from the dock off P.F. Gioia.

Linee Marittime Partenopee (☎089 87 41 83) runs ferries to **Capri** (1½hr., 3 per day 8:40am-9:10pm, L1000/€0.52) and hydrofoils to: **Capri** (35min.; 4 per day 8:30am-5:30pm; L20,000/€10.33); **Ischia** (1½hr.; 3:30pm; L30,000/€15.50); **Positano** (20min.; 7 per day 8:30am-6pm; L13,000/€6.71); **Salerno** (30min.; 9 per day 8:40am-7pm; L16,000/€8.26).

Travelmar (☎089 847 31 90) runs hydrofoils to: **Positano** (1¼hr., 7 per day 8:40am-6pm, L9000/€4.65); **Salerno** (30min., 7 per day 8:40am-7pm, L6000/€3.10); **Sorrento** (25min.; 3 per day 8:30am-3:30pm; L15,000/€7.75).

Taxis: ☎089 87 22 39.

ORIENTATION AND PRACTICAL INFORMATION

Amalfi's main street is **via Lorenzo d'Amalfi,** which leads from the port to the hills above. Ferries and buses stop in **Piazza Flavio Gioia** on the waterfront. **Piazza del Duomo** lies up V. d'Amalfi through the white arch. **Piazza Municipio** is 100m up Corso delle Repubbliche Marinare toward **Atrani** from P. Gioia, on the left. Go through the tunnel to reach **Atrani,** 750m down the coast or follow the public path through the restaurant next to the tunnel.

Tourist Office: AAST, Corso delle Repubbliche Marinare, 27 (☎089 87 11 07), through a gate on the left as you head up the road. Free maps and brochures. Open May-Oct. daily 8am-2pm and 3-8pm; Nov.-Apr. M-Sa 8am-2pm.

Police: Carabinieri, V. Casamare, 19 (☎089 87 10 22), on the left up V. d'Amalfi.

Medical Emergency: American Diagnostics Pharmaceutics (☎0335 45 58 74). On-call 24hr. Clean and modern. Blood tests, lab procedures, and English-speaking docs.

Post Office: C. delle Repubbliche Marinare, 35 (☎089 87 13 30), next to the tourist office. Offers currency exchange with good rates. Commission L1000/€0.52, L5000/€2.58 on checks over L100,000/€51.65. Open M-F 8:15am-7:20pm.

Postal Code: 84011.

ACCOMMODATIONS

Staying in Amalfi can be expensive, but you get what you pay for. Accommodations fill up in August, so reserve at least one month in advance.

Beata Solitudo Campeggio Ostello (HI), P. Generale Avitabile 6, Agerola (☎/fax 081 802 50 48; www.beatasolitudo.it). 30min. bus ride from Amalfi. Get off at the *piazza* in Agerola. The only hostel in the area, with 3 rooms and 16 beds, a kitchen, laundry facilities, Internet, and TV. A favorite among travelers to Amalfi.

Hotel Lidomare, V. Piccolomini, 9 (☎089 87 13 32; fax 87 13 94; lidomare@amalfi-coast.it/hotel/lidomare), through the alley across from the *duomo,* left up the stairs, then cross the *piazzetta*. Big rooms with terraces. Halls and common areas decked with local antiques. 30 rooms with bath, TV, phone, fridge, and A/C. Breakfast included. Singles L75,000/€38.73; doubles L150-170,000/€77.47-87.80. AmEx/MC/V.

A'Scalinatella, P. Umberto, 6 (☎089 87 19 30 or 87 14 92), up V. dei Dogi in Atrani. Look for arrows painted on wall to the right. Genial brothers Filippo and Gabriele have rooms in Atrani, as well as campsites and scenic rooms above Amalfi. Laundry L10,000/€5.16. Seasonal variations in prices, highest in August. Dorms L20-35,000/€10.33-18.08; doubles L50-70,000/€25.82-36.15, with bath L70-120,000/€36.15-61.97. Camping L15,000/€7.75 per person.

Hotel Amalfi, V. dei Pastai, 3 (☎089 87 24 40; fax 87 22 50), left off V. Lorenzo onto Salita Truglio, uphill. A 3-star establishment with 42 immaculate rooms, attentive management, terraces, and citrus gardens with restaurant. Bar, telephone, safe, and TV in all rooms. English spoken. Continental breakfast included. With *Let's Go:* singles L90-170,000/€46.48-87.80; doubles L120-200,000/€61.97-103.29. AmEx/MC/V.

Villagio Vettica, V. Muista dei Villaggi, 92 (☎089 87 18 14). Call from the SITA bus stop in Amalfi for directions. Amidst lemon groves in a small village high in the cliffs above nearby Amalfi. Rooms offer great panoramas and a quiet retreat. Kitchens available. *Alimentari* nearby. Doubles L50,000/€25.82 per person, with bath L100,000/€51.65. Camping L35,000/€18.08.

Hotel Fontana, P. Duomo, (☎089 87 15 30). A bit noisy with a friendly staff, Hotel Fontana provides 16 comfortable, clean rooms with shared baths. Breakfast included. Singles L75,000/€38.73; doubles L140,000/€72.30.

◖ FOOD

Food in Amalfi is good, but expensive. Indulge in seafood, *scialatelli* (a coarsely cut local pasta), and the pungent lemon liqueur *limoncello*. The town's many **paninoteche** (sandwich shops) are perfect for a tight budget.

◪ Da Maria, P. Duomo (☎089 87 18 80). In the quest for quality Neapolitan cuisine, Da Maria should be your one and only stop. In this spacious eatery, owners instruct the adventurous on the daily specials. *Primi* from L12,000/€6.20 and pizza from L7000/€3.62. Closed mid-Nov. Open Tu-Su noon-3:30pm and 7pm-midnight. Reservations recommended. AmEx/MC/V.

Trattoria La Perla, Salita Truglio, 5 (☎089 87 14 40), around corner from the Hotel Amalfi. Moderately priced. Try the bountiful *scialatielli ai frutti di mare* (with seafood; L14,000/€7.32), or the *bigné al limone* (pastry with lemon cream; L6000/€3.10). *Menù turistico* L26,000/€13.91. Cover L3500/€1.81. Open Mar.-Nov. daily noon-3:30pm and 7pm-midnight; Apr.-Oct. W-M noon-3:00pm and 7-11:30pm. AmEx/MC/V.

Lo Sputino, Lgo. Scavio, 3, on the left as you walk up C. delle Repubbliche Marinare. Hearty and imaginative *panini* (L4-6000/€2.07-3.10). Beer from L2000/€1.03. Mar.-Oct. Open daily 10am-3am.

Al Teatro, V.E. Marini, 19 (☎089 87 24 73). From V. d'Amalfi, turn left up the staircase (Salita degli Orafi) with a sign immediately after a shoe store, then follow the signs. Al Teatro is proud to present a pleasant locale, starring authentic atmosphere, and introducing good, cheap food. Try the *scialatelli al Teatro* (with tomato and eggplant) for L11,000/€5.68. *Primi* and *secondi* from L8000/€4.13. *Menù* L25,000/€12.91. Open Th-Tu 11:30-3:15pm and 7:30-11:30pm. Closed early Jan. to mid-Feb. AmEx/MC/V.

Royal, V. Lorenzo d'Amalfi, 10 (☎089 87 19 82), near the *duomo*. Follow the smell to Amalfi's best ice cream and Neapolitan pastries. Cones L3-5000/€1.55-2.58. Delectable *gelato* made from the local wine. Lip-smacking crêpes with *nutella* for L6000/€3.10. Open June-Sept. daily 7am-2am; Oct.-May Tu-Su 7am-midnight. AmEx/MC/V.

Andrea Pansa, P. del Duomo, 40 (☎089 87 10 65). This pastry shop has been making local specialties since 1830, and you'll know it with your first bite of their delicious confections. In winter, ask for *sprocollati* (fig with ground almond); all year round the *Baba au limon* (L3000/€1.55) is delicious. Open daily 7am-midnight.

◉ SIGHTS

The 9th-century Duomo di Sant'Andrea imparts grace, elegance, and dignity to the P. del Duomo. The *piazza* may need it; the nearby **Fontana di Sant'Andrea** features a marble female nude squeezing her breasts as water spews from her nipples. Those who can put their Freudian complexes aside drink from the fountain. Rebuilt in the 19th century according to the original medieval plan. The cathedral features a facade of varied geometric designs typical of the Arab-Norman style.

The **bronze doors,** crafted in Constantinople in 1066, started a bronze door craze that spread through Italy. (Open daily 8:30am-8pm. Appropriate dress required.)

To its left, the **Chiostro del Paradiso** (Cloister of Paradise), a 13th-century cemetery, has become a graveyard for miscellaneous columns, statues, and sarcophagus fragments. The elegant interlaced arches, like the *campanile* in the square, show the Middle Eastern influence. Its museum houses mosaics, sculptures, and the church's treasury. (Open daily June-Sept. 8:30am-8pm. Free multilingual guides available. L3000/€1.55 for cloister, museum, and crypt.)

The 9th-century **Arsenal** on the waterfront, by the entrance to the city center, contains relics of Amalfi's former maritime glory. Up on V. D'Amalfi, several signs point to a path to the **Valle dei Mulini** (Valley of the Mills). Hike along a stream bed by the old paper mills for a pastoral view of lemon groves and rocky mountains. At the start of the valley is the **Paper Museum,** and its collections of, surprisingly, sundry paper items. (Open Tu-Su 9am-1pm. L2000/€1.03.)

◪ ▧ BEACHES, HIKING, AND DRAGONS

While there is a small beach in Amalfi itself, a five- to ten-minute trip will bring you to a much better (and free) beach in **Atrani.** A beachside village of 1200 inhabitants just around the bend from Amalfi, Atrani used to be home to the Republic's leaders; today it's a quiet place to escape from Amalfi's crowds. After the tunnel, descend a small winding staircase to the beach and P. Umberto. Atrani's one cobbled road, V. dei Dogi, leads from the beach up past P. Umberto, at which point a white stairway leads to **Chiesa di San Salvatore de Bireto,** with its 11th-century bronze doors from Constantinople. The name refers to the ceremonial hat placed on the Republic's doge when he was inaugurated.

Hikers often tackle paths that head up from Amalfi into the imposing Monti Lattari, winding through lemon groves and mountain streams, suddenly emerging onto beautiful vistas. From Amalfi, you can head up the **Antiche Scale** toward Pogerola. Trek through the **Valley of the Dragons,** named for the torrent of water and mist (like smoke from a dragon) exploding out to sea every winter. Another favorite is the three-hour **Path of the Gods,** which takes you from Bomerano to Positano, with great views along the way. Naturally, the hikes can get steep, and a good map is essential to find specific locations.

If you just want a short walk, a path leads up through the streets clinging to the cliffs up to the cave where the famous rebel Masaneillo hid from Spanish police. Although the cave is sporadically closed, the view of Atrani alone is worth the hike, which takes about an hour both ways.

▨ DAYTRIPS FROM AMALFI

MINORI

SITA buses from Amalfi stop on V.G. Capone, which changes its name to V.G. Amendola as it heads north to Minori, 1km away. Roman villa (☎089 85 28 43. Open daily 9am-1hr. before sunset. Free.)

Although Minori's downtown is better preserved than Maiori's, its main attraction is its beaches. Hotels are more expensive than in Maiori, so it's best to stay there and brave the 1km walk along the coastal road. Unlike Maiori, where only a tiny section of the beach is public, a large swath of Minori's waterfront is free to all. Minori also has the remains of a Roman villa, with monochrome mosaics of a hunt, well-preserved arcades, and a small museum. The site is several blocks up from the beach on V.S. Lucia.

MAIORI

The pedestrian-only Corso Regina intersects V.G. Capone by the SITA bus stop. Several blocks up C. Regina, inside a garden on the left, is the tourist office, C. Regina, 73. (☎089 877 452; fax 853 672. Open M-Sa 8am-2pm.) The nearest medical facilities are in Amalfi; however, there are carabinieri (☎089 87 72 07).

Only a few kilometers from well-known and touristed Amalfi, this beachfront town has few foreign visitors among the many Italians drawn to its shores. Though it lacks neither the style of Positano nor the history of Amalfi, Maiori has low priced hotels and excellent beaches, as well as several historical sights.

Much of Maiori was damaged during World War II, and what was left was destroyed in a flood several decades ago, so most of its buildings are modern.

Most visitors come to Maiori to lounge on the beaches. Although much of the beach is privately owned, with a L10-15,000/€5.16-7.75 fee for access with chair and umbrella, there is a small public section near the SITA bus stop. Keep hydrated and score snacks from the nearby stands.

If you'd rather see sights than sun, the town's main attraction is **Chiesa di S. Maria a Mare,** up a flight of stairs in the left side of a mini *piazza* three blocks up C. Regina from the beach. In addition to a great view of the town, it has a beautiful 15th-century alabaster altar kept in front of the crypt. Maiori has several inexpensive hotels near the beach. **Albergo De Rosa,** V. Orti, 12 (turn left two blocks up C. Regina from the beach), has English-speaking management and rooms with bath and breakfast included. (☎/fax 089 87 70 31. Singles L55,000/€28.41; doubles L110,000/€56.81; triples L140,000/€72.30.) An inexpensive local restaurant is **Dedalo,** on V. Cerasuoli just off C. Regina one block up from the beach. They serve up a L20,000/€10.33 *menù* and L6-10,000/€3.10-5.16 pizzas in an air-conditioned interior. (☎ 089 87 70 84. Open daily noon-3pm and 4:30pm-3am.)

RAVELLO   ☎089

Ravello and its lush villas perch 330m atop the cliffs, gazing down on a patchwork of villages and ravines extending to the sea. Settled in AD 500 by Romans fleeing barbarian invasions, it grew into an opulent town of 70,000 during the heyday of the Amalfi Republic and later under Norman rule. But epidemics and raiding Saracens left only 2700 people. Though plague and civil war sapped its strength, the town's natural beauty and romantic decay drew artists and intellectuals alike. The exquisite gardens of Villa Rufolo inspired Giorgio Boccaccio's literary masterpiece, *The Decameron,* as well as Richard Wagner's opera, *Parsifal.* In fact, Ravello is still known as "*La Città della Musica,*" thanks to the many concert series and performances it hosts throughout the year. For those needing creative inspiration, Ravello is well worth the trip up the mountain.

🖪🖪 TRANSPORTATION AND PRACTICAL INFORMATION. Take the blue SITA bus from Amalfi (20min., 18 per day 6:45am-10pm, L1800/€0.92). If you're an adventurous scamp, hike the footpaths along the hills and lemon groves from Minori (1hr.), Atrani (2hr. via Scala), or Amalfi (2½hr. via Pontone). The **AAST Information office,** P. Duomo, 10 (☎ 089 85 70 98), is to the left of the **Piazza Duomo** as you face it. The English-speaking staff provides brochures, event and hotel listings, and a map. More maps are available at magazine or book shops; the best one is published by the *Club Alpino Italiano.* For a **taxi,** call ☎ 089 85 79 17. If the taxi hits you, the **carabinieri** (☎ 089 85 71 50) are close by on V. Roma. For pain-killers, a **pharmacy,** P. Duomo, 14, is on the left side of the *piazza* as you face the *duomo.* (☎ 089 85 71 89. Open in summer daily 9am-1:30pm and 5-8:30pm.) And to write home and complain to everyone that your leg is broken, the **post office** is at P. Duomo, 15. (Open M-Sa 8am-1:30pm.) **Postal Code:** 84010.

🖪🖪 ACCOMMODATIONS AND FOOD. Ravello offers several affordable options. **Hotel Villa Amore,** V. dei Fusco, 5, on the road to Villa Cimbrone, has 12 cute, tidy rooms and a garden overlooking cliffs and the sea. As their welcome sign says, "A stay at Villa Amore gives peace to the soul and joy to the heart." All rooms have terraces and views; some have bath. Reserve a month in advance. (☎/fax 089 85 71 35. Breakfast included. L105,000/€54.23 per person. AmEx/MC/V.) **Albergo Garden,** V.G. Boccaccio, 4, before the tunnel into Ravello, by the SITA bus stop, offers a great view of the cliffs. All 10 rooms have bath and balcony. English is spoken. (☎089 85 72 26; fax 85 81 10. Breakfast included. Reservations recommended one month in advance for August. Doubles L145,000/€74.87; low-season L125,000/€64.56. Extra bed L30,000/€15.50. AmEx/MC/V.)

Although many wines savored around the globe appear under a Ravello label, actual wine from the area is neither common nor commercially available—make friends in the town if you hope to try some. **Cumpà Cosimo,** V. Roma, 44/46 (☎089 85 71 56), caters to the indecisive. Savor a variety of local specialties with an *assaggio di primi*, a sampler of all the available pasta dishes (L6000/€3.10), or try the house specialty *mista di pasta fatta in casa*, a mix of five homemade pastas for L25,000/€12.91. (Open noon-3pm and 6:30pm-midnight. AmEx/MC/V.)

🅖🅙 **SIGHTS AND ENTERTAINMENT.** The beautiful churches, ivy-covered walls, and meandering paths of **Villa Rufolo** inspired Wagner's magic garden in the second act of *Parsifal*. In the summer, ugly stages are often erected in the most picturesque spots, spoiling their beauty (but making for great concerts). A medieval **tower** with Norman-Saracen vaulting and statues representing the four seasons serves as the entry to the famous Moorish cloister. Enter through the arch off P. Duomo near the tunnel. (☎089 85 76 57. Open daily 9am-sunset. L6000/€3.10, under 12 or over 65 L4000/€2.07, groups of more than 10 L5000/€2.58 per person.)

In the portal of Ravello's **duomo** you can see the Amalfi Coast's third set of famous bronze doors, cast by Barisano of Trani in 1179. Inside, a group of antique columns sets off two pulpits with elaborate mosaics. To the left of the altar stands the Cappella di S. Pantaleone, the town's patron saint. Behind the painting you can see his blood, preserved in a cracked vessel. Saint Pantaleone was beheaded on July 27, AD 290, at Nicomedia. Every year on this day the city holds a **festival,** when the saint's blood purportedly liquefies. The **museum** within depicts the *duomo's* history during pagan and Christian eras. (*Duomo* open Mar.-Nov. daily 9:30am-1pm and 3-7pm; Dec.-Feb. Sa-Su 9am-1pm and 2-5pm. Museum L2000/€1.03.)

Follow Viale dei Rufo out of P. Duomo to **Villa Cimbrone.** Renovated by Lord Grimmelthorpe in the 19th century in an attempt to draw attention away from his name, the villa sports floral walkways and majestic gardens. Greek temples and statued grottoes hide among Cimbrone's twisty paths, which harbor some of the most magnificent views on the Amalfi coast. A procession of notables made it a retreat, including Greta Garbo and Leopold Stokowski, who had romantic interludes here, and Jackie Kennedy, resident in 1962. (Open daily 9:30am-7:30pm. L8000/€4.13, children under 12 L5000/€2.58.)

Ravello deserves its "Città della Musica" moniker. During the year, internationally renowned musicians come to perform at the **classical music festivals** held around New Year's Day, Easter, and throughout the summer. Concerts are performed in the gardens of the Villa Rufolo (in winter concerts move indoors, into the Villa or the *duomo*). Tickets are usually around L20-35,000/€10.33-18.08, and can be purchased at the AAST Information Office. Call the *Società di Concerti di Ravello* (☎089 85 81 49) for more information.

SALERNO ☎089

The capital of the Norman Empire from 1077 to 1127 and home to Europe's first medical school, Salerno is more recently famous as the site of an Allied landing during World War II. After being blasted to bits, it was rebuilt with a big-city atmosphere: the urban landscape of postwar buildings may shock those accustomed to the Amalfi Coast's peaceful coastal villages. Though lacking notable sights, Salerno is a cheap base from which to visit the Amalfi coast and Paestum.

▛ TRANSPORTATION

Trains: arrive at and depart from the station in P. Veneto. Luggage storage available (p. 529). To: **Florence** (5½-6½hr., 7 per day, L49-79,500/€25.31-41.06); **Naples** (45min., 32 per day, L5100-17,100/€2.63-8.83); **Paestum** (40min., 9 per day 6am-

9:30pm, L4700/€2.43); **Rome** (2½-3hr., 18 per day, L22-45,000/€11.36-23.24); **Reggio Calabria** (3½-5hr., 20 per day, L31-60,000/€16.01-30.99); and **Venice** (9hr., 1am, L64,000/€33.05).

Buses: Blue **SITA** buses leave from the train station for **Naples** (1hr., 47 per day 6am-9pm, L5100/€2.63) and **Amalfi** (1¼hr., 23 per day 6am-10:30pm, L5100/€2.63). Purchase tickets from a bar or *tabacchi*.

Ferries and **hydrofoils:** One dock is in P. della Concordia, 2 blocks from the train station. Another is in M. Marittimo Manfredi, a 15min. walk up the waterfront. **Linee Marittime Partenopee** (☎089 22 79 79) runs ferries to **Capri** (2hr., 3 per day 7:30am-8:30pm, L15,000/€7.75) and hydrofoils to **Capri** (1hr., 3 per day 8am-5pm, L26,000/€13.43) and **Ischia** (1½hr., 7:30am, L34,000/€17.56). **Travelmar** (☎089 87 31 90) runs ferries to **Amalfi** (1hr., 3 per day 7:30am-8:30pm, L9000/€4.65) via **Positano** (40min., L7000/€3.62) and hydrofoils to **Amalfi** (30min., 3 per day 8am-5pm, L6000/€3.10) via **Positano** (20min., L5000/€2.58).

Local Transportation: The orange **city buses** connect the train station neighborhood to the rest of the city. For routes and schedules, check the ticket booth in P. Veneto. Tickets L1300/€0.67 for 1hr., L2500/€1.29 for an all-day pass.

Taxis: ☎089 22 91 71 or 22 99 47.

ORIENTATION AND PRACTICAL INFORMATION

From the train station on **Piazza Vittorio Veneto,** the expansive, remarkably clean, pedestrian **Corso Vittorio Emanuele** veers to the right. C.V. Emanuele becomes V. dei Mercanti in the **old quarter,** the most historically interesting and lively part of Salerno. **Via Roma** runs parallel to C.V. Emanuele one block toward the waterfront. Along the waterfront from the train station is P. della Concordia and the **Lungomare Trieste,** which runs to the **Molo Marittimo Manfredi.**

TOURIST, FINANCIAL, AND LOCAL SERVICES

Tourist Office: EPT (☎800 21 32 89 or 23 14 32), in P. Veneto to the right as you leave the train station. The *Agenda del Turista* has practical info for Salerno and the Amalfi coast, while the biweekly *MEMO* guide has hotel, restaurant, club, and special events listings. English spoken. Open M-Sa 9am-2pm and 3-8pm.

Car Rental: Hertz, P. Veneto, 33 (☎089 22 21 06; fax 22 02 07), L130,000/€67.14 per day, L300,000/€154.94 for 3 days. Open M-F 8:30am-1pm and 4-7:30pm, Sa 8:30am-2pm, Su 9am-noon.

Luggage Storage: In train station. L5000 for 12hr. Open daily 7:30am-3pm.

English-Language Bookstore: Libreria Leggenda, V. Settimnio Mobilio, 38 (☎089 40 51 59), near hostel. Classics and new fiction. Open M-Sa 9am-1:30pm and 5-8:30pm.

Laundromat: Onda Blu, V. Mauri, 128 (☎089 33 32 26), in Salerno's Mercatello neighborhood. City's only self-service laundry. Take bus from C. Garibaldi, opposite the train station, to P. Grasso. Walk 1 block down on V. Mauri. L6000/€3.10 wash, L6000/€3.10 dry for up to 7kg. Soap L1000/€0.52. Open daily 8am-10pm.

EMERGENCY AND COMMUNICATIONS

Emergency: ☎113. **Police:** ☎113 or 112.

Hospital: S. Leonardo (☎089 67 11 11).

First Aid: ☎089 23 33 30.

Internet Access: Mailboxes, Etc., V. Diaz, 19 (☎089 23 12 95), off C.V. Emanuele, 500m from the station. With *Let's Go* L3000/€1.55 for 30min. Also offers FedEx, UPS, Western Union, and fax service. Open M-F 8:30am-2pm and 4-8:30pm, Sa 8:30am-1pm and 5:30-8:30pm.

Post Office: C. Garibaldi, 203 (☎089 22 99 70). Open M-Sa 8:15am-6:15pm. **Branch office** (☎089 22 99 98) at P. Veneto. Open M-Sa 8:15am-1:30pm. **Currency exchange** only at the main office.

Postal Code: 84100.

ACCOMMODATIONS

Ostello della Gioventù "Irno" (HI), V. Luigi Guercio, 112 (☎089 79 02 51). Exit train station and turn left onto V. Torrione and left under the bridge onto V. Mobilio. It's 700m ahead, across from gas station. Free daytrips in the summer to Paestum, Pompeii, and Amalfi. Hot showers, restaurant, TV, spacious rooms, and Internet for L7000/€3.62 per hr. Breakfast and sheets included. Curfew 2am. Dorms L17,500/€9.04.

Albergo Santa Rosa, C.V. Emanuele, 14 (☎/fax 089 22 53 46), 1 block from the train station, on the right. 12 clean, comfortable rooms. The helpful proprietors are full of crafty tips that will help you save money and heartache. Singles L45,000/€23.24, with bath L65,000/€33.57; doubles L75,000/€38.73, L95,000/€49.06.

Hotel Salerno, V. Vicinanza, 42 (☎089 22 42 11; fax 22 44 32), the 1st left off C. Emanuele. Close to the train station. Some of the 27 rooms have phone and TV. Singles L50,000/€25.82, with bath L75,000/€38.73; doubles L66-75,000/€34.09-38.73, L87,000/€44.93. AmEx/MC/V.

FOOD

Salerno serves typical Campanian cuisine, including *pasta e fagioli* (pasta and bean soup), as well as unusual specialties of its own, such as *milza* (spleen).

Hosteria Il Brigante, V.F. Linguiti, 4 (☎089 22 65 92). From P. Duomo, head up the ramp and look on the left. Join the locals for a delicious *pasta alla Sangiovannara*, a steal at L6500/€3.36. Open daily 9pm-midnight.

Taverna del Pozzo, V. Roma, 216 (☎089 25 36 36), serves some of the street's best pizza at truly reasonable prices on a pleasant patio. Pizzas L3-14,000/€1.55-7.23. Cover L2000/€1.03. Open M-Sa 1-3:30pm and 8pm-2am.

Cueva del Sol, V. Roma, 218 (☎089 23 73 91), serves delicious Mexican food and exotic drinks. Tacos L7000/€3.62. *Agave spinosa*, tequila, papaya juice, and lime L7000/€3.62. Open daily 8pm-3am.

SIGHTS AND ENTERTAINMENT

Though most of Salerno is dominated by aesthetically uninteresting modern buildings, there are a handful of interesting things to see in the old quarter. V. dei Mercanti and its tiny side streets afford a taste of life in the Middle Ages. The city was already considered "ancient" in the 9th century, and this area of Salerno was once the capital of the Norman empire (1077-1127).

Started in 845 and rebuilt 200 years later by Norman leader Robert Guiscard, **Duomo San Matteo** is decorated in the cosmopolitan style of the Norman regime. The arches of the portico, floor of the apse, and two pulpits in the nave are decorated with beautiful geometric mosaics and patterns influenced by those of the Islamic world. The **crypt**, with vaulted ceiling and beautiful frescoes, houses the **holy tooth** of the city's patron saint, S. Matteo. His holy filling and holy toothbrush are nowhere to be found. (Turn right off V. Mercanti or V. Roma onto V. Duomo and walk uphill. Open daily 10am-noon and 4-6:30pm.) One block down V. Duomo from the *duomo*, the **Museo della Ceramica** exhibits local ceramic art. (☎089 22 77 82. Open M-W and F-Sa 9am-1pm, Th 9am-1pm and 4-7pm. Free.) Climb L. Plebiscito on its far side to reach **Museo Diocesano**, which displays religious paintings and the fine work of medieval ivory-carvers from Amalfi. (Open daily 9am-6:30pm. Free.) Exotic plants grow in the **Parco del Mercatello** east of the city. CTSP bus #6 (L1000/€0.52) runs to the gardens. If you want to soak up some rays, there is a sandy beach after the sailboat harbor (take the bus along Lungomare Trieste).

During the month of July, the **Salerno Summerfestival**, includes a concert series (mostly jazz and blues) at the Arena del Mare, near the Molo Marittimo Manfredi. (Concerts usually start at 10pm; prices vary. Call ☎089 66 51 76 for more info.)

At night, the youngest crowd gathers at **Bar-Gelateria Nettuno,** V. Lungomare Trieste, 136-138 (☎089 22 83 75), near the fountain. Discos rock the area around Salerno, but prices are steep without the free passes often dispensed at random. Women can often enter for free, but let that be its own warning. In summer, locals flock to gigantic open-air discos on the western and southern coasts. **Movida, Villaggio del Sole, Morgana,** and **Mermaid's Tavern** along the southern coast are difficult to reach without a car. From June through September, the nighttime hotspot **Fuenti,** in Cetara (4km west of Salerno), has three floors of open-air dancing on the coastal cliffs. (☎089 26 18 00. Cover L20-25,000/€10.33-12.91. Open F-Sa 10:30pm-5am.) **Africana,** the most spectacular club around but far away in Praiano, sometimes charters boats to Salerno and back in the summer (see **Praiano,** p. 522). Check the magazine *MEMO* (at the tourist office or the hostel) for special events and club listings, including those outside Salerno.

Nearby **Vietri sul Mare** is home to hundreds of artisans and a pleasant beach to Salerno. Bus #4 or 9 runs from the station (10min.). Check out the neon-lit **Café degli Artisti,** V.C. Colombo, 35. Live Latin lyrics see salsa swingers swill shameful sums of sangria. (☎089 76 18 42. Open nightly 7:30pm-3am. Cover L15,000/€7.75.)

▨ DAYTRIP FROM SALERNO: CERTOSA DI SAN LORENZO

Without a car, the Certosa is best reached from Salerno, and can be seen in an easy daytrip. A bus leaves from Concodia Sq. at 6:25am, 10:30am, noon, and 2:30pm. The last bus returning to Salerno leaves Padula at 5:45pm. (2½hr., L9500/€4.91 each way.) Buses do not stop at Padula itself, but at the crossroads about 2km away. From the crossroads, follow the signs for 1km to the monastery.

Beneath the small town of **Padula** in the beautiful hilly farmland of southern Campania sits the magnificent Certosa di San Lorenzo, one of the largest monasteries in Europe and a magnificent example of Baroque architecture. The monastery was founded for Carthusian monks in the early 14th century to help the Angevin kings maintain control over routes into Calabria, but it was beautifully redecorated in a lavish Baroque style in the 17th century. Charles V stopped here, and he and his court were served an omelette made from 1000 eggs; though you won't be able to eat the embryos of 1000 chickens today, the splendid architecture and beautiful setting of the Certosa make it well worth a visit.

The *certosa* is divided into two sections, "Upper" and "Lower." Lay people could visit the lower section, which is the 1st courtyard through the main gate, but only the monks could pass through the ornate facade into the main body of the monestary. (Open daily 9am-5:30pm. L6000/€3.10.) The path through the monastery leads through two halves of the chapel, with choir stalls covered in inlaid wood depicting landscapes and Biblical scenes, along with a delicately inlaid marble altar. The path leads through the dining hall and kitchen, decorated in colorful majolica tiles, to the staircase to the library, which winds precariously up, without railings or pillars for support. Pass the staircase into the huge and serenely beautiful **Great Cloister,** decorated with carved miniatures of religious symbols in the entablature. At the far end of the cloister, the Grand Staircase, a wonderfully designed double staircase, curves up to the upper level.

Although you can easily see the *certosa* as a daytrip from Salerno, if you want to relax (or because you missed the last bus), **Albergo La Rosa,** attached to a farm, offers six clean rooms with a kitchen for L25,000/€12.91 per person. Call to be picked up from anywhere in Padula, or when exiting the *certosa* turn right, take the 1st right, then the 2nd right, then follow the road until the next intersection, turn left, and continue a short way. The *albergo* is on the left. (☎0975 77 81 04.)

PAESTUM   ☎082

Not far from the Roman ruins of Pompeii and Herculaneum, the three Greek temples of Paestum are among the best-preserved in the world, even rivaling those of Sicily and Athens. Paestum's perfectly constructed temples remained standing even after the great earthquake of AD 69 reduced Pompeii's to a pile of rubble.

Greek colonists from Sybaris founded Paestum as Poseidonia in the 7th century BC, in an attempt to curry favor with the sea god. Apparently it worked, as the city quickly became a flourishing commercial and trade center. After a period of Lucanian (native Italian) control in the 5th and 4th centuries BC, Poseidonia fell to the Romans in 273 BC, was renamed Paestum, and remained a Roman town until the deforestation of nearby hills turned the town into a swampy mush. Plagued by malaria and pirates, Paestum's ruins lay relatively untouched until they were rediscovered in the 18th century. Because Paestum is not urbanized, you may think that you missed your stop as you step off the train and nervously scan the sky for vultures. Fear not the dearth of modern urban squalor; the ruins alone are a must-see, especially when the *Sovrintendenza Archeologica* lets visitors walk around on the temples (sometimes they are fenced off).

🚍 TRANSPORTATION AND PRACTICAL INFORMATION. CTSP buses from Salerno (1hr., every hr. 7am-7pm, L4700/€2.43) stop at **via Magna Graecia,** the main modern road. The tourist office in Salerno provides a helpful list of all return buses from Paestum. **Trains** run from **Naples** (1¼hr., 9 per day 5:30am-10pm, L8200/€4.24) via **Salerno** (35min., L4700/€2.43). The **AAST Information Office,** V. Magna Graecia, 155, is next to the museum. (☎082 81 10 16; fax 872 23 22. Open July-Sept. 15 M-Sa 8am-2pm and 3:30-7:30pm, Su 9am-noon; Sept. 16-June M-Sa 8am-2pm.)

🛏 ACCOMMODATIONS. There is really no reason to stay in Paestum. The "nearby" hotels and restaurants are overpriced, and the site can be visited as a day-trip. However, the beachside **Ostello "La Lanterna" (HI),** V. Lanterna, 8, in Agropoli, is the nearest budget option. (☎/fax 0974 83 83 64. Sheets and shower included. 56 beds. Dorms L17,000/€8.78; quads L68,000/€35.12.) To get to Agropoli take the **CTSP buses** from Paestum (10min., 1 per hr. 7am-7pm, L2000/€1.03) or from Salerno (1hr., L4700/€2.43). Agropoli is also connected by train to Paestum (10min., L2200/€1.14); Salerno (45min., L4700/€2.43); and Naples (1½hr., L8200/€4.23).

📷 SIGHTS. Paestum's three Doric temples rank among the best-preserved in the world. Built without any mortar or cement, the buildings were originally covered by roofs of terra-cotta tiles supported by wooden beams. When excavators first uncovered the three temples, they misidentified (and thus misnamed) them. Although recent scholarship has provided new information about the temples's dedications, the old names have stuck. Restoration work on the temples occasionally leaves them fenced off or obscured by scaffolding. (Temples open daily 9am-1hr. before sunset. Closed 1st and 3rd Monday of each month. Last admittance 2hr. before sunset. L8000/€4.13, EU citizens over 60 and under 18 free).

There are three entrances to the ruins. The northernmost entrance leads to the **Temple of Ceres.** Built around 500 BC, this temple became a church in the early Middle Ages but was abandoned in the 9th century. The ancient Greeks built Paestum on a north-south axis, marked by the paved V. Sacra. Farther south on V. Sacra is the Roman **forum,** which is even larger than the one at Pompeii. The Romans leveled most of the older structures in the city's center to build this proto-*piazza*, the commercial and political arena of Paestum. To the left, a shallow pit marks the pool of an ancient **gymnasium.** East of the gymnasium lies the Roman **amphitheater.**

South of the forum lies the 5th-century BC **Temple of Poseidon** (actually dedicated to Hera), which incorporates many of the optical refinements that characterize the Parthenon in Athens. Small lions' heads serve as gargoyles on the temple roof. The southernmost temple, known as the **basilica,** is the oldest, dating to the 6th century BC. Its unusual plan, with a main interior section split by a row of columns down the middle, has inspired the theory that the temple was dedicated to two gods, Zeus and Hera, rather than one. A **museum** on the other side of V. Magna Graecia houses an extraordinary collection of pottery, paintings, and artifacts taken primarily from Paestum's tombs with outstanding bilingual descriptions and essays on site. It also includes samples of 2500-year-old honey and paintings from the famous **Tomb of the Diver,** dating to 475 BC. (Museum open daily 9am-6:30pm.

Ticket office open daily 9am-5:30pm. Closed 1st and 3rd Monday of each month. L8000/€4.13, EU citizens over 60 and under 18 free.)

If visiting the temples puts you in a worshipful mood, bow down on golden sand toward the sun at the **beach** 2km to the west. Unfortunately, much of it is owned by resorts that charge for beach access and chair rental. For a free dip in the Mediterranean, head to a *spiaggia pubblica*—ask for directions.

APULIA (PUGLIA)

Welcome to absolute Italy, where the sun's scorching rays and the people's intense passions continually threaten to bring things to a boil. Conversations, complete with elaborate hand gestures, quickly progress from pleasant joking to frenzied yelling and then back again. Some travelers interpret the South's mercurial passion as rudeness, but you'll have a better understanding (and a better time) if you try to see it as part of an uninhibited zest for life. Women may find the persisting legacy of *machismo* a little too much zest for them, especially in large cities where the 'alpha' males appear especially threatening.

The heel of Italy's boot, Apulia has been prized throughout the centuries for its fertile plains and numerous natural ports. The Greeks, and later the Romans, controlled the region as a vital stop on the trade route to the East. With the Middle Ages came an onslaught of invaders who shaped the culture. Modern Apulia, having served its time on "skid row," is regaining stature as a wealthy and educated region. Within its borders, remote medieval villages and cone-roofed *trulli* houses dot a cave-ridden plain, and ports have a distinctly Middle Eastern flair.

Direct train lines run from Naples to Bari and from Bologna to Lecce, and rail service is supplemented within the region by several private train and bus companies. Eurail passes and *cartaverde* are not valid on these private carriers.

HIGHLIGHTS OF APULIA

GO BAROQUE in **Lecce's churches** (p. 548) without losing a *lira*.

TAKE A BREATHER in **Bari** (p. 534). It's free.

MARVEL at Alberobello's mortarless houses, *trulli* (p. 540).

BARI   ☎ 080

Se Parigi ci avesse lo mare, sarebbe una piccola Bari.
(If Paris had the sea, it would be a little Bari.)
— An Italian proverb

Vibrant, modern, and indisputably Italian, Apulia's capital is a chaotic melange of seemingly incompatible ingredients. Begin with a tiny old city, the monuments dating from its days as a Byzantine stronghold. Add a well-organized, modern city grid, a port with ferries to Greece, hip nightlife fueled by a large university population, and vast quantities of delectable Puglian cuisine. Sprinkle in Rome's drivers and Naples's pickpockets, and broil the whole mishmash in some scorching southern Italian weather. The city is often called dirty, violent, and nightmarishly inefficient, and while most tourists stay in Bari only long enough to buy a ferry ticket to Greece, the reputation's bark is worse than Bari's bite. The old city is home to several great monuments and excellent prices. Bari can be a little intimidating and is certainly not for everybody, but the city strives to make tourists feel welcome.

▐▀ TRANSPORTATION

Airport: Bari Palese Airport (☎080 92 12 172), 8km west of the city. Alitalia, Air-France, British Airways, and Lufthansa fly to major European cities. A **shuttle bus** (L8000/€4.13) leaves 1¼hr. before flights.

Trains: Bari is connected to 4 different railways, all of which leave from P. Aldo Moro. The higher prices listed below are for InterCity (IC) or EuroStar (ES) trains.

> **FS** to: **Brindisi** (1-1¾hr.; 26 per day 6am-midnight; L10,100-25,100/€5.22-12.96); **Foggia** (1-1¾hr.; 35 per day 4:30am-12:30am; L10,300-25,100/€5.32-12.96); **Lecce** (1¾-2¼hr.; 26 per day 5am-midnight; L12,100-28,100/€6.25-14.51); **Milan** (9hr.; 9 per day 5am-midnight; L67,500-91,000/€34.86-47); **Naples** (4½hr.; 8:30am; L25,500/€13.17); **Reggio Calabria** (7½hr.; 3 per day noon-9pm; L45,500-65,000/€23.50-33.57); **Rome** (5-7hr.; 6 per day 6:30am-11:39pm; L47-65,500/€24.27-33.83); **Termoli** (2-3hr.; 6 per day 10am-10pm; L19-28,500/€9.81-14.72).

> **FSE** (☎080 546 24 44) from the main station to **Alberobello** (1½hr., 14 per day 5:30am-7:15pm, L5900/€3.05), sometimes via **Castellana Grotte** (1hr., 3 per day 8:25am-7:15pm, L4700/€2.43).

> **Ferrotramviaria Bari Nord** (☎080 521 35 77), next to the main station. Trains run to: **Andria** (1¼hr., L5100/€2.63); **Barletta** (1¼hr., 19 per day 6am-10pm, L5900/€3.05) via **Bitonto** (30min., L3000/€1.55); **Ruvo** (45min., L3900/€2.01). On Su the route is served by a bus leaving from P. Aldo Moro.

> **FAL** (☎080 524 48 81) runs Su to **Matera** (1½hr., 8 per day 6:30am-9pm, L6700/€3.46) via **Altamura** (1¼hr., 8 per day, L5700/€2.94). Across the ATS Viaggi Tours agency on V. Capruzzi, near the tunnel from the station.

Buses: SITA (☎080 556 24 46) usually leaves from V. Capruzzi on the other side of the tracks. Call ahead for fares and schedules. **Marozzi** buses to **Castel del Monte** leave from near the Teatro Petruzzelli on C. Cavour (1hr., M-Sa 2:10pm, L6000/€3.14).

Public Transportation: Local buses leave from P. Aldo Moro, in front of the train station. Tickets cost L1500/€0.77.

Taxis: ☎080 55 43 33.

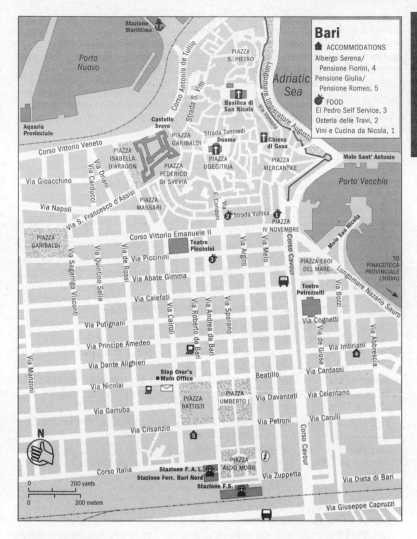

Bari

♠ ACCOMMODATIONS
Albergo Serena/
  Pensione Fiorini, 4
Pensione Giulia/
  Pensione Romeo, 5
🍴 FOOD
El Pedro Self Service, 3
Osteria delle Travi, 2
Vini e Cucina da Nicola, 1

🔲 FERRIES

Although there are no discounts for InterRail or Eurail pass holders (as there are in Brindisi), Bari is an important port for ferries to Greece, Turkey, Albania, and Israel. Because Bari's **Stazione Marittima** and the surrounding area can be intimidating, you should take one of the many buses to the port rather than walking the 2km through the old city. **Check in at least two hours before departure.** Many lines offer special student rates and discounts on round-trip tickets (Poseidon discounts 30% on return-trips). The list of companies below includes the lowest prices (deck class) for each destination on weekdays. The higher figure denotes high-season (July-Aug.) prices, while the lower figure represents low-season prices. Call ahead as schedules and prices vary, especially on weekends. Obtain tickets and information at the Stazione Marittima or at the offices listed below.

Poseidon Lines, c/o Morfimare, C. de Tullio, 36/40 (☎080 521 00 22; fax 521 12 04). Window #11 at the port. To **Turkey** and **Israel.**

Ventouris Ferries, c/o P. Lorusso & Co., V. Piccinni, 133 (☎080 521 76 99; fax 521 77 34). Windows #7-10. To: **Cefalonia** (15hr.; July 26-Aug. 21 every other day; L63-87,000/€32.54-44.93, students L57-77,000/€29.44-39.77); **Corfu** (11hr.; June 27-Sept. 29 1 per day; L53-73,000/€27.37-37.70, students L47-67,000/€24.27-34.60); **Igoumenitsa** (13hr.; in summer 1 per day; L53-73,000/€27.37-37.70, students L47-67,000/€24.27-34.60); **Patras** (18hr.; 1 per day; L63-87,000/€32.54-44.93, students L57-77,000/€29.44-39.77).

Marlines (☎080 523 18 24; fax 523 02 87). To **Igoumenitsa** (13hr.; 4 per week, in winter 2 per week; L50-70,000/€25.82-36.15, return L35-49,000/€18.08-25.31).

Superfast Ferries (☎080 528 28 28), to **Greece.**

■ ⚡ ORIENTATION AND PRACTICAL INFORMATION

Via Sparano runs straight from the train station to **Piazza Umberto I,** Bari's main square. Farther along V. Sparano, fancy boutiques line the street and provide some of the city's best window-shopping. The end of V. Sparano intersects **Corso Vittorio Emanuele II** and the edge of the **old city** (Bari Vecchia). Those attempting the long walk to the **port** should skirt the old city's winding streets by turning left on C.V. Emanuele and right at P. della Libertà onto **via Giuseppe Massari.** Walk around the castle, head right, and follow the coast. Otherwise, take the bus from the station (1 per hr.). For a more leisurely stroll, turn right off V. Sparano onto C.V. Emanuele; this path takes you past **Corso Cavour** to **Piazza Eroi del Mare.**

TOURIST, FINANCIAL, AND LOCAL SERVICES

Tourist Office: APT, P. Aldo Moro, 33a, 2nd fl. (☎080 524 23 61; fax 524 23 29), to the right as you leave the station. Has maps of Apulia and Bari. English spoken. Open M-F 8am-2pm, Tu and Th also 3-6pm.

Currency Exchange: At window #4 in the FS train station. Open daily 7am-9:30pm.

American Express: Morfimare, C. de Tullio, 36/40 (☎080 521 00 22), near the port. Open M-F 9am-1pm and 3:30-7:30pm, Sa 9am-noon.

English-Language Bookstores: Libreria Mondadori, V. Sparano, 158 (☎080 521 8343). Open M-F 9-8:30pm, Sa 9am-1:30pm.

Laundromat: V. Toma, 35 (☎080 556 70 56). Take the underpass past the last track, turn left on V. Capruzzi and right on C. Croce, continue, then turn left on V. Toma, and walk for 3 blocks. L10,000/€5.16 per load. Open July-Aug. 21 M-F 9am-1pm and 4-8pm, Sa 9am-1pm; Aug. 22-June M-Sa 9am-1pm and 4-8pm.

EMERGENCY AND COMMUNICATIONS

Emergency: ☎113. **Police:** ☎113. **Carabinieri:** ☎112.

Late-Night Pharmacy: Lojacono di Berrino, V. Cavour, 47 (☎080 521 26 15), across from Teatro Petruzzelli. Open M-F 4:30-11pm, Sa-Su 4:30-8pm. **De Cristo,** V. Kennedy, 75 (☎080 513 138).

Internet Access:

Mailboxes Etc., V. Roberto da Bari, 133 (☎080 521 39 53; fax 572 01 40). L5000/€2.58 per 30min. Open M-F 9am-8pm, Sa 9am-12:30pm.

Libreria Palomar, V. Nicolai 8 (☎080 521 28 45). Turn left on the 1st street after P. Umberto. L5000/€2.58 per 30min., L8000/€4.13 per hr. Open M-F 8:30am-1:30pm and 4:30-8:30pm, Sa 8:30am-1:30pm.

Post Office: (☎080 575 71 87; fax 575 70 07), in P. Battisti, behind the university. From P. Umberto, turn left on V. Crisanzio, then take the 1st right on V. Cairoli. Recently discovered, to everyone's shock, to be Italy's most efficient. Open M-F 8:20am-8pm, Sa 8:20am-1pm.

Postal Code: 70100.

▐ ACCOMMODATIONS

Most travelers don't stay long in Bari, but cheap accommodations are plentiful.

▨ Albergo Serena, V. Imbriani, 69 (☎080 554 09 80; fax 558 66 13). The most spacious option, all 14 rooms with shower. Singles L50,000/€25.82; doubles L80,000/€41.32; triples L120,000/€62.

Pensione Fiorini, V. Imbriani, 69 (☎080 554 07 88), a 10min. walk from the station. Walk straight past P. Umberto I and turn right onto V. Dante, which becomes V. Imbriani. Some rooms have balconies. Shower L5000/€2.58. Dorms L19,000/€9.81; singles L30,000/€15.50; doubles L59,000/€30.47, with bath L69,000/€35.64.

Pensione Romeo, V. Crisanzio, 12 (☎080 521 63 52; fax 523 72 53). Below his star-crossed love, Pensione Giulia. 25 rooms. Singles with bath L65,000/€33.57; doubles with bath L95,000/€49.06.

Pensione Giulia, V. Crisanzio, 12 (☎080 521 66 30; fax 521 82 71), above her star-crossed love. 13 spacious rooms with balcony (of course). Singles L70,000/€36.15, with bath L80,000/€41.32; doubles L90,000/€46.48, L120,000/€62. AmEx/MC/V.

▐ FOOD

Bari offers delicious Apulian food at outrageously low prices. Restaurants in the old town give a taste of old-world style, often providing neither menus nor itemized checks. Purchase food for the ferry ride at **Super CRAI,** V. de Giosa, 97, three streets to the right of P. Umberto I while facing away from the station. (☎080 524 74 85. Open M-Sa 8am-2pm and 5-8:30pm.) There is a daily **vegetable market** in P. del Ferrarese, closer to the port.

Vini e Cucina Da Nicola, Strada Vallisa, 23, in the old city. From P. IV November, enter the old city to the left; the restaurant is on the left. Inexpensive dining at its best. Don't let the no-frills service intimidate you. Dishes change daily. The fried calamari is exquisite. *Menù* L15,000/€7.75, drinks included. Open Tu-Su noon-3pm and 8:30-10pm.

El Pedro Self-Service, V. Piccini, 152 (☎080 521 12 94), off V. Sparano. Turn left (when heading away from the station) a block before C.V. Emanuele. Not a Mexican restaurant, but a busy cafeteria serving authentic Apulian specialties. Expect to wait in line. Complete meal with drink L14,000/€7.32. Open M-Sa 11am-3:30pm and 6-10pm.

Osteria delle Travi, Largo Chiurlia, 12 (☎080 84 04 38), at the end of V. Sparano. Turn left through the arches at the entrance to the old city. True *mezzogiorno* cuisine including pasta with arugula. Full meal L20,000/€10.33 with drinks. Open Tu-Sa 12:30-3pm and 7:30-10:30pm, Su 12:30-3pm.

▐ SIGHTS

As a strategic port on the Italian coast, Bari has always been a favorite target for invading armies. To help defend against approaching troops, Bari's citizens built the old city as a labyrinth; residents could hide in the twisting streets or use them to ambush those less familiar with the city. Thieves have learned to use this maze of streets to their advantage, and careless tourists are their favorite victims. **Do not venture alone into the old city, especially at night.** Avoid flashy watches and jewelry, keep valuables inside front pockets, and hold on tightly to purses, bags, and cameras. Stick to the larger streets and use a map (*Stop-Over's* enlarged map of the old city is great). At the same time, you should not let petty criminals scare you off entirely. The old city is of great historic interest and well worth visiting.

▨ BASILICA DI SAN NICOLA. Yes, Virginia, there is a **Santa Claus,** but he's dead. In 1087, 60 *Baresi* sailors stole the remains of St. Nicholas from Demre, Turkey—they don't call Bari *scippolandia* (land of the petty thieves) for nothing. Although the victorious sailors refused to hand over the saint to the local clergy, the Catholic Church built the Chiesa di San Nicola as Santa's final resting place. The church's spartan appearance would be better suited to a fortress—in fact, the tower on the right survives from a Byzantine castle that originally occupied the site. Inside, an 11th-century Episcopal throne hides behind the high altar, and 17th-century paintings with gaudy trim adorn the ceiling. The **crypt,** with its windows of translucent marble, holds the remains of Kris Kringle. To the left of the entrance, a Greek Orthodox shrine welcomes pilgrims visiting from the east. On the back wall several 17th-century paintings commemorate the saint's life, including a scene of the resurrection of three children sliced to bits and plunged into a barrel of brine by a nasty butcher. On a third wall, stockings are hung by the chimney with care. *(Open daily 7am-noon and 4-7:30pm, except during mass.)*

CASTELLO SVEVO. Fortifying the old maze of streets near the port is the colossal Swabian Castle, built in the 13th century by Frederick II on Norman and Byzantine foundations. Isabel of Aragon and Sona Sforza added bulwarks in the 16th century. Although you can't climb the ramparts, you can see the frequent art exhibits inside the medieval keep. *(Just outside the old city, off C.V. Veneto near the water. ☎ 080 528 61 11. Open daily 9am-12:30pm and 3:30-6:30pm. L4000/€2.07, under 18 and over 60 free.)*

DUOMO. Bari's most important monument, this Apulian-Romanesque cathedral was built in the late-12th century, during years of peaceful Norman rule. The *duomo* displays a typically austere tripartite Romanesque facade, augmented by rose windows on the transepts and Baroque decorations around the doors. *(In the old city at P. Odegitria. Open daily 8am-12:30pm and 7:30pm.)*

OTHER SIGHTS. The 17-room **Pinacoteca Provinciale** displays paintings by Veronese, Tintoretto, Bellini, and the Impressionist Francesco Netti, Bari's most acclaimed artist. The collection of 18th- and 19th-century Apulian landscapes is also refreshing. *(Down Lungomare N. Sauro, past P.A. Diaz, 4th fl. ☎ 080 521 24 22. Open Tu-Sa 9am-1pm and 4-7pm, Su 9am-1pm. L5000/€2.58, students L2000/€1.03.)*

The **Acquario Provinciale** sports a large collection of, well, live fish. No paintings, no chapels, just fish. Big fish. Not cooked. No fish and chips. Just fish. *(On Molo Pizzoli across P. Garibaldi. ☎ 080 541 22 84. Open M-Sa 9am-12:30pm. Free.)*

ᴵ ENTERTAINMENT

Pubs and **clubs** pepper this university town. Most are open daily from around 8pm until 1 or 2am (3am on Saturdays); they are generally closed during the August holidays. On weekends, students cram into Largo Adua and the other *piazze* along the *lungomare* east of the old city, where **Deco,** P. Eroi del Mare, 18 (☎ 080 524 60 70), serves American food and has live music.

Bari is the cultural nucleus of Apulia. **Teatro Piccinni** offers a spring concert season and opera year-round (purchase tickets at the theater). Consult the *Stop-Over* newsletter or the *Bari Sera* section of *La Gazzetta del Mezzogiorno* (the local newspaper) for the latest information.

Bari's **soccer** team was successful enough in 1997 to move up to Serie A, but since has been booted back down to Serie B. For true Italian culture, catch a game any Sunday (and often other days of the week) from September through June. Tickets, starting at L18,000/€9.30, are available at the stadium or in bars. The great commercial event of the year, the **Levante Fair,** runs for 10 days in mid-September. The largest fair in southern Italy, it displays goods from all over the world in the huge fairgrounds by the municipal stadium. May 7, 8, and 9 bring the **Festival of San Nicola.** Every Sunday *Baresi* carry an image of the saint from church to church.

⯈ DAYTRIPS FROM BARI

The numerous train lines that radiate from Bari make daytripping easy and affordable. Nearby towns are arranged in groups along five routes: Barletta, Trani, and Bisceglie to the northwest along the coast; Bitonto, Ruvo di Puglia, and Castel del Monte to the west; Altamura and Gravina in Puglia in the southwest; Castellana Grotte, Alberobello, and Martina Franca to the south; and Polignano a Mare, Monopoli, Egnazia, Fasano, and Ostuni to the southeast.

CASTEL DEL MONTE

*In summer, take Ferrotramviaria Bari Nord **train** (☎ 0883 59 26 84) to Andria (1¼hr. 19 per day 6am-10pm, L5100/€2.63) and then take **bus** from station to the castle, 17km away (30min.; 8:30am and 4:40pm, returns 10:50am and 7pm; L3300/€1.70). Call ☎ 0883 29 03 29 or contact Pro Loco tourist office (☎ 0883 59 22 83) to confirm the schedule. Miccolsi buses from Bari, near the Teatro Petruzzelli, also stop 2km from the castle (1 per day, M-Sa 2:10pm, L6000/€3.10). Castel del Monte (☎ 0883 56 98 48), is open Apr.-Sept. daily 9am-1:30pm and 2:30-7pm; Oct.-Mar. 9am-1pm. L6000/€3.10.*

Halfway between the High Murge and the sea, Castel del Monte sits majestically atop a hill surrounded by rolling farmlands. It is easily the most impressive of the castles of Frederick II, the Swabian king who ruled southern Italy in the 13th century. According to legend, the castle housed the Holy Grail; in reality, it served as a hunting lodge and, later, a prison. Check out the majestic gateway, inspired by a Roman triumphal arch—Frederick tried to revive classical principles of art and good government, and many Neoclassical details can be seen throughout the castle. The striking octagonal layout is aligned astronomically, leading scholars to hypothesize that the castle was designed as an observatory rather than a military structure. Atop one of the spiral staircases sits a small room used as a roost for hunting hawks, one of the emperor's hobbies.

CASTELLANA GROTTE

The FSE train from Bari toward Alberobello stops at "Grotte di Castellana Grotte" (1hr., 8 per day 8:30am-7:15pm, L4700/€2.43). Do not disembark at "Castellana Grotte," the city, which is 2km away down V. Grotte. Check schedules carefully because not all trains stop here. To get to the caves walk across the parking lot and turn left. Short tour (45min.; every hr. 8:30am-7pm, in winter 8:30am-1pm; L15,000/€7.75); longer tour (2hr.; every hr. 9am-6pm, in winter 9am-noon; L25,000/€12.91). English tours (long tour 11am and 4pm; short tour 1pm and 6:30pm; schedules may change).

The breathtaking, natural caverns of ◪**Castellana Grotte,** discovered in 1938, are famed for their size, age, and beauty. Stalactites and stalagmites have developed over time into all sorts of whimsical shapes, including a Madonna, a camel, a wolf, an owl, and an ice cream cone. Even if you don't see the resemblances, the various formations invite the imagination to run wild. Those with time to kill can even watch them grow—at the rate of 3cm per century. Visiting the caverns is expensive but worthwhile. To enter, you must join one of two **guided tours** (☎ 0167 21 39 76 or 0804 98 55 11). A short 1km jaunt and a longer 3km trek both start at La Grave, an enormous pit that superstitious locals feared was an entrance to hell. The longer tours culminate in the stunning Grotta Bianca (White Cave), a giant cavern filled with white stalactites. Tours in English are offered less frequently.

THE GARGANO MASSIF

*For Siponto, take the **train** to Foggia from Bari (1-1¾hr.; 35 per day 4:30am-12:30am; L10,100-25,100/€5.22-12.96) or Termoli (1-1¼hr.; 29 per day 4am-2:30am; L7400-12,400/€3.82-6.40). From there, another train will take you to Siponto (20min., 24 per day 5am-10:30pm, L3500/€1.81). To get to the church, take the path that starts across the tracks next to the (small) amusement park. For **Monte Sant'Angelo,** take the SITA bus from the train station in Foggia (40min., 9 per day 5:30am-5:30pm, L7000/€3.62). Ferrovie del Gargano buses (☎ 167 29 62 47) also run to Vieste (2hr., 8am and 12:30pm, L9000/€4.65), via Pugnochiuso (1¾hr., L9000/€4.65). SITA buses also run to San Giovanni Rotondo, home of the famous Padre Pio—his tomb and the church built in his honor draw droves of Italian pilgrims. Crypt open daily 9:30am-1:30pm and 4-7pm.*

The Gargano Massif once ranked among the most popular pilgrimage destinations in Europe. The Archangel Michael was said to have appeared in a cave in **Monte Sant'Angelo** in the 5th century, and in ancient times a respected oracle supposedly occupied the same cavern. Now the peninsula is renowned for its stretches of sand (65km) on the north and east coasts. Popular beach destinations include **Vieste, San Menaio,** and **Pugnochiuso.** Unfortunately, the Gargano is gradually succumbing to the twin blights of the southern coastal areas—smokestacks and beach umbrellas—so visit soon. Inland from the shore is the **Foresta Umbra,** which abruptly gives way to classic Mediterranean terrain in the south.

Residents of **Siponto,** 3km southwest of Manfredonia, abandoned the ancient city after a 12th-century earthquake and plague. The sole remains of Siponto surround the remarkable **Chiesa di Santa Maria di Siponto,** built during the 11th century in the Apulian-Romanesque style. The blind arcade shows strong Pisan influence and the square plan and cupola reveal Byzantine roots. Ask the caretaker to allow you to visit the 7th-century **crypt.**

RUVO

For Ruvo, 40min. by train from Bari on the Ferrovie Bari Nord Line, by the main FS station in P. Aldo Moro (14 per day 6:30am-8pm, reduced service by bus Su, L3200/€1.65). For Bitonto, take a train from Ruvo (20min., L2200/€1.140 or Bari (30min., L2200/€1.14).

An easy half-day trip from Bari, Ruvo is home to one of the most beautiful Romanesque cathedrals of medieval Puglia. Exit the station, take a right on V. Scarlatti, then a left on V. Fornaci, which turns into C. Cavour; the ▨**cathedral** is to the left when you reach the public gardens. Built in the 13th century, it has one of Puglia's most beautiful doorways, ornamented with a wild assortment of motifs derived from the Saracen, German, and French conquerors who ruled Puglia.

Midway between Ruvo and Bari on the Ferrovie Bari Nord line, **Bitonto** is home to another impressive Romanesque cathedral. From the train station head up V. Matteotti until you reach a squat tower—turn left and continue until you reach the large *piazza* with the church. Modeled after the church of San Nicola in Bari (p. 537), the exterior of the church is decorated with an array of carved details. At the central portal, carved scenes from the life of Christ contrast with abstract patterns. Inside, be sure to check out the beautifully carved pulpit and its reliefs of Frederick II. (Open daily 8am-noon and 4-7pm.)

ALBEROBELLO AND THE TRULLI DISTRICT ☎0804

Hundreds of *trulli*, unusual white-stone dwellings with cone-shaped roofs, crowd the **Valley of Itria,** between Bari and Taranto, like a scene out of Tolkien. The first recorded *trulli* were built in the 1400s, but the peculiar buildings did not take their well-known, mortarless form until 1654. Sometime that year, the local court heard of an impending royal inspection and ordered the *trulli*—regarded as substandard peasant housing—razed to the ground in order to avoid fines. After the inspection, the Court had the buildings rebuilt without mortar so that they could be easily dismantled before future royal visits to the farming community. Today, dismantling the *trulli* is illegal (the ones in Alberobello are a UNESCO World Heritage Site).

The largest, most-celebrated conglomeration of ▨*trulli* is in Alberobello, which features more than 1000 dwellings, a *trullo* church, and the two-domed **Trullo Siamese.** It's nearly impossible to escape Alberobello without buying one of the omnipresent replicas from the gift shops.

▣⁊ TRANSPORTATION AND PRACTICAL INFORMATION. Alberobello is just south of Bari. Take the **FSE train** from **Bari** (1½hr., 14 per day 5:30am-7:15pm, L5900/€3.05). To reach the *trulli* masses from the train station (☎080 432 33 08), bear left and take V. Mazzini (which becomes V. Garibaldi) to P. del Popolo. The staff at the **tourist information office** (☎080 432 51 71), in P. Fernando IV, off P. del Popolo, provides helpful maps marked with all the sights. **Postal code:** 70011.

▛▢ ACCOMMODATIONS AND FOOD. Eating and sleeping in Alberobello can be expensive; it's less costly to visit the *trulli* as a daytrip. Perhaps the most memorable way to spend the night is to rent a *trullo* from the aptly named **Trullidea,** V. Montenero, 18. As you face the *trulli* district, V. Montenero leads uphill from your left. Spacious *trulli* include kitchen and breakfast. (☎/fax 080 432 38 60; info@trullidea.com; www.trullidea.com. Singles L80,000/€41.32; doubles L120,000/€62; triples L150,000/€77.47. Prices 20% higher Aug. MC/V.) **Albergo da Miniello,** V.

Balenzano, 14, a block down V. Bissolati from P. del Popolo, is one of the only hotels in town without the word *trullo* in its name, and it's also the least expensive. The *albergo* has 15 rooms, all with bath, TV, phone, and fridge, many with great views of the you-know-whats. (☎/fax 080 43 11 88. Singles L50,000/€25.82; doubles L75,000/€38.73. MC/V). The local restaurant, **L'Olmo Bello**, V. Indipendenza, 33, to the left before entering the *trulli* district, serves local specialties under a century-old *trullo*. Try the *orechiette alla buongustaio*, ear-shaped pasta in a gourmet sauce. (☎080 432 36 07. *Primi* and *secondi* from L8000/€4.13. Cover L2000/€1.03. Open W-M noon-3pm and 7-10pm.)

🔘 **SIGHTS.** V. Monte S. Michele leads up the hill to the *trullo* **Church of St. Anthony.** To reach the **Trullo Sovrano** (Sovereign Trullo), take C.V. Emanuele from P. del Popolo and continue past the church at the end. This two-story structure, the largest *trullo* in Alberobello, was built in the 16th century as a seminary. It's decorated to show what the *trulli* were like when farmers inhabited them. (Open M-Sa 10am-1pm and 3-8pm. L2500/€1.29, includes tour in Italian.) Even if Alberobello isn't the most unique town you've ever visited, perhaps the **Museo del Territorio** will be the strangest museum you've ever seen. Composed of 23 *trulli* linked together, the museum has various temporary exhibits and a permanent display explaining the history and structure of the *trulli*. From P. del Popolo, turn left by the Eritrea store to P. XXVII Maggio. (Open daily 10am-1pm and 4:30-7:30pm. L2500/€1.29.)

BRINDISI   ☎ 0831

Everyone comes to Brindisi to leave Italy—here Pompey beat a hasty retreat from Caesar's armies, and Crusaders set forth to retake the Holy Land. Today those passing through Brindisi have more peaceful intentions. Backpackers headed for Greece crowd the town, stopping only to pick up their ferry tickets. Despite the traffic, Brindisi is a safe and pleasant town, and nearby towns of Ostuni and Lecce amply repay travelers who stop to explore—Corfu will still be there tomorrow.

🔘 FERRIES

Brindisi is Italy's major departure point for ferries to Greece. Ferries leave for **Corfu** (8hr.), **Igoumenitsa** (10hr.), **Kephalonia** (16½hr.), and **Patras** (17hr.). Ferries usually follow the Corfu-Igoumenitsa-Patras route, occasionally stopping in Kephalonia. From **Patras**, buses (2½hr., buy tickets at the *stazione marittima*) and trains service **Athens.** Ferries run to **Çesme**, in Turkey (30hr.) and **Durres**, in Albania (9hr.), but there are no InterRail or Eurail discounts to those destinations.

All passengers leaving from Brindisi pay a port tax (usually L10-14,000/€5.16-7.32) in addition to the regular fare. Whether or not you have an InterRail or Eurail pass, any agency in Brindisi can sell you a ticket for any particular ferry, and all charge the same rates. Ask about all options—a store owner who says there is only one way lies like a yellow dog and has a son-in-law who runs the suggested ferry line. **Delta Shipping,** Corso Umberto, 116 (☎0831 52 03 67), has a friendly, English-speaking staff. The cheapest option is deck passage (*passagio semplice*). The downside; hard wooden decks don't make for soft comfortable beds. Nights at sea are often cold and wet. If you'd rather be inside, a supplemental fee brings a little comfort. Food and drink are available on board, but stocking up for the ride is cheaper. If you plan to snack at the restaurant or while away the hours at the bar (a surefire recipe for sea-sickness), make sure the boat accepts *lire*.

If you have bought tickets somewhere other than Brindisi, you may lose your reservations if you do not **check in at least two hours before departure.** Allow plenty of time for late trains and for the 1km walk from the train station to the ferry embarkation terminal, and then for a shuttle to the dock. At the port and on the ferries, be sure to take appropriate precautions with your belongings—bolt down your bags, sit on your money, and sleep with one eye open (like a pirate).

INTERRAIL AND EURAIL TRAVELERS

Some Eurail/InterRail travelers arrive in Brindisi expecting to hop on a free ferry to their destination. Sadly, ferry service is intermittent or interrupted, causing the loss of a day of Eurail travel. Many opt to purchase non-Eurail/Interrail ferry tickets for the sake of convenience, despite cost. Some go directly to Bari to avoid the hassle, even though **no Bari ferries accept Eurail/InterRail passes.** Companies that accept Eurail/Interrail will find seats on other lines when their ferries are full.

InterRail and Eurail passes are only valid on **Hellenic Mediterranean Lines.** Their tickets can be obtained at any agency, but Hellenic Mediterranean Lines, C. Garibaldi, 8, has an efficient main office (☎0831 52 85 31; fax 52 68 72; www.hml.it). Eurail pass holders, however, will have to pay a L19,000/€9.81 fee for travel between June 10 and September 30. InterRail pass holders are exempt from this fee. The pass will only get you deck passage. A seat inside costs L29,000/ €14.98 extra; cabins start at L45,000/€23.24. The port tax is L12,000/€6.20 on Hellenic Mediterranean Lines. May through October, Hellenic Mediterranean ferries leave every other day between 7am and 8pm. Call to verify departure times.

TRAVELING WITHOUT INTERRAIL OR EURAIL

Traveling to Greece without a pass is only slightly more expensive. Hellenic Mediterranean Lines charges L45-55,000/€23.24-28.41 for deck passage, depending on the season. Prices fluctuate throughout the year and are highest on weekends in late July and early August, while Eurailers pay a supplement during the entire high season. As with Eurail/InterRail tickets, most agencies also sell non-Eurail/InterRail tickets, and all charge the same price. The company offices, as opposed to general agents, will give you information only on their ships, while general agents present a variety of options. Three of the more reliable ferry companies are **Strintzis Lines,** C. Garibaldi, 65, which has newer boats (☎0831 56 22 00); **Fragline,** c/ o Discovermare, C. Garibaldi, 88 (☎0831 59 01 96); and **Med Link Lines,** c/o Discovery, C. Garibaldi, 49 (☎0831 52 76 67). At each office, ask for the total price (including taxes and fees) and for access to the **free shuttle bus.** Most companies offer a 10-20% discount on round-trip tickets and offer youth/student fares and "bargain" tickets on certain days. A speedier option is **Italian Ferries'** catamarans, C. Garibaldi, 97 (☎0831 59 03 05; fax 59 01 91), which run to **Corfu** in half the time (3¼hr.; July 24-Aug.15 at 2pm; L100,000/€51.65, under 26 L60,000/€31).

▐▘ TRANSPORTATION

Trains: (☎0831 166 105 050) in P. Crispi. Open daily 8am-8pm. Luggage storage available (p. 544). Prices higher for Intercity trains. **FS** to: **Bari** (1¼-1¾hr.; 24 per day 4am-11pm; L10,100-25,100/€5.22-12.96); **Lecce** (20-30min., 28 per day 5:30am-1am, L3900-15,900/€2.01-8.21); **Milan** (10hr.; 6:30pm and 9:40pm; L62,000/€32.02); **Naples** (7hr.; 5 per day; L31,000/€16.01); **Reggio Calabria** (8¾hr.; 9:30pm; L42,000/€21.69); **Rome** (6-9hr.; 4 per day 7am-9:45pm; L49-79,500/€25.31-41.06); **Taranto** (1¼hr., 12 per day 5am-8:30pm, L5900/€3.05); **Venice** (11hr.; 7:50pm; L67,500/€34.86); **Zurich** (14hr.; 8:40pm; L85,000/€43.90).

Buses: FSE, at the train station, handles buses throughout Apulia. Buy tickets for both companies at **Grecian Travel,** C. Garibaldi, 75 (☎0831 56 83 33; fax 56 39 67). Open M-F 9am-1pm and 3:30-8pm, Sa 9am-1pm. **Marozzi buses** travel to **Rome** (7½-8½hr.; 3 per day 11am-10pm; L55-65,000/€28.41-33.57). **Miccolis** runs to **Naples** (5hr.; 3 per day 6:35am-6:35pm; L41,000/€21.17).

Public Transportation: City buses (☎0831 54 92 45) run between train station and port and to destinations around city. Buy tickets (L1200/€0.62) from bars and *tabacchi.*

Taxis: (☎0831 22 29 01). Brindisi's virtually unregulated taxi drivers have a terrible reputation for swindling foreigners. Some say that the only English many of them know is the phrase "queekly, queekly, de boat is leeving." Buses (or feet) are a better option between the train station and port.

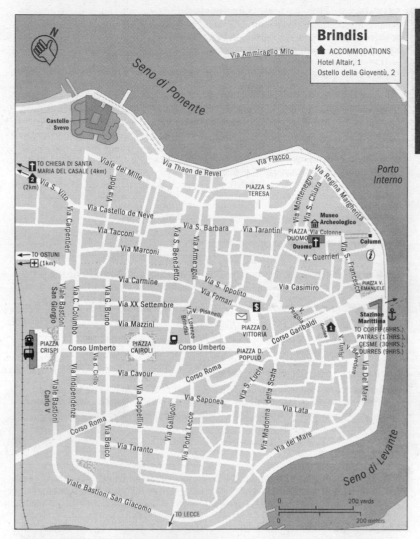

Brindisi

⌂ ACCOMMODATIONS
Hotel Altair, 1
Ostello della Gioventù, 2

ORIENTATION AND PRACTICAL INFORMATION

Corso Umberto runs from the train station, through **Piazza Cairoli** and to **Piazza D. Populo** and **Piazza D. Vittorio** where it becomes Corso Garibaldi and heads to the port. The **Stazione Marittima** is to the right on **via Regina Margherita**. V. Regina Margherita curves around the waterfront past the column that once marked the end of the Appian Way and becomes **via Flacco** and then **via Revel,** which are full of bars, restaurants, food stands, and, in summer, carnival rides.

Tourist Office: APT Information Office, V. Regina Margherita, 5 (☎0831 52 30 72). From C. Garibaldi, turn left on V. Margherita. Pretty useless for ferry info, but the staff provides a free map and advice about hotels, local services, and sights. Open M-Sa 8am-7pm; in winter M-F 9am-1pm and 4-6pm. Despite the signs, there is no info office at the *stazione marittima.*

Currency Exchange: Banca Nazionale del Lavoro, V. Santi, 11, uphill from P. Vittoria. Open M-F 8:20am-1:35pm and 2:45-4pm. For other exchanges try C. Umberto or C. Garibaldi; all offer dollar-*drachma-lire* conversions.

Luggage Storage: At the train station. L5000/€2.58 per 12hr. Open daily 6:30am-10:30pm. Also at the port.

Emergency: ☎113.

Municipal Police: ☎0831 22 95 22. **Carabinieri:** ☎112 or 0831 52 88 48.

Medical Emergency: Pronto Soccorso (☎0831 52 14 10) at **Ospedale Di Summa** (☎0831 51 01).

Internet Access: Foto Center, C. Umberto, 114 (☎0831 52 84 25). L12,000/€6.20 per hr. Open M-F 9am-1pm and 4:45-8:45pm, Sa 9am-1pm. **Jumbo Store,** V. Bastori S. Giorgio, 14/16, the 1st left after the station. Slow connection at peak times. L6000/€3.10 per 30min. Open daily 8:30am-8:30pm.

Post Office: P. Vittoria, 10 (☎0831 52 39 56). Open M-F 8:10am-6:30pm, Sa 8:10am-1:30pm.

Postal Code: 72100.

ACCOMMODATIONS

▨ **Ostello della Gioventù,** V. Brandi, 2 (☎0831 41 31 23; hostelbrindisi@hotmail.com), in Casale, 2km from train station. Call and have hostel's free shuttle pick you up. Lively atmosphere and fun-loving, multilingual owner Maurizio. Shower and sheets included. Laundry L9500/€4.91. L23,000/€11.88 per person. Also rents 80 beds during the day for L9000/€4.65.

Hotel Altair, V. Giudea, 4 (☎/fax 0831 56 22 89), near the port and center. From *stazione marittima*, walk up C. Garibaldi and take the 2nd left. 15 big rooms with high ceilings. Singles L40,000/€20.66, with bath L60,000/€30.99; doubles L60,000/€30.99, L90,000/€46.48. AmEx/MC/V.

Hotel Venezia, V. Pisanelli, 4 (☎0831 52 75 11). After the fountain, take the 2nd left off C. Umberto onto V.S. Lorenzo da Brindisi, then right onto V. Pisanelli. Brindisi's cheapest, but be prepared to share a bath. 12 rooms. Reserve 4 days in advance. Singles L25,000/€12.91; doubles L45,000/€23.24.

FOOD

An open-air **market,** on V. Fornari off P. Vittoria, sells fresh fruit by the ton. (Open M-Sa 7am-1pm.) Pick up supplies for your ferry ride at the **Maxi Sidis supermarket,** C. Garibaldi, 106, a block from the port. (Open M-Sa 8am-1:15pm and 4:15-8:30pm, Su 9am-1pm and 5:30-8:30pm.) Across the street, **Il Fornaio,** C. Garibaldi, 93, stocks fresh bread and pastries at bargain prices. (Open daily 7am-10pm.) Avoid the restaurants and cafes on the main strip, where advertised "tourist *menùs*" mean small portions and steep drink prices. Better options lie on nearby side streets. **Il Foccaceria,** V. Cristoforo Colombo, 5 (☎0831 56 09 30), offers much more than what its name implies. Take out pizza and lasagne on the quick. Try the lasagne for only L5000/€2.58. (Open daily 8am-11pm. AmEx/MC/V.)

SIGHTS AND ENTERTAINMENT

From the port, V. Regina Margherita leads three blocks to stairs facing the water. The column here marked the end of the **Appian Way.** The marble capital is graced by the figures of Jove, Neptune, Mars, and eight tritons. The column's twin, which once stood on the adjacent base, now resides in Lecce. V. Colonne runs from behind the column to P. Duomo. In the 11th-century **duomo** (rebuilt in the 18th-century) Emperor Frederick II married Jerusalem's Yolande. (Open daily 7am-noon and 4-7pm.) The small **Museo Archeologico** next door traces Brindisi's rich history though pottery, tablets, and other artifacts. (☎ 0831 22 14 01. Open M-F 9:30am-1:30pm, Tu 9:30am-1:30pm and 3:30-6:30pm, Sa-Su 9:30am-1:30pm. Free.)

From the hostel, follow the signs for 15min. to the pride of Brindisi, the **Chiesa di Santa Maria del Casale.** The interior is decorated with 13th-century frescoes, including one of Mary blessing Crusaders. (Open daily 7am-noon and 4-7pm.)

◪ DAYTRIP FROM BRINDISI: OSTUNI

Ostuni is on the train line between Brindisi (30min., 20 per day 7am-10:30pm, L3900/ €2.01) and Bari (1hr., 20 per day 7am-10:30pm, L6700/€3.46). From train station (☎ 0831 30 12 68), take city bus to Piazza della Libertà, the center of town (5min.; M-Sa every 30min., Su every hr. 7am-9:30pm; L1000/€0.55). Buy tickets at train station bar.

Rising out of a landscape of sea, dark red earth, and olive trees, Ostuni's *città bianca* (white city) appears ethereal. The *centro storico*'s white walls protect the city from the elements and lend a fairy-tale touch to the serpentine streets. The terrace at the top of C.V. Emanuele boasts a beautiful view of the old city. Just off the *piazza*, the little church of **Santo Spirito** has a doorway with impressive late-medieval reliefs. From the *piazza*, V. Cattedrale rises through the old town center. The **Convento delle Monacelle** (Convent of Little Nuns), V. Cattedrale, 15, has a Baroque facade and a colorful white-tiled dome of Moorish inspiration. (☎ 0831 33 63 83. Museum inside open daily 9am-1pm and 4:30-10:30pm. L3000/€1.55.) Crowning Ostuni's hill, the **duomo** (1437) was the last Byzantine building erected in southern Italy and has a remarkable facade in the Spanish Gothic style. (Open daily 7:30am-12:30pm and 4-7pm.) On August 26 and 27, Ostuni celebrates St. Oronzo with the **Cavalcata,** a parade of costumed horses and riders. Many praise Ostuni's nearby **beach,** accessible from P. della Libertà (15min., every 30min. 8am-7:30pm, L1500/ €0.77). Buses are unnumbered; ask the driver if you're on the right one.

Ostuni's **AAST Information Office,** C. Mazzini, 6, just off P. della Libertà, provides both assistance and a booklet entitled *Ostuni.* Catchy. (☎ 0831 30 12 68. Open June-Aug. M-Sa 9:30am-1:30pm and 3-8pm; Sept.-May M-F 9:30am-noon and 4-7pm, Sa 9:30am-noon.) If you choose to stay the night, try the 26 large rooms at **Hotel Orchidea Nera,** C. Mazzini, 118, about half a kilometer from P. della Libertà. (☎ 0831 30 13 66. Singles L45,000/€23.24, with bath L60,000/€30.99; doubles L70,000/ €36.15, L90,000/€46.48. AmEx/MC/V.)

There are a great many rustic taverns and *osterie* in the old city. One of the favorites is **Porta Nova,** V. Gaspare Petrolo, 38. Enjoy the panoramic view of the countryside from the elegant dining room. L25,000/€12.91 *menù* includes *primo, secondo, contorno,* water, service, and cover. (☎ 0831 33 89 83. Open Th-Tu 10am-4pm and 7pm-1am.) **Locanda dei Sette Peccati,** on Vco. F. Campana, has pizza from L5000/€2.58, *primi* L7000/€3.62, and *panini* L5-7000/€2.58-3.62. (Open Tu-Su 10:30am-3:30pm and 7pm-2am. Open M July-Aug. In winter, live music (soft jazz) Th 8:30pm-closing in Sette Peccati's stylish back room. AmEx/MC/V.

LECCE ☎ 0832

The hidden pearl of Italy, Lecce is where Italians go when foreign tourists invade their country. Once here, they marvel at the city's architecture, a spectacularly ornate style known as Leccese Baroque. Made from *tufigna,* a soft local stone that hardens when exposed to air, most of Lecce's perfectly preserved *palazzi* and elaborate churches are covered with intricate floral carvings, lavishly embellished balconies, and finely decorated portals. At night, the lighted buildings are extraordinary. Although a succession of conquerors—Cretans, Romans, Saracens, Swabians, and more—passed through here, the Spanish Hapsburgs solidified the old city's current form in the 16th and 17th centuries. Lecce, the "Florence of the Mezzogiorno," is a great starting point for a tour of the Salento Peninsula, the heel of Italy's boot. Thanks to its university, the city also has a vibrant nightlife.

☐ TRANSPORTATION

Trains: P. Stazione, 1km from the town center. Buses #24 and 28 run from the train station to the center of town. Lecce is the southeastern terminus of the state railway. **FS** trains (☎0832 30 10 16) to: **Bari** (1½-2hr.; 22 per day 5am-10:30pm; L12,100-29,000/€6.25-14.98); **Brindisi** (20-40min., 29 per day 5am-10:30pm, L3900-16,000/€2.01-8.26); **Reggio di Calabria** (9hr.; 9pm; L45,500/€23.50); **Rome** (6-9½hr.; 5 per day 6:30am-9pm; L67,100-79,500/€34.65-41.06); **Taranto** (2½hr.; 3 per day 1-9:30pm; L10,100/€5.22). **FSE** trains (☎0832 66 81 11) criss-cross the Salento. To **Gallipoli** (1hr., 12 per day 5:30am-8pm, L5100/€2.63) and **Otranto** (1¼hr., 9 per day 7am-7:30pm, L4700/€2.43) via **Maglie.**

Buses: FSE V. Boito (☎0832 34 76 34), easily accessible by bus #4 (L1000/€0.55) from the train station. To **Gallipoli** (1hr., 5 per day, L4500/€2.32) and **Taranto** (2hr., 5 per day 7am-2:30pm, L8000/€4.13). **STP** (☎0832 30 28 73), V. Adua, heads to the smaller towns of the Salento Peninsula. Pick up a schedule at the tourist office.

Taxis: at P. Stazione (☎0832 24 79 78) or P.S. Oronzo (☎0832 30 60 45).

Bike Rental: Giringiro (☎0347 871 07 17), Porta Napoli. L2-3000/€1.03-1.55 per hr. Open M-F 9am-1pm. **P.S. Oronzo.** L12,000/€6.20 per hr. Open daily 6pm-midnight.

✴☐ ORIENTATION AND PRACTICAL INFORMATION

Lecce lies 35km south and inland from Brindisi. From the train station, take **Viale Quarta** straight into V. Cairoli, which turns left onto **via Paladini** and winds around the *duomo*, stopping at V. Vittorio. To the left, V. Libertini passes the **Piazza Duomo** and **Chiesa di San Giovanni Battista** and exits the old city walls through Porta Rudiae. To the right lies **Piazza Sant'Oronzo,** Lecce's main square, with the **castello** beyond. Three blocks beyond the castello on V. Trinchese is **Piazza Mazzini.** On the other side of the city, **V. dell'Università** runs parallel to the old city walls.

TOURIST, FINANCIAL, AND LOCAL SERVICES

Tourist Office: AAST Information Office, V.V. Emanuele, 24 (☎0832 31 41 17). Maps and info. Open M-F 9am-1:45pm and 4-7:30pm.

Budget Travel: Centro Turistico Studentesco, V. Palmieri, 91 (☎0832 33 18 62). From P. Sant'Oronzo take V. Emanuele and turn right on V. Palmieri. Provides flight and train info and sells tickets. Open M-F 9am-1pm and 4:30-7:30pm.

Laundromat: Lavanderia Self-Service, V. dell'Università, 47 (☎0339 683 63 96), halfway between Porta Rudiae and Porta Napoli. Wash L5000/€2.58; dry L1000/€0.55 per 10 min. Soap L1000/€0.55. Open M-F 9am-1pm and 5-9pm, Sa 9am-2pm.

EMERGENCY AND COMMUNICATIONS

Police: V. Otranto, 5 (☎113).

Pronto Soccorso: (☎0832 66 14 03), at **Ospedale Vito Fazzi** (☎0832 66 11 11), on V.S. Cesario.

Internet Access: Cliocom, V. 95° Regimento Fanteria, 89 (☎0832 34 40 41; www.clio.it). A 5min. walk from castle. First time users must bring passport. L5000/€2.58 per 30min. Open M-Sa 9am-1pm and 4-8pm. Closed Sa afternoons in Aug.

Post Office: (☎0832 24 27 12), in P. Libertini, behind the castle. **Currency exchange** available. Open M-F 8:15am-7:15pm.

Postal Code: 73100.

☐ ACCOMMODATIONS & CAMPING

Lecce lacks ultra cheap accommodations. The tourist office lists *affittacamere.*

Hotel Cappello, V. Montegrappa, 4 (☎0832 30 88 81; fax 30 15 35; hcappello@tin.it). From the station, take the 1st left off V. Quarta onto V. Don Bosco and follow the signs.

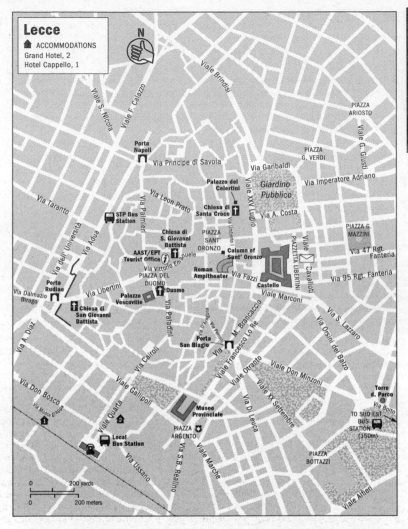

Lecce

🏠 ACCOMMODATIONS
Grand Hotel, 2
Hotel Cappello, 1

Modern, comfortable, and convenient. All 35 rooms with A/C, bath, phone, TV, and fridge. Singles L53,000/€27.32; doubles L85,000/€43.90. AmEx/MC/V.

Grand Hotel, V. Quarta, 28 (☎0832 30 94 05; fax 30 98 91), half a block from the train station. A little faded, but still as elegant as the name suggests. All 70 rooms with phone and TV. Breakfast L10,000/€5.16. Singles L55,000/€28.41, with bath L80,000/€41.32; doubles L90,000/€46.48, L140,000/€72.30. AmEx/MC/V.

Camping: Torre Rinalda (☎0832 38 21 61), on the beach, 15km from town. Bus #32 from P.S. Oronzo. Virtually every amenity. July 19-Aug. 29 L10,800/€5.58 per person; Oct.-Mar. L5800/€3 per tent.

🍴 FOOD

Regional specialties range from the hearty *cicerietria* (chickpeas and pasta) and *pucce* (sandwiches made with olive-bread rolls) to *confettoni* (chocolate candies made from a top-secret recipe). For a century, cheese-loving women and men have bought picnic supplies at **Salumeria Loiacono,** V. Fazzi, 11, in P. Sant'Oronzo, a long-established cheese establishment. (Open daily 7am-2pm and 4:20-8:30pm.) The indoor **market** behind the post office provides a chance to haggle over meat and fruit. (Open M-F 4am-2:30pm, Sa 4am-2:30pm and 3:30-9pm.)

■ **Ristorante Re Idomeneo,** V. Libertini, 44 (☎0832 24 49 73), just a few blocks from the *duomo*. Reasonably priced with endearing staff and salads fit for the king of Crete (or you). In the winter, enjoy traditional *cicerietria* (L8000/€4.13). Pizza L5-15,000/€2.58-7.75; *primi* L8-11,000/€4.13-5.68; *secondi* L9-14,000/€4.65-7.32. Open W-M noon-3pm and 7:30pm-1am. AmEx/MC/V.

La Capannina, V. Cairoli, 13 (☎0832 30 41 59), between the train station and P. Duomo. Excellent outdoor dining in the tranquil *piazza* opposite the restaurant. Pizza L4-8000/€2.07-4.13; *primi* L6-10,000/€3.14-5.16; *secondi* L8-12,000/€4.13-6.20. Cover L2500/€1.29. Open Tu-Su 9am-2:30pm and 6:30pm-midnight.

De Matteis Oronzo, V. Marconi, 51 (☎0832 30 28 00), near the castle. This fantastic candy store sells *confettoni* (L500/€0.26) and *cotognata leccese* (dried fig candies so delicious that they're ordered by the Pope; L500/€0.26). Open daily 6am-10:30pm.

Natale Pasticceria, V. Trinchese, 7 (☎0832 25 60 60), close to the McDonalds (in proximity, anyway). Pastry shop is full of Leccenese pastries, gelati, and candies. Try local cream-filled delights for L1500/€0.77. Open daily 9am-4pm.

⊙ SIGHTS

Lecce has an endless supply of **churches,** and the best are all within a 15-minute walk of each other. *(Churches open daily 8-11:30am and 5-7:30pm unless otherwise stated.)*

■ **BASILICA DI SANTA CROCE.** The most outstanding of Lecce's churches, this *chiesa* (1549-1695) is the supreme expression of Leccese Baroque. Most of the area's accomplished architects contributed their efforts to this church at some time or another; if you look closely, you can see the profile of Gabriele Riccardi, the original designer, hidden between the upper window and the column to its left. Inside you'll find two rows of massive Corinthian columns. A wonderfully animated altar (1614) by F. A. Zantimbalo adorns the chapel to the left of the apse. *(From P.S. Oronzo, head down V. Templari toward the basilica's extravagant facade.)*

PALAZZO CELESTINI. Giuseppe Zimbalo—nicknamed "Lo Zingarello" (the gypsy) due to his penchant for wandering from one church project to another—designed the lower half of the *palazzo's* facade. His pupil, Giuseppe Cino, finished the upper part. Visitors can view the inner courtyard of the building now used for offices. In the summer classical music concerts are held in the courtyard; keep an eye out for posters advertising the concerts or ask at the AAST office for more information. *(Next to Chiesa d.S. Croce. Concerts L10,000/€5.16, students L3000/€1.55.)*

PIAZZA DEL DUOMO. Constructed in 1114, the *duomo* was "Zingarelloed" between 1659 and 1670. The interior dates from the 18th century, with the exception of two Leccese altars. The **campanile** (bell tower, 1682) rises from the left side of the cathedral. Opposite, the **Palazzo Vescovile** (Bishop's Palace) has been remodeled several times since construction in 1632. On the right, with a Baroque well in its center, stands the **seminary** (1709) designed by Cino. Small yellow signs in the *piazza* chatter about the construction of the church in Italian. Be sure to come at night, when the lighting on the building facades is spectacular. *(From P.S. Oronzo, take V. Emanuele. Duomo open daily 8-11am and 4:30-7:30pm.)*

ANCIENT RUINS. Lecce also offers an array of ancient ruins. The **Column of Sant'Oronzo,** one of two that marked the termination of the Appian Way in Brindisi (see p. 544), towers over P. Sant'Oronzo. A statue of the saint now tops the column. Also in P.S. Oronzo lie the ruins of a 2nd-century amphitheater, thought to have held 20,000 spectators (at least that many young people gather here on summer nights to flirt). Half of the structure was filled in to build the nearby church. Near the station, the **Museo Provinciale** is home to Apulian ceramics from the 5th century BC. *(V. Gallipoli, 30. ☎ 0832 24 70 25. Open M-F 9am-1:30pm and 2:30-7:30pm, Sa-Su 9am-1:30pm. Wheelchair accessible. Free.)*

OTHER SIGHTS. The complex **Chiesa di San Giovanni Battista** (Church of the Rosary) was Lo Zingarello's last work. Here, the artist seemed to surrender to the Baroque with reckless abandon. *(Take V. Libertini from P. del Duomo).* The ornate **Port Napoli** once stood on the road from Naples. This arch was erected in 1548 in honor of Holy Roman Emperor Charles V, whose coat of arms adorns the front. *(From P. del Duomo, take V. Palmieri.)*

🎵 ENTERTAINMENT

In 1999, Lecce's soccer team (after one shame-ridden year in Serie B) managed to make it back to Serie A, the country's highest division. (Games held Sept.-June. Stadium ☎ 0832 45 38 86. Tickets from L17,000/€8.78. Buy at *tabacchi* and lottery agencies.) The AAST office distributes *Calendario Manifestazioni*, which describes seasonal events of the province and Lecce's annual summer festivals. Every night, crowds gather outside the many bars, pseudo-Irish pubs (very popular among Italian university students), and pizzerias along V.V. Emanuele and P. Oronzo. Dancing picks up at **Torre di Merlino,** V.G. Battista del Tufoi, 10, near the Roman Theater. (Open Th-Tu 8pm-3am.) Most nightclubs, especially during the summer, are on the coast and are only accessible by car. For current information on nighttime hotspots, ask for the monthly *Balocco* at local bars.

SALENTO PENINSULA

Foreign tourists often overlook Italy's sun-baked high heel, home to beautiful sandy beaches on two seas, hidden grottoes, medieval fortresses, and some of Italy's oldest and best-preserved art and architecture. With cultural roots stretching back to the Greeks, the peninsula is worthy of exploration. Roam an enchantingly varied coastline, or venture to inland villages to sample wine and olives.

OTRANTO ☎ 0836

Although Otranto is a congested mess in August, its winding streets, crystal-clear waters, and medieval sights make it tranquil and picturesque during the rest of the summer. Once the stage of a famous medieval battle, the town was conquered by Ottoman Turks who killed most of the inhabitants. Rather than convert to Islam, the town's 800 survivors opted to join their fellow Christians in death. The Turkish executioners were so impressed that they too converted to Christianity, at which point they were decapitated. The bones of the *Martiri d'Otranto* (Martyrs of Otranto), in glass cases in the *duomo*, are a popular tourist attraction, but most visitors are content to wade in the warm waters of Otranto's gorgeous beaches.

🏛 TRANSPORTATION AND PRACTICAL INFORMATION. Otranto is 40km southeast of Lecce on the Adriatic coast and is downright hard to get to by public transportation during the year. Rustic (read: turn-of-the-century) **FSE trains** run from Lecce (1¼hr., 9 per day 7am-7:30pm, L5000/€2.58) to Maglie. Get off and take the waiting bus to Otranto. The FSE ticket to Lecce covers both. In July and August, the bus will take you straight to the castle (30min., L6000/€3.10. Pick the bus up in Lecce in front of the Grand Hotel in front of the train station). At the end of the hill is the **Lungomare d'Otranto,** with the beach and turquoise waters beyond. Three blocks beyond the **public gardens** on V.V. Emanuele is **Piazza de Donno** and the entrance to the *centro storico.* Enter through the city gate and turn right on **via Basilica** to reach the **duomo.** Past the *duomo*, in the *piazza* in front of the castle, the **APT tourist office** provides advice on lodgings and transportation to towns on the peninsula. (☎0836 80 14 36. Open daily 8am-2pm and 4-9pm.) The **carabinieri** can be reached at ☎0836 80 10 10. **Pronto Soccorso,** V. Pantaleone, 4 (☎0836 80 16 76), is downhill from the information office. **Pharmacy Ricciardi** is at V. Lungomare, 101. (Open daily 8:30am-1pm and 4:30-9pm.) The **post office** is at the stoplight on V. Pantaleone (☎0836 80 10 02. Open M-Sa 8:15am-6pm). **Postal Code:** 73028.

▉▉ ACCOMMODATIONS AND FOOD. Lodging in Otranto is very expensive from mid-July through August, when most hotels require half-pension. The tourist office can help find rented rooms in local homes. The monolithic, recently renovated **Hotel Miramare,** Lungomare, 55, has 55 well-furnished rooms, some with balconies and TVs, right on the beach. Call in March for a room in July or August. (☎0836 80 10 23; fax 80 10 24; www.cliotranto.clio.it/hotelmiramare. Singles L80,000/€41.32; doubles L120,000/€62. AmEx/MC/V.)

The **market** by P. de Donno sells fruit, meat, and fish. (Open daily 8am-1pm.) Across from the public gardens, **Boomerang Self-Service,** V.V. Emanuele, 14, offers tasty Italian dishes served cafeteria-style. (☎/fax 0836 80 26 19; www.otrantovacanze.it. Pizza L6-10,000/€3.10-5.16. Full meal and drink L20,000/€10.33. Open Mar.-Sept. daily 12:30-3pm and 7:30pm-2am.) For dining with a view, **Acmet Pasia** at the end of V. Emanuele provides covered, outdoor dining with a gorgeous view of the water. (☎0836 80 12 82. *Primi* L10-15,000/€5.16-7.75; fish *secondi* L17,000/€8.78. Open Tu-Su 10am-4pm and 7:30pm-1am.)

▉▉ SIGHTS AND ENTERTAINMENT. Otranto's picturesque old city is surrounded by fortifications. Lending a majestic air to this enclosed city is the famous **duomo,** paved with a phenomenal 11th-century floor mosaic of the Tree of Life. Dante visited here while he wrote *The Divine Comedy.* The mosaic extends the entire length of the nave and depicts religious, mythological, and historical figures from Adam to Alexander the Great to King Arthur. And that's just the "A"s. Another section shows the 12 zodiac signs and the farm work done each month. Among the dead bodies and columns pilfered from Greek, Roman, and Arab sites, the crypt also houses the **Capella dei Martiri,** a small chapel with large glass display cases housing the skulls and bones of all 800 who died for their faith. (*Duomo* open daily 8am-noon and 4-6pm, excluding mass times. Modest dress required.)

Red, pink, and blue mosaics of the Garden of Eden brighten the intimate interior of 8th-century Byzantine **Chiesa di San Pietro.** (Take C. Garibaldi to P. del Popolo and follow the signs up the stairs on the left. Open on request 9:30am-1pm and 3:30-7:30pm.) The 16th-century **Aragonese castle,** with its imposing walls and newly excavated moat, casts a shadow over the town. You can't see much of the castle besides the courtyard, but a gate in the ramparts on a side street leads down to a pier that runs along the small boat harbor, offering views of the old town and anchored sailboats. (Open M-Su 9am-1:30pm.)

In August, Otranto's **beaches** are packed; the fine sand and light-blue waters are even more enjoyable during the first part of the summer. The public strips along the *lungomare* and farther along on V. degli Haethey are the most popular and accessible. The beach closest to V. Pantaleone will neatly extract L6-8000/€3.10-4.13 from your wallet, but the beach one block down the road is free. Both of these beaches are just as nice as the more crowded ones along the *lungomare,* although some may not enjoy swimming in sight of rusty old freighters belching out smoke as they dock at the port. In the evenings, vendors arrive in droves to feed the crowds—try the delicious *noccioline zuccherate* (candy coated peanuts).

After dark, Otranto's *lungomare* fills with people walking the waterfront and patronizing the pubs, but those with cars head to the *discoteche* 5-6km away. On August 13, 14, and 15, Otranto welcomes tourists with the **Festa dei Martiri d'Otranto,** a feast in honor of the martyrs. On the first Sunday in September, the town celebrates again with the **Festa della Madonna dell'Altomare** (Festival of the Virgin of the High Seas). Every Wednesday the castle is surrounded by a **market** that sells everything from shirts to jewelry, shoes to music. (Open 9am-1pm.)

TARANTO ☎ 0994

In ancient times, Taranto was a proud Greek city-state with a navy ruling the seas and 300,000 seafaring citizens prospering on numerous merchant routes. Today Taranto still houses 300,000 citizens, a busy, dirty port, and Italy's fine naval fleet. The downward spiral of high unemployment, government corruption, welfare dependency, and mafia control has taken its toll. Young, entrepreneurial Tarantinos head to Milan to stake their fortunes, as there are few opportunities here. However, Taranto is beginning to experience an urban renewal, and well-to-do young professionals pack trendy downtown cafes and restaurants. Reasonably priced accommodations aren't hard to find, and a world-famous archaeological museum, shady public gardens, wide *piazze*, delicious and inexpensive seafood, sailboat-packed beaches, and a swinging bridge give this city a resort feel today.

☞ TRANSPORTATION

Trains: (☎ 1478 880 88), in P. Liberta, across the old city from the center of town. **FS** to: **Bari** (1¾hr.; 16 per day 4:41am-10:22pm; L11,000/€5.68); **Brindisi** (1¼hr., 13 per day 5am-10pm, L6500/€3.36); **Naples** (4hr.; 3 per day 6:40am-4pm; L27,000/€13.94); **Rome** (6-7hr.; 9per day 6am-midnight; L83,000/€42.87).

Buses: Buses stop at P. Castello (near the swinging bridge); buy tickets at the **Marozzi Ticket Office,** C. Umberto, 67 (☎ 0994 59 40 89), 1 block up from P. Garibaldi. **SITA buses** run to **Matera** (1¾hr., 5 per day 6am-7pm, L8300/€4.29). **CTP buses** (☎ 0997 32 42 01) run to **Bari** (1¾hr.; 20 per day 5:30am-10pm; L10,000/€5.16) and **Lecce** (1¾hr., 7 per day 6am-6pm, L9000/€4.65). Buses stop at Discesa Vasto in the old city, downhill from the swinging bridge.

Public Transportation: Tickets on local AMAT buses cost L1300/€0.67 (L1600/€0.93 for 90min. or L3200/€1.65 for full-day).

✴ ☞ ORIENTATION AND PRACTICAL INFORMATION

Taranto's old city is on a small island between two promontories. Bridges join the old city to the new port area and the train station. Be wary of pickpockets during the day, and avoid the old city at night. From the station, buses to the new city take you near P. Garibaldi, the main square. On foot, take V. Duca d'Aosta over Ponte Porta Napoli into P. Fontana in the old city. Walk 10min. along the shore to P. Castello and across the bridge to reach the new city; P. Garibaldi is a block ahead.

Tourist office: APT Information Office, C. Umberto, 113 (☎ 0994 53 23 92; fax 52 04 17; apt99@libero.it; www.pugliaturismo.com), 4 blocks from P. Garibaldi. Good maps available. Open May-Oct. M-F 9am-1pm and 5-7pm, Sa 9am-noon; Nov.-Apr. 9am-1pm and 4:30-6:30pm, Sa 9am-noon. The **Info booth** in the station stocks city maps.

Emergency: ☎ 113. **Police:** ☎ 112.

Internet Access: Chiocciolin@it, C. Umberto I, 85. (☎/fax 0994 53 80 51.) Next to P. Garibaldi. Sony Playstation and Dreamcast available to delight of those hungering for the Final Fantasy comforts of home. Open daily 9am-1pm and 4:30-9:30pm, May-Oct. closed Sa 9am-1pm; Nov.-Apr. closed M. AmEx/MC/V. **Mare Mare Mare, Voglio Annegare,** Lungomare V. Emanuele, 27. Walk up V. d'Aquino from P. Garibaldi, turn right on V. Acclavio, and walk to waterfront. L10,000/€5.16 per hr. Open daily 6:30pm-1am.

Post office: (☎ 0994 359 51), on Lungomare V. Emanuele. Open M-Sa 8:15am-6pm.

Postal Code: 74100.

☞ ✿ ACCOMMODATIONS AND FOOD

Albergo Pisani, V. Cavour, 43, off P. Garibaldi, is conveniently located, reasonably priced, and provides comfortable accommodations. (☎ 0994 53 40 87; fax 70 75 93. Breakfast included. Singles with bath L43,000/€22.20; doubles L75,000/€38.73, with bath L85,000/€43.90.) **Albergo Sorrentino,** P. Fontana, 7, has 13 rooms over-looking the sea. Although cheap, it is inconveniently located and the neighbor-hood doesn't scream "walk through me at 2am." (☎0994 71 83 90. Singles L35,000/€18.08; doubles L50,000/€25.81, with bath L60,000/€30.99.)

Taranto's prosperous fishing industry translates into delicious, plentiful, and inexpensive seafood. Try *cozze* (mussels) in basil and olive oil or spaghetti with *vongole* (clams). Grab your bread, sandwiches, and pizza at the **Panificio** between P. Garibaldi and the swinging bridge. (Open daily 7am-11pm.) Fruit is available at the **market** in P. Castello. (Open daily 7am-1:30pm.) **Queen,** V. di Cesare, 20, offers delectable seafood, local specialties, impeccable service, and affordable prices. The L20,000/€10.33 meal lasts the entire next day and includes wine. The *menù* changes daily, but the ace is the Queen pizza with everything on it for L9000/€4.65. (☎099 459 10 11. Beer from L2500/€1.29. *Primi* L4000/€2.07; *secondi* L6-12,000/€3.10-6.20. Evening cover L2000/€1.03. Open M-Sa 7:30am-midnight.)

👁 SIGHTS

▓ **MUSEO NAZIONALE ARCHEOLOGICO.** This museum houses the world's larg-est terra-cotta figure collection. The museum also has a plethora of ancient pots, marble and bronze sculptures, mosaics, jewelry, and coins. *(C. Umberto, 41, in P. Garibaldi. ☎099 453 21 12. Open M-F 8:30am-1:30pm and 2:30-7:30pm, Sa 9am-midnight. Undergoing renovations and scheduled to reopen in 2002. Part of the museum's collection is on display at Palazzo Pantaleone, to the right along C.V. Emanuele when crossing the bridge from the station. Open daily 8:30am-7:30pm. Free)*

SWINGING BRIDGE. From P. Garibaldi, a bridge built in 1887 hangs over the ship-ping canal to the *città vecchia*. It was the first of its kind, opening sideways to let ships through. The bridge still swings with the best of 'em, and is fun to watch—check the daily schedule of opening times posted on either side.

🎵 ENTERTAINMENT

Every night between 6 and 11pm, **via d'Aquino** pulses with crowds. On P. Garibaldi, the navy band accompanies the lowering of the flag at sundown. Taranto's **Holy Week Festival** draws hordes from around the country. In a ceremony rooted in medieval Spanish ritual, sheet-covered men carrying papier-maché statues parade to all the churches. Festivities begin the Sunday before Easter.

BASILICATA

Uncovered in Carlo Levi's *Christ Stopped at Eboli* as a land of poverty and pagan mysticism, small, sparsely populated Basilicata is seldom visited. It begins in the rugged Lucan Apennines and stretches across the Murge to the Ionian and Tyrrhe-nian coastlines. Mountainous, almost landlocked, and lacking natural resources, it never attained the strategic importance or prominence of neighboring coastal regions. Fortunately for travelers, its fascinating prehistoric caves, breathtaking vistas, colorful local culture, and smooth beaches remain unspoiled.

MATERA   ☎ 0835

Matera's claim to fame are the *sassi*, ancient homes carved directly in the rocks of the Materan terrain. The settlements remained livable until 1952, when the govern-ment deemed the 7000-year-old homes unsafe and unsanitary, displacing the resi-dents. Yuppies and several high-tech firms recently went slumming and restored and occupied several *sassi*. Strikingly beautiful and oddly captivating, the city that calls itself "The Heritage of Humanity" has expanded to become the 2nd-larg-est in Basilicata, earning it the nickname "Capital of Nowhere." The city is still relatively isolated, but remains the only provincial capital in Italy not connected by FS trains. Nonetheless, its extraordinary sights, inexpensive accommodations, and engaging local culture, including the exhilarating **Festa di Santa Maria della Bruna** (see **Entertainment,** p. 555), make getting to Matera worth the trouble.

⌐ TRANSPORTATION

Trains: Station at P. Matteotti. **FAL** trains run to **Altamura** (30min., 13 per day 6:30am-9pm, L6700/€3.46) and **Bari** (1½hr., 8 per day 6:30am-9pm, L6700/€3.46).

Buses: FAL buses leave from P. Matteotti for **Bari** on Sunday, when train service is suspended (1¾hr., 6 per day 6am-2pm, L6700/€3.46). Buy tickets at train station. **SITA buses** leave from the same *piazza;* buy tickets at P. Matteotti, 3 (☎0835 38 50 70). Buses run to: **Altamura** (30min., 4 per day 12:30-6:30pm, L3100/€1.60); **Gravina** (50min., 3 per day 1-6:30pm, L4700/€2.43); **Metaponto** (1hr., 5 per day 8:15am-5:30pm, L5100/€2.63); **Taranto** (1½hr.; 6 per day 6am-5pm; L10,000/€5.16).

✷🛈 ORIENTATION AND PRACTICAL INFORMATION

Matera's grottoes split into two small valleys overlooking a deep canyon in the **Parco della Murgia Materana.** From the train and bus stations at **Piazza Matteotti,** head down **via Roma** to **Piazza V. Veneto,** the heart of the city. The first valley, **Sasso Barisano,** the more modern area, is straight ahead; descend through the stairway across from the Banco di Napoli. To reach the nearby **Sasso Caveoso,** the cavernous *sassi,* continue to the right down V. del Corso, which bears right to V. Ridola, and descend to the left at P. Pascoli. Some of the more important *chiese rupestri* (rock churches) are on the other side of the ridge opposite the Sasso Caveoso. A detailed map of the *sassi* can be found at the tourist office and hotels.

TOURIST AND LOCAL SERVICES

Tourist Office: APT, V. di Viti de Marco, 9 (☎0835 33 19 83; fax 33 34 52). From the station, walk down V. Roma and take the 2nd left. Some English spoken. Open M and Th 8:30am-1:30pm and 4-6pm, Tu-W and F-Sa 8:30am-1:30pm. The city has an **information office** on V. Madonna della Virtù, with better maps of the *sassi.* Open Apr.-Sept. 9:30am-12:30pm and 3:30-6:30pm.

Emergency: ☎113.

Police: 0835 37 81.

Ambulance: ☎0835 24 32 70.

Hospital: (☎0835 24 31), on V. Lanera.

Internet Access: Biblioteca, P. Vittorio Veneto (☎0835 33 06 61; www.biblioteca.metar.it). Buy a phone card next to the computer and follow the prompts. L10,000/€5.16 per hr. Open M-F 8:30am-6:30pm, Sa 8:30am-1:30pm.

Post Office: (☎0835 33 25 91), on V. del Corso off P. Veneto. Open M-Sa 8:30am-6pm.

Postal Code: 75100.

⌂ ACCOMMODATIONS

Matera has a great hostel, making it an inexpensive base for regional exploration.

▓ **Sassi Hostel (HI),** V.S. Giovanni Vecchio, 89 (☎0835 33 10 09). From the station, take V. Roma to P. Veneto and continue on V.S. Biagio to the church, where signs leading to the hostel appear on the right. This hostel and hotel, amid the prehistoric caves, will fulfill your troglodyte fantasies. The rooms are renovated *sassi,* each with private bath. Sheets and towels included. Curfew midnight. Dorms L30,000/€15.50. AmEx/MC/V.

Albergo Roma, V. Roma, 62 (☎0835 33 39 12), by tourist office. 10 rooms at reasonable prices. Singles L40,000/€20.66; doubles L60,000/€30.99, with bath L70,000/€36.15.

SOUTHERN ITALY

Hotel De Nicola, V. Nazionale, 158 (☎/fax 0835 38 51 11). Follow V.A. Moro from P. Matteotti to V. Anunziatella on the left, which becomes V. Nazionale, or take orange city bus #7 or 10 from the station (every 10min., L1000/€0.52). 99 modern rooms, all with bath, TV, and phone. Pay a supplement for a room with a fridge and A/C. Singles L80,000/€41.32; doubles L125,000/€64.56. AmEx/MC/V.

 FOOD

Try some of Matera's specialties: *favetta con cicore* (a soup of beans, celery, chicory, and croutons, mixed in olive oil) or *frittata di spaghetti* (pasta with anchovies, eggs, bread crumbs, garlic, and oil). Experience true Materan grit by gnawing on *pane di grano duro*—made of extra-hard wheat, this bread has a shelf-life as long as a Twinkie. Also try the **Divella supermarket,** V. Spine Bianche, 6. (Open M-W and F-Sa 8:30am-1:30pm and 5-8:30pm, Th 8:30am-1:30pm.)

Ristorante Pizzeria La Terrazzina, V.S. Giuseppe, 7 (☎0835 33 25 03), off P. Veneto near Banco di Napoli. Savor immense portions of local delicacies in a cave dug into the cliffs. Cave below doubles as wine cellar. Try handmade pasta like *cavatelli alla boscaiola* (with a sauce of tomatoes, mushrooms, and *prosciutto* for L10,000/€5.16). Pizza L4-10,000/€2.07-5.16. Cover L3000/€1.55. *Menù* L25,000/€12.91. Open W-M noon-3:30pm and 7pm-midnight. AmEx/MC/V.

Ristorante il Casino del Diavolo, V. La Martella (☎0835 26 19 86). With great food at moderate prices, this huge restaurant is always packed with locals. Main courses L10-20,000/€5.16-10.33. Open Tu-Su 12:30-3:30pm and 8pm-1am.

Carpe Diem, V. Minzoni, 32/4 (☎0835 24 03 59), between the station and P. Veneto. *Tavola calda,* a stylish interior, and great *foccaccia.* Open daily 7am-9:30pm.

Gran Caffè, P. Veneto, 6. No seating. Grab a sandwich, soda, and *cannoli* for less than L6000/€3.10 and eat on the pleasant benches in the *piazza.* Open daily 7am-10pm.

Trattoria Lucana, V. Lucana, 48 (☎0835 33 61 17), off V. Roma. Begin with the *orecchiette alla materana* (ear-shaped pasta with tomatoes and fresh veggies for L8000/€4.13) and continue with their specialty, the *bocconcini alla lucana* (thinly sliced veal with mushrooms for L12,000/€6.20). Cover L2000/€1.03. Service 10%. Open M-Sa 12:30-3pm and 8-10:30pm. Closed early Sept. AmEx/MC/V.

 SIGHTS

ALONG THE WAY TO...THE SASSI. The 7000-year-old homes lie amid a maze of stone pathways, so you will need a **detailed map** to negotiate them properly. The ones from the information office on V. Madonna della Virtù (or the booth near the train station) are the best. Enter the heart of *sassi* zone from P. Veneto by taking V. del Corso past the Chiesa di S. Francesco d'Assisi to P. Sedile. From there, V. Duomo leads to the Apulian-Romanesque **duomo** in P. del Duomo—check out the beautiful carving on the outside portals. Inside, the 15th-century carved choir stalls compete with the 16th-century **Cappella dell'Annunziata.** *(Open daily 9am-1pm and 4:30-6pm.)* From P.S. Francesco, V. Ridola leads past the creepy **Chiesa del Purgatorio,** with its skeleton and skull-covered facade, to the **Museo Ridola,** which displays the area's archaeological treasures. The museum houses excellent prehistoric and early Classical art in a 17th-century monastery. *(V. Ridola, 24. ☎0835 31 12 39. Open daily 9am-7pm. L4000/€2.07, but often free.)*

THE SASSI. From P. Sedile, two well-marked paths *(itinerari turistici)* head to the *sassi* in the valleys of **Sasso Caveoso** (through the arch at the left) and **Sasso Barisano** (past the Conservatory at the right). Of obscure origin, the *sassi* are carved from a soft limestone (calcarenite) in several styles. The oldest, inhabited around 7000 years ago, are crumbling structures that line Sasso Barisano along V. Addozio. The second type, dating from 2000 BC, includes the carved nooks around Sasso Caveoso in the valley to the east of the *duomo.* The more elaborately carved homes in the rock around V. Buozzi (which stems from V. Madonna delle Virtù near the *duomo*) are about 1000 years old. In addition, most of the 6th-century *chiese rupestri* (rock churches) remain unmodified, and all still display remnants of 12th- through 16th-century frescoes.

As you roam the Sasso Caveoso, you may be approached by children offering "tours"; the organized ones are more valuable. **Tour Service Matera,** P. Veneto, 42 (☎0835 33 46 33), offers tours (L10,000/€5.16 per person). For a comprehensive, self-guided tour, pick up a book at any bookstore or magazine stand.

CHURCHES...WITH SASSI. Churches carved into the rock and decorated with centuries old frescoes dot the *sassi*. From the *piazza* past the museum, head down the narrow street to the right of the *palazzo*, continue down V. Buozzi, and follow the signs to reach the Convicino di S. Antonio, a large complex of painted rock churches with a great view of the *sassi*. (*Open in summer 8am-7pm; in winter reduced hours. L2000/€1.03.*) From here follow the path along the cliffs to reach the churches of San Pietro Caveoso, Santa Maria d'Idris, and Santa Lucia alle Malve, which preserve beautiful 11th-century Byzantine frescoes in their caves. (*Caveoso open daily 9am-noon and 3:30-8pm. Idris closed unless you ask at Malve. Malve open daily in summer 8am-7pm; reduced hours in winter. Tours of Malve L2000/€1.03.*) A nearby **sasso** is furnished as it was when ten people and two horses shared its two small rooms. (*L2000/€1.03, includes English tour.*) Further along is the multilevel complex of Madonna delle Virtu and S. Nicola dei Greci, where the ancient frescoes and rough-hewn houses are juxtaposed against modern sculpture exhibited within. (*Open daily 9am-9pm. L4000/€2.07, students L2000/€.03, includes a guided tour in English.*)

PARCO DELLA MURGIA METERANA. Home to spectacular hiking, this park inhabits the ridge across the canyon from the *sassi*. The entrance to the park is off Strada Statale, 7, a healthy walk down V. Annunziatella and then V. Marconi.

♫ ENTERTAINMENT

Matera celebrates the ▨**Festa di Santa Maria della Bruna** during the last week of June and the first week of July. The festival, one of Italy's best, includes numerous musical and cultural events, nightly fireworks displays, and open-air markets where you can buy power tools or have a parakeet predict your future. The culmination of the festival comes on July 2nd during the **Assalto al Carro.**

YOU WANT A PIECE OF ME? The frenzied excitement of the *Festa di Santa Maria della Bruna* reaches its apex during the thrilling *"Assalto al Carro,"* in which a beautiful papier-maché cart is led through the town by people in medieval garb; as it reaches P.V. Veneto, melee sets in, and the cart is destroyed by reveling natives in no longer than ten seconds. Dating back to the Middle Ages, what seems like a simple exercise in mob violence actually possesses an interesting etiquette: the cart is not to be touched until it has made it all the way into P.V. Veneto (a SWAT team of terrified *carabinieri* tries to ensure this), and once the bullies who fought their way to the center of the *piazza* have grabbed themselves a piece of the cart, they run out as quickly as possible, holding the best fragments high over their heads, to the applause of the crowd. Occasionally, though, the first rule is broken, and the cart is attacked before it has quite entered the *piazza*. The first person gets the best piece (actually, the second person usually gets the best piece, while the first person gets trampled), and the *carabinieri*, true to their stereotype, melt away at the first inkling of resistance. When this happens, the people who have gotten chunks of the cart still run out of the *piazza* with their prizes high over their heads and broad smiles on their faces. Scowls and muttered curses, rather than applause, greet the premature evacuators, who have made off with prized cart booty.

▓ DAYTRIPS FROM MATERA

ALTAMURA

The city is on the FAL line between Bari (1hr., 8 per day, L5700/€2.94) and Matera (40min., 8 per day 6:30am-9pm, L4000/€2.07).

The urban center for the farm country of inland Puglia, Altamura boasts an impressive Romanesque **cathedral**. The beautiful rose window sits above one of the best decorated church portals in Puglia. Scenes from the life of Christ surround the main carving showing the last supper. (Cathedral in P. Duomo, on V. Frederico in the old city.) Altamura also has an interesting (and free) museum in P.S. Theresa, documenting the life and customs of the Apulian countryside, including more agricultural implements than you can shake a scythe at. (Open M-Sa 8am-2pm. Free.)

Viale Regina Margerita runs from the station to the old city, where it becomes V. Frederico di Svevia. Just after the old city, V. Federico di Svevia splits into via Pietro Colletta and via Matera. A **hospital** is on V. Regina Margerita (☎ 0803 108 11), and **Guardia Medica** can be reached at ☎ 080 310 82 01. The **carabinieri** (☎ 0803 10 29 92) are in P.S. Teresa, down V.N. Melodia from P. Duomo.

GRAVINA

Gravina is most accessible from Altamura by FAL train (15min., 13 per day 7:15am-9pm, L2200/€1.14), while FS trains run to Barletta (1¾hr., 7:50am-10:58pm, L8600/€4.44); Brindisi (1½hr., 16 per day 7:01am-11:57pm, L7100/€3.67); and Taranto (1½hr., 7 per day 6:34am-midnight, L7000/€3.62). Museum ☎ 080 325 10 21. Open Tu-Su 9am-1pm.

Gravina is perched along a steep gorge which gives the town its name. The town's highlight is the beautiful view of the city and Apulian countryside from the ravine.

Both train stations are at the end of **Corso Aldo Moro,** which runs to the old city, becoming **V.V. Veneto** midway down. V.V. Veneto dissolves into a tangled mass of streets in the old city—keep heading downhill to reach P. Notar Domenico and the **Chiesa del Purgatorio,** decorated with leering statues of reclining skeletons. The bears supporting the columns represent the Roman Orsini family, feudal lords of Gravina. Next to the church in a large *palazzo* is the small **Archaeological Museum.** Free admission includes tours of the collection of Lucanian grave goodies. Farther downhill sits a small park which leads to the bottom of the ravine and its abandoned caves and rock-carved churches. Locals superstitiously avoid this area, and the gates are often locked. Though you may be able to persuade some local boys to track down someone with a key, the area is sometimes inaccessible. Next to the stations, **Chiesa di Madonna di Grazie** has Italy's largest relief of an eagle spreading its wings across the facade. On C.A. Moro heading away from the stations, turn left down V. Fontana La Stella to the stone bridge leading across the ravine to the cliffs on the other side and a lovely pastoral view of town. Check out the caves dug into the cliffs, used by locals in the 5th century to hide from attacking barbarians. If Gravina's got your stomach growling, head to the **Old River Pub,** V.S. Giuseppe, 92 (☎ 080 326 90 23), for pizza and beer (pizza from L6000/€3.10).

METAPONTO   ☎ 0835/0831

Metaponto consists of a few campsites along the beach, some lonely Greek ruins, a museum, and a train station 3km inland. Although the undulating sand along the sparkling Ionian is a beach-lover's delight, it is better enjoyed in early July or September. Metaponto feels like a ghost town for most of the year, but from mid-July through August the campsites burst with hordes of Italians scrambling to the sea.

▐ TRANSPORTATION. Metaponto is most easily reached by train, although both the beach and the ruins are a short bus ride away from the station. **Trains** to: **Bari** (2-2½hr., 4 per day 5:30am-3pm); **Reggio di Calabria** (4½-5½hr.; 2 per day 10am-2pm;

L36,000/€18.60); **Rome** (5½-6hr., 3 per day 6:30am-3:30pm); **Salerno** (3-3½hr.; 5 per day 6:30am-midnight; L21,000/€10.85); **Taranto** (30-45min., 25 per day 5am-11pm, L6000/€3.10). Blue **SITA buses** run from the train station to **Matera** (1hr., 5 per day 7:05am-4:30pm, L5300/€2.74).

⬛🔓 **ORIENTATION AND PRACTICAL INFORMATION.** The town can be divided into four areas: *scalo* (the train station), *borgo* (the museum), *lido* (beach and hotels), and the **ruins** of an archaeological park. While Scalo, Borgo, and the ruins are all 1-2km apart, the *lido* is farther away. Metaponto's best reserved ruin, the **Tavole Palatine**, is 5km from Borgo. Local **Chiruzzi buses** serve the area. Bus #1 runs between the train station, the museum, and *lido* (14 per day 7:30am-9:30pm), while the less frequent #2 runs between the train station and the ruins (7 per day 8am-7pm, L1000/€0.52 tickets on the bus). The *lido* district is a small area around P. Nord, where the bus stops and bicycles can be rented. In case of **medical emergency**, contact the **Pronto Soccorso** (☎0835 74 19 97), off the beach. The **post office** is near the Museo Archeologico. (Open M-Sa 8am-1:15pm.) **Postal Code:** 75010.

📷📇 **ACCOMMODATIONS, CAMPING, AND FOOD.** Metaponto's many cheap campgrounds host most of its beachgoers. **Camping Magna Grecia**, V. Lido, 1, is on the right of the highway Viale Jonio toward the *lido* (connecting the *lido* to the station). The campground's noisy *discoteca* offers a sharp contrast to the quiet national forest next door. There are also tennis courts, game rooms, bars, a swimming pool, and a shuttle to the beach. (☎0831 74 18 55. July 21-Aug. 25 L12,000/€6.20 per person, L12,000/€6.20 per tent, L4000/€2.07 per parking space. Electricity L5000/€2.58.) There are no inexpensive hotels near the *lido*, and prices rise dramatically in August. The **Hotel Turismo**, in P. Lido, features a penitentiary facade that will bring back your days in Attica. The hotel also showcases authentic 70s furniture, private baths, A/C, and proximity to the beach. (☎0835 74 19 18. Open June to mid-Sept. 50 rooms. Singles L70,000/€36.15; doubles L110,000/€56.81. Extra bed L27,000/€13.94.) Numerous beachside pizzerias and restaurants compete for your tourist dollar—try **Lido self-service restaurant** on P. Lido right by the beach. (Pizza L5-9000/€2.58-4.65. Open daily noon-3pm and 8pm-midnight.) **Maria's** mini-market off P. Nord makes good sandwiches. (Open daily 7am-6pm.)

🎫 **SIGHTS.** Most people go to Metaponto for the beach, and with good reason: the sand is powdery-fine, the water bright turquoise and clean, and large stretches are public. If the sun starts to get to you, catch the #1 bus from the *lido* or the train station to the **Museo Archeologico**. The museum displays ancient jewelry, vases, and figurines, most of which are related to the ruins. (☎0831 74 53 27. Open daily 9am-7pm. L5000/€2.58, ages 18-26 L2500/€1.29, under 18 and over 60 free.) From the museum head through the park, past the post office down a country road to the **ruins** of the Doric **Temple of Apollo Licius** and a **Greek Theater** (6th century BC). It's another 5km to the **Tavole Palatine**, the ruins of a Greek temple of Hera and the best-preserved temple in Metaponto. Greek triangle-man Pythagoras taught here until his death in 479 BC. (The #2 bus connects the train station with all the ruins.)

TYRRHENIAN COAST

MARATEA ☎0973

Two hours south of Naples by train and 180° away in the pace of local life, Maratea is a collection of quiet towns along the Tyrrhenian Sea. This 30km coastline is the only portion of west Basilicata on water, but the beauty and diversity of Maratea's landscape make up for its small size. Each town presents manages to present a unique aspect of coastal life to the southern traveler. The sea is not all there is to see, however. The rocky landscape is improbably covered with trees and vibrant, perfumed flowers and dotted with dozens of inviting churches. From mid-July to mid-August tourists flock to Maratea to take part (and upset just a little) the tranquil lifestyle the towns enjoy the rest of the year.

Maratea Centro is closest to the train station and has many secrets to give up to the explorer, but if the sea is why you came to Maratea, **Fiumicello (Santavenere)** and **Maratea Porto** are the places to be. Fiumicello melts down to the hillside in the form of small *ristorante* and shops until joining the sea in a near-perfect beach. Maratea Porto's cove houses boats, not bathers, and another array of restaurants and shops. Visible from all of Maratea though difficult to reach is the 22m white statue of *Redentore* (Christ the Redeemer) placed in 1963 atop 'San Baglio' in **Maratea Anziana**. Second in height only to the similar statue in Rio de Janeiro—a point the Marateani love to refute—it stands over the ruins of the ancient city and is an other-worldly sight in moonlight.

⌷ TRANSPORTATION. Trains run from **Maratea Station** to Cosenza, Naples, and Reggio di Calabria. (☎ 0973 87 69 06. Open 7:30am-noon, 3:30-6pm, and 8:50-11pm; AmEx/MC/V.) Fiumicello, Maratea Centro, and Maratea Anziana are all accessible by **bus** from Cosenza during the summer (June-Aug., every hr. 9am-midnight; Sept.-May service more erratic). Local buses are far less frequent and run on no particular schedule, and run only between the station, Fiumicello, and Porto. Though the main bus stop is down the road from the train station, don't hesitate to flag down a bus—they will generally stop anywhere. If you prefer to walk, **Maratea Porto** (4km) and **Fiumicello** (2km) may be reached on foot from the train station. Exit the station, turn right, and continue down V. Profiti under the bridge. Turn left down the hill to Fiumicello. Porto is farther down the same road. Taxis are available through **Taxi Maratea** (☎ 0973 87 00 84 or 0337 90 15 79). Use them if arriving at Maratea Station in the evening or to travel to other towns.

⏹ PRACTICAL INFORMATION. The **AAST tourist office**, 40 V. Santa Venere, is on the far side of P. Gesù as you curve down the hill on V. Santa Venere. (☎ 0973 87 69 08. Open June-Aug. M-Su 8am-2pm and 3-10pm; Sept.-May M, W, F-Sa 8am-2pm, Tu and Th 8am-2pm and 3-6pm.) From mid-May to October, **Porto Turistico di Maratea** (☎ 0973 87 73 07), in Maratea Porto rents out **motorboats** for L150,000/€77.47. There is a Banco di Napoli with an **ATM** at V.S. Venere, 161. The closest **post office** is in Maratea Porto, via Porto, 27 (☎ 0973 87 67 11. Open M-Sa 8am-1:15pm).

⌂ ▣ ACCOMMODATIONS, CAMPING, AND FOOD. The perfect beach of Fiumicello creates less-than-perfect prices the closer you get to the water. **Hotel Fiorella**, V. Santa Venere, 21, is on the hill on the right as you enter Fiumicello. The bus from the train station drives by the hotel; ask the driver to drop you off. With spacious rooms and nifty prices, the Fiorella will let you enjoy your hard-earned sojourn in the sun. (☎ 0973 87 69 21; fax 87 73 43. Lockout 2-5pm. Singles with bath L50,000/€25.82; doubles with bath L80,000/€41.32. Comparable rooms L70-L100,000/€36.15-51.65 from July 25 to Aug. 21. AmEx/MC/V.) **Maratea Castrocucco**, 8km down the coastal road from Maratea's port, is the site of Camping Maratea, Localita Castrocucco, 72 (☎ 0973 87 75 80 or 87 16 99). Because it is close to the sea and usually busy, make reservations early in the summer.

Around the corner from Hotel Fiorella, the friendly pizzeria **Osteria La Bussola**, V.S. Venere, 43, offers a casual atmosphere and large pizzas starting at L6000/€3.10. (☎ 0973 87 68 63. Open June-Sept. 7pm-1:30am; Oct.-May W and F-S 7pm-1:30am.) The more chic **El Sol**, V.S. Venere, 151, serves expensive restaurant fare and cheap pizza (L7-12,000/€3.62-6.20). (☎ 0973 87 69 28. Open Nov. to mid-Mar. until 2am; only dinner. AmEx/MC/V.) Locals gather on beneath the wisteria vines on the patio of **Da Felicia**, V. Fiumicello, 13., to enjoy pasta, fresh seafood, and each other's company. The white linen and attentive service of the chuckling owner is well worth the L2000/€1.03 cover, as are the inexpensive meals, with *primi* starting at L7000/€3.62. (☎ 0973 87 68 00. Open noon-3pm and 7:30-10:30pm.)

The **Supermercato Pick-Up,** V.S. Venere, 143, is an inexpensive alternative for picnickers and beach-goers. This new facility has a wide range of standard market items, including fresh produce and toiletries. (☎0973 87 78 24. Open Mar.-Nov. 8am-1:30pm and 4:30-8:30pm.) Listen for **Rosario's Fruit Stand,** as well. The charming self-promoter broadcasts over a loud-speaker from his truck as he drives all over Maratea selling juicy delights.

CALABRIA

Calabria is the most under-developed of Italy's provinces, but it is also the most under-appreciated. Shunned by tourists in favor of the flashier and more expensive North, Calabria has developed an isolated culture of its own. But two and a half millennia ago, Calabria was the center of the world, home to its leading philosophers, artists, and athletes—all this while the northern cities that laugh at her today were small backwaters, unworthy of any note. Fortunately, however, for the Calabrese pride, traces of this illustrious past remain in delightful abundance, from the Greek ruins at Locri to the Norman Castle at Cosenza.

HIGHLIGHTS OF CALABRIA

ENCOUNTER wildlife in the parks of the **Sila Massif** (p. 562).

GLIMPSE at the remarkable Riace Bronzes in Reggio's **National Museum** (p. 565).

LOLL on the beautiful **beaches** of Scilla (p. 568).

COSENZA
☎0984

Around AD 410, Cosenza received its first tourist group. Unlike today's well-mannered backpackers, these men were true barbarians—Visigoths actually, ten thousand of them, led by King Alaric I. Upon arriving in Cosenza, the king died of malaria and was buried in the Busento River, along with the treasure he plundered from the Goth sacking of Rome. Today the Busento divides the city into historic and modern sections, thus giving Consenza its characteristic split personality between past and present. Cosenza's seven hills slope downward into the legendary **Sila Massif,** great forests that offer southern Italy's greatest hiking. During the winter the short trip to **Camigliatello** rewards visitors with excellent ski slopes. In warmer weather, the nearby beaches of **Paola** provide sun and surf.

⌐ TRANSPORTATION

Public transportation shuts down on Sundays, so be sure to plan ahead.

Trains: Stazione Cosenza (☎0984 39 47 46), V. Popilia, at the *superstrada*. Ticket office open daily 6:30am-8:25pm. **FS** (☎1478 880 88; 7am-9pm) trains run to: **Naples** (3½-4hr., 7 per day); **Paola** (30min., 15 per day); **Reggio** (3hr., 4 per day); **Rome** (6½hr., 2 per day); **Sibari** (1hr., 9 per day). Station serviced by **Ferrovie della Calabria** trains (Camigliatello, 1½hr, 2 per day, L3,300/€1.70) and buses (most blue buses stop at train station; wait at the blue "fermata" sign in front of station.)

Buses: Autostazione (☎0984 41 31 24), on V. Autostazione. Where C. Mazzini ends in P. Fera, turn right and walk down the marked sloping street to the station. **Ferrovie della Calabria** regional buses for inland destinations leave from here and the train station, where you can buy bus tickets at windows opposite those for train tickets (Camigliatello and San Giovanni, 10 per day, L3400/€1.76; Villagio Palumbo, L5800/€3.00).

Public Transportation: All orange **buses** stop at P. Matteotti; buy tickets (L1300/€0.67) at any one of the magazine stands (main stand where V. Trieste crosses C. Mazzini near P. dei Bruzi) and at most *tabacchi*. Buses #22 and 23 serve the old city, stopping in P. Prefettura (every 30min. 5:30am-11pm). Buses #27 and 28 go between P. Matteotti and the train station (every 7min. 5am-midnight.) For more detailed bus routes look for yellow hanging street signs in P. Matteotti and at all bus stops. A word of caution: posted schedules are your only clue to what bus stop you're at. Ask the driver or a fellow passenger to tell you when your stop comes up.

ORIENTATION AND PRACTICAL INFORMATION

The **Busento River** divides the city into two distinct regions: the traffic-plagued "new city," north of the Busento, and the "old city," with its ancient buildings, south of the river. **Corso Mazzini,** the main thoroughfare and shopping center, begins in **Piazza dei Bruzi,** continues through the small **Piazza Kennedy,** and ends in **Piazza Fera.** To get to C. Mazzini, hop on any bus to **Piazza Matteotti** and with your back to the bus stop walk a block up C. Umberto into **P. dei Bruzi.** The central bus station is on **via Autostazione,** just to the right off P. Fera at the end of C. Mazzini, where the *corso* splits seven ways.

Cosenza Centro Storico rests across the Ponte Mario Martiri, three blocks to the right from P. Matteoti when facing away from P. dei Bruzi. A labyrinth of medieval multi-level stone buildings, the old city features winding "roads," some of which are just elaborate, winding, cobblestone staircases. Its only identifiable street, narrow **Corso Telesio,** begins in the petite Piazza Valdesi, near the Busento, and climbs through the recently revived section of the old city to the statue of the philosopher Telesio himself in the well lit and immaculate Piazza Prefettura (Piazza XV Marzo).

EMERGENCY AND COMMUNICATIONS

Emergency: ☎ 113. **Carabinieri:** ☎ 112.

Police: Municipale (☎ 0984 268 02), in P. dei Bruzi, behind the town hall. Open 24hr.

Ambulance: Croce Bianca, V. Beato Angelo d'Acri, 29 (☎ 0984 39 35 28). **Red Cross:** V. Popilia, 35 (☎ 0984 41 11 55).

Late-Night Pharmacy: P. Kennedy, 7 (☎ 0984 241 55). Open 24hr., Su 10pm-8am; closed M-Sa 1-2:30pm. **Farmacia Berardelli,** C. Mazzini, 40. Open 8:30am-1pm and 4:30-8pm. MC/V.

Hospital: Ospedale Civile dell'Annunziata (☎ 0984 284 09), on V. Felice Migliori.

Internet Access: Casa delle Culture, C. Telesio, 98. With your back to the *duomo,* exit the *piazza* to the left. It's a few blocks down on right, set back from road. Only 7 terminals. Reservation an hour ahead of time recommended.

Post Office: V.V. Veneto, 41, (☎ 0984 252 84; fax 732 37), at the end of V. Piave, off C. Mazzini. Open M-F 8:10am-4pm, Sa 8:10am-1:30pm.

Postal Code: 87100.

ACCOMMODATIONS

■ **Albergo Bruno,** C. Mazzini, 27 (☎ 0984 73 889). With your back to P. dei Bruzi, walk 1 block up C. Mazzini. Entrance on left under small yellow sign. High quality family-run establishment. 23 rooms with high ceilings and luxurious beds, and some have televisions and flower-covered balconies. Free piano practice. Recommended check-in 10pm. Reservations suggested. Singles L40,000/€20.66, with bath L50,000/€25.82; doubles L60,000/€31.00, L80,000/€41.32; triples with bath L90,000/€46.48.

Hotel Grisaro, V. Monte Santo, 6 (☎ 0984 279 52). Walk 1 block up C. Mazzini from P. dei Bruzzi, then make a left onto V. Trieste. V. Monte Santo is 1 block up on the right. Hotel is well advertised by large signs. Spacious rooms with TV and comfy beds are easily accessible, courtesy of the Grisaro elevator. Friendly common room downstairs with TV and comfy armchairs. Wheelchair accessible. Reservations suggested. Singles L50,000/€25.82, with bath L60,000/€31; doubles L85,000/€43.90, L90,000/€46.48; triples L120,000/€62; quads L140,000/€72.30. MC/V.

IS THAT A PHONE IN YOUR POCKET OR ARE YOU HAPPY TO SEE ME? Newspapers cover scandalous events, but in Southern Italy this phrase has literal meaning. The old newspapers that cover the windshields of parked cars often serve not to keep out the sun's heat but to conceal the more torrid heat produced from within. Beware, virgin eyes—this is the age-old art of *l'amore*.

FOOD

Cosenza is a well-fed city, and the city's bounty of restaurants draw on the rich mushrooms and fresh *prosciutto* of the Sila forests, plentiful fish from the sparkling Tyrrhenian, and the fruit of the region's orchards. For sumptuously fresh fruits and vegetables stop into **Cooper Frutta**, Viale Trieste, 28, a block from C. Mazzini, and acquire everything else from **Cooperatore Alimentare** next door at Viale Trieste 35; have yourself a picnic in nearby P. Vittoria—just you, a peach, a loaf, and the old men playing *Gioca Tresete*, a local card game. For artistic fruit handiwork, check out the tiny **Dolcezze di Calabria**, C. Mazzini, 92, next to the entrance to the tourist office, which sells candied tangerines and figs cooked in fig honey and wrapped in fig leaves.

Gran Caffè Renzelli, C. Telesio, 46 (☎0984 268 14). 200 years history. Once official confectioner of the king. The Bandiera brothers, famous patriots of the Risorgimento, stopped by for a cup of Renzelli's excellent coffee; an hour later Bourbon troops caught and executed them beneath the Valle di Rovina aqueduct. Find out if the cappucino is really to die for. Mini *pizza rustica* L2000/€1.03. Table service L1000/€0.52. Open W-Su, from early afternoon to late night, depending on the crowd and the owner's fancy.

Taverna L'ArcoVecchio, P. Archi di Ciaccio, 21 (☎0984 72564). Take 4T bus to hillside village, or follow signs along V. Petrarca. Combines elegance (royal blue table cloths) with rustic (crumbling stone village locale) to great effect. Large wine selection and a *menù* with *piatti* from L13,000/€6.71 that changes daily. Cover L3000/€1.55. Open daily until 10:30pm or later. MC/V.

Da Giocondo, V. Piave, 53 (☎0984 29 81 00). Left off of C. Mazzini, then 2 blocks up on left. For worldly style, Calabrian casualness, and feisty character, head to this 3 room restaurant. Bow-tied waiters serve local fish, regional specialties, and tasty fruit desserts to go with the long wine list. Cover L3500/€1.81. *Piatti* from L8000/€4.13. Open daily noon-3pm, M-Sa 7-10pm. AmEx/MC/V.

Yankee, V. Piave, 17-19 (☎0984 27 032). Left off C. Mazzini, then 1 block up on left. Ever wonder what Italians really think of America? The decor of this establishment throws together such random elements as Coca-Cola, Popeye cartoons, a wall mural of the wild west, Pokemon, and radio hits from five years ago. But don't worry; you're still in Italy. The pizza is cheap (from L4800/€2.48), Italian-style, and quite good. Open daily noon-3pm and 5pm-midnight.

SIGHTS

CHIESA DI SAN FRANCESCO D'ASSISI. This smallish church's plain exterior hides a lavish but tired white Baroque interior. Paintings by the Flemish William Borremons chronicle the life of Christ. In the chorus chamber at the church's far end lies the angelic—but shriveled—body of a 500-year-old Franciscan monk on full display. The chambers above (reached by a stairway from the adjoining sacristy) contain astounding views of the city, but are not normally accessible to the public—so ask nicely. Cosenza's greatest treasure, however, lies just below the church. When the *duomo* was reconsecrated in 1222 following an earthquake, Frederick II gave the city a gilt **Byzantine crucifix** containing a splinter said to come from the True Cross. A skilled work in fine gold, the cross is truly exquisite. Once on public display in the *duomo*, then moved to the Archbishopric, it is now safe and sound in the basement of the Convento di San Francesco d'Assisi. *(Cross the Mario Martiri bridge, turn left up narrow C. Telesio to the Duomo. Continue on C. Telesio just past the cathedral's facade, then turn right onto V. del Seggio (don't be fooled by its staircase-like appearance; it is a street). Take a right at the top; church is around the corner. For the cross, follow the church's left flank down to the last door and press the buzzer for "Laboratorio di Restauro." Call in advance to see the cross ☎0984 755 22. Free.)*

DUOMO. On weekend nights, young Cosentini and people from surrounding provinces relax in the triangular *piazze* before and behind the *duomo*. Inside is Cosenza's second most-prized artwork after the famed cross: *La Madonna del Pilerio*, a 12th-century painting in the Byzantine style with Sicilian influences. The work is framed by an ornate baroque chapel, the first on the left side of the church as you enter. The next chapel belongs to the *Arciconfraternità della Morte* (Archbrotherhood of Death). Not to be confused with a heavy metal band, the brothers actually belonged to a religious order charged by ancient privilege to aid the condemned. Many Cosentini executed for their part in the Risorgimento lie buried in the chapel. *(Cross the M. Martini bridge into the old city, and head left up C. Telesio into P. Parrasio. Or take bus #22 or 23 up to P. Prefettura, and with your back to P. del Governo, turn right down C. Telesio. Open mornings and late afternoons.)*

CASTELLO NORMANNO-SVEVO (NORMAN CASTLE). This fairytale structure on the hill high above the city predates most of the *Centro Storico* and in its ruined state provides a silent and meditative testament to the city's tumultuous past. Originally built by the Saracens but refurbished by Frederick II after the Cosentini tried to overthrow him, the castle offers impressive views of the surprisingly compact city. Now overrun with grass and a few trees, the castle has been a barracks for the armies of three different monarchs, a prison, and a seminary. Though three earthquakes have destroyed most of its ornaments, the castle's flowered columns and roofless, open-ended chambers still remain. *(Take bus #22 or 23 to P. Prefettura, and with your back to Rendano Theater, walk up the curved road to the right. Or take bus 4T to the elevated village and follow signs 10-15min. uphill. Open daily 9am-1:30pm. Free. Word of caution: the climb is very steep, without shade, and the light colored roads reflect the harsh sunlight; be extra cautious on hot days and bring water.)*

RENDANO THEATER. Calabria's most prestigious venue, the Rendano Theater was originally constructed in 1895 but was destroyed by World War II bombing. It has since been rebuilt to its former glory. Crimson, white, and gold, its plush interior has hosted the likes of José Carreras. Reservations for non-Calabresi are extremely difficult to get during the opera season (Oct.-Dec.); you might have more luck stopping in during the theater season (Jan.-May). If it's performance itself you want, the Rendano hosts regional performance groups during the summer with tickets in ready availability. *(☎0984 81 32 20. Behind the statue of Telesio in P. Prefettura. For plays, tickets may be available 10am-1pm and 5-8pm on day of performance, but cannot check by phone. L35,000/€18.08. Student discounts.)*

CAMIGLIATELLO AND SILA MASSIF ☎0984

The Sila Massif, outside the tiny town of Camigliatello, translates roughly from its ancient Greek and Latin origins to "large, pristine ancient forest (overrun by wild pigs.)" Sila may best be left undefined by words. The glorious landscape involves woods, lakes, mountains, and valleys, all ready and waiting to be explored by intrepid independent travelers. The national park is *the* spot for Calabria's hikers, campers, and skiers (who converge on the Sila's cross-country trails). Oft-neglected by foreign tourists, the Sila is as worthwhile a destination as the coast.

◨◪ TRANSPORTATION AND PRACTICAL INFORMATION. Camigliatello is the best base to visit elsewhere in the Sila. Ferrovie della Calabria **trains** travel to Camigliatello from Cosenza, which is served by **FS** trains (1½hr., 2 per day, L3300/

€1.70) from Reggio as well as points north and by **bus** (40-45min., 10 per day, L3400/€1.76). Service is drastically reduced on Sundays.

Get your bearings with the maps and expertise provided at the **Pro Loco tourist office,** V. Roma, 5, uphill to the right from the train station and bus stop. Information on area attractions and events, including local trails. Three well-marked trails (2.2km, 3.3km, and 6½km), leaving the picnic area down V. Roma past Hotel Tassio, make for easier day-hikes without missing any of Sila's beauty.

The **bank,** Banca Carime, is at V. del Turismo, 73. (☎0984 57 80 27. Open M-F 8:30am-1:20pm and 2:35-3:35pm.) For **medical emergencies,** call ☎0984 57 83 28. Camigliatello's **post office,** at the intersection of V. del Turismo and V. Roma, is next to Hotel Tasso; walk uphill on V. Roma and the office is on the left, past the sign for Hotel Tasso, V. Tasso. (☎0984 57 80 76. Open M-Sa 9am-1pm.)

▐▌ ACCOMMODATIONS, CAMPING, AND FOOD. Prices for local lodgings are mountainous. You can snuggle under a neon bedspread at **La Baita,** V. Roma, 99, 100m from the train station, without worrying about the bill. Each of the rooms has a bath. (☎0984 57 81 97. Singles L40,000/€20.66; doubles L70,000/€36.15. During August and ski season singles L50,000/€25.82; doubles, L90,000/€46.48.) The **La Fattoria** campsite (☎0984 57 82 41), by a vineyard, is a bargain at L8000/€4.13 per person, tent provided. Buses service La Fattoria from Camigliatello.

From the walls embellished with wine bottles and prints to the listings of prices and specialties, the restaurants in Camigliatello vary little. **Le Tre Lanterne,** V. Roma, 142, is a popular family-run spot that serves everything piled high with mushrooms, Sila-style. Pizza, from L7000/€3.62, is served only at dinner. (☎0984 57 82 03. Cover L3000/€1.55. Open daily noon-3:30pm and 7pm-midnight.) **La Stragola,** V. Roma, 160, offers fresh mushroom pasta and other local favorites. (☎0984 57 83 16. *Primi* from L10,000/€5.16; *secondi* from L12,000/€6.20. Cover L2000/€1.03.) For a change of pace, try the *salumerie* (deli-like eateries) that overflow with smoked cheeses, cured meats, and marinated mushrooms. Picnic grounds lie 10 minutes from the *centro*, up V. Tasso past the post office.

◙♫ SIGHTS AND ENTERTAINMENT. If it's snow you want, you'll get plenty of it at the **Tosso Ski Trail,** on Monte Curcio, about 2km from town up V. Roma and left at Hotel Tosso. In winter, minibuses leave for the trailhead from Camigliatello's bus stop (buy tickets at Bar Pedaggio, next door to the stop). Though Tosso offers 35km of beautiful cross-country skiing, it has only two downhill trails (2km each). (☎0984 57 81 36 or 57 94 00. Lifts open daily 8am-5pm. Round-trip lift ticket L5000/€2.58, full-day pass L30,000/€15.50.) The slopes, however, are only open for skiing when snow is on the ground (between December and March).

Getting to the **Parco Nazionale di Calabria** (☎0984 57 97 57), 10km northwest is not quite so easy. The state bus service sends just two buses into the park per day, in the morning and afternoon at varying times. **Altrosud,** V. Corado, 20, (☎0984 57 81 54) offers guided tours of the park in Italian for large groups. Arrange times and prices through reservation.

If you seek traditional Calabrian culture, ignore the stores filled with knick-knacks. Instead, hop on the bus for **San Giovanni in Fiore** (33km from Camigliatello), where you can view a 12th-century abbey, exhibitions of handicrafts at the museum, and traditional festivals (including the world-renowned **Potato Festival**).

REGGIO DI CALABRIA ☎0965

More than two thousand years ago, Reggio was one of the greatest cities of Magna Graecia, the western end of the ancient Greek world. Those days of glory are now only to be found in the city's prized **Museo Nazionale.** Reggio has since fallen on hard times. Repeated raids and sacks for hundreds of years left the region in disarray. Finally a devastating earthquake in 1908 provided the city with a chance to renew and rebuild. From the rubble arose a new town, lacking in old-world charm but brimming with designer stores and ornate turn-of-the-century *palazzi*.

Though often regarded as merely a jumping off point for reaching Sicily, Reggio and its environs encompass some of the finest landscapes in Italy. With the Tyrrhenian Coast to the north and the Ionian to the east, amazing beaches are easily accessible in all directions. Be sure to check out the nearby towns of **Scilla** (see p. 567) and **Gerace** (see p. 566): the former has a beach paramount to any in Italy, and the latter is one of the best-preserved medieval towns in the country.

TRANSPORTATION

Flights: Svincolo Aeroporto (☎0965 64 05 17), 5km south of town. Orange bus #113, 114, 115, 125, or 131 from P. Garibaldi outside Stazione Centrale (L1000/€0.52). Service to Milan, Rome, Florence, Torino, and Bologna.

Trains: Reggio has 2 train stations. All trains stop at **Stazione Centrale** (☎0965 89 81 23), on P. Garibaldi at southern end of town. The less-frequented **Stazione Lido** (☎0965 86 36 64) sits at the northern end of town off V. Zerbi, close to museum, port, and beaches. To: **Cosenza** (2½hr.; 3 per day; L22,000/€11.36); **Naples** (5hr.; 10 per day; L59,000/€30.47, *rapido* L70,000/€36.15); **Rome** (7hr.; 10 per day; L78,000/€40.28, *rapido* L88,000/€45.45); **Scilla** (30min., 20 per day, L4400/€2.27); **Tropea** (2hr., 5 per day, L9000/€4.65).

Ferries: From Reggio's port, at the northernmost end of the city, boats and hydrofoils service Messina as well as the Aeolian Islands (Lipari, Salina, Vulcano). **FS** (☎0965 295 68), all the way to left, against the water as you enter the port, shares Reggio's hydrofoil service with **SNAV** (☎0965 295 68), just to right of FS. FS open daily 6:30am-8:15pm; SNAV's hours less concrete. **NGI** (☎0335 842 77 84), across from the "Onda Marina" bar to the right of the port's entrance, runs a ferry service (M-F 12:20am-10:20pm, Sa 12:20am-8:20pm). **Meridiano** (☎0965 81 04 14) is on the corner of the water nearest the port entrance (Su-Sa 2:10am-11:50pm, fewer on Su).

ORIENTATION AND PRACTICAL INFORMATION

Reggio's main artery is **Corso Garibaldi**, which runs 1km parallel to the sea and to all the major sights. With your back to **Stazione Centrale**, walk straight through **Piazza Garibaldi** to C. Garibaldi; a left turn leads to the heart of the town. At the end of C. Garibaldi and down V.le G. Zerbi is Reggio's **port**, from which hydrofoils and boats zip off to Messina and the Aeolian Islands. One block to the left of the station, the twin roads **Corso Vittorio Emanuele III** and **Viale Matteotti** trace the **Lungomare** on the sea. City buses (L1000/€0.52) run continuously up and down C. Garibaldi and along the two roads toward the **Stazione Lido,** 1½km to the north.

TOURIST AND FINANCIAL SERVICES

Tourist Office: APT booth (☎0965 271 20), at the central train station. Free maps detail hotels, sights, public services, and agencies. Open M-Sa 8am-2pm and 2:30-8pm. Other branches with similar hours at the **airport** (☎0965 64 32 91) and **main office,** V. Roma, 3 (☎0965 211 71 or 0965 89 25 12), with some staff proficient in English. Another **APT office** lies at C. Garibaldi, 329 (☎0965 89 20 12), next to theater.

Currency Exchange: Banca Nazionale del Lavoro, C. Garibaldi, 431 (☎0965 805 11). Open M-F 8:20am-1:20pm and 2:35-4:05pm. The **FS ticket window** in the station is not as good. Open daily 7am-9pm. C. Garibaldi is amply supplied with **ATMs.**

EMERGENCY AND COMMUNICATIONS

Emergency: ☎113. **Carabinieri:** ☎112.

Police: (☎0965 41 11), on C. Garibaldi near central station.

First Aid: ☎0965 34 71 06.

Hospital: Ospedale Riuniti (☎0965 39 71 11), on V. Melacrino.

24-Hour Pharmacy: Farmacia Caridi, C. Garibaldi (☎0965 240 13); **Farmacia Curia,** C. Garibaldi, 327 (☎0965 33 23 32).

Internet Access: Agen Service (☎0965 581 87 62) At port, next to FS ticket office. L2000/€1.03 per 15min. Open 8am-12:40pm and 5:30-7:30pm. **PuntoNet,** C. Garibaldi, 70 (☎/fax 0965 33 16 68). L8000/€4.13 per hr. Open daily 3:30-8:30pm.

Post Office: V. Miraglia, 14 (☎0965 31 52 68), rear left from P. Italia on C. Garibaldi in an airy and official early 20th-century building. Open M-Sa 8am-7pm.

Postal Code: 89100.

ACCOMMODATIONS

■ **Hotel Diana,** V. Diego Vitrioli, 12 (☎0965 89 15 22), off C. Garibaldi 4 blocks past and across the street from *duomo*. Elegantly furnished rooms and 18ft. ceilings. Chandeliers and marble floors whisper of past grandeur. Rooms with TV, bath, and phone. 1-month advance reservation required Aug. Singles L50,000/€25.82; doubles L100,000/€51.65; triples L135,000/€69.72; quads L170,000/€87.80. A/C 20% more.

Albergo Noel, V. Genoese Zerbi, 13 (☎0965 33 00 44 or 89 09 65), near port at opposite end of C. Garibaldi from Stazione Centrale. With the sea behind you, turn left from station. Dusty rooms and plastic furniture. Great location. The port, beach and museum are within a few blocks. Reduced baths and color TV. Reservations recommended July-Sept. Wheelchair accessible. Singles L50,000/€25.82; doubles L70,000/€36.15.

FOOD

In Reggio, they like it hot and meaty. Chefs serve *spaghetti alla calabrese* (with pepper sauce), *capocollo* ham (spiced with local hot peppers), and *pesce spada* (local harpoon-hunted swordfish). Reggio's restaurants vary little, and can be pricey. You cn avoid over paying, and stock up for the beach at **Dì par Dì supermarket,** opposite the train station on C. Garibaldi. (Open M-Sa 8am-1:30pm and 5-8:30pm, Tu 8am-2pm.) Bars along C. Garibaldi often include top-flight bakeries. Pick up a few of the region's favorite *biscotti* to make your outings a little sweeter.

■ **Pizzeria Rusty,** V. Crocefisso, 14 (☎0965 8925 30), to the right of the *duomo*. Nothing rusty about this fine eatery. Double-folded Neapolitan slices the size of Fiats come with mushrooms, anchovies, eggplant, prosciutto, or artichokes. Slices priced by weight. Another branch on V. Romeo, next to the museum and near the Antica Gelateria. Both restaurants open daily 3:30-11pm.

Shanghai Ristorante Cinese, V. Giulia, 2/C (☎0965 33 06 42), off C. Garibaldi. A dynasty of delights and a delicious respite from food *all'italiana* served amongst elegant eastern decor. Vegetarian options from L4000/€2.07. Pork and chicken dishes from L6000/€3.10. The spicy dishes will knock your socks off. A/C. Takeout available. Open Tu-Su 11am-3pm and 6pm-midnight.

La Pignata, V. Demetrio Tripepi, 122 (☎0965 278 41), up V. Giutecca from C. Garibaldi. A sparkling interior and sociable waiters create the perfect atmosphere to sample specialties. Nicer than it has to be, La Pignata is the place to go when you want a little luxury at a little price. *Primi* from L10,000/€5.16; *secondi* from L16,000/€8.26. MC/V.

SIGHTS

■ **MUSEO NAZIONALE.** Reggio's famed **museo** commemorates and celebrates the city's past as a great ancient Greek *polis*. The preeminence the city enjoyed in antiquity may have passed, but the Nazionale preserves the Reggio's historical claim to fame with one of the world's finest collections of art and artifacts from Magna Graecia ("Greater Greece.") In the first floor galleries, a wealth of *amphorae* and *pinakes*, wine jars and votive tablets, show scenes from mythology and daily life. The floor above the gallery contains a large coin collection and a 2300-year-old novelty sarcophagus shaped like a large, sandaled foot.

DO YOU HEAR THE PEOPLE SING? Poor Reggio.

First the earthquakes, now this. The Reggesi are fiercely proud of their city—and keenly aware of its millenial decline. In 1971, when Italy's central government decided to move the Calabrian *capoluogo,* or administrative seat, from Reggio to Catanzaro, it was the last straw. The plan was that while Catanzaro got the *capoluogo,* Reggio would get an industrial factory center. But the Reggesi would have none of it. Citizens took to the streets, setting up makeshift barricades and bombarding the nationally-administered carabinieri with stones. After about a year of these shenanigans, the central government got fed up and sent in riot troops, causing a full-scale street war. The ensuing battles, involving everything from sticks to tear gas canisters, created a couple of Reggesi martyrs, though no one is sure how they died or who killed them. One is commemorated by a plaque on the small street leading upward opposite P. Italia; it reads "Fallen for the Capoluogo." Down on his luck, Reggio lost the *capoluogo* to Catanzaro anyway, and the promised center of industry never materialized.

The centerpiece of the collection is in the **Sezione Subacquea,** downstairs. The Ionian Sea continuously yields submerged treasures to the surprise of scuba divers and the delight of the archaeologists. The discoveries often have consisted of pottery, anchors, and broken statues, which are all on display. Some finds have proven to be more monumental. The **Bronze di Riace** (Riace Bronzes), arguably the most valuable and important of known Greek sculptures, stand casually in all their muscular glory in a gallery shared with the **Head of the Philosopher,** thought to be the first life-like portrait in the Greek tradition. The Bronzes, two male nude warriors of stunning anatomical detail, date from the 5th century BC and are thought to be greek originals, as opposed to roman copies. Discovered by chance in 1972 near Riace, they have since stood guard in Reggio. A comprehensive display before you enter the gallery documents the bronzes's nine year restoration process. *(P. de Nave, on C. Garibaldi toward the Stazione Lido. ☎ 0965 81 22 55; www.museodella-calabria.com. Open daily May-Oct. 9am-11pm; Nov.-Apr. 9am-7:30pm. Closed 1st and 3rd Monday of the month. L8000/€4.13; ages 18-25. L4000/€2.07; under 18 and over 65 free.)*

🏖🎵 BEACHES AND ENTERTAINMENT

As the day cools, Reggesi and their *gelati* intermingle on the **lungomare,** a long, narrow botanical garden stretching along the seaside. When they want to make like a nude bronze warrior and take a dip, pale travelers sprawl on the beach near **Lido Communale.** Playgrounds, an elevated boardwalk, and monuments to the city's more famous citizens dot the *lungomare,* and a sunset behind the misty blue mountains of nearby Sicily is a sight not to be missed. Calabrians finish the summer with the **Festival of the Madonna della Consolazione.** The four-day festival, celebrated in mid-September, concludes with an astonishing display of fireworks.

🔁 DAYTRIPS FROM REGGIO DI CALABRIA

LOCRI AND GERACE

From Reggio, trains (2hr.; 23 per day; L9600/€4.96) run to and from Locri on the coast. From the station, the Audino bus (L1800/€0.93) runs 7:20am-5:30pm up to Gerace and back; to avoid getting stuck find out from the driver when he'll stop by again.

An easy and relaxing vacation from the urban energy of Reggio, **Locri** features the very best qualities of Ionian Coast: expansive beaches and ancient ruins. Between Bianco and Siderno, Locri is at the center of the coast's most pleasant and explorable beaches. The long and under-populated stretches of sand and stone allow for low-key and private afternoons lolling in the sun. Despite its location, Locri is not a "beach town." At the end of the last century, the regional government moved all public offices to Locri from nearby Gerace. The grand **Communale** (now being refurbished but expected to be open in 2002) presides over a square that is more park than *piazza*. With flowers, trees, grass, and benches, **Piazza Re Umberto** is a pleasant spot to watch the locals play cards and just relax.

On the outskirts of town, **Locri Epizephyri** offers those up to the 2km stroll a remarkable expanse of ancient Greek ruins. Various remaining foundations and supports give a sense of the Locri of old. Visitors can explore the Sanctuary of Persephone, the Necropolis, and the Ionic Temple of Marasa. The highlight of the site is the theatre, built into the hillside. Much of the seats and the stage remain, moving some visitors to give impromptu performances. The nearby museum (☎ 0964 39 04 33) displays objects and maps of the site. There is a **Pro Loco** office on V. M. di Savoia, 1 block to the left as you exit the *piazza* in front of the station, with helpful maps of the town. (Open 8am-2pm, 4-8pm.) A 24hr. Banco di Napoli **ATM** is on V. Mileto. After a right out of the station's *piazza*, take the first left.

Gerace is among the best-preserved medieval towns in Italy. Since losing the government seat to Locri, Gerace has become something of a "ghost town," but this has only served to maintain its medieval beauties in pristine, untouched splendor. The bus from Locri drops passengers off uphill from the *duomo* beside **Largo delle Tre Chiese**, a *piazza* enclosed by three churches. **The Chiesa di San Francesco** (to your left if you stand facing the Largo from the street) has a beautiful portal decorated in the Arabic-Norman style; inside is an elegant wooden altar fully decorated with exquisite black and white marble. Take a short walk up Gerace's pinnacle for the astounding view from **Castello di Roberto il Guiscardo.** Down V. Caduti sul Lavoro from the bus stop, Gerace's immense **cathedral**—the largest in Calabria—occupies most of P. Duomo. Twenty-six Greek columns pilfered from Locri support the grand Romanesque interior. Highlights of the church are ancient Greek graffiti and Bishop Calceopulo's 16th-century tombstone.

There is a **Banca Carical** with an **ATM** and currency exchange in Largo Barlaam, downhill from the *duomo* on toward P. del Tocco. (Open M-F 8:20am-1:20pm and 2:35-3:35pm, Sa 8:20-11:50am.) The **post office** is in P. del Tocco. In **medical emergencies,** call the **Guardia Medica** (☎ 0964 39 91 11).

SCILLA

You can access Scilla from Reggio by train (30min, 20 per day, L4400/€2.27) or by bus (20min., 12 per day, L2500/€1.29).

Homer immortalized the town's great cliffs in *The Odyssey* as the home of the terrible monster Scylla (Italian: Scilla), whose six heads, 12 feet, and foul temper destroyed many a ship that steered away from Charybdis, a whirlpool in the straits where the oceans meet. Tourists today need not fear being devoured by a scaly monster, but beware of being seduced by Scilla the town. This fishing village-cum-beach resort is just 23km from Reggio, but its slow pace, white sands, and turquoise waters feel a world away. About ten times a year, however, the world can seem a lot closer as the *Fata Morgana*—a meteorological oddity wherein the light on the ocean air creates a natural magnifying glass—make the Aeolian Islands seem to be within walking distance. The town is built directly into the cliffs enclosing the beach, creating level after level of incredible vistas. In quiet moments, listen for the soft music of the merfolk. Scilla may be gone, but local legend contends that beautiful mermaids still grace the waters.

If Scilla proves too enticing to leave, consider spending the night at the seaside **Pensione Le Sirene,** V. Nazionale, 57,(☎ 0965 75 40 19 or 75 41 21; www.svagocalabria.com/pensionelesirene) across from the train station. A clean, cozy haven with nine rooms, Le Sirene is sandwiched between the station and the beach. (Breakfast included in summer. Reservations recommended during the summer. Singles L46,000/€23.76; doubles L82,000/€42.35.) Being eaten by Scylla is not fun, but eating in Scilla can be most enjoyable. The cheapest meals are served at the air-conditioned **Pizzeria San Francesco,** V. Cristoforo Colombo, 29, (☎ 0349 32 60 670) along the beach. This family-run establishment prides itself on its specialty, the Pizza Stefania. (Pizza L5-10,000/€2.58-5.16.) To dine with a Homerian epic view, climb the stairs to **Vertigine,** P. San Rocco, 14 (☎ 0965 75 40 15) at the top of the town.

Devour some speciality seafood as it gazes out to the water for a last glimpse of home. (*Primi* from L7000/€3.62; *secondi* from L10,000/€5.16. Drinks from L2500/€1.29. Cover L2500/€1.29. Open daily noon-3pm and 7:30pm-midnight. MC/V.)

Scilla's most famous cliff now supports the 17th-century **Castello Ruffo,** evidence of Scilla's important historical role as a control base for the Straits of Messina. For over 2000 years, the cliffs have been valuable real estate when it comes to controlling the region, and everyone from the Italiots to Garibaldi himself has fought to take possession. Just down hill from the castle, **Chiesa di Maria S. S. Immacolata** is the largest and most impressive of Scilla's many churches. An enormous altarpiece and 14 bronze sculptures of Christ cannot contend with the beauty of the landscape, but are well worth the trip uphill. In August, Scilla celebrates the Festival of S. Rocco, the town's patron saint, with a grand fireworks display.

TROPEA   ☎0963

Tropea delivers all that its postcards promise: breathtaking turquoise water, white sand beaches, gleaming rock cliffs, and aging stone streets. The town acts as a focused portal for the best beach on the Tyrrhenian. Winding streets discover hidden *piazzas* at every turn; dignified churches reflect the water's glimmer. By day, the gentle town is abandoned as everyone heads to the beach. By night, the streets become a brimming ocean of bronzed bodies, especially during the high season when the town is filled past capacity.

▐▍ TRANSPORTATION AND PRACTICAL INFORMATION. Trains run from the Reggio train station (2hr., 10 per day; Open M-Sa 9am-1:50pm and 4:30-6pm. AmEx/MC/V). **Autoservizi** (☎0963 611 29) operates obliging *pullmini* (blue minivans), which pick up passengers on V. Stazione all summer every 30min. For L1000/€0.52 per person, the vans travel 27 different routes, going as far as 24km out, and are often the easiest or only way to access some of the more remote attractions and accommdations around Tropea. For exact stops, ask the English-speaking staff at the **Pro Loco tourist office** (☎0963 614 75), down V. Stazione at P. Ercole. It has maps showing historical sites. **Banca Carime,** V. Stazione, has an **ATM** and an automatic money exchange machine (Open M-F 8:20am-1:20pm and 2:35-3:35pm.) In an **emergency,** call the **police** (☎113 or 0964 612 21) or the **Carabinieri** (☎112). For medical *emergencies,* call **Pronto Soccorso** (☎0963 613 66). The **post office** is on C. Rigna. From V. Stagione take the far left street; it is on the corner. (Open M-Sa 8:15am-7pm.) **Postal Code:** 89861.

▐▌ ACCOMMODATIONS AND FOOD. As long as you make reservations, staying in Tropea need not be expensive. The best deal in town is ▧**Da Litto,** V. Carmine, 26. Exit the train station and walk down V. Stazione past the gas station at left. Turn right onto the angular V. degli Orti, then a right onto V. Carmine. Follow a full S-curve of the road; driveway is the fourth unmarked left. Each bungalow in the garden is independent, with patio, kitchenette, and bathroom. (☎0963 60 33 42 or 0339 332 15 35; www.tropea.it/deluca. July-Aug. L47-65,000/€24.27-33.57, Sept.-June L25,000/€12.91.) For camping by the sea, try the tree-shaded **Campeggio Marina dell'Isola,** below sandstone cliffs to the left of Santuaria di Santa Maria. (☎0963 619 70; www.italiaabc.it/a/marinaisola. L15,000/€7.75 per person, L5000/€2.58 per light and car. Hot showers included, tents provided. MC/V.)

Tropea's sweet red onions are reputed to keep eaters thin and healthy. Delight in the delicious aroma of *rigatoni alla Tropea* at **Ristorante Tropea Vecchia** (☎0349 2923 953), in a flowery private *piazza* on Largo Barone, just down a narrow corridor behind the fountain at the Pro Loco. **Il Bocconcino,** C. Emanuele, 29, directly across the street from Pro Loco, serves tasty Calabrian rice balls for L2500/€1.29 and calzones for L3000/€1.55. To dine on local fish with an ocean view, try **Pimm's Restaurant,** Largo Migliarese. (☎0963 66 61 05), next to the lookout at the end of C. Emanuele. The *alimentare* on V. Stazione in the center of town across from V.V. Veneto is great for grabbing snacks on the way to the beach.

◙ SIGHTS. The gleaming **Santuaria di Santa Maria** presides over the white cliffs at the edge of town. In its isolated beauty, the church mirrors Tropea's character as it reflects the crystal water below. Townsmen take the church's pink-clad *Madonna and Child* out to sea every August 15. Up the cliff is Tropea's graceful **Norman cathedral.** Besides some nice polychrome marble work and several dead sword-bearing Tropeans, the elegant interior houses two bombs that miraculously failed to destroy Tropea when an American warplane dropped them in 1943. To reach the **beach,** take a winding set of stairs down the cliffs at the end of V. Umberto (turn off V. Stazione to the left).

THE IONIAN COAST

From Reggio to Riace, the Ionian Coast offers miles of beaches. Ranging in type from white sand to rocks to dunes, the beaches cater to every taste and contrast the mountains visible in the distance. Though the ancient Greeks once made these shores as crowded as modern Tropea, the beaches are now frequented primarily by locals. Even the more established sites at **Bovalino Marina, Bianca,** and **Soverato** are largely unknown and waiting to be enjoyed. A train ride along the coast is a pleasant trip in itself. Since trains along the Ionian coast often have erratic schedules and multiple connections, allow ample time to reach your destination.

SICILY (SICILIA)

Without Sicily, Italy cannot be fully understood. It is here one finds the key to all things.
—J.W. von Goethe

Sicily is a land of sensuous sunshine and sinister shadows. Ancient Greek influences lauded the golden island as the second home of the Gods; now eager tourists seek it as the home of *The Godfather*. While the *Cosa Nostra* does remain a presence in Sicilian life, it makes up only the smallest part of the vivacious and varied island's culture. The boiling sun has melted together the traditions, dialects, and architecture of the countless peoples who have coveted the island's beauty to create a diverse society. Evidence of prehistoric, Carthaginian, Greek, Roman, Arab, Norman, Bourbon, and Argonese eras are to be found in exquisite temples, local foods, hilltop castles, and dialects. On the whole, Sicily has very little to do with Italy. Its physical separation from the mainland literalizes Sicilians' determined independence. The many volcanoes that cover Sicily and its lesser isles seem to inspire Sicilian character: timeless and beautiful, but prone to passionate volatility. The volcanoes are just one element of this exciting landscape. A 1000km coastline encompasses rocky shores, intriguing grottoes, impossible cliffs, and beaches whose sand ranges from pure white to dirty black. Inland, the view changes from a sea of turquoise waters to one of golden grain and craggy jutting cliffs to gentle whitecapped waves. Orchards of olive, citrus, and almond trees alternate with vineyards to produce some of Italy's sweetest culinary delights. The locals working the rich soil do so with love and tradition, creating a postcard image of a Sicily untouched by time. As Palermo and other cities illustrate, however, Sicily is hardly behind the times. Vespas, cell phones, chic boutiques, and high rises are as much a part of Sicilian life as the farms that lie just outside- and sometimes inside- the city limits. Sadly, modernization has had negative effects as well. As unemployment rises, petty crime and poverty mar the island's progress. Nevertheless, Sicily remains an extraordinary island, full of myth and mystery, traditions and history.

HIGHLIGHTS OF SICILY

VISIT Grecian glories at **Segesta, Selinunte, Syracuse,** and the world famous **Valle dei Tempii** (p. 622) in Agrigento.

VENTURE into Sicily's many volcanoes: Stromboli and Vulcano of the Aeolian Islands and the volatile **Mt. Etna,** Europe's tallest (p. 604).

ENJOY Enna (p. 610), the best all around little medieval hilltop city, anywhere.

APPLAUD Palermo's traditional puppet shows in local theaters and world-class performances in the newly-restored **Teatro Massimo** (p. 579).

NORTHERN SICILY

PALERMO ☎091

The largest city in Sicily, Palermo is like a concentrated version of the region's most potent wine. It retains the overall flavor, but is strong and works faster on your poor, befuddled mind. A gritty urban environment with over a million inhabitants, the pace of life here dispels any myth of a sleepy Sicily. Cars, buses, scooters, and horse-drawn carriages infest the streets day and night, except for Sundays, when the city is all but abandoned to baby strollers and roller skaters. Despite Sicilians' best attempts to make Palermo seem like a slightly run-down

Sicily (Sicilia)

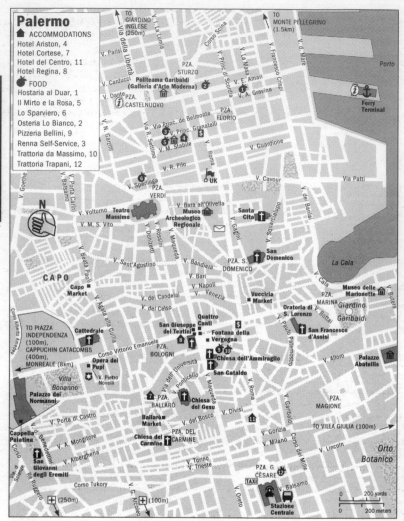

Palermo

ACCOMMODATIONS
Hotel Ariston, 4
Hotel Cortese, 7
Hotel del Centro, 11
Hotel Regina, 8

FOOD
Hostaria al Duar, 1
Il Mirto e la Rosa, 5
Lo Sparviero, 6
Osteria Lo Bianco, 2
Pizzeria Bellini, 9
Renna Self-Service, 3
Trattoria da Massimo, 10
Trattoria Trapani, 12

version of Berlin or Madrid, the city is still very much grounded in both its medieval and its more recent *Cosa Nostra* identities. The knotted tiny streets in the old sections wind past ancient ruins, Norman structures, and bombed-out buildings. The 1993 election of a publicly anti-Mafia mayor, however, brought an end to the mob's knee-bashing control. Much of Palermo backs the mayor's efforts, and with political clean-up underway, the city is now restoring its architectural treasures.

⌫ TRANSPORTATION

Flights: Punta Raisi/Falcone & Borsellino airport (domestic info ☎ 091 601 92 50; international info ☎ 702 01 11). 40min. from central Palermo. **Prestia & Comande** buses (☎ 091 58 04 57) run every 30 min. from P. Castelnuovo (45min.) and the central station (1hr. L9000/€4.65). Taxis charge at least L65,000/€33.57.

Trains: Stazione Centrale, in P. Giulio Cesare. At the foot of V. Roma and V. Maqueda. Ticket office open 6:45am-8:40pm. Luggage storage available (p. 574). To: **Agrigento**

(2hr.; 13 per day; L13,200/€6.82); **Catania** (3½hr.; 8:15am and 2:40pm; L21,700/ €11.21); **Cefalù** (1hr., 23 per day, L7000/€3.62); **Firenze** (16hr.; 3 per day; L82,000/€42.35); **Messina** (3hr.); **Milan** (19½hr.; 2 per day; L95,000/€49.06); **Milazzo** (2½hr.; every hr.; L17,400/€8.99); **Rome** (11hr.; 7 per day; L75,000/ €38.73); **Termini** (30min., 12 per day, L4500/€2.32); **Torino** (21hr.; 11:20am, 1:35, 2:33pm; L95,000/€49.06); **Trapani** (2½hr.; 11 per day; L13,200/€6.82).

Ferries and Hydrofoils:

Tirrenia (☎091 60 21 111). On the waterfront, off V. Francesco Crispi, within the port gates. Open M-F 8:30am-12:45pm and 3:30-8:45pm, Sa 3:30-8:45pm, Su 5-8:45pm. Ferries to **Naples** (11hr.; 2 per day; armchair *"poltrona"* L68-77,000/€35.12-39.77, cabin L99,000/€51.13) and **Sardinia** (14hr.; *poltrona* L60,500-78,000/€31.25-40.28, cabin L107,000/€55.26).

Siremar, V. Francesco Crispi, 118 (☎091 690 25 55). On the last street before the waterfront, just in front of port. Ferries to **Ustica** (2½hr.; 1 per day; L19,000/€9.81). From July-Aug. Siremar also runs hydrofoils (1¼hr.; 2 per day; L31,000/€16.01). Open daily 8:30am-1pm and 4-6:30pm.

SNAV (☎091 33 33 33 or 611 85 25). Off V. Francesco Crispi, inside the port gates; the office is at the far end of Stazione Marittima. Runs hydrofoils twice a day to the Aeolian Islands. All hydrofoils stop in **Lipari** and **Vulcano;** check schedule for other islands. More erratic in winter.

Grimaldi Group (☎091 58 74 04). 100m before Tirrenia with the sea to your left. Luxury ships have gyms and discos. Office open M-F 8:45am-1pm/ferry leaves at 2:15pm; Sa 9am-noon/ferry leaves at 4:30pm. Ferries to **Livorno** (17hr.; Tu, Th, Sa 11pm; *poltrona* L103-161,000/€53.20-31.50) and **Genoa** (20hr.; 6 per week M-Sa; *poltrona* L123-181,000/€63.52-93.48).

Buses: All 4 lines run along V. Balsamo, by the train station. With your back to the tracks, turn right; exit with McDonald's on your left and newspaper stands on your right; V. Balsamo is straight ahead, hidden by an army of buses. After purchasing tickets, ask exactly where your bus will be arriving and find out its logo—there is no order in busland.

Cuffaro, V. Balsamo, 13 (☎091 616 15 10). Opposite Segesta. To **Agrigento** (2½hr.; M-Sa 7 per day Su 3 per day; L13,000/€6.71).

Segesta, V. Balsamo, 14 (☎091 616 79 19). Sometimes uses buses confusingly marked "Sicilbus," "EtnaTransport," or "Interbus." To: **Alcamo** (1hr.; M-Sa 10 per day, Su 11:30am-11:30pm; L8000/€4.13); **Rome** (12hr.; daily 6:30pm; L69,000/€35.64); **Syracuse** (3hr.; 5 per day; L26,000/€13.43); **Terrasini** (1hr.; M-Sa 6 per day 6:30am-8pm; L13,000/€6.71); **Trapani** (2hr.; M-F 26 per day, Sa every hr., Su 13 per day; L12,000/€6.20).

SAIS Transporti, V. Balsamo, 16 (☎091 617 11 41). To **Corleone** (1¼hr., 5 per day 6am-6pm, L7500/€3.87).

SAIS, V. Balsamo, 16 (☎091 616 60 28). On the right from the train station and just next door to SAIS Transporti. To: **Catania Airport** (3¼hr.; 8 per day; L22,500/€11.82); **Catania** (2½hr.; every hr. 5am-8pm; L22,500/€11.82); **Messina** (3¼hr.; every hr. 5am-9pm; L24,000/€12.39); **Piazza Armerina** (1½hr.; 8 per day; L18,500/€9.55).

Public Transportation: Orange **city buses (AMAT).** Main terminal in front of train station, under a dark green overhang. L1500/€0.77 for 1½hr., L5000/€2.58 per day. Buy tickets from any *tabacchi* or on-site mini offices. 17 **metropolitana** stations around the city are useful for getting to spots north or south of the **centro storico. Metro trains** to suburbs use normal train tracks. Catch trains at the central station. Ticket prices are the same bus fares. Ask at one of the mini offices or info booths for a combined metro and bus map. Most bus stops are labeled and have route maps posted.

Taxis: (☎091 22 54 55), in front of the central station next to the bus stop.

✴🛈 ORIENTATION AND PRACTICAL INFORMATION

Palermo, Italy's fourth largest city, is Sicily's most urban. The newer half of the city follows a regular grid pattern, but the older sections to the south, near the train station, are a crazy knot hundreds of years old. The **station** dominates **Piazza Giulio Cesare,** from which the city's two primary streets define Palermo's central axis. **Via Roma** begins directly across from the station and passes the **post office.** Parallel to V. Roma, to the left from the front of the station, **via Maqueda** runs to the Teatro Massimo and **Piazza Verdi,** where it becomes **via Ruggero Settimo.** After 300m, it runs into **Piazza Castelnuovo (Politeama),** home to the tourist office and the **Politeama Theater.** The stylish **via della Libertà** signals the beginning of the new city

A CRASH COURSE IN SICILIAN STREET SMARTS Palermo shuts down at night and its streets are poorly lit. Knowing where to go and how to get there is essential, especially after dark. When possible, stay on the main streets of V. Roma, V. Maqueda, or C.V. Emanuele—you may feel like the only pedestrian, but the stream of cars and scooters, which continues into the night, is reassuring. The areas behind the train station and around the port are particularly sketchy after shops close in the evening. Daylight hours are safer, but still be cautious— don't carry cameras around your neck or wear backpacks, flashy jewelry, or watches. Women should not carry purses slung sideways across the body. Walk with a purposeful stride at all times and avoid openly consulting maps.

and leads to the **Giardino Inglese.** At **Quattro Canti, via Vittorio Emanuele** intersects V. Maqueda, connecting **Piazza Independenza** to the sea. **Via Cavour** travels in the same direction from P. Verdi toward the port.

TOURIST, LOCAL, AND FINANCIAL SERVICES

Tourist Office: P. Castelnuovo, 34 (☎091 605 83 51 or 58 38 47; fax 58 63 38) on 3rd floor of the Banco di Sicilia building opposite Teatro Politeama. From the train station, take a bus to P. Politeama at the end of V. Maqueda. Cross the *piazza.* English spoken. Detailed maps and brochures. Ask for the monthly *Agenda.* Open daily 8am-5pm. Hours change slightly with season. 2 other **branches,** at the train station (☎091 616 59 14) and airport (☎091 59 16 98), keep the same hours. Smaller info kiosks with maps scattered throughout the city, at most parks and at the port.

Consulates: UK, V.C. Cavour, 117 (☎091 32 64 12). **US,** V. Re Federico, 18 (☎091 611 00 20), off Viale della Libertà. Take bus #28 from V. della Libertà. Emergencies only. Open M-F 8am-12:30pm and 3-5pm.

Currency Exchange: *Cambios* at the central post office and train station. **Banca Nazionale del Lavoro,** V. Roma, 201, and **Banco di Sicilia,** on V. R. Settimo, both open M-F 8:20am-1:20pm. **ATMs** on V. Roma and V. Maqueda often reject international cards; **Bankomat 3-plus** ATMs are newer and more reliable.

American Express Representative: G. Ruggieri and Figli Travel, V.E. Amari, 40 (☎091 58 71 44). From P. Castelnuovo (Politeama), follow V.E. Amari toward the water. Cashes **traveler's checks** for card holders only. Ask for the red city map "Palermo in your pocket." Open M-F 9am-1pm and 4-7pm, Sa 9am-1pm.

Luggage Storage: In the train station at the end of track #8. L5000/€2.58 per bag for 12hr. Open daily 6am-10pm.

English-Language Bookstore: Feltrinelli, V. Maqueda, 395 (☎091 58 77 85), a few blocks before Teatro Massimo from the train station. A selection of classics and mysteries occupies the 2nd fl. foreign titles island upstairs. Open M-Sa 9am-8pm. **Mondadori,** on the corner of V. Roma and P.S. Domenico, adjacent to a department store. 7 shelves of mystery, romance, classics, and sci-fi. Internet available. L5000/€2.58 per 30min.

Gay and Lesbian Resource Center: ARCI-GAY and **ARCI-Lesbica,** V. Genova, 7 (☎091 33 56 88), off V. Roma. Info on events. Open M-F 5-7pm.

EMERGENCY AND COMMUNICATIONS

Carabinieri: ☎112.

First Aid: (☎118 or 091 666 22 07), in Ospedale Civico.

Late-Night Pharmacy: Lo Cascio, V. Roma, 1 (☎091 616 21 17). Look for a green cross near the train station. Open daily 4:30pm-8:30am. **Di Naro,** V. Roma, 207 (☎091 58 58 69), on the right after C.V. Emanuele. Open M-F 4pm-1pm, Sa-Su 8pm-8:30am.

Hospital: Policlinico Universitario, V. del Vespro (☎091 655 11 11), or **Ospedale Civico** (☎666 11 11), on V. Lazzaro, near the train station.

Internet Access:

Mondadori, V. Roma, across from post office. 2 computers at L5000/€2.58 per 30min.

Nick Carter, V. Roma, 182/188 (☎091 33 12 72), is a burger joint/Internet cafe with 2 computers. L10,000/€5.16 per hr.

Informatica Commerciale, V. Notarbartolo (☎091 34 36 46). Walk down V. Libertà from P. Politeama/Castelnuovo and turn left past the English Gardens. 3 computers with speedy connections. L10,000/€5.16 for 1st 30min., L5000/€2.58 each additional 30min. Open M-F 9:30am-1pm and 4-7:30pm, Sa 9:30am-1pm.

Candelai (see **Entertainment**, p. 579). L8000/€4.13 per hr. Open F-Sa 7pm-late.

Post Office: V. Roma, 322 (☎091 160 or 695 91 11). Massive white-columned building 5 blocks up V. Roma past V.E. Emanuele. Open M-Sa 8:10am-7pm.

Postal Code: 90100.

ACCOMMODATIONS & CAMPING

Palermo is packed with places to stay at all levels of price and luxury, though the two seldom have any discernible relationship; always see the room before accepting. V. Roma and V. Maqueda have high concentrations of budget accommodations, but the neighborhoods near the train station are dangerous at night. Women especially should use caution at night when staying in this area.

Hotel Regina, C.V. Emanuele, 316 (☎091 611 42 16; fax 612 21 69), at the intersection of V. Maqueda and C.V. Emanuele across from the larger Hotel Centrale. Carved bureaus, ornate tables, light pine, and glass light fixtures adorn lengthy corridors at the top of worn marble staircases. Central location makes all of Palermo easily accessible. Small courtyard helps filter out the street noise. Free use of kitchen. 7 singles L30,000/€15.50; doubles L70,000/€36.15, with bath L80,000/€41.32.

Hotel del Centro, V. Roma, 72 (☎091 617 03 76; fax 617 36 54; hoteldelcentro@libero.it; www.hoteldelcentro.it), 5 blocks up V. Roma from the station, on 2nd fl. Old-world style rooms have few furnishings and stratospheric ceilings. Classy curtains and cream-colored details create ambience. Rooms with TV and A/C. Singles L50,000/€25.82, with bath L70,000/€36.15; doubles L70,000/€36.15, L95,000/€49.06.

Hotel Cortese, V. Scarparelli, 16 (☎/fax 091 33 17 22; hotelcortese@Tiscalinet.it; www.paginegialle.it/hotelcortese). From train station, walk 10min. down V. Maqueda to V. dell'Università; look for yellow sign on left (alternative entrance on Corso V. Emanuele is better for night arrivals; same yellow sign 200m on left). Direct access to Ballarò market. Small rooms with ample furnishings and TV. Solarium terrace has views of warm terracotta rooftops. Breakfast L8000/€4.13. Singles L45,000/€23.24, with bath L55,000/€28.41; doubles L70,000/€36.15, L85,000/€43.90. AmEx/D/MC/V.

Hotel Ariston, V.M. Stabile, 139 (☎091 33 24 34). Take V. Roma 4 blocks past V. Cavour, or take bus #122 and get off before V. Amari. Bright, modern rooms in impeccable minimalist style. Classy and comfortable. Hotel is in the middle of town between Teatros Massimo and Politeamo. All 7 rooms with bath, A/C, and TV, 6 floors above small courtyard. Single L60,000/€30.99; doubles L95,000/€49.06.

Camping: Campeggio dell'Ulivi, V. Pegaso, 25 (☎/fax 091 53 30 21), 35min. outside Palermo. Take bus #101 from Palermo's central station to P. de Gasperi; then take bus #628 to V. Sferracavallo. Walk downhill a block and turn right on V. dei Manderini just after the post office. Campground is on the right. Neurotically clean facilities. Bungalows available. L10,000/€5.16 per person, tent included. Hot showers free.

FOOD

Palermo is famous for its *spaghetti ai broccoli affogati alla palermitana* (with spicy fried broccoli), *pasta con le sarde* (with sardines and fennel), and *rigatoni alla palermitana* (with meat and peas). *Arancini* (fried balls filled with rice, spinach, or meat) and *panini con panelle* (fried balls of chick pea flour sliced and sandwiched) are also rich Sicilian delicacies. Try the popular *pesce spada* (swordfish). Palermitans claim to have invented their own *cassata* (a sweet ricotta pastry), discovered *paste con gelo di melone* (pastries with watermelon-paste filling), and perfected *gelato*. The best restaurants in town are positioned between Teatro Massimo and Politeama. Palermo's bustling markets provide better budget opportunities than most supermarkets, and more interesting selections. **Ballarò** sprawls through the intricate streets behind V. Maqueda and C.V. Emanuele, while **Capo** covers the streets behind Teatro Massimo. **Vucciria** completes the trio in the area between C.V. Emanuele and P. San Domenico. All three are open M-Sa during daylight hours. Saturday mornings are the most chaotic.

■ **Lo Sparviero,** V. Sperlinga, 23 (☎091 33 11 63), 1 block toward P. Politeama from the Teatro Massimo. This local secret is kept hidden by its dark interior and cloudy brown glass walls. Antique atmosphere envelops dark wood tables. Pizza from L4000/€2.07; *primi* from L10,000/€5.16. A/C. Open daily noon-3pm and 6:30am-midnight.

■ **Pizzeria Bellini,** P. Bellini, 6 (☎091 616 56 91), to left of P. Pretoria in the shadow of the Teatro Bellini. Outdoor umbrella-shaded dining creates one of Palermo's more romantic spots. Quality brick-oven pizzas from L7000/€3.62 (take-out available for picnics); *primi* from L10,000/€5.16. Cover L2000/€1.03. Open W-M 6am-1am. MC/V.

Il Mirto e la Rosa, V. Principe di Granatelli, 30 (☎091 32 43 53). Upscale vegetarian fare amid cathedral-like arches and 30-something Palermitans. Try *fettuccine al profumo d'estate* (in an aromatic sauce of tomatoes, pine nuts, peppers, garlic, and basil). Giganitic portions of *primi* (L8000/€4.13); simple *Secondi* from L8000/€4.13. 52 styles of pizza from L8000/€4.13. Open daily 12:30-3pm and 8-11pm.

Trattoria da Massimo, (☎091 616 75 20) behind Pizzeria Bellini. Solid budget fare with *primi* and *secondi* from L2000/€1.03. Indoor dining in the tiny restaurant or outside on street tables. Easily Palermo's most inexpensive full-blown meal: *primo, secondo, contorno*, and drink for L13,000/€6.71. Cover L2000/€1.03.

Hostaria al Duar, V. Ammiraglio Gravina, 31 (☎0347 473 57 44). Off V. Roma, 3 blocks north toward the port. Sicilian and Arabic flavors mingle on the menu as a living reminder of Sicily's conquests. Complete meals starting at L13,000/€6.71. Cover L2000/€1.03. Service 10%. Open Tu-Su 10am-3:30pm and 7pm-midnight.

Osteria Lo Bianco, V.E. Amari, 104 (☎091 58 58 16), off V. Roma. Sicilian favorites, eclectic regional decor, and a good reputation have kept locals flocking to this little restaurant for 95 years. *Primi* from L6500/€3.36; *secondi* from L9000/€4.65. Open daily 8:30am-3:30pm and 6:30-10:30pm.

Renna Self-Service, V. Principe di Granatelli, 29 (☎091 58 06 61). Fast food joint as crowded as a high school cafeteria. Bright decor makes it feel like one. Only difference is the food—Renna doesn't skimp on taste or portions. *Primi* from L3500/€1.81; *secondi* from L6000/€3.10. Open daily noon-3:30pm and 7-10pm. AmEx/MC/V.

Trattoria Trapani, P. Giulio Cesare, 16 (☎091 61 61 642), on the right of the station as you exit. Simple light wood interior serves quality budget food to those on the go. *Primi* from L4500/€2.32; *secondi* from L5500/€2.84. Cover L3000/€1.55. Open 11:45am-3pm and 6:30-10pm.

☎ SIGHTS

Ancient glory, seven centuries of neglect, and heavy World War II bombing have made Palermo a city of splendor and deterioration, where the beauty of the past hides behind the face of urban blight. The bizarre sight of Palermo's half-crumbled, soot-blackened 16th-century *palazzi* startles visitors accustomed to the cleaner historic districts of northern Italy. For much of the 20th century, corrupt politicians and Mafia activity diverted funds and attention from the dilapidated landmarks. In the past several years, however, cleaning and rebuilding efforts have slowly begun to reopen structures, like the magnificent Teatro Massimo.

■ **MONREALE.** Palermo's greatest treasure actually rests 8km outside of the city. The extraordinary **Monreale Cathedral** is a somewhat standard example of the Sicilian take on Norman architecture, mixing Arabic and local styles with the northern template. The interior, however, is a complete original. The cathedral's walls glisten with 6340 sq. meters of golden mosaics, the largest display of Byzantine religious art outside the Hagia Sofia. The series of 130 panels depict the massive **Christ Pantocrator** (Ruler of All) over the main altar, the mystical flavor of the locale emphasized by the minimal light from the cathedral's small windows. Every few minutes, someone pays the L2000/€1.03 necessary to activate electric lighting in a portion of the church. The sudden illumination never fails to startle. From the side entrance, visitors face the beginning of Genesis at the upper left of the central aisle. The two-tiered Old Testament narrative continues clockwise, with especially interesting and moving images of Adam and Eve. Christ's miracles are shown in marvelous detail along both the side aisles. *(Bus #389 leaves from Palermo's P. Indipendenza for Monreale's P.V. Emanuele (40min., 3 per hr., L1500/€0.77). To get to P. Indipendenza take bus #109 or 118 from Palermo's Stazione Centrale. Tourist info (☎ 091 656 45 70) to left of the church. Modest dress required. Cathedral open daily 8am-noon and 3:30-6pm.)*

Just next to the cathedral, the quiet, light-flooded **cloisters** offer a contrast to the solemn shadows of the cathedral. Though seemingly simple and empty, this courtyard contains one of the best and most unusual collections of Sicilian sculpture. Alternately plain and inlaid with Arabic tiles, 228 paired columns ring the interior. Each capital is unique, constructed alternately in Greco-Roman, Islamic, Norman, Romanesque, and Gothic styles. In the corner by the lesser colonnade and its fountain, a capital shows William II offering the Cathedral of Monreale to the Virgin. A balcony along the cathedral's apse looks over the cloisters and beyond to all of Palermo. Two doors down from the cloister is the entrance to a series of quiet **gardens** that survey Palermo. *(Open daily 9:30am-5:45pm. Cloister open M-Sa 9am-7pm, Su 9am-1pm. L8000/€4.13, students L4000/€2.07. Roof access L3000/€1.55.)*

■ **CAPPELLA PALATINA.** This chapel, in the monstrous conglomerate **Palazzo dei Normanni**, houses a smaller and more local version of the mosaics at Monreale. The Norman kings imported artists from Constantinople to cover every inch of the interior with gold, glass, gold, wood carvings, gold, sculpture, and, oh yes, gold. Many Palerimitans and their city pride claim to prefer this local treasure to that of Monreale, citing this Christ Pantocrator as being softer and more compassionate. Local Arab craftsman created the artful wooden ceilings and the geometric designs on the walls. Upstairs, guards lead tours through the **Sala di Ruggero,** King Roger's Hall. *(Follow C.V. Emanuele all the way up to Palazzo dei Normanni; entrance on the far right from P. Independenza. Chapel open M-Sa 9am-noon and 3-5pm, Su 9-10am and noon-1pm.)*

■ **CAPPUCHIN CATACOMBS.** The set of a horror movie or the backstage of the most macabre puppet show in history? No matter how you try to classify them, these murky subterranean chambers plunge skull-first into the grotesque. Over the course of 350 years, the friars of the Cappuchin order preserved the remains of over 8000 bodies. Attached to wall niches by wires and nails, grimacing, sneering skeletons in varying degrees of decomposition scream silently at visitors. The bodies are dressed in their finest clothes and sorted by sex and profession. Several bishops and the painter Velázquez also inhabit these corridors. *(Take bus #109 or 318 from Stazione Centrale to P. Indipendenza. From there hop on #327 to catacombs. P. Cappuccini. ☎ 091 21 21 17. Open M-Su 9am-noon and 3pm. L2500/€1.29.)*

TEATRO MASSIMO. Constructed between 1875 and 1897 in a robust Neoclassical style, the **Teatro Massimo** is the largest indoor stage in Europe after the Paris Opera House. After undergoing foot-dragging renovation since 1974, the theater opened in grand Sicilian style (with trumpets and confetti) for its 100th birthday in 1997. The word on the street is that the 23-year restoration was not a question of artistry but of Mafia feuding. Cleaned, polished, and shined, the exterior has now regained its light sand castle-colored appearance, and the interior its former gleam. It was here that Francis Ford Coppola shot the climactic opera scene of *The Godfather Part III*. The Massimo performs operas, plays, and ballets throughout the year. The **Festival di Verdura,** from late June to mid-August, brings famous international performers for one or two night shows. Performances are very accesible and run year-round. *(Across V. Maqueda from the Museo Archeologico, 500m up V. Maqueda from the Quattro Canti intersection with C.V. Emanuele. Toll free ☎ 800 65 58 58; box office ☎ 091 605 35 15. Open Tu-Su 10am-4pm for 20min. tours in English, French, and German.)*

PALERMO'S CATHEDRAL. During the 12th- and 13th-centuries, Palermo and Monreale raced to complete their cathedrals in hopes of gaining the archbishop's seat for the region. Palermo lost to the magnificent Monreale, and the loss still hangs over this strange hybrid of a church. Continually renovated from the 13th through 18th centuries, the cathedral's enormous exterior shows every addition and stylistic clash. Arab columns, Norman turrets, and an inexplicable 18th-century dome crowd the facade and walls. Note the inscription from the Qu'ran on the first left column before the entrance; in 1185 the Palermitan archbishop chose to plunk his cathedral down on top of a mosque, and this column was part of its stonework. The interior is that of a by-the-book Neoclassical church, with ornate chapels lining the sides. The chapels on the left contain six royal tombs (four canopied and two set in the wall) of Norman kings and the Hohenstaufen emperors from the 12th to 14th centuries. The *cattedrale* is connected by flying buttresses to the former archbishop's palace (1460), more massive and opulent than the church itself. *(On C.V. Emanuele. Open daily 9:30am-5:30pm. Closed Su mornings. Archbishop's Palace closed for restoration. Treasury and crypts L3000/€1.55.)*

QUATTRO CANTI AND THE FOUNTAIN OF SHAME. 630m down V. Maqueda from the train station, the intersection of V. Maqueda and C.V. Emanuele forms the **Quattro Canti** (the four corners). Each sculpted angle of this little 17th-century *piazza* celebrates either a season, a king of Spain (that once ruled the region), or one of the city's patron saints. Covered in soot and smog for decades, the sculptural works are now benefitting from Palermo's city-wide restoration. Large posted drawings give a picture of what lies beneath the scaffolding. **Piazza Pretoria,** down V. Maqueda, houses the oversized **Fontana della Vergogna** (Fountain of Shame) under **Teatro Bellini.** The statue-bedecked fountain was given its name by irate churchgoers who didn't like staring at mythological monsters and nude figures as they left **Chiesa di San Giuseppe dei Teatini** (1612), across the street. An even more shameful story explains its inappropriate size—the Fountain of Shame was not intended for the small *piazza*. In the early-16th century, a rich Florentine commissioned the fountain for his villa, sending a son to the Carrara marble quarries to ensure its safe delivery. The son, in need of some quick cash, shipped it to Palermo and sold the fountain to the city senate. Restoration scheduled to finish by 2002.

MUSEO ARCHEOLOGICO REGIONALE. Housed at a quiet *palazzo* in the center of town, this museum features an impressive collection of archeological finds from all over Sicily. The collection has several fine Greek and Roman works, including a large section of the Punic Temple of Himera, whose grinning lion heads stick out their tongues in celebration of a victory over Greece, and the Greek *Ram of Syracuse* (3rd century BC), notable for its realist sneer. The top floor features prehistoric cave carvings, and large Roman mosaic floors. *(P. Olivella, 4. Head away from the train station on V. Roma, and turn left onto V. Bara all'Olivella across from Teatro Massimo. ☎ 091 662 02 20. Open daily 8:30am-1:45pm, and T-W and F afternoons 3-6:45pm. L8000/€4.13, students L4000/€2.07, under 18 free.)*

LA FAMIGLIA Pin-striped suits, machine guns, and *The Godfather* are a far cry from the reality of the **Sicilian Mafia.** The Mafia system has its roots in the *latifondi* (agricultural estates) of rural Sicily, where land managers and salaried militiamen protected their turf and people. Powerful because people owed them favors, strong because they supported one another, and feared because they did not hesitate to kill offenders, they were the founders of a tradition that has dominated Sicilian life since the late-19th century. Since the mid-80s, the Italian government has worked to curtail Mafia influence. Today, Sicilians shy away from any Mafia discussion, referring to the system as *Cosa Nostra* (our thing). For more information see **Organized Crime,** p. 32.

PALAZZO ABATELLIS. Signs in P. Marina point toward this 15th-century *palazzo* (1495), which houses one of Sicily's most superb art museums, the **Galleria Regionale della Sicilia.** Dozens of religious panel paintings and sculptures from the Middle Ages through to the Baroque period, culminate with Antonello da Messina's unusual *Annunciation.* The massive and morbid fresco *The Triumph of Death* merits a room of its own on the lower level. *(V. Alloro, 4. From P.G. Cesare in front of train station, take V. Abramo Lincoln, then go left for 2 blocks on V.N. Cervello. ☎ 091 16 50 74. Open M-Sa 9am-12:30pm, Tu and Th afternoons also 3-7:30pm, Su 9am-1pm. L8000/€4.13.)*

CHIESA DEL GESÙ (CASA PROFESSA). Via Ponticello winds through a crowded neighborhood to this church, crowned by a green mosaic dome, colloquially called Il Gesù (1363-1564). Stucco conceals a dazzling multicolored marble interior and an almost surrealist depiction of the Last Judgment. The courtyard shows the effects of World War II bombing. Next to Il Gesù, the **Quartiere dell'Albergheria** droops with shattered buildings and bomb-blackened facades. *(On V. Ponticello, across V. Maqueda. Open M-F 7-11:30am and 5-6:30pm; Su 7am-12:30pm and 5-6:30pm.)*

OTHER CHURCHES. The famous **Santa Maria dell'Ammiraglio** ("La Martorana"), was built for an admiral of the Norman king Roger II. The Byzantine mosaics inside are the 12th-century equivalent of celebrity photos: Roger I stands with Jesus, and Admiral George admires the Mother of God. *(P. Bellini, a few steps from P. Pretoria. Open M-F 8:30am-3pm, Sa-Su 8:30am-1pm.)* Next door lies the **Chiesa di San Cataldo** (1154), whose red domes and arches give it the appearance of a mosque. *(Open M-F 8:30am-1pm and 3:30-7pm, Sa-Su 8:30am-1pm.)* Perhaps the most romantic spot in Palermo, the garden and cloister of the **Chiesa di San Giovanni degli Eremiti** (St. John of the Hermits) comes complete with fanciful bulbous pink domes designed by Arab architects. Gazebos and little fountains dot this vine-wreathed paradise. *(V. dei Benedettini, 3. Walk west from the train station on C. Tukory to Porta Montalto, and hang a right. Open M-Sa 9am-7pm, Su 9am-1pm. L8000/€4.13.)*

PUPPETS. The **Museo Internazionale delle Marionette** offers a playful glimpse at Sicilian culture. There are no small parts, only small actors. For three hundred years puppets have taken the main stage at this little museum, while their retired counterparts, clad in amazing costumes, manipulate from behind the curtains. Listen closely as the puppets tell you stories from days gone by of swashbuckling and dragon-slaying. (*Let's Go* recommends that if you actually do hear the puppets speak, seek help as soon as possible). Viewing galleries also display puppets of different traditions from India, Africa, Burma, China, Thailand, France, and Britain. *(V. Butera, 1. Follow signs from P. Marina. ☎ 091 32 80 60. Open M-F 9am-1pm and 4-7pm. L5000/€2.58, students L3000/€1.55. Demonstrations on request.)* Catch an authentic Palermo puppet show at Vincenzo Argenti's **Opera dei Pupi.** Three-foot tall armored puppets wail away at each other, fight dragons and behead saracens, reenacting scenes from the chivalric romance of Orlando Furioso. *(V. Pietro Novelli, 1, opposite duomo. ☎ 091 611 36 80. Shows daily 6pm require min. audience of 15. L15,000/€7.75.)*

GARDENS. Relief from Palermo's dense urban environment is found in the fresh air of the city's gardens and parks. The large and refined **Giardino Inglese** off V. della Libertà harbors many a picnicker under its shady palms and marble busts. During the summer, the park hosts free concerts. Down C.V. Emanuele toward the port, **Giardino Gaibaldi** features several enormous and strange banyan trees, whose limbs and roots seem to drip down from leaf to land. The large **Villa Giulia,** at the end of V. Lincoln from the station, is a Parisian-style park with white sand pathways, meticulous flower beds, and large fountains. *(All open daily 8am-8pm.)*

🔳 BEACHES AND ENTERTAINMENT

As part of Palermo's recent attempts to better its tourism, the city has established **Mondello Lido** as a free, tourist-only beach. All registered hotels have tickets for guests, which are good for the day and must be shown at the beach entrance. From Teatro Politeama, take bus #806 to the beach. Near the "Charleston" stop.

Palermo packs buses every weekend to seaside **Mondello**, a beach by day and playground of clubs and bars by night. Take bus #833 from P. Castelnuovo to reach Mondello. **Addaura** entertains the young jet-setters. Take bus #101 or 107 from Stazione Centrale to De Gasperi and then #614, 615, or 677 to reach Mondello.

Palermo's nightlife centers around bars that are hard to find and even harder to stagger home from. For information on cultural events and nightlife, pick up a copy of *Un Mese a Palermo*, a monthly brochure available at any APT office, or the far-from-redundant *News-News*. **Fuso Orario**, in P. Olivella, and **Champagneria**, a block from the Teatro Massimo, are home to the mob of young Palermitani that floods the street opposite Teatro Massimo every weekend night. **Candelai**, V. Candelai, 65, tends to pick up around midnight. It has one of central Palermo's few dance floors, with live, mainstream rock. The place is usually packed, so arrive early if you want some time on Candelai's three net-connected computers. (☎091 32 71 51. L8000/€4.13 per hr. Open F-Su 7pm-late.) **Exit** (☎0347 800 74 88 or 781 46 98), in P. San Francesco di Paola up V. Aragona from P. Verdi, has outdoor tables that serve a friendly, exclusively gay clientele.

Finish the night crooning Italian vocals in the quiet *piazza* at **Havana's** outdoor tables (☎091 320 608), in P.S. Onofrio. Follow tiny Vicolo dei Fiovenchi off V. Maqueda, just opposite the intersection of V. Maqueda and V. Bari. The crowd is older and more sedate than those in many of Palermo's other bars.

◪ DAYTRIPS FROM PALERMO: M. PELLEGRINO & USTICA

◪**Monte Pellegrino**, an isolated mass of limestone rising from the sea, is Palermo's principal natural landmark, separating the city from the beach at Mondello. Near its peak, the **Santuario di Santa Rosalia** marks the site where Rosalia, a young Norman princess, sought ascetic seclusion. When her bones were brought to Palermo in 1624, they ended a raging plague. The present sanctuary stands over the cave where Rosalia performed her ablutions; its trickling waters are said to have miraculous powers. The summit of Monte Pellegrino (30min. climb from sanctuary) offers a gorgeous view of Palermo, Conca d'Oro, the Aeolian Islands, and Mount Etna. *(Take bus #812 from P. Castelnuovo.)* The volcanic island of **Ustica** lies 36 miles off the coast. Settled first by the Phoenicians, then by pirates and exiled convicts, it features prime snorkeling and grotto exploration. **Siremar** runs ferries and hydrofoils to Ustica (see **Ferries**, p. 573).

CEFALÙ   ☎0921

Dominated by its grand *duomo*, Cefalù is a labyrinth of cobblestone streets curling around the base of Rocca, an enormous stone promontory. The city's love of the sea draws its aging *terracotta* and stone buildings right up to the water's edge and its people to the social *lungomare* (beaches). The Sicilian proverb "good wine comes in small bottles" captures the timeless nature of little Cefalù, whose paradisal qualities were featured in the Academy Award-winning film *Cinema Paradiso*. Be warned: Cefalù's charms do not come cheaply. The city's reputation as a beach resort and its close proximity to Palermo allow *pensione* to charge what they please (and more often, what you displease).

▤ TRANSPORTATION

Trains: At P. Stazione, 1 (☎0921 42 11 69). From the intersection of V. Roma, V. Mazzini, and V. Matteotti, take V.A. Moro. Station is 3 blocks up on the left. Open daily 6:45am-8:50pm. AmEx/D/MC/V. To: **Messina** (3hr.; 11 per day; L14,500/€7.49); **Milazzo** (2hr.; 7 per day; L11,500/€5.94); **Palermo** (1hr, 36 per day, L7000/€3.62); **S. Agata di Militello** (50 min., 16 per day, L6000/€3.14).

Buses: Spisa buses run from train station and the waterfront P. Colombo to 26 local towns for L2000/€1.03. Schedules posted in station bar's window and tourist office.

Taxis: Kefautoservizi (☎0921 42 25 54), in P. Stazione or near P. Colombo.

ORIENTATION AND PRACTICAL INFORMATION

From the station, **via Aldo Moro** curves downhill to the city's biggest intersection. To the left, **via Roma** cuts through the center of the new city. At the left, **via Matteotti** leads into the **old city**, changing at **Piazza Garibaldi** into **Corso Ruggero. Via Cavour,** across the intersection from V.A. Moro, turns down to the **lungomare.**

Tourist Office: C. Ruggero, 77 (☎0921 42 10 50; fax 42 23 86), in the old city. English-speaking staff has a vast supply of brochures, maps, hotel listings, and schedules. Open M-F 8am-2:30pm and 3:30-7pm, Sa 9am-1pm.

Currency Exchange: Banca S. Angelo (☎0921 42 39 22), near the station at the corner of V. Giglio and V. Roma. Open M-F 8:30am-1:30pm and 2:45-3:45pm. The **ATM** at the **Banca di Sicilia** (☎0921 42 11 03), in P. Garibaldi has 24hr. access.

Carabinieri: ☎112. **Municipal Police:** ☎0921 42 01 04.

First Aid: ☎0921 42 45 44. **Guardia Medica:** V. Roma, 15 (☎0921 42 36 23), in a modern yellow building in the new city, behind an iron fence. Open daily 8pm-8am.

Late-Night Pharmacies: Dr. V. Battaglia, V. Roma, 13 (☎0921 42 17 89), in the new city. Open M-Sa 9am-1pm and 4-8pm. MC/V. **Cirincione,** C. Ruggero, 144 (☎0921 42 12 09). Open M-F 9am-1pm and 4:30-8:30pm, Sa-Su 4:30-11pm. Call ahead in Aug.

Hospital: V.A. Moro (☎0921 92 01 11), at the intersection with V. Matteotti.

Internet Access: Kefaonline, P.S. Francesco, 1 (☎0921 92 30 91), where V. Umberto meets V. Mazzini. L10,000/€5.16 per hr. Open M-Sa 9:30am-1:30pm and 3:30-7:30pm. **Bacco On-Line,** C. Ruggero, 36, across from the tourist office. Would you like red, white, or rosé with your email? Slow connection gives time to decide. Wine store has 2 IBM computers in back. L5000/€2.58 per 30min. Open daily 9am-midnight.

Post Office: V. Vazzana, 2 (☎0921 42 15 28). In a modern concrete building on the right off the *lungomare,* 2 long blocks down from P. Colombo. Open M-Sa 8am-6:30pm.

Postal Code: 90015.

ACCOMMODATIONS & CAMPING

Cangelosi Rosaria, V. Umberto I, 26 (☎0921 42 15 91), off P. Garibaldi. Cefalù's only budget accommodation in the city. Private residence has 4 large, simply furnished rooms just off a dining room with communal fridge and TV. Separate sex bathrooms just down the hall. Reserve ahead. Single L50,000/€25.82; doubles L70,000/€36.15.

Hotel Mediterraneo, V.A. Gramsci, 2 (☎/fax 0921 92 26 06 or 92 25 73), 1 block left when exiting the station. 13 classy, well-furnished rooms boast heavenly beds, A/C, TV, and sparkling baths with hairdryers. Breakfast buffet included. Oct.-May singles L90,000/€46.48, doubles L120,000/€62; June singles L95,000/€49.06, doubles L130,000/€67.14; July and Sept. singles L105,000/€54.23, doubles L150,000/€77.47; Aug. singles L140,000/€77.47, doubles L200,000/€103.29.

Camping: Costa Ponente (☎0921 42 00 85; fax 42 44 92), 3km west at Contrada Ogliastrillo. 45min. walk or short ride on Cefalù-Lascari bus (L2000/€1.03) from P. Colombo. Swimming pool and tennis court. July-Aug. L11,500/€5.94 per person, L9500-11,500/€4.91-5.94 per tent; Sept.-June L10,500/€5.42 per person, L8500-10,500/€4.39-5.42 per tent.

FOOD

Several affordable *trattorie* in the old city beckon the hungry with sizzling Sicilian scents. Prices increase in the new city, however, and some appealing restaurants on the *lungomare* feature prices that are clearly a result of the view. Just off the *lungomare,* next door to the post office on V. Vazzana, a **MaxiSidis** supermarket sells all the basics. (☎0921 42 45 00. Open M-Sa 8am-6:30pm.)

▨**Trattoria la Botte,** V. Veterani, 6 (☎0921 42 43 15), off C. Ruggero, 2 blocks past P. Duomo. Intimate interior and candle-lighted exterior whisper of romance and history. Leather-bound menus overflow with *primi* and *secondi* from L9000/€4.62, but the friendly owner's family recommends the house special, *casarecce alla Botte,* a traditional Sicilian pasta with meat sauce (L10,000/€5.16). Cover L2000/€1.03. Open Tu-Su 12:30-3pm and 7:30-11:30pm. AmEx/D/MC/V.

L'Arca di Noé, V. Vazzana, 7/8 (☎0921 92 18 73), across from the post office. Crowded wooden booths docked among nautical maps, anchors, and ropes fill half of this popular nightspot, while a fully stocked bar and gelateria serve those on the run. Pizza from L7000/€3.61; *primi* from L8000/€4.13; *menù* L23,000/€11.88. Open M-F 6am-5am, Sa-Su all day. AmEx/MC/V.

L'Antica Corte, Cortele Pepe, 7 (☎0921 42 32 28), at the end of C. Ruggero past the *duomo*. Dine on Cefalesi cuisine in the columned interior or quiet courtyard. A/C. Pizza from L7000/€3.61; *primi* from L8000/€4.13; *menù* L23,000/€11.88. Open daily noon-3pm and 7pm-midnight. AmEx/MC/V.

Pasticceria Serio Pietro, V.G. Giglio, 29 (☎0921 42 22 93), a well-advertised first left from the train station when heading into town. 30 flavors of *gelato*, a dozen cakes, and piles of cookies make this sleek bar a palace of delights equal to the magnificent marzipan *duomo* on display. Open Sept.-July daily 7am-1pm and 3-10pm; Aug. 7am-10pm.

👁🌀 SIGHTS AND BEACHES

DUOMO. The grand *duomo* appears suddenly to those traveling the city's narrow streets. This dramatic off-white structure combines Arabic, Norman, and Byzantine architectural styles, a result of the diverse craftsman King Roger II hired for its construction in AD 1131. Legend has it that the king promised to build a great monument to the Saviour if he lived through a terrible shipwreck. Keen eyes will note that Roger carried the theme of survival all the way up to the crenellated towers, which are punctuated with firing outposts. Once a potential fortress, the cathedral now serves to protect the king's body. The *duomo*'s more famous and heavenly contents, however, are the enormous Byzantine mosaics covering the bowl of the apse. The great ▨**Christ Pantocrator** surveys with glistening calm all who enter the cathedral's walls. *(Open daily 8am-noon and 3:30-7pm. Modest dress required. If a woman's shoulders are not covered, she'll be handed a shawl, or the boot.)*

MUSEO MANDRALISCA. Stuffed alligator cases and ancient vases are presented with equal flourish in this museum, the chaotic collection of Baron Mandralisca. The 19th-century connoisseur amassed an impressive array of medieval and early Renaissance Sicilian paintings by anonymous artists, many of which are undergoing restoration. For every good painting, however, there are a few hundred seashells, a shelf of old books, and a half-dozen lamps of questionable taste. A 4th-century BC Greek *krater* showing a cartoon-like tuna vendor merits attention, but the collection's centerpiece is the ▨**Ritratto di un Ignoto** (Portrait of an Unknown) by Sicilian master Antonello da Messina. The image is inescapable in Cefalù, smirking at tourists from every postcard rack and hotel wall, but in its actual presentation is surprisingly fresh and lively, albeit small. *(V. Mandralisca, 13, opposite the duomo. ☎0921 42 15 47. Open daily 9am-7pm. L8000/€4.13.)*

ROCCA. The massive cliffs above Cefalù have always stood at the center of the city's history. They now offer extraordinary vistas and serene ruins. Medieval walls from long-abandoned fortifications lace the edges, while crumbling cisterns and ovens line forgotten avenues. Ancient foundations cluster under trees and lead to the monolithic **Tempio di Diana** (Temple of Diana). The nimble huntress's temple, surrounded by pines and overlooking the city and the sea, was used first as a place of sea worship and later as a defensive outpost. Morning is the best time for pictures, when the sun's direction does not dull the vivid colors of the city below. *(Accessible by the Salita Saraceni, a ½hr. hike up the side. From P. Garibaldi, follow the*

STICKS AND STONES MAY BREAK MY BONES, BUT WHIPS AND CHAINS EXCITE ME

As the home of the mythical giant Gargantua, Cefalù has a history of monstrous associations. Perhaps this is why the notorious English occultist and sadist Aleister Crowley (rhymes with "holy") chose to found his new "abbey" (nicknamed Thelema) here in 1920. "Do what thou wilt shall be the whole of the law" was the motto of Crowley and his followers. It was in Cefalù that the "magician," or the "Purple Sacerdote," as he liked to be called, practiced his particular flavor of sexual occultism. "All [sexual] acts are allowed, if they injure not others; approved, if they injure not self," he proclaimed from Cefalù.

When one of Crowley's students died in the 1920s, his widow claimed that her husband's death was caused by drinking cat's blood during a Black Mass in Thelema. Suffice it to say, Crowley and his followers were expelled from Italy in 1923. Thelema is known among students of the occult for the grotesque, demonic frescoes that cover its walls. Though the site is closed for the moment, the regional department of Cultural Resources promises to restore and reopen the abbey soon.

signs for 'Pedonale Rocca' from between the fountain and the Banco di Sicilia. The volcanic rock path is quite slippery when wet; use caution. Gates close 1 hr. before sunset.)

BEACHES. Cefalù's most attractive beaches, **Spiaggia Mazzaforno** and **Spiaggia Settefrati,** lie west of town on Spisa's Cefalù-Lascari bus line. Popular **Spiaggia Attrezzata** lies just off the *lungomare*. Crowded for good reason, Attrezzata has white sand, gradual turquoise shallows, and free showers. At the beach in Cefalù, seven stones protrude from the waves. Legend has it that seven brothers died here while trying to save their sister from pirates.

▶ DAYTRIP FROM CEFALÙ: THE RUINS OF TYNDARIS

*Tyndaris is a popular destination, but difficult to reach without **private transportation.** Sarri **buses** leave the train station in Patti 5 times each morning (L6000/€3.10 round-trip; schedule varies; ask at station and double-check return times with driver). Tyndaris can also, with effort, be reached on **foot.** Take the **train** to Oliveri-Tindari and hike 40min. uphill. Take 1st right from station, and bear left under the highway and right past a grove of lemon trees. At the green gate, turn left (following the white arrows). Finally, bear right when path forks. **Tourist office** in Patti, P.G. Marconi, 11. ☎0941 24 62 18. Office also at the site, V. Teatro Greco, 15. ☎0941 36 91 84. Both have maps and brochures about Tyndaris and information about performances. **Ruins** open daily 9am-1hr before sunset. L4000/€2.07, students L2000/€1.03. **Santuario** ☎0941 36 90 03. Open M-F 6:45am-12:30pm and 2:30-7pm. Sa-Su 6:45am-12:30pm and 2:30-8pm. Proper attire required.*

The ancient ruins of Tyndaris sit in majesty atop an enormous rock promontory. A view that stretches from Patti to Milazzo over the Aeolian Islands has made this site a valuable strategic position since the 4th century BC, and a popular tourist destination. The ancient Greeks first adopted Tyndaris as a refuge from the onslaughts of the Peloponnesian War. Excavated at the beginning of the 20th century, the site is in surprisingly good condition. A large **theater** is cut into the hill at one end of the town. Over the years the original stone seats have witnessed theatrical performances and gladiator fights, as well as the original Greek plays are still performed in front of the buildings during the summer. From behind the stage the **decumanus,** the main thoroughfare, passes through the center of town to the **Agora,** the old marketplace and town center. At right are the foundations of the **Villa Romana,** of which just a few columns and walls remain. Stylish mosaic floors whisper of the life once lived among its crumbling walls. The **Gymnasium (Basilica),** currently under restoration, retains many harmonious arches and columns.

The ruins of Tyndaris share their rocky perch with a more modern marvel, the **Santuario di Tindari,** erected less than 30 years ago for the **Madonna Nera** (Black

Madonna). Local legend has it that a statue of this Byzantine Madonna washed up on the shores of Tindari hundreds of years ago, and the current sanctuary stands on the site where the first church in her name once stood. The designers did not miss an inch when covering the interior with marble, gilt, pastels, sculpture, painting, and stained glass. Solemn statues ask visitors to turn off their cellphones.

AEOLIAN ISLANDS (ISOLE EOLIE)

Residents refer to this archipelago as *Le Perle di Mare* (the pearls of the sea), and each summer boatloads of visitors second the motion. Homer thought the **Aeolian** (or **Lipari**) **Islands** to be the second home of the gods, and indeed these unspoiled shores border on the divine. Sparkling seas, incomparable beaches, and fiery volcanoes all contribute to the area's stunning beauty. **Lipari,** the central and largest island, has ancient ruins, a bustling port, and one of the finest museums in Italy. Visit nearby **Vulcano** for bubbling mud baths and a sulfurous crater; **Stromboli** for spectacular colors and a restless volcano; **Panareab** for inlets and an elite clientele; and **Salina** for cliffs and luxurious vegetation. The more remote sister islands of **Filicudi** and **Alicudi** feature untouched wilderness and intriguing rock formations. Although pleasantly affordable in the off-season, the islands suffer an exponential rise in prices at the end of July and August. Those planning a summer excursion should make reservations no later than May.

Before traveling to any of the other islands, buy food at the **UPIM supermarket** on C.V. Emanuele in Lipari (see p. 587) in order to avoid dishing out L1000/€0.52 for a roll in the meagerly stocked *alimentari* or L30,000/€15.50 for dinner at a *pensione*. Bargaining is always helpful. Though Aeolian residents are charged three times less than tourists when buying hydrofoil tickets, *Let's Go* does not recommend asking a friendly local to purchase them. That would be breaking the law.

FERRY SCHEDULE

DESTINATION	TIME	OFF-SEASON	HIGH-SEASON
Vulcano	1½hr.	5 per day; L10,000/€5.16	3-5 per day L11,000/€5.68
Lipari	2hr.	8 per day; L10,500/€5.42	3-6 per day; L11,500/€5.94
Salina	3hr.	5 per day; L13,000/€6.71	2-4 per day; L15,000/€7.75
Panarea	3½hr.	3 per week; L12,300/€7.75	1-2 per day; L14,000/€7.23
Alicudi	4hr.	6 per week; L22,000/€11.36	W-M 1 per day; L22,000/€11.36
Filicudi	4½hr.	6 per week; L18,000/€9.3	W-M 1 per day; L20,500/€10.59
Stromboli	5hr.	3 per week; L16,500/€8.52	M-Tu and Th-Sa 1-2 per day; L19,000/€9.81

HYDROFOIL SCHEDULE

DESTINATION	TIME	OFF-SEASON	HIGH-SEASON
Vulcano	40min.	8-9 per day; L18,000/€9.3	15 per day, L20,000/€10.33
Panarea	2hr.	6-8 per day; L23,500/€12.14	7 per day; L25,000/€12.91
Lipari	50min.	9-11 per day; L19,500/€10.07	15 per day; L21,500/€11.1
Salina	1½hr.	8-9 per day; L24,000/€12.4	8 per day; L24,500/€12.65
Stromboli	2hr.	7-8 per day; L30,000/€15.5	7 per day; L31,000/€16.01
Filicudi	2hr.	4 per day; L31,500/€16.27	2-3 per day; L33,500/€17.3
Alicudi	3½hr.	4-5 per day; L40,000/€20.66	2-3 per day; L41,000/€21.17

▐ TRANSPORTATION

The archipelago lies off Sicily, north of **Milazzo,** the principal and least expensive embarkation point. **Trains** run to Milazzo from **Messina** (40min., 18 per day, L4500/€2.32) and **Palermo** (3hr.; L15,500/€8.01). **Giuntabus** (☎ 090 67 37 82 or 090 67 57 49) brings you directly to Milazzo's port from **Messina** (45min., M-Sa 14 per day, Su 1 per day, L5000/€2.58) and from the **Catania airport** (Apr.-Sept. daily 4pm, L16,000/€9.30). From the Milazzo train station, you can buy a ticket for the orange **AST bus** to the seaport (10min., every hr., L1200/€0.62). **Ferries** leave less frequently from Molo Bevellero in **Naples. Hydrofoils** *(aliscafi)* run regularly in late July and August from **Messina, Naples, Cefalù, Palermo,** and **Reggio Calabria** for twice the price of a hydrofoil. Rates vary from each destination; check with local offices.

Three hydrofoil and ferry companies service the islands, and all three have ticket offices in Milazzo on V. dei Mille, directly across from the docks in the port. Hydrofoils run twice as often as ferries for twice the price (and half the time). Off-season runs from Sept.-June 30. High-season is July-Aug. 31.

Navigazione Generale Italiana (NGI): V. dei Mille, 26 (☎090 928 40 91; fax 928 34 15), in **Milazzo**; V. Ten. Mariano Amendola, 14 (☎090 981 19 55), in **Lipari;** Molo di Levante (☎090 985 24 01), in **Vulcano;** and P. Santa Marina (☎090 984 30 03), in **Salina.** Sends ferries to the islands.

SNAV: (☎090 928 45 09), V. dei Mille, sends hydrofoils to the islands.

Siremar: (☎090 928 32 42; fax 928 32 43), V. dei Mille, sends both ferries and hydrofoils to the islands. Also has offices in Lipari (☎090 981 22 00) and in Naples (☎081 551 21 12) from which it services the Aeolian islands (see Naples, p. 484).

LIPARI ☎090

...a floating island, a wall of bronze and splendid smooth sheer cliffs.
　　—Homer

Centuries ago, wild-eyed pirates ravaged Lipari's shores. Today, boats and hydrofoils let loose swarms of equally ravenous visitors. Lipari is, and has always been, the most developed of the islands off the coast of Sicily. Because it is the largest of the Aeolians, however it was always the first to get burned, razed, sacked, and depopulated during 2000 years of invasions. You can hear the influence of the raiding civilizations in the local dialect, which is interspersed with French adjectives, Arabic nouns, and Spanish verbs. In the town, pastel colored houses and bright shops surround the base of a medieval *castello*, the site of an ancient Greek acropolis. From the busy port, crowds move to Spiaggia Bianca and Spiaggia Porticello, the most popular beaches, to splash idly in the waves and bask in luxurious sunshine. For those who prefer the colors of the surrounding sea and mountains to neon umbrellas and swimsuits, short hikes often lead to private beaches. Inexpensive hotels, luscious beaches, and one of Italy's best museums have made Lipari the ideal launching point for daytrips to the six neighboring islands.

▐ TRANSPORTATION

Public Transportation: Autobus Urso Guglielmo (☎090 981 12 62 or 090 981 10 26), V. Cappuccini, 9. Ticket office open daily 9am-1pm; tickets also available on the bus. Hits most spots on the island.

Bike/Moped Rental: ▧ **De. Sco.,** V. Stradale Pianoconto, 5 (☎090 981 32 88), at the end of C.V. Emanuele closest to the hydrofoil docks. Flamenco music and shiny scooters lined up showroom-style. 24hr. rental includes gas. Helmets provided. L35-50,000/€18.08-25.62. Nov.-Mar. L25,000/€12.91; Apr.-May L30,000/€15.50. Open 8:30am-8pm. June-Aug. MC/V. **Carbonara** (☎090 981 19 94), on C.V. Emanuele just a few steps away from De. Sco., offers 12hr. rental. July-Aug. L45,000/€23.24; Sept-June L30,000/€15.50.

Taxis: Ready and waiting at either port (☎0338 563 29 21 or 0339 577 64 37 or 090 988 06 16).

✳❷ ORIENTATION AND PRACTICAL INFORMATION

Two ports are on either side of the large rock promontory supporting the *castello* and **museum.** Restaurants, hotels, and shops are along or between the roughly parallel **Corso Vittorio Emanuele II** and **via Garibaldi.** V. Garibaldi runs from the hydrofoil port around the base of the *castello*, and is accessible by large stone stairs up the street. C.V. Emanuele is Lipari's main thoroughfare and ends at the ferry docks.

TOURIST, FINANCIAL, AND LOCAL SERVICES

Tourist Office: AAST delle Isole Eolie, C.V. Emanuele, 202 (☎090 988 00 95; fax 98 11 190; infocast@netnet.it; www.netnet.it/aasteolie). From the hydrofoil docks, take a right up V. Garibaldi for 200m, then turn left on V. XXIV Maggio, following the traffic. Turn right onto C.V. Emanuele—the office is 100m down on the right. The information hub for all 7 islands. Offices elsewhere are nonexistent, or they perform a disappearing act at the end of Aug. English-speaking staff offers a comprehensive color-coded booklet, *Ospitalita in blu*, in several languages. Pick up a map at any *tabacchi*. Open July-Aug. M-Sa 8am-2pm and 4-10pm, Su 8am-2pm; Sept.-June M-F 8am-2pm and 4:30-7:30pm, Sa 8am-2pm.

Currency Exchange: C.V. Emanuele is lined with banks and ATMs. **Banco Antonveneta** (☎090 9812 117; open M-F 8:20am-1:20pm and 2:35-3:35pm) and **Banco di Roma** (open M-F 8:25am-1:35pm and 2:10-4:10pm; Sa 8:25am-1:35pm) exchange money, as does the post office (cash only). ATMs are not common on the other islands—be sure to stock up here.

Books: La Stampa (☎090 98 11 282), on C.V. Emanuele near the port. 4 shelves of various novels in English. Open M-Sa 9am-2pm and 4:30-10pm. MC/V.

EMERGENCY AND COMMUNICATIONS

Emergency: ☎113.

Carabinieri: (☎112 or 090 981 13 33) in emergencies.

Ambulance: (☎090 98 95 267). **First Aid:** ☎090 988 52 67. **Night Doctor: Guardia Medica** (☎090 988 52 26), office 50m up V. Garibaldi from the waterfront, on the left under the Italian flag. Open M-F 8:30am-1pm; Tu and Th 3:30-5:30pm.

Pharmacies: Farmacia Internazionale, C.V. Emanuele, 128 (☎090 981 15 83). Open M-F 9am-1pm and 5-9pm. MC/V. **Farmacia Cincotta,** V. Garibaldi, 60 (☎090 981 14 72). Open M-F 9am-1pm and 5-9pm. AmEx/D/MC/V. Mini-computer screen on storefront window of every pharmacy lists the pharmacist on call 24hr.

Hospital: (☎090 988 51), on V. Santana, off the southern end of C.V. Emanuele. At end of C.V. Emanuele, descend the side street between scooter rental places and take a right up V. Roma. V. Santana is the 2nd left.

Internet Access: NetNet, V. Marte, 3 (☎090 981 24 62; www.net.net.it). With your back to water, turn left off the port and continue up to the church. Turn right on V. Mare. It's the 2nd door on the left. 4 computers. L7000/€3.62 for 30min., L10,000/€5.16 per hr. Open 9am-noon; afternoons by appointment. **Net C@fe,** V. Garibaldi, 61 (☎090 98 135 27), offers 2 computers and a cool atmosphere. L15,000/€7.75 per hr.

Post Office: C.V. Emanuele, 207 (☎090 981 13 79). From the tourist office, 40m up C.V. Emanuele to the left, in the building that looks like 2 stacked steam-pipes. Exchanges cash. Open M-F 8:15am-6:30pm, Sa 8:15am-1:20pm.

Postal Code: Lipari 98055; Canneto-Lipari 98052; all other islands 98050.

◤ ACCOMMODATIONS & CAMPING

Three steps down the swaying hydrofoil exit ramp and you will be swamped with offers for *affittacamere* (private rooms for rent). If you have not yet booked a room, especially in July and August, these are often worth checking out. Ask to see the room before accepting, and don't be afraid to show a bit of hesitation, as prices tend to drop a few thousand *lire*. Because many private rooms are not registered (and thus are technically illegal), it is always a good idea to politely **ask for your price quote in writing.** As the summer progresses, Lipari is increasingly invaded by tourists, and the island reaches its saturation point in August. Hotels fill almost instantaneously and owners raise their prices by as much as 25%. Make reservations far in advance, even for early July.

■ **Pensione Enso Il Negro,** V. Garibaldi, 29 (☎090 981 31 63), 20m up V. Garibaldi and up 3 flights. Painted tiles lead the way into 8 rooms with patio, fridge, A/C, and roomy baths. Elegant archways, blond wood furniture, and a location 3min. from the hydrofoil dock add class to comfort. Singles L70,000/€36.15; doubles L120,000/€62.

Casa Vittorio, Vico Sparviero, 15 (☎/fax 090 981 15 23). Take V. Garibaldi from the hydrofoil dock and make a U-turn around the first possible left. From the small alley, turn right at first chance onto Vico Sparviero. The Casa is the yellow building with blue window frames. If door is locked, continue to the end of the street and turn right. At the red iron gate, ring the top white button on the left for the owner. Spacious rooms are scattered among staircases in this sprawling *casa*. Rooms vary in size and style from intimate singles to 5-person penthouses. Top-floor communal kitchen and open terrace with an ocean view. May-July singles L30-40,000/€15.50-20.66; doubles L60-70,000/€31-36.15, with kitchen L80,000/€41.32.

Tivoli (Quatropani) (☎/fax 090 988 60 31 or 0339 263 08 76), V. Quartara, 17. Take bus to Quatropani and follow signs to hotel. Former newly-wed resort has 5 double rooms, 3 separate apartments, and the best views on the island. June L60,000/€31; July-Aug. L80,000/€41.32; half-pension L80,000/€41.32. Discounts for children.

Hotel Europeo, C.V. Emanuele, 98 (☎090 981 15 89). Convenient location at the center of C.V. Emanuele and near both ports almost makes up for the dizzying staircases. Small bright rooms have few furnishings, but comfortable beds. Top floor has external doors and terrific view of the city. Sept.-June singles L30,000/€15.50; doubles L60,000/€31. July-Aug. singles L55,000/€28.41, with bath L60,000/€31; doubles L110,000/€56.81, L120,000/€62.

Camping: Baia Unci, V. Marina Garibaldi, 2 (☎090 981 19 09 or 981 25 27 in low season; fax 981 17 15), 2km from Lipari at the entrance to the beachfront town Canneto. 10m from the beach. Amiable management and an inexpensive self-service restaurant Restaurant open daily noon-3pm and 7pm-midnight; Reserve for Aug. Open Mar. 15-Oct. 15. Mar.-May L11-14,000/€5.68-7.32 per person with tent; June-Aug. L15-27,000/€7.75-13.94 per person with tent.

🍴 FOOD

Legions of lovers have sprinkled sauces, garnished salads, and spiced meats with the island's *capperi* (capers), renowned for their aphrodisiac powers. The sweet local Malvasia dessert wine perfectly complements dinner. Unfortunately, eating cheaply on Lipari is something of a challenge. The *alimentari* (food stores) lining C.V. Emanuele are open daily and sell cheap fruit. Traditional dinners in Lipari feature the island's *capperi*, renowned for their aphrodisiac powers, on everything, followed by some of the region's sweet Malvasia dessert wine. Lipari's lip-licking love gets a little expensive, however, and the budget-minded may want to self-cater at the **UPIM supermarket,** C.V. Emanuele, 212, (☎090 981 15 87. Open M-Sa 8:30am-1:30pm and 4-9:30pm. AmEx/D/MC/V.) C.V. Emanuele is also lined with *fruttivendoli*, who sell their juicy wares late into the evening.

■ **Da Gilberto,** V. Garibaldi, 22-24 (☎090 981 27 56), has become famous nationwide for what may well be Italy's best sandwiches. Into the hot *panini* go any of the ingredients on Gilberto's shelves: prosciutto, capers, fresh and dried tomatoes, olives, garlic, mint, the kitchen sink, etc. Construct whatever you want, starting from L5000/€2.58. Gilberto also stocks everything needed for a complete picnic. Panini from L6000/€3.10. Open 7am-midnight or closing, 7pm-2am in low season. MC/V.

La Cambusa, V. Garibaldi, 72. Checkered tablecloths spill out into the street along with the voices of happy diners. The intimate *trattoria* is a family affair, service courtesy of the owner and his wife. Exceptionally tasty pasta from L8000/€4.32 earns raves from the regulars. Cover L2000/€1.03. Open daily 7-11pm.

SICILY

Il Galeone, C.V. Emanuele, 220 (☎090 981 14 63 or 981 26 35), close to the ferry dock. Outdoor dining on a shaded terrace makes for a mellow evening. Pizza, pasta, and all things Aeolian served by an attentive wait staff. Pizza from L7000/€3.62; *primi* from L7000/€3.62; *menú* from L7000/€3.62. Open June-Sept. daily 8am-midnight; Oct.-May Th-Tu 8pm-midnight. MC/V.

Kasbah, V. Maurolico, 25 (☎090 981 10 75), on a sidestreet connecting C.V. Emanuele and V. Garibaldi. She said goodbye for the last time and passed through the carved Arabic archways into the street. He remained behind at the tiled table in the garden, drinking sweet Malvasia (L4000/€2.07) alone and thinking "we'll always have pizza Casablanca" (L7000/€3.62). In the background, Sam played it again. Mellow jazz, that is. Cover L3000/€1.55. Open daily 7:30pm-midnight.

Pasticceria Subba, C.V. Emanuele, 92 (☎090 981 13 52). The archipelago's oldest *pasticceria* is considered one of Italy's best. Indulge in the heavenly *paradiso*, a lemon-stuffed dumpling topped with almonds. Pastries from L2000/€1.03. Open daily May-Oct. 7am-3am; Nov.-Apr. 7am-midnight.

👁 🎵 SIGHTS AND ENTERTAINMENT

Lipari's best sights, aside from its beaches, are all to be found in the *castello* on the hill between the ports. The gigantic fortress with ancient Greek foundations supports the medieval and 16th-century fortifications and enclose prehistoric ruins. A splendidly rebuilt medieval fortress dwarfs the surrounding town. It shares the hill with an archaeological park, the **San Bartolo church,** and the **Museo Eoliano.**

■ **MUSEO ARCHEOLOGICO EOLIANO.** Highlights of the collection include several gigantic *Liparite* burial urns, galleries full of Greek and Sicilian red figureware pottery from the 4th and 5th centuries BC, and the treasures of underwater exploration around the Aeolians. An entire building, the **Serione Geologico-Vulcanologica,** is devoted to the island's natural history. (☎090 988 01 74. *Up the stone steps off V. Garibaldi. Turn left at the church. Open May-Oct. M-Su 9am-1:30pm and 4-7pm; Nov.-Apr. M-Su 9am-1:30pm and 3-6pm. L8000/€4.32.)*

CHURCH AND ARCHEOLOGICAL PARK. All around the church and museum, ancient ruins beckon to be explored. Comprehensive charts show the process of excavation and the age of structures. The centerpiece of the park—and the best preserved site—is the theater, which still functions as a performance space. *(Both sites are across from the museum. Open daily 9am-1pm. Church L1000/€0.52.)*

🎵 ENTERTAINMENT

Lipari's summer excitement reaches its height (and surpasses the island's capacity) each August 24 during the **Feast of St. Bartholomew.** Processions, parties, and pyrotechnics take over the city in celebration. The quieter **Wine and Bread** festival in mid-November, in the Pianoconte district, features more delectable activities.

⚐ BEACHES, BATHING, AND BUMMING AROUND

Lipari is known for its beaches and its hillside views. Take the Lipari-Cavedi bus to Canneto, a couple of kilometers north, for the popular beaches at **Spiaggia Bianca** (White Beach) and **Porticello.** Spiaggia Bianca is *the* spot for topless (and sometimes bottomless) sunbathing. Protect your flesh—the pebbles are sharp and the sun is hot. From Canneto's center, the secluded, sandy coves flanking Spiaggia Bianca can be explored by renting one of the rafts, kayaks, or canoes that line the beach at V.M. Garibaldi (L6-8000/€3.10-4.32 per hr.; L25-35,000/€12.91-18.08 per day). The sand isn't as white now that environmentalists have decided to ruin everyone's fun and stopped the dumping of pumice into the sea. Just a few kilometers north of Canneto lies **Pomiciazzo,** where white pumice mines line the road. On clear days, spectacular views of Salina, Panarea, and Stromboli adorn the horizon. A few kilometers north at Porticello, you can bathe at the foot of the mines while small flecks of stone float on the sea's surface. Dive beneath the waves for polished obsidian. For the island's finest view, take the Lipari-Quattropani bus to the Pianoconte stop, and head over to **Monte S. Angelo.** The path to Monte S. Angelo is tiny and hidden; ask or you'll never find it.

From July to September, **Bus Tours of the Isle of Lipari** (L5000/€2.58) run from **Autobus Urso Guglielmo** (☎090 981 12 62) on V. Cappuccini. The best way to see the island's many beaches is a leisurely day aboard a rented **boat** from the hydrofoil port in Lipari. **Menalda Tours,** V.V. Emanuele, 247 (☎090 988 05 73; fax 988 01 59), runs excursions to **Lipari** or **Salina** (L35,000/€18.08), **Panarea** (L30,000/€15.50), **Stromboli** (L45,000/€23.24), and **Vulcano** (L20,000/€10.33). Times and frequency vary. For lower prices, try contacting privately with a fishing boat. Bargain for a decent price—L15,000/€7.75 per person per hour is fairly reasonable.

VULCANO ☎090

Stretch out and immerse yourself; the hand of the god Vulcan will hold you gently, transforming thoughts into bubbles of music and culture.
—A signpost in Vulcano

Thought at various points in the past to be the home of Aeolus, Hephaestus (Vulcan), and the gate to Hell, the island's four volcanoes now play host to 470 *vulcanarí* and some wild landscapes. Vulcano is dormant during the winter, but there is a population explosion during the summer when the weather heats up and the tourists come a' flocking. Black beaches, bubbling seas, and natural mud spas attract them like flies from all over the world. The largest volcano—Fossa di Vulcano—is crowded by any standard. Beware of another small inconvenience—some geologists think the gurgling volcano will burst its top within the next 20 years. For now, the great furnace lies dormant at the island's center. Its proximity to Lipari and pervading sulfur perfume make a day in Vulcano time enough.

▐ TRANSPORTATION

Ferries: N.G.I. Biglietteria (☎090 985 24 01), under a blue awning on V. Provinciale, just off P. Levante. To **Lipari** (30min., 2 per day, L2500/€1.29) and **Milazzo** (1½hr.; 3 per day; Sept.-June L11,000/€5.68, July-Aug. L12,000/€6.20).

Hydrofoils: SNAV (☎090 985 22 30), in a tiny cranny directly off the port, next to Cantine Stevenson; **Siremar** (☎090 985 21 49), at the top of an elevated stone walkway at the Porto Levante intersection. Both run to **Lipari** (7min., 20 per day, L4500/€2.32); **Milazzo** (40min.; 18 per day; L20,000/€10.33). SNAV makes the hike to **Palermo** (4hr.; 2 per day; L27,000/€13.94).

Buses: Scaffidi Tindaro (☎090 985 30 47), in front of the Ritrovo Remigio bar, just off the port on V. Provinciale. Infrequent buses run to Vulcano Piano (L3500/€1.81).

Taxis: (☎0339 600 57 50 or 0347 813 06 31), or at the stand in the port. Call **Centro Nautico Baia di Levante** (☎090 982 21 97 or 0339 337 27 95) (see **boat rental,** below) for 24hr. watertaxi service.

✴ ⃞ ORIENTATION AND PRACTICAL INFORMATION

Vulcano's casual atmosphere is marked—or, rather, unmarked—by an almost complete lack of posted street names and numbers. Large and frequent directional signs, however, make this pedestrian island easy to navigate. All ferries and hydrofoils dock at **Porto di Levante** on the eastern side of Vulcanello, one of four volcanoes on the island. With your back to the hydrofoil dock at the far left of the port, **via Provinciale** heads left toward the largest volcano and the **Gran Cratere.** Straight ahead is **via Porto Levante,** a semicircular road that loops through the center of town and reconnects to the part of the ferry side. From the hydrofoil docks, V. Porto Levante stretches straight until splitting in three directions at the small statue of Aeolus at rest. The pharmacy is straight ahead, while the famed **acqua-**

calda and **Laghettodi Fanghi** are on the right. When V. Porto Levante splits again, the left road will lead you to the luxurious black shore of **Sabbie Nere.**

TOURIST, FINANCIAL, AND LOCAL SERVICES

Tourist Office: AAST, V. Provinciale, 41 (☎090 985 20 28). Open May-Aug. daily 8am-1:30pm and 3-5pm. For info on **rented rooms** *(affittacamere),* call ☎090 985 21 42. Otherwise, get info from the Lipari tourist office (see p. 586).

Bank: Banco Sicilia (☎090 9852 335), 100m down from the port on V. Provinciale, has an **ATM.** Open M-F 8:30am-1:30pm and 2:45-3:45pm.

Currency Exchange: SNAV Office (☎090 985 22 30), at Porto di Levante.

Boat Rental: Centro Nautico Baia di Levante (☎090 982 21 97 or 0339 337 27 95) in a shed on the beach behind the Ritrovio Remigio bar, near the hydrofoil dock. 4-person motorboats (L150-200,000/€77.47-103.29 plus gas). Open 8am-9pm.

Scooter and Bicycle Rentals: *Noleggio* nemeses **da Paolo** (☎090 98 52 112 or 0338 139 28 09) and **Sprint** (☎090 98 52 208 or 0347 760 02 75), just a block apart at the intersection of V. Provinciale and V. Porto Levante, battle a constant rate war. May L25-30,000/€12.91-15.50; June L30-35,000/€15.50-18.08; July-Aug. L35-50,000/€18.08-25.62; Sept. L30,000/€15.50. Bicycles L10,000/€5.16. Sprint has a novelty tandem surrey bike for L15,000/€7.75 per hr.

EMERGENCY AND COMMUNICATIONS

Police: ☎090 985 21 10.

First Aid: ☎090 985 22 20.

Late-Night Pharmacy: Farmacia Bonarrigo (☎090 985 22 44), straight ahead from the port, at the far end of the *piazzetta.* Open M-F 9am-1pm and 5-8pm, Sa 9am-1pm. MC/V. For emergencies ☎090 98 53 113.

Post Office: down V. Provinciale; at Vulcano Piano. Open M-F 8:30am-1pm, Sa 8:30am-12:30pm.

Postal Code: 98050.

█ ACCOMMODATIONS & CAMPING

As the temperature rises, so do hotel prices, and the chance you won't find a room. Reasonable rooms are in abundance in winter, but call ahead in July and August.

▨ **Hotel Torre** (☎/fax 090 985 23 42), straight down V. Porto Levante from the hydrofoil docks, near the pharmacy. This centrally located hotel is a perfect retreat after a day at the nearby *acquacalda.* All 8 enormous rooms come fully-equipped with terrace, kitchen, TV, A/C, and grand, airy bathrooms. Many of the rooms offer extraordinary views. Cribs available. Extra person 35% more. Doubles Jan.-May L70,000/€36.15, June L80-100,000/€41.32-51.65, Aug. L140,000/€72.30. Solo travelers should seek discounts of up to L20,000/€10.33 in off season.

Pensione La Giara (☎090 985 22 29 or 0333 437 08 02), down V. Provinciale, on the way to the crater from the hydrofoils. Breezy A/C rooms with private patios contain adequately sized baths, TV, and candy cane-striped bedcovers. Includes breakfast served on open rooftop terrace. Apr.-May and Oct. L41,000/€21.17; June L53,000/€27.37; July L59-65,000/€30.47-33.57; Aug. L85-110,000/€43.90-56.81; Sept. L45-62,000/€23.24-32.02. Half pension L30,000/€15.50 more.

Camping: Campeggio Togo Togo (☎090 985 23 03), at Porto Ponente on the opposite side of Vulcanello's isthmus neck, 1½km from the hydrofoil dock and adjacent to *Sabbie Nere* (black beach). Showers and hot water included. In summer, the pizzeria is open and Internet access is available. Open Apr.-Sept. Reserve in Aug. L20,000/€10.33 per person. 5 double and 14 quad bungalows with TV, fridge and kitchenette Apr.-June and Sept. L35,000/€18.08 per person; July-Aug. bungalow L140,000/€72.30 for up to 4 people.

🔲 FOOD

The **Tridial Market** in the little white *piazza* off the Aeolus center, has all the basics, including an inexpensive sandwich counter. (Open daily 8am-1pm and 5-8pm.) For fruit and vegetables, there is an *alimentari* on V. Provinciale, toward the crater from the port. (☎090 985 22 22. Open 8am-1pm and 5-8pm. MC/V.) *Granitas* (crushed ice drinks) and *gelato* are in abundance at the port, but take a plunge off the main roads for a good full meal.

🔲 **Il Sestante-Ritrovo Remigio** (☎090 985 20 85), at end of hydrofoil dock. Popular with tourists and locals alike, this large bar offers hot and cold made-to-order sandwiches (from L4000/€2.07) and a beguiling terrace on the port to eat them in. The *gelato* is delicious, but skip it in favor of any of the delicious desserts from the largest selection on the islands. *Tiramisu* (L3000/€1.55), *cassata* (L4000/€2.07), *cannoli* (L2500/€1.29) and a dazzling display of marzipan fruit. Open daily 6am-1am.

Ristorante Il Castello (☎090 985 21 17), on Vulcano Porto, near *acquacalda*, has Sicilian specialties served cafeteria-style on sprawling terraces near the beaches. Pizza from L7000/€3.62. Self-service lunch L15,000/€7.75. Open June-Oct. daily noon-midnight.

Ristorante Faraglione (☎090 985 21 80 or 985 20 54). Whether it's your first or your 40th *granita* on the islands, cool down at this popular bar on the port between the hydrofoil and ferry docks. L4500/€2.32 buys any combination of 20 standard to surprising flavors, from strawberry and grape to onion, cucumber, and rose petal.

🔲 SIGHTS

Vulcano's natural wonders are perfect for casual thrill-seeking. The aura of danger coupled with ancient tradition makes for unusual and relaxing experiences.

🔲 **GRAN CRATERE.** Anyone visiting Vulcano for more than a day should tackle the one hour hike to the inactive crater, up a snaking footpath along the mountainside. The top rewards trekkers with unsurpassed views of the island, the sea, and the great crater itself. The hike takes you past bright yellow *fumaroli*, fuming noxious smoke, and across bizarre orange rock formations powdered with white moon dust. The hot smoke is reputedly safe to breathe, and is even thought to be good for the lungs by some locals. Between 11am and 3pm the sun transforms the volcano into a furnace, so head out in the early morning or late afternoon. Bring sunscreen, a hat, plenty of water, and sturdy climbing shoes. Portions of the trail are quite strenuous and difficult and should be approached with caution by the inexperienced. Obey the signs, and don't sit or lie down, as poisonous gases are heavy and tend to accumulate close to the ground. Though you risk taking an unpleasant spill, 🔲sprinting straight down the side of the volcano shaves a good 30 minutes off the time required for descent (and is quite a rush to boot). *(With your back to the water at the port turn left onto V. Provinciale, and follow it until you reach a path with "Cratere" signs. The notices point the way to a dirt turn off 300m down on the left.)*

LAGHETTO DI FANGHI. The water's murky grey-brown color blends right in with the volcanic rock formations that surround it, but the putrid smell makes this natural spa impossible to miss. Hundreds of visitors flock to the pit to spread grey goo all over their bodies for its therapeutic effects. Therapeutic or not, the mud is high in sulfuric acid and is radioactive. Remove all silver and leather accessories, and keep the actual mud away from your eyes. If some should happen to get in, *immediately* rinse them with running water and a few drops of lemon juice from a nearby restaurant. *(Up V. Porto Levante and to the right from the port. L1500/€0.77 per day.)*

ACQUACALDA. Double, double, mud and trouble, sulfur burn and ocean bubble. Just behind the mud pits, Vulcano's shoreline bubbles like a jacuzzi, courtesy of volcanic *fumarole* beneath the surface. You'll get used to the heat, but not to the sulfurous holes in your bathing suit; wear something you don't mind destroying. **Ugly bathing suits** (L20,000/€10.33) are available nearby.

BEACHES

If sulfur burns and radioactive mud don't sound so appealing, join carefree sun-bathers on Vulcano's best beach, **Sabbie Nere**. Black sands, blue water, white crests, and colorful swimsuits make for a rainbow of relaxation. To enjoy yourself a bit farther out to sea, hire **boats** from C. La Cava (☎ 090 981 33 00), on V. Porto Levante across from the *tabacchi*. (Near the statue of Aeolus.)

OTHER ISLANDS

STROMBOLI   ☎ 090

Stromboli has the Aeolians' only active volcano, a fact that keeps residents few (pop. 370) and visitors many. Though the great Stromboli is always active, the island itself is quiet until the summer. For those intimidated by the volcano's dangers, renting a boat is a great alternative method of visiting the island. The deluge is at its height from mid-June to September, making cheap accommodations almost impossible to find. In the off-season, many *pensioni* are closed and owners are reluctant to rent rooms for fewer than three nights at a time. Ferries are rare, so it is worthwhile to call ahead.

▐ TRANSPORTATION. Along the shorefront, **Siremar** (☎ 090 98 60 11; open daily 2:30-6pm), **SNAV** (☎ 090 98 60 03), and **N.G.I.** (☎ 090 98 30 03) run infrequent ferries and hydrofoils to the islands. Boat rentals are available at the port from the **Società Navigazione Pippo.** (☎ 090 98 61 35. Open only 9am-noon and 2-10pm. L70-130,000/€36.15-67.14 per 4hr. rental, 10am-2pm or 2-6pm, gas not included.)

◼▐ ORIENTATION AND PRACTICAL INFORMATION. On the calmer slopes of smoking Stromboli, the three towns of Scari, Ficogrande, and Piscita have melded into one continuation of whitewash known as the town of Stromboli. From the ferry docks, the wide *lungomare* is on the right, while the narrow **via Roma** heads toward the center of town from the corner where all the ticket offices are located. Twisting uphill to the left, the hike up V. Roma passes the following: the **carabinieri** station (☎ 090 98 60 21), the island's **only ATM,** and the **pharmacy** (☎ 090 98 67 13; open June-Aug. 8:30am-1pm and 4-9pm; Sept.-May 8:30am-1pm and 4-7:30pm; AmEx/MC/V), before finally reaching **Piazza San Vincenzo.** V. Roma then dips downhill becoming **via Vittorio Emanuele,** running past the **Guarda Medica** (☎ 090 98 60 97) to the end of town.

▐ ACCOMMODATIONS. Stromboli's hotels are booked solid in August, and your best bet may be one of the *affittacamere.* You should expect to pay between L30,000/€15.50 and L50,000/€25.82 for your room. Ask to see the room before paying, and don't be afraid to check for hot water and good beds. As for hotels, the best value is ▮**Casa del Sole,** V. Giuseppe Cincotta, off V. Regina at the end of town. At the St. Bartholomew's, take a right down the stairs and go straight down the alley. Large hostel-style rooms with antique beds and tables face a shaded terrace and communal kitchen. Private doubles painted in sea colors upstairs. Four separate bathrooms downstairs. (☎/fax 090 98 60 17. Apr.-May and Oct. singles L25,000/€12.91; June and Sept. L30,000/€15.50 downstairs, L35,000/€18.08 upstairs; July L35,000/€18.08; Aug. L40,000/€20.66.) Another option is **Locanda Stella,** V.F. Filzi, 14, on the left off C.V. Emanuele as you descend from the *piazza*. Large whitewashed rooms with blue doors look onto a communal, reed-roofed ter-razza with a sea view. (☎ 090 198 67 22; www.netnet.it/locandastella/index.html. All doubles. Apr.-May, Oct. L70-80,000/€36.15-41.32; June-July L80,000/€41.32; Aug. L140-150,000/€72.30-77.47.) More rudimentary is the **Pensione Roma,** which shares an address with Da Luciano restaurant. Escher-like stairs lead in all directions to small rooms, some with tiny baths, many with excellent views. (☎ 090 98 60 88. May-June singles L30-40,000/€15.50-20.66; doubles L70,000/€36.15. July-Aug. singles L60-70,000/€31-36.15.)

FOOD. Stuff your pack at the **Duval Market,** on V. Roma just before the church. (☎ 090 98 60 52. Open daily 8am-1pm and 4-9pm. AmEx/MC/V.) **Ristorante da Luciano,** V. Roma, 15, offers the delicious caper-spiced *pasta strombolana.* The terrace offers a tremendous view of the sea and the hulking Strombolicchio. (☎ 090 98 60 88. Pizza from L8000/€4.13; *primi* from L12,000/€6.20; *secondi* from L20,000/€10.33. Open daily noon-2pm and 6-11:30pm.) At the rosticceria **La Trattola,** V. Roma, 34, delve into the *pizza Stromboli,* a cone-shaped creation bursting with mozzarella, tomatoes, and olives. (☎ 090 98 60 46. Pizza from L7000/€3.62. Open daily 8am-2pm and 4-11pm.)

The plateau of **Piazza San Vincenzo** is Stromboli's geographic center, its highest point and its most happening 500 square feet (besides the crater itself). Each night around 10pm, islanders flock to **Bar Ingrid** (☎ 090 986 385; open 8am-1am) for drinks, *gelato* (L3000/€1.55), and conversation. The *piazza* is abuzz with voices, occasional singing, and half the town. The moon rising directly over the *piazza* is quite a sight, and from behind the church there's a great view of the *volcano.*

SIGHTS. At the **volcano** each evening, orange cascades of lava and molten rock spill over the slope, lighting the **Sciara del Fuoco** (trail of fire) at 10-minute intervals. The **Società Navigazione Pippo** (☎ 090 98 61 35), at the port, runs a boat trip for the very adventurous (1hr.; 10pm; L25,000/€12.91).

> ▌ **STOP IN THE NAME OF LAVA.** *Let's Go* does not recommend, advocate, or take responsibility for anyone hiking Stromboli's volcano, with or without a guide. A red triangle with a black, vertical bar means "danger."

An ordinance passed in 1990 made hiking the volcano without a guide officially illegal, and with good reason: not long ago a photographer was burnt to death after getting too close to the volcanic opening; in 1998, a Czech diplomat, lost in the fog, walked off the cliff's edge. So if such criminality is not your cup of lava, look into a trip with the island's authorized guides through the **Guide Alpine Autorizzate** (☎ 090 98 62 11), down a flight of steps across from the P. Vincenzo church. The hike (L35,000/€18.08) leaves from P. Vincenzo on M, W, Sa, and Su and by request at 5:30pm with a midnight return. Those who choose to ignore the law (feigning ignorance of the four languages on the warning signs) and head up alone can arrange to do the more dangerous descent with a returning GAA group. Hikers should take sturdy shoes, a flashlight, extra batteries, snacks, lots of water, and warm clothes for the exposed summit. Don't wear contact lenses, as the wind sweeps ash and dust everywhere. Excess weight can make for an unpleasant three-hour hike. During the day only smoke is visible, so plan to reach the summit around dusk to snuggle into a rock dugout and watch the brilliant lava bursts. Climbing shoes, daypacks, flashlights, and walking sticks can be rented at the GAA office. Helmets are also available; every two years someone gets hit by a piece of flying rock.

To reach the volcano, follow C.V. Emanuele from P. Vincenzo for a kilometer until you reach a large warning sign; bear right at the fork in the road. The path turns upward when a secluded stretch of beach comes into view and (after 400m) cuts between two white houses. Smart hikers take only the well-trodden shortcuts—anything else will lead to a maze of thick brambles and reeds. Halfway up the slope, the trail degenerates into a scramble of volcanic rock and ash; follow the striped red, orange, and white rock markings. Follow markings very carefully or you'll end up stranded in a landslide of loose volcanic ash, sand, and soil. The warning signs at the top ridge are sincere. At all costs, avoid climbing with heavy loads or in the dark. The risk of walking off the edge is greater during the spring and fall fogs. The most important rule of all: **when hiking down the volcano at night, use the same path you took up.** The professional guides' shortcuts are tempting but infinitely easier to get lost on. For an overnight trip (which *Let's Go* does *not* recommend), bring a sturdy food bag, plastic to place on the wet sand, warm clothing, and foul-weather gear for the frigid fogs that can envelop the peak.

Strombolicchio, a gigantic rock with a small lighthouse, rises 2km in the distance from the black beach at **Ficogrande.** The ravages of the sea have eroded the rock from 56m to a mere 42m in the past 100 years.

PANAREA ☎ 090

Panarea, the smallest of the Aeolian islands, has a reputation as an elite playground for celebrities. The *gliteratti* come to leave the world behind, but they bring their money with them. Panarea's reputed snobbishness and high prices keeps many budget travelers away, but the island's golden beaches and jeweled seas offer free tastes of *la dolce vita.* It's an easy daytrip from Lipari.

⚑ ☎ ORIENTATION AND PRACTICAL INFORMATION. Panarea is accessible by ferry and hydrofoil (See **Ferry Schedules,** p. 584). Its small size and relaxed attitude make Panarea a pedestrian island. Scooters are limited to the small window between 8-11am. The only other method of transportation here is the golf cart, many of which are owned by hotels. All directional signs are listed not in kilometers or miles, but in minutes by foot. Street signs are nowhere to be found, but for the sake of formality, **V. San Pietro** runs past Chiesa San Pietro and, along an undulating stone path to **Punta Milazzese. Banca Antonveneta,** up V.S. Pietro from the port and left at the first large crossing, has an **ATM.** The **post office,** on V.S. Pietro, past the bank and on the right, changes cash and AmEx traveler's checks. (☎ 090 98 32 83. Open daily 8:30am-1:30pm.) In an **emergency** call the **carabinieri** (July-Aug. ☎ 090 31 81; Sept.-June in Lipari ☎ 090 981 13 33) or the **Guardia Medica** (☎ 090 98 30 40).

⚑ ☐ ACCOMMODATIONS AND FOOD. Though expensive year-round, hotel prices skyrocket in August when rooms are solidly booked. During the rest of the year, the reasonably priced **Pensione Pasqualino,** which shares space and management with **Trattoria da Francesco,** has spacious rooms and a friendly management. From the port, turn right and follow signs up the stairs. (☎ 090 98 30 23. Breakfast included. Apr.-June L40-70,000/€20.66-36.15; July-Aug. L100,000/€51.65.) Half a block from the port, **Hotel Tesoriero,** on V.S. Pietro, has big rooms with tiled floors, each connected to a bamboo-shaded terrace with an ocean view. (☎ 090 98 30 98 or 98 31 44; fax 98 30 07; www.hoteltesorio.it. Breakfast included. TV, A/C, and bath. Mar. 15-June 15 and Sept. 9-30 singles L70,000/€36.15, doubles L90,000/€46.48; June 16-July 15 and Sept. 1-15 singles L90,000/€46.48, doubles L135,000/€69.72; July 16-Aug. 31 singles L140,000/€72.30, doubles L240,000/€123.95. MC/V.)

The **Da Bruno supermarket** is on V.S. Pietro by the post office. (☎ 090 98 30 02. Open July-Aug. daily 8am-9pm; off-season 8am-1pm and 4:30-9pm.) At the *panificio* next door to Da Bruno, locals line up for baked goods including *biscotti, foccacia,* and pizza slices. (Open Sept.-July daily 7am-1:30pm and 5-8pm; Aug. 7am-8pm.) Hold out for a filling *panino* (L3500-5000/€1.81-2.58) at **Ritrovo da Tindero,** on V. Comunale Iditella. Feast on huge salads for L8000/€4.13 and *cannoli* that ooze with fresh *ricotta* for L4000/€2.07. (☎ 090 98 30 27. *Primi* from L11,000/ €5.68; *secondi* L15-18,000/€7.75-9.30. Open Apr.-Oct. daily 8am-1am.)

◉ ♫ SIGHTS AND ENTERTAINMENT. From Punta Milazzese, Panarea's three famous beaches extend along the coastline. Gradually changing from rocks to sand, this trio gives a wide spectrum of Aeolian shores. Taking two rights from the center of town to **Calcara** (also known as **"Spiaggia Fumarole"**), you'll reach a beach near the thermal springs at **Acquacalda.**

Panarea lights up at night during summer, when pricey Bohemian cafes spill out onto the shorefront, with clientele lazing on oversized pillows and drinking champagne. Up the short *lungomare* past the bars, the **Raya Discoteca** sits right smack in the middle of Panarea's most drippingly posh hotel. The disco fevered come from as far away as Milan to party in the glass-walled, ceiling-less laser-beam paradise under the stars. (☎ 090 98 30 13. Open mid-July to Aug. daily 1-6am.)

SALINA
☎ 090

Though close to Lipari in both size and distance, Salina is far removed from its more developed neighbor. Untouched landscapes, quiet villages, and the most dramatic beaches in the Aeolian Islands make Salina a lush paradise. With its vast variety of plants and flowers, Salina's natural wonders equal those of the more boisterous volcanic isles. The island's most astounding rock formations are found at **Semaforo di Pollara**, the enchanting setting of Massimo Troisi's *Il Postino*. The lack of steady tourism has its downside, however, for there are few budget accommodations to be found, making Salina more suited to daytrips.

▣ TRANSPORTATION. From Lipari, Salina is accessible by **hydrofoil** (25min.; 14 per day; L10,000/€5.16) and **ferry** (4 per day, L5500/€2.84). Salina's main port is the **Porto Santa Marina**, but the smaller port of **Rinella** on the opposite side of the island also receives hydrofoils (at an additional 15min. and L1500/€0.77) and ferries (extra 30min., L1000/€0.52). **SNAV** (☎ 090 984 30 03) and **Siremar** (☎ 090 984 30 04) have offices on either side of the church of S. Marina, in front of the port. The island's blue **buses** stop in front of the church (monthly schedules posted at SNAV office), with 13 daily runs to Levi, Valdichiesa, Malfa, Pollara, Gramignazzi, Rinella, and Lingua (L2000-3500/€1.03-1.81).

▣▣ ORIENTATION AND PRACTICAL INFORMATION. Rent scooters from **Buongiorno Antonio**, V. Risorgimento, 240. Facing away from the hydrofoil docks, turn left up the curving road uphill. Turn left up the first side street past a row of parked scooters to reach the office. **Caution:** Salina's roads are extremely narrow, high, and riddled with blind curves and fast-moving cars and buses. Only those with experience should attempt to engage a vehicle with wheels. (Scooters L35-50,000/€18.08-25.82 per day; mountain bikes L15-20,000/€7.75-10.33. Open daily 8:30am-8pm.) In case of emergency, call the **police** (☎ 090 984 30 19). The **Farmacia Comunale**, V. Risorgimento, 111, is at the bottom of the street. (☎ 090 984 30 98. Open M 5:30-8:30pm, Tu-F 9am-1pm and 5:30-8:30pm, Sa 9am-1pm.) **Banco di Sicilia**, V. Risorgimento, cashes **traveler's checks, exchanges money,** and has an **ATM.** (☎ 090 984 33 63. Open M-F 8:30am-1:30pm and 2:45-3:45pm.) There is a **post office,** at V. Risorgimento, 13, which changes AmEx traveler's checks. (☎ 090 984 30 28. Open daily 8am-1:20pm.) **Postal Code:** 98050.

▣▣ ACCOMMODATIONS AND FOOD. Restaurants are crowded into Santa Marina, the town by the docks, but most accommodations are farther afield in neighboring towns. Lingua, 2km down the coast from Santa Marina, offers **Il Delfino**, V. Garibaldi, 19, whose breezy blue rooms are accented with hand-painted tiles. All rooms have bath. Reserve ahead for July and August. (☎ 090 984 30 24 or 984 32 98. Doubles L60-80,000/€30.99-41.32; triples L70-100,000/€36.15-51.65.) A few steps up the price ladder, **Pensione Mamma Santina**, V. Sanità, 40, offers first-rate rooms painted in traditional Aeolian colors. Guests mingle on the melon-colored terrace, and the enthusiastic owner makes everyone feel at home. Consider a half or whole pension--the owner/chef has been featured in *Cucina Italiana*. (☎ 090 984 30 54; fax 984 30 51. Singles L30-50,000/€15.50-25.82; doubles L60-100,000/€30.99-51.65, with bath L70-130,000/€36.15-67.14. Half-pension additional L20,000/€10.33; full-pension L40,000/€20.66. AmEx/D/MC/V.) Take the bus or aliscafo to Rinella for Salina's only true budget accommodations. **Campeggio Tre Pini**, V. Rotabize, 1, which has a market, bar, and restaurant. Terraced sites drop down to the sea. (☎ 090 980 91 55 or 980 90 41. Reserve July-Aug. L8-12,000/€4.13-6.20 per person, L20-25,000/€10.33-12.91 per tent.)

The menu at **Ristorante da Franco** promises "courtesy, hospitality, and quality" from "the best of nature." That is exactly what this family-run restaurant serves in the dining room and garden. The 15min. walk uphill works up a healthy appetite and rewards the intrepid with the best views in Salina. *Antipasti* and *primi* (from L15,000/€7.75) overflow with home-grown vegetables. (☎ 090 984 32 87. Open

June-Sept. daily 1-2:30pm and 8pm-midnight; Jan.-May closed M. AmEx/MC/V.) At night, **Ni Lausta,** V. Risorgimento, 188, crowds locals and tourists into the bar downstairs for quick drinks and the latest gossip. Evening diners come upstairs to enjoy *pasta modo mio*, an ever-changing original pasta dish, in the more relaxed garden terrace. (☎090 984 34 86. Open Apr.-Oct. daily noon-3:30pm and 8pm-midnight. (Restaurant only open for dinner.) As always, the cheapest way to eat is the cold lunch route; assemble a beach picnic at any *alimentari* on V. Risorgimento.

◪ **SIGHTS.** Seeing Salina's finest sight involves a harrowing hour-long bus ride from Santa Marina to the dramatic ◪**beach** at Pollara, which lies 100m straight down from the town's cliffs, in the middle of a half-submerged volcanic crater. The trip is worth every twist and turn. Black sand, crumbling boulders, and raked sandstone walls create the rough crescent of land that embraces impossibly blue water. To the far right, a natural rock archway bursts out of the water, sunning itself against the cliff. On the other side of the island, **Valdichiesa** rests at the base of **Monte Fossa delle Felci,** the highest point in the Aeolians. Trails lead from the town 962m up the mountain to superb vistas. Those not willing to climb relax at Malfa's luxurious beach, offering views of the *sconcassi* and huge sulfur bubbles.

FILICUDI AND ALICUDI   ☎090

Filicudi and its distant neighbor Alicudi are the best-kept secret of the Aeolians. Outside the summer rush, Filicudi is left entirely to its 250 inhabitants, though even in July and August the island is seldom found on the standard Sicilian itinerary. The lack of developed towns makes Filicudi ideal for outdoor exploration and hiking. A thick tangle of cacti, fruit trees, and flowers, climb up lush slopes and rocky terraces. The rewarding climb up Fossa delle Felci (774m) takes visitors to the rewarding view of La Canna, the impressive rock spike that bursts 71m out of the sea. Enchanting beaches and grottoes encircle the mountainous terrain. Some sandy stretches, including the Grotta del Bue Marino, lie in front of interesting caves. Exploration by water is also a great way to see Filicudi's charms from a distance. Contact **I Delfini** (☎/fax 090 988 90 77) in Pecorini Mare, a small town near the port, for boat, moped, and scuba diving rentals and information.

Even reaching accommodations in FIlicudi is an adventure. Filicudi has few hotels for the budget traveler. The two most affordable hotels are perched atop a cliff directly above the port. The island's one paved road reaches it eventually, but the most direct route is a steep, 20min. climb up the crumbling rock steps. Facing away from the water, the steps begin behind the SNAV office. **Villa La Rosa,** V. Rossa, is the island's social center, crowded day and night with locals and visitors alike. Twelve uniquely decorated doubles make up only a portion of this restaurant/bar/arcade/discoteche conglomerate. (☎090 988 99 65; fax 988 92 91; villalarosa@netnet.it. May-June L75,000/€38.73 per person; July 1-20 L95,000/€49.06; July 21-Aug. 31 L115,000/€59.39; Sept. L70-85,000/€36.15-43.90. Half-pension L30,000/€15.50.) The luxurious **Hotel La Canna,** V. Rossa, 43, offers exquisite views from its comfortable, airy rooms. All rooms have bath, A/C, and TV. Communal terracotta terrace, Internet, and a restaurant round out the hotel's amenities. (☎090 988 99 56; fax 988 99 66; vianast@tin.it. Singles L110-140,000/€56.81-72.30; doubles L130-160,000/€67.14-82.63.) In case of emergency call the **carabinieri** (☎090 988 99 42) or **Guardia Medica** (☎090 988 99 61). The **post office** (☎090 98 80 53) is uphill to the right of the port. Filicudi does not have an ATM.

EASTERN SICILY

MESSINA   ☎090

Messina is a transportation hub, as its breakneck pace serves to remind; better airconditioning and a duty-free shop would turn this fast-paced town into an airport.

The hubbub lets up only on the weekends, when the Messinese loll on neighboring beaches. Strangely, Messina's history is marked by disaster rather than glorious victory. The Carthaginians first razed the site in 4th century BC. Thereafter, legions of conquerors, from the Mamertines to the Normans to Richard the Lion-Heart, followed. Under Norman rule, Messina blossomed as a crusader port, and for 600 years it proudly sat as a bastion of civilization. After the 17th century, however, the economy dried up as the gods frowned upon the land: the city was devastated by the plague in 1743, demolished by an earthquake in 1783, bombarded from the sea in 1848, struck with cholera in 1854, slammed with earthquakes again in 1894 and 1908, and flattened by both Allied and Axis bombs during World War II. *Terremotto* (earthquake) is probably the most frequently uttered word within the city's boundaries. The earthquake of 1908 shaped the city skyline with buildings that hug the ground. The churches in Messina are most spectacular. The *duomo*, with its gorgeous artwork, is a must-see, while the clock tower, with a gallery of moving figures, may be the world's most allegorical timepiece.

⌐ TRANSPORTATION

Trains: Central station (☎ 090 67 97 95 or info 147 88 80 88), on P. della Repubblica. To: **Naples** (4½hr.; 7 per day; L41,800/€21.59); **Palermo** (3½hr.; 15 per day; L19,500/€10.07); **Rome** (9hr.; 7 per day; L57,000/€29.44 and less-frequent rapido trains L78,300/€40.28); **Syracuse** (3hr.; 14 per day; L17,000/€6.71); **Taormina** (1hr., 26 per day, L5500/€2.84). Trains to the west stop in **Milazzo,** the main port of the Aeolian Islands (45min., L4500/€2.32). Luggage storage available (p. 598).

Buses: Messina has 4 parallel and overlapping bus carriers.

SAIS, P. della Repubblica, 6 (☎ 090 77 19 14). The ticket office is behind the trees, across from the far left tip of the train station. To: **Airport** (1-2hr.; 6 per day; L13,000/€6.71); **Catania** (1½hr.; 9 per day; L12,000/€6.20); **Florence** (19hr.; 1 per day Su; L56,000/€28.92); **Naples** (22hr.; 3 per week; L49,000/€25.31); **Palermo** (1½hr.; 8 per day; L24,000/€12.39).

Interbus (☎ 090 66 17 54), has blue offices left of train station, beyond the line of buses. To **Giardini Naxos** (1½hr., 9 per day, L5000/€2.58); **Naples** (1 each Su; L39,500/€20.40); **Rome** (2 per day; L50,000/€12.91); **Taormina** (1½hr., 12 per day, L5000/€2.58).

Giuntabus, V. Terranova, 8 (☎ 090 67 37 82 or 67 57 49), 3 blocks up V. 1 Settembre, left onto V. Bruno, right onto V. Terranova. To: **Catania Airport** (Apr.-Sept. 4pm; L20,000/€10.33); and **Milazzo:** from Terranova (45min.; M-Sa 14 per day, Su 1 per day; L6000/€3.10).

AST (☎ 090 66 22 44, ask for "informazioni"). The province's largest carrier; their *biglietteria* is in an orange minibus across P. Duomo from the cathedral. They service all destinations including smaller and less-touristed areas all over Southern Italy and Sicily.

Ferries: NGI (☎ 0335 842 77 85) and **Meridiano** (☎ 0347 910 01 19 or 64 13 234), under the 1st pair of yellow cranes on the waterfront, 300m from the FS station. Both send ferries to **Reggio. NGI:** (40min.; M-F 12 per day, Sa 10 per day, Su 1 per day; L1000/€0.52). **Meridiano:** (40min.; M-F 15 per day, Sa 11 per day, Su 3 per day; L3000/€1.55.

Hydrofoils: From the waterfront wing of the central rail station, Messina Marittima, **FS** sends hydrofoils to **Reggio** (25 min., 12 per day, L5000/€2.58) and **Villa S. Giovanni** (30min., 3 per hr., L1800/€0.93). **SNAV** (ticket office ☎ 0903 640 44; fax 28 76 42), has offices in a blue building on the waterfront side of C.V. Emanuele, 2km north of the train station off C. Garibaldi. Hydrofoils to: **Aeolian Islands** (2hr., 3-6 per day for each destination from June-Sept.); **Lipari** (40min.; 6 per day; L32,000/€16.53); **Salina** (1¼hr.; 4 per day; L37,000/€19.11); **Panarea** (1¾hr.; 3 per day; L37,000/€19.11).

Public Transportation: Orange **ATM** buses leave either from P. della Repubblica or from the bus station, 2 blocks up V. 1 Settembre from the station, on the right. Purchase tickets (L1200/€0.62) at any *tabacchi* or newsstand. Detailed bus info on yellow-bordered signs outside the *autostazione*. Note that bus #79, stopping at the *duomo*, museum, and aquarium, can only be taken from P. della Repubblica.

Taxis: Taxi Jolli (☎ 090 65 05), to the right of the *duomo* when facing its entrance.

SICILY

ORIENTATION AND PRACTICAL INFORMATION

Messina's transportation center is **Piazza della Repubblica,** in front of the train station, home to the tourist office and headquarters for several bus lines. Along the waterfront perpendicular to the station runs the boat dock, **via G. la Farina** runs directly in front of the train station; beyond the highrises to the left, **via Tommaso Cannizzaro** leads to the center of town, meeting palm tree-lined **Viale S. Martino** at **Piazza Cairoli.** Enter P. della Repubblica from the train station and at the far right end begins **via Primo Settembre,** which intersects **Corso Garibaldi.** Corso Garibaldi runs along the harbor to both the hydrofoil dock and C. Cavour.

> **SAFETY FIRST.** Women should **not** walk alone in Messina at night, and no one should roam the streets near the train station or the harbor after 10pm. Stay near the more populated streets around the *duomo* and the university. Be wary of pickpockets and purse-snatchers, and keep money in a secure place.

TOURIST AND FINANCIAL SERVICES

Tourist Office: Azienda Autonoma Per L'Incremento Turistico (AAPIT), V. Calabria, 301 (☎090 640 22). The office is on the right corner facing P. della Repubblica from the train station. Well-staffed, and offers a deluge of maps and helpful info on Messina, the Aeolian Islands, and even Reggio Calabria. Pick up a map, and ask nicely for a mini Italian grammar guide. English spoken. Open M-F 9am-1:30pm, M-Th 3-5pm.

Currency Exchange: Cambio/Ufficio Informazioni (☎090 67 52 34 or 090 67 52 35), just inside the train station. Good rates and info on trains and buses. Open 7am-9pm. There are **ATMs** just outside the train station, to the right and at V. Cannizzaro, 24. There is a **Banco di Napoli** on V. Emanuele facing the port.

English-Language Bookstore: Libreria Nunnari e Sfameri, V. Cannizzaro, 116 (☎090 71 04 69), has 4 shelves of your high school reading list and English classics. Open M-F 8:30am-1pm and 4-8pm, Sa 8:30am-1pm.

Luggage Storage: Central station L7500/€3.87 per day. Open daily 6am-10pm (see p. 597).

EMERGENCY AND COMMUNICATIONS

Emergency: ☎113. **Police:** ☎113. **Carabinieri:** ☎112. **First Aid:** ☎118.

Guardia Medica: (☎090 34 54 22), V. Garibaldi, 242.

Late-Night Pharmacy: Farmacia Abati (☎090 71 75 89 for info on all pharmacies in town), Viale S. Martino, 39. Up V. del Vespro 4 blocks, then left, from the station. All pharmacies open M-F 8:30am-1pm and 4:30-8pm. Posted schedules show weekly late-night rotation among local pharmacies.

Hospital: Ospedale Policlinico Universitario (☎090 22 11), V.C. Valeria.

Internet: Stamperia, V.T. Cannizzaro, 170 (☎090 64 094 28. stamperi@tin.it). L10,000/€5.16 per hr. Open M-F 8:30am-1:30pm and 3:30-8pm.

Post Office: (☎0906 68 64 15), on P. Antonello, off C. Cavour and across from Galleria. Open M-Sa 8:30am-6:30pm.

Postal Code: 98100.

♦ ACCOMMODATIONS

Messina continues to be a fly-by, not a stop-over, on the travel itinerary. The handful of hotels the city does possess cater not to cost-minded travelers, but to businessmen with deep pockets. Messina's cheaper hostels tend to be in a shadier neighborhood near the train station; be extremely careful during the evening.

Hotel Mirage, V.N. Scotto, 3 (☎090 293 88 44). Turn left from the train station, pass the buses, and continue under the *autostrata* bridge onto V. Scotto. Mission-style simplicity in airy rooms with tall windows. Curfew midnight. Singles L40,000/€20.66, with bath and TV L65,000/€33.57; doubles L70,000/€36.15, L90,000/€46.48. MC/V.

Hotel Touring, V.N. Scotto, 17 (☎090 293 88 51), up one block from Hotel Mirage. Mirrors and faux marble-lined halls lead to simple rooms with dark wood furniture and armoirs. Midnight curfew. Singles L40,000/€20.66, with bath and TV L70,000/€636.15; doubles L70,000/€36.15, L120,000/€62; triples L90,000/€46.48, L135,000/€69.72; quads with bath and TV L160,000/€82.63.

Hotel Cairoli, V.S. Martino, 63 (☎090 67 37 55). From the station, 4 blocks up V. del Vespro and left 1 block. At the intersection of two main streets, this converted *palazzo* is deceptively large, with grand staircases and mini-greenhouse beyond the lobby. The small rooms are plain and minimally furnished, but come fully equipped with TV, A/C, and phone. Breakfast included. Singles L70,000/€36.15, with bath L86,000/€44.42; doubles L116,000/€59.91, L140,000/€72.30. MC/V.

🖸 FOOD

Ristorante and *trattorie* cluster in the area around V. Risorgimento, reached by following V. Cannizzaro two blocks past P. Cairoli. Messina is hooked on swordfish, whether baked, fried, or stewed *(pesce stocco)*. Creative chefs stuff eggplants and mix *caponata* (fried eggplant, onion, capers, and olives in a red sauce), producing sensual and nourishing feasts. The sinfully rich *cannoli* and sugary *pignolata* will fix any sweet tooth. The **STANDA supermarket,** P. Cairoli, 222, in the center of town, is a great place to stock up on the basics. (☎090 292 77 38. Open M-Sa 9am-8pm.) Fresh fruit and vegetables are cheaper and readily available on nearly every street. Messina may be large, but restaurants and nightlife are only beginning to flourish, as students continue to flock outside the town for clubbing.

▨ Osteria del Campanile, V. Loggia dei Mercanti, 9 (☎090 71 14 18), behind the *duomo*. Locals flock to the elegant dining room or the sidewalk tables for *linguini all'inferno marina* and other *cucina tipica messinese*. Superb wine list. *Primi* from L6000/€3.10; *secondi* from L7000/€3.62. Open Tu-Su noon-3pm and 7pm-midnight. AmEx/MC/V.

Osteria Etnea, V. Cannizzaro, 139 (☎090 67 29 60), near the university. Simplified art-deco rooms contain fancy tablecloths and signature plates that are eager to host delicious pasta and fish dishes from L8000/€4.13. Cover and bread L3000/€1.55. Open noon-4:00pm and 8:30-midnight.

Pizza e Coca, V.C. Battisti, N47 (☎090 67 36 79). Take V. Primo Settembre 1 block down from the *duomo* and turn right. The pizza (from L7000/€3.62) in this little cola-centered local hangout is especially good, and the *bruschetta* (L2000/€1.03) especially cheap. Open daily 7:30-midnight.

🖸 SIGHTS

Though Messina has lost many of its monuments to earthquakes, invasions, and bombings, the town features a number of great sights, many of which have been recently restored. Messina's wealth of churches, ranging from the Romanesque to the Baroque, cover the city and reveal both its religious fervor and an indomitable will to survive. Some of the churches on the outskirts of town, such as **Montalto,** offer sweeping views of the city and port.

PIAZZA DEL DUOMO. Bright flagstones and shady trees provide a relaxing respite from the bustling city that surrounds this central *piazza*. The great *duomo* dominates the square with an enormous sandstone face that can be blinding in the afternoon sun. The surprisingly long nave rolls past 14 niche sculptures of saints to arrive at a massive altar dedicated to *Madonna della Lettera*, the city's patroness. O *Il Tesoro* (The Treasury), a modern two-story museum, houses the church's most valuable possessions, including gold reliquaries, chalices, and candlesticks.

The highlight of the collection is the ornate *Manta d'Oro* (Golden Mantle), a special cover for the Madonna and Child in the church's altar, now on display for the first time in three centuries. The ■**clock tower** built in 1933 at the order of Archbishop Paino displays man's arduous ascension from a base being to a noble creature. The structure features an astrological wheel, a menagerie of animals, several biblical scenes, and Messina's legendary female heroes. At noon, a grand spectacle takes place as a creaky recording of Schubert's *Ave Maria* booms and the gigantic lion lets out a mechanical roar. Below the clock tower, mythology and local lore meet in stone at the **Fontana di Orione** (1547). Designed by Angelo Montorsoli, a pupil of Michelangelo, the intricate fountain glorifies Orion, the mythical founder of Messina. *(Duomo open daily 8am-6:30pm. Guided tours of Il Tesoro in English, French, and German available. L5000/€2.58, under 18 and over 65 L3000/€1.55.)*

MUSEO REGIONALE. Founded in the early 20th century in a converted mill, the museum houses artwork salvaged from the monastery of St. Gregory and churches throughout the city after the devastating earthquakes of 1894 and 1908. A series of galleries enclosing a quiet courtyard display the chronological development of the surprisingly rich Messinese artistic tradition. The collection includes everything from many medieval *Madonna and Childs* to an ornate Baroque carriage worthy of Cinderella. The most notable pieces are *The Polyptych of the Rosary* (1473) by local master Antonello da Messina, Andrea della Robbia's terracotta of the *Virgin and Child*, and Caravaggio's life-size *Adoration of the Shepherds* (1608) and *Resurrection of Lazarus* (1609). Inside the entrance, bronze door panels tell the story of the Madonna della Lettera for the ignorant, illiterate peasant folk and you. *(Down from the hydrofoil port on V. della Libertà. Take bus #8 or #79 from the station or P. Duomo to P. Museo.* ☎ *090 36 12 92. Open Oct.-May M, W, F 9am-1:30pm; Tu, Th, Sa 9am-1:30pm and 3-5:30pm; Su 9am-12:30pm; June-Sept. M, W, F 9am-1:30pm; Tu, Th, Sa 9am-1:30pm and 4-6:30pm; Su 9am-12:30pm. L8000/€4.13.)*

PORT. Messina's history and character largely centers on its naval prowess. The modern port is more than a place to catch a hydrofoil; it is a destination in itself. The impossibly blue waters are protected by the city's most important icons: the enormous **La Madonnina,** a 6m golden statue, watches over the comings and goings of the city from a 60m column across the water in the port's center; while on the city side, the pristine **Fontana di Nettuno** by Montorsoli graces the intersection of V. Garibaldu and V. della Libertà. The muscular marble god extends one arm to calm the seas and stands above the monsters Scylla and Charybdis. Locals crowd the sides of the docks for leisurely afternoons fishing and sunning, or lounge at the outdoor cafes. The port becomes dangerous during the evening and night, however, so be sure to make this a daytime visit.

▣ ENTERTAINMENT

The *Festa di Madonna della Lettera* (June 3) celebrates the city's protector. Parades throughout the town end at the *duomo*, where the *Manta d'Oro* is restored to the altar for one day per year. Messina overflows with sightseers and approximately 150,000 white-robed pilgrims during the nationally celebrated **Ferragosto Messinese** festival (August 13-15). During the first two days of Ferragosto, two huge human effigies and a giant camel are motored around the city in the *Processione dei Gianti* (Procession of the Giants).

MILAZZO ☎ 090

Ready, set, hydrofoil; Milazzo is more of an embarkation point than a destination. Hydrofoils and ferries set sail for the seven Aeolian Islands several times daily. If time is of the essence, you can be bused from the train station, dropped at the docks, packed onto a sprightly young hydrofoil, and skipping to the archipelago in just over an hour. If the islands's easygoing pace has already charmed you from across the bay, more infrequent (and inexpensive) ferries might grant an opportunity to take a load off and leave fresh in the morning.

⚟⚟ TRANSPORTATION AND PRACTICAL INFORMATION. Trains run to **Messina** (45min., every hr., L4500/€2.32) and **Palermo** (2½hr.; L17,000/€8.78). Milazzo's center is a 10min. orange bus ride from the train station (L12,000/€6.20). Giuntabus (☎090 67 37 82 or 067 57 49) runs **buses** to Messina (45min., every hr. 14 per day, L6000/€3.10). Both Giuntabuses and city buses arrive in **Piazza della Repubblica** at the center of the port. **Lungomare Garibaldi** runs the length of the port. Take a left down **via Crispi** and right into **Piazza Caio Duilio** and follow the yellow signs to the **tourist office,** P. C. Duillo, 20. (☎090 922 28 65. Open July-Aug. M-F 8am-2:30pm and 3-6:30pm.) Milazzo's **castello** in the old center is considered one of Sicily's best. Hourly guided tours run from 9am-8pm in summer.

⚟⚟ ACCOMMODATIONS AND FOOD. Milazzo has a surprising number of reasonably priced accommodations. **Pensione Cosenz,** V.E. Cosenz, 5, is out of the way but has excellent rooms with TV, fridge, and bath. Take V. del Sole from the Agip Station on Lungomare Garibaldi and take the fourth right onto V.E. Cosenz. (☎090 928 2996. Singles L50,000/€25.62; doubles L90,000/€46.48.) The **Hotel Central,** V. del Sole, 8, has 12 rooms with a cheery ambience. (☎090 928 10 43. Singles L40,000/€20.66; doubles L70,000/€36.15. Communal baths and TV.) If the Central doesn't suit you, **Hotel California,** V. del Sole, 9, is just across the street. A few lumpy pillows never hurt anyone. (☎090 922 13 89. Singles L30-40,000/€15.50-20.66; doubles with bath L60-80,000/€31-41.32.) **Campground: Riva Smerelda** (☎090 928 29 80) is out on Capo Milazzo, 6km out of town (take the bus from P. della Repubblica).

Milazzo is designed for eating on the go. Bars line the *lungomare* and fruit vendors set up along V. Regis in Piazza Natasi and at the intersection with V. del Sole. There is a large **supermarket** at V. del Sole, 34, a block away from the **Hotels Central** and **California.** Locals flock to **Biscotti Focacce Panificio,** V. Umberto, 41, for the finest bread in town. Take a right at the supermarket from V. del Sole, and left at the *piazza;* there's a yellow sign 200m down on the left. To relax in air-conditioned turquoise splendor, head to **Pizzeria da Tonino,** V. Manzoni, 4 (☎090 928 38 39). Thirty varieties of pizza (from L7000/€3.62) served in a wavy New Mexican-designed restaurant make for a tasty break from Milazzo's hectic pace.

TAORMINA ☎0942

According to legend, Neptune wrecked a Greek boat off the eastern coast of Sicily in the 8th century BC, and only one soul survived to climb ashore. He was so inspired by the spectacular scenery that he founded a city; Taormina was born. Historians, however, tell a different tale: the Carthaginians founded Tauromenium at the turn of the 4th century BC, only to have it wrested away by the Greek tyrant Dionysius. Regardless of its origin, Taormina is a city of unsurpassed beauty—mansions, pines, and flowers crown a cliff above the sea. Disoriented fanny-packed foreigners, hearty backpackers, and elite VIPs all come for what millions of photographic flashes and hyperbolic statements can't seem to dull: a panorama dizzily sweeping from boiling Etna to the straights of Messina.

⚟ TRANSPORTATION

Taormina is accessible by bus from Messina or Catania. Although trains from Catania and Messina are more frequent, the train station lies far from Taormina. Buses run from the train station to Taormina (every 30min. 6:50am-midnight) and Giardini-Naxos (M-Sa 6:50am-midnight, Su 9am-midnight).

Trains: (☎0942 510 26 or 515 11). At the bottom of the hill in Giardini-Naxos. To: **Catania** (45min., 35 per day 1:20am-9:36pm, L5500/€2.84); **Messina** (50min., 26 per day 4am-11:25pm, L5500/€2.84); **Syracuse** (2hr.; 17 per day 4:10am-9:36pm; L12,500/€6.46).

Buses: Interbus (☎0942 62 53 01). Ticket office open daily 6am-8:15pm. **CST** (☎0942 233 01) offers *Etna Tramonto,* a sunset trip up the volcano (June-Oct. M-W L80,000/€41.32). To **Catania** (M-F 12 per day 7am-6pm; Su 8 per day 7am-6pm; L6500/€3.36) and **Messina** (M-Sa 13 per day 6:30am-7:20pm, Su 8:50am, 12:30, 6pm; L5000/€2.58). Same bus runs to **Giardini-Naxos** and **train station** (dir: "Recanti" or "Catania"; M-F every 30min. 6:50am-midnight; L2500/€1.29). Also to **Gole Alcantara** (M-Sa 9:30am, 1:15, 4:30pm; Su 9:30am) and **Isola Bella, Mazzaro, Spisone** (M-Sa 14 per day 6:30am-7:30pm; Su 8:50am, 12:30, 6pm).

Moped and Car Rental: Autonolo "City," P. Sant'Antonio, 5 (☎0942 231 61), around corner from post office at the end of C. Umberto. **Scooters:** L45,000/€23.24 per day, L280,000/€144.61 per week. **Vespas:** L70,000/€36.15 per day, L455,000/€235 per week (18+, with Vespa license). **Cars:** L113-250,000/€58.36-129. 11 per day, L526-950,000/€271.66-490.63 per week. 21+. Must have a license for 1yr. Open May-Sept. daily 8am-noon and 4-8pm.

✴❷ ORIENTATION AND PRACTICAL INFORMATION

To reach the city from the train station, hop on the blue Interbus that makes the trip uphill (10min., every 30min. 7:45am-11:45pm, L2500/€1.29). Taormina's steep and narrow streets are closed to cars; all automobiles are shooed into a small lot at the base of **via Pirandello.** From the bus depot, the center is a brief walk left up V. Pirandello to **Corso Umberto I,** which runs the length of town. Beginning under a stone archway, the *corso* runs left through four principal *piazze.* Small stairways and sidestreets wind downhill to countless restaurants, shops, and bars. **Via Naumachia** leads downhill to **via Bagnoli Croci,** which continues to the public gardens.

TOURIST, FINANCIAL, AND LOCAL SERVICES

Tourist Office: AAST, P. Corvaja (☎0942 232 43; fax 249 41), off C. Umberto across from P.V. Emanuele. English-speaking staff provides several pamphlets but their standard map is useless; ask instead for the turquoise fold-out "SAT Sicilian Airbus Travel" map. Open M-F 8am-2pm and 4-7pm, Sa 9am-1pm and 4-7pm.

Currency Exchange: Dozens of banks line C. Umberto and V. Pirandello. **ATMs** are in great supply as are **currency exchange** offices, including **Cambio Valute,** C. Umberto, 224, right before P. Sant'Antonio. Open M-Sa 9am-1pm and 4-8pm.

American Express: La Duca Viaggi, V. Don Bosco, 39 (☎0942 62 52 55), on P. IX Aprile. Mail held for 1 month. Open M-F 9am-1pm and 4-7:30pm, Sa 9am-noon.

EMERGENCY AND COMMUNICATIONS

Emergency: ☎ 113 or 0942 537 45.

Police: ☎ 112 or 0942 232 32.

Medical Assistance: Guardia Medica (☎0942 62 54 19).

Late-Night Pharmacy: Farmacia Ragusa, P. Duomo, 9 (☎0942 23 231), posts the weekly rotation. Open Th-Tu 8:30am-1pm and 5-8:30pm.

Hospital: Ospedale San Vincenzo (☎0942 57 91), in P.S. Vincenzo.

Internet: Internet Cafe, C. Umberto, 214 (☎0942 62 88 39). L5000/€2.58 for 20min., L10,000/€5.16 per hr.

Post Office: (☎0942 230 10), on P. Sant'Antonio at the very top of C. Umberto near the hospital. Cashes **traveler's checks.** Open M-Sa 8:15am-6:30pm.

Postal Code: 98039.

▐ ACCOMMODATIONS & CAMPING

Taormina's resort-popularity makes cheap accommodations difficult to find. Many find Taormina's Sicilian charm priceless, but if your budget is tight, consider staying in the nearby Mazzarò, Spisone, and Giardini-Naxos (see p. 604). Hike down steep trails to Mazzarò and Spisone or take the bus; service stops around 9pm.

Pensione Svizzera, V. Pirandello, 26 (☎0942 237 90; fax 62 59 06. panki@tao.it), 100m up from the bus station. Pricey, but worth every *lira*. Magnificent sea views. Clean rooms with bath and TV. Breakfast buffet (included) sets up on garden terrace by the sea. Reservations recommended Aug. Open Feb.-Nov. and during Christmas. Singles L100,000/€51.65; doubles L160,000/€82.63; triples L180,000/€92.96. MC/V.

La Campanella, V. Circonvallazione, 3 (☎0942 233 81; fax 62 52 48), just around the bend of the middle road at the end of V. Pirandello. The hallways and lobby are cluttered with Sicilian memorabilia, but rooms are as tidy as can be. Singles L80,000/€41.32; doubles L135,00/€69.72.

Inn Piero, V. Pirandello, 20 (☎0942 231 39), near base of C. Umberto after gas station, in 2 buildings overlooking the sea. Pristine, small, white rooms. All 10 with bath. Reserve in summer. Singles L90,000/€46.48; doubles L145,000/€74.90. Half-pension L113,000/€58.36 per person required in summer. AmEx/D/MC/V.

Camping: Campeggio San Leo (☎0942 246 58), on V. Nazionale along the cape, 800m up the hill from the train station, in the shadow of the Grand Albergo Capo Taormina. Campground wrapped around the terraced cliff. Earthen sites and dazzling views. Take any bus from Taormina that passes the station (L2500/€1.29). Reserve ahead July and Aug. L8000/€4.13 per person; L12,000/€6.20 per tent; L5000/€2.58 per car.

⬛ FOOD

Taormina's restaurants are of consistently high quality but also offer consistently high prices. Even buying bread, cheese, and fruit can be expensive. Try **STANDA supermarket,** V. Apollo Arcageta, 49, at the end of C. Umberto, one block up from the post office. (☎0942 237 81. Open M-Sa 8:30am-1pm and 5-9pm.)

▨ Trattoria da Nino, V. Pirandello, 37 (☎0942 212 65), between the buses and town center. Trust Nino to guide you through extensive and delicious menu. The fish and pasta creations are the best in town. *Primi* L7-14,000/€3.62-7.23; *secondi* L9-18,000/€4.65-9.30. Student discounts available; lay your *Let's Go* on the table. AmEx/MC/V.

▨ Bella Blu, V. Pirandello, 28 (☎0942 242 39). Descend through a tunnel of purple flowers to a terrace dining room with seaside view. Waiters burst into song regularly and perform Sicilian classics on guitar. *Primi* from L7000/€3.62; *secondi* from L12,000/€6.20. Complete tourist *menù* L26,000/€13.43. Cover L2000/€1.03. Open 10am-3:30pm and 6pm until the last person leaves. MC/V.

San Pancrazio, P. San Pancrazio, 3 (☎0942 231 84), at the end of V. Pirandello. Crowded outdoor tables *piazza* attest to the high quality of the food. Pizza from L9000/€4.65; *primi* L9-13,000/€4.65-6.71; *secondi* L11-20,000/€5.68-10.33. Cover L2000/€1.03. Open W-M noon-3pm and 7-11pm. AmEx/D/MC/V.

Gastronomia la Fontana, V. Constantino Patricio, 28 (☎0942 234 78), up the hill (middle street, to the right of the archway) from the end of V. Pirandello. Follow the smell of rotisserie chicken uphill to this popular spot for people on the go. A variety of pizzas, *panini,* and savory snacks including *cipolline* and *arancine,* each L2-2500/€1.03-1.29. Open Tu-Su 11:30am-11pm.

⬤ SIGHTS

▨ GREEK THEATER. This almost perfectly preserved theater is Taormina's greatest treasure. The theater offers an unsurpassed view of Etna, whose sultry smoke and occasional eruptions can be more dramatic than the works of Sophocles and Euripedes combined. In ancient days, the 3rd-century cliffside arena seated 5000 spectators; today that number packs in for the annual summer-long festival performances of Taormina Arte. *(Walk up V. Teatro Greco, off C. Umberto at P.V. Emanuele. Open daily 9am-1hr. before sunset. L8000/€4.13, EU residents under 18 and over 65 L4000/€2.07.)*

DUOMO. Up C. Umberto, at P. del Duomo, this 13th-century cathedral, rebuilt during the Renaissance, takes center stage. The Gothic interior shelters paintings by Messinese artists and an alabaster statue of the Virgin Mary. An two-legged female centaur, Taormina's mascot, crowns the nearby fountain. *(Reopens Feb. 2002.)*

OTHER SIGHTS. Behind the tourist office, the **Church of Santa Caterina** protects a small theater, the **Roman Odeon.** Slip into the **Church of St. Augustine** in Piazza IX Aprile, now the town library. The short walk down V. di Giovanni leads to one of Taormina's most enjoyable and least visited sights, the **Villa Comunale.** These lush gardens look out over Giardini-Naxos below and Etna in the distance. A trek to the **piccolo castello** offers an escape from boisterous crowds. V. Circonvallazione, which runs parallel to and above C. Umberto, leads to a small stairway that snakes up the mountainside to the castle.

🎵🎧 ENTERTAINMENT AND BEACHES

While the wildest nights are spent below in Giardini-Naxos, Taormina also stays up well past its bedtime. Chic bars line C. Umberto and its tributary side streets. **Mediterraneo,** V. di Giovanni, 6, packs in a lively crowd, alternatively devouring crèpes and cocktails. By the time the packed dance floor closes, it will be time for breakfast at **Tiffany Club,** V.S. Pancrazio, 5 (☎0942 62 54 30). With Arabic tents and treats, **Cafe Marrakech,** P. Garibaldi, 2 (☎0942 62 56 92), seduces party-goers until 3am. A 30-minute jaunt down the hill leads to **Tout Va,** V. Pirandello, 70 (☎0942 238 24), an open-air club with good food and great views. **Shateulle,** a popular mixed club, sits directly behind Cafe Marrakech. (☎0942 62 61 75. Open July-Aug. 7pm-5am; Sept.-Feb. 5pm-2am; Mar.-June 9am-3am.)

Every summer from late July to September the city pleases crowds with **Taormina Arte,** an international festival of theater, ballet, music, and film. Performances attract the likes of Jose Carreras, Bob Dylan, and Ray Charles. (☎0942 62 87 49. Ticket office at C. Umberto, 19. Tickets L20-100,000/€10.33-51.65.)

Tourists and locals lounge on beach **Lido Mazzarò,** just below town. Shallow sparkling waters flow around the tiny **Isola Bella,** a national nature preserve, 100m off-shore. **Cable cars** (☎0942 236 05) zip from V. Pirandello to Lido (in summer every 15min., 7:45am-1:30am, L3000/€1.55). The island beach is just a 200m walk uphill to the right. The strong-stomached can travel the narrow, winding route to **Castelmola** and other nearby towns on buses. **Gole Alcantura** is a nearby haven of wonderful waterfalls, gorgeous gorges, and ravishing rapids. The Gole Alcantara office has a monopoly on tours. (☎0942 98 50 10. Entrance L8000/€4.13; wetsuit L15,000/€7.75.) Bring a towel, sunscreen, a change of clothes, and a pair of sturdy shoes for climbing the rapids. Restaurants and a bar are on the premises.

GIARDINI-NAXOS ☎0942

As any resident and dozens of signs will tell you, Giardini-Naxos was the site of the first Greek colony in Sicily (734 BC). Naxos enjoyed moderate success, reaching a population of 10,000 at its height. Choosing sides poorly in an Athenian-Syracusan clash in the late 5th-century BC resulted in the devastation of the city. The modern town is now less Naxos and more Giardini, with fertile slopes, shady palms, and wild flowers clinging to volcanic cliffs, and one long *lungomare*. The eastern coast's ultimate beach town, Giardini-Naxos swims all day and swings all night.

🛈 **PRACTICAL INFORMATION.** Only 5km away from Taormina, Giardini-Naxos shares a train station with its neighbor. **Interbus** runs frequently from Giardini to the train station and Taormina's central bus station (25 per day, last bus 11:30pm, L3000/€1.55). Signs throughout town point the way to the **AAST tourist office,** V. Tysandros, 54. (☎0942 510 10; fax 528 48. English spoken. Open M-F 8:30am-2pm and 4-7pm, Sa-Su 9:30am-1:30pm; in winter M-F 8:30am-2pm, 3:30-5:30pm, Sa-Su 9:30am-1:30pm.) In an **emergency,** call the **carabinieri** (☎113) or the **hospital** (☎0942 537 45). There is a **post office** at V. Erice, 1 (☎0942 510 90).

▐▌ ACCOMMODATIONS AND FOOD. As in Taormina, hotels in Giardini are often filled in August, but prices are better. Make reservations in advance. The beachfront V. Tysandros is packed with hotels, but they vary considerably in quality and price. The ▓**Hotel Villa Mora,** V. Naxos, 47, is set back from the *lungomare* promenade, with direct access to the beach. Ask for a room with a view. (☎/fax 0942 51 839; hotelvillamora@tin.it. All rooms with bath, TV, and fan; some with A/C. Singles L65-78,000/€33.57-40.28; doubles L110-140,000/€56.81-72.30. Half-pension L80,000/€41.32 required in Aug.) In the **Pensione Otello,** V. Tysandros, 62, watch your back while walking the small hallways to the bare rooms that lie on the beach. (☎0942 510 09. L60,000/€30.99 per person. Half-pension L80,000/€41.32.) Campers head to **Campeggio San Leo** in Taormina.

Buy staples at **Sigma supermarket,** V. Dalmazia, 31, down from the central bus stop. (Open M-Sa 8:30am-1pm and 5-10pm.) Central **Calypso,** V. IV Novembre, 267 (☎0942 51 289), serves Sicilian specialties. Sidewalk tables afford pleasant sea views interrupted by zipping vespas. (Pizza from L7000/€3.62; *primi* L6500-9500/€3.36-4.91; *menù* L20,000/€10.33. Open Th-Tu noon-4pm and 6pm-midnight. AmEx/MC/V.) **Angelina,** V. Calcide Eubea, 2, specializes in seafood. Found at the tip of Giardini-Naxos's curved port, the dining room has ocean views on two sides. (☎0942 514 77. *Primi* L8-10,000/€4.13-5.16; *secondi* L10-20,000/€5.16-10.33, pizza from L8000/€4.13. Open daily noon-2am. AmEx/MC/V.)

▣▐▌ SIGHTS AND ENTERTAINMENT. Excavations in the 1960s unearthed outlines of a **Greek city,** with walls built of solidified lava blocks. The two-room **Museo Archeologico** records the city's earliest days, and includes an inscribed ceramic cup, the earliest writing that survived from the colony. (☎0942 510 01. Open daily 9am-7pm. L4000/€2.07, ages 18-25 L2000/€1.03, under 18 and over 65 free.)

Beach by day, fluorescent-lit pub/promenade strip by night, Giardini-Naxos seems to casually lose the hours in between. Things light up around 11pm, as busloads of glitzed-up revelers disperse among pubs, restaurants, and flashy *discoteche.* The party starts 20m from the bus stop at pizzeria/karaoke bar **Mister Roll,** V. Jannuzzo, 31. (☎0942 65 30 87. Open daily 8:30pm-5am; in winter closed Tu.) Disco-happy folk should hang a left down to **Marabù,** on V. Jannuzzo. Follow back-lit palm trees and the neon blue cursive sign to this red-carpeted complex, complete with rotating techno, oldies, Latin, and international pop music. (☎0942 540 76. Live piano before 1am. Cover L25,000/€12.91. Open 11:30pm until morning.) Let your dancing shoes and inner child fly at **Discoteca Peter Pan,** V. Stracina, 6. (Cover L20,000/€10.33. Open May-Sept. daily 11pm-4am; Oct.-May Sa-Su 11pm-4am.) Farther to the left, a poorly lit but well trafficked road leads down to the all-night party of *lungomare* V.S. Naxos/V. Tysandros. It's an extra-sensory experience with bumping live music, wafting popcorn and cotton candy, whizzing pre-teen in-line skaters, and people, people, people.

CATANIA ☎095

With the smoking Etna looming above and a reputation as Sicily's crime capital, Catania is a city seemingly fraught with danger. Beneath the squalid veneer of sooty *palazzi*, however, Catania is elegant. Leveled repeatedly, most often by the nearby volcano, it has been rebuilt several times since its founding as a Greek colony in 729 BC. After the monstrous 1693 earthquake, G. B. Vaccarini recreated the city with his Baroque *piazze* and *duomo*. The virtuoso composer Vincenzo Bellini brought another type of harmony to Catania: the opera and his eternal arias.

▐ TRANSPORTATION

Flights: Fontanarossa (☎34 05 05). Take the *alibus* from train station or pay L35,000/€18.08 for the 15min. cab ride. 2 daily flights to Malta with **Air Malta,** V. Libertà, 188 (☎095 31 33 08; fax 31 65 58). Open daily 8:30am-1pm and 2:30-7pm. Round-trip flights in Aug. from L255,000/€131.70, plus L40,000/€20.66 in taxes.

Trains: P. Papa Giovanni XXIII (☎ 095 730 62 55). To: **Agrigento** (4hr.; 5 per day 5:55am-1:35pm; L18,000/€9.30); **Enna** (1½hr., 4 per day 5:55am-1:35pm, L8500/€4.39); **Florence** (12hr.; 3 per day; L75,000/€38.73); **Messina** (2hr., 27 per day 3:15am-10:40pm, L9500/€4.91); **Palermo** (3½hr.; 3 per day, 2:21, 4, 7pm; L21,500/€11.10); **Ragusa** (4hr., 1 per day 5:47am, L6000/€3.10); **Rome** (10hr.; 4 per day 8:25am-10:40pm; L65,000/€33.57); **Syracuse** (1½hr., 19 per day 5am-10:22pm, L8500/€4.39); **Taormina/Giardini-Naxos** (1hr., 18 per day 3:15am-8:30pm, L5500/€2.84).

Buses: All companies are on V. D'Amico, across the city-bus filled *piazza* in front of train station, behind the construction. Reduced service Su. **SAIS Trasporti** (☎ 095 53 62 01) to **Agrigento** (3hr.; 11 per day; L19,000/€9.81) and **Rome** (14 hr.; 2 per day 5 and 6:15pm; L65-75,000/€33.57-38.73). **SAIS Autolinee** (☎ 095 53 61 68) to: **Enna** (1¼hr.; 7 per day; L11,500/€5.40); **Messina** (1½hr.; 27 per day; L12,000/€6.20); **Palermo** (2¾hr.; 17 per day; L22,500/€11.62). **Interbus** and **Etna** (☎ 095 53 27 16), both to: **Brindisi** (8hr.; 2 per day 1 and 10pm; L65,000/€33.57); **Giardini-Naxos** (1hr., 12 per day 7am-7:30pm, L5000/€2.58); **Noto** (1½-2hr.; 6 per day 9:30am-5:45pm; L11,000/€5.68); **Piazza Armerina** (2hr., 6 per day 8:15am-7:30pm, L9500/€4.91); **Ragusa** (2hr.; 11 per day 6am-8pm; L12,000/€6.20); **Rome** (14hr.; 4 per week; L49-58,500/€25.05-30.12); **Taormina** (1¼hr.).

Ferries: La Duca Viaggi, P. Europa, 1 (☎ 095 72 22 295). Walk up Viale Africa from train station. Ferry tickets to **Malta** (high season L200,000/€103.27, under 25 L165,000/€85.22).

Public Transportation: AMT buses leave from train station. *Alibus* goes to airport and bus #27 to beach. Tickets (L1300/€0.67) valid for 1½hr. at *tabacchi* and newsstands.

◼ 🛈 ORIENTATION AND PRACTICAL INFORMATION

Via Etnea, running from the **duomo** to the **Giardini Bellini,** is Catania's chic main street. From the **train** and **bus stations** in the waterfront Piazza Giovanni XXIII, **Corso Martiri della Libertà** heads west into the city center, changing into **Corso Sicilia** in P. della Repubblica. C. Sicilia bisects V. Etnea in P. Stesicoro, under the watchful eye of a pigeon-covered Bellini monument. A right on V. Etnea leads to budget accommodations, fashionable boutiques, the post office, and the gardens; the **Teatro Bellini** and city **University** cluster around the *duomo* to the left. Although notorious for petty thievery, Catania can be conquered by the cautious traveler. At night, stick to the populated and well lit areas along V. Etnea. Be wary of staged distractions. For further information, see **Safety and Security** (p. 43) and **Women Travelers** (p. 70).

Tourist Office: AAPIT (☎ 095 730 62 33 or 730 62 22), on V. Cimarosa. From V. Etnea, turn on V. Pacini before post office and follow signs. English-speaking staff offers brochures on city, region, and Etna. Open daily 9am-7pm. **Branches** at station (☎ 095 730 62 55) and airport (☎ 095 730 62 66 or 730 62 77). Open M-Sa 9am-7pm.

Budget Travel: CTS, V. Ventimiglia, 153 (☎ 095 53 02 23), where C. Sicilia becomes C. Martiri della Libertà. Useful info on travel in Sicily, Italy, and beyond. Take a number and be prepared to wait. Open M-F 9:30am-1pm and 4:30-7pm; Sa 9:30am-12:30pm.

American Express: La Duca Viaggi, P. Europa, 1 (☎ 095 72 22 295) up Viale Africa from train station. Mail held for 1 month. Open M-F 9am-1pm and 3-6:30pm, Sa 9am-noon.

Emergency: ☎ 113.

Police: ☎ 112 or 095 736 71 11.

First Aid: (☎ 095 32 02 29). **Guardia Medica:** C. Italia, 234 (☎ 095 37 71 22).

Late-Night Pharmacy: Croceverde, V.G. D'Annunzio, 43 (☎ 095 44 16 62), at the intersection of C. Italia and C. della Provincia. **Crocerossa,** V. Etnea, 274.

Hospital: Garibaldi (☎ 095 31 16 66 or 759 43 71), on P. Santa Maria del Gesù.

Internet: Hi-Tech Cafe, V.A. di S. Giovanni, 230-236 (☎ 095 31 23 24). 3 computers upstairs with decent connections. L5000/€2.58 per hr.

Post Office: V. Etnea, 215 (☎ 095 715 51 11), in the big building next to the Villa Bellini gardens. Open M-Sa 8:15am-7:30pm.

Postal Code: 95125.

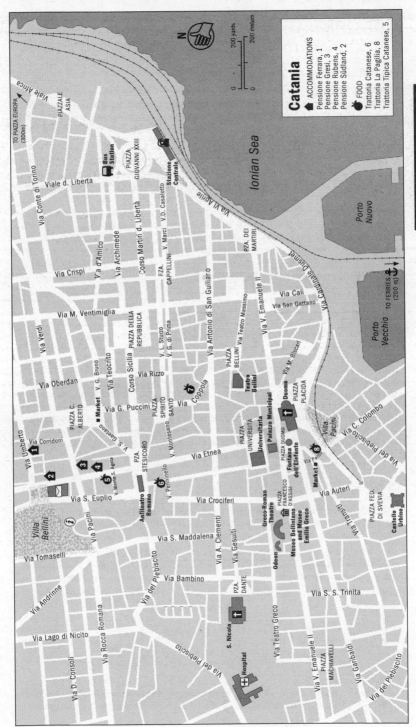

SICILY

Ionian Sea

Catania

ACCOMMODATIONS
Pensione Ferrara, 1
Pensione Gresi, 3
Pensione Rubens, 4
Pensione Südland, 2

FOOD
Trattoria Catanese, 6
Trattoria La Paglia, 8
Trattoria Tipica Catanese, 5

▌ ACCOMMODATIONS

Though the plethora of posh stores lining the streets suggests high *pensione* prices, many hotels along V. Etnea can be surprisingly affordable. Make reservations early for late-July through September.

▓ **Pensione Rubens,** V. Etnea, 196 (☎095 31 70 73; fax 71 51 713). Amicable owner's lifetime in hotel business shows in 9 well-kept, spacious rooms, all with A/C, TV, and phone. Mismatched furniture in welcoming common spaces gives a cozy shade of local color. Singles L50,000/€25.82, with bath L60,000/€30.99; doubles L65,000/€33.57, L85,000/€43.90; extra bed L25,000/€12.91. AmEx/MC/V.

Pensione Gresi, V. Pacini, 28 (☎095 32 27 09; fax 715 30 45), off V. Etnea before Villa Bellini and the post office. Hallways lead to bar, breakfast room, and reading room. A/C, TV, phone, minibar, and large bathrooms. Upper rooms superior. Singles L70,000/€36.15; doubles L100,000/€51.65; triples L120,000/€62. AmEx/D/MC/V.

Pensione Ferrara, V. Umberto, 66 (☎095 31 60 00), off V. Etnea across from the gardens. Clean, rosy rooms vary in noise and light levels, but are comfortable and appealing. Singles L49,000/€25.31, with bath L62,000/€32.02; doubles L75,000/€38.73, L94,000/€48.55.

Pensione Südland, V. Etnea, 270 (☎095 31 24 94; fax 31 13 43), opposite post office. Those with bath have little half-tubs and old TVs. Reserve a week in advance in summer. Singles L40,000/€20.66, with bath L55,000/€28.41; doubles L60,000/€30.99, L75,000/€38.73; triples L78,000/€40.28, L98,000/€50.61.

▐ FOOD

When Catanians ring the dinner bell, they enjoy eggplant- and ricotta-topped *spaghetti alla Norma,* named for Bellini's famous opera. Other local favorites are fresh anchovies known as *masculini.* Vendors at the **market** that extends from the end of V. Pacini (off V. Etnea) to C. Sicilia hawk everything from fist-sized figs to kitschy T-shirts. (Open M-Sa early morning-2pm.) Another market on V. Pardo off P. del Duomo specializes in fish and meat. The **SMA supermarket** is at C. Sicilia, 50. (Open M-Sa 8:30am-10:30pm.) **Bar Savia,** V. Etnea, 304, across from Bellini Gardens, displays *pizzete* and *arancini* and serves the city's best *granite di Gelsi.* (Open Th-Tu 8am-9pm.) The **Gelateria del Duomo,** across from the elephant fountain, serves 24 flavors from L2500/€1.29. The *latte di mandorla* (almond milk) makes a cool treat. (☎095 715 05 56. Open Su-F 5am-midnight, Sa 5am-3am.)

Trattoria Tipica Catanese, V. Monte S. Agata, 13 (☎095 31 54 53), off V. Etnea just after the Stefanel store on P. Stesicoro. Authentic Catanese charm accompanies the food. Vegetarian *primavera* draws "mmms." Cover L2000/€1.03. *Primi* L8-12,000/€4.13-6.20; *secondi* from L12,000/€6.20. Open daily noon-3pm and 7-11pm.

Trattoria la Paglia, V. Pardo, 23 (☎095 34 68 38). Lunch in the heart of the bustling market near P. del Duomo. Solo women may be uncomfortable in this area after dark. Tired of tomatoes? Trade red sauce for black with *spaghetti al nero di seppia* (with squid ink; L9000/€4.65). *Primi* from L8000/€4.13; *secondi* L8-12,000/€4.13-6.20. Open M-Sa 10am-4pm and 6pm-1am.

De Fiore, V. Coppola, 24/26 (☎095 31 62 83), near Teatro Bellini. Enthusiastic chef serves excellent pasta and homemade desserts to loyal regulars. Checkered tables are always packed. The *boccacina di ricotta* (pastry with ricotta) melts in your mouth. *Primi* and *secondi* from L8000/€4.13. Open M-Sa 11am-midnight. AmEx/MC/V.

Trattoria Catanese, V. Penninello, 34 (☎095 32 24 61), off V. Etnea near the amphitheater. Family-run restaurant. Variety of fish and Catanese cuisine for over 50 years. *Primi* L8-15,000/€4.13-7.75; *secondi* L10-15,000/€5.16-7.75. Open M-Sa 9am-10pm.

BEWARE THE ANIMAL SPIRITS! According to Catanian legend, each of the city's many animal fountains is inhabited by an animal spirit. Anyone who falls asleep by one of these fountains will lose his soul to the resident animal spirit and never wake up. *Let's Go* does not recommend losing your soul to a resident animal spirit, so nap elsewhere.

◐ SIGHTS

PIAZZA DEL DUOMO. In P. del Duomo, Giovan Battista Vaccarini's little lava **Fontana dell'Elefante** (Elephant Fountain; 1736) commands the city's attention. Vaccarini carved his elephant (the symbol of the city) without visible testicles. When the statue was unveiled, horrified Catanian men, who concluded that this omission was an attack on their virility, demanded corrective measures. Vaccarini's acquiescence was, um, monumental. Residents claim that visitors may attain citizenship by smooching the elephant's tush, but the height of the pachyderm's backside precludes such aspirations. The other buildings on the *piazza*, the 18th-century **Palazzo del Municipio** on the left and the former **Seminario dei Chierici** on the right, are striped black and white to mirror the *duomo*'s side.

DUOMO. Restoration in 1950 revealed glimpses of the *duomo's* interior before its Baroque makeover. Teams discovered stumps of old columns and tall, pointed arches of the original three apses. In the Norman **Cappella della Madonna**, on the right, every surface sparkles with precious metals surrounding a beautiful Roman sarcophagus and a 15th-century statue of the Virgin Mary. Nine meters from the chapel, the body of Catania's beloved priest, the Beato Cardinal Dusmet, lies with his bronze head and bony fingers protruding from his vestments. To the right as you enter through the main door is **Bellini's tomb,** guarded by a life-size marble angel. The words and music from *Sonnambula,* one of the composer's four principal works, are inscribed above the tomb and translate as "Ah, I didn't think I'd see you wilt so soon, flower." *(Modest dress required.)*

OTHER SIGHTS. Uphill from P. del Duomo lies the entrance to the **Greco-Roman Theater,** built in 415 BC. Behind the theater is the similar but smaller **Odeon,** with an entrance around the back. Mt. Etna's 1669 eruption coated the marble of both theaters in lava. *(V.V. Emanuele, 266. Open daily 9am-1hr. before sunset. Free.)* The centerpiece of Catania's restoration efforts rests just up V. Etnea. The **Bellini Gardens** sprawl over several small hills, around tiny ponds, and through miniature forests. Below an elegant Victorian bandstand, the day's date is replanted daily. Sunday afternoons find half the city strolling here with *gelato* in hand. A few blocks away in P. Stesicoro, the ruins of a 2nd-century AD **Roman amphitheater** have been integrated into the surrounding hustle and bustle. Below street level, the amphitheater is in good condition, with its gladiator tunnels still visible.

♫ ENTERTAINMENT

The **Teatro Massimo (Bellini)** mesmerizes audiences with opera and concerts. Sink into plush red seats during symphony season (Sept.), or wait for the thrill of the opera (Oct.-June). Student discounts are available for all tickets; contact the tourist office. (☎ 095 71 50 921. Box office open M-F 9:30am-12:30pm, Tu-F 5-7pm.) The AAPIT's free monthly bulletin, *Lapis,* available at bars and the tourist office, details Catania's hot nightlife, movies, concerts, and festivals.

Participants in the nightly *passeggiata* promenade around P. del Duomo and swarm near Teatro Bellini. Cafes liven up on weekends, drawing a sometimes raucous crowd. Local university students, urban thirty-somethings, and eager travelers all enjoy the bounty of drinking holes that fill this area. **Mythical Pub,** V. Michele Rapisardi, 8, in the shadow of Teatro Bellini, is where Catania's beautiful people watch one another on weekend nights. (Imaginative cocktails L7000/€3.62. Open

9pm.) From the *centro*, locals drive to the dance floor of **Banacher,** V. XXI Aprile S.S., 114, a 15min. taxi ride from Catania. Lights capture dancing crowds until 5am at what is reputed to be Europe's largest outdoor *discoteca*. (☎095 27 12 57. Cover L15,000/€7.75. Open daily 10pm-4am.) Weekend summer crowds also scooter 20min. away to the nightly destination of *passagiate*, seaside bars, and general mayhem known as **Aci Castello.** This side of Catania's coast is far from the city chaos, but it isn't out of reach of Etna's fury; huge black boulders thrown from boiling Etna line the jagged shore.

Catania's biggest feast day is that of **Saint Agata,** the city's patron saint. The first five days of February are saved from winter gloom by a non-stop fireworks display and partying. The pleasant but crowded beach **La Plaja** has a view of a nearby power plant (bus #27; June-Sept. #D). Farther from the port is the better **La Scogli-era,** with fiery cliffs and a bathing area (30min., bus #34 from P. del Duomo).

▓ DAYTRIP FROM CATANIA: MOUNT ETNA

An AST bus leaves from Catania's central train station at 8:30am for Rifugio Sapienza. The bus returns to Catania at 4:45pm (times subject to change; round-trip L6900/€3.56).

At 3350m, Mt. Etna is one of the world's largest active volcanoes and the tallest in Europe. The Greek poet Hesiod envisioned Etna as the home of Typhon, the last monster conceived by Earth to fight the gods before the dawn of the human race. Apparently Typhon isn't done yet; a 1985 eruption destroyed much of the summit tourist station. Increasingly frequent activity in 1999 and 2000 led to an eruption in late July of 2001, sending lava rolling down the hillside at 100m per hour.

From Sapienza (1900m), where the AST bus stops, the hike up to **Torre del Filosofo** (Philosopher's Tower; 2920m) and back takes five hours. From here, the looming peaks of Etna's craters and their rising steam are in full view. Anyone wearing sturdy shoes can safely maneuver around the crater in front of the parking area for a 30min. taste of the peaks. An expensive cable-car service runs to 2500m (daily 9am-4pm, last return 4:30pm; L16,000/€8.26, under 10 L8000/€4.13). To climb farther (2950m), a jeep and guide are necessary (L62,000/€32.02).

From the Philosopher's Tower, a two-hour hike leads to the **craters** themselves. While the view of the hardened lava, huge boulders, and unearthly craters is incredible, the trail is so difficult and the volcanic activity so unpredictable that all guided tours have been suspended. Eleven tourists died several years ago when one of the craters erupted unexpectedly. Those who brave the trip should take precautions; notify someone when you leave, don't go alone, carry water, and bring warm clothing as winds are ferocious, and even in mid-July pockets of snow remain. Returning from the tower, you will pass the **Valle de Bove,** Etna's original crater. For tour information, call **CIT,** C. Umberto, 101 (☎0942 233 01) or **Gruppo Guide Alpine,** V. Etna, 49 (☎095 53 98 82). **SAT** (☎0942 24 653; www.sat-group.it) operates day-long tours from Taormina. (M 8:30am. L45,000/€23.24 per person.) In an **emergency,** call ☎0942 53 17 77.

CENTRAL SICILY

ENNA   ☎0935

Enna, *l'ombelico della Sicilia* (the navel of Sicily), is far more charming than its ancient nickname implies. Stone streets curve up and down arriving at stunning vistas. Ennesi enjoying their evening *passegiate* occupy the intimate *piazze* and simple churches that rest behind every corner. The hilltop city's remote location in the island's center and the popularity of distant beaches have isolated Enna from the tourist circuit for years, but the great fortress town is not impenetrable to visitors. The voyage inland travels through one of the most beautiful, though poorest, of Sicily's provinces. Golden grain fields climbing craggy hillsides stretch as far as the eye can see, even from Enna's 948m heights.

TRANSPORTATION

Enna is serviced by both buses and trains, but arriving by bus saves you the 8km uphill hike from the train station.

Trains: (☎0935 50 09 10). Buses connect station to town center (M-Sa 11 per day 6:50am-8:55pm, L2500/€1.29). Schedule posted in station. To: **Agrigento** (7:12, 9:50am, 2:59pm; L9800/€5.06); **Catania** (1hr., 9 per day 6:17am-7:55pm, L7200/€3.72); **Palermo** (2hr.; 11am, 3:58, 5:17, 8:19pm; L12,700/€6.56).

Buses: All buses depart from the *autostazione* on V. Diaz, a short walk uphill from P. Matteotti. **Interbus** (☎0935 50 23 90) and **SAIS** (☎0935 50 09 02) are under one roof, with an additional Interbus office on V. Roma by the tourist office. To: **Catania** (2¼hr.; M-Sa 5-7 per day 6:15am-5pm; Su 5 and 6pm; L12,500) continuing to **Noto, Ragusa,** and **Syracuse; Palermo** (2hr.; M-Sa 9 per day 5:45am-5:45pm, Su 6 per day; L15,000/€7.75); **Piazza Armerina** (40min., 10 per day, L5500/€2.84).

Taxis: ☎0935 689 50.

ORIENTATION AND PRACTICAL INFORMATION

The bus station lies outside Enna's central historic district. **Via Vittorio Emanuele** runs from the station to **P. Matteotti,** where **via Roma** branches in two directions. Straight ahead, V. Roma passes **Piazza Vittorio Emanuele** and the **duomo,** ending at the **Castello di Lombardia.** To the right, V. Roma cuts an arc through residential areas to the **Torre di Federico II.**

Tourist Office: AAPIT, V. Roma, 411 (☎0935 52 82 28). English-speaking staff cheerfully provides maps, brochures, pamphlets, and many other goodies from the well-stocked shelves. Open M-Sa 9am-1pm and 3-7pm.

Currency Exchange: Banks, including a Monte dei Paschi di Siena and a Banca Mercantile, line V. Roma between P.V. Emanuele and P. Umberto I. Exchange currency at the post office. **ATMs:** there is a Bankomat 3 in P. Umberto on V. Roma.

Emergency: ☎113.

Police: ☎0935 50 12 89. **Carabinieri:** (☎112 or 0935 50 13 21), in P. Europa.

Ambulance: ☎0935 219 33. **First Aid/Emergency Room:** ☎0935 50 08 99. **Guardia Medica:** (☎0935 52 04 89 or 50 08 96). Open daily 8pm-8am.

Late-Night Pharmacy: Farmacia del Centro, V. Roma, 315 (☎0935 50 06 50), posts the rotation schedule of the city's late-night pharmacies.

Hospital: Ospedale Umberto I (☎0935 45 245), on V. Trieste.

Internet Access: Bar Panorama, Viale Belvedere, 16 (☎0935 24 803) has 1 net-connected computer. L10,000/€5.16 per hr. Open daily 9-11am and 4pm-midnight.

Post Office: V. Volta, 1 (☎0935 56 23 27). Take a left off V. Roma just before the AAPIT and walk to the right behind "Provincia" building. Open M-Sa 8:20am-7:20pm.

Postal Code: 94100.

ACCOMMODATIONS

Enna's only accommodation is Hotel Sicilia, forcing many to the nearby town of Pergusa which can be reached from Enna proper by **bus #5** (L5000/€2.58). It makes the 7km trip every hour from Enna's bus station and from in front of Agenzia Viaggi Loppola in the chaotic little *piazza* not far down V. Roma from P.V. Emanuele. In Pergusa, buses normally stop at the town gas station, but drivers will drop you at the hotel if you ask.

Hotel Sicilia, P. Colajanni, 7 (☎0935 50 08 50), just up V. Roma from AAPIT in Enna. Posh rooms with TV, hairdryer, phone, bathroom, and antiqued furniture. Excellent views. Breakfast L10,000/€5.16. Singles L99-109,000/€51.13-56.29; doubles L155-170,000/€80.05-87.80; triples L180,000/€92.96. AmEx/DC/MC/V.

Hotel Miralago (☎0935 54 12 72), 3km outside Pergusa's center on V. Nazionale. Area's only budget accommodation. Fluffy towels don't really redeem remote location and noise from the *discoteca* next door. Breakfast L5000/€2.58. Singles L50,000/€25.82; doubles L70,000/€36.15; triples L100,000/€51.65.

FOOD

Enna's relaxed pace makes eating an enjoyable and lengthy affair. Good restaurants cluster along the aptly titled Viale Belvedere (beautiful view) behind V. Roma and P. Crispi. **F.lli Caruso,** V. Roma, 374, sells the essentials. (Open M-Sa 8:30am-2pm and 5-8:30pm.) A sweeter option is the **Bar del Duomo,** in P. Mazzini next to the *duomo,* whose glass shelves boast rows of perfect cookies. Picnickers may want to wander through **via Mercato Sant'Antonio,** filled with *alimentari,* fruit stands, and bakeries.

San Gennaro da Gino, Viale Belvedere Marconi, 8 (☎0935 240 67). Serves fabulous food with a view to match. Start with extensive *antipasti* buffet and finish with delicious *pannacotta* (L5000/€2.58), their specialty. Cover L1500/€0.77. Service 15%. *Primi* from L9000/€4.65; pizza from L5000/€2.58. Open daily 1-3pm and 8pm-2am. MC/V.

Ristorante La Fontana, V. Volturo, 6 (☎0935 254 65), in P. Crispi. Has indoor dining area, but the wise will opt for the flower-covered terrace to enjoy *ravioli siciliani.* Cover L2000/€1.03. Service 15%. Open daily noon-4pm and 7pm-closing. AmEx/MC/V.

◉ SIGHTS

CASTELLO DI LOMBARDIA AND ENVIRONS. Enna's history as a defensive city is most apparent at the **Castello di Lombardia.** The enclosed courtyards are now covered with grass and vines, but most of the thick walls and towers remain. A view of the entire province and Mt. Etna is worth fending off roosting pigeons for in *La Pisana,* the tallest of the towers. Named for a Lombardian siege, the castle was constructed by the Swabians in the Norman period and later by Federico II. Fred really liked to feel secure; one of the city's other architectural marvels is the **Torre di Federico II.** Next to the castle, a natural fortress offers excellent views of the city. The **Rocca di Cerere** is supposedly where the weeping Ceres mourned the loss of her daughter Persephone to Hades. *(From the duomo, V. Roma curves uphill and becomes V. Lombardia before ending at the castle. Castle ☎0935 50 09 62. Open daily 9am-1pm and 3-5pm, though gates often stay open later. Torre closed for restorations summer 2001. Turn left onto V. IV Novembre for the public gardens. Open daily 9am-8pm. Free.)*

DUOMO. Over a dozen religious fraternities throughout the city each have their own church, but all share the curious *duomo,* which combines as many architectural styles as there are brotherhoods. Construction began in the early 14th century, but the cathedral was remodeled throughout the 15th and 16th centuries. The result is a walking tour through three centuries of Italian architectural movements. The interior sports Gothic doors, medieval walls, Renaissance paintings, and gilded Baroque flourishes to encompass them all. The sacrilegious stretch out on wooden pews to appreciate the marvelous wood-paneled ceiling.

The **Museo Alessi** is housed in the rectory immediately behind the cathedral. The eclectic collection mirrors the *duomo* in its veneration of variety. Oil paintings and ancient coins and pottery share space with the *duomo's* treasures, including a remarkable fine silver model cathedral. Look for Paolo Vetri's work (the first left on the ground floor): watercolor plans for cathedral frescoes and the exquisite *Portrait of an Elder Man.* (☎0935 50 31 65. Open July-Sept. daily 8am-10pm; Oct.-June Tu-Su 9am-1pm and 4-7pm. L5000/€2.58.)

♪ ENTERTAINMENT

For the **Festa della Madonna** (July 2), the entire town turns out to watch men dressed in white with blue sashes strapped around their middles carry three enormous votive statues through the city. Ennesi celebrate by enjoying fireworks, music, and *mastazzoli* (apple cookies). The party continues through the summer, with similar festivities for the feasts of **Sant'Anna** and **San Valverde**, the last Sundays of July and August, respectively. The largest festival in Enna is Easter, when each fraternity dons their hoods and capes to parade through the streets.

Processions of a faster sort take place down the hill at the Autodromo di Pergusa (☎ 0935 256 60; fax 258 25), where the city hosts **Grand Prix auto races** from March through October. The most important are the Formula 3 in July. In other months, you can catch everything from motorcycle races to dog shows there.

PIAZZA ARMERINA ☎ 0935

Like the neighboring Ennesi, the founders of Piazza Armerina headed for the hills. Dominated by its green-domed *duomo* and King Martino's *Castello Aragonese*, the medieval city is perched in the Erei Mountains. Time has changed little here, and many streets are no more than twisting stone staircases. The city's greatest attraction, however, lies in the foothills below. The famed Villa Romana at Casale has the largest and finest collection of ancient mosaics in the world.

🖅 TRANSPORTATION AND PRACTICAL INFORMATION. Piazza Armerina is a bus ride from Enna (45min.; 8 per day; L3700/€1.91). **Buses** arrive at P. Senatore Marescalchi at the city's northern end. From the *piazza*, V. D'Annunzio becomes first V. Chiaranda and then V. Mazzini before arriving at **Piazza Garibaldi**, the historic center. The **tourist office**, V. Cavour, 15, is in the courtyard of a *palazzo* just off P. Garibaldi. (☎ 0935 68 02 01. Open M-Sa 8am-2pm.) In P. Garibaldi **Farmacia Quattrino** posts the night-shift rotations. (☎ 0935 68 00 44. Open daily 9am-1pm and 4-8pm.) In **emergencies,** call the **carabinieri** (☎ 0935 68 20 14).

🖪 ACCOMMODATIONS AND FOOD. For the best budget accommodation, follow the yellow signs to **⬛Ostello del Borgo,** Largo S. Giovanni, 6, a recently renovated 14th-century monastery in the heart of historic P. Armerina. Yellow-tiled hallways lead to 20 rooms with dignified dark wood furniture and excellent beds. (☎ 0935 68 70 19; fax 68 69 43; www.ostellodelborgo.it. Breakfast included. Singles L65,000/€33.57; doubles L85,000/€43.90; triples L115,000/€59.39; quads L140,000/€72.30; L5000/€2.58 each additional person.)

Only a handful of restaurants sprinkle Piazza Armerina's streets; a *panino* from **Spaccio Alimentari,** P. Garibaldi, 15 (☎ 0935 68 10 84), is a possible alternative. If only a restaurant will do, the centrally located **Pepito**, V. Roma, 140, just off P. Garibaldi, serves quality local dishes. The house specialty, *agnello al forno* (baked lamb) is especially popular. (☎ 0935 827 37. *Primi* from L11,000/€5.68; *secondi* from L18,000/€9.30. Open W-M noon-4pm and 7-11pm. AmEx/MC/V.)

⬛ SIGHTS. ⬛ Villa Romana "Del Casale" lies 5km southwest of town in a fertile green valley. This remarkable site, known locally as *"I Mosaici,"* is thought to have been constructed at the turn of the 4th century AD, but a landslide in the 12th century kept it mostly hidden for 800 years. In 1916, the famed archaeologists Paolo Orsi and Giuseppe Culterra unearthed 40 rooms of extraordinary stone mosaics, the largest and best-preserved collection of their kind in the world. Glass walls and shaded ceilings now cover the mosaics but still allow for a sense of what the villa would have looked like at the height of its glory. A guidebook from a nearby vendor helps to appreciate the finer points of the villa's construction. The entrance passes first through the baths, where gods and goddesses frolic about, taking the waters warmed by visible hot air vents that run under the entire structure. A large ovoid hall on the left just past the baths depicts an eternal chariot race; flying legs at left are all that remain of the poor driver who has been thrown from his ride. While the owner is not certainly identified, many believe it to have been Maximenius Herculeus, co-ruler of the western half of the Roman Empire with Diocletian. Max's great wealth, fondness for the hunt, and side business, as an importer of exotic animals, are all apparent in the tiles. One of the largest rooms shows the dramatic capture and exportation of lions, and tigers, and bulls (oh my!), while the enormous Triclinium, with its Battle of the Giants and the Feats of Hercules, offers more bloody evidence of Maximanius's ownership; he was publicly associated with Hercules. The mosaics show both the exotic and the erotic: the famed **Salle delle Dieci Raggazze** (Room of Ten Girls) shows buff bikini-clad beauties in various aerobic activities. While the **Cubicolo Scena Erotica** is not quite as racy as the title suggests, the bare tush and intimate kiss have kept people talking for centuries. A room off the great hall showcases the battle between Odysseus and Polyphemus, but the artist was a bit confused on the finer details of the story; the cyclops has three eyes instead of one. (☎0935 68 00 36. *No public transportation to villa from P. Armerina. The 5km walk from town is well-marked. Bring plenty of water on hot days. Check with tourist office to see if any private tour groups have available space. Open daily 9am-1:30pm and 3:30pm-sunset. L8000/€4.13, under 18 and over 65 L4000/€2.07.)*

SOUTHERN SICILY

SYRACUSE (SIRACUSA)   ☎0931

The most beautiful and noble of the Greek cities.
  —Titus Livius (Livy), on Syracuse

Modern Syracuse is a sum of its parts, with each area adding a certain quality of its own to the collective character. At its height, Syracuse rivaled Athens as one of the greatest cities in the west, cultivating such luminaries as Theocritus, Archimedes, and the great Greek lyric poet Pindar. Hard times followed in 211 BC, however, when the Romans conquered the city, and again in AD 668, when the bathing emperor Constans was bludgeoned to death with a soap dish. The city's prominence was perhaps most seriously undermined in AD 879, when Arabs conquered Sicily and established Palermo as the capital of the island. Though no longer the titan of its youth, today's city is hardly crestfallen. Modern Syracuse is content to rest upon laurels long since won. Pride has always been one of the city's most noticeable qualities, a characteristic over a millennium of decline has yet to tarnish. Ask a citizen to point to the pride of Syracuse and a tanned arm may gesture wordlessly toward the stunning archaeological park, with its extraordinary theater, or toward Ortigia and its elegant churches.

◨ TRANSPORTATION

Trains: V. Francesco Crispi, halfway between Ortigia and archaeological park. To: **Catania** (1½hr., 20 per day 4:50am-9:10pm, L8500/€4.39); **Florence** (14hr.; 3 per day; L85,000/€43.90); **Messina** (3¼hr.; 18 per day 4:50am-9:10pm; L16,000/€8.26); **Milan** (19hr.; 3 per day; L96,000/€49.78); **Noto** (30min., 11 per day 5:20am-7:50pm, L9500/€4.91); **Ragusa** (2¼hr.; 6 per day 5:20am-3:32pm; L11,000/€5.68); **Rome** (12hr.; 5 per day 7:15am-9:10pm; L73,000/€37.70); **Taormina** (2hr.; 12 per day 4:50am-9:10pm; L12,500/€6.46); **Turin** (20hr.; 2 per day 1:28 and 2:30pm; L96,100/€49.63). Luggage storage available (p. 616).

Buses: AST office (☎0931 46 48 20), next to the post office on Ortigia, to left after stone bridge. While construction continues, blue buses leave from P. Marconi on the mainland side of the stone bridge. To: **Gela** (4hr.; 2 per day 7am and 1:30pm; L14,000/€7.23); **Piazza Armerina** (3hr.; 1 per day 7am; L14,000/€7.23); **Ragusa** (3hr.; 7 per day; L10,500/€5.42). **Interbus**, V. Trieste, 28 (☎0931 66 710), 1 or 2

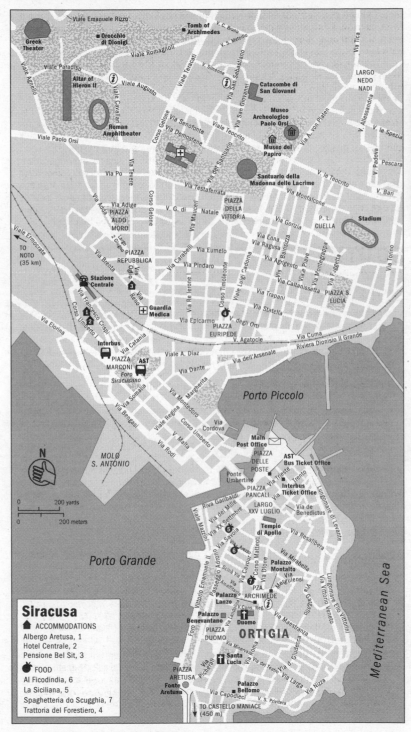

Siracusa

🏠 **ACCOMMODATIONS**
Albergo Aretusa, 1
Hotel Centrale, 2
Pensione Bel Sit, 3

🍴 **FOOD**
Al Ficodindia, 6
La Siciliana, 5
Spaghetteria do Scugghia, 7
Trattoria del Forestiero, 4

blocks from P. delle Poste toward center of Ortigia, 2nd street to left after stone bridge. To: **Catania** (1¼hr.; M-F 17 per day 5:45am-6:30pm, Sa-Su 8 per day 6:45am-6:30pm; L8000/€4.13); **Giardini-Naxos** (2hr.; 1 per day; L14,000/€7.23); **Noto** (1hr., 9 per day, L5000/€2.58); **Palermo** (3¼hr.; M-Sa 4 per day, Su 1 per day, 3:30pm; L26,000/€13.43); **Rome** (12hr.; 1 per day 7:45am; L73,500/€37.96); **Taormina** (2hr.; 1 per day; L14,000/€7.23).

Local Transportation: Orange AST buses depart from P. delle Poste. Bus #21, 22, and 24 run past Fontane Bianche. #23 to Aranella. Tickets L1000/€0.52 in *tabacchi*.

Taxis: (☎0931 697 22 or 609 80). From train station to Ortigia about L15,000/€7.75.

✳🛈 ORIENTATION AND PRACTICAL INFORMATION

The **Ponte Umbertino** connects the island of **Ortigia** to mainland Syracuse. **Corso Umberto I** links the bridge to the **train station** and passes through **Piazza Marconi**, from which **Corso Gelone** courses through town up to the **archaeological park**. A bridge joins the island of **Ortigia** to mainland Syracuse. This bridge becomes **Corso Umberto I**, leading to **Foro Siracusano** at the base of the town. As you stand on C. Umberto I in the Foro, the city's main artery, **Corso Gelone**, is to the right, accessible through a gap in some unused railway tracks. C. Umberto continues past Foro Siracusano to the train station.

Tourist Office: APT, V.S. Sebastiano, 43 (☎0931 67 710). From the station, take V.F. Crispi to C. Gelone V.V. Catania on the left. Turn right onto Viale Teocrite after 400m, then left onto V.S. Sebastiano; the office is 150m up on the left. Useful tourist map includes a mini-guide. English spoken. **AAT Office, Ortigia,** V. Maestranza, 33 (☎0931 65 201 or 46 42 55). After crossing Umbertino Bridge, turn right through P. Pancali to uphill C. Matteotti. Turn left onto V. Maestranza at fountain in P. Archimede; office in courtyard of *palazzo* across from pharmacy. Open M-Sa 8am-2pm and 3:30-5:30pm.

Luggage Storage: In train station. L7500/€3.87 for 24hr. Open daily 7am-11pm.

Emergency: ☎113.

Police: ☎0931 46 35 66.

Guardia Medica: ☎0931 48 46 39. From P. Archimede on Ortigia, turn down V. Maestranza; take 1st left onto V.S. Coronati. Open M-F 8pm-8am, Sa-Su 8am-8pm.

Late-Night Pharmacy: Mangiafico Farmacia, C. Matteotti, 33 (☎0931 65 643). Open M-Sa 8:30am-1pm and 4:30-8pm. MC/V.

Hospital: Ospedale Generale Provinciale (☎0931 72 41 11), a beige brick monstrosity on V. Testaferrata, off C. Gelone toward the *corso's* end.

Internet Access: W@W: Web and Work, V. Roma, 16/18 (☎0931 46 59 60), in Ortigia. Take V. Roma from P. Archimede at end of C. Matteoti. Fast connections. Many other multimedia services available. L5000/€2.58 per 30min.; L8000/€4.13 per hr. Open M-Sa 10am-10pm, Su 5-10pm.

Post Office: P. delle Poste, 15 (☎0931 684 16). Turn left after crossing the bridge to Ortigia. BancoPosta **currency exchange.** Open M-Sa 8:15am-7:40pm.

Postal Code: 96100.

⌂ ACCOMMODATIONS & CAMPING

Many budget accommodations have staked out the area between the station and the bridge to Ortigia. While prices are good, the quality is not. This area can be dangerous at night. Ortigia's few options are more expensive, but of higher quality.

Albergo Aretusa, V. Francesco Crispi, 75 (☎/fax 0931 242 11), down the street from the train station. 50 rooms crowd a well-maintained palazzo with original marble floor tiling. Rooms vary in size and lighting. English spoken. Breakfast L5000/€2.58. Reserve Aug. Singles L30,000/€15.50, with bath L40,000/€20.66; doubles

L40,000/€20.66, L50,000/€25.82; triples L75,000/€38.73, L90,000/€46.48. Prices rise L10-15,000/€5.16-7.75 July-Aug. AmEx/MC/V.

Hotel Centrale, C. Umberto I, 141 (☎0931 60 528), near train station. Low prices and stupendous sea views have made this hotel popular with Anglo-American backpackers. Best views: singles #18, 20 and doubles #19, 21. Singles L30,000/€15.50; other rooms L25,000/€12.91 per person.

Pensione Bel Sit, V. Oglio, 5 (☎0931 602 45; fax 46 28 82). Follow signs from C. Gelone, close to the train station. Large bare rooms, all with bath, occupy two floors of a mini-high rise. Upstairs rooms with A/C and TV. Reserve 1 week ahead July-Aug. Singles L40,000/€20.66; doubles L65,000/€33.57.

Camping: Fontane Bianche, V. dei Lidi, 476 (☎0931 79 03 33), 30km from Syracuse, near the beach of the same name. Take bus #21 or 22 (L1000/€0.52) from the post office. Open May-Sept. L11,000/€5.68 per person. No tents.

◨ FOOD

While hotel prices can run fairly high, restaurants are affordable. On the mainland, the area around the station and the archaeological park offers some of the best deals. Ortigia has an **open air market** on V. Trento, off P. Pancali (Open M-Sa 8am-1pm), as well as several budget options on V. Savoia and V. Cavour.

◪ La Siciliana, V. Savoia, 17 (☎0931 689 44), in Ortigia, next door to Hotel Gran Bretagna. Perky staff serves 58 varieties of excellent thin-crust pizza to tables in the memorabilia-laden dining room or outdoor tables. Cover L2000/€1.03. Pizza L6-10,000/ €3.10-5.16; *primi* from L8000/€4.13. Open Tu-Su 10am-4pm and 6pm-midnight.

Spaghetteria do Scugghiu, V.D. Scinà, 11, a tiny street off P. Archimede, on Ortigia. This eatery boasts 17 different spaghetti dishes (L10,000/€5.16). Wide selection of vegetarian options. Wine L8000/€4.13 per liter. Open Tu-Su noon-3pm and 5pm-midnight.

Al Ficodindia, V. Arezzo, 7/9 (☎0931 46 28 38), off V. Cavour in Ortigia. A/C interior off the main roads but popular with tourists. *Antipasto* buffet (L8000/€4.13), 29 kinds of pizza, and *cucina tipica siciliana*. *Menù* (L15,000/€7.75) includes pizza, drink, and *gelato*. Open Th-Tu noon-3pm, 7-11pm. D/MC/V.

Trattoria Del Forestiero, C. Timoleonte, 2 (☎0931 46 12 45), on mainland. From the start of C. Gelone, take V. Agatocle to P. Euripede; restaurant on far side at start of C. Timoleonte. High quality food served in big portions with small prices. *Primi* from L6000/€3.10; *secondi* from L9000/€4.65. 21 kinds of pizza (L4-9000/€2.07-4.65) for evening take-out. Cover L2000/€1.03. Open W-M noon-3pm and 7pm-midnight.

◙ SIGHTS

▧ SIGHTS WITHIN ARCHAEOLOGICAL PARK. Syracuse's three centuries as the most important city on the Mediterranean left behind a collection of immense monuments. The Greek ruins are the most impressive, but Roman remains also attest to a rich heritage. Two theaters, an ancient quarry, and the world's largest altar share a fenced compound, visited with a single ticket. Take a deep breath before plowing through the paper fan- and bead-hawking tourist tunnel. *(Follow C. Gelone to V. Teocrito; park entrance down V. Augusto to the left. Open daily 9am-7pm. Ticket office closes 1hr. before park. L8000/€4.13, EU residents under 18 or over 60 L4000/€2.07.)*

GREEK THEATER. While sitting in one of the theater's rows, carved into the hillside in 475 BC, it's easy to understand why Syracuse became such a successful Greek colony. If the 15,000 spectators watching Aeschylus's original production of *The Persians* got bored, they could lift their eyes over the now-ruined scenic building to look out over green fields, colorful flowers, the sparkling sea in the distance, and oncoming attackers. Original Greek inscriptions line the walls along the mid-level aisles and the track for the *deus ex machina*, a large crane that made the gods "fly," is still visible around the orchestra.

PARADISE QUARRY. The floral valley next to the theater derives its name from the fertile gardens that line the base of large, chalky cliffs. It is from these quarries that most of the characteristic gray stone that built old Syracuse was taken. Two large artificial caves now cut into the walls, the **Orecchio di Dionigi** (Ear of Dionysius) and the **Grotta dei Cordari** (Ropemakers's Cave). The latter is closed to the public for safety reasons, but visitors can still see the former. Legend claims the tyrant Dionysius put his prisoners here in order to eavesdrop on their rebellious conversations. Even if the story were true, Dionysius certainly wouldn't dare to spend long hours listening now: the cave rings with the delighted high-pitched shrieks of visiting children.

OTHER SIGHTS IN THE PARK. Outside this area lies Ara di Ierone II, the altar of Heiron II (241-215 BC), once used for public sacrifices. At 198mx23m, this is the world's largest altar. Walk up the hill and through the other gate to reach the Roman amphitheater. Constructed in the 2nd century AD, the theater is well-preserved. Visitors can also see the tunnels through which wild gladiators and brave animals entered.

MUSEO ARCHEOLOGICO PAOLO ORSI. Named for the most famous archaeologist in Sicily, this museum has an overwhelming collection of objects from prehistory through to the ancient Greeks. From the circular introductory room at the museum's core, hallways branch out into chronologically arranged galleries that wind through time and place. Exquisite *kouroi* torsos, grimacing Gorgons, elegant vases, and a couple of Pygmy elephant skeletons rest in dimly-lit galleries. (*V. Teocrito.* ☎ *0931 46 40 22. Open Tu-Sa 9am-2pm; M, W, and F-Sa 3:30-7:30pm. Ticket office closes 1hr. before museum. L8000/€4.13.*)

CATACOMBE DI SAN GIOVANNI. Dating from AD 415-460, this subterranean maze has over 20,000 tombs carved into the walls. Fear not, o ye of little stomach: there are no corpses to be seen here; only ghostly frescoes, an occasional sarcophagus, and a few wall-carvings remain. The 4th-century **Cripta di San Marziano** (the first bishop of Syracuse) lies below the ruins. (*Across from tourist office on V.S. Giovanni, off Viale Teocrito from C. Gelone. Open Mar. 15-Nov. 14 Th-Tu 9am-12:30pm and 2-5pm; Nov. 15-Mar. 14 Th-Tu 9am-1pm. L6000/€3.10, under 10 L1000/€0.52. Guided tours mandatory.*)

SANTUARIO DELLA MADONNA DELLE LACRIME. This concrete cone in the center of the city celebrates three days in 1953 when a mass-produced statuette of the Madonna cried for Argentina, er Syracuse. Chemical tests proved the liquid to be similar to human tears, and as word spread, the number of pilgrims grew too large for the Syracusan home in which the event occurred; the larger sanctuary was built in 1966 on the competition-winning plans of Frenchmen Michel Arnault and Pierre Parat. (*☎ 0931 214 46. Open daily 6:30am-12:30pm and 4-7:30pm.*)

MUSEO DEL PAPIRO. Up the street from the Orsi museum, this collection of papyrus texts and woven objects displays four or five pages from the ancient Egyptian Book of the Dead, containing invocations (translated into Italian) to the Eater of Souls and the Snake-that-Rises. (*☎ 0931 221 00. Open Tu-Su 9am-2pm. Free.*)

ORTIGIA. The Greeks first landed in Ortigia, using the island as an embarkation point for their attack on the mainland. At the end of the Ponte Umbertino, the fenced in ruins of the Tempio di Apollo catch the golden evening sun and many a tourist's eye. The temple, dating from 575 BC, is the oldest peripteral (columns on all sides) Doric temple in Sicily. The island flourished in the Baroque period, leaving a smattering of elegant churches all over the place as well as the Palazzo Impellizzeri, V. Maestranzo, 22. As any Siracusan will tell you, the island is best enjoyed during the evening *passegiata*, when citizens from all over the city and their rambunctious children take to strolling in the streets.

DUOMO. Don't judge a *duomo* by its facade. The 18th-century exterior of Syracuse's cathedral may look like the standard Baroque compilation of architectural fancies, but the interior is anything but. The *duomo* was built upon the site of the

5th-century BC Temple of Athena, but rather than demolishing the pagan structure, the architects incorporated it directly into their own construction. Fluted columns line both sides of the interior in an unusual but aesthetically effective design scheme. According to legend, the temple became a church with the arrival of St. Paul. Large, shiny letters proclaim this the first Christian church in the west. The first chapel on the right as you enter the church is dedicated to St. Lucia, the light-bearer and Syracuse's patron saint. The elaborate reliquary in the glass case holds a piece of her left arm. Hidden from view above the reliquary is a masterpiece of Sicilian silver work. A life-size statue of Lucia that is paraded through the street on her feast day (see **Entertainment,** below). Lest you forget to remember how she died, the silversmiths kindly included a dagger sticking out of her throat. *(Down V. Minerva from P. Archimede. Open daily 8am-noon and 4-7pm. Modest dress required.)*

FONTE ARETUSA. This small, ancient pond fed by a "miraculous" fresh-water spring near the sea overlooks Porta Grande. Siracusani believe that the nymph Arethusa escaped the enamored river god Alpheus by diving into the ocean and that the goddess Diana rescued her by transforming her into this fountain. Alpheus, pining for his love, transformed himself into a subterranean river, so their waters could mingle eternally. The river surfaces here at the Fonte Aretusa. *(P. Aretusa. From P. Duomo, walk down V. Picherale.)*

■ ENTERTAINMENT

Siracusani, like all Italians, fall prey in summer to powerful ancestral instincts that force them from the cities to the beach. **Fontane Bianche** is a glitzy, fleshy beach with many discos by night; staying at the *campeggio* there ensures you a place to sleep when the buses stop. Take bus #21, 22, or 24 (30min., L1000/€0.52). On Ortigia, nightlife consists of a grand tour of the island, stopping at any of several bars along the way. In winter, check out **Troubador,** off P.S. Rocco. In summer, the Ortigia hotspot is **Nonsolobar Bar** behind the Fonte Aretusa. Patrons drink in a mossy natural grotto below street level. (Open W-M 7am-2am; cave open after 6pm.)

In May and June, the city stages **classical Greek drama.** The APT office has all the details. Tickets for **Istituto Nazionale del Dramma Antico** (☎ 0931 48 35 31) are available at the theater box office M-F 3:30-6:30pm. General admission is L25,000/€12.91; reserved seats start at L45,000/€23.24.

Syracuse's biggest festival is the **Festa di Santa Lucia,** Dec. 13. Local men carry the silver statue of the city's patron saint in a six-hour procession from the *duomo* to S. Lucia al Sepolcro on the mainland. The statue stays on the mainland for a week and is carried back to the *duomo* on Dec. 20.

■ DAYTRIP FROM SYRACUSE: NOTO

Interbus and AST buses head from Syracuse in a steady stream (40min., 12 per day, L5000/€2.58). Ticket office opposite bus stop in the Bar Efirmmedio. Also reach Noto by train (30min., 9 per day, L3200/€1.65). The station is 20min. uphill from town.

After the 1693 earthquake shook Sicily's shore, the Laudlino family made Noto their favorite renovation project. Its architecture epitomizes Baroque elegance, with monumental staircases, chubby cupid moldings, and pot-bellied balconies. Things have slowed to a more relaxed pace since the earthquake, making Noto a calm retreat from frenzied tourist destinations.

From the bus stop at the **Giardini Pubblici** (Public Gardens), cross the paved way with the fountain on the right. Turn left through the tunnel of low hanging trees and pass under the **Porta Nazionale** (built in 1838) onto **Corso Vittorio Emanuele.** The **APT tourist office,** in P. XVI Maggio, is 500m ahead, to the right behind the octagonal red wall around Fontana d'Encole. (☎ 0931 57 37 79. English spoken. Free map. Open summer Su-F 8:15am-1:45pm and 4:45-6:20pm.) To reach the town center from the train station, follow the road leading uphill and to the right; at the second traffic light, turn right, and then right again.

Toward the city center from C.V. Emanuele stands the immense **Chiesa di San Francesco all'Immacolata,** built in 1704, which houses one of the bloodiest crucifixes you'll find in Sicily. (Open daily 9:30am-12:30pm, 4-7pm.) From C.V. Emanuele turn right on V. Niccolaci, and pause to gawk at the balconies of the **Palazzo Niccolaci,** supported by cherubs, griffins, and sirens. The noteworthy *duomo* contains captivating frescoes, currently under renovation. Fine **beaches** are 7km away at **Noto Marina.** Buses depart from the **Giardini Pubblici** (July-Aug. M-Sa; 2 per day 8:30am and 12:45pm; L2500/€1.29).

Trattoria al Buco, V.G. Zanardelli, 1, provides *affittacamere* of varying quality, most in the historic district. All units have kitchen, bath, eccentric furnishings, and mohair bedspreads. (☎ 0931 83 81 42. Singles L30-35,000/€15.50-18.08; doubles L60-70,000/€30.99-36.15; quads L140,000/€72.30.) The *trattoria* serves excellent homemade pasta. Feast on *tagliatelle alle melanzane* (egg noodles with eggplant) for L5000/€2.58. (*Menù* L18,000/€9.30. Cover L1000/€0.52. Open daily 10am-3:30pm and 7:30-11:30pm.) **Pasticceria La Vecchia Fontana,** C.V. Emanuele, 150, scoops sinfully good *gelato* (L2000/€1.03). We're talking immaculate confection. (☎ 0931 83 94 12. Open W-M 7am-1 or 2am.)

RAGUSA ☎ 0932

Hot Ragusa's lethargic pace contrasts with the frantic modernity of other Sicilian cities. The city, settled comfortably in the interior, is distant from even its nearest neighbors. The language cascading off the Baroque buildings has little to do with Italian, and it is rare that a tourist tongue is heard. The craggy valley that divides **Ragusa Ibla** from the modern **Ragusa Superiore** is the city's most unusual feature, with its verdant cliffs and winding paths. Antique buildings and wide vistas make Ragusa the retreat even time could not be troubled to visit.

⌐ TRANSPORTATION

Trains: New town end of V. Roma, off P. della Libertà, behind the bus stop. To: **Caltanissetta** (3hr.; 3 per day 6:10am-5:16pm; L16,000/€8.26); **Gela** (1½hr., 7 per day 4:08am-8:20pm, L8000/€4.13); **Palermo** (5hr.; 3 per day, 11:03am, 2:53, 4:17pm; L25,000/€12.91); **Syracuse** (2hr.; 13 per day 6:05am-6:32pm; L11,000/€6.71).

Buses: Beside train station, just above P. della Libertà, at new town end of V. Roma. Schedules posted on wall facing stop. To: **Catania** (2hr.; M-Sa 8 per day 5:45-7pm, Su 5pm; L12,500/€6.46); **Gela** (1½hr., M-F 9:45am and 4:15pm, L6500/€3.36); **Noto** (1½hr.; M-Sa 7 per day, Su 2 per day; L7500/€3.87); **Palermo** (4hr.; M-F 4 per day 5:30am-5:30pm, Sa-Su 2:15 and 5:30pm; L22,500/€11.62); **Syracuse** (2hr.; M-F 7 per day 6:50am-7pm; L10,500/€5.42). Connections to **Agrigento** and **Enna** via **Gela.** Tickets at **Bar Puglisi,** across the street. Open daily 5am-10pm.

✴❼ ORIENTATION AND PRACTICAL INFORMATION

The **train** and **bus stations** are in P. del Popolo and neighboring P. Gramsci. To reach the center from either of these adjacent *piazze,* turn left on Viale Tenente Lena, walk through P. Libertà on V. Roma and over the Ponte Senatore F. Pennavaria, the northernmost of three bridges crossing the Vallata Santa. **Corso Italia,** off V. Roma, leads downhill for several blocks, passing the **post office** in P. Matteotti, and becomes **via XXIV Maggio.** It ends at the **Chiesa di Santa Maria della Scala.** Here stairs and roads wind down to Ragusa Ibla.

Tourist Office: AAPIT, V. Capitano Bocchieri, 33 (☎ 0932 62 14 21 or 65 48 23), in lower Ragusa Ibla beyond the *duomo* from the new city; look for signs in P. del Duomo. Red-carpet treatment accompanies brochures, maps, and info on nearby beaches and sights. English spoken. Open M-Sa 9am-1pm.

Emergency: ☎ 113. **Police:** ☎ 112. **Medical emergency:** ☎ 118.

First Aid: ☎ 0932 60 02 69. **Guarda Medica:** (☎ 0932 62 39 46), in P. Igea.

Hospital: Ospedale Civile (☎ 0932 60 01 11), in a peach building on V. da Vinci.

Post Office: (☎ 0932 62 40 43), in P. Matteotti, 2 blocks down C. Italia from V. Roma. Open Oct.-June M-Sa 8:15am-6:30pm, last day of the month 8:15am-noon.

Postal Code: 97100.

ACCOMMODATIONS

Hotel San Giovanni (☎ 0932 62 10 13; fax 62 12 94), V. Transpontino, 3. From P. del Popolo, take Viale L. da Vinci to V. Transpontino; the hotel is to the left before the bridge. Decent rooms with ceiling fans and Ragusa Ibla views in a central location. Singles L60,000/€30.99, with bath L70,000/€36.15; doubles L100,000/€51.65, L120,000/€62. AmEx/MC/V.

Hotel Jonio (☎ 0932 62 43 22), V. Risorgimento, 49. Facing away from the train station entrance, walk across the *piazza* to V. Sicilia. Turn right, and walk past the gas station. Fine rooms and a location near the train station and several restaurants. Singles L35,000/€18.08, with bath L55,000/€28.41; doubles L80,000/€41.32, with bath L90,000/€46.48; triples with bath L110,000./€56.81. AmEx/MC/V.

Baia del Sole (☎ 0932 62 31 84), in Marina, near the beach. Tumino buses run from P. Gramsci in Ragusa to P. Duca degli Abruzzi in Marina (30min., every hr., L4000/€2.07). 1km down from the main *piazza* (with the water to your right) on Lungomare Andrea Doria. L10,000/€5.16 per tent. Hot showers until 6pm L4000/€2.07.)

FOOD

While in Ragusa, try some *panatigghie* (thin pastries filled with the unholy trio of cocoa, cinnamon, and ground meat). Unfortunately, they aren't cheap, and neither are the meals at the quality *trattorie* where they're sold.

La Valle (☎ 0932 22 93 41), V. Risorgimento, 66-70. Waiters sport retro 30s-style uniforms as they whisk tasty pizzas to tables in the curious mint-green dining room. *Primi* from L7500/€3.87; *secondi* from L10,000/€5.16; pizza from L6000/€3.10. Cover L2500/€1.29. AmEx/D/MC/V.

Pizzeria La Grotta (☎ 0932 22 73 70), on V.G. Cartia, the second right off V. Roma with your back to the bridge, serves standard *tavola calda* favorites, plus a few original creations. (Th-Tu 5:30pm-midnight.)

SIGHTS AND ENTERTAINMENT

The dual hilltop locations of Ragusa Superiore and Ragusa Ibla offer great views of the countryside. The latter is accessible by a steep but lovely 10min. climb down from the church at the very bottom of C. Italia (a.k.a. V. XXIV Maggio) and by the #3 city bus (L1000/€0.52) from the *duomo* or P. del Popolo. The stairs at S. Maria offer a stellar view of Ragusa Ibla, crowned by a monastery and the 18th-century dome of **San Giorgio,** which glows an unearthly turquoise at night. (Modest dress required.) Walk down 200m of tricky steps to P. Repubblica. The road to the left circumvents the town, passing abandoned monasteries and lush farmland. P. del Duomo di San Giorgio sits at the top of the city. C. XXV Aprile runs downhill from the *piazza* and ends at the **Giardino Ibleo,** and passes two churches, ending in views of the surrounding countryside. Ragusa Superiore's **Museo Archeologico,** below the Ponte S. Pennavaria, has a collection of pottery from the nearby Syracusan colony of Camarina (☎ 0932 62 29 63. Open daily 9am-1:30pm and 4-7:30pm. L8000/€4.13.)

In summer, any citizen with a swimsuit spends the weekend at **Marina di Ragusa,** a bikini-packing, Vespa-roaring, booty-shaking stretch of sand. **Autolinee Tumino** (☎ 0932 62 31 84) runs buses to Marina from P. Gramsci (40min.; 14 per day; L3500/€1.81, round-trip L6500/€3.36). A schedule is posted in Polleria Giarrosto in Marina's P. Duca degli Abruzzi. In the same *piazza,* savor Marina's best *gelato* at **Delle Rose** (L2400/€1.24 per scoop). Every year since 1990, Ragusa has hosted an **International piano/voice/composition** competition from late-June to early-July. Performances are held in the theater of Palazzo Comunale.

WESTERN SICILY

AGRIGENTO   ☎ 0922

Agrigento's skyline of fabulous temples and standard city high rises seems like a surreal juxtaposition out of one of local celebrity Luigi Pirandello's plays. Originally founded in the 6th century BC by Greek colonists, Agrigento now prides itself on being impeccably modern, as if to make up for the traces of the past that rest just below the city in the fantastic Valley of the Temples. A compromise between the ancient and the new, the *centro storico* offers its causal charms to those who stroll down the winding cobblestone streets. With excellent museums, stunning ruins, and plenty of character, Agrigento is a city that should find itself on a list of Italy's most under-appreciated locations.

▟ TRANSPORTATION

Trains: In P. Marconi, below P. Moro. Ticket office open M-Sa 5:45am-8pm, Su 7am-8pm. To **Catania** (3¼hr.; 12:20, 2:05, 5:55pm) via **Enna** (2hr.; L11,100/€5.73) and **Palermo** (2hr.; 11 per day 4:50am-8pm; L12,500/€6.46)

Buses: From P. Vittorio, buses are to left in P. Roselli. **Interbus** ticket booth (☎ 0922 59 64 90), is in back of the parking lot. Office open M-Sa 5:30am-6:10pm. Luggage storage available (p. 622). Buses to: **Palermo** (2hr.; M-Sa 4 per day 5:45am-2:30pm, Su 7am and 5pm; L13,000/€6.71); **Sciacca** (1¾hr.; M-F 12 per day 7:55am-8:40pm, Su 9:40am, 5, 6pm; L9000/€4.65); **Syracuse** (5hr.; daily 8, 11am, 5, 5:45pm, M also 8:30am; L27,000/€13.94); **Trapani** (4hr.; M-Sa 6:20, 8:30am, 1:55pm, Su 9:40am, 5, 6pm; L18,000/€9.30). **SAIS Trasporti**, V. Ragazzi, 99 (☎ 0922 59 59 33), behind the ticket office. To: **Caltanissetta** (1hr., 9 per day, L9000/€4.65); **Catania** (2¾hr.; 11 per day; L19,000/€9.81); and **airport**. Also indirectly to **Rome** and **Messina**.

Public Transportation: Orange **TUA city buses** depart from the train station. Ticket (L1500/€0.77) valid 1½hr. Buses #2 and 2/ run to the beach at San Leone; #1, 2, and 2/ run to the Valley of Temples; #1/ runs to Pirandello's house. Alternatively, take the bus to **Porto Empedocle** (L2000/€1.03) and get off at "La Casa di Pirandello." Tickets available at the cream-colored bar cart in the parking lot. Ask for schedules on board.

Taxis: At stand in front of station.

✴ ◪ ORIENTATION AND PRACTICAL INFORMATION

The middle of Agrigento is a string of large *piazze*. The **train station** is in **Piazza Marconi,** which spills into **Piazza Moro** at the far left corner when facing away from the station. From P. Moro, **via Atenea** leads straight through the **centro storico**. At the far side of P. Moro is **Piazza Vittorio Emanuele**, home of the post office and the **bus station.** The temples are a short bus ride (#1 or 2) or a long walk below the town.

Tourist Office: Ufficio Informazioni Assistenza Turisti (AAST), V. Battista, 13 (☎ 0922 204 54), the 1st left off V. Atenea. Staff will outfit you with maps and brochures. Open in summer M-F 9am-1:30pm. Another summer office in **Valle dei Tempii,** adjacent to car park and bar. English spoken. Open daily 8am-7:30pm.

Luggage Storage: in bus station. L7500/€3.87 per bag per 24hr. Open daily 8am-9:30pm.

Emergency: ☎ 113.

Carabinieri: (☎ 0922 59 63 22), in P. Moro opposite V. Atenea.

Late-Night Pharmacy: Farmacia Averna Antonio, V. Atenea, 325 (☎ 0922 26 093). Posts late-night rotation. Open daily 9am-1:30pm and 5-8:30pm.

Hospital: Ospedale Civile (☎ 0922 49 21 11), on S. Giovanni XXII.

Internet Access: Libreria Multimediale, V. Celauro, 7 (☎ 0922 40 85 62), off V. Atenea, 2 blocks down from P. Moro. L6000/€3.10 per hr. Open M-Sa 9am-1pm and 4:30-8:30pm.

Post Office: P.V. Emanuele. Open M-F 8:10am-6:30pm, with a break at 1:30pm when the shifts change; Sa 8:10am-1:20pm.

Postal Code: 92100.

ꙮ ACCOMMODATIONS & CAMPING

Agrigento's hotels are central and cheap, but so are many park benches; in this case, "low price" and "good value" are not synonymous. Consider spending a little more or heading to one of the easily accessible campgrounds.

▨ **Hotel Belvedere,** V.S. Vito, 20 (☎/fax 0922 200 51). Follow the hotel signs in front of the train station, left to P. Moro. With Banco di Sicilia behind you and the stand of trees to your left, look for a yellow sign on the right pointing up a flight of stone steps. Agrigento's nicest 2-star hotel, with sleek, colorful, eccentrically painted rooms, funky antique furniture, and a garden overlooking P. Moro and the valley. Ask for a room with a view. Breakfast L4000/€2.07. Singles L60,000/€30.99, with bath L80,000/€41.32; doubles L75,000/€38.73, with bath L110,000/€56.81; triples with bath L160,000/€62.

Hotel Bella Napoli, P. Lena, 6 (☎/fax 0922 204 35), off V. Bac Bac. Take V. Atenea 1km uphill and turn right after you pass the Justice Building. Institutional hallways lead to clean white rooms with mismatched wood furniture, and large, bare bathrooms. Rooftop terrace overlooks the valley. 20 rooms, all with bath. Singles L40,000/€20.66; doubles L85,000/€43.90; triples L100,000/€51.65.

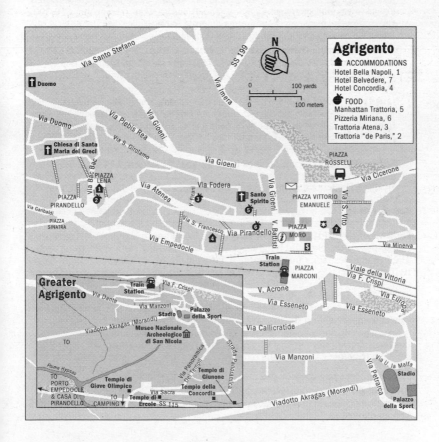

Agrigento

🏠 ACCOMMODATIONS
Hotel Bella Napoli, 1
Hotel Belvedere, 7
Hotel Concordia, 4

🍴 FOOD
Manhattan Trattoria, 5
Pizzeria Miriana, 6
Trattoria Atena, 3
Trattoria "de Paris," 2

Hotel Concordia, V.S. Francesco, 11 (☎0922 59 62 66). At end of V. Pirandello in historic district, just after the church. Sleepy white dog greets visitors. Hot, small rooms with brown tile floors have small baths. Some with TV. Late risers may not appreciate early-morning shouting from the street market below. Rooms on far side have less noise and more light. Singles L30,000/€15.50, with bath L40,000/€20.66; doubles L65,000/€33.57, with bath L80,000/€41.32; triples with bath L80,000/€41.32.

Camping: 2 campgrounds lie on the beach, 3km from San Leone in **Le Dune.** Buses #2 and 2/ go to the campsites from the train station. **Camping Nettuno** (☎0922 41 62 68), on V. L'Acquameno at the bus stop. Reasonable market, restaurant, bar, and pizzeria. L9000/€4.65 per person, L8000/€4.13 per tent. Showers L1000/€0.52. Up the road, the shaded and better-equipped **Camping Internazionale San Leone,** V. Alessandro Giuliana Alaimo, 2 (☎/fax 0922 41 61 21), is run by a family of extroverts. July-Aug. L10,000/€5.16 per person, L8000/€4.13 per tent, L5000/€2.58 per car; Sept.-June L9000/€4.65 per person, L7000/€3.62 per tent, L4000/€2.07 per car.

▶ FOOD

The vegetable market in front of the Hotel Concordia is open Monday through Saturday mornings, and plenty of small *alimentari* line V. Pirandello and V. Atenea. Indulge a sweet tooth at the candy stalls along V. della Vittoria. The local specialty is *torrone*, a nut-filled nougat. Authentic, inexpensive *trattorie* lie off V. Atenea.

Trattoria Atenea, V. Ficani, 32 (☎0922 202 47), 4th right off V. Atenea from P. Moro, just beyond the Stefanel store. Like grandma's kitchen—huge portions with no-fuss. Extensive seafood offerings. *Calamari* (squid) and *gamberi* (shrimp) for L10,000/€5.16. House specialty *grigliata mista di pesce* (mixed grilled fish; L9000/€4.65). Smooth local wine L4000/€2.07 per liter. Open M-Sa noon-3pm and 7pm-midnight.

Manhattan Trattoria/Pizzeria, Salita M. degli Angeli, 9 (☎0922 209 11), up steps to the right off V. Atenea near P. Moro. Spiral pasta with swordfish, eggplant, and tomato (L12,000/€6.20). *Primi* from L8000/€4.13; *secondi* from L10,000/€5.16. Cover L2000/€1.03. Open M-Sa noon-3pm and 7:30-11pm.

Trattoria "de Paris," P. Lena, 7 (☎0922 254 13), next to Hotel Bella Napoli. White and blue embroidered table cloths share small crowded rooms with odd figurines and sculptures. Tasty *rigatoni alla Pirandello* (with tomatoes, *prosciutto*, mushrooms, and cream). *Primi* L8000/€4.13; *secondi* from L10,000/€5.16. *Menù* L20,000/€10.33. Service charge 10%. Open M-Sa 12:30-3pm and 7:30-10:30pm. AmEx/D/MC/V.

Pizzeria Miriana, V. Pirandello, 6 (☎0922 22 828), at the start of V. Pirandello off P. Moro. Friendly chefs serve small pizzas (from L1500/€0.77) and *panini* (from L3000/€1.55) for budget eating on the go. Open daily 8am-10pm.

◉ SIGHTS

VALLE DEI TEMPII. Not so much a valley as a lesser ridge below Agrigento's hilltop perch, the elevated temples create a breathtaking vista from every angle. The five temples along this impressive panorama have been named official World Heritage Landmarks, a well-deserved distinction. Today the temples are in various degrees of ruin, a function of time, earthquakes, the vicious Punic Wars, and the rise of Christianity. Weathered by time to glowing golden hues, the temples are best viewed at sunset as crowds thin and temperatures cool. The transition from sunset to moonlight on the massive columns is not to be missed.

From the entrance, a wide avenue heads uphill along the ridge, first passing the **Tempio di Ercole** (Hercules). One row of solid, squat columns are all that remain standing from the earliest of the temples. Further along, the **Tempio della Concordia** stands as the proud victor in the battle against fate. With 34 columns, walls intact, and evident metopes and stylobates, this temple is one of the best preserved of the Greek world. Erected in the mid-5th century BC from limestone, it owes its preserved state to an early conversion to Christianity by the archbishop of Agrigento. Though the temple is fenced off from the public, the niches carved into the interior walls are still visible. The road ends at the contemporary 5th-century BC **Tempio di Giunone** (Juno). Elegant columns and part of the pediment remain to create one of the more interesting sunset silhouettes. To the left during the ascent, holes in the ground mark an early Christian burial ground.

Across the street lies the entrance to the unfinished **Tempio di Giove Olimpico** (Jupiter). Had its construction not been interrupted by Carthaginian troops in 406-405 BC, it would have been one of the largest Greek temples ever built. The toppled jigsaw puzzle of partitioned columns and walls has challenged archaeologists for years. The temple's most interesting features are the gigantic *telamones*, 8m sculpted male figures, one of which has been reconstructed at the site. These massive figures would have encircled the temple, holding up the roof and entablature. At the far end of the ride, past the Tempio di Giove, four columns of the long-gone **Tempio di Catore e Polluce** (Castor and Pollux) stand eternal guard in case the Carthaginians should choose to come back.

The excellent **Museo Nazionale Archeologico di San Nicola,** 1km uphill from the parking lot, has a fabulous collection of red- and black-figureware vases, terracotta votive figures, and funerary vessels from the area's necropolis. The newly renovated interior boasts light-filled display cases and English explanations. A gallery features an upright telamon, as well as model projections of how a completed Tempio di Giove may have looked. *(Valle dei Tempii is several km from city. Starting on V.F. Crispi, it's a 30min. walk from the train station to the entrance, following signs downhill and left at the lower intersection. Or, take bus #1, 2, or 27 from train station; it stops in a dirt lot car park with a snack bar and many tour buses. Tempii di Giove open 8:30am-sunset. L4000/€2.07; all other temples free. Museum open daily 9am-1:30pm, W-Sa 2-6pm. L8000/€4.13.)*

CHIESA DI SANTA MARIA DEI GRECI. Built atop a 5th-century BC Greek temple, this church is the most interesting building in medieval Agrigento. The interior contains a Norman wooden ceiling, original Doric columns, and 14th-century frescoes of a strangely wizened Christ child. *(Follow the signs up the hill from V. Bac Bac off V. Atenea. Open 9am-7pm or until the curator leaves. Ring the bell for entrance. Donation expected.)*

CHIESA DEL PURGATORIO (S. SPIRITO). The legendary Serpotta employed all of his wizardry in making this church's stucco doodads look like marble. The statues of the "Virtues" are meant to help you stay out of purgatory, but most of the imagery reminds you how imminent purgatory actually is—note the unusual skull and crossbones on the confessional and the countless depictions of roasted sinners (Mmmm...tasty). To the left of the church, below a sleeping lion, lies a 5th-century BC Greek entrance to a network of underground channels. *(In P. Purgatorio off V. Atenea in the centro storico.)*

SIX TOURISTS IN SEARCH OF AN AUTHOR. Those with their eyes open need not search long—Agrigentan playwright **Luigi Pirandello** is an omnipresent figure in Agrigento. Literature aficionados will want to visit his birthplace, now a small museum of books, notes, and family photographs. Pirandello's ashes are buried below a large boulder under his favorite pine tree, a few hundred meters from the house. Though currently undergoing restoration, the museum will reopen in fall 2001. *(Take the Lumia bus #1 to P. Kaos. ☎0922 51 11 02. Open daily 8am-1:30pm. L4000/€2.07.)* The **Settimana Pirandelliana,** a week-long outdoor festival of plays, operas, and ballets in P. Kaos, occurs in late July and early August. *(Info ☎0922 235 61. Tickets L15-30,000/€7.75-15.50.)* The **Teatro Pirandello** recently reopened inside the town hall. Built in 1870, the interior was created by G. Battista Basile, who also designed the decor for La Fenice in Venice.

🎵 ENTERTAINMENT

The first Sunday in February brings the **Almond Blossom Festival,** an international folk-dancing fest, to the Valle dei Tempii. In early July, town folk throw bread to the effigy of St. Calogero, thanking him for having spared them from food poisoning during the plague. During summer months, Agrigentans move to the beach and nightlife strip at **San Leone,** 4km from Agrigento by bus #2 or 2/.

MARSALA ☎0923

When Garibaldi and his red-shirted devotees landed at Marsala, the city provided them with men and means, making itself the *Risorgimento*'s proud launchpad. Today, the streets are more full of remnants of the hot and dusty *scirocco* wind from Africa than with revolutionary fever. The city is best known for its exquisite Marsala wine, which gained fame thanks to Englishman John Woodhouse. Despite its small size, the city has several worthwhile sights, including the ruins of Lilybaeum and a famed Carthaginian warship.

🖪🛈 TRANSPORTATION AND PRACTICAL INFORMATION. Trains service the town from **Trapani** (20min., 16 per day, L4500/€2.32), as do **buses** (30min., 4 per day, L5000/€2.58). **Taxis** answer to ☎0923 71 29 92. With your back to the train station, a first right facing V.A. Fazio and another slight right through the intersection onto **via Roma** leads to Marsala's historic center. V. Roma turns into **via XI Maggio** and then **via Veneto**. The **Pro Loco tourist office** is at V. XI Maggio, 100, in the old city, just before Palazzo Comunale and the *duomo*. The staff checks bus schedules and suggests housing but doesn't speak English. (☎0923 71 40 97 or 71 44 77; www.prolocomarsala.org. Open M-Sa 8am-8pm, with a break around 2pm as shifts change, Su 9am-noon.) In an **emergency,** call the **carabinieri** (☎0923 95 10 10 or 112), **first aid** (☎0923 95 14 10), or **Guardia Medica** (☎0923 78 23 43). There is a **pharmacy** with the nighttime rotation posted one block away from the Pro Loco office at V. XI Maggio, 114. (☎0923 95 32 54. Open Su-F 9am-1:30pm and 4:30-8pm.)

🖪🍴 ACCOMMODATIONS AND FOOD. Marsala has few hotels of any kind, and very few budget accommodations. The best bet is **Hotel Garden,** V. Gambini, 36. The gritty station neighborhood and drab exterior hides a sparkling interior with marble, mirrors, and shiny communal bathrooms. The tidy rooms have TV, fans, and woven rugs. (☎0923 98 23 20. Singles L55,000/€28.41, with bath L65,000/€33.57; doubles with bath L95,000/€49.06, triples with bath L128,000/€66.11. AmEx/D/MC/V.) Those planning to spend a few days wine tasting might check out **Andrea's affittacamere.** Though quite a distance from the center, the series of rooms (100 spots in all) scattered about the countryside near the old salt mills and the lagoon can be great values. Call ahead for free pickup at the bus or train station. (☎0923 74 57 47; ring the tourist office if there's no answer. Aug. L50,000/€25.82 per person; Sept.-July L25,000/€12.91.)

Trattoria da Pino, V. San Lorenzo, 27, offers a wide range of local seafood and wine specialties. An excellent *antipasto* buffet precedes *primi* and *secondi* from L9000/€4.65. Facing the cathedral's main door, head left through the Porta Garibaldi arch into P. Garibaldi. Take your first right and look for a sign several blocks down. (☎0923 71 56 52. Open M-Sa 12:30-3pm and 7pm-late. AmEx.) **E & N Cafe,** V. XI Maggio, 130, serves delectable delicacies to crowds from dawn until drop. (☎0923 95 19 69. *Cannoli* from L2500/€1.30; *gelato* L2500/€1.29. Open Su-F 7:30am-10pm, Sa 7:30am-midnight.) Self-caterers should head to the **STANDA supermarket,** V. Cammareti Scurtil, 10. (☎0923 71 54 76. Open M 4-7:30pm, Tu-Sa 9am-1pm and 4-7:30pm.)

🖪🎵 SIGHTS AND ENTERTAINMENT. The **Museo Archaeologico Regional "Baglio Anselmi"** guards the famed **Carthaginian warship,** stylishly presented in its own specially-designed gallery. The now-skeletal vessel sank in the devastating final battle (241 BC) of the First Punic War, in which Rome defeated Carthage and established its permanent naval supremacy. The few wooden planks, preserved for over 2000 years in underwater sand off Marsala, are the largest existing portion of this type of ship. Other galleries in the museum display objects from Lilybaeum and the isle of Motya. To reach the museum, follow V. XI Maggio through its portal end to P. della Libertà. Facing the bright pink cinema, take the flower-filled road slightly to the left, continuing right at its end. (☎0923 95 25 35. L4000/€2.07, EU residents free. Open daily 9am-2pm and W-Su 4-7pm.)

Also down V. XI Maggio and left down V. Sauro, the **Chiesa di San Giovanni** conceals the **Groita della Sibilla** (reached via a trapdoor), where an ancient oracle spent 28 years preaching to believers through a hole in the ceiling. Early Christians staked out the cave in the 4th century AD (hence the frescoes of fish and doves); St. Paul is said to have baptized converts in the pool here, and a statue of St. John covers the reclusive sibyl's grave. (Open daily, but hours vary.)

Just behind the *duomo* at V. Garraffa, 57, the **Museo degli Arazzi (Flemish Tapestry Museum)** contains eight violent 16th-century Flemish tapestries illustrating Titus's war against the Jews in AD 66-67. (☎ 0923 71 29 03. L2000/€1.03. Open Tu-Su 9am-1pm and 4-6pm.) A few steps down from P. Reppubblica and the *duomo*, the **Museo Civico** houses several of the thousand red shirts, as well as Garibaldi's own rather snazzy uniform. (Open Tu-Su 9am-1pm and 4-8pm.)

Visitors can watch the Marsala grapes be crushed during a free tour (with free samples) of the monstrous **Cantine Florio** facilities, still distilling on Lungomare V. Florio. Take V. Francesco Crispi toward the water from the main intersection of V. Roma next to the train station. At the end, follow Lungomare Mediterraneo until the painted Florio sign. (☎ 0923 78 11 11. Open Sept.-July M-Th 3-6pm, F 11am-1pm. Call ahead for monthly tour times.) On the way back, stop by the **Fontana del Vino** (Fountain of Wine), where a wine-loving lady drinks gustily with a barrel-bearing donkey. The *piazza* surrounding the fountain, with a brick pattern that mimics the Union Jack, is a subtle poke at the British presence in Marsala.

The ⬛**Marsala DOC Jazz Festival** whips it up in the last two weeks of July, attracting the greats of the international jazz scene. The festival emblem colorfully depicts a mellowed-out bass player strumming his six-foot wooden stained bottle of Marsala (apparently, he's already been sampling).

TRAPANI ☎ 0923

A vast blue sea defines the peninsular Trapani. The city is bordered on both sides by sparkling waters, such that most streets in the old section end in delightful ocean views. Everything from fishing boats to ferries line the docks. Easy transportation and solid lodgings make Trapani a desirable launching point for adventures to Segesta's ancient ruins, medieval Erice, the lush Lo Zingaro nature reserve, the islands of Sicily's western coast, Sardinia, and even Tunisia.

▐ TRANSPORTATION

Flights: V. Florio Airport, (☎ 0923 84 25 02) in Birgi en route to Marsala. 16km outside the city. Buses from P. Malta are timed to coincide with flights. Daily flights to Rome and Pantelleria. Not a heavily used airport.

Trains: P. Stazione (☎ 0924 280 71). Luggage storage available (p. 628). Office open M-Sa 5:40am-7:50pm. AmEx/MC/V. To: **Castelvetrano** (1hr., 20 per day 4:40am-8:40pm, L8000/€4.13); **Marsala** (30min., 16 per day 6:10am-8:40pm, L4500/€2.32); **Palermo** (2hr.; 16 per day 4:40am-8pm; L11,500/€5.94).

Buses: AST (☎ 0923 21 021). Main bus station at P. Malta. Buses to **Erice** (45min.; M-Sa 11 per day 6:30am-7:30pm, Su 4 per day 9am-6pm; L3500/€1.81) and **San Vito Lo Capo** (1½hr.; M-Sa 8 per day 7am-8:30pm, Su 4 per day 8am-6:45pm; L6000/€3.10). Service to all destinations reduced Su. **Segesta** (☎ 0923 20 066) runs buses to local towns and to **Rome** (15hr.; 1 per day 5:30pm; L74,000/€38.22).

Ferries: Ferries and *aliscafi* (hydrofoils) leave Trapani for the **Egadi Islands** (Levanzo, Favignana, and Marettimo), **Ustica, Pantelleria** (an Italian island off the Tunisian coast), and **Tunisia.** All boats leave from the docks across from P. Garibaldi and along V.A. Staiti, which runs the length of the southern side of the peninsula. 4 companies operate ticket offices in front of the hydrofoil/ferry dock: **Ustica** (☎ 0923 222 00; www.usticalines.it), in a yellow booth on the waterfront; **Siremar** (☎ 0923 54 54 55; www.siremar.it. Open M-F 6:15am-noon, 3-7pm and 9pm-midnight. AmEx/D/MC/V.),

SICILY

with ticket offices both at a blue and white striped waterfront booth and in Stazione Marettima; **Tirrenia** (☎0923 52 18 96; www.tirrenia.it. Open M 6:30am-1pm and 3-6pm, Tu 9am-1pm and 4-9pm, W-F 9am-1pm and 3-6pm, Sa 9am-noon. AmEx/D/MC/V), in Stazione Marettima; and **Lauro** (☎092 392 40 73. Open W-M 9am-1pm and 4-7pm, Tu from 7am), on the waterfront near Ustica. You can also purchase tickets for these lines from the travel agents along V.A. Staiti. Keep in mind that the schedules for inter-island ferries can be unreliable. Off-season frequency and prices may fluctuate from those in the chart. Schedules are available at all ticket offices.

DESTINATION	COMPANY	DURATION	FREQUENCY	PRICE
Favignana (Egadi Islands)	Siremar (ferry)	1hr.	2 per day	L6000/€3.10
Favignana (E.I.)	Ustica (hydrofoil)	25min.	11 per day	L10,000/€5.16
Favignana (E.I.)	Siremar (hydrofoil)	25min.	10 per day	L10,000/€5.16
Levanzo (E.I)	Siremar (ferry)	1hr.	7 per day	L6000/€3.10
Levanzo (E.I.)	Siremar (hydrofoil)	20min.	10 per day	L10,000/€5.16
Levanzo (E.I.)	Ustica (hydrofoil)	20min.	10 per day	L10,000/€5.16
Marettimo (E.I.)	Siremar (ferry)	3hr.	2 per day	L12,500/€6.46
Marettimo (E.I.)	Siremar (hydrofoil)	1hr.	3 per day	L22,500/€11.62
Marettimo (E.I.)	Ustica (hydrofoil)	1hr.	2 per day	L22,500/€11.62
Pantelleria	Siremar (ferry)	6hr.	Midnight	L43,500/€22.47
Pantelleria	Ustica (hydrofoil)	2hr.	1:35pm	L65,000/€31
Ustica via Favignana	Ustica (hydrofoil)	2hr.	3 per week	L36,000/€18.60
Cagliari (Sardinia)	Tirrenia (ferry)	11½hr.	Tu 9pm	L57,500/€29.70
Tunis	Tirrenia (ferry)	8½hr.	M 10am	L95,000/€49.06
Tunis	Linee Lauro (ferry)	12hr.	2 per week	L90,000/€46.48

Public Transportation: SAU, the orange city bus, has its main terminal at P.V. Veneto, down V. Osorio from the station right on V. XXX Gennaio and straight ahead all the way to the water. Office at left when facing water. Has posted schedules of all bus routes. Tickets sold at most *tabacchi* (L1100/€0.57).

Taxis: (☎0923 232 33 or 228 08), often in P. Umberto, outside the train station.

✴ 🛈 ORIENTATION AND PRACTICAL INFORMATION

Trapani sits on a peninsula two hours west of Palermo by bus or train. The old city began at the outer tip of the hook, growing in cautious backward steps until it tripped and spilled new wide streets and cement high-rises onto the mainland. The **train station** is in **Piazza Umberto,** with the **bus station** just to the left in **Piazza Malta.** From the train station, **via Osorio** passes the **Villa Margherita Gardens** to end at the perpendicular **via XXX Gennaio.** A right onto this racy road leads to **Piazza V. Veneto,** the city bus station. A left goes down to **via A. Staiti,** which runs along the port. The **tourist office** is at the end of **Corso Italia,** off V. XXX Gennaio. From P.V. Veneto **via Garibaldi** becomes **via Libertà** and moves into the old city.

Tourist Office: Ufficio Informazioni Turistiche (☎0923 290 00; fax 240 04), at P. Saturno, up V. Torrearsa from the port. English-speaking staff. Train and bus schedules. Map of Trapani and info on cultural events and surrounding towns. Open M-Sa 8am-8pm, Su 9am-noon. Second office in Stazione Marittima keeps same hours.

Currency Exchange: Banks on C. Italia have better rates than the train station. Open daily 8:10am-1pm. Post office also exchanges money and cashes traveler's checks. **ATMs** are at Stazione Marettima in the old city and along V.M.V. Scontrino in front of the train station. Withdrawal in L50,000/€25.82 increments.

Luggage Storage: In train station. L7500/€3.87 per bag for 24hr. Open 8am-9:30pm.

Police: (☎113), in P.V. Veneto. **Carabinieri:** V. Orlandini, 19 (☎0923 59 811).

Guardia Medica: (☎0923 29 629). **Pronto Scorso:** (☎0923 80 94 50).

Late-Night Pharmacy: Check rotating schedule on the door of any pharmacy. All open Su-F 9am-1:30pm and 4:30-8pm. Pharmacy at V. Garibaldi, 9, next to P.V. Veneto.

Hospital: Ospedale Sant'Antonio Abate (☎ 0924 80 91 11), on V. Cosenza, far northeast of the city center.

Internet Access: Phone Center GGE (☎ 0923 54 98 40), in Stazione Marittima, has one net-connected laptop at L7000/€3.62 per 30min. **Mondial Phone SAS,** V. Scontrino, 13 (☎ 0923 21 952), has 1 slow computer. L10,000/€5.16 per hr.

Post Office: P.V. Veneto (☎ 0923 219 96 or 43 44 04). With your back to the train station, turn right down V.M.V. Scontrino and left through the small fountain park. Continue left down V. Fardella, with iron fenced public gardens on the left. Post office on left after Palazzo del Governo. *Cambio* booth is number 18. Open M-Sa 8:20am-6:30pm.

Postal Code: 91100.

▌ ACCOMMODATIONS & CAMPING

▨ **Pensione Messina,** C.V. Emanuele, 71 (☎ 0923 211 98), through a Renaissance courtyard and up 4 flights of steps. Welcome to grandma's house, complete with ticking of a baby grandfather clock, eclectic bric-a-brac, garden statues, and familial vibes. Communal bathrooms contribute to this feeling. Sept.-June singles L25,000/€12.91; doubles L50,000/€25.82. July-Aug. singles L30,000/€15.5; doubles L60,000/€30.99.

▨ **Albergo Maccotta,** V. degli Argentieri, 4 (☎ 0923 284 18 or 43 76 93; albergo-maccotta@comeg.it), behind the tourist office. Soft beds in cool, tiled, white, and impeccably modern rooms with A/C. Lobby has Internet. July 15-Aug. 31 singles L60,000/€30.99, with bath L80,000/€41.32; doubles L80,000/€41.32, L100,000/€51.65. Sept. 1-July 14 singles L35,000/€18.08, with bath L45,000/€23.24; doubles L60,000/€30.99, L80,000/€41.32. AmEx/MC/V.

Albergo Moderno, V. Genovese, 20 (☎ 0923 212 47). From P.S. Agostino on C.V. Emanuele, go left on V. Roma, then right on V. Genovese after Cafè Moderno. Clean, white rooms with TV are made perkier by puzzling framed jigsaws of famous artworks. All but 2 rooms with sparkling tiled bathrooms. Singles L45,000/€23.24; doubles L70,000/€36.15; triples L94,000/€48.55. MC/V.

Ostello per la Gioventù (HI) (☎ 0923 55 29 64), Strada Provinciale, Trapani-Erice. The hostel is a good 6km from the station. Take city bus #23 from the train station (2 per hr., L1100/€0.57) and tell the driver your destination. Follow signs from the stop to the hostel, about 900m. The hostel's distance from Trapani is both its greatest selling point and its worst feature. A peaceful, wooded setting with cheery red bunk beds and the scent of evergreen and cappuccino. Many English-speaking travelers. HI members only. Meals L15,000/€7.75. Showers and sheets included. Lock-out 10am-4pm, even for check-in. Curfew midnight (keys otherwise available). 6-bed dorms L21,000/€10.85. Free camping space available; shower and bathroom L5000/€2.58 per person.

Camping: Campeggio Lido Valderice (☎ 0923 57 30 86), on V. del Detince, in seaside town of the same name. Take bus for Bonegia or San Vito La Capo (L5000/€2.58) and tell driver your destination. Follow flower-lined road opposite bus stop and perpendicular to the highway, and turn right at its end. Well-shaded campground near a couple of beaches. Gravel flooring for mobile campers and packed earth sites for tents. L6500/€3.36 per person, L7-15,000/€3.62-7.75 per tent. Hot showers L1000/€0.52.

▐ FOOD

In Trapani, couscous is actually touted as a Sicilian dish, with local fish added to the North African favorite. Bakeries carry *biscotti con fichi*, the Italian Fig Newton, for about L400/€0.21 each. The old city has lots of small *alimentari*, and a daily fish and fruit market springs up each morning along the northern *lungomare*, at the intersection of V. Maggio and V. Garibaldi in the old city. Almost everything in Trapani closes on Sunday.

Pizzeria Calvino, V.N. Nasi, 77 (☎0923 21 464), 1 street portside behind C.V. Emanuele. If the line out the door every night doesn't convince you that these are the best pizzas in town, take a seat in the labyrinth of peekaboo backrooms and dig into any one of 30 varieties. Pro chefs present each pizza for the customer's approval. Small pizzas from L6500/€3.37; medium from L10,000/€5.16; large from L13,000/€6.71. Pizza only at night. Open W-M noon-2pm and 6pm-late.

Trattoria da Salvatore, V.N. Nasi, 19 (☎0923 54 65 30), 1 street toward the port from C.V. Emanuele. Small and authentic, this family-run restaurant offers perfect pasta to a regular local crowd. Debates over soccer games on the overheard TV are as hot as the house couscous. Menu changes daily. *Primi* from L7000/€3.62; *secondi* L12-16,000/€6.20-8.26. Cover L2000/€1.03. Open Sept.-June M-Sa noon-3:30pm and 7-11pm; July-Aug. daily noon-3:30pm and 7-11pm. AmEx.

Trattoria Miramare (☎0923 200 11), on the port side *lungomare,* at the end of V. Torrearsa. Features a small dining room and a huge wine list. Couscous is their specialty, in a fish sauce so spicy that they won't serve it to foreigners unless prodded. Locals dive right in without preliminaries. *Tortellini con panna* (with cream) L11,000/€5.68. *Primi* from L8000/€4.13; *secondi* L8-22,000/€4.13-11.21. Cover L2000/€1.03. A non-smoking Italian anomaly. Open daily noon-5pm and 7pm-midnight.

Pizza Sport, V. Libertà, 16 (☎0923 87 37 51). Sports-themed interior has lots of trophies, some of which could be for the pizza. The chef displays pictures from the marathons he has run while you wait for take-out only pies. Small pizza from L6000/€3.10; medium from L8500/€4.39; large from L15,000/€7.75. Open M-Sa 7pm-late.

⊙ SIGHTS

CHIESA DEL PURGATORIO. This 17th-century Baroque church in the heart of the old city houses *I Misteri*, the city's greatest treasures. Sixteen separate groups of almost life-size sculptures depict the passions and the crucifixion in agonizing, bloody detail. Each year on Good Friday, local guildsmen carry the floats in an elaborate procession through the city, each guild bearing a float with special significance. Suffocating incense, dramatic lighting, and low music create a somewhat forced viewing atmosphere. *(1 block up V.D.G. Giglio from P. Garibaldi across from Stazione Marettima. Open daily 8:30am-12:30pm and 4-8pm.)*

SANTUARIO DELL'ANNUNZIATA/MUSEO NAZIONALE PEPOLI. The only attraction in the modern part of town, the enormous *santuario* is a lavishly decorated church housing a 14th-century statue of the Madonna of Trapani. In the same complex is the Museo, which features a collection of local sculptures and paintings, coral carvings, and folk-art figurines, including a frighteningly violent collection portraying the biblical story of Herod's baby hunt. *(Take SAU buses #24, 25, or 30 from P.V. Emanuele (L1100/€0.57), 2 blocks to the right of the train station. ☎0923 55 32 69. Open daily 9am-12:30pm. Call to make sure it's open. L8000/€4.13.)*

TORRE DI LIGNY. A mini-peninsula, the Torre is at the end of wide jetty off the tip of Trapani. Wild coastal winds stream past the tower, from which both sides of Trapani's ports are visible. The tower itself houses the **Museo di Preistoria/Museo del Mare,** with its collection of shells, prehistoric artifacts, and underwater excavation pieces. *(☎0923 223 00. Open daily 9:30am-12:30pm and 4-7:30pm. L3000/€1.55.)*

VILLA MARGHERITA. At the cusp of the old and new cities, the Villa or Public Gardens, offers a delightful change of pace from the bustling cobblestone and cement that is Trapani. Palms, banyans, and fountains rest behind flower-lined avenues. Playgrounds and statues complete the picture of the perfect city park. Each July the villa is the center of the **Luglio Musicale Trapanese,** an annual festival of opera, ballet, and cabaret that draws national and international stars to the temporary stage among the trees. *(☎0923 214 54; fax 229 34. Shows 9pm. Info booth inside park gates. Tickets from L25,000/€12.91.)*

◪ DAYTRIPS FROM TRAPANI

SAN VITO LO CAPO

Buses to San Vito Lo Capo, the closest town to the reserve, leave from Trapani at P. Malta (1¼hr.; 8 per day 7am-8:35pm, Su 4 per day 8am-6:45pm; L6000/€3.10)

Superb San Vito sports one of the best beaches in all of Sicily. Separated from hectic Trapani by 40km and a huge rock outcropping, the white arc of smooth sand is paradise found. Italians from far and wide stay for an afternoon or several days enjoying turquoise, shallow water and silky sun. Make sure to bring or rent an umbrella, as shade is minimal. San Vito proper is nothing without its beach. Perfectly flat and composed of large avenues, the town hugs the *lungomare* while pedestrians in bathing suits walk idly from the *gelaterie* to cafes. The main road is V. Savoia, on which the local tourist office is at #57 (☎ 0923 97 43 00). **Albergo Costa Gaia**, V. Savoia, 123-125, on the main street four blocks from the beach, has rooms with A/C and bath. (☎ 0923 97 22 68 or 97 23 75. Breakfast included. Sept.-June singles L50,000/€25.82; doubles L95,000/€49.06. July-Aug. L95,000/€49.06 per person. Half-pension L95,000/€49.06; full pension L110,000/€51.65. AmEx/MC/V.) San Vito has several excellent nearby camping options. **Camping La Fata**, V.B. Napoli, 68, 2 blocks from the beach, is right in town. Complete with bar and disco, the site has a secluded, bamboo-shaded rectangle for tenting. (☎ 0923 97 21 33. Open June-Sept. Reservations recommended. L10,000/€5.16 per person, L9000/€4.65 per tent, L7000/€3.62 per car. One person, tent, and car L25,000/€12.91. AmEx/D/MC/V.) **Campeggio La Pineta**, V. del Secco, 88, is on the town's edge. (☎ 0923 97 28 18. Reservations recommended in Aug. L10,800/€5.58 per person, L9500/€4.91 per tent. AmEx/MC/V.) In case of an emergency, call the **beach police** (☎ 0923 97 43 71) or **Guardia Medica** (☎ 0923 97 20 91).

RISERVA DELLO ZINGARO

Inquire in San Vito at Mare Monti, V. Amadeo, 15 (☎ 0923 97 22 31. info@sanvitomare-monti.com), about private van service to the reserve (L15,000/€12.91). English guidebooks available. Reserve entrance free.

For shade and seclusion, drive 10km outside of San Vito to the green mountains of Riserva dello Zingaro. One unfinished half mile of a four-lane highway hangs perilously close to the pristine reserve. A 1981 environmentalist rally march halted the highway in its tracks, sending jackhammering workers on a permanent lunch break and leaving the province of Trapani holding Sicily's (and Italy's) first nature reserve, complete with Bonelli's eagles, mountain trails, prehistoric caves, and almost alpine scenery. Follow the yellow brick road (umber dirt for grown-ups lacking imagination) to a succession of secluded pebble beaches. With entrances on both sides of the coast, the middle two are most private. Camping is officially illegal, and motor vehicles are prohibited, but hiking is encouraged and superb.

SEGESTA

Trains from Trapani head to the station at Segesta, from which the site is a short walk. (25min., 11 per day 7:30am-8pm, L4500/€2.32.) Ticket office for temple closes 1hr. before park. L8000/€4.13, under 18 and over 65 L4000/€2.07. Open daily 9am-7pm.

Isolated and untouched, the extraordinary ▧**Doric temple** at Segesta is one of the best-preserved examples of ancient Greek architecture. The golden stones dominate a surprisingly green landscape, sculpted by sudden valleys, tall trees, and lush vineyards. Dating from the 5th century BC, the unfinished temple has aided archaeologists in determining the way such temples were built. The structure lacks a roof and cellar, and the gigantic columns are un-fluted. Visitors are now free to roam among the great columns and contemplate the classical lifestyle (minus oil lamps and nude youths wrestling on the ground). Picnic areas by the ticket office and gift shop host many an impromptu symposium, while many take advantage of the absent roof by sunning in the temple's center. Segesta's second great treasure is a large **theater** carved into the top of Mount Barbaro. The L2000/ €1.03 ticket fare for the bus ride (2 per hr.) is well worth avoiding the trek up the steep mountain. The theater holds 4000 and is used for performances of modern and classical plays that take place from mid-July to early-August every other year (ask at the ticket office or tourist offices in Trapani for details). Both the temple and theater are best in the morning and late afternoon, when the temperatures are low and the light brings out the stone's golden and silver hues.

ERICE   ☎ 0923

Medieval Erice is a fairy-tale setting, complete with a majestic castle, enchanting streets, and mysterious fogs. The physical restrictions of a 750m hilltop have kept modern construction at a minimum, leaving the city almost untouched. Traveling here is more like taking a time machine than hopping on a bus. Though somewhat old and tired today, the city was (in its wild, untamed youth) a powerful and wealthy force in the region. Its *richesse* dwarfed that of neighboring Segesta in the 5th century BC, and throughout its history the mountain was considered the mythical home of several fertility goddesses. Cults to the Phoenician Tanit-Astarte, the Greek Aphrodite, and the Roman Venus all sought sanctuary on the cliffs. Now reverence and piety should be saved for the views, which are spectacular. On a clear day you can see forever...or at least to Pantelleria, near Tunisia. When the evening *passegiate* have ended, little Erice locks up for the night, and only howling wind runs through the quiet streets, lulling everyone to sleep.

🖃🔋 TRANSPORTATION AND PRACTICAL INFORMATION. The **AAST** tourist office is a tiny stone cottage at V.C.A. Pepoli, 11, uphill from the first bus stop. (☎ 0923 86 93 88. Open M-Sa 8am-2pm.) The bus from Trapani departs from P. Malta to **Erice/Montalto** (45min.; M-Sa 11 per day, Su 4 per day; L3500/€1.81).

🏠🍴 ACCOMMODATIONS AND FOOD. Lofty hotel prices make Erice more affordable as a daytrip, but if you're enamoured with Erice's medieval streets, try the small and white, clean and bright accommodations at **Albergo Edelweiss,** Cortile P. Vincenzo, 9, where they'll look happy to greet you. (☎ 0923 86 91 58; a.edelweiss@libero.it. Breakfast included. Singles with bath L100,000/€51.65; doubles L130,000/€67.14.

Erice's few restaurants can have prices as steep as the town's cliffs, but offer enough charm enough to make them worthwhile. **Ulysse,** V. Chiaromonte, 45, serves excellent pizzas in air-conditioned splendor. Getting there need not be an odyssey; follow the signs from the city entrance closest to the bus stop. (☎ 0923 86 93 33. Cover L4000/€2.07. Pizza from L8000/€4.13, *primi* and *secondi* from L12,000/€6.20. Open daily noon-3pm and 8-11pm. AmEx/D/MC/V.) At **La Vetta,** V.G. Fontana, 5, off P. Umberto I., *primi* and *secondi* at sidewalk tables start at L10,000/€5.16. Decent pizzas run from L6000/€3.10. (☎ 0923 86 94 04. Open daily noon-5pm and 7:30pm-midnight. AmEx/D/MC/V.) The **Balio Gardens,** up Viale Conte Pepoli from the bus stop, have stone benches carved directly into the hillside that look out over the whole valley and make an ideal location for an enchanting picnic. The **Antica Pasticceria del Convento,** V. Guarnotta, 1, concocts wonderful sweets for L20,000/€10.33 per kg. Despite their name, the *bellibrutti* (pretty-ugly) almond paste cookies are quite tasty, as are their cousins, *sospiri* (lemon and almond). (☎ 0923 86 97 77. Open daily 9am-1:30pm and 3-9pm.)

◎ SIGHTS. Erice fits a surprising number of sites inside the 8th-century BC **Elymian walls** that encircle the city. At the hilltop's highest point, the **Norman Castle (Castello di Venere)** towers over the city. Covered with thick, healthy vines, the castle was built upon the site of several ancient temples to the fertility goddesses; a large altar and several walls from the original ruins were incorporated into the fortification's foundations. At the castle's base, the flowering **Giardni del Balio** spreads its boughs over natural stone benches. The views from the gardens and the castle are incomparable, with most of the western countryside, the Egadi Islands, Pantelleria, and occasionally Tunisia clearly visible. On the other side of town, the 14th-century Gothic **duomo** features original delicate lacy stonework in its large windows. The nearby **bell tower** offers still more exquisite Erice-exclusive views for a small price (L2000/€1.03). Throughout the city, 60 quiet churches await exploration. In P. Museo, the **Museo Comunale di Erice** houses a small but interesting collection of treasures and trinkets from Erice's illustrious history as a city of sacred fertility goddesses. (Open M-Sa 8:30am-7:30pm, Su 9am-1pm. Free.)

EGADI ISLANDS (ISOLE EGADI)

Inhabited since prehistoric times, the Egadi Islands have long been treasured for their natural wonders and exquisite seas. Lying just off the coast of Trapani, the islands of Favignana, Levanzo, and Marettimo are easily accessible by frequent ferries and hydrofoils (see **Trapani Ferries**, p. 627). Consider passing over Favignana in favor of the other two; it is by far the most trafficked, touristed, and tainted by modernity. Levanzo and Marettimo, on the other hand, are largely untouched, with tiny port towns as the sole man-made intrusions. Extraordinary unspoiled natural beauty reveals at once the history and heart of the Egadis. Mules and sheep share plains with cacti, as rugged mountainous cliffs burst upward in all directions. Lush and green, these islands offer some of the best outdoor adventures in Sicily. The best way to see the islands is to choose one and spend an entire day, as the finest beaches and most intriguing discoveries lie far from the ports. Stop by the **bankomat** before leaving; Levanzo and Marretimo have no ATMs.

LEVANZO   ☎ 0923

Levanzo's town is little more than a row of white-washed buildings hugging the cliffs on the port. The bar directly above the docks is the social center of the island. The Ustica office is in the bar (ah, the perfect Italian town). Up to the left, Albergo Paradiso has the island's best accommodations. Newly renovated rooms have ocean views, bath, and lightwood furniture. (☎/fax 0923 92 40 80. Booked solid for Aug. by mid-Mar. Reservations crucial. July-Aug. singles L45,000/€23.24; doubles L85,000/€43.90; *mezza-pensione* L100,000/€51.65. Sept.-June singles L40,000/€20.66; doubles L80,000/€41.32. AmEx/MC/V.) Head down the *lungomare* past the Siremar office to bus #27 to access the island's primary attraction, the **Grotta del Genovese,** a cave containing Paleolithic incisions and ochre-grease paintings depicting ancient tuna-fishing rituals. (☎ 0923 92 40 32 or 74 18 800; nacasti@tin.it. L20,000/€10.33 includes admission and transportation in boat or bumpy jeep. Reserve a week in advance. Tours daily 10:30am and 3pm.) The cave is kept under lock and key to preserve the artworks, but can be conquered with a difficult 2hr. hike (L10,000/€5.16, ages 5-11 L5000/€2.58). A few kilometers along the coastal road to the left of the town, secluded grottoes and beaches await. The crystal-clear water between the rounded rock beach and the neighboring island has a ripping current when the winds pick up; snorkel carefully.

MARETTIMO   ☎ 0923

The most physically remote of the Egadi Islands, Marettimo is equally distant in spirit. Pristine white cubic buildings with bright blue shutters line the curve of the port, introducing visitors to Marettimo's relaxed way of life. The town itself is actually larger than Levanzo and has a few *piazze*. Ask at **Il Pirate** about renting a room. (☎ 0923 92 30 27; follow signs from the hydrofoil dock. L30-35,000/€15.50-18.08 per night, but be ready to haggle.) Because there are few roads, you'll need a boat to see the island's most intriguing caves. The port is filled with boats to rent. Beyond the port and village, the only intrusion into Marettimo's rugged environment is an outstanding new set of stone hiking trails crossing the island. The 2hr. hike (71 min., 32 seconds if you run) to ◼**Pizzo Falcone** (884m), the highest point on any of the islands, is worth every minute. The trailhead is on the sea road, past the

Siremar office and Il Pirate. Around 6pm is prime time to take on the ascent; it makes for one helluva *passagiata*. Sunset from the peak over the wild and uninhabited far side of the island is unforgettable. Along the way, snuggled between dramatic cliffs and lush greenery, stand the **Case Romane,** domestic and sacred ruins dating back to Roman domination. To the right of the little village and past an arc of beach sand at **Punta Traia,** a 17th-century Spanish castle tops the cliff.

PANTELLERIA   ☎ 0923

Seven thousand years ago, this island of thickly wooded mountains, terraced hillsides, and jagged rock was inhabited by Neolithic people in search of **obsidian,** black, petrified lava that was once as valuable as gold. Today the volcanic island is home to dazzling natural phenomena, including a natural sauna, a myriad of hot springs, and the best capers in the Mediterranean. Attracted by its isolation and natural beauty, several celebrities, including Giorgio Armani and Sting, have set up camp on the island. Although Pantelleria lies six hours off the coast from Trapani, it's just five hours from Kelibia, Tunisia. If you come to Pantelleria, expect to linger; many of the best accommodations require a minimum stay of several days, and the nighttime ferry ride means you'll spend much of your first day face down. Once you get behind the wheel of your moped, you'll never want to leave.

▐ TRANSPORTATION

The midnight ferry from Trapani may save money, but it costs one exhausting day. Opt for the hydrofoil and relax on the noon return ferry.

Hydrofoils: Ustica Lines (☎ 0923 91 15 02) has a mini ticket office at #66 on the *lungomare.* Open M-Sa 9am-noon and 5:30-10:45pm. Hydrofoil tickets only 3-4:20pm. Tickets also available at **La Cossira travel agency** (☎ 0923 91 10 78), left of Khamma Hotel, where V. Catania meets the *lungomare.* Open daily 9am-1pm and 5:30-7:30pm. To **Trapani** (2hr.; 4:40pm; L65,000/€33.57).

Ferries: Siremar (☎ 0923 91 11 04), on the waterfront, runs to **Trapani** (5hr.; noon; Mar.-June L39,500/€20.40, July-Aug. L43,500/€22.47). The return journey is a bit more practical than its nocturnal counterpart—it arrives in Trapani at 5pm.

Island Buses: Infrequent buses run weekdays from P. Cavour to 5 island towns (L1500/ €0.77) and the airport (L2500/€1.29). Schedules at tourist office.

Scooter and Car Rental: Autonoleggio Policardo, V. Messina, 31 (☎ 0923 91 28 44, 91 17 41, or 35 56 973; noleggiopolicar@tiscalinet.it), just off the port, up the small street to the right after giant fenced-in scooter lot. Gianni and Maria at your service. Scooters Sept.-July L35,000/€18.08 per day, L210,000/€108.46 per week; Aug. L70,000/€36.15 per day. Cars Sept.-July L50,000/€25.82 per day, L280,000/ €144.61 per week; Aug. L80,000/€41.32 per day.

✴ ▐ ORIENTATION AND PRACTICAL INFORMATION

Ferries and hydrofoils deposit visitors at the northwestern tip of the teardrop shaped island. The curved port is bordered by Pantelleria. A long *lungomare,* first **via Borgo Italia** then **Lungomare Paolo Borsellino,** suns itself from the docks to the private sailboat moorings. At the end of L.P. Borsellino, **Piazza Almanza,** beneath the **Castello,** becomes **Piazza Cavour,** where most services are located, including the **Pro Loco Office.** Roads at either end of the *lungomare* head backward along the coast to other towns. Facing away from the water, the coastal road to the left leads to **Bue Marino, Gadir, Lago Specchio di Venere,** and **Arco dell'Elefante.** The right leads toward the **airport,** the **Sesi, Scauri town,** and **Rekhale.** An inland road (above and to the right of the southwest sea highway, past the dockside Agip station) leads to the **airport, Sibà,** and **Montagna Grande.** Be sure to get a road map from the Pro Loco office before making excursions.

Tourist Office: Pro Loco (☎0923 91 18 38), in P. Cavour in the corner of the municipal building closest to Banco di Sicilia. Look for the language flags. Office is stuffed with brochures, maps, and bus schedules. Open M and W 8am-2pm and 3:30-8pm; Tu and Th 8am-2pm and 6-8pm; F-Sa 9:30am-12:30pm and 6-8pm; hours vary Aug.-May.

Currency Exchange: Banca del Popolo (☎0923 91 27 32), up V. Catania from the *lungomare*. Open M-F 8:20am-1:20pm and 2:50-3:50pm, Sa 8:20-11:50am. Has a Bankomat, as does **Monte dei Paschi di Siena** across the street and **Banco di Sicilia**, in P. Cavour across from the municipal building.

Carabinieri: (☎0923 91 11 09), on V. Trieste.

Guardia Medica: (☎0923 91 11 10), in P. Cavour, on the far right side of the Municipal building (opposite Banco di Sicilia). Separate tourist and resident services. English-speaker available. Open M-F 8pm-8am, Sa 10am-8pm, Su 8am-8pm.

Late-Night Pharmacy: Farmacia Greco, P. Cavour, 28 (☎0923 91 13 10). Open M-F 9:10am-12:20pm and 4:15-8:25pm. Posts late-night rotation.

Hospital: (☎0923 91 18 44), on V. Almanza.

Internet Access: Cossyra Computer Center/Meditel, V. Salibi, 5 (☎0923 91 31 11). As you face the water, the inconspicuously marked pink building is on the right, 600m up the road marked airport to the left of the coastal highway. Come in the morning around 9 or 10am and the proprietor may provide use of the front room computer for free. Open M-Sa 9am-1pm and 5-7:30pm.

Post Office: (☎0923 69 52 33), on V. de Amicis, adjacent to the municipal building and across from Banco di Sicilia (off P. Cavour). Changes cash and traveler's checks. Open M-Sa 8:15am-1:30pm.

Postal Code: 91017.

▚ ACCOMMODATIONS

Dammusi, the square-shaped, domed dwellings of Arab descent unique to this island, are one of the most interesting sleeping options available. Their one meter-thick black lava stone walls keep the interior cool, and water is drawn from a cistern filled by tubes running from the rain-trapping roof. The classic *dammuso* is whitewashed inside and simply furnished, with a sleeping alcove or two and several niches for storage. There are over 3000 *dammusi* on Pantelleria, and nearly every resident rents one out or knows someone who does. There are also very reasonable *affitacamere* (room rental) options available in Pantelleria town (many compare to furnished apartments). Room quality varies considerably and landing a pad often requires patient perseverance. For both *dammusi* and *affitacamere* options, the best places to start are the bars lining the beach. Flyers fill the windows advertising available rooms. Walk up to the counter and state your situation and price—singles L35-50,000/€18.08-25.82; doubles L60-80,000/€30.99-41.32.

▨ **La Vela** (☎0923 91 18 00), on Scauri Scalo. Follow the sea road 10km west from Pantelleria town to these 12 luxurious *dammusi*, with kitchen, bath, and terrace. Black volcanic stone, white domed roofs, brilliant purple bougainvillea, and bamboo-shaded porches. Small beach and sea-view restaurant just below. Reserve 3 months in advance for July and Aug. July-Aug. L50,000/€25.82 per person; Sept-June L40,000/€20.66.

Hotel Khamma (☎0923 91 25 70), on the *lungomare* at end of docks. Not strictly budget, but offers central location and some rooms with sea views. Polished rooms with bath, TV, A/C, phone, and minibar. 7-day min. stay in Aug. Reserve far ahead. Breakfast included. Sept.-July singles L70-80,000/€36.15-41.32, doubles L130-150,000/€67.14-77.47, triples L170-210,000/€87.80-108.46; Aug. singles L110,000/€56.81; doubles L180,000/€92.96; triples L250,000/€129.11. AmEx/D/MC/V.

▜ FOOD

Arab domination in the 8th century AD turned Pantelleria away from fishing to the cultivation of its rich volcanic soil. A local specialty, *pesto pantesco*, is a sauce of tomato, capers, basil, and garlic, eaten with pasta or *bruschetta*. The local variety of *zibbibi* grape yields the island's yellowish grape jelly and the sweet amber *passito* or *muscato* dessert wine (delicious Pantelleria gold). The **SISA supermarket** in Pantelleria town sits above the *lungomare*. Hike up two flights of stairs at the 90 degree bend of the *lungomare*, passing Banco de Popolo on the right. (Open M-Tu and Th-F 8am-1pm and 5:30-8:30pm, W 8am-1pm. MC/V.)

La Risacca, V. Roma, 36 (☎0923 91 29 75). Open-air dining room shaded by reed mats and decorated with small lanterns. Extensive pizza options from L7000/€3.62 served only for dinner. For local flavor try the *cappero*, with tuna, capers, and oregano. Cover L3000/€1.55. *Primi* from L9000/€4.65; *secondi* from L12,000/€6.20. Open daily 12:30-2pm and 7:30-late. Closed M Oct.-May.

Ristorante Il Dammuso (☎0923 91 14 22), on the waterfront before Banco del Popolo, at the 90 degree turn in the port-facing *lungomare*. Popular *trattoria* serves fish in a petite pink dining room on the port. Pasta with *pesto pantesco* (L12,000/€6.20). *Primi* from L12,000/€6.20; *secondi* from L10,000/€5.16. Fills up by 8pm on weekends. Open noon-3pm and 8pm-midnight. D/MC/V.

👁 SIGHTS

Most of Pantelleria's sights are of the spend-an-afternoon-here-with-a-book kind, rather than the peek-in-and-move-on variety, so don't plan to hit more than two of them in a single day. The island is deceptively large, and if you crave liberation from the tyranny of Pantelleria's bus system (which may leave you waiting in the sun for up to five hours, *poverino*), a colorful portside line of free-flying mopeds await your motor-revving inner speed demon. Motorized transportation is an absolute necessity for most destinations inland and to the south; even some coastal spots are a good hour's walk from the scattered bus stops.

▧ BAGNO ASCIUTTO AND MONTAGNA GRANDE. Far away from the port near the inland town of Sibà, a natural rock sauna and the summit of Pantelleria's highest mountain await. Signs guide you through and beyond Sibà to the sauna; the last 10 minutes or so must be traveled on foot. Inside, Panteschi lie face down in a deep, low cave. Bring water and a towel; the oven-like heat is hard to stand, and it's normal to leave and reenter several times. Farther along the sauna path, at the foot of Monte Gibole, the **Favara Grande** is a fumarole that still emits clouds of hot smoke. Many trails, most pretty but short, lead off the asphalt road, and a shady picnic area in a pine grove near the summit is the perfect place to relax after a *bagno asciutto*. If the midday heat is already steamy enough, head to Montagna Grande just for the view. The mountain road past Sibà leads almost to the top, with fantastic views of the second half of the lush *Piano di Ghirlanda*. (*To get to Sibà, take the marked bus from P. Cavour at 6:40am, 12:40, 2, and 7:40pm. Both the Bagno and the mountain are clearly marked. By car, follow signs from Pantellria Town for Sibà.*)

THE SESI AND PUNTO DI SATARIA. The Bronze Age people who inhabited Pantelleria 5000 years ago have left behind the **sesi**, dome-shaped funerary monuments built without mortar. Tunnels in the *sesi* gave access to the womb-shaped chambers where kneeling corpses were placed. The largest remaining *sese* (many have been torn down for building material) contains chambers. (*Take a left off the western sea road, when you see a yellow sign past the posh Mursia Hotel.*) Past the prehistoric village is **Punto di Sataria**, where stairs lead down to the cement-lined Cave of Calypso. A bath in the thermal pools (37°C) is relaxing. From the pools, you can hop directly into the sea two feet away.

LO SPECCHIO DI VENERE (THE MIRROR OF VENUS). Legend has it that Venus used this lake as a mirror before her dates with Bacchus, a frequenter of Pantelleria for its superb (and powerful) *zabbibo* wine. Mere mortals will likewise be unable to resist a long look down into this startlingly aquamarine pool, fringed with firm white mud and surrounded by its bowl of green hillsides. Sulfur springs warm the water and enrich the mud. According to local practice, you're supposed to let the sun dry the therapeutic mud to a white cake on your skin. (*Take the bus to*

Bugeber from P. Cavour and ask the driver to drop you off. Be sure to ask about return times. Buses depart Pantelleria Town M-F at 7:50am, noon, and 2pm. By car or scooter, head toward Bugeber and follow signs for the turnoff.)

THE NORTHEAST COAST AND THE ARCO DELL'ELEFANTE. The best swimming off Pantelleria is along the Northeastern coast in three small inlets. The first of the three, Gadir, is one of the more popular *acquacalda* spots on the island. Cement encloses the bubbly natural pool next to the sea. Superior swimming spots, however, are just down the coast at Cala di Tramontana and Cala di Levante, amazingly uncovered by the omnipresent concrete that rings the island. Perfect for sunbathing, these twin coves are actually one, split by a rocky outcropping. Cala di Levante offers a view of the ░Arco dell'Elefante off to the right. The unofficial symbol of the island, this unusual rock formation looks like a large elephant guzzling up the surf. *(All 3 inlets are on the Khamma/Tracino bus line. Buses leave P. Cavour daily at 6:40, 8, 9:15am, noon, 2, and 6:40pm. Be sure to check return times. Drivers should follow signs for Khamma and Tracino, then follow sign for the coastal roads.)*

IL PIANO DI GHIRLANDA. Surrounded by its own crumbled lip, this fertile crater makes a perfect 2hr. hike from Tracino. The area is one of Pantelleria's prettiest, and a reminder that the island makes its living by farming. Here, terraced hills and caper fields are tended by peasants working out of small, utilitarian *dammusi*. Explore this region by taking the road that leads out of Tracino's P. Perugio. *(Take Tracino bus to the Byzantine tombs, then follow signs to the trails. Ask locals for help)*

▣ BEACHES AND BOAT TOURS

Though surrounded with luscious turquoise water and covered with dramatic rock formations and unusual bathing opportunities, standard definition "beaches" are a rarity on Pantelleria. What sandy stretches there may have been were inexplicably replaced by concrete blocks. Swimming areas around the coast are rated on a three point scale maps by difficulty of access. Rocky coves and swimming grottoes abound, but require some seeking out. The closest swimming to Pantelleria can be found at **Grotta del Bue Marino**, just 2km to the east (to the right when facing the water) along the *lungomare*. Snorkelers prowl the coast, sunbathers perch on volcanic rock, and maniacal young boys hurl themselves off cliffs into the deep waters below. While these feats of derring-do may look exciting, use **extreme caution.** The water becomes shallow at will and the bottom is lined with jagged rocks.

░**Boat tours** are one of the best, fastest, and most relaxing ways to see Pantelleria. Sailing over liquid glass waters provide an excellent looks at hidden grottoes, caves, colorful marine life, and various volcanic remains. Passengers slip demurely in with mask and flippers or dive recklessly off top decks for an unrivaled *bagno dolce* ("sweet swim"). Boats also offer a view of some of Pantelleria's greatest (and otherwise inaccessible) delights, including *Cinderella's slippers*, *L'Arco dell'Elefante*, and *I cinque denti* (the five teeth). The colorful portside line of boats offer various advantages; while smaller boats make it into a few grottoes, their larger cousins provide bamboo shade, napping cushions, and room for young ones to play. Expect to pay L40-50,000/€20.66-25.82 for a full day at sea.

▣ NIGHTLIFE

Pantelleria's most obvious nightlife is at the port, where Panteschi take 24hr. *passagiate* at either of two popular, but interchangeable bars: **Tikirriki** (☎ 0923 91 10 79. Open 5am-3am) and **Il Goloso** (☎ 0923 91 18 14. Open Th-Tu 5:30am-11pm). Twelve kilometers away in the small town of Scauri is the sleek, clubbish **U Frisco** (☎ 0923 91 60 52), on the western seaside road from Pantelleria.

The one *discoteca* open on Pantelleria during the summer is **Oxidana**, on the western seaside road near Hotel Mursía-Cossira; look for a huge electronic scrolling banner that reads "Tutte le Sere." Come midsummer, tourists pack the protozoan seating pods and multi-level outdoor dance floor. (☎ 0923 91 23 19. Open July-Sept. 15. Cover L20,000/€10.33 includes 1 drink.)

SARDINIA (SARDEGNA)

When the boyish vanity of highly cultivated mainland Italians starts to wear thin, when one more church interior will send you into the path of the nearest speeding Fiat, Sardinia's savage coastline and rugged people are bound to soothe your soul. D. H. Lawrence sought respite from the "deadly net of European civilization" that plagued him even in the outermost reaches of Sicily, and he found his escape among the wild horses, wind-carved rock formations, and pink flamingos of this remote island. An old Sardinian legend says that when God finished making the world, he had a handful of dirt left over, which he threw into the Mediterranean and stepped on, creating Sardinia. The contours of that divine foot formed some of the world's most spectacular landscapes. The haphazard, rough-hewn coastlines, tiny rivers, rolling hills, and mighty mountain ranges today support about a million Sardinians, a people some describe as too sturdy and macho to be Italians.

The ancient feudal civilizations of warring shepherd-kings that settled in Sardinia some 3500 years ago left about 8000 scattered *nuraghe* ruins, gutted coneshaped tower-houses built of stone blocks and assembled without mortar. The first recorded invaders of this land were the Phoenicians, followed by the equally belligerent Carthaginians. Sardinia finally settled down when the Romans pacified the island and made it an agricultural colony. In the 13th century, Sardinia became a stomping ground for the Pisans, the Aragonese, the newly united Spanish, and the Piemontese. From this exploited island, Vittorio Emanuele, Italy's first king, began his campaign to unify Italy in 1861. In 1948, the island regained some autonomy, establishing its own administration. Only decades ago, *padroni* (landlords) still held Sardinia's land, and farmers toiled under a system akin to serfdom. Italian Communism leapt to the rescue, and today much of the land is owned by those who till it. But even here, capitalism has infiltrated the coastline, where tourists relax in resorts, lounge on the beaches, and sip fruity drinks.

 Sardinia's cuisine, like its terrain, is rustic and rugged. Hearty dishes like *sa fregula* (pasta in broth with saffron), *malloreddus* (shell-shaped pasta), *culurgiones* (ravioli stuffed with cheese, beets, tomato sauce, lamb, and sausage), and *pane frattau* (thin bread covered with eggs, cheese, and tomato sauce) frequent the island's menus. Celebrated dishes include *cardo* (lamb entrails), pork cooked in lamb's stomach, and grilled pig, horse, donkey, and goat. The infamous product of Sardinian shepherds, *casu fatizzu* (cheese with worms) and savory *pecorino* (sheep's milk cheese) are considered delicacies. Local wines are often sweet and strong. Try *vernaccia d'uva* (for its almond aftertaste) with fish or the robust *cannonau di Sardegna* with red meat.

✈ TRANSPORTATION

FLIGHTS
Flights link Alghero, Cagliari, and Olbia to major Italian cities. Flights are faster than water travel, but exorbitant fares discourage most travelers.

FERRIES
The cheapest way to get to Sardinia is by ferry to Olbia from Civitavecchia, Genoa, or Livorno; expect to pay around L40,000/€20.66 and as much as L133,000/€68.70

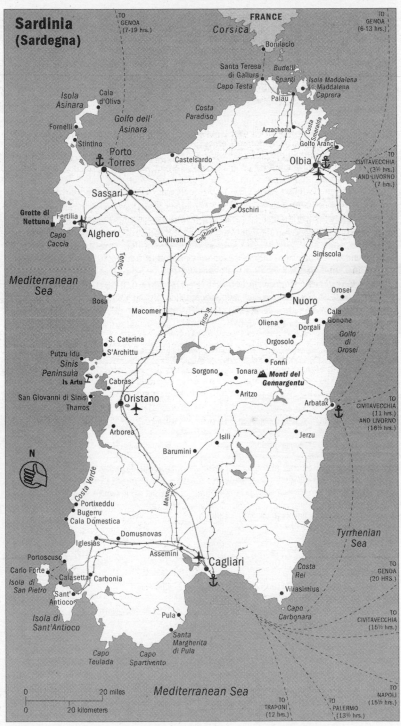

**Sardinia
(Sardegna)**

FRANCE

Corsica

Bonifacio

Santa Teresa
di Gallura
Capo Testa

Budelli
Spargi
Isola Maddalena
La Maddalena
Caprera

*Isola
Asinara*

Cala
d'Oliva

*Golfo dell'
Asinara*

Palau

Fornelli

Stintino

*Costa
Paradiso*

Arzachena

Costa
Smeralda

Porto
Torres

Castelsardo

Golfo Aranci

Olbia

TO
CIVITAVECCHIA
(3½ hrs.)
AND LIVORNO
(7 hrs.)

Sassari

Oschiri

S A R D I N I A

**Grotte di
Nettuno**

Fertilia

Chilivani

Coghinas R.

Siniscola

Alghero

*Capo
Caccia*

Tirso R.

Orosei

*Mediterranean
Sea*

Bosa

Macomer

Nuoro

Cala
Gonone

Oliena

Dorgali

*Golfo
di
Orosei*

S. Caterina

Orgosolo

Putzu Idu

S'Archittu

*Sinis
Peninsula*

Is Artu

Cabras

Sorgono

Tonara

Fonni

▲ *Monti del
Gennargentu*

San Giovanni di Sinis
Tharros

Oristano

Aritzo

Arbatax

TO
CIVITAVECCHIA
(11 hrs.)
AND LIVORNO
(16½ hrs.)

Arborea

Isili

Jerzu

Barumini

*Tyrrhenian
Sea*

N

Costa Verde

Portixeddu
Bugerru
Cala Domestica

Domusnovas

Mannu R.

Iglesias

Assemini

Cagliari

Portoscuso

Carlo Forte

*Isola di
San Pietro*

Calasetta

Carbonia

Carbonia

*Costa
Rei*

TO
GENOA
(20 HRS.)

Villasimius

Sant'
Antioco

Pula

*Capo
Carbonara*

*Isola di
Sant'Antioco*

Santa
Margherita
di Pula

TO
CIVITAVECCHIA
(15½ hrs.)

*Capo
Teulada*

*Capo
Spartivento*

0   20 miles

0   20 kilometers

Mediterranean Sea

TO
NAPOLI
(15½ hrs.)

TO
TRAPONI
(12 hrs.)

TO
PALERMO
(13½ hrs.)

depending on the season, speed of the boat, and departure time (night trips cost more). The cheapest tickets are for daytime *posta ponte* (deck class) slots on the slow-moving boats, but most ferry companies require that the *poltrone* (reserved armchairs) be sold to capacity before they open *posta ponte* for sale. In the price ranges in the table below, the low number is the low-season *poste ponte* fare, and the high number is the high-season *poltrone* fare. Expect to pay an additional L10-60,000/€5.16-30.99 depending on the season, duration, and compartment size. Travelers with cars, mopeds, animals, or children should arrive one to two hours before departure; everyone else should arrive 45 to 90 minutes early.

Tirrenia (☎ 199 123 199 or toll-free 800 824 079; www.tirrenia.it) runs the most ferries to and from Sardinia, has the most offices, and almost always costs the least. *Bravo*, Tirrenia. Offices are in the *stazione marittima* in most cities, including **Cagliari** (☎070 66 60 65), **Civitavecchia** (☎0766 217 03), **Genoa** (☎010 269 82 28), and **Olbia.** There are also Tirrenia offices in **Livorno** (☎0586 42 47 30), on Calata Addis Abeba–Varco Galvani; **Palermo** (☎091 33 33 00), on Calata Marinai d'Italia; **Porto Torres,** V. Mare, 38; and **Rome,** V. Bissolati, 41 (☎06 474 20 41).

Sardinia Ferries (☎019 215 511; fax 215 53 00; www.sardiniaferries.com). Offices in **Livorno,** at the *stazione marittima* (☎0586 881 380; fax 89 61 03), and in **Civitavecchia** (☎0766 50 07 14; fax 50 07 18), at Calata Laurenti.

Moby Lines has offices in **Olbia**'s *stazione marittima* (☎0789 279 27) and in **Livorno** (☎0586 42 67 88; fax 44 39 40), at Varco Galvani.

Grand Navi Veloci has offices in **Genoa**, V. Fieschi, 17 (☎010 58 93 31), and in **Porto Torres** (☎0795 160 34), in the *Porto Industriale*.

Tris (www.tris.it) has offices in **Genoa**, at P. della Vittoria, 12/14 (☎010 576 24 11; fax 576 24 02), in **Porto Torres** (☎079 51 26 34), and in **Palau** (☎0789 70 86 31), at the port terminal.

ROUTE	COMPANY	DURATION	FREQUENCY	PRICE
Civitavecchia-Olbia	Tirrenia (Rapido)	4hr.	2-4 per day	L46-61,500/ €23.76-37.76
Civitavecchia-Olbia	Tirrenia (Traditional)	8hr.	1 per day	L28-44,500/ €14.46-22.98
Civitavecchia-Cagliari	Tirrenia (Traditional)	15-18hr.	2 per day	L48-77,000/ €24.79-39.77
Genoa-Olbia	Tirrenia (Rapido)	6hr.	5-7 per week	L87-137,500/ €44.93-71.01
Genoa-Olbia	Tirrenia (Traditional)	13½hr.	July-Sept. 1 per day	L50-83,000/ €25.82-42.87
Genoa-Porto Torres	Tirrenia (Rapido)	6hr.	1-2 per day in summer	L87-137,500/ €44.93-71.01
Genoa Porto Torres	Tirrenia (Traditional)	13hr.	5-7 per week	L50-83,000/ €25.82-42.87
Genoa-Cagliari	Tirrenia (Traditional)	20hr.	July-Sept. 2 per week	L86-102,000/ €44.42-52.68
Naples-Cagliari	Tirrenia (Traditional)	16hr.	Jan.-Sept. 1 per week	L48-78,000/ €24.79-40.28
Palermo-Cagliari	Tirrenia (Traditional)	13½hr.	1 per week	L45-73,000/ €23.24-37.70
La Spezia-Golfo Aranci	Tirrenia (Rapido)	5½hr.	1 per day in summer	L119,000/ €61.46
Trapani-Cagliari	Tirrenia (Traditional)	11hr.	1 per week	L45-73,000/ €23.24-37.70
Civitavecchia-G. Aranci	Sardinia Ferries	3½-7hr.	1-3 per day in summer	L32-95,000/ €16.53-49.06
Livorno-Golfo Aranci	Sardinia Ferries	10hr.	2 per day in summer	L40-86,000/ €20.66-44.42
Olbia-Livorno	Moby Lines	10hr.	2 per day	L54-106,000/ €27.89-54.74

ROUTE	COMPANY	DURATION	FREQUENCY	PRICE
S. Teresa-Bonifacio	Moby Lines	1hr.	10 per day in summer	L14-18,000/ €7.23-9.3
Genoa-Palau	Tris	12hr.	1-2 per day	L52-84,000/ €26.86-43.38
Genoa-Olbia	Grand Navi Veloci	10hr.	1 per day	L79-133,000/ €40.8-68.69
Genoa-Port Torres	Grand Navi Veloci	10hr.	1 per day	L79-133,000/ €40.8-68.69

CAGLIARI PROVINCE

CAGLIARI ☎070

Cagliari combines the bustle and energy of a modern Italian city with the endearing rural character of the rest of Sardinia. Downtown, regal tree-lined streets run past rows of tiny boutiques and stately *piazze*. By the port, arcades shelter cafes, cinemas, and chic stores from the midday sun. Above the port, the 13th-century Castello district winds up and down the hillside with twisting cobblestoned streets. Medieval Pisan towers overshadow bewildered map-clutching tourists, and an ancient Roman amphitheater welcomes modern-day opera lovers to performances of *Carmen*. It's little wonder that the devil chose to ride Cagliari's mountains and that the Savoy king briefly made the city his home.

▐ TRANSPORTATION

Flights: (☎070 210 51), in the village of **Elmas.** ARST buses run from airport to the city terminal at P. Matteotti (30min., 23 per day 6:15am-midnight, L1300/€0.67).

Trains: FS (☎070 65 62 93 or 84 88 88 088), in P. Matteotti. Open daily 6am-8:30pm. 24hr. ticket machines. To: **Olbia** (4hr.; L24,400/€12.60), via **Oristano** or **Macomer; Oristano** (1½hr., 21 per day 6:30am-10:40pm, L8600/€4.44); **Porto Torres** (4hr.; 6:45am-2:25pm; L24,400/€12.60); **Sassari** (4hr.; 2 per day 6:40am and 4:28pm; L22,800/€11.78). **Ferrovie della Sardegna** (☎070 580 075), in P. della Repubblica. Info office open daily 7:30am-8:45pm. Private railroad with supplementary services to **Arbatax** (6:45am and 1:45pm; L33,100/€17.09).

Buses: Station open M-Sa 8-8:30am, 9am-2:15pm, and 5:30-7pm; Su 1:30-2:15pm and 5:30-7pm. When office is closed, buy tickets on bus. **PANI,** ticket booth in Stazione Marittima. To: **Nuoro** (3½hr.; 4 per day 5:30am-6:15pm; L21,900/€11.31); **Oristano** (1½hr.; 8 per day 5:30am-6:15pm; L11,300/€5.84); **Sassari** (3hr.; 7 per day 5:30am-7pm; L24,400-26,000/€12.39-13.43). **ARST**, P. Matteotti, 6 (☎070 40 98 324), serves local towns, including: **airport** (10min.; 23 per day 5:45am-9:45pm, return 6:15am-midnight; L1300/€0.67); **Arbatax** (10:25am-3pm; L14,800/€7.64); **Barumini** (3 per day 2-7pm, L8600/€4.44); **Pula** (dir: Anna Azzesi, 19 per day 5:25am-8:35pm, L3900/€2.01); **Uta** (12 per day 6:15am-8:30pm, L2800/€1.45); . Open daily 5:45am-10:15pm. **FMS** (☎800 0445 53) runs to: **Bugerru** (3hr., 5 per day 5:40am-5:50pm, L10,400/€5.37); **Calasetta** and **Sant'Antioco** (both 2hr., 2 per day 10am-4pm). Buy tickets at newsstand across from Farmacia Spanno on V. Roma. Buy tickets a day in advance if traveling on Su.

Ferries: Tirrenia (☎070 66 60 65 or 800 82 40 79), in Stazione Marittima. Luggage storage available (p. 642). Open M-F 8:30am-8pm, Sa 8:30am-6pm, Su 4-7pm.

Car Rental: Ruvioli, V. dei Mille, 11 (☎070 65 89 55; fax 65 79 69; ruvioli@essenet.it; www.ruvioli.it). All cars with A/C. Insurance included. You can make reservations here, but must pick up the car at the **airport branch** (☎070 24 03 23). English speaking staff. 21+. Major credit card required. Web reservations preferred. L121,000/€62.49 per day; L586,000/€302.64 per week. Both open daily 8am-11pm. AmEx/D/MC/V.

Local Transportation: Orange **CTM** buses run from P. Matteotti. Tickets sold at ARST station's newsstand. L1500/€0.77 per 1½hr.; L2500/€1.29 per 2hr.; L4000/€2.07 per 24hr.; L15,000/€7.75 for 12 tickets. Buses **P, PQ,** and **PF** go to beach from **Il Poetto.**

✦ 🔃 ORIENTATION AND PRACTICAL INFORMATION

Sandwiched in between the harbor, Stazione Marittima, and the PANI bus stop on one side and outdoor cafes on the other, **via Roma** stretches before those arriving by train, boat, or bus. At one end of V. Roma, **Piazza Matteotti** houses the train station, the ARST station, and the tourist office. Across from P. Matteotti, **Largo Carlo Felice** climbs the steep hill leading to the *castello* and the historic center of town.

TOURIST, FINANCIAL, AND LOCAL SERVICES

Tourist Office: (☎070 66 92 55), in P. Matteotti, in park across from train and bus stations. Oddly shaped wooden cabin with a multilingual staff. Substantial info on local sights. Open M-Sa 8am-8pm; in winter M-Sa 8am-7pm. If you can't get the answers (or maps) you need, the **Stazione Marittima branch,** open daily 8am-7pm.

Budget Travel: CTS, V. Cesare Balbo, 12 (☎070 48 82 60). Info on student discounts and packages. Open M-F 9am-1pm and 4-7:30pm, Sa 9am-1pm. **Memo Travel,** V. Pitzolo, 1a (☎070 40 09 07). Open M-F 9am-1pm and 4-7:30pm, Sa 9am-1pm.

Laundry: Lavanderia Self-Service, V. Sicilia, 20 (☎070 565 521), off V. Bayle. 6kg wash L6000/€3.10; 20min. dry L5000/€2.58. Prices decrease by L1000/€0.52. Open daily 8am-10pm (last wash at 9pm).

Bookstore: Cocco, V. Roma, 65 (☎070 65 02 56). Well-stocked in classics and current best-sellers. Open M-Sa 9am-9pm. MC/V.

Luggage Storage: At the Stazaione Marittima. Free. Open daily 7am-7pm.

EMERGENCY AND COMMUNICATIONS

Emergency: ☎113. **First Aid/Ambulance:** ☎118.

Police: V. Amat, 9 (☎070 492 169).

Pharmacy: Farmacia Dr. Spano, V. Roma, 99 (☎070 65 56 83). Open M-F 9am-1pm and 4:50-8:10pm; in winter M-F 9am-1pm and 4:30-7:50pm.

Hospital: V. Ospedale, 46 (☎070 66 32 37), by Chiesa di S. Michele.

Internet Access: Mail Boxes Etc., V. Trieste, 65B (☎070 673 704), near the post office. L15,000/€7.75 per hr. Open M-F 9am-1pm and 3:30-7:30pm. MC/V. **V@ssel,** V. Tigellio, 22A/B (☎070 67 20 20). From V. Porto Scalas, turn right on V. San Ignazio da Laconi and take 2nd left onto V. Tigellio. Take right fork and it's on the right. L6000/€3.10 per 30min.; L10,000/€5.16 per hr. Open M-F 10am-1pm and 4-9pm.

Post Office: (☎070 65 82 57), in P. del Carmine. Take V. Sassari from P. Matteotti. Fermo Posta, phone cards, and **currency exchange.** Open M-F 8am-6:40pm, Sa 8:10am-1:20pm.

Postal Code: 09100.

🏠 ACCOMMODATIONS

🏨 **Pensione Vittoria,** V. Roma, 75 (☎070 65 79 70). Cross V. Roma from train station or ARST station and turn right. Check in on 3rd fl. 14 majestic rooms, Venetian chandeliers, bathrooms, and A/C. Possibly the nicest in Cagliari. Breakfast L9000/€4.65. Wheelchair accessible. Reserve ahead. Singles L60-65,000/€31-33.57, with bath L70-75,000/€36.15-38.73; doubles L90-95,000/€46.48, L100-110,000/€51.65-56.81.

Hotel Quattro Morii, V.G.M. Angioj, 27 (☎070 668 535; fax 666 087). Set back a little from the noisy port, and handy to P. Yenne, this hotel is modern and attractively decorated. The staff helpful and polite. A nice, but relatively expensive break from the standard *pensione*. All rooms with A/C, bath, phone, and TV. Reservations recommended. Singles L90,000/€46.48; doubles L130,000/€67.14. AmEx/D/MC/V.

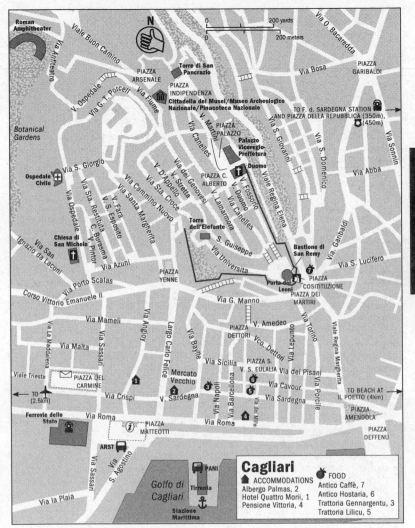

Cagliari

🏠 ACCOMMODATIONS
Albergo Palmas, 2
Hotel Quattro Morii, 1
Pensione Vittoria, 4

🍅 FOOD
Antico Caffè, 7
Antico Hostaria, 6
Trattoria Gennargentu, 3
Trattoria Lilicu, 5

Albergo Palmas, V. Sardegna, 14 (☎ 070 65 16 79). Cross V. Roma and turn right. Take 1st left on Largo Carlo Felice, and 1st right on V. Sardegna. Excellent location and accommodating management. 14 rooms have chair, sink, and bed. Singles L40,000/€20.66; doubles L60,000/€31, with shower L70,000/€36.15.

🍴 FOOD

Along V. Sardegna, many small shops provide fruit, cheese, and bread. Try **Panetteria Mura,** V. Sardegna, 40 (☎ 070 66 38 64; MC/V), a small market, and a heavenly bakery. (Open M-Sa 7:30am-1:30pm and 4:30-8:30pm.) The colossal **Iper Pan La Plaia,** V. la Plaia, 15, sells groceries. (Open daily 9am-9pm.) On Sundays, explore the **market** on the far side of the stadium in Borgo S. Elia for fresh fruit and seafood. There's a down-to-earth **self-service restaurant** at V. Sassari, 16, with a

AIO? EIA! If you've just sat down with a hearty plate of horse and tentacles and suddenly realize that your four years of college Italian aren't helping you eavesdrop effectively on the people at the table next to you, chances are that you've just had your first encounter with Sardo. The German linguist Weher divided it into four main dialects, if matters weren't already complicated enough for poor tourists from the mainland: Logudorese (from Logudo, near the center of the island), Campidanese (from the plains of Campidano around Cagliari in the south), Sasserese (from Sassari, in the northwest), and Gallurese (from Gallura, in the north). Sardo is influenced by Italian, but also by the tongues of its ancient conquerors: Arabs, Germans, Spanish, and the Romans. On the street of Sardinian towns, you're likely to hear locals greeting each other with "Eia" (pronounced eh-yah), which means "yes" but is used more like "ciao", and "Aio" ("ay-yoh") meaning–you guessed it–let's go.

L13,000/€6.71 *menù* and A/C. For a very basic pizza in a very basic setting, try **Pizzeria 744** at V. Roma, 181. (Across from the train station. ☎070 666 626.)

🞐 **Trattoria Lilicu,** V. Sardegna, 78 (☎070 65 29 70). Established 80 years ago and still run by the same family. Simple *trattoria* serves traditional Sardi dishes like *lacetti di agnelle* (lamb; L10,000/€5.16) and expertly prepared seafood (L15-20,000/€7.75-10.33) at clamorous communal tables. Full meal L35-40,000/€18.08-20.66. Cover L3000. Open M-Sa 1-3pm and 8:30-11pm. Reservations necessary. D/MC/V.

🞐 **Antica Hostaria,** V. Cavour, 60 (☎070 66 58 70; fax 66 58 78). Reputedly one of Cagliari's best restaurants, but still within the budget traveler's reach. This beautiful restaurant maintains an art nouveau decor, clothes its waitstaff in tuxes, and starts your meal with a basket of bread and glass of a tasty yellow drink made of white whine, pear juice, and a little drop of gin. Classy, huh? Tasty *malloreddus gnocchetti* (L15,000/€7.75) are far from malodorous. Veal in *vernaccia* sauce L18,000/€9.30. Cover L4000/€2.07. Open M-Sa 12:45-3pm and 8-11pm; closed Aug. AmEx/MC/V.

Trattoria Gennargentu, V. Sardegna, 60 (☎070 65 82 47). Join the locals in this *salumeria* and restaurant for a Sardinian feast of *spaghetti alle arselle e bottarga* (with baby clams and seasoned with ground fish eggs) for L12,000/€6.20 and a zesty *salsiccia arrosto* for L7000/€3.62. The wine list is as long as the menu. Cover L2500/€1.29. Open M-Sa 12:30-3pm and 8-11pm. AmEx/MC/V.

Antico Caffè, P. Costituzione, 10/11 (☎070 65 82 06). The haunt of Nobel Prize winners, Italian presidents, and flashy Italian TV stars; this elegant, snobbish cafe has over 150 years of history. Reserve a table outside. Delicious crêpes (L5500-10,000/€2.84-5.16), decadent ice cream sundaes (L8-10,000/€4.13-5.16), and bountiful salads (L6-9000/€3.10-4.64). Breakfast L6-13,000/€3.1-6.71; *primi* L7-9000/€3.62-4.65. 20% service charge. Open daily 8am-3am. AmEx/MC/V.

👁 SIGHTS

ROMAN AMPHITHEATER. This 2nd-century theater was constructed after the Carthaginians succumbed to the Roman juggernaut in 238 BC. Built into a rocky hillside, the amphitheater conforms beautifully to the natural slope. Underground cages once hosted ferocious animals, and the arena itself was used for gladiatorial combat. Today summer performances in the refurbished theater are a little more civilized. From July to September, the city hosts an **arts festival.**

BASTIONE DI SAN REMY. When you get to **Piazza Costituzinoe,** you'll be dwarfed by an enormous arch and a staircase that seems to be carved into the hillside. Climb up the graceful (though graffiti-covered) double stairway, through the archway, to the terraces of the 19th-century *bastione* for a spectacular view of Cagliari spread out below. Take particular notice of the Golfo degli Angeli, the pink flamingos, and the **Sella del Diavolo** (Devil's Saddle), a rock formation within the mountains surrounding the city. The *bastione* was destroyed during World War II but was rebuilt and today continues to divide the modern city and the medieval *castello* district. For a stroll through medieval Cagliari, start at the top of the Bastione, follow narrow streets as they wind past Aragonese churches and Piedmontese palaces, and stop at the Pisan wall that runs about the hill.

DUOMO. This stunning cathedral was modeled after the one in Pisa (p. 373). Below the solemn inscription on the facade ("Sanctae Mariae Sardorum"), dazzling gold mosaics sit atop each entryway. The pulpits on either side of the main entrance and the four wrestling lions at the base of the 12th-century altar are the works of Guglielmo Pisano. The ornate wooden balcony to the left and in front of the altar served as the seat of the Piedmontese king—he refused to sit among the people for fear of regicide. The **sanctuary** below the *duomo* was carved into the rock in 1618. Colorful marble inlays cover the 292 niches that contain the relics of early Christian martyrs. *(P. Palazzo, 3. ☎ 070 66 38 37. Open daily 8am-12:30pm and 4-8pm.)*

MUSEUMS. Although the menacing spear above the entrance recalls the building's original purpose, today the Arsenale houses a modern complex of research museums that includes the vaguely inspiring **Museo Archeologico Nazionale.** Among the Phoenician statuettes and Roman glass works are impressive armies of tiny, 1000-year-old bronze figurines. *(Take V. Buoncammino to P. Arsenale and pass under the Torre di S. Pancrazio to the Arsenale. ☎ 070 65 59 11. Open May-Aug. Tu-Su 9am-8pm; Sept.-Apr. 9am-1:30pm and 3-7:30pm. Wheelchair accessible. L5000/€2.58, over 65 and under 18 free.)*

The **Pinacoteca Nazionale,** in the same complex as the archaeological museum, displays medieval and Baroque religious paintings. The labyrinthine museum is built around the remains of a 16th-century city fortification, visible on the ground floor. Works include portraits by the most influential Sardinian painter of the 19th century, Giovanni Marghinotti. *(☎ 070 66 24 96. Open Tu-Su 8:30am-7:30pm. Wheelchair accessible. L4000/€2.07, ages 18-25 L2000/€1.03, over 60 and under 18 free.)*

BOTANICAL GARDENS. A perfect spot for a picnic, the university gardens protect over 500 species of plants, many of which are unique to Sardinia. Chill out by the fountain and forget that you're anywhere near a city. *(V. Fra Ignazio, 11. Head down V.S. Ignazio da Laconi to the university. ☎ 070 675 35 22. Open daily Apr. 1-Sept. 30 8am-1:30pm and 3-8pm; Oct. 1-Mar. 31 8am-1:30pm. L1000/€0.56, under 6 and over 60 free.)*

BEACHES. **Il Poetto,** Cagliari's most popular stretch of pure white sand and emerald-sapphire water spans 10km from the massive Devil's Saddle to the Margine Rosso (Red Bluff). Locals claim it's ugly, but only because the nearby treasures of **Villasimus** and **Chia** put most beaches in Sardinia to shame. Behind Il Poetto, the salt-water **Stagno di Molentargius** (Pond of Molentargius) provides habitat for flamingos and their fair-skinned admirers. City buses P, PQ, and PF run to the beaches (20min., L1500/€0.77). To avoid more crowded areas, hold off for a few stops once you see the beach. For more private sunning and swimming head to the less crowded **Cala Mosca,** a smaller beach surrounded by dirt paths leading to isolated coves. Take city bus #5 to Stadio Amsicora and then bus #11 to the beach.

🎵 ENTERTAINMENT

Most bars and clubs in the city are open from 9pm to 5am, but they shut down in August when dancing moves outdoors. Some bars are members-only digs—you'll have to shell out a one-time L10-25,000/€5.16-12.91 for a nifty AICS card; look for a sticker on the window to see if that's necessary. **De Candia,** V. De Candia, 1, on top of the Bastione de San Remy, serves expensive drinks to an older crowd. (☎ 070 65 58 84. Cocktails L8000/€4.13. Open in the summer M-Sa 8am-2am, Su 7am-1:30pm and 4pm-2am.) On summer evenings, **Piazza Yenne** is packed full of locals chatting, drinking, and flirting. **Caffè Forum** and **Bar Centrale** are both hopping, as is **L'Isola del Gelato,** P. Yenne, 35, a *gelateria* with an impressive selection and a waterfall in the wall that feeds a river running beneath the transparent floor.

Discos don't require AICS cards and are generally more lively. If you have a car or moped at your disposal and appreciate big pick-up scenes, you'll enjoy a night at the beach with the young local crowd. If you don't have a car, take the PQ bus before 10:30pm to Il Poetto and return by cab. Bronzed Italians fill **Pandemonium** (the last stop on Il Poetto) on weekends.

Outdoor movies are shown (without subtitles) in July and August (around 9pm) at the Marina Piccola off Spiaggia del Poetto. Buy tickets (L5-10,000/€2.58-5.16) at the Marina. Merchants converge on the terraces of the Bastione di S. Remy for a **flea market** on Sunday mornings and a smaller daily flea market in P. del Carmine.

On the 1st of May, Sardinians flock to Cagliari for the **Festival of Sant'Efisio**, honoring a deserter from Diocletian's army who saved the island from the plague but couldn't save himself from a beheading. A costumed procession escorts his effigy from the capital down the coast to the small church that bears his name.

▓ DAYTRIP FROM CAGLIARI: BARUMINI

*The only direct service from Cagliari to **Barumini** is the **ARST bus** (1½hr., 2 and 5pm, L7200/€3.72). Buses return to Cagliari in the morning. If you want to return in the evening, take the ARST bus (40min., 6:05pm, L3500/€1.81) to **San Luri**. In San Luri, take commuter **train** to Cagliari (50min.; 7:04pm; L4200/€2.17, L5000/€2.58 if purchased on the train). If bus is late, the next train is 9:01pm. To see the **ruins:** after you get off of the bus, walk to the intersection and take a left in front of the bar. Site is about 10min. down the road. Open daily 9am-7pm. L8000/€4.13. Free tours every 30min. in Italian.*

An agricultural village in the rolling countryside 60km north of Cagliari, Barumini is 1km west of Sardinia's most complex set of *nuraghi* ruins, at ◪**Su Nuraxi.** Here you can see the remains of a defensive castle-like structure and the village that surrounded it. Construction of the first of five towers began in 1500 BC; the central tower grew to 14m over the course of several centuries, and the walls reached a thickness of 6m in many parts, reflecting the expanding power of the prehistoric fortress's rulers. The surrounding village huts multiplied in response. Much of the architecture is ingenious for its era, and despite the best efforts of archaeologists and historians, the procedure used to construct the castles remains a mystery. In AD 238, well after the decline of *nuraghi* civilization, Romans built over the silt-covered village. Their usurpation altered little, and superstitious farmers left the mound of earth-covered ruins untouched (except for use as a burial pit) through 1851, when archaeologists excavated them.

NEAR CAGLIARI

CALASETTA   ☎0781

On the northwestern tip of Sant'Antioco Island, Calasetta has Nuraghic, Punic, and Roman roots. Over the course of Tabarcan, Piemontese, French, and Spanish occupation, these roots have long withered away, and nothing but a small, nondescript, quiet Sardinian town remains. Fairly modern and uninteresting concrete buildings are laid out upon a simple grid of streets centered around **via Roma** (the main thoroughfare). A few beaches lie on either side of the port.

Saremar Ferries (☎0781 884 30) has a ticket office at the port and runs boats to **Carloforte** (30min.; 13-17 per day 7:35am-11:50pm; L3-4000/€1.55-2.07, children L1500-2000/€0.77-1.03, cars L8600-21,700/€4.44-11.21). Buy **FMS** (☎0781 882 91) tickets at the *tabacchi* on the corner of V. Roma and V. Sicilia. **Buses** leave from the port to **Cagliari** (3hr.; 10 per day 4:54am-5:45pm; L10,400/€5.37) and **Sant'Antioco** (30min., 16 per day 4:54am-9:38pm, L1300-3800/€0.67-1.96).

The **Pro Loco Tourist Office** (☎0781 885 34; prolocal@tin.it; www.prolococalasetta.it), on V. Lungomare Colombo, in the same building as the *biblioteca*, has lots of historical information and maps. In case of an **emergency,** call the **police** (☎113), **carabinieri** (☎0781 884 22), **medical emergency hotline** (☎0781 884 40), or the **hospital** (☎0781 66 83 44). For **Internet access,** try the *Biblioteca Comunale*

(☎0781 883 78) on V. Lungomare Colombo below the tourist office. No charge if you can assure the librarian you'll only use it once or twice. (The **post office** is found at V.R. Margherita, 53. (☎0781 884 24. Open M-Sa 9am-1pm.)

The sheets at **Hotel Cala di Seta,** V.R. Margherita, 61, may not be silk, but the bedspreads sure are pink. Twenty-one feminine rooms, all with A/C, bath, and phone. (☎0781 883 04; fax 315 38. Singles L60-100,000/€31-51.65; doubles L90-160,000/€46.48-82.63. Half-pension L85-135,000/€43.90-69.72 per person, required in Aug. AmEx/MC/V.) The **Nonna Isa Supermarket,** at the corner of Lungomare Colombo and V. Barcelona, is just the place to restock. (Open M-Sa 8am-1pm and 5-8pm, Su 8am-noon.) If you get stuck waiting for the ferry, you can grab a drink or a bite to eat at **Kambusa,** right next to the port; a plate of spaghetti will run you L10-12,000/€5.16-6.20. **FMS buses** leave from the port to Spiaggia Grande, Calasetta's biggest and most appealing beach (10min.; 7 per day 10:15am-7pm; L1300/€0.67).

CARLOFORTE ☎0781

On the eastern coast of the Isola S. Pietro, Carloforte was founded by Ligurians. Today it's a relatively upscale resort town that offers a beach, a port, beautiful blue water, and the occasional casual daytrip. Massive salt ponds support flocks of flamingos, fields of grass are littered with crumbling towers, and lighthouses lead to several lovely beaches, including **La Caletta.**

Saremar Ferries (☎0781 85 40 05) runs boats to **Carloforte** (30min.; 13 per day 6:55am-11:10pm; L3-4000/€1.55-2.07, children L1500-2000/€0.77-2.07, cars L8600-21,700/€4.44-11.21). **Marinatour Noleggio,** V. Porcile, 12 (☎0781 44 29 41 or 854 110; marinatour@tiscalinet.it), rents scooters and organizes diving excursions.

Services include: the **Pro Loco Tourist Office** in P. Carlo Emanuele (☎0781 85 40 09; open M-Sa 9:30am-12:30pm and 5-7pm); a **Banca Commerciale Italiana,** C. Cavour, 1, with **currency exchange** and a 24hr. **ATM** (open M-F 8:20am-1:40pm and 2:50-4:15pm, Sa 8:20am-11:50pm); the **carabinieri** (☎0781 85 58 21); **Guardia Medica** (☎0781 85 62 28); an **ambulance** (☎0781 85 52 70); and a **post office,** on Porto Paglia off P. dei Galanzieri (☎0781 85 40 38; open M-F 9am-1pm and Sa 9am-12:30pm).

In a refurbished old town home on the water, the ◪**Hieracon Hotel,** C. Cavour, 63, caters to a mature crowd that appreciates the backyard garden, dignified interior, and prices. (☎0781 85 40 28. Half-pension included. Singles and doubles L125,000/€64.56 per person; triples L108,000/€55.78. AmEx/MC/V.) Welcome to the **Hotel California,** V. Cavallera, 15, such a lovely place, such a lovely face, and always plenty of room (except May-Oct., when you should reserve ahead). It's far from port, but the rooms are airy and clean. (☎0781 854 470 or 855 539. Doubles with bath L85-150,000/€43.90-77.47.) For **camping,** catch the bus toward La Caletta and ask to be let off at the **Campeggio "La Caletta."** (☎0781 85 21 12. Open June 15-Sept. 15. L20,000/€10.33 per person, children L12,000/€6.20.)

Beaches line the shores south of Carloforte and are only a 15-minute bus ride away (11 per day 9:25am-7:14pm; L1300/€0.67, buy tickets from Saremar office in P. Carlo Emanuele). The drive takes you past the *Saline di Carloforte,* some saltwater ponds awash with pink flamingos, to La Caletta, on the western side of the island. Here dark cliffs enclose an underpopulated mini-bay.

ORISTANO PROVINCE

ORISTANO ☎0783

In the 7th century, the stoic inhabitants of Tharros repelled invasion after invasion until a band of merciless Moorish pirates finally forced them to abandon their homes. With nowhere else to go, they set up camp around nearby Oristano. Today, Oristano has developed into a modest-sized city, complete with the island's largest *duomo*. Still, as in the 7th century, it would take nothing less than an angry mob of Moorish pirates to convince you to stay in Oristano much longer than a day. It's most notable as a base for exploring the natural and historical splendor of the nearby Sinis Peninsula, where the enticing Phoenician and Roman ruins at Tharros, the awe-inspiring arch at S'Archittu, and the beaches of Is Arutas all beckon.

▐ TRANSPORTATION

Trains: (☎0783 722 70), on P. Ungheria, 1km from town center. Luggage storage available (p. 648). To: **Cagliari** (1-2hr., 26 per day, L8600/€4.44); **Macomer** (9 per day, 6:45am-9:21pm, L5500/€2.84); **Olbia** (2½hr.; 1:20pm; L16,600/€8.57) via **Ozieri Chilvani.** To get to **Sassari,** go to Macomer for connection.

Buses: PANI, V. Lombardia, 30 (☎0783 21 22 68), inside Bar Blu. Open daily 7am-10pm. To: **Cagliari** (1½hr.; 4 per day 8:55am-9:34pm; L11,300/€5.84); **Nuoro** (2hr.; 4 per day 7:05am-7:50pm; L11,300/€5.84); **Sassari** (2¼hr.; 4 per day 7:05am-7:50pm; L13,900/€7.18). **ARST,** on V. Cagliari, runs local routes (☎0783 711 85 or 71 776). Ticket office open daily 7:30am-2pm and 4:30-6pm. To: **Putzu Idu** (dir: Su Pallosu; 50min., 2 per day 6:10am-1:50pm, L4500/€2.32); **Santa Caterina** (dir: Porto Alabe; 40 min., 6 per day 7:10am-7:10pm, L3400/€1.76); **San Giovanni di Sinis** (July 1-Sept. 31, dir: Is Arutas; 40min., 5 per day 8:25am-6:30pm, L2800/€1.45). **ARST** runs to **Cagliari** (2hr.; 2 per day 6:15am-2:10pm; L11,700/€6.04).

Taxis: At P. Roma (☎0783 70 280), the train station (☎0783 74 328), and from PANI (☎0330 43 04 98).

Car Rental: Avis, V. Liguria, 17 (☎0783 31 06 38). Cars from L127,000/€65.59 per day. 21+. Open Su-F 9am-1pm and 4-7:30pm, Sa 9am-1pm.

Scooter Rental: Marco Moto, V. Cagliari, 99/101. Scooters and tandems L50-75,000/€25.82-38.73 per day. 18+. Open M-F 8:30am-1pm and 3:30-8pm. AmEx/MC/V.

✹ ORIENTATION

To get to the city center from the ARST bus station, take the back exit and turn left. Continue past the *duomo* and head straight onto V. De Castro, which spills into **Piazza Roma,** the heart of the city. From the train station, follow **via Vittorio Veneto,** the street farthest to the right, to **Piazza Mariano.** Then take **via Mazzini** to P. Roma. From the PANI station on V. Lombardia on the other side of town, face the Blu Bar and turn right. At the end of the street, turn right onto **via Tirso,** left onto **via Cagliari,** and left on **via Tharros,** which leads directly into P. Roma.

▐ PRACTICAL INFORMATION

Tourist Office: Pro Loco, V.V. Emanuele, 8 (☎/fax 0783 30 32 12; proloco.oris@tiscalinet.it). Maps and info on local festivals. Conveniently located. Open M-F 9am-12:30pm and 4:30-8pm, Sa 9am-12:30pm. Mobile tourist info booth in **P. Roma.** Open July-Sept. M-F 9am-1pm and 9-11pm, Sa 9am-1pm.

Currency Exchange: Banca Nazionale del Lavoro, Banca di Napoli, and **Credito Italiano** are in P. Roma. All open M-Sa 8:30am-1:20pm and 3-4:30pm, Su 8:20-11:50am.

Luggage storage: In the train station. L3000/€1.55 per day. Open daily 6am-7:30pm.

Emergency: ☎113.

Ambulance: ☎0783 743 18. **First Aid:** ☎0783 317 213.

Pharmacy: V. Umberto 49/51 (☎0783 05 07 00). Open M-F 9am-1pm and 5-8:20pm.

Hospital: (☎0783 31 71), on V. Fondazione Rockefeller.

Internet Access: Center for Cultural Services at the **Community Library,** V. Carpaccio, 9 (☎0783 21 16 56). Free access. Open M-F 9am-1pm and 4-7pm. **Internet Point,** V. Calgiari, 283, outside of ARST bus station, across the street to the left. Slow connection L7500/€3.87 per hr. Open M-Sa 10am-1pm and 5-11pm.

Post Office: V. Liguria, 60 (☎0783 21 17 78). Open M-Sa 8:15am-6:40pm.

Postal Code: 09170.

▟ ACCOMMODATIONS & CAMPING

Oristano caters primarily to travelers on their way to the beaches, and low competition maintains high prices. For attractive *agriturismo* options in the surrounding countryside, ask at the tourist office or **Consorzio Agriturismo di Sardegna**, P. Cattedrale, 17. (☎0783 739 54; fax 739 24; cas.agriturismo@tiscali.net. Open Apr.-Oct. M-F 9am-1pm and 4-7pm, Sa 9am-noon; Nov.-Mar. M-F 9am-1pm.)

ISA, P. Mariano, 50 (☎/fax 0783 36 01 01; isarose@tiscalinet.it). Exit from back of ARST station, turn left, and turn right on V.V. Emanuele. Walk through edge of P. D'Arborea and through the adjoining P. Martini, and then follow V. Lamarmora to the end. Turn right, then immediately left. Take 1st right down V. Mazzini to P. Mariano. Immaculate baths, phones, TV, and A/C. Breakfast included in high season. Reservations recommended July-Aug. Singles L85,000/€43.90; doubles L140,000/€72.30. Extra bed L20,000/€10.33. Half-pension L90,000/€46.48. AmEx/MC/V.

Piccolo Hotel, V. Martignano, 19 (☎0783 715 00). From the ARST station take the back exit, turn right, and continue across P. Mannu. Head down the street to the left (it runs east to west) and take the 1st left. Turn right at the end of this street. From the PANI station, call a cab. Town's best budget option. Clean rooms, and firm beds. Mosquitoes are everywhere—close your windows and lather on plenty of repellent. All 10 rooms with bath, many with balconies. Singles L50,000/€25.82; doubles L100,000/€51.65.

Camping: Marina di Torregrande (☎/fax 0783 222 28), on V. Stella Maris, near the beach and 100m out of Torre Grande toward Oristano (7km). Orange local buses leave from V. Cagliari in front of the ARST station (10min., 2 per hr. 7:30am-12:30am, L1500/€0.78). Clean bathrooms, hot showers, a restaurant/pizzeria, bar, and small market with fresh produce. Unpleasant fumes may waft over from the nearby tar plant. Packed during the summer. 400 lots. Check-in 8am-2pm and 4-9pm. Open May-Sept. L10,000/€5.16 per person, L6000/€3.10 for children, L10-12,000/€5.16-6.20 per tent. Tent rental L55,000/€28.41 for 4-person capacity. Bungalows available, prices vary seasonally. Camper L60,000/€31. Electricity L3000/€1.55 per day.

▟ FOOD

The **Euro-Drink market**, P. Roma, 22, sells inexpensive basics and special *Sarde* products. (Open M-Sa 8am-1:30pm and 5-9pm. MC/V.) A **STANDA supermarket**, V. Diaz, 53, is at the corner of V. XX Settembre. (Open daily 9am-9pm. AmEx/MC/V.) A **SiSA supermarket** is at V. Amiscora, 26. (Open M-Sa 8am-8pm.)

Ristorante Craf da Banana, V. De Castro, 34 (☎0783 706 69). Slightly more expensive than other restaurants near the town center, but far more elegant. Low arched brick ceilings, earthy lighting, and fine cuisine. *Primi* L13,000/€6.76; *pesce* from L8000/€4.15 per *etto*. Reservations necessary. Open M-Sa 1-4:30pm and 8-11:30pm. AmEx/MC/V.

La Torre, P. Roma, 52 (☎0783 707 84). Local favorite serves Sardinian fare. Pizza L6500-11,000/€3.36; *gnocchetti all'orgosolese* (pasta with tomato meat sauce; L10,000/€5.16). Cover L2000/€1.03. Open Tu-Su noon-3pm and 7-11pm. Pizzeria open daily 6:30-11pm. D/MC/V.

La Muraglia, P. Mariano, 2 (☎0783 71 309). If your desire to eat cheaply overrides your interest in local cuisine, this Chinese restaurant's lunchtime menu (plenty of food for L12,500/€6.46) is only slightly more expensive than a picnic—and you get to sit in an air-conditioned room. Chat with the bus drivers who hang out at the bar. *Primi* L5-8000/€2.58-4.13; *secondi* L8-12,000/€4.13-6.20.

◉ ▟ SIGHTS AND HIKING

CHIESA DI SAN FRANCESCO. This pastel church was heavily remade in Neoclassical fashion during the 19th century, leaving little of the original interior intact. A notable remnant is the gruesome wooden crucifix draped with the emaciated and

> **THE LORD IS MY SHEPHERDESS** Unlike most Italian cities, Oristano is heir to a matriarchal tradition, with roots in the 14th-century reign of Eleonora d'Arborea. Not only did Eleonora develop the progressive *Carta de Logu* legal code (which was in use from 1392-1897), but she also helped her people fight off the Aragonese for five years (she eventually signed a truce) and paved the way for future female leaders. In contrast to other cities, dotted with marble Vittorio Emanueles and Gramscis, Oristano's *piazze* are guarded by statues of powerful *donne*. This estrogen-rich tradition still continues—every second Saturday of September, crowds of women don yellow flowers and march on Oristano's streets, celebrating this legacy.

tortured body of Christ. Though the artist was actually a 16th-century teacher of Catalán culture, the townspeople originally attributed the cross to Nicodemus; they felt that such a vivid image could only have been captured by an actual eyewitness to the Crucifixion. The sacristy houses a 16th-century polyptych of *St. Francis Receiving the Stigmata* and Nino Pisano's 14th-century marble statuette of San Basilio. It's the largest cathedral in Sardegna. (*In P.E. d'Arborea at the end of V. de Castro. Open M-Sa 8am-1pm, Su 7am-noon and 4-7:15pm. Free.*)

TOWER OF SAN MARIANO II. Once a fortified entrance to the medieval city, this 13th-century tower dominates P. Roma. On summer evenings, young *oristanesi* gather in this *piazza* and the adjoining C. Umberto to flirt, drink Ichnusa (Sardinian beer), and chatter away on their *telefonini*.

ANTIQUARIUM ARBORENSE. This museum shelters a small collection of Nuraghic, Punic, Phoenician, and Roman artifacts unearthed at Tharros. On display are urns, cups, containers, and earthenware of all shapes and sizes, as well as a tabletop model of ancient Tharros. (*In P. Corrias, near P.E. d'Aborea. ☎ 0783 744 33. Open daily 9am-2pm and 6:30-11pm. Wheelchair accessible. L4000/€2.07.*)

BASILICA OF SANTA GIUSTA. In its synthesis of Lombard and Pisan influences, this 12th-century basilica is typically Sardinian. Far from inspiring pious tranquility, the sculpted facade depicts two tiny lions dismembering and devouring a deer. (*V. Manzoni, 2, on the road to Cagliari, 3km out of town. Take the ARST pullman toward "Arborea" and get off at 1st stop (5min., every hr. 6:15am-8:05pm, L1300/€0.67). Basilica ☎ 0783 35 92 05. Open daily 7:30am-12:30pm and 4-7:30pm*)

OUTDOOR ACTIVITIES. Maneggio Ippocamo in Rimedio leads full-day horseback tours. (*☎ 333 479 49 55. Open M-Sa 9am-5:30pm. Tours including lunch L150,000/€77.47. Lessons L20,000/€10.33 per hr. Discounts for groups of 5 or more.*)

🎵 ENTERTAINMENT

On the last Sunday of Carnevale and the following Tuesday (usually in March), Oristano's biggest festival, the **Sartiglia,** the citizens of Oristano don traditional finery (horse-riding gear, expressionless masks, and small top-hats) and ride on horseback through the strects. One of the festive days is sponsored by the *falegnami* (wood workers) and the other by the *contadini* (farmers); at the Sartiglia's climax, they charge down the street on horseback, trying to pierce six-inch metal stars with their spears. The more stars pierced, the better the upcoming harvest.

▶ DAYTRIP FROM ORISTANO: SINIS PENINSULA

*To reach **Tharros** take the ARST bus to San Giovanni di Sinis (dir: Is Aruttas, July-Aug. 40min.; 4 per day 8:25am-5:30pm, last return 6:05pm; L2800/€1.45). Ruins open daily 9am-7:30pm. L8000/€4.13. For **S'archittu** take the ARST bus (30min., 7 per day 7:10am-7:10pm, L2800/€1.45). For **Is Arutas** (July-Aug. only; 50min., 5 per day 8:25am-6:30pm, L3200/€1.65). For **Putzu Idu** (dir: Su Pallosu; July-Aug. only; 1hr., 2 per day 8:15am-12:30pm, last return 6:45pm; L3200/€1.65). Take local orange bus and follow locals to **Torregrande's** coarser sands (Sept.-June; 15-20min., 2 per hr., L1200/€0.62).*

Visiting Oristano and missing the Sinis Peninsula is like visiting Italy without trying the pasta. Tranquil beaches, stark-white cliffs, rolling country hills and ancient ruins, all within an easy day's drive, make the trip unforgettable. Public transportation is poor and infrequent, but don't let that deter you. Summon up all of your courage (and a little cash), and rent a moped or a car.

The peninsula's southernmost tip, a narrow finger of land rising into a hill 17km west of Oristano, holds the ruins of the ancient Phoenician and Roman port of ◼Tharros. Much of the city remains submerged, but excavations have revealed Punic fortifications, a Roman temple dedicated to Demeter, a Christian baptistery, and a Phoenician shrine. Two white columns, one decapitated, rise above the rest of the ruins, framed by the blue sea in the background. A medieval Spanish watchtower crowns the hill, offers comprehensive views.

Gracing the coast slightly to the north of the peninsula proper (off the road to Cuglieri) is ◼S'Archittu, a sleepy town with a beautiful seaside where young locals lounge on and leap 15m from a massive, naturally formed limestone arch into the waters of a beautiful rocky inlet.

Also well-worth the trip is the secluded, but well-exploited, beach of ◼Is Arutas, on the coast north of San Giovanni di Sinis. With no town for miles around, white quartz sand the texture of fine caviar, and an endless stretch of Sardinia's famous blue water, this is the place to go for a relaxing day away from civilization. The shallow, sloping waters of Putzu Idu are dotted with bobbing fishing boats, seaweed, and sun-worshippers. The beach is on the northern tip of the peninsula, accessible by car or bus.

NUORO PROVINCE

Of all the provinces in Sardinia, Nuoro is by far the least frequented by tourists. Few realize that, as the heart of Sardinia, Nuoro contains some of the most spectacular terrain in the country. Nuoro spans from Bosa on the west coast to the Golfo di Orosei on the east. Between these two towns lie smooth plateaus, rolling hills, and the island's highest mountain.

NUORO   ☎0784

Although it is set against a dramatic backdrop of Sardinian mountains, the unimaginative architecture of this provincial capital betrays its agricultural heritage. A few parts of the town—notably, C. Garibaldi—are lively during the day, but Nuoro is still relatively small and underdeveloped, and offers little more than a couple of decent museums. The really attractive quality of the town is its proximity to more interesting destinations in the surrounding countryside.

▐ TRANSPORTATION

Trains: on V. Lamarmora at V. Stazione (☎0784 301 15). Buy tickets M-Sa 7:30am-7pm. To **Cagliari** (3½-5hr.; 6 per day 6:14am-6:44pm; L20,400/€10.54).

Buses: The following bus companies serve the island.

ARST (☎0784 322 01). Buses stop along V. Sardegna between the intersection with V. Toscana and the intersection with V. Lamarmora. Tickets available at bar next door or at corner of V. Lamarmora and V. Stazione. Open M-F 6:30am-8pm, Sa-Su 6:30am-2pm. To: **Cagliari** (2 per day 7:40am-2:05pm; L20,100/€10.38); **Dorgali** (1hr., 6 per day 6:53am-7pm, L3900/€2.01); **Olbia** (7 per day 5:30am-8:50pm; L12,200-14,800/€6.30-7.64); **Oliena** (30min., 12 per day 6:53am-7:45pm, L1700/€0.89); **Orgosolo** (30min., 8 per day 5:30am-6:30pm, L2800/€1.45).

F. Deplanu (☎0784 20 15 18) runs buses from the ARST station to the **Olbia airport** (1½hr.; 5 per day 5:45am-5pm; L18,000/€9.30). **Redentours** offers the same service to the **Alghero airport** (2¾hr.; 2 per day; L24,000/€12.39).

PANI, V.B. Sassari, 15 (☎0784 368 56). Walk up V. Stazione and follow it to the right. Ticket office open 9am-noon, 5-7:30pm, and 30min. before each departure. Buses to: **Cagliari** (3½hr.; 4 per

day 6:52am-7:31pm; L21,900/€11.31); **Oristano** (2hr.; 4 per day 6:52am-7:31pm; L11,300/
€5.84); **Sassari** (2½hr.; 6 per day 5:52am-7:31pm; L13,100/€6.77).

Local Transportation: Buy tickets (L1100/€0.57) for the local buses at a *tabaccheria*.
Bus #4 runs from P.V. Emanuele to train station (3 per hr.), **bus #3** to V. Sardegna.

Car Rental: Autonoleggio Maggiore, V. Convento, 32 (☎/fax 0784 304 61; www.mag-
giore.it). L135,000/€69.72 per day. 23+. Affiliated with National Car Rental. Open M-
F 8:30am-1pm and 3:30-7pm, Sa 8am-1pm. AmEx/MC/V.

✳🛈 ORIENTATION AND PRACTICAL INFORMATION

Facing the PANI bus stop, turn left and take V.B. Sassari directly into **Piazza Italia,**
where you'll find the friendly tourist office and a pleasant park. As you exit the
ARST bus stop, take a left down V. Sardegna (continuing in the direction of the
bus), and then take the first right onto V. Lamarmora and follow it to **Piazza delle
Grazie.** Turn left and follow V. IV Novembre uphill to P. Italia. V. Roma leads from
P. Italia to P. San Giovanni and the town's social hub, **Piazza Vittorio Emanuele,**
known to the locals simply as **"giardini."**

Tourist Office: EPT, P. Italia, 7 (☎0784 300 83), on street level in summer and on the
4th floor in winter. Stocked with brochures. Enthusiastic staff is eager to offer hiking
info. Open Th-Su 8:30am-1:30pm and 2:30-8pm, Tu-W 9am-1pm and 3-8pm.

Punto Informa, C. Garibaldi, 155 (☎/fax 0784 387 77; www.viazzos.it), is a private
tourist office with extensive brochures and published guides. Staff will help sort through
Sardinia's transportation system, and will set you on the right track for hikes, bike tours,
and other countryside diversions. Open June-Sept. M-Sa 10am-1pm and 4-7pm.

Emergency: ☎113. **Medical Emergency:** ☎118.

Red Cross: ☎0784 312 50.

Internet Access: Rigenera Toner Internet Service, C. Garibaldi, 156 (☎0784 372 89).
L10,000/€5.16 per hr. Open M-F 9am-1pm and 4-8pm, Sa 9am-1pm.

Post Office: P. Crispi, 8 (☎0784 302 78), off V. Dante. Open M-F 8:15am-6:30pm, Sa
8:15am-12:45pm. **Currency exchange** L5000/€2.58.

Postal Code: 08100.

🛏 ACCOMMODATIONS

Inexpensive hotels are rare in Nuoro, and campgrounds are in distant towns; take
the hint and head for smaller hamlets in the hills. If you're really stuck for a room,
give the tourist office a call, explain your budget constraints, and hope they can
help. The only real option in the city is **Hotel Sandalia,** V. Einaudi, 14. Follow the
roadsigns for Cagliari and Sassari to the outskirts of town; as you near the hospital, you'll see Sandalia sitting atop a hill with a big sign. From the ARST station, go
as far as V. Lamarmora (see directions above) and take a left, following road signs
as above. The singles are grim, but the doubles nice in this modern three-star
hotel. It's a bit of a schlep to the town center, but all of the rooms have a TV, a
phone, and A/C. (☎0784 312 00; fax 383 53. Singles L75,000/€38.73; doubles
L105,000/€54.23. MC/V.) Nearby *agriturismo* options include **Testone,** to the
northeast of the city. The owner can be reached at V. Verdi, 8100. (☎0784 23 05 39.)
There's also a hostel in **Tonara** at V. Muggianeddu, 2. (☎0784 610 005.) Buses to
Tonara are infrequent, so plan ahead or rent a car.

🍴 FOOD

For provisions, head to the **Comprabene supermarket** in P. Mameli. (Open M-Sa
8:30am-1:30pm and 5-8:30pm. MC/V.) **Mercato Civico,** P. Mameli, 20, off V. Manzoni
and across from Comprabene, is the place to look for fresh fruit, cheese, and meat.
(Open M-Sa 7am-1:30pm and 4:30-8pm. Closed Sa afternoon in July and Aug.) An

old-fashioned, wood-oven bakery, **Antico Panifico,** V. Ferraccio, 71, off P. delle Grazie, sells hot, fresh rolls, the Sardinian bread *pane caratau,* and scrumptious *panzerotti,* filled with cheese, tomato, and your choice of eggplant, mushroom, or ham for L3000/€1.55. (Open M-Sa 8am-1am.)

Il Portico, V.M. Bua, 15. Excellent rustic cuisine in one of Sardinia's few smoke-free restaurants. Try the L18,000/€9.30 *menù,* including *primo, secondo, contorno,* fruit, and drink. Or sample the house specialty, *ravioli di ricotta alla crema di carciofi* (ricottastuffed pasta in a cream of artichoke sauce; L10,000/€5.16). *Secondi* from L15,000/ €7.75. Excellent fish L6000/€3.10 per *etto.* Cover L2500/€1.29. Open Tu-Su 12:30-2:30pm and 8-10:30pm. AmEx/MC/V.

Canne Al Vento, V. Repubblica, 66 (☎0784 20 17 62), a 15min. walk down V. Lamarmora from P. delle Grazie. Handsome decor, livened by bright flowers. Generous servings of classic Sardinian *pane frattau* (cheese, egg, and tomato sauce on a bed of thin, crisp bread; L9000/€4.65), or the house specialty *porcetto* (chicken-based staple; L17,000/€8.78). Menu of *cucina tipica* for L32,000/€16.53 is part of a province-wide tourist incentive; you'll get a list of other participating restaurants and a L2000/€1.03 discount at any one of them with your check. Cover L2500/€1.29. Open M-Sa 12:30-3pm and 8-10:30pm. AmEx/MC/V.

🔄 🎵 SIGHTS AND ENTERTAINMENT

Nuoro has a surprising shortage of restaurants, but no lack of bars. The cement P. V. Emanuele—*giardini* for short—is the hangout spot of choice for younger locals who come to sit, talk, and smoke in the evenings. A more mature crowd converges upon C. Garibaldi, as *chic* as Sardegna gets, to do much the same thing.

MUSEUM OF THE ART OF THE PROVINCE OF NUORO. The striking white building that houses the MAN stands out among its dimmer surrounding, as does the local contemporary art found inside. Special exhibits change regularly. *(V. Manara, 1. ☎0784 25 21 10. Open Tu-Su 10am-1pm and 4:30-8:30pm. L5000/€2.58, students L3000/ €1.55, under 18 and over 60 free.)*

MUSEO ETNOGRAFICO (MUSEO DELLA VITA E DELLE TRADIZIONI POPOLARI SARDE). If the MAN is cutting-edge, this place is in serious need of a grindstone. It showcases masks, ceremonial costumes, and a lot of wool that harkens back to the days when men and sheep weren't afraid to get intimate. *(V. Mereu, 56. ☎0789 24 29 00 or 314 26; renuoro@interbusiness.it. Open daily June 15-Sept. 30 9am-8pm; Oct. 1-June 14 9am-1pm and 3-7pm. L5000/€2.58, under 18 and over 60 L3000/€1.55.)*

MONTE ORTOBENE. A mind-blowing view, a bronze statue of Christ the Redeemer, and a shady park overlooking the neighboring hamlets await at the peak of this hill. From the bus stop on Monte Ortobene, walk 20m down the road for a view of Monte Corrasi, which dwarfs neighboring Oliena. *(To reach the summit, take the orange ATP bus #8 from P. V. Emanuele, 15 per day 8:15am-8pm, last return 8:15pm; L1100/€0.55. Or hike about 6km up the hillside. Beware: Cinghiali, wild boar, haunt the hills.)*

SAGRA DEL REDENTORE. Nuoro celebrates The Feast of the Redeemer in the last week of August. This spartan religious procession during which the townfolk contemplate the Resurrection takes place on August 29. A colorful parade of revelers dressed in traditional Sardinian garb and lively productions of traditional folk dances and choral performances precede it.

📷 DAYTRIP FROM NUORO: ORGOSOLO

Entrust your life to an ARST driver (40min.; 8 per day 5:50am-6:30pm, last return 7:05pm; L2800/€1.45).

The bus ride alone merits a trip to sleepy ▧**Orgosolo.** With its comparatively Spartan architecture and its shaded *piazza,* Orgosolo is the quintessential Sardinian mountain town. You'll find your eyes drawn away from the mountain vistas and toward the Picasso-esque murals that dot the buildings. **Francesco del Casino,** a local teacher, initiated this ongoing outdoor art project in the 1960s, after studying in Latin America. His work focuses on everything from imperialism to fascism to commercialism. Del Casino drew inspiration from the 1963 film *The Bandits of Orgosolo*, which immortalized the blood "banditismo" in the south of Oliena.

Exit the bus at the third stop and follow the signs to the **Hotel Sa'e Jenna,** V.E. Lussu, 17, a family-run establishment offering enormous rooms with bath. Even the room numbers are painted with colorful designs. The restaurant downstairs serves solid Sarde food with inventive *primi* for L6-9000/€3.10-4.65 and *secondi* for L12-13,000/€6.20-6.71. (☎0784 401 247; fax 402 437. Singles L57,000/€29.44; doubles L80,000/€41.32. Half-pension L75,000/€38.73 per person; full-pension L85,000/€43.90.) More del Casino architecture decorates the less glamorous but homier **Petit Hotel,** V. Mannu, 9, off C. Repubblica. Back track from the bus stop at the small park (keeping the police station to your right), then head up the incline on the left and follow the signs. (☎/fax 0784 402 009. Breakfast L6000/€3.10. Singles L40-45,000/€20.66-23.24; doubles L60-65,000/€30.99-33.57. AmEx/MC/V.)

DORGALI ☎0748

Placed on a sloping hillside, the little town of Dorgali has learned one of the essential lessons of Italian tourism: training its locals to make business out of the regional tradition of making handicrafts. Comprised almost entirely of tourist-oriented shops offering carved wooden masks, pottery, tapestries, Spanish-Arabian style cutlery, and tons of tacky T-shirts that will assure your friends that yes, Sardinians Do It Better, Dorgali is more of a convenient stop on the way to the spectacular beach at Cala Gonone than a place to stay for its own merit.

🖪🗗 TRANSPORTATION AND PRACTICAL INFORMATION. Buy tickets at **Blues Bar,** V. La Marmora, 154. (Open daily 8am-10pm.) Buses stop at corner of V. La Marmora and C. Umberto. **ARST buses** run to **Cala Gonone** (20min., 10 per day 6:20am-7:45pm, L1300/€0.67); **Nuoro** (50min., 7-9 per day 6:05am-7:50pm, L3900/€2.01) via **Oliena** (30min.); and **Olbia** (3hr.; 2 per day 6:35am-5:25pm; L12,200/€6.30). The main commercial street is **via La Marmora,** which winds along the hillside, where it is eventually intersected by Corso Umberto. C. Umberto runs perpendicular to V. La Marmora, and it's your best bet for a cold drink or *gelato*. Services include: the **Pro Loco tourist office,** V. La Marmora, 108B, with maps, their own attractive guidebook to Dorgali and Cala Gonone (L5000/€2.58) and information on hotels, *agriturismo*, and rooms for rent (☎0784 962 43; Oct. 1-June 30 M-F 9am-1pm and 3:30-7pm; Oct. 20-Jan. 1 M-F 9am-1pm; Jan.-June 29 9am-1pm and 4-8pm); a **Banco di Sardegna,** V. La Marmora, 152, with **currency exchange** and an **ATM** (open M-F 8:20am-1:20pm and 3:05-4:05pm); **carabinieri** (☎112 or 0784 961 14); an **ambulance** (☎0337 81 81 80); the **Farmacia Mundula,** V. Mannu, 1, off V. La Marmora (open M-F 8:30am-1pm and 4:30-8pm); and a **post office** at the corner of V. La Marmora and V. Ciusa (☎0784 974 12; open M-F 8:10am-1:15pm). **Postal Code:** 08022.

🖪🗖 ACCOMMODATIONS AND FOOD. It makes more sense to stay in nearby Cala Gonone (see below), where the tourist office will help you find reasonably priced accommodations if you call or stop by. However, the **Hotel S'Adde,** V. Concordia, 38, has spacious rooms with bathrooms, A/C, TV, and phone. At the intersection of C. Umberto and C. La Marmora, take V. Mare and follow the signs. The hotel runs a shuttle to **Cala Gonone** (1 per day; L10,000/€5.16), has a restaurant and pizzeria downstairs, and organizes excursions to nearby *nuraghi* and archaeological sites. (☎0784 944 12; fax 943 15. Breakfast L15,000/€7.75. Singles L60-100,000/€30.99-51.65; doubles L100-150,000/€51.65-77.47.) Bars and *gelaterie* line C. Umberto; for a solid meal or a quick pizza, try **Restaurant S'Udulu,** C. Umberto, 20. (☎ 0784 952 39. Pizza from L6500/€3.36. *Primi* L9-15,000/€4.65-7.75; *secondi* from L12,000/€6.20. Cover L3000/€1.55. Open 12:30-3pm and 7:30-11:30pm. MC/V.)

◙ SIGHTS. The **Museo Arceologico,** V. La Marmora, past the post office and next to the elementary school, houses some provocative pottery shards discovered in and around Dorgali and Cala Gonone, including items from 70 or so surrounding *nuraghe* village sites. (Open daily 9:30am-1pm and 4-7pm; in winter 9:30am-1pm and 2-4:30pm. L4000/€2.07, under 12 L2000/€1.03.)

▨ DAYTRIP FROM DORGALI: CALA GONONE. The bus ride to Cala Gonone may well be the most spectacular one on an island full of beautiful, bouncy bus journeys. The town, situated where the hills roll into the sea, has pebbly sand and crowded beaches. It is the gateway to several spectacular beaches and caves, many only accessible by boat. **Boats** (7 per day 9am-6pm, L10-12,000/€5.16-6.20) travel to the stunning **Grotta del Bue Marino** (Cave of the Monk Seal), one of the last haunts of the elusive creature. The seals rarely appear during the day, and stampeding crowds and a locked gate succeed in marring the experience. Just down the coast lies the cast beach of **Cala Luna.** Encircled by marshes and caverns, the beach is accessible only by boat (L10-27,000/€5.16-13.94; combined ticket for cave and beach L32,000/€16.53). Boats (L32,000/€16.53) also run to the more remote beaches of **Cala Sisina** and **Cala Marilou.**

Cala Gonone lies just over an hour east of Nuoro by **ARST bus** (5-7 per day, 6:40-5:05pm, L5000/€2.58) and 20min. from Dorgali (7-10 per day, 6:40am-8:10pm, L1300/€0.67). Buy tickets at Bar Fronte del Porto, V. Aquadolce, 5. **Consorzio Marittimo Transport** (☎0784 933 052) has monopolized the market for beach access. **Pesca Turismo Delfino** offers day-long fishing and beach cruises starting from L100,000/€51.65. (☎0784 493 330. Consider reserving ahead.) You can also rent a boat from one of several agencies at the port (from L100,000/€51.65).

Be sure to stop by the helpful and friendly **Pro Loco Tourist Office** at V. Umberto, 37 (☎0784 926 200; fax 942 88). They are particularly useful to those looking for accommodations; in addition to hotel listings, they can contact local bed and breakfasts and town residents who rent rooms. If you're interested in renting bikes, scooters, or kayaks, or in bike tours and trekking, check out **Prima Sardegna,** V. Lungomare Palmasera, 32. (☎/fax 0784 933 67; prima.sardegna@tiscalinet.it. Scooters from L60,000/€30.99 per day; kayaks L45,000/€23.24 per day. Internet access. Open Apr.-Oct. 9am-1pm and 4-8pm. AmEx/MC/V.) They are affiliated with a mountain biking, trekking, and spelunking firm called **Nature Adventure,** V. Colombo, 62 (☎338 810 541).

SASSARI PROVINCE

SASSARI   ☎079

Founded as the first free commune of Sardinia in 1294, Sassari held onto its medieval walled-town layout until the late 1800s. In the last 100 years, it has become an important petrochemical center and Sardinia's second largest city. The city continues to have a strong student presence thanks to its university, which draws youths from the surrounding area as well as neighboring countries. Congregating along the wide boulevards and the refurbished 18th-century P. d'Italia, pink-haired rebels roll their eyes at grim religious processions (where participants carry Christ's instruments of passion closer to their heart than their cell phones). When the preaching's done, the kids switch their phones back on and city-dwellers say "Pronto" to the highest standard of living on the island.

▐ TRANSPORTATION

Flights: (☎079 93 50 39), near **Fertilia,** 35km south of Sassari. Allow about 1 hr. to get there from the bus station (see **ARST,** below). Domestic flights year-round, charter flights to European destinations only in summer.

Trains: (☎079 26 03 62), in P. Stazione, 1 block from P. Sant'Antonio. Take the #8 bus from P. d'Italia. Tickets (L1100/€0.57) available at newsstands. Luggage storage available (p. 656). To: **Alghero** (40min., 11 per day 6:09am-8:55pm, L3500/€1.81); **Cagliari** (3½hr.; 6 per day 7:04am-6:45pm; L22,700/€14.04); **Olbia** (2hr.; 4 per day 8:02am-8:40pm; L10,600/€5.47); **Porto Torres** (20min., 9 per day 6am-6:40pm, L2300/€1.19).

Buses:

ARST (info ☎079 26 39 220). Tickets at Tonni's Bar, C. M. Savoia, 11. Buses depart from V. Italia in public gardens to **Nuoro** (2hr.; 2 per day 9:35am and 2:50pm; L12,200-14,800/€6.30-7.64) and **Porto Torres** (35min., 1-2 per hr. 5:20am-9:15pm, L2300/€1.19). Buses to **Castelsardo** (1hr., 11 per day 7:20am-7:45pm, L3900/€2.01) and **Fertilia Airport** (40min., 5-6 per day 5:10am-4:55pm, last return 10:55pm, L3400/€1.76) leave from in front of Tonni's bar.

FDS (☎079 24 13 01), with buses leaving from Emiciclo Garibaldi, serves the local area. Tickets are sold at Bar Garibaldi, Emiciclo Garibaldi, 26. Destinations include **Alghero** (1½hr., 13 per day 5:35am-7pm, L4500-5000/€2.32-2.58).

PANI, V. Bellieni, 25 (☎079 23 69 83; fax 26 00 66; www.comune.sassari.it/vivere_sassari/ trasporti/autolinee_pani.htm), 1 block from P. d'Italia. Office open M-F 5:30-6:35am, 8:30am-2:15pm, and 5-7:15pm, Sa-Su 5:30-6:35am, 9-9:30am, noon-2:15pm, and 5-7:15pm. Buses leave from P. Italia to: **Cagliari** (3-4hr.; 7 per day 6am-7:15pm; L26,000/€13.43) via **Oristano** (2¼hr.; 4 per day 6:36am-7:15pm; L13,900/€7.18); **Nuoro** (2½hr.; 6 per day 6:36am-7:15pm; L13,100/€6.77); **Torralba** (40-60min., 6 per day 6:36am-7:15pm, L4500/€2.32).

Taxis: Radiotaxi (☎079 26 00 60). Open 24hr.

Car Rental: Avis, V. Mazzini, 2 (☎ 079 23 55 47). L130,000/€67.14 per day. 25+. Open M-Sa 8:30am-12:30pm and 4-7pm. MC/V. **Eurorent,** V. Roma, 56 (☎079 23 23 35). Fiats L105,600/€54.54 per day. 21+. Open M-Sa 8:30am-1pm and 3-7pm.

✦ 🔒 ORIENTATION AND PRACTICAL INFORMATION

All buses stop in the *giardini publici* before heading to the bus station. Since these gardens are much closer to Sassari's attractions, get off at **via Italia** in the park (unless you've made reservations at a hotel near the station). **Emiciclo Garibaldi** lies ahead, past **via Margherita di Savoia.** To reach the town center, head straight through Emiciclo Garibaldi onto **via Carlo Alberto,** which spills into **Piazza Italia.** To the right, **via Roma** runs to the tourist office and the Museo Sana. To the left lies **Piazza Castello,** an eatery-packed, people-watching playground, 200m from **Corso Vittorio Emanuele,** a major thoroughfare.

TOURIST, FINANCIAL, AND LOCAL SERVICES

Tourist Office: V. Roma, 62 (☎079 23 17 77), a few blocks to the right of and behind P. d'Italia when facing the provincial administration building. Go through the gate and then the doorway on your right; the door is on the right hand side of the hallway. Ring the bell to be let in. The English-speaking staff provides a map and bus and train schedules. Open M-Th 9am-1pm and 4-6pm, F 9am-1pm.

Budget Travel: CTS, V. Manno, 35 (☎079 20 04 00). Also assists students in finding accommodations. Open M-F 9:30am-1pm and 4:30-7pm, Sa 9:30am-1pm. MC.

Ferry Tickets: Ajo Viaggi, P. Fiume, 1 (☎079 20 02 22; fax 23 83 11). **Agitour,** P. Italia, 13 (☎079 2 317 67; fax 23 69 52).

Currency Exchange: Banca Commerciale D'Italia, in P. D'Italia, has an **ATM** outside. Open M-F 8:20am-1:50pm and 3-4:45pm, Sa 8:20-11:50am.

Luggage Storage: (☎079 26 03 62) in the train station. L5000/€2.58 per 12hr. Open daily 6:50am-8:50pm.

English-Language Bookstores: Demetra di Sassari, V. Cavour, 16 (☎079 20 13 118). Best-sellers and classics; relatively big selection. Open daily 9am-8pm; in winter closed Su. AmEx/MC/V. **Gulliver Librerie,** V. Portici Crispo, 4 (☎079 23 44 75). Mostly classics. Open M-Sa 9am-9pm, Su 9am-1pm and 5-9pm. AmEx/MC/V.

EMERGENCY AND COMMUNICATIONS

Emergency: ☎113.

Police: V. Coppino, 1 (☎079 28 30 500).

Ambulance: Red Cross, C. Vico, 4 (☎079 23 45 22). **First Aid: Ospedale Civile** (☎079 20 61 000), on V. Italia and V. Nicola.

Late-Night Pharmacy: Simon, V. Brigata Sassari, 2 (☎079 23 32 38). Open May-Oct. M-Sa 5pm-1pm, Su 8:30pm-1:10am; Nov.-Apr. M-Sa 4:30pm-1pm, Su 8pm-1:10am. Posts list of 24hr. pharmacies.

Internet Access: Buffetti (☎079 215 10 55), at V. Italia, 21. L10,000/€5.16 per 30min. Open daily 9am-1pm and 4:30-8pm. **PC Mainia,** V. Cavour, 71A (☎079 23 49 71). L10,000/€5.16 per hr. Open daily 9am-1pm and 4:30-8pm.

Post Office: V. Brigata Sassari, 13 (☎079 28 21 267), off P. Castello. Open M-F 8:15am-6:15pm, Sa 8:15am-1pm. **Currency exchange,** phone cards, Fermo Posta.

Postal Code: 07100.

ACCOMMODATIONS

Budget accommodations in Sassari are not easy to come by. Call ahead (the tourist office is helpful) or make the city a daytrip from the countryside or Alghero.

Hotel Giusy, P. Sant'Antonio, 21 (☎079 23 33 27; fax 23 94 90), near the train station. Mom always said that it's the little things, like toilet seats and shower curtains, that really count. That's why she never stayed here. Travelers on a budget will find its low rates attractive, but bring insect repellent and earplugs. Breakfast (a cup of coffee) included. Singles L55,000/€28.41; doubles L75,000/€38.73.

Hotel Leonardo da Vinci, V. Roma, 79 (☎079 28 07 44; fax 28 07 44). All rooms have A/C, phone, minibar, bath, and TV. Singles L100-130,000/€51.65-67.14; doubles L153-180,000/€79.02-92.96. AmEx/D/MC/V.

FOOD

A wide selection of pizzerias line **Corso Emanuele.** Any college ID and a ticket affords you a meal at the **University Mensa,** V. dei Mille. A ticket costs L4800/€2.49. Meals include *primo, secondo, contorno,* and fruit. (☎079 21 64 83 or 25 82 11. Open M-Sa 12:15-2:30pm and 7:30-9pm. Closed the last week of July-Aug.) Another university cantine is on V. dei Manzella, 2, but is only open for lunch in the summer. A large, enclosed **market** occupies P. Mercato, down V. Rosello from V.V. Emanuele. (Open M-F 8am-1pm and 5-8pm, Sa 8am-1pm.) **Multimarkets supermarket** is on the corner of V. Cavour and V. Manno. (☎079 23 72 78. Open M-Sa 8am-8:30pm.) Dining in Sassari is not credit card-friendly, so bring plenty of cash.

Trattoria Da Antonio, V. Arborea, 2B (☎079 23 42 97), behind the post office. The wood-paneled, arched interior and the subdued ambience is a refreshing alternative to P. Castello. No menus, just amazing food. If there's one place to be adventurous, it's here. Expect the waitstaff to recommend horse, donkey, and tentacled creatures. Menu L25,000/€12.91 (including L2000/€1.03 cover). Open daily 1-3pm and 8:30-11pm.

Trattoria Da Peppina, V. Pigozzi, 1 (☎079 23 61 46), off C. Emanuele. The *menù* (with everything from horse to tripe) is delicious but unfriendly to vegetarians. The waitstaff conducts lively lunchtime banter with the patrons in rapid-fire Italian. *Primi* L5-9000/€2.58-4.65; *secondi* L9-15,000/€4.65-7.75. You must order something else with a *primo.* Open M-Sa 12:30-2:30pm; dinner starts at 7:30pm.

SIGHTS

MUSEO GIOVANNI ANTONIO SANNA. This museum houses models portraying *nuraghi* (towers) dating from 1500 BC, Sardinian paintings, skulls with holes drilled into them (a case of medieval patients lacking proper medical insurance), and petrified tree stumps. *(V. Roma, 64.* ☎*079 27 22 03. Open Oct.-May Tu-Su 9am-8pm; June-Sept. Tu-F and Su 9am-11:30pm. L4000/€2.07, ages 18-25 L2000/€1.03. EU citizens under 18 and over 60 free.)*

CATTEDRALE DI SAN NICOLÒ. Sassari's *duomo*, dubbed "an immense flower of stone" by Elio Vittorini, is a 13th-century Romanesque structure with a 17th-century Spanish colonial facade. Renovations have uncovered vibrant, early frescoes sunk into the church walls. For those looking for 16 men on a dead man's chest, the reliquary of St. Benedetta masquerades as a skull-and-crossbones. *(Walk down C. Emanuele from P. Castello and turn left on V. al Duomo to P. Duomo.)*

🎵 ENTERTAINMENT

The lavish **Sardinian Cavalcade,** held on the second to last weekend in May, is Sardinia's most notable folk festival. Festivities include a procession of costumed emissaries from Sardinian villages, a *palio* (horse race), singing, and dancing. I **Candelieri,** the festival of the candlesticks, takes place on the Day of Assumption (Aug. 14). The *Gremi*, or farmers' guilds, sport traditional Spanish dress and carry huge wooden columns (in the shape of enormous tapers) through the streets.

If it weren't for the **University Pub,** V. Amendola, 49/A, Sassari would be devoid of a hip youth scene. A favorite among locals, the subdued pub offers dirt-cheap drinks (beer from L2500/€1.29) and overflows with students when school's in session. Request (but don't inhale) the cannabis beer (L7000/€3.62) or the super-secret Sardinia Island mixed drink (L10,000/€5.16), whose recipe is more closely guarded than Coca Cola's. (☎079 20 04 23. Open W-M 8:30pm-1am; closed Aug.)

📷 DAYTRIP FROM SASSARI: CASTELSARDO

To reach Castelsardo, take ARST bus from Sassari. From P. Pianedda, face uphill and walk up stairs. Open M-Sa 9:30am-1pm and 2:30-9pm. Castle and museum L3000/€1.55.

Castelsardo's striking location atop a lofty crest, and proximity to sandy beaches, make it a popular stop along the Costa Paradiso. Renowned across the island for its beauty, the town was once described by a Sardinian poet as a "flower of light that smiles from the top of a sharp promontory upon the glimmering sea." (He wasn't known for mincing on the compliments). This large, well-preserved, and well-situated castle (containing a dull wicker-work museum) crowns the village.

PORTO TORRES ☎079

Founded in 27 BC, the village of Turris Libissonis, on the mouth of the river Mannu, was the first Sardinian outcropping of the Roman Empire and served as one of Rome's principal ports along the corn-trading routes between Sicily and Africa. Today the town's ancient spice can be savored in its Roman ruins and Romanesque 12th-century church—but good luck getting rid of the bitter taste of the outlying industrial zones. This modern port town is best sampled as a stopover and as a point of access to luscious Stintino.

📟 **TRANSPORTATION. Trains** (☎079 243 01), synchronized with ferries, leave from the port to **Sassari** (20min., 8 per day 5:50am-8:10pm, L2300/€1.19), continuing on to **Olbia,** while **ARST** buses (☎079 26 39 200 or 800 86 50 42) run from the ferry port in Porto Torres. Schedule restricted on Sundays. Tickets available in the cafe at C.V. Emanuele, 38. To: **Alghero Fertilia Airport** (40min., 5 per day 6:05am-10:05pm, L2800/€1.45); **Sassari** (35min., 1-2 per hr. 5:55am-10pm, L2300/€1.19); **Stintino** (40min., 6 per day 5:51am-8:10pm, last return 8:20pm, L3400/€1.76).

🔲🎯 **ORIENTATION AND PRACTICAL INFORMATION.** Porto Torres has one major thoroughfare, **Corso Vittorio Emanuele,** which runs perpendicular to the ocean from the port. The first stop you should make in Porto Torres is the **Pro Loco**

Tourist Office, P. XX Settembre, 2, about 20m up on the left. The multilingual staff will provides bus schedules and information on local sights, beaches, and mountain biking. (☎/fax 079 51 50 00. Open July-Sept. M-Sa 9am-1pm and 4-8pm; Oct.-June M-Sa 8:30am-12:30pm.) Farther up the street, the bank **BNL,** C.V. Emanuele, 18, has an **ATM** outside. (Open M-F 8:30am-1:30pm and 2:15-2:45pm, Sa 8:30am-noon.) In case of **emergency,** call the **police** (☎112, 079 50 24 32, or 070 51 01 19), **Guardia Medica** (☎079 51 03 92), or an **ambulance** (☎079 51 60 68). The town's **pharmacy,** C.V. Emanuele, 76, is down the block. (☎079 51 40 88. Open M-Sa 9am-1pm and 5-11pm.) The **post office** is at V. Sachi, 113. (☎079 51 49 05. Open M-F 8:15am-6:15pm, Sa 8:15am-noon.) **Postal Code:** 07046.

▐▐ ACCOMMODATIONS AND FOOD. Albergo Royal, V.S. Satta, 8, has comfortable decor, TV, and private bathrooms. From the port or bus stop, walk up C.V. Emanuele away from the water until you reach a yellow "Albergo Royal" sign hanging overhead. Turn left and walk about 300m along V. Petronia and then follow the signs; it'll be another 200m or so. (☎079 50 22 78; 20 beds. Singles L50-70,000/€25.82-36.15; doubles L90-110,000/€46.48-56.81.) The lodging closest to the ferry port is the **Hotel Elisa,** V. Mare, 2. A bland exterior masks what is in fact one lovely lady. This three-star joint is all class. 27 rooms all have private baths, TV, phone, and a small refrigerator. It's pricier than the average budget digs, but it's worth it. Ask the amicable Alessandro about the local beaches and nightlife. (☎079 51 32 60; fax 51 37 68. Breakfast included. Singles L95,000/€49.06; doubles L140,000/€72.30. Meals L30,000/€15.50. MC/V.)

In the mornings, an **outdoor market** is at the intersection of V. Delle Vigne and V. Sacchi. Try **Bar Trattoria Pedoni Teresa,** V.G. Bruno, 5, off P. XX Settembre, but only if you are daring enough to sample real Sardinian cuisine; donkey, horse, and octopus are standard fare. There's no written menu, but you get a whole meal for L15,000/€7.75. (Lunch at noon and dinner at 7:30pm. Closed Su evenings.) For less-challenging cuisine, fun waitstaff, and good, fast food, go to **Poldiavolo,** in P. Settembre XX. Ask the cook to make you a fresh *poldiavolo panino* (eggplant, ham, tuna, cheese, and veggies; L6000/€3.10). Sandwiches and pizza start at L5000/€2.58, pasta from L6000/€3.10. (Open daily noon-3pm and 6pm-1:30am.)

◙◪ SIGHTS AND BEACHES. The 11th-century **Basilica di San Gavino,** up the stairs in P. Marconi at the end of C.V. Emanuele, houses the crypt of local Saints Gavino, Proto, and Gianuario. Proto and Gianuario were Christians persecuted by the Romans around AD 300. Gavino was a Roman soldier who, while holding the Christians captive, was converted and then set them free. All three were eventually captured and beheaded. The holy bones of murdered martyrs aren't the church's only Roman remnant—the mismatched columns supporting the church were salvaged from nearby Roman ruins. (Open 7am-noon and 4-7:30pm.) The ruins of the **Roman Thermal Baths,** along V. Ponte Romane, five minutes from the center of town, were ravaged in the 19th century by the evil railway planners and dynamite-wielding quasi-archaeologists searching for the site of the martyrs' decapitation. (☎079 51 44 33. Open Tu-Su 9am-8pm. Sa May-Oct. until 11pm. L6000/€3.10. Discount ages 18-25, under 18 or over 65 free.)

Soak up some rays (read: cancer) at the two beaches along Porto Torres's shore. **Scoglio Lungho Spiaggia,** a sandy beach 250m from the port, is family-friendly, complete with rock-diving and plastic-dolphins. **Acquedolci,** right down the road, is more one for the craggy coral and emerald waters.

▐ DAYTRIP FROM PORTO TORRES: STINTINO. Northwest of Porto Torres on the Capo del Falcone, Stintino was once a legitimate fishing village; then came the Eurotourist deluge. The winter population of fewer than 1000 swells to almost 20,000 in summer. Exploitation of the captivating ▨**Spiaggia di Pelosa,** a beach 4km outside town, spawned Stintino's transformation. Sardinia's legendary blue water is at its best at Pelosa, which is framed by an island in the distance and a blend of sandy beaches and rocky shores close up. Here children fondle captured baby octopi along the rocky shore and sparkling waters glisten against the bone-dry Isola Piana. On the other side of Piana lies **Isola Asinara**, which was used as a penal colony until very recently. Considering the gorgeous surroundings, maybe crime does have its benefits. To reach a more accessible island (graced with an 18th-century Aragonese tower), walk all the way along the beach, and either tackle the 500m swim from the beach or strap on sandals and make a wet scramble 50m over the rocks. Octopi aren't the beach's only marine life; be wary of sea urchins lurking within small crevices along the way (forget your shoes and you'll feel like a captive once you get to the other side).

Stintino has a **tourist office**, V. Sassari, 77, that provides a map and helps find activities and accommodations that suit your interests and budget. (☎/fax 079 52 37 88; stintoturismo@tin.it. Open daily 9:30am-1pm and 5-8pm.) Orange line **A buses** run from the beach back to Stintino (every hr. 8-12:30am, L1100/€0.57). **Buses** run from Pelosa to **Sassari** (1¼hr., 6 per day 6:45am-8:15pm, L5400/€2.79) via **Porto Torres** (40min., L3700/€1.91). In Stintino you can catch the bus in P. Municipio (6:50am-8:20pm). If you get stuck waiting for a bus, head to **Lu Funali**, Lungomare C. Colombo, 89 (☎079 52 30 54), along the water. Admire the tiny port's collection of sailboats, have a drink to the sounds of Bob Marley, and feel all right.

ALGHERO ☎079

Salty sea breezes flatten oceanfront sand dunes into fabulous beaches for sun-filled serenity during the day. After dark, the same breezes whip through the twisting medieval streets and Gothic arches of the *centro storico*, grazing its three surrounding towers, cooling the passions of *lungomare* lovers, and swirling the sounds of live music through the night air. Vineyards, ruins, and horseback rides are all a short trip away from Alghero's palm-lined parks and cobbled streets. If you prefer to stay in town, however, you'll have plenty to see. Alghero's history spans centuries of occupation by everyone from native Sardinians to the Aragonese and the Genovese. The result is a fascinating *centro storico* with fragments of different cultures around every corner. In addition to Italian, you're likely to hear a dialect of Catalán, left in Alghero's streets by Pere I of Aragon after his 14th-century conquest. In fact, Alghero is sometimes known as *Barcelonetta*. The Aragonese influence is also reflected in the architecture (check out S. Francesco) and the cuisine (lots of restaurants offer *paella* as well as pasta).

▇ TRANSPORTATION

Flights: (☎079 93 50 39), near **Fertilia**, 6km north of Alghero. Domestic flights year-round, charter flights to European destinations only in summer.

Trains: (☎079 95 07 85), on V. Don Minzoni, in northern part of city. Take **AP** or **AF** bus from front of the Casa del Caffè in the park (3 per hr.), or walk 1km along port. Open daily 5:45am-9pm. Buy ticket at **FS** stand in the park and you can ride the city bus to the station for free. Luggage storage available (p. 661). To **Sassari** (40min.; 11 per day 6:01am-8:47pm, fewer trains on Su; L3500/€1.81, round-trip L6000/€3.10).

Buses:

　ARST: (☎079 95 01 79 or 800 865 042). Blue buses depart from V. Catalogna next to the park. Buy tickets at the tiny stand in the park. To: **Bosa** (1½hr., 4 per day 6:35am-7:30pm, L3400-7200/€1.76); **Porto Torres** (1hr., 8 per day 4:50am-8:50pm, L5000/€2.58); **Sassari** (1hr., 18 per day 5:35am-7pm, L5000/€2.58).

　FS: Orange city buses (info ☎079 95 04 58). Buy tickets (L1100/€0.57) at *tabacchi*. Book of 12 tickets L11,000/€5.68. Buses run from V. Cagliari in front of Casa del Caffè to the **airport** (20min., 6 per day 5:45am-8:30pm, last return from airport 11:45pm). **Line AF** travels between **Fertilia** and V. Cagliari, with a stop at the port (every 40min., 7:10am-9:30pm, return from Fertilia 7:50am-9:50pm). **AP** (from P. Della Mercede) runs to the train station (3 per hr. 6:20am-9pm). **AO** (from V. Cagliari) heads to the *lido* (beach) and the hospital (2 per hr. 7:15am-8:45pm). **AC** (from V. Liguria) runs to Carmine on the hour and half-hour (2 per hr. 7:30am-8pm).

Taxis: (☎079 97 53 96) in Alghero, can be caught on V.V. Emanuele across from the BNL bank and (☎079 935 035) at the airport.

Car Rental: Avis, Piazza Sulis, 7 (☎079 979 577), or Fertilia airport (☎079 935 064). Cars for L110-140,000/€56.81-72.30 per day for unlimited mileage. 25+. Credit card required. AmEx/D/MC/V. **Europcar** (☎079 93 50 32), at the airport. From L150,000/ €77.47 per day, including insurance. 150km per day limit. Open daily 8am-11pm.

Bike/Moped Rental: Cycloexpress di Tomaso Tilocca (☎/fax 079 98 69 50), at the harbor near the intersection of V. Garibaldi and V. La Marmora. Bikes L15,000/€7.75; mountain bikes L20-25,000/€10.33-12.91; tandem bikes L25,000/€12.91; scooters L50,000/€25.82. L300,000/€154.90 security deposit required for scooters. Bring your credit card. Open M-Sa 9am-1pm and 4-8:30pm. AmEx/MC/V.

■✻🛈 ORIENTATION AND PRACTICAL INFORMATION

ARST buses stop at the corner of **via Catalogna** and **via Cagliari,** on the waterfront one block from the port. The tourist office, in **Piazza Porta Terra,** lies diagonally across the small park, on the right beyond the easily visible towers of the *centro storico.* The train station is a hike from the town center, but is accessible by local orange buses (lines AF and AP). If you'd rather walk from the station, follow **via Don Minzoni** until it turns into **via Garibaldi** along the waterfront.

TOURIST, FINANCIAL, AND LOCAL SERVICES

Tourist Office: P. Porta Terra, 9 (☎079 97 90 54; fax 97 48 81; infotourism@infoalghero.it; www.infoalghero.it), on the right from the bus stop (toward the old city). Cheerful, multilingual staff offers an indexed street map, tours of the city, and daytrips to local villages. Open Apr.-Oct. M-Sa 8am-8pm, Su 9am-1pm; Nov.-Mar. M-Sa 8am-2pm.

Horseback Riding: Club Ippico Capuano (☎079 97 81 98), 3km from Alghero on Strada Villanova. Afternoon guided excursions. They will pick you up in Alghero for L15,000/€7.75 per carload. Reserve 2-3 days in advance. L30,000/€15.50 per hr.

Vineyard tours: Sella and Mosca (☎079 99 77 00), 11km up the road to Porto Torres. Has a shop (open M-Sa 8:30am-1pm and 3-7:30pm; June-Aug. daily) and offers tours of their facilities (June 15-Sept. 30 M-Sa 5:30pm; in winter by request). **Santa Maria La Palma Wine Growers' Cooperative** (☎079 99 90 44) has a shop and offers tours on request. (Open M-Sa, 7:30am-1pm and 2:30-5:30pm.)

Currency Exchange: Banca Nazionale del Lavoro, V. Emanuele, 5 (☎079 980 122), across from the tourist office, has 24hr. **ATM.** Open M-F 8:20am-1:20pm and 3-4:30pm. Exchange also at the **post office** for L5000/€2.58.

Luggage Storage: In train station L1500/€0.77 per day.

English-Language Bookstore: Mondolibro, V. Roma, 50 (☎079 981 555) has classics and best-sellers. Open daily 9:30am-1pm and 4:30pm-midnight; Nov.-Apr. closed Su.

EMERGENCY AND COMMUNICATIONS

Emergency: ☎113. **Carabinieri:** ☎112.

Police: P. della Mercede, 4 (☎113 or 97 20 00).

Ambulance: ☎118, 079 97 66 34, or 98 05 87. **First Aid:** ☎079 99 62 33.

Late-Night Pharmacy: All pharmacies, including **Farmacia Puliga di Mugoni,** V. Sassari, 8 (☎079 97 90 26), across from market. Open May-Oct. M-Sa 9am-1pm and 5-9pm; Feb.-Apr. M-Sa 9am-1pm and 4:30-8:30pm; Nov.-Jan. 9am-1pm and 4-8pm. AmEx/MC/V.

Hospital: Ospedale Civile (☎079 99 62 00), Regione la Pietraia, V. Don Minzoni.

Internet Access: Soft, V. Tarragona, 22 (☎079 97 00 57). L15,000/€7.75 per hr. Open M-Sa 9am-1pm. Also see listings for **Caffe Teatro** and **Libreria Labadinto.**

Post Office: V. XX Settembre, 112 (☎079 97 93 09; fax 98 10 29). Fermo Posta (next door to main office). Open M-F 9:30am-1:30pm and 2:30-6:15pm. **Currency exchange** M-F 8:15am-5pm, Sa 8:15am-1pm. Open M-F 8:15am-6:15pm, Sa 8:15am-1pm.

Postal Code: 07041.

▐ ACCOMMODATIONS & CAMPING

Prices escalate and rooms vanish in July and August. Unless you've made a reservation far in advance or are willing to pay for half-pension, consider staying at the youth hostel in Fertilia or redirecting your search to the hotels along the beach.

▨ **Ostello dei Giuliani (HI),** V. Zara, 3 (☎/fax 079 93 03 53), 6km from Alghero in Fertilia. Take the orange AF city bus from V. Cagliari outside the Nuova Case bar in the park or from V. La Marmora next to train station (25min., every 40min. 7:10am-9:30pm, L1100/€0.57). ARST pullman buses bound for Sassari and Porto Conte also stop in Fertilia (last bus 7pm, L1300/€0.67). From bus stop in Fertilia, face the church (with your back to the water), and take the street on left out of the *piazza* (by the church). Take 1st right onto V. Zara, and hostel is on left. Walk through the rose garden and up the steps into the loving arms of Mamma Margherita. 70 beds are a short walk from a small, odoriferous beach and 4km from the fabulous Spiaggia Bombarda. Delicious and filling lunch or dinner L15,000/€7.75. Curfew 11:30pm, not strictly enforced. Reserve ahead July-Aug. Dorms L19,000/€9.81.

▨ **Hotel San Francesco,** V. Machin, 2 (☎/fax 079 98 03 30; hostfran@tin.it). Walk straight from the tourist office and take the 3rd right. 21 rooms in the church cloister, all with bath, phone, and beautiful stone walls. Pray to St. Francis for sweet dreams. Breakfast included. Reservations necessary June-Aug. Singles L65-80,000/€33.57-41.32; doubles L100-140,000/€51.65-72.30; triples L135-189,000/€69.72-97.61. MC/V.

Hotel San Guian, V.G. M. Angioy, 2 (☎079 95 12 22; fax 95 10 73), 1 block east from the beach and the *lido*. Firm beds and immaculate bathrooms. Breakfast included. All rooms with bath, TV, and phone. Rooftop terrace with a view. Reserve June-Aug. 22 rooms. Singles L60-75,000/€30.99-38.73; doubles L100-130,000/€51.65-67.14; triples 128-166,000/€66.11-85.73. MC/V.

Camping: La Mariposa (☎079 95 03 60; fax 984 489; campmari@tin.it; www.lamariposa.it), on V. Lido, near the beach and 3km away from town on the Alghero-Fertilia road. Reservations suggested in summer. Open Mar.-Oct. L14-22,000/€7.32-11.36 per person, children ages 3-13 L7-15,000/€3.62-7.75. 4-person bungalow L80-120,000/€41.32-61.97. L6000/€3.10 per tent, L3400/€1.76 per car. Apr.-June. Tents and cars free. Discount roughly 10% for very large groups.

▐ FOOD

On V. Sassari, two blocks from the tourist office, a **market** offers fresh produce every morning. On Wednesdays, the **open-air market** on V. de Gasperi floods with crowds. Take the *linea mercato* bus from V. Cagliari. Be sure to stop by the **Antiche Cantine del Vino Sfuso,** C.V. Emanuele, 80, a *cantina sociale* that shoots inexpensive (but decent) table wine from giant space-age machines for a piddling L2100/€1.09 per liter. (Open M-Sa 8:30am-1pm and 4:30-8pm. MC/V.) Beware of the *algherese menù*. Most cost upward of L30,000/€15.50 and consist of little more than spaghetti with tomato sauce and the unavoidable fried calamari.

Ristorante La Muraglia, Bastioni Marco Polo, 7 (☎079 97 55 77), offers a sweeping view of the sea from its upstairs balcony. Rather touristy, but the food is excellent. Make sure you get a seat with a view; you'll pay for it either way. Curry *penne* with mixed seafood L15,000/€7.75. Other *primi* L12-22,000/€6.20-11.36; meat *secondo* L13-18,000/€6.71-9.30; fish *secondo* L14-25,000/€7.32-12.91 and up. Finish off the meal with *seadas*, a Sardinian cheese pastry doused in honey. Cover L3000/€1.55. Open daily June-Sept. noon-3:30pm and 7pm-2am. AmEx/D/MC/V.

Ristorante La Piconia, V. Principe Umberto, 27 (☎079 97 80 01). Low stone-vaulted ceilings and walls decorated with poppies and garlic make for pleasant dining in the midst of the *centro storico*. *Spaghetti al nero* L12,000/€6.2; pizzas L7-13,000/€3.62-6.71. No pizza at lunch. Cover L2000/€1.03. Open Tu-Su noon-3pm and 7pm-midnight. AmEx/D/MC/V.

Ristorante Pizzeria Pesce d'Oro, V. Catalonga, 12 (☎079 95 26 02). Handy to park and ARST bus stop. Relaxed, airy, and less touristy than restaurants in the *centro storico.* Serves pizza at lunch. *Primi* L9-18,000/€4.65-9.30; meat *secondo* L5-13,000 (€5.16-9.30); fish *secondo* L12-24,000/€6.20-12.39); pizza L5-13,000/€2.58-6.71. Cover L2500/€1.29. Open Tu-Su 7am-2:30pm and 5:30pm-midnight. D/MC/V.

⊙ SIGHTS

A leisurely walk through the *centro storico* reveals tiny alleyways, half-hidden churches, and the ancient town walls. Unlike many of its counterparts elsewhere in Italy, it's also very clean and safe. The old city is intricate and hard to navigate without a map, so stop by the tourist office before heading inside. Don't leave without seeing Alghero's **Chiesa di San Francesco.** The heavy Neoclassical facade of this church conceals a graceful Gothic presbytery. Originally erected in the 14th century, the church was partially rebuilt in the 16th century. The colored stones mark where the original ends and the reconstruction begins. *(From P. Sulis, take V. Carlo Alberto to the intersection with V. Machin. Open 7:30am-noon and 5-8pm. Free.)* Nearby is the **duomo.** Begun in 1552, this cathedral took 178 years to construct, resulting in a motley Gothic-Catalán-Renaissance facade. Rebuilt in the 19th century, the cathedral retains its striking Gothic choirs and a mosaic of John the Baptist. *(On V. Roma.)*

♫ ENTERTAINMENT

Alghero truly comes alive at night—with revelers streaming through the cramped streets of the *centro storico* and pouring onto the promenade until the early hours of the morning (be wary of indulging in the late-night scene if you're staying at the hostel; the last bus to Fertilia is at 11:30pm). Lungomare Dante is lined with open-air bars that attract locals in search of warm evening breezes and decent bands. Closer to the water, **Bar del Trò,** Lungomare Valencia, 3, offers live music after 11:30pm. (Open daily May-Oct. 9pm-6am; Nov.-Apr. 7:30pm-3am.) To escape from the nighttime stampede in P. del Teatro, duck into the cool confines of **Caffe Teatro,** V. Principe Umberto, 23, where buying a drink is your ticket to free Internet access. (☎079 97 32 119. Open daily 5am-3am.) In July and August, the town has **outdoor movies** in Forte della Maddalena. Call ☎079 97 63 44 for information.

▶ DAYTRIP FROM ALGHERO: GROTTE DI NETTUNO

FDS buses run to Capo Caccia and Porto Conte (☎079 95 01 79; 50min.; 3 per day 9:15am-5:15pm, last return 6:05pm, L3400/€1.76). Or take the more frequent and pleasant Navisarda Grotte di Nettuno boat tour. Boats (☎079 97 62 02, 95 06 03, or 97 89 61) leave Alghero's Bastione della Maddalena hourly (1hr.; 8 per day 9am-5pm, fewer in winter; L18,000/€9.30, under 13 L10,000/€5.16).

The Duke of Buckingham dubbed the ▨**Grotte di Nettuno** "the miracle of the gods." The majestic caves have been around for 60 to 70 million years and today are one of Sardinia's most coveted tourist attractions. Respect your elders and watch where you bump your head—one cubic centimeter of stalactite took 100 years of dripping rain water to form. Well-run tours are conducted in just about any language. The caves are in **Capo Caccia,** a steep promontory that juts out from **Porto Conte.** Once there, descend the 632 steps that plunge to the sea between massive white cliffs. (☎079 94 65 40. Open daily Apr.-Sept. 9am-7pm; Oct. 10am-5pm; Nov.-Mar. 9am-2pm. Groups admitted hourly. L15,000/€7.75, under 12 L8000/€4.13.)

ARST buses to Capo Caccia stop along the way at the **nuraghe of Palmavera** (☎079 95 32 00), where a central tower surrounded by several huts forms a limestone complex dating from 1500 BC. (Ruins open daily Apr.-Oct. 9am-7pm; Nov.-Mar. 9:30am-4pm. L4000/€2.07, with guided tour L7000/€3.62. Call ☎079 95 32 00 for information on the tours offered by the S.I.L.T. cooperative; tours available in English, French, German, and Spanish if you reserve in advance.)

BOSA
☎0785

It's unusual that a town with a 12th-century castle this charming, perched atop a hill overlooking the sea, could remain relatively untouristed—but Bosa pulls it off. The town has two identities. The first, Bosa proper, is home to the castle and the accompanying *città vecchia* and its fair share of photogenically dilapidated buildings. The second, a ten-minute bus ride away, is Bosa Marina, where a lengthy *lungomare*, complete with relatively unpopulated beaches and the usual assortment of seaside bars, resides. Bosa may seem strangely deserted though: so much so that you might wonder what the locals know that you don't.

▉▐ ORIENTATION AND TRANSPORTATION. **Bosa**, the larger of the two cities, and the one with the *centro storico*, is about 3km inland from the ocean, while **Bosa Marina** is across the **River Temo**, on the beach. Buses stop in Bosa's **Piazza Angelico Zanetti**. Buses run from Bosa to **Piazza Palmiro Togliatti** in Bosa Marina (5min., 22 per day, L1300/€0.67). Additionally, Pullman buses from **Alghero** or **Oristano** often continue to Bosa Marina. **ARST** buses run from Bosa to **Oristano** (1½hr., 4 per day 7:30am-4:50pm, L8600/€4.44) and **Sassari** (2hr.; 4 per day 6:20am-6pm; L10,400-18,600/€5.37-9.61). Buy tickets from the *tabacherria* at V. Alghero, 7A. **FDS buses** run to **Alghero** (11 per day; *linea mare* 55min., L5600/€2.89; *linae montagna* 1½hr., L7200/€3.72) and **Nuoro** (1¾hr., 3 per day 6:06am-7:31pm, L9500/€4.91). Tickets can be bought at the FDS office in P. Zanetti. (Open 5:30-8:30am, 9:30am-3:20pm, and 4:10-8:25pm; in winter 5:30-8:30am and 9:30am-7:35pm.)

▊ PRACTICAL INFORMATION. The **Pro Loco tourist office**, V. Zuni, 5, at the intersection of V. Francesco Romagna and V. Azuni, has a good map of the city (L1000/€0.55), but you can pick one up for free at the hostel (☎0785 37 61 07; proloco@bosa.net; www.bosa.net. Open daily 10am-1pm and 5-8pm.) For **currency exchange** head to **Credito Italiano**, C.V. Emanuele, 62, or its 24hr. **ATM**. (Open M-F 8:20am-1:20pm and 2:35-4:05pm.) In case of **emergency**, dial ☎113 or call **Red Cross** (☎0785 37 38 18) or **carabinieri** (☎0785 37 31 16). Get some **Internet access** with all the toppings at **Al Gambero Rosso**, V. Nazionale, 12, in Bosa on the Bosa Marina side of the river. This cyber-pizzeria charges L10,000/€5.16 per hr. (☎0785 37 41 50. Access available M-Sa 12:45-3pm and 7:30pm-1am.) The **post office**, V. Pischetta, 1, offers fax service and **currency exchange**. (☎0785 37 31 39. Open M-F 8:20am-6:30pm, Sa 8:20am-12:45pm.) **Postal Code:** 08013.

▊▌ ACCOMMODATIONS AND FOOD. Bosa Marina is home to a well-run ▐Youth Hostel at V. Sardegna, 1. Ask the bus driver to let you off near the hostel. From P. Palmiero Togliatti, take V. Sassari to V. Grazia Deledda and turn right. After two blocks, turn left and look for the hostel at the end of the street. Fifty meters from the beach, this hostel has a restaurant, a bar that's open until midnight, and an amicable staff. (☎0785 375 009. Meals L15,000/€7.75; breakfast L2000/€1.03. Lockout Sept.-June noon-6pm. Midnight curfew. 50 beds. 6- to 8-bed dorms L20,000/€10.33; doubles available if reserved.) For something classier, try **Albergo Perry Clan**, V. Alghero, 3, in Bosa. From the bus stop, walk along V.D. Manin and turn right. The hotel is on the left after P. Dante Alighieri. All rooms have bath, A/C, and phone; some have a TV. (☎0785 37 30 74. 32 beds. Singles L30-50,000/€15.50-25.82; doubles L60-100,000/€30.99-51.65.) If you can afford to shell out the clams, **Tattore**, in P. Monumento, sates the appetite with savory, fresh seafood. (☎0785 37 31 04. Open Tu-Sa noon-3pm and 8:15pm-midnight.)

◎▐ SIGHTS AND OUTDOORS. Walk around the town's historic area, **Quartiere Sa Costa,** and inhale the history. One of the largest in Sardinia, it has serpentine alleys, cobbled streets, and small squares. A large, free **beach** awaits in Bosa Marina, with a *lungomare* lined with bars and its very own **Aragonese Tower**. (Open occasionally; check with tourist office.) The **Bosa Diving Center**, V. Colombo, 2 (☎0785 37 56 49; fax 37 56 33), in Bosa Marina, offers snorkeling (L45,000/€23.24)

and scuba trips (L50-95,000/€25.82-49.06 per dive plus accessory costs), 4km river boat rides with exceptional views of the city (L15,000/€7.75), and ocean sightseeing in nearby grottoes and a white sand beach (2hr.; L25,000/€12.91).

OLBIA ☎0789

Most visitors only stop in Olbia while en route to other Sardinian destinations. Although there are archaeological sites in the area, the town itself has but a single, unremarkable medieval church and nary a beach in sight. Unless you're willing to rent a moped or bike to explore some of the surrounding countryside, Olbia offers little more than convenient ferry connections to Corsica and the rest of Italy.

⌐ TRANSPORTATION

Trains: (☎0789 84 88 or 88 088), on V. Pala. Turn off C. Umberto, pass through the bus station to the tracks, and turn right. Trains run to the port to meet departing ferries. Ticket office open M-Sa 6am-12:40pm and 1:50-8:30pm. Luggage storage available (p. 665). To: **Cagliari** (4hr.; 4 per day 6:43am-6:17pm; L24,400/€12.6); **Golfo Aranci** (20min., 7 per day 7:03am-8:04pm, L3300/€1.70); **Sassari** (2hr.; 4 per day 6:43am-8:22pm; L10,600/€5.47).

Buses: ARST, C. Umberto, 168 (☎0789 55 30 00). Waiting room open daily 7am-8pm. Tickets and schedule at train station ticket window. Fewer buses on Su. To: **Arzachena** (30min., 13 per day 6:30am-11pm, L3400/€1.76); **Nuoro** (2½hr.; 7 per day 8am-7:55pm; L12,200-14,000/€6.3-7.32); **Palau** (1hr., 13 per day 6:30am-1pm, L5000/€2.58); **Santa Torosa di Gallura** (2½hr., 7 per day 6:30am-5:22pm, L7200/€3.72).

Ferries: All of the ferry companies have offices in the Stazione Marittima. **Port office** open when ferries are running. Check-in 1½hr. before departure. **Tirrenia** (☎0789 207 100). Open M-Sa 7am-1pm and 5:30pm-midnight. To **Civitavecchia** (4-8hr.; L28,500-64,500/€14.72-33.31) and **Genoa** (6-13½hr., L52,500-103,00/€27.11-53.19). **Moby Lines** (☎0789 27 927). Open daily 8am-12:30pm and 3-10pm. To: **Civitavecchia** (4-8hr.; L35-70,000/€18.08-36.15); **Genoa** (6-13½hr.; L45-100,000/€23.24-51.65); **Livorno** (10hr.; L41-90,000/€21.17-46.48). **Grand Nave Veloci** (☎0789 20 01 26). Open daily 8:30am-12:30pm and 4-8pm. To **Genoa** (L84-140,000/€43.37-72.30). **Lloyd Sardegna** (☎0789 21 411). To **Livorno** (11hr.; L31-64,000/€16.01-33.05) and **Piombino** (8hr.; L31-64,000/€16.01-33.05).

Car and Moped Rental: Avis (☎0789 695 40), in the airport. MC/V. **Gallura** (☎0789 275 70 or 51 518), on V. Aldo Moro. Cars from L90,000/€46.48 per day plus VAT and insurance. Open daily 8:30am-1pm and 3:30-6pm.

✴⁊ ORIENTATION AND PRACTICAL INFORMATION

Blue intercity **ARST buses** and a train timed to meet incoming passengers greet **ferries** arriving at the port. To reach Olbia's *centro*, take the waiting train to the first stop. To find the tourist office, walk directly from the train station up **via Pala** until it intersects **Corso Umberto**. The ARST bus station is 200m to the right. Turn left and continue past **Piazza Margherita** until you reach **via Catello Piro.**

TOURIST, FINANCIAL, AND LOCAL SERVICES

Tourist Office: V. Catello Piro, 1 (☎0789 214 53; fax 222 21), off C. Umberto. Look for the modern white building. Ask for *Annuario Hotels and Camping.* Open in summer M-Sa 8:30am-1pm and 4-6pm. Hours vary with staff availability.

Currency Exchange: Credito Italiano, C. Umberto, 167. Open M-F 8:20am-1:20pm and 2:50-4:20pm, Sa and holidays 8:20-11:50am. **ATM** outside. **Banco di Sardegna,** C. Umberto, 142, off P. Margherita and **Banca Popolare di Sassari,** C. Umberto, 3, have **ATMs** outside.

Luggage Storage: In train station. L5000/€2.58 per 12hr.

American Express: Avitur, C. Umberto, 142B (☎0789 243 27), will cash checks (9am-1pm) and hold mail for AmEx cardholders. Also books ferry and plane tickets. Friendly, English-speaking staff. Open M-F 9am-1pm and 4-7pm, Sa 9am-1pm.

English-Language Bookstore: La Libreria dell'Isola, C. Umberto, 154 (☎0789 21 386). House an impressive selection of English titles (best-sellers and classics). Stock up before you depart for other island destinations. Open May.-Oct. daily 9am-1pm and 4:30-8:30pm; Nov.-Apr. daily 9am-1pm and 4-8pm. AmEx/D/MC/V.

EMERGENCY AND COMMUNICATIONS

Emergency: ☎113.

First Aid: Guarda Medica (☎0789 55 24 31), on V. Canova, facing the hospital.

Late-Night Pharmacy: Farmacia Lupacciolu, C. Umberto, 134 (☎0789 213 10), at the corner of V. Porto Romano. Open M-Sa 9am-1pm and 5-8:20pm. Local papers, *La Nuova Sardegna* and *L'Unione Sarda*, list pharmacies open on Su.

Hospital: Ospedale Civile (☎0789 55 22 00), V. Aldo Moro.

Internet Access: Mailboxes, Etc., V.R. Elena, 24 (☎0789 260 00). L12,000/€6.2 per hr. Also offers Western Union, UPS, and FedEx services. Open M-F 9:30am-1pm and 4:30-8pm, Sa 9:30am-1pm.

Post Office: V. Acquedotto (☎0789 23 151), 2 blocks from P. Matteotti. Open M-F 8:15am-6:15pm, Sa 8:15am-1pm.

Postal Code: 07026.

⌂ ACCOMMODATIONS

Albergo Terranova, V. Garibaldi, 3 (☎0789 223 95; fax 272 55; htlterraova@tiscalinet.it; www.paginegialle.it/terranova-07), off P. Margherita. This labor of love has been run by the same family for 40 years. Recent renovations make it the best option in the city for the budget traveler. All rooms with bathroom, TV, and A/C. Some doubles have balconies. Breakfast L8000/€4.13. Singles L95-125,000/€49.06-64.56; doubles L130-190,000/€67.14-98.13. Half-pension L115-140,000/€72.30. AmEx/MC/V.

Hotel Minerva, V. Mazzini, 6 (☎/fax 0789 211 90). From P. Margherita, walk C. Umberto toward water and take 1st right. Friendly management and bright rooms. Some rooms have bathrooms. Most pets allowed, free (children under 3 ft. or 1m do not count as pets; neither do children taller than this). Breakfast L6000/€3.10. Singles L50-65,000/€25.82-33.57; doubles L70-100,000/€36.15-51.65.

⬛ FOOD

For bargains, shop at **Mercato Civico,** on V. Acquedotto (open M-Sa 8am-1:30pm and 5-8:30pm), **Superpan,** P. Crispi, 2, off V. R. Elena at the waterfront (open M-Sa 8:30am-9pm and Su 8am-1:30pm; MC/V), or **Supermercato Sisa,** V. Dettori, 10 (open daily 8am-1pm and 5-8pm; MC/V).

▨ **La Datcha,** V. Cavour, 3 (☎0789 25 784). Sit outside and watch the world go by as you enjoy good food at reasonable prices. In addition to *primi* (L9-13,000/€4.65-7.32), and *secondi* (L13-24,000/€6.71-12.39), you can enjoy a crêpe, starting at L6000/€3.20, and finish it all off with some *mirto*, a traditional Sardinian berry liquor. Call ahead and they'll prepare you *paella* or couscous. Sardinian specialty *menú* for L40,000/€20.66. Open daily for lunch at noon, dinner at 7:30pm. MC/V.

▨ **Ristorante da Paolo,** V. Garibaldi, 18 (☎0789 216 75). The combination of rugged brown stone, soft pastel tablecloths, and pleasantly kitschy wall murals creates a soft and self-indulgent air. Try the house specialty *porcetta* (L13,000/€6.71). *Primi* L10-15,000/€5.16-7.75; *secondi* L12-20,000/€6.20-10.33; fish L15-25,000/€7.75-12.91. Cover L3000/€1.55. Open daily noon-2:30pm and 7-10:30pm. MC/V.

⊙ SIGHTS

A walk along the water in Olbia takes you through an industrial area, sadly obscuring Sardinia's peaks and blue coasts. Nearly all traces of Olbia's Greek, Roman, and medieval past have disappeared. The sole exception is the relatively boring 12th-century **Chiesa di San Simplicio,** behind the train station. Built in the Pisan-Romanesque style, the imposing facade is etched in off-white granite.

If you have a car or feel up to a bike ride, think about taking an excursion from Olbia to **S'Abe,** an archaeological site 6km away or to the **Giants' Tombs of Su Monte** (prehistoric burial grounds with megaliths emerging from the ground). The bus to Nuoro passes **Isola Tavolara,** an prism of rock protruding 450m out of the sea.

ARST buses run to **San Teodoro** (1hr.; 5 per day 6:40am-7:25pm, last return 8:15pm; L3400/€1.76), where a long, luxurious beach eases into aquamarine water. **Hotel La Palma,** on V. del Tirreno, offers 18 budget rooms. (☎0784 86 59 62. Doubles L150,000/€77.47; half-pension L110,000/€56.81 per person. AmEx/MC/V.) One kilometer from San Teodoro, the **Cala d'Ambra campground** has satisfactory facilities and 100 lots just 250m from the beach. (☎0784 86 56 50. Open Apr.-Oct. L12-21,000/€6.20-10.85 per person, L3-10,000/€1.55-5.16 per tent.)

PALAU   ☎0789

Palau's most famous inhabitant, the *roccia dell'orsù*, is an enormous rock that the tireless Mistral winds have carved into the shape of a bear. It was an object of intrigue even in Homer's day, when he immortalized it in his *Odyssey* (Tenth Chant) by warning of the ferocious *Lestrigoni* people that once lived around it. The locals have mellowed a bit since then, and Palau is now a sleepy, harmless coastal town composed of modern buildings done in typically Sardinian pastel shades of yellow and pink. The real attraction these days is the coast. Convenient ferry shuttles that transport passengers across the bay to the beautiful islands of La Maddalena and Caprera attract visitors; it was as a transfer point to La Maddalena that Palau was developed during the 18th century.

🛈 **PRACTICAL INFORMATION.** The port end of **via Nazionale**—Palau's single thoroughfare—contains a white building that houses a bar, several ferry ticket offices, and a newsstand that also sells ARST bus tickets (the buses stop outside). **ARST buses** head to **Olbia** (16 per day; L4500/€2.32 to the *centro*, L5000/€2.58 to the port) and **Santa Teresa di Gallura** (6 per day 7:15am-9:25pm, L3400/€1.72). The **Trenino Verde** (little green train) provides a slow, indirect, and expensive means of transportation to Sassari—the train goes to Tempio in July and August (2 hr.; 2 per day 9:50am-7pm; L18,000/€9.30) and on Thursdays a train runs from Tempio to Sassari (2hr., 4:54pm, L20,000/€10.33). **TRIS** (☎0789 70 86 31) and **Saremar Ferries** (☎0789 70 92 70) serve the island of **La Maddalena** (15min., 1-3 per hr. 7:15am-11:50pm, round-trip L8000/€4.13, under 12 L4000/€2.07, locals L3000/€1.55, cars L7600-15,700/€3.93-8.11, moped/motorcycle L3-7500/€1.55-3.87, bicycles free). For **car rental** head to **Centro Servizio Autonoleggio,** P. Chiesa, 2. (☎0789 70 85 65. From L80,000/€41.32 per day, including insurance and unlimited mileage. 20+. Open daily 8:30am-12:30pm and 4:30-7:30pm. AmEx/MC/V.)

Palau's **tourist office,** V. Nazionale, 96, slightly uphill from the center of town, offers information on nearby beaches, outdoor activities, and tours of neighboring islands. (☎/fax 0789 70 95 70. Open M-Sa 8am-1pm and 4-8pm; off-season 8am-1pm and 3-6pm.) **Banca di Sassari,** V. Roma, 9, has **currency exchange** and **ATMs** in front. (Open M-F 8:20am-1:20pm and 2:30-3:30pm, Sa 8:20-11:50am.) In an **emergency,** dial ☎113, contact the **carabinieri** (☎0789 70 95 03), call the **Guarda Medica** (☎0789 70 93 96), or ring the **hospital** in Olbia (☎0789 22 279) or Tempio (☎079 63 17 01). **Farmacia Nicolai** (☎0789 70 95 16; for urgent medical emergencies only call 0329 95 34 693) is at V. Delle Ginestre, 19. (Open M-Sa 9am-1pm and 5-8pm. AmEx/MC/V.) The **post office** is at the intersection of V. Garibaldi and V. La Maddalena. (☎0789 70 85 27. Open M-F 8:15am-1:15pm, Sa 8:15am-12:45pm.)

KILLER CLOWNS FROM OUTER SPACE

Ancient Sardinian lore warns of the dangers that lurk in the waters between Sardinia and Corsica. Just as mainland Italians look down upon native Sardinians as a bit brutish, Sardinians consider all Corsicans to be descended from fools. It is said that after God spread mankind throughout the world, the island of Corsica remained empty and uninhabited, because all right-minded folk headed to Sardinia first and found no reason to leave. Only the fishermen of the clan *Shearer* ventured to the shores of the island to the North, in search of the legendary *Matt Ben,* the waters of plenty. According to legend, one particularly foolish fisherman cast his net too high and brought a star crashing down into his boat. He managed to paddle to shore before the boat collapsed and sank. There, the star—which had been part of a constellation known to Sardinians as 'The Idiot Jester'—spawned the first Corsicans. A band of celestial clowns followed, descending from the sky to take their revenge on the poor fisherman for unbalancing the heavens. After dispatching the poor sap, they submerged themselves in the waters between the two islands, becoming deadly enforcers waiting patiently for the next foolish fisherman to cast his net too high.

ACCOMMODATIONS & CAMPING. Accommodations in Palau are often prohibitively expensive. The best of the lot is **Hotel Serra**, V. Nazionale, 17, close to the port. The hotel provides 20 simple, clean rooms, all with bath, and the lobby is bedecked with thank-yous and photographs of various US Naval vessels. (☎0789 70 95 19; fax 70 97 13. Reserve in summer. Singles L55-60,000/€28.41-30.99; doubles L80-85,000/€41.32-43.90. AmEx/MC/V.) **Hotel La Roccia**, V. dei Mille, 15, is modern and has a lobby designed around an enormous boulder. All 20 rooms have bathrooms, A/C, and TV Private parking available. (☎0789 70 95 28; fax 70 71 55. Breakfast included. Call ahead. Singles L90-120,000/€46.48-61.97; doubles L130-196,000/€67.14. AmEx/MC/V.) For camping try **Acapulco**, Loc. Punta Palau. The facility has a private beach, nightly piano music (live singer in Aug.), and a bar and restaurant. Bring your own tent. (☎0789 70 94 97; fax 70 63 80. Open Easter-Oct. 15. Reservations necessary in summer for bungalows. L12-26,000/€6.20-13.43 per adult, L10-16,000/€5.16-9.30 per child ages 4-12. Bungalows L35-40,000/€18.08-20.66 per person, 4-person caravans L90-150,000/€46.48-77.47. AmEx/MC/V.)

FOOD. Numerous **bakeries** and **alimentari** line V. Nazionale. The friendly, attentive waitstaff of **L'Uva Fragola**, P.V. Emanuele, 2, serves a variety of crisp, refreshing salads (L10-12,000/€5.16-6.20), pizzas (L6-12,000/€3.10-6.20), and desserts in a relaxed, shaded outdoor setting. (☎0789 70 87 65. Cover L2000/€1.03. Open daily noon-3pm and 7-11:30pm.) **Ristorante Robertino,** V. Nazionale, 20, dishes out flavorful spaghetti with scallops or *zuppa marinara* for around L20,000/€10.33. (☎0789 70 96 10. Cover L3000/€1.55. Open Tu-Su 1-2:30pm and 8-11:30pm. MC/V.) If you want a drink while you're waiting for the ferry and you don't mind sitting next to sailors, check out **Guido's** by the Stazione Marittima, where you buy the ferry tickets. (☎0789 709 465. US currency accepted. Open daily 5:30am-midnight.)

SIGHTS. Tiny **Spiaggia Palau Vecchia** is the beach to the left of the port when facing the water. Palau's main draw is the *roccia dell'orsù*. **Caramelli buses** (15min., 5per day 7:30am-6pm, last return 6:20pm, L1200/€0.62) run to the rock at **Capo d'Orso** from the port. Caramelli also runs to **Porto Pollo**, a beautiful beach brimming with big-bottomed tourists and baby-blue water (30min., 5 per day 8:15am-7:20pm, last return 7:55pm, L2300/€1.19). An **antique steam-engine tour** departs in July and August for Tempio (9:50am, return 5pm; round-trip L23,000/€11.81). Several private boat companies run all-day tours of the archipelago, including the islands of **Budelli** and **Spargi** (see La Maddalena, below).

LA MADDALENA ARCHIPELAGO   ☎0789

Corsica and Sardinia were once joined by a massive land bridge; La Maddalena, Caprera, and the 50-plus smaller islands that surround them are its fragmented remains. La Maddalena is clean, safe, and unambiguously oriented toward its visitors, drawing an interesting mix of tourists (mostly an upscale crowd) and soldiers as the beautiful coastline is also a strategically important one, and one-fifth of La Maddalena's inhabitants are members of the Italian or US Navy. Although US tourists are still a rarity, plenty of sailors jog through the streets, kayak in the waters, and enjoy drinks at the bars of La Maddalena. You'll run into more shopkeepers and waiters who speak English here than anywhere else in Sardinia. Italian patriots mob La Maddalena for their own reasons: their national hero, Giuseppe Garibaldi, made the nearby island of Caprera his home while he was in exile.

⚑ PRACTICAL INFORMATION. Tris (☎0789 73 54 65) runs ferries between Palau and La Maddalena (15min., 2-3 per hr. 7:15am-11:20pm, L8000/€4.13), as does **Saremar** (☎0789 73 76 60; 1-2 per hr. 4:30am-11:45pm, L8000/€4.13). For a **taxi**, call ☎0789 73 65 00. For **scooter rental**, the people at **Nicol Sport**, on V. Amendola, will hook you up for L35-60,000/€18.08-30.99 per day (plus a hefty L200,000/€103.29 deposit). Half-day rates available. (☎0789 73 54 00. Open daily 9am-8pm.) Services include: a **tourist office** in P. Barone de Geneys (☎0789 73 63 21; open May-Oct. M-Sa 9am-1pm and 5-8pm, Su 9:30am-12:30pm and 5-8pm; Nov.-Apr. M-Sa 9am-1pm. Times may vary according to daylight); a **Banco di Sardegna**, on V. Amendola off P. XXIV Febbraio, with **currency exchange** and a 24hr. **ATM** (open M-F 8:45am-1:30pm and 2:45-6pm); **carabinieri** (☎0789 73 69 43); **Pronto Soccorso** (☎0789 79 12 18); **pharmacy (Farmacia Russino)**, V. Garibaldi, 5 (☎0789 73 73 90; open Su-F 9am-1pm and 5-8:30pm); a **hospital** (☎0789 79 12 00); **Internet** access at **Sotta Sopra Internet Cafe**, V. Garibaldi, 48 (☎0789 73 50 07; L12,000/€6.20 per hr.; open F-W 11am-3:30pm and 5:30pm-late); and a **post office**, in P. Umberto (☎0789 73 75 95; open M-F 8:15am-6:15pm, Sa 8:15am-noon).

ⒻⒸ ACCOMMODATIONS AND FOOD. Hotel Arcipelago, V. Indepedenza, 2, is the best deal, though it's a 20min. walk from the town itself. From P. Umberto, follow V. Mirabello along the water until you reach the intersection with the stoplight (it's quite a ways—persevere). Take a left here and then a right at the Ristorante Sottovento. Continue uphill to the sign directing you to your left; take the left indicated by the sign, and then take a left and a right after the grocery store. The brown stucco hotel is on your right. Or, catch the bus to Caprera from the Garibaldi column, ask to be let off at the *semaforo* (stoplight), and proceed as above. All 12 rooms have bath and TV; some have balconies. (☎0789 72 73 28. Breakfast and cup of coffee included. Reservations necessary in July and Aug. Singles L70-90,000/€36.15-46.48; doubles L100-135,000/€51.65-69.72.) Pick up the basics at the **Dimeglio Supermarket**, V. Amendola, 6. (☎0789 73 90 05. Open M-Sa 8am-1:30pm and 5-8pm, Su 8:30am-1pm. MC/V.) The **Gastronomia Terra Mare**, V. Amendola, 35 (☎0789 73 10 25; open daily 9:30am-10:30pm), offers a taste of some of the most unusual fare around, from octopus *(polpa)* to horse *(cavallo)*, measured out by the kilogram. A full meal can be devoured here for under L15,000/€7.75. **Mangana**, V. Mazzini, 2 (☎0789 738 477) is decent and not too expensive; try the *primi* (L10-16,000/€5.16-8.20) and pizzas (L5-12,000/€2.58-6.20), though they're only available at dinner. If you're looking for a night out, La Maddalena's seafaring citizens support enough bars to satisfy the thirstiest of tourists. For Guinness on tap (small L5000/€2.58) and tartan wall-decorations that seem oddly misplaced in Sardinia, check out **The Penny Drops**, an Irish pub on V. Nazionale in front of the church. (☎0333 349 9372. Open daily 11am-3am.)

◪ SIGHTS. The islands of **⬛Spargi, ⬛Budelli, Razzoli**, and **Santa Maria** are a paradise of uninhabited natural beauty. Some time ago, National Park status was conferred upon the islands to protect them from development and to curb the throngs of tourists. Some spots, including the infamous **Spiaggia Rosa**, have been closed off altogether. However, boatloads of swimsuit-wearing sightseers still pack large tour ships to take all-day cruises around the archipelago, stopping along the way at Spargi's **Cala Connari** and Budelli's **Spiaggia Cavaliere**. To avoid the crowds, you have to hike along the thorny, glittering granite cliffsides that cascade down to the beaches. Even then, you're bound to share the crystalline waters with swimmers diving off anchored yachts and tiny power boats. Ticket sellers clamor along the docks of both La Maddalena and Palau every morning until the boats begin to depart (10-10:30am). Purchase tickets the day before, especially in summer, as they do sell out. The tour should include a meal and two or three two-hour stops at beaches along the way. Most boats return around 5-6:30pm. Though expensive (L50-60,000/€25.82-30.99), the tour is the cheapest way to reach the islands.

Pine groves shade picnic tables on the quiet island nature reserve of **Caprera.** With few inhabitants, the calm is interrupted only by carloads of tourists coming for a stay at Caprera's Club Med or for a visit to the much-adored **House of Garibaldi.** (☎0789 72 71 62. Open 9am-6:30pm. L4000/€2.07. Discounts for children, senior citizens, and EU citizens.) **Buses** run from the Garibaldi column in P. XXIV Febbraio in La Maddalena to Caprera (13 per day 8:45am-6:45pm, last return 7:15pm; one-way L1300/€0.67). During the *Risorgimento*, Garibaldi was forced into exile in Tunisia, the US, and finally Caprera in 1854. Two years later he built a home here, spending the rest of life commuting back and forth between his Caprera home and the mainland in pursuit of his patriotic endeavors. The house contains much of Garibaldi's original furniture and possessions.

SANTA TERESA DI GALLURA ☎0789

Although the crowds here might make you forget you ever left the mainland, Santa Teresa's beautiful view and surrounding countryside will soon convince you that you could be nowhere but Sardinia. The little town makes a lovely launching point for exploring coves, inlets, and the Capo Testa, a rocky plain with magnificent beaches overlooking the sea. It boasts its own small (and rather crowded) beach, Rena Bianca, from which the hazy shores of Corsica are visible over the shoulders of the tall German tourists who will inevitably stand in front of you.

▐▀ TRANSPORTATION

Buses: ARST (☎0789 211 97) buses depart from V. Eleonora d'Arborea, adjacent to post office off V. Nazionale. Buy tickets at Baby Bar on V. Nazionale, 100m to left from bus stop. To: **Olbia** (2hr., 6 per day, L7200/€3.72); **Palau** (40min., 6 per day 6:10am-8:50pm, L3400/€1.76); **Sassari** (2½hr.; 5 per day 5:15am-7:15pm; L11,300/€5.83); **Tempio** (1½hr., 3 per day, L6700/€3.46).

Ferries: Moby Lines (☎0789 75 40 05). Tickets can be purchased at the office on V. del Porto. Open daily 6:30am-10pm. For ferry details, see p. 638. To **Bonifacio, Corsica** (1hr.; 10 per day 7am-9:10pm, last return 10pm; L13-16,500/€6.71-8.52 plus additional L6000/€3.10 port tax for entrance into Corsica).

Taxis: (☎0789 75 42 86), on V. Cavour. Open 6am-midnight.

✷ⁿ ORIENTATION AND PRACTICAL INFORMATION

The ARST bus stops in front of the post office. Facing the post office, turn right, head to the intersection, and turn right onto **via Nazionale.** Head for the church at the end of the street (in **Piazza San Vittorio**) and turn right again to reach **Piazza Vittorio Emanuele.** The tourist office is on the opposite side of the *piazza.*

TOURIST, FINANCIAL, AND LOCAL SERVICES

Tourist Office: The Consorzio Operatori Turistici, P.V. Emanuele, 24 (☎0789 75 41 27). List of rooms for rent. Ask about horse, moped, and boat rentals. Open June-Sept. daily 8:30am-1pm and 3:30-8pm; Oct.-May M-Sa 8am-1pm and 3:30-6:30pm.

Boat Tours: Consorzio delle Bocche, P.V. Emanuele, 16 (☎0789 75 51 12), tours the islands of the archipelago. Daily tours lasting from 9:30am until 5pm with lunch (L55-

60,000/€28.41-30.99 per person, ages 3-10 L30-35,000/€15.50-18.08). Alternative itineraries can be requested. Office open daily 10am-1pm and 6-11pm.

Horseback Riding: Scuola di Turismo Equestre/Caddhos Club (☎0789 75 16 40), in nearby Marazzino (4km away). Guided excursions L35,000/€18.08 per hr. Closed Su.

Scuba Diving: No Limits Diving Center, V. del Porto, 16 (☎/fax 0789 75 90 26), offers a 7-day course for PADI and SSI certification (L600,000/€309.87), guided excursions (L60-90,000/€30.99-46.48), and help in finding accommodations. AmEx/D/MC/V.

Car Rental: Avis, V. Maria Teresa, 41 (☎0789 75 49 06). 23+. About L163,000/ €84.20 per day. Open daily 8:30am-12:30pm and 4:30-7:30pm. AmEx/D/MC/V. **GULP,** V. Nazionale, 58 (☎0789 75 56 98; info@gulpimmobiliare.it). Cars from L126,000/€65.07 per day. 25+. Credit card necessary. AmEx/MC/V.

Scooter and Bike Rental: Top Service Noleggio, V. Nazionale, 15/17 (☎0789 754 533 or 328 48 88 757; topservice@tiscalinet.it). Bikes from L10,000/€5.16 per day; scooters from L40,000/€20.66 per day; 4-wheeler L120,000/€61.97 per day. Discounts available for long-term rental; 18+. Open daily 9am-1pm and 4-8pm. MC/V.

EMERGENCY AND COMMUNICATIONS

Emergency: ☎113. **Medical Emergency:** ☎118.

Police: Carabinieri (☎0789 75 41 27), V. Nazionale.

First Aid: Guarda Medica (☎0789 75 40 79), V. Carlo Felice. Open 24hr.

Late-Night Pharmacy: P.S. Vittorio, 2 (☎0789 75 53 38). Open June-Aug. daily 9am-1pm and 5-8pm; reduced hours in the off-season.

Internet Access: Infocell (☎/fax 0789 75 54 48), V. Nazionale, off V. D'Arborea. L10,000/€5.16 per hr. Open daily 9am-1pm and 4:30-8pm.

Post Office: (☎0789 73 53 24), on V. Eleonora D'Arborea, across from the bus stop. Open M-F 8am-12:45pm, Sa 8am-12:30pm.

Postal Code: 07028.

◢ ACCOMMODATIONS

▨ **Hotel Moderno,** V. Umberto, 39 (☎0789 75 42 33), off V. Nazionale. Central location, 16 white rooms, big, bright bathrooms, and a bright smile from the dapper proprietor make this hotel a jewel. The prices may seem high, but they're reasonable for this area. Ask about the deal for a L30,000/€15.50 *menú* at the restaurant Da Thomas (see below). Breakfast included. Reservations required. Singles with bath L60-90,000/ €30.99-46.48; doubles L100-150,000/€51.65-77.47. AmEx/MC/V.

Hotel Bellavista, V. Sonnino, 8 (☎/fax 0789 75 41 62), 2 blocks past P.V. Emanuele. Incredible views of the sea. 16 bright, airy rooms with balconies and baths. Breakfast L8000/€4.13. Singles L55-60,000/€28.41-30.99; doubles L85-105,000/€43.88-54.22. Half-pension L80-110,000/€41.32-56.81; full pension L100-128,000/ €51.65-66.09. 30% more for an extra bed.

Hotel del Porto, V. del Porto, 20 (☎/fax 0789 75 41 54). From ARST stop on V. Nazionale, face post office and go left. At the intersection, take another left and then a right. Follow V. del Porto down the hill. Likely to have vacancies. 20 large rooms, some with bathrooms and views of the nearby rocks, all close to the ferry horns. Breakfast L10,000/€5.16. L25,000/€12.91 per meal at the restaurant downstairs. Singles L50-60,000/€25.82-30.99; doubles L70-100,000/€36.15-51.65. AmEx/MC/V.

◖ FOOD

Alimentari scattered along V. Aniscara, off P. V. Emanuele sell inexpensive basics. A fruit and clothing **market** by the bus station opens on Thursday mornings. If you're on a really tight budget, head to the **Gastronomia** (see below), or make a picnic with food from the **SISA supermarket,** on V. Nazionale next to the Banco di Sardegna. (Open M-Sa 8am-1pm and 4:30-8pm, Su 9am-noon.)

Papé Satan, V. Lamarmora, 22 (☎0789 75 50 48). Look for the sign off V. Nazionale. You wouldn't think the Prince of Darkness would be such a good cook, but this home of Lucifer is ranked among the top 100 Neapolitan pizzerias in all of Italy and among the top 4 in Sardinia. Try the devilishly rich *pizza alla Papé Satan* (L12,500/€6.46), or, if you don't mind anchovies, the *quattro stagione* (L14,000/€7.32), divided into 4 parts with strips of crust. Cover L4000/€2.07. Open daily noon-2:30pm and 7-11pm.

Da Thomas, V. Val d'Aosta, 22 (☎0789 75 51 33). Eat outdoors with some space between you and the madding crowd that floods the *piazza* and the seaside at dinner-time. On the inexpensive side for Santa Teresa. *Primi* L10-27,000/€5.16-13.94; meat *secondi* from L12,000/€6.2; fish L18,000/€9.30. If staying at the Moderno, ask about the L30,000/€15.50 *menù*. Open daily for lunch from 12:30pm, dinner 7:30pm.

BEACHES AND HIKING

V. XX Settembre leads toward the sea. As the road forks, veer left and continue past Hotel Miramar to reach **Piazza Libertà.** Words cannot do justice to the perfect **Aragonese Tower** framed by the deep blue of the wide ocean, with the shores of Corsica just barely visible through the mist across the sea. Take a walk down the stairs in the *piazza* to reach **Spiaggia Rena Bianca.** Those seeking a more off-the-beaten-path sunbathing experience must sacrifice sand for rock. Above the beach, an unkempt trail winds up and around the rocks along the coast, giving the more adventurous traveler access to the coves and lagoons. The trek is thorny and overgrown, so proper footwear is a must. Farther up, the path offers glimpses of the impressive beaches of ■**Capo Testa.** If you prefer flip-flops to hiking boots but still want to get to the beach, either take the **Sardabus** from the post office to Capo Testa (10min.; 5 per day; L1300/€0.67, round-trip L2400/€1.24) or brave the traffic and walk the 3km along **V. Capo Testa** from V. Nazionale.

ENTERTAINMENT

Groove's Cafe, V. XX Settembre, 2, offers a limited pub menu, cushioned booths, and outdoor balcony seating where you can nod your head to acid jazz and deep house after 11pm. **Conti** (☎0789 75 42 71), on the other side of the *piazza,* has similar music with an upstairs dance floor and loft beds where you can nod your bod to the sounds of a live DJ. (Both open 7am-late). If you just want to hang out and shoot some pool or surf the net, head to **Poldo's Pub.** While a cocktail anywhere else in town will run about L10,000/€5.16, a little Corona at Poldo's will set you back L3000/€1.55. (☎0789 75 58 60. Open all night.)

APPENDIX

TEMPERATURE AND CLIMATE

°CELSIUS	-5	0	5	10	15	20	25	30	35	40
°FAHRENHEIT	23	32	41	50	59	68	77	86	95	104

To convert from °C to °F, multiply by 1.8 and add 32. For a rough approximation, double the Celsius and add 25. To convert from °F to °C, subtract 32 and multiply by 0.55. For a rough approximation, subtract 25 from Fahrenheit and cut it in half.

AVERAGE TEMPERATURE AND PRECIPITATION

	JANUARY			APRIL			JULY			OCTOBER		
	°C	°F	cm/in	°C	°F	cm/in	°C	°F	cm/in	°C	°F	cm/in
Florence	2/10	35/50	6.4/2.5	8/19	46/66	7.1/2.8	17/31	62/87	3.4/1.3	10/21	50/69	10.3/4
Milan	-4/6	25/42	5.2/2.0	5/17	40/63	12.5/5	15/28	59/82	6.4/2.5	6/18	43/63	8.4/3.3
Rome	3/14	38/56	8.1/3.2	7/19	45/66	5.6/2.2	17/30	62/86	1.8/0.7	11/22	52/73	12/4.6
Venice	-1/6	31/42	5.6/2.2	8/16	46/61	7.3/2.9	18/27	63/81	6.8/2.7	9/18	48/64	7.7/3.0

ABBREVIATIONS

Throughout the book, address titles have been abbreviated:

ABBREVIATIONS	
C.	Corso
D.	De
Loc.	Locanda
P.	Piazza
Pta.	Porta
V.	Via
Vco.	Vicolo

INTERNATIONAL CALLING CODES

To call internationally without a calling card, dial the international access number ("00") + country code (for the country you are calling) + number. For operator-assisted and calling card calls, dial the international operator: 170. For directory assistance, dial 12.

TELEPHONE CODES		TELEPHONE CODES	
Australia	61	Monaco	377
Austria	43	New Zealand	64
Canada	1	Slovenia	386
France	33	South Africa	27
Germany	49	Spain	34
Greece	30	Switzerland	41
Ireland	353	UK	44
Italy	39	US	1

TIME ZONES

Italy is one hour later than Greenwich Mean Time (GMT), six hours later than US Eastern Standard Time (EST), 10 hours ahead of Vancouver and San Francisco time, the same as Johannesburg time, 12 hours behind Sydney time, and 14 hours behind Auckland time. From the last Sunday in March to the last Sunday in September, Italy and Malta both switch to Daylight Savings Time and are two hours later than GMT but still six hours later than US EST.

MEASUREMENTS

Italy uses the metric system. Below are metric units and English system equivalents.

MEASUREMENT CONVERSIONS

1 inch (in.) = 25.4 millimeters (mm)	1 millimeter (mm) = 0.039 in.
1 foot (ft.) = 0.30m	1 meter (m) = 3.28 ft.
1 yard (yd.) = 0.914m	1 meter (m) = 1.09 yd.
1 mile (mi.) = 1.61km	1 kilometer (km) = 0.62 mi.
1 ounce (oz.) = 28.35g	1 gram (g) = 0.035 oz.
1 pound (lb.) = 0.454kg	1 kilogram (kg) = 2.202 lb.
1 fluid ounce (fl. oz.) = 29.57ml	1 milliliter (ml) = 0.034 fl. oz.
1 gallon (gal.) = 3.785L	1 liter (L) = 0.264 gal.
1 acre (ac.) = 0.405ha	1 hectare (ha) = 2.47 ac.
1 square mile (sq. mi.) = 2.59km^2	1 square kilometer (km^2) = 0.386 sq. mi.

ITALIAN

PRONUNCIATION

VOWELS

There are seven vowel sounds in standard Italian. **A, i,** and **u** each have one pronunciation. **E** and **o** each have two pronunciations, one tense and one lax, depending on the vowel's placement in the word, the stress, and the regional accent (some don't incorporate this distinction). It is difficult for non-native speakers to predict the quality of vowels—don't worry so much about **e** and **o.** You may hear a difference, especially with **e.** Below is the *approximate* pronunciation of vowels.

THE BASICS	
a:	*a* as in father *(casa)*
e: tense e: lax	*ay* as in bay *(sete)* *eh* as in set *(bella)*
i:	*ee* as in cheese *(vino)*
o: tense o: lax	*o* as in bone *(sono)* between *o* of bone and *au* of caught *(zona)*
u:	*oo* as in droop *(gusto)*

CONSONANTS

Save a few quirks, Italian consonants are easy. **H** is always silent, **r** is always rolled.

- **C and G:** Before **a, o,** or **u, c** and **g** are hard, as in *cat* and *goose* or as in the Italian word *colore* (koh-LOHR-eh), "color," or *gatto* (GAHT-toh), "cat." They soften into **ch** and **j** sounds, respectively, when followed by **i** or **e,** as in English *cheese* and *jeep* or Italian *ciao* (chow), "goodbye," and *gelato* (jeh-LAH-toh), "ice cream."

CH and GH: H returns **c** and **g** to their "hard" sounds in front of **i** or **e** (see above): *chianti* (ky-AHN-tee), the Tuscan wine, and *spaghetti* (spah-GEHT-tee), the pasta.

GN and GLI: Pronounce **gn** like the **ni** in *onion*, thus *bagno* ("bath") is "BAHN-yoh." **Gli** is like the **lli** in *million*, so *sbagliato* ("wrong") is said "zbal-YAH-toh."

SC and SCH: When followed by **a, o,** or **u, sc** is pronounced as **sk.** *Scusi* ("excuse me") yields "SKOO-zee." When followed by an **e** or **i, sc** is pronounced **sh** as in *sciopero* (SHOH-pair-oh), "strike." H returns **c** to its hard sound **(sk)** before **i** or **e,** as in *pesche* (PEHS-keh), "peaches," not to be confused with *pesce* (PEH-sheh), "fish."

Double consonants: The difference between double and single consonants in Italian is likely to cause problems for English speakers. When you see a double consonant, pronounce it twice or hold it for a long time. English phrases like "dumb man" or "bad dog" approximate the double consonant sound. Failing to make the distinction can lead to confusion; for example, *penne all'arrabbiata* is "short pasta in a spicy red sauce," whereas *pene all'arrabbiata* means "penis in a spicy red sauce."

STRESS

In many Italian words, stress falls on the next-to-last syllable. When stress falls on the last syllable, accents indicate where stress falls: *città* (cheet-TAH) or *perchè* (pair-KAY). Stress can fall on the third-to-last syllable, but this occurs less often.

PLURALS

Italians words form the plural by changing the last vowel. Words ending in an **a** in the singular (usually feminine) end with an **e** in the plural; *mela* (MAY-lah), "apple," becomes *mele* (MAY-lay). Words ending with **o** or **e** take an **i** in the plural; *conto* (KOHN-toh), "bill," is *conti* (KOHN-tee), and *cane* (KAH-neh), "dog," becomes *cani* (KAH-nee). Words with a final accent, like *città* and *caffè*, and words that end in consonants, like *bar* and *sport*, do not change in the plural.

PHRASEBOOK

ENGLISH	ITALIAN	ENGLISH	ITALIAN
NUMBERS			
one	uno	twenty-one	ventuno
two	due	twenty-three	ventitre
three	tre	twenty-eight	ventotto
four	quattro	thirty	trenta
five	cinque	forty	quaranta
six	sei	fifty	cinquanta
seven	sette	sixty	sessanta
eight	otto	seventy	settanta
nine	nove	eighty	ottanta
ten	dieci	ninety	novanta
eleven	undici	one hundred	cento
twelve	dodici	one hundred five	cento cinque
thirteen	tredici	two hundred	duecento
fourteen	quattordici	eight hundred	ottocento
fifteen	quindici	one thousand	mille
sixteen	seidici	two thousand	due mila
seventeen	diciasette	eight thousand	otto mila
eighteen	diciotto	hundred thousand	cento mila
nineteen	dicianove	million	un millione
twenty	venti	billion	un milliardo

DAYS			
Monday	lunedì	Friday	venerdì
Tuesday	martedì	Saturday	sabato
Wednesday	mercoledì	Sunday	domenica
Thursday	giovedì		

MONTHS			
January	gennaio	July	luglio
February	febbraio	August	agosto
March	marzo	September	settembre
April	aprile	October	ottobre
May	maggio	November	novembre
June	giugno	December	dicembre

ENGLISH	ITALIAN	PRONUNCIATION
GENERAL		
Hello/So long (informal)	Ciao	chow
Good day/Hello	Buongiorno	bwohn JOHR-noh
Good evening	Buona sera	BWOH-nah SEH-rah
Good night	Buona notte	BWOH-nah NOHT-teh
Goodbye	Arrivederci/ ArrivederLa (formal)	ah-ree-veh-DAIR-chee/ah-ree-veh-DAIR-lah
Please	Per favore/Per piacere	pehr fah-VOH-reh/pehr pyah-CHEH-reh
Thank you	Grazie	GRAHT-see-yeh
How are you?	Come stai? sta (formal)	COH-meh st-EYE/stah
I am well.	Sto bene	stoh BEH-neh
You're welcome	Prego	PREY-goh
May I help you?	Prego?	PREY-goh
Go right ahead!	Prego!	PREY-goh
Excuse me	Scusi	SKOO-zee
I'm sorry	Mi dispiace	mee dees-PYAH-cheh
My name is...	Mi chiamo...	mee key-YAH-moh
What's your name?	Come ti chiami?	COH-meh tee key-YAH-mee
Yes/ No/ Maybe	Sì/ No/ Forse	see/no/FOHR-seh
I don't know	Non lo so	nohn loh soh
I have no idea	Boh.	boh
Could you repeat that?	Potrebbe ripetere?	poh-TREHB-beh ree-PEH-teh-reh
What does this mean?	Cosa vuol dire questo?	Coh-za vwohl DEE-reh KWEH stoh
I understand	Ho capito	Oh kah-PEE-toh
I don't understand	Non capisco	nohn kah-PEES-koh
I don't speak Italian	Non parlo italiano	nohn PAR-loh ee-tahl-YAH-noh
Is there someone who speaks English?	C'è qualcuno che parla inglese?	cheh kwahl-KOO-noh keh PAR lah een-GLAY-zeh
Could you help me?	Potrebbe aiutarmi?	poh-TREHB-beh ah-yoo-TAHR mee
How do you say...?	Come si dice...?	KOH-may see DEE-chay
What do you call this in Italian?	Come si chiama questo in italiano?	KOH-may see key-YAH-mah KWEH-stoh een ee-tahl-YAH-no
this/that	questo/quello	KWEH-sto/KWEHL-loh
who	chi	kee
where	dove	DOH-vay
which	quale	KWAH-lay
when	quando	KWAN-doh
what	che/cosa/che cosa	kay/KOH-za/kay KOH-za
how	come	koh-meh

why/because	perchè	pair-KEH
more/less	più/meno	pyoo/MEH-noh
good luck (literally, in the mouth of the wolf)	in bocca al lupo	in BOHKA al lOO-po

TIME		
At what time...?	A che ora...?	ah keh OHR-ah
What time is it?	Che ore sono?	keh OHR-ay SOH-noh
It's 3:30 (Remember, Italians often use the 24-hour clock, so add twelve to afternoon/evening arrival times.)	Sono le tre e mezzo.	SOH-noh leh tray eh MEHD-zoh
It's noon.	È mezzogiorno.	eh MEHD-zoh-JOHR-noh
midnight	mezzanotte	MEHD-zah-NOT-eh
now	adesso/ora	ah-DEHS-so/OH-rah
tomorrow	domani	doh-MAH-nee
today	oggi	OHJ-jee
yesterday	ieri	YAYR-ee
right away	subito	SU-bee-toh
soon	fra poco/presto	frah POH-koh/ PREH-stoh
already	già	jah
after(wards)	dopo	DOH-poh
before	prima	PREE-mah
late/later	tardi/più tardi	TAHR-dee/pyoo TAHR-dee
early (before scheduled arrival time)	presto	PREHS-toh
late (after scheduled arrival time)	in ritardo	een ree-TAHR-doh
daily	quotidiano	kwoh-tee-dee-AH-no
weekly	settimanale	seht-tee-mah-NAH-leh
monthly	mensile	mehn-SEE-leh
vacation	le ferie	leh FEH-ree-eh
weekdays	i giorni feriali	ee JOHR-nee feh-ree-AH-lee
Sundays and holidays	i giorni festivi	ee JOHR-nee fehs-TEE-vee
day off (at store, restaurant, etc.)	riposo	ree-POH-zo

DIRECTIONS AND TRANSPORTATION		
Where is...?	Dov'è...?	doh-VEH
How do you get to...?	Come si arriva a...	KOH-meh see ahr-REE-vah ah
Do you stop at...?	Ferma a...?	FEHR-mah ah
...the beach	la spiaggia	lah spee-AH-jah
...the building	il palazzo/l'edificio	eel pah-LAHT-zo/leh-dee-FEE-choh
...the bus stop	la fermata d'autobus	lah fehr-MAH-tah DAOW-toh-boos
...the center of town	in centro	een CHEN-troh
...the church	la chiesa	lah kee-AY-zah
...the consulate	il consolato	eel kohn-so-LAH-toh
...the grocery store	l'alimentari/il supermercato	lah-lee-men-TAH-ree/eel SOO-pehr mer-CAT-oh
...the hospital	l'ospedale	los-peh-DAH-leh
...the market	il mercato	eel mehr-KAH-toh
...the office	l'ufficio	loo-FEE-choh
...the post office	l'ufficio postale	loo-FEE-choh poh-STAH-leh
...the station	la stazione	lah staht-see-YOH-neh
near/far	vicino/lontano	vee-CHEE-noh/lohn-TAH-noh
turn left/right	gira a sinistra/destra	JEE-rah ah see-NEE-strah/DEH-strah

APPENDIX

straight ahead	sempre diritto	SEHM-pray DREET-toh
here	qui/qua	kwee/kwah
there	lì/là	lee/lah
the street address	l'indirizzo	leen-dee-REET-soh
the telephone	il telefono	eel teh-LAY-foh-noh
street	strada, via, viale, vico, vicolo, corso	STRAH-dah, VEE-ah, vee-AH-leh, VEE-koh, VEE-koh-loh, KOHR-soh
Take the bus from/to...	Prenda l'autobus da/a...	PREN-dah LAOW-toh-boos dah... ah...
What time does the... leave?	A che ora parte...?	ah kay OHR-ah PAHR-tay
...the (city) bus	l'autobus	LAOW-toh-boos
...the (intercity) bus	il pullman	eel POOL-mahn
...the ferry	il traghetto	eel tra-GHEHT-toh
...the plane	l'aereo	lah-EHR-reh–oh
...the train	il treno	eel TRAY-no
How much does it cost?	Quanto costa?	KWAN-toh CO-stah
How much does...cost?	Quanto costa...?	KWAN-toh CO-stah
I would like...	Vorrei...	VOH-ray
...a ticket	un biglietto	oon beel-YEHT-toh
...a pass (bus, etc.)	una tessera	OO-nah TEHS-seh-rah
one-way	solo andata	SO-lo ahn-DAH-tah
round-trip	andata e ritorno	ahn-DAH-tah ey ree-TOHR-noh
reduced price	ridotto	ree-DOHT-toh
student discount	uno sconto studentesco	oon-oh SKOHN-toh stoo-dehn-TEHS-koh
What time does the train for...leave?	A che ora parte il treno per...?	ah kay OH-rah PAHR-tay eel TRAY-noh pair
What platform for...?	Quale binario per...?	qwal-eh bee-NAH-ree-oh pair
From where does the bus leave...?	Da dove parte l'autobus per...?	dah DOH-vay PAHR-tay LAU-toh-boos pair
Is the train late?	È in ritardo il treno?	eh een ree-TAHR-doh eel TRAY-no
the arrival	l'arrivo	la-REE-voh
the departure	la partenza	la par-TENT-sah
the track	il binario	eel bee-NAH-ree-oh
the terminus (of a bus)	il capolinea	eel kah-poh-LEE-neh-ah
the flight	il volo	eel VOH-loh
the reservation	la prenotazione	la pray-no-taht-see-YOH-neh
the entrance/the exit	l'ingresso/l'uscita	leen-GREH-so/loo-SHEE-tah
I need to get off here.	Devo scendere qui.	DEH-vo SHEN-der-ay qwee

EMERGENCY		
I lost my passport/wallet	Ho perso il passaporto/portafoglio.	oh PEHR-soh eel pahs-sah-POHR-toh/por-ta-FOH-lee-oh
I've been robbed.	Sono stato derubato.	SOH-noh STAH-toh deh-roo-BAH-toh
Wait!	Aspetta!	ahs-PEHT-tah
Stop!	Ferma!	FAIR-mah
Help!	Aiuto!	ah-YOO-toh
Leave me alone!	Lasciami stare!	LAH-shah-mee STAH-reh
Don't touch me!	Non mi toccare!	NOHN mee tohk-KAH-reh
I'm calling the police!	Telefono alla polizia!	tehl-LEH-foh-noh ah-lah poh-leet-SEE-ah
Go away, idiot!	Vattene, cretino!	VAH-teh-neh creh-TEE-noh

MEDICAL		
I have...	Ho...	OH
...allergies	delle allergie	DEHL-leh ahl-lair-JEE-eh

...a blister	una bolla	lah BOH-lah
...a cold	un raffreddore	oon rahf-freh-DOH-reh
...a cough	una tosse	OO-nah TOHS-seh
...the flu	l'influenza	lenn-floo-ENT-sah
...a fever	una febbre	OO-nah FEHB-breh
...a headache	mal di testa	mahl dee TEHS-tah
...an itch	un prurito	eel pru-REE-toh
...a lump (on the head)	un bernoccolo	eel bear-NOH-koh-loh
...menstrual pains	delle mestruazioni dolorose	DEH-leh meh-stroo-aht-see-OH-nee doh-lor-OH-zay
...a rash	un'esantema/un sfogo/ un'eruzione	oo-NEH-zahn-TAY-mah/ eel SFOH-goh/ loo-NEH-root-see-OHN-eh
...a stomach ache	mal di stomaco	mahl dee STOH-mah-koh
...a swelling/growth	un gonfiore	oon gohn-fee-OR-ay
...a venereal disease	una malattia venerea	OO-nah mah-lah-TEE-ah veh-NAIR-ee-ah
...a vaginal infection	un'infezione vaginale	oon-een-feht-see-OH-neh vah-jee-NAH-leh
...a wart	una verruca	OO-nah veh-ROOK-kah
My foot hurts.	Mi fa male il piede.	mee fah MAH-le eel PYEHD-deh
I'm on the pill.	Prendo la pillola.	PREHN-doh lah PEE-loh-lah
I haven't had my period for (2) months.	Non ho le mestruazioni da (due) mesi.	nohn oh leh meh-stroo-aht-see-OH-nee dah (DOO-eh) may-zee
I'm (3 months) pregnant.	Sono incinta (da tre mesi).	SOH-noh een-CHEEN-tah (dah treh MAY-zee)
You're (a month) pregnant.	Lei è incinta (da un mese).	lay eh een-CHEEN-tah (dah oon MAY-zeh)
the bladder	la vescica	lah veh-SHEE-cah
the gall bladder	la cistifellea	lah sees-tee-fehl-LAY-ah
the blood	il sangue	eel SAHN-gweh
the appendix	il appendice	eel ap-pen-DEE-chay
a gynecologist	un ginecologo	oon jee-neh-KOH-loh-goh
the skin	la pelle	lah PEHL-leh

HOTEL AND HOSTEL RESERVATIONS

Hello? (used when answering the phone)	Pronto?	PROHN-toh
Do you speak English?	Parla inglese?	PAHR-lah een-GLAY-zeh
Could I reserve a single room/double room for (the second of August)?	Potrei prenotare una camera singola/doppia per (il due agosto)?	POH-tray pray-noh-TAH-reh OO-nah CAH-meh-rah SEEN-goh-lah/DOH-pee-yah pair eel DOO-ay ah-GOH-stoh?
Is there a free bed for tonight?	C'è un posto libero stasera?	chay oon POHS-toe LEE-ber-oh sta-SER-ah?
with bath/shower	con bagno/doccia	kohn BAHN-yo/DOH-cha
with bathroom	con un gabinetto/un bagno	kohn ooh gah-bee-NEHT-toh/oon BAHN-yoh
Is there a cheaper room without a bath/shower?	C'è una stanza più economica senza bagno/doccia?	chay oo-nah STAN-zah pyoo eko-NOM-ika sen-zah BAHN-yo/DOH-cha?
open/closed	aperto/chiuso	ah-PAIR-toh/KYOO-zoh
a towel	un asciugamano	oon ah-shoo-gah-MAH-noh
sheets	le lenzuola	leh lehn-SUO-lah
a blanket	una coperta	OO-nah koh-PEHR-tah
heating	il riscaldamento	eel ree-skahl-dah-MEHN-toh
How much is the room?	Quanto costa la camera?	KWAHN-toh KOHS-ta lah KAM-eh-rah
I will arrive (at 2:30pm).	Arriverò alle (quattordici e mezzo).	ah-ree-vehr-OH ah-lay (kwah-TOHR-dee-chee eh MED-zoh)
Certainly!	Certo!	CHAIR-toh
We're closed during August.	Chiudiamo ad agosto.	kyu-dee-AH-moh ahd ah-GOH-stoh

No, we're full.	No, siamo al completo.	no, see-YAH-moh ahl cohm-PLAY-toh
We don't take telephone reservations.	Non si fanno le prenotazioni per telefono.	nohn see FAHN-noh leh pray-noh-tat-see-YOH-nee pair teh-LAY-foh-noh
You'll have to send a deposit/check.	Bisogna mandare un anticipo/un assegno.	bee-ZOHN-yah mahn-DAH-reh oon ahn-TEE-chee-poh/oon ahs-SAY-nyoh
You must arrive before 2pm.	Deve arrivare primo delle quattordici.	DAY-veh ah-ree-VAH-reh PREE-moh day-leh kwah-TOHR-dee-chee
Okay, I'll take it.	Va bene. La prendo.	vah BEHN-eh. lah PREHN-doh
What is that funny smell?	Che cos'è il odore curioso?	kay kohz-EH eel oh-DOOR-eh kyoor-ee-OH-so

RESTAURANTS		
breakfast	la colazione	lah coh-laht-see-YO-neh
lunch	il pranzo	eel PRAHND-zoh
dinner	la cena	lah CHEH-nah
appetizer	l'antipasto	lahn-tee-PAH-stoh
first course	il primo	eel PREE-moh
second course	il secondo	eel seh-COHN-doh
side dish	il contorno	eel cohn-TOHR-noh
dessert	il dolce	eel DOHL-cheh
fork	la forchetta	lah fohr-KEH-tah
knife	il coltello	eel cohl-TEHL-loh
spoon	il cucchiaio	eel koo-kee-EYE-yoh
teaspoon	il cucchiaino	eel koo-kee-EYE-ee-noh
bottle	la bottiglia	lah boh-TEEL-yah
glass	il bicchiere	eel bee-kee-YAIR-eh
napkin	il tovagliolo	eel toh-vahl-YOH-loh
plate	il piatto	eel pee-YAH-toh
waiter/waitress	il/la cameriere/a	eel/lah kah-meh-ree-AIR-reh/rah
the bill	il conto	eel COHN-toh
cover charge	il coperto	eel koh-PAIR-toh
service charge/tip	il servizio	eel sehr-VEET-see-oh
included	compreso/a	KOHM-preh-zoh/ah

LOVE		
You're cute.	Sei carino/a (bello/a).	SAY cah-RIN-oh/ah (BEHL-loh/lah)
I'm married.	Sono sposato/a	soh-noh spo-ZA-to/-ta
Save a dance for me.	Lasciami un ballo.	LAH-shah-mee oon BAH-loh
I don't dance.	Non ballo.	nohn BAH-loh
Your friend is cute.	Tuo amico/tua amica è bello.	TOO-oh ah-MEE-coh ay BEHL-loh
She dances poorly, why don't you dance with me?	Lei balla male, perchè non balli con me?	lay BAH-lah mal-eh, pair-KEH nohn BAH-lee con meh
Kiss me.	Baciami.	BAH-cha-mee
I love you, I swear.	Ti amo, te lo giuro.	tee AH-moh, teh loh JOO-roh
Let's get a room.	Prendiamo una camera.	prehn-DYAH-moh oo-nah CAH-meh-rah
I only have safe sex.	Pratico solo sesso sicuro.	PRAH-tee-coh sohl-oh SEHS-so see-COO-roh
Is it okay if I touch you there?	Va bene se ti tocco là?	vah BEH-neh seh tee toh-coh lah
I have a boyfriend/a girlfriend.	Ho un ragazzo/una ragazza.	oh oon rah-GAHT-soh/oo-nah rah-GAHT-sah
Would you touch me here?	Puoi toccarme qui?	poy toc-CAR-meh qwee?
Leave her alone, she's mine.	Lasciala stare, è mia.	LAH-shah-lah STAH-reh eh mee-ah
I'm leaving tomorrow.	Vado via domani.	VAH-doh vee-ah doh-MAH-nee
Leave right now.	Vai via subito.	vai VEE-ah SOO-bit-oh.
I'll never forget you.	Non ti dimenticherò mai.	nohn tee dee-men-tee-ker-OH my
heterosexual/straight	etero (sessuale)	EH-teh-roh (ses-SOOAH-leh)

bisexual	bisessuale	bee-ses-SOOAH-leh
gay	gay	GAH-ee
lesbian	lesbica	LEH-sbee-cah
celibate	celibe	CHEH-lee-beh
a transvestite	uno/a travestito/a	OO-noh/nah trah-veh-STEE-toh/tah

AT THE BAR		
May I buy you a drink?	Posso offrirle qualcosa da bere?	POHS-soh ohf-FREER-leh kwahl-COH-zah dah BAY-reh
I'm drunk.	Sono ubriaco/a.	SOH-noh oo-BRYAH-coh/cah
Would you buy me a drink?	Può mi offriresti qualcosa da bere?	pwoh mee ohf-freer-ES-tee kwahl-COH-zah dah BEH-reh
Are you drunk?	Sei ubriaco/a?	SAY oo-BRYAH-coh/cah
Let's drink some more!	Beviamo più!	beh-vee-AH-moh pyoo
I don't drink.	Non bevo.	nohn BEH-voh
Can I have a sip?	Mi fai fare un sorso?	mee fah-ee FAH-reh oon SOHR-soh
Cheers!	Cin cin!	chin chin
Do you have a light?	Mi fai accendere?	mee fah-ee ah-CHEN-deh-reh
No thank you, I don't smoke.	No grazie, non fumo.	noh GRAH-zye nohn FOO-moh
Do you have an ashtray?	Hai un portacenere?	ah-ee oon pohr-tah-CHEH-neh-reh
I was here before this lady!	C'ero io prima io di questa signora!	CHEH-roh EE-oh PREE-mah dee QHEH-stah see-nyoh-rah
Do you believe in aliens?	Credi negli extraterrestri?	CREH-dee neh-lyee ehx-trah-teh-REH-stree
I feel like throwing up.	Mi viene di vomitare.	mee VYE-neh dee voh-mee-TAH-reh
beer	una birra	OO-nah BEER-rah
a glass of wine	un bicchiere di vino	oon bee-KYE-reh dee VEE-noh
a liter of wine	un litro di vino	oon LEE-troh di VEE-noh

MENU READER

PRIMI	
pasta aglio e olio	garlic and olive oil
pasta all'amatriciana	in a tangy tomato sauce with onions and bacon
pasta all'arrabbiata	in a spicy tomato sauce
pasta alla bolognese	in a meat sauce
pasta alla boscaiola	egg pasta, served in a mushroom sauce with peas and cream
pasta alla carbonara	in a creamy sauce with egg, cured bacon, and cheese
pasta alle cozze	in a tomato sauce with mussels
pasta al forno	oven-baked pasta, like lasagna
pasta alla pizzaiola	tomato-based sauce with olive oil and red peppers
pasta al pomodoro	in tomato sauce
pasta alla puttanesca	in a tomato sauce with olives, capers, and anchovies
pasta alla romana	cooked in milk, butter, cheese, and then baked
pasta alle vongole	in a clam sauce; bianco for white, rosso for red
polenta	deep fried cornmeal
risotto	rice dish, comes in nearly as many flavors as pasta sauce
PIZZA	
ai carciofi	with artichokes
ai fiori di zucca	with zucchini blossoms
ai funghi	with mushrooms
alla capriciosa	with ham, egg, artichoke, and more
con acciughe	with anchovies

PIZZA

con bresaola	with cured beef
con melanzana	with eggplant
con prosciutto	with ham
con prosciutto crudo	with cured ham (also called simply *crudo*)
con rucola (rughetta)	with arugala (rocket for the Brits)
margherita	plain ol' tomato, mozzarella, and basil
peperoncini	chillies
polpette	meatballs
quattro formaggi	with four cheeses
quattro stagioni	four seasons; a different topping for each quarter of the pizza, usually mushrooms, *crudo*, artichoke, and tomato

SECONDI

agnello	lamb
anatra	duck
animelle alla griglia	grilled sweetbreads
anguila	eel
arrosto misto di pesce	mixed grilled seafood
asino	donkey (served in Sicily and Sardinia)
bistecca	steak
cavallo (sfilacci)	horse (a delicacy throughout the South and Sardinia)
carciofi alla giudia	fried artichokes
carne alla valdostana	cutlets fried in lemon butter, baked with cheese and ham
coda alla vaccinara	stewed oxtail with herbs and tomatoes
coniglio/pollo cacciatore	rabbit/chicken served in a tomato sauce; varies widely by region
coppa	cured pork shoulder
cotoletta	breaded veal cutlet with cheese
cozze	mussels
fegato alla veneziana	chicken liver cooked with onions
filetto di baccalà/merluzzo	fried cod
fiori di zucca	zucchini flowers filled with cheese, battered, and lightly fried
gamberi	prawns
granchi	crabs
involtini al sugo	veal cutlets filled with ham, celery, and cheese, with tomato sauce
manzo	beef
oca	goose
orata	sea bream
osso buco	braised veal shank
pasta e ceci	pasta with chick peas
polpo	octopus
salsiccia	sausage
saltimbocca alla romana	slices of veal and ham cooked together and topped with cheese
seppia	cuttlefish, usually served grilled in its own ink
sogliola	sole
speck	smoked raw ham, lean but surrounded by a layer of fat
supplì	fried rice ball filled with tomato, meat, and cheese
tonno	tuna
trippa	tripe; chopped, sautéed cow intestines, usually in a tomato sauce
vitello	veal
vongole	clams

CONTORNI

broccoletti	broccoli florets

CONTORNI

cavolo	cabbage
cipolle	onion
fagioli	beans (usually white)
fagiolini	green beans
funghi	mushrooms
insalata caprese	tomatoes with mozzarella cheese and basil, drizzled with olive oil
insalata mista	mixed green salad
lattuga	lettuce
melanzana	eggplant
piselli	peas
radicchio	radish
sottaceti	pickled vegetables
tartufi	truffles

ANTIPASTI

antipasto rustico	assortment of cold appetizers
bresaola	sliced cold cuts of meat, served with olive oil, lemon, salt, pepper, and *parmigiano*
bruschetta	large, crisp slices of garlic-rubbed, baked bread, sometimes served with raw tomatoes
carpaccio	extremely thin slices of lean, raw beef
crostini	small pieces of toasted bread usually served with chicken liver or mozzarella and anchovies, though other toppings abound
prosciutto e melone	cured ham and honeydew melon

FRUTTA

anguria/cocomero	watermelon
arancia	orange
ciliege	cherries
fragole	strawberries
lamponi	raspberries
pesca	peach
prugna	plum
uva	grape

DOLCE

cannoli	sicilian tube pastries filled with sweet ricotta
cassata siciliana	sponge cake, sweet cream, cheese, chocolate, and candied fruit
confetti	candied almonds
fragole con panna	strawberries with cream
gelato	italian-style ice cream
panforte	round, flat, honey-coated, candied fruit cakes originally from Siena
panna cotta	flan
sfogliatelle	sugar-coated layers of crunchy pastry with ricotta
tiramisù	marscapone, eggs, and lady fingers dipped in *espresso*
zuppa inglese	alternating layers of chocolate, egg cream, and biscuits soaked in liqueur and coffee.

PREPARATION

al dente	firm to the bite (pasta)
al diavolo	very spicy, made with *fra diavolo* chili peppers
al forno	baked
al sangue	rare
al vino	in wine sauce
alla griglia	grilled
aromatica/o	spicy

PREPARATION	
ben cotta/o	well done
condita/o	seasoned
cruda/o	raw
fresca/o	fresh
fritta/o	fried
marinata/o	marinated
non troppo cotta/o	medium rare
piccante	spicy
poco cotta/o	undercooked
raffermo	stale
resentin	coffee in a grappa-rinsed mug
ripieno	stuffed
scottata	scorched
secca	dry
stracotta	overcooked

GLOSSARY

abbazia	also badia, an abbey
agriturismo	tourist accommodations on farms
affittacamere	rooms for rent (usually privately owned and cheaper than a hotel)
albergo	hotel
alimentari	grocery store, often the cheapest place in town to get food
aliscafi	hydrofoil
anfiteatro	amphitheater
APT	Azienda Promozione Turistica (tourist office)
architrave	the lowermost part of an entablature, resting directly on top of a column
arco	arch
apse	a semicircular, domed niche projecting from the altar end of a church
atrium	an open central court, usually an ancient Roman house
baldacchino	stone or bronze canopy supported by columns over the altar of a church
basilica	a rectangular building with aisle and apse; no transepts. Used by ancient Romans for public administration, later used by Christians for their churches.
battistero	a baptistry, usually a separate building near the town's duomo, where the town's baptisms were performed
Berber	non-Arab native inhabitants of North Africa
borgo	ancient town or village
campanile	a bell tower, usually freestanding
cappella	chapel
carabinieri	military police
cartoon	full-sized drawing used to transfer a preparatory design to the final work, especially to a wall for a fresco.
castrum	the ancient Roman military camp. Many Italian cities were originally built on a rectilinear plan with straight streets, the chief of which was called the decumanus maximus.
Cenacolo	"Last Supper;" a depiction of Christ at dinner on the evening before his crucifixion, often found in the refectory of an abbey or convent
chancel	the space around the altar reserved for clergy and choir
chiaroscuro	the balance between light and dark in a painting, and the painter's ability to show the contrast between them
chiesa	church
cloister/chiostro	a courtyard; generally a quadrangle with covered walkways along its edges, often with a central garden, forming part of a church or monastery
comune	the government of a free city of the Middle Ages
condottiere	a leader of mercenary soldiers in Italy in the 14th and 15th centuries, when wars were almost incessant here
corso	a principal street or avenue
cosmati work	mosaic on marble, found in early Christian churches
cupola	a dome
diptych	a painting in two parts or panels
duomo	cathedral; the official seat of a diocesan bishop, and usually the central church of an Italian town
etto	330 grams
facade	the front of a building, or any wall given special architectural treatment
fiume	a river
forum	in an ancient Roman town, a square containing municipal buildings and/or market space. Smaller towns have one forum, larger cities can have several.
fresco	a painting made on wet plaster. When it dries, the painting becomes part of the wall.
frieze	a band of decoration. Architecturally, this can also refer to the middle part of an entablature (everything above the columns of a building) between the architrave and the cornice.

FS	Ferrovie dello Stato (Italian State Railways)
fumarole	a hole in the ground from which volcanic vapor is released
giardino	garden
gabinetto	toilet, WC
Greek Cross	a cross with arms of equal length
grotesque	painted, carved, or stucco decorations of fantastic, distorted human or animal figures, named for the grotto work from Nero's buried Golden House
in restuaro	under restoration; a key concept in Italy
intarsia	inlay work, usually of marble, metal, or wood
Latin Cross	a cross with the vertical arm longer than the horizontal arm
largo	(small) square
loggia	a covered gallery or balcony
lungo, lung	literally "along," so that a lungomare is a boardwalk or promenade alongside the mare (ocean)
lunette	a semicircular frame in a ceiling or vault, holding a painting or sculpture
mausoleum	a large tomb or building with places to entomb the dead above ground
mithraeum	a temple to the Roman god Mithras
nave	the central body of a church
nuraghe	cone-shaped tower-houses built of stone and assembled without mortar
palazzo	an important building of any type, not just a palace
passeggiata	a ritual evening stroll (see p. 27)
piazza	a city square
piazzale	(large) open square
Pietà	a scene of the Virgin mourning the dead Christ
pietra serena	gray to bluish stone commonly used in Renaissance constructions
pilaster	a rectangular column set into a wall as an ornamental motif
polyptych	altarpiece with more than three panels
ponte	bridge
presepio	nativity scene
putto	(pl. putti) the little nude babies that flit around Renaissance art occasionally and Baroque art incessantly
reliquary	holding place for a saint's relics, usually the bones, but often much stranger
sinopia drawing	a red pigment sketch made on a wall as a preliminary study for a fresco
scalinata	stairway
settimana bianca	literally "white week," a winter package that combines lodging, food, and skiing
sottoportico	street or sidewalk continuing under a building (like an extended archway)
spiaggia	beach
stigmata	miraculous body pains or bleeding resembling Christ's crucifix wounds
thermae	(terme in Italian) ancient Roman baths and, consequently, social centers
telamoni	large, often sensual, statues of men used as columns in temples
tessera	one of the small colored pieces of stone or glass used in making mosaics
transept	in a cruciform church, the arm of the church that intersects the nave or central aisle (i.e. the cross-bar of the T)
travertine	a light colored marble or limestone
triptych	a painting in three panels or parts
trompe l'oeil	literally, "to fool the eye," a painting or other piece or art whose purpose is to trick the viewer, as in a flat ceiling painted so as to appear domed
tufa	a soft stone composed of volcanic ash (tufo in Italian)
via	a street or road
villa	a country house, usually a large estate with a formal garden

A

abbazia 685
Abruzzo 427–434
Abruzzo National Park 432
accommodation information 49
acid 45
Acqui Terme 186
adapters
  see converters.
Aeneas 7
Aeolian Islands 584–596
aerogrammes 54
affittacamere 51
Africa 455
Agrigento 622–625
agriturismo 685
AIDS 47
airplane travel
  fares 58
airports
  Alghero-Fertilia 660
  Bari 534
  Bologna 273
  Cagliari 641
  Catania 605
  Elba 383
  Florence 306
  Genoa 135
  Milan 79
  Naples 484
  Palermo 572
  Parma 290
  Pisa 306, 373
  Reggio di Calabria 564
  Rimini 299
  Rome 437
  Sardinia 638
  Sassari 656
  Trapani 627
  Trieste 243
  Turin 172
  Venice 196
Albanese 29
albergo 685
Alberobello 540
Alberti, Leon Battista 18, 21, 108, 302
alcohol 45
  see also wines
Alexander Mosaic 15, 495, 506
Alghero 660–663
Alicudi 596
Aligheri, Dante
  disciple of xv
Alighieri, Dante 21, 226, 330, 350, 378
  Casa di 466

empty tomb 333
full tomb 298
alimentari 685
aliscafi 685
Alleanza Nazionale 13
Altamura 556
alte vie 263
altitude, high 46
Alzo 133
Amalfi 523–526
Amalfi Coast 520–533
Amato, Giuliano 14
American Express 41, 42, 54
  Bari 536
  Catania 606
  Florence 315
  Milan 84
  Naples 490
  Olbia 666
  Palermo 574
  Taormina 602
  Venice 206
  Verona 234
Amiternum 429
Anacapri 510
Ancient Rome 7
Ancona 421
anfiteatro 685
Angelico, Beato 332, 341
antique festivals
  Arezzo 345
  Mantua, Mercato dell'Antiquariato 109
  Orta, Mercato Antiquariato 134
Antonioni, Michelangelo 26
Aosta 189–192
apartments 445
apse 685
APT 685
Apulia 533–552
L'Aquila 428
Aquileia 249
Ara Pacis 15
arabica 29
Arch of Beneventum 503
Archangel Michael 539
architectural history 14–20
architrave 685
ARCI-GAY 72
  Bologna 280
  Milan 85
  Naples 500
  Palermo 574
  Pisa 374
  Ravenna 296
  Rome 476
arco 685
Arena Chapel 17
Aretino, Pietro 22
Arezzo 342–345

Arola 133
art
  Baroque and Rococo 19
  Byzantine 16
  Etruscan 14
  Gothic 16
  Greek 15
  Mannerism 19
  modern 19
  Renaissance 16
  Romanesque 16
art exhibitions 478
art history 14–20
art, inevitability of in Italy 14
Ascoli Piceno 423–426
Assisi 16, 397–403
ass-kissing 609
Asti 183–186
ATM cards 41
atrium 685
au pair 76
Augustus 8, 15, 457, 459, 460, 463, 469
Augustus of Primaporta 15
Australian consulates 35
  Milan 84
  Venice 205
Australian embassies
  Italy 35, 36
auto races 613

B

Babylonian Captivity 10
backpacks 52
bad wind 502
Baia 501
baldacchino 685
ballet, Spoleto festival 410
Baptistery of San Giovanni 17, 326
Bar Da Benito 456
bargaining 43
Bari 534–538
barista 29
Baroque 19
baroque music 24
Barumini 646
basilica 685
  San Lorenzo, Genoa 143
basilicas
  Asti 185
  Cattedrale di San Giovanni, Turin 177
  Chiesa dei Francescani, Bolzano 260
  Duomo di San Martino, Lucca 371
  Milan 90
  Monreale, Palermo 576

San Francesco, Arezzo 344
San Francesco, Assisi 401
San Gennaro, Naples 495
San Lorenzo, Florence 332
San Marco, Venice 216
San Michele, Pavia 101
San Romano, Ferrara 284
Santa Croce, Lecce 548
Santa Maria del Fiore,
    Florence 325
Santa Maria Maggiore,
    Bergamo 114
Syracuse 618
Basilicata 552–559
Bassani, Giorgio 285
Bassano del Grappa 241
Bassano, Jacopo da 242
battistero 685
Bay of Naples 503–510
Bellagio 125
Bellini, Giovanni 18
Bellini, Vincenzo 605
Belluno 263
Benetton, birthplace of 239
Benevento 502
Benigni, Roberto 27
Berber 685
Bergamo 109–115
Berio, Luciano 24
Berlusconi, Silvio 13, 14, 72
Bernini
    baldacchino 465
Bernini, Gianlorenzo 19, 461,
    462, 463, 464, 465, 467, 471
Bertolucci, Bernardo 26
The Bicycle Thieves 26
bicycling 32
biking
    Abruzzo National Park 434
    Porto Torres 659
    Valle d'Aosta 188
Black Death 10
Blacks and Whites (political
    factions) 10
boat rentals 481
Boccaccio, Giovanni 21, 496
Bologna 272–281
Bolzano 258–261
Bominaco 429
Bond, James 131
bones of death
    see desserts
Bordighera 165–167
borgo 685
Borromean Islands 132
Borromini, Francesco 19
Bosa 664
Bossi Umberto 13
Botticelli, Sandro 18, 295
Bozen
    see Bolzano

Bramante, Donato 19
Brescia 115–119
Bressanone 262
Breuil-Cervinia 188, 192
Brindisi 541–545
Brixen
    see Bressanone
Brunate 123
Brunelleschi, Filippo 18,
    325, 326, 367
Brusson 193
bungee jumping
    highest in the world,
    Locarno 131
Buonarroti, Michelangelo
    see Michelangelo
buses 67
Busseto 293
Byzantine Empire 9
    in Italy 9, 16

C

Caesar, Julius 8, 20, 457, 460
caffè 29
    Americano 29
    di orto 241
    latte 29
    macchiato 29
Cagliari 641–646
Cagliari province 641–647
Cala Gonone 654
Cala Mosca 645
Calabria 559–569
Calasetta 646
Caligula 9
calling cards 54
Calvino, Italo 22
Camigliatello 562
Camogli 144
Campania 483–533
campanile 16, 685
Campi Flegrei 500
camping 51, 450
Canada. See consulates.
Canadian consulates
    Naples 490
    Rome 36
    Venice 205
Canadian embassies
    Italy 36
Canelli 186
Cannabis beer 658
Cannabis Restaurant 386
canoeing
    see kayaking 271
Canossa 10
Canova 19
Il Capellaio Matto 455
capers 587

Capo Testa 670
cappella 685
cappuccino 29
Caprera 667
carabinieri 685
Caravaggio 19, 462, 463,
    471, 472, 474
Carloforte 647
Carnevale 33, 94
carta d'argento 64
cartaverde 64
Carthage 8
cartoon 685
Caruso 477
Caserta 502
cash cards 41
Castel del Monte 429
Castellana Grotte 539
Castelsardo 658
Castiglione, Baldassare 21
castrati 23
castrum 685
catacombs 16
    Naples 497, 498
    Priscilla 464
    Rome 469
Catania 605–610
Catullus 20
Cavour, Camillo 12, 171
CDC 46
Cefalù 580–583
Cellini, Benvenuto 22
Cenacolo 685
Centers for Disease Control
    (CDC) 46, 47
Cernobbio 123
Certosa di Pavia 102
Certosa di San Lorenzo 531
Cerveteri 480
Cervia 299
Cervino
    see Matterhorn
Champoluc 193
chancel 685
Charlemagne 10, 101
Chianti (region) 353
chiaroscuro 18, 685
chiesa 685
Chiessi 387
children and travel 74
chiostro 685
de Chirico, Giorgio 20
Chirico, Giorgio de 20
Christian art 16
Christian Democratic Party
    12
CIA World Factbook 77
Cicero 20
Cimabue 16, 17, 401
cinema 25
Cinema Paradiso 27

INDEX

Cinque Terre 150–155
Cirrus 41
Citicorp 41
city festivals
  Agrigento, Almond
    Blossom Festival 625
  Aosta, Fiera di Sant'Orso
    192
  Ascoli, Carnevale 426
  Assisi, Festa di
    Calendimaggio 402
  Asti, Festivale delle Sagre
    186
  Asti, Palio di Asti 186
  Bari, Festival of San Nicola
    538
  Bari, Levante Fair 538
  Bologna, Made in Bo 280
  Cagliari, Festival of
    Sant'Efisio 646
  Gubbio, Corsa dei Ceri 406
  Gubbio, Palio della
    Balestra 406
  Livorno, Palio Marinaro
    381
  Lucca, Settembre
    Lucchese 372
  Mantua, Festivaletteratura
    109
  Matera, Festa di Santa
    Maria della Bruna 555
  Milan, Carnevale 94
  Montepulciano, Bravio
    delle Botti 359
  Naples, Festa di San
    Gennaro 499
  Naples, Madonna del
    Carmine 499
  Nuoro, Sagra del
    Redentore 653
  Oristano, Sartiglia 650
  Orvieto, Festa della
    Palombella 414
  Otranto, Festa dei Martiri
    d'Otranto 550
  Otranto, Festa della
    Madonna dell'Altomare
    550
  Ravello, blood liquefying
    528
  Ravenna, Dante Festival
    298
  Ravenna, Ravenna
    Festival 298
  Rome, Saturnalia 457
  Sassari, Sardinian
    Cavalcade 658
  Siena, Palio 350, 353
  Spoleto, Spoleto Festival
    410
  Turin, Giorni d'Estate 180

Udine, Udine d'Estate 252
Venice, Biennale 223
Venice, Carnevale 223
Venice, Festa del
  Redentore 223
Venice, *regata storica* 223
civic humanism 11
Cividale del Friuli 252
Civitella Alfedena 434
Claus, Santa 537
Clinton, Bill 493
cloister 685
coagulated blood 496
cocaine 45
Colosseum 15, 17, 458
Columbus, Christopher 101
commedia dell'arte 223
communi 10
Como 120–123
comune 685
concentration camp, Trieste
  248
concrete 15
condottiere 685
Congress of Vienna 12
Constantine 9
Constantinople 9
Constitution, Italian 12
consulates 35, 84
  see Australian consulates
  see Irish consulates
  see South African
    consulates
  see UK consulates
  see US consulates
consulates. See UK
  consulates.
converters and adapters 49
Copernicus 226
Corniglia 150
Corriere della Sera 25
corso 685
Cortina d'Ampezzo 265
Cortona 340–342
cosa nostra 570
Cosenza 559–562
cosmati work 685
Costigliole 186
Council Travel 58
counterculture 478
country codes
  Switzerland 126
courier flights 60
Courmayeur 194
Crassus, Marcus 8
Craxi, Bettino 13
credit cards 41
crema 29
Cremona 102–105
cross-country trails
  Val di Cogne 193

CTS Travel 58
cuisine
  Emilia-Romagna 28
  Lombardese 28
  Piemontese 28
  regional specialties 27
Cumae (Cuma) 501
cupola 685
currency 40
current events 14
customs 38

D

d'Alema, Massimo 14
D'Annunzio, Gabriele 22,
  266, 268
d'Arborea, Eleonora 650
da Vinci, Leonardo 18, 92,
  293, 329, 338
Dallapiccola, Luigi 24
dammusi 635
Dante
  see Alighieri, Dante
David 327
  Donatello's 16
  Marian's xv
  Michelangelo's 17, 18
dazzling *digestif* 32
de Sica, Vittorio,*The Bicycle
  Thieves* 26
deadly sins 2
death's-head-cow-skull 97
della Francesca, Piero 420
  birthplace of 345
Desenzano 266
desserts
  bones of death 361
  confetti 430
  confettoni 547
  pampepato 283
  torrone 429
dialect 32
Dictator 8
dietary concerns 74
Diocletian 9
diptych 685
disabled travelers 72
diseases
  food- and water-borne 47
  insect-borne 47
dog museum 192
La Dolce Vita 26
Dolceacqua 171
Dolomites 257–266
Dolomiti
  see Dolomites
Domaso 126
Donatello 16, 226, 330
donkey races

see Palio
Dorgali 654
Dorms 50
dragons 526
Dreas 14
driving permits 68
drugs 45
Duccio 16, 17
duomo 685
dynamite-wielding quasi-
archaeologists 659

E

earliest inhabitants 7
Earthly Paradise 2
Eco, Umberto 22, 181
ecstasy 45
Edict of Milan 9
Egadi Islands 633–637
Elba 382–387
Elderhostel 71
electronic banking 41
elevation, high 46
email 56
embassies 35
  see Irish embassies
  see Italian embassies
  see New Zealand
  embassies
emergency medical services
  46
Emiglia-Romagna 272–303
ENIT 35
Enjoy Rome 445
Enna 610
Entrance requirements 35
Ercolano
  see Herculaneum
Eremo delle Carceri 403
Erice 632
espresso 29
espresso
  see *caffè espresso*
essentials 35–77
ethnic foods
  Ethiopian 455
Etna 610
Etruria 479
Etruscans 7, 14, 338, 362,
  387, 411, 414
  art and architecture 14
etto 685
Eugabian Tables 405
Eurailpass 64
Euro 40
Europass 65
exchange rates
  Italy 40
  Switzerland 126

F

facade 685
Facist Regime 12
Fall of the Roman Empire of
  the West 9
Fano 418
Farinelli 23
Farnese Bull 495
Farnese Collection 498
Fascism 12
fat Frenchman 493
Fattori, Giovanni 19
feces, catapulted 346
Federal Express 53
Fellini, Federico 26, 463
Fermo Posta 53
Ferrara 281–285
Ferrari factory 289
ferries 68
  Brindisi 541
  to Albania 541
  to Capri 488
  to Corsica 156, 379
  to Croatia 421
  to Egadi Islands 627
  to Elba 383
  to Greece 421, 535, 541
  to Ischia 488
  to Israel 536
  to Lake Trasimeno 394
  to Pantelleria 627
  to Procida 488
  to Reggio 597
  to Sardinia 135, 156, 379,
    488, 638
  to Sicily 135, 564, 638
  to Spain 135
  to Tunisia 135, 627, 638
  to Turkey 536, 541
Ferrovie dello Stato (FS) 63,
  686
festivals 33
  see antique festivals
  see city festivals
  see film festivals
  see food festivals
  see medieval festivals
  see music festivals
  see theatrical festivals
Fiesole 337
Filicudi 596
Filippo Lippi 328, 331
film 25
film festivals
  Pesaro, Mostra
    Internazionale del Nuovo
    Cinema 418
  Taormina Arte 604
  Venice International Film

Festival 223
Finale Ligure 159–162
financial matters 38
firsts
  bikini, Positano 520
  modern violin, Cremona
    102
  nature preserve in Italy,
    Riserva dello Zingaro 631
  novelist in Italy, Bosone
    Novello Raffaelli 404
  swingin' bridge, Taranto
    552
fish
  and chips 538
  big 538
  cooked 538
  just 538
fiume 685
Flagellation of Christ 420
flamingos, in Sardinia 645
Flavian 9
Florence
  accommodations 316
  duomo 325
  food 321
  intercity transportation
    306
  local transportation 307
  orientation 307
  Ponte Vecchio 329
  practical information 314
  shopping 336
  sights 325
  The Uffizi 328
  walking tours 314
Fo, Dario 23
food 27–29
  Milan 87
food festivals
  Abruzzo National Park,
    Sagra degli Gnocchi 433
  Camogli, Sagra del Pesce
    146
  Cortona, Festa dei Porcini
    342
  Cortona, Sagra della
    Bistecca 342
  Florence, Festival of the
    Cricket 336
  Ischia, Festa del Limone
    519
  Sila Massif, Potato
    Festival 563
food orgies, Roman 451
Foot and Mouth disease 47
Foreign Rule (1540-1815)
  11
fortified abbey 436
forum 685
Forza Italia 13

Founding of Rome 7
Fra Angelico 18, 332, 392
Franchi 454
Francis, St., of Assisi 10
Franks 10
fresco 15, 685
frieze 685
Friuli-Venezia Giulia 242–253
fumarole 686
Futurism 19

G

gabinetto 686
Galilee, Galileo 226, 230
  tomb of 334
Gallipoli 551
Gardone Riviera 268
Gargano Massif 539
Garibaldi, Giuseppe 12, 626
gay travelers 72
general delivery 53
Genoa 134–144
Gerace 569
gestures, useful but
  dangerous 33
getting around safely 44
Ghiberti, Lorenzo 18, 326
Ghirlandaio 365
Giardini-Naxos 604
giardino 686
Gioia, Flavia 523
Giorgione 19
Giotto 16, 17, 226, 229, 326, 333, 401
GO25 card 38
Godfather, The 570
gods, Olympian 20
Goldoni, Carlo 22, 101
golfing, Riva del Garda 271
Gothic 16
Gran Caffè Rossi Martini 451
Gran Sasso 430
grappa 32
Grattachecca da Bruno 456
Gravina 556
grayboxes
  Aio? Eia! 644
  And the Winner Is... 280
  Beware the Animal Spirits!
    609
  Can You Hear The People
    Sing? 566
  Devils Defeated by the
    Holy Skeletor 134
  Eat Your Heart Out, Chef
    Boyardee 277
  Good Thing He Didn't
    Catch a Porcupine 514

I Found Jesus in Turin 178
Killer Clowns from Outer
  Space 668
La Famiglia 578
Sticks and stones may
  break my bones, but
  whips and chains excite
  me 583
The 2½ Billion Lire Bed
  123
The Lord is my
  Shepherdess 650
Travelin' Italy Lactose-
  Intolerant Style 241
Walk Like an Italian 95
You want a Piece of Me?
  555
Great Schism 10
Greek art and architecture
  15
Greek Cross 686
Gregory, Pope, The Great 10
Gregory, pope, VII 10
grotesque 686
grottoes
  Grotta Gigante 248
  Grotte di Nettuno 663
  Grotto Smeralda 523
  Orecchio di Dionigi 618
  Grottoes of Stiffe 430
Gruppo Speleologico
  Aquilano 430
Guarneri, Giuseppe 102
Gubbio 403–406
Guelphs and Ghibellines
  see Blacks and Whites

H

Hadrian 9
hang-gliding, Valle d'Aosta
  188
Hannibal 8, 394
H-bomb 45
health
  heatstroke 46
  women 47
hearts and lungs of popes
  463
heat exhaustion 46
heatstroke 46
help lines 445
Herculaneum 507
heroin 45
high altitude 46
hiking 32
  Abruzzo National Park 434
  Amalfi 526
  Cinque Terre 154
  Dolomites 257

Egadi Islands 633
Gole Alcantura 604
Gran Sasso 430
Ischia 518
Matera 555
Mont Blanc 195
Mt. Etna 610
Riva del Garda 271
Santa Teresa di Gallura
  672
Stromboli 593
Vulcano 591
hiking equipment 52
history and politics 7–14
hitchhiking 70
HIV 47
holidays 33
holy tooth 530
home exchange 51
Homer 522, 585, 667
Horace 20
horseback riding
  Alghero 661
  Menaggio 124
  Santa Teresa di Gallura
    671
Hostelling International (HI)
  49
hostels 49
hot springs
  see thermal springs
hotels 50
hydrofoils
  to Aeolian Islands 597
  to Reggio 597

I

ibex, 5000 193
Ice Man 260
identification 37
Il Poetto 645
Illy 29
immunizations 45
IMPACT Model Mugging 71
in restuaro 686
innoculations 45
L'Insalata Ricca 453
insulae 15
insurance 48
intarsia 686
International Driving Permit
  (IDP) 68
International Student
  Identity Card (ISIC) 38
International Teacher
  Identity Card (ITIC) 38
International Youth Travel
  Card 38
internet 56

Ionian Coast 569
Irish consulates 35
Irish embassies 35
Italy 36
Is Arutas 651
Ischia 515–518
ISIC 38
  see International Student
  Identity Card
Isola Bella 132
Isola di San Giulio 133
Isola Madre 132
Isola Maggiore 395
Isola Tavolara 667
Isole Egadi
  see Egadi Islands
Isole Eolie
  see Aeolian Islands
Italian Cultural Institute 35
Italian Government Tourist
  Board (ENIT) 35
ITIC 38
ITIC card 38

J

James, Henry 379, 514
Jason and the Argonauts
  382
joke, bad 24, 350, 377, 429,
  460
Jonathan's Angels 476
Julio-Claudians 9
Julius Caesar 8, 477
Jungle 478
Jupiter 20

K

kayaking
  Lipari 588
  Riva del Garda 271
  Valle d'Aosta 188
Keats, John
  dying place 463
  resting place 469
keeping in touch 53–56
kosher 74
Kringle, Kris 538

L

L'Aquila 428
La Dolce Vita 463
La Maddalena 668
La Repubblica 25
La Scala 91
La Spezia 156
La Stampa 25

lactose intolerance 241
Lake Bracciano 480
Lake Campotosto 429
Lake Como 119–126
Lake Garda 266–272
Lake Maggiore 128–132
Lake Orta 132–134
Lake Trasimeno 394
language schools 75
Laocoön 17
largo 686
Last Supper, The 92
Latin Cross 686
latte
  see caffè latte
Law of the Twelve Tables 8
Lazio 437–481
Le Marche 415–427
le Nôtre, Louis 179
Leaning Tower of Pisa 377
Lecce 545–549
Lega Nord 13
Leghorn 379
Leonardo da Vinci
  see da Vinci, Leonardo
lesbian travelers 72
Lesselyong 10
Levanto 155
Levanzo 633
Levi, Primo 22
light whipping 420
Liguria 134–171
limoncello 509
Lipari 585–589
Lipari Islands
  see Aeolian Islands
Lippi, Fra Filippo, tomb of
  409
literary highlights 21
literature 20–23
Litt, Jordan 21
Livorno 379–381
Livy 20
Zimbalo, Giuseppe 548
Locarno 131
loggia 686
Lombardia. See Lombardy
Lombardy 78–119
lost passports 37
LSD 45
Lucca 368–372
Lucretia 7
Ludovisi Throne 473
Lugano 126
lunette 686
lungo 686

M

Macchiaioli 335, 381

Macchiaioli group 19
macchiato 29
Machiavelli, Niccolo 22
  tomb of 334
La Maddalena 667
Madonna 328
  interactive 378
  pregnant 346
Madonna Enthroned 17
Maestà Altar 17
Mafia 578
magazines and newspapers
  25
Magna Graecia 7, 15
Maiori 526
Malatesta, Sigismondo 302
Manarola 151
Mannerism 19, 289
Mantegna, Andrea 18, 108,
  109, 226
Mantua 105–109
Manzoni, Alessandro 22
Maratea 557
The Marches
  see Le Marche
Marcus Aurelius 9
Marettimo 633
marijuana 45, 136, 500
Marina di Campo 385
Marini, Marino 367
Marsala 626
Masaccio 18
Massimo D'Alema 14
MasterCard 41
Matera 552–556
Matterhorn 192
mausoleum 686
Mazzini, Giuseppe 12, 135
McGnocchi 28
MDMA 45
Medic Alert 46
medical assistance 46
Medici 11, 334
Medici, Cosimo 11
Medici, Lorenzo (il
  Magnifico) 11
medieval festivals
  Arezzo, Giostra del
  Saraceno 345
  Ascoli Piceno, Tournament
  of Quintana 426
  Ferrara, Palio di San
  Giorgio 285
  Ostuni, Cavalcata 545
  Palio di Asti 186
  Pisa, Gioco del Ponto 378
  Pistoia, Giostra dell'Orso
  368
  San Marino 305
  Sulmona, Giostra
  Cavalleresca 431

Urbino,Revocation of the
   Duke's Court 421
Menaggio 123
Menotti, Gian Carlo 24
menù 28
Merano 261
Messina 596–600
methamphetamine 45
Michael, Archangel 539
Michelangelo 18, 22, 330,
   332, 460, 467
Milan 78–99
   accommodations and
      camping 86
   entertainment 94
   food 87
   intercity transportation 79
   La Scala 91
   local transportation 82
   practical information 83
   shopping 94
   sights 90
   University of 93
Milazzo 600
Minori 526
minority travelers 73
Misena 501
mithraeum 468, 686
Model Mugging 44
Modena 285–289
modern music 24
Modern Period 12
Modigliani, Amadeo 381
Modigliani, Amedeo 20
Molise 427–434
money 38–43
Monreale 576
Mont Blanc (Monte Bianco)
   194
Montalcino 354
Monte Bianco
   see Mont Blanc
Monte Ingino 406
Montecatini Terme 368
Montepulciano 356–359
Monterosso 150
Montesarchio 503
Monteverdi, Claudio 23, 102
Moravia, Alberto 22
Moro, Aldo 13
mosaic 15, 16
mosquitoes 47
Mt. Vesuvius 507
movies
   outdoor film festivals 475
Mt. Epomeo 518
Mt. Etna 610
museums
   Accademia 332
   Galleria Nazionale
      dell'Umbria, Perugia 392

Gallerie dell'Accademia,
   Venice 218
Museo and Gallerie di
   Capodimonte, Naples
   498
Museo Archaeologico
   Regional "Baglio
   Anselmi", Marsala 626
Museo Archeologico
   Nazionale, Naples 495
Museo Archeologico
   Regionale, Palermo 578
Museo del Opera del
   Duomo, Florence 325
Museo dell'Opera
   Metropolitana, Siena 351
Museo di Storia e d'Arte,
   Trieste 247
Museo Diocesano,
   Cortona 341
Museo Egizio and Galleria
   Sabauda, Turin 177
Pinacoteca Nazionale 279
Pinacoteca Nazionale,
   Sardinia 645
Stradivariano, Cremona
   104
Uffizi, Florence 328
music festivals
   Bergamo, Festivale
      Pianistico Internazionale
      115
   Brescia, Festivale
      Pianistico Internazionale
      119
   Cremona, Cremona Jazz
      105
   Cremona, Estate in Musica
      105
   Cremona, Festival di
      Cremona 105
   E'grandeEstate, Parma
      293
   Ferrara, Busker's Festival
      285
   Fiesole, Estate Fiesolana
      336
   Florence, Festa dell'Unità
      336
   Florence, Maggio Musicale
      336
   Marsala DOC Jazz Festival,
      Marsala 627
   Montepulciano, Cantiere
      Internazionale d'Arte 359
   Perugia, jazz 342
   Perugia, Sagra Musicale
      Umbra 394
   Perugia, Umbria Jazz
      Festival 394
   Pesaro, Rossini Opera

   Festival 418
   Pistoia, Pistoia Blues 367
   Ragusa, International
      Piano and Voice
      Competiton 621
   Salerno, Salerno
      Summerfestival 530
   Siena, Settimana
      Musicale Sienese 353
   Stresa, Settimane
      Musicali 130
   Taormina Arte 604
   Turin, Settembre Musica
      180
   Umbria, Jazz Winter 414
   Urbino, Antique Music
      Festival 421
   Verona, Verona Opera
      Festival 238
Mussolini, Benito 12, 461

N

Naples 484–500
   accommodations 491
   food 493
   intercity transportation
      484
   local transportation 488
   orientation 488
   practical information 489
   Roman roads 496
   sights 495
Napoleon 11, 254, 382, 385
Napoleonic Kingdom of Italy
   93
Napoli
   see Naples
Napoli by Bus 488
national parks
   see parks
nature reserves
   Isola Bella 604
   Portofino 149
   Riserva dello Zingaro 631
   see also parks
nave 686
neo-classicism 19
Nero 9
New Zealand consulates 35,
   84
   Venice 205
New Zealand embassies 35
New Zealand. See New
   Zealand consulates.
Northern Sicily 570–584
Noto 619
nuns, cemetery of 517
Nuoro 651–653
nuraghi 638, 657, 686

O

Olbia 665–667
Ollomont 192
omica 158
opera 23, 24
  Bergamo 115
  Bologna 280
  brief history of 23
  Catania 609
  Cremona 105
  La Scala, Milan 91
  Parma 293
  Pesaro, Rossini Opera
    Festival 418
  Spoleto 410
  Trieste 248
  Venice 223
  Verona 238
Opi 433
Orgosolo 653
Oristano 647–651
Orta San Giulio 132
Orvieto 411–414
Ostuni 545
Otranto 549
Our Lady of Mercy 496
Ovid 20
Oyace 192

P

packing 49
Padua 226–230
Paestum 531
Palau 667
palazzo 686
Palazzo Ducale, Venice 16
Palazzo Vecchio 11
Palermo 570–580
  sights 576
  transportation 572
Palestrina, Giovanni 23
Palio
  Asti 186
  Gubbio 406
  Livorno 381
  Orvieto 414
  Siena 346, 350, 353
Palladio, Andrea 19, 21, 221,
  231, 232, 240
Pallanza 130
Palmarola 481
Panarea 594
Pantelleria 634–637
Pantheon 15, 17
paragliding, Brescia 116
parks
  Abruzzo National Park 432

Gran Paradiso National
  Park, Val di Cogne 193
Parco della Murgia
  Materana, Matera 553
Parco Nazionale di
  Calabria 563
  see also nature reserves
Parma 289–293
parmigian cheese 293
Parmigianino 19, 289
Pasolini, Pier Paolo 26
passeggiata 686
Passignano sul Trasimeno
  395
passports 36
patricians 8
Pavarotti, Luciano 24, 285,
  289
Pavese, Cesare 22
Pavia 99–101
Pavia, University of 101
Pazzi, Francesco (inept
  assassin) 11
peacocks, Borromean
  Islands 132
pensions 51
Personal Identification
  Number (PIN) 41
perspective 18
Perugia 388–394
Pesaro 416–418
Petacci, Claretta 12
Petrarch 21, 101, 226
Petronius 20
phalli
  bull's 353
  detachable 219
  in spicy red sauce 675
  Priapus's member 506
Phidias 17
phone cards 54
phone codes
  see country codes
phrases, hip 33
Piacenza 294
pickled body (in a glass
  case) 406
pickpockets 437
Piedmont 171–187
Piemonte
  see Piedmont
Pietà 686
pietra serena 686
pigs
  little 331
pilaster 686
PIN numbers 41
Pirandello, Luigi 22, 625
Pisa 373–379
Pisano, Giovanni 144, 367,
  378

Pistoia 365–368
Pizzeria Corallo 452
plainchant 23
Plautus 20
plebeians 8
PLUS 41
Policlinico Umberto I 446
La Pollarola 453
poltrone 70
Polyclitus 17
polyptych 686
Pompeii 17, 503–507
Pompey the Great 8
ponte 686
Ponte Vecchio 16, 329
Portinari Chapel, Milan 93
Porto Azzurro 386
Porto Torres 658
Portoferraio 383–385
Portofino 149
poste restante 53
  see also Fermo Posta 53
posterior, sore
  see poltrone
Il Postino 27
Pozzuoli 501
pre-Roman history 7
presepio 686
Procida 518
Prodi, Romano 14
Puccini, Giacomo 24, 372
Puglia
  see Apulia
Pulcino Ballerino 455
Punic Wars 8
Punta del Capo 510
putto 686
Pythagoras 557

R

rafting, Valle d'Aosta 188
Ragusa 620–621
railpasses
  Eurailpass 64
  Europass 65
Raphael 19, 334, 392
  Double Portrait 474
Ravello 527
Ravenna 16, 295–299
Recent Politics 13
Reggia 502
  see also Caserta 502
Reggio di Calabria 563–566
relics
  heads of St. Peter and St.
    Paul 468
  holy tooth 530
religious festivals
  Assisi, Festival of St.

Francis 403
Bordighera, Festival of Sant'Ampelio 167
Messina, Ferragosto Messinese festival 600
Reggio di Calabria, Festival of the Madonna della Consolazione 566
Taranto, Holy Week Festival 552
Venice, Festa della Salute 223
reliquary 686
Remus 7, 459
Rena Bianca 670
Renaissance 11
  early 16
  high 18
Republic 12
Respighi, Ottorino 24
Riace Bronzes 17
rifugi alpini 188
Rimini 299–303
Riomaggiore 151
Riserva dello Zingaro 631
Risorgimento 12
Risorgimento 12, 178
Riva del Garda 269
Riviera
  see Liguria
Riviera di Levante 144–158
Riviera di Ponente 158–171
robusta 29
rock climbing
  Dolomites 257
  Finale Ligure 162
  Riva del Garda 269
  Valle d'Aosta 188
Rococo 19
Rolling Venice Card 204
Roma, pet rooster 9
Romanesque 16
Romano, Giulio 19
Rome 437–478
  accommodations 446
  catacombs 469
  entertainment 474
  food 451
  orientation 444
  practical information 445
  sights 456
  Vatican City 464
  wine bars 456
Romulus 7, 459
Rosi, Francisco 26
Rossellini, Roberto 26
Rossini, Gioacchino 24
  birthplace 418
Rovereto 271
Ruvo 540

S

Sabbioneta 109
Sacra di San Michele 181
Sacro Monte 134
safety 43, 44
sailing, Elba 385
saints
  Anthony 229
  Cecilia 469
  Cyril 468
  David xv
  Francis 387
  Gavino 659
  Geminiano 288
  Gennaro 496
  Gianuario 659
  Paul 468
  Peter 468
  Proto 659
  Sarah xv
  Shannon xv
Salento Peninsula 549–551
Salerno 528–531
Salina 595
Salò 266
Salvatore, Gabriele 27
Samaritans 446
San Benedetto del Tronto 426
San Francesco d'Assisi
  see saints, Francis
San Galgano 353
San Gimignano 362–365
San Marino 303–305
San Remo 163–165
San Teodoro 667
San Vitale 16
San Vito lo Capo 631
Sansepolcro 345
Sant'Ambrogio 16
Santa Teresa di Gallura 670
Santo Stefano di Sessanio 429
Sardinia 638–672
Sassari 655
sassi 554
Satan's restaurant 672
Saturnia 359
Savona 158
Savonarola, Girolamo 11
  Bonfire of the Vanities 327
  prison cell 332
Savoy family 171, 178, 179
scalinata 686
Scarlatti, Alessandro 23
School of Athens 19
scooter, ubiquity 32
scuba diving
  Bosa 664

Cinque Terre 155
Santa Teresa di Gallura 671
Trieste 248
Secret Collection 495
security 43
Segesta 631
self defense 44
Serie A 32
sesi 636
Sestriere 182
settimana bianca 686
sexy leather outfits 9
Shakespeare, William 233, 239
  Romeo and Juliet 238
Shelley, Percy Bysshe 378
  resting place 469
Shroud of Turin 177
Sicilia
  see Sicily
Sicily 570–637
Siena 346–353
  Palio 350, 353
Sinis Peninsula 650
sinopia drawing 686
Siracusa
  see Syracuse
Sirmione 266
Sistine Chapel 470
skiing
  Abruzzo National Park 434
  Alagna Valsesia 183
  Dolomites 257
  Gran Sasso 430
  Macugnaga 183
  Sestriere 182
  Sila Massif 563
  Turin 183
  Valle d'Aosta 188
snails and oysters - relative merits 9
soccer 32
Sorrento 507–510
sottoportico 686
South African consulates 36
  Naples 490
  Venice 205
South African embassies
  Italy 36
Spartacus 8
spear guns 436
specific concerns
  bisexual, gay, and lesbian travelers 72
  children and travel 74
  dietary concerns 74
  disabled travelers 72
  minority travelers 73
  women travelers 70
SPECTRE agents 436

spiaggia 686
Spoleto 406–410
sports and recreation 32
St. Bernard Passes 187
STA Travel 58
Stairway of the Dead 182
Stiffe, Grottoes of 430
stigmata 686
Stintino 659
Stradivarius, Antonio 102
    see also firsts, mordern
    violin
Stresa 128
Stromboli 592
studying abroad 74
Su Monte 667
Su Nuraxi 646
Suetonius 20
Sulla 8
Sulmona 430
sunscreen 46
superlatives
    best capers in the
    Mediterranean,
    Pantelleria 634
    best monastic building in
    the world, Certosa di
    Pavia 102
    best place to rent a
    moped, Pantelleria 634
    best place to rent a
    scooter, Elba 383
    best preserved temples,
    Paestum 532
    best summer meal, Capri
    513
    deepest lake, Lake Como
    119
    Europe's largest outdoor
    disco, Catania 610
    Europe's oldest indoor
    theater, Vicenza 232
    greatest Italian work of the
    8th century, Cividale del
    Friuli 253
    largest fair in southern
    Italy, Bari 538
    largest known altar,
    Syracuse 618
    largest man-made lake in
    Italy, L'Aquila 429
    largest music store in Italy,
    Milan 91
    largest oil painting in the
    world, Venice 217
    largest *piazza* in Italy,
    Trieste 247
    largest relief of an eagle
    556
    largest terra-cotta figure
    collection, Taranto 552

largest zodiacal sundial,
    Bologna 278
most active volcano in
    Europe, Mt. Etna 610
oldest ampitheater,
    Pompeii 506
oldest cableway in the
    world, Bolzano 258
oldest library in Europe,
    Verona 238
oldest university in
    Europe, Bologna 272
shortest river in Italy,
    Varenna 126
tallest *campanile in Italy*,
    Cremona 104
world's 3rd-longest nave,
    Florence 325
world's largest pizzeria,
    Sorrento 510
worst pun ever, Ferrara
    281
Susa 182
Sybil 501
syphilis 10
Syracuse 614–619

T

Tacca, Pietro 381
Tacitus 20
Talented Mr. Bright, The 518
Talented Mr. Ripley, The 163
Tangentopoli 13
Taormina 600–604
Taranto 551
Tarquin 7
Tarquinia 479
tartufo 456
Taverna dei Quaranta 451
taxes 43
telamoni 686
Tempio della Concordia 17
tenors, three 298
Termoli 435
tesserae 15, 686
testicles, lack of
    castrati 23
    elephant 609
Tharros 651
The Colosseum 458
The Pantheon 461
theatrical festivals
    Asti, Asti Teatro 185
    Brescia, Stagione di Prosa
    119
    Syracuse, Greek classical
    drama 619
thermae 686
thermal springs

Acqui Terme 186
Aquacalda 594
Pantelleria 634
Vulcano 589
three orders of Greek
    architecture 15
three tenors
    see tenors, three
Thunderball-inspired
    spearfishing 436
Ticket Consolidators 62
Tiepolo 19
Tiepolo, Giovanni Battista
    19, 250
tifosi (soccer fans) 32
Tindari
    see Tyndaris
Tintoretto, Jacopo 19, 206,
    217, 218, 219, 221, 233
tipping 29, 43
tiramisù 240
Titian 19, 206, 218, 229, 238,
    281
Tivoli 478
Todi 396
Tomba, Alberto 182
topless sunbathing 588
Torino
    see Turin
Tornatore, Giuseppe 27
Torregrande 650
Torrone 429
Toscana
    see Tuscany
Touring Club Italiano 450
trains 63
Trajan 9, 460, 503
Trajan's Column 17
transept 16, 686
transportation
    bus 67
    ferry 70
    plane 58
    train 63
transvestite prostitutes 336
Trapani 627–630
Trattoria da Sergio 452
travel agencies 58
traveler's checks 40
travertine 686
Tre Scalini 456
trees
    see marijuana
Tremiti Islands 435
Trent 254–256
    Council of 256
Trentino Alto-Adige 254
Trevi 410
Treviso 239–241
Trieste 243–248
Trinity College 476

triptych 686
trompe l'oeil 15, 686
Tropea 568
trulli 540
Trulli District 540
tufa 686
Turin 172–181
  Holy Shroud 177
Tuscany 339–387
Tyndaris 583
Tyrrhenian Coast 557

U

Uccello, Paolo 18, 326, 331
Udine 250–252
The Uffizi 328
UK consulates 36
  Florence 315
  Genoa 136
  Milan 84
  Naples 490
  Palermo 574
  Venice 206
UK embassies
  Italy 36
Umbria 387–414
Unification 12
universities
  Bologna 272
  Catania 605
  Messina 598
  Milan 93
  Padua 226, 230
  Pavia 101
  student housing 451
  Verona 234
unusual two-legged female
  centaur 604
Urbino 418–421
US consulates 36
  Florence 315
  Genoa 136
  Milan 84
  Palermo 574
  Venice 205
US embassies
  Italy 36
Usit world 58

V

vaccinations 45
Val d'Ayas 193
Val di Cogne 193
Valle D'Aosta 187–195
Valley of Itria 540
Valnontey 193
valuables, protecting 44
Varenna 125

Vasari 21, 378
Vatican City 464–465
  Museums 470
The Veneto 225–242
Venice 196–224
  accommodations 207
  disabled visitors 205
  entertainment 222
  food 212
  gelaterie and pasticcerie
    215
  intercity transportation
    196
  local transportation 204
  orientation 197
  practical information 205
  sights 215
  vaporetti 204
  Venice International Film
    Festival 223
  wines 212
Ventimiglia 167–170
Verdi, Giuseppe 24, 289,
  293, 294
Vernazza 150
Verona 233–239
  Juliet's tomb 238
  University of 234
Vespa bandits 43
Vesuvius 507
via 686
Viareggio 381
Vicenza 231
villa 686
Villa Ada 464
Villa Borghese 464
Villa d'Este 123, 478
Villa Rotonda 233
Villa Rotunda 19
Virgil 20, 105, 498, 501
  tomb of 498, 499
Visa 41
Visconti 11
Visconti, Lucino 26
Vittorio Emanuele II 12, 171
Vivaldi, Antonio 24
volcanoes
  Mt. Etna 610
  Mt. Vesuvius 507
  Stromboli 593
Volta, Alessandro 101
Volterra 359–362
Volto Santo 371
volunteering abroad 77
vomitorium 451
Vulcano 589–592

W

water taxis 481

waterfalls
  Gole Alcantara 604
  L'Aquila 430
  Lo Sorgente del
    Fiumelatte, Varenna 126
  Riva del Garda 271
  Sass Corbee Gorge,
    Menaggio 125
watersports 32
Western Union 42
Whore of Babylon 413
wilderness 53
wines 30
  Acqui Terme 187
  Asti, *Asti Spumante* 186
  Bassano del Grappa,
    grappa 241
  Brescia, *Tocai di San
    Martino della Battaglia,
    Groppello,* and *Botticino*
    117
  Capri, *Tiberio* and
    Caprense 513
  Cortona, *Bianco vergine di
    Valdichiana* 341
  Dolceacqua, *Rossese* 166
  Emilia-Romagna,
    Lambruschi 229
  Florence, *Chianti* 321
  Marsala 626
  Montalcino, *Brunello* 354
  Montelpulciano, *Vino
    Nobile* 356
  Orvieto, *Orvieto Classico*
    412
  Pantelleria, *Muscato and
    Passito* 636
  Parma, *Malvasia* 289
  Piedmont, *Barolo,
    Barbaresco and Barbera*
    176
  San Gimignano, *Vernaccia*
    362
  Venice, *Proseco della
    Marca, Tocai, Merlot, and
    Valpolicella* 212
  Verona, *Soave,
    Valpolicella, Bardolino,
    and Recioto* 236
wine-tastings
  Modena 289
wolf-children 7
women travelers 47, 70
work 75
World Wide Web 77

Y

YWCA 451

Z

zoo
 Villa Borghese 464

Maps

Abruzzo National Park 433
Agrigento 623
Aosta 190
Apulia, Basilicata, &
 Calabria 533
Ascoli Piceno 425
Assisi 398
Bari 535
Bergamo 111
Bologna 275
Brindisi 543
Cagliari 643
Campania 483
Catania 607
Central Florence 310-311
Central Florence key 314
Central Genoa 139
Central Naples 486-487
Central Venice 200-201
Centro Storico & Trastevere
 440-441
Chapters ix
Cinque Terre 151

Country Map x-xi
Dolomites 257
Emilia-Romagna 273
Ferrara 283
Florence 308-309
Genoa 137
Italian Riviera 135
Lake Area East 267
Lake Area West 118
Lazio 479
Le Marche, Abruzzo, and
 Molise 415
Lecce 547
Lombardy 79
Lucca 369
Mantua 106
Milan 80-81
Milan: Around Stazione
 Centrale 84
Milan Metro 83
Modena 287
Montepulciano 358
Naples 485
Orvieto 413
Padua 227
Palermo 572
Parma 290
Perugia 389
Piemont, Valle d'Aosta, and
 Liguria 172
Pisa 375

Pompeii 505
Rimini 301
Sardinia 639
Sicily 571
Siena 347
Siracusa 615
Spoleto 407
Termini and San Lorenzo
 438-439
Transportation Map xii-xiii
Trieste 245
Turin 174
Tuscany and Umbria 339
Veneto & Friuli-Venezia
 Giulia 225
Venice 198-199
Venice: Vaporetti 197
Verona 235
Walking Tour: Florence
 312-313
Walking Tour: Rome 442-443
Walking Tour: Venice 202-203

Mooooore Room.

Real American Airlines deals for students and faculty, online at StudentUniverse. Earn AAdvantage miles and enjoy *more room throughout Coach only on American**.

StudentUniverse.com

featuring
AmericanAirlines

ABOUT LET'S GO

FORTY-TWO YEARS OF WISDOM

For over four decades, travelers crisscrossing the continents have relied on *Let's Go* for inside information on the hippest backstreet cafes, the most pristine secluded beaches, and the best routes from border to border. *Let's Go: Europe*, now in its 42nd edition and translated into seven languages, reigns as the world's bestselling international travel guide. In the last 20 years, our rugged researchers have stretched the frontiers of backpacking and expanded our coverage into the Americas, Australia, Asia, and Africa (including the new *Let's Go: Egypt* and the more comprehensive, multi-country jaunt through *Let's Go: South Africa & Southern Africa*). Our new-and-improved City Guide series continues to grow with new guides to perennial European favorites Amsterdam and Barcelona. This year we are also unveiling *Let's Go: Southwest USA*, the flagship of our new outdoor Adventure Guide series, which is complete with special roadtripping tips and itineraries, more coverage of adventure activities like hiking and mountain biking, and first-person accounts of life on the road.

It all started in 1960 when a handful of well-traveled students at Harvard University handed out a 20-page mimeographed pamphlet offering a collection of their tips on budget travel to passengers on student charter flights to Europe. The following year, in response to the instant popularity of the first volume, students traveling to Europe researched the first full-fledged edition of *Let's Go: Europe*. Throughout the 60s and 70s, our guides reflected the times—in 1969, for example, we taught you how to get from Paris to Prague on "no dollars a day" by singing in the street. In the 90s we focused in on the world's most exciting urban areas to produce in-depth, fold-out map guides, now with 20 titles (from Hong Kong to Chicago) and counting. Our new guides bring the total number of titles to 57, each infused with the spirit of adventure and voice of opinion that travelers around the world have come to count on. But some things never change: our guides are still researched, written, and produced entirely by students who know first-hand how to see the world on the cheap.

HOW WE DO IT

Each guide is completely revised and thoroughly updated every year by a well-traveled set of nearly 300 students. Every spring, we recruit over 200 researchers and 90 editors to overhaul every book. After several months of training, researcher-writers hit the road for seven weeks of exploration, from Anchorage to Adelaide, Estonia to El Salvador, Iceland to Indonesia. Hired for their rare combination of budget travel sense, writing ability, stamina, and courage, these adventurous travelers know that train strikes, stolen luggage, food poisoning, and marriage proposals are all part of a day's work. Back at our offices, editors work from spring to fall, massaging copy written on Himalayan bus rides into witty, informative prose. A student staff of typesetters, cartographers, publicists, and managers keeps our lively team together. In September, the collected efforts of the summer are delivered to our printer, who turns them into books in record time, so that you have the most up-to-date information available for your vacation. Even as you read this, work on next year's editions is well underway.

WHY WE DO IT

We don't think of budget travel as the last recourse of the destitute; we believe that it's the only way to travel. Our books will ease your anxieties and answer your questions about the basics—so you can get off the beaten track and explore. Once you learn the ropes, we encourage you to put *Let's Go* down and strike out on your own. You know as well as we that the best discoveries are often those you make yourself. When you find something worth sharing, please drop us a line. We're Let's Go Publications, 67 Mount Auburn St., Cambridge, MA 02138, USA (feedback@letsgo.com). For more info, visit our website, www.letsgo.com.

Will you have enough stories to tell your grandchildren?

<u>Yahoo! Travel</u>

CHOOSE YOUR DESTINATION SWEEPSTAKES

No Purchase Necessary.

**Explore the world with Let's Go® and StudentUniverse!
Enter for a chance to win a trip for two to a Let's Go destination!**

Separate Drawings! May & October 2002.

GRAND PRIZES:
Roundtrip StudentUniverse Tickets

✓ Select one destination and mail your entry to:

☐ Costa Rica
☐ London
☐ Hong Kong
☐ San Francisco
☐ New York
☐ Amsterdam
☐ Prague
☐ Sydney

* Plus Additional Prizes!!

Choose Your Destination Sweepstakes
St. Martin's Press
Suite 1600, Department MF
175 Fifth Avenue
New York, NY 10010-7848

Restrictions apply; see offical rules for
details by visiting Let'sGo.com or sending SASE
(VT residents may omit return postage) to the address above.

Name: _____

Address: _____

City/State/Zip: _____

Phone: _____

Email: _____

Grand prizes provided by:

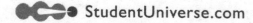 StudentUniverse.com   Real Travel Deals

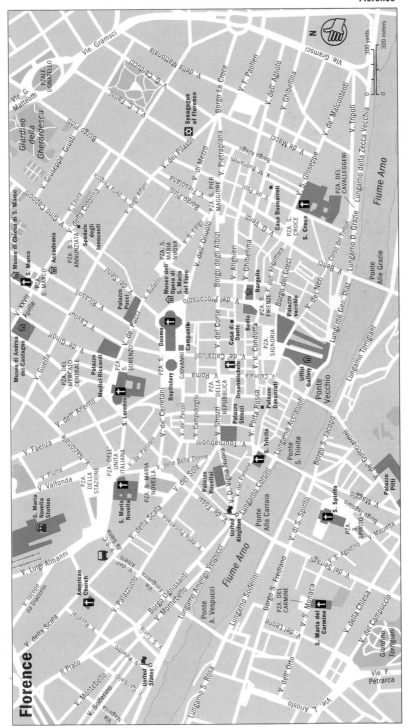

Florence

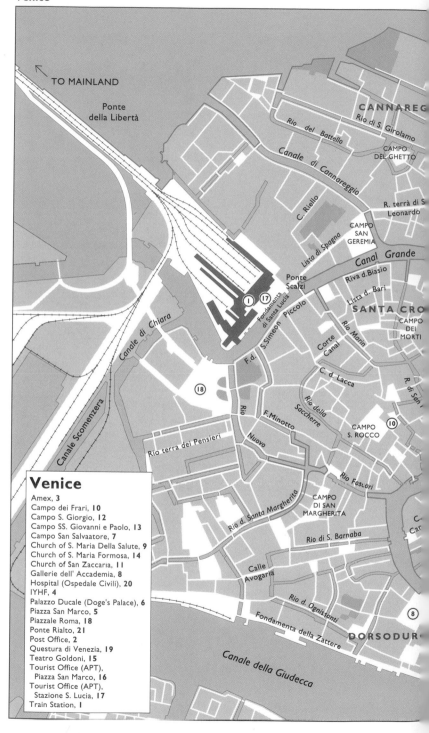

Venice

TO MAINLAND

Ponte
della Libertà

CANNAREG

Rio del Battello

Rio di S. Girolamo

CAMPO
DEL GHETTO

Canale di Cannareggio

C. Riello

R. terrà di S
Leonardo

CAMPO
SAN
GEREMIA

Lista di Spagna

Canal Grande

Ponte
Scalzi

Riva d.Biasio

Lista d. Bari

① ⑰

Fondamenta di Santa Lucia

F.d. S.Simeon Piccolo

SANTA CRO

CAMPO
DEI
MORTI

Rio Marin

Corte
Canal

Canale di Chiara

C. d. Lacca

R. di San

⑱

Rio

F.Minotto

Rio della Sacchere

CAMPO
S. ROCCO

⑩

Canale Scomenzera

Rio terra dei Pensieri

Nuova

Rio Foscari

CAMPO
DI SAN
MARGHERITA

Rio d. Santa Margherita

C.
Car

Rio di S. Barnaba

Calle Avogaria

Rio d. Ognissonti

⑧

Fondamenta della Zattere

DORSODUR

Canale della Giudecca

Venice

Amex, **3**
Campo dei Frari, **10**
Campo S. Giorgio, **12**
Campo SS. Giovanni e Paolo, **13**
Campo San Salvaatore, **7**
Church of S. Maria Della Salute, **9**
Church of S. Maria Formosa, **14**
Church of San Zaccaria, **11**
Gallerie dell' Accademia, **8**
Hospital (Ospedale Civili), **20**
IYHF, **4**
Palazzo Ducale (Doge's Palace), **6**
Piazza San Marco, **5**
Piazzale Roma, **18**
Ponte Rialto, **21**
Post Office, **2**
Questura di Venezia, **19**
Teatro Goldoni, **15**
Tourist Office (APT),
  Piazza San Marco, **16**
Tourist Office (APT),
  Stazione S. Lucia, **17**
Train Station, **1**

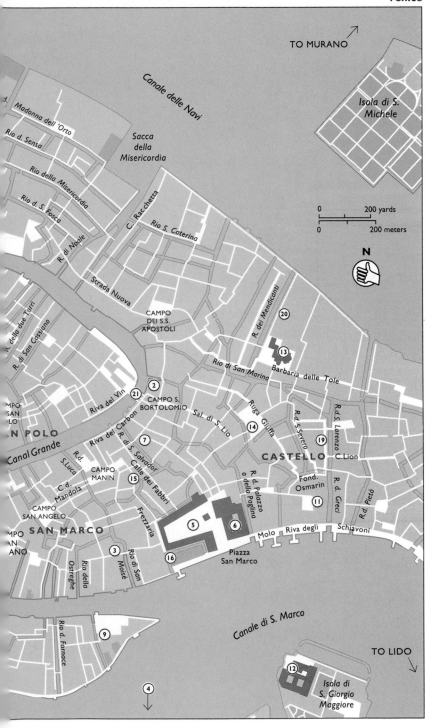

Venice

TO MURANO

Isola di S. Michele

Canale delle Navi

Madonna dell 'Orto

Rio d. Sensa

Rio della Misericordia

Rio d. S. Fosca

Sacca della Misericordia

R. di Noale

C. Racchetta

Rio S. Caterina

0   200 yards
0   200 meters

N

R. della due Torri

R. di San Crassiano

Strada Nuova

CAMPO DEI S.S. APOSTOLI

R. dei Mendicanti

20

13

Barbaria delle Tole

Rio di San Marina

Riva del Vin

21

2

CAMPO S. BORTOLOMIO

Sal. di S. Lio

Ruga Giuffa

R.d. S.Severo

R.d.S. Lorenzo

Canal Grande

Riva del Carbon

R. di S. Salvador

7

14

19

CASTELLO

C.Lion

N POLO

MPO SAN LO

S.Luca

R.d.

CAMPO MANIN

15

Calle dei Fabbri

R. d. Palazzo o della Paglina

Fond. Osmarin

R. d. Greci

R. d. Pietà

C d' Mandola

CAMPO SAN ANGELO

11

MPO AN ANO

SAN MARCO

3

Frezzaria

Rio di San

5

6

Molo   Riva degli   Schiavoni

16

Piazza San Marco

Ostreghe

Rio della

Moisè

Canale di S. Marco

Rio d. Fornace

9

TO LIDO

4

12

Isola di S. Giorgio Maggiore

Milan

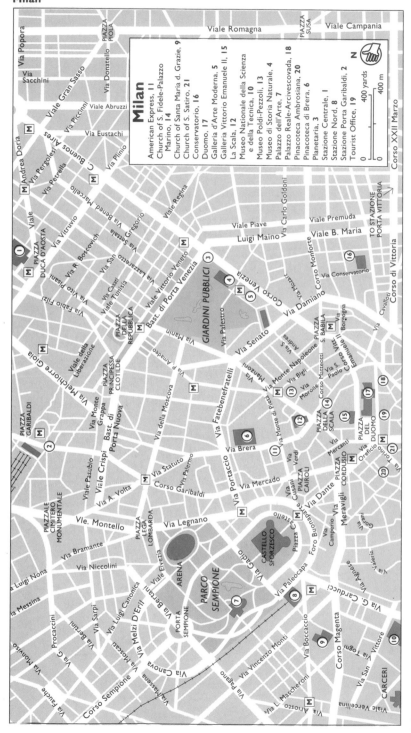

Milan

American Express, 11
Church of S. Fidele-Palazzo Marino, 14
Church of Santa Maria d. Grazie, 9
Church of S. Satiro, 21
Conservatorio, 16
Duomo, 17
Galleria d'Arte Moderna, 5
Galleria Vittorio Emanuele II, 15
La Scala, 12
Museo Nazionale della Scienza e della Tecnica, 10
Museo Poldi-Pezzoli, 13
Museo di Storia Naturale, 4
Palazzo dell'Arte, 7
Palazzo Reale-Arcivescovada, 18
Pinacoteca Ambrosiana, 20
Pinacoteca di Brera, 6
Planetaria, 3
Stazione Centrale, 1
Stazione Nord, 8
Stazione Porta Garibaldi, 2
Tourist Office, 19

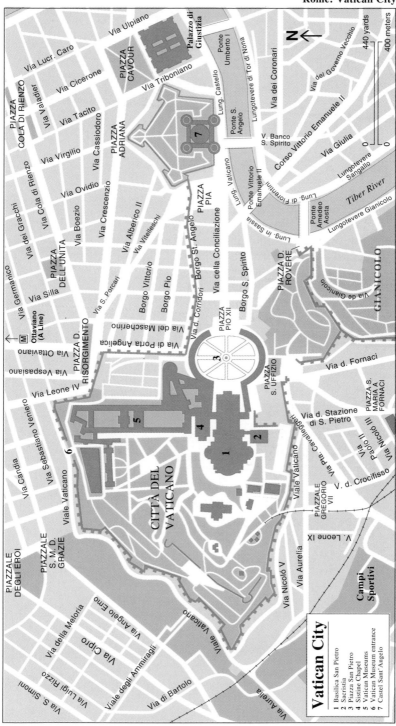

Rome: Vatican City

Palazzo di Giustizia

Via Ulpiano
Via Lucr. Caro
Via Cicerone
Via Valadier
Via Tacito
Via Virgilio
Via Cassiodoro
Via Cola di Rienzo
Via Ovidio
Via dei Gracchi
Via Boezio
Via Crescenzio
Via Germanico
Via Silla
Via Vespasiano
Via Ottaviano
Via Leone IV
Via Sebastiano Veniero
Via Candia
Via della Meloria
Via Cipro
Via Luigi Rizzo
Via S. Simoni
Via Angelo Emo
Viale degli Ammiragli
Via di Bartolo

PIAZZA CAVOUR
Via Triboniano
PIAZZA COLA DI RIENZO
PIAZZA ADRIANA
PIAZZA DELL'UNITÀ
PIAZZA D. RISORGIMENTO
PIAZZALE S. M. D. GRAZIE
PIAZZALE DEGLI EROI

Ponte Umberto I
Lung. Castello
Ponte S. Angelo
Lungotevere di Tor di Nona
Via dei Coronari
Via del Governo Vecchio
Via Giulia
Corso Vittorio Emanuele II
V. Banco S. Spirito
Lungotevere Sangallo
Ponte Vittorio Emanuele II
Lung. Vaticano
Lung. in Sassia
Ponte Amedeo Aosta
Lungotevere Gianicolo
Lung. di Florenni

Tiber River

Via S. Porcari
Via Alberico II
Via Vitelleschi
Borgo Vittorio
Borgo Pio
Via d. Corridori
Borgo St. Angelo
Via della Conciliazione
Borgo S. Spirito
Via del Mascherino
Via di Porta Angelica

PIAZZA PIA
PIAZZA PIO XII
PIAZZA D. ROVERE
GIANICOLO
Via de Gianicolo

7

3

PIAZZA S. UFFIZIO

Via d. Fornaci
Via d. Stazione di S. Pietro
PIAZZA S. MARIA A FORNACI
Via Cavalleggeri
Via Paolo III
Via Nicolò III
V. d. Crocifisso
PIAZZALE GREGORIO VII
V. Leone IX

5
4
1
2
6

CITTÀ DEL VATICANO

Viale Vaticano

Via Nicolò V
Via Aurelia
Viale Vaticano
Via Aurelia

Campi Sportivi

M Ottaviano (A Line)

N

440 yards
400 meters
0
0

Vatican City

1 Basilica San Pietro
2 Sacristia
3 Piazza San Pietro
4 Sistine Chapel
5 Vatican Museums
6 Vatican Museum entrance
7 Castel Sant'Angelo

Rome: Overview

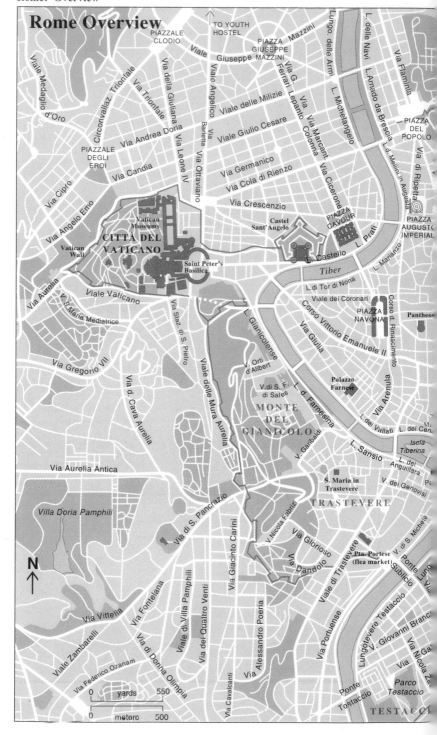

Rome Overview

TO YOUTH HOSTEL

PIAZZALE CLODIO

PIAZZA GIUSEPPE MAZZINI

Viale Giuseppe Mazzini

Lungo. delle Armi

L. Arnado da Brescia

L. delle Navi

Via Flaminia

PIAZZA DEL POPOLO

Viale Medaglio d'Oro

Circonvallaz. Trionfiale

Via Trionfiale

Via della Giuliana

Via Andrea Doria

Via Angelico

Viale Angelico

Via G. Ferrari

Via Lepanto

Viale delle Milizie

Via Marcanti

L. Michelangelo

L.d Melilin in Augusta

Via di Ripetta

PIAZZALE DEGLI EROI

Via Leone IV

Via Barletta

Viale Giulio Cesare

Via Cicerone

Via Colonna

Via Candia

Via Ottaviano

Via Germanico

Via Cola di Rienzo

Via Crescenzio

PIAZZA CAVOUR

L. Prati

PIAZZA AUGUSTO IMPERIAL

Via Cipro

Via Angelo Emo

Vatican Museums

Castel Sant'Angelo

L. Castello

L. Marianzo

Via Aurelia

CITTÀ DEL VATICANO

Saint Peter's Basilica

Tiber

Vatican Wall

V. S. Maria Mediatrice

Viale Vaticano

Via Staz. di S. Pietro

L. di Tor di Nona

Viale dei Coronari

Corso Vittorio Emanuele II

PIAZZA NAVONA

Corso d. Rinascimento

Pantheo

Via Gregorio VII

Via d. Cava Aurelia

Viale delle Mura Aurelia

L. Gianicolense

Via Giulia

V. Orti d'Alibert

V. di S. F. di Sales

MONTE DEL GIANICOLO

L. d. Farnesina

Palazzo Farnese

Via Arenula

L. dei Vallati

L. dei Cen

Via Aurelia Antica

V. Garibaldi

L. Sansio

L. dei Anguillara

Isola Tiberina

Villa Doria Pamphili

Via di S. Pancrazio

Via Giacinto Carini

Via Nicola Fabrizi

S. Maria in Trastevere

V. dei Genovisi

TRASTEVERE

Via Glorioso

Via Dandolo

Pta. Portese (flea market)

V. di S. Michele

Ponte Lung

Via Vitelia

Via Fontelana

Via di Villa Pamphili

Viale dei Quattro Venti

Via Alessandro Poeria

Viale di Trastevere

Via Portuense

Lungotevere Testaccio

Sublicio

Viale Zambarelli

Via Cavalcanti

Via

V. Giovanni Branc

Via Nicola Za

Via Federico Ozanam

Via di Donna Olimpia

Ponte Testaccio

Parco Testaccio

TESTACC

N

| 0 | yards | 550 |
| 0 | meters | 500 |

Rome: Transportation

Rome Transport

Rome: Transportation map showing A-Line and B-Line metro routes with stations including VITTORIO, TERMINI, CAVOUR, REPUBBLICA, BARBERINI, SPAGNA, FLAMINIO, LEPANTO, OTTAVIANO, and S. PIETRO.

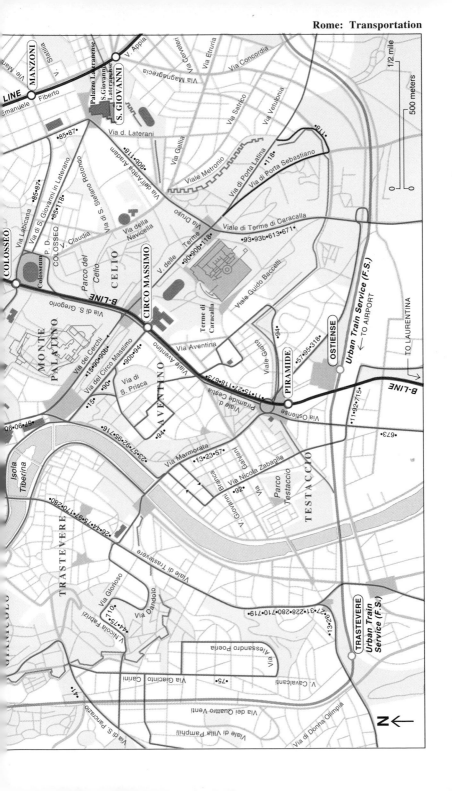

Rome: Transportation

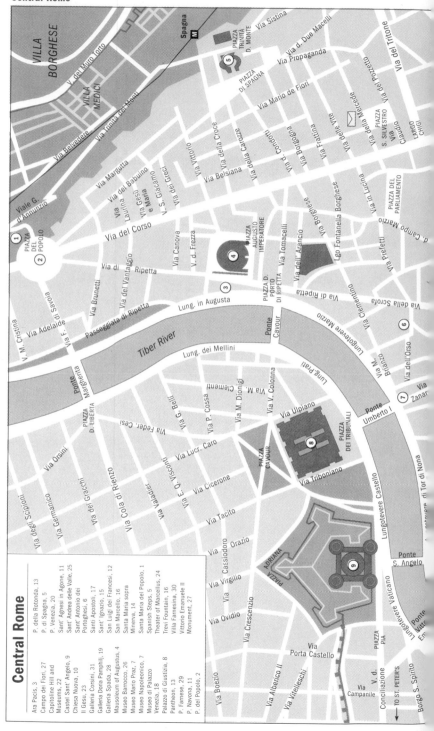

Central Rome

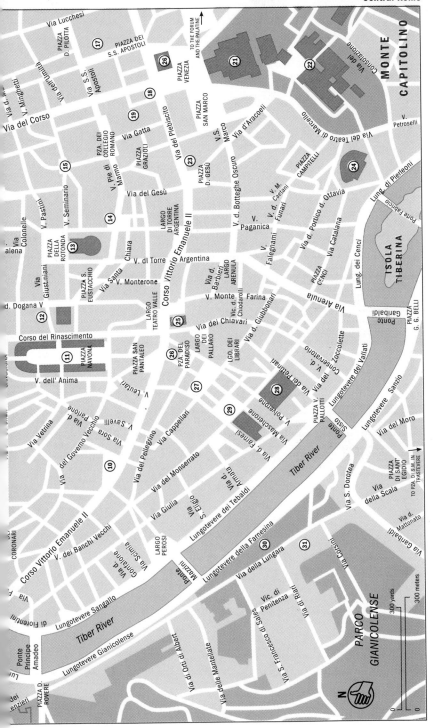

Rome: Villa Borghese

200 yards
200 meters

Giovanni Paisiello
V. Giovannelli
Via S. Mercadante
Via P. Raimondi
Viale dei Daini
PIAZZALE DEI RAIMONDI
Via Po
Via di S. Teresa
Corso d'Italia
V. Puglia
V. Romagna
Via Bancompagni
Via Quintina
Via Sardegna
Via Sicilia
Via Piemonte
Via dell'Uccelleria
V. Pupazzi
Museo Borghese
PIAZZA E. SIENKIEWICZ
Via Pinciana
Via Toscana
Via Marche
GIARDINO ZOOLOGICO
Zoologico
Viale Museo Borghese
Via Vittorio Veneto
Viale dei Cavalli Marini
PIAZZA DI SIENA
Pineta
Viale P. Canonica
Viale Casina
V. d. Goethe
Viale di Raffaello
V. di S. Paolo del Brasile
PIAZZALE BRASILE
Via Emilia
Via Aurora
Via Ludovisi
Via Liguria
Viale del Giardino
Via Ulisse Aldrovandi
PIAZZA CANESTRE
D. CANESTRE
VILLA BORGHESE
Via Porta Pinciana
V. dell'Aranciera
V. F. Laguardia
Viale P. Canestre
Viale Galoppatoio
Viale del Muro Torto
Via del Babuino
Spagna
A LINE
M
Viale delle Belle Arti
Bernadotte
Via Bernadotte
PIAZZALE PAOLA BORGHESE
PIAZZALE DEL FIOCCO
Via Raimondi
Viale d. Belvedere
VILLA MEDICI
Galleria Nazionale d'Arte Moderne
Viale Madama
Via Washington
PIAZZALE DEI MARTIRI
Viale Valadier
Viale Trinita dei Monti
Via del Babuino
Via della Croce
Museo di Villa Giulia
VILLA STROHL FERN
VILLA RUFFO
Flaminio
M
PIAZZA DEL POPOLO
Via del Corso
Via Vittoria
V. A. Canova
PIAZZA AUGUSTO IMPERATORE
V. di S. Eugenio
Via Flaminia
PIAZZALE FLAMINIO
Via Brunetti
Via de. Vantaggio
Via di Villa Giulia
Via Flaminia
PIAZZA DELLA MARINA
V. G. Pisanelli
V. Romanosi
V. D. Azuni
V. Savoia
V. Disavoia
Via Ripetta
Lungotevere in Augusta
Lungotevere delle Navi
Lungotevere Arnaldo da Brescia
Ponte Margherita
Lungotevere d. Mellini
Ponte G. Matteotti
Fiume Tevere
Ponte d. Risorg
Ponte Nenni
Lungotevere Michelangelo
Via Fed. Cesi
Via G. Belli
PIAZZA MONTE GRAPPA
PIAZZA DELLE CINQUE GIORNATE
Lungotevere delle Armi
Via Giulio Cesare
Via degli Scipioni
Via Pompeo Magno
Via dei Gracchi
PIAZZA D. LIBERTA
PIAZZA Viale Valadier
PIAZZA COLA DI RIENZO
Via E. Q. Visconte
Viale Giuseppe Mazzini
Via G. Nicotera
Viale della Milizie
Via Settembrini
Lepanto
M
A LINE
Via Marc. Colonna
Via Ezio
Via Boezio

N

Villa Borghese